CASES

EFFECTIVE SMALL BUSINESS MANAGEMENT • 8/E

Case #	Company Name	Related Topics	ESBM Chapter Reference
1	Yes, We Care Landscaping	Board of advisors	2
		Profit planning and cost control	8
		Pricing	10
		Target market and marketing	7
2	Techline Studio	Strategic management	2
		Web site design and marketing	13
		Location analysis	16
3	id Software	Strategic management	2
		Exit strategy	20
4	Blue Man Group	Marketing	7
5	D.G. Yuengling & Son	Management succession	20
		Management and organizational structure	19
		Marketing	7
6	Eclipse Aviation	Entrepreneurship	1
		Marketing	7
		Marketing communications	
		Personal selling	11
7	Lynn Wilson's Dolls	Pricing	10
		Staffing and leading	19
		Ethics	21
		Business plan	6
8	Triple Point Technology	Legal environment	22
		Ethics	21
9	Henderson Paint & Wallpaper Inc.	Financial analysis	8
		Risk management	20
		Forms of ownership	3
10	Google Inc.	Sources of equity financing	14
		Sources of debt financing	15

Effective Small Business Management

An Entrepreneurial Approach

EIGHTH EDITION

Norman M. Scarborough

Presbyterian College

Thomas W. Zimmerer

Saint Leo University

PEARSON

Prentice Hall

Upper Saddle River, New Jersey 07458

Library of Congress Cataloging-in-Publication Data

Scarborough, Norman M.
   Effective small business management : an entrepreneurial approach / Norman M.
Scarborough, Thomas W. Zimmerer.—8th ed.
     p. cm.
  Includes bibliographical references and index.
  ISBN 0-13-146984-3
    1. Small business—Management. 2. New business enterprises—Management.
  3. Small business—United States—Management. 4. New business enterprises—United
States—Management. I. Zimmerer, Thomas, II. Title.

HD62.7.S27 2005
658.02'2—dc22   2004053364

Acquisitions Editor: David Parker
Editorial Director: Jeff Shelstad
Editorial Assistant: Richard Gomes
Media Project Manager: Nancy Welcher
Marketing Manager: Anke Braun
Marketing Assistant: Patrick Danzuso
Senior Managing Editor (Production): Judy Leale
Production Editor: Kelly Warsak
Permissions Supervisor: Charles Morris
Manufacturing Buyer: Diane Peirano
Design Director: Maria Lange
Art Director: Pat Smythe
Interior Design: Rebecca Silber, Seven Worldwide
Cover Design: Rebecca Silber, Seven Worldwide
Cover Photo: Paul Barton/Corbis
Illustrator (Interior): BookMasters, Inc.
InTote Composition: Judy Allan Book Design
Director, Image Resource Center: Melinda Reo
Manager, Rights and Permissions: Zina Arabia
Manager, Visual Research: Beth Brenzel
Manager, Cover Visual Research & Permissions: Karen Sanatar
Photo Researcher: Stephen Forsling
Image Permission Coordinator: Debbie Latronica
Manager, Print Production: Christy Mahon
Full-Service Project Management: Jennifer Welsch/BookMasters, Inc.
Composition: Integra Software Services
Printer/Binder: Courier-Westford
Cover Printer: Lehigh Press
Typeface: 10.5 pt. Minion

Credits and acknowledgments borrowed from other sources and reproduced, with
permission, in this textbook appear on pages 811–812.

Pearson Education LTD.   Pearson Education Australia PTY, Limited
Pearson Education Singapore, Pte. Ltd   Pearson Education North Asia Ltd
Pearson Education, Canada, Ltd   Pearson Educación de Mexico, S.A. de C.V.
Pearson Education–Japan   Pearson Education Malaysia, Pte. Ltd

10 9 8 7 6 5 4 3 2
ISBN 0-13-146984-3

In memory of Lannie H. Thornley

To Louise T. Scarborough, Mildred Myers,
and John Scarborough. Your love, support,
and encouragement have made all the difference.

N.M.S.

To my wife, Linda, whose many hours of work on this
project helped make the book a reality, and to Jesse and Minnie
Williams, whose simple life and love of learning will inspire
many generations to come.

T.W.Z.

❚❚❚ Brief Contents

▌▌▌ Contents

▌▌▌ Preface

The field of entrepreneurship is experiencing incredible rates of growth, not only in the United States but across the world as well. People of all ages, backgrounds, and nationalities are launching businesses of their own and, in the process, are reshaping the global economy. Entrepreneurs are discovering the natural advantages that result from their companies' small size—speed, agility, flexibility, sensitivity to customers' needs, creativity, a spirit of innovation, and many others—that give them the ability to compete successfully with companies many times their size with budgets to match. As large companies struggle to survive wrenching changes in competitive forces by downsizing, merging, and restructuring, the unseen army of small businesses continues to flourish and to carry the nation's economy on its back. Entrepreneurs willing to assume the risks of the market to gain its rewards are at the heart of capitalism. These men and women, with their bold entrepreneurial spirits, have led our nation into prosperity throughout history. Entrepreneurship is a significant force throughout the world. We need look no farther than those nations that are throwing off decades of control and central planning in favor of capitalism to see where the entrepreneurial process begins. In every case, it is the entrepreneurs creating small companies that lead those nations out of the jungles of economic oppression to higher standards of living and hope for the future.

In the United States, we can be thankful that the small business sector is strong and thriving. Small companies deliver the goods and services we use every day, provide jobs and training for millions of workers, and lead the way in creating the products and services that will make our lives easier and more enjoyable in the future. Small businesses were responsible for introducing to the world the elevator, the airplane, FM radio, the zipper, the personal computer, and a host of other marvelous inventions. The imaginations of the next generation of entrepreneurs—of which you may be a part—will determine which other fantastic products and services may lie in our future! Whatever those ideas may be, we can be sure of one thing: Entrepreneurs will be there to make them happen.

The purpose of this book is to excite you about the possibilities, the challenges, and the rewards of owning your own business and to provide the tools you will need to be successful if you choose the path of the entrepreneur. It is not an easy road to follow, but the rewards—both tangible and intangible—are well worth the risks. Not only may you be rewarded financially for your business idea, but also like entrepreneurs the world over, you will be able to work at doing something you love!

Effective Small Business Management: An Entrepreneurial Approach, Eighth Edition, brings to you the material you will need to launch and manage a small business successfully in the hotly competitive environment of the twenty-first century. In writing this edition, we have worked hard to provide you with plenty of practical, "hands-on" tools and techniques to make your business venture a success. Many people launch businesses every year, but only some of them succeed. This book teaches you the right way to launch and manage a small business with the staying power to succeed and grow. Perhaps one day we'll be writing about your success story in future editions of this book!

New to This Edition

1. *Fully integrated into text Business Plan Pro.* Professors also can choose to bundle with this edition Business Plan Pro, the best-selling business plan software on the market. To many entrepreneurs, preparing a business plan seems at first to be an overwhelming task, but Business Plan Pro makes the job much easier by providing an easy-to-use template that guides students through the process of building a solid business plan. The Web site that accompanies *Effective Small Business Management*, Eighth Edition, also includes additional exercises designed to help students get the most out of using Business Plan Pro.

2. *A sample business plan.* Many courses in entrepreneurship and small business management require students to write business plans. Students of entrepreneurship find it helpful to have a model to guide them as they build their own plans, and they can access a sample plan from our Web site. The plan is one written for InTote, a business that designs and makes tote bags and other accessories, that was started and is operated by a college student.

3. *Case studies.* This edition includes an exciting new feature: 10 cases, most of them about actual small businesses students can research online. These cases are designed to give students the opportunity to apply the concepts they have learned throughout the course. They challenge students on a variety of topics that are covered in the text, and they are ideal for either individual or group assignments. In addition, professors can choose to bundle Cases in Entrepreneurship and Small Business Management, a collection of 13 comprehensive cases written by experts in the field and edited by Kirk Heriot, with this edition of *Effective Small Business Management*. Instructors may download case teaching notes at the Instructor's Resource Center at www.prenhall.com/zimmerer.

4. *Updated coverage of important topics such as:*
   - E-commerce
   - Strategic management
   - Guerrilla marketing techniques
   - Sources of financing, both equity and debt
   - Business strategies for global markets
   - Values-based leadership

Hallmark Features

Effective Small Business Management, Eighth Edition, contains many unique features that make it the ideal book for entrepreneurs who are serious about launching their businesses the right way. These features include the following:

- *A complete chapter on e-commerce and thorough coverage of the World Wide Web as a business tool.* One of the most important business tools today is the World Wide Web. Still in its infancy, it is already proving to be a powerful force in reshaping the face of business. *Effective Small Business Management*, Eighth Edition, offers the most comprehensive coverage of e-commerce of any book on the market. In these pages, you'll find many references to the Web, ideas for using the Web as a business tool, and examples of entrepreneurs who are unleashing the power of the Web in creative ways.
- *Real company examples.* Because examples help people learn more effectively and efficiently, you'll find plenty of examples in this edition set off in italics, which illustrate how entrepreneurs are using the concepts covered in the text to make their businesses more successful. These examples are also a great way to stimulate creativity.

- *Emphasis on building and using a business plan.* Chapter 6 is devoted to building a business plan, and features in many other chapters reinforce the business planning process.
- *Features in every chapter that help students master the material more readily.* Learning objectives introduce each chapter, and they appear in the text margins at appropriate places to keep students' attention focused on what they are learning. Chapter summaries are organized by learning objectives as well.
- *Boxed features in every chapter that follow two important themes:*
  - "In the Footsteps of an Entrepreneur," which offer in-depth, interesting examples of entrepreneurs who are using the concepts covered in the text and which reinforce the learning objectives.
  - "Gaining a Competitive Edge," a "hands-on, how-to" feature designed to offer practical advice on a particular topic that students can use to develop a competitive edge for their businesses.

  Each feature presents thought-provoking issues that will produce lively class discussions and enhance students' learning experiences by asking them to (1) identify, (2) analyze, and (3) evaluate key issues related to entrepreneurship.

Resources

OneKey for convenience, simplicity, and success

OneKey offers the best teaching and learning online resources all in one place. OneKey is all instructors need to plan and administer their course. OneKey is all students need for anytime, anywhere access to online course material. Conveniently organized by textbook chapter, these compiled resources help save time and help students reinforce and apply what they have learned. OneKey is available in three course management platforms: BlackBoard, CourseCompass, and WebCT.

For the Student OneKey includes:

- **Learning Modules** for each chapter composed of a pretest, chapter review, learning activities, and a post-test.
- **Student PowerPoints**
- **Current News Articles Powered by** *Research Navigator* *Research Navigator* helps your students make the most of their research time. From finding the right articles and journals, to citing sources; drafting and writing effective papers; and completing research assignments, this site simplifies and streamlines the entire process.

For the Instructors OneKey includes: The complete Instructor Resource Center as well as access to all student resources.

Instructor's Resource Center available online or on CD-ROM

The Instructor's Resource Center, available on CD, online at www.prenhall.com, or your OneKey online course, provides presentation and other classroom resources. Instructors can collect the materials, edit them to create powerful class lectures, and upload them to an online course management system.

Using the Instructor's Resource Center on CD-Rom, instructors can easily create custom presentations. Instructors can select a chapter from the contents to see a list of available resources or simply search by keyword. Desired files can be exported to the instructor's hard drive for use in classroom presentations, and online courses.

With the Instructor's Resource Center, you will find the following faculty resources:

- **PowerPoints** A comprehensive package allowing access to the figures of the text, these PowerPoint presentations are designed to aid the educator and supplement in-class lectures.

- **TestGen Test-Generating Software** The printed test bank contains approximately 125 questions per chapter including multiple choice, true/false, and scenario-based questions. (*Print version available in Instructor's Manual*)
- **Instructor's Manual** Designed to guide the educator through the text, each chapter in the Instructor's Manual contains learning objectives, a highly detailed instructor's outline, a chapter review, and suggested answers to discussion questions. (*Print version also available*)

Video

Video clips highlight small business and entrepreneurial issues at a variety of both large and small companies.

Companion Web Site

The text Web site www.prenhall.com/scarborough features chapter quizzes, student PowerPoints, a Business Plan Evaluation Scale, a "Before you Start" checklist, and a list of hundreds of links to useful small business sites (organized by chapter).

Business Plan Pro Software 0-13-100836-6

Step-by-step instruction of the Windows-based Business PlanPro software walks students through the process of creating a business plan. Students examine sample plans from a variety of businesses and personalize their own professional business plan.

Acknowledgments

Partnering with every author team is a staff of professionals who work extremely hard to bring a book to life. They handle the thousands of details involved in transforming a rough manuscript into the finished product you see before you. Their contributions are immeasurable, and we appreciate all they do to make this book successful. We have been blessed to work with the following outstanding publishing professionals:

David Parker, acquisitions editor, is one of the finest editors we have had the pleasure of working with over the course of more than two decades. David's vision, dedication, and support made the process of creating this edition flow quite smoothly. He truly is an asset to the publishing industry.

Rich Gomes, editorial assistant, who so capably handled a seemingly infinite number of details related to getting this edition ready for production and managed all of the components of the teaching package that plays such a vital role in the success of this book. Rich has a bright future in publishing.

Kelly Warsak, our production editor, who skillfully coordinated the production schedule for this edition of *Effective Small Business Management* and all of the ancillaries that accompany it. Kelly kept this project on schedule, which in publishing is never an easy task, and she always managed to do so in a friendly, caring manner.

Jennifer Welsch, our project director at BookMasters, who was always ready to answer questions and whose organization and dedication helped to guide this project through the production process.

Donna Mulder, our copy editor, who caught our mistakes and helped us polish the manuscript and transform it into the finished product you see before you.

Stephen Forsling, our photo researcher, who took our suggestions for photographs and made them come to life.

Shannon Moore and Anke Braun, marketing managers, who gave us many ideas based on their extensive contact with those who count the most: our customers.

We also extend our appreciation to the army of Prentice Hall sales representatives, who work so hard to get our books into our customers' hands and who represent the front line in our effort to serve our customers' needs. They are the unsung heroes of the publishing industry.

Especially important in the development of the eighth edition of this book were the following professors, who reviewed the manuscript and provided valuable input that improved the final product:

Ralph Jagodka–Mt. San Antonio College
Marcella Norwood–University of Houston
Khaled Sartawi–Fort Valley State University
H. Lon Addams–Weber State University
John Moonen–Daytona Beach Community College
Jack Sheeks–Broward Community College
Linda M. Newell–Saddleback College
James H. Browne–University of Southern Colorado
John F. McMahon–Mississippi County Community College
Charles N. Toftoy–George Washington University
Ben Powell–University of Alabama
Kyoung-Nan Kwon–Michigan State University
Judy Dietert–Southwest Texas State University

We also are grateful to our colleagues who support us in the sometimes grueling process of writing a book: Foard Tarbert, Sam Howell, Jerry Slice, Meredith Holder, Suzanne Smith, Jody Lipford, and Kristy Hill of Presbyterian College and Dr. Aurthur F. Kirk Jr. and Dr. Douglas Astolfi of Saint Leo University.

A very special acknowledgment to Pat Guinn, whose talent in manuscript typing is legendary. Finally, we thank Cindy Scarborough and Linda Zimmerer for their love, support, and understanding while we worked many long hours to complete *Effective Small Business Management*, Eighth Edition. For them, this project represents a labor of love.

Norman M. Scarborough
William Henry Scott III Associate
Professor of Information Science
Presbyterian College
Clinton, South Carolina
e-mail: nmscarb@presby.edu

Thomas W. Zimmerer
Dean, School of Business
Professor of Management
St. Leo University
Tampa, Florida
e-mail: tom.zimmerer@saintleo.edu

Chapter 1

Entrepreneurs: The Driving Force Behind Small Business

It's kind of fun to do the impossible.
—WALT DISNEY

Fall down seven times. Stand up eight.
—JAPANESE PROVERB

Upon completion of this chapter, you will be able to:

1. Define the role of the entrepreneur in the U.S. economy.
2. Describe the entrepreneurial profile.
3. Describe the benefits of owning a small business.
4. Describe the potential drawbacks of owning a small business.
5. Explain the forces that are driving the growth in entrepreneurship.
6. Discuss the role of diversity in small business and entrepreneurship.
7. Describe the contributions small businesses make to the U.S. economy.
8. Explain the reasons small businesses fail.
9. Put business failure into the proper perspective.
10. Explain how small business owners can avoid the major pitfalls of running a business.

1. Define the role of the entrepreneur in the U.S. economy.

Welcome to the world of the entrepreneur! Every year, entrepreneurs in the United States launch nearly 6 million businesses.[1] These people from diverse backgrounds are striving to realize that Great American Dream of owning and operating their own businesses. Some of them have chosen to leave the security of the corporate hierarchy in search of independence, others have been forced out of large corporations as a result of downsizing, and still others have from the start dreamed of the autonomy that owning a business offers. The impact of these entrepreneurs on the nation's economy goes far beyond their numbers, however. This resurgence of the entrepreneurial spirit is the most significant economic development in recent business history. These heroes of the new economy are rekindling an intensely competitive business environment that had once disappeared from the landscape of U.S. business. With amazing vigor, their businesses have introduced innovative products and services, pushed back technological frontiers, created new jobs, opened foreign markets, and, in the process, sparked the U.S. economy into regaining its competitive edge in the world.

Scott Cook, cofounder of Intuit Inc., a highly successful publisher of personal financial software, explains the new attitude toward entrepreneurship and the vital role small businesses play:

> Small business is cool now, and I don't mean that lightly. . . . People are seeing that the stuff that makes our lives better comes from business more often than it comes from government. It used to be that there was an exciting part of big business that attracted people. But today it's the reverse; small companies are the heroes . . . and now the entrepreneurs get the attention.[2]

The past several decades have seen record numbers of entrepreneurs launching businesses. In 1969, entrepreneurs created 274,000 new corporations; today, the number of new incorporations exceeds 600,000 in a typical year![3] Another indicator of the popularity of entrepreneurship is the keen interest expressed by students in creating their own businesses. Increasing numbers of young people are choosing entrepreneurship as a career rather than joining the ranks of the pinstriped masses in major corporations. In short, the probability that you will become an entrepreneur at some point in your life has never been higher!

Current conditions suggest that entrepreneurial activity, although not at record levels, remains strong—not only in the United States but across the globe as well. According to the Global Entrepreneurship Monitor (GEM), a study of entrepreneurial activity across the globe, 10.5 percent of the U.S. population aged 18 to 64 is engaged in entrepreneurial activity. The study also found that 12 percent of people in the 37 GEM countries analyzed are involved in starting a new business (see Figure 1.1).[4] Even in countries rocked by war, entrepreneurs manage to persist in their efforts to build businesses. *After Allied forces removed Saddam Hussein from power in Iraq in 2003, Walid Mahmoud saw the opportunity to realize his dream of opening a pizza shop, even though order had not yet been restored to the city. After learning to make pizza at a relative's shop in Jordan, Mahmoud returned to Iraq after its liberation and opened his shop near the "green zone" in central Baghdad where thousands of Allied officials and soldiers lived and worked. Word about his business spread quickly, and soon Mahmoud was selling more than 200 pizzas a day, mainly to Americans stationed in nearby compounds. The small pizza shop displaying an Italian flag decorated with Arabic writing began earning profits of $1,000 a week, an astronomical sum in postwar Iraq.[5]*

Productivity gains in recent years have made it possible for companies to accomplish more with fewer people, and America's largest companies have engaged in massive downsizing campaigns, dramatically cutting the number of managers and workers on their payrolls. This flurry of "pink slips" has spawned a new population of entrepreneurs—"castoffs" from large corporations (many of whom thought they would be lifetime ladder-climbers in their companies) with solid management experience and many productive years left before retirement. This downsizing has all but destroyed the long-standing notion of job security

Company Example →

Figure 1.1

Entrepreneurial Activity Across the Globe

Persons per 100 Adults, 18–64 Years Old, Engaged in Entrepreneurial Activity

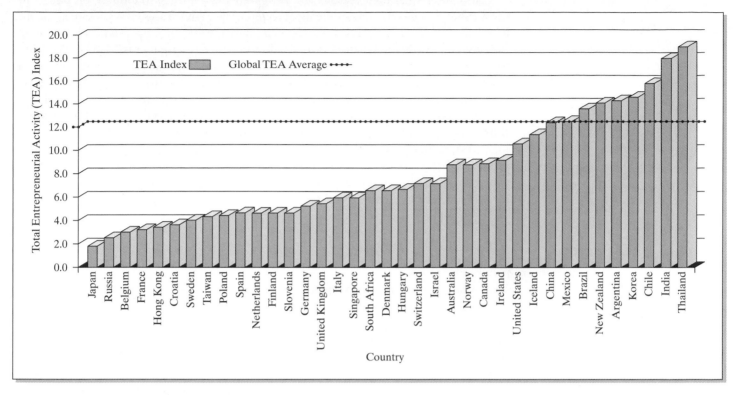

Source: Adapted from "Total Entrepreneurial Activity (TEA) By Country," 2002 *Global Entrepreneurship Monitor,* fig.1, pg. 10. Used by Permission.

in large corporations. As a result, people who once saw launching a business as being too risky now see it as the ideal way to create their own job security.

This downsizing trend among large companies has created a significant philosophical change. It has ushered in an age in which "small is beautiful." Twenty-five years ago, competitive conditions favored large companies with their hierarchies and layers of management; today, with the pace of change constantly accelerating, fleet-footed, agile, small companies have the competitive advantage. These nimble competitors can dart into and out of niche markets as they emerge and recede, they can move faster to exploit opportunities the market presents, and they can use modern technology to create within a matter of weeks or months products and services that once took years and all of the resources a giant corporation could muster. The balance has tipped in favor of small entrepreneurial companies.

Entrepreneurship also has become mainstream. Although launching a business is never easy, the resources available today make the job much simpler now than ever before. Thousands of colleges and universities offer courses in entrepreneurship, the Internet hosts a sea of information on launching a business, sources of capital that did not exist just a few years ago are now available, and business incubators hatch companies at impressive rates. Once looked down on as a choice for people unable to hold a job, entrepreneurship is now an accepted and respected part of our culture.

Another significant shift in the bedrock of our nation's economic structure is influencing this swing in favor of small companies. The nation is rapidly moving away from an industrial economy to a knowledge-based one. What matters now is not so much the factors of production as *knowledge* and *information*. The final impact of this shift will be as dramatic as the move from an agricultural economy to an industrial one that occurred

200 years ago in the United States. A knowledge-based economy favors small businesses because the cost of managing and transmitting knowledge and information is very low, and computer and information technologies are driving these costs lower still.

No matter what their reasons are, entrepreneurs continue to embark on one of the most exhilarating—and one of the most frightening—adventures ever known: launching a business. It's never easy, but it can be incredibly rewarding, both financially and emotionally. One successful business owner claims that an entrepreneur is "anyone who wants to experience the deep, dark canyons of uncertainty and ambiguity and wants to walk the breathtaking highlands of success. But I caution: Do not plan to walk the latter until you have experienced the former."[6] True entrepreneurs see owning a business as the real measure of success. Indeed, entrepreneurship often provides the only avenue for success to those who otherwise might have been denied the opportunity.

Who are these entrepreneurs, and what drives them to work so hard with no guarantee of success? What forces lead them to risk so much and to make so many sacrifices in an attempt to achieve an ideal? Why are they willing to give up the security of a steady paycheck working for someone else to become the last person to be paid in their own companies? This chapter will examine the entrepreneur, the driving force behind the U.S. economy.

What Is an Entrepreneur?

2. Describe the entrepreneurial profile.

Company Example →

Each year, entrepreneurs in the United States start nearly 6 million businesses. An **entrepreneur** is one who creates a new business in the face of risk and uncertainty for the purpose of achieving profit and growth by identifying opportunities and assembling the necessary resources to capitalize on those opportunities. Entrepreneurs usually start with nothing more than an idea—often a simple one—and then organize the resources necessary to transform that idea into a sustainable business. One business writer says that an entrepreneur is "someone who takes nothing for granted, assumes change is possible, and follows through; someone incapable of confronting reality without thinking about ways to improve it; and for whom action is a natural consequence of thought."[7] *Ava DuVernay is one entrepreneur who spotted a business opportunity and acted on it. During a marathon hairstyling session in a Los Angeles salon, DuVernay had an idea: Why not provide specialized programming, some paid for by advertisers and some original content, for customers in salons across the country? Just a few months later, she launched Urban Beauty Collective Television (UBC TV) and produced her first two-hour video, which targets African American and Hispanic women, and distributed it to 10,000 salons in 16 major cities, including Miami and Detroit. That video generated a profit for the small company, and advertisers already are clamoring to get into DuVernay's next video. DuVernay is talking with 2,000 more salons interested in picking up UBC TV and is in the process of launching UBC Radio.*[8]

Many people dream of owning their own businesses, but most of them never actually launch a company. Those who do take the entrepreneurial plunge, however, will experience the thrill of creating something grand from nothing; they will also discover the challenges and the difficulties of building a business "from scratch." Whatever their reasons for choosing entrepreneurship, many recognize that true satisfaction comes only from running their own businesses the way they choose.

Researchers have invested a great deal of time and effort over the last decade studying these entrepreneurs and trying to paint a clear picture of the entrepreneurial personality. Although these studies have identified several characteristics entrepreneurs tend to exhibit, none of them has isolated a set of traits required for success. We now turn to a brief summary of the entrepreneurial profile.[9]

1. *Desire and willingness to take initiative.* Entrepreneurs feel a personal responsibility for the outcome of ventures they start. They prefer to be in control of their resources

and to use those resources to achieve self-determined goals. They are willing to step forward and build businesses based on their creative ideas.

2. *Preference for moderate risk.* Entrepreneurs are not wild risk takers but are instead *calculating* risk takers. Unlike "high-rolling, riverboat gamblers," they rarely gamble. Entrepreneurs often have a different perception of the risk involved in a business situation. The goal may appear to be high—even impossible—from others' perspective, but entrepreneurs typically have thought through the situation and believe that their goals are reasonable and attainable. David Neeleman launched a new low-cost airline, JetBlue, just when the industry was retrenching and suffering some of the greatest setbacks in its history. Many thought Neeleman was foolish to launch an airline in such a turbulent environment, but JetBlue is one of the few airlines that has been able to maintain its profitability.

This attitude explains why so many successful entrepreneurs failed many times before finally achieving their dreams. For instance, Milton Hershey, founder of one of the world's largest and most successful chocolate makers, started four candy businesses, all of which failed, before he launched the business that would make him famous. One successful entrepreneur who has launched six companies explains entrepreneurs' view of risk:

> Contrary to popular myth, entrepreneurs do not enjoy taking risks. Granted, a certain amount of risk is unavoidable in business, but the thrill of the start-up doesn't come from defying the odds. It comes from creating a viable company, and you improve your chances of doing that if you keep the level of risk as low as possible.[10]

Good entrepreneurs become risk *reducers*, and one of the best ways to minimize the risk in any entrepreneurial venture is to create a sound business plan, which is the topic of Chapter 6.

3. *Confidence in their ability to succeed.* Entrepreneurs typically have an abundance of confidence in their ability to succeed, and they tend to be optimistic about their chances for business success. Entrepreneurs face many barriers when starting and running their companies, and a healthy dose of optimism can be an important component in their ultimate success.

4. *Self-reliance.* Entrepreneurs do not shy away from the responsibility for making their businesses succeed. Perhaps that is why many entrepreneurs persist in building businesses even when others advise them of the folly of their ideas. Their views reflect those of Ralph Waldo Emerson in his essay "Self Reliance":

> You will always find those who think they know what is your duty better than you know it. It is easy in the world to live after the world's opinion; it is easy in solitude to live after our own; but the great man is he who in the midst of the crowd keeps with perfect sweetness the independence of solitude.[11]

5. *Perseverance.* Even when things don't work out as they planned, entrepreneurs don't give up. They simply keep trying. *J. Peterman (who was portrayed as Elaine's eccentric boss on the long-running situation comedy* Seinfeld) *started selling cowboy dusters with a small ad in the* New Yorker *and built a successful upscale catalog business offering unique items that eventually hit $75 million in sales in 1998. Rapid growth, over-expansion, and an inundation of orders after an appearance on* Oprah *created serious growing pains that the young company could not handle, and J. Peterman declared bankruptcy in 1999. Two years later, Peterman bought back the rights to his company's name for $1 million and relaunched a more streamlined—and profitable—company. Sales from the company's eight catalogs now generate more than $8 million in annual sales, and Peterman is glad that his perseverance paid off.[12]*

Company Example →

6. *Desire for immediate feedback.* Entrepreneurs like to know how they are doing and are constantly looking for reinforcement. Tricia Fox, founder of Fox Day Schools, Inc., claims, "I like being independent and successful. Nothing gives you feedback like your own business."[13]

7. *High level of energy.* Entrepreneurs are more energetic than the average person. That energy may be a critical factor given the incredible effort required to launch a start-up company. Long hours—often 60 to 80 hours a week—and hard work are the rule rather than the exception. Building a successful business requires a great deal of stamina.

8. *Competitiveness.* Entrepreneurs tend to exhibit competitive behavior, often early in life. They enjoy competitive games and sports and always want to keep score!

9. *Future orientation.* Entrepreneurs tend to dream big and then formulate plans to transform those dreams into reality. They have a well-defined sense of searching for opportunities. They look ahead and are less concerned with what they accomplished yesterday than what they can do tomorrow. Ever vigilant for new business opportunities, entrepreneurs *observe* the same events other people do, but they *see* something different.

Taking this trait to the extreme are **serial entrepreneurs** who create multiple companies and often run more than one business simultaneously. *Lori Hon, who at age 34 already has started two successful businesses and is working on a third, is always alert to new business opportunities. "I rarely get through a day without some sort of business idea," says Hon, who admits that she enjoys starting businesses much more than running them. After graduating from college, she took a job with a retail snowboard company that she soon learned was in financial trouble. Hon responded to the challenge and turned the company's fortunes around, consolidating three stores into one and paying off creditors. Four years later, she launched her own snowboard shop financed with capital from a Japanese firm. Before long, Hon was inspired to start a sushi restaurant, Hapa. The restaurant was a huge success, growing to three locations with total annual sales of $4 million. She recently sold her ownership in the restaurants to launch Gray V,*

Company Example

a subscription music service for restaurants. Gray V customizes play lists for its customers not only by type of music but also by the pace of business and the desired mood.[14]

10. *Skill at organizing.* Building a company from scratch is much like piecing together a giant jigsaw puzzle. Entrepreneurs know how to put the right people and resources together to accomplish a task. Effectively combining people and jobs enables entrepreneurs to bring their visions to reality.

11. *Value of achievement over money.* One of the most common misconceptions about entrepreneurs is that they are driven wholly by the desire to make money. To the contrary, *achievement* seems to be the primary motivating force behind entrepreneurs; money is simply a way of "keeping score" of accomplishments—a *symbol* of achievement. "Money is not the driving motive of most entrepreneurs," says Nick Grouf, the 28-year-old founder of a high-tech company. "It's just a very nice by-product of the process."[15]

Other characteristics entrepreneurs exhibit include:

- *High degree of commitment.* Launching a company successfully requires total commitment from the entrepreneur. Business founders often immerse themselves completely in their businesses. "The commitment you have to make is tremendous; entrepreneurs usually put everything on the line," says one expert.[16] That commitment helps overcome business-threatening mistakes, obstacles, and pessimism from naysayers, however. Entrepreneurs' commitment to their ideas and the businesses those ideas spawn determine how successful their companies ultimately become.

- *Tolerance for ambiguity.* Entrepreneurs tend to have a high tolerance for ambiguous, ever-changing situations—the environment in which they most often operate. This ability to handle uncertainty is critical because these business builders constantly make decisions using new, sometimes conflicting, information gleaned from a variety of unfamiliar sources.

- *Flexibility.* One hallmark of true entrepreneurs is their ability to adapt to the changing demands of their customers and their businesses. In this rapidly changing world economy, rigidity often leads to failure. As our society, its people, and their tastes change, entrepreneurs also must be willing to adapt their businesses to meet those changes. *When Bill Hewlett and Dave Packard founded their company in a garage in the late 1930s, they had no clear idea what to make. They knew that they wanted to create a business in the vaguely defined field of electronic engineering. Their company, Hewlett-Packard (now one of the most successful electronics companies in the world), probably survived because of the founders' flexibility. Some of their early product ideas included a clock drive for a telescope, a bowling foul-line indicator, a device to make urinals flush automatically, and a shock machine to make people lose weight!*[17]

- *Tenacity.* Obstacles, obstructions, and defeat typically do not dissuade entrepreneurs from doggedly pursuing their visions. Successful entrepreneurs have the willpower to conquer the barriers that stand in the way of their success.

> **Company Example** →

What conclusion can we draw from the volumes of research conducted on the entrepreneurial personality? Entrepreneurs are not of one mold; no one set of characteristics can predict who will become entrepreneurs and whether they will succeed. Indeed, *diversity* seems to be a central characteristic of entrepreneurs. As you can see from the examples in this chapter, *anyone*—regardless of age, race, gender, color, national origin, or any other characteristic—can become an entrepreneur. There are no limitations on this form of economic expression. Entrepreneurship is not a genetic trait; it is a skill that is learned. The editors of *Inc.* magazine claim, "Entrepreneurship is more mundane than it's sometimes portrayed. . . . You don't need to be a person of mythical proportions to be very, very successful in building a company."[18]

IN THE FOOTSTEPS OF AN ENTREPRENEUR . . .

The Seeds of Entrepreneurship

Two hallmarks of entrepreneurs are their creativity and their ability to spot opportunities where others see nothing. Many entrepreneurs start their businesses in humble surroundings—a spare bedroom, basement, or garage—with only an idea and a passion for making it work. Not all succeed, but those who do are never the same, and in some cases, neither is the world. Walt Disney began making cartoon reels of his first creation, Oswald the Rabbit, in his uncle's Los Angeles garage in 1923, before going on to create the company that would entertain the world with movies, television programs, and theme parks. Steve Wozniak and Steve Jobs developed the first personal computer in Jobs's parents garage and changed the world forever. In 1986, Jobs launched Pixar with a former Disney animator, and the company went on to create computer-animated hit movies such as *Toy Story*, *A Bug's Life*, and *Finding Nemo*.

The current generation of entrepreneurs continues to push back the frontiers of creativity and innovation. After cofounding Orbital Sciences Corporation, a company that launches low-orbit satellites, as a Harvard Business School student, Bruce Ferguson became fascinated by plants and their ability to clean up a variety of toxins in the environment, a field known as phyto-remediation. After researching botanical technology, Ferguson launched Edenspace Inc., a company that develops hybrid plants designed to remove harmful substances such as lead, arsenic, nickel, and others through absorption. "Plants, through their roots, operate like little solar-powered pumps and filters," he observes. Edenspace's primary customer to date has been the U.S. government, but corporations and individuals now buy the company's hardworking plants. Edenspace's plants have cleaned the water surrounding the Chernobyl nuclear power plant in the Ukraine and have purged the soil of lead at an army firing range. Edenspace now is developing a plant that glows when it detects the presence of land mines or other explosives.

Gord Black takes a different approach to harvesting trees that ultimately become beautiful hardwood floors. Rather than cut down live trees (that's too easy!), Black, an experienced diver, discovered hundreds of thousands of trees that foresters had cut in the 1800s sitting at the bottom of the 310-mile-long Ottawa River. Because of the cold water, the logs are in pristine condition, and Black's company, Logs End Inc., salvages about 20,000 of them each year. Using a special process, the company dries, cuts, and then mills the logs into unique and beautiful planks for hardwood floors.

Julian Bayley transformed his hobby as an ice sculptor into a full-time business in 1989. In addition to providing the spectacular ice carvings for private and corporate parties and events (Elton John is a loyal customer), Bayley also has developed numerous inventions that his company, Ice Culture, sells to other ice sculptors. The Canadian-based company sells to customers all across the globe 300-pound blocks of ice made using a special technique that results in clear ice that is ideal for carving. Ice Culture currently is developing a process that injects foam around finished sculptures, creating an inexpensive but effective shipping container that keeps a sculpture frozen even without a refrigerated transport truck. Bayley also has developed a computerized ice router that enables artists to mass produce intricate ice sculptures in a fraction of the normal time. Two of Ice Culture's most challenging—and expensive—jobs were creating a $17,000 full-scale ice model of a BMW Mini Cooper and a 17-foot-tall model of the CN Tower, one of the world's tallest buildings!

Winning ideas for creating successful businesses abound. Achieving success requires an entrepreneur's vision, passion, creativity, and enthusiasm to transform an idea into a viable business. Look around. Can you spot any areas that could be the genesis of a successful business?

1. How have entrepreneurs such as those described here and others changed the world?
2. What role do entrepreneurs play in raising the world's standard of living?
3. Use the resources of your library and the Internet to research the story of an entrepreneur whose idea led to an important product, service, business, or innovation. Prepare a brief report describing the entrepreneur's story.

Sources: Maggie Overfelt, "The California Garage Start-Me-Up," *FSB*, September 2003, p. 118; Rob Turner, "Here Comes the New Gold Rush: Bruce Ferguson," *FSB*, June 2003, p. 78; Geoff Williams, "Salvage Operation," *Entrepreneur*, November 2003, p. 32; Chana R. Schoenberger, "The Small Chill," *Forbes*, October 13, 2003, pp. 128–129.

The Benefits of Owning a Small Business

3. Describe the benefits of owning a small business.

Surveys show that owners of small businesses believe they work harder, earn more money, and are happier than if they worked for a large company. Before launching any business venture, every potential entrepreneur should consider the benefits and opportunities of small business ownership.

Opportunity to Gain Control over Your Own Destiny

Entrepreneurs cite controlling their own destinies as one of the benefits of owning their own businesses. Owning a business provides entrepreneurs the independence and the opportunity to achieve what is important to them. Entrepreneurs want to "call the shots" in their lives, and they use their businesses to bring this desire to life. A study by the Hartford Financial Services Group found that 53 percent of entrepreneurs cited "being my own boss" as the major incentive for starting their businesses (second only to "setting my own hours," which was cited by 62 percent of respondents).[19] Entrepreneurs reap the intrinsic rewards of knowing they are the driving forces behind their businesses.

Opportunity to Make a Difference

Increasingly, entrepreneurs are starting businesses because they see an opportunity to make a difference in a cause that is important to them. Whether it is providing low-cost, sturdy housing for families in developing countries or creating a company that educates young people about preserving the earth's limited resources, entrepreneurs are finding ways to combine their concerns for social issues and their desire to earn good livings.

Company Example →

Judy Wicks, owner of the White Dog Café in Philadelphia, uses her business to support a variety of social causes that are important to her and her customers, ranging from environmental issues to diversity in the workplace. Still, Wicks recognizes the importance of earning a profit. "I would describe myself as an activist businessperson," she says. The White Dog started as a muffin shop catering primarily to nearby University of Pennsylvania students and faculty and just kept growing. Today the restaurant seats 200 and serves a casual bistro menu of sandwiches, pasta, and salads. Whenever possible, Wicks buys organic produce and fresh products from local farmers. The White Dog also was the first business in Philadelphia to generate 100 percent of its electricity from wind power. "I believe that you can do well and do good at the same time," says Wicks.[20]

Opportunity to Reach Your Full Potential

Too many people find their work boring, unchallenging, and unexciting. But to most entrepreneurs, there is little difference between work and play: Roger Levin, founder of Levin Group, the largest dental practice management consulting firm in the world, says, "When I come to work every day, it's not a job for me. I'm having fun!"[21]

Entrepreneurs' businesses become the instrument for self-expression and self-actualization. Owning a business challenges all of an entrepreneur's skills, abilities, creativity, and determination. The only barriers to success are self-imposed. Entrepreneurs' creativity, determination, and enthusiasm—not limits artificially created by an organization (e.g., the "glass ceiling")—determine how high they can rise.

Opportunity to Reap Impressive Profits

Although money is *not* the primary force driving most entrepreneurs, the profits their businesses can earn are an important motivating factor in their decisions to launch companies. If accumulating wealth is high on your list of priorities, owning a business is usually the best way to achieve it. When a survey asked the wealthiest 1 percent of Americans to identify the career path that offers young people the greatest potential for financial success, the number-one response (46 percent) was starting a business.[22] Indeed, self-employed people are four times more likely to become millionaires than those who work for someone else. In fact, self-employed business owners make up two-thirds of the nation's millionaires![23] According to researchers Thomas Stanley and William Danko, the typical American millionaire is first-generation wealthy, owns a small business in a less-than-glamorous industry such as welding, junkyards, or auctioneering, and works between 45 and 55 hours per week.[24]

> Company Example →

Marc Benioff has reaped financial rewards from his entrepreneurial efforts. As a teenager, Benioff made enough money designing computer games to buy a car and to pay for his college education. After college, he went to work for software giant Oracle, where he became the youngest vice president in the history of the company. Living up to his reputation as a "big-idea guy," Benioff left Oracle to launch Salesforce.com, a company that sells customer relationship management (CRM) software over the Web. Salesforce.com (where Benioff's golden retriever, Koa, is the CLO, "chief love officer") has become the industry leader, with annual sales of more than $100 million and projections of $10 billion a year by 2012. Benioff, who owns 30 - percent of the company's stock, has a net worth of hundreds of millions of dollars. When the company completes its initial public offering, Benioff's net worth will climb even higher. Benioff also runs a global philanthropic organization based on the "1 percent solution." Salesforce.com gives 1 percent of its profits, 1 percent of its net worth, and 1 percent of its employee hours back to the communities it serves.[25]

Opportunity to Contribute to Society and Be Recognized for Your Efforts

Often small business owners are among the most respected—and most trusted—members of their communities. Business deals based on trust and mutual respect are the hallmark of many established small companies. These owners enjoy the trust and the recognition they receive from the customers they have served faithfully over the years. Playing a vital role in their local business systems and knowing that the work they do has a significant impact on how smoothly our nation's economy functions is yet another reward for entrepreneurs.

Opportunity to Do What You Enjoy Doing

A common sentiment among small business owners is that their work *really* isn't work. Most successful entrepreneurs choose to enter their particular business fields because they have an interest in them and enjoy those lines of work. They have made their avocations (hobbies) their vocations (work) and are glad they did. These entrepreneurs are living the advice Harvey McKay offers: "Find a job doing what you love, and you'll never have to work a day in your life."

> Company Example →

When he was just 12 years old, Greg Martin bought an 1863 Colt revolver at a San Jose, California, junk store for just $15. Enthralled by the beautiful engraving on the cylinder, he became an avid collector and trader of antique guns. Before he was old enough to drive, Martin was combing flea markets, antique stores, and junk shops in search of antique guns, which he would advertise in specialty publications. Soon he was shipping antique guns all across the nation. Martin went on to manage the arms and armor *division of San Francisco's Butterfields auction house for 16 years before leaving to turn his love of collecting and trading antique guns into a business. In 2002, he launched Greg Martin Auctions, a company that specializes in fine antique arms and weaponry. The company generates more than $16 million in annual sales, but Martin's real reward is owning a business in a field that he loves and that continues to fascinate him.*[26]

The Potential Drawbacks of Entrepreneurship

4. Describe the potential drawbacks of owning a small business.

Although owning a business has many benefits and provides many opportunities, anyone planning to enter the world of entrepreneurship should be aware of its potential drawbacks. "If you aren't 100 percent sure you want to own a business," says one business consultant, "there are plenty of demands and mishaps along the way to dissuade you."[27]

Uncertainty of Income

Opening and running a business provides no guarantees that an entrepreneur will earn enough money to survive. Some small businesses barely earn enough to provide the owner-manager with an adequate income. In fact, the median income of small business owners is the same ($30,000) as that of wage and salary workers. (However, business owners are more likely to earn high incomes than wage and salary workers.)[28] In the early days of a business, entrepreneurs often have trouble meeting financial obligations and may have to live on savings. The regularity of income that comes with working for someone else is absent. The owner is always the last one to be paid. The owner of a flavor and fragrances manufacturing operation recalls the time his bank unexpectedly called the company's loans just before Thanksgiving, squeezing both the company's and the family's cash flow. "We had planned a huge Christmas party, but we canceled that," recalls his wife. "And Christmas. And our usual New Year's trip."[29]

Risk of Losing Your Entire Invested Capital

The small business failure rate is relatively high. According to a study by the Small Business Administration, 34 percent of new businesses fail within two years, and 50 percent shut down within four years. Within six years, 60 percent of new businesses will have folded.

A failed business can be financially and emotionally devastating. Before launching their businesses, entrepreneurs should ask themselves if they can cope financially and psychologically with the consequences of failure. They should consider the risk/reward trade-off before putting their personal assets and their mental well-being at risk:

- What is the worst that could happen if I open my business and it fails?
- How likely is the worst to happen? (Am I truly prepared to launch a business?)
- What can I do to lower the risk of my business failing?
- If my business were to fail, what is my contingency plan for coping?

Long Hours and Hard Work

Business start-ups often demand that owners keep nightmarish schedules. In many start-ups, 10- to 12-hour days and six- or seven-day workweeks with no paid vacations are the norm. For example, restaurateurs face not only traditionally high failure rates (one in two new restaurants fails within two years) but also long work hours; one in ten owners work more than 80 hours a week.[30]

Because they often must do everything themselves, owners experience intense, draining workdays. "I'm the owner, manager, secretary, and janitor," says Cynthia Malcolm, who owns a salon called the Hand Candy Mind and Body Escape in Cheviot, Ohio.[31] Many business owners start down the path of entrepreneurship thinking that they will own a business only to discover later that the business owns them!

Lower Quality of Life until the Business Gets Established

The long hours and hard work needed to launch a company can take their toll on the rest of an entrepreneur's life. Business owners often find their roles as husbands and wives or fathers and mothers take a back seat to their roles as company founders. Marriages and friendships are too often casualties of small business ownership. Part of the problem is that most entrepreneurs launch their businesses between the ages of 25 and 34, just when they start their families. *When Anthony DeHart was in the process of building his precision-cutting tool company, DeHart Tooling Components, he was also about to be married. After a romantic wedding in Greece, DeHart whisked his new bride off to Germany for a less-than-romantic honeymoon at a machine-tool trade show. "I actually tried to make vacations out of business trips for the first two years we were married," he recalls. Perhaps DeHart's biggest mistake was underestimating how much time getting his business established would take away from his home life. "I was literally never home," he recalls, leaving his wife, Dottie, who had a full-time job, to care for their young son and to handle household duties. When the DeHarts discovered they were going to have a second child, Anthony reassessed his priorities and saved the marriage. Now he is at home almost every night by 6 P.M., when he and his family cook dinner and spend time together.*[32]

Figure 1.2 provides a breakdown of the ages at which entrepreneurs start their businesses.

Company Example

Figure 1.2

Owner Age at Business Formation

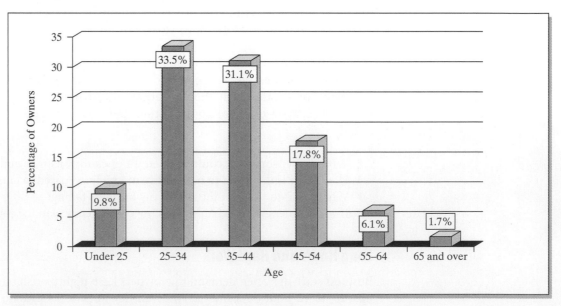

Source: © 2004 National Federation of Independent Businesses (NFIB).

High Levels of Stress

Launching and running a business can be an extremely rewarding experience, but it also can be a highly stressful one. Most entrepreneurs have made significant investments in their companies, have left behind the safety and security of a steady paycheck, and mortgaged everything they own to get into business. Failure often means total financial ruin as well as a serious psychological blow, and that creates high levels of stress and anxiety.

Complete Responsibility

Owning a business is highly rewarding, but many entrepreneurs find that they must make decisions on issues about which they are not really knowledgeable. When there is no one to ask, pressure can build quickly. The realization that the decisions they make are the cause of success or failure of the business has a devastating effect on some people. Small business owners realize quickly that *they* are the business.

Discouragement

Launching a business requires much dedication, discipline, and tenacity. Along the way to building a successful business, entrepreneurs will run headlong into many obstacles, some of which may appear to be insurmountable. Discouragement and disillusionment can set in, but successful entrepreneurs know that every business encounters rough spots and that perseverance is required to get through them.

IN THE FOOTSTEPS OF AN ENTREPRENEUR...

The Story of Tupperware

Almost every household in the United States has at least one Tupperware container in its kitchen cabinets. This common product traces its ancestry to two creative entrepreneurs—inventor Earl Tupper and master marketer Brownie Wise. Earl Tupper (1907–1983) was a prolific inventor, always tinkering with a variety of inventions (including pants that would not lose their crease and a fish-powered boat), keeping meticulous notes and drawings about what worked and what did not and looking for the one idea that would make him famous. After working in DuPont's plastics division for a year, Tupper decided to start his own plastics company in 1938. Initially, the company made plastic products for the military, but Tupper soon began shifting his focus to the consumer market. Tupper made a significant breakthrough in 1942 when he invented a method for making a drastically improved clear plastic. In 1946, he developed a way to mold his containers so that they produced an airtight seal. His idea for creating the airtight seal was patterned after the inverted

rim on paint cans. The result was the "Wonderbowl," a container that could keep food fresh longer.

Tupper tried to market his kitchen containers through traditional outlets, but skeptical consumers were not convinced. Plastic was an unfamiliar substance to most people in those days, and consumers needed a product demonstration to show them how to use Tupperware containers and to understand their benefits. Sales languished.

The struggling company's fortune changed, however, when Tupper met Brownie Wise (1913–1992), a single mother from Detroit who had been racking up impressive sales of Tupperware products using a unique concept. He invited Wise to Massachusetts and, after hearing her ideas, hired her as the vice president of sales and completely changed his company's marketing strategy. Tupper dropped the notion of selling Tupperware through retail outlets to focus on selling exclusively through home parties, where groups of housewives would

convene in a friend's home for product demonstrations and a sales pitch. The "Tupperware party" was born and remained the sole method of selling until the company began selling its products from its Web site in 1999.

Although she had no formal training in business, Brownie Wise was a natural salesperson. She turned the company around by enlisting a legion of women to become the in-home sales force for Tupperware. In the 1950s, Tupperware parties were the rage in suburban America, and by 1954, Tupperware's revenues reached $25 million. Wise became the first woman to appear on the cover of *Business Week*. Because female executives were a rare breed in the 1950s, Wise received lots of publicity, attention, and credit for Tupperware's success.

In 1958, tensions between the geniuses behind Tupperware led Tupper to fire Wise and sell the company to Rexall Drugs for $16 million. Although both launched other companies after Tupperware, neither of them ever achieved the level of success they did at Tupperware. Their company lives on today, however. Tupperware products generate sales of more than $1.1 billion from more than 100 countries, and a Tupperware party takes place on average every 2.5 seconds.

1. Use the Internet to research Earl Tupper, Brownie Wise, and Tupperware. Identify the entrepreneurial traits that Tupper and Wise exhibited.
2. How important is creativity and innovation to the success of a small business? Describe how Tupper and Wise demonstrated these characteristics.

Sources: Paul Lukas, "Party Like It's 1951," *FSB*, July/August 2003, p. 118; "A Trailblazer Rediscovered," *Inc.*, September 2003, p. 26 ; "Five Decades of Change," Tupperware order.tupperware.com/pls/htprod_www/tup_company.decades?fv_item_category_code = 80000; "Inventor of the Week: Earl Tupper," Lemelson-MIT Program, web.mit.edu/invent/iow/tupper.html; "Tupperware!" *American Experience*, PBS, www.pbs.org/wgbh/amex/tupperware/peopleevents/p_wise.html.

Why the Boom: The Fuel Feeding the Entrepreneurial Fire

5. Explain the forces that are driving the growth of entrepreneurship.

What forces are driving this entrepreneurial trend in our economy? Which factors have led to this age of entrepreneurship? Some of the most significant ones follow.

Entrepreneurs as Heroes

An intangible but very important factor is the attitude that Americans have toward entrepreneurs. As a nation, we have raised them to hero status and have held out their accomplishments as models to follow. Business founders such as Michael Dell (Dell Computers), Lillian Vernon (Lillian Vernon Catalogs), Howard Schultz (Starbucks Coffee), Robert Johnson (BET Holdings—Black Entertainment Television), and Phil Knight (Nike) are to entrepreneurship what Shaquille O'Neil and Eddie George are to sports.

Entrepreneurial Education

People with more education are more likely to start businesses than those with less education, and entrepreneurship is an extremely popular course of study among students at all levels. A rapidly growing number of college students see owning a business as an attractive career option, and in addition to signing up for entrepreneurship courses, many of them are launching companies while in school. Today, more than 1,600 colleges and universities offer more than 2,200 courses in entrepreneurship and small business, up from just 16 in 1970.[33] More than 500 colleges and universities now offer entrepreneurship majors at both undergraduate and graduate levels, up from just 175 in 1990.[34] Many colleges and universities are having trouble meeting the demand for courses in entrepreneurship and small business management.

Economic and Demographic Factors

Most entrepreneurs start their businesses between the ages of 25 and 44, and the number of U.S. citizens in that age range stands at nearly 85 million. The economic growth over the past 20 years has created many business opportunities and a significant pool of capital for launching companies to exploit them.

Shift to a Service Economy

The service sector now accounts for about 89 percent of the jobs (up from 70 percent in the 1950s) and 80 percent of the gross domestic product (GDP) in the United States. Because of their relatively low start-up costs, service businesses have been very popular with entrepreneurs. The booming service sector has provided entrepreneurs with many business opportunities, from hotels and health care to translation services and computer maintenance.

Company Example →

Stephanie Firchau began preparing and freezing her homemade meals for use on those nights when her family members' schedules made cooking a challenge. One day, she and several friends rented a commercial kitchen so they could prepare meals en masse. Word spread, and before she knew it, Firchau had filled eight "prepare and freeze" sessions! Spotting a business opportunity, Firchau invited longtime friend Tina Kuna to help her launch Dream Dinners Inc. At each Dream Dinners class, 12 customers, each paying $160, move around the 12 food stations, preparing any 12 of the 14 featured menus. Because all of the food items are laid out for them, "All they need to do is follow the recipe and they are done in two hours," says Kuna. With five locations, Dream Dinners, which has been featured in Entrepreneur *magazine and on the Food Network, brings in more than $2 million in sales a year.*[35]

Technological Advancements

With the help of modern business machines—personal computers, tablet computers, personal digital assistants, fax machines, copiers, color printers, answering machines, and voice mail—even one person working at home can look like a big business. At one time, the high cost of such technological wizardry made it impossible for small businesses to compete with larger companies that could afford the hardware. Although entrepreneurs may not be able to manufacture heavy equipment in their spare bedrooms, they can run a service- or information-based company from their homes very effectively and look like any *Fortune* 500 company to customers and clients. *For example, Scott Adams, creator of the* Dilbert *cartoon strip that appears in more than 2,000 newspapers worldwide, runs his entire business from a home office that resembles nothing of the cubicles in which his cartoon characters exist. His custom-made desk ("the world's coolest desk," according to Adams) and a host of high-tech gadgetry enable Adams to manage his cartoon strip, his books, and many Dilbert-related products as well as to stay in touch with Dilbert fans via e-mail.*[36]

Company Example →

Independent Lifestyle

Entrepreneurship fits the way Americans want to live—independently and self-sustaining. Increasingly, entrepreneurs are starting businesses for lifestyle reasons. They want the freedom to choose where they live, the hours they work, and what they do. Although financial security remains an important goal for most entrepreneurs, lifestyle issues such as more time with family and friends, more leisure time, and more control over work-related stress are also important. To these "lifestyle entrepreneurs," launching businesses that give them the flexibility to work the hours they prefer and live where they want to live are far more important than money.

E-Commerce and the World Wide Web (WWW)

The proliferation of the **World Wide Web**, the vast network that links computers around the globe via the Internet and opens up endless oceans of information to its users, has spawned thousands of entrepreneurial ventures since its beginning in 1993. Although estimates of the volume of global e-commerce sometimes vary significantly, experts expect worldwide e-commerce sales to climb from $6.8 trillion in 2004 to $12.8 billion in 2006.[37] Small businesses have been slow to capitalize on the opportunity the Web presents, however. A recent survey of small companies found that just 33 percent have Web sites; however, of those companies with Web sites, 78 percent said that their companies benefit from having a site. The most commonly cited benefits were company credibility and more powerful marketing efforts.[38]

Company Example → *Mark Walerstein started GroomsOnline to tap into the market segment that spends more time and more money online than any other: men. As the company's name suggests, GroomsOnline offers grooms advice on everything from selecting a honeymoon location and planning a bachelor party to tips on wedding toasts and choosing gifts for groomsmen, which the site happens to sell. Walerstein says that his best-selling gift for groomsmen is a $56 black personalized Louisville Slugger baseball bat! "I sell close to 100 bats a month," he says.[39]*

International Opportunities

No longer are small businesses limited to pursuing customers within their own borders. The dramatic shift to a global economy has opened the door to tremendous business opportunities for those entrepreneurs willing to reach across the globe. Although the United States is an attractive market for entrepreneurs, approximately 95 percent of the world's population lives outside its borders. With so many opportunities in international markets, even the smallest businesses can sell globally. Small businesses account for 97 percent of all exporters; however, they account for just 33 percent of total export sales. Most small businesses do not take advantage of exporting opportunities; less than 2 percent of the nation's small businesses export their goods and services.[40] As business becomes increasingly global in nature, international opportunities for small businesses will continue to grow rapidly in the future.

Company Example → Although "going global" can be fraught with many dangers and problems, especially for small companies, many entrepreneurs are discovering that selling their products and services in foreign markets is not really as difficult as they originally thought. Patience, diligence, and a management commitment to exporting are essential elements. *In 1955, Betsy and Dave Wilcox developed a recipe for a marinade they used to spice up their meals. In 1978, they launched a business, Allegro Fine Foods, and began selling their line of marinades, first in their hometown of Paris, Tennessee, and ultimately throughout the United States. In 2000, the 25 employees of Allegro recognized the company's potential to expand into global markets and, with the help of the U.S. Commercial Service, began exporting the spicy marinades to shops in Asia and Mexico. Allegro's small town approach, which is based on building personal relationships* *with customers and understanding the nuances of local cultures, has been a key to its exporting success. Bolstered by its early accomplishments in reaching global markets, Allegro managers are exploring export opportunities in Australia, New Zealand, and several European countries.*[41]

IN THE FOOTSTEPS OF AN ENTREPRENEUR...

Under Armour Scores Big!

Kevin Plank may not have been a star when he played college football at the University of Maryland, but he has become an entrepreneurial superstar with the success of Under Armour, the company he founded during his senior year in college. As a special teams captain, Plank grew weary of wearing a heavy, sweat-soaked cotton T-shirt under his football pads. He began to research the properties of various fabrics and produced sample shirts that fit snugly and were extremely lightweight, durable, and capable of wicking away perspiration so that they stayed dry. He tested early prototypes himself and, at first, his teammates laughed at him because the fabric resembled lingerie. Before long, however, those teammates were asking for shirts of their own!

After graduating, Plank received a trademark for the name Under Armour and launched a business from the basement of his grandmother's townhouse in Washington, D.C., which served as the company's first office, warehouse, distribution center—and bedroom. He started the company with $20,000 of his own money and $40,000 in credit card debt that he ran up on five cards before landing a $250,000 loan guaranteed by the U.S. Small Business Administration. Plank used a network of contacts he had developed during his years of playing football to get Under Armour shirts into the hands of top college and professional football players such as Eddie George and Frank Wychek.

Sales for Plank's company started slowly, but he managed to land accounts with the football teams at the University of Arizona and Georgia Technology Institute. "In the summer of 1997," he recalls, "I was totally broke—so broke that I went to my mom's house to see if she minded cooking dinner for me." Then enough orders for Under Armour shirts came in for the company to support itself. The NFL's Atlanta Falcons' equipment manager called and said, "I love the product. Do you make the shirts in long sleeve?" Plank replied, "Of course, we make it in long sleeve." Actually, the company had not yet developed a long sleeve version, but Plank got in his car, drove to the company that was producing the shirts,

and promptly designed a long sleeve version for the Falcons.

Under Armour's first big break came in 1999, when its shirts appeared in the film *Any Given Sunday.* Before the film aired, Plank took out a $25,000 ad in *ESPN* magazine, counting on the movie to attract attention for the small company's products. It worked. Today, thousands of athletes in a variety of sports wear Under Armour clothing, generating more than $110 million in annual sales. The company has since developed six distinct product lines for every playing condition and every season. Athletes from Little League to the pros are dedicated to their Under Armour clothing. Plank's company does not have to pay superstar athletes millions of dollars to wear Under Armour, yet the company gets tremendous amounts of publicity when Barry Bonds, Roger Clemens, Allen Iverson, LaVar Arrington, and others display Under Armour garments on national television.

Plank's bold entrepreneurial moves, aggressive advertising and public relations campaign, and superior product quality have enabled Under Armour to capture nearly 90 percent of the market for compression performance apparel, far surpassing industry giants Nike, Reebok, and Adidas. When asked what the future holds for Under Armour, Plank replies, "We just want to be a great company." It looks as though Under Armour is off to a great start!

1. What risks did Kevin Plank take when he started Under Armour?

2. What obstacles did he have to overcome to achieve success?

3. Work with a group of your classmates to develop a list of lessons you can learn from Kevin Plank and Under Armour about how small companies can compete with much larger firms that have more resources.

Sources: Karen E. Spaeder, "Beyond Their Years: Kevin Plank," *Entrepreneur,* November 2003, p. 76; Kevin Plank and Mark Hyman, "How I Did It," *Inc.,* December 2003, pp. 102–104; "Company Overview," Under Armour, www.underarmour.com/ua2/biz/pages/company_overview.asp.

The Cultural Diversity of Entrepreneurship

6. Discuss the role of diversity in small business and entrepreneurship.

As we have seen, virtually anyone has the potential to become an entrepreneur. The entrepreneurial sector of the United States consists of a rich blend of people of all races, ages, backgrounds, and cultures. It is this cultural diversity that is one of entrepreneurship's greatest strengths. We turn our attention to those who make up this diverse fabric we call entrepreneurship.

Young Entrepreneurs

Young people are setting the pace in entrepreneurship. Disenchanted with their prospects in corporate America and willing to take a chance to control their own destinies, scores of young people are choosing entrepreneurship as their primary career path. Generation X, made up of those people born between 1965 and 1980, is the most entrepreneurial generation in history. Because members of this generation are responsible for 70 percent of all business start-ups, Generation X might be more appropriately called "Generation E."[42] There is no slowdown in sight as Generation Y, the millenials, also begins to flex its entrepreneurial muscles. The Global Entrepreneurship Monitor reports that globally one in six young men and one in 18 young women between the ages of 18 and 29 is involved in starting or running a new business.[43] Surveys also show that more than 80 percent of teenagers in the United States say they hope to launch their own businesses (see Figure 1.3).[44]

Company Example

Randy Eisenman began his entrepreneurial adventures at the age of 16 when he started a fitness training business in his house. He earned a stock brokerage license at the age of 19 and went on to lead the venture capital division Q Investments before launching Handango when he was just 23 years old. Eisenman's experience and contacts in the venture capital business helped him raise $18 million to start Handango, which produces software for mobile computing and communications devices. Eisenman's company is growing rapidly and has partnered with industry giants Microsoft, Palm, and Nokia to reach more than 6 million customers a month![45]

Women Entrepreneurs

Despite years of legislative effort, women still face discrimination in the workforce. However, small business has been a leader in offering women opportunities for economic expression through employment and entrepreneurship. Increasing numbers of women are discovering that the best way to break the "glass ceiling" that prevents them from rising to the top of many organizations is to start their own companies (see Figure 1.4). In fact, women now own 46 percent of all businesses in the United States, many of them in fields that traditionally have

Figure 1.3

Aspiring Teenage Entrepreneurs

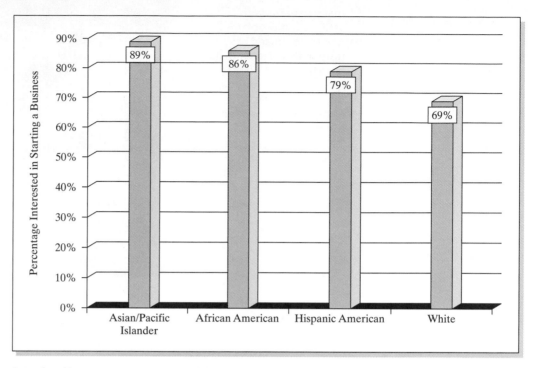

been male dominated.[46] Women entrepreneurs have even broken through the comic strip barrier. Blondie Bumstead, long a typical suburban housewife married to Dagwood, now owns her own catering business with her best friend and neighbor, Tootsie Woodly!

Although the businesses women start tend to be smaller than those that men start, their impact is anything but small. The 10.1 million women-owned companies across the

Figure 1.4

Women-Owned Businesses in the United States

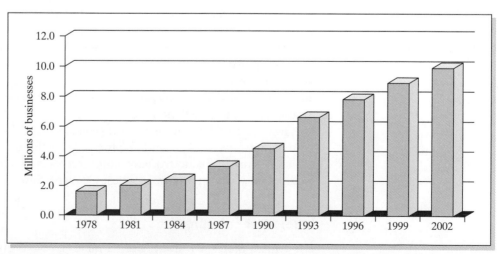

Formally trained as an orthopedic surgeon, Dr. Taryn Rose treated many patients with serious foot problems that were caused by fashion footwear, with its high heels and pointed toes. Spotting a business opportunity, this entrepreneur changed the footwear industry in 1998 by creating a line of luxury shoes that are as comfortable as they are beautiful.

Company Example →

United States employ 18.2 million workers—one-seventh of the nation's workforce—and generate approximately $2.32 trillion in revenues each year.[47]

When she was practicing as an orthopedic surgeon, Taryn Rose saw many patients with serious foot problems caused by high-fashion footwear, many of them women who spent hours each day in high heels with pointed toes. Spotting a business opportunity, Rose created a line of luxury shoes for both men and women that are as comfortable and functional as they are stylish and beautiful. "I targeted a niche—the luxury market—with comfort as a philosophy," she explains. In 1998, she left her medical practice to start a company, Taryn Rose International, which has been featured on CNN, Oprah, Discovery Channel, National Public Radio, and in a host of magazines. Taryn Rose International has grown rapidly, now generating annual sales in excess of $20 million and is exporting its line of shoes to specialty retailers in Japan.[48]

Minority Enterprises

Like women, minorities also are choosing entrepreneurship more often than ever before. Asians, Hispanic Americans, and African Americans, respectively, are most likely to become entrepreneurs. Like women, minorities cite discrimination as a principal reason for their limited access to the world of entrepreneurship. Minority-owned businesses have come a long way in the past decade, however. Increasingly, minorities are finding ways to overcome the barriers to business ownership. A recent study by the Ewing Marion Kaufman Foundation found that African Americans are 50 percent more likely to start a business than whites, and Hispanic Americans are 20 percent more likely.[49] Studies show that the nation's minority entrepreneurs own nearly 3.5 million businesses that generate $600 billion in revenues and employ nearly 4.5 million workers.[50] The future is promising for this new generation of minority entrepreneurs who are better educated, have more business experience, have more entrepreneurial role models, and are better prepared for business ownership than their predecessors.

Immigrant Entrepreneurs

The United States has always been a melting pot of diverse cultures, and many immigrants have been lured to this nation by its economic freedom. Unlike the unskilled

Company Example	→

"huddled masses" of the past, today's immigrants arrive with more education and experience. Although many of them come to the United States with few assets, their dedication and desire to succeed enable them to achieve their entrepreneurial dreams. *Chai Ling's leadership role in the uprising against the Chinese government at Tiananmen Square in 1989 landed her on the government's most wanted list. Hidden inside a cargo crate, she escaped to the United States, where she earned degrees from Princeton and Harvard and was nominated twice for the Nobel Peace Prize. When she graduated from Harvard in 1998, Ling launched Jenzabar (loosely translated from Mandarin as "best and brightest"), a company that provides Web-based software products and services for colleges. The company survived the dot-com implosion and other business obstacles, and its products are used in 20 percent of the universities across the United States, generating more than $50 million in annual sales.*[51]

Part-Time Entrepreneurs

Starting a part-time business is a popular gateway to entrepreneurship. Part-timers have the best of both worlds. They can ease into a business without sacrificing the security of a steady paycheck. Nearly 16 million Americans are self-employed part-time. A major advantage of going into business part-time is the lower risk in case the venture flops. Many part-timers are testing the entrepreneurial waters to see whether their business ideas will work and whether they enjoy being self-employed. As they grow, many part-time enterprises absorb more of the entrepreneur's time until they become full-time businesses.

Home-Based Business Owners

Home-based businesses are booming. A study by Business Communications Inc. estimates that 14 million people in the United States operate businesses from their homes.[52] Indeed, 53 percent of all businesses are home based, but about 80 percent of them are very small with no employees. However, one study reported more than 55,000 home-based businesses generating sales of more than $1 million per year.[53] The biggest advantage home-based businesses offer entrepreneurs is the cost savings of not having to lease or buy an external location. Home-based entrepreneurs also enjoy the benefits of flexible work hours and lifestyles.

In the past, home-based businesses tended to be rather unexciting cottage industries such as crafts or sewing. Today's home-based businesses are more diverse; modern home-based entrepreneurs are more likely to be running high-tech or service companies with millions of dollars in sales. The average home-based entrepreneur works 61 hours a week and earns an income of just over $50,000.[54] Studies by Link Resources Corporation, a research and consulting firm, suggest that the success rate for home-based businesses is high: 85 percent of these businesses are still in operation after three years.[55] Less costly and more powerful technology, which is transforming many ordinary homes into "electronic cottages," will continue to drive the growth of home-based businesses.

Company Example	→

Dorn Kennison launched his business, DMK Productions, a company that creates 3-D computer animations and sound effects for a variety of applications, from his kitchen table. "It was a way to keep costs down during the time my new venture was taking form—and it sure was handy for snacks," he says. As a set designer and visual effects expert in the movie industry, Kennison saw plenty of opportunities for a business creating special effects and animations for movies as well as for architects needing 3-D graphics of the buildings they designed. His first step was to create a business plan, and then he began calling on prospective clients. Although Kennison's business has experienced tremendous growth, he still runs the company from his home in Simi Valley, California.[56]

Table 1.1 offers 18 guidelines home-based entrepreneurs should follow to be successful.

Table 1.1

Managing a Successful Home-Based Business

Eighty-five percent of home-based entrepreneurs are satisfied with their working arrangement. Yet, working from home poses several unique challenges, including feelings of isolation and learning to separate work and home life. How do those who succeed do it? They follow these guidelines.

1. *Do your homework.* Much of a home-based business's potential for success depends on how much preparation an entrepreneur makes *before ever opening for business.* The library is an excellent source for research on customers, industries, competitors, and the like.

2. *Find out what your zoning restrictions are.* In some areas, local zoning laws make running a business from home illegal. Avoid headaches by checking these laws first. You can always request a variance from the local zoning commission.

3. *Choose the most efficient location for your office.* About half of all home-based entrepreneurs operate out of spare bedrooms. The best way to determine the ideal office location is to examine the nature of your business and your clients. Avoid locating your business in your bedroom or your family room.

4. *Focus your home-based business idea.* Avoid the tendency to be "all things to all people." Most successful home-based businesses focus on a particular customer group or in some specialty.

5. *Discuss your business rules with your family.* Running a business from your home means you can spend more time with your family . . . and that your family can spend more time with you. Establish the rules for interruptions up front.

6. *Select an appropriate business name.* Your first marketing decision is your company's name, so make it a good one! Using your own name is convenient, but it's not likely to help you sell your product or service.

7. *Buy the right equipment.* Modern technology enables a home-based entrepreneur to give the appearance of any *Fortune* 500 company—but only if you buy the right equipment. A well-equipped home office should have a separate telephone line, a computer, a laser or inkjet printer, a fax machine (or board), a copier, a scanner, and an answering machine (or voice mail), but realize that you don't have to have everything from day one.

8. *Dress appropriately.* Being an "open-collar worker" is one of the joys of working at home. But when you need to dress up (to meet a client, make a sale, meet your banker, close a deal), do it! Avoid the tendency to lounge around in your bathrobe all day.

9. *Learn to deal with distractions.* The best way to fend off the distractions of working at home is to create a business that truly interests you. Budget your time wisely. Avoid leaving your office except for prescheduled breaks. Your productivity determines your company's success.

10. *Realize that your phone can be your best friend or your worst enemy.* As a home-based entrepreneur, you'll spend lots of time on the phone. Be sure you use it productively. Install a separate phone line for the exclusive use of your business.

11. *Be firm with friends and neighbors.* Sometimes friends and neighbors get the mistaken impression that because you're at home, you're not working. If one drops by to chat while you're working, tactfully ask him or her to come back "after work."

12. *Take advantage of tax breaks.* Although a 1993 Supreme Court decision tightened considerably the standards for business deductions for an office at home, many home-based entrepreneurs still qualify for special tax deductions on everything from computers to cars. Check with your accountant.

13. *Make sure you have adequate insurance coverage.* Many homeowner's policies provide minimal coverage for business-related equipment, leaving many home-based entrepreneurs with inadequate coverage on their business assets. Ask your agent about a business owner's policy (BOP), which may cost as little as $300 to $500 per year.

14. *Understand the special circumstances under which you can hire outside employees.* Sometimes zoning laws allow in-home businesses, but they prohibit hiring employees. Check zoning laws carefully.

15. *Be prepared if your business requires clients to come to your home.* Dress appropriately (no pajamas!). Make sure your office presents a professional image.

16. *Get a post office box.* With burglaries and robberies on the rise, you're better off using a "P.O. Box" address rather than your specific home address. Otherwise, you may be inviting crime.

17. *Network, network, network.* Isolation can be a problem for home-based entrepreneurs, and one of the best ways to combat it is to network. It's also a great way to market your business.

18. *Be proud of your home-based business.* Merely a decade ago there was a stigma attached to working at home. Today, home-based entrepreneurs and their businesses command respect. Be proud of your company!

Sources: Susan Biddle Jaffo. "Balancing Your Home Business," *Nation's Business,* April 1997, pp. 56–58; Ronaleen Roha, "Home Alone," *Kiplinger's Personal Finance Magazine,* May 1997, pp. 85–89; Lynn Beresford, Janean Chun, Cynthia E. Griffan, Heather Page, and Debra Phillips, "Homeward Bound," *Entrepreneur,* September 1995, pp. 116–118; Jenean Huber, "House Rule," *Entrepreneur,* March 1993, pp. 89–95; Hal Morris, "Home-Based Businesses Need Extra Insurance," *AARP Bulletin,* November 1991, p. 16; Stephanie N. Mehta, "What You Need," *Wall Street Journal,* October 14, 1994, p. R10.

Family Business Owners

A **family-owned business** is one that includes two or more members of a family with financial control of the company. They are an integral part of the U.S. economy. Of the 25.5 million businesses in the United States, 90 percent are family owned and managed. These companies account for 60 percent of total employment in the United States, 78 percent of all new jobs, and generate more than 50 percent of the U.S. gross domestic product (GDP). Not all of them are small; 37 percent of the *Fortune* 500 companies are family businesses.[57]

"When it works right," says one writer, "nothing succeeds like a family firm. The roots run deep, embedded in family values. The flash of the fast buck is replaced with long-term plans. Tradition counts."[58] Despite their magnitude, family businesses face a major threat—a threat from within: management succession. Only 33 percent of family businesses survive to the second generation; just 12 percent make it to the third generation; and only 3 percent survive to the fourth generation and beyond.[59] Business periodicals are full of stories describing bitter disputes among family members that have crippled or destroyed once-thriving businesses, usually because the founder failed to create a succession plan. To avoid the senseless destruction of valuable assets, founders of family businesses should develop plans for management succession long before retirement looms before them. We will discuss family businesses and management succession in more detail in Chapter 20.

Copreneurs

Copreneurs are entrepreneurial couples who work together as co-owners of their businesses. The National Federation of Independent Businesses (NFIB) estimates that more than 1.2 million husband-and-wife teams are running companies in the United States.[60] Unlike the traditional "mom and pop" business (Pop as "boss" and Mom as "subordinate"), copreneurs divide their business responsibilities on the basis of their skills, experience, and abilities rather than on gender. Studies suggest that companies co-owned by spouses represent one of the fastest-growing business sectors.

Managing a small business with a spouse may appear to be a recipe for divorce, but most copreneurs say not. "There are days when you want to kill each other," says Mary Duty, who has operated Poppa Rollo's Pizza with her husband for 20 years. "But there's nothing better than working side-by-side with the [person] you love."[61] Successful copreneurs learn to build the foundation for a successful working relationship *before* they ever launch their companies. Some of the techniques they rely on include:

- an assessment of how well their personalities will mesh in a business setting.
- mutual respect for each other and one another's talents.
- compatible business and life goals—a common "vision."
- a view that they are full and equal partners, not a superior and a subordinate.
- complementary business skills that each acknowledges in the other and that lead to a unique business identity for each spouse.
- a clear division of roles and authority—ideally based on each partner's skills and abilities—to minimize conflict and power struggles.
- the ability to keep lines of communication open, talking and listening to each other about personal as well as business issues.
- the ability to encourage each other and to "lift up" a disillusioned partner.
- separate work spaces that enable them to "escape" when the need arises.

- boundaries between their business life and their personal life so that one doesn't consume the other.
- a sense of humor.
- an understanding that not every couple can work together.

Company Example → Although copreneuring isn't for everyone, it works extremely well for many couples and often leads to successful businesses. *Terry and Stella Henry started Vista Del Sol, a long-term-care and assisted-living center in Culver City, California, in 1979. Stella, an experienced registered nurse, manages patient care and employees; Terry handles the company's financial and business matters. The Henrys trust one another to run their respective parts of the business but are careful not to intrude on each other's turf. "In our own spheres," says Stella, "our decisions are final." Although their offices are on different floors of the same building, they discuss business matters over a quiet dinner each day. In the evenings at home, they can focus on family matters and leave their work at the office.*[62]

Corporate Castoffs

Concentrating on trying to operate more efficiently, corporations have been downsizing, shedding their excess bulk, and slashing employment at all levels in the organization. Downsizing victims or "corporate castoffs" have become an important source of entrepreneurial activity. Skittish about experiencing more downsizing at other large companies, many of these castoffs are choosing instead to create their own job security by launching their own businesses. They have decided that the best defense against future job insecurity is an entrepreneurial offense. Armed with years of experience, a tidy severance package, a working knowledge of their industries, and a network of connections, these former managers are setting out to start companies of their own. Some 20 percent of these discharged corporate managers become entrepreneurs, and many of those left behind in corporate America would like to join them.

Company Example → *When Peter Rinnig worked as the art director for Lycos, he earned a large salary, received stock options, and worked on cool projects such as designing the Lycos-sponsored NASCAR race car. Then he was laid off as part of the company's downsizing initiative. Rather than risk becoming a layoff statistic again, Rinnig decided to launch his own business, and it has nothing to do with the high-tech industry. Rinnig started QRST's LLC, a five-person company in Somerville, Massachusetts, that produces screen-printed T-shirts for a wide range of customers. He has already nearly matched his former Lycos salary and, more important, enjoys the excitement and the independence he has running his own business. "I only have to answer to myself," says Rinnig.*[63]

Corporate "Dropouts"

The dramatic downsizing in corporate America has created another effect among the employees left after restructuring: a trust gap. The result of this trust gap is a growing number of dropouts from the corporate structure who then become entrepreneurs. Although their workdays may grow longer and their incomes may shrink, those who strike out on their own often find their work more rewarding and more satisfying because they are doing what they enjoy and they are in control. When one dropout left his corporate post, he invited his former coworkers to a bonfire in the parking lot—fueled by a pile of his expensive business suits! He happily passed out marshmallows to everyone who came. Today, he and his wife run an artists' gallery in California's wine country.[64]

Because they often have college degrees, a working knowledge of business, and years of management experience, both corporate dropouts and castoffs may ultimately increase

Company Example → the small business survival rate. Better-trained, more experienced entrepreneurs are less likely to fail in business. *Kevin Green left a secure career as marketing director for a large architectural and engineering company to purchase The Virginia Florist, a small flower shop that had been in the same location in Alexandria for 43 years. Green recalled that his grandfather had owned a flower shop and had been able to earn a good living even during the Great Depression. When Green and his wife Kathy bought The Virginia Florist, it was generating less than the national average in annual sales. The changes the Greens have made since buying the shop have more than doubled its sales, and they now employ 26 workers, including two full-time floral designers.*[65]

IN THE FOOTSTEPS OF AN ENTREPRENEUR . . .

Not Just Another "Lowly" Business

In 1992, Helene Stone started a computer supply company, Data-Link Associates, from the basement of the Long Island, New York, home she shared with her husband Bobby and their two children. The company sold a wide variety of computer supplies, ranging from storage devices to cleaning kits. Bobby wanted to join the home-based business after he was fired from a sales job he had held for 14 years, but Data-Link Associates was generating only $162,300 in annual sales and was incurring a loss. With the help of a friend who was an experienced entrepreneur, the Stones made changes in their operation and, within two years, the company was generating enough cash flow to support itself and was growing at a healthy pace.

Much of the company's growth is the result of the Stones' strategic use of the Internet as a selling tool. Shortly after their son Steven joined the family business, the Stones turned him loose to set up a company Web site and to learn the finer points of Web-based marketing, including techniques to get Data-Link Associates' products listed in premier placement in key search engines. The move paid off; 98 percent of the company's new business comes from the Web, which enables the Stones to focus on selling—following up on leads from the Web site and contacting existing customers via e-mail and fax using the 23,000 names in the company's customer database.

In 2002, Bobby learned that a Canadian manufacturer of high-quality media storage cabinets was looking for distributors in the United States. The cabinets fit perfectly with Data-Link Associates' product line, so Bobby contacted the company's international sales manager, who was coming to the United States to interview candidates. The sales manager agreed to put Data-Link Associates on the list of companies and set up an appointment.

Accustomed to dealing with businesses located in office buildings or industrial parks, the sales manager was quite surprised when he stopped his rental car in front of the Stones' house in the middle of a residential section. Helene answered the door, holding her three-year-old granddaughter in her arms. Bobby then escorted the sales manager to the "business entrance" at the rear of the house and into company headquarters, the basement, which also served as the packing and shipping dock. Winding their way through the clutter of computer equipment to which Bobby was oblivious and into a dining room that doubled as the company's conference room, the sales manager didn't know what to think—or to say. "He was in shock," recalls Helene. "He kept looking at us like, 'What's going on here?' He couldn't believe the numbers we were churning out. It just blew him away that we were running the business out of a basement with no sales force. He had a million questions."

The Stones answered them all.

It began to dawn on the sales manager that what the Stones' business lacked in polish and panache, it more than made up for in creativity and resourcefulness. Bobby and Helene explained how they had used the Internet to develop relationships with customers all over the world by landing superior placement in Web search engines, how they identify key trends and use that information to decide which promotions to run, and how they had improved the collection rate on their accounts receivable. Ninety minutes later, the Stones escorted their guest out the front door of their home.

Back in Canada, the sales manager told his colleagues about his unusual visit to Data-Link Associates. They shook their heads and laughed. Then the sales manager shocked them all when he said, "I'm choosing Data-Link as one of our five U.S. distributors." They thought he had lost his mind, but he assured them that there was something about the Stones, the way they had explained their business strategy, and the passion they had for their home-based business that convinced him that the relationship would be a successful one. He was right: In the first year, Data-Link Associates outsold the other four distributors the Canadian company had selected! Today, Data-Link Associates has six employees, generates $2.6 million in sales, and is still located right where it began: in the basement of the Stones' home on Long Island.

1. What benefits have the Stones realized by running their business out of their basement?

2. What risks do entrepreneurs encounter when they operate a home-based business?
3. What implications does the World Wide Web have for home-based businesses?

Sources: Norm Brodsky, "Street Smarts: Ya Gotta Love It," *Inc.,* November 2003, pp. 43–44; Brodsky, "An Internet Model That Works," *Inc.,* May 2001, pf.inc.com/magazine/20010501/22481.html.

The Contributions of Small Businesses

7. Describe the contributions small businesses make to the U.S. economy.

Of the 25.5 million businesses in the United States today, approximately 25.1 million, or 98.5 percent, can be considered "small." Although there is no universal definition of a small business, a common delineation of a **small business** is one that employs fewer than 100 people. They thrive in virtually every industry, although the majority of small companies are concentrated in the service and retail industries (see Figure 1.5). Their contributions to the economy are as numerous as the businesses themselves. For example, small companies employ 52 percent of the nation's private sector workforce, even though they possess less than one-fourth of total business assets.[66] Small companies also pay 45 percent of the total private payroll in the United States. Because they are primarily labor intensive, small businesses actually create more jobs than do big businesses. The Small Business Administration estimates that small companies created 75.8 percent of the nation's net new jobs.[67] David Birch, president of the research firm Cognetics, says that the ability to create jobs is not distributed evenly across the small business sector, however. His research shows that just 6 percent of these small companies created 70 percent of the net new jobs, and they did so across all industry sectors—not just in "hot" industries. Birch calls these job-creating small companies "gazelles," those growing at 20 percent or more per year with at least $100,000 in annual sales. His research also identified "mice," small companies that never grow much and don't create many jobs. The majority of small companies are "mice." Birch tabbed the country's largest job-shedding businesses "elephants," which continued to cut jobs through the past decade.[68]

Not only do small companies lead the way in creating jobs, but they also bear the brunt of training workers for them. Small businesses provide 67 percent of workers with their first jobs and basic job training. Small companies offer more general skills instruction and training than large ones, and their employees receive more benefits from the training than do those in larger firms. Although their training tends to be informal, in-house, and on-the-job programs, small companies teach employees valuable skills—from written communication to computer literacy.[69]

Figure 1.5

A Profile of Small Business by Industry

Source: U.S. Small Business Administration, 2002.

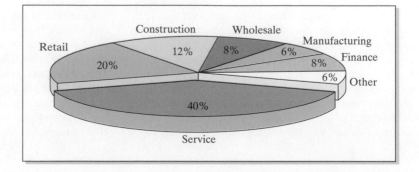

Small businesses also produce 51 percent of the country's private sector gross domestic product (GDP) and account for 47 percent of business sales.[70] In fact, the U.S. small business sector is the world's third largest economy, trailing only the economies of the United States and Japan.[71] Small businesses also play an integral role in creating new products, services, and processes. Two-thirds of all new inventions are created by small companies.[72] Research conducted for the National Science Foundation concluded that small firms create four times more innovations per research and development (R&D) dollar than medium-sized firms and 24 times as many as large companies. Another study found that small companies produce 13 to 14 times more patents per employee than do large firms, and many of those patents are among the most significant inventions in their fields.[73] Many important inventions trace their roots to an entrepreneur; for example, the zipper, the personal computer, FM radio, air conditioning, the escalator, the lightbulb, and the automatic transmission all originated in small businesses. Entrepreneurs continue to create innovations in many important areas ranging from energy to communications. Earthfirst Technologies has developed a system that produces both a clean-burning fuel called MagneGas from contaminated water or sewage and irrigation-quality water.[74] ActiveSky Inc. is developing a compression technology that squeezes data down to a size that can be sent to a multitude of wireless portable devices such as cell phones, personal digital assistants, and others. Users will be able to receive video and multimedia images practically anywhere in the world.[75]

Eleven Deadly Mistakes of Entrepreneurship

8. Explain the reasons small businesses fail.

The median age of U.S. companies is 12 years, and nearly half of the companies in the United States have been in business for at least 15 years.[76] Many businesses don't last that long, however. Studies by the Small Business Administration (SBA) suggest that 50 percent of new businesses will have failed within four years. Because of their limited resources, inexperienced management, and lack of financial stability, small businesses suffer relatively high mortality rates. Exploring the causes of business failure may help to avoid it.

Management Incompetence

In most small businesses, management inexperience or poor decision making ability is the chief problem of the failing enterprise. Sometimes the manager of the small business does not have the capacity to operate it successfully. The owner lacks the leadership ability and knowledge necessary to make the business work. Many managers simply do not have what it takes to run a small enterprise. *Andrew Kay was a pioneer in the earliest days*

Company Example ➤ *of the portable computer with his Kaypro model (which in 1981 weighed in at a hefty 25 pounds and had 64 KB of RAM). Unfortunately, he had no experience in running a high-tech start-up and despite the popularity of his computer, Kay made a series of managerial blunders that ultimately forced the company into bankruptcy.*[77]

Lack of Experience

Small business managers need to have experience in the field they want to enter. For example, those who want to open a retail clothing business should first work in a retail clothing store. This will give them practical experience as well as help them learn the nature of the business. This type of experience can spell the difference between failure and success. One West Coast entrepreneur had always wanted to own a restaurant, but he had no experience in the restaurant business. He later admitted that he thought that running a restaurant consisted primarily of dressing up in black tie, greeting his regular customers at the door, and showing them to his best tables. He invested $150,000 of his own money and found a partner to put up more capital and to help manage the restaurant. They opened and immediately ran into trouble because they knew nothing about running a restaurant. Eventually, the restaurant closed, and the partners lost their original investments, their homes, and their cars; they also spent the next several years paying off back taxes.[78]

Ideally, a prospective entrepreneur should have adequate technical ability; a working knowledge of the physical operations of the business; sufficient conceptual ability, the power to visualize, coordinate, and integrate the various operations of the business into a synergistic whole; and the skill to manage the people in the organization and motivate them to higher levels of performance.

Forcing a Flawed Idea

Another cause of business failure is launching a business based on a concept that is fundamentally flawed. Thousands of dot-com entrepreneurs folded their companies when they discovered that merely drawing people to a Web site was insufficient for business success. Their business models simply made no sense because there was no way for them to generate a profit without producing a sale. Other entrepreneurs launch businesses without identifying how they will reach their customers efficiently and profitably. *For instance, after he and his brother launched and then sold the highly successful Borders Book Store chain, Louis Borders launched the ill-fated Web-based grocery store Webvan. Customers would order groceries over the Web, and delivery crews would deliver them to customers' homes. The model required Webvan to build a large, highly automated warehouse in every city in which it would operate and to assemble a fleet of vans and trucks for home delivery. Unfortunately, customers stayed away in droves, and Webvan burned through $1 billion of investors' money before crashing.*[79] Preparing a solid business plan, the topic of Chapter 6, enables entrepreneurs to measure their ideas against the yardstick of reality and avoid such costly mistakes.

Company Example

Undercapitalization

Sound management is the key to a small company's success, and effective managers realize that any successful business venture requires proper financial control. The margin for error in managing finances is especially small for most small businesses, and neglecting to install proper financial controls is a recipe for disaster. Two pitfalls affecting a small business's financial health are common: undercapitalization and poor cash management. Many small business owners make the mistake of beginning their businesses on a shoestring, a fatal error which may lead to business failure. Entrepreneurs tend to be overly optimistic and often underestimate the financial requirements of launching a business or the amount of time required for the company to become self-sustaining. As a result, they start off undercapitalized and can never seem to catch up financially as their companies consume increasing amounts of cash to fuel their growth. One key to success with a business start-up is to begin with enough capital to get the company to the point at which it can support itself with its own cash flow.

Poor Cash Management

Insufficient cash flow due to poor cash management is a common cause of business failure. Many entrepreneurs believe that profit is what matters most in a new venture, but cash is the most important financial resource a business owns. Companies need adequate cash flow to thrive; without it, a company is out of business. Maintaining adequate cash flow to pay bills in a timely fashion is a constant challenge for small companies, especially those in the turbulent start-up phase or more established companies experiencing rapid growth. Fast-growing companies devour cash fast! Poor credit and collection practices on accounts receivable, sloppy accounts payable practices that exert undue pressure on a company's cash balance, and uncontrolled spending are common to many small business bankruptcies. When it comes to managing expenses, one experienced business owner advises entrepreneurs to "throw nickels around like manhole covers."[80]

Company Example →

The founders of Boo.com, a highly publicized Internet clothing retailer, failed to establish adequate financial controls in the business, and it ultimately caused the company to run out of cash and fold. Boo.com had little trouble attracting capital, but its founders were careless in their spending habits, pouring millions into a complex Web site that launched late and failed to meet customer expectations. Although the company's sales reached $1.1 million per month, its expenses were running 10 times that amount! The company's cash drained away, and by the time the company went into bankruptcy, it had burned through more than $135 million of investors' capital and had become one of the highest-profile failures in the "dot-com" crash.[81]

Lack of Strategic Management

Too many small business managers neglect the process of strategic management because they think that it is something that benefits only large companies. "I don't have the time" or "We're too small to develop a strategic plan," they rationalize. Failure to plan, however, usually results in failure to survive. Without a clearly defined strategy, a business has no sustainable basis for creating and maintaining a competitive edge in the marketplace. Building a strategic plan forces an entrepreneur to assess *realistically* the proposed business's potential. Is it something customers are willing and able to purchase? Who is the target customer? How will the business attract and keep those customers? What is the company's basis for serving customers' needs better than existing companies? We will explore these and other vital issues in Chapter 2.

Weak Marketing Effort

Sometimes entrepreneurs make the classic *Field of Dreams* mistake. Like Kevin Costner's character in the movie, they believe that if they build it, customers automatically will come. Although the idea makes for a great movie plot, in business, it almost never happens.

Company Example →

Stephen Mason and Alan Davis, cofounders of Catamount Brewery, one of New England's first microbreweries, discovered the importance of marketing the hard way. Early on, customers who were intrigued by the romance and mystique of microbreweries flocked to Catamount's unique beers. The company's marketing efforts amounted to no more than Davis "getting in a car and calling on [customer] accounts." Within six years, Catamount's production had climbed from 3,500 barrels a year to 12,000 barrels a year. Unfortunately, its marketing efforts did not keep pace. Sales slipped as customers drifted away, and the company could not generate enough cash to repay the debt it took on to expand its plant, forcing it into bankruptcy.[82]

Business success requires a sustained, creative marketing effort to draw a base of customers and to keep them coming back. This is especially true for start-up companies. As you will see in Chapter 7, that does *not* mean that entrepreneurs must spend vast amounts of money on costly marketing and advertising campaigns. Creative entrepreneurs find ways to market their businesses effectively to their target customers without breaking the bank. One technique many small business owners find particularly valuable is listening to their customers. Asking for their suggestions and paying attention to what they say can give a small company an edge over much larger competitors.

Uncontrolled Growth

Growth is a natural, healthy, and desirable part of any business enterprise, but it must be planned and controlled. Management expert Peter Drucker says that start-up companies can expect to outgrow their capital bases each time sales increase 40 to 50 percent.[83] Ideally, entrepreneurs finance the expansion of their companies by the profits they generate (retained earnings) or by capital contributions from the owner(s), but most businesses wind up borrowing at least a portion of the capital investment.

Expansion usually requires major changes in organizational structure, business practices such as inventory and financial control procedures, personnel assignments, and other areas. But the most important change occurs in managerial expertise. As the business increases in size and complexity, problems tend to increase in proportion, and the manager must learn to deal with this. Sometimes entrepreneurs encourage rapid growth, and the business outstrips their ability to manage it. *Shortly after Lyle Bowin launched his Web-based bookstore, Positively You, his home-based business was featured in the* New York Times, Time *magazine,* Good Morning America, *and Fox News. Almost overnight, sales skyrocketed from $2,000 a month to more than $50,000 a month. Bowlin and his small staff were overwhelmed by the sales volume, and the company lacked the capital base and the cash flow to finance the unplanned growth. Even worse, Bowlin's lack of experience in running a growing business left a leadership void. "Nobody knew who was in charge or who answered to whom," says one former employee. Within months, Positively You had become just another business failure statistic.*[84]

Company Example

Poor Location

For any business, choosing the right location is partly an art and partly a science. Too often, entrepreneurs select their locations without adequate research and investigation. Some beginning owners choose a particular location just because they noticed a vacant building. But the location question is much too critical to leave to chance. Especially for retailers, the choice of a location influences heavily the lifeblood of the business—sales. One small merchandiser located in a rural area was heavily dependent on the customers of a nearby restaurant for her clientele. When the restaurant folded, sales at the small retail store suffered, and the business failed.

Another factor to consider in selecting location is the rental rate. Although it is prudent not to pay an excessive amount for rent, business owners should weigh the cost against the location's effect on sales. Location has two important features: what it costs and what it generates in sales volume.

Lack of Inventory Control

Normally, the largest investment the small business owner must make is in inventory; yet, inventory control is one of the most neglected of all managerial responsibilities. Insufficient inventory levels result in shortages and stockouts, causing customers to become disillusioned and not return. A more common situation is that the manager not only has too much inventory but also too much of the wrong type of inventory. Many small firms have an excessive amount of working capital tied up in an accumulation of needless inventory. Poor inventory management translates directly into strains on a company's cash flow.

One entrepreneur who had managed several service companies successfully for many years became a partner in a business that sold gift items to high-end retail outlets and gift stores. He had never operated a business that carried inventory, however, and his inexperience showed. The six-month inventory supply the company had planned to maintain quickly blossomed to a 12-month supply, and the cost of carrying that extra inventory was a drag on cash flow. With $750,000 invested in the business, the entrepreneur began looking for someone to buy the company at a bargain price, one that would yield a $350,000 loss for him, which he would "chalk up to my ongoing business education," he says.[85] We will discuss both purchasing and inventory control techniques in Section VII.

Inability to Make the Entrepreneurial Transition

If a business fails, it is most likely to do so in its first five years of life. Making it over the "entrepreneurial start-up hump," however, is no guarantee of business success. After the start-up, growth usually requires a radically different style of leadership and management. Many businesses fail when their founders are unable to make the transition from entrepreneur to manager and are unwilling to bring in a professional management team. The very abilities that make an entrepreneur successful often lead to *managerial* ineffectiveness. Growth requires entrepreneurs to delegate authority and to relinquish hands-on control of daily operations, something many entrepreneurs simply can't do. Their business's success requires that they avoid micromanaging and become preservers and promoters of their companies' vision, values, and culture.

When the founder of a successful software company needed capital to fund his company's growth, he turned to professional venture capital firms. With the capital infusion, the company founder successfully guided the company past the $10 million sales level. When the business shifted its focus from government contracts to commercial sales, however, the founder's skills and experience were lacking. Investors asked him to step aside for another CEO who was able to manage that transition and take the company public.[86]

Putting Failure into Perspective

9. Put business failure into proper perspective.

Because they are building businesses in an environment filled with uncertainty and shaped by rapid change, entrepreneurs recognize that failure is likely to be a part of their lives; yet, they are not paralyzed by that fear. "The excitement of building a new business from scratch is far greater than the fear of failure," says one entrepreneur who failed in business several times before finally succeeding.[87] Instead, they use their failures as a rallying point and as a means of defining their companies' reason for being more clearly. They see failure for what it really is: an opportunity to learn what doesn't work! Successful entrepreneurs have the attitude that failures are simply stepping-stones along the path to success. Walt Disney was fired from a newspaper job because, according to his boss, he "lacked ideas." Disney also went bankrupt several times before he created Disneyland.

Failure is a natural part of the creative process. The only people who never fail are those who never do anything or never attempt anything new. Baseball fans know that Babe Ruth held the record for career home runs (714) for many years, but how many know that he also held the record for strikeouts (1,330)? Successful entrepreneurs realize that hitting an entrepreneurial home run requires a few strikeouts along the way, and they are willing to accept that. Lillian Vernon, who started her mail-order company with $2,000 in wedding present money, says, "Everybody stumbles. . . . The true test is how well you pick yourself up and move on, and whether you're willing to learn from that."[88]

One hallmark of successful entrepreneurs is the ability to fail *intelligently*, learning why they failed so that they can avoid making the same mistake again. They know that business success does not depend so much on their ability to avoid making mistakes as on being open to the lessons each mistake brings. They learn from their failures and use them as fuel to push themselves closer to their ultimate target. Entrepreneurs are less worried about what they might lose if they try something and fail than about what they miss if they fail to try.

Entrepreneurial success requires both persistence and resilience, the ability to bounce back from failures. Thomas Edison discovered about 1,800 ways *not* to build a lightbulb before hitting on a design that worked—and revolutionized the world. Entrepreneur Bryn Kaufman explains this "don't quit" attitude by saying, "If you are truly an entrepreneur, giving up is not an option."[89]

How to Avoid the Pitfalls

10. Explain how small business owners can avoid the major pitfalls of running a business.

As valuable as failure can be to the entrepreneurial process, no one sets out to fail. We have seen some of the most common reasons behind small business failures. Now we must examine the ways to avoid becoming another failure statistic and gain insight into what makes a start-up successful. Entrepreneurial success requires much more than just a good idea for a product or service. It also takes a solid plan of execution, adequate resources (including capital and people), the ability to assemble and manage those resources, and perseverance. The following suggestions for success follow naturally from the causes of business failures.

Know Your Business in Depth

We have already emphasized the need for the right type of experience in the business. Get the best education in your business area you possibly can *before* you set out on your own. Read everything you can—trade journals, business periodicals, books, Web pages—relating to your industry. Personal contact with suppliers, customers, trade associations, and others in the same industry is another excellent way to get important knowledge.

Company Example →

Before she launched Stephanie Anne Room to Grow, a chain of stores selling upscale furniture for babies and children, Stephanie Anne Kantis had career stints at a major department store and a small interior design/furniture store. In both jobs, she picked up many valuable tips on everything from how to check in merchandise to establishing employee policy manuals and identified the key factors required for success in her industry.[90] Like Kantis, successful entrepreneurs are like sponges, soaking up as much knowledge as they can from a variety of sources, and they continue to learn about their businesses, markets, and customers as long as they are in business.

Prepare a Business Plan

To wise entrepreneurs, a well-written business plan is a crucial ingredient in business success. Without a sound business plan, a company merely drifts along without any real direction and often stalls out when it faces its first challenge. Yet, entrepreneurs, who tend to be people of action, too often jump right into a business venture without taking time to prepare a written plan outlining the essence of the business. "Most entrepreneurs don't have a solid business plan," says one business owner. "But a thorough business plan and timely financial information are critical. They help you make the important decisions about your business; you constantly have to monitor what you're doing against your plan."[91]

Although uncertainty is a part of any business start-up, preparing a business plan enables entrepreneurs to replace "I think" with "I know" in many important areas of a business. In many cases, entrepreneurs attempt to build businesses on faulty assumptions such as "I think there are enough customers in town to support a health food store." Experienced entrepreneurs investigate these assumptions and replace them with facts before making the decision to go into business. We will discuss the process of developing a business plan in Chapter 6.

Manage Financial Resources

The best defense against financial problems is developing a practical financial information system and then using this information to make business decisions. No entrepreneur can maintain control over a business unless he or she is able to judge its financial health.

The first step in managing financial resources effectively is to have adequate start-up capital. Too many entrepreneurs begin their businesses with too little capital. One experienced business owner advises, "Estimate how much capital you need to get the business going and then double that figure." His point is well taken; it almost always costs more to launch a business than any entrepreneur expects. Establishing a relationship early on with at least one reliable lender who understands your business is a good way to gain access to financing when your company needs capital for growth or expansion.

The most valuable financial resource to any small business is *cash*; successful entrepreneurs learn early on to manage it carefully. Although earning a profit is essential to long-term survival, a business must have an adequate supply of cash to pay its bills and meet its obligations. Some entrepreneurs count on growing sales to supply their company's cash needs, but it almost never happens. Growing companies usually consume more cash than they generate, and the faster they grow, the more cash they gobble up! We will discuss cash management techniques in Chapter 9.

Understand Financial Statements

Every business owner must depend on records and financial statements to know the condition of his or her business. All too often, these records are used only for tax purposes and are not employed as vital control devices. To truly understand what is going on in the business, an owner must have at least a basic understanding of accounting and finance.

When analyzed and interpreted properly, these financial statements are reliable indicators of a small firm's health. They can be quite helpful in signaling potential problems. For example, declining sales, slipping profits, rising debt, and deteriorating working capital are all symptoms of potentially lethal problems that require immediate attention. We will discuss financial statement analysis in Chapter 8.

Learn to Manage People Effectively

No matter what kind of business you launch, you must learn to manage people. Every business depends on a foundation of well-trained, motivated employees. No business owner can do everything alone. The people an entrepreneur hires ultimately determine the heights to which the company can climb—or the depths to which it can plunge. Attracting and retaining a corps of quality employees is no easy task, however; it remains a challenge for every small business owner. One entrepreneur alienated employees with a memo chastising them for skipping lines on interoffice envelopes (the cost of a skipped line was two-thirds of a penny) while he continued to use a chauffeur-driven luxury car and to stay at exclusive luxury hotels while traveling on business.[92] Entrepreneurs quickly learn that treating their employees with respect, dignity, and compassion usually translates into their employees treating customers in the same fashion. Successful entrepreneurs value their employees and constantly find ways to show it. We will discuss the techniques of managing and motivating people effectively in Chapter 19.

Set Your Business Apart from the Competition

The formula for almost certain business failure involves becoming a "me-too business"—merely copying whatever the competition is doing. Most successful entrepreneurs find a way to convince their customers that their companies are superior to their competitors even if they sell similar products or services. It is especially important for small companies going up against larger, more powerful rivals with greater financial resources. Ideally, the basis for differentiating a company from its competitors is founded in what it does best. For small companies, that basis often is customer service, convenience, speed, quality, or whatever else is important to attracting and keeping happy customers. We will discuss the strategies for creating a unique footprint in the marketplace in Chapter 7.

Keep in Tune with Yourself

"Starting a business is like running a marathon. If you're not physically and mentally in shape, you'd better do something else,'" says one business consultant.[93] Managing a successful business, especially in the early days, requires *lots* of time, energy, and enthusiasm. Therefore, good health is essential. Stress is a primary problem for many entrepreneurs, especially if it is not kept in check.

Achieving business success also requires an entrepreneur to be maintain a positive mental attitude toward business and the discipline to stick with it. Successful entrepreneurs recognize that their most valuable resource is their time, and they learn to manage it effectively to make themselves and their companies more productive. None of this, of course, is possible without passion—passion for their businesses, their products or services, their customers, their communities. Passion is what enables a failed business owner to get back up, try again, and make it to the top! One business writer says that growing a successful business requires entrepreneurs to have great faith in themselves and their ideas, great doubt concerning the challenges and inevitable obstacles they will face as they build their businesses, and great effort—lots of hard work—to make their dreams become reality.[94]

As you can see, entrepreneurship lies at the heart of this nation's free enterprise system; small companies truly are the backbone of our economy. Their contributions are as many and as diverse as the businesses themselves. Indeed, diversity is one of the strengths of the U.S. small business sector. Although there are no secrets to becoming a successful entrepreneur, there are steps that entrepreneurs can take to enhance the probability of their success. The remainder of this book will explore those steps.

▌▌▌ Chapter Review

1. Define the role of the entrepreneur in the U.S. economy.
   - Record numbers of people have launched companies over the past decade. The boom in entrepreneurship is not limited solely to the United States; many nations across the globe are seeing similar growth in the small business sector. Various competitive, economic, and demographic shifts have created a world in which "small is beautiful."
   - Society depends on entrepreneurs to provide the drive and risk taking necessary for the business system to supply people with the goods and services they need.

2. Describe the entrepreneurial profile.
   - Entrepreneurs have some common characteristics, including a desire for responsibility, a preference for moderate risk, confidence in their ability to succeed, desire for immediate feedback, a high energy level, a future orientation, skill at organizing, and a value of achievement over money. In a phrase, they are high achievers.

3. Describe the benefits of owning a small business.
   - Driven by these personal characteristics, entrepreneurs establish and manage small businesses to gain control over their lives, become self-fulfilled, reap unlimited profits, contribute to society, and do what they enjoy doing.

4. Describe the potential drawbacks of owning a small business.
   - Small business ownership has some potential drawbacks. There are no guarantees that the business will make a profit or even survive. The time and energy required to manage a new business may have dire effects on the owner and family members.

5. Explain the forces that are driving the growth in entrepreneurship.
   - Several factors are driving the boom in entrepreneurship, including entrepreneurs portrayed as heroes, better entrepreneurial education, economic and demographic factors, a shift to a service economy, technological advancements, more independent lifestyles, and increased international opportunities.

6. Discuss the role of diversity in small business and entrepreneurship.
   - Several groups are leading the nation's drive toward entrepreneurship—women, minorities, immigrants, part-timers, home-based business owners, family business owners, copreneurs, corporate castoffs, and corporate dropouts.

7. Describe the contributions small businesses make to the U.S. economy.
   - The small business sector's contributions are many. They make up 99 percent of all businesses, employ 53 percent of the private sector workforce, create 75.8 percent of the new jobs in the economy, produce 51 percent of the country's private gross domestic product (GDP), and account for 47 percent of business sales.

8. Explain the reasons small businesses fail.
   - The failure rate for small businesses is higher than for big businesses, and profits fluctuate with general economic conditions. SBA statistics show that 60 percent of new businesses will have failed within six years. The primary cause of business failure is incompetent management. Other reasons include poor financial control, failure to plan, inappropriate location, lack of inventory control, improper managerial attitudes, and inability to make the "entrepreneurial transition."

9. Put business failure into the proper perspective.
   - Because they are building businesses in an environment filled with uncertainty and shaped by rapid change, entrepreneurs recognize that failure is likely to be a part of their lives; yet, they are not paralyzed by that fear. Successful entrepreneurs have the attitude that failures are simply stepping stones along the path to success.

10. Explain how small business owners can avoid the major pitfalls of running a business.
    - There are several general tactics small business owners can employ to avoid failure. Entrepreneurs should know the business in depth, develop a solid business plan, manage financial resources effectively, understand financial statements, learn to manage people effectively, set the business apart from the competition, and keep in tune with themselves.

▌▐▐▐ Discussion Questions

1. What forces have led to the boom in entrepreneurship in the United States?
2. What is an entrepreneur? Give a brief description of the entrepreneurial profile.
3. *Inc.* magazine claims, "Entrepreneurship is more mundane than it's sometimes portrayed . . . you don't need to be a person of mythical proportions to be very, very successful in building a company." Do you agree? Explain.
4. What are the major benefits of business ownership?
5. Which of the potential drawbacks to business ownership are most critical?
6. Briefly describe the role of the following groups in entrepreneurship: women, minorities, immigrants,

part-timers, home-based business owners, family business owners, copreneurs, corporate castoffs, and corporate dropouts.

7. What contributions do small businesses make to our economy?

8. Describe the small business failure rate.

9. Outline the causes of business failure. Which problems cause most business failures?

10. How can the small business owner avoid the common pitfalls that often lead to business failures?

11. Why is it important to study the small business failure rate?

12. Explain the typical entrepreneur's attitude toward failure.

13. One entrepreneur says that too many people "don't see that by spending their lives afraid of failure, they *become* failures. But when you go out there and risk as I have, you'll have failures along the way, but eventually the result is great success if you are willing to keep risking . . . For every big 'yes' in life, there will be 199 'nos.'" Do you agree? Explain.

14. What advice would you offer an entrepreneurial friend who has just suffered a business failure?

15. Noting the growing trend among collegiate entrepreneurs launching businesses while still in school, one educator says, "A student whose main activity on campus is running a business is missing the basic reason for being here, which is to get an education." Do you agree? Explain.

Entrepreneurs: The Driving Force Behind Small Business

Business PlanPro

Your copy of this book may have come with the best-selling business planning software package Business Plan Pro, which serves as a valuable guide for you as you begin to build a business plan. Business Plan Pro includes a series of simple questions for you to answer concerning your proposed business venture. It also provides advice for making key business decisions and contains a number of "wizards" that make creating financial forecasts very easy. At the end of each chapter in this book, you will find a Business Plan Pro activity relating to the concepts in that chapter. By completing these activities, you will build your plan one step at a time. At first, creating a business plan may seem like an overwhelming task. However, by building your plan one step at a time, you will find it to be a manageable and perhaps even enjoyable process. Use Business Plan Pro as your business planning guide, and complete your plan across the course of the semester.

Install and launch Business Plan Pro according to the instructions included on the CD. When you launch Business Plan Pro for the first time, you may want to open the Sample Plan Browser, which enables you to preview sample business plans created with this software package. We encourage you to take some time to look over several of these sample plans so that you get a clear understanding of the form your finished plan will take. You'll find plenty of samples in all types of industries, from an accounting firm to a yoga center.

Once you've reviewed several sample plans, return to the main program and open a file for a new business plan. This will take you to the Plan Setup portion of Business Plan Pro's EasyPlan Wizard. This wizard lays the foundation for your business plan by asking you a variety of basic questions about the nature of the business you plan to launch. The wizard asks you the following series of questions about your proposed business venture:

- Do you sell products, services, or both?
- Is your business a profit or a nonprofit organization?
- Is your business a start-up operation or an ongoing business?
- Do you want to create a more detailed or a less detailed business plan?
- Do you plan to import financial data from QuickBooks?
- Do you want to include a second year of forecasts for your financial statements?
- Under Table Settings, the wizard asks you several questions about the forecasted financial statements in your plan. Answer each question.
- Do you have a Web site?
- Do you want to prepare a standard-term (one year of monthly financial forecasts and two years of annual forecasts) or a long-term plan (one year of monthly financial forecasts and four years of annual forecasts)?

- What is the target date for starting your business?
- What title do you want to give your business plan?

The final screen in the wizard asks you to provide the name, address, telephone number, fax number, and e-mail address for your company. Now that you have provided this information, you are on your way to building a business plan for your company. Completing the process takes time and perseverance, but the payoffs are well worth everything you invest. You have a better chance at building a successful business if you take the time to create a winning business plan.

Business Plan Pro will help you build your plan one step at a time. Congratulations on getting off to a great start! Business Plan Pro will have some more questions for you when you finish reading Chapter 2.

Chapter 2

Strategic Management and the Entrepreneur

> *A rock pile ceases to be a rock pile the moment a single man contemplates it, bearing within him the image of a cathedral.*
> —ANTOINE DE SAINT-EXUPERY

> *If you do not think about the future, you cannot have one.*
> —JOHN GALSWORTHY

Upon completion of this chapter, you will be able to:

1. Understand the importance of strategic management to a small business.

2. Explain why and how a small business must create a competitive advantage in the market.

3. Develop a strategic plan for a business using the nine steps in the strategic planning process.

4. Discuss the characteristics of three basic strategies: low cost, differentiation, and focus.

5. Understand the importance of controls, such as the balanced scorecard, in the planning process.

1. Understand the importance of strategic management to a small business.

ew activities in the life of a business are as vital—or as overlooked—as that of developing a strategy for success. Too often, entrepreneurs brimming with optimism and enthusiasm launch businesses destined for failure because their founders never stop to define a workable strategy that sets them apart from their competition. Because they tend to be people of action, entrepreneurs often find the process of developing a strategy dull and unnecessary. Their tendency is to start a business, try several approaches, and see what works. Without a cohesive plan of action, however, these entrepreneurs have as much chance of building a successful business as a defense contractor attempting to build a jet fighter without blueprints. Companies lacking clear strategies may achieve some success in the short run, but as soon as competitive conditions stiffen or an unanticipated threat arises, they usually "hit the wall" and fold. Without a basis for differentiating itself from a pack of similar competitors, the best a company can hope for is mediocrity in the marketplace.

In today's global competitive environment, any business, large or small, that is not thinking and acting strategically is extremely vulnerable. Every business is exposed to the forces of a rapidly changing competitive environment, and in the future small business executives can expect even greater change and uncertainty. From sweeping political changes around the planet and rapid technological advances to more intense competition and newly emerging global markets, the business environment has become more turbulent and challenging to business owners. Although this market turbulence creates many challenges for small businesses, it also creates opportunities for those companies that have in place strategies to capitalize on them. Historically important, entrepreneurs' willingness to create change, to experiment with new business models, and to break traditional rules has become more important than ever.

Perhaps the biggest change business owners face is unfolding now: the shift in the world's economy from a base of *financial to intellectual* capital. "Knowledge is no longer just a factor of production," says futurist Alvin Toffler. "It is the *critical* factor of production."[1] Today, a company's intellectual capital is likely to be the source of its competitive advantage in the marketplace. **Intellectual capital** is comprised of three components:[2]

1. *Human capital,* the talents, skills, and abilities of a company's workforce.
2. *Structural capital,* the accumulated knowledge and experience that a company possesses. It can take many forms including processes, software, patents, copyrights, and, perhaps most important, the knowledge and experience of the people in a company.
3. *Customer capital,* the established customer base, positive reputation, ongoing relationships, and goodwill a company builds up over time with its customers.

Increasingly, entrepreneurs are recognizing that the capital stored in these three areas forms the foundation of their ability to compete effectively and that they must manage this intangible capital base carefully. Every business uses all three components in its strategy, but the emphasis they place on each component varies.

This knowledge shift will create as much change in the world's business systems as the Industrial Revolution did in the agricultural economies of the 1800s. The Knowledge Revolution will spell disaster for those companies that are not prepared for it, but it will spawn tremendous opportunities for those entrepreneurs equipped with the strategies to exploit these opportunities. Management legend Jack Welch, who masterfully guided General Electric for many years, says, "Intellectual capital is what it's all about. Releasing the ideas of people is what we've got to do if we are going to win."[3] However, in practice, releasing people's ideas is much more difficult than it appears. The key is to encourage employees to generate a large volume of ideas, recognizing that only a few (the best) will survive. According to Gary Hamel, author of *Inside the Revolution,* "If you want to find a few ideas with the power to enthrall customers, foil competitors, and thrill investors, you must first generate hundreds and potentially thousands of unconventional strategic ideas. Put simply, you have to crush a lot of rock to find a diamond."[4]

In short, the rules of the competitive game of business have changed dramatically. To be successful, entrepreneurs can no longer do things the way they've always done them. Fortunately, successful entrepreneurs have at their disposal a powerful weapon to cope with such a hostile environment: the process of strategic management. **Strategic management** is a process that involves developing a game plan to guide the company as it strives to accomplish its vision, mission, goals, and objectives and to keep it from straying off its desired course. The idea is to give the owner a blueprint for matching the company's strengths and weaknesses to the opportunities and threats in the environment.

Building a Competitive Advantage

2. Explain why and how a small business must create a competitive advantage in the market.

Company Example

The goal of developing a strategic plan is to create for the small company a **competitive advantage**—the aggregation of factors that sets the small business apart from its competitors and gives it a unique position in the market. From a strategic perspective, the key to business success is to develop a unique competitive advantage, one that creates value for customers and is difficult for competitors to duplicate. No business can be everything to everyone. In fact, one of the biggest pitfalls many entrepreneurs stumble into is failing to differentiate their companies from the crowd of competitors. Entrepreneurs often face the challenge of setting their companies apart from their larger, more powerful competitors (who can easily outspend them) by using their creativity, speed, flexibility, and special abilities their businesses offer customers.

The fast-food business has become brutal as the industry giants pound one another in battles for miniscule gains in market share with offers of 99-cent value items that serve mainly to lower profit margins across the entire sector. Yet a California-based hamburger chain called In-N-Out Burger is thriving because its strategy, which is built on what the company does best, gives it a competitive advantage over its rivals, whatever their size. Started in 1948 by Harry and Esther Snyder as a single drive-through stand in Baldwin Park, a Los Angeles suburb, In-N-Out has grown to 175 locations in three western states by sticking to its basic formula for success: top-quality, freshly ground beef on buns baked daily with side orders of hand-cut potatoes served quickly. In other words, simplicity reigns—no chicken, no salads, no desserts, no kiddie toys—just really good basic burgers, fries, soft drinks, and milk shakes. Unlike its larger competitors, In-N-Out does not rely on 99-cent items to generate customer traffic; devoted In-N-Out customers happily wait in line to pay full price for a double-double combo (two beef patties and two slices of cheese on a fresh-baked bun with an order of fries and a soft drink). Despite dozens of offers, the Snyders have refused to franchise their operation. Their reasoning: They would have to focus on selling businesses rather than the best hamburgers. Another significant component of In-N-Out's strategy for success lies in the area of human resources management, an unusual approach in the fast-food industry. Part-time workers start at $8.25 an hour and get paid vacation time, ample training opportunities, and the ability to participate in the company's retirement plan! The result is a satisfied workforce and a low employee turnover rate. The multiple components of the Snyder family's strategy combine to make In-N-Out a huge success in a very competitive industry.[5]

As In-N-Out demonstrates, over the long run, a company gains a sustainable competitive advantage through its ability to develop a set of core competencies that enables it to serve its selected target customers better than its rivals. **Core competencies** are a unique set of capabilities that a company develops in key areas, such as superior quality, customer service, innovation, team building, flexibility, speed, responsiveness, and others that enable it to vault past competitors. They are the things that a company does best and does better than its competitors. Typically, a company is likely to build core competencies in no more than five or six (sometimes fewer) areas. These core competencies become the nucleus of a company's competitive advantage and are usually quite enduring over time. Markets, customers, and competitors may change, but a company's core competencies are more durable, forming the building blocks for *everything* a company does. To be effective,

Started in 1948 by Harry and Esther Snyder at a single location, In-N-Out Burger has grown to 175 stores in three western states by sticking to a strategy in which simplicity reigns: really good basic burgers, fries, soft drinks, and milk shakes served quickly. The company has created a competitive advantage with its human resource strategy that focuses on building a satisfied work force and a low employee turnover rate.

these competencies should be difficult for competitors to duplicate, and they must provide customers with a valuable perceived benefit. Small companies' core competencies often have to do with the advantages of their size—agility, speed, closeness to customers, superior service, or ability to innovate. In short, their smallness is an advantage, enabling them to do things that their larger rivals cannot. The key to success is building these core competencies (or identifying the ones a company already has) and then concentrate on them to provide superior service and value for its target customers.

Developing core competencies does *not* necessarily require a company to spend a great deal of money. It does, however, require an entrepreneur to use creativity, imagination, and vision to identify those things that the business does best and that are most important to its target customers. Building a company's strategy around its core competencies enables a business to gain a sustainable competitive edge over its rivals and to ride its strategy to victory. *For example, Fastenal Company, a supplier of fasteners such as nuts and bolts, has achieved an impressive annual growth rate in excess of 20 percent for the past two decades by focusing on its core competencies and the value they offer customers. Founded in 1967 by Bob Kierlin and four friends, Fastenal targets factories, builders, and others with a complete line of fasteners and tools. Kierlin recognized that even though fasteners literally are "nuts and bolts" items, their absence can cause a multimillion-dollar factory or construction project to grind to a halt. As a result, Fastenal maintains a vast fleet of delivery trucks that can supply materials on short notice, a highly valuable service to customers. Capitalizing on its mastery of controlling inventories of vast numbers of small parts, Fastenal offers to manage customers' hardware parts inventory as well. Fastenal relies on yet another core competency it has developed over time: its efficient purchasing process that uses electronic data interchange (EDI) and makes buying its products simple, convenient, and inexpensive for its customers.*[6]

When it comes to developing a strategy for establishing a competitive advantage, small companies have a variety of natural advantages over their larger competitors. The typical small business has fewer product lines, a better-defined customer base, and a limited geographic market area. Entrepreneurs usually are in close contact with their markets, giving them valuable knowledge on how to best serve their customers' needs and wants. Because of the simplicity of their organizational structures, small business owners are in touch with employees daily, often working side by side with them,

Company Example

allowing them to communicate strategic moves firsthand. Consequently, small businesses find that strategic management comes more naturally to them than to larger companies with their layers of bureaucracy and far-flung operations.

Strategic management can increase a small company's effectiveness, but entrepreneurs first must have a process designed to meet their needs and their business's special characteristics. It is a mistake to attempt to force a big company's strategic management process onto a small business because a small business is not a little big business. Because of their size and their particular characteristics—limited resources, a flexible managerial style, an informal organizational structure, and adaptability to change—small businesses need a different approach to the strategic management process. The strategic management process for a small business should incorporate the following features:

- Use a relatively short planning horizon—two years or less for most small companies.
- Be informal and not overly structured; a shirtsleeve approach is ideal.
- Encourage the participation of employees and outside parties to improve the reliability and creativity of the resulting plan.
- Do not begin with setting objectives because doing so extensively early on may interfere with the creative process of strategic management.
- Maintain flexibility; competitive conditions change too rapidly for any plan to be considered permanent.
- Focus on strategic *thinking*, not just planning, by linking long-range goals to day-to-day operations.

✦ GAINING *a* COMPETITIVE EDGE ✦

A Chinese Warrior and Business Strategy

In China around 400 B.C., a general named Sun Tzu rose to fame because of his incredible ability to win victories for his commanders. To pass along the wisdom of his battle strategies and experience, Sun Tzu wrote a book, *The Art of War,* that has become a popular handbook not only for military strategists but also for business strategists. His book is a masterpiece on developing and implementing strategy primarily because Sun Tzu's approach, to the surprise of some, emphasizes the notion of winning battles *without fighting.* Success in battle—and in business—is determined by proper preparation before the battle ever (or better yet, never) begins. Centuries after Sun Tzu recorded his doctrine of military strategy, author Mark McNeilly organized those strategies into six principles that apply to business. They are explained in his book, *Sun Tzu and the Art of Business.* Excerpts from *The Art of War* and the six principles from *Sun Tzu and the Art of Business* that are based on them follow:

"For to win one hundred victories in one hundred battles is not the acme of skill. To subdue the enemy without fighting is the acme of skill."

—Sun Tzu

Principle 1. Capture your market without destroying it.

To be successful, businesses must capture their markets, but they must do so in a way that does not destroy them. For small companies, this means refraining from attacking a competitor head on. The most successful strategy is a more subtle, low-key approach that does not draw a response from competitors. For instance, rather than attacking a market by launching a price war, which draws the swiftest and most severe responses from competitors, a company would be better off focusing on segments of the market that are underserved or overlooked by larger, stronger rivals. Find an opening (niche) in the market that competitors are overlooking and position your company there.

"Just as flowing water avoids the heights and hastens to the lowlands, so an army avoids strengths and strikes weaknesses."

—Sun Tzu

Principle 2. Avoid your competitors' strengths and attack their weaknesses.

Attacking competitors at their points of strength is a recipe for failure in battle and in business. Direct attacks are costly to both parties because they lead to battles of attrition. A much more effective strategy involves attacking competitors at their points of weakness. Companies whose strategies focus on a competitor's weaknesses can maximize their gains while minimizing the use of their own resources. Although a small retail store cannot compete on price with giant retailers that buy in volume, it can compete successfully by offering unique products and services, exceptional knowledge, deeper product lines, and other extras that customers value.

"Know the enemy, and know yourself; in a hundred battles you will never be in peril."

—Sun Tzu

Principle 3. Use foreknowledge and deception to maximize the power of business intelligence.

Before an entrepreneur can attack a competitor's weaknesses, he or she must be able to identify the competitor's weaknesses, and that requires information. It is vitally important for business owners to survey the "battlefield of business" by monitoring overall competitive and industry trends as well as key competitors' individual moves. Knowledge management is a vital strategic activity as is masking as much as possible about your own company's strategic intent.

"Rush to places the enemy least expects."

—Sun Tzu

Principle 4. Use speed and preparation to swiftly overcome the competition.

The notion that large organizations are stronger than small ones is a myth. Small companies can use their size to their advantage; it enables them to use speed, flexibility, and focus to gain an edge over their larger rivals. In the market for small, (relatively) inexpensive corporate jets, Adam Aircraft Industries has emerged as the leader because of its ability to bring its A700 jet to market two years faster and with a smaller investment than any of its competitors. The company uses rapid prototyping (a topic discussed in Chapter 6) and as many off-the-shelf parts as possible to speed its double-tailfin jet to market and gain an edge over its rivals.

"Those skilled in war bring the enemy to the battlefield and are not brought there by him."

—Sun Tzu

Principle 5. Use alliances and strategic control points in the industry to "shape" your opponents and make them conform to your will.

This principle suggests changing the rules of the competitive game to make rivals play against your strengths, enabling you to take control of the battle. For instance, when Netflix introduced the idea of using the Web as the mechanism for making video rentals easier and more convenient for customers, it rewrote the rulebook of competition in the industry in its favor. Although bigger and more established, Blockbuster had to develop its own online video rental process to remain competitive. Innovations and strategic alliances are important ways of reshaping an industry and staying ahead of competitors.

"When one treats people with benevolence, justice, and righteousness and reposes confidence in them, the army will be united in mind and all will be happy to serve their leaders."

—Sun Tzu

Principle 6. Develop your character as a leader to maximize the potential of your employees.

Sun Tzu emphasized that leaders must put the needs of their troops ahead of their own needs, a concept known today as servant leadership. Leaders with character garner the respect of followers and are able to get the greatest performance from them. Discipline is an important part of an organization because it establishes order.

1. Relate the six principles described here to the nine steps of the strategic management process described in this chapter.

Sources: Mark McNeilly, "The Six Principles from Sun Tzu and the Art of Business: Six Principles for Managers," *Sun Tzu and the Art of Business*, www.suntzu1.com/business/sixprin.shtml; "The Ancient Bing-Fa," *Sun Tzu's Art of War Plus*, www.clearbridge.com/basic_principles.htm; Rich Karlgaard, "Small-Jet Shocker," *Forbes*, September 15, 2003, p. 35.

The Strategic Management Process

3. Develop a strategic plan for a business using the nine steps in the strategic planning process.

One of the most important tasks a business owner must perform is to look ahead—to peer into the future—and then devise a strategy for meeting the challenges and opportunities the future presents. Strategic management, the best way to accomplish this vital task, is a continuous process that consists of nine steps:

Step 1   Develop a clear vision and translate it into a meaningful mission statement.
Step 2   Assess the company's strengths and weaknesses.

Step 3   Scan the environment for significant opportunities and threats facing the business.

Step 4   Identify the key factors for success in the business.

Step 5   Analyze the competition.

Step 6   Create company goals and objectives.

Step 7   Formulate strategic options and select the appropriate strategies.

Step 8   Translate strategic plans into action plans.

Step 9   Establish accurate controls.

Step 1: Develop a Clear Vision and Translate It into a Meaningful Mission Statement

Vision. Throughout history, the greatest political and business leaders have been visionaries. Whether the vision is as grand as Martin Luther King, Jr. expressed in his "I Have a Dream" speech or as simple as Ray Kroc's devotion to quality, service, cleanliness, and value at McDonald's, the purpose is the same: to focus everyone's attention and efforts on the same target. The vision touches everyone associated with the company—employees, investors, lenders, customers, and community. It is an expression of what entrepreneurs believe in and the values on which they build their businesses. A vision statement addresses the questions, "What do we stand for?" and "What do we want to become?" In his book, *Daring Visionaries: How Entrepreneurs Build Companies, Inspire Allegiance, and Create Wealth,* Ray Smilor describes the importance of vision:

> Vision is the organizational sixth sense that tells us why we make a difference in the world. It is the real but unseen fabric of connections that nurture and sustain values. It is the pulse of the organizational body that reaffirms relationships and directs behavior.[7]

Highly successful entrepreneurs are able to communicate their vision and their enthusiasm about that vision to those around them. One study of more than 500 "hidden champions"—little-known superperforming companies that hold worldwide market shares of at least 50 percent—identified the presence of a clear vision as an important factor in the competitive edge these companies had established. The founders of these companies adhere strongly to their own fundamental vision and purpose, while giving employees the freedom to handle daily activities within the context of that vision.[8]

Vision is based on an entrepreneur's values. Successful entrepreneurs build their businesses around a set of three to six core values, which might range from respect for the individual and encouraging innovation to creating satisfied customers and making the world a better place. Indeed, truly visionary entrepreneurs see their companies' primary purpose as much more than just "making money." One writer explains, "Almost all workers are making decisions, not just filling out weekly sales reports or tightening screws. They will do what they think best. If you want them to do as the company thinks best too, then you must [see to it that] they have an inner gyroscope aligned with the corporate compass."[9] That gyroscope's alignment depends on entrepreneurs' values and how well they transmit them throughout the company.

The best way to put values into action is to create a written mission statement that communicates those values to everyone the company touches.

Mission Statement. A mission statement addresses the first question of any business venture: "What business am I in?" Establishing the purpose of the business in writing must come first in order to give the company a sense of direction. The mission is the mechanism for making it clear to everyone the company touches "why we are here" and "where we are going." It helps create an emotional bond between a company and its stakeholders, especially its employees and its customers. Without a concise, meaningful mission statement, a small business risks wandering aimlessly in the marketplace, with no idea of where to go or how to get there. *Julian Gordon, founder of Gordon Industries, watched his Boston-based company grow during the construction boom of the 1980s, supplying fabricated metal stairs and grates for buildings. When the boom came to a sudden halt, the business struggled to survive, and Gordon was forced to lay off half of his employees. Sales plummeted to less than $1 million from more than $3 million. By 1996, Gordon noticed that customers were placing increasing numbers of orders for wheelchair ramps and he began experimenting with different designs. In 1998, he earned a patent on a low-cost, modular metal ramp that could be assembled easily and taken apart with only a wrench. His unique design meant that institutions needing to provide short-term access for disabled persons or people with temporary disabilities could rent ramps at a reasonable cost, a real benefit to insurance companies. This breakthrough saved the company and led Gordon to transform completely his definition of his company's business. No longer is the company in the metal fabrication sector of the construction business. With sales exceeding $5 million and growing fast, Gordon Industries is now in the medical care business, providing low-cost wheelchair access to an aging population in need of a practical solution.*[10]

A good mission statement essentially sets the tone for the entire company and guides the decisions its people make. Tom's of Maine, a successful small company that sells all natural consumer products such as toothpaste, deodorant, and soap, has relied heavily on its mission statement (which was written collaboratively by employees and owners in 1989) as a strategic and ethical compass. The statement expresses the importance of earning a profit while meeting the company's social responsibility. When Tom's of Maine modified one of its deodorants, the company discovered that the new formula did not work. When deciding how to handle the problem, Chappell and his employees turned to the mission statement for guidance. They decided to contact every customer who had purchased the deodorant and replace it with a newly formulated one. "We [made the decision] because our mission statement says that we will serve customers with safe, effective, and natural products," says Chappell.[11]

Tom Chappell and his wife Kate left the corporate world for Kennebunk, Maine, where they co-founded Tom's of Maine, a company that sells all natural consmer products such as toothpaste, deodorant, and soap. The company relies heavily on its mission statement (which was written collaboratively by employees and owners in 1989) as a strategic and ethical compass.

Elements of a Mission Statement. A sound mission statement need not be lengthy to be effective. Some of the key issues entrepreneurs and their employees should consider as they develop a mission statement for their companies include:

- What are the basic beliefs and values of our company? What do we stand for?
- Who are our company's target customers?
- What are our core products and services? What customer needs and wants do they satisfy?
- Why should customers do business with us rather than the competitor down the street (or across town, on the other coast, on the other side of the globe)?
- What constitutes value to our customers? How can we offer them better value?
- What is our competitive advantage? What is its source?
- In which markets (or market segments) will we choose to compete?
- Who are the key stakeholders in our company and what effect do they have on it?
- How does our company and its products and services affect these key stakeholders?
- What benefits should we be providing our customers five years from now?
- What business do we want to be in five years from now?

By answering these basic questions, a company will have a much clearer picture of what it is and what it wants to be.

A firm's mission statement may be the most essential and basic communication that it puts forward. If the people on the plant, shop, retail, or warehouse floor don't know what a company's mission is, then, for all practical purposes, it does not have one! The mission statement expresses the company's character, identity, and scope of operations, but writing it is only half the battle, at best. The most difficult part is living that mission every day. *That's* how employees decide what really matters. To be effective, a mission statement must become a natural part of the organization, embodied in the minds, habits, attitudes, and decisions of everyone in the company every day. Consider the mission statement of Fetzer Vineyards, a vineyard whose own acreage is 100 percent organic with no chemical pesticides, herbicides, fungicides, or fertilizers, and the message it sends to company stakeholders:

> We are an environmentally and socially conscious grower, producer, and marketer of wines of the highest quality and value.
>
> Working in harmony with respect for the human spirit, we are committed to sharing information about the enjoyment of food and wine in a lifestyle of moderation and responsibility.
>
> We are dedicated to the continuous growth and development of our people and our business.[12]

A company may have a powerful competitive advantage, but it is wasted unless (1) the owner has communicated that advantage to workers, who, in turn, are working hard to communicate it to customers and potential customers and (2) customers are recommending the company to their friends because they understand the benefits they are getting from it that they cannot get elsewhere. *That's* the real power of a mission statement.

Step 2: Assess the Company's Strengths and Weaknesses

Having defined the vision and the mission of the business, entrepreneurs can turn their attention to assessing company strengths and weaknesses. Competing successfully demands that a business create a competitive strategy that is built on and exploits its strengths and overcomes or compensates for its weaknesses. **Strengths** are positive internal factors that contribute to the accomplishment of a company's mission, goals, and

© 2000 Randy Glasbergen.

GLASBERGEN

**"Now that we've celebrated our diversity,
embraced a new spirit of creativity, made a fresh
commitment to excellence, and given something
back to the community,** *does anyone here remember
what it is we're supposed to manufacture and sell?"*

objectives. **Weaknesses** are negative internal factors that inhibit the accomplishment of its mission, goals, and objectives.

Identifying strengths and weaknesses helps an entrepreneur understand his or her business as it exists (or will exist). An organization's strengths should originate in its core competencies because they are essential to its ability to remain competitive in each of the market segments in which it competes. The key is to build a successful strategy by using the company's underlying strengths as its foundation and matching those strengths against competitors' weaknesses. In-N-Out Burger, for instance, uses the quality and the freshness of its products and loyalty of its customers as major strengths in its strategy for competing against much larger and more financially capable competitors.

One effective technique for taking a strategic inventory is to prepare a balance sheet of the company's strengths and weaknesses (see Table 2.1). The positive side should reflect important skills, knowledge, or resources that contribute to the company's success. The negative side should record honestly any limitations that detract from the company's ability to compete. This balance sheet should analyze all key performance areas of the business—human resources, finance, production, marketing, product development, organization, and others. This analysis should give owners a more realistic perspective of their business, pointing out foundations on which they can build future strengths and obstacles that they must remove for business progress. This exercise can help owners move from their current position to future actions.

Table 2.1

Identifying Company
Strengths and
Weaknesses

Strengths (Positive Internal Factors)	Weaknesses (Negative Internal Factors)

Step 3: Scan the Environment for Significant Opportunities and Threats Facing the Business

Opportunities. Once entrepreneurs have taken an internal inventory of company strengths and weaknesses, they must turn to the external environment to identify any opportunities and threats that might have a significant impact on the business. **Opportunities** are positive external options that the firm could employ to accomplish its objectives. The number of potential opportunities is limitless, so managers need to analyze only factors significant to the business (probably two or three at most). Otherwise, they may jeopardize their core business by losing focus and trying to do too much at once.

When identifying opportunities, entrepreneurs must pay close attention to new potential markets. Are competitors overlooking a niche in the market? Is there a better way to reach customers? Are customers requesting new products or product variations? Have environmental changes created new markets? *After spending years working for large companies selling skin care and makeup to women, Emily Dalton and Curran Dandurand recognized the potential to sell similar products to men. "We knew there was a huge opportunity with men," says Dandurand. Before launching their business, Jack Black, Dalton and Dandurand conducted extensive research on their target customers to discover exactly what men wanted and would buy. According to Dalton, their target customer "cares about how he looks, but he's not going to go through a five-step skin-care regimen." Recognizing their customers' needs, the partners built their product line around simplicity and multifunctionality; for example, the company's All-Over Wash is suitable for face, hair, and body. Their packaging, which is distinctively upscale and masculine, has helped Jack Black's sales climb to more than $5 million a year.*[13]

> Company Example

Threats. **Threats** are negative external forces that inhibit the firm's ability to achieve its objectives. Threats to the business can take a variety of forms, such as new competitors entering the local market, a government mandate regulating a business activity, an economic recession, rising interest rates, technological advances making a company's product obsolete, and many others. *For instance, Patricia Potts, CEO of Harbison Brothers, a third-generation company that is in the unglamorous business of refurbishing used 55-gallon steel drums for resale to manufacturers, faces a serious threat from plastic drums that are lighter and easier to transport. Since 1990, steel drums' market share has fallen from 80 percent to 57 percent, and Harbison Brothers' sales reflect that decline.*

> Company Example

The owners of birthday and souvenir newspaper businesses (companies that sell old newspapers to commemorate a birthday, anniversary, or special life event) face a different type of threat: Their raw materials are becoming increasingly difficult to find. Most libraries and newspaper publishers, the major sources of newspaper supply for companies in this business, long ago completed the transition from actual newsprint to microfilm or electronic storage media. Philip Druce, owner of Newspaper Archives, says that his supply of newspapers printed between 1945 and 1955, particularly the New York Times, *is running dangerously low.* Although these entrepreneurs cannot control the threats their businesses face, they must prepare a strategic plan that will shield their businesses from these threats.

> Company Example

Figure 2.1 illustrates that opportunities and threats are products of the interactions of forces, trends, and events outside the direct control of the business. These external forces will have direct impact on the behavior of the markets in which the business operates, the behavior of competitors, and the behavior of customers. By monitoring demographic trends as well as trends in their particular industries, entrepreneurs can sharpen their ability to spot most opportunities and threats well in advance, giving themselves time to prepare for them. *Christian Martin, sixth-generation president of C.F. Martin and Company, a famous maker of high-quality acoustic guitars for more than 170 years, made an*

> Company Example

Figure 2.1

External Market Forces

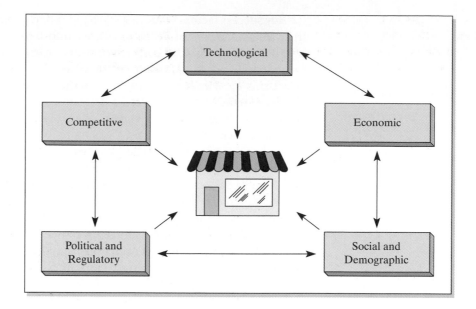

important strategic decision after observing the rapid growth in the low end of the guitar market. Martin's specialty has always been luxury guitars. Guitars in the under-$1,000 price range now account for about 65 percent of total acoustic guitar sales, but C.F. Martin, whose guitars normally sell for $1,500 to $100,000 (a limited edition Dreadnought), had no guitars in the lower price range. Martin decided to enhance his company's product line by introducing the X series of guitars that starts at $600. The challenge for Martin is to boost sales in the low end of the market without diluting its reputation for quality among customers in the luxury end of the market.[14]

Table 2.2 provides a form that enables business owners to take a strategic inventory of the opportunities and threats facing their companies.

Step 4: Identify the Key Factors for Success in the Business

Key Success Factors. Every business is characterized by a set of controllable factors that determine the relative success of market participants. Identifying, understanding, and manipulating these factors allows a small business to gain a competitive advantage in its market segment. By focusing efforts to maximize their companies' performance on these key success factors, entrepreneurs can achieve dramatic market advantages over their competitors. Companies that understand these key success factors tend to be leaders of the pack, whereas those who fail to recognize them become also-rans.

Table 2.2

Identifying Opportunities
and Threats

OPPORTUNITIES (POSITIVE EXTERNAL FACTORS)	THREATS (NEGATIVE EXTERNAL FACTORS)

Key success factors come in a variety of different patterns depending on the industry. Bruce Milletto, owner of Bellissimo Coffee Info-Group, a coffee business consulting firm, says that to be successful coffee shops must focus on three key success factors: high-quality coffee products, stellar customer service, and a warm, inviting ambience that transforms a coffee house into a destination where people want to gather with their friends. Martin Mayorga started a coffee roasting business with his wife in 1998 and recently opened a retail coffee store in Silver Springs, Maryland, that focuses on specialty imported coffee beans. The shop looks more like a lounge than a retail store, with plush leather family-style seating. The Mayorgas also have added an entertainment factor by including musical entertainment and allowing customers to view the entire roasting process on its custom-made bean roaster, attractive extras for customers looking for a way to relax after a busy day at work.[15]

Simply stated, key success factors determine a company's ability to compete in the marketplace. Sometimes these sources of competitive advantages are based on cost factors such as manufacturing cost per unit, distribution cost per unit, or development cost per unit. More often these key success factors are less tangible but are just as important, such as level of product quality, customer services offered, convenient store locations, availability of customer credit, and others. For example, one restaurant owner identified the following key success factors for his business:

> Tight cost control (labor, 15–18 percent of sales and food costs, 35–40 percent of sales)
> Trained, dependable, honest in-store managers
> Close monitoring of waste
> Convenient location
> High food quality
> Consistent food
> Clean restaurants
> Friendly and attentive service from a well-trained waitstaff

These controllable variables determine the ability of any restaurant in his market segment to compete. Restaurants lacking these key success factors are not likely to survive, whereas those that build these factors into their strategies will prosper. However, before entrepreneurs can build a strategy on the foundation of the industry's key success factors, they must identify them. Table 2.3 presents a form to help entrepreneurs identify the most important success factors and their implications for the company.

Entrepreneurs must use the information gathered to analyze their businesses, their competitors, and their industries to isolate these sources of competitive advantage. They must then determine how well their companies meet these criteria for successfully competing in the market. Highly successful companies know and understand these relationships, but marginal competitors are mystified by which factors determine success in that particular business. For example, a small manufacturer of cosmetics may discover that shelf space, brand recognition, innovative products, efficient distribution,

Table 2.3

Identifying Key Success Factors

List the key success factors that your business must possess if it is to be successful in its market segment.

	Key Success Factor	How Your Company Rates
1		Low 1 2 3 4 5 6 7 8 9 10 High
2		Low 1 2 3 4 5 6 7 8 9 10 High
3		Low 1 2 3 4 5 6 7 8 9 10 High
4		Low 1 2 3 4 5 6 7 8 9 10 High
5		Low 1 2 3 4 5 6 7 8 9 10 High
Conclusions:		

and high quality are crucial to business success. On the other hand, a small retail chain owner may find that broad product lines, available customer credit, personalized service, capable store management, and a high-volume location determine success in his or her business.

Step 5: Analyze the Competition

Ask small business owners to identify the greatest challenge they face, and one of the most common responses is *competition*. Small companies increasingly are under fire from larger, more powerful rivals, including general retailers such as Wal-Mart and specialty stores such as Home Depot, PetSmart, and Office Depot. Keeping tabs on rivals' strategic movements through competitive intelligence programs is a vital strategic activity. Indeed, in a recent study of fast-growing companies, 84 percent of entrepreneurs said that information about their competitors is an important factor in the growth of their companies' profits.[16] According to one small business consultant, "Business is like any battlefield. If you want to win the war, you have to know who you're up against."[17] The primary goals of a competitive intelligence program include the following:

- Avoiding surprises from existing competitors' new strategies and tactics
- Identifying potential new competitors
- Improving reaction time to competitors' actions
- Anticipating rivals' next strategic moves

Unfortunately, most small companies fail to gather competitive intelligence because their owners mistakenly assume that it is too costly or simply unnecessary. A study by Stanford University and UCLA found that nearly 80 percent of business owners had no idea what their competitors were up to![18] In reality, the cost of collecting information about competitors typically is minimal, but it does require discipline.

Competitor Analysis. Sizing up the competition gives a business owner a more realistic view of the market and his or her company's position in it. Yet not every competitor warrants the same level of attention in a strategic plan. *Direct competitors* offer the same products and services, and customers often compare prices, features, and deals from these competitors as they shop. *Significant competitors* offer some of the same products and services. Although their product or service lines may be somewhat different, there is competition with them in several key areas. *Indirect competitors* offer the same or similar products or services only in a small number of areas, and their target customers seldom overlap yours. Entrepreneurs should monitor closely the actions of their direct competitors, maintain a solid grasp of where their significant competitors are heading, and spend only minimal resources tracking their indirect competitors. For instance, two of Philadelphia's landmark businesses, Pat's King of Steaks and Geno's Steaks, are direct competitors in the market for Philly cheese-steaks. Their locations—across the street from one another—make it easy for each to keep track of the other. Pat's and Geno's charge the same prices for their sandwiches, and both claim to be the home of the original Philly cheese-steak sandwich.[19]

A competitive intelligence exercise enables entrepreneurs to update their knowledge of competitors by answering the following questions:

- Who are your major competitors and where are they located? Bob Dickinson, president of Carnival Cruise Lines, considers his company's main competition to be land-based theme parks and casinos rather than other cruise lines. Why? Because 89 percent of American adults have never been on a cruise![20]

- What distinctive competencies have they developed?
- How do their cost structures compare to yours? Their financial resources?
- How do they market their products and services?
- What do customers say about them? How do customers describe their products or services, their way of doing business, and the additional services they might supply?
- What are their key strategies?
- What are their strengths? How can your company surpass them?
- What are their primary weaknesses? How can your company capitalize on them?
- Are new competitors entering the market?

A small business owner can collect a great deal of information about competitors through low-cost competitive intelligence (CI) methods including the following:

- Read industry trade publications for announcements from competitors.
- Ask questions of customers and suppliers on what they hear competitors may be doing. In many cases, this information is easy to gather because some people love to gossip.
- Talk to your employees, especially sales representatives and purchasing agents. Experts estimate that 70 to 90 percent of the competitive information a company needs already resides with employees who collect it in their routine dealings with suppliers, customers, and other industry contacts.[21]
- Attend trade shows and collect competitors' sales literature.
- Watch for employment ads from competitors; knowing what types of workers they are hiring can tell you a great deal about their future plans.
- Conduct patent searches for patents that competitors have filed. This gives important clues about new products they are developing.
- Environmental Protection Agency reports can provide important information about the factories of manufacturing companies, including the amounts and the kinds of emissions released. A private group, Environmental Protection, also reports emissions for specific plants.[22]
- Learn about the kinds and amounts of equipment and raw materials competitors are importing by studying the *Journal of Commerce Port Import Export Reporting Service (PIERS)* database. These clues can alert an entrepreneur to new products a competitor is about to launch.
- If appropriate, buy the competitors' products and assess their quality and features. Benchmark their products against yours. The owner of an online gift-basket company periodically places orders with his primary competitors and compares their packaging, pricing, service, and quality to his own.[23]
- Obtain credit reports on each of your major competitors to evaluate their financial condition. Dun & Bradstreet and other research firms also enable entrepreneurs to look up competitors' profiles that can be helpful in a strategic analysis.
- Publicly held companies must file periodic reports with the Securities and Exchange Commission (SEC), including quarterly 10-Q and annual 10-K reports. These are available at the SEC's Web site.
- Check out the resources of your local library, including articles, computerized databases, and online searches. Press releases, which often announce important company news, can be an important source of competitive intelligence. Many companies supply press releases through the *PR Newswire*. For local competitors, review back issues of the area newspaper for articles on and advertisements by competitors.
- Use the vast resources of the World Wide Web to learn more about your competitors. The Web enables entrepreneurs to gather valuable competitive information at

little or no cost. Refer to our Web site at www.prenhall.com/scarborough for an extensive listing of more than 1,000 useful small business Web sites.

- ■ Visit competing businesses periodically to observe their operations. Sam Walton, founder of Wal-Mart, was famous for visiting competitors' operations to see what he could learn from them.

Using the information gathered, a business owner can set up teams of managers and employees to evaluate key competitors and make recommendations on strategic actions that will improve the company's competitive position against each one.

Entrepreneurs can use the results of the competitor intelligence analysis to construct a competitive profile matrix for each market segment in which the firm operates. A **competitive profile matrix** enables entrepreneurs to evaluate their firms against the major competitor on the key success factors for their market segments (refer to Table 2.4). The first step is to list the key success factors identified in Step 4 of the strategic planning process and to attach weights to them reflecting their relative importance. (For simplicity, the weights in this matrix sum add up to 1.00). In this example, notice that product quality is the most important key success factor, which is why its weight (0.25) is the highest.

The next step is to identify the company's major competitors and to rate each one (and your company) on each of the key success factors:

If factor is a:	Rating is:
Major weakness	1
Minor weakness	2
Minor strength	3
Major strength	4

Once the rating is completed, the owner simply multiplies the weight by the rating for each factor to get a weighted score, and then adds up each competitor's weighted scores to get a total weighted score. Table 2.4 shows a sample competitive profile matrix for a small company. The results will show which company is strongest, which is weakest, and which of the key success factors each one is best and worst at meeting. By carefully studying and interpreting the results, small business owners can begin to envision the ideal strategy for building a competitive edge in their market segment. Figure 2.2 shows a radar chart created from the competitive profile matrix in Table 2.4. Such a chart shows entrepreneurs how their companies measure up against competitors on the key success factors they have identified.

Knowledge Management. Most small companies have significant stockpiles of valuable knowledge that can help them gain an edge in the marketplace—from a key customer's purchasing criteria to how one department uses Excel to forecast product

Table 2.4

Sample Competitive
Profile Matrix

Key Success Factor	Weight	My Company Score	My Company Weighted Score	Competitor 1 Score	Competitor 1 Weighted Score	Competitor 2 Score	Competitor 2 Weighted Score
Quality	0.25	4	1.00	2	0.50	2	0.50
Customer Retention	0.20	3	0.60	2	0.40	3	0.60
Location	0.15	4	0.60	3	0.45	4	0.60
Perception of Value	0.20	4	0.80	2	0.40	3	0.60
Cost Control	0.20	3	0.60	1	0.20	4	0.80
	100%		3.60		1.95		3.10

Figure 2.2

Key Success Factors:
Competitive Analysis

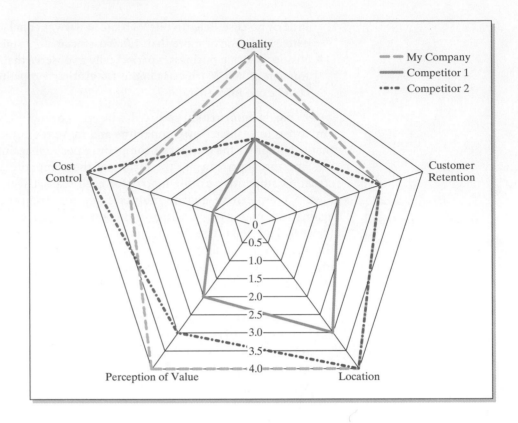

demand. Unfortunately, that knowledge most often sits idle or is shared only by happenstance on an informal basis. This scenario is the equivalent of having a bank account without a checkbook or an ATM card to access it! The key is learning how to manage and utilize the knowledge a company accumulates over time. **Knowledge management** is the practice of gathering, organizing, and disseminating the collective wisdom and experience of a company's employees for the purpose of strengthening its competitive position. "Organizations that harness knowledge and put it to good use are able to gain a clear competitive advantage," says Eric Lesser, a consultant at IBM's Institute for Knowledge Management.[24] Knowledge management enables companies to get more innovative products to market faster, respond to customers' needs faster, and solve (or avoid altogether) problems more efficiently. Because of their size and simplicity, small businesses have an advantage over large companies when it comes to managing knowledge. Knowledge management requires that a small company identify what its workers know, incorporate that knowledge into the business and distribute it where it is needed, and leverage it into more useful knowledge.

The first step in creating a knowledge management program is to take an inventory of the special knowledge a company possesses that gives it a competitive advantage. This involves assessing the knowledge bank that a company and its employees have compiled over time. One of the most valuable assets available to companies is their customer databases, information that, when analyzed properly, can give amazing insight into customers' likes, dislikes, and buying habits and patterns. Increasingly, software companies are providing business information software that links to simple applications such as Excel and Access, enabling small business owners to extract meaningful information from their computerized databases. *The Ben & Jerry's Homemade factory in Waterbury, Vermont, produces 190,000 gallons of ice cream each day, and the company uses specialized software to track every pint from the factory floor to the grocer's aisle. Sales managers can generate*

Company Example

reports on which flavors are selling best, the marketing department can determine when sales of each product trigger a donation to the philanthropic organizations the company supports, and finance managers can pull relevant data to complete financial statements and forecasts faster than ever before. If a customer complaint arises, managers can match the contents of a particular pint back to the suppliers of the raw materials that went into it. The company's analysis of these data contributes to its success.[25]

The second step in knowledge management is to organize the essential knowledge and disseminate it throughout the company to those who need it. High-tech solutions such as e-mail, computerized databases, and software that enable many different employees to work on a project simultaneously are important tools, but low-tech methods such as whiteboards, Post-it notes, and face-to-face meetings can be just as effective in small

Company Example →

companies. The final step in creating a knowledge management program is to continue to add to the knowledge base the company has assembled. *Heather Hesketh, owner of hesketh.com, a Web-consulting firm, realized that a knowledge management program was essential to her fast-growing company's success. Not only is Hesketh hiring a new employee every two months, but she also is selling her employees' collective knowledge to her clients! When employees left the company, Hesketh realized that a valuable base of information went out the door with them. To avoid this brain drain, she created a constantly growing database of employees' knowledge on the company intranet, where it is available to any employee at any time. She claims it is her way of preserving the company's past and preparing for its future.*[26]

Step 6: Create Company Goals and Objectives

Before entrepreneurs can build a comprehensive set of strategies, they must first establish business goals and objectives, which give them targets to aim for and provide a basis for evaluating their company's performance. Without these goals and objectives, entrepreneurs cannot know where the business is going or how well it is performing. Creating goals and objectives is an essential part of the strategic management process.

Goals. Goals are the broad, long-range targets that a business seeks to accomplish; they tend to be general and sometimes even abstract. Goals are not intended to be specific enough for a manager to act on but simply state the general level of accomplishment sought. Do you want to boost your market share? Does your cash balance need strengthening? Would you like to enter a new market or increase sales in a current one? What return on your investment do you seek? Researchers Jim Collins and Jerry Porras studied a large group of businesses and determined that one of the factors that set apart successful companies from unsuccessful ones was the formulation of very ambitious, clear, and inspiring long-term goals. Collins and Porras called them BHAGs ("Big Hairy Audacious Goals," pronounced "bee-hags") and say that their main benefit is to inspire and focus a company on important actions that are consistent with its overall mission.[27]

Addressing these broad issues will help you focus on the next phase—developing specific, realistic objectives.

Objectives. Objectives are more specific targets of performance. Common objectives address profitability, productivity, growth, efficiency, markets, financial resources, physical facilities, organizational structure, employee welfare, and social responsibility. Jim Collins suggests that the objectives a company sets determine the level of success it achieves. Establishing profitability targets is *not* enough. Instead, entrepreneurs must set objectives and measure performance in those critical areas that determine their companies' ability to be profitable—a concept he calls a company's true economic denominators. Those denominators might be the cost of acquiring a customer, sales per labor hour, the customer retention rate, the rate of inventory turnover, or some other factor. Dell Computer, for instance, has left most of its competitors in the dust by focusing on one of its true economic denominators, achieving a phenomenal inventory turnover ratio of 73 times a year! Unfortunately, Collins claims fewer than 10 percent of all companies understand what their true economic denominators are. Because objectives in one area of the company might conflict with those in another area of the company, entrepreneurs must establish priorities. Which objectives are most important? Arranging objectives in a hierarchy according to their priority can help business owners resolve conflicts when they arise.

Well-written objectives have the following characteristics:

They are specific. Objectives should be quantifiable and precise. For example, "to achieve a healthy growth in sales" is not a meaningful objective, but "to increase retail sales by 12 percent and wholesale by 10 percent in the next fiscal year" is precise and spells out exactly what management wants to accomplish.

They are measurable. Managers should be able to plot the organization's progress toward its objectives; this requires a well-defined reference point from which to start and a scale for measuring progress.

They are assignable. Unless an entrepreneur assigns responsibility for an objective to an individual, it is unlikely that the company will ever achieve it. Creating objectives without giving someone responsibility for accomplishing them is futile.

They are realistic, yet challenging. Objectives must be within the reach of the organization or motivation will disappear. In any case, managerial expectations must remain high. In other words, the more challenging an objective is (within realistic limits), the higher the performance will be. Set objectives that will challenge your business and its employees.

They are timely. Objectives must specify not only what is to be accomplished but also when it is to be accomplished. A time frame for achievement is important.

They are written down. This writing process does not have to be complex; in fact, the manager should make the number of objectives relatively small, from five to fifteen.

The strategic planning process works best when managers and employees are actively involved jointly in setting objectives. Developing a plan is top management's responsibility, but executing it falls to managers and employees; therefore, encouraging them to participate broadens the plan's perspective and increases the motivation to make the plan work. In addition, managers and employees know a great deal about the organization and usually are willing to share this knowledge.

IN THE FOOTSTEPS OF AN ENTREPRENEUR...

A Billion Dollars in Sales—99 Cents at a Time

While working at the liquor store that he and his sister had purchased from their father, Dave Gold had an epiphany about a retail store in which every item sold for just 99 cents. After retiring from the liquor business in 1982 at age 50, Gold decided to open his 99-cent store at the encouragement of family and friends who had grown tired of hearing him talk about it. Gold leased a building that had once housed a Mexican restaurant near the Los Angeles airport and opened the first 99¢ Only Store. As a low-cost, guerrilla marketing tactic, he offered the first 13 customers (the store opened on Friday the 13th) the chance to buy TVs for just 99 cents. Customers flocked to the store, and within six months, Gold knew he had hit on a successful business idea. Over the next few years, he purchased or leased nine other retail sites from businesses that were closing and began building a chain of stores.

Today, 99¢ Only Stores operates 147 stores, mainly in California, Nevada, and Arizona, and, true to Gold's original concept, everything sells for just 99 cents. Unlike many discount stores, 99¢ Only Stores are clean, brightly lit, organized, and large—about the size of a small supermarket. At least half of the brands the company stocks are well known, such as Yoplait, Neutrogena, Dole, Häagen-Daz, and others; yet all are priced at 99 cents. The inventory mix changes depending on the deals that Gold's 12 buyers can find from suppliers with product overruns, canceled orders, or slow-moving items. On a typical day, customers can shop for tools and cosmetics, kitchen gadgets and cleaners, personal care items and food (from shitake mushrooms to wine), and many other items as well. Recently, when an article in the *Los Angeles Times* mentioned that 99¢ Only Stores were selling a cabernet for 99 cents (its original retail price was $15), customers poured in and bought 17,000 bottles in just two hours!

Customers on limited incomes are the chain's primary target customer, but its appeal is much broader. A survey by WSL Strategic Retail found that 75 percent of all consumers shop at discount "dollar" stores, half of them at least once a month. Celebrities such as Richard Gere, Vanna White, and Martha Stewart have been spotted strolling down 99¢ Only aisles. The stores are such an important part of West Coast culture that the Rolling Stones and the Goo Goo Dolls have shot music videos in them.

Although competition at the discount end of the market can be intense, the 99¢ Only Stores are thriving by sticking to the strategy that Gold originally defined for the company. Gold pinches pennies whenever he can. No one in the company has a secretary, and company headquarters is located in Commerce City, California, where property values are lower than in Los Angeles. The executive conference table cost $15, and everyone drinks coffee from small cups because Gold got a deal on them years ago! Gold is smart enough to spend money where it counts, however. He pays his buyers, who are a vital component in the company's success, double the salaries they would earn at more upscale stores. He also offers all employees a generous stock option program. The stock options are so valuable that many shelf-stockers and truck drivers have used them to buy their homes—*for cash!* A few years ago, Gold purchased a plastic manufacturing business that was folding, enabling him to make most of the company's plastic products (baskets, storage containers, cutting boards, and other items) far more cheaply than he can buy them. Gold's low-cost strategy works; 99¢ Only Stores' gross profit margin is 40 percent, the highest in the discount business.

Even though the company made an initial public offering in 1996, the Gold family still owns 35 percent of the business. 99¢ Only Stores remains very much a family business; Dave Gold is the CEO, his sons Howard and Jeff are senior vice presidents, and son-in-law Eric Schiffer is president. As 99¢ Only Stores begins a national expansion effort, it will run into stiff competition from Dollar General, Dollar Tree, and Family Dollar stores. If the company's track record is any indication of its future success, 99¢ Only Stores will compete successfully with its low cost strategy. "This is a penny business," says Schiffer, "but those pennies add up to millions of dollars."

1. Describe the components of 99¢ Only Stores' low-cost strategy.
2. What strategic advice can you offer Dave Gold to ensure 99¢ Only Stores' future success?
3. What are the sources of 99¢ Only Stores' competitive advantage? Are these sources likely to be sustainable as the company expands nationally?

Sources: Carlye Adler, "The 99¢ Empire," *FSB,* July/August 2003, pp. 86–92; "99¢ Only Stores Corporate Information," 99¢ Only Stores, www.99only.com/corpInfo.htm.

Step 7: Formulate Strategic Options and Select the Appropriate Strategies

4. Discuss the characteristics of three basic strategies: low cost, differentiation, and focus.

By this point in the strategic management process, entrepreneurs should have a clear picture of what their business does best and what its competitive advantages are. Similarly, they should know their firm's weaknesses and limitations as well as those of its competitors. The next step is to evaluate strategic options and then prepare a game plan designed to achieve the company's objectives.

Strategy. A **strategy** is a road map an entrepreneur draws up of the actions necessary to fulfill a company's mission, goals, and objectives. In other words, the mission, goals, and objectives spell out the *ends,* and the strategy defines the *means* for reaching them. A strategy is the master plan that covers all of the major parts of the organization and ties them together into a unified whole. The plan must be action oriented—that is, it should breathe life into the entire planning process. An entrepreneur must build a sound strategy based on the preceding steps that uses the company's core competencies as the springboard to success. Joseph Picken and Gregory Dess, authors of *Mission Critical: The 7 Strategic Traps That Derail Even the Smartest Companies,* write, "A flawed strategy—no matter how brilliant the leadership, no matter how effective the implementation—is doomed to fail. A sound strategy, implemented without error, wins every time."[28]

A successful strategy is comprehensive and well integrated, focusing on establishing the key success factors that the owner identified in Step 4. For instance, if maximum shelf space is a key success factor for a small manufacturer's product, the strategy must identify techniques for gaining more in-store shelf space (e.g., offering higher margins to distributors and brokers than competitors do, assisting retailers with in-store displays, or redesigning a wider, more attractive package). When building their strategies, successful companies avoid going toe-to-toe with more powerful rivals, choosing instead to be the dominant player in a specific market segment. They focus their resources on serving the customers in their corner of the market better than anyone else rather than trying to compete for market leadership with companies that are much stronger.

Three Strategic Options. The number of strategies from which entrepreneurs can choose is infinite. When all the glitter is stripped away, however, three basic strategies remain. In his classic book, *Competitive Strategy,* Michael Porter defines these strategies: (1) cost leadership, (2) differentiation, and (3) focus.

Cost Leadership. A company pursuing a **cost leadership strategy** strives to be the lowest-cost producer relative to its competitors in the industry. Low-cost leaders have a competitive advantage in reaching buyers whose primary purchase criterion is price, and they have the power to set the industry's price floor. This strategy works well when buyers are sensitive to price changes, when competing firms sell the same commodity products, and when companies can benefit from economies of scale. Not only is a low-cost leader in the best position to defend itself in a price war, but it also can use its power to attack competitors with the lowest price in the industry. "You have to be the lowest-cost producer in your patch," says the president of a company that sells the classic commodity product—cement.[29]

Company Example →

Google, the well-known Web search engine, relies on a low-cost strategy to stay on top in a fiercely competitive industry. Google's Web site receives 170 million page views a day and is the fourth most visited site in the world. Yet the company's information technology budget is just 10 percent of the industry average. Google's secret: Google's hardware system consists of more than 12,000 inexpensive servers linked together that, without monitors (no need!), cost just $2,000 each. Google's real cost savings, however, lies in its IT maintenance; if a server breaks, Google simply throws it away and replaces it! The company has no need for costly service contracts or an extensive in-house IT department.[30]

There are many ways to build a low-cost strategy, but the most successful cost leaders know where they have cost advantages over their competitors, and they use these as the foundation for their strategies. For example, because their workforces currently are nonunion, airlines JetBlue and AirTran have a significant advantage in labor costs, but not in fuel costs, over their larger, unionized competitors. For instance, AirTran's labor cost, the largest single cost in the airline business, is 29 percent of its operating expenses, compared to the industry average of 40 percent. AirTran also gets more out of its employees' time than its competitors through cross-utilization, giving workers multiple assignments and job duties. JetBlue keeps its maintenance costs low by flying only two types of jets—Airbus A320s on long routes and Embraer 190s on short routes. All of these factors mean that JetBlue and AirTran airplanes are in the air (the only place they can make money!) longer than their competitors' planes are. The result is a successful low-cost strategy for both companies. Customers are responding; sales at both airlines are climbing fast.[31]

Of course, there are dangers in following a cost leadership strategy. Sometimes a company focuses exclusively on lower manufacturing costs, without considering the impact of purchasing, distribution, or overhead costs. Another danger is misunderstanding the firm's true cost drivers. For instance, one furniture manufacturer drastically underestimated its overhead costs and, as a result, was selling its products at a loss. Finally, a company may pursue a low-cost leadership strategy so zealously that it essentially locks itself out of other strategic choices.

Differentiation. A company following a **differentiation strategy** seeks to build customer loyalty by positioning its goods or services in a unique or different fashion. In other words, a company strives to be better than its competitors at something that its customers value. The primary benefit of successful differentiation is the ability to generate higher profit margins because of customers' heightened brand loyalty and reduced price sensitivity. There are many ways to create a differentiation strategy, but the key is to be special at something that is important to customers and offers them unique value such as quality, convenience, flexibility, performance, or style. "You'd better be on top of what it is your customers value and continually improve your offerings to better deliver that value," advises Jill Griffin, a strategic marketing consultant.[32] If a small company can offer products or services that larger competitors do not, improve a product's or service's performance, reduce the customer's risk of purchasing it, or both, it has the potential to differentiate. For instance, at Petco, a chain of pet supply stores selling luxury pet products and services, only 40 of its more than 10,000 product offerings overlap the pet supply offerings of industry giant Wal-Mart.[33]

Even in industries in which giant companies dominate, small companies that differentiate themselves can thrive even when they cannot compete effectively on the basis of price. *For example, the success of Audiophile International, a Web-based vintage record business founded by John and Marianne Turton, depends on the entrepreneurs' ability to differentiate their company from the dozens of large music retailers that control the industry. The copreneurs have spent years educating themselves about hard-to-find vinyl LPs and CDs of all types of music (from Bella Fleck to Procol Harem), and customers say that the Turtons' expertise and customer-friendly attitude, not their prices, are what sets their business apart from competitors. Audiophile International removes the risk of buying online, allowing customers to return any product for any reason. The Turtons also spend hours listening to recordings, writing commentaries on them, and then sharing their knowledge with customers through a newsletter and individual e-mails.* Like Audiophile International, small companies can use their size to their advantage and build their differentiation strategies on the notion that small entrepreneurial businesses are friendlier, more responsive to customers, and more genuine than their larger rivals.

The key to a successful differentiation strategy is to build it on a *distinctive competency*—something the small company is uniquely good at doing in comparison to its competitors. Common bases for differentiation include superior customer service, special product features, complete product lines, a custom-tailored product or service, instantaneous parts availability, absolute product reliability, supreme product quality, extensive product knowledge, and the ability to build long-term, mutually beneficial relationships with customers. To be successful, a differentiation strategy must create the perception of value to the customer. No customer will purchase a good or service that fails to produce a *perceived* value, no matter how *real* that value may be. One business consultant advises, "Make sure you tell your customers and prospects what it is about your business that makes you different. Make sure that difference is in the form of a true benefit to the customer."[34] For instance, travelers in England can book accommodations at one of 34 different fully

Company Example →

operational lighthouses, many of which were built in the eighteenth and nineteenth centuries, offering panoramic views of pounding surf, rugged cliffs, and fascinating wildlife in out-of-the-way locations. For rates ranging from $480 to $1,700 for a minimum three-night stay, the cottages include thoroughly modern amenities, including telephones, high-definition televisions, central heat and air conditioning, and others. Travelers who stay at these lighthouses get more than just comfortable accommodations (which are available at thousands of "regular" hotels); they indulge themselves in a sense of history, adventure, and beauty unavailable at most hotels and bed-and-breakfasts inns.[35]

Pursuing a differentiation strategy includes certain risks. One danger is trying to differentiate a product or service on the basis of something that does not boost its performance or lower its cost to the buyer. Another pitfall is overdifferentiating and charging so much that a company prices its products out of its target customers' reach. Another risk is focusing only on the physical characteristics of a product or service and ignoring important psychological factors—status, prestige, image, and style. For many successful companies, psychological factors are key elements in differentiating their products and services from those of competitors.

Focus. A **focus strategy** recognizes that not all markets are homogeneous. In fact, in any given market, there are many different customer segments, each having different needs, wants, and characteristics. The principal idea of this strategy is to select one (or more) segment(s); identify customers' special needs, wants, and interests; and approach them with a good or service designed to excel in meeting these needs, wants, and interests. Focus strategies build on *differences* among market segments. Using a focus strategy, entrepreneurs concentrate on serving a niche in the market rather than trying to reach the entire market.

A successful focus strategy depends on a small company's ability to identify the changing needs of its targeted customer group and to develop the skills required to serve them. That means the owner and everyone in the organization must have a clear understanding of how to add value to the product or service for the customer. How does the product or service meet the customer's needs at each stage—from raw material to final sale?

Rather than attempting to serve the total market, a company pursuing a focus strategy specializes in serving a specific target segment or niche that larger companies are overlooking or underestimating. A focus strategy is ideally suited to many small businesses, which often lack the resources to reach a national market. Their goal is to serve their narrow target markets more effectively and efficiently than do competitors that pound away at the broad market. Common bases for building a focus strategy include zeroing in on a small geographic area, targeting a group of customers with similar needs or interests (e.g., left-handed people), or specializing in a specific product or service (e.g., petite clothing). *For example, Wayne and Marty Scott, owners of Clown Shoes and Props, have captured about 20 percent of the U.S. market for clown shoes! The copreneurs learned their craft while working at the Ringling Brothers Circus in the 1960s and now fill orders from across the country for wingtips that are two feet long. The Scotts offer nine basic clown shoe styles, each a shoe within a shoe, and add accessories such as squirting flowers, trains, and mouths that open and close with each step. Making clown shoes is serious business for the Scotts, however; the average pair sells for $225. Before making a pair of shoes, the Scotts insist on a description of the clown's character and a picture of the clown in costume. "A clown isn't complete without the right shoes," says Peggy Williams, a former clown and now a manager at Ringling Brothers, "and you can't get these at the mall."*[36]

Like the Scotts, the most successful focusers build a competitive edge by concentrating on specific market niches and serving them better than any other competitor can. Essentially, this strategy depends on creating value for the customer either by being the lowest-cost producer or by differentiating the product or service in a unique fashion, but doing so in a narrow target segment. Speedy service, a unique product or service, superior customer service, and convenience are important strengths for companies using focus strategies. Consider the following examples of small companies competing successfully in small, yet profitable, niches:

Company Example

In 1949, Frank Zamboni created the machine that bears his name and is recognized by hockey fans across the globe. The maker of "the coolest machine on ice," Zamboni dominates the ice resurfacing market by implementing a focus strategy that emphasizes continuous improvement and superior quality. Here Frank Zamboni (center) works on experimental Prototype No. 3 in 1947.

- Brian Workman and Paul Rodgers, owners of Blind Corners and Curves, design and make custom window coverings for oddly shaped windows. Launched in 1999 in Denver, Colorado, their business now generates sales of more than $1 million a year.
- Donna Quinn's company, Tall Walls Inc., specializes in selling art, sculpture, tapestries, lighting, and other decorations for homes with large walls.[37]
- The Zamboni Company is the market leader in ice resurfacing machines with a famous product that bears the founder's name. In 1949, Frank Zamboni invented the first ice resurfacing machine in an attempt to reduce the amount of time spent manually resurfacing the ice at his rink. The time-consuming resurfacing process involved five workers and took up to an hour and a half to complete. Today, the company sells machines all around the world and hockey fans know that the Zamboni machine comes out to resurface the ice in between periods.[38]
- David Wilson's company, Wilson Audio, occupies a niche at the very top of the market for stereo speakers. The company, which targets real audiophiles who have the resources to indulge their desire for the supreme musical experience, manufactures and sells the world's highest-quality—and most expensive—speakers. The hardware that holds the speakers together is made of austenitic stainless steel (often used in the aerospace industry), and workers fashion their own speaker wire out of raw copper rather than buy off-the-shelf wiring. Wilson Audio holds a commanding 50 percent share of the ultra-high-end niche in the market for speakers, with many of its models selling for more than $100,000! Its "low-end" speakers (the Sophia line) sell for $11,700, and its top-of-the-line WAMMs are listed at $225,000. "We've selected a small slice of the market where the big predators aren't interested in going," says Wilson, explaining his company's focus strategy.[39]

The rewards of dominating a niche can be huge, but pursuing a focus strategy does carry risks. Companies sometimes must struggle to capture a large enough share of a small market to be profitable. A niche must be big enough for a company to generate a profit. A successful focus strategy also brings with it a threat. If a small company is successful in its niche, there is the danger of larger competitors entering the market and eroding or controlling it. Sometimes a company with a successful niche strategy gets distracted by its success and tries to branch out into other areas. As it drifts farther away from its core strategy, it loses its competitive edge and runs the risk of confusing or alienating its customers. Muddying its image with customers puts a company in danger of losing its identity.

An effective strategic plan identifies a complete set of success factors—financial, operating, and marketing—that, taken together, produce a competitive advantage for the small business. The resulting action plan distinguishes the firm from its competitors by exploiting its competitive advantage. The focal point of this entire strategic plan is the customer. The customer is the nucleus of any business, so a competitive strategy will succeed only if it is aimed at serving customers better than the competitor does. An effective strategy draws out the competitive advantage in a small company by building on its strengths and by making the customer its focus. It also defines methods for overcoming a company's weaknesses, and it identifies opportunities and threats that demand action.

Step 8: Translate Strategic Plans into Action Plans

No strategic plan is complete until it is put into action. Entrepreneurs must convert strategic plans into operating plans that guide their companies on a daily basis and become a visible, active part of their businesses. No small business can benefit from a strategic plan sitting on a shelf collecting dust.

Implement the Strategy. To make the plan workable, business owners should divide the plan into projects, carefully defining each one by the following:

Purpose. What is the project designed to accomplish?
Scope. Which areas of the company will be involved in the project?
Contribution. How does the project relate to other projects and to the overall strategic plan?
Resource requirements. What human and financial resources are needed to complete the project successfully?
Timing. Which schedules and deadlines will ensure project completion?

Once entrepreneurs assign priorities to these projects, they can begin to implement the strategic plan. Involving employees and delegating adequate authority to them is essential because these projects affect them most directly.

If an organization's people have been involved in the strategic management process to this point, they will have a better grasp of the steps they must take to achieve the organization's goals as well as their own professional goals. Early involvement of the workforce in the strategic management process is a luxury that larger businesses cannot achieve. Commitment to achieve the objectives of the firm is a powerful force for success, but involvement is a prerequisite for achieving total employee commitment. Without a committed, dedicated team of employees working together to implement strategy, a company's strategy, no matter how well planned, usually fails.

When putting their strategic plans into action, small companies must exploit all of the competitive advantages of their size by:

■ Responding quickly to customers' needs.
■ Remaining flexible and willing to change.
■ Continually searching for new emerging market segments.
■ Building and defending market niches.

- Erecting "switching costs" through personal service and special attention.
- Remaining entrepreneurial and willing to take risks.
- Acting with lightning speed to move into and out of markets as they ebb and flow.
- Constantly innovating.

Although it is possible for competitors to replicate a small company's strategy, it is much more difficult for them to mimic the way in which it implements and executes its strategy.

IN THE FOOTSTEPS OF AN ENTREPRENEUR...

A Strategy Set in Stone

Since launching his business, Rhodes Architectural Stone, in 1984, Richard Rhodes has traveled the world in search of quarries to supply the unusual stone his clients want to use in the construction of their homes and landscape features. In 1997, his business took a turn into a unique segment of the market. Rhodes was at a quarry in China looking for a particular type and color of granite for a house for Oracle CEO Larry Ellison that recreated a fifteenth-century Japanese temple complex. He took a side trip to see the famous gorges of the Yangtze River, where he saw many ancient Chinese villages with buildings made of beautiful stone. Because of the construction of Three Gorges Dam, all of these monuments, temples, houses, and buildings—literally tons of irreplaceable antique material—would soon be under 600 feet of water. The dam would flood an area about the size of Los Angeles, covering nearly 1,700 villages, some of which had remained virtually unchanged for hundreds of years.

Looking at the soon-to-be lost villages, Rhodes saw a business opportunity. "To see these beautiful materials lost seemed like a tragedy," he says. So he bought them. He and his employees began salvaging and shipping stone roads, walls, pavers, staircases, battlements, sills, lintels, and other items, all tinged and veined with beautiful colors from the iron and magnesium found in the soil. Some even contained fossilized remains of ancient sea creatures.

Rhodes Architectural Stone began selling the antique stone material to upscale customers in the United States and around the world for whom price is not the major factor in a purchase decision. "Our customers are not building for shelter," explains Rhodes. "Our customers want beauty. More than that, they want emotional resonance." Rhodes estimates that the recovered stone he sells "is three times the price" of standard quarried stone. In addition to Larry

Ellison, Rhodes counts as customers other notable names such as Oprah Winfrey and Wall Street financier Steve Steinman, who is building a 37,000-square-foot mansion made completely out of stone salvaged from the Three Gorges area. Rhodes estimates that this project alone will require 4,000 tons of stone!

The World Wide Web has enabled Rhodes to operate his company, which now generates sales of more than $10 million annually, more effectively and efficiently. He and his employees are traveling the globe, often in remote locations that make taking standard photographs of objects and mailing them to potential customers impractical if not impossible. Now equipped with digital cameras and laptop computers, Rhodes and his 14 international scouts can take pictures of ancient Indonesian roads, Chinese walls, or Indian barracks and e-mail them to customers or post them on the company's Web site. The company has even developed a character-based "language" making it possible to communicate with the 600 stonecutters located around the world, many of whom are illiterate. "We're an eighteenth century business using twenty-first century information technology," says Rhodes.

1. Which of the three strategies described in this chapter is Richard Rhodes using? Explain.
2. What advantages does successful execution of this strategy produce for Rhodes Architectural Stone?
3. What are the risks associated with this strategy?

Sources: April Y. Pennington, "Richard Rhodes," *Entrepreneur,* August 2003, p. 19; "Stones Salvaged from Dam Site in Three Gorges Adorn Homes of Wealthy in U.S.," MSNBC, June 26, 2003, www.rhodes.org/Press_Coverage/msnbc/6–26–2003.pdf ; Guy Trebay, "From Ming to the Patio," *New York Times,* June 26, 2003, www.rhodes.org/Press_Coverage/nytimes/nytimes%206–26–2003.pdf ; "Rock Star," *Inc.,* December 2002, www.rhodes.org/Press_Coverage/inc/december%202002.pdf.

5. Understand the importance of controls, such as the balanced scorecard, in the planning process.

Step 9: Establish Accurate Controls

So far, the planning process has created company objectives and has developed a strategy for reaching them, but rarely, if ever, will the company's actual performance match stated objectives. Entrepreneurs quickly realize the need to control actual results that deviate from plans.

Controlling the Strategy. Planning without control has little operational value, and so a sound planning program requires a practical control process. The plans created in this process become the standards against which actual performance is measured. It is important for everyone in the organization to understand—and to be involved in—the planning and controlling process.

Controlling projects and keeping them on schedule means that the owner must identify and track key performance indicators. The source of these indicators is the operating data from the company's normal business activity; they are the guideposts for detecting deviations from established standards. Accounting, production, sales, inventory, and other operating records are primary sources of data the manager can use for controlling activities. For example, on a customer service project, performance indicators might include customer complaints, orders returned, on-time shipments, and order accuracy.

To evaluate the effectiveness of their strategies, some companies are developing **balanced scorecards,** a set of measurements unique to a company that includes both financial and operational measures and gives managers a quick yet comprehensive picture of the company's total performance. One writer says that a balanced scorecard:

> is a sophisticated business model that helps a company understand what's really driving its success. It acts a bit like the control panel on a spaceship—the business equivalent of a flight speedometer, odometer, and temperature gauge all rolled into one. It keeps track of many things, including financial progress and softer measurements—everything from customer satisfaction to return on investment—that need to be managed to reach the final destination: profitable growth.[40]

Rather than sticking solely to the traditional financial measures of a company's performance, the balanced scorecard gives managers a comprehensive view from *both a financial and an operational perspective.* The premise behind such a scorecard is that relying on any single measure of company performance is dangerous. Just as a pilot in command of a jet cannot fly safely by focusing on a single instrument, an entrepreneur cannot manage a company by concentrating on a single measurement. The complexity of managing a business demands that an entrepreneur be able to see performance measures in several areas simultaneously. Those measures might include traditional standards such as financial ratios or cash flow performance and gauges of product innovation; customer satisfaction, retention, and profitability; as well as measures of vendor performance and inventory management.

When the balanced scorecard is properly used, an entrepreneur can trace the elements on the company's balanced scorecard back to its mission, goals, and objectives. The goal is to develop a reporting system that does not funnel meaningful information only to a few decision makers but that makes it available in a timely manner throughout the entire company, enabling employees at all levels to make decisions based on strategic priorities. A balanced scorecard reporting system should collect, organize, and display meaningful information that managers and employees need to make daily decisions that are congruent with the company's overall strategy and it must do so in a concise,

Figure 2.3

The Balanced Scorecard
Links Performance
Measures

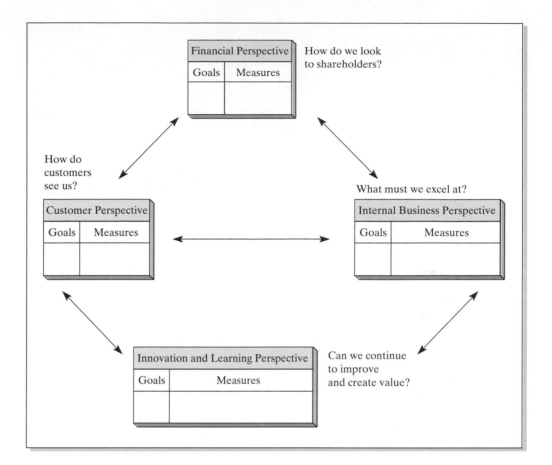

easy-to-read, timely manner. When creating a balanced scorecard for a company, the key is to establish goals for each critical indicator of company performance and then create meaningful measures for each one. Although some elements will apply to many businesses, a company's scorecard should be unique. The balanced scorecard looks at a business from four important perspectives (see Figure 2.3):[41]

> *Customer perspective:* How do customers see us? Customers judge companies by at least four standards: time (how long it takes the company to deliver a good or service), quality (how well a company's product or service performs in terms of reliability, durability, and accuracy), performance (the extent to which a good or service performs as expected), and service (how well a company meets or exceeds customers' expectations of value). Because customer-related goals are external, managers must translate them into measures of what the company must do to meet customers' expectations.

> *Internal business perspective:* What must we excel at? The internal factors that managers should focus on are those that have the greatest impact on customer satisfaction and retention and on company effectiveness and efficiency. Developing goals and measures for factors such as quality, cycle time, productivity, costs, and others that employees directly influence is essential.

> *Innovation and learning perspective:* Can we continue to improve and create value? This view of a company recognizes that the targets required for success are never static; they are constantly changing. If a company wants to continue its pattern of success, it cannot stand still; it must continuously improve. A company's ability to innovate, learn, and improve determines its future. These goals and measures

emphasize the importance of continuous improvement in customer satisfaction and internal business operations.

Financial perspective: How do we look to shareholders? The most traditional performance measures—financial standards—tell how much the company's overall strategy and its execution are contributing to its bottom line. These measures focus on such factors as profitability, growth, and shareholder value. On balanced scorecards, companies often break their financial goals into three categories: survival, success, and growth.

Company Example →

John Garrett, copresident of Triad Distributing-Northwest Inc., a building supplies wholesaler in Idaho, monitors hourly the balanced scorecard his company has developed. It incorporates an array of measures, including cash on hand, accounts payable and accounts receivable balances, inventory levels, new customer accounts, and several measures unique to both the industry and the company. As he sees key measures change, Garrett can act immediately, working with people throughout the company to address them. Recently when he opened the balanced scorecard, he noted a $9,000 sale to a new customer. Garrett called to congratulate the salesperson and then called the customer to introduce himself, starting off the new relationship on a positive note. "It's a great way to keep in touch with the pulse of the company," he says. "It gives you that quick overview of your business so, on the fly, you can see where your business is going."[42]

Although the balanced scorecard is a vital tool that helps managers keep their companies on track, it is also an important tool for changing behavior in an organization and for keeping everyone focused on what really matters. As conditions change, managers must make corrections in performance policies, strategies, and objectives to get performance back on track. Increasingly, companies are linking performance on the metrics included in their balanced scorecards to employees' compensation. A practical control system is also economical to operate. Most small businesses have no need for a sophisticated, expensive control system. The system should be so practical that it becomes a natural part of the management process.

Conclusion

The strategic planning process does *not* end with the nine steps outlined here; it is an ongoing procedure that a small business owner must repeat. With each round, he or she gains experience, and the steps become much easier. The planning process outlined here is designed to be as simple as possible. No small business should be burdened with an elaborate, detailed, formal planning process that it cannot easily use. Such programs require excessive amounts of time to operate, and they generate a sea of paperwork. The small business manager needs neither.

What does this strategic planning process lead to? It teaches a entrepreneurs a degree of discipline that is important to their business's survival. It helps them to learn about their business, their competitors, and, most important, their customers. It forces small business owners to recognize and evaluate their company's strengths and weaknesses as well as the opportunities and threats facing it. It also encourages entrepreneurs to define how they will set their business apart from the competition. Although strategic planning cannot guarantee success, it does dramatically increase the small firm's chances of survival in a hostile business environment. Unfortunately, most business owners forgo the benefits of strategic planning. A recent survey of family businesses by Arthur Andersen Consulting and MassMutual Life Insurance Company found that just 30 percent of the companies had a written strategic plan.[43] Don't let that happen to you!

▌ ▌ ▌ Chapter Review

1. Understand the importance of strategic management to a small business.

   ▪ Strategic planning, often ignored by small companies, is a crucial ingredient in business success. The planning process forces potential entrepreneurs to subject their ideas to an objective evaluation in the competitive market.

2. Explain why and how a small business must create a competitive advantage in the market.

   ▪ The goal of developing a strategic plan is to create for the small company a competitive advantage—the aggregation of factors that sets the small business apart from its competitors and gives it a unique position in the market. Every small firm must establish a plan for creating a unique image in the minds of its potential customers.

3. Develop a strategic plan for a business using the nine steps in the strategic planning process.

   ▪ Small businesses need a strategic planning process designed to suit their particular needs. It should be relatively short, be informal and not structured, encourage the participation of employees, and not begin with extensive objective setting. Linking the purposeful action of strategic planning to an entrepreneur's ideas can produce results that shape the future.

   Step 1 Develop a clear vision and translate it into a meaningful mission statement. Highly successful entrepreneurs are able to communicate their vision to those around them. The firm's mission statement answers the first question of any venture: What business am I in? The mission statement sets the tone for the entire company.

   Step 2 Assess the company's strengths and weaknesses. Strengths are positive internal factors; weaknesses are negative internal factors.

   Step 3 Scan the environment for significant opportunities and threats facing the business. Opportunities are positive external options; threats are negative external forces.

   Step 4 Identify the key factors for success in the business. In every business, key factors determine the success of the firms in it, and so they must be an integral part of a company' strategy. Key success factors are relationships between a controllable variable (e.g., plant size, size of sales force, advertising expenditures, product packaging) and a critical factor influencing the firm's ability to compete in the market.

   Step 5 Analyze the competition. Business owners should know their competitors almost as well as they know their own company. A competitive profile matrix is a helpful tool for analyzing competitors' strengths and weaknesses.

   Step 6 Create company goals and objectives. Goals are the broad, long-range targets that the firm seeks to accomplish. Objectives are quantifiable and more precise; they should be specific, measurable, assignable, realistic, timely, and written down. The process works best when subordinate managers and employees are actively involved.

   Step 7 Formulate strategic options and select the appropriate strategies. A strategy is the game plan the firm plans to use to achieve its objectives and mission. It must center on establishing for the firm the key success factors identified earlier.

   Step 8 Translate strategic plans into action plans. No strategic plan is complete until the owner puts it into action.

   Step 9 Establish accurate controls. Actual performance rarely, if ever, matches plans exactly. Operating data from the business serve as guideposts for detecting deviations from plans. Such information is helpful when plotting future strategies.

   The strategic planning process does not end with these nine steps; rather, it is an ongoing process that the owner must repeat.

4. Discuss the characteristics of three basic strategies: low cost, differentiation, and focus.

   ▪ Three basic strategic options are cost leadership, differentiation, and focus. A company pursuing a cost leadership strategy strives to be the lowest-cost producer relative to its competitors in the industry.

   A company following a differentiation strategy seeks to build customer loyalty by positioning its goods or services in a unique or different fashion. In other words, the firm strives to be better than its competitors at something that customers value.

   A focus strategy recognizes that not all markets are homogeneous. The principal idea of this strategy is to select one (or more) segment(s), identify customers' special needs, wants, and interests, and approach them with a good or service designed to excel in meeting these needs, wants, and interests. Focus strategies build on differences among market segments.

5. Understand the importance of controls, such as the balanced scorecard, in the planning process.

   ▪ Just as a pilot in command of a jet cannot fly safely by focusing on a single instrument, an entrepreneur cannot manage a company by concentrating on a single measurement. The balanced scorecard is a set of measurements unique to a company that includes both financial and operational measures and gives managers a quick yet comprehensive picture of the company's total performance.

▌▌▐ Discussion Questions

1. Why is strategic planning important to a small company?
2. What is a competitive advantage? Why is it important for a small business to establish one?
3. What are the steps in the strategic management process?
4. What are strengths, weaknesses, opportunities, and threats? Give an example of each.
5. What is knowledge management? What benefits does it offer a small company?
6. Explain the characteristics of effective objectives. Why is setting objectives important?
7. What are business strategies? Explain the three basic strategies from which entrepreneurs can choose. Give an example of each one.
8. Describe the three basic strategies available to small companies. Under what conditions is each most successful?
9. How is the controlling process related to the planning process?
10. What is a balanced scorecard? What value does it offer entrepreneurs who are evaluating the success of their current strategies?

Strategic Management and the Entrepreneur

Business PlanPro

Chapter 2 is designed to help you think about your business from a strategic perspective. You may find it helpful to review the concepts in the chapter before completing this portion of Business Plan Pro.

In this part of the EasyPlan Wizard, you will develop the first draft of a mission statement for your business, identify your company's strengths and weaknesses, define the principal opportunities and threats facing your business, and identify the key success factors in your industry. You also will have the opportunity to assess your competitors based on their strengths and weaknesses in these key success factors. Then based on the key success factors you have identified, you will establish meaningful goals and objectives that your company must accomplish to be successful. Recall that the weights you assign to the key success factors reflect their relative importance (you can have them sum to 1.00 for simplicity, but that's not necessary). Review Chapter 2 for tips on assigning the scores (1 to 4) on each key success factor. Calculate the weighted score for each company on each key success factor by multiplying the weight by the score, and then get the total weighted score for each company. Which company has the highest total weighted score? Consider the scores for each company on each of the key success factors (i.e., scan across the table). What are the strategic implications of these scores?

Based on your strategic analysis, which of the three business strategies—low cost, differentiation, or focus—will you use to give your company a competitive advantage? How will you customize this strategy to capitalize on your company's strengths and to appeal to your customers" needs? Finally, how do you plan to review the success of your company's strategic plan? How often will you conduct a strategic performance review?

Chapter 3
Choosing a Form of Ownership

"
By the time a partnership dissolves, it has dissolved.
—John Updike

Some regard private enterprise as if it were a predatory tiger to be shot. Others look upon it as a cow that they can milk. Only a handful see it for what it really is: the strong horse that pulls the whole cart.
—Sir Winston Churchill
"

Upon completion of this chapter, you will be able to:

1. Discuss the issues entrepreneurs should consider when evaluating different forms of ownership.

2. Describe the advantages and disadvantages of the sole proprietorship.

3. Describe the advantages and disadvantages of the partnership.

4. Describe the advantages and disadvantages of the corporation.

5. Describe the features of the alternative forms of ownership such as the S corporation, the limited liability company, joint venture, and syndicate.

Entrepreneurs must recognize that, with rare exception, they are not trained in the finer points of business law. Consequently, before selecting the form of ownership for a new business venture, it is imperative that an entrepreneur review the types of legal ownership and then consult an attorney and/or accountant to verify whether the choice best addresses the specific needs of the entrepreneur. Although any choice is not irreversible, changing the form of ownership can be expensive and often complicated.

Each form of ownership has its own unique set of advantages and disadvantages. The key to choosing the "right" form of ownership is the ability to understand the characteristics of each and knowing how they affect an entrepreneur's business and personal circumstances.

Before we examine the different legal forms of ownership, the following are typical issues an entrepreneur should consider in the evaluation process:

1. Discuss the issues entrepreneurs should consider when evaluating different forms of ownership.

- *Tax considerations.* Because of the graduated tax rates under each form of ownership, the government's constant tinkering with the tax code, and the year-to-year fluctuations in a company's income, an entrepreneur should calculate the firm's tax bill under each ownership option every year. Changes in federal or state tax codes may have a significant impact on the firm's bottom line.

- *Liability exposure.* Certain forms of ownership offer business owners greater protection from personal liability due to financial problems, faulty products, and a host of other difficulties. Entrepreneurs must weigh the potential for legal and financial liabilities and decide the extent to which they are willing to assume personal responsibility for their companies' obligations. Individuals with significant personal wealth or a low tolerance for the risk of loss may choose a form of ownership that provides greater protection of personal assets.

- *Start-up and future capital requirements.* The form of ownership can impact an entrepreneur's ability to raise start-up capital. Depending on how much capital is needed and the source from which it is to be obtained, some forms of ownership are better when obtaining start-up capital. Also, as a business grows, capital requirements increase, and some forms of ownership make it easier to attract outside financing.

- *Control.* By choosing certain forms of ownership, an entrepreneur automatically gives up some control over the company. Each individual must decide early on how much control he or she is willing to sacrifice in exchange for help from other people or organizations. *For example, the founder of an Internet health portal site diligently labored for more than a year to build the operational "skeleton" of a very impressive Web site. This work was done utilizing existing resources and volunteer labor from a large medical organization but was stopped once the existing resources were exhausted. The reason: The founder did not want to give up control to investors who were willing to financially back the venture!* Some ventures, when beginning to grow rapidly, require a great deal of financial capital.

  Company Example →

- *Managerial ability.* Entrepreneurs must assess their own ability to manage their companies successfully. If they lack skill or experience in certain areas, they may need to select a form of ownership that enables them to bring individuals who possess those needed skills or experience into the company. The decline and failure of many high-profile Internet companies during the 2001 economic downturn can in many cases be directly linked to the lack of managerial and basic business skills, resulting in a series of bad business decisions. Approximately 31 million Americans have been directly or indirectly affected by the dot-com downturn. According to a survey by the Pew Internet and American Life Project, more than 56 percent of Americans who are aware of dot-coms' financial woes say the dot-coms' business plans were a problem; cyber companies did not have a clear plan for profitability, and this contributed to subsequent financial problems. Another 38 percent of Americans who are aware of dot-coms' financial woes say the youth and inexperience of those running Internet companies was a reason behind the dot-com downturn.[1]

- *Business goals.* How big and how profitable an entrepreneur plans for the business to become will influence the form of ownership chosen. Businesses often evolve into a different form of ownership as they grow, but moving from some formats can be complex and expensive. Legislation can change in ways that make current options to convert ownership type no longer viable.
- *Management succession plans.* When choosing a form of ownership, business owners must look ahead to the day when they will pass their companies on to the next generation or to a buyer. Some forms of ownership make this transition easier. In other cases, when the owner dies, so does the business.
- *Cost of formation.* Some forms of ownership are much more costly and complex to create. Entrepreneurs must weigh carefully the benefits and the costs of the particular form they choose.

Business owners have traditionally had three major forms of ownership from which to choose: the sole proprietorship, the partnership, and the corporation. (See Figure 3.1 for a breakdown of the major forms of ownership.) In recent years, various hybrid forms of ownership have developed, including the S corporation, the limited liability company, and the joint venture.

Figure 3.1

Forms of Business Ownership

Source: Statistics of Income Bulletin, Internal Revenue Service, October 2003.

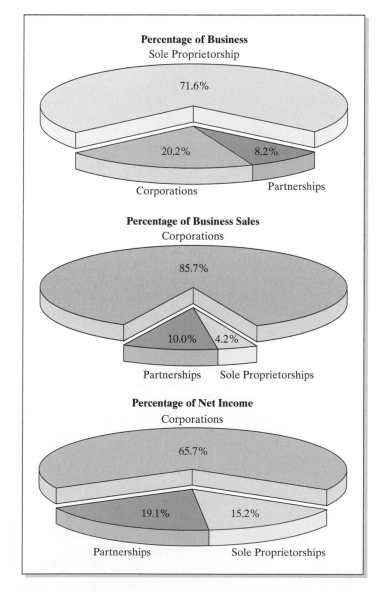

✦ Gaining *a* Competitive Edge ✦

What Does the Name of Your Business Convey to Potential Customers?

For some people, something as simple as naming the business seems totally irrelevant. But for one company in Stamford, Connecticut, the choice of a name became the company's worst nightmare. GHB Marketing Communications started getting numerous e-mails and phone calls requesting a certain product. Sounds harmless. Right? Wrong! The product that individuals were seeking was GHB—an illegal drug known as ecstasy. "Imagine having a 30-year-old company named LSD, Inc. in the late 60s," says company President Mark Bruce. "Then you can begin to understand what we went through. "The new name (HiTechPR) cost the owners $20,000.

Choosing a memorable name can be one of the most fun—and most challenging—aspects of starting a business. Large companies spend hundreds of thousands of dollars researching names. Although small businesses do not normally have unlimited resources at their disposal, you can use the same tools and development process that large companies use to catch the customer's eye.

Look at your name from the perspective of potential customers. The customer may want to be reassured (Gentle Dentistry) or may prefer a bit of humor (The Barking Lot Dog Grooming). Other choices might be to convey an image to your customers that is compatible with your business strategy. For example: Discount Hair Products, Quality Muffler, or Pay Less Auto Detailing. In addition, most of us are familiar with the upscale practice of including foreign phrases (especially French) to convey an exclusive image. La Petite Day Care sounds more upscale than Small Day Care.

Whatever the image you wish to communicate to an audience of potential customers, the process of choosing the "perfect" name involves a series of steps.

1. Decide the most appropriate single quality of the business that you wish to convey. Avoid sending a mixed or inappropriate message. Remember: A name is the single most visible attribute of your company. It will be displayed on all of your advertising and printed material, it portrays a personality, stands out in a crowd, and sticks in the minds of consumers if done properly.

2. Avoid names that are hard to spell, pronounce, or remember. This is especially true if your business is an Internet company or if you plan on having a Web site. Try typing in posiesbythedozenandthensomefromrosie.com a few times before you decide this is *the* name for your online flower store!

3. Select a name that is short, attention getting, and memorable. The name can be your initial marketing tool to attract new customers. Rosiesposies.com may be a better choice than the preceding example.

4. Be creative but in good taste!

5. Make sure your choice of a name won't get dated quickly. Big Stiff Hair Salon might have been a great name in the 1950s, but it would have died a horrible death in the 1960s as long straight locks became the norm.

6. Be careful that the name, while catchy and cute, doesn't create a negative image. Ask yourself: Does Rent-a-Wreck attract you because you think you'll save money on a car rental or does the name put you off because you question the reliability of its cars?

7. Once you have selected a suitable name, practice using it for a few days. Try it out on friends and family. "Hello, I am the CEO of FlubberDuds" may get on your nerves after the first few times.

8. Finally, after all is said and done and you are comfortable with your choice, conduct a name search to make sure that no one else in your jurisdiction has already claimed the name. This is an especially tedious chore if you are starting an Internet company. Registering a domain name can be daunting because quite often you will find that your brilliant idea is already taken—but it just might be available for the tidy sum of $1.9 million!

There are millions of names in the marketplace. Coming up with the one that is just right can help greatly in creating a brand image for your business. Choosing a name that is distinctive, memorable, and positive can go a long way toward helping you achieve success in your business venture. What's in a name? Everything!

Sources: Elizabeth Weinstein, "GHB Marketing Finds Its Name Is One Thing It Doesn't Want to Plug," *Wall Street Journal,* June 7, 2001 p. A1, A8. Andrew Raskin, "The Name of the Game," *Inc.,* February, 2000, pp. 31–32; Rhonda Adams, "Sometimes Business Success Is All In the Name," *Business,* July 23, 2000, p. 3; Thomas Edmark, "What's in a Name?" *Entrepreneur,* October 1999, pp. 163–165.

Sole proprietor Juan "Punchy" Gonzalez at work in Diet of Worms Studios (DOW) in Tampa, Florida. Artists recording at DOW include Morbid Angel, As Under, Diabolic, and others. Because of its simplicity and ease of formation, the sole proprietorship is by far the most popular form of business ownership in the United States.

The Sole Proprietorship

A sole proprietorship is a business owned and managed by one individual. Because of its simplicity and ease of formation, this is by far the most popular form of ownership in the United States.

2. Describe the advantages and disadvantages of the sole proprietorship.

Advantages of a Sole Proprietorship

Simple to Create. One attractive feature of a proprietorship is the ease and speed of its formation. If entrepreneurs want to form a business under their own name (e.g., J. Jolly Financial Consulting), they obtain the necessary business licenses from state, county, and/or local governments and begin operation. In most cases, entrepreneurs can complete all of the necessary paperwork in a single day because few barriers exist to creating a sole proprietorship.

Least Costly Form of Ownership to Establish. In addition to being quick and easy to create, the proprietorship is generally the least expensive form of ownership to establish. There is no need to create and file the legal documents that are recommended for partnerships and are required for corporations. An entrepreneur simply goes to the city or county government, states the nature of the business, and pays the appropriate fees and license costs. Paying these fees and license costs gives the entrepreneur the right to conduct business in that particular jurisdiction.

In many jurisdictions, entrepreneurs planning to conduct business under a trade name are usually required to acquire a Certificate of Doing Business under an Assumed Name from the secretary of state. An entrepreneur functioning as a sole proprietor may want to use his or her own name for the company name, such as Bob Smith Towing Service. On the other hand, many entrepreneurs view their company names as a way of

Company Example → using creativity to distinguish themselves in the market. *Kenneth Wolf resolved to find a name for his New York City–based software company that would distinguish it from the bland monikers so many companies pick. He and his partner settled on the name Revelwood for the company. The name alludes to a favorite series of novels, the Chronicles of Thomas*

Covenant the Unbeliever, by Stephen R. Donaldson. The fictional Revelwood is a village in the trees where characters study the knowledge and lore of the land. Because Revelwood fosters knowledge acquisition—its software helps companies gather business intelligence—Wolf boasts that the name fits the business perfectly.[2]

The fee for the Certificate of Doing Business under an Assumed Name is usually nominal. Acquiring this certificate involves conducting a search to determine that the name chosen for the business is not already registered as a trademark or service mark with the secretary of state. Filing this certificate also notifies the state of who owns the business. Additionally, most states now require notice of the trade name to be published in a newspaper serving the trading area of the business.

Profit Incentive. One major advantage of the proprietorship is that once owners have paid all of the company's expenses, they can keep the remaining profits (less taxes, of course). The profit incentive is a powerful one, and among entrepreneurs profits represent an excellent way of "keeping score" in the game of the business.

Total Decision-Making Authority. Because sole proprietors are in total control of operations, they can respond quickly to changes. The ability to respond quickly is an asset in a rapidly shifting market, so the freedom to set the company's course of action is both a major motivational and strategic force. For people who thrive on seeking new opportunities, the freedom of fast, flexible decision making is vital. The entrepreneur alone directs the operations of the business.

No Special Legal Restrictions. The proprietorship is the least regulated form of business ownership. In a time when government requests for information seem never-ending, this feature has much merit.

Easy to Discontinue. If the entrepreneur decides to discontinue operations, he or she can terminate the business quickly, even though he or she will still be liable for all of the business's outstanding debts and obligations.

Although these advantages of a proprietorship are extremely attractive to most individuals contemplating starting a new business, it is important to recognize that this form of ownership has some significant disadvantages.

IN THE FOOTSTEPS OF AN ENTREPRENEUR...

A Brief History

Many environmental factors must be analyzed when trying to decide which form of ownership is best. Over the past two decades, fluctuating tax rates and changes in the legal environment have had a significant impact on the popularity of certain forms of ownership. For example, prior to 1981, maximum individual marginal tax rates exceeded the maximum rates for C corporations. This made C corporations an appealing choice from a tax standpoint. However, the 1981 Tax Act lowered the maximum individual tax rate from 70 percent to 50 percent. At the same time,

the maximum corporate rate decreased from 48 percent to 46 percent. Then in 1986, the Tax Reform Act (TRA 86) established a maximum rate for individuals that was lower than the tax rate for C corporations. The maximum individual rate became 28 percent, compared to the maximum corporate rate of 34 percent. TRA 86 led to an increased popularity of conduit entities such as partnerships and S corporations, vis-à-vis C corporations. Today, the individual rate once again exceeds the corporate rate, though not at the magnitude prior to 1981.

In addition to the impact of changing tax laws on the choice of form of ownership, liability or limiting exposure has become a major factor in business planning. Many accounting firms learned a bitter lesson about personal liability in the early 1980s. Accounting firms organized as general partnerships were devastated by their legal responsibility for the savings and loan crisis. Plaintiffs attached the personal assets of partners regardless of direct responsibility for malfeasance. As a result, the S corporation became a viable choice as owners sought to limit their personal legal liability. However, restraints on ownership and capital structure limited the usefulness of the S corporation. Demand rose for a hybrid form of ownership that would offer more flexibility to maximize individual taxpayers' advantage and, at the same time, increase liability protection for owners. In 1988, the IRS issued Revenue Ruling 88–76, which provided a guide for states to follow the lead of Wyoming (which adopted the first LLC statute in 1977) and develop their own LLC laws. Then, in 1991, Texas enacted the first LLP statute. Many states initially restricted the use of LLCs by professionals such as physicians and attorneys. LLPs filled this void and provided better liability protection than general partnerships but somewhat less than LLCs.

1. For many entrepreneurs, taxation and personal liability concerns often cloud their reasoning when deciding on a form of ownership. The following is a series of business conditions that are unique to Jody Jeffers and her potential business. You have been asked to evaluate these specific conditions and make a recommendation to her about the most appropriate form of ownership. The conditions are:

a. Three years ago Jeffers inherited a large sum of money and, although invested, her earnings place her in the highest federal tax bracket.
b. Jeffers plans to use the invested funds as collateral to borrow 20 percent of what she needs to start a new business venture.
c. Jeffers has eight close friends who indicate that they are each willing to invest in the business to cover the remaining 80 percent of financial capital requirements.
d. The business will involve a fleet of automobiles on the road 10–15 hours each day.
e. A legal question exists as to whether the drivers are company employees or contract workers.
f. Because this new venture is a dramatic new concept, there is honest debate as to its economic viability.
g. In the event the business fails, an issue to the ownership of some of the firm's inventory would be in question.

Source: Adapted from "C Corporation, LLC, or Sole Proprietorship: What Form Is Best for Your Business?" *Management Accounting Quarterly,* Spring 2000.

Disadvantages of a Sole Proprietorship

Unlimited Personal Liability. Probably the greatest disadvantage of a sole proprietorship is the unlimited personal liability of the owner; the sole proprietor is personally liable for all of the business's debts. As stated before, in a proprietorship the owner *is* the business. The proprietor owns all the business's assets, and if the business fails, creditors can force the sale of those assets to cover its debts. If unpaid business debts remain, creditors can also force the sale of the proprietor's *personal* assets to cover repayment. In short, the company's debts are the owner's debts. Laws vary from one state to another, but most states require creditors to leave the failed business owner a minimum amount of equity in a home, a car, and some personal items. The reality: *Failure of the business can ruin the sole proprietor financially.*

Limited Access to Capital. If the business is to grow and expand, a sole proprietor often needs additional financial resources. However, many proprietors have already put all they have into their business and have used their personal resources as collateral on existing loans, so it is difficult for them to borrow additional funds. Sole proprietorships are limited to whatever capital the owners can contribute and whatever money they can borrow. In short, proprietors, unless they have great personal wealth, often find it difficult to raise additional money while maintaining sole ownership. Most banks and other lending institutions have well-defined formulas for determining a borrower's eligibility. Unfortunately, many sole proprietors cannot meet those borrowing requirement, but loan programs such as those from the U.S. Small Business Administration (SBA) help some entrepreneurs gain access to capital.

[Company Example →]

One entrepreneur, Tammy Reger, owner of Thompson Brothers Greenhouse, received an SBA loan through Fleet Bank to make improvements on some of her 16 greenhouses. Reger sells mostly annuals to commercial customers, and her staff fluctuates seasonally from three to twenty employees. Though she had never applied for a loan, she had tried to qualify for various government programs but was refused. She initially asked for $150,000 to repair a greenhouse that had collapsed from heavy snow but was told the most she qualified for was $30,000. "They told me they wouldn't give me any more because it was too risky a business and I wasn't qualified," she says.[3]

Limited Skills and Abilities. A sole proprietor may not have the wide range of skills running a successful business requires. Each of us has areas in which our education, training, and work experiences have taught us a great deal; yet there are other areas in which our decision-making ability is weak. Many business failures occur because owners lack skills, knowledge, and experience in areas that are vital to business success. Owners tend to push aside problems they do not understand or do not feel comfortable with in favor of those they can solve more easily. Unfortunately, the problems they set aside seldom solve themselves. By the time an owner decides to ask for help in addressing these problems, it may be too late to save the company.

Feelings of Isolation. Running a business alone allows an entrepreneur maximum flexibility, but it also creates feelings of isolation; there is no one to turn to for help in solving problems or getting feedback on a new idea. Most small business owners report that they sometimes feel alone and frightened when they must make decisions knowing that they have nowhere to turn for advice or guidance. The weight of each critical decision rests solely on the proprietor's shoulders.

[Company Example →]

New companies, such as My Home Tech of Rancho Cordova, California, are focused on the needs of small business owners dealing with feelings of isolation. According to founder and co-owner Darren Hans Bobella, the company handles any type of computer hardware or software problem at any location. Although large IT services companies are sometimes reluctant to visit home offices, his company isn't. My Home Tech offers its services seven days a week and hands out its emergency phone number to repeat customers, offering them round-the-clock service. And it provides something many sole proprietors need but never get: one-on-one instruction.[4]

Lack of Continuity for the Business. Lack of continuity is inherent in a sole proprietorship. If the proprietor dies, retires, or becomes incapacitated, the business automatically terminates. Unless a family member or employee can take over, the business could be in jeopardy. Because people look for secure employment and an opportunity for advancement, proprietorships, being small, often have trouble recruiting and retaining good employees. If no one is trained to run the business, creditors can petition the court to liquidate the assets of the dissolved business to pay outstanding debts.

For founders who have no intention of ultimately creating a large, complex business, a sole proprietorship may be ideal. Some entrepreneurs, however, find that forming partnerships is one way to overcome the disadvantages of the sole proprietorship. For instance, a person who lacks specific managerial skills or has insufficient access to needed capital can compensate for those weaknesses by forming a partnership with someone who has complementary management skills or money to invest.

The Partnership

3. Describe the advantages and disadvantages of the partnership.

A **partnership** is an association of two or more people who co-own a business for the purpose of making a profit. In a partnership the co-owners (partners) share a business's assets, liabilities, and profits according to the terms of an established partnership agreement.

The law does not require a written partnership agreement (also known as the articles of partnership), but it is wise to work with an attorney to develop one that spells out the exact status and responsibility of each partner. All too often the parties think they know what they are agreeing to, only to find later that no real meeting of the minds took place. The **partnership agreement** is a document that states in writing all of the terms of operating the partnership for the protection of each partner involved. Every partnership should be based on a written agreement. When problems arise between partners, the written document becomes invaluable.

When no partnership agreement exists, the Uniform Partner Act (discussed later) governs the partnership, but its provisions may not be as favorable as a specific agreement hammered out among the partners. Creating a partnership agreement is not costly. In most cases, the partners can discuss each of the provisions in advance. Once they have reached an agreement, an attorney can draft the formal document. Banks will often want to see a copy of the partnership agreement before lending the business money. Probably the most important feature of the partnership agreement is that it addresses in advance sources of conflict that could result in partnership battles and the dissolution of a business that could have been successful. Spelling out details—especially sticky ones such as profit splits, contributions, workloads, decision-making authority, dispute resolution, and others—at the outset will help avoid tension in a partnership that could lead to business failure or dissolution of the partnership.

A partnership agreement can include any terms the partners want (unless they are illegal). The standard partnership agreement will likely include the following:

1. *Name of the partnership.*
2. *Purpose of the business.* What is the reason the partners created the business?
3. *Domicile of the business.* Where will the business be located?
4. *Duration of the partnership.* How long will the partnership last?
5. *Names of the partners and their legal addresses.*
6. *Contributions of each partner to the business at the creation of the partnership and later.* This would include each partner's investment in the business. In some situations a partner may contribute assets that are not likely to appear on the balance sheet. Experience, sales contracts, or a good reputation in the community may be some reasons for asking a person to join a partnership.
7. *Agreement on how the profits or losses will be distributed.*
8. *Agreement on salaries or drawing rights against profits for each partner.*
9. *Procedure for expansion through the addition of new partners.*
10. *Distribution of the partnership's assets if the partners voluntarily dissolve the partnership.*
11. *Sale of the partnership interest.* How can partners sell their interests in the business?
12. *Absence or disability of one of the partners.* If a partner is absent or disabled for an extended period of time, should the partnership continue? Will the absent or disabled partner receive the same share of profits as he or she did before his or her absence or disability? Should the absent or disabled partner be held responsible for debts incurred while unable to participate?
13. *Voting rights.* In many partnerships, partners have unequal voting power. The partners may base their voting rights on their financial or managerial contributions to the business.

14. *Decision-making authority.* When can partners make decisions on their own, and when must other partners be involved?
15. *Financial authority.* Which partners are authorized to sign checks, and how many signatures are required to authorize bank transactions?
16. *Handling tax matters.* The Internal Revenue Service requires partnerships to designate one person to be responsible for handling the partnership's tax matters.
17. *Alterations or modifications of the partnership agreement.* No document is written to last forever. Partnership agreements should contain provisions for alterations or modifications. As a business grows and changes, partners often find it necessary to update their original agreement. As stated before, in the event there is no written partnership agreement and a dispute arises, the courts will apply the body of law entitled the Uniform Partnership Act.

The Uniform Partnership Act

The **Uniform Partnership Act (UPA)** codifies the body of law dealing with partnerships in the United States. Under the UPA, the three key elements of any partnership are common ownership interest in a business, sharing the business's profits and losses, and the right to participate in managing the operation of the partnership. Under the act, each partner has the right to:

1. Share in the management and operations of the business.
2. Share in any profits the business might earn from operations.
3. Receive interest on additional advances made to the business.
4. Be compensated for expenses incurred in the name of the partnership.
5. Have access to the business's books and records.
6. Receive a formal accounting of the partnership's business affairs.

The UPA also sets forth the partners' general obligation. Each partner is obligated to:

1. Share in any losses sustained by the business.
2. Work for the partnership without salary.
3. Submit differences that may arise in the conduct of the business to majority vote or arbitration.
4. Give the other partner(s) complete information about all business affairs.
5. Give a formal accounting of the partnership's business affairs.

Rights and Duties of Partners. Because of the power of any one partner to influence the financial viability of the partnership, partnership law has established certain rights and duties. The following are the rights that exist among partners.

1. *The right to participate in the management of the business.* Unless there is an agreement to the contrary, in a general partnership *all* partners have a right to participate in the active management of the business. All partners, irrespective of financial contribution, have an equal vote on critical issues, with a simple majority needed to decide.
2. *The right to an accounting.* Because a partner does not, under law, have a right to sue the partnership or other partner(s), the Uniform Partnership Act provides any partner the right to bring an action for an accounting against other partners. If such a request is made, the courts have the authority to review the partnership and the transactions made by all partners and award each partner his or her share of the partnership assets.

Partners also have a defined set of duties to the partnership and the other partners. Business laws that deal with the behaviors of partners spell out the duties of each partner and include the following:

a. *Duty of loyalty.* Each partner has a fiduciary responsibility to the partnership and, as such, must always place the interest of the partnership above his or her personal interest.

b. *Duty of obedience.* This duty requires each partner to adhere to the provisions of the partnership agreement and the decisions made by the partnership.

c. *Duty of care.* As the name implies, each partner is expected to behave in ways that demonstrate the same level of care and skill that a reasonable manager in the same position would use under the same circumstances.

d. *Duty to inform.* All information relevant to the management of the business must be made available to all partners.

Beyond what the law prescribes, a partnership is based above all else on mutual trust and respect. Any partnership missing those elements is destined to fail. Like sole proprietorships, partnerships have advantages and disadvantages.

IN THE FOOTSTEPS OF AN ENTREPRENEUR...

Trust Me, It's Not Junk

Some family businesses are not exactly hightech or trendy, fashionable, or even clean. The Hugh Neu Corporation is a family-held steel scrap exporter. The firm's founder, Hugh Neu, began turning trash to cash in 1945 when he started trading surplus equipment and material left over from both the Allies and Axis powers at the end of World War II. Now his son John leads the business. In 2002, the Hugh Neu Corporation won the bid to recycle all of the cans and bottles collected in New York City. The winning bid was $5.10 per ton.

Over its five-decade history, the company has grown into one of America's largest and most successful scrap processors and the number-one exporter of scrap from the United States. Because manufacturers have grown and expanded into Southeast Asia, Mexico, and Turkey, the company now ships 3.5 million tons of steel scrap each year, which return to our shores as cans, appliances, and other metal items.

Over the life of this family business, its leadership aggressively followed the new emerging markets for scrap. In 1953, founder Hugh Neu became a supplier to Japan. By 1962, the company had purchased its own ships to better meet the demands of its Japanese customers. In today's global economy the major international market is China, and the Hugh Neu Corporation has been trading in China since the mid-1970s. In 2003, the company exported 1.6 million tons of steel to China.

The Hugh Neu Corporation is an example of a family business that is a privately held corporation that has successfully undergone a transition to a second generation of family leadership.

1. Find another successful family-owned business that operates as a privately held company. Prepare a brief summary of its history.

Source: Adapted from John Turrettini, "One Man's Junk," *Forbes,* December 22, 2003, pp. 118–120.

Advantages of the Partnership

Easy to Establish. Like the proprietorship, the partnership is easy and inexpensive to establish. The owners must obtain the necessary business license and submit a minimal number of forms. In most states, partners must file a Certificate for Conducting Business as Partners if the business is run under a trade name.

Complementary Skills. In a sole proprietorship, the owner must wear lots of different hats, and not all of them fit well. In successful partnerships, the parties' skills and abilities complement one another, strengthening the company's managerial foundation. The

Company Example →

synergistic effect created when partners of equal skill and creativity collaborate effectively results in outcomes that reflect the contributions of all involved. *In the mid-1980s, Santhana Krishnan and Yash Shah were roommates at Clarkson University in Potsdam, New York. A few years after graduation, the friends lived together in Waltham, Massachusetts, where each worked. Shah became an IT consultant for Hewlett-Packard (HP) and a year later Krishnan joined Shah's division. In March 1995 the two men left HP to start their own IT consulting business. Today, as partners at InteQ based in Burlington, Massachusetts, the verbally polished Krishnan is CEO, and the technically adept Shah is president and chief technology officer.*[5]

When it comes to the many new technology-oriented businesses, it is beneficial if at least one of the partners has knowledge and experience at operating a business. Understanding the technological aspects of building a technology-based business must be equally supported by a sound understanding of the principles that govern marketing, finance, business management, human resources, logistics, and a myriad of other factors. Many technology-based firms fail because their founders lack basic business skills, even though they may otherwise have the technological expertise to succeed.

Division of Profits. There are no restrictions on how partners distribute the company's profits as long as they are consistent with the partnership agreement and do not violate the rights of any partner. The partnership agreement should articulate the nature of each partner's contribution and proportional share of profits. If the partners fail to create an agreement, the UPA says that the partners share equally in the partnership's profits, even if their original capital contributions are unequal.

Larger Pool of Capital. The partnership form of ownership can significantly broaden the pool of capital available to a business. Each partner's asset base will support a larger borrowing capacity than either partner would have had alone. Undercapitalization is a common cause of business failures.

Ability to Attract Limited Partners. Not every partner need take an active role in the operation of a business. Partners who take an active role in managing a company and who share in its rewards, liabilities, and responsibilities are **general partners**. Every partnership must have at least one general partner (although there is no limit on the number of general partners a business can have). General partners have unlimited personal liability for the company's debts and obligations and are expected to take an active role in managing the business.

Limited partners, on the other hand, cannot take an active role in the operation of the company. They have limited personal liability for the company's debts and obligations. If the business fails, they lose only what they have invested in it and no more. Essentially, limited partners are financial investors who do not want to participate in the day-to-day affairs of the partnership. If limited partners are "materially and actively" involved in a business (defined as spending more than 500 hours a year in the company), they will be treated as general partners and will lose their limited liability protection. Silent partners and dormant partners are special types of limited partners. **Silent partners** are not active in a business but generally are known to be members of the partnership. **Dormant partners** are neither active nor generally known to be associated with the business.

A limited partnership can attract many investors by offering them limited liability and the potential to realize a substantial return on their investments if the business is successful. Many individuals find it very profitable to invest in high-potential small businesses, only if they avoid the disadvantages of unlimited liability while doing so. Limited partnerships will be discussed in greater detail later in this chapter.

Little Governmental Regulation. Like the proprietorship, the partnership form of operation is not burdened with red tape.

Flexibility. Although not as flexible as sole proprietorships, partnerships can generally react quickly to changing market conditions. In large partnerships, however, getting all partners' approval on key decisions can slow down a company's strategic actions.

Taxation. The partnership itself is not subject to federal taxation. It serves as a conduit for the profit or losses it earns or incurs; its net income or losses are passed through the individual partners as personal income, and the partners, not the business, pay income tax on their distributive shares. The partnership, like the proprietorship, avoids the *double taxation* disadvantage associated with the corporate form of ownership.

Disadvantages of the Partnership

Unlimited Liability of at Least One Partner. At least one member of every partnership must be a general partner. The general partner has unlimited personal liability, even though he or she is often the partner with the fewest personal resources. In most states, certain property belonging to a proprietor or a general partner is exempt from attachment by creditors of a failed business. The most common is the homestead exemption, which enables the debtor's home to be sold to satisfy debt but stipulates that a certain dollar amount be reserved to enable the debtor to find other shelter. Some states require that the debtor have a family before the homestead exemption is allowed. Also, state laws normally exempt certain personal property items from attachments by creditors. For example, household furniture (up to a specified amount), clothing and personal possessions, government or military pensions, and bonuses are protected and cannot be taken to satisfy an outstanding business debt. Make a point to know your state laws regarding these issues.

Capital Accumulation. Although the partnership form of ownership is superior to the proprietorship when it comes to attracting capital, it is generally not as effective as the corporate form of ownership, which can raise capital by selling shares of ownership to outside investors.

Difficulty in Disposing of Partnership Interest Without Dissolving the Partnership. Most partnership agreements restrict how partners can dispose of their shares of the business. Often a partner is required to sell his or her interest to the remaining partner(s). Even if the original agreement contains such a requirement and clearly delineates how the value of each partner's ownership will be determined, there is no guarantee that other partners will have the financial resources to buy the seller's interest. If the money is not available to purchase a partner's interest, the other partner may be forced to either accept a new partner or to dissolve the partnership, distribute the remaining assets, and begin again. If a partner withdraws from the partnership, the partnership ceases to exist unless there are specific provisions in the partnership agreement for a smooth transition. If a general partner dies, becomes incompetent, or withdraws from the business, the partnership automatically dissolves, although it may not terminate (the difference is discussed later). Even when there are numerous partners, if one wishes to disassociate his or her name from the business, the remaining partners will probably form a new partnership.

Lack of Continuity. If one partner dies, significant complications arise. Partnership interest is often nontransferable through inheritance because remaining partners may not want to be in a partnership with the person who inherits the deceased partner's interest. Partners can make provisions in the partnership agreement to avoid dissolution due to death only if all parties agree to accept as partners those who inherit the deceased's interest.

"I'm going to be up-front with you Kong. If you work with me, I'm the King."

Potential for Personality and Authority Conflicts. Being in a partnership is much like being married. Making sure partners' work habits, goals, ethics, and general business philosophy are compatible is an important step in avoiding a nasty business divorce. Friction among partners is inevitable and can be difficult to control. The key is having a mechanism such as a partnership agreement and open lines of communication for controlling it. The demise of many partnerships can often be traced to interpersonal conflicts and the lack of a partnership agreement for resolving those conflicts. Knowing potential partners well and having a conflict resolution plan in place can result in better outcomes when dealing with the inevitable conflicts that eventually occur when there is a fundamental difference of opinion on one or more critical business decisions. *Aliza Sherman is an entrepreneur and author of* Cybergrrl: A Woman's Guide to the World Wide Web. *Sherman is currently working on her next book and a new company. What has she learned from a failed past partnership? "My most vivid memories of disputes with my own business partner are money related," she says. "It wasn't until after we worked together in the same office that I realized how different our communication styles were—something that not only led to trivial arguments between us but also major issues in terms of how we communicated with clients and staff." She now realizes that planning out and discussing the partnership, individual expectations, roles and responsibilities, and so on is crucial before actually getting the business venture underway.*[6]

Company Example

Partners Are Bound by the Law of Agency. A partner is like a spouse in that decisions made by one in the name of the partnership bind all. Each partner is an agent for the business and can legally bind the other partners to a business agreement. Because of this agency power, all partners must exercise good faith and reasonable care in performing their responsibilities. Consider the case of a partner who dramatically increased the cost of the business when, in the name of the company, she signed a three-year lease for a business jet. Decisions such as this ultimately forced the partners to file for bankruptcy.

Some partnerships survive a lifetime, whereas others experience the difficulties described previously. In a general partnership, the continued exposure to personal liability for partners' actions can wear entrepreneurs down. Knowing that they could lose their personal assets because of a partner's bad business decision is a fact of life in partnerships. Conflicts between or among partners could force a business to close. Few partnerships ever put into place a mutually agreed upon means for conflict resolution. An arbitration of conflict mechanism is always valuable and may keep the business operating. Without such a mechanism, disagreements can escalate to the point where the partnership is dissolved and the business ceases to operate.

Dissolution and Termination of a Partnership

Partnership dissolution is not the same as partnership termination. **Dissolution** occurs when a general partner ceases to be associated with the business. **Termination** is the final act of winding up the partnership as a business. Termination occurs after the partners have expressed their intent to cease operations and all affairs of the partnership have been concluded. In other words, dissolution ends the partnership as a business; termination winds up its affairs.

Dissolution occurs as a result of one or more of the following events:

- Expiration of a time period or completion of the project undertaken as delineated in the partnership agreement.
- Expressed wish of any general partner to cease operation.
- Expulsion of a partner under the provisions of the agreement.
- Withdrawal, retirement, insanity, or death of a general partner (except when the partnership agreement provides a method of continuation).
- Bankruptcy of the partnership or of any general partner.
- Admission of a new partner resulting in the dissolution of the old partnership and establishment of a new partnership.
- A judicial decree that a general partner is insane or permanently incapacitated, making performance or responsibility under the partnership agreement impossible.
- Mounting losses that make it impractical for the business to continue.
- Impropriety or improper behavior of any general partner that reflects negatively on the business.

Limited Partnerships

A **limited partnership**, which is a modification of a general partnership, is composed of at least one general partner and at least one limited partner. In a limited partnership the general partner is treated, under law, exactly as in a general partnership. Limited partners are treated as investors in the business venture, and they have limited liability. They can lose only the amount they have invested in the business.

Most states have ratified the Revised Uniform Limited Partnership Act. To form a limited partnership, the partners must file a Certificate of Limited Partnership in the state in which the partnership plans to conduct business. The Certificate of Limited Partnership should include the following information:

- The name of the limited partnership.
- The general character of its business.
- The address of the office of the firm's agent authorized to receive summonses or other legal notices.
- The name and business address of each partner, specifying which ones are general partners and which are limited partners.
- The amount of cash contributions actually made, and agreed to be made in the future, by each partner.
- A description of the value of noncash contributions made or to be made by each partner.
- The times at which additional contributions are to be made by any of the partners.
- Whether and under what conditions a limited partner has the right to grant a limited partner status to an assignee of his or her interest in the partnership.

■ If agreed upon, the time or the circumstances when a partner may withdraw from the firm (unlike the withdrawal of a general partner, the withdrawal of a limited partner does not automatically dissolve a limited partnership).

■ If agreed upon, the amount of, or the method of determining, the funds to be received by a withdrawing partner.

■ Any right of a partner to receive distributions of cash or other property from the company and the circumstances for such distributions.

■ The time or circumstances when the limited partnership is to be dissolved.

■ The rights of the remaining general partners to continue the business after the withdrawal of a general partner.

■ Any other matters the partners want to include.

Although limited partners do not have the right to take an active role in managing the business, they can make management suggestions to general partners, inspect the business, and make copies of business records. A limited partner is, of course, entitled to a share of the business's profits as agreed on and specified in the Certificate of Limited Partnership. The primary disadvantage of limited partnerships is the complexity and cost of establishing them.

Master Limited Partnerships

A relatively new form of business structure, **master limited partnerships (MLPs)**, are just like regular limited partnerships, except their shares are traded on stock exchanges. They provide most of the same advantages to investors as a corporation—including limited liability. A master limited partnership behaves like a corporation and trades on major stock exchanges like a corporation. Congress originally allowed MLPs to be taxed as partnerships. However, in 1987, it ruled that any MLP not involved in natural resources or real estate would be taxed as a corporation, eliminating their ability to avoid the double taxation disadvantage. Master limited partnership profits typically must be divided among thousands of partners.

Limited Liability Partnerships

Many states now recognize **limited liability partnerships (LLPs)** in which all partners in the business are limited partners, having only limited liability for the debts and obligations of the partnership. Most states restrict LLPs to certain types of professionals such as attorneys, physicians, dentists, and accountants. Just as with any limited partnership, the partners must file a Certificate of Limited Partnership in the state in which the partnership plans to conduct business. Also, like a partnership, an LLP does not pay taxes; its income is passed through to the limited partners, who pay taxes on their shares of the company's net income.

✦ GAINING *a* COMPETITIVE EDGE ✦

"Disguised Dividends"

The corporate form of ownership places one potentially significant limitation on the owners, and that is the ability to arbitrarily compensate themselves at a level that is more than ordinary, necessary, and reasonable. The reason is that the IRS believes that extremely high levels of compensation, which are an expense on the income statement, are an attempt to avoid the payment of corporate income taxes. The

IRS contends that a portion of the compensation that it deems to be disproportionately high in comparison with that of other firms of similar size in the same industry should be declared as corporate dividends.

To avoid this potential source of conflict, it would be better to select an S corporation form of ownership in which all profits are able to be transferred to the owners and in which the tax liability is that of the recipients (taxed only once).

Being greedy and attempting to wrongfully avoid federal corporate taxes will gain the attention of the IRS. Being aware of the regulations regarding compensation and what the IRS calls "disguised dividends" might be a factor in selecting an S corporation over a C corporation. Always remember that it is critical to evaluate the pros and cons of each form of ownership prior to starting a business.

1. What steps can a business owner take to prove that his or her salary is "ordinary, necessary, and reasonable?"

Source: Adapted from Joan Szabo, "Greed Isn't Good," *Entrepreneur,* September 2000, pp. 85–87.

The Corporation

4. Describe the advantages and disadvantages of the corporation.

The corporation is the most complex of the three major forms of business ownership. A **corporation** is an artificial entity created by the state that can sue or be sued in its own name, enter into and enforce contracts, hold title to and transfer property, and be found civilly and criminally liable for violations of the law.[7] Because the life of the corporation is independent of its owners, the shareholders can sell their interest in the business.

Corporations (also known as C corporations) are creations of the state. When a corporation is founded, it accepts the regulations and restrictions of the state in which it is incorporated and any other state in which it chooses to do business. A corporation that conducts business in the state in which it is incorporated is a **domestic corporation**. When a corporation conducts business in another state, that state considers it to be a **foreign corporation**. Corporations that are formed in other countries but do business in the United States are **alien corporations**.

Corporations have the power to raise large amounts of capital by selling shares of ownership to outside investors, but many corporations have only a handful of shareholders. **Publicly held corporations** have a large number of shareholders, and their stock is usually traded on one of the large stock exchanges. **Closely held corporations** have shares that are controlled by a relatively small number of people, often family members, relatives, or friends. Their stock is not traded on any stock exchange but instead is passed from one generation to the next. Many small corporations are closely held.

In general, a corporation must report annually its financial operations to its home state's attorney general. These financial reports become public record. If the corporation's stock is sold in more than one state, the corporation must comply with federal regulations governing the sale of corporate securities. There are substantially more reporting requirements for a corporation than for other forms of ownership.

Requirements for Incorporation

Most states allow entrepreneurs to incorporate without the assistance of an attorney. Some states even provide incorporation kits to help in the incorporation process. Although it is cheaper for entrepreneurs to complete the process themselves, it may not be the best idea as some provisions of incorporation may be overlooked. In some states, the application process is complex, and the required forms are confusing. Unless the incorporation process is extremely complicated, entrepreneurs can usually employ an attorney to incorporate their business for a nominal fee. Most new corporations are a great deal less complex than their larger "cousins." Obtaining the advice of a qualified professional is a wise decision for all entrepreneurs to consider when creating or expanding a business.

Once the owners decide to form a corporation, they must choose the state in which to incorporate. If the business will operate in a single state, it usually makes sense to incorporate in that state. States differ—sometimes dramatically—in the requirements they place on the corporations they charter and in how they treat corporations chartered in other states. They also differ in the tax rate imposed on corporations, the restrictions placed on their activities, the capital required to incorporate, and the fees or organization tax charged to incorporate.

Every state requires a Certificate of Incorporation or charter to be filed with the secretary of state. The following information is generally required to be in the Certificate of Incorporation:

- *The corporation's name.* The corporation must choose a name that is not so similar to that of another firm in that state that it causes confusion or lends itself to deception. It must also include a term such as *corporation, incorporated, company,* or *limited* to notify the public that they are dealing with a corporation.
- *The corporation's statement of purpose.* The incorporators must state in general terms the intended nature of the business. The purpose must, of course, be lawful. An illustration might be "to engage in the sale of office furniture and fixtures." The purpose should be broad enough to enable some expansion in the activities of the business as it develops.
- *The company's time horizon.* Most corporations are formed with no specific termination date; they are formed "for perpetuity." However, it is possible to incorporate for a specific duration (e.g., 50 years).
- *Names and addresses of the incorporators.* The incorporators must be identified in the articles of incorporation and are liable under the law to attest that all information in the articles of incorporation is correct. In some states, one or more of the incorporators must reside in the state where the corporation is being created.
- *Place of business.* The post office address of the corporation's principal office must be listed. This address, for a domestic corporation, must be in the state in which incorporation takes place.
- *Capital stock authorization.* The articles of incorporation must include the amount and class (or type) of capital stock the corporation wants to be authorized to issue. This is not the number of shares it must issue; a corporation must also define the different classification of stock and any special rights, preferences, or limits each class has.
- *Capital required at the time of incorporation.* Some states require a newly formed corporation to deposit in a bank a specific percentage of the stock's par value before incorporating.
- *Provisions for preemptive rights, if any, that are granted to stockholders.*
- *Restrictions on transferring share.* Many closely held corporations—those owned by a few shareholders, often family members—require shareholders interested in selling their stock to offer it first to the corporation. (Shares the corporation itself owns are called **treasury stock**.) To maintain control over their ownership, many closely held corporations exercise this right, known as **the right of first refusal**.
- *Names and addresses of the officers and directors of the corporation.*
- *Rules under which the corporation will operate.* **Bylaws** are the rules and regulations the officers and directors establish for the corporation's internal management and operation.

Once the attorney general of the incorporating state has approved a request for incorporation and the corporation pays its fees, the approved articles of incorporation become its charter. With the charter in hand, the next order of business is to hold an organizational meeting for the stockholders to formally elect directors, who, in turn, will appoint the corporate officers.

Corporations may dominate sales and profitability in our economy, but, like the preceding forms of ownership, they have advantages and disadvantages.

Advantages of the Corporation

Limited Liability of Stockholders. The primary reason most entrepreneurs choose to incorporate is to gain the benefit of limited liability, which means that investors can limit their liability to the total amount of their investment. This legal protection of personal assets beyond the business is of critical concern to many potential investors. The shield of limited liability may not be impenetrable, however. Because start-up companies are so risky, lenders and other creditors require the owners to *personally* guarantee loans made to the corporation. Experts estimate that 95 percent of small business owners have to sign personal guarantees to get the financing they need. By making these guarantees, owners are putting their personal assets at risk (just as in a proprietorship) despite choosing the corporate form of ownership. Court decisions have extended the personal liability of small corporation owners beyond the financial guarantees that banks and other lenders require, "piercing the corporate veil" much more than ever before. Courts are increasingly holding entrepreneurs personally liable for environmental, pension, and legal claims against their corporations. Courts will pierce the corporate veil and hold owners liable for the company's debts and obligations if the owners deliberately commit criminal or negligent acts when handling corporate business. Corporate shareholders most commonly lose their liability protection, however, because owners and officers have commingled corporate funds with their own personal funds. Failing to keep corporate and personal funds separate is most often a problem in closely held corporations. Positive steps that entrepreneurs should take to avoid legal difficulties include the following:

- *File all of the reports and pay all of the necessary fees required by the state in a timely manner.* Most states require corporations to file reports with the secretary of state on an annual basis. Failing to do so will jeopardize the validity of the corporation and will open the door for personal liability problems for its shareholders.
- *Hold annual meetings to elect officers and directors.* In a closely held corporation, the officers elected may *be* the shareholders, but that does not matter.
- *Keep minutes of every meeting of the officers and directors, even if it takes place in the living room of the founders.* It is a good idea to elect a secretary who is responsible for recording the minutes.
- *Make sure that the corporation's board of directors makes all major decisions.* Problems arise in closely held corporations when one owner makes key decisions alone without consulting the elected board.
- *Make it clear that the business is a corporation by having all officers sign contracts, loan agreements, purchase orders, and other legal documents in the corporation's name rather than their own names.* Failing to designate their status as agents of the corporation can result in the officers being held personally liable for agreements they think they are signing on the corporation's behalf.
- *Keep corporate assets and the personal assets of the owners separate.* Few things make courts more willing to hold shareholders personally liable for a corporation's debts

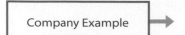

than commingling corporate and personal assets. In some closely held corporations, owners have been known to use corporate assets to pay their personal expenses (or vice versa) or to mix their personal funds with corporate funds in a single bank account. Don't do it! Protect the corporation's identity by keeping it completely separate from the owners' personal identities. *John Lathrop, a former Arthur Andersen accountant, took many flights aboard airplanes owned by Western Resources, Inc., including once flying to a football game with CEO David Wittig. Lathrop later said he never imagined that company executives one day would face criminal charges for personal use of the planes. In 2003, former CEO Wittig and former Executive Vice President Douglas Lake made an initial court appearance to hear 40 criminal charges handed down by a grand jury. "Personal use of corporate assets should certainly be reported to the audit committee when first discovered by an auditing firm," said Steve Erickson, a New Mexico–based consultant to auditing firms. "I think Arthur Andersen reported all significant matters it was aware of to the Western audit committee," Lathrop said. "We met with the audit committee several times each year, and I do not recall the airplanes being one of the items we talked about."*[8]

Ability to Attract Capital. Because of the protection of limited liability, corporations have proved to be the most effective form of ownership for accumulating large amounts of capital. Limited only by the number of shares authorized in its charter (which can be amended), the corporation can raise money to begin business and expand as opportunity dictates by selling shares of its stock to investors. A corporation can sell its stock to a limited number of private investors (a private placement) or to the public (a public offering).

Ability to Continue Indefinitely. Unless limited by its charter, a corporation is a separate legal entity and can continue indefinitely. Unlike a proprietorship or partnership, in which the death of a founder ends the business, the corporation lives beyond the lives of those who created it. This perpetual life gives rise to the next major advantage, transferable ownership.

Transferable Ownership. If stockholders in a corporation are displeased with the business's progress, they can sell their shares to someone else. Millions of shares of stock representing ownership in companies are traded daily on the world's stock exchanges. Shareholders can also transfer their stock through inheritance to a new generation of owners. During all of these transfers of ownership, the corporation continues to conduct business as usual.

Unlike that of large corporations, whose shares are normally traded on organized stock exchanges, the stock of many small corporations is held by a small number of people ("closely held"), often company founders, family members, or employees. Because only a small number of people hold the stock, the resale market for shares is limited, so the transfer of ownership might be difficult.

Disadvantages of the Corporation

Cost and Time Involved in the Incorporation Process. Corporations can be costly and time consuming to establish. The owners are giving birth to an artificial legal entity, and the gestation period can be prolonged for the novice. In some states, an attorney must handle incorporation, but in most states entrepreneurs can complete all of the required forms alone. However, an owner must exercise great caution when incorporating without the help of an attorney. Also, incorporating a business requires fees that are not applicable to proprietorships or partnerships. Creating a corporation can cost between $500 and $3,000, with the average cost around $1,500.

Double Taxation. Because a corporation is a separate legal entity, it must pay taxes on its net income to the federal, most state, and some local governments. Before stockholders receive a penny of its net income as dividends, a corporation must pay these taxes at the corporate tax rate. Then stockholders must pay taxes on the dividends they receive from these same profits at the individual tax rate. Thus, a corporation's profits are taxed twice—once at the corporate level and again at the individual level. This **double taxation** is a distinct disadvantage of the corporate form of ownership.

Potential for Diminished Managerial Incentives. As corporations grow, they often require additional managerial expertise beyond that which the founders can provide. Because they created their companies and often have most of their personal wealth tied up in them, entrepreneurs have an intense interest in ensuring their success and are willing to make sacrifices for their businesses. Professional managers an entrepreneur brings in to help run the business as it grows do not always have the same degree of interest or loyalty to the company. As a result, the business may suffer without the founder's energy, care, and devotion. One way to minimize this potential problem is to link managers' (and even employees') compensation to the company's financial performance through profit-sharing or bonus plans. Corporations can also stimulate managers' and employees' incentive on the job by creating an employee stock ownership plan (ESOP) in which managers and employees become owners in the company.

Legal Requirements and Regulatory Red Tape. Corporations are subject to more legal and financial requirements than other forms of ownership. Entrepreneurs must resist the temptation to commingle their personal funds with those of the corporation and must meet more stringent requirements for recording and reporting business transactions. They must also hold annual meetings and consult the board of directors about major decisions that are beyond day-to-day operations. Managers may be required to submit some major decisions to the stockholders for approval. Corporations that are publicly held must file quarterly and annual reports with the Securities and Exchange Commission (SEC). Failure to follow state and federal regulations has led to the demise of many firms. *PCT Services was a provider of janitorial services, primarily to military installations and hospitals. Until 1995, it operated throughout the United States and paid almost no employment taxes, while it incurred tax liabilities totaling almost $2.5 million in addition to significant penalties and interest. In June 1995, the IRS collected $1.5 million from the company. Soon after, PCT filed for Chapter 11 bankruptcy protection. PCT's debt to the IRS was part of the bankruptcy proceeding. In February 1997, the bankruptcy court approved a plan for PCT to repay its debts, including those to the IRS. Until June 1999, PCT made payments according to the plan; it defaulted on the plan soon after.*[9]

Company Example	→

Potential Loss of Control by the Founders. When entrepreneurs sell shares of ownership in their companies, they relinquish some control. Especially when they need large capital infusions for start-up growth, entrepreneurs may have to give up significant amounts of control, so much, in fact, that they become minority shareholders. Losing majority ownership—and, therefore, control—in their companies leaves founders in a precarious position. They no longer have the power to determine the company's direction; "outsiders" do. In some cases, founders' shares have been so diluted that majority shareholders actually choose to vote them out of their jobs!

The Professional Corporation

A **professional corporation** is designed to offer professionals such as lawyers, doctors, dentists, accountants, and others the advantage of the corporate form of ownership. Corporate ownership is ideally suited for licensed professionals, who must always be concerned about malpractice lawsuits, because it offers limited liability. For example, if three doctors form a professional corporation, none of them would be liable for the malpractice of the other. (Of course, each would be liable for his or her own actions.) Professional corporations are created in the same way as regular corporations. They often are identified by the abbreviation P.C. (professional corporation), P.A. (professional association), or S.C. (service corporation).

Alternative Forms of Ownership

5. Describe the features of the alternative forms of ownership such as the S corporation, the limited liability company, joint venture, and syndicate.

In addition to the sole proprietorship, the partnership, and the corporation, entrepreneurs can choose other forms of ownership, including the S corporation, the limited liability company, the joint venture, and the syndicate.

The S Corporation

In 1954, the Internal Revenue Service Code created the Subchapter S corporation. In recent years the IRS has changed the title to S corporation and has made a few modifications in its qualifications. An S corporation is a distinction that is made only for federal income tax purposes and is, in terms of legal characteristics, no different from any other corporation. In 1996, Congress passed legislation to simplify or eliminate some of the restrictive rules and requirements for S corporations so that a business seeking "S" status must meet the following criteria:

1. It must be a domestic (U.S.) corporation.
2. It cannot have a nonresident alien as a shareholder.
3. It can issue only one class of common stock, which means that all shares must carry the same rights (e.g., the right to dividends or liquidation rights). The exception is voting rights, which may differ. In other words, an S corporation can issue voting and nonvoting common stock.
4. It cannot have more than 75 shareholders (increased from 35).
5. No more than 20 percent of the corporation's income can be from passive investment income.
6. Corporations and partnerships cannot be shareholders.

By increasing the number of shareholders allowed in S corporations to 75, the current law makes succession planning easier for business owners. Aging founders now can pass their stock on to their children and grandchildren without worrying about exceeding the maximum allowable number of owners. The larger number of shareholders also granted S corporations a greater ability to raise capital by attracting more investors. The law includes another provision that enables S corporations to raise money more readily. It permits them to sell shares of their stock to certain tax-exempt organizations such as pension funds. (Previous rules limited ownership strictly to individuals, estates, and certain trusts.) The new law also allows S corporations to own subsidiary companies. Previously, the owners of S corporations had to establish separate businesses if they wanted to launch new ventures, even those closely related to the S corporation. This change is especially beneficial to entrepreneurs with several businesses in related fields. They can establish an S corporation as the "parent" company and then set up multiple subsidiaries as either C or S corporations as "offspring" under it. Because they are separate corporations, the liabilities of one business cannot spill over and destroy the assets of another.

Violating any of the requirements for an S corporation automatically terminates a company's S status. If a corporation satisfies the definition of an S corporation, the owners must actually elect to be treated as one. The election is made by filing IRS Form 2553 (within the first 75 days of the tax year), and all shareholders must consent to have the corporation treated as an S corporation.

Advantages of an S Corporation. S corporations retain all of the advantages of a regular corporation, such as continuity of existence, transferability of ownership, and limited personal liability for their owners. The most notable provision of the S corporation is that it passes all of its profits or losses through to the individual shareholders and its income is taxed only once at the individual tax rate. Thus, electing S corporation status avoids a primary disadvantage of the regular (or C) corporation—double taxation. In essence, the tax treatment of an S corporation is exactly like that of a partnership; its owners report their proportional shares of the company's profits on their individual income tax returns and pay taxes on those profits at the individual rate (even if they never take the money out of the business). See Figure 3.2 for an example of the effects of tax rate changes on these two forms of ownership.

Figure 3.2

Effects of Tax Rate Changes—C Corporation and S Corporation

The total tax of an S corporation is generally considerably lower than that of a C corporation. Recently passed tax legislation reduced the capital gains tax rate from 20 percent to 15 percent and reduced personal tax rates up to 3.6 percent at the top rate (from 38.6 percent to 35 percent). In addition, the tax rate on dividends has been reduced to 15 percent under the new law. Corporate rates remain unchanged.

The following example illustrates the effect of these rate changes. Scenario 1 assumes that after-tax C corporate earnings will be taxed to the shareholder at capital gains rates and Scenario 2 assumes such earnings will be taxed to the shareholder as dividends. Under both scenarios, the S corporate shareholder is taxed at ordinary income rates on the S corporate income. It is assumed that the shareholder files married filing jointly.

Source: Adopting the Business Structure-An Exercise with Care by Jonathan Chapman, "Construction Accounting & Taxation." Boston: Sep./Oct. 2003, Vol. 13, Iss. 5; pg. 5.

SCENARIO 1
CAPITAL GAINS RATES

	OLD LAW		NEW LAW	
	C CORP.	S CORP.	C CORP.	S CORP.
Corporate income	$500,000	$500,000	$500,000	$500,000
Corporate tax	(170,000)	-0-	(170,000)	-0-
After-tax income	330,000	500,000	330,000	500,000
Shareholder tax	(66,000)	(163,300)	(49,500)	(150,200)
Net after-tax income	$264,000	$336,700	$280,500	$349,800
S savings	$72,700		$69,300	

SCENARIO 2
DIVIDEND RATES

	OLD LAW		NEW LAW	
	C CORP.	S CORP.	C CORP.	S CORP.
Corporate income	$500,000	$500,000	$500,000	$500,000
Corporate tax	(170,000)	-0-	(170,000)	-0-
After-tax income	330,000	500,000	330,000	500,000
Shareholder tax	(97,700)	(163,300)	(49,500)	(150,200)
Net after-tax income	$232,300	$336,700	$280,500	$349,800
S savings	$104,400		$69,300	

Another advantage of the S corporation is that it avoids the tax C corporations pay on the assets that have appreciated in value and are sold. Also, owners of S corporations enjoy the ability to make year-end payouts to themselves if profits are high. In a C corporation, owners have no such luxury because the IRS watches for excessive compensation to owners and managers.

Disadvantages of an S Corporation. Tax rates are established by laws passed by legislators and signed by the president or state governors. An S corporation would lose its attractiveness if either or both of the following occurred:

1. Personal income tax rates rose above those of C corporation rates, or
2. C corporation rates were lowered below personal income tax rates.

Currently neither of these conditions exists, but it is never possible to predict the actions of federal or state governments.

In addition to the tax implications of making the switch from an S corporation, owners should consider the size of the company's net income, the tax rates of its shareholders, plans (and their timing) to sell the company, and the impact of the C corporation's double taxation penalty on income distributed as dividends. These recent reductions in personal tax rates may alter the calculations used to decide if the S corporation is superior to the C corporation.

When Is an S Corporation a Wise Choice? Choosing S corporation status is usually beneficial to start-up companies anticipating net losses and to highly profitable firms with substantial dividends to pay out to shareholders. In these cases, the owner can use the loss to offset other income or is in a lower tax bracket than the corporation, thus saving money in the long run. Companies that plan to reinvest most of their earnings to finance growth also find S corporation status favorable. Small business owners who intend to sell their companies in the near future will prefer S over C status because the taxable gains on the sale of an S corporation are generally lower than those on the sale of a C corporation.

On the other hand, small companies with the following characteristics are *not* likely to benefit from S corporation status:

- Highly profitable personal-service companies with large numbers of shareholders, in which most of the profits are passed on to shareholders as compensation or retirement benefits.
- Fast-growing companies that must retain most of their earnings to finance growth and capital spending.
- Corporations in which the loss of fringe benefits to shareholders exceeds tax savings.
- Corporations in which the income before any compensation to shareholders is less than $100,000 a year.
- Corporations with sizable net operating losses that cannot be used against S corporation earnings.

The Limited Liability Company (LLC)

Like an S corporation, the limited liability company (LLC) is a cross between a partnership and a corporation. The 1995 Uniform Limited Liability Company Act codified limited liability company law. LLCs are gaining in popularity because, like S corporations, they combine many of the benefits of the partnership and the corporate forms of ownership but are not subject to many of the restrictions imposed on S corporations. For example, S corporations cannot have more than 75 shareholders, and they are limited to only one class of stock. Those restrictions do not apply to LLCs. Although an LLC can have one owner, most have multiple owners (called members). An LLC offers its owners limited liability without imposing any requirements on their characteristics or any ceiling on their numbers. Unlike a limited partnership, which prohibits limited partners from participating in day-to-day management of the business, an LLC does not restrict its members' ability to become involved in managing the company.

In addition to offering its members the advantage of limited liability, LLCs also avoid the double taxation imposed on C corporations. Like an S corporation, an LLC does not pay income taxes; its income flows through to the members, who are responsible for paying income taxes on their shares of the LLC's net income. Because they are not subject to the many restrictions imposed on other forms of ownership, LLCs offer entrepreneurs another significant advantage: flexibility. Like a partnership, an LLC permits its members to divide income (and, thus, tax liability) as they see fit.

These advantages make the LLC an ideal form of ownership for small companies in many diverse industries. Moviegoers will recognize the production company Dream Works SKG, which was formed by Steven Spielberg, Jeffery Katzenberg, and David Geffen ("SKG") as a limited liability company.

Creating an LLC is much like creating a corporation. Forming an LLC requires an entrepreneur to file two documents with the secretary of state: the articles of organization and the operating agreement. The LLC's **articles of organization**, similar to the corporation's articles of incorporation, establish the company's name, its method of management (board managed or member managed), its duration, and the names and addresses of each organizer. In most states, the company's name must contain the words *limited liability company, limited company,* or the letters *LLC* or *LC.* An LLC can have a defined term of duration (term LLC), or it can elect to be an "at-will" LLC that has no specific term of duration. However, the same factors that would cause a partnership to dissolve would also cause a term LLC to dissolve before its charter expired.

The **operating agreement**, similar to a corporation's bylaws, outlines the provisions governing the way the LLC will conduct business. To ensure that their LLCs are classified as a partnership for tax purposes, entrepreneurs must draft the operating agreement carefully. The operating agreement must create an LLC that has more characteristics of a partnership than of a corporation to maintain this favorable tax treatment. Specifically, an LLC cannot have any more than two of the following four corporate characteristics:

1. *Limited liability.* Limited liability exists if no member of the LLC is personally liable for the debts or claims against the company. Because entrepreneurs choosing this form of ownership usually get limited liability protection, the operating agreement almost always contains this characteristic.
2. *Continuity of life.* Continuity of life exists if the company continues to exist despite changes in stock ownership. To avoid continuity of life, any LLC member must have the power to dissolve the company. Most entrepreneurs choose to omit this characteristic from their LLC's operating agreements. Thus, if one member of an LLC resigns, dies, or declares bankruptcy, the

LLC automatically dissolves and all remaining members must vote to keep the company going.

3. *Free transferability of interest.* Free transferability of interest exists if each LLC member has the power to transfer his or her ownership to another person without the consent of other members. To avoid this characteristic, the operating agreement must state the recipient of a member's LLC stock cannot become a substitute member without the consent of the remaining members.

4. *Centralized management.* Centralized management exists if a group that does not include all LLC members has the authority to make management decisions and to conduct company business. To avoid this characteristic, the operating agreement must state the company elects to be "member managed."

Despite their universal appeal to entrepreneurs, LLCs have some disadvantages. For example, they can be expensive to create. Although an LLC may be ideally suited for an entrepreneur launching a new company, it may pose problems for business owners who are considering converting an existing business to an LLC. Switching to an LLC from a general partnership, a limited partnership, or a sole proprietorship reorganizing to bring in new owners is usually not a problem. However, owners of corporations and S corporations would incur large tax obligations if they converted their companies to LLCs.

Joint Ventures and Syndicates

The **joint venture** is very much like a partnership, except that it is formed for a specific, limited purpose. For instance, suppose that you have a 500-acre tract of land 60 miles from Chicago. This land has been cleared and is normally used for farming. One of your friends has solid contacts among major musical groups and would like to put on a concert. You expect prices for your agricultural products to be low this summer, so you and your friend form a joint venture for the specific purpose of staging a three-day concert. Your contribution will be the exclusive use of the land for one month, and your friend will provide all the performers, as well as the technicians, facilities, and equipment. All costs will be paid out of receipts, and the net profits will be split, with you receiving 20 percent for the use of your land. When the concert is over, the facilities removed, and the accounting for all costs completed, you and your friend will split the profits 20–80, and the joint venture will terminate. The "partners" form a new joint venture for each new project they undertake. The income derived from a joint venture is taxed as if it had arisen from a partnership.

In any endeavor in which neither party can effectively achieve the purpose alone, a joint venture becomes the common form of ownership. That's why joint ventures have become increasingly popular in global business dealings. For instance, a small business in the United States may manufacture a product that is in demand in Brazil, but the U.S. firm has no knowledge of how to do business in Brazil. Forming a joint venture with a Brazilian firm that knows the customs and laws of the country, has an established distribution network, and can promote the product effectively could result in a mutually beneficial joint venture.

Much like a joint venture, a **syndicate** is a private investment group that is formed for the purpose of financing a large commercial project whose scope is larger than the capacity of a single investor to finance alone. The members of the investment syndicate can come together quickly to seize an opportunity. On the downside, if the project fails, the members of the syndicate may be held liable for a breach of agreement by a third party.

Table 3.1 summarizes the key features of the sole proprietorship, the partnership, the C corporation, the S corporation, and the limited liability company.

Table 3.1

Characteristics of the Major Forms of Ownership

Feature	Sole Proprietorship	Partnership	C Corporation	S Corporation	Limited Liability Company
Owner's personal liability	Unlimited	Unlimited for general partners Limited for limited partners	Limited	Limited	Limited
Number of owners	1	2 or more (at least 1 general partner required)	Any number	Maximum of 75 (with restriction on who they are)	2 or more
Tax liability	Single tax: proprietor pays at individual rate	Single tax: partners pay on their proportional shares at individual rate	Double tax: corporation pays tax and shareholders pay tax on dividends distributed	Single tax: owners pay on their proportional shares at individual rate	Single tax: members pay on their proportional shares at individual rate
Maximum tax rate	39.6%	39.6%	35% (39.6% on distributed dividends)	39.6%	39.6%
Transferability of ownership	Fully transferable through sale or transfer of company assets	May require consent of all partners	Fully transferable	Transferable (but transfer may affect S status)	Usually requires consent of all members
Continuity of business	Ends on death or insanity of proprietor or upon termination by proprietor	Dissolves upon death, insanity, or retirement of a general partner (business may continue)	Perpetual life	Perpetual life	Perpetual life
Cost of formation	Low	Moderate	High	High	High
Liquidity of owner's investment in business	Poor to average	Poor to average	High	High	High
Complexity of formation	Extremely low	Moderate	High	High	High
Ability to raise capital	Low	Moderate	Very high	Moderate to high	High
Formation procedure	No special steps required other than buying necessary licenses	No written partnership agreements required (but highly advisable)	Must meet formal requirements specified by state law	Must follow same procedures as C corporation, then elect S status with IRS	Must meet formal requirements specified by state law

Source: www.bizstats.com.

Chapter Review

1. Discuss the issues entrepreneurs should consider when evaluating different forms of ownership.

   - The key to choosing the "right" form of ownership is understanding the characteristics of each form and knowing how they affect an entrepreneur's personal and business circumstances.
   - Factors to consider include: tax implications, liability expense, start-up and future capital requirements, control, managerial ability, business goals, management succession plans, and cost of formation.

2. Describe the advantages and disadvantages of the sole proprietorship.

   - A sole proprietorship is a business owned and managed by one individual and is the most popular form of ownership.
   - Sole proprietorships offer these advantages:
     - Simple to create
     - Least costly form to begin
     - Owner has total decision-making authority
     - No special legal restrictions
     - Easy to discontinue
   - Sole proprietorships suffer from these disadvantages:
     - Unlimited personal liability of owner
     - Limited managerial skills and capabilities
     - Limited access to capital
     - Lack of continuity

3. Describe the advantages and disadvantages of the partnership.

   - A partnership is an association of two or more people who co-own a business for the purpose of making a profit.
   - Partnerships offer these advantages:
     - Easy to establish
     - Complementary skills of partners
     - Division of profits
     - Larger pool of capital available
     - Ability to attract limited partners
     - Little government regulation
     - Flexibility
     - Tax advantages
   - Partnerships suffer from these disadvantages:
     - Unlimited liability of at least one partner
     - Difficulty in disposing of partnership interest
     - Lack of continuity
     - Potential for personality and authority conflicts
     - Partners bound by the law of agency

4. Describe the advantages and disadvantages of the corporation.

   - A limited partnership operates like any other partnership except that it allows limited partners (primary investors who cannot take an active role in managing the business) to become owners without subjecting themselves to unlimited personal liability for the company's debts.
   - A corporation, the most complex of the three basic forms of ownership, is a separate legal entity. To form a corporation, an entrepreneur must file the articles of incorporation with the state in which the company will incorporate.
   - Corporations offer these advantages:
     - Limited liability of stockholders
     - Ability to attract capital
     - Ability to continue indefinitely
     - Transferable ownership
   - Corporations suffer from these disadvantages:
     - Cost and time in incorporating
     - Double taxation
     - Potential for diminished managerial incentives
     - Legal requirements and regulatory red tape
     - Potential loss of control by the founders

5. Describe the features of the alternative forms of ownership such as the S corporation, the limited liability company, the joint venture, and syndicate.

   - An S corporation offers its owners limited liability protection but avoids the double taxation of C corporations.
   - A limited liability company, like an S corporation, is a cross between a partnership and a corporation. However, it operates without the restrictions imposed on an S corporation. To create an LLC, an entrepreneur must file the articles of organization and the operating agreement with the secretary of state.
   - A joint venture is like a partnership, except that it is formed for a specific purpose.
   - Much like a joint venture, a syndicate is a private investment group formed for the purpose of a large commercial project whose scope is larger than the capacity of an investor to finance alone.

▌▐▐ Discussion Questions

1. What factors should an entrepreneur consider before choosing a form of ownership?
2. Why are sole proprietorships so popular as a form of ownership?
3. How does personal conflict affect partnerships? How can co-owners avoid personal conflict?
4. What issues should the articles of partnership address? Why are the articles important to a successful partnership?
5. Can one partner commit another to a business deal without the other's consent? Why?
6. Explain the differences between a domestic corporation, a foreign corporation, and an alien corporation.
7. What issues should the Certificate of Incorporation cover?
8. How does an S corporation differ from a regular corporation?
9. How does a joint venture differ from a partnership?
10. What role do limited partners play in a partnership? What will happen if a limited partner takes an active role in managing the business?
11. What advantages does a limited liability company offer over an S corporation? Over a sole proprietorship?
12. How is an LLC created?
13. What criteria must an LLC meet to avoid double taxation?

Forms of Ownership

Business PlanPro

Launch the Business Plan Pro CD and go to the exercises for Chapter 3. There you will find a series of questions designed to help you decide which form of ownership is best for you. Remember: There is no one "best" form of ownership. The key is to understand the characteristics of each form of ownership and how those characteristics fit your particular needs. Based on this analysis, you will choose to create a sole proprietorship, a partnership, a corporation, an S corporation, a limited liability company, or a business modeled after one of the other forms of ownership.

When you complete this exercise, you are ready to go to the Your Company section of Business Plan Pro and describe the form of ownership you have chosen and your reasons for selecting it.

Chapter 4

Franchising and the Entrepreneur

> *One thorn of experience is worth a whole wilderness of warning.*
> —JAMES RUSSELL LOWELL

> *The big print giveth, the fine print taketh away.*
> —BISHOP FULTON J. SHEEN

Upon completion of this chapter, you will be able to:

1. Explain the importance of franchising in the U.S. economy.
2. Define the concept of franchising and describe the different types of franchises.
3. Describe the benefits and limitations of buying a franchise.
4. Describe the legal aspects of franchising, including the protection offered by the FTC's Trade Regulation Rule.
5. Explain the right way to buy a franchise.
6. Describe a typical franchise contract and some of its provisions.
7. Explain current trends shaping franchising.

1. Explain the importance of franchising in the U.S. economy.

Franchising is booming! Much of its popularity arises from its ability to offer those who lack business experience the chance to own and operate a business with a high probability of success. Franchising's growth in recent years has been phenomenal (see Figure 4.1), reaching far beyond the traditional auto dealerships and fast-food outlets. Through franchised businesses, consumers can buy nearly every good or service imaginable—from singing telegrams and home cleaning services to waste-eating microbes and tax preparation services. One franchise, Lifestyle Improvements Centers, LLC, offers motivation centers based on hypnosis![1] "Franchising is the most successful marketing concept ever created," says trend-tracker John Naisbitt.[2]

Because of the many benefits it offers both franchisers and franchisees, franchising has experienced exponential growth rates in the United States and abroad. A new franchise opens somewhere in the United States every 8 minutes and somewhere in the world every $6^1/_2$ minutes![3] Approximately 1 out of 12 retail businesses in the United States is a franchised operation. Franchises now account for 40 percent of all retail sales, totaling more than $1 trillion, and they employ more than 8 million people in more than 100 major industries.[4] Franchising has become an important part of the U.S. economy and its culture and has had a significant impact on global markets as well. More than 500 franchisers operate internationally, and since 1994 almost half of all new franchise units sold by all U.S. franchisers were in foreign lands.[5]

What Is Franchising?

2A. Define the concept of franchising.

Franchising can be traced to the post–Civil War era when Isaac M. Singer devised a more efficient, less expensive way to sell his Singer sewing machines through franchised outlets. From this meager beginning as a distribution system, franchising has become a major force in the U.S. economy, expanding into a broad range of retail and service businesses. The concept has reached beyond its traditional fast-food roots (which still accounts for about 40 percent of all the goods sold by franchisees) into businesses as diverse as diamond jewelry, on-site furniture repair, in-home pet care, and management training for executives. Retail outlets dominate franchising, accounting for about 85 percent of all franchise sales. However, increasing demand for business and consumer services is producing a boom among service-oriented franchises.

Figure 4.1

Franchising Growth

Source: "Top Reasons People Want to Become Franchises" and "The Big Bang," January 2004, www.entrepreneur.com. "Reprinted with permission from Entrepreneur Media, Inc.

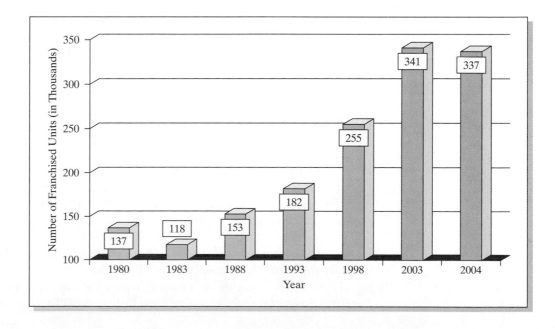

In **franchising,** semi-independent business owners (franchisees) pay fees and royalties to a parent company (franchiser) in return for the right to sell its products or services under the franchiser's trade name and often to use its business format and system. Franchisees do not establish their own autonomous businesses; instead, they buy a "success package" from the franchiser, who shows them how to use it. Ulf Schaefer, who operates a highly successful Play It Again Sports franchise with partner T. J. Western, says, "Buying a franchise is like buying a cookbook: The recipe is there, but you have to do the cooking yourself. A good franchiser gives you a system—advertising support, group buying power, continuing training, market research and so on. That support . . . is like a little insurance policy."[6]

Franchisees, unlike independent business owners, don't have the freedom to change the way they run their businesses—for example, shifting advertising strategies or adjusting product lines—but they do have a formula for success that the franchiser has worked out. Rich Premec, who invested $65,000 of his savings in a Sanford Rose executive recruiting franchise, recouped his investment and was earning a six-figure income from his franchise within two years. The secret, according to Premec, is "following the recipe." Premec recalls another Sanford Rose franchisee who decided to "go his own way" rather than follow the franchiser's system and failed.[7] Successful franchisers claim that not following the recipe is one of the chief reasons that franchisees fail. Franchisers develop the business systems their franchisees use to create a uniform level of quality and service. This standardization lies at the core of franchising's success as a method of distribution. One writer explains:

> The science of franchising is an exacting one; products and services are delivered according to tightly-wrapped operating formulas. There is no variance. A product is developed and honed under the watchful eye of the franchiser, then offered by franchisees under strict quality standards. The result: a democratization of products and services. Hamburgers that taste as good in Boston as in Beijing. Quick lubes available to everyone, whether they drive a Toyota or a Treblinka.[8]

Types of Franchising

2B. Describe the different types of franchises.

More than 1,500 franchisers operate nearly 337,000 outlets in the United States using three basic types of systems: trade name franchising, product distribution franchising, and pure franchising.[9] **Trade name franchising** involves a brand name such as True Value Hardware or Western Auto. Here, the franchise purchases the right to become identified with the franchiser's trade name without distributing particular products exclusively under the manufacturer's name. **Product distribution franchising** involves licensing the franchisee to sell specific products under the manufacturer's brand name and trademark through a selective, limited distribution network. This system is commonly used to market automobiles (Chevrolet, Honda, Chrysler), gasoline products (Exxon, Sunoco, Texaco), soft drinks (Pepsi-Cola, Coca-Cola), bicycles (Schwinn), appliances, cosmetics, and other products. Both of these forms of franchising enable franchisees to acquire some of the parent company's identity.

Pure (or **comprehensive** or **business format**) **franchising** involves providing the franchisee with a complete business format, including a license for a trade name, the products or services to be sold, the physical plant, the methods of operation, a marketing strategy plan, a quality control process, a two-way communications system, and the necessary business services. The franchisee purchases the right to use all the elements of a fully integrated business operation. Pure franchising is the most rapidly growing of all types of franchising and is common among fast-food restaurants, hotels, business service firms, car rental agencies, educational institutions, beauty aid retailers, and many others.

IN THE FOOTSTEPS OF AN ENTREPRENEUR...

America's First Business Format Franchise

Martha Matilda Harper probably never knew that the word franchising is derived from the French word that means "to free from servitude," yet this determined, visionary woman, who had spent 25 years as a domestic servant, created the first business format franchise in the United States. Born in 1857 in Ontario, Canada, and hired out as a servant at age 7, Harper never had the opportunity to be formally educated, but she quickly learned the skills required for entrepreneurial success. As a young woman, Harper emigrated to Rochester, New York, bringing with her a secret formula for a special shampoo (known as hair tonic in those days) and the lessons learned from years of caring for the hair of the women for whom she had worked.

In 1888, with her life savings of $360, Harper opened Rochester's first hair- and skin-care salon in the most prestigious building in town. A woman opening a business was a major accomplishment in the Victorian era, and the fact that Harper had spent most of her life as a servant made her entrepreneurial move all the more remarkable. (She had to hire an attorney to negotiate the lease after the building's owner refused to deal with her because she was a woman.) Despite stringent Victorian standards that encouraged women to have their hair done in the privacy of their homes, Harper's salon was highly successful. One of her most effective marketing tools was her own hair, which flowed in beautiful waves to the floor! Superior customer service, something Harper learned during her years of domestic work, became a hallmark of her company. "Base everything on customer service," she preached.

As her business's reputation grew, Harper saw the opportunity to expand her business as out-of-town customers begged her to open salons in their hometowns. Harper encouraged these satisfied customers to recruit other potential clients before she would consider opening a shop in their towns. Knowing that her new shops had to maintain the same standards as the one in Rochester and recognizing that she could not manage each one herself, Harper came up with a new way to do business: franchising! By franchising her salons, she would be able to expand rapidly without draining the capital from her existing business and she could change the destinies of other women as well, helping them get into business for themselves. Harper wanted women who would follow precisely the formula for success she had worked out in her Rochester, New York, salon, so she targeted former domestic servants as her franchisees. She understood that high standards that guaranteed customers consistency and quality were keys to expanding her business empire. Her system became known as the Harper Method.

In 1891, the first franchise opened in Buffalo, New York, followed by another in Chicago's Marshall Field's department store. Franchisees not only sold the hair- and skin-care products Harper manufactured, but they also attended her beauty training schools, which sprang up in cities ranging from Calgary, Canada, to Georgia. Harper also taught her franchisees how to collect information from their customers and to use it to create effective direct-mail advertising campaigns. Harper encouraged her franchisees to establish child care centers in their salons so that customers could relax and enjoy their visits. She also saw the centers as a way to recruit the children as future customers! Harper's customer-focused business practices paid off, and her list of clients grew to include many famous people of the day, including Susan B. Anthony and first ladies Wilson and Coolidge. Even during the Great Depression, customers continued to visit Harper's franchises, and every one of her salons survived the economic downturn. When she died in 1950, Harper had more than 350 salons bearing her name in the United States, Canada, South America, and Europe.

Martha Matilda Harper truly was a woman ahead of her time, creating a method of doing business that has become one of the most successful in the world!

1. How does business format franchising work?
2. How important was standardization and consistent quality to Harper's franchises?

How important are these factors to modern franchisers?
3. What can franchisers do to ensure standardization and consistent quality? What impact do these steps have on franchisees?

Sources: Adapted from Jane R. Plitt, "Ahead of Her Time," *Success,* July/August 2000, pp. 84–86; "Martha Matilda Harper," www.winningthevote.org/MMHarper.html.

The Benefits of Buying a Franchise

3A. Describe the benefits of buying a franchise.

Perhaps the most important reason franchising has been so successful is the mutual benefits it offers franchisers and franchisees. In a franchising relationship, each party depends on the other for support. The ideal franchising relationship is a partnership based on trust and a willingness to work together for mutual success. Over the long run, the most successful franchisers are those that see their franchisees as partners. They know that *their* success depends on their *franchisees'* success. Noting the importance of maintaining a solid relationship with the company's franchisees, McDonald's founder Ray Kroc said, "None of us is as good as all of us."[10]

Franchisees get the opportunity to own a small business relatively quickly, and, because of the identification with an established product and brand name, a franchise often reaches the break-even point faster than an independent business would. Still, most new franchise outlets don't break even for at least six to eighteen months.

Franchisees also benefit from the franchiser's business experience. In fact, *experience* is, in essence, what a franchisee buys from a franchiser. The franchiser's knowledge, experience, and expertise in the industry serve as the basis for a competitive advantage for franchisees. Too often entrepreneurs go into business by themselves and make many costly mistakes. Given the thin margin for error in the typical start-up, a new business owner cannot afford to make many mistakes. In a franchising arrangement, the franchiser already has worked out the kinks in the system, often by trial and error, and franchisees benefit from that experience. Franchisers have climbed up the learning curve and can share with franchisees the secrets of success they have discovered in the industry. For franchisees, the ability to draw on the franchiser's experience is like having a safety net under them as they build their businesses.

Franchisees also earn a great deal of satisfaction from their work. According to a recent Gallup survey of franchise owners, 71 percent of franchisees said their franchises either met or exceeded their expectations. Plus, 65 percent said they would purchase their franchises again if given the opportunity (compared to just 39 percent of Americans who say they would choose the same job or business again).[11]

Before jumping at a franchise opportunity, an entrepreneur should consider carefully the following question: "What can a franchise do for me that I cannot do for myself?" The answer to the question will depend on the entrepreneur's particular situation and is just as important as a systematic evaluation of any franchise opportunity. After careful deliberation, a potential franchisee may conclude that a franchise offers nothing that she could not do on her own; on the other hand, it may turn out that the franchise is the key to success as a business owner. Table 4.1 shows the top six reasons people want to become franchisees.

Let us investigate the specific advantages of buying a franchise.

Table 4.1

The Top Reasons People Want to Become Franchisees

1. They want to be entrepreneurs.
2. They want to own a second business.
3. They seek more flexible schedules or want to work from their homes.
4. They are corporate castoffs with severance packages looking for new business opportunities.
5. They have retired from their jobs and want to keep working.
6. They have just graduated from college.

Source: "Top Reasons Why People Want to Become Franchises," January 2004 issue of *Enterpreneur Magazine* and "The Big Bang," January 2004 issue of *Entrepreneur Magazine.* Reprinted with permission from Entrepreneur Media, Inc.

A Business System

One major benefit of joining a franchise is gaining access to a business system with a proven track record. In many instances, franchisers provide their franchisees with turnkey operations, enabling them to get their businesses up and running much faster, more efficiently, and more effectively than if they launched their own companies. Because franchisees have a business system to follow, they can succeed in business without having many years of experience in the industry. They have the advantage of relying on the franchiser's experience and the business system that results from that experience to build successful businesses. *For instance, when Lori Somley became a single mother, she worried that her modest salary as a dental assistant would not be sufficient for raising her four children. Although she was intrigued by the idea of becoming an entre- preneur, she had no experience running a business and dismissed the idea of starting her own company from scratch. Somley realized that a franchise might be ideal for her and began exploring her options. After evaluating her own skills and interests, Somley decided to purchase a Curves International franchise, one of the fastest-growing franchises in the nation. Curves is an exercise franchise that offers busy women on tight schedules short (30-minute) workouts available on flexible schedules. Because she had no business experience, Somley knew she needed a franchise system that provided her with a solid business system and managerial support. She launched the Curves franchise in her home- town of Goffstown, New Hampshire, and in her first year of operation, she was able to double the salary she was earning as a dental assistant. In addition to greater earning power, Somley also enjoys a more flexible personal schedule that enables her to spend more time with her children, and she has lost 24 pounds by exercising in her gym!*[12]

Company Example

Management Training and Support

Recall from Chapter 1 that a leading cause of business failure is incompetent management. Franchisers are well aware of this and, in an attempt to reduce the number of franchise casualties, offer managerial training programs to franchisees prior to opening a new outlet. Many franchisers, especially the well-established ones, also provide follow-up training and counseling services. This service is vital because most franchisers do not require a fran- chisee to have experience in the business. "Just putting a person in business, giving him a trademark, patting him on the [back], and saying, 'Good luck,' is not sufficient," says one franchise consultant.[13]

Training programs often involve both classroom and on-site instruction to teach franchisees the basic operations of the business—from producing and selling the goods or services to purchasing raw materials and completing paperwork. Before beginning opera- tions, Subway franchisees take a 55-hour course and then spend an additional 34 hours in on- the-job training at Subways near company headquarters in Milford, Connecticut. Toward the end of their training, franchisees manage a store by themselves, and they must pass a final exam before Subway gives them final approval to become franchisees.[14] Franchisees at Golden Corral learn how to manage a restaurant as well as how to perform every job in a typical 100-employee location, and Dunkin' Donuts trains franchisees for as long as five weeks in everything from accounting to dough making. Franchisees at Plato's Closet, a chain of resale shops that focuses on clothing for teens and young adults, spend two weeks learning how to develop a business plan, secure financing, hire and manage employees, buy and sell inventory, and use the company's proprietary computer software system to manage their stores. The strength of that training program is one factor that gave Charlotte Knowles, a former schoolteacher with no experience in retail clothing, the confidence to open a Plato's Closet franchise in Greenville, South Carolina.[15] Although these training programs are beneficial to running a successful franchise, franchisees should not expect a two- to five-week program to make them management experts. Management is much too complex to learn in any single crash course.

To ensure franchisees' continued success, many franchisers supplement their start-up training programs with ongoing instruction and support. Franchisers commonly provide field support to franchisees in customer service, quality control, inventory management, and general management. Some franchisers assign field consultants to guide new franchisees through the first week or two of operation after the grand opening. Franchisers offer this support because they realize that their ultimate success depends on the franchisee's success. Because the level of field support provided is one of the most common causes of franchisee–franchiser lawsuits, prospective franchisees should know exactly what the franchise contract says about the nature, extent, and frequency of field support they can expect.

Despite the positive features of training, inherent dangers exist in the trainer–trainee relationship. Every would-be franchisee should be aware that, in some cases, "assistance" from the franchiser tends to drift into "control" over the franchisee's business. Also, some franchisers charge fees for their training services, so the franchisee should know exactly what he or she is agreeing to and what it costs.

Brand Name Appeal

Franchisees purchase the right to use a nationally known and advertised brand name for a product or service, giving them the advantage of identifying their businesses with a widely recognized name, which provides a great deal of drawing power. Customers recognize the identifying trademark, the standard symbols, the store design, and the products of an established franchise. Jeff McCoy, who converted his independent electronics store into a Radio Shack franchise, explains, "Name recognition means a lot because it brings in customers who know what they're going to get as soon as they walk through the door."[16] Indeed, one of franchising's basic tenets is cloning the franchiser's success. Nearly everyone is familiar with the golden arches of McDonald's or the red roof of the Red Roof Inn, and the standard products and quality offered at each. A customer is confident that the quality and content of a meal at McDonald's in Fort Lauderdale will be consistent with a meal at a San Francisco McDonald's. One franchising expert explains, "The day you open a McDonald's franchise, you have instant customers. If you choose to open [an independent] hamburger restaurant, . . . you'd have to spend a fortune on advertising and promotion before you'd attract customers."[17]

Standardized Quality of Goods and Services

Because a franchisee purchases a license to sell the franchiser's product or service and the privilege of using the associated brand name, the quality of the goods or services sold determines the franchiser's reputation. Building a sound reputation in business is not achieved quickly, although destroying a good reputation takes no time at all. If some franchisees were allowed to operate at substandard levels, the image of the entire chain would suffer irreparable damage; therefore, franchisers normally demand compliance with uniform standards of quality and service throughout the entire chain. In many cases, the franchiser conducts periodic inspections of local facilities to assist in maintaining acceptable levels of performance. Maintaining quality is so important that most franchisers retain the right to terminate the franchise contract and to repurchase the outlet if the franchisee fails to comply with established standards.

National Advertising Programs

An effective advertising program is essential to the success of virtually all franchise operations. Marketing a brand name product or service over a wide geographic area requires a far-reaching advertising campaign. A regional or national advertising program benefits all franchisees. Normally, such an advertising campaign is organized and controlled by the franchiser. It is financed by each franchisee's contribution of a percentage of monthly sales, usually 1 to 5 percent or a flat monthly fee, into an advertising pool. For example, Subway franchisees pay 3.5 percent of gross revenues to the Subway national advertising program. The franchiser uses this pool of funds to create a cooperative advertising program, which has more impact than if the franchisees spent the same amount of money separately.

Most franchisers also require franchisees to spend a minimum amount on local advertising. To supplement their national advertising efforts, both Wendy's and Burger King require franchisees to spend at least 3 percent of gross sales on local advertising. Some franchisers assist franchisees in designing and producing local ads. Many companies help franchisees create promotional plans and provide press releases, advertisements, and special materials such as signs and banners for grand openings and special promotions.

Financial Assistance

Because they rely on their franchisees' money to accelerate the growth of their businesses, franchisers, as a general rule, typically do not provide any extensive financial help for franchisees. Few franchisers make loans to enable franchisees to pay the initial franchise fee. However, once a franchiser locates a suitable prospective franchisee, it may offer the qualified candidate direct financial assistance in specific areas, such as purchasing equipment, inventory, or even the franchise fee. Because the total start-up costs of some franchises are already at breathtaking levels, some franchisers find that they must offer direct financial assistance. *For example, when Stanley Wong purchased his first International House of Pancakes (IHOP) franchise in 1967, he had only $10,000 to invest, and the company's franchise fee alone was $40,000. However, IHOP's financing program enabled Wong to finance the franchise fee and other costs associated with starting the franchise. Today, Wong owns 23 IHOP restaurants, and IHOP continues to finance 80 percent of the franchise fee and 100 percent of the leases on the buildings and equipment. The company-sponsored financing programs translate into much lower up-front costs for franchisees.*[18]

Entrepreneur magazine reports that nearly three-fourths of its Franchise 500® companies offer some type of financing for their franchisees. However, only about 16 percent offer direct, "in-house" financial assistance.[19] In most instances, financial assistance takes a form other than direct loans, leases, or short-term financing. Many franchisers offer to help franchisees prepare a business plan or apply for a loan from

Company Example

a bank, the Small Business Administration, or another lender. Franchisers usually are willing to assist qualified franchisees in establishing relationships with banks, private investors, and other sources of funds. In many instances, franchisers have established alliances with third-party lenders to make it easier for their franchisees to get financing. For instance, the parent company of Baskin-Robbins, Dunkin' Donuts, and Togo's franchises has created an arrangement with three national small business lending programs in which its franchisees can qualify for up to 75 percent of the cost of a franchise. Through this preferred lender relationship, franchisees can obtain loans to cover the initial franchise fee, fixtures, vehicles, working capital, and equipment purchases by completing a shorter, customized loan application designed just for them.[20] Support from the franchiser enhances a franchisee's chances of getting the financing they seek because most lenders recognize the lower failure rate among reputable franchises.

The Small Business Administration (SBA) has simplified the loan application process for franchisees by working with FRANdata to create the Franchise Registry, a central database of information about participating franchises that the SBA has certified and whose franchisees benefit from a streamlined loan review process. Since 1993, the SBA has guaranteed more than 12,000 loans to franchisees in more than 1,200 franchise systems.[21]

Proven Products and Business Formats

What a franchisee essentially is purchasing is the franchiser's experience, expertise, and products. A franchise owner does not have to build the business from scratch. Instead of being forced to rely solely on personal ability to establish a business and attract a clientele, the franchisee can depend on the methods and techniques of an established business. These standardized procedures and operations greatly enhance the franchisee's chances of success and avoid the most inefficient type of learning—trial and error. "When we say 'Do things our way,' " says an executive at Subway Sandwiches and Salads, "it's not just an ego thing on the part of the franchiser. We've proven it works."[22]

Company Example →   Also, franchisees do not have to struggle for recognition in the local marketplace as much as an independent owner might. *Concerned that an independent pet shop would have difficulty competing with much larger stores with greater visibility and name recognition, Stephen Adams decided to take the franchising route into business. After researching their options, Adams and his wife purchased a Pet Valu franchise and are extremely pleased with the results. The business became profitable just a few months after they launched it, and sales are growing at 46 percent a year!*[23]

Reputable franchisers also invest resources in researching and developing new products and services (or improvements on existing ones) and in tracking market trends that influence the success of the product line. In fact, many franchisees cite this as one of the primary benefits of the franchising arrangement.

Centralized Buying Power

A significant advantage a franchisee has over the independent small business owner is participation in the franchiser's centralized and large-volume buying power. If franchisers sell goods and materials to franchisees (not all do), they may pass on to franchisees any cost savings from quantity discounts they earn by buying in volume. For example, it is unlikely that a small, independent ice cream parlor could match the buying power of Baskin-Robbins with its 3,000 retail ice cream stores. In many instances, economies of scale simply preclude independent owners from competing head-to-head with franchise operations.

Site Selection and Territorial Protection

A proper location is critical to the success of any small business, and franchises are no exception. In fact, franchise experts consider the three most important factors in franchising to be location, location, and location. Becoming affiliated with a franchiser may be the best way to get into prime locations. McDonald's, for example, is well known for its ability to obtain prime locations in high-traffic areas. Although choosing a location is the franchisee's responsibility, the franchiser usually reserves the right to approve the final site. Many franchisers will make an extensive location analysis for each new outlet (for a fee), including studies of traffic patterns, zoning ordinances, accessibility, and population density. Even if the franchiser does not conduct a site analysis, the franchisee must. A thorough demographic and statistical analysis of potential locations is essential to selecting the site that offers the greatest potential for success. We will discuss these topics in more detail in Chapter 7.

Franchisers also may offer a franchisee territorial protection, which gives the franchisee the right to exclusive distribution of brand name goods or services within a particular geographic area. Under such an agreement, a franchiser agrees not to sell another franchised outlet or to open a company-owned unit within the franchisee's assigned territory. The size of a franchisee's territory varies from company to company. For example, one fast-food restaurant agrees not to license another franchisee within a mile and a half of existing locations. A soft-serve ice cream and yogurt franchiser defines its franchisees' territories on the basis of ZIP code designations. The purpose of this protection is to prevent an invasion of existing franchisees' territories and the accompanying dilution of sales. Unfortunately for franchisees, fewer franchisers now offer their franchisees territorial protection.

As the competition for top locations has escalated over the past decade, disputes over the placement of new franchise outlets have become a source of friction between franchisers and franchisees. Existing franchisees charge that franchisers are encroaching on their territories by granting new franchises in such close proximity that their sales are diluted. Franchise experts consistently cite territorial encroachment as the number-one problem for franchisees. Although the new outlets franchisers grant lie outside the boundaries of existing franchisees' territories, their market coverage and reach overlap those of existing territories, causing sales and profits to decline. A ruling by a court of appeals in California has given franchisees greater protection from encroachment. *When Naugles Inc., a Mexican restaurant chain, opened a company-owned outlet within 1.5 miles of an existing franchisee's location, the franchisee, Vylene Enterprises, charged that Naugles' opening of the new restaurant breached the franchise agreement and violated the implied requirement of fair dealing. Vylene testified that the new outlet caused a 35 percent sales decline at its store. Even though the franchise agreement did not grant Vylene an exclusive territory, the court ruled in Vylene's favor, stating that "Naugles' construction of a competing restaurant within a mile and a half of Vylene's restaurant was a breach of the covenant of good faith and fair dealing."[24]*

Company Example →

Greater Chance for Success

Investing in a franchise is not risk free. Between 200 and 300 new franchise companies enter the market each year, and many of them do not survive. A study by Scott Shane at the University of Maryland found that one-fourth of new franchisers fail within 10 years and that the failure rate is highest within the first four years.[25] Still, available statistics suggest that franchising is less risky than building a business from the ground up. Approximately 46 percent of independent businesses fail by the third year of operation; in contrast, only about 18 percent of all franchises fail by the third year. A study by the Small

Business Administration found that the failure rate among franchisees of small franchise systems was 38 percent after five years, compared to a five-year failure rate of 60 percent among independent businesses.[26] The higher success rate for franchises is attributed to the broad range of services, assistance, guidance, and the business system most franchisers provide. Still, most new franchises take two years to start earning a profit.

Franchising's success statistics must be interpreted carefully, however, because when a franchise outlet is in danger of failing, the franchiser often repurchases or relocates the outlet and does not report it as a failure. According to the American Bar Association's Franchise Committee, one-third of the franchisees in a typical franchise system are making a decent profit, one-third are breaking even, and one-third are losing money.[27]

The risk of purchasing a franchise is two-pronged: success—or failure—depends on an entrepreneur's managerial skills and motivation and on the franchiser's business experience and system. "Don't think that because you become a franchisee you'll automatically be successful," warns one franchise consultant. "The franchiser is only providing the tools; the rest is up to you."[28] Many owners are convinced that franchising has been a crucial part of their success. The business system they get serves as a safety net when launching a business. Many franchisees say that buying a franchise is like going into business *for* yourself but not *by* yourself.

Drawbacks of Buying a Franchise

3B. Describe the limitations of buying a franchise.

The benefits of franchising can mean the difference between success and failure for a small business. However, franchisees must sacrifice some freedom to the franchiser. Prospective franchisees must explore other limitations of franchising before buying into this business system. Thoroughly researching potential franchise opportunities is the only way an entrepreneur can find a franchise that is a good match with his or her personality, likes, and dislikes.

Franchise Fees and Profit Sharing

Virtually all franchisers impose some type of fees and demand a share of a franchisee's sales revenues in return for the use of the franchiser's name, products or services, and business system. Franchise fees and initial capital requirements vary among the different franchisers. The average total start-up cost for a franchise is about $200,000, and nearly 80 percent of franchise opportunities include initial investments of $250,000 or less (excluding real estate).[29] The Commerce Department reports that total investments for franchises range from $1,000 for business services up to $10 million for hotel and motel franchises. For example, Jani-King, a home-based commercial cleaning business, sells franchises for $8,200 to $33,500, depending on the territory's size; Molly Maid franchisees invest between $63,000 and $93,000 to own one of the company's residential cleaning outlets; and McDonald's requires an investment of $506,000 to $1,600,000 (but McDonald's owns the land and the building).

Start-up costs for franchises often include numerous additional fees. Most franchisers impose a franchise fee ranging from $5,000 to $50,000 up front for the right to use the company name. The average franchise fee is $25,000.[30] Molly Maid, for example, charges a franchise fee of $6,900, and McDonald's up-front franchise fee is $45,000. Other additional start-up costs might include site purchase and preparation, construction, signs, fixtures, equipment, management assistance, and training. Some franchise fees include these costs whereas others do not. Before signing any contract, a prospective franchisee should determine the total cost of a franchise, something every franchiser is required to disclose in item 10 of its Uniform Franchise Offering Circular (see "Franchising and the Law" on pages 113 to 115).

Franchisers also impose ongoing royalty fees as profit-sharing devices. The royalty usually involves a percentage of gross sales with a required minimum or a flat fee levied on the franchise. Royalty fees typically range from 1 percent to 12 percent of sales, although most franchisers assess a rate between 3 and 7 percent. Subway Sandwiches and Salads charges a franchise fee of $10,000 and a royalty of 8 percent of sales, payable weekly. Krispy Kreme's franchise fee is $40,000, and its royalty is 5.5 percent of each unit's sales. These fees can increase a franchisee's overhead expenses significantly. Because franchisers' royalties and fees are calculated as a percentage of a franchisee's *sales,* they get paid even if the franchisee fails to earn a profit. Sometimes unprepared franchisees discover (too late) that the franchiser's royalties and fees are about what the normal profit margin is for a franchise. To avoid this problem, a prospective franchisee should find out which fees are required (some are merely recommended) and then determine what services and benefits the fees cover. One of the best ways to do this is to itemize what you are getting for your money and then determine whether the cost is reasonable. Be sure to get the details on all expenses—amount, time of payment, and financing arrangements; find out which items, if any, are included in the initial franchise fee and which ones are extra.

Strict Adherence to Standardized Operations

Although franchisees own their businesses, they do not have the autonomy of independent owners. The terms of the franchise agreement govern the franchiser–franchisee relationship. That agreement requires franchisees to operate their outlets according to the principles spelled out in the franchiser's operations manual. Typical topics covered in the manual include operating hours, dress codes, operating policies and procedures, product or service specifications, and confidentiality requirements.

To protect its public image, franchisers require franchisees to maintain certain operating standards. If a franchise constantly fails to meet the minimum standards established for the business, the franchiser may terminate its license. Determining compliance with standards is usually accomplished by periodic inspections. At times, strict adherence to franchise standards may become a burden to the franchisee.

Restrictions on Purchasing

In the interest of maintaining quality standards, franchisers sometimes require franchisees to purchase products, supplies, or special equipment from the franchiser or from an approved supplier. For example, KFC requires that franchisees use only seasonings blended by a particular company. A poor image for the entire franchise could result from some franchisees using inferior products to cut costs. The franchise contract spells out the penalty for using unapproved suppliers, which usually is termination of the franchise agreement.

Franchisees at some chains have filed antitrust suits alleging that franchisers overcharge their outlets for supplies and equipment and eliminate competition by failing to approve alternative suppliers. A franchiser can legally set the prices paid for the products it sells to franchisees but cannot establish the retail prices franchisees charge. Franchisers may suggest retail prices but cannot force the franchisee to abide by them.

Limited Product Line

In most cases, the franchise agreement stipulates that franchisees can sell only those products approved by the franchiser. Unless they are willing to risk license cancellation, franchisees must avoid selling any unapproved products through their outlets. Franchisers strive for standardization in their product lines so that customers, wherever they may be, know what to expect. Some companies allow franchisees to modify their product or service offerings to suit regional or local tastes, but only with the franchiser's approval. When Heavenly Hams franchisee Felix Mirando spotted an opportunity to sell ready-made box lunches to employees at corporate offices near his franchise, he asked for and received approval from the franchiser to add the item to his menu.[31]

A franchise may be required to carry an unpopular product or be prevented from introducing a desirable one by the franchise agreement. Some franchises discourage franchisees from deviating from the standard formula in any way, including experimenting with new products and services. However, other franchisers encourage and even solicit new ideas and innovations from their franchisees. *In fact, a McDonald's franchisee, Herb Peterson, created the highly successful Egg McMuffin while experimenting with a Teflon-coated egg ring that gave fried eggs rounded corners and a poached appearance. Peterson put his round eggs on English muffins, adorned them with Canadian bacon and melted cheese, and showed his creation to McDonald's chief, Ray Kroc. Kroc devoured two of them and was sold on the idea when Peterson's wife suggested the catchy name. In 1975, McDonald's became the first fast-food franchise to open its doors for breakfast, and the Egg McMuffin became a staple on the breakfast menu.[32] McDonald's franchisees also came up with the ideas for the Filet-O-fish sandwich and the popular Big Mac.[33]*

> Company Example

Unsatisfactory Training Programs

Every would-be franchisee must be wary of unscrupulous franchisers who promise extensive services, advice, and assistance but deliver nothing. For example, one owner relied on a franchiser to provide what had been described as an "extensive, rigorous training program" after paying a handsome technical assistance fee. The program was nothing but a set of pamphlets and do-it-yourself study guides. Common prey for dishonest franchisers are those impatient entrepreneurs who purchase franchises without investigating the business and never hear from the franchiser again. Although disclosure rules have reduced the severity of the problem, dishonest characters still prey on unprepared prospective franchisees.

Market Saturation

As the owners of many fast-food and yogurt and ice cream franchises have discovered, market saturation is a very real danger. Although some franchisers offer franchisees territorial protection, many do not. Territorial encroachment has become a hotly contested issue in franchising as growth-seeking franchisers have exhausted most of the prime locations and are now setting up new franchises in close proximity to existing ones. The biggest challenge to the growth potential of franchising is the lack of satisfactory locations. In some areas of the country, franchisees are upset, claiming that their markets are oversaturated and their sales are suffering.

Another challenge to territorial protection for franchisees is the Internet. Increasingly, franchisers are setting up Web sites, which some franchisees say are taking sales from their outlets and are in violation of their exclusive territory agreements. Franchisees of one drugstore chain recently filed arbitration claims to block the franchiser from competing with them by selling products over its Web site. The franchiser denied that its Web site was cannibalizing sales of its franchised outlets and claimed that the site would promote the entire company's brand.[34]

Table 4.2

A Franchise Evaluation Quiz

Taking the emotion out of buying a franchise is the goal of this self-test developed by Franchise Solutions, Inc., a franchise consulting company in Portsmouth, New Hampshire. Circle the number that reflects your degree of certainty or positive feelings for each of the following 12 statements; 1 is low; 5 is high.

	Low				High
1. I would really enjoy being in this kind of business.	1	2	3	4	5
2. This franchise will meet or exceed my income goals.	1	2	3	4	5
3. My people-handling skills are sufficient for this franchise.	1	2	3	4	5
4. I understand fully my greatest challenge in this franchise, and I feel comfortable with my abilities.	1	2	3	4	5
5. I have met with the company management and feel compatible.	1	2	3	4	5
6. I understand the risks with this business and am prepared to accept them.	1	2	3	4	5
7. I have researched the competition in my area and feel comfortable with the potential market.	1	2	3	4	5
8. My family and friends think this is a great opportunity for me.	1	2	3	4	5
9. I have had an adviser review the disclosure documents and the franchise agreement.	1	2	3	4	5
10. I have contacted a representative number of the existing franchisees; they were overwhelmingly positive.	1	2	3	4	5
11. I have researched this industry and feel comfortable about the long-term growth potential.	1	2	3	4	5
12. My background and experience make this franchise an ideal choice.	1	2	3	4	5

The maximum score on the quiz is 60. A score of 45 or below means that either the franchise opportunity is unsuitable or that you need to do more research on the franchise you are considering.

Source: Reprint by permission, *Nation's Business,* October 1996, Copyright 1996, U.S. Chamber of Commerce and October 1997, Copyright 1997, U.S. Chamber of Commerce.

Less Freedom

When franchisees purchase their franchises and sign the contract, they agree to sell the franchiser's product or service by following its prescribed formula. When McDonald's rolls out a new national product, for instance, all franchisees put it on their menus. Franchisers want to ensure success and most monitor their franchisees' performances closely. Strict uniformity is the rule rather than the exception. Entrepreneurs who want to be their own bosses and to avoid being subject to the control of others will most likely be frustrated as franchisees. Highly independent, "go-my-own-way" individuals probably should not choose the franchise route to business ownership. Table 4.2 offers a Franchise Evaluation Quiz designed to help potential franchisees decide whether a franchise is right for them.

IN THE FOOTSTEPS OF AN ENTREPRENEUR...

Better ButterBurgers

When he was a teenager, Craig Culver learned the restaurant business from the bottom up, working in the A&W restaurant his parents owned in Sauk City, Wisconsin. In 1984, he transformed that same business into the first Culver's restaurant, specializing in frozen custard and ButterBurgers (modeled after the homemade ones his mother prepared with a dollop of butter on the top of each bun before toasting it). He lost money the first year, but within two years, Culver was earning a healthy profit and began expanding. As the chain became increasingly popular, Culver fielded many requests from loyal customers about franchising the operation. In 1988, the company sold its first franchise and now has more than 200 locations, most of which are in the Midwest and in Texas.

This highly profitable company's sales are growing at a rate that is seven times faster than the fast-food industry as a whole, and its per-store sales volume is an impressive $1.6 million, an amount that exceeds that of McDonald's! Buying a Culver's franchise is not easy, however. The screening process is intense, and candidates must have a net worth of at least $500,000, including liquid assets of at least $200,000 to be considered. For those with the right numbers on their personal financial statements, the cost of opening an average Culver's franchise is $1.9 million: $800,000 for a 4,500 square-foot building, $600,000 for 1.5 acres of land, $450,000 for restaurant equipment, and a $50,000 franchise fee. The 15-year contract also requires franchisees to pay an ongoing 4 percent royalty on sales and to contribute 3 percent of their sales to an advertising program. Because the cost of opening a franchise is steep, the company often steers those who qualify to private lenders who offer loans guaranteed by the Small Business Administration with interest rates at one or two points above the prime interest rate.

Buying a Culver's franchise takes more than just money, however. Before becoming franchisees,

candidates must work for 60 hours—without pay—at one of the five company-owned restaurants to become familiar with the Culver system. The next step is an intense four-month "boot camp" at company headquarters in Wisconsin, all at the franchisee's expense (an estimated $20,000). Six days a week for 12 hours a day, franchisees learn everything they can about running a successful restaurant—how to handle the accounting software, mop the floors properly, fix the equipment, work the front counter, and prepare the items on the menu, which includes everything from ButterBurgers and Norwegian cod filet sandwiches to fried cheese curds and malted milk shakes. When they graduate from the Culver program, franchisees get two things from Culver: his cell phone number and some advice—"Never leave your post." Justin Obriecht, who bought his Culver's franchise at age 24 with all of his savings plus money from his mother, his aunt, and a $2 million bank loan, says, "If he calls your restaurant and you're not there, he's going to want to know why."

A stickler for detail, Culver spends half his time visiting his franchisees' restaurants (which now cover 12 states) and inspecting them much like a drill sergeant inspects his troops' barracks. Often arriving unannounced, he checks the condition of the counters and the carpet as well as the cleanliness of the windows, doors, and parking lot.

Culver's rigorous franchisee screening and selection process means that most candidates don't make the cut. For those who do, however, the rewards can be significant. Most franchisees become profitable within 12 to 24 months and on average recover their initial investments in seven years. "I want to create millionaires," explains Culver, who estimates that, so far, he's done exactly that for more than two dozen of his franchisees.

1. Explain the advantages and disadvantages of opening and operating a franchise such as Culver's.
2. What steps does Culver take to ensure standardization and consistent quality? What impact do these steps have on Culver's franchisees? On Culver's customers?
3. Would a Culver's franchise suit your personality, goals, and interests? Explain.

Sources: Adapted from Erin Killian, "Butter'Em Up," *Forbes,* June 9, 2003, pp. 175–176; Rob Kaiser, "Custard That's Far from Last Stand," *Chicago Tribune,* September 7, 2002, www.culvers.com/AdminToolFiles/Documents/Document190/Article-ChicagoTribune.pdf; "Culver's Press Kit," Culver Franchising System, www.culvers.com/PressRoom/PressKit.aspx; "Culver Franchising System," *Entrepreneur's* Franchise Zone, www.entrepreneur.com/franzone/details/0,5885, 12-12—282264-0,00.html?section=profile.

Franchising and the Law

4. Describe the legal aspects of franchising, including the protection offered by the FTC's Trade Regulation Rule.

The franchising boom spearheaded by McDonald's in the late 1950s brought with it many prime investment opportunities. However, the explosion of legitimate franchises also ushered in with it several fly-by-night franchisers who defrauded their franchisees. In response to these specific incidents and to the potential for deception inherent in a franchise relationship, California in 1971 enacted the first Franchise Investment Law. This law and those of 13 other states* that have since passed similar laws require franchisers to register a **Uniform Franchise Offering Circular (UFOC)** and deliver a copy to prospective franchisees before any offer or sale of a franchise. The UFOC establishes full disclosure guidelines for the franchising company and gives potential franchisees the ability to protect themselves from unscrupulous franchisers running fly-by-night operations.

In October 1979, the Federal Trade Commission (FTC) enacted the **Trade Regulation Rule**, requiring all franchisers to disclose detailed information on their operations at the first personal meeting or at least 10 days before a franchise contract is signed or any money is paid. The FTC rule covers all franchisers, even those in the 36 states lacking franchise disclosure laws. The purpose of the regulation is to assist the potential franchisee's investigation of the franchise deal and to introduce consistency into the franchiser's disclosure statements. In 1993, the FTC modified the requirements for the UFOC with a "plain English" requirement, making more information available to prospective franchisees and making the document easier to read and understand. The FTC's philosophy is not so much to detect and to prosecute abusers as to provide information to prospective franchisees and help them make intelligent decisions. Although the FTC requires each franchiser to provide a potential franchisee with this information, it does not verify the UFOC's accuracy. Even though the UFOC is an extremely important part of investigating any franchise, prospective franchisees should use this document only as a starting point for the investigation. The Trade Regulation Rule requires a franchiser to include in its disclosure statement a sample franchise contract, audited financial statements for three years, and information on the following 23 major topics:

1. Information identifying the franchiser and its affiliates and describing their business experience and the franchises being sold.
2. Information identifying and describing the business experience of each of the franchise's officers, directors, and management personnel responsible for the franchise program.
3. A description of the lawsuits in which the franchiser and its officers, directors, and managers have been involved in the past 10 years.
4. Information about any bankruptcies in which the franchiser and its officers, directors, and/or managers have been involved.
5. Information about the initial franchise fee and other payments required to obtain the franchise, including the intended use of the fees.
6. A description of any other continuing payments franchisees are required to make after start-up, including royalties, service fees, training fees, lease payments, advertising charges, and others.
7. A detailed description of the payments a franchisee must make to fulfill the initial investment requirement and how and to whom they are made. The categories covered are initial franchise fee, equipment, opening inventory, initial advertising fee, signs, training, real estate, working capital, legal, accounting, and utilities.

---

*The 14 states requiring franchise registration are California, Hawaii, Illinois, Indiana, Maryland, Michigan, Minnesota, New York, North Dakota, Rhode Island, South Dakota, Virginia, Washington, and Wisconsin.

8. Information about quality restrictions on goods and services used in the franchise and where they may be purchased, including restricted purchases from the franchises. Franchisers often require franchisees to purchase goods, services, and supplies only from approved suppliers (including the franchiser).

9. A cross-reference chart that shows where the description of the franchisee's obligations under the contract is contained in the text of the UFOC.

10. A description of any financial assistance available from the franchiser in the purchase of the franchise.

11. A description of all obligations the franchiser must fulfill in helping a franchisee prepare to open and operate a unit, with information covering location selection methods and the training program provided to franchisees. This typically is the longest section of the UFOC.

12. A description of any territorial protection that will be granted to the franchise and a statement as to whether the franchiser may locate a company-owned store or other outlet in that territory. Because market saturation and territorial encroachment have become such controversial issues in franchising, prospective franchisees should pay special attention to this section.

13. All relevant information about the franchiser's trademarks, service marks, trade names, logos, and commercial symbols, including where they are registered.

14. Similar information on any patents and copyrights the franchiser owns and the rights to these that are transferred to franchisees.

15. A description of the extent to which franchisees must participate personally in the operation of the franchise.

16. A description of any restrictions on the goods or services franchises are permitted to sell and with whom franchisees may deal.

17. A description of the conditions under which the franchise may be repurchased or refused renewal by the franchiser, transferred to a third party by the franchisee, and terminated or modified by either party. This section also spells out the process for resolving disputes between franchisees and the franchiser.

18. A description of the involvement of celebrities and public figures in the franchise.

19. A complete statement of the basis for any earnings claims made to the franchisee, including the percentage of existing franchises that have actually achieved the results that are claimed. New rules put two requirements on franchisers making earnings claims: (a) Any earnings claim must be included in the UFOC, and (b) the claim must "have a reasonable basis at the time it is made." However, franchisers are not required to make any earnings claims at all; in fact, 80 percent of franchisers don't make earnings claims in their circulars, primarily because of liability concerns about committing such numbers to paper.[35]

20. Statistical information about the expansion or the contraction of the franchise over the past three years. This section also includes the present number of franchises, the number of franchises projected for the future and the states in which they are to be sold, the number of franchises terminated, the number of agreements the franchiser has not renewed, the number of outlets repurchased in the past, and a list of the names and addresses of other franchises. This section is particularly useful for the next phase of investigating a franchise: talking to existing franchisees about their experience with the franchiser.

21. The audited financial statements of the franchisers.

22. A copy of all franchise and other contracts (leases, purchase agreements, etc.) the franchisee will be required to sign.

23. A standardized, detachable "receipt" to prove that the prospective franchisee received a copy of the UFOC.

The typical UFOC is about 100 pages long, but every potential franchisee should take the time to read and understand it. Unfortunately, most do not, which often results in unpleasant surprises for uninformed franchisees. The information contained in the UFOC neither fully protects potential franchisees from deception, nor does it guarantee success. It does, however, provide enough information to begin a thorough investigation of the franchiser and the franchise deal. Many experts recommend that potential franchisees have an experienced franchise attorney or consultant review a company's UFOC before they invest. The UFOC is a valuable tool for prospective franchisees, giving them the information they need to make informed decisions, saving them time, and providing them with more complete information about a franchise.

The Right Way to Buy a Franchise

5. Explain the right way to buy a franchise.

If used, the UFOC can help potential franchises avoid dishonest franchisers. The best defenses a prospective entrepreneur has against making a bad investment decision or against unscrupulous franchisers are preparation, common sense, and patience. By investigating thoroughly before investing in a franchise, potential franchisees eliminate the risk of being hoodwinked into a nonexistent business. Asking the right questions and resisting the urge to rush into an investment decision help a potential franchisee avoid unscrupulous franchisers.

Despite existing disclosure requirements, dishonest franchisers that take unsuspecting people's money and disappear still operate, often moving from one state to another just ahead of authorities. Potential franchisees must beware. Franchise fraud has destroyed the dreams of many hopeful franchisees and has robbed them of their life savings. Because dishonest franchisers tend to follow certain patterns, well-prepared franchisees can avoid getting burned. The following clues should arouse the suspicion of an entrepreneur about to invest in a franchise:

- Claims that the franchise contract is "the standard one" and that "you don't need to read it." There is no standard franchise contract.
- A franchiser who fails to give you a copy of the required disclosure document, the UFOC, at your first face-to-face meeting.
- A marginally successful prototype store or no prototype at all.
- A poorly prepared operations manual outlining the franchise system or no manual (or system) at all.
- An unsolicited testimonial from "a highly successful franchisee." Scam artists will hire someone to pose as a successful franchisee, complete with a rented luxury car and expensive-looking jewelry and clothing to "prove" how successful franchisees can be and to help close the sale. Use the list of franchisees in item 20 of the UFOC to find real franchisees and ask them plenty of questions.
- An unusual amount of litigation brought against the franchiser. In this litigious society, companies facing lawsuits is a common situation. However, too many lawsuits is a sign that something is amiss. This information is found in item 3 of the UFOC.
- Verbal promises of large future earnings without written documentation. Remember: If franchisers make earnings claims, they must document them in item 19 of the UFOC.
- A high franchisee turnover rate or a high termination rate. This information is described in item 20 of the UFOC.
- Attempts to discourage you from allowing an attorney to evaluate the franchise contract before you sign it.

- No written documentation to support claims and promises.
- A high-pressure sale—sign the contract now or lose the opportunity. This tactic usually sounds like this: "Franchise territories are going fast. If you hesitate, you are likely to miss out on the prime spots."
- Claims of exemption from federal laws requiring complete disclosure of franchise details in a UFOC. If a franchiser has no UFOC, run—don't walk—away from the deal.
- "Get-rich-quick schemes," promises of huge profits with only minimum effort.
- Reluctance to provide a list of present franchisees for you to interview.
- Evasive, vague answers to your questions about the franchise and its operation.

Not every franchise "horror story" is the result of dishonest franchisers. More often than not, the problems that arise in franchising have more to do with franchisees who buy legitimate franchises without proper research and analysis. They end up in businesses they don't enjoy and that they are not well suited to operate. The following steps will help any franchisee make the right franchise choice.

Evaluate Yourself

Henry David Thoreau's advice to "know thyself" is excellent advice for prospective franchisees. Before looking at any franchise, entrepreneurs should examine their own personalities, experiences, likes, dislikes, goals, and expectations. Will you be comfortable working in a structured environment? What kinds of franchises fit your desired lifestyle? Do you want to sell a product or a service? Do you want to work with the public? Do you enjoy selling? What hours do you expect to work? Do you mind getting dirty? Do you want to work with people or do you prefer to work alone? Which franchise concepts mesh best with your past work experience? What activities and hobbies do you enjoy? What income do you expect a franchise to generate? How much can you afford to invest in a franchise? Will you be happy with the daily routine of operating the franchise? Most franchise contracts run for 10 years or more, making it imperative that prospective franchisees conduct a complete inventory of their interests, likes, dislikes, and abilities before buying a franchise.

Research the Market

Before shopping for a franchise, entrepreneurs should research the market in the areas they plan to serve. How fast is the overall area growing? In which areas is that growth occurring fastest? Is the market for the franchise's product or service growing or declining? Investing some time in the library or on the World Wide Web developing a profile of the customers in the target area is essential; otherwise the potential franchisee is flying blind. Who are your potential customers? What are their characteristics? What are their income and education levels? What kinds of products and services do they buy? What gaps exist in the market? These gaps represent potential franchise opportunities for you.

Solid market research should tell a prospective franchisee whether a particular franchise is merely a passing fad. Steering clear of fads and into long-term trends is a key to sustained success in franchising. The secret to distinguishing between a fad that will soon fizzle and a meaningful trend that offers genuine opportunity is finding products or services that are consistent with fundamental demographic and lifestyle patterns of the population. That requires sound market research that focuses not only on local market opportunities but also on the "big picture." For instance, the prevalence of dual-career couples, available disposable income, and hectic schedules is creating a booming business for maid service and home improvement and repair franchises.

Consider Your Franchise Options

Tracking down information on prospective franchise systems is easier now than ever before. Many cities host franchise trade shows throughout the year, where hundreds of franchisers gather to sell their franchises. Many business magazines such as *Entrepreneur, Inc., FSB,* and others devote at least one issue and a section of their Web sites to franchising, where they often lists hundreds of franchises. Plus, most franchisers now publish information about their systems on the World Wide Web. These listings can help potential franchisees find a suitable franchise within their price ranges.

Get a Copy of the Franchiser's UFOC and Study It

Once you narrow down your franchise choices, you should contact each franchise and get a copy of its UFOC. Then read it! This document is an important tool in your search for the right franchise, and you should make the most of it. When evaluating a franchise opportunity, what should a potential franchisee look for? Although there's never a guarantee of success, the following characteristics make a franchise stand out.

- *A unique concept or marketing approach.* "Me-too" franchises are no more successful than "me-too" independent businesses. Pizza franchiser Papa John's has achieved an impressive growth rate by emphasizing the quality of its ingredients, whereas Domino's is known for its fast delivery.
- *Profitability.* A franchiser should have a track record of profitability and so should its franchisees. If a franchiser is not profitable, its franchisees are not likely to be either. Franchisees who follow the business format should expect to earn a reasonable rate of return.
- *A registered trademark.* Name recognition is difficult to achieve without a well-known and protected trademark.
- *A business system that works.* A franchiser should have in place a system that is efficient and is well documented in its manuals.
- *A solid training program.* One of the most valuable components of a franchise system is the training it offers franchisees. The system should be relatively easy to teach.
- *Affordability.* A franchisee should not have to take on an excessive amount of debt to purchase a franchise. Being forced to borrow too much money to open a franchise outlet can doom a business from the outset. Respectable franchisers verify prospective franchisees' financial qualifications as part of the screening process.
- *A positive relationship with franchisees.* The most successful franchises are those that see their franchisees as partners—and treat them accordingly.

The UFOC covers the 23 items discussed in the previous section and includes a copy of the company's franchise agreement and any contracts accompanying it. Although the law requires a UFOC to be written in plain English rather than "legalese," it is best to have an attorney experienced in franchising to review the UFOC and discuss its provisions with you. The franchise contract summarizes the details that will govern the franchiser–franchisee relationship over its life. It outlines exactly the rights and the obligations of each party and sets the guidelines that govern the franchise relationship. Franchise contracts typically are long term; 50 percent run for 15 years or more, so it is extremely important for prospective franchisees to understand their terms before they sign them.

Particular items in the UFOC that entrepreneurs should focus on include the franchiser's experience (items 1 and 2), the current and past litigation against the franchiser (item 3), the fees and total investment (items 5, 6, and 7), and the franchisee turnover rate for the past three years (item 20). The **franchisee turnover rate,** the rate at which franchisees leave the system, is one of the most revealing items in the UFOC. If the turnover rate is less than 5 percent, the franchise is probably sound. However, a rate approaching 20 percent is a sign of serious, underlying problems in a franchise. Although virtually every franchiser has been involved in lawsuits, an excessive amount of litigation against a franchiser over a particular matter should also alert a prospective franchisee to potential problems down the road. Determining what the cases were about and whether they have been resolved is important.

Talk to Existing Franchisees

Although the UFOC contains much valuable information, it is only the starting point for researching a franchise opportunity thoroughly. Perhaps the best way to evaluate the reputation of a franchiser is to interview (in person) several franchise owners who have been in business at least one year about the positive and the negative features of the agreement and whether the franchiser delivered what it promised. Knowing what they know now, would they buy the franchise again? *After investment banker Todd Recknagel narrowed the field of franchises he was considering, he spent time interviewing several franchisees about their experiences with the franchisers. Based on his findings, Recknagel decided to purchase a Blimpie Subs and Salads franchise. Recknagel's research paid off; in less than six years, he has built eight outlets and was named Franchisee of the Year both by Blimpie and the International Franchise Association.*[36] Item 20 of the UFOC lists all of a company's franchisees and their addresses by state, making it easy for potential franchisees to contact them.

Company Example →

It is also wise to interview former franchisees to get their perspectives on the franchiser–franchisee relationship. (UFOC item 20 also lists those franchisees who have left the system within the past fiscal year.) Why did they leave? Franchisees of some companies have formed associations, which might provide prospective franchisees with valuable information. Other sources of information include the American Association of Franchisees and Dealers, the American Franchise Association, and the International Franchise Association.

Ask the Franchiser Some Tough Questions

Take the time to visit the franchiser's headquarters and ask plenty of questions about the company and its relationship with its franchisees. You will be in this relationship a long time, and you need to know as much about it as you possibly can beforehand. What is its philosophy concerning the relationship? What is the company culture like? How much input do franchisees have into the system? What are the franchiser's future expansion plans? How will they affect your franchise? What kind of profits can you expect? (If the franchiser made no earnings claims in item 19 of the UFOC, why not?) Does the franchiser have a well-formulated strategic plan?

Make Your Choice

The first lesson in franchising is "Do your homework before you get out your checkbook." Once you have done your research, you can make an informed choice about which franchise is right for you. Then it is time to put together a solid business plan that will serve as your road map to success in the franchise you have selected. The plan is also a valuable tool to use as you arrange the financing for your franchise. We will discuss the components of a business plan in Chapter 6.

Table 4.3 offers practical advice on selecting the right franchise.

Table 4.3

Make Sure You Select the Right Franchise

Finding the right franchise is no easy task, but the results are well worth the effort—*if* you make the right choice. First-time franchisees often make the following mistakes:

Mistake 1. Not knowing what they want in franchise. Failing to define their goals increases the chance they will make the wrong choice.

Mistake 2. Buying a franchise they cannot afford. Franchises are expensive, and potential franchisees must know what they can afford before they begin reviewing franchises.

Mistake 3. Failing to ask existing and former franchisees about the franchise. This is one of the best ways to determine what the franchise experience will be.

Mistake 4. Failing to read the fine print. The UFOC is a valuable document for potential franchisees but only if they read it and use it to make the decision.

Mistake 5. Failing to get professional help. Inexperienced frachise shoppers believe that paying attorneys and accountants to help them understand the UFOC is waste of money. Wrong!

Mistake 6. Buying in too early. Some new franchise operations simply have not worked the bugs out of their business systems or are not prepared to teach the system effectively.

Mistake 7. Falling for exaggerated earnings claims. Remember: Any earnings claims franchisers make must be backed by facts.

Mistake 8. Neglecting to check the escape clause. Most franchise contracts include options for getting out of a franchise. Franchisees must know what they are.

Franchisees who have made both wise and ill-advised franchise purchases offer the following advice to avoid making these common mistakes:

- Start by evaluating your own personal and business interests. What activities do you enjoy?
- Establish a budget. Know how much can afford to spend before you ever go shopping for a franchise.
- Do your research. Study broad trends to determine which franchise concepts are likely to be most successful in the future.
- Identify potential franchise candidates. Create a profile of the most promising franchises that best fits both your interests and market trends.
- Review candidates' marketing literature and narrow your search to the top five or six.
- Get these companies' UFOCs and review them thoroughly. Get an experienced attorney to review the "fine print" in each UFOC.
- Visit existing franchisees and ask them lots of questions about the franchise system, the franchiser and the franchiser–franchisee relationship.
- Study your local market. Use what you learned from existing franchisees to determine whether the concept would be successful in the area you are considering. Don't forget to evaluate the level of competition present.
- Meet with company officials to discuss the details of buying a franchise. Look for depth and experience in the management team.
- Complete negotiations with the franchiser and close the deal.

Sources: Adapted from Andrew A Caffey, "Watch Your Step," *Entrepreneur B.Y.O.B.,* August 2002, p. 82; Todd D. Maddocks, "Write the Wrong," *Entrepreneur B.Y.O.B.,* January 2001, pp. 152–155; Kerry Pipes, "Franchise Lifestyles," Franchise UPDATE, www.franchise-update.com/fuadmin/articles/rticleFranchiseeLifestyles5.htm.

Franchise Contracts

6. Describe a typical franchise contract and some of its provisions.

The amount of franchiser–franchisee litigation has risen steadily over the past decade. A common source of much of this litigation is the interpretation of the franchise contract's terms. Most often, difficulties arise after the agreement is in operation. Because the franchiser's attorney prepares franchise contracts, the provisions favor the franchiser. Courts have relatively little statutory law and few precedents on which to base decisions in franchise disputes, resulting in minimal protection for franchisees. The problem stems from the tremendous growth of franchising, which has outstripped the growth of franchise law.

The contract summarizes the details that will govern the franchiser–franchisee relationship over its life. It outlines exactly the rights and the obligations of each party and sets the guidelines that govern the franchise relationship. To protect potential franchisees from having to rush into a contract without clearly understanding it, the Federal Trade Commission requires that the franchisee receive the completed contract with all revisions at least five business days before it is signed. Despite such protection, one study by the FTC suggests that 40 percent of new franchisees sign contracts *without reading them!*[37]

Every potential franchisee should have an attorney evaluate the franchise contract and review it with the investor before he or she signs anything. Too many franchisees don't discover unfavorable terms in their contracts until *after* they have invested in a franchise. By then, however, it's too late to negotiate changes. Although most large, established franchisers are not willing to negotiate the franchise contract's terms, many smaller franchises will, especially for highly qualified candidates. *Because Gary Gramkow was only the seventh franchisee to open a Foot Solutions store, he was able to negotiate a royalty rate below the company's standard 5 percent, rate, saving himself thousands of dollars over the life of the 10-year agreement. Gramkow used a home equity loan to get the $150,000 he needed to open his first store, which proved to be so successful that within two years he opened a second location to which the lower royalty rate also applied.*[38]

Table 4.4 describes the advantages and the disadvantages of buying a new versus an established franchise.

Although franchise contracts cover everything from initial fees and continuing payments to training programs and territorial protection, three issues are responsible for most franchiser–franchisee disputes: termination of the contract, contract renewal, and transfer and buyback provisions.

Company Example →

Termination

Probably the most litigated subject of a franchise agreement is the termination of the contract by either party. Most contracts prohibit termination "without just cause." However, prospective franchisees must be sure they know exactly when and under what conditions they—and the franchiser—can terminate the contract. Generally, the franchiser has the right to cancel a contract if a franchisee declares bankruptcy, fails to make required payments on time, or fails to maintain quality standards.

Terminations usually are costly to both parties and are seldom surrounded by a sense of goodwill. Most attorneys encourage franchisees to avoid conditions for termination or to use alternative routes to resolve disputes, such as formal complaints through franchise associations, arbitration, or ultimately selling the franchise.

Table 4.4

Advantages and Disadvantages of Buying a New Versus an Established Franchise

	Pros	Cons
New Franchise	▪ Can be new and exciting ▪ Business concept can be fresh and different in the market ▪ Possibility of getting lower fees as a "pioneer" of the concept ▪ Potential for a high return on investment	▪ Business is not tested or established in the market ▪ Unknown brand and trademark ▪ Possibility that the concept is a fad with no staying power ▪ Franchiser may lack the experience to deliver valuable services to franchisees
Established Franchise	▪ Business concept likely is well known to consumers and market for the products or services is already established ▪ Franchiser has experience in delivering services to franchisees ▪ Franchiser has had time to work the "bugs" out of the business system	▪ High franchise fees and costs that often are nonnegotiable ▪ Concept may be on the wane in the market ▪ Franchiser's brand and trademark may remind customers of an outdated concept ▪ Franchiser's "trade dress" may be in need of updating and redesigning

Source: Based on Andrew A. Caffey, "Age Issues," *Entrepreneur,* January 2002, p. 118.

Renewal

Franchisers usually retain the right to renew or refuse to renew franchisees' contracts. If a franchisee fails to make payments on schedule or does not maintain quality standards, the franchiser has the right to refuse renewal. In some cases, the franchiser has no obligation to offer contract renewal to the franchisee when the contract expires.

When a franchiser grants renewal, the two parties must draw up a new contract. Frequently, the franchisee must pay a renewal fee and may be required to fix any deficiencies of the outlet or to modernize and upgrade it. The FTC's Trade Regulation Rule requires the franchiser to disclose these terms before any contracts are signed.

Transfer and Buybacks

At any given time, about 10 percent of the franchisees in a system have their outlets up for sale.[39] Franchisees typically are not free to sell their businesses to just anyone, however. Under most franchise contracts, franchisees cannot sell their franchise to a third party or will it to a relative without the franchiser's approval. In most instances, franchisers do approve a franchisee's request to sell an outlet to another person. *American Leak Detection, a system with more than 300 franchisees, lists the company's resale opportunities on its Web site. That's how Jim Dickson found the two Florida-based territories he purchased when he decided to leave his job in corporate America to operate a business of his own. After finding the franchises listed for sale on the Web, Dickson began his research in earnest, poring over the company's financial records and operating history. "I . . . knew there was no way the [previous owner] was tapping the potential of the franchise," he says.*[40]

Most franchisers retain the right of first refusal in franchise transfers, which means the franchisee must offer to sell the franchise to the franchiser first. For example, McDonald's Corporation recently repurchased 13 restaurants under its first refusal clause from a franchisee wanting to retire. If the franchiser refuses to buy the outlet, the franchisee may sell it to a third party who meets the franchiser's approval (essentially the same standards buyers of new franchises must meet).

Company Example

✦ GAINING *a* COMPETITIVE EDGE ✦

The Hole Story

When the "Hot Doughnuts Now" sign at a Krispy Kreme franchise lights up, it's a good idea to step away from the door; otherwise, you may be run over by the throng of customers storming in to buy those sugary sweet, addictive orbs that one 5-year-old says taste like "glazed fluffy clouds." Krispy Kreme sells more than *2 billion* doughnuts a year, rivaling the volume of its competitor Dunkin' Donuts, even though Krispy Kreme has a mere 300 stores in operation compared to Dunkin' Donuts' 5,500 stores. Krispy Kreme is expanding rapidly both in the United States and around the globe, having come a long way from its humble roots in Winston-Salem, North Carolina.

The company began in the mid-1930s when doughnut maker Vernon Rudolph bought a secret recipe for yeast doughnuts from a French pastry chef in New Orleans. Rudolph moved to Winston-Salem and, on July 13, 1937, opened a wholesale business, selling doughnuts to local grocery stores. People who passed by Rudolph's factory in the downtown could smell the lovely aroma coming from the plant and began pounding on the door, wanting to buy doughnuts. Recognizing a business opportunity, Rudolph cut a hole in the factory wall, installed a window, and launched the retail division of Krispy Kreme's business. By the early 1950s, Rudolph had built a small, regional chain of stores—some company owned and some franchised. Each store made its own doughnuts using the Krispy Kreme recipe, but the results were not as consistent as Rudolph wanted, so the company built its own mix plant to make the powdered doughnut mix that was then delivered to the stores, where the fresh doughnuts were made. Krispy Kreme still uses that same system today, although company engineers have improved the process dramatically.

The opening of a Krispy Kreme franchise is a major media event in the local market. Television crews show up, as do mobs of customers, many of whom have camped out to be among the first to buy a doughnut. In its first week, a new Krispy Kreme store takes in almost as much in sales as the typical Dunkin' Donuts store takes in over an entire year! Franchisee Gerard Centioli, who owns stores in the northwestern part of the United States, holds the current record for first-week sales in the chain; his Issaquah, Washington, store took in $454,000 in sales its first week! The average Krispy Kreme store generates $43,000 in sales each week, or $2.2 million a year. To accelerate its growth, Krispy Kreme now emphasizes multiunit franchisees, "area developers" in company lingo. Sales at outlets owned by area developers average $3.4 million per year. Applying the company's profit margin of 20 percent translates into a net profit of about $750,000 per year for each area developer's store.

Krispy Kreme is able to generate those rather impressive numbers with a national advertising budget of zero! Don't assume, however, that Krispy Kreme does not emphasize marketing. When stores first open, franchisees inundate television and radio stations and newspapers with free doughnuts. The company also is famous for selling its doughnuts to charitable and non-profit organizations at a discount to help them raise money. Perhaps Krispy Kreme's best marketing tool is the "doughnut theater" that appears in every store.

Stores are designed so that all of the doughnut making equipment is clearly visible, allowing drooling customers to watch as the doughnuts are cooked for exactly 115 seconds in 365-degree vegetable oil before passing under the glaze waterfall. With the "Hot Doughnuts Now" sign in the window illuminated (another simple, yet highly effective marketing tool), employees pluck hot doughnuts right off the assembly line and hand them straight to customers.

Before you pick up the phone to ask for the Krispy Kreme franchise offering circular, however, you need to know that qualifying to become a franchisee is a daunting task. The cost to open a franchise is about $2 million. The company's franchise contract, which runs for 15 years, is not that much different from most franchise contracts. The franchise fee is $40,000, the royalty rate is 4.5 percent of sales, and the public relations/brand development fee is 2 percent of sales. Candidates must have a net worth of $5 million and "ownership and operating experience of multi-unit food serve operations," which narrows considerably the list of those who qualify. For example, Jim Morrisey, who owns 15 Krispy Kreme stores in six states, sold nearly 100 other restaurant franchises to join the Krispy Kreme team. "It was an easy decision," he says. "I still shake my head over the sales-per-unit numbers. I've never seen anything like it."

1. Explain the advantages franchising offers franchisers. What disadvantages do franchisers face by licensing their operations to franchisees?
2. What questions would you ask existing Krispy Kreme franchisees before purchasing a franchise?

Sources: Adapted from "History, Krispy Kreme Doughnuts and Coffee," www.krispykreme.com/history.html; Carlye Adler, "Would You Pay $2 Million for This Franchise?" *FSB,* May 2002, pp. 36–39; Andy Serwer, "The Hole Story," *Fortune,* July 7, 2003, pp. 53–62; Krispy Kreme Doughnuts Annual Report, 2003.

Trends in Franchising

7. Explain current trends shaping franchising.

Franchising has experienced three major growth waves since its beginning. The first wave occurred in the early 1970s when fast-food restaurants used the concept to grow rapidly. The fast-food industry was one of the first to discover the power of franchising, but other businesses soon took notice and adapted the franchising concept to their industries. The second wave took place in the mid-1980s as our nation's economy shifted heavily toward the service sector. Franchises followed suit, springing up in every service business imaginable—from maid services and copy centers to mailing services and real estate. The third wave began in the early 1990s and continues today. It is characterized by new, low-cost franchises that focus on specific market niches. In the wake of major corporate downsizing and the burgeoning costs of traditional franchises, these new franchises enable would-be entrepreneurs to get into proven businesses faster and at lower costs. These companies feature start-up costs from $2,000 to $250,000 and span a variety of industries—from leak detection in homes and auto detailing to day care and tile glazing.

Other significant trends affecting franchising include the following.

International Opportunities

Currently, one of the hottest trends in franchising is the globalization of American franchise systems. Increasingly, franchising is becoming a major export industry for the United States. In fact, 25 percent of all franchisees of U.S.-based franchise companies are located outside of the United States.[41] For most franchisers, markets outside the borders of the United States offer the greatest potential for growth. Faced with extremely competitive conditions in domestic markets that are already saturated, franchisers increasingly are moving into international markets to boost sales and profits. Others are taking their franchise systems abroad simply because they see tremendous growth potential there. According to a report by Arthur Andersen, 44 percent of U.S. franchisers have international locations, up from 34 percent in 1989. International expansion is a relatively new phenomenon in franchising, however; approximately 75 percent of franchisers established their first foreign outlet within the past 10 years.[42] Canada is the primary market for U.S. franchisers, with Mexico, Japan, and Europe following. These markets are most attractive to franchisers because they are similar to the U.S. market—rising personal incomes, strong demand for consumer goods, growing service economies, and spreading urbanization. However, most franchisers recognize the difficulties of developing franchises in foreign markets and start slowly. According to Arthur Andersen, 79 percent of franchisers doing business internationally have fewer than 100 outlets in foreign countries.[43]

As they move into foreign markets, franchisers have learned that adaptation is one key to success. Although they keep their basic systems intact, franchises that are successful in foreign markets quickly learn how to change their concepts to adjust to local cultures and to appeal to local tastes. For instance, fast-food chains in other countries often must make adjustments to their menus to please locals' palates. In Venezuela, diners prefer mayonnaise with their french fries, and in Chile, customers want avocado on their hamburgers. In Japan, McDonald's (known as "Makudonarudo") outlets sell teriyaki burgers, rice burgers, seaweed soup, vegetable croquette burgers, and katsu burgers (cheese wrapped in a roast pork cutlet topped with katsu sauce and shredded cabbage) in addition to their traditional American fare. In the Philippines, the McDonald's menu includes a spicy Filipino-style burger, spaghetti, and chicken with rice.

Smaller, Nontraditional Locations

As the high cost of building full-scale locations continues to climb, more franchisers are searching out nontraditional locations in which to build smaller, less expensive outlets. Based on the principle of **intercept marketing,** the idea is to put a franchise's products or services directly in the paths of potential customers, wherever that may be. Franchises are putting scaled-down outlets on college campuses, in sports arenas, in hospitals, on airline flights, and in zoos. Today, customers are likely to find a mini-Wendy's inside the convenience store at a Mobil gas station, a Subway sandwich shop in a convenience store, a Dunkin' Donuts outlet in the airport, or a Maui Wowi kiosk at a sports stadium or arena. Twins Jason and Jeff Jokerst purchased their first Maui Wowi franchise straight out of college and are expanding their business with locations at several California sports arenas and a major exposition center.[44] Auntie Anne's Pretzels has outlets inside some Wal-Mart stores, and the 7,000-member Brentwood Baptist Church in Houston recently opened a McDonald's franchise in its lifelong learning center. The church co-owns the franchise with one of its members, who owns six McDonald's franchises.[45] Many franchisees have discovered that smaller outlets in these nontraditional locations generate nearly the same sales volume as full-sized outlets at just a fraction of the cost. Establishing outlets in innovative locations will be a key to continued franchise growth in the domestic market. One franchise expert explains, "Years ago, we never dreamed you could purchase pizza over the Internet or be served a McDonald's hamburger on an airplane. There are so many ways of franchising now, there's no telling what the future might bring."[46]

Conversion Franchising

The trend toward **conversion franchising**, in which owners of independent businesses become franchisees to gain the advantage of name recognition, will continue. One study found that 72 percent of North American franchise companies use conversion franchising in their domestic markets, and 26 percent use the strategy in foreign markets.[47] In a franchise conversion, the franchiser gets immediate entry into new markets and experienced operators; franchisees get increased visibility and often a big sales boost. In fact, the average

Company Example

sales gain in the first year for converted franchisees is 20 percent.[48] *Seven years after starting his own travel agency, Travel Discounters, Neal Dembo decided to convert his independent business into a Carlson-Wagonlit travel franchise. At the time, the travel industry was changing as customers increasingly were using the Web to research and book travel, bypassing travel agents altogether. The airline industry also began limiting agents' commissions. "We needed to increase our profits," recalls Dembo, and joining a franchise seemed to be the best way to accomplish that goal. Dembo realized that the franchiser's name would make his company more visible to corporate customers, whom he wanted to target because they offered greater sales and profit potential. With the name recognition of the franchise and direct referrals from Carlson-Wagonlit, Dembo says that his company has increased sales by 59 percent.*[49]

Multiple-unit Franchising

Multiple-unit franchising (MUF) became extremely popular in the early 1990s, and the trend has accelerated rapidly since then. According to the International Franchise Association, 34 percent of franchisees own multiple outlets.[50] In multiple-unit franchising, a franchisee opens more than one unit in a territory within a specific time period. In recent years, franchising has attracted more professional, experienced, and sophisticated entrepreneurs who have access to more capital—and who have their sights set on big goals that owning a single outlet cannot meet. Twenty-five years ago, a franchisee owning 10 or more outlets was rare; today, it is becoming increasingly common for a single franchisee to own 50 or more outlets. The typical multiunit franchisee owns between three and six outlets, but some franchisees own many more units.

For franchisers, multiple-unit franchising is an efficient way to expand quickly. Multiple-unit franchising is especially effective for franchisers targeting foreign markets, where having a local representative who knows the territory is essential. For a franchiser, the time and cost of managing 10 franchisees each owning 12 outlets are much less than managing 120 franchisees each owning one outlet. For franchisees, multiple-unit franchising offers the opportunity for rapid growth without leaving the safety net of the franchise. Also, because franchisers usually offer discounts of about 25 percent off their standard fees on multiple units, franchisees can get fast-growing companies for a bargain.

Company Example

After earning advanced degrees at Wharton and at Harvard, Charles Smithgall became one of Ted Turner's first employees in the early 1980s before striking out on his own as an entrepreneur, ultimately owning several radio stations. Smithgall sold his stations at age 54 and began looking for something to do in his "retirement," never considering a career in franchising. After meeting Charlie Loudermilk, chairman and CEO of Aaron's Rental and Leasing, Smithgall was impressed with the franchise, which rents and leases furniture and electronics. He soon purchased his first Aaron's franchise, and today is a multiple-unit franchisee, owning 40 outlets with 325 employees.[51]

Master Franchising

A **master franchise** (or **subfranchise** or **area developer**) gives a franchisee the right to create a semi-independent organization in a particular territory to recruit, sell, and support other franchisees. A master franchisee buys the right to develop subfranchises within a broad geographic area or, sometimes, an entire country. Like multiple-unit franchising, subfranchising "turbocharges" a franchiser's growth. *After founding five companies of his own, Tom Watson decided to become an area developer for Steak Out, a delivery and take-out restaurant. Using master franchising, Watson plans to create 102 new stores in his area within five years.*[52]

Many franchisers use master franchising to open outlets in international markets because the master franchisees understand local laws and the nuances of selling in local markets. *One master franchisee with TCBY International, a yogurt franchise, has opened 21 stores in China and in Hong Kong. Based on his success in these markets, the company has sold him the master franchise in India.*[53]

Piggybacking (or Co-Branding)

Some franchisers also are discovering new ways to reach customers by teaming up with other franchisers selling complementary products or services. A growing number of companies are **piggybacking** (or **co-branding**) outlets—combining two or more distinct franchises under one roof. This "buddy system" approach works best when the two franchise ideas are compatible and appeal to similar customers. At one location, a Texaco gasoline station, a Pizza Hut restaurant, and a Dunkin' Donuts—all owned by the same franchisee—work together in a piggyback arrangement to draw customers. Doughnut franchiser Dunkin' Donuts, ice cream franchiser Baskin-Robbins, and sandwich shop Togo's are working together to build hundreds of combination outlets, a concept that has proved to be highly successful.[54] Properly planned, piggybacked franchises can magnify many times the sales and profits of individual, self-standing outlets.

Serving Aging Baby Boomers

Now that dual-career couples have become the norm, especially among baby boomers, the market for franchises offering convenience and timesaving services is booming. Customers are willing to pay for products and services that will save them time or trouble, and franchises are ready to provide them. Franchisees of Around Your Neck go into the homes and offices of busy male executives to sell men's apparel and accessories ranging from shirts and ties to custom-made suits. An executive at a franchise consulting firm points out that "by 2010, 39 million Americans will be 65 or older; that's almost 20 percent of the population."[55] Franchises offering home delivery of meals, house-cleaning and repair services, continuing education (especially computer and business training), leisure activities (crafts, hobbies, health spas, and travel-related activities), products and services aimed at home-based businesses, and health care (ranging from fitness and diet products and services to in-home elder care and medical services) will see sales grow rapidly.

Conclusion

Franchising has proved its viability in the U.S. economy and has become a key part of the small business sector because it offers many would-be entrepreneurs the opportunity to own and operate a business with a greater chance for success. Despite its impressive growth rate to date, the franchising industry still has a great deal of room left to grow, especially globally. Describing the future of franchising, one expert says, "Franchising has not yet come close to reaching its full potential in the American marketplace."[56]

▌▌▌ Chapter Review

1. Explain the importance of franchising in the U.S. economy.

   ▪ Through franchised businesses, consumers can buy nearly every good or service imaginable—from singing telegrams and computer training to tax services and waste-eating microbes.

   ▪ A new franchise opens somewhere in the United States every 8 minutes and somewhere in the world every $6^{1}/_{2}$ minutes! Franchises account for more than 50 percent of all retail sales, totaling more than $1 trillion, and they employ more than 8 million people in more than 100 major industries.

2. Define the concept of franchising and describe the different types of franchises.

   ▪ Franchising is a method of doing business involving a continuous relationship between a franchiser and a franchisee. The franchiser retains control of the distribution system, whereas the franchisee assumes all of the normal daily operating functions of the business.

   ▪ There are three types of franchising: trade name franchising, where the franchisee purchases only the right to use a brand name; product distribution franchising, which involves a license to sell specific products under a brand name; and pure franchising, which provides a franchisee with a complete business system.

3. Describe the benefits and limitations of buying a franchise.

   ▪ The franchiser has the benefits of expanding his or her business on limited capital and growing without developing key managers internally. The franchisee also receives many key benefits: management training and counseling, customer appeal of a brand name, standardized quality of goods and services, national advertising programs, financial assistance, proven products and business formats, centralized buying power, territorial protection, and greater chances for success.

   ▪ Potential franchisees should be aware of the disadvantages involved in buying a franchise: franchise fees and profit sharing, strict adherence to standardized operations, restrictions on purchasing, limited product lines, possible ineffective training programs, and less freedom.

4. Describe the legal aspects of franchising, including the protection offered by the FTC's Trade Regulation Rule.

   ▪ The FTC's Trade Regulation Rule is designed to help the franchisee evaluate a franchising package. It requires each franchiser to disclose information covering 23 topics at least 10 days before accepting payment from a potential franchisee. This document, the Uniform Franchise Offering Circular (UFOC) is a valuable source of information for anyone considering investing in a franchise.

5. Explain the right way to buy a franchise.

   ▪ To buy a franchise the right way requires that you evaluate yourself, research your market, consider your franchise options, get a copy of the franchiser's UFOC and study it, talk to existing franchisees, ask the franchiser some tough questions, and make your choice.

6. Describe a typical franchise contract and some of its provisions.

   ▪ The amount of franchiser–franchisee litigation has risen steadily over the past decade. Three reasons are responsible for most franchiser–franchisee disputes: termination of the contract, contract renewal, and transfer and buyback provisions.

7. Explain current trends shaping franchising.

   ▪ Trends influencing franchising include international opportunities; the emergence of smaller, nontraditional locations; conversion franchising; multiple-unit franchising; master franchising; piggyback franchising (or co-branding); and products and services targeting aging baby boomers.

▌▌▌ Discussion Questions

1. What is franchising?
2. Describe the three types of franchising and give an example of each.
3. How does franchising benefit the franchiser?
4. Discuss the advantages and the disadvantages of franchising for the franchisee.
5. How beneficial to franchisees is a quality training program? Explain.
6. Compare the failure rates for franchises with those of independent businesses.
7. Why might an independent entrepreneur be dissatisfied with a franchising arrangement?
8. What are clues to detect an unreliable franchiser?
9. Should a prospective franchisee investigate before investing in a franchise? If so, how and in what areas?
10. What is the function of the FTC's Trade Regulation Rule?
11. Outline the rights the Trade Regulation Rule gives all prospective franchisees.
12. What is the source of most franchiser–franchisee litigation? Whom does the standard franchise contract favor?
13. Describe the current trends affecting franchising.
14. One franchisee says, "Franchising is helpful because it gives you somebody (the franchiser) to get you going, nurture you, and shove you along a little. But the franchiser won't make you successful. That depends on what you bring to the business, how hard you are prepared to work, and how committed you are to finding the right franchise for you." Do you agree? Explain.

Franchising and the Entrepreneur

Business PlanPro

If you are considering purchasing a franchise, go to the exercises for Chapter 4 of Business Plan Pro, where you will find a series of questions that will help you decide whether a franchise is right for you. The primary question to keep in mind as you work through this analysis is, "What can a franchise do for me that I cannot do for myself?"

If you discover that a franchise is an ideal way for you to become a business owner, you will need to gather information about potential franchises to complete the analysis. Franchisers' Web sites, small business magazines, and franchise showcases are excellent sources of information, but the Uniform Franchise Offering Circular (UFOC) is probably the best and most reliable source of the data you will need to make an informed decision.

Remember that the first step in buying the right franchise is to evaluate yourself, examining your personality, experience, likes, dislikes, goals, and expectations. Only then are you ready to begin looking at the advantages and disadvantages of various franchise operations.

When you complete this exercise, you are ready to complete the Your Company section of Business Plan Pro.

Chapter 5
Buying an Existing Business

> "
>
> *What we obtain too cheap, we esteem too lightly; it is dearness only that gives everything its value.*
> —THOMAS PAINE

> *The best we can do is size up the chances, calculate the risks involved, estimate our ability to deal with them, and then make our plans with confidence.*
> —HENRY FORD
> "

Upon completion of this chapter, you will be able to:

1. Understand the advantages and disadvantages of buying an existing business.

2. Define the steps involved in the *right* way to buy a business.

3. Describe the various methods used in the valuation of a business.

4. Discuss the process of negotiating the deal.

How often in our lives are we asked to be patient? Well, this chapter begins by making the same recommendation when it comes to buying a business. Be patient, don't rush and, above all, do your homework before buying a business. Time spent in the evaluation process is certainly time well spent if it saves you from failure later.

In too many cases, the excitement of getting started and the attraction of being able to implement a "fast entry" into the market cause entrepreneurs to make unnecessary mistakes in judgment. Buying an existing business requires a great deal of analysis and evaluation to ensure that what you are purchasing really meets your needs. Don't rush—be sure that you know absolutely everything that can be learned about the business and the market you wish to serve before you buy. According to Russell Brown, author of *Strategies for Successfully Buying or Selling a Business,* "You have access to the company's earnings history, which gives you a good idea of what the business will make and an existing business has a proven track record; most established organizations tend to stay in business and keep making money."[1]

If vital information such as audited financial statements and legal clearances are not available, be especially diligent. Do your homework before you even begin to negotiate a purchase price. For starters, be sure that you have considered answers to each of the following questions:

- Is this the type of business you would like to operate? Do you know the negative aspects of this business? Are there any skeletons in the company closet that might come back to haunt you?
- Is this the best market and the best location for this business?
- Do you know the critical factors that must exist for this business to be successful?
- Do you have the experience required to operate this type of business? If not, will the current owner be willing to stay on for three to six months to teach you the "ropes"?
- Will you need to make any changes to the business or its operating procedures to be successful and, if so, at what expense? Does the present facility meet all state and federal accessibility guidelines, and if not, what will it take to bring the facility up to code?
- If the business is currently in a decline, do you have a plan to return the business to profitability? Justify your plan—what makes you certain it will work?
- If the business is profitable, why does the current owner want to sell? Does the reason given for selling the business make sense to you? If not, can you verify the *real* reason?
- Have you examined other similar businesses that are currently for sale or that have sold recently to determine what a fair market price should be?

These basic questions ask you to be honest with yourself about your ability to operate the business successfully. It is one thing to watch others manage a business successfully, and another to know why they make the decisions they do and the actions they take. Chapter 1 highlighted the reasons for business failure. Before making any decision to purchase an existing business, review the primary reasons for failure and ensure that you have taken all the steps necessary to reduce the risk of failure. Whatever time and energy you invest in the evaluation of the business opportunity will earn significant dividends if you acquire a business that becomes successful or avoid purchasing a business that will fail.

Buying an Existing Business

1. Understand the advantages and disadvantages of buying an existing business.

Advantages of Buying an Existing Business

The following are a few of the factors that can make the purchase of an existing business an advantage.

An Established Successful Business May Continue to Be Successful. A business that has been profitable for some time may reflect an owner who has established a solid customer base, developed successful relationships with critical suppliers, and mastered the day-to-day operational components of the business. All of these factors are positive and may be keys to continued success. In such cases, it is important to make changes slowly and to take extra care to retain the relationships with customers, suppliers, and staff that have made the business a success. This advantage often goes hand in hand with the second advantage, using the experience of the previous owner.

The New Owner Can Use the Experience of the Previous Owner. In many cases in which a business has a long history of success, you may negotiate with the current owner to stay on for a short time to introduce you to the customers or clients, the vendors or suppliers, and to show you how the policies and procedures they developed actually operate. Additionally, the previous owner can be very helpful in unmasking the unwritten rules of business in the area: whom to trust, expected business behavior, and many other critical intangibles. Most owners who have built a successful business want the buyer to succeed. Hiring the previous owner as a consultant for the first few months can be a valuable investment. When this option is not possible, at a minimum, you should review with the owner the key financial records to ensure that you can recognize the relationships between expenses and revenues. Learning from the previous owner's experience is extremely valuable.

✦ GAINING *a* COMPETITIVE EDGE ✦

Preparing to Sell Your Business

As a business owner, you should take the following actions before putting the "For Sale" sign in front of your business.

1. Have a qualified professional conduct a valuation of your business.
2. Have your financial statements up-to-date and in order.
3. Have the financial statements reflect the true profitability of the business. If you have been charging personal expenses to the business, you are reducing the profitability of the business and, although you may have avoided some taxes, the value of the business as a multiple of profitability has been reduced.
4. Work with a financial adviser to determine which financial structure of the sale of the business is most advantageous in your tax and estate situation.
5. Clean up the appearance of your business. Beauty might be only skin deep—but that outer layer is important when trying to entice potential buyers. Get rid of unnecessary clutter, use a little fresh paint here and there, and remember—first impressions count!

6. Organize your legal papers to reduce confusion at the time of the sale.
7. Consider all aspects of management succession and have a workable plan in place.
8. Write down the reasons why you want to sell and then question the assumptions behind each reason. Once the sale is complete, it's too late to play "what if." It's best to do this up front.
9. Work with your advisory board to ensure that you have not missed any critical aspects of your plan. If you do not have a formal advisory board, seek the help of associates who have successfully sold their businesses or professionals that get paid to guide sellers through the process.
10. Be sure that the business remains profitable while you are attempting to sell it. You have a better chance to get your asking price when profits are up.

Based on your readings and experience, discuss any other steps that a seller could take to create an environment conducive to the successful sale of a business.

Source: Adapted from Loraine McDonald, "Preparing to Sell Your Business," *Entrepreneur,* May 7, 2001, www.entrepreneur.com/article/0,4621,289171,00.html.

"Let's take a minute to allow
the bad karma of the old regine to lift."

The New Business Owner Hits the Ground Running. Buying a business is one of the fastest pathways to entrepreneurship. The entrepreneur who purchases an existing business saves the time, costs, and energy required to plan and launch a new business. The buyer gets a business that is already generating cash and sometimes profits. The day he takes over the ongoing business is the day his revenues begin. In this way, he earns while he learns. Tom Gillis, who has spent 50 years as a business owner, entrepreneur, lawyer, CPA, and management consultant in Houston, Texas, says, "Acquisition of an established company becomes attractive in three situations: when you haven't found 'the idea' which really turns you on and you find it in an existing business; when you have more money than you have time to start a business from scratch; when you want to grow but lack a compatible product, service, location, or particular advantage that is available from an owner who wants out." According to Gillis, the critical question is: What do I gain by acquiring this business that I wouldn't be able to achieve on my own?[2]

An Existing Business May Already Have the Best Location. When the location of the business is critical to its success, it may be wise to purchase a business that is already in the right place. Opening a second-choice location and hoping to draw customers often proves fruitless. In fact, the existing business's greatest asset may be its location. If this advantage cannot be matched in other locations, an entrepreneur may have little choice but to buy instead of build.

Employees and Suppliers Are Already in Place. An existing business already has experienced employees who can help the company earn money while the new owner learns the business. In addition, an existing business has an established set of suppliers with a history of business transactions. Vendors can continue to supply the business while the new owner assesses the products and services of other vendors. Thus, the new owner is not pressured to choose suppliers quickly without thorough investigation.

Equipment Is Installed and Productive Capacity Is Known. Acquiring and installing new equipment exerts a tremendous strain on a fledgling company's financial resources. In an existing business, a potential buyer can determine the condition of the plant and equipment and its capacity before buying the business. The previous owner may have established an efficient production operation through trial and error although the new owner may need to make modifications to improve it. In many cases, the entrepreneur can purchase physical facilities and equipment at prices significantly below replacement costs.

Inventory Is in Place and Trade Credit Has Been Established. The proper amount of inventory is essential to both cost control and sales volume. If the business has too little inventory, it will not have the quantity and variety of products to satisfy customer demand. But if the business has too much inventory, it is tying up excessive capital, increasing costs, reducing profitability, and increasing the danger of cash flow problems. Many successful established businesses have learned a balance between these extremes. Previous owners also have established trade credit relationships of which the new owner can take advantage. The business's proven track record gives the new owner leverage in negotiating favorable trade credit terms. No supplier wants to lose a good customer.

Finding Financing Usually Is Easier. Because investors or bankers often perceive the risk associated with buying an existing business as lower than that of a start-up, financing for the purchase is easier. With 16 years of business brokerage experience, Bill Broocke is considered an authority on business valuation and the buying and selling of small businesses. According to Broocke, founder and CEO of The Success Connection Inc., "Businesses like these (existing businesses), with a record of growth, trained employees, a good customer base, proper equipment, and an established inventory, are excellent business opportunities. In fact, the failure rates of businesses that have been around for at least five years are quite low."[3] A buyer can point to the existing company's track record and to the plans he or she has for improving it to convince potential lenders to finance the purchase. Also, in many buy–sell agreements the buyer uses a "built-in" source of financing: the seller!

It's a Bargain. Some existing businesses may be real bargains. If the current owners want to sell quickly, they may sell the business at a low price. The more specialized the business is, the greater the likelihood is that a buyer will find a bargain. Any special skills or training required to operate the business limit the number of potential buyers. If the owner wants a substantial down payment or the entire selling price in cash, there may be few qualified buyers; those who do qualify may be able to negotiate a good deal.

Disadvantages of Buying an Existing Business

It's a Loser. A business may be for sale because it has never been profitable. Such a situation may be disguised; owners can use various creative accounting techniques that make the firm's financial picture appear much brighter than it really is. The reason that a business is for sale will seldom be stated honestly as "It's losing money." If there is an area of business in which the maxim "let the buyer beware" still prevails, it is in the sale of a business. Any buyer unprepared to do a thorough analysis of the business may be stuck with a real loser.

Although buying a money-losing business is risky, it is not necessarily taboo. If your analysis of a company indicates that it is poorly managed or suffering from neglect, you may be able to turn it around. However, buying a struggling business without a well-defined plan for solving the problems it faces is an invitation to disaster. *One entrepreneur, Ira Jackson Jr., thought he had done all his due diligence when he bought Perfect Image, an Atlanta printing company, but he was in for a few surprises. The company was facing slumping sales, and employee morale was way down. Jackson did know going in that the previous*

Company Example

Despite conducting what he thought was adequate due diligence before buying a small printing business, Ira Jackson found himself the owner of a company in need of a major turnaround, which he was able to execute successfully.

owner had lost his largest customer right before the purchase was completed. However, Jackson underestimated the impact it would have on the company. "I didn't know how much [that customer] accounted for the company's success," he says. Suddenly Jackson found himself with a company in need of a major turnaround. The quality of its printing service was the greatest virtue of the struggling company. To boost sales, Jackson pushed that quality aggressively and went after Fortune 500 companies as well as companies with in-house print purchasing divisions. "We wanted to focus on doing business with accounts that brought in a significant amount of printing over the course of the year," Jackson says. He also had to trim fat from the business. He streamlined production, updated machinery, and eliminated brokers and third parties. Jackson also got employees involved in the turnaround, attacking a growing morale problem the previous owner had left him with. Perfect Image has become a strong company with more than $2 million in sales annually.[4]

The Previous Owner May Have Created Ill Will. Just as proper business dealings create goodwill, improper business behavior or unethical practices create ill will. The business may look great on the surface, but customers, suppliers, creditors, and/or employees may have extremely negative feelings about it. Too many business buyers discover (after the sale) that they have inherited undisclosed credit problems, poor supplier relationships, soon-to-expire leases, lawsuits, building code violations, and/or other problems created by the previous owner. Vital business relationships may have begun to deteriorate, but the long-term effects may not yet be reflected in the business's financial statements. Ill will can permeate a business for years. The only way to avoid these problems is to investigate a prospective purchase target thoroughly *before* moving forward in the negotiation process.

Company Example ⟶ *For example, when Norman Savage was negotiating to buy a small mortgage company, the deal seemed just right. The seller had provided three years of audited financial statements, all of them pointing toward a rosy future for North American Equity Corp. The company was exactly the next step Savage wanted, a jump from distressed mortgages to conventional home financing. A sharp, well-chosen staff was already in place. It looked as if Savage could just step in and glide along with North American Equity as it continued on its way. Reality struck in the first few weeks after closing the sale, however. The new owner was hit with a string of problems. The seller had given some employees 20 percent pay increases after the deal was made—effectively buying for himself the credit for being a generous boss and leaving the cost of that generosity for Savage to pay. A printer stopped working, and in getting it repaired, Savage learned that one of the office computers had needed to be replaced for some time. Some of North American Equity's business licenses were about to expire, and the necessary documents to renew them weren't easy to locate. On top of all that, several important clients let Savage know they needed to meet with him right away to determine whether he'd be giving them the same kind of service they had been getting from the company under the previous owner.*[5]

Current Employees May Not Be Suitable. If the new owner plans to make changes in a business, the present employees may not suit the new owner's needs. Some workers may have a difficult time adapting to the new owner's management style and vision for the company. Previous managers may have kept marginal employees because they were close friends or because they started off with the company. The new owner, therefore, may have to make some very unpopular termination decisions. For this reason, employees often do not welcome a new owner because they feel threatened. Furthermore, employees who may have wanted to buy the business themselves but could not afford it are likely to see the new owner as the person who stole their opportunity. Bitter employees are not likely to be productive workers.

The Business Location May Have Become Unsatisfactory. What was once an ideal location may be in the process of becoming obsolete as market and demographic trends change. Large shopping malls, new competitors, or highway reroutings can spell disaster, especially for a small retail shop. Prospective buyers should always evaluate the current market in the area surrounding an existing business as well as its potential for future growth and expansion. Always check with the state and local highway departments about new road projects that are planned.

Equipment and Facilities May Be Obsolete or Inefficient. Potential buyers sometimes neglect to have an expert evaluate a company's building and equipment before they purchase it. Only after it's too late do they discover that the equipment is obsolete and inefficient, pushing operating expenses to excessively high levels. Modernizing equipment and facilities is seldom inexpensive. Employing these experts to provide an objective assessment of the equipment and facilities is essential unless the buyer has that expertise.

Change and Innovation Are Difficult to Implement. It is easier to plan for change than it is to implement it. Methods and procedures the previous owner used created precedents that can be difficult or awkward for a new owner to change. For example, if the previous owner granted a 10 percent discount to customers purchasing 100 or more units in a single order, it may be impossible to eliminate that discount without losing some of those customers. The previous owner's policies, even those that are unwise, can influence the changes the new owner can make. Implementing changes to reverse a downward sales trend in a turnaround situation can be just as difficult as eliminating unprofitable procedures. Convincing alienated customers to return can be an expensive and laborious process that may take years.

Inventory May Be Obsolete. Inventory is valuable only if it is salable. Too many potential owners make the mistake of trusting a company's balance sheet to provide them with the value of its inventory. The inventory value reported on a company's balance sheet is seldom an accurate refection of its real market value. In some cases, a company's inventory may actually appreciate during periods of rapid inflation, but more likely it has depreciated in value. The value reported on the balance sheet reflects the original cost of the inventory, not its actual market value. Most businesses for sale include inventory and

Table 5.1

Valuing Accounts
Receivable

A prospective buyer asked the current owner of a business about the value of the accounts receivable. The owner's business records showed $101,000 in receivables. But when the prospective buyer aged them and then multiplied the resulting totals by his estimated probabilities of collection, he discovered their *real* value

AGE OF ACCOUNTS (DAYS)	AMOUNT	PROBABILITY OF COLLECTION	VALUE (AMOUNT × PROBABILITY OF COLLECTION)
0–30	$ 40,000	.95	$38,000
31–60	25,000	.88	22,000
61–90	14,000	.70	9,800
91–120	10,000	.40	4,000
121–150	7,000	.25	1,750
151+	5,000	.10	500
Total	$101,000		$76,050

Had the prospective buyer blindly accepted the book value of these accounts receivable, he would have overpaid nearly $25,000 for them!

other assets that may be absolutely worthless because they are outdated and obsolete! It is the buyer's responsibility to discover the real value of the assets before negotiating a purchase price for the business.

Accounts Receivable May Be Worth Substantially Less Than Face Value. Like inventory, accounts receivable rarely are worth their face value. A prospective buyer should age the accounts receivable to determine their collectibility. The older the receivables are, the less likely they are to be collected and, consequently, the lower their value is. Table 5.1 shows a simple but effective method of evaluating accounts receivable once the buyer ages them.

The Business May Be Overpriced. Most business are acquired based on the purchase of the firm's assets rather than the purchase of its stock, and a buyer must be sure which assets are included in the deal and what their real value is. Each year, many people purchase businesses at prices far in excess of their value. A buyer who correctly values a business's accounts receivable, inventories, and other assets will be in a good position to negotiate a price that will enable the business to be profitable. Making payments on a business that was overpriced is a millstone around the new owner's neck; it will be difficult to carry this excess weight and keep the business afloat.

How to Buy a Business

2. Define the steps involved in the *right* way to buy a business.

Although it may sound easy, purchasing an existing business is a time consuming process that requires a great deal of concentration and is often difficult to complete. Repeated studies report that more than half of all business acquisitions fail to meet the buyer's expectations. This statistic alone should provide a warning about the need to conduct a systematic and thorough analysis prior to negotiating any deal. The recommended process includes the following steps:

- Look first at yourself; objectively analyze your skills, abilities, and personal interests to determine the type(s) of business for which you are best suited.
- Based on this self-analysis, develop a list of the criteria that define your ideal business.
- Seek the help of others in developing a list of potential businesses for acquisition that meet your criteria.

Conducting adequate research before purchasing an existing business will help a business buyer avoid unexpected—and unpleasant—surprises.

■ Thoroughly investigate the potential acquisition targets that best meet your criteria. This is called the *due diligence process,* which will be discussed in detail later in the chapter. This process involves some fairly obvious steps such as analyzing financial statements and making certain that the facilities are structurally sound. Less obvious factors include how the company has traditionally paid its bills, problems with any unhappy vendors, and employee morale. Remember that your goal is to minimize the many pitfalls and problems that may arise.

■ When you select the most acceptable candidate, begin the negotiation process with the existing owner.

■ Explore various financing options that are beneficial to creating a profitable business.

■ When the deal is completed, be careful to ensure a smooth transition of ownership.

Let's briefly expand on each of these steps.

Self-Analysis of Skills, Abilities, and Interests

The first step in buying a business is conducting a self-audit to determine the ideal business for you. Consider, for example, how the following questions could produce valuable insights into the best type of business for you. These answers will provide important guidelines that might help you avoid a costly mistake.

■ What business activities do you enjoy most? Least?

■ Which industries interest you most? Least? Why?

■ What kind of business do you want to buy?

■ What kinds of businesses do you want to *avoid*?

■ In what geographic area do you want to live and work?

■ What do you expect to get out of the business?

■ How much can you put into the business—in both time and money?

■ What business skills and experience do you have? Which ones do you lack?

■ How easily can you transfer your existing skills and experience to other types of businesses? In what kinds of businesses would that transfer be easiest?

- How much risk are you willing to take?
- What size company do you want to buy?

Answering these and other questions *beforehand* will allow you to develop a list of criteria that a company must meet before you will consider it to be a purchase candidate.

IN THE FOOTSTEPS OF AN ENTREPRENEUR...

Ready, Aim, Aim, Aim . . .

Too often, entrepreneurs who buy businesses rush into deals, discovering later that they should have been more patient and spent more time doing their due diligence, the process of analyzing the details of a business and its financial position before opening negotiations to purchase it. Matt McGinnes, age 32 and currently employed at a Boston software company, is intent on avoiding that mistake. Having been laid off from a previous job and unable to find work for six months, McGinnes's goal is to purchase a business before he turns 40. "I don't want to be subject to this [another layoff] again," he says. "What do I need to do to make [owning my own company] happen in the future?"

McGinnes wants be sure that he purchases the right business for him and that he avoids any unpleasant surprises, so he is extremely thorough—some say obsessed—when conducting due diligence on prospective businesses. "You can do due diligence until you are blue in the face," says McGinnes's father-in-law, Jim McCready, himself a successful business owner." [Matt] can do it for 20 years. There's no perfect deal out there," he says, the exasperation over what he considers Matt's tedious approach to due diligence showing in his voice.

McGinnes learned his methodical, exhaustive approach from his father Sandy, who left a successful career at a Boston advertising agency at age 40 to purchase a microfilming business. A business broker friend guided the elder McGinnes through the process of buying the company, which he operated for two years before selling it at a handsome profit. During his search, Sandy McGinnes kept detailed records of every potential candidate in a three-ring binder he called "the black book." Each carefully organized section recounts the leads he received from

bankers, accountants, attorneys, business brokers, venture capitalists, and others. He even launched his own direct mail campaign, contacting the owners of 200 businesses to see if they were inclined to sell. "I went first to the interviews where I knew I was *not* interested," he recalls. "For practice."

Matt McGinnes says that he needs more experience managing people before he buys a business. "Until I get a taste of that, I won't be ready," he admits. After reflecting on his interests, abilities, and experience, McGinnes has determined that the ideal company for him is one that sells a service to other businesses, enjoys strong gross profit margins ("so I have some room to screw up initially," he says), and has been too cautious in its growth plans.

Now compiling a black book of his own, Matt McGinnes is willing to wait for the right business opportunity to come along. He has managed to reduce his plan for buying a business to one page. Since Matt began searching for a business to buy, he and his father make it a point to spend some time on their annual father-son canoeing trip talking about his plan and how to improve it and ultimately implement it. For now, Matt is content with his methodical approach to buying a business.

1. How much effort should an entrepreneur put into the due diligence process? Why?
2. Do you believe that it is possible to find "the perfect business"? Explain.
3. What advantages do you see in McGinnes's approach to buying a business? Disadvantages?

Source: Adapted from Jeff Bailey, "A Potential Owner Prefers the Studied Approach," *Wall Street Journal,* April 29, 2003, p. B6.

Develop a List of Criteria

Based on your answers to the preceding questions, the next step is to develop a list of criteria that a potential business acquisition must meet. Looking at every business you find for sale is a huge waste of time. The goal is to identify the characteristics of the ideal business for you. Addressing these issues early in your search will save a great deal of time and trouble as you wade through a multitude of business opportunities. These criteria will provide you and anyone helping you with specific parameters against which you can evaluate potential acquisition candidates.

Prepare a List of Potential Candidates

Once you know the criteria and parameters for the ideal candidate, you can begin your search. One technique is to start at the macro level and work down. Drawing on the resources in the library, the World Wide Web, government publications, and industry trade associations and reports, buyers can discover which industries are growing fastest and offer the greatest potential in the future. For entrepreneurs with a well-defined idea of what they are looking for, another effective approach is to begin searching in an

Company Example →

industry in which they have experience or one they understand well. *To narrow the field of businesses he and his partners would consider, Mitchell Mondy conducted extensive research on a variety of industries that met the criteria they had established. He discovered that many of the fastest-growing industries were in high-tech areas (something the group was not interested in), but his research also showed that the staffing industry was growing rapidly and had very bright projections. Focusing on the staffing industry, Mondy and his partners soon found four companies that met their purchase criteria. They purchased all four businesses and merged them into one. Their staffing company, Teamplayers, based in Birmingham, Michigan, generates $9 million in annual revenues.*[6]

Typical sources for identifying potential acquisition candidates include the following:

- Business brokers
- Bankers
- Accountants
- Investment bankers
- Industry contacts: suppliers, distributors, customers, and others
- Knocking on the doors of businesses you would like to buy (even if they're not advertised "for sale")
- Newspaper and trade journal listings of businesses for sale (e.g., the Business Opportunities section of the *Wall Street Journal*)
- Trade associations
- The World Wide Web, where several sites include listings of companies for sale
- Networking: through social and business contacts with friends and relatives

Buyers should consider every business that meets their criteria, even those that may not be listed for sale. Just because a business does not have a "for sale" sign in the window does not mean it is not for sale. In fact, the hidden market of companies that might be for sale but are not advertised as such is one of the richest sources of top-quality businesses. By getting the word out that you are seeking a specific type of business, you often discover opportunities that must be negotiated in complete confidence. The existing owners may not want anyone to know that they are considering selling the business.

The Due Diligence Process: Investigating and Evaluating the Acquisition Candidates

The next step is to investigate the candidates in more detail through the process of due diligence. **Due diligence** involves studying, reviewing, and verifying all of the relevant information concerning the top acquisition candidates. The goal is to discover exactly what you will be buying and to avoid any unpleasant surprises after the deal is closed.

Thoroughly exploring a company's character and condition through the Better Business Bureau, credit-reporting agencies, the company's banker, its vendors and suppliers, your accountant, your attorney, and other resources is a vital part of making sure you get a good deal on a business with the capacity to succeed.

Conducting a thorough analysis of a potential acquisition candidate usually requires an entrepreneur to assemble a team of advisers. Finding a suitable business, structuring a deal, and negotiating the final bargain involves many complex legal, financial, tax, and business issues, and good advice can be a valuable tool. Many entrepreneurs bring in an accountant, an attorney, an insurance agent, a banker, and a business broker to serve as consultants during the due diligence process.

The due diligence process involves investigating five critical areas of the business and the potential deal.

1. Why does the owner want to sell?
2. What is the true nature of the firm's assets?
3. What is the market potential for the company's products or services?
4. What legal aspects of the business are hidden risks?
5. Is the business financially sound?

Why Does the Owner Want to Sell? Every prospective business owner should investigate the *real* reason the business owner wants to sell. Two of the most common reasons that owners give for selling are boredom and burnout. Others decided to cash in their business investments and diversify into other types of assets. Other less obvious reasons that a business owner might have for selling his or her venture include a major competitor's move into the market, highway rerouting, frequent burglaries and robberies, expiring lease agreements, cash flow problems, and a declining customer base. Every prospective buyer should investigate *thoroughly* any reason the seller gives for selling the business. Remember, "let the buyer beware!"

Businesses do not last forever, and most owners know when the time has come to sell. Some owners think ethical behavior requires not making false or misleading statements, but they may not disclose the whole story. In most business sales, the buyer bears the responsibility of determining whether the business is a good value. Visiting local business owners may reveal general patterns about the area and its overall vitality. The local chamber of commerce also may have useful information. Suppliers and competitors may be able to shed light on why the business is up for sale. By combining this information with an analysis of the company's financial records, a potential buyer should be able to develop a clear picture of the business and its real value.

What Is the True Nature of the Firm's Assets? A prospective buyer should evaluate the business's assets to determine their value. Are they reasonably priced? Are they obsolete? Will they need to be replaced soon? Do they operate efficiently? The potential buyer should check the condition of both the equipment and the building. It may be necessary to hire a professional to evaluate the major components of the building: its structure and its plumbing, electrical, and heating and cooling systems. Renovations are rarely inexpensive or simple, and unexpected renovations can punch a gaping hole in a buyer's budget.

How fresh is the firm's inventory? Is it consistent with the image the new owner wants to project? How much of it would the buyer have to sell at a loss? A potential buyer may need to get an independent appraisal to determine the value of the firm's inventory and other assets because the current owner may have priced them far above their actual value.

These items typically constitute the largest portion of a business's value, and a potential buyer should not accept the seller's asking price blindly. Remember: *Book value is not the same as market value.* Usually, a buyer can purchase equipment and fixtures at substantially lower prices than book value. Value is determined in the market, not on a balance sheet.

Other important factors that the potential buyer should investigate include the following.

1. *Accounts Receivable.* If the sale includes accounts receivable, the buyer should check their quality before purchasing them. How creditworthy are the accounts? What portion of them is past due? By aging the accounts receivable, the buyer can judge their quality and determine their value. (Refer to Table 5.1.)

2. *Lease Arrangements.* Is the lease included in the sale? When does it expire? What restrictions does it have on renovation or expansion? The buyer should determine beforehand what restrictions the landlord has placed on the lease and should negotiate any change before purchasing the business.

3. *Business Records.* Well-kept business records can be a valuable source of information and can tell a prospective buyer a lot about the company's pattern of success (or lack of it). Unfortunately, many business owners are sloppy record keepers. Consequently, the potential buyer and his or her team may have to reconstruct some critical records. It is important to verify as much information about the business as possible. For instance, does the owner have customer or mailing lists? These can be valuable marketing tools for a new business owner.

4. *Intangible Assets.* Does the sale include any intangible assets such as trademarks, patents, copyrights, or goodwill? Determining the value of such intangibles is much more difficult than computing the value of the tangible assets, yet intangible assets can be one of the most valuable parts of a business acquisition. Edward Karstetter, director of valuation services at USBX, says, "The value placed on intangible assets such as people, knowledge, relationships, and intellectual property is now a greater proportion of the total value of most businesses than is the value of tangible assets such as machinery and equipment."[7]

5. *Location and Appearance.* The location and the overall appearance of the building are important. What had been an outstanding location in the past may be totally unacceptable today. Even if the building and equipment are in good condition and are fairly priced, the business may be located in a declining area. What kinds of businesses are in the area? Every buyer should consider the location's suitability several years into the future. The potential buyer should also check local zoning laws to ensure that any changes he or she wants to make are legal. In some areas, zoning laws are very difficult to change and, as a result, can restrict the business's growth.

IN THE FOOTSTEPS OF AN ENTREPRENEUR...

In Search of the Perfect Business: Part 1

After becoming a victim of corporate downsizing, Hendrix Neimann decided to buy an existing business rather than start one from scratch. At the time, his wife, Judi, was expecting their third child, and Neimann did not want to risk all of the family's personal assets or to commit to the time and emotional demands of a start-up company. He had no idea what kind of business he was looking for, but he believed he would know the right company when he found it. "When I started looking for a company," he says, "I decided that I'd be very clever and find one to buy *before* anyone knew it was on the market."

For months, Neimann found nothing, so he began calling business brokers. As the weeks slipped by and the end of his severance pay approached, Neimann became discouraged and nervous. "Is this what I should be doing?" he asked himself. Then he found a promising company through a blind ad in the *Wall Street Journal:* an access control and security company with sales of nearly $2 million whose owner was retiring. He met with the owner, Peter Klosky, and the broker, Lauren Finberg. In their initial meeting, Klosky told Neimann that there was nothing wrong with the company that a little sales-manship and marketing muscle wouldn't cure. He thought his employees would stay on if he asked them to, and he promised to tell Neimann every-thing he wanted to know.

On his first visit to Automatic Door Specialists [ADS], Neimann was shocked. "I had never seen such a dirty building," he recalls. "The walls were filthy, and inventory, files, and notebooks were stacked every-where." His first thought: "This is a mistake." Still, the business intrigued him. The price was affordable, and Neimann's severance pay was about to run out.

Klosky sent Neimann a proposal showing how he could buy ADS with 100 percent financing, while keeping the debt service at manageable levels and tak-ing out 75 percent of what his previous salary was. The deal appealed to Neimann, and he and Klosky signed a letter of intent, that, although not legally binding, indi-cated that they had a serious deal in the works.

The next step was for Neimann to meet with ADS employees. What they told him was unsettling: The company was going downhill *fast.* Neimann asked the

employees if they thought he should go ahead with the deal. Their response: "Yes, but only if the price is rock-bottom." Neimann's accountant brought more bad news: ADS was losing money, and there were scads of bad accounts receivable on the books; nearly half were more than 90 days old. Also, the accountant told him, after paying the debts from the purchase, there would be *nothing* left for Neimann's salary! "I was despondent," says Neimann. "And furious. And scared."

Despite his reservations, Neimann went ahead with the purchase, but only after offering Klosky just 50 percent of the amount stated in the letter of intent. Klosky accepted the offer the next day. The final step was the actual closing, which was scheduled to occur three days after Neimann's severance pay ended. Neimann was astonished when Klosky and his attor-ney suddenly wanted to rewrite the entire deal at the closing. Both Neimann and Klosky came close to walk-ing out, but seven hours—and more negotiations— later, they signed the deal. Hendrix Neimann had bought himself a business.

1. Critique the way in which Neimann went about buying Automatic Door Specialists.
2. Suppose that Neimann is a friend of yours and that he has come to you for advice about whether to purchase ADS. What will you tell him? Explain.

Source: Adapted from Hendrix F. C. Neimann, "Buying a Business," *Inc.* February 1990, pp. 28–38.

What Is the Market Potential for the Firm's Products or Services? No one wants to buy a business with a dying market. A thorough market analysis can lead to an accurate and realistic sales forecast. This research should tell a buyer whether he or she should consider a particular business and help define the trend in the business's sales and customer base.

Customer Characteristics and Composition. Before purchasing an existing business, a business owner should analyze both the existing and potential customers. Discovering why customers buy from the business and developing a profile of the entire customer base can help the buyer identify a company's strengths and weaknesses. The entrepreneur should determine the answers to the following questions:

- Who are my customers in terms of race, age, gender, and income level?
- What do the customers want the business to do for them? What needs are they satisfying?
- How often do customers buy? Do they buy in seasonal patterns?
- How loyal are present customers?
- Why do some potential customers *not* buy from the business?
- Will it be practical to attract new customers? If so, will the new customers be signifi-cantly different from existing customers?
- Does the business have a well-defined customer base? Is it growing or shrinking? Do these customers come from a large geographic area, or do they all live near the business?

Analyzing the answers to these questions can help the potential owner develop a marketing plan. He or she will most likely try to keep the business attractive to existing customers but also change some features of its marketing plan to attract new customers.

Competitor Analysis. A potential buyer must identify the company's direct competition, the businesses in the immediate area that sell the same or similar products or services. The potential profitability and survival of the business may well depend on the behavior of these competitors. In addition to analyzing direct competitors, a buyer should identify businesses that compete indirectly. For example, supermarkets and chain retail stores often carry a basic product line of automobile supplies (oil, spark plugs, and tune-up kits), competing with full-line auto parts stores. These chains often purchase bulk quantities at significant price reductions and do not incur the expense of carrying a full line of parts and supplies. As a result, they may be able to sell such basic products at lower prices. Even though these chains are not direct competitors, they may have a significant impact on local auto parts stores. Indirect competitors frequently limit their product lines to the most profitable segments of the market and, by concentrating on high-volume or high-profit items, they can pose a serious threat to other businesses.

A potential buyer should also evaluate the trend in the competition. How many similar businesses have entered the market in the past five years? How many similar businesses have closed in the past five years? What caused these failures? Has the market already reached the saturation point? Being a latecomer in an already saturated market is not the path to long-term success.

When evaluating the competitive environment, the prospective buyer should answer other questions:

- Which competitors have survived, and what characteristics have led to the success of each one?
- How do the competitors' sales volumes compare with those of the business the entrepreneur is considering?
- What unique services do the competitors offer?
- How well organized and coordinated are the marketing efforts of competitors?
- What are the competitors' reputations?
- What are the strengths and weaknesses of the competitors?
- How can you gain market share in this competitive environment?

The intent of competitor analysis is to objectively determine the firm's current competitive situation, as well as the competitive landscape that is evolving and in which the firm will be forced to compete.

What Legal Aspects of the Business Present Hidden Risks? Business buyers face myriad legal pitfalls. The most significant legal issues involve liens, bulk transfers, contract assignments, covenants not to compete, and ongoing legal liabilities.

Liens. The key legal issue in the sale of any asset is typically the proper transfer of good title from seller to buyer. However, because most business sales involve a collection of assorted assets, the transfer of a good title is complex. Some business assets may have liens (creditors' claims) against them, and unless those liens are satisfied before the sale, the buyer must assume them and become financially responsible for them. One way to reduce this potential problem is to include a clause in the sales contract stating that any liability not shown on the balance sheet at the time of sale remains the responsibility of the seller.

A prospective buyer should have an attorney thoroughly investigate all of the assets for sale and their lien status before buying any business.

Bulk Transfers. A **bulk transfer** is a transaction in which a buyer purchases all or most of a business's inventory (as in a business sale). To protect against surprise claims from the seller's creditors after purchasing a business, the buyer should meet the requirements of a bulk transfer under Section 6 of the Uniform Commercial Code. Suppose that an owner owing many creditors sells his or her business. The seller, however, does not use the proceeds of the sale to pay his or her debts to business creditors. Instead, the seller "skips town," leaving creditors unpaid. Without the protection of a bulk transfer, those creditors could make claim (within six months) to the assets that the buyer purchased in order to satisfy the previous owner's debts.

To be effective, a bulk transfer must meet the following criteria:

- The seller must give the buyer a sworn list of existing creditors.
- The buyer and the seller must prepare a list of the property included in the sale.
- The buyer must keep the list of creditors and the list of property for six months.
- The buyer must give notice of the sale to each creditor at least 10 days before taking possession of the goods or paying for them (whichever is first).

By meeting these criteria, a buyer acquires free and clear title to the assets purchased, which are not subject to prior claims from the seller's creditors. Because Section 6 can create quite a burden on a business buyer, 16 states have repealed it, and more may follow. About a half-dozen states have revised Section 6 to make it easier for buyers to notify creditors. Under the revised rule, if a business has more than 200 creditors, the buyer may notify them by public notice rather than by contacting them individually.

Contract Assignments. A buyer must investigate the rights and the obligations he or she would assume under existing contracts with suppliers, customers, employees, lessors, and others. To continue the smooth operation of the business, the buyer must assume the rights of the seller under existing contracts. For example, the current owner may have 4 years left on a 10-year lease and so will need to assign this contract to the buyer. In general, the seller can assign any contractual right, unless the contract specifically prohibits the assignment or the contract is personal in nature. For instance, loan contracts sometimes prohibit assignments with **due-on-sale clauses.** These clauses require the buyer to pay the full amount of the remaining loan balance or to finance the balance at prevailing interest rates. Thus, the buyer cannot assume the seller's loan at a lower interest rate. Also, a seller usually cannot assign his or her credit arrangements with suppliers to the buyer because they are based on the seller's business reputation and are personal in nature. If such contracts are crucial to the business operation and cannot be assigned, the buyer must negotiate new contracts.

The prospective buyer also should evaluate the terms of any other contracts the seller has, including the following:

- Patent, trademark, or copyright registrations
- Exclusive agent or distributor contracts
- Real estate leases
- Insurance contracts
- Financing and loan arrangements
- Union contracts

Covenants Not to Compete. One of the most important and most often overlooked legal considerations for a prospective buyer is negotiating a **covenant not to compete** (or a **restrictive covenant**) with the seller. Under a restrictive covenant, the seller agrees not to

An attorney is an important adviser to an entrepreneur looking to buy a business. Understanding the legal aspects of the deal and the company itself are vital to completing a successful purchase.

open a new competing store within a specific time period and the geographic area of the existing one. (The covenant should be negotiated with the owner, not the corporation, because if the corporation signs the agreement, the owner may not be bound.) However, the covenant must be a part of a business sale and must be reasonable in scope in order to be enforceable. Without this protection, a buyer may find his new business eroding beneath his feet.

Ongoing Legal Liabilities. Finally, a potential buyer must look for any potential legal liabilities the purchase might expose. These typically arise from three sources: (1) physical premises, (2) product liability claims, and (3) labor relations. First, the buyer must examine the physical premises for safety. Is the employees' health at risk because of asbestos or some other hazardous material? If a manufacturing environment is involved, does it meet Occupational Safety and Health Administration (OSHA) and other regulatory agency requirements?

Second, the buyer must consider whether the product contains defects that could result in **product liability lawsuits,** which claim that a company is liable for damages and injuries caused by the products or services it sells. Existing lawsuits might be an omen of more to follow. In addition, the buyer must explore products that the company has discontinued, for he or she might be liable for them if they prove to be defective. The final bargain between the parties should require the seller to guarantee that the company is not involved in any product liability lawsuits.

Third, what is the relationship between management and employees? Does a union represent employees in a collective bargaining agreement? The time to discover sour management–labor relations is before the purchase, not after.

The existence of liabilities such as these does not necessarily eliminate a business from consideration. Insurance coverage can shift such risks from the potential buyer, but the buyer should check to see whether the insurance covers lawsuits resulting from actions taken before the purchase. Despite conducting a thorough search, a buyer may purchase a business only to discover later the presence of hidden liabilities such as unpaid back taxes or delinquent bills, unpaid pension fund contributions, undisclosed lawsuits, or others.

Including a clause in the purchase agreement that imposes the responsibility for such hidden liabilities on the seller can protect a buyer from unpleasant surprises after the sale.

Is the Business Financially Sound? A prospective buyer must analyze the financial records of the business to determine its health. The buyer shouldn't be afraid to ask an accountant for help. Accounting systems and methods can vary tremendously from one type of business to another and can be quite confusing to a novice. Current profits can be inflated by changes in the accounting procedure or in the method for recording sales. For the buyer, the most dependable financial records are audited statements, those prepared by a certified public accountant in accordance with generally accepted accounting principles (GAAP). Any investment in a company should produce a reasonable salary for the owner and a healthy return on the money invested. Otherwise, it makes no sense to purchase the business.

A buyer also must remember that he or she is purchasing the future profit potential of an existing business. To evaluate the firm's profit potential, a buyer should review past sales, operating expenses, and profits as well as the assets used to generate those profits. The buyer must compare current balance sheets and income statements with previous ones and then develop pro forma statements for the next two or three years. Sales tax records, income tax returns, and financial statements are valuable sources of information.

Are profits consistent over the years or are they erratic? Is this pattern typical in the industry or is it a result of unique circumstances or poor management? Can the business survive if serious fluctuation in revenues, costs, and profits are present? If these fluctuations are caused by poor management, can a new manager turn the business around? Some of the financial records that a potential buyer should examine are discussed next.

Income Statements and Balance Sheets for the Past Three to Five Years. It is important to review data from several years because creative accounting techniques can distort financial data in any single year. Even though buyers are purchasing the future profits of a business, they must remember that many businesses intentionally show low profits in order to minimize the owners' tax bills. Low profits should prompt a buyer to investigate their causes.

Income Tax Returns for the Past Three to Five Years. Comparing basic financial statements with tax returns can reveal discrepancies of which the buyer should be aware. Some small business owners "skim" from their businesses; that is, they take money from sales without reporting it as income. Owners who skim will claim their businesses are more profitable than their tax returns show. However, buyers should not pay for "phantom profits."

Owner's Compensation (and That of Relatives). The owner's compensation is especially important in small companies; and the smaller the company is, the more important it will be. Although many companies do not pay their owners what they are worth, others compensate their owners lavishly. Buyers must consider the impact of fringe benefits—company cars, insurance contracts, country club memberships, and the like. It is important to adjust the company's income statements for the salary and fringe benefits that the seller has paid himself or herself and others.

Cash Flow. Most buyers understand the importance of evaluating a company's profit history, but few recognize the need to analyze its cash flow. They assume that if profits are adequate, there will be sufficient cash to pay all of the bills and to fund an adequate salary for themselves. *That is not necessarily the case!* Before closing any deal, a buyer should sit down with an accountant and convert the target company's financial statements into a cash flow forecast. This forecast must take into account not only existing debts and obligations but also any modifications or additional debts the buyer plans to make in the business. It should reflect the repayment of financing the buyer arranges to purchase the company. The telling question is: Can the company generate sufficient cash to be self-supporting? How much cash will it generate for the buyer?

A potential buyer must look for suspicious deviations from the average (in either direction) for sales, expenses, profits, assets, and liabilities. Have sales been increasing or decreasing? Is the equipment really as valuable as it is listed on the balance sheet? Are advertising expenses unusually high? How is depreciation reflected in the financial statements?

This financial information gives the buyer the opportunity to verify the seller's claims about the business's performance. Sometimes, however, an owner will take short-term actions that produce a healthy financial statement but weaken the firm's long-term health and profit potential. For example, a seller might lower costs by gradually eliminating equipment maintenance or might boost sales by selling to marginal businesses that will never pay their bills. Such techniques can artificially inflate assets and profits, but a well-prepared buyer should be able to see through them. Finally, a potential buyer should always be wary of purchasing a business if the present owner refuses to disclose his or her financial records. Table 5.2 lists the records that a potential buyers should review before

Table 5.2

Records a Business Buyer Should Review Before Committing to a Deal

At a minimum, a business buyer should examine the following documents:

- *Organizational documents*—documents that show how the business is organized, such as partnership agreements, articles of incorporation, and business certificates, should be examined to determine how the business is structured and capitalized.
- *Contracts and leases*—documents such as property and machinery leases, sales contracts, and purchase contracts should be examined to determine the exact obligations the business is subject to.
- *Financial statements*—examine the financial statements for the past three years (and longer if available) to determine the financial condition of the business.
- *Tax returns*—examine the tax returns for the past three years (and longer if available) to determine the profitability of the business and whether any tax liability is outstanding.

However, a more complete investigation is recommended and should include the following:

- Asset list including real estate, equipment, and intangible assets such as patents, trademarks, and licenses
- Real and personal property documents (e.g., deeds, leases, appraisals, mortgages, loans, insurance policies)
- Bank account list
- Financial statements for the last three to five years
- Tax returns for as many years as possible
- Customer list
- Sales records
- Supplier/purchaser list
- Contracts that the business is a party to
- Advertisements, sales brochures, product packaging and enclosures, and any other marketing materials
- Inventory receipts (also take a look at the inventory itself to check the amount and condition)
- Organizational charts and résumés of key employees
- Payroll, benefits, and employee pension or profit-sharing plan information
- Certificates issued by federal, state, or local agencies (e.g., certificate of existence, certificate of authority to transact business, liquor license)
- Certificates, registration articles, and any amendments filed with any federal, state, or local agency (e.g., articles of incorporation for a corporation, articles of organization for a limited liability company)
- Organizational documents (e.g., corporate bylaws, partnership agreements, operating agreements for limited liability companies)
- List of owners, if more than one (e.g., all shareholders if a corporation, all partners if a partnership, all members if a limited liability company)

Source: Adapted from *Business Owner's Toolkit* at www.toolkit.cch.com/text/P01_0860.asp, 2004.

making a final decision about buying a business. Too often, potential buyers fail to review many of these important financial documents, records, and contracts. Such an oversight can result in a negative series of surprises after the deal is completed and the new owner discovers the liabilities that went undisclosed due to poorly conducted due diligence.

Methods for Determining the Value of a Business

3. Describe the various methods used in the valuation of a business.

Business valuation is partly an art and partly a science. What makes establishing a reasonable price for a privately owned business so difficult is the wide variety of factors that influence its value. These include the nature of the business itself, its position in the market or industry, the outlook for the market or industry, the company's financial status and stability, its earning capacity, any intangible assets it may own (e.g., patents, trademarks, and copyrights), the value of other similar companies that are publicly owned, and many other factors.

Computing the value of the company's tangible assets normally poses no major problem, but assigning a price to the intangibles, such as goodwill, almost always creates controversy. The seller expects goodwill to reflect the hard work and long hours invested in building the business. The buyer, however, is willing to pay extra only for those intangible assets that produce exceptional income. So how can the buyer and the seller arrive at a fair price? There are few hard-and-fast rules in establishing the value of a business, but the following guidelines can help.

- There is no single best method for determining a business's worth, because each business sale is unique. The wisest approach is to compute a company's value using several techniques and then to choose the one that makes the most sense.
- The deal must be financially feasible for both parties. The seller must be satisfied with the price received for the business, but the buyer cannot pay an excessively high price that would require heavy borrowing and would strain cash flow from the outset.
- Both the buyer and the seller should have access to the business records.
- Valuations should be based on facts, not fiction.
- The two parties should deal with one another honestly and in good faith.

The main reason that buyers purchase an existing business is to capture the firm's earnings potential. The second most common reason is to obtain an established asset base. It is often much easier to buy assets than to build them. Although evaluation methods should take these characteristics into consideration, too many business sellers and buyers depend on rules of thumb that ignore the unique features of many small companies. There is no rule of thumb or universal valuation method that fits every type of business.

This section describes three basic techniques—the balance sheet method, the earnings approach, and the market approach—and several variations on them for determining the value of a hypothetical business, Lewis Electronics.

Balance Sheet Method: Net Worth = Assets – Liabilities

The **balance sheet technique** is one of the most commonly used methods of evaluating a business, although it is not highly recommended because it oversimplifies the valuation process. This method computes the book value of a company's **net worth**, or **owner's equity** (net worth = assets – liabilities), and uses this figure as the value. The problem with this technique is that it fails to recognize reality: Most small businesses have market values that exceed their reported book values.

The first step is to determine which assets are included in the sale. In most cases, the owner has some personal assets that he or she does not want to sell. Professional business brokers can

Figure 5.1

Balance Sheet for Lewis
Electronics, June 20, 200X

ASSETS		
CURRENT ASSETS		
Cash	$11,655	
Accounts receivable	15,876	
Inventory	56,523	
Supplies	8,574	
Prepaid insurance	5,587	
Total current assets		$ 98,215
FIXED ASSETS		
Land	$24,000	
Buildings	$141,000	
less accumulated depreciation	51,500	89,500
Office equipment	$ 12,760	
less accumulated depreciation	7,159	5,601
Factory equipment	$ 59,085	
less accumulated depreciation	27,850	31,235
Trucks and autos	$ 28,730	
less accumulated depreciation	11,190	17,540
Total fixed assets		$167,876
Total Assets		$266,091
LIABILITIES		
CURRENT LIABILITIES		
Accounts payable	$19,497	
Mortgage payable	5,215	
Salaries payable	3,671	
Note payable	10,000	
Total current liabilities		$ 38,383
LONG-TERM LIABILITIES		
Mortgage payable	$54,542	
Note payable	21,400	
Total long-term liabilities		$ 75,942
Total Liabilities		$114,325
OWNER'S EQUITY		
Owner's Equity [net worth]		$151,766
Total Liabilities + Owner's Equity		$266,091

help the buyer and the seller arrive at a reasonable value for the collection of assets included in the deal. Remember that net worth on a financial statement will likely differ significantly from actual net worth in the market. Figure 5.1 shows the balance sheet for Lewis Electronics. Based on this balance sheet, the company's net worth is $151,766, ($266,091 − $114,325).

Variation: Adjusted Balance Sheet Technique. A more realistic method for determining a company's value is to adjust the book value of net worth to reflect the actual market value. The values reported on a company's books may either overstate or understate the true value of assets and liabilities. Typical assets in a business sale include notes and accounts receivable, inventories, supplies, and fixtures. If a buyer purchases notes and accounts receivable, he or she should estimate the likelihood of their collection and adjust their value accordingly (refer to Table 5.1).

In manufacturing, wholesale, and retail businesses, inventory is usually the largest single asset in the sale. Taking a physical inventory count is the best way to determine accurately the quantity of goods to be transferred. The sale may include three types of inventory, each having its own method of valuation: raw materials, work-in-process, and finished goods.

The buyer and the seller must arrive at a method for evaluating the inventory. First in, first out (FIFO), last in, first out (LIFO), and average costing are three frequently used techniques, but the most common methods use the cost of last purchase and the replacement value of the inventory. Before accepting any inventory value, the buyer should evaluate the condition of the goods.

To avoid problems, some buyers insist on having a knowledgeable representative on an inventory team to count the inventory and check its condition. Nearly every sale involves merchandise that cannot be sold, but by taking this precaution, a buyer minimizes the chance of being stuck with worthless inventory. Fixed assets transferred in a sale might include land, buildings, equipment, and fixtures. Business owners frequently carry real estate and buildings on their books at prices well below their actual market value. Equipment and fixtures, depending on their condition and usefulness, may increase or decrease the true value of the business. Appraisals of these assets on insurance policies are helpful guidelines for establishing market value. Also, business brokers can be useful in determining the current value of fixed assets. Some brokers use an estimate of what it would cost to replace a company's physical assets (less a reasonable allowance for depreciation) to determine value. For Lewis Electronics, the adjusted net worth is $274,638 − $114,325 = $160,313 (see the adjusted balance sheet in Figure 5.2), indicating that some of the entries on its books did not accurately reflect market value.

Business valuations based on balance sheet methods suffer one major drawback: They do not consider the future earnings potential of the business. These techniques value assets at current prices and do not consider them as tools for creating future profits. The next method for computing the value of a business is based on its expected future earnings.

Earnings Approach

The buyer of an existing business is essentially purchasing its future income. The **earnings approach** is more refined than the balance sheet method because it considers the future income potential of the business.

Variation 1: Excess Earnings Method. This method combines both the value of the firm's existing assets (over its liabilities) and an estimate of its future earnings potential to determine its selling price. One advantage of the **excess earnings method** is that it offers an estimate of goodwill. Goodwill is an intangible asset that often creates problems in a business sale. In fact, the most common method of valuing a business is to compute its tangible net worth and then to add an often arbitrary adjustment for goodwill. In essence, goodwill is the difference between an established, successful business and one that has yet to prove itself. Goodwill is based on the company's reputation and its ability to attract customers. A buyer should not accept blindly the seller's arbitrary adjustment for goodwill because it is likely to be inflated.

The excess earnings method provides a fairly consistent and realistic approach for determining the value of goodwill. It measures goodwill by the amount of profit the business earns above that of the average firm in the same industry. It also assumes that the owner is entitled to a reasonable return on the firm's adjusted tangible net worth.

Step 1 *Compute adjusted tangible net worth.* Using the excess earnings method of valuation, the buyer should compute the firm's adjusted tangible net worth.

ASSETS

CURRENT ASSETS

Cash	$11,655	
Accounts receivable	10,051	
Inventory	39,261	
Supplies	7,492	
Prepaid insurance	5,587	
Total current assets		$ 74,046

FIXED ASSETS

Land		$36,900	
Buildings	$177,000		
less accumulated depreciation	51,500	125,500	
Office equipment	$ 11,645		
less accumulated depreciation	7,159	4,486	
Factory equipment	$ 50,196		
less accumulated depreciation	27,850	22,346	
Trucks and autos	$ 22,550		
less accumulated depreciation	11,190	11,360	
Total fixed assets			$200,592
Total Assets			$274,638

LIABILITIES

CURRENT LIABILITIES

Accounts payable	$19,497	
Mortgage payable	5,215	
Salaries payable	3,671	
Note payable	10,000	
Total current liabilities		$ 38,383

LONG-TERM LIABILITIES

Mortgage payable	$54,542	
Note payable	21,400	
Total long-term liabilities		$ 75,942
Total Liabilities		$114,325

OWNER'S EQUITY

Owner's Equity [net worth]	$160,313
Total Liabilities + Owner's Equity	$274,638

IN THE FOOTSTEPS OF AN ENTREPRENEUR . . .

In Search of the Perfect Business: Part 2

Two years after purchasing Automatic Door Specialists (ADS), Hendrix Neimann was well aware of the dark side of buying a business. "Never, but never, had an owner known so little about his business," he says, "or been so totally at the mercy of his employees. What's more, I barely even knew what business we were in. I had always thought we were in the security/access control industry. It turned out we were a subset of the construction industry. I had never had any desire to be in construction or anything remotely resembling construction." he says.

Neimann discovered that a substantial portion of ADS sales came from government contracts, where the lowest bidder got the job. Under Neimann, however, ADS was focusing on quality product lines and full installation and service practices. Unfortunately, Neimann also discovered that potential customers saw ADS's products as commodities and made their purchase decisions on the basis of price, not quality and service. "I couldn't, or wouldn't, do business that way," says Neimann. As government jobs became more scarce, competition became more intense. Sales slumped, and ADS lost $53,000 in Neimann's first year.

Neimann's attempts to change the company's culture met with no more success than did his marketing strategies. He tried all of the latest management philosophies, but they never seemed to work. "The staff nodded, smiled, asked a few questions—and then proceeded to ignore everything I had said and go about their business," he says. Several longtime employees decided to leave what they saw as a sinking ship.

As in many small companies, cash flow was a constant problem. On two occasions, Neimann barely made payroll—with $37 to spare one week and $95 the other. "We just couldn't seem to develop any momentum," Neimann says. Slipping into panic, he

took virtually all decision-making authority away from his workers, further alienating them. Paying creditors soon became a problem, and Neimann was forced to juggle the company's bills. Unpaid telephone bills, vendor invoices, even the payments to former owner Peter Klosky were piling up.

Looking back on his purchase of ADS, Neimann says, "Before I bought the business, I never really, truly assembled enough information to tell if I was actually going to like what I was doing. I got so caught up in the details of negotiating the deal and in checking out all the facts that I didn't take enough time to figure out if I'd be happy. It took a year for me to admit that I didn't like the industry I had joined or what I had to do to be successful in it." Neimann felt trapped. "Here I was," he says, "not having any fun, in fact hating a lot of what I was doing, with every personal asset on the line, and unable to get out. That's as trapped as you get."

1. Review the sections in this chapter entitled "How to Buy a Business" and "In Search of the Perfect Business: Part 1" Which steps did Neimann violate?
2. What could Neimann have done to avoid the problems at ADS?
3. What is your forecast for ADS and Hendrix's future?

Source: Adapted from Hendrix F. C. Neimann, "How to Buy a Business," *Inc.,* October 1991, pp. 38–46.

Total tangible assets (adjusted for market value) minus total liabilities yields adjusted tangible net worth. In the Lewis Electronics example, adjusted tangible net worth is $274,638 − $114,325 = $160,313 (refer to Figure 5.2).

Step 2   *Calculate the opportunity costs of investing in the business.* **Opportunity costs** represent the cost of forgoing a choice. If the buyer chooses to purchase the assets of a business, he or she cannot invest his or her money elsewhere. Therefore, the opportunity cost of the purchase would be the amount that the buyer could have earned by investing the same amount in a similar-risk investment.

There are three components in the rate of return used to value a business: (1) the basic, risk-free return, (2) an inflation premium, and (3) the risk allowance for investing in the particular business. The basic, risk-free return and the inflation premium are reflected in investments such as U.S. Treasury bonds. To determine the appropriate rate of return for investing in a business, the buyer must add to this base rate a factor reflecting the risk of purchasing the company. The greater the risk is, the higher the rate of return will be. A normal-risk business typically indicates a 25 percent rate of return. In the Lewis Electronics example, the opportunity cost of the investment is $160,313 \times 25\% = \$40,078$.

The second part of the buyer's opportunity cost is the salary that he or she could have earned working for someone else. For the Lewis Electronics example, if the buyer purchases the business, the buyer must forgo the

$25,000 that he or she could have earned working elsewhere. Adding these amounts yields a total opportunity cost of $65,078.

Step 3   *Project net earnings.* The buyer must estimate the company's net earnings for the upcoming year before subtracting the owner's salary. Averages can be misleading, so the buyer must be sure to investigate the trend of net earnings. Have they risen steadily over the past five years, dropped significantly, remained relatively constant, or fluctuated wildly? Past income statements provide useful guidelines for estimating earnings. In the Lewis Electronics example, the buyer and an accountant project net earnings to be $74,000.

Step 4   *Compute extra earning power.* A company's extra earning power is the difference between forecasted earnings (step 3) and total opportunity costs (step 2). Many small businesses that are for sale do not have extra earning power (i.e., excess earnings) and they show marginal or no profits. The extra earning power of Lewis Electronics is $74,000 − $65,078 = $8,922.

Step 5   *Estimate the value of intangibles.* The owner can use the business's extra earning power to estimate the value of its intangible assets: that is, its goodwill. Multiplying the extra earning power by a years-of-profit figure yields an estimate of the intangible assets' value. The years-of-profit figure for a normal-risk business ranges from three to four. A high-risk business may have a years-of-profit figure of one, whereas a well-established firm might use a figure of seven. For Lewis Electronics, the value of intangibles (assuming normal risk) would be $8,922 × 3 = $26,766.

Step 6   *Determine the value of the business.* To determine the value of the business, the buyer simply adds together the adjusted tangible net worth (step 1) and the value of the intangibles (step 5). Using this method, the value of Lewis Electronics is $160,313 + $26,766 = $187,079.

Both the buyer and seller should consider the tax implications of transferring goodwill. The amount that the seller receives for goodwill is taxed as ordinary income. Because the *buyer* can amortize both the cost of goodwill and a restrictive covenant over 15 years, the tax treatment of either would be the same for him or her. However, the *seller* would prefer to have the amount of the purchase price in excess of the value of the assets allocated to goodwill, which is a capital asset. The gain on the capital asset would be taxed at the lower capital gains rates. If that same amount were allocated to a restrictive covenant (which is negotiated with the seller personally, not the business), the seller must treat it as ordinary income, which would be taxed at regular rates that are higher than the capital gains rates.

Variation 2: Capitalized Earnings Approach. Another earnings approach capitalizes expected net profits to determine the value of a business. The buyer should prepare his or her own pro forma income statement and should ask the seller to prepare one also. Many appraisers use a five-year weighted average of past sales (with the greatest weights assigned to the most recent years) to estimate sales for the upcoming year.

Once again, the buyer must evaluate the risk of purchasing the business to determine the appropriate rate of return on the investment. The greater the perceived risk, the higher the return the buyer will require. Risk determination is always somewhat subjective, but it is necessary for proper evaluation.

The **capitalized earnings approach** divides estimated net earnings (after subtracting the owner's reasonable salary) by the rate of return that reflects the appropriate risk level. For Lewis Electronics, the capitalized value (assuming a reasonable salary of $25,000) is:

$$\frac{\text{Net earnings (after deducting owner's salary)}}{\text{Rate of return}} = \frac{\$74,000 - \$25,000}{25\%} = \$196,000$$

Clearly, firms with lower risk factors are more valuable (a 10 percent rate of return would have yielded a value of $499,000) than are those with higher risk factors (a 50 percent rate of return would have yielded a value of $99,800). Most normal-risk businesses use a rate-of-return factor ranging from 25 to 33 percent. The lowest risk factor that most buyers would accept for any business ranges from 15 to 20 percent.

Variation 3: Discounted Future Earnings Approach. This variation of the earnings approach assumes that a dollar earned in the future will be worth less than that same dollar today. Therefore, using the **discounted future earnings approach**, the buyer estimates the company's net income for several years into the future and then discounts these future earnings back to their present value. The resulting present value is an estimate of the company's worth.

The reduced value of future dollars has nothing to do with inflation. Instead, present value represents the cost of the buyer giving up the opportunity to earn a reasonable rate of return by receiving income in the future instead of today. To visualize the importance of the time value of money, consider two $1 million sweepstakes winners. Rob wins $1 million in a sweepstakes, and he receives it in $50,000 installments over 20 years. If Rob invests every installment at 15 percent interest, he will have accumulated $5,890,505.98 at the end of 20 years. Lisa wins $1 million in another sweepstakes, but she collects her winnings in one lump sum. If Lisa invests her $1 million today at 15 percent, she will have accumulated $16,366,537.39 at the end of 20 years. The dramatic difference in their wealth is the result of the time value of money.

The discounted future earnings approach has five steps:

Step 1   *Project earnings for five years into the future.* One way is to assume that earnings will grow by a constant amount over the next five years. Perhaps a better method is to develop three forecasts—optimistic, pessimistic, and most likely—for each year and then find a weighted average using the following formula:

$$\text{Forecasted earnings for year } i = \frac{\text{Optimistic earnings for year } i + (\text{Most likely earnings for year } i \times 4) + \text{Pessimistic earnings for year } i}{6}$$

For Lewis Electronics, the buyer's forecasts are:

Year	Pessimistic	Most Likely	Optimistic	Weighted Average
XXX1	$65,000	$74,000	$92,000	$75,500
XXX2	74,000	90,000	101,000	89,167
XXX3	82,000	100,000	112,000	99,000
XXX4	88,000	109,000	120,000	107,333
XXX5	88,000	115,000	122,000	111,667

The buyer must remember that the further into the future he or she forecasts, the less reliable the estimates will be.

Step 2   *Discount these future earnings using the appropriate present value factor.* The appropriate present value factor can be found by looking in published present value tables, by using modern calculators or computers, or by solving the equation $1/(1 + k)^t$, where k = rate of return and t = time (year 1, 2, 3 . . . n). The rate that the buyer selects should reflect the rate he or she could earn on a similar-risk investment. Because Lewis Electronics is a normal-risk business, the buyer chooses 25 percent.

Year	Income Forecast (Weighted Average)	Present Value Factor (at 25 percent)	Net Present Value
XXX1	$75,500	0.8000	$ 60,400
XXX2	89,167	0.6400	57,067
XXX3	99,000	0.5120	50,688
XXX4	107,333	0.4096	43,964
XXX5	111,667	0.3277	36,593
Total			$248,712

Step 3 *Estimate the income stream beyond five years.* One technique suggests multiplying the fifth-year income by 1/(rate of return). For Lewis Electronics, the estimate is:

Income beyond year 5 = $111,667 × (1 / 25%) = $446,668

Step 4 *Discount the income estimate beyond five years using the present value factor for the sixth year.* For Lewis Electronics:

Present value of income beyond year 5 = $446,668 × 0.2622 = $117,116

Step 5 *Compute the total value of the business.*

Total value = $248,712 + $117,116 = $365,828

The primary advantage of this technique is that it evaluates a business solely on the basis of its future earnings potential, but its reliability depends on making forecasts of

IN THE FOOTSTEPS OF AN ENTREPRENEUR . . .

Would You Buy This Business, and If So, for What Price?

Many people can enjoy the fantasy of owning a vineyard and winery where they might enjoy the pleasures derived by sipping a glass of cabernet while enjoying a warm, scenic sunset. If you are one of these people, what would you pay for the Southern Illinois Vineyard?

Here's the opportunity: The vineyard was first planted in 1991 and encompasses 625 acres. By now the plants are mature and in peak productivity. In addition to the vineyard, there is a 4,000-square-foot winery featuring state-of-the-art production technology. The winery currently produces 10 types of wines and several of the varieties have won silver and bronze medals at the state fair.

Other vineyards and wineries have come "on line" in the region and there has been an active marketing campaign to attract visitors to the area. The majority of the sales occur through this direct-to-consumer channel. The following are some recent financial numbers for your review:

Year	Gross Revenue	EBITDA	Owner's Compensation
2000	$19,727	($57,675)	-0-
2001	49,679	7,441	-0-
2002	70,000	27,441	-0-

For comparison purposes, a 15-acre Napa Valley property recently sold for $3.5 million, a 74-acre Italian property sold for $1.5 million, and a 79-acre New Zealand property sold for $5.5 million.

1. What are the pros and cons of a business such as this?
2. What additional information would you need to make a decision, and where would you obtain that information?
3. If you were to make an offer for the business, how much would it be?

Source: Adapted from Kate O'Sullivan, "Little Napa on the Prairie," *Inc.,* December 2002, p. 38.

future earnings and on choosing a realistic present value factor. The discounted future earnings approach is especially well suited for valuing service businesses (whose asset bases are often small) and for companies experiencing high growth rates.

Market Approach

The **market** (or **price/earnings**) **approach** uses the price/earnings ratios of similar businesses to establish the value of a company. The buyer must use businesses whose stocks are publicly traded in order to get a meaningful comparison. A company's **price/earnings ratio** (or **P/E ratio**) is the price of one share of its common stock in the market divided by its earnings per share (after deducting preferred stock dividends). To get a representative P/E ratio, the buyer should average the P/Es of as many similar businesses as possible.

To compute the company's value, the buyer multiplies the average price/earnings ratio by the private company's estimated earnings. For example, suppose that the buyer found four companies comparable to Lewis Electronics but whose stock is publicly traded. Their price/earnings ratios are:

Company 1	3.300
Company 2	3.800
Company 3	4.700
Company 4	4.100
Average	3.975

Using this average P/E ratio produces a value of $294,150:

Value average P/E ratio × Estimated net earnings = 3.975 × $74,000 = $294,150

The biggest advantage of the market approach is its simplicity. But this method does have several disadvantages, including the following:

1. *Necessary comparisons between publicly traded and privately owned companies.* The stock of privately owned companies is illiquid and, therefore, the P/E ratio used is often subjective and lower than that of publicly held companies.
2. *Unrepresentative earnings estimates.* The private company's net earnings may not realistically reflect its true earnings potential. To minimize taxes, owners usually attempt to keep profits low and rely on fringe benefits to make up the difference.
3. *Finding similar companies for comparison.* Often it is extremely difficult for a buyer to find comparable publicly held companies when estimating the appropriate P/E ratio.
4. *Applying the after-tax earnings of a private company to determine its value.* If a prospective buyer is using an after-tax P/E ratio from a public company, he or she must use the after-tax earnings from the private company.

Despite its drawbacks, the market approach is useful as a general guideline to establishing a company's value.

Which of these methods is best for determining the value of a small business? Simply stated, there is no single best method. These techniques will yield a range of values. Buyers should look for values that might cluster together and then use their best judgment to determine their offering price. The final price will be based on both the valuation used and the negotiating skills of both parties.

Negotiating the Deal

4. Discuss the process of negotiating the deal.

Placing a value on an existing business represents a major hurdle for many would-be entrepreneurs. Once an entrepreneur has a realistic value for the business, the next challenge in making a successful purchase is negotiating a suitable deal. Although most buyers do not realize it, the price they pay for a company typically is not as crucial to its continued success as the terms on which they make the purchase. In other words, *the structure of the deal is more important than the actual price the seller agrees to pay.* Of course, wise business buyers will try to negotiate a reasonable price, but they are much more focused on negotiating favorable terms: how much cash they must pay out and when, how much of the price the seller is willing to finance and for how long, the interest rate at which the deal is financed, which liabilities they will assume, and other such terms. The buyer's primary concern should be to make sure that the deal does not endanger the company's financial future and that it preserves the company's cash flow.

Figure 5.3 sets forth the detailed sequence of events in a successful acquisition negotiation process.

Figure 5.3

Steps in the Acquisition Process

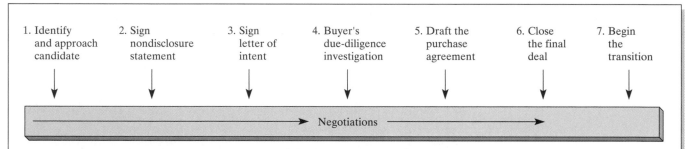

| 1. Identify and approach candidate | 2. Sign nondisclosure statement | 3. Sign letter of intent | 4. Buyer's due-diligence investigation | 5. Draft the purchase agreement | 6. Close the final deal | 7. Begin the transition |

Negotiations

Step 1 *Approach the candidate company.* If a business is advertised for sale, the proper approach is through the channel defined in the ad. Sometimes buyers will contact business brokers to help them locate potential target companies. If you have targeted a company in the "hidden market," an introduction from a banker, accountant, or lawyer often is the best approach. During this phase, the seller checks out the buyer's qualifications, and the buyer begins to judge the quality of the company.

Step 2 *Sign a nondisclosure document.* If the buyer and the seller are satisfied with the results of their preliminary research, they are ready to begin serious negotiations. Throughout the negotiation process, the seller expects the buyer to maintain strict confidentiality of all of the records, documents, and information he or she receives during the investigation and negotiation process. The nondisclosure document is a legally binding contract that ensures the secrecy of the parties' negotiations.

Step 3 *Sign a letter of intent.* Before a buyer makes a legal offer to buy the company, he or she typically will ask the seller to sign a letter of intent. The letter of intent is a nonbinding document that says that the buyer and the seller have reached a sufficient "meeting of the minds" to justify the time and expense of negotiating a final agreement. The letter should state clearly that it is nonbinding, giving either party the right to walk away from the deal. It should also contain a clause calling for "good faith negotiations" between the parties. A typical letter of intent addresses terms such as price, payment terms, categories of assets to be sold, and a deadline for closing the final deal. Typically, a letter of intent includes a "no-shop" clause. This clause states that the seller cannot use the deal that you are negotiating as leverage to raise the offer from other potential buyers for a given time frame, usually 90 days.

Step 4 *Conduct buyer's due diligence.* While negotiations are continuing, the buyer is busy studying the business and evaluating its strengths and weaknesses. In short, the buyer must do his or her homework to make sure that the business is a good value. The buyer should obtain an independent valuation of the business and conduct a detailed review of all company records, employment agreements, leases, pending litigation, and even current or past compliance with federal, state, and local regulations.

(Continued)

Figure 5.3   Continued

Step 5   *Draft the purchase agreement.* The purchase agreement spells out the parties' final deal. It sets forth all of the details of the agreement and is the final product of the negotiation process. Typical purchase agreement provisions include:

- Definitions for terms in the agreement.
- Description of assets, property, and timing of payment.
- Purchase price.
- Special conditions that the parties must satisfy to close the deal.
- Allocation of purchase price to specific assets.
- Whether the purchaser assumes any liabilities and, if so, which ones.
- Lease transfers and their terms.
- Warranties, representations, and agreements.
- A clause addressing bulk transfer provisions, if appropriate.
- Conduct of the business between the date of the purchase agreement and the closing date.
- Conditions necessary to close the deal.
- Provisions specifying procedures for resolving postclosing disputes and breaches of seller's warranties and representations.
- Covenants restricting competition.
- Miscellaneous matters regarding escrows, payment of broker commissions, and various legal and regulatory provisions.
- Time and place of closing.

Step 6:   *Close the final deal.* Once the parties have drafted the purchase agreement, all that remains to make the deal "official" is the closing. Both buyer and seller sign the necessary documents to make the sale final. The buyer delivers the required money, and the seller turns the company over to the buyer.

Step 7:   *Begin the transition.* For the buyer, the real challenge now begins: making the transition to a successful business owner!

Sources: Adapted from *The Buying and Selling a Company Handbook* (New York: Price Waterhouse, 1993), pp. 38–42; "Small Business Practices: How to . . . Buy a Business," Edgeonline, www.edgeonline.com|maInlbizbuilders/BIZ/Sm_business/buybus.shtml; "Buying a Business," www.ptbo.igs.net/~lbk/bab.htm <http://www.ptbo.igs.net/~lbk/bab.htm>; Ronaleen R. Roha, "Don't Start It, Buy It," *Kiplinger's Personal Finance Magazine*, July 1997, pp. 74–78.

On the surface, the negotiation process appears to be strictly adversarial. Although each party may be trying to accomplish objectives that are at odds with those of the opposing party, the negotiation process does not have to turn into a nasty battle with overtones of "If you win, then I lose." The negotiation process will go much more smoothly and much faster if the two parties work to establish a cooperative relationship based on honesty and trust from the outset. A successful deal requires both parties to examine and articulate their respective positions while trying to understand the other party's position. Recognizing that neither of them will benefit without a deal, both parties must work to achieve their objectives while making certain concessions to keep the negotiations alive. To avoid a stalled deal, both buyer and seller should go into the negotiation with a list of objectives ranked in order of priority. Prioritizing increases the likelihood that both parties will get most of what they want from the bargain. Knowing which terms are most important (and which are least important) to them enables the parties to make concessions without "giving away the farm" and without getting bogged down in nit-picking. If, for instance, the seller insists on a term that the buyer cannot agree to, the buyer can explain why he or she cannot concede on that term and then offer to give up something in exchange. The following negotiating tips can help parties reach a mutually satisfying deal:

- *Know what you want to have when you walk away from the table.* What will it take to reach your business objectives? What would the perfect deal be? Although it may not be possible to achieve the perfect deal, defining it helps you identify which issues are most important to you.
- *Develop a negotiation strategy.* Once you know where you want to finish, decide where you will start, and remember to leave some room to give. Try not

to be the first one to mention price. Let the other party do that; then negotiate from there.

- *Recognize the other party's needs.* For a bargain to result, both parties must believe that they have met at least some of their goals. Asking open-ended questions can clue you in to the other side's position and why it's important.
- *Be an empathetic listener.* To truly understand what the other party's position is, you must listen attentively.
- *Focus on the problem, not on the person.* If the negotiation reaches an impasse, a natural tendency is to attack the other party. Resist! Instead, focus on developing a workable solution.
- *Avoid seeing the other side as "the enemy."* Such an attitude reduces the negotiation to an "I win, you lose" mentality that only hinders the process.
- *Educate; don't intimidate.* Rather than trying to bully the other party into accepting your point of view, try explaining your reasoning and the logic behind your proposal.
- *Be patient.* Resist the tendency to become angry and insulted at the proposals the other party makes. Similarly, don't be in such a hurry to close the deal that you give in on crucial points.
- *Remember that "no deal" is an option.* What would happen if the negotiations failed to produce a deal? In most negotiations, walking away from the table is an option. In some cases, it may be the best option.
- *Be flexible and creative.* Always have a fall-back position—an alternative that, although not ideal, satisfies you and is acceptable to the other party.

Before beginning negotiations, a buyer should take stock of some basic issues. How strong is the seller's desire to sell? Is the seller willing to finance part of the purchase price? What terms does the seller suggest? Which ones are most important to the seller? Is it urgent that the seller close the deal quickly? What deal structure best suits the buyer's needs? What are the tax consequences for both parties? Will the seller sign a restrictive covenant? Is the seller willing to stay on with the company for a time as a consultant? What general economic conditions exist in the industry at the time of the sale? Sellers tend to have the upper hand in good economic times, and buyers will have an advantage during recessionary periods in an industry.

In general, the seller of the business is looking to:

- Get the highest price possible for the company.
- Sever all responsibility for the company's liabilities.
- Avoid unreasonable contract terms that might limit his or her future opportunities.
- Maximize the cash he or she gets from the deal.
- Minimize the tax burden from the sale.
- Make sure the buyer will make all future payments.

The buyer seeks to:

- Get the business at the lowest price possible.
- Negotiate favorable payment terms, preferably over time.
- Get assurances that he or she is buying the business he or she thinks it is.
- Avoid enabling the seller to open a competing business.
- Minimize the amount of cash paid up front.

Entrepreneurs who are most effective at acquiring a business know how important it is to understand the many emotions that influence the seller's behavior and decisions. For some sellers this business has, to a very large degree, been their life. They may have been the original founder and the person who breathed life into the business. They nurtured the business through its infancy, matured it, and now it's time to "let go." Sellers may be asking themselves, "What will I do now? Where will I go each morning? Who will I be without my business?" During the negotiation process, sellers may discover that their business is the focal point in their life and an essential element of their identity. The negotiation process requires sellers to, in effect, put a price tag on their life's work. For these reasons, the potential buyer must negotiate in a manner that displays patience and respect.

On the other hand, before selling their business, entrepreneurs must themselves address some important questions so that the negotiation process will move more smoothly. Following are some of these critical questions:

■ Do I want to continue my involvement with the business if the new owner asks me to stay on?

■ If I decide to stay on to help in the transition, how involved do I want to be, especially if the new owner has plans to make significant change?

■ Before I sell this business and lose my source of income, how much must this business sell for to earn me a comparable income?

■ Before I sell to an outside individual, are there internal candidates who both want to purchase the business and can afford to do so? Do I want my children or others to take over the business?

■ Which professionals (attorneys, accountants, business brokers, etc.) do I need to assemble as a team to help me sell the business?

■ What financial terms and conditions do I prefer? What financial terms or conditions are unacceptable?

■ Do I feel any pressure to sell in a specific time frame?

When sellers take this proactive approach to the process, they are almost always better prepared to negotiate.

✦ GAINING *a* COMPETITIVE EDGE ✦

Know When It's Time to End the Negotiations

Marc Diener, author of the book *Deal Power*, provides some tips as to when you should cut your losses and leave the negotiating table. The obvious reasons are normally financial in nature, such as the opponent's last, and final, offer was not financially viable. Some of the nonfinancial reasons for leaving the table are as follows:

The opponent is overly difficult. "If you find the person an insufferable, time-wasting nuisance at the bargaining table, remember, it's only a preview of coming attractions." Some people will drive you crazy.

The transaction costs are too high. This sometimes happens because the simple deal continues to evolve into a dark hole of complexities as a legion of lawyers, accountants, bankers, brokers, consultants, and appraisers muddy the deal with contingencies, complications, fees, and commissions. When the anticipated rising tide of expenses becomes disproportionate to the size of the deal, cut the negotiations and avoid the cost.

In some cases it's best to not do the deal to teach some less scrupulous individuals a lesson. Diener states that some dealmakers are "a blight on the business community." Denying them a deal might teach them a valuable lesson.

Your gut instinct may be right when it tells you to stop. Intuition may be defined as knowing without knowing why you know. Intuition about a bad deal may be worth listening to.

1. What are other signs that it is time to walk away from negotiations?
2. Can you give at least two examples of entrepreneurs who have walked away from a deal based on a "gut" feeling? How did they explain their decisions?

Source: Adapted from Marc Diener, "Deals Unplugged," *Entrepreneur,* August 2003, p. 69.

The "Art of the Deal"

Both buyers and sellers must recognize that no one benefits without an agreement. Both parties must work to achieve their goals while making concessions to keep the negotiations alive. Figure 5.4 is an illustration of two individuals prepared to negotiate for the purchase and sale of a business. The buyer and seller both have high and low bargaining points in this example. The buyer would like to purchase the business for $900,000 but would not pay more than $1,300,000. The seller would like to get $1,500,000 for the business but would not take less than $1,000,000. If the seller insists on getting $1,500,000, the business will not be sold to this buyer. Likewise, if the buyer stands firm on an offer of $900,000, there will be no deal. The bargaining process will eventually lead both parties into the *bargaining zone,* the area within which an agreement can be reached. It extends from above the lowest price the seller is willing to take to below the maximum price the buyer is willing to pay. The dynamics of this negotiation process and the needs of each party will ultimately determine whether the buyer and seller can reach an agreement and for what price.

Learning to negotiate successfully means mastering "the art of the deal." The following guidelines will help the parties involved see the negotiation as a conference, likely to produce positive results, rather than as a competition, likely to spiral downward into conflict.

Establish the proper mind-set. Successful negotiations are built on a foundation of trust. The first step in any negotiation should be to establish a climate of trust and communication. Too often, buyers and sellers rush into putting their chips on the bargaining table without establishing a rapport with one another.

Recognize the "rules" of successful negotiations.

- Everything is negotiable.
- Take nothing for granted.
- Ask for as much as possible.
- Consider the other party's perspective.
- Explore a variety of options.
- Seek solutions that are mutually beneficial.

Develop a negotiating strategy. One of the biggest mistakes business buyers can make is entering negotiations with only a vague notion of the strategies they will employ. To be successful, it is necessary to know how to respond to a variety of situations that are likely to arise. Every strategy has an upside and a downside, and effective negotiators know what they are.

Figure 5.4

Identifying the Bargaining Zone

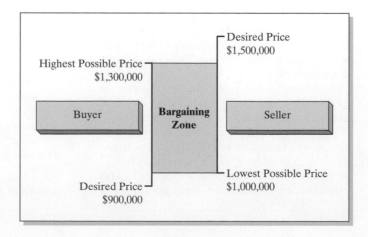

Be creative. When negotiations stall or come to an impasse, negotiators must seek creative alternatives that benefit both parties or, at a minimum, get the negotiations started again.

Keep temper in check. A short temper and an important negotiation make ill-suited partners. The surest way to destroy trust and to sabotage a negotiation is to lose one's temper and lash out at the other party. Anger leads to poor decisions.

Be patient. Sound negotiations often take a great deal of time, especially when one is buying a business from the entrepreneur who founded it. The seller's ego is woven throughout the negotiation process, and wise negotiators recognize this. Persistence and patience are the keys to success in any negotiation involving the sale of the business.

Don't become a victim. Well-prepared negotiators are not afraid to walk away from deals that are not right for them.

IN THE FOOTSTEPS OF AN ENTREPRENEUR...

In Search of the Perfect Business: Part 3

"How could I possibly have been so foolish?" asks Hendrix Neimann. "I thought I had done a decent job of checking out [Automatic Door Specialists] during the summer-long due diligence process." After Neimann and his accountant discovered the unpaid bills, inflated inventory values, and past-due accounts receivable, they discounted heavily the price they offered Peter Klosky for the company. "The good news is that I didn't pay much," says Neimann. "The bad news is that I didn't get much."

Yet he went ahead with the deal, and, in the process, put all of his family's personal assets at risk. Looking back, Neimann says, "I really thought I was a smart, talented, hard-working guy and that I could fix whatever was wrong with the company. Never mind that I didn't have a technical bone in my body and that this was a technical business in a technical industry. Never mind that the company turned out to be struggling and, in fact, losing money when I bought it. I, Neimann the Great, could do it."

But he couldn't. On February 12, 1997, Neimann closed the company, now called ADS Systems, that he had purchased nearly eight years before. He contacted the company's banker and its creditors and told them that he was ceasing operations. Preparing a summary of the company's financial position shone a spotlight on just how bleak the situation was. ADS had $473,000 in debt and accounts payable and only $142,000 in assets and receivables. Neimann explained to his creditors that he did not want to declare bankruptcy and that he intended to pay everything he owed, even if it took years. The bank stood first in line and had the right to claim all of the company's assets and, if those

were insufficient (and they were), to claim the Neimanns' personal assets (including their home and personal bank accounts) as well.

For Neimann, the next few months were a nightmare. "[The banker] called me daily (sometimes twice daily) for no particular reason other than to let me know he was there and, unlike a bad dream, was not going to go away. Creditors called every day by the dozen." Concerned customers called wanting to know who would finish their jobs and who would service the equipment ADS had already installed. The landlord served notice that ADS would be evicted on March 24. The telephone and electric bills were more than two months past due, and the utility companies were threatening to shut off service.

From the time Neimann had bought ADS, the company was struggling financially and was never able to recover. The company was constantly in a cash flow bind, was usually behind in paying its bills, and rarely had a payables-to-receivables ratio of less than 2.5 to 1. When the company fell behind on employee withholding taxes, the Internal Revenue Services swept its bank account, taking out the $7,200 ADS owed.

To raise as much cash as possible to pay off some of the company's debts, Neimann advertised a business liquidation sale in the local newspaper. As friends and family pitched in to organize the sale, Neimann reflected on the path that had brought him to this point. Looking around at the condition he had allowed his company to degenerate into, Neimann was embarrassed. "Like the former owner, I no longer had noticed the dirt, the grease, the grime, the disorganization. I had allowed the men's offices, their desks, their vans to become no better than the inside of garbage cans. I had let the shop remain in a state of chaos since we had moved in there. The technicians and I never connected—ever. My lack of technical experience and knowledge grated on them—and rightly so. But the worst part of the seven and a half years was the overwhelming sense of hopelessness, of fearing that I would never, ever be able to dig out of the hole. I hated the business, hated the industry, hated the job. Yet I would not, could not, give up or in. My house was the ultimate collateral for the loan I'd taken out to buy the business. Therefore, lose the business, lose the house. I was trapped."

Finally, on March 24, 1997, with the building completely cleared out and all of ADS's assets sold off, Neimann's wife Judi, unplugged the office clock at exactly 5 P.M. and took it off the wall. "We were finished," says Neimann.

1. Using Hendrix Neimann's experience with ADS, develop a list of "red flags" that should alert a buyer that a particular business is not for him or her.
2. Looking back at Neimann's experience, what advice would you give to someone who is considering buying a business?

Source: Adapted from Hendrix F. C. Neimann, "The End of the Story," *Inc.*, October 1997, pp. 68–77.

The Structure of the Deal

To make negotiations work, the two sides must structure the deal in a way that is acceptable to both parties.

Straight Business Sale. A straight business sale may be best for a seller who wants to step down and turn over the reins of the company to someone else. A recent study of small business sales in 60 categories found that 94 percent were asset sales; the remaining 6 percent involved the sale of stock. About 22 percent were for cash, and 75 percent included a down payment with a note carried by the seller. The remaining 3 percent relied on a note from the seller with no down payment. When the deal included a down payment, it averaged 33 percent of the purchase price. Only 40 percent of the business sales studied included covenants not to compete.

Although selling a business outright is often the safest exit path for an entrepreneur, it is usually the most expensive one. Sellers who want cash and take the money up front may face an oppressive tax burden. They must pay a capital gains tax on the sale price less their investments in the company. Nor is a straight sale an attractive exit strategy for those who want to stay on with the company or for those who want to surrender control of the company gradually rather than all at once.

Ideally, a buyer has already begun to explore the options available for financing the purchase. (Recall that many entrepreneurs include bankers on their team of advisers.) Traditional lenders often shy away from deals involving the purchase of an existing business. Those who are willing to finance business purchases normally lend only a portion of the value of the assets, so buyers often find themselves searching for alternative sources of funds. Fortunately, most business buyers discover an important source of financing built into the deal: the seller. Typically, a deal is structured so that the buyer makes a down payment to the seller, who then finances a note for the balance. The buyer makes regular principal and interest payments over time, perhaps with a larger balloon payment at the end, until the note is paid off. In most business sales, the seller is willing to finance 40 percent to 70 percent of the purchase price over time, usually 3 to 10 years. The terms and conditions of such a loan are vital to both buyer and seller. They cannot be so burdensome that they threaten the company's continued existence; that is, the buyer must be able to make the payments to the seller out of the company's cash flow. Defining reasonable terms is the result of the negotiation process between the buyer and the seller.

Sale of Controlling Interest. Sometimes business owners sell the majority interest in their companies to investors, competitors, suppliers, or large companies with an agreement that the owner will stay on after the sale. In this way a potential buyer might feel more confident about the acquisition if he or she knows the owner will commit to an intermediate-term management contract for two to four years. Additionally, for the seller who does not want to retire or start a new business, the management contract can be an excellent source of income. This type of flexibility by the seller may result in negotiating a more lucrative final deal.

Restructure the Company. Another way for business owners to cash out gradually is to replace the existing corporation with a new one, formed with other investors. The owner essentially is performing a leveraged buyout of his or her own company. For example, assume that you own a company worth $15 million. You form a new corporation with $12 million borrowed from a bank and $3 million in equity: $1.5 million of your own equity and $1.5 million in equity from an investor who wants you to stay on with the business. The new company buys your company for $15 million. You net $13.5 in cash ($15 million minus your $1.5 million equity investment) and still own 50 percent of the new leveraged business. For a medium-sized business whose financial statement can justify a significant bank loan, this is an excellent alternative. This can be an option in cases in which both parties agree that the seller should remain involved in the business.

Use a Two-Step Sale. For owners wanting the security of a sales contract now but not wanting to step down from the company's helm for several years, a two-step sale may be ideal. The buyer purchases the business in two phases, getting 20 to 70 percent today and agreeing to buy the remainder within a specific time period. Until the final transaction takes place, the entrepreneur retains at least partial control of the company.

Other Alternatives

Form a Family Limited Partnership. Entrepreneurs who want to pass their businesses on to their children should consider forming a family limited partnership. Using this exit strategy, entrepreneurs can transfer their business to their children without sacrificing control over it. Owners take the role of general partners while their children become limited partners. General partners keep just 1 percent of the company, but the partnership agreement gives them total control over the business. The children own 99 percent of the company but have little or no say over how to run the business. Until the founders decide to step down and turn the reins of the company over to the next generation, they continue to run the business and set up significant tax savings for the ultimate transfer of power.

Establish an Employee Stock Ownership Plan (ESOP). Some owners cash out by selling to their employees through an employee stock ownership plan (ESOP). An ESOP is a form of employee benefit plan in which a trust created for employees purchases their employers' stock. Here's how an ESOP works: The company transfers shares of its stock to the ESOP trust, and the trust uses the stock as collateral to borrow enough money to purchase the shares from the company. The company guarantees payment of the loan principal and interest and makes tax-deductible contributions to the trust to repay the loan. The company then distributes the stock to employees' accounts on the basis of a predetermined formula (see Figure 5.5). In addition to the tax benefits an ESOP offers, the plan permits the owner to transfer all or part of the company to employees as gradually or as suddenly as preferred.

To use an ESOP successfully, a small business should be profitable (with pretax profits exceeding $100,000) and should have a payroll of at least $500,000 a year. In general, companies with fewer than 15 to 20 employees do not find ESOPs beneficial. For companies that prepare properly, however, ESOPs offer significant financial and managerial benefits.

Figure 5.5

A Typical Employee Stock Ownership Plan (ESOP)

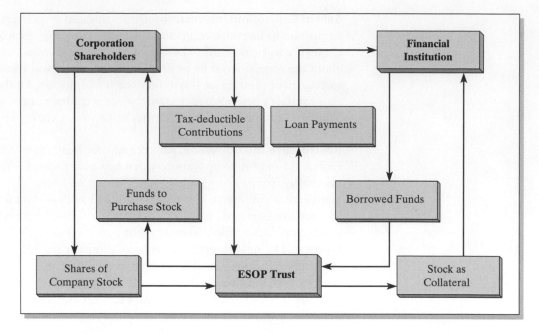

Owners get to sell off their stock at whatever annual pace appeals to them. There's no cost to the employees, who eventually get to take over the company, and for the company the cost of the buyout is fully deductible.

Sell to an International Buyer. In an increasingly global marketplace, small U.S. businesses have become attractive buyout targets for foreign companies. Foreign buyers—mostly European—buy more than 1,000 U.S. businesses each year. In most instances, foreign companies buy U.S. businesses to gain access to a lucrative growing market. They look for a team of capable managers, whom they typically retain for a given time period. They also want companies that are profitable, stable, and growing.

Selling to foreign buyers can have disadvantages, however. They typically purchase 100 percent of a company, thereby making the previous owner merely an employee. Relationships with foreign owners also can be difficult to manage.

Ensure a Smooth Transition

Once the parties have negotiated a deal, the challenge of making a smooth transition immediately arises. No matter how well planned the sale is, there are always surprises. For instance, the new owner may have ideas for changing the business—perhaps radically—that cause a great deal of stress and anxiety among employees and the previous owner. Charged with such emotion and uncertainty, the transition phase is always difficult and frustrating and sometimes painful. To avoid a bumpy transition, a business buyer should do the following:

- *Concentrate on communicating with employees.* Business sales are fraught with uncertainty and anxiety, and employees need reassurance. Take the time to explain your plans for the company.
- *Be honest with employees.* Avoid telling them only what they want to hear.
- *Listen to employees.* They have intimate knowledge of the business and its strengths and weaknesses and usually can offer valuable suggestions. Keep your door and your ears open and come in as somebody who's going to be good for the entire organization.

> ■ *Devote time to selling your vision for the company to its key stakeholders, including major customers, suppliers, bankers, and others.*
> ■ *Consider asking the seller to serve as a consultant until the transition is complete.* The previous owner can be a valuable resource.

▌ ▐ ▐ Chapter Review

1. Understand the advantages and disadvantages of buying an existing business.
   - The *advantages* of buying an existing business include obtaining a successful business that may continue to be successful; the business may already have the best location; employees and suppliers are already established; equipment is installed and its productive capacity known; inventory is in place and trade credit established; the owner hits the ground running; the buyer can use the expertise of the previous owner; and the business may be a bargain.
   - The *disadvantages* of buying an existing business include obtaining an existing business that may be for sale because it is deteriorating; the previous owner may have created ill will; employees inherited with the business may not be suitable; its location may have become unsuitable; equipment and facilities may be obsolete; change and innovation are hard to implement; inventory may be outdated; accounts receivable may be worth less than face value; and the business may be overpriced.

2. Define the steps involved in the *right* way to buy a business.
   - Buying a business can be a treacherous experience unless the buyer is well prepared. The right way to buy a business is by analyzing your skills, abilities, and interests to determine the ideal business for you; preparing a list of potential candidates, including those that might be in the "hidden market"; investigating and evaluating candidate businesses and evaluating the best one; exploring financing options before you actually need the money; and, finally, ensuring a smooth transition.
   - Rushing into a deal can be the biggest mistake a business buyer can make. Before closing a deal, every business buyer should investigate five critical areas: (1) Why does the owner wish to sell? Look for the *real* reason. (2) Determine the physical condition of the business. Consider both the building and its location. (3) Conduct a thorough analysis of the market for your products or services. Who are the present and potential customers? Conduct an equally thorough analysis of competitors, both direct and indirect. How do they operate and why do customers prefer them? (4) Consider all of the legal aspects that might constrain the expansion and growth of the business. Did you comply with the provisions of a bulk transfer? Negotiate a restrictive covenant? Consider ongoing legal liabilities? (5) Analyze the financial condition of the business, looking at financial statements, income tax returns, and especially cash flow.

3. Describe the various methods used in the valuation of a business.
   - Placing a value on a business is partly an art and partly a science. There is no single best method for determining the value of a business. The following techniques (with several variations) are useful: the balance sheet technique (adjusted balance sheet technique); the earnings approach (excess earnings method, capitalized earnings approach, and discounted future earnings approach); and the market approach.

4. Discuss the process of negotiating the deal.
   - Selling a business takes time, patience, and preparation to locate a suitable buyer, strike a deal, and make the transition. Sellers must always structure the deal with tax consequences in mind. Common exit strategies include a straight business sale, forming a family limited partnership, selling a controlling interest in the business, restructuring the company, selling to an international buyer, using a two-step sale, and establishing an employee stock ownership plan (ESOP).
   - The first rule of negotiating is never confuse price with value. In a business sale, the party who is the better negotiator usually comes out on top. Before beginning negotiations, a buyer should identify the factors that are affecting the negotiations and then develop a negotiating strategy. The best deals are the result of a cooperative relationship based on trust.

▌▌▌ Discussion Questions

1. What advantages can an entrepreneur who buys a business gain over one who starts a business from scratch?
2. How would you go about determining the value of the assets of a business if you were unfamiliar with them?
3. Why do so many entrepreneurs run into trouble when they buy an existing business? Outline the steps involved in the *right* way to buy a business.
4. When evaluating an existing business that is for sale, what areas should an entrepreneur consider? Briefly summarize the key elements of each area.
5. How should a buyer evaluate a business's goodwill?
6. What is a restrictive covenant? Is it fair to ask the seller of a travel agency located in a small town to sign a restrictive covenant for one year covering a 20-square-mile area? Explain.
7. How much negative information can you expect the seller to give you about the business? How can a prospective buyer find out such information?
8. Why is it so difficult for buyers and sellers to agree on a price for a business?
9. Which method of valuing a business is best? Why?
10. Outline the different exit strategies available to a seller.
11. Explain the buyer's position in a typical negotiation for a business. Explain the seller's position. What tips would you offer a buyer about to begin negotiating the purchase of a business?

Buying an Existing Business

Business PlanPro

If you are considering buying an existing business, go to Chapter 5 of Business Plan Pro, where you will find a series of questions to guide you through the process of analyzing prospective businesses for sale. Buying a business is a process filled with potential pitfalls, and the best way to circumvent them is to avoid rushing into a decision. Buying a business the right way requires you to take the time to thoroughly investigate the prospective business by conducting due diligence. The analysis in this section of Business Plan Pro will guide you through this process, which involves investigating five critical areas of the business and the potential deal.

1. Why does the owner want to sell?
2. What is the true nature of the firm's assets?
3. What is the market potential for the company's products and/or services?
4. What legal aspects of the business are hidden risks?
5. Is the business financially sound?

When you complete this exercise, you are ready to complete the Your Company section of Business Plan Pro.

Chapter 6
Crafting a Winning Business Plan

*In preparing for battle, I have always found that plans
are useless, but planning is indispensable.*
—DWIGHT EISENHOWER

Often the search proves more profitable than the goal.
—E. L. KONIGSBURG

Upon completion of this chapter, you will be able to:

1. Explain why every entrepreneur should create a business plan.

2. Describe the elements of a solid business plan.

3. Explain the three tests every business plan must pass.

4. Understand the keys to making an effective business plan presentation.

5. Explain the "five Cs of credit" and why they are important to potential lenders and investors reading business plans.

S tarting a business requires lots of planning, and one of the most important activities an entrepreneur should undertake before launching a company is building a solid business plan. It is the best insurance against becoming just another business failure statistic. A large body of evidence suggests that, whatever their size, companies that engage in business planning outperform those that do not. For entrepreneurs, a business plan is:

- a systematic, realistic evaluation of a venture's chances for success in the market.
- a way to determine the principal risks facing the venture.
- a game plan for managing the business successfully.
- a tool for comparing actual results against targeted performance.
- an important tool for attracting capital in the challenging hunt for money.

This chapter describes how to build and use this vital business document, and it will help entrepreneurs create business plans that will guide them on their entrepreneurial journey and will help them attract the capital they need to launch and grow their businesses.

Why Develop a Business Plan?

1. Explain why every entrepreneur should create a business plan.

A **business plan** is a written summary of an entrepreneur's proposed business venture, its operational and financial details, its marketing opportunities and strategy, and its managers' skills and abilities. There is no substitute for a well-prepared business plan, and there are no shortcuts to creating one. The plan serves as an entrepreneur's road map on the journey toward building a successful business. One writer says that "a business plan should be the place where the map is drawn, for, as every traveler knows, a journey is a lot less risky when you have directions."[1] In essence, a business plan describes the direction the company is taking, what its goals are, where it wants to be, and how it's going to get there. The plan is written proof that an entrepreneur has performed the necessary research and has studied the business opportunity adequately. A business plan is an entrepreneur's best insurance against launching a business destined to fail or mismanaging a potentially successful company.

The business plan serves two essential functions. First and more important, it guides the company's operations by charting its future course and devising a strategy for following it. The plan provides a battery of tools—a mission statement, goals, objectives, budgets, financial forecasts, target markets, and strategies—to help managers lead the company successfully. It gives managers and employees a sense of direction, but only if everyone is involved in creating or updating it. As more team members become committed to making the plan work, it takes on special meaning. It gives everyone targets to shoot for, and it provides a yardstick for measuring actual performance against those targets, especially in the crucial and chaotic start-up phase. Plus, writing a plan requires entrepreneurs to get an in-depth understanding of the industries in which they plan to compete and how their companies fit into them. Finally, creating a plan forces entrepreneurs to subject their ideas to the test of reality: Can this business actually produce a profit and sustain itself?

The greatest waste of a completed business plan is to let it sit unused on a shelf collecting dust. When properly done, a plan becomes an integral and natural part of a company. In other words, successful entrepreneurs actually *use* their business plans to help them

Company Example →

build strong companies. *Every month Craig Knouf, CEO of Associated Business Systems (ABS), an office-equipment supplier in Portland, Oregon, distributes the company's business plan to the seven vice presidents who report to him, and in the resulting planning session, they compare their divisions' and the overall company's actual results to the goals set forth in the*

Craig Knouf, CEO of Associated Business Systems, uses his business plan to make his company more competitive. Every month, Knouf and the company's top managers meet to compare actual results with the objectives established in the plan and to make managerial adjustments based on what they learn.

plan. When the plan and the actual results don't match, the managers try to determine why and then rewrite the business plan accordingly. Knouf and his top managers also devote two full days each year to a planning retreat where they discuss, evaluate, and revise ABS's mission and long-term goals. Knouf says this dedicated approach to actually using the business plan the management team develops has been a vital part of helping the 110-employee company reach $21.5 million in annual sales. For example, when the monthly planning sessions began to show that demand for scanning software was climbing, Knouf and his team spotted the trend and were able to broaden that part of ABS's product line quickly. With the help of the revised business plan, ABS saw sales of scanning software double to $3.1 million in just one year.[2]

The second function of the business plan is to attract lenders and investors. Too often small business owners approach potential lenders and investors without having prepared to sell themselves and their business concept. "Lenders [and investors] want to see solid, incisive business plans that clearly demonstrate an entrepreneur's creditworthiness and his ability to build and manage a profitable company," says a partner in a venture capital firm.[3] Simply scribbling a few rough figures on a note pad to support a loan application is not enough. Applying for loans or attempting to attract investors without a solid business plan rarely attracts needed capital. The best way to secure the necessary capital is to prepare a sound business plan. The quality of an entrepreneur's business plan weighs heavily in the final decision to lend or invest funds. It is also potential lenders' and investors' first impression of the company and its managers. Therefore, the finished product should be highly polished and professional in both form and content.

Company Example →

William Hyman, owner of Comprehensive Automotive Reclamation Services (CARS), the largest auto salvage yard in the nation, used a detailed business plan to attract $24 million in capital to purchase and install the equipment he needed to create his one-of-a-kind salvage operation. Hyman's plan showed the special equipment his business would need, how much it would cost, and the unique advantages his design would give the company. The CARS "disassembly line" can dismantle up to 30,000 vehicles a year, compared to about 600 at the average junkyard, and can reclaim 99 percent of the material in them, compared to just 75 percent at a typical salvage operation. After reviewing Hyman's business plan and meeting the entrepreneur, a top manager at one large company was so impressed with the company's competitive edge that he invested $2 million![4]

A plan is a reflection of its creator. It should demonstrate that an entrepreneur has thought seriously about the venture and what will make it succeed. Preparing a solid plan demonstrates that an entrepreneur has taken the time to conduct the necessary research and to commit the idea to paper. Building a plan also forces an entrepreneur to consider both the positive and the negative aspects of the business. A detailed and thoughtfully developed business plan makes a positive first impression on those who read it. In most cases, potential lenders and investors read a business plan before they ever meet with the entrepreneur behind it. Sophisticated investors will not take the time to meet with an entrepreneur whose business plan fails to reflect a serious investment of time and energy in defining a promising business opportunity. They know that an entrepreneur who lacks the discipline to develop a good business plan likely lacks the discipline to run a business.

Entrepreneurs should not allow others to prepare a business plan for them because outsiders cannot understand the business or envision the proposed company as well as the entrepreneurs can. Entrepreneurs are the driving force behind the business idea and are the ones who can best convey the vision and the enthusiasm they have for transforming their ideas into a successful business. Also, because the entrepreneurs will make the presentation to potential lenders and investors, they must understand every detail of the business plan. Otherwise, entrepreneurs cannot present it convincingly and in most cases the financial institution or investor will reject it. Answering the often difficult questions potential lenders and investors ask requires that entrepreneurs completely understand the details of their plans. Alice Medrich, cofounder of Cocolat, a manufacturer of specialty candies and desserts, recalls her first attempt at presenting her business plan:

> First of all, I went to the bank, and I was so ill-prepared and so insecure about what I was asking about . . . I was extremely insecure with a banker. I didn't know how to describe what I was doing with any confidence. I did not know how to present a business plan. And he was condescending to me. Looking back on it, I can understand why: I wasn't prepared . . . We didn't get the loan.[5]

Investors want to feel confident that an entrepreneur has realistically evaluated the risk involved in the new venture and has a strategy for addressing it. They also want to see proof that a business will become profitable and produce a reasonable return on their investment.

Perhaps the best way to understand the need for a business plan is to recognize the validity of the "two-thirds rule," which says that only two-thirds of the entrepreneurs with a sound and viable new business idea will find financial backing. Those who do find financial backing will only get two-thirds of what they initially requested, and it will take them two-thirds longer to get the financing than they anticipated.[6] The most effective strategy for avoiding the two-thirds rule is to build a business plan!

Sometimes the greatest service a business plan provides an entrepreneur is the realization that "it just won't work." The time to find out that a business idea won't succeed is in the planning stages *before* committing significant money, time, and effort to the venture. It is much less expensive to make mistakes on paper than in reality. In other cases, a business plan reveals important problems to overcome before launching a company. Exposing these flaws and then addressing them enhances the chances of a venture's success.

The real value in preparing a plan is not so much in the plan itself as it is in the *process* the entrepreneur goes through to create the plan. Although the finished product is useful, the process of building the plan requires entrepreneurs to subject their ideas to an objective, critical evaluation from many different angles. What entrepreneurs learn about their industries, target markets, financial requirements, competition, and other factors is essential to making their ventures successful. Simply put, building a business plan reduces the risk and uncertainty of launching a company by teaching an entrepreneur to do it the right way!

Table 6.1 describes the four bases every business plan should cover.

Table 6.1

Covering the Bases in a Business Plan

What do potential lenders and investors look for in a business plan? Although there's no surefire method for satisfying every lender or investor, entrepreneurs who emphasize the following four points will cover their bases.

- *Key people.* Potential lenders and investors want to see proof of the experience, skills, and abilities of a venture's key players. Even though the company may be new, it helps for potential lenders and investors to see that it's not being run by a bunch of amateurs.
- *Promising opportunity.* A basic ingredient in the success of any business venture is the presence of a real market opportunity. The best way to show that such an opportunity exists is with facts. Smart entrepreneurs use the results of market research and an industry analysis to prove that the market for a business is rapidly expanding or that it is already large enough to support a niche profitably. It is also important to show how a venture will gain a competitive advantage in its market segment.
- *Business context.* A business plan should also demonstrate that an entrepreneur understands how macroeconomic factors such as inflation and interest rates affect the business. Another important issue for many businesses is the role that government regulation plays.
- *Risks and rewards.* A business plan should cover the risks a venture faces without dwelling on them. Investors and lenders like to see plans that describe the most serious threats to a venture and how entrepreneurs will deal with them. A plan should address the rewards investors can expect from the company's success. That means defining lenders' and investors' exit paths. How will the company repay lenders and "cash out" investors? Is an initial public offering in the future? A sale to a larger company?

Source: Adapted from Brent Pollock, "Remember the Investor," *Success,* October 1997, p. 24.

The Elements of a Business Plan

2. Describe the elements of a solid business plan.

Smart entrepreneurs recognize that every business plan is unique and must be tailor-made. They avoid the off-the-shelf, "cookie-cutter" approach that produces look-alike plans. The elements of a business plan may be standard, but how entrepreneurs tell their story should be unique and reflect their personal excitement about the new venture. If this is a first attempt at writing a business plan, it may be very helpful to seek the advice of those with experience in this process. Consultants with Small Business Development Centers, accountants, business professors, business planning professionals, and attorneys can be excellent sources of advice in refining a business plan. Remember, however, not to allow someone else to write your plan!

Business planning software, such as Business Plan Pro that is available with this book, has become quite popular in recent years. These software packages provide entrepreneurs with templates—and examples—for creating a plan for their businesses; entrepreneurs respond to an extensive series of questions that guide them through the process of developing a business plan. Business Plan Pro, for example, covers every aspect of a business plan from the executive summary to the cash flow forecasts. One danger of using business planning software is that these packages tend to produce uniform plans that do little to set a creative business idea apart from the competition. Used properly, however, they can be a helpful way to organize the information needed for the solid plan and can prevent an entrepreneur from overlooking crucial parts of the plan.

Initially, the prospect of writing a business plan may appear to be overwhelming. Many entrepreneurs would rather launch their companies and "see what happens" than invest the necessary time and energy defining and researching their target markets, defining their strategies, and mapping out their finances. After all, building a plan is hard work! However, it is hard work that pays many dividends, and not all of them are immediately apparent. Entrepreneurs who invest their time and energy building plans are better prepared to face the hostile environment in which their companies will compete than those who do not. Earlier we said that a business plan is like a road map that guides an entrepreneur on the journey to building a successful business. If you were making a journey to a particular destination through unfamiliar, harsh, and dangerous territory, would you rather ride with someone equipped with a road map and a trip itinerary or with someone who didn't believe in road maps or in planning trips, layovers, and destinations? Although building a business plan does not guarantee success, it does raise an entrepreneur's chances of succeeding in business.

A business plan typically ranges from 25 to 50 pages in length. Shorter plans usually are too sketchy to be of any value, and those much longer than this run the risk of never getting used or read! This section explains the most common elements of a business plan. However, entrepreneurs must recognize that, like every business venture, every business plan is unique. Entrepreneurs should view the following elements as a starting point for building a plan and should modify them as needed to better tell the story of their new venture.

The Executive Summary

To summarize the presentation to each financial institution or potential investor, the entrepreneur should write an executive summary. It should be concise—a maximum of two pages—and should summarize all of the relevant points of the proposed deal. After reading the executive summary, anyone should be able to understand the entire business concept and what differentiates the company from the competition. The executive summary is a synopsis of the entire plan, capturing its essence in a capsulized form. It should explain the basic business model and the problem the business will solve for customers, briefly describing the owners and key employees, target market(s), financial highlights (e.g., sales and earnings projections, the dollar amount requested, how the funds will be used, and how and when any loans will be repaid or investments cashed out), and the company's competitive advantage.

The executive summary is a written version of what is known as "the elevator pitch." Imagine yourself on an elevator with a potential lender or investor. Only the two of you are on the elevator, and you have that person's undivided attention for the duration of the ride, but the building is not very tall! To convince the investor that your business idea is a great investment, you must boil your message down to its essence—key points that you can communicate in a matter of one or two minutes.

The executive summary is designed to capture the reader's attention. If it misses, the chances of the remainder of the plan being read are minimal. A coherent, well-developed summary introducing the rest of the plan establishes a favorable first impression of the business and the entrepreneur behind it and can go a long way toward obtaining financing. A good executive summary should enable the reader to understand the business concept and how it will make money as well as answering the ultimate question from an investor or lender: "What's in it for me?" Although the executive summary is the first part of the business plan, it should be the last section written.

IN THE FOOTSTEPS OF AN ENTREPRENEUR...

A Short Ride and a Focused Pitch

As she stepped onto the elevator, graduate student Margaret Price felt her stomach twinge. She wasn't worried about the short elevator ride in the 28-story Wachovia Center in Winston-Salem, North Carolina; she was more concerned with making sure her presentation to the venture capitalist who was sharing the ride would go smoothly. Price wasn't about to confront a total stranger with her business idea;

it was all part of a unique entrepreneurial competition. Unlike a typical business plan competition, however, this one involves no PowerPoint presentations, props, displays, or handouts. Plus, it actually takes place in an elevator! When the elevator reaches the top floor, entrepreneurs can leave nothing with the venture capitalist except a business card.

Sound a bit strange?

It's the Babcock Elevator Competition sponsored by the Angell Center for Entrepreneurship at Wake Forest University, where students actually ride an elevator with a venture capitalist and have the opportunity to pitch their business ideas in just two minutes. "The competition was designed to simulate reality," says Stan Mandel, creator of the event and director of the Angell Center for Entrepreneurship. The object of the competition is to hone a two-minute "elevator pitch" presentation and deliver it to a venture capitalist during an actual elevator ride. Unlike some business plan competitions, winners do not actually receive any money. However, they do win the chance to spend 30 minutes in face-to-face conversations with the venture capitalists who judge the competition. This more formal presentation often leads to financing for the winners' business ventures. Since the competition began in 2000, judging venture capitalists and others have invested millions of dollars in the companies students have created.

A winner in a recent Babcock Elevator Competition that involved 25 teams from 17 of the nation's top universities, Price pitched Altadonics, the company she formed with her husband and father-in-law that offers a unique method of "cloning" dentures so that lost or broken dentures can be replaced in one to three days rather than the normal four to six weeks. Altadonics manufactures a device that duplicates a person's dentures by creating a mold from the wearer's existing dentures. "[The elevator competition] was nerve-wracking," says Price. "The challenge was getting all of that information presented in such a short time. We spent two or three weeks just preparing the material, making sure all the questions were answered," she says. "It goes by real fast."

Winning the competition paid off for the Prices and Altadonics. With funding that came from winning the elevator competition, the Prices completed their first phase of product testing and launched their venture in 2002. That's exactly the outcome Mandel wants to see. "This is the opportunity of a lifetime for entrepreneurial students with the right business plan," says Mandel. "In addition to making an outstanding formal presentation—as brilliant as it is concise—the students need an exceptional entrepreneurial team with a compelling plan."

1. Why is it important for an entrepreneur to develop an elevator pitch?
2. Assume that you are a judge in the elevator competition. What characteristics would you look for in a business as you take that elevator ride?
3. Use the resources in the library and on the World Wide Web to develop a list of suggestions and advice for entrepreneurs presenting their business plans to lenders and investors.

Sources: Adapted from Dusty Donaldson, "Entrepreneurial MBA Students Pitch Winning Business Plans During Two-Minute Elevator Ride with Venture Capitalists," *Babcock News and Events,* March 26, 2003, www.mba.wfu.edu/prlib/prelev0303b.html; Lori L. Riley, "Rising to the Top," *Venture,* July 2003, http://altadonics.com/newsroom2.shtml; Nichole L. Torres, "Movin' On Up," *Entrepreneur,* September 2002, http://altadonics.com/newsroom1.shtml; Laura Hilgers, "Going Up?" *Attaché,* January 2004, pp. 43–45.

Mission Statement

As you learned in Chapter 2, a mission statement expresses an entrepreneur's vision for what his or her company is, what it is to become, and what it stands for. It is the broadest expression of a company's purpose and defines the direction in which it will move. It serves as the thesis statement for the entire business plan.

Company History

The owner of an existing small business should prepare a brief history of the operation, highlighting the significant financial and operational events in the company's life. This section should describe when and why the company was formed, how it has evolved over time, and what the owner envisions for the future. It should highlight the successful accomplishment of past objectives and should convey the company's image in the marketplace.

Business and Industry Profile

This section should provide an overview of the industry or market segment in which the new venture will operate. Industry data such as market size, growth trends, and the relative economic and competitive strengths of the major firms in the industry all set the stage for a better understanding of the viability of a new product or service. Strategic issues such as ease of market entry and exit, the ability to achieve economies of scale or scope, and the existence of cyclical or seasonal economic trends further help to evaluate a new venture. This part of the plan also should describe significant industry trends and an overall outlook for its future. Information about the evolution of an industry may reveal insights into its competitive dynamics.

Industry trade associations can provide much of the background information required for the industry analysis portion of a plan. Trade associations collect and publish valuable statistical information on their industries as well as studies and reports about emerging trends that affect companies in those industries. Also, the *U.S. Industrial Outlook Handbook* is an excellent reference that profiles a variety of industries and offers projections for future trends in them. Another useful resource of industry and economic information is the *Summary of Commentary on Current Economic Conditions,* more commonly known as *The Beige Book.* Published eight times a year by the Federal Reserve, it provides detailed statistics and trends in key business sectors and in the overall economy. *The Beige Book* offers valuable information on topics ranging from tourism and housing starts to consumer spending and wage rates and is available on the World Wide Web. Articles in business periodicals can be useful in identifying key success factors in an industry, forces shaping competition in it, forecasts for its future sales, and other useful information. Online searches often reveal hundreds (sometimes thousands) of articles that can help an entrepreneur write a thorough industry analysis.

The industry analysis should also address the profitability of the businesses in the targeted market segment. This section also should contain a discussion of the significance of the entry or exit of firms or the effect that consolidations and mergers have had on the competitive behavior in the market. An entrepreneur also should mention any events that have significantly altered the industry in the past 10 years. For example, the owner of a travel agency that specializes in planning adventure vacations would include the impact that online travel services have had on the industry and how her business will deal with online competition.

When summarizing their companies' backgrounds, entrepreneurs should describe the present state-of-the-art products in the industry. They should also identify the current applications of the product or service in the market and include projections for future applications.

This section also should include a statement of the company's general business goals and a narrower definition of its immediate objectives. Together they should spell out what the business plans to accomplish, how, when, and who will do it. **Goals** are broad, long-range statements of what a company plans to do in the distant future that guide its overall direction and express its raison d'être. In other words, they answer the question: "Why am I in business?" Answering such a basic question appears to be obvious, but, in fact, many entrepreneurs cannot define the basis of their businesses.

Objectives are short-term, specific performance targets that are attainable, measurable, and controllable. Every objective should reflect some general business goal and include a technique for measuring progress toward its accomplishment. To be meaningful, an objective must have a time frame for achievement. Both goals and objectives should relate to the company's basic mission. In other words, accomplishing each objective should move a business closer to achieving its goals, which, in turn, should move it closer to its mission.

Business Strategy

An even more important part of the business plan is the owner's view of the strategy needed to meet—and beat—the competition. In the previous section, entrepreneurs defined where they want to take their business by establishing goals and objectives. This section addresses the question of how to get there—business strategy. Here entrepreneurs must explain how they plan to gain a competitive edge in the market and what sets their business apart from the competition. They should comment on how they plan to achieve business goals and objectives in the face of competition and government regulation and should identify the image the business will project. An important theme in this section is what makes the company unique in the eyes of its customers. One of the quickest routes to business failure is trying to sell "me-too" products or services that offer customers nothing newer, better, bigger, faster, or different. The foundation for this part of the business plan comes from the material in Chapter 2.

This section of the business plan should outline the methods the company can use to meet the key success factors cited earlier. If, for example, making sales to repeat customers is critical to success, an entrepreneur must devise a plan of action for achieving a customer retention rate that exceeds that of existing companies in the market.

Description of Firm's Product/Service

An entrepreneur should describe the company's overall product line, giving an overview of how customers use its goods or services. Drawings, diagrams, and illustrations may be required if the product is highly technical. It is best to write product and service descriptions so that laypeople can understand them. A statement of a product's position in the product life cycle might also be helpful. An entrepreneur should include a summary of any patents, trademarks, or copyrights protecting the product or service from infringement by competitors. Finally, the plan should include an honest comparison of the company's product or service with those of competitors, citing specific advantages or improvements that make its goods or services unique and indicating plans for creating the next generation of goods and services that will evolve from the present product line. What competitive advantage does the venture's product or service offer? Ideally, a product or service offers high-value benefits to customers and is difficult for competitors to duplicate.

One danger entrepreneurs must avoid in this part of the plan is the tendency to dwell excessively on the features of their products or services. This problem is the result of the "fall-in-love-with-your-product" syndrome, which often afflicts inventors. Customers, lenders, and investors care less about how much work, genius, and creativity went into a product or service than about what it will do for them. The emphasis of this section should be on defining the benefits customers get by purchasing the company's products or services, rather than on just a "nuts and bolts" description of the features of those products or services. A **feature** is a descriptive fact about a product or service (e.g., "an ergonomically designed, more comfortable handle"). A **benefit** is what the customer gains from the product or service feature (e.g., "fewer problems with carpal tunnel syndrome and increased productivity"). Advertising legend Leo Burnett once said, "Don't tell the people how good you make the goods; tell them how good your goods make them."[7] This part of the plan must describe how a business will transform tangible product or service features into important but often intangible customer benefits—for example, lower energy bills, faster access to the Internet, less time writing checks to pay monthly bills, greater flexibility in building floating structures, shorter time required to learn a foreign language, or others. Remember: *Customers buy*

Table 6.2

Transforming Features
into Meaningful Benefits

For many entrepreneurs, there's a big gap between what a business is selling and what its customers are buying. The following worksheet is designed to eliminate that gap.

First, develop a list of the features your company's product or service offers. List as many as you can think of, which may be 25 or more. Consider features that relate to price, performance, convenience, location, customer service, delivery, reputation, reliability, quality, features, and other aspects.

Next, group features with similar themes together by circling them with the same color ink. Then translate those groups of features into specific benefits to your customers by addressing the question "What's in it for me?" from the customer's perspective. (Note: It usually is a good idea to ask actual customers why they buy from you. They usually give reasons that you never thought of.) As many as six or eight product or service (or even company) features may translate into a single customer benefit, such as saving money or time or making life safer. Don't ignore intangible benefits such as increased status; they can be more important than tangible benefits.

Finally, combine all of the benefits you identify into a single sentence or paragraph. Use this statement as a key point in your business plan and to guide your company's marketing strategy.

Features	Benefits

Benefit Statement:

Source: Adapted from Kim T. Gordon, "Position for Profits," *Business Start-Ups,* February 1998, pp. 18–20.

benefits, not product or service features. Table 6.2 offers an easy exercise designed to help entrepreneurs translate their products' or services' features into meaningful customer benefits.

Company Example ➡

Adam Rizika, his brother Bob, and friend Scott Brazina found the basis for their business in a product that Adam's employer had rejected. The product was based on a new type of reflective technology that enabled fabrics to be coated with a material that reflects light. An improvement on traditional reflective garments that rely on light-reflecting stripes, the new fabric, called illumiNITE, provides a full reflective silhouette of the person wearing it, making it ideal for runners, cyclists, children, highway workers, firefighters, and others. After forming their company, Reflective Technologies, and applying for a patent, the entrepreneurs focused on marketing their unique material. They spent a year preparing their business plan, and their first step was to develop a matrix that highlighted the advantages illumiNITE offered over existing products and the customer benefits it provided. "New technology isn't a plus if it doesn't translate into a consumer benefit," says Adam Rizika.[8]

Manufacturers should describe their production process, strategic raw materials required, sources of supply they will use, and their costs. They should also summarize the production method and illustrate the plant layout. If the product is based on a patented or proprietary process, a description (including diagrams, if necessary) of its unique market advantages is helpful. It is also helpful to explain the company's environmental impact and how the entrepreneur plans to mitigate any negative environmental consequences the process may produce.

Marketing Strategy

One of the most important tasks a business plan must fulfill is proving that a real market exists for a company's goods or services (or showing that one does not exist and that launching a business would be a mistake). A business plan must identify and describe a company's target customers and their characteristics and habits. Defining the target audience and its potential is one of the most important—and most challenging—parts of building a business plan. Narrowing its target market enables a small company to focus its limited resources on serving the needs of a specific group of customers rather than attempting to satisfy the desires of the mass market. Creating a successful business depends on an entrepreneur's ability to attract real customers who are willing and able to spend real money to buy its products or services. Perhaps the worst marketing error entrepreneurs can commit is failing to define their target market and trying to make their business "everything to everybody." Small companies usually are much more successful focusing on a specific market niche or niches where they can excel at meeting customers' special needs or wants.

Company Example ➡️

In 1985, Peter Capolino, owner of Mitchell & Ness Nostalgia Company, a sporting goods company founded in 1904, spotted an opportunity to make and sell high-quality replicas of the jerseys of famous sports figures. Capolino's idea proved to be so successful that, by the end of the year, he dropped all of the other items in the company's product line and focused exclusively on selling the jerseys. Initially, Capolino targeted college-educated men in the 35 to 75 age group with his product offerings, and flourished. Before long, he discovered an entirely different target audience for his vintage jersey replicas when members of the rap group Outkast wore the company's jerseys in one of their music videos. Capolino realized that his company also could target young urban customers as well. Priced from $300 to $500, the jerseys have become part of the wardrobes of older fans who remember watching sports legends Gale Sayers, Johnny Unitas, and Hank Aaron as well as those of the new generation of sports fans who simply like the look of a vintage jersey.[9]

Successful entrepreneurs know that a solid understanding of their target markets is the first step in building an effective marketing strategy. Indeed, every other aspect of marketing depends on their having a clear picture of their customers and their unique needs and wants. Proving that a profitable market exists involves two steps: showing customer interest and documenting market claims.

Showing Customer Interest. An important element of any business plan is showing how a company's product or service provides a customer benefit or solves a customer

Peter Capolino, owner of Mitchell & Ness Nostalgia Company, originally targeted men in the 35 to 75 age range as the primary customers for his company's vintage sports jerseys. After the members of the rap group Outkast wore the company's jerseys, however, Capolino shifted his marketing strategy to include young urban customers who appreciate the look of a vintage sports jersey.

problem. Entrepreneurs must be able to prove that their target customers actually need or want their goods or services and are willing to pay for them. Venture capitalist Kathryn Gould, who has reviewed thousands of business plans, says that she looks for plans that focus on "target customers with a compelling reason to buy. The product must be a 'must-have.' "[10] *When Marc Shuman launched Garage-Tek in 2000, his business plan defined "garage clutter" as the customer problem that his product, a garage organizational system, would solve. (How many homeowners never park their cars in their garages because they are so cluttered with junk?) The Garage-Tek system consists of patented slotted wall panels and a collection of modular attachments, including cabinets, shelves, bike racks, workbenches, and other items made of gray steel and plastic that, says Shuman, can transform a garage. Because the average Garage-Tek installation is $4,500, Shuman defines the company's target market as owners of homes worth an average of $350,000, which includes the top 20 percent of the nation's 50 million houses with garages.[11]*

Company Example

Proving a viable market exists for a product or service is relatively straightforward for a company already in business but can be quite difficult for an entrepreneur with only an idea or a prototype. In this case an entrepreneur might offer the prototype to several potential customers in order to get written testimonials and evaluations to show to investors. Or the owner could sell the product to several customers at a discount. This would prove that there are potential customers for the product and would enable demonstrations of the product in operation. Getting a product into customers' hands is also an excellent way to get valuable feedback that can lead to significant design improvements and increased sales down the road.

Documenting Market Claims. Too many business plans rely on vague generalizations such as, "This market is so huge that if we get just 1 percent of it, we will break even in eight months." Statements such as these usually reflect nothing more than an entrepreneur's unbridled optimism, and in most cases, are quite unrealistic! *When Dave and Dan Hanlon relaunched the Excelsior-Henderson motorcycle brand in 1993, they hoped to carve a profitable niche in a market dominated by Harley-Davidson. With their business plan, the Hanlons raised $15 million in venture capital before making an initial public offering that brought in an additional $28 million. Despite rave reviews about their motorcycles, Excelsior-Henderson filed for bankruptcy after seven years of development and eight months of production. One industry expert says the company failed because the Hanlons "overestimated the market, and they didn't do enough market research to determine the styling, the performance elements, and the price points that would stand the best chance [of success]."[12]*

Company Example

Entrepreneurs must support claims of market size and growth rates with *facts*, and that requires market research. Results of market surveys, customer questionnaires, and demographic studies lend credibility to an entrepreneur's frequently optimistic sales projections. (Refer to the market research techniques and resources in Chapter 7.) Quantitative market data are important because they form the basis for all of the company's financial projections in the business plan. *When Ken and Debra Hey were considering launching a company that sold boatlifts for high-end boats, his original plan was to sell five boatlifts in five months. They decided to test the entrepreneurial waters at a Seattle boat show and came away with orders for 50 lifts, tangible proof that the demand for his product was strong even though the Heys priced their lifts 30 percent higher than their competitors by emphasizing quality. Today, the Heys' company, Sunstream Corporation, has sales of more than $7 million and is one of the fastest growing companies in the state of Washington.[13]*

Company Example

One effective documentation technique involves **business prototyping**, in which entrepreneurs test their business models on a small scale before committing serious resources to a business that might not work. Business prototyping recognizes that every business idea is a hypothesis that needs to be tested before an entrepreneur takes it to full scale. If the test supports the hypothesis and its accompanying assumptions, it is time to launch a company. If the prototype flops, the entrepreneur scraps the business idea with only minimal losses and turns to the next idea.

Company Example →

The World Wide Web makes business prototyping practical, fast, and easy. *Adam Ginsburg was selling billiard tables from a retail store in Los Angeles when the idea of selling billiard tables on eBay, the online auction house, struck him. To test the validity of his idea, Ginsburg listed one of his pool tables on eBay, which, much to his surprise, sold quickly. He listed another table on the auction site, which also sold quickly. Within a year, Ginsburg's online sales effort was so successful that he decided to close his retail shop and sell his line of billiard tables and accessories exclusively online through eBay. Today, Zbilliards generates sales of more than $15 million a year—thanks to Ginsburg's online business prototyping approach.*[14]

One of the main purposes of the marketing section of the plan is to lay the foundation for financial forecasts that follow. Sales, profit, and cash forecasts must be founded on more than wishful thinking. An effective market analysis should identify the following:

Target market: Who are the company's target customers? How many of them are in the company's trading area? What are their characteristics (age, gender, educational level, income, and others)? What do they buy? Why do they buy? When do they buy? What expectations do they have about the product or service? Will the business focus on a niche? How does the company seek to position itself in the market(s) it will pursue? Knowing customers' needs, wants, and habits, what should be the basis for differentiating this new business in their minds?

Advertising and promotion: Only after entrepreneurs understand their companies' target markets can they design a promotion and advertising campaign to reach those customers most effectively and efficiently. Which media are most effective in reaching the target market? How will they be used? How much will the promotional campaign cost? How will the promotional campaign position the company's products or services? How can the company benefit from publicity? How large is the company's promotional budget?

Market size and trends: How large is the potential market? Is it growing or shrinking? Why? Are customers' needs changing? Are sales seasonal? Is demand tied to another product or service?

Location: For many businesses, choosing the right location is a key success factor. For retailers, wholesalers, and service companies, the best location usually is one that is most convenient to their target customers. Using census data and other market research, entrepreneurs can determine the sites with the greatest concentrations of their customers and locate there. Which sites put the company in the path of its target customers? Maps showing customer concentrations (available from census maps and other sources), traffic counts, the number of customers using a particular train station and when, and other similar types of information provide evidence that a solid and sizable customer base exists. Do zoning regulations restrict the use of a site? For manufacturers, the location issue often centers on finding a site near their key raw materials or near their primary customers. Using demographic reports and market research to screen potential sites takes the guesswork out of choosing the "right" location for a business. We will discuss the location decision in more detail in Chapter 16.

Figure 6.1

The Link Between Pricing,
Perceived Quality,
and Company Image

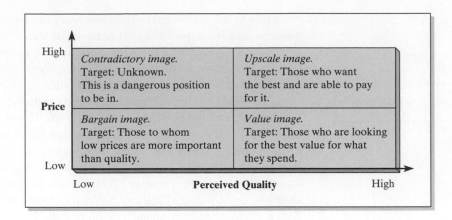

Pricing: What does the product or service cost to produce or deliver? Before opening a restaurant, for example, an entrepreneur should know *exactly* what it will cost to produce each item on the menu. Failing to know the total cost (including the cost of the food as well as labor, rent, advertising, and other indirect costs) of putting a plate in front of a customer is a recipe for failure. As we will discover in Chapter 10 cost is just one part of the pricing equation. Another significant factor to consider is the image a company is trying to create in the market. "Price really is more of a marketing tool than it is a vehicle for cost recovery," says Peter Meyer, author of *Creating and Dominating New Markets.* "People will pay more for a high value product or solution, so be sure to research your [product's or service's] total value."[15]

Other pricing issues: What is the company's overall pricing strategy? Will the planned price support the company's strategy and desired image? (See Figure 6.1.) Given the company's cost structure, will the price produce a profit? How does the planned price compare to those of similar products or services? Are customers willing to pay it? What price tiers exist in the market? How sensitive are customers to price changes? Will the business sell to customers on credit? Will it accept credit cards? Will the company offer discounts? If so, what kinds and how much?

Distribution: How will the product or service be distributed? Will distribution be extensive, selective, or exclusive? What is the average sale? How large will the sales staff be? How will the company compensate its sales force? What are the incentives for salespeople? How many sales calls does it take to close a sale? What can the company do to make it as easy as possible for customers to buy?

This portion of the plan also should describe the channels of distribution that the business will use (the Internet, direct mail, in-house sales force, sales agents, retailers, or others). An entrepreneur should summarize the company's overall pricing strategies and its warranties and guarantees for its products and services.

Competitor Analysis

Entrepreneurs should honestly assess their new ventures' competition. Failing to assess competitors realistically makes entrepreneurs appear to be poorly prepared, naive, or dishonest. Gathering information on competitors' market shares, products, and strategies is usually not difficult. Trade associations, customers, industry journals, sales representatives, and sales literature are valuable sources of data. This section of the plan should focus on demonstrating that the entrepreneur's company has an advantage over its competitors. Who are the company's key competitors? What are their strengths and weaknesses? What are their strategies? What images do they have in the marketplace?

How successful are they? What distinguishes the entrepreneur's product or service from others already on the market, and how will these differences produce a competitive edge?

Firsthand competitor research is particularly valuable. *When Tonya Davis was developing a business plan for the day care center she planned to launch, she visited other day care centers to determine their strengths and weaknesses. She was also able to assess the competition's pricing policies and the range of services they offered, which helped her differentiate her company in the minds of her target customers.*[16]

[Company Example →]

Owners' and Managers' Résumés

The most important factor in the success of a business venture is its management. In financing decisions, financial officers and investors weight heavily the ability and experience of a company's managers. A plan should include the résumés of business officers, key directors, and any person with at least 20 percent ownership in the company. This is the section of the plan in which entrepreneurs have the chance to sell the qualifications and the experience of their management team. Remember: *Lenders and investors prefer experienced managers.* Ideally, they look for managers with at least two years of operating experience in the industry they are targeting.

A résumé should summarize each individual's education, work history (emphasizing managerial responsibilities and duties), and relevant business experience. When compiling a personal profile, an entrepreneur should review the primary reasons for small business failure (refer to Chapter 1) and show how the management team will use its skills and experience to avoid them. Lenders and investors look for the experience, talent, and integrity of the people who will breathe life into the plan. This portion of the plan should show that the company has the right people organized in the right fashion for success. One experienced private investor advises entrepreneurs to remember the following:

■ Ideas and products don't succeed; people do. Show the strength of your management team. A top-notch management team with a variety of proven skills is crucial. Arthur Rock, a legend in the venture capital industry, says, "I invest in people, not ideas."[17]

■ Show the strength of key employees and how you will retain them. Most small companies cannot pay salaries that match those at large businesses, but stock options and other incentives can improve employee retention.

■ Enhance the strength of the management team with a capable, qualified board of advisers. A board of directors or advisers consisting of industry experts lends credibility and can complement the skills of the management team.

Plan of Operation

To complete the description of the business, an entrepreneur should construct an organizational chart identifying the business's key positions and the people occupying them. Assembling a management team with the right stuff is difficult, but keeping it together until the company is established may be even harder. Thus, the entrepreneur should describe briefly the steps taken to encourage important officers to remain with the company. Employment contracts, shares of ownership, and perks are commonly used to keep and motivate key employees.

Finally, a description of the form of ownership (partnership, joint venture, S corporation, LLC, and others), and of any leases, contracts, and other relevant agreements pertaining to the operation is helpful.

Financial Forecasts

To potential lenders and investors, one of the most important sections of the business plan is the financial forecasts an entrepreneur makes. Lenders and investors use past financial statements to judge the health of an existing small company and its ability to repay loans or generate adequate returns. Owners of existing businesses should supply copies of their companies' major financial statements from the past three years. Ideally, these statements should be audited by a certified public accountant because most financial institutions prefer that extra reliability, although a financial review of the statements by an accountant sometimes may be acceptable.

Preparing financial forecasts for a proposed business is more challenging, but with the help of published industry statistics, information from trade associations, and discussions with industry experts or existing business owners in other locations, entrepreneurs can develop reliable forecasts for start-up companies. We will discuss the techniques involved in developing financial forecasts from these and other resources in Chapter 8.

Whether assembling a plan for an existing business or a start-up, an entrepreneur should carefully prepare monthly projected (or pro forma) financial statements for the venture for one year and by quarter for the next two to three years using past operating data, published statistics, and judgment to derive three sets of forecasts of the income statement, balance sheet, cash flow, and schedule of planned capital expenditures. The first stop for most potential lenders and investors is the income statement, which shows the company's revenues, expenses, and the resulting profit. Although they recognize that start-ups often lose money in their early stages, investors and lenders expect to see positive trends in earnings. They also look to see if the gross, operating, and net income margins on the forecasted income statements are consistent with industry averages. From there, investors typically move on to the cash flow statement to judge whether the company is viable over time. Earnings are important, but staying in business requires a company to generate positive cash flow. Entrepreneurs must make sure that they have accumulated enough capital to carry the company until it generates enough cash to support itself. Finally, potential lenders and investors examine the balance sheet, where they see the company's assets (everything it owns), its liabilities (everything it owes), and its net worth (the difference in assets and liabilities). They view intangible assets somewhat suspiciously, especially in start-up companies, and look for potential problems with inventory, which can absorb a company's cash.

There should be forecasts under pessimistic, most likely, and optimistic conditions to reflect the uncertainty of the future. Preparing a set of financial forecasts can be a daunting task for an inexperienced entrepreneur, but spreadsheets can make the job much easier. Entrepreneurs who lack financial aptitude should not hesitate to get help from accountants or consultants when preparing their financial analysis. *Tonya Davis did not have a financial background and was having difficulty creating realistic financial projections for her proposed day care center. She worked with a local accountant to develop financial statements based on most likely, pessimistic, and optimistic sales forecasts.*[18]

It is essential that all three sets of forecasts be realistic. Entrepreneurs must avoid the tendency to "fudge the numbers" just to make their businesses look good. Financial officers compare these projections against published industry standards and can detect unreasonable forecasts. In fact, some venture capitalists automatically discount an entrepreneur's financial projections by as much as 50 percent. Upon completing these forecasts, an entrepreneur should perform a break-even analysis. At what point does the business begin to earn a profit? More important, when will the company's cash flow become positive?

> Company Example

Finally, it is also important to include a statement of the assumptions on which these financial projections are based. Potential lenders and investors want to know how the entrepreneur derived forecasts for sales, cost of goods sold, operating expenses, accounts receivable, collections, inventory, and other such items. Spelling out such assumptions gives a plan more credibility.

In addition to providing valuable information to potential lenders and investors, these projected financial statements help entrepreneurs run their businesses more effectively and more efficiently. They establish important targets for financial performance and make it easier for an entrepreneur to maintain control over routine expenses and capital expenditures. These projected financial statements should *not* outweigh the rest of the plan, however. A common mistake among entrepreneurs creating plans for business start-ups is devoting too much space to financial forecasts that are uncertain at best and spending too little time on the people, the marketing research, and the strategies that will generate the financial results.

The Request for Funds

If an entrepreneur is seeking external financing, the loan or investment proposal section of the business plan should state the purpose of the loan or investment, the amount requested, and the plans for repayment or cashout. One important by-product of preparing a business plan is discovering how much money it will take to launch the business. When describing the purpose of the loan, entrepreneurs must specify how they plan to use the money they are seeking and how it will produce a reasonable return. "You'd be surprised how many people request a loan for a specific amount but can't articulate what they would use the money for," says one banker.[19] General requests for funds such as "for modernization," "working capital," or "expansion" are unlikely to win approval. Instead, descriptions such as "to modernize production facilities by purchasing five new, more efficient looms that will boost productivity by 12 percent" and "to rebuild merchandise inventory for fall sales peak, beginning in early summer" are much more likely to win approval. Entrepreneurs should state the precise amount of money they are requesting and include relevant backup data, such as vendor estimates of costs or past production levels. They also should not hesitate to request the amount of money needed; however, inflating the amount of a loan request in anticipation of the financial officer trying to "talk them down" is a mistake. Remember: *Lenders and investors are familiar with industry cost structures.*

Another important element of the loan or investment proposal is the repayment schedule and exit strategy. A lender's main consideration in granting a loan is the reassurance that the applicant will repay, whereas an investor's major concern is earning a satisfactory rate of return. Financial projections must reflect the firm's ability to repay loans to lenders and to produce adequate yields for investors. Without this proof, a request for funding stands little chance of being accepted. It is necessary for an entrepreneur to produce tangible evidence showing the ability to repay loans or to generate attractive returns. The plan should propose an exit strategy for investors—how they will get their money back (plus an attractive return on their investment), perhaps by selling the company to a larger business or by making an initial public offering. "When we sit down with company owners to talk about funding growth," says one experienced business lender, "I want to see a defined repayment source with an eventual exit strategy."[20]

It is beneficial to include an evaluation of the risks of a new venture. Evaluating risk in a business plan requires an entrepreneur to walk a fine line. Dwelling too much on everything that can go wrong will discourage potential lenders and investors from financing the venture. Ignoring a project's risks makes those who evaluate the plan tend to believe the entrepreneur to be either naive, dishonest, or unprepared. The best strategy is to identify the most significant risks the venture faces and then to describe the plans the entrepreneur has developed to avoid them altogether or to overcome the negative outcome if the event does occur. The accompanying "Gaining a Competitive Edge" feature explains how two simple diagrams can communicate to investors both the risks and the rewards of a business venture.

✦ GAINING *a* COMPETITIVE EDGE ✦

Visualizing a Venture's Risks and Rewards

When reviewing business plans, lenders and investors naturally focus on the risks and the rewards of a business venture. Rather than taking dozens of pages of text and charts to communicate these important concepts to investors, entrepreneurs can use the following simple graphs to convey accurately both the potential risk and the returns of their proposed businesses. The first diagram shows the amount of money an entrepreneur needs to launch the business, the time required to reach the point of positive cash flow, and the anticipated amount of the payoff.

longer cash chasms *as long as their founders have a plan in place to carry the company through until cash flow does become positive.*

The second diagram complements the first. It shows investors the range of possible returns and the probability of achieving them. In the following example, investors can see that there is a 15 percent chance that their investments will be complete losses. The flat section shows that there is a very small chance that investors will lose only a small amount of money. The hump in the middle says that investors have a significant chance of earning between 15 percent and 45 percent on their money. (Note the probability of these returns is about the same as that of a total loss.) Finally, there is a small chance that their initial investments will yield a 200 percent rate of return.

In this diagram, the depth of hole shows lenders and investors how much money it will take to start the business, and the length of the chasm shows how long it will take to reach positive cash flow. Experienced business owners know that cash flow is the lifeblood of any business. As you will learn in Chapter 9, a company can operate (at least in the short run) without earning a profit, but it cannot survive without cash flow. Shallow cash holes and short times to positive cash flow are ideal, but businesses can tolerate deeper holes and

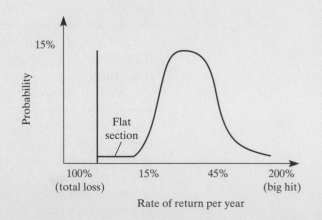

This diagram portrays what investors intuitively understand: Most companies either fail big or achieve solid success.

Source: Adapted from William A. Sahlman, "How to Write a Great Business Plan," *Harvard Business Review,* July/August 1997, pp. 98–108.

Finally, entrepreneurs should have a timetable for implementing the plan. They should present a schedule showing the estimated start-up date for the project and note any significant milestones along the way. Entrepreneurs tend to be optimistic, so it is important that the timetable of events be realistic.

There is a difference between a working business plan—one entrepreneurs are using to guide their business—and the presentation business plan—the one they are using to attract capital. Although coffee rings and penciled-in changes in a working plan don't matter (in fact, they're a good sign that the entrepreneur is actually using the plan), they have no place on a plan going to someone outside the company. A business plan is usually the tool that an entrepreneur uses to make a first impression on potential lenders and investors. To make sure that impression is favorable, entrepreneurs should follow these tips:

- Make sure the plan is free of spelling and grammatical errors and "typos." It is a professional document and should look like one.
- Make it visually appealing by creating an attractive layout. Use color charts, figures, photographs, and diagrams to illustrate key points. Don't get carried away, however, and end up with a "comic book" plan.
- Leave ample white space in margins.
- Create an attractive (but not extravagant) cover that includes the company's name and logo.
- Include a table of contents to enable readers to navigate the plan easily.
- Write in a flowing, conversational style and use bullets to itemize points in lists.
- Support claims with facts and avoid generalizations.
- Avoid overusing industry jargon and acronyms with which readers may not be familiar.
- Make it interesting. Boring plans seldom get read.
- Use computer spreadsheets to generate financial forecasts. They enable entrepreneurs to perform valuable "what if" (sensitivity) analysis in just seconds.
- Always include cash flow projections. Entrepreneurs sometimes focus exclusively on their proposed venture's profit forecasts and ignore cash flow projections. Although profitability is important, lenders and investors are much more interested in cash flow because they know that's where the money to pay them back or to cash them out comes from.
- The ideal plan is "crisp"—long enough to say what it should but not so long that it is a chore to read.
- Tell the truth. Absolute honesty is always critical in preparing a business plan.

As you can see, business plans are forecasts about the future that an entrepreneur plans to create, something that one expert compares to "taking a picture of the unknown," which is quite a feat! As uncertain and difficult to predict as the future may be, an entrepreneur who launches a business without a plan arguing that "trying to forecasting the future is pointless" is misguided. In the *Harvard Business Review,* William Sahlman says that "the best business plans . . . are like movies of the future. They show the people, the opportunity, and the context from multiple angles. They offer a plausible, coherent story of what lies ahead. They unfold the possibilities of action and reaction."[21] That's the kind of "movie" an entrepreneur should strive to create in a plan.

Can Your Plan Pass These Tests?

3. Explain the three tests every business plan must pass.

Preparing a sound business plan clearly requires time and effort, but the benefits greatly exceed the costs. Building the plan forces potential entrepreneurs to look at their business ideas in the harsh light of reality. It also requires entrepreneurs to assess the venture's chances of success more objectively. A well-assembled plan helps prove to outsiders that a business idea can be successful. To get external financing, an entrepreneur's plan must pass three tests with potential lenders and investors: the reality test, the competitive test, and the value test.[22] The first two tests have both an external and an internal component.

>   *Reality test.* The external component of the reality test revolves around proving that a market for the product or service really does exist. It focuses on industry attractiveness, market niches, potential customers, market size, degree of competition, and similar factors. Entrepreneurs who pass this part of the reality test prove in the marketing portion of their business plans that there is strong demand for their business idea.
>
>   The internal component of the reality test focuses on the product or service itself. Can the company really build it for the cost estimates in the business plan? Is it truly different from what competitors are already selling? Does it offer customers something of value?
>
>   *Competitive test.* The external part of the competitive test evaluates the company's relative position to its key competitors. How do the company's strengths and weaknesses match up with those of the competition? How are existing competitors likely to react when the new business enters the market? Do these reactions threaten the new company's success and survival?
>
>   The internal competitive test focuses on the management team's ability to create a company that will gain an edge over existing rivals. To pass this part of the competitive test, a plan must prove the quality of the venture's management team. What other resources does the company have that can give it a competitive edge in the market?
>
>   *Value test.* To convince lenders and investors to put their money into the venture, a business plan must prove to them that it offers a high probability of repayment or an attractive rate of return. Entrepreneurs usually see their businesses as good investments because they consider the intangibles of owning a business—gaining control over their own destinies, freedom to do what they enjoy, and others. Lenders and investors, however, look at a venture in colder terms: dollar-for-dollar returns. A plan must convince lenders and investors that they will earn an attractive return on their money.

Appendix A at the end of this book contains a sample business plan for InTote, a company started by a college student that makes stylish tote bags.

Making the Business Plan Presentation

4. Understand the keys to making an effective business plan presentation.

Lenders and investors are favorably impressed by entrepreneurs who are informed and prepared when requesting a loan or investment. When entrepreneurs try to secure funding from lenders or investors, the written business plan almost always precedes the opportunity to meet face-to-face. The written plan must first pass muster before an entrepreneur gets the opportunity to present the plan in person. Usually, the time for presenting a business opportunity is short, often no more than just a few minutes. (When presenting a plan to a venture capital forum, the allotted time is usually less than 20 minutes, 30 minutes at the maximum.) When the opportunity arises, an entrepreneur must be well prepared. It is important to rehearse, rehearse, and then rehearse some more. It is a mistake to begin by presenting the audience with a long-winded explanation about the technology on which the product or service is based. Within minutes most of the audience will be lost, and so is any chance the entrepreneur has of obtaining the necessary financing for the new venture. A business plan presentation should cover five basic areas:

- The company's background and its products or services.
- A market analysis and a description of the opportunities it presents.
- The company's competitive edge and the marketing strategies it will use to promote that edge.
- The management team and its members' qualifications and experience.
- A financial analysis that shows lenders and investors an attractive payback or payoff.

Company Example →

No matter how good a written business plan is, entrepreneurs who muff the presentation to potential lenders and investors will blow the deal. *For example, the founder of an Internet company wanted to show a group of potential investors how cutting edge his business was by conducting a live demonstration of his company's product on a portable computer and a projection system. Initially, the presentation went well, but then the computer failed to make the connection to the Internet. That caused the presentation program to lock up, forcing the entrepreneur to reboot the entire system while trying to hold the audience's attention and get the presentation back on track. The technological glitch occurred at the most crucial part of the entrepreneur's presentation, making his company look like a minor league player in a major league industry. His company's prospects for an initial public offering failed to connect to his audience the second his computer failed to connect to the Internet!*[23]

Entrepreneurs who are successful raising the capital their companies need to grow have solid business plans and make convincing presentations of them. Some helpful tips for making a business plan presentation to potential lenders and investors include:

- Prepare. Good presenters prepare their presentations well in advance and know the points they want to get across to their audiences.
- Demonstrate enthusiasm about the business but don't be overemotional.
- Fight the temptation to launch immediately into a lengthy discourse about the details of your product or service or how much work it took to develop it. Focus instead on communicating the dynamic opportunity your idea offers and how you plan to capitalize on it. Otherwise, you'll never have the chance to describe the details to lenders and investors.
- Hook investors quickly with an up-front explanation of the new venture, its opportunities, and the anticipated benefits to them.
- Use visual aids. They make it easier for people to follow your presentation. Don't make the mistake of relying on visuals to communicate the entire message. Visual aids should punctuate your spoken message and focus the audience's attention on what you are saying.
- Hit the highlights; specific questions will bring out the details later. But don't get caught up in too much detail in early meetings with lenders and investors.
- Keep the presentation "crisp" just like your business plan. Otherwise, says one experienced investor, "Information that might have caused an investor to bite gets lost in the endless drone."[24]
- Avoid the use of technological terms that will likely be above most of the audience. Do at least one rehearsal before someone who has no special technical training. Tell him to stop you anytime he does not understand what you are talking about. When this occurs (and it likely will), rewrite that portion of your presentation.
- Remember that every potential lender and investor you talk to is thinking, "What's in it for me?" Be sure to answer that question in your presentation.
- Close by reinforcing the nature of the opportunity. Be sure you have sold the benefits the investors will realize when the business is a success.

- Be prepared for questions. In many cases, there is seldom time for a long "Q&A" session, but interested investors may want to get you aside to discuss the details of the plan.
- Anticipate the questions the audience is most likely to ask and prepare for them in advance.
- Be sensitive to the issues that are most important to lenders and investors by reading the pattern of their questions. Focus your answers accordingly. For instance, some investors may be interested in the quality of the management team where as others are more interested in marketing strategies. Be prepared to offer details on either.
- Follow up with every investor to whom you make a presentation. Don't sit back and wait; be proactive. They have what you need—investment capital. Demonstrate that you have confidence in your plan and have the initiative necessary to run a business successfully.

IN THE FOOTSTEPS OF AN ENTREPRENEUR...

Once Upon a Time . . .

Once upon a time, there was an entrepreneur, Andy, who launched a technology company with two friends, Zen and Shanti. Pooling their limited financial resources, they were able to get the company off the ground, but for the business to grow and succeed, they needed a serious cash infusion. They developed a business plan and began sending it to venture capitalists—lots of venture capitalists, most of whom lived in a mystical land called Silicon Valley. The results were always the same—rejection—but at least the rejection letters they received were usually kind. One rejection letter cited "vague direction and exit strategy for investors. Product viability . . . doubtful." Most letters ended the same way: "Best of luck in building your company."

After so many rejections, Andy was troubled, wondering if he would have to return to his life as a corporate minion, working for someone else. One day as he walked along Broadway, he noticed in the window of a bookstore a book called *Story: Substance, Structure, Style, and the Principles of Screenwriting*. A promotional poster claimed that students of the author had used the secrets to write and produce screenplays that had garnered 17 Oscars and 79 Emmys. The dust jacket said it was a step-by-step guide for screenwriters who wanted to turn "great ideas into great stories." Flipping through the pages, Andy realized that Hollywood producers and Silicon Valley investors both make risky investments in projects in hopes of earning big returns when those projects become blockbusters. In other words, both wanted a good story.

So Andy and his partners set out to give the venture capitalists a good story as part of their business plan. First, they added what the book called

"spine," an inciting incident such as a ship hitting an iceberg or a villain disrupting a city that creates an opportunity for a hero—or a start-up company—to set things right. They described how their company's software would encourage and reward Web users with frequent-flier miles for passing along commercial and promotional messages to their friends.

Next, they added conflict. Given that they had never battled villains, aliens, or monsters, the entrepreneurs described how after launching their company, so many people had used their software that the volume crashed their server! They didn't have the money to buy a larger server, so they gave all of their users 100 free frequent-flier miles as an apology. The story brought to life the proof that their business idea actually worked!

Finally, the trio added a happy ending, what the book called "the object of desire." They described how marketers, recommenders, and others could reap the benefits of the fledgling company's word-of-mouth networks and how large the payoff for any investors who helped them build their business would be.

The intrepid entrepreneurs sent their business plan out again, and that very day a venture capitalist came to see them. Three months later, they had negotiated a deal with that investor, had the money in the bank, and had their company running wide open. The company grew, and the brave entrepreneurs decided to sell out and pursue other entrepreneurial ventures, living happily ever after.

Their story emphasizes the power of a story. As part of either your business plan or your business plan presentation, consider telling a story, which will enable you to communicate the essence of your business naturally, clearly, and persuasively. It also helps entrepreneurs get across to investors concepts that can be highly abstract in a concrete and entertaining way. Also, when told well, stories create an emotional connection with readers or listeners and help them remember the key components longer. After all, isn't that what entrepreneurs want to their plans to do?

1. Why are stories such powerful ways of communicating?
2. Develop a compelling story for your business plan.

Sources: Adapted from Andy Raskin, "Letter from Silicon Valley," *Inc.,* April 2002, pp. 62–64; "What Are the Potential Benefits of Storytelling?" Storytelling: Passport to the 21st Century, www.creatingthe21stcentury.com/Intro6-benefits-story.html.

What Lenders and Investors Look for in a Business Plan

5. Explain the "five Cs of credit" and why they are important to potential lenders and investors reading business plans.

To increase their chances of success when using their business plans to attract capital, entrepreneurs must be aware of the criteria lenders and investors use to evaluate the credit-worthiness of entrepreneurs seeking financing. Lenders and investors refer to these criteria as the **five Cs of credit**: capital, capacity, collateral, character, and conditions.

Capital

A small business must have a stable capital base before any lender will grant a loan. Otherwise the lender would be making, in effect, a capital investment in the business. Most lenders refuse to make loans that are capital investments because the potential for return on the investment is limited strictly to the interest on the loan, and the potential loss would probably exceed the reward. In fact, the most common reasons that banks give for rejecting small business loan applications are undercapitalization or too much debt. Investors also want to make sure that entrepreneurs have invested enough of their own money into the business to survive the tenuous start-up period.

Capacity

A synonym for *capacity* is *cash flow*. Lenders and investors must be convinced of a company's ability to meet its regular financial obligations and to repay a bank loan, and that takes cash. In Chapter 9, you will see that more small businesses fail from lack of cash than from lack of profit. It is possible for a company to be showing a profit and still have no cash—that is, to be technically bankrupt. Lenders expect a business to pass the test of liquidity, especially for short-term loans. Lenders study closely a small company's cash flow position to decide whether it has the capacity required to succeed.

Collateral

Collateral includes any assets an entrepreneur pledges to a lender as security for repayment of the loan. If an entrepreneur defaults on the loan, the bank has the right to sell the collateral and use the proceeds to satisfy the loan. Typically, lenders make very few unsecured loans (those not backed by collateral) to business start-ups. Bankers view an entrepreneur's willingness to pledge collateral (personal or business assets) as an indication of dedication to making the venture a success.

Character

Before putting money into a small business, lenders and investors must be satisfied with the owner's character. An evaluation of character frequently is based on intangible factors such as honesty, competence, polish, determination, knowledge, experience, and ability. Although the qualities judged are abstract, this evaluation plays a critical role in a lender's or investor's decision.

Lenders and investors know that most small businesses fail because of poor management, and they try to avoid extending loans to high-risk entrepreneurs. Preparing a solid business plan and a polished presentation can go far in convincing potential lenders and investors of an entrepreneur's ability to manage a company successfully.

Conditions

The conditions surrounding a loan request also affect the owner's chance of receiving funds. Banks consider factors relating to the business operation such as potential growth in the market, competition, location, form of ownership, and loan purpose. Again, the owner should provide this relevant information in an organized format in the business plan. Another important condition influencing the banker's decision is the shape of the overall economy, including interest rate levels, the inflation rate, and demand for money. Although these factors are beyond an entrepreneur's control, they still are an important component in a banker's decision.

The higher a small business scores on these five Cs, the greater its chance will be of receiving a loan or an investment. Wise entrepreneurs keep this in mind when preparing their business plans and presentations.

Conclusion

Although there is no guarantee of success when launching a business, the best way to insure against failure is to create a business plan. A good plan serves as a strategic compass that keeps a business on course as it travels into an uncertain future. Also, a solid plan is essential to raising the capital needed to start a business; lenders and investors demand it. "There may be no easier way for an entrepreneur to sabotage his or her request for capital than by failing to produce a comprehensive, well-researched, and, above all, credible business plan," says one small business expert.[25] Of course, building a plan is just one step along the path to launching a business. Creating a successful business requires entrepreneurs to put the plan into action. The remaining chapters in this book focus on putting your business plan to work.

Suggested Business Plan Format

Although every company's business plan will be unique, reflecting an entrepreneur's individual circumstances, certain elements are universal. The following outline summarizes these components.

I. Executive Summary (not to exceed two pages)
   A. Company name, address, and phone number
   B. Name, address, and phone number of all key people
   C. Brief description of the business, its products and services, and the customer problems they solve
   D. Brief overview of the market for the company's products and services
   E. Brief overview of the strategies that will make the firm a success
   F. Brief description of the managerial and technical experience of key people
   G. Brief statement of the financial request and how the money will be used
   H. Charts or tables showing highlights of financial forecasts

II. Vision and Mission Statement
    A. Entrepreneur's vision for the company
    B. "What business are we in?"
    C. Values and principles on which the business stands
    D. What makes the business unique? What is the source of its competitive advantage?

III. Company History (for existing businesses only)
    A. Company founding
    B. Financial and operational highlights
    C. Significant achievements

IV. Industry Profile and Overview
    A. Industry analysis
        1. Industry background and overview
        2. Major customer groups
        3. Regulatory restrictions, if any
        4. Significant trends
        5. Growth rate
        6. Barriers to entry and exit
        7. Key success factors in the industry
        8. Outlook for the future
    B. Stage of growth (start-up, growth, maturity)

V. Business Strategy
    A. Desired image and position in market
    B. Company goals and objectives
        1. Operational
        2. Financial
        3. Other
    C. SWOT analysis
        1. Strengths
        2. Weaknesses
        3. Opportunities
        4. Threats
    D. Competitive strategy
        1. Cost leadership
        2. Differentiation
        3. Focus

VI. Company Products and Services
    A. Description
        1. Product or service features
        2. Customer benefits
        3. Warranties and guarantees
        4. Uniqueness
    B. Patent or trademark protection
    C. Description of production process (if applicable)
        1. Raw materials
        2. Costs
        3. Key suppliers
        4. Lead times
    D. Future product or service offerings

VII. Marketing Strategy
    A. Target market
        1. Problem to be solved or benefit to be offered

      2. Complete demographic profile

      3. Other significant customer characteristics

    B. Customers' motivation to buy

    C. Market size and trends

      1. How large is the market?

      2. Is it growing or shrinking? How fast?

    D. Personal selling efforts

      1. Sales force size, recruitment, and training

      2. Sales force compensation

      3. Number of calls per sale

      4. Amount of average sale

    E. Advertising and promotion

      1. Media used—reader, viewer, listener profiles

      2. Media costs

      3. Frequency of usage

      4. Plans for generating publicity

    F. Pricing

      1. Cost structure

        a. Fixed

        b. Variable

      2. Desired image in market

      3. Comparison against competitors' prices

      4. Discounts

      5. Gross profit margin

    G. Distribution strategy

      1. Channels of distribution used

      2. Sales techniques and incentives for intermediaries

    H. Test market results

      1. Surveys

      2. Customer feedback on prototypes

      3. Focus groups

VIII. Location and Layout

    A. Location

      1. Demographic analysis of location versus target customer profile

      2. Traffic count

      3. Lease/rental rates

      4. Labor needs and supply

      5. Wage rates

    B. Layout

      1. Size requirements

      2. Americans with Disabilities Act compliance

      3. Ergonomic issues

      4. Layout plan (suitable for an appendix)

IX. Competitor Analysis

    A. Existing competitors

      1. Who are they? Create a competitive profile matrix.

      2. Strengths

      3. Weaknesses

    B. Potential competitors: companies that might enter the market

      1. Who are they?

      2. Impact on the business if they enter

X. Description of Management Team
    A. Key managers and employees
        1. Their backgrounds
        2. Experience, skills, and know-how they bring to the company
    B. Résumés of key managers and employees (suitable for an appendix)
    C. Future additions to management team
    D. Board of directors or advisers
XI. Plan of Operation
    A. Form of ownership chosen and reasoning
    B. Company structure (organization chart)
    C. Decision making authority
    D. Compensation and benefits packages
XII. Financial Forecasts (suitable for an appendix)
    A. Key assumptions
    B. Financial statements (year 1 by month, years 2 and 3 by quarter)
        1. Income statement
        2. Balance sheet
        3. Cash flow statement
    C. Break-even analysis
    D. Ratio analysis with comparison to industry standards (most applicable to existing businesses)
XIII. Loan or Investment Proposal
    A. Amount requested
    B. Purpose and uses of funds
    C. Repayment or "cash out" schedule (exit strategy)
    D. Timetable for implementing plan and launching the business
XIV. Appendices (supporting documentation, including market research, financial statements, organization charts, résumés, and other items)

▌▌▌ Chapter Review

1. Explain why every entrepreneur should create a business plan.

   ▪ A business plan serves two essential functions. First and more important, it guides the company's operations by charting its future course and devising a strategy for following it. The second function of the business plan is to attract lenders and investors. Applying for loans or attempting to attract investors without a solid business plan rarely attracts needed capital. Rather, the best way to secure the necessary capital is to prepare a sound business plan.

2. Describe the elements of a solid business plan.

   ▪ Although a business plan should be unique and tailor-made to suit the particular needs of a small company, it should cover these basic elements: an executive summary, a mission statement, a company history, a business and industry profile, a description of the company's business strategy, a profile of its products or services, a statement explaining its marketing strategy, a competitor analysis, owners' and officers' résumés, a plan of operation, financial data, and the loan or investment proposal.

3. Explain the three tests every business plan must pass.

   ▪ Reality test. The external component of the reality test revolves around proving that a market for the product or service really does exist. The internal component of the reality test focuses on the product or service itself.

   ▪ Competitive test. The external part of the competitive test evaluates the company's relative position to its key competitors. The internal competitive test focuses on the management team's ability to create a company that will gain an edge over existing rivals.

   ▪ Value test. To convince lenders and investors to put their money into the venture, a business plan must prove to them that it offers a high probability of repayment or an attractive rate of return.

4. Understand the keys to making an effective business plan presentation.

   ■ Lenders and investors are favorably impressed by entrepreneurs who are informed and prepared when requesting a loan or investment.

   ■ Tips include demonstrating enthusiasm about the venture but not being overemotional; "hooking" investors quickly with an up-front explanation of the new venture, its opportunities, and the anticipated benefits to them; using visual aids; hitting the highlights of your venture; not getting caught up in too much detail in early meetings with lenders and investors; avoiding the use of technological terms that will likely be above most of the audience; rehearsing the presentation before giving it; closing by reinforcing the nature of the opportunity; and being prepared for questions.

5. Explain the "five Cs of credit" and why they are important to potential lenders and investors reading business plans.

   ■ Small business owners needs to be aware of the criteria bankers use in evaluating the creditworthiness of loan applicants—the five Cs of credit: capital, capacity, collateral, character, and conditions.

   ■ *Capital.* Lenders expect small businesses to have an equity base of investment by the owner(s) that will help support the venture during times of financial strain.

   ■ *Capacity.* A synonym for *capacity* is *cash flow.* The bank must be convinced of the firm's ability to meet its regular financial obligations and to repay the bank loan, and that takes cash.

   ■ *Collateral.* Collateral includes any assets the owner pledges to the bank as security for repayment of the loan.

   ■ *Character.* Before approving a loan to a small business, the banker must be satisfied with the owner's character.

   ■ *Conditions.* Conditions such as interest rates, the health of the nation's economy, and industry growth rates surrounding a loan request also affect the owner's chance of receiving funds.

▮▮▮ Discussion Questions

1. Why should an entrepreneur develop a business plan?
2. Why do entrepreneurs who are not seeking external financing need to prepare business plans?
3. Describe the major components of a business plan.
4. How can an entrepreneur seeking funds to launch a business convince potential lenders

and investors that a market for the product or service really does exist?

5. How would you prepare to make a formal presentation of your business plan at a venture capital forum?
6. What are the five Cs of credit? How do lenders and investors use them when evaluating a request for financing?

Crafting a Winning Business Plan

Business PlanPro

Building a business plan is one of the most important activities an entrepreneur will undertake before launching a business. Simply put, there's a right way and a wrong way to launch a business, and developing a business plan definitely is the right way! Many entrepreneurs never create a business plan because they don't think it is necessary, they don't want to invest the time and energy to build one, or they don't know where to start. Business Plan Pro is

an easy to use tool that guides you through the process of building a plan.

If you are using Business Plan Pro, by this point, you are well on your way to building a winning plan. The exercises for Chapter 6 that accompany Business Plan Pro are designed to help you determine the following:

■ How to make the best use of your plan once you complete it.
■ Whether your plan can pass three important tests: the reality test, the competitive test, and the value test.
■ How to convert your plan into a brief but powerful presentation capable of convincing potential lenders and investors that your business idea is sound.

Chapter 7
Building a Guerrilla Marketing Plan

> *Customer satisfaction is when you sell something that does not return to someone who does.*
> —STANLEY MARCUS, COFOUNDER, NEIMAN MARCUS

> *There is less to fear from outside competition than from inside inefficiency, discourtesy, and bad service.*
> —ANONYMOUS

Upon completion of this chapter, you will be able to:

1. Describe the components of a guerrilla marketing plan and explain the benefits of preparing one.

2. Explain how small businesses can pinpoint their target markets.

3. Explain how to determine customer needs through market research and outline the steps in the market research process.

4. Describe the guerrilla marketing strategies on which a small business can build a competitive edge in the marketplace.

5. Discuss marketing opportunities the World Wide Web offers and how entrepreneurs can take advantage of them.

6. Discuss the "four Ps" of marketing—product, place, price, and promotion—and their role in building a successful marketing strategy.

Too often, business plans describe in great detail what the entrepreneur intends to accomplish (e.g., "the financials") and pay little, if any, attention to the strategies to achieve those targets. Others fail miserably because they are not willing to invest the time and energy to identify and research their target markets and to assemble a business plan. These entrepreneurs squander enormous effort pulling together capital, staff, products, and services because they neglect to determine what it will take to attract and retain a profitable customer base. To be effective, a solid business plan must contain both a financial plan and a marketing plan. Like the financial plan, an effective marketing plan projects numbers and analyzes them, but from a different perspective. Rather than focus on cash flow, net income, and owner's equity, the marketing plan concentrates on the customer.

This chapter is devoted to creating an effective marketing plan, which is an integral part of a total business plan. Before producing reams of computer-generated spreadsheets of financial projections, entrepreneurs must determine what to sell, to whom and how often, on what terms and at what price, and how to get the product or service to the customer. In short, a marketing plan identifies a company's target customers and describes how it will attract and keep them.

Creating a Guerrilla Marketing Plan

> 1. Describe the components of a guerrilla marketing plan and explain the benefits of preparing one.

Marketing is the process of creating and delivering desired goods and services to customers and involves all of the activities associated with winning and retaining loyal customers. The secret to successful marketing is to understand what the company's target customers' needs, demands, and wants are before competitors can; to offer them the products and services that will satisfy those needs, demands, and wants; and to provide those customers with quality, service, convenience, and value so that they will keep coming back. The marketing function cuts across the entire organization, affecting every aspect of its operation from finance and production to hiring and purchasing. As the global business environment becomes more turbulent, small business owners must understand the importance of developing relevant marketing strategies; they are not just for megacorporations competing in international markets. Although they may be small in size and cannot match their larger rivals' marketing budgets, entrepreneurial companies are not powerless when it comes to developing effective marketing strategies. By building a guerrilla marketing plan using unconventional, low-cost, creative techniques, small companies can wring as much or more "bang" from their marketing bucks.

> Company Example →

Facing industry giants Coca-Cola and Pepsi-Cola as well as a host of other competitors in the beverage industry, tiny Jones Soda has relied on a guerrilla marketing strategy since Peter van Stolk founded the company in 1996. When Jones Soda had trouble landing shelf space from traditional beverage outlets, van Stolk turned to what he calls "an alternative distribution strategy" for his company's uniquely flavored drinks that carry names such as Blue Bubble Gum and Green Apple. The company lured customers by stocking its colorful drinks (neon-bright reds, yellows, blues, purples, and greens) with their retro long-necked bottles and unusual labels in nontraditional venues such as surf, skate, and snowboarding shops, music stores, tattoo parlors, and clothing stores—all places where Jones Soda's target customers were likely to be. Once customers started requesting the products, more traditional beverage outlets were willing to stock the company's drinks. Convenience stores and supermarket chains such as Safeway and Albertson's now sell Jones Soda products. To keep demand strong, the company has signed an array of extreme athletes, including BMX rider Matt Hoffman, surfer Kahea Hart, and skateboarder Willie Santos, to promote its line of drinks. Employees also travel through cities in RVs handing out Jones Sodas and talking up the product line among customers. Van Stolk keeps customers interested in the brand with the help of a contest that encourages them to send in pictures of themselves for use on product labels! With its innovative guerrilla strategy, Jones Soda has built a brand with cult status among its customer base.[1]

Jones Soda Company founder Peter van Stolk relies on a guerrilla marketing strategy to sell the company's unique soft drinks in the fiercely competitive soft drink industry, where Jones Soda competes with industry giants such as Coca-Cola and Pepsi.

Developing a winning marketing strategy requires a business to master three vital resources: people, information, and technology. People are the most important ingredient in formulating a successful marketing strategy. Hiring and retaining creative, talented, well-trained people to develop and implement a marketing strategy is the first step. Just as in sports, implementing a successful marketing strategy relies on an entrepreneur's ability to recruit people with the talent to do the job and to teach them to work together as a team.

In today's more sophisticated and competitive markets, successful marketing relies on a company's ability to capture data and transform it into useful, meaningful information. Information is the fuel that feeds the marketing engine. Without it, a marketing strategy soon sputters and stops. Collecting more data than competitors, putting it into a meaningful form faster, and disseminating it to everyone in the business, especially those who deal with customers, can give a company a huge competitive edge. Unfortunately, too many small business owners fail to see the importance of capturing the information needed to drive a successful marketing strategy.

Technology has proved to be a powerful marketing weapon; yet, technology alone is not the key to marketing success. Competitors may duplicate or exceed the investment a small business makes in technology, but that may not guarantee their marketing success. The way a company integrates the use of technology into its overall marketing strategy is

Company Example →

what matters most. *For instance, the Progressive Insurance Company is setting itself apart from the competition by putting to use technology that enables its claims adjusters to serve their customers faster and more efficiently. Delays in processing claims and issuing checks are common complaints in the insurance industry, and Progressive's use of technology is aimed at eliminating those complaints. The company employs a fleet of immediate response vehicles (IRVs), loaded with a battery of communications equipment—laptop computers with wireless connectivity, cell phones, digital cameras, and ink-jet printers—allowing adjusters to settle claims and issue checks on the spot. At some companies, settling a claim can take weeks or even months! Progressive says that the IRVs not only have improved customer retention by 20 percent but also have helped the company reduce its labor costs.*[2]

A marketing plan focuses the company's attention on the customer and recognizes that satisfying the customer is the foundation of every business. Its purpose is to build a strategy of success for a business from the customer's point of view. Indeed, the customer is the central player in the cast of every business venture. According to marketing expert Theodore Levitt, the primary purpose of a business is not to earn a profit; instead, it is "to create and keep a customer. The rest, given reasonable good sense, will take care of itself."[3]

Every area of the business must practice putting the customer first in planning and actions. A **guerrilla marketing plan** should accomplish four objectives:

1. It should pinpoint the target markets the small company will serve.
2. It should determine customer needs, wants, and characteristics through market research.
3. It should analyze a company's competitive advantages and build a marketing strategy around them.
4. It should help create a marketing mix that meets customer needs and wants.

This chapter focus as on building a customer orientation into these four objectives of the small company's marketing plan.

Market Diversity: Pinpointing the Target Market

2. Explain how small businesses can pinpoint their target markets.

Company Example

One of the first steps in building a marketing plan is identifying a small company's **target market**, the group of customers at whom the company aims its products and services. The more a business learns from market research about its local markets, its customers and their buying habits and preferences, the more precisely it can focus its marketing efforts on the group(s) of prospective and existing customers who are most likely to buy its products or services. *Blane Nordahl, one of the most successful cat burglars ever (until he was caught), specialized in stealing only the finest sterling silver. What made Nordahl so difficult for police to catch was his meticulous market research that allowed him to target exactly the right homes to rob. Nordahl used local libraries and publications such as the duPont* Registry *and Sotheby's* Previews *to identify and learn about upscale neighborhoods. Then he would scout out the most likely "old money" homes in those neighborhoods, carefully selecting his targets to maximize his take and to minimize the likelihood of getting caught. Nordahl's systematic approach to selecting his target market worked for more than 15 years, netting him millions of dollars' worth of ill-gotten gain before a footprint left in a hasty exit allowed police to nab him. "Of all the burglars I've ever gone up against," says one police officer, "he is absolutely the best."[4]*

Although Nordahl used a creative marketing approach to achieve illegal gain, small businesses can use a similar approach to make their businesses more successful. Unfortunately, most marketing experts contend that the greatest marketing mistake small businesses make is failing to define clearly the target market to be served. In other words, most small businesses follow a "shotgun approach" to marketing, firing marketing blasts at every customer they see, hoping to capture just some of them. Most small companies simply cannot use shotgun marketing to compete successfully with larger rivals and their deep pockets. These small businesses develop new products that do not sell because they failed to target them at a specific audience's needs; they broadcast ads that attempt to reach everyone and end up reaching no one; they spend precious resources trying to reach customers who are not the most profitable; and many of the customers they manage to attract leave because they don't know what the company stands for.

Failing to pinpoint their target markets is especially ironic because small firms are ideally suited to reaching market segments that their larger rivals overlook or consider too small to be profitable. Why, then, is the shotgun approach so popular? Because it is easy and does not require market research or a marketing plan! The problem is that the shotgun approach is a sales-driven rather than a customer-driven strategy. To be customer

Company Example → driven, an effective marketing program must be based on a clear, concise definition of an entrepreneur's targeted customers. *David Lance Schwartz, founder of David Lance New York (DLNY), targets upscale professional men, mainly corporate CEOs and Wall Street barons, with his private-label line of top-quality men's clothing and premier service. Before the clothier will sell a suit, shirt, or tie to a client, a representative schedules a consultation either at the store or the client's office or home to take the necessary measurements and to "gather the details we'll use in creating [his] new wardrobe," says Lance. "Before an inch of fabric is cut, we want to know [a client's] profession, work habits, traveling schedule, lifestyle and what he keeps in his closet." The result is a customized wardrobe that fits each client's lifestyle. That customization isn't cheap, however. DLNY's suits sell for $3,250 to $15,000 each (the $15,000 suit has pinstripes made from real gold!), and shirts cost $275 to $625. DLNY's product line, prices, and service fit the company's target market perfectly.*[5]

A "one-size-fits-all" approach to marketing no longer works because the mass market is rapidly disappearing. The population of the United States, like that of many countries, is becoming increasingly diverse. The mass market that dominated the business world 30 years ago has been replaced by an increasingly fragmented market of multicultural customers including Hispanic American, African American, Asian Pacific, Native American, and many other populations. In fact, by 2010, Hispanics, African Americans, Asian Americans, and other minorities will account for one-third of the nation's population. To be successful, businesses must be in tune with the multicultural nature of the modern marketplace. Small businesses that take the time to recognize, understand, and cater to the unique needs, experiences, and preferences of these multicultural markets (and their submarkets) will reap immense rewards.

The nation's increasingly diverse population offers businesses of all sizes tremendous marketing opportunities if they target specific customers, learn how to reach them, and offer goods and services designed specifically for them. The key to success is understanding those target customers' unique, needs, wants, and preferences. The largest and fastest growing minority sector in the United States today is the Hispanic population. More than 35 million Hispanic Americans now comprise the nation's single largest minority group, edging out African Americans. With $926 billion in purchasing power, the Hispanic American population is an extremely attractive target market for many entrepreneurs selling everything from groceries and perfumes to houses and entertainment.[6]

Company Example → *When Ruben and Rosalinda Montalvo moved to the United States from Mexico, they noted the rapidly rising Hispanic population in their area and left their corporate jobs to launch a string of businesses aimed at serving this market. In addition to their small chain of authentic Mexican restaurants, the Montalvos launched Salsatheque, a nightclub aimed specifically at young, upscale Hispanic professionals. The club's music, food, drinks, décor, and ambiance are designed to appeal to the Montalvos' target customers, whom they know well because of their firsthand experience and their market research.*[7]

Like Salsatheque, the most successful businesses have well-defined portraits of the customers they are seeking to attract. From market research, they know their customers' income levels, lifestyles, buying patterns, likes and dislikes, and even their psychological profiles. For instance, companies that target Hispanic customers should advertise in Spanish because, even though most also speak English quite well, their target customers see the effort as an important accommodation to their cultural identity and pride. In short, at successful companies, the target customer permeates the entire business—from the merchandise the company purchases and the ads it uses to the layout and décor of the store. They have an advantage over their rivals because the images they have created for their companies appeal to their target customers, and that's why they prosper. *One Miami homebuilder specializing in developing retirement communities that target baby boomers shifted his company's marketing approach after he learned that his target customers avoid anything that reminds them that they are aging. (Research shows that the "reality gap" between baby*

Company Example →

boomers' chronological age and their perceived age is 15 years.) Wanting to hold on to their youth as long as possible, baby boomers are attracted to products and services that make them feel and look younger. In its residential developments, the company has added computer labs, exercise facilities, concierge services, and restaurants to enhance the residents' living experience. In one location, the builder teamed up with a local university to add a large educational center with classrooms, a lecture hall, a library, and a Starbucks outlet. The company also stopped calling its developments "retirement communities" and opted for the more youthful "active adult communities."[8] Without a clear picture of its target market, a small company will try to reach almost everyone and usually will end up appealing to almost no one.

Determining Customer Needs and Wants Through Market Research

3A. Explain how to determine customer needs through market research.

The changing nature of the U.S. population is a potent force altering the landscape of business. Shifting patterns in age, income, education, race, and other population characteristics (which are the subject of demographics) have a major impact on companies, their customers, and the way they do business with those customers. Entrepreneurs who ignore demographic trends and fail to adjust their strategies accordingly run the risk of their companies' becoming competitively obsolete. "It's important at the top levels of an organization to spend time looking for big new ideas," says one retail consultant.[9]

A demographic trend is like a train; an entrepreneur must find out early on where it's going and decide whether to get on board. Waiting until the train is roaring down the tracks and gaining speed means it's too late to get on board. However, by checking the schedule early and planning ahead, an entrepreneur may wind up at the train's controls wearing the engineer's hat! Similarly, small companies that spot demographic trends early and act on them can gain a distinctive edge in the market. An entrepreneur's goal should be to align his or her business with as many demographic, social, and cultural trends as possible. Staying on trend means staying in synchronization with the market as it shifts and changes over time. The more trends a business converges with, the more likely it is to be successful. Conversely, a business moving away from significant trends in society is in danger of losing its customer base.

By performing some basic market research, entrepreneurs can detect key demographic, social, and cultural trends and zero in on the needs, wants, preferences, and desires of its target customers. Indeed, every business can benefit from a better understanding of its market, customers, and competitors. **Market research** is the vehicle for gathering the information that serves as the foundation for the marketing plan. It involves systematically collecting, analyzing, and interpreting data pertaining to the small company's market, customers, and competitors. Businesses face the challenge of reaching the highly fragmented markets that have emerged today, and market research can help them. Market research allows entrepreneurs to answer such questions as: Who are my customers and potential customers? What is their gender? To which age group(s) do they belong? What is their income level? What kind of people are they? Where do they live? Do they rent or own their own homes? What are they looking for in the products or services I sell? How often do they buy these products or services? What models, styles, colors, or flavors do they prefer? Why do or don't they buy from my store? How do the strengths of my product or service serve their needs and wants? What hours do they prefer to shop? How do they perceive my business? Which advertising media are most likely to reach them? How do customers perceive my business versus competitors? This information is an integral part of developing an effective marketing plan.

When marketing its goods and services, a small company must avoid mistakes because there is no margin for error when funds are scarce and budgets are tight. Small businesses simply cannot afford to miss their target markets, and market research can help them zero in on the bull's eye. That usually requires conducting market research up front, *before* launching a company. One of the worst—and most common—mistakes entrepreneurs make is *assuming* that a market exists for their products or services. The time to find out if customers are likely to buy a product or a service is before investing thousands of dollars to launch it! Market research can tell entrepreneurs whether a sufficient customer base exists and how likely those customers are to buy their products and services. In addition to collecting and analyzing demographic data about their target customers, entrepreneurs can learn a great deal by actually observing, mingling with, and interviewing customers as they shop. *For instance, researchers for Maker's Mark, a Kentucky bourbon distillery, have gathered some of their most meaningful data while talking to customers and potential customers in bars across the country. Their up-close-and-personal approach allows them to get a handle on customers' attitudes and behavior in a way that more traditional techniques cannot.*[10] Other companies videotape their customers while they are shopping to get a clear picture of their buying habits. This hands-on market research allows entrepreneurs to get past the barriers that customers often put up and to uncover their true preferences and hidden thoughts.

> **Company Example** →

Many entrepreneurs are discovering the speed, the convenience, and the low cost of conducting market research over the World Wide Web. Online surveys, customer opinion polls, and other research projects are easy to conduct, cost virtually nothing, and help companies connect with their customers. With Web-based surveys, businesses can get real-time feedback from customers, often using surveys they have designed themselves.

Market research does *not* have to be time consuming, complex, or expensive to be useful. *At Newbury Comics, a 21-year-old chain of music and novelty stores in New England, managers see the necessity of keeping up with the rapidly changing tastes of their young target customers who are typically in their twenties. To stay plugged in, the company hosts small groups of customers at informal dinners of hamburgers and beers, where managers learn what their customers are thinking. Based on feedback from these meetings, Newbury Comics has shifted its advertising from newspapers and radio to transit ads and movie theater advertising.* Market research for a small business can be informal; it does not have to be highly sophisticated nor expensive to be valuable.

> **Company Example** →

How to Conduct Market Research

> **3B.** Outline the steps in the market research process.

The goal of market research is to reduce the risks associated with making business decisions. It can replace misinformation and assumptions with facts. Opinion and hearsay are not viable foundations on which to build a solid marketing strategy. Successful market research consists of four steps:

Step 1: Define the Objective

The first and most crucial step in market research is defining the research objective clearly and concisely. A common flaw at this stage is to confuse a symptom with the true problem. For example, dwindling sales is not a problem—it is a symptom. To get to the heart of the matter, an entrepreneur must consider all the possible factors that could have caused it. Is there new competition? Are the firm's sales representatives impolite or unknowledgeable? Have customer tastes changed? Is the product line too narrow? Do customers have trouble finding what they want? In other cases, an owner may be interested in researching a specific type of question. What are the characteristics of my customers? What are their income levels? What radio stations do they listen to? Why do they shop here? What factors are most important to their buying decisions? What impact do in-store displays have on their purchasing patterns? Do they enjoy their shopping experience? If so, why? If not, why not? What would they like to see the store do differently?

Business owners also can use market research to uncover new market opportunities as well. For example, when the owner of a fitness center surveyed his customers, he discovered that many had an interest in aerobic exercise. He added an aerobics program, and within a year his revenues had grown by 25 percent.

Step 2: Collect the Data

The marketing approach that companies of all sizes strive to achieve is **individualized** (or **one-to-one**) **marketing**, a system of gathering data on individual customers and then developing a marketing plan designed specifically to appeal to their needs, tastes, and preferences. Its goal is not only to attract customers but also to keep them and to increase their purchases. In a society in which people feel so isolated and transactions are so impersonal, one-to-one marketing gives a business a competitive advantage. Companies following this approach know their customers, understand how to give them the value they want, and perhaps most important, know how to make them feel special and important. The goal is to treat each customer as an individual. Hilton Hotels uses an extensive computer network that provides information to all of the hotels in the chain to track its guests' preferences and spending habits with the company and to provide them individual attention. Hilton also uses the huge database to offer customized promotional offers to which individual customers are most likely to respond.[11]

Individualized marketing requires business owners to gather and assimilate detailed information about their customers. Fortunately, owners of even the smallest companies now have access to affordable technology that creates and manages computerized databases, allowing entrepreneurs to develop close, one-to-one relationships with their customers. Much like gold nuggets waiting to be discovered, significant amounts of valuable information about customers and their buying habits is hidden *inside* many small businesses, tucked away in computerized databases. For most business owners, collecting useful information about their customers and potential new products and markets is simply a matter of sorting and organizing data that are already floating around somewhere in their companies. "Most companies are data rich and information poor," claims one marketing expert.[12] The key is to mine those data and turn them into useful information that allows the company to "court" its customers with special products, services, ads, and offers that appeal most to them.

Entrepreneurs have at their disposal two basic types of market research: *primary research* (data you collect and analyze yourself), and *secondary research* (data that have already been compiled and are available, often at a very reasonable cost or even free). Primary research techniques include:

- *Customer surveys and questionnaires.* Keep them short. Word your questions carefully so that you do not bias the results, and use a simple ranking system (e.g., a 1-to-5 scale, with 1 representing "unacceptable" and 5 representing "excellent"). Test your survey for problems on a small number of people before putting it to use. Web surveys are inexpensive, easy to conduct, and provide feedback fast. Femail Creations, a mail-order company that sells clothing, accessories, and gifts to women, uses Web surveys to gather basic demographic data about its customers and to solicit new product ideas as well. Customer responses have led to profitable new product lines for the small company.[13]
- *Focus groups.* Enlist a small number of customers to give you feedback on specific issues in your business—quality, convenience, hours of operation, service, and so on.

Listen carefully for new marketing opportunities as customers or potential customers tell you what is on their minds. Once again, consider using the Web. One small bicycle company conducts 10 online focus groups each year at virtually no cost and gains valuable marketing information from them.

■ *Daily transactions.* Sift as much data as possible from existing company records and daily transactions—customer warranty cards, personal checks, frequent-buyer clubs, credit applications, and others.

■ *Other ideas.* Set up a suggestion system (for customers and employees) and use it. Establish a customer advisory panel to determine how well your company is meeting needs. Talk with suppliers about trends they have spotted in the industry. Contact customers who have not bought anything in a long time and find out why. Contact people who are not customers and find out why. Teach employees to be good listeners and then ask them what they hear.

Secondary research, which is usually less expensive to collect than primary data, includes the following sources:

■ *Business directories.* To locate a trade association, use *Business Information Sources* (University of California Press) or the *Encyclopedia of Associations* (Gale Research). To find suppliers, use *The Thomas Register of American Manufacturers* (Thomas Publishing Company) or *Standard and Poor's Register of Corporations, Executives, and Industries* (Standard and Poor Corporation). *The American Wholesalers and Distributors Directory* includes details on more than 18,000 wholesalers and distributors.

■ *Direct-mail lists.* You can buy mailing lists for practically any type of business. *The Standard Rates and Data Service (SRDS) Directory of Mailing Lists* (Standard Rates and Data) is a good place to start looking.

■ *Demographic data.* To learn more about the demographic characteristics of customers in general, use *The Statistical Abstract of the United States* (U.S. Government Printing Office). Profiles of more specific regions are available in *The State and Metropolitan Data Book* (U.S. Government Printing Office). *The Sourcebook of Zip Code Demographics* (CACI, Inc.) provides detailed breakdowns of the population in every zip code in the country. *Sales and Marketing Management's Survey of Buying Power* (Bill Communications) has statistics on consumer, retail, and industrial buying.

■ *Census data.* The Bureau of the Census publishes a wide variety of reports that summarize the wealth of data found in its census database, which is available at most libraries and at the Census Bureau's Web site (www.census.gov).

■ *Forecasts.* The *U.S. Global Outlook* traces the growth of 200 industries and gives a five-year forecast for each one. Many government agencies including the Department of Commerce offer forecasts on everything from interest rates to the number of housing starts. A government librarian can help you find what you need.

■ *Market research.* Someone may already have compiled the market research you need. *The FINDex Worldwide Directory of Market Research Reports, Studies, and Surveys* (Cambridge Information Group) lists more than 10,600 studies available for purchase. Other directories of business research include *Simmons Study of Media and Markets* (Simmons Market Research Bureau Inc.) and the *A.C. Neilsen Retail Index* (A.C. Neilsen Company).

■ *Articles.* Magazine and journal articles pertinent to your business are a great source of information. Use the *Reader's Guide to Periodical Literature*, the *Business Periodicals Index* (similar to the *Reader's Guide* but focused on business periodicals), and *Ulrich's Guide to International Periodicals* to locate the ones you need.

■ *Local data.* Your state Department of Commerce and your local chamber of commerce will very likely have useful data on the local market of interest to you. Call to find out what is available.

■ *World Wide Web.* Most entrepreneurs are astounded at the marketing information that is available on the World Wide Web (WWW). Using one of the search engines, you can gain access to a world of information—literally!

Thanks to advances in computer hardware and software, data mining, once available only to large companies with vast computer power, is now possible for even very small businesses. **Data mining** is a process in which computer software that uses statistical analysis, database technology, and artificial intelligence finds hidden patterns, trends, and connections in data so that business owners can make better marketing decisions and predictions about their customers' behavior. Finding relationships among the many components of a data set, identifying clusters of customers with similar buying habits, and predicting customers' buying patterns, data mining gives entrepreneurs incredible marketing power. Popular data mining software packages include ACT!, Clementine, DataScope Pro, GoldMine, MineSet, Nuggets, and many others.

For an effective individualized marketing campaign to be successful, business owners must collect and mine three types of information:

1. *Geographic.* Where are my customers located? Do they tend to be concentrated in one geographic region?
2. *Demographic.* What are the characteristics of my customers (age, education levels, income, sex, marital status, and many other features)?
3. *Psychographic.* What drives my customers' buying behavior? Are they receptive to new products or are they among the last to accept them? What values are most important to them?

Company Example →

Harrah's Entertainment Inc., which operates 21 casinos around the United States, uses data mining to develop sophisticated demographic and psychographic profiles of its customers. Using its Total Gold frequent gambler card (much like the cards supermarkets distribute to shoppers) to collect information about its customers and their gambling habits, ranging from which games they play to how fast they play them, Harrah's was able to pinpoint its best customers, whom managers dubbed "avid experienced players," and to develop individual marketing strategies for them. Unlike many casinos that court "high rollers," wealthy gamblers who gamble hundreds of thousands of dollars at a time, with expensive "comps" such as free air fare and luxury suites, Harrah's best and most profitable customers are low rollers with modest incomes who spend between $100 and $499 per trip. With the help of its data mining system, Harrah's targets individual customers with promotional offers, ranging from free meals and show tickets to cash vouchers and free rooms, designed to get them back into the casino. The payoff has been exceptional; Harrah's sales, profits, market share, and customer response rate to promotions have climbed dramatically.[14]

Figure 7.1 explains how to become an effective individualized marketer.

Step 3: Analyze and Interpret the Data

The results of market research alone do not provide a solution to the problem; the owner must attach some meaning to them. What do the facts mean? Is there a common thread running through the responses? Do the results suggest any changes needed in the way the business is run? Are there new opportunities the owner can take advantage of? There are no hard-and-fast rules for interpreting market research results; the owner must use judgment and common sense to determine what the numbers mean. *William Pulte, owner of what has become the second largest home-building company in the United States, relies*

Company Example →

Figure 7.1

How to Become an Effective One-to-One Marketer

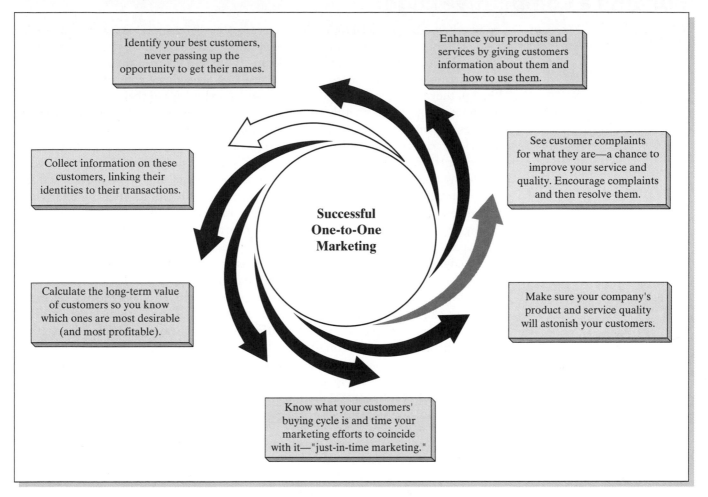

Source: Adapted from Susan Greco, "The Road to One-to-One Marketing," *Inc.*, October 1995, pp. 56–66.

extensively on market research to reveal where to build housing developments and how to design the homes in them. Pulte's research has identified 11 distinct customer segments and the features they most want in their homes. Market research also tells him in which markets these target segments are most underserved, enabling him to build homes there and sell them quickly, one of the keys to success in the industry. For instance, in San Francisco, Pulte recently identified an underserved market for first-time homeowners. Further research showed that these young professionals wanted stylish housing with a unique flair that was low maintenance. Pulte purchased and renovated an old fruit-processing plant in a suburban area, transforming it into chic row houses and lofts. The night before the units went on sale, hopeful buyers camped out so they could be first in line to buy their dream homes.[15]

Step 4: Put the Information to Work

The market research process is not complete until business owners act on the information collected. Based on their understanding of what the facts really mean, owners must then decide how to use the information in their businesses. For example, the owner of a retail shop discovered from a survey that her customers preferred evening shopping hours over early morning hours. She made the schedule adjustment and sales began to climb.

Plotting a Guerrilla Marketing Strategy: Building a Competitive Edge

4. Describe the guerrilla marketing strategies on which a small business can build a competitive edge in the marketplace.

A competitive edge is crucial for business success. A small business has a competitive edge when customers perceive that the company and its products or services are superior to those of its competitors. The right marketing strategy, not size or financial resources, is a key determinant of how successful a business is at achieving a competitive advantage. Although they may be smaller and lack the marketing budgets of their larger rivals, small companies can gain a competitive advantage using creative, low-cost guerrilla marketing strategies that hit home with their target customers. Independent bookstores have discovered that large chains use their buying power to get volume discounts and undercut the independents' prices. Individual shop owners are finding new ways, such as special ordering, adult reading groups, children's story hours, newsletters, autograph parties, and targeting unique niches to differentiate themselves and to retain loyal customers. These entrepreneurs are finding that the best way to gain a competitive advantage is to create value by giving customers what they really want that they cannot get elsewhere.

Successful businesses often use the special advantages they have to build a competitive edge over their larger rivals. Their close contact with the customer, personal attention, focus on service, and organizational and managerial flexibility provide a solid foundation from which to build a towering competitive edge in the market. Small companies can exploit their size to become more effective than their larger rivals at **relationship marketing** or **customer relationship management** (**CRM**)—developing, maintaining, and managing long-term relationships with customers so that they will want to keep coming back to make repeat purchases. CRM puts the customer at the center of a company's thinking, planning, and action and shifts the focus from a product or service to customers and their needs and wants. CRM requires business owners to take the following steps:

- Collect meaningful information about existing customers and compile it in a database.
- Mine the database to identify the company's best and most profitable customers, their needs, and their buying habits. In most companies, a small percentage of customers account for the majority of sales and profits. These are the customers on whom a business should focus its attention and efforts.
- Focus on developing lasting relationships with these customers. This often requires entrepreneurs to "fire" some customers that require more attention, time, and expense than they generate in revenue for the business. Failing to do so reduces a company's return on its CRM effort.
- Attract more customers who fit the profile of the company's best customers.

Business owners are discovering that even though they may be providing their customers with satisfactory service and value, many of their customers do not remain loyal, choosing instead to buy from other companies. Businesses that provide poor customer service are in grave danger. Hepworth, a consulting firm that specializes in customer retention, measures its clients' **revenue at risk**, which calculates the sales revenue a company would lose by measuring the percentage of customers who would leave because of poor service. According to Hepworth's research, for companies that score in the top 25 percent on customer loyalty, revenue at risk averages just 3 percent. However, for companies that rate loyalty scores in the bottom 25 percent, poor customer service puts at risk an average of more than 12 percent of company revenue.[16] Today, earning customers' loyalty requires businesses to take customer focus and service to unprecedented levels, and that requires building long-term relationships with customers.

✦ GAINING *a* COMPETITIVE EDGE ✦

FISHing for Success

If you ever find yourself in Pike Place in Seattle, Washington, and you hear yelling, boisterous laughter and thunderous applause, then step closer and you'll see an animated crowd of people from all walks of life at the Pike Place Fish market having a blast! You'll see tourists who wandered by, amazed at the energy of the show they are enjoying, and the yogurt crowd, businesspeople from local offices who come by almost every day to eat their cups of yogurt (which they often hoist into the air as they cheer the fishmongers on). Most people's first reaction is "What is going on here? Is this place for real?" Indeed, it is for real, and the Pike Place Fish market offers entrepreneurs a valuable lesson in employee relations and motivation and in creating a base of loyal customers.

Pike Place Fish is famous for its playful, bustling, and raucous atmosphere and for its success at creating an environment that has transformed its employees from bored fishmongers who took little pride in their smelly, monotonous work into fish-selling dynamos who derive a great deal of pleasure from their work in the joyful setting they have created for themselves. Pike Place Fish has become widely known as the subject of popular books, including *FISH!* and *FISH! TALES,* and of videos based on the best-selling books. Companies of all sizes and in a multitude of industries have become students of this humble fish market so they can learn the principles that have made it wildly successful. What are those principles?

FISH! Principle 1. Choose your attitude

There is always a choice about the way you do your work, even if there is not a choice about the work itself. The employees at the Pike Place Fish market discovered that even though they cannot change the nature of their work (i.e., selling fish is smelly, hard work with days that start very early and can stretch for long hours), they do have control about the attitudes they brought to work. "We can bring a grouchy attitude and irritate our coworkers and customers," says one employee, "or we can bring a sunny, playful, cheerful attitude and have a great day."

FISH! Principle 2. Play

At the Pike Place Fish market, flying fish are a common occurrence! When a customer places an order, one of the employees yells out, "One salmon flying away to Minnesota!" All the other employees repeat in unison, "One salmon flying away to Minnesota!" The employee, decked out in his black rubber boots and white apron, grabs the salmon and then flings the fish through the air toward a coworker behind the counter, who makes an amazing one-handed catch before wrapping the fish for the customer. The crowd loves it, giving the cast of "fish performers" an enthusiastic round of applause. The scene is reminiscent of a playground—the only difference is that it's a group of adults at work who look like they're at recess. Still, the energy is electric.

FISH! Principle 3. Make their day

The playful attitude of the employees at the Pike Place Fish market allows them to engage their customers. These workers don't stand back; they mingle with the crowd, making eye contact with potential customers and talking with them. They engage their customers! "We try not to stand apart from our customers," says one worker, "but to find ways to respectfully include them in our fun. When we are successful, it makes their day."

FISH! Principle 4. Be present

The "fish guys" stay focused while working with customers. They are vigilant, focused on customers, looking for the next opportunity for action. *That's* what enables them to make a customer's day. They put their customers' needs before their own. Customers recognize that and respond.

Although most businesses can't throw fish around for fun, any business can use the FISH! principles to become a better place. At a small hospital, nurses were having a difficult time with an elderly patient who was near death. He was incoherent, agitated, and trying to pull out his intravenous tubes. When nurse assistant Leo Carter found out that the man had been an orchestra conductor for many years, his FISH! training took over. He had an idea. "I have my clarinet in my car," he told a nurse, who offered to cover for him while he retrieved the instrument. Leo assembled the instrument, practiced for a few minutes, and then went into the elderly patient's room. He played a classical piece, "Peter and the Wolf," and then the theme from *The Muppet Show*. Almost immediately, the man stopped thrashing and began to settle down. He lay on his back, raised his hands, and began to move them as if conducting *his* orchestra as Leo played. After a few

minutes, the man slowly moved his arms to his side, and he slept peacefully for the rest of the night. Leo had the next few days off, and when he returned to work, he learned that the man had died—peacefully, something for which his family credited Leo's kind gesture.

1. Research the FISH! principles in more detail. Using a job you have had or currently have, develop a strategy for applying these principles at work.
2. Explain the benefits of putting the FISH! philosophy into practice in a company.

Sources: Adapted from Stephen C. Lundin, Harry Paul, and John Christensen, *FISH!* (New York: Hyperion Publishing Company, 2000); Stephen C. Lundin, Harry Paul, and John Christensen, *FISH!* (New York: ChartHouse Learning Publishers, 2002).

Guerrilla Marketing Principles

To be successful guerrilla marketers, entrepreneurs must be as innovative in creating their marketing strategies as they are in developing new product and service ideas. The following 11 guerrilla marketing principles can help business owners develop a competitive edge: niche-picking, entertailing, building a consistent branding strategy, emphasizing their uniqueness, connecting with their customers, focusing on customers' needs, emphasizing quality, paying attention to convenience, concentrating on innovation, dedicating themselves to service, and emphasizing speed.

Find a Niche and Fill It. As we saw in Chapter 2, "Strategic Management and the Entrepreneur," many successful small companies choose their niches carefully and defend them fiercely rather than compete head-to-head with larger rivals. A niche strategy enables a small company to maximize the advantages of its smallness and to compete effectively even in industries dominated by giants. Focusing on niches that are too small to be attractive to large companies or in which entrepreneurs have unique expertise are

Company Example →

common recipes for success among thriving small companies. *Newkirk Environmental Inc. is an environmental consulting firm whose founders have used their expertise and experience to create a highly successful business in a small but fast-growing niche. The group of foresters, biologists, environmental planners, and former environmental regulators at Newkirk Environmental offers a full array of services, from environmental studies and protected species surveys to securing environmental permits and consulting services on how to meet the requirements of various environmental regulatory agencies. The company's clients range from developers of golf courses and residential housing complexes to marinas and large companies looking for locations to build new factories.*[17] "Small business is uniquely positioned for niche marketing," says marketing expert Philip Kotler. "If a small business sits down and follows the principles of targeting, segmenting, and differentiating, it doesn't have to collapse to larger companies."[18]

Don't Just Sell; Entertain. Numerous surveys have shown that consumers are bored with shopping and that they are less inclined to spend their scarce leisure time shopping than ever before. Winning customers today requires more than low prices and wide merchandise selection; increasingly, businesses are adopting strategies based on **entertailing**, the notion of drawing customers into a store by creating a kaleidoscope of sights, sounds, smells, and activities, all designed to entertain—and, of course, sell (think Disney). The primary goal of entertailing is to catch customers' attention and engage them in some kind of entertaining experience so that they shop longer and buy more goods or services. Entertailing involves "making [shopping] more fun, more educational, more interactive," says one retail consultant.[19] Research supports the benefits of entertailing's hands-on, interactive, educational, approach to selling; one study found that, when making a purchase, 34 percent of consumers are driven more by emotional factors such as fun and excitement than by logical factors such as price and convenience.[20]

Company Example → Entertailing's goal, of course, is not only to entertain but also to sell. *One small company that has successfully blended show business with the retail business is Build-A-Bear Workshop, a chain of retail stores where children of all ages can go to design and build their own teddy bears. As children enter a Build-A-Bear Workshop, they become Guest Bear Builders, and their first stop is the "Choose Me" station, where they select the unstuffed skin that will become their teddy bear (or monkey, frog, bunny, or other animal). The next stop is the "Hear Me" area, where children pick the sounds their animals will make. The message can be prerecorded or the children can record the sounds themselves. Next, guests go to the "Stuff Me" station, where with the help of an employee (a Master Bear Builder), they fill their animals to just the right volume on a machine that resembles a large popcorn popper. Each child then picks a tiny pillowy heart to be inserted before the stuffed animal is stitched up. Kids groom their new creations into just the right shape at the "Fluff Me" station before moving on to a row of computers where they name their animals and complete a birth certificate for them. Prices for each bear range from $10 to $25, but kids can choose from an assortment of clothing options—from argyle sweaters to athletic shoes—and accessories such as toy cell phones for their stuffed animals at prices ranging from $8 to $15. Just as in any clothing store, new styles arrive regularly. At the cash register, each guest receives a printed birth certificate signed by "Maxine Clark, C.E.B (Chief Executive Bear)." The child's new friend is packed safely into a house-shaped box, ready for the journey to its new home. Clark's unique brand of entertailing has made Build-A-Bear Workshops incredibly successful! The chain averages sales of $600 per square foot of store space, twice that of the average mall store. "When customers have fun, they spend more money," says Clark.* [21]

Build a Consistent Branding Strategy. Branding involves creating a distinct identity for a business and requires a well-coordinated effort at every touch point a company has with its customers. In an age where companies find standing out from the crowd of competitors increasingly difficult, branding strategies have taken on much greater importance. One way to do this is by defining exactly how your company's product or service solves a problem customers face, preferably in a unique fashion. Although entrepreneurs don't have the resources to invest in building a brand that Coca-Cola and Nike do (Nike's brand alone is estimated to be worth more than $1 billion), they can take steps to create value for their companies' images through branding. One way is to develop logos, letterheads, and graphics that serve as visual ambassadors for the company, communicating its desired image, values, and personality at a glance. Another aspect of creating a successful brand is to transform existing customers into evangelists for the company and its products by keeping them happy. Convincing celebrities to become customers also helps. Chrissy Azzaro, founder of My-Tee, a Los Angeles–based fashion company that sells its own line of T-shirts, tank tops, and accessories, has seen the value of her brand rise after stars such as Courtney Cox and Hilary Duff were photographed in My-Tee designs.[22]

Company Example → Ideally, an entrepreneur will spell out a company's brand strategy in the business plan. *Shelly Mars is the founder of Ecoluxe, an upscale organic dry-cleaning business with four locations in the Boston area. Mars spent $60,000 on establishing her company's brand name in its first year of operation, including creating a unified identity strategy that linked everything* *from Ecoluxe's logo and letterhead to its graphics and public relations efforts. Mars carefully selects her stores' locations with her target customers in mind, and her marketing efforts steer clear of discount coupons to avoid diluting the image and the value of the brand. In addition, she supports community events such as Earth Day to cement the environmentally friendly nature of her operation in the minds of her target customers. Her branding strategy is working; sales have climbed from $85,000 to more than $1 million in just four years!*[23]

Strive to Be Unique. One of the most effective guerrilla marketing tactics is to create an image of uniqueness for your business. Entrepreneurs can achieve a unique place in the market in a variety of ways, including through the products and services they offer, the marketing and promotional campaigns they use, the store layouts they design, and the business strategies they employ. The goal is to stand out from the crowd; few things are as uninspiring to customers as a "me-too" business that offers nothing unique.

Company Example →

One company that holds a unique place in the market is Hot Topic, a fast-growing chain of retail stores targeting angst-filled teenagers with products ranging from gothic clothing and offbeat T-shirts to CDs from up-and-coming bands and multitudes of body jewelry. One key to Hot Topic's success is its ability to understand its target customers, most of whom are members of Generation Y and the Millenials, and their fast-changing preferences. Everyone in the company, including store clerks, buyers, and the CEO, conducts market research by attending rock concerts and raves that its "alternative" customers frequent to see and to photograph what performers and fashion-forward fans are wearing. Every store keeps comment cards near the cash register for shoppers to fill out, and the company's Web site encourages customer comments, a tactic that produces more than 1,000 e-mails a month. When employees spot an emerging trend, Hot Topic moves fast, testing a small quantity of a new item in a small number of stores. If the product sells, managers roll it out nationwide. By using domestic suppliers, Hot Topic moves from the idea stage for a product to putting it on store shelves in as little as six to eight weeks, something that requires most retailers six to nine months! The result: Hot Topic marks down less than 10 percent of its merchandise, far lower than the average 40 percent markdown in the retail industry.[24]

Connect with Customers on an Emotional Level. Some of the most powerful marketers are those companies that have a clear sense of who they are, what they stand for, and why they exist. Defining their vision for their companies in a meaningful way is one of the most challenging tasks facing entrepreneurs. As we learned in Chapter 2, that vision stems from the beliefs and values of the entrepreneur and is reflected in a company's culture, ethics, and business strategy. Although it is intangible, this vision is a crucial ingredient in a successful guerrilla marketing campaign. Once this vision is firmly planted, guerrilla marketers can use it to connect with their customers. *ESPN Zone,*

Company Example →

a chain of restaurants that draws on the popularity of the parent company's widely recognized brand name, has succeeded in establishing an emotional connection with its core target audience of males between the ages of 25 and 39. Step into one of these restaurants, and you quickly realize that it is a shrine to sports! Giant HDTV screens play nonstop ESPN sports broadcasts (further reinforcing the brand), and a 10,000-square-foot section called the Sports Arena offers interactive games such as air hockey, NASCAR simulators, and a glacier climbing wall. Regular customers receive frequent diner cards that designate them as "Season Ticket Holders." Diners have plenty of opportunity to shop for merchandise emblazoned with the ESPN logo in the Studio Store section of the restaurant. The music, the décor, the attractions, and, of course, the food are all aimed squarely at ESPN's core customers. The menu includes hearty fare such as a full slab of barbecued ribs, the Zone Cheesesteak, and a full pound of chicken wings.[25]

Companies that establish a deeper relationship with their customers than one based merely on making a sale have the capacity to be exceptional guerrilla marketers. These

Managers at ESPN Zone understand that its target customers' world revolves around sports. The restaurant chain relies on the parent company's well-known brand name and features such as giant television screens broadcasting nonstop sports events and interactive games to connect with its core target audience of males age 25 to 39.

businesses win because customers receive an emotional boost every time they buy the company's product or service. Companies connect with their customers emotionally by supporting causes that are important to their customer base, taking exceptional care of their customers, and making it fun and enjoyable to do business with them. Harley-Davidson, the maker of classic motorcycles with that trademark throaty rumble, has established an emotional connection with its customers that makes many other businesses jealous.

Focus on the Customer. Too many companies have lost sight of the most important component of every business: the customer. Research shows that the average U.S. company loses about half of its customer base every five years, and many of those defections are the result of companies failing to take care of their customers.[26] Businesses are just beginning to discover the true costs of poor customer relations. For instance:

- Sixty-seven percent of customers who stop patronizing a particular store do so because an indifferent employee treated them poorly.[27]
- Customers are five times more likely to leave because of poor service than they are for product quality or price.[28]
- Ninety-six percent of dissatisfied customers never complain about rude or discourteous service, but . . .
- Ninety-one percent of these dissatisfied customers will not buy from the business again.
- One hundred percent of these unhappy customers will tell their "horror stories" to at least nine other people.
- Thirteen percent of those unhappy customers will tell their stories to at least 20 other people.[29]

According to the authors of *Keeping Customers for Life,* "The nasty result of this customer indifference costs the average company from 15 to 30 percent of gross sales."[30] Because 70 percent of the average company's sales come from existing customers, few can afford to alienate any customers. In fact, the typical business loses one-third of its customers each year.[31] But a recent study by the consulting firm Bain & Company shows that businesses that retain just 5 percent more customers experience

profit increases of at least 25 percent, and in some cases, as much as 95 percent![32] Increasing a company's retention rate by just 2 percent has the same impact as cutting expenses by 10 percent![33] Studies by the Boston Consulting Group also show that companies with high customer retention rates produce above-average profits and superior growth in market share.[34]

Because about 20 to 30 percent of a typical company's customers account for about 70 to 80 percent of its sales, it makes more sense to focus resources on keeping the best (and most profitable) customers than to spend them trying to chase "fair weather" customers who will defect to any better deal that comes along. Suppose that a company increases its customer base by 20 percent each year, but it retains only 85 percent of its existing customers. Its effective growth rate is just 5 percent per year [20% − (100% − 85%) = 5%]. If this same company can raise its customer retention rate to 95 percent, its net growth rate *triples* to 15 percent [20% − (100% − 95%) = 15%].[35] Shrewd entrepreneurs recognize that the greatest opportunity for new business often comes from existing customers.

Although winning new customers keeps a company growing, keeping existing ones is essential to success. Attracting a new customer actually costs five times as much as keeping an existing one. Table 7.1 shows the high cost of lost customers. Given these statistics, small business owners would be better off asking, "How can we improve customer value and service to encourage our existing customers to do more business with us?" rather than "How can we increase our market share by 10 percent?" Retailers have learned that allowing shoppers to customize their products has the power to increase customer retention, satisfaction, and profits. *When retailer Lands' End introduced a service that enabled customers to create made-to-order pants and dress shirts by answering a few questions online, managers thought the products, which sell for $15 to $20 more, would make up about 10 percent of sales.*

> Company Example

Table 7.1

The High Cost of Lost Customers

If you lose . . .	Spending $5 weekly	Spending $10 weekly	Spending $50 weekly	Spending $100 weekly	Spending $200 weekly	Spending $300 weekly
1 customer a day	$ 94,900	$ 189,800	$ 949,000	$ 1,898,000	$ 3,796,000	$ 5,694,000
2 customers a day	189,800	379,600	1,898,000	3,796,000	7,592,000	11,388,000
5 customers a day	474,500	949,000	4,745,000	9,490,000	18,980,000	28,470,000
10 customers a day	949,000	1,898,000	9,490,000	18,980,000	37,960,000	56,940,000
20 customers a day	1,898,000	3,796,000	18,980,000	37,960,000	75,920,000	113,880,000
50 customers a day	4,745,000	9,490,000	47,450,000	94,900,000	189,800,000	284,700,000
100 customers a day	9,490,000	18,980,000	94,900,000	189,800,000	379,600,000	569,400,000

Instead, custom-made garments account for 30 percent of online garment sales! Based on the customer's answers to the questions, software calculates the exact dimensions of the resulting garment, which are transmitted electronically to the factory. Two to three weeks later, the custom-made garment arrives on the customer's doorstep.[36]

The most successful small businesses have developed a customer orientation and have instilled a customer satisfaction attitude throughout the company. Companies with world-class customer attitudes set themselves apart by paying attention to the little things. For example, at one dentist's office, staff members take photos on a patient's first visit. The photo, placed in the patient's file, enables everyone in the office to call him by name on subsequent visits. A small flower shop offers a special service for customers who forget that special event. The shop will insert a card reading, "Please forgive us! Being shorthanded this week, we were unable to deliver this gift on time. We hope the sender's thoughtfulness will not be less appreciated because of our error. Again, we apologize." [37]

How do these companies focus so intently on their customers? They follow basic principles:

- When you create a dissatisfied customer, fix the problem fast. One study found that, given the chance to complain, 95 percent of customers will buy again if a business handles their complaints promptly and effectively.[38] The worst way to handle a complaint is to ignore it, to pass it off to a subordinate, or to let a lot of time slip by before dealing with it.
- *Encourage* customer complaints. You can't fix something if you don't know it's broken. Table 7.2 describes nine ways to turn complainers into satisfied customers.
- Ask employees for feedback on improving customer service. A study by Technical Assistance Research Programs (TARP), a customer service research firm, found that frontline service workers can predict nearly 90 percent of the cases that produce customer complaints.[39] Put that expertise to work by involving frontline employees in process improvement efforts. Emphasize that *everyone* is part of the customer satisfaction team.

Table 7.2

Ways to Turn Complainers into Satisfied Customers

When faced with a complaining customer, business owners naturally defend their companies. Don't do it! Here are nine ways to turn disgruntled buyers into loyal customers.

1. Let unhappy customers vent their feelings; don't interrupt; maintain eye contact and listen to them.
2. Remain objective; avoid labeling customers' emotions or passing judgment on them.
3. Promptly apologize and accept responsibility for the problem. Ask customers what they need to correct the error.
4. See the complaint for what it is. The customer is upset about something; zero in on what it is so you can fix it.
5. Wait until the customer finishes expressing a complaint and then respond with a solution.
6. Thank the customer; let him or her know you appreciate being told about the situation. Listen for suggestions the customer might have about resolving the complaint. Try to win a friend, not an argument.
7. Fix the problem quickly. The longer a business delays in resolving the problem, the less likely the customer is to be satisfied with the solution.
8. Follow up with the customer. Tell him or her what you're doing about a problem and make sure he or she is satisfied with the result. This shows that you really do care.
9. Ask yourself, "What changes do I need to make to our business system so this complaint does not occur again with this customer or other customers in similar situations?"

Sources: Adapted from Brian Caufield, "How to Win Customer Loyalty," *Business 2.0,* March 2004, pp. 77–78; Shirley Bednarz, "Fine Whine," *Entrepreneur,* February 1999, pp. 103–105; "Five Ways to Turn Complaints into Satisfied Customers," *Personal Selling Power,* April 1991, p. 53; "Handling Disgruntled Customers," *Your Company,* Spring 1993, p. 5.

- Get total commitment to superior customer service from top managers and allocate resources appropriately.
- Allow managers to wait on customers occasionally. It's a great dose of reality. Dell CEO Michael Dell and his team of top managers meet periodically with the company's major customers to get a better understanding of how to serve their needs more effectively.[40]
- Develop a service theme that communicates your attitude toward customers. Customers want to feel they are getting something special.
- Reward employees "caught" providing exceptional service to customers. At ScriptSave, a company that manages prescription-drug benefit programs, managers hand out Bravo Bucks that are redeemable for gifts to employees who excel in providing superior customer service.[41]
- Carefully select and train everyone who will deal with customers. View training for what it is: an investment rather than an expense. *Never* let rude employees work with customers. Charlie Horn, CEO of ScriptSave, requires all customer service representatives to go through three weeks of training before taking their first telephone call from a customer. Each representative also gets an additional 60 hours of classroom training in customer service techniques.[42]

Company Example

Devotion to Quality. In this intensely competitive global business environment, quality goods and services are a prerequisite for success—and even survival. According to one marketing axiom, the worst of all marketing catastrophes is to have great advertising and a poor-quality product. Customers have come to expect and demand quality goods and services, and those businesses that provide them consistently have a distinct competitive advantage. *Schreiner's Fine Sausage, now owned by Nancy Schiller, has remained a fixture in Phoenix, Arizona, by emphasizing the quality of the sausage products the company has sold since Hugo Schreiner started the company in 1955. Schiller cites the company's top-quality ingredients, high level of customer service, and family atmosphere as the keys that have enabled Schreiner's to thrive while many other small businesses have failed. Only the best ingredients go into the 65 varieties of sausage that are made by hand in the tiny factory behind the storefront. Employees still use the recipes that founder Hugo Schreiner brought from Germany five decades ago; others, such as chicken apple sausage and chorizo links, Schiller, who has a degree in food and nutrition, developed herself. Although sales are growing fast, Schiller is committed to keeping the operation small, which, she says, "has allowed us to keep our focus."* [43]

Today, quality is more than just a slogan posted on the company bulletin board; world-class companies treat quality as a strategic objective and an integral part of the company culture. This philosophy is called **total quality management** (**TQM**)—quality not just in the product or service itself but also in *every* aspect of the business and its relationship with the customer and in continuous improvement in the quality delivered to customers. Companies achieve continuous improvement by using statistical techniques to discover problems, determine their causes, and solve them; then they must incorporate what they have learned into improving the process. It is a never-ending system of improvement that relies on the DMAIC process shown in Figure 7.2.

Companies on the cutting edge of the quality movement are developing new ways to measure quality. Manufacturers were the first to apply TQM techniques, but retail, wholesale, and service organizations have seen the benefits of becoming champions of quality. They are tracking customer complaints, contacting "lost" customers, and finding new ways to track the cost of quality and their return on quality (ROQ). ROQ recognizes that although any improvement in quality may improve a company's competitive ability, only those improvements that produce a reasonable rate of return are worthwhile. In essence,

Figure 7.2

The Quality DMAIC Process

Source: Adapted from Walter H. Ettinger, MD, "Six Sigma," *Trustee,* September 2001, p.14.

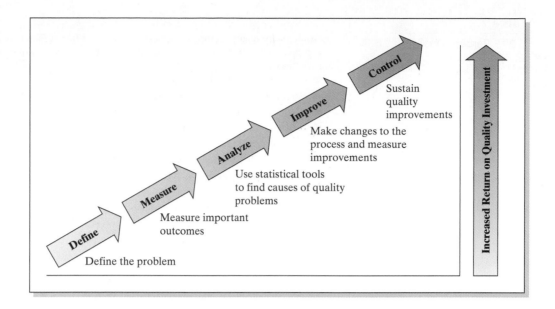

ROQ requires managers to ensure that the quality improvements they implement will more than pay for themselves.

Company Example

Dean Dunaway, president of Capweld Inc., a small gas distributor in Jackson, Mississippi, turned to a TQM philosophy known as poka-yoke (which comes from two Japanese words meaning "avoid errors") when the cost of lost gas tanks began to cause the company's profits to decline. When Capweld sells $20 worth of oxygen, it is delivered in a $200 tank. Although all of Capweld's tanks are numbered, keeping up with 15,000 to 20,000 transactions each month was difficult and inevitably led to missing tanks. Losing just one tank erased the profits on a huge number of sales. Putting together a team of employees to study the causes of the problem revealed that employees misreading tanks' identification numbers was the source of many lost tanks. The quality team suggested a computerized solution to solve the lost tank problem. Capweld now uses a computerized database to track the location of every one of its 40,000 tanks and has attached scannable microchips to them to avoid employee input errors. The company's poka-yoke efforts have more than paid for themselves by significantly lowering the number of lost tanks. Dunaway, who hopes to keep whittling away at the small errors that have a big impact at Capweld says, "It's just hundreds of little bitty things." [44]

The key to developing a successful TQM philosophy is seeing the world from the customer's point of view. In other words, quality must reflect the needs and wants of the customer. How do customers define quality? According to one survey, Americans rank quality components in this order: reliability (average time between failures), durability (how long it lasts), ease of use, a known or trusted brand name, and, last, a low price. [45] In services, customers are likely to look for similar characteristics: tangibles (equipment, facilities, and people), reliability (doing what you say you will do), responsiveness (promptness in helping customers), and assurance and empathy (conveying a caring attitude). Companies successful in capturing a reputation for top-quality products and services follow certain guidelines to "get it right the first time":

■ Build quality into the process; don't rely on inspection to obtain quality.
■ Emphasize simplicity in the design of products and processes; it reduces the opportunity for errors to sneak in.
■ Foster teamwork and dismantle the barriers that divide disparate departments.
■ Establish long-term ties with select suppliers; don't award contracts on low price alone.

Table 7.3

Is 99.9 Percent Quality
Good Enough?

In the battle for quality, companies quickly discover just how difficult zero defects are to achieve. Isn't 99.9 percent defect free good enough? Consider the following consequences of 99.9 percent quality and then decide:

- 1 hour of unsafe drinking water every month
- 730 unsafe landings at Chicago's O'Hare Airport each year
- 16,000 pieces of mail lost by the U.S. Postal Service every hour
- 20,000 incorrect drug prescriptions processed each year
- 500 incorrect surgical procedures each week
- 22,000 checks deducted from the wrong bank accounts each hour
- 2 million documents lost by the IRS every year
- 12 babies delivered to the wrong parents each day
- 1,314 telephone calls misrouted every minute
- 2,488,200 magazines published with the wrong covers each year
- 5,517,200 cases of soft drinks produced without any snap, sparkle, or fizz each year

Most entrepreneurs would love for their companies to operate at the 99.9 percent level of quality. However, unless business leaders and their companies continuously strive for 100 percent quality, there is little chance that they will ever achieve 99.9 percent quality. The goal, says one quality expert, "is to move away from the toleration of failure to the idea that we're going to be as perfect as we can be."

Sources: Adapted from Mark Henricks, "Is It Greek to You?" *Entrepreneur,* July 1999, p. 67; Sal Marino, "Is 'Good Enough' Good Enough?" *Industry Week,* February 3, 1997, p. 22; "Why 99.9% Just Won't Do," *Inc.,* April 1989, p. 276.

- Provide managers and employees the training needed to participate fully in the quality improvement program.
- Empower workers at all levels of the organization; give them authority and responsibility for making decisions that determine quality.
- Get managers' commitment to the quality philosophy. Otherwise, the program is doomed. Describing his role in his company's TQM philosophy, one CEO says, "People look to see if you just talk about it or actually do it." [46]
- Rethink the processes the company uses now to get its products or services to customers. Employees at Analog Devices redesigned its production process and significantly lowered the defect rate on its silicon chips, saving $1.2 million a year. [47]
- Reward employees for quality work. Ideally, employees' compensation is linked clearly and directly to key measures of quality and customer satisfaction.
- Develop a company-wide strategy for constant improvement of product and service quality.

The goal of these procedures is to achieve 100 percent quality. Table 7.3 offers insight into why 99.9 percent quality simply isn't good enough.

Attention to Convenience. Ask customers what they want from the businesses they deal with and one of the most common responses is "convenience." In this busy, fast-paced world of dual-career couples and lengthy commutes to and from work, consumers have more disposable income but less time in which to enjoy it. A generation ago, married couples worked an average of 3,331 hours a year; today, the typical married couple combines to put in 3,719 hours a year, an average of 71.5 hours a week. [48] Anything a business can do to enhance convenience for its customers will give it an edge. Several studies have found that customers rank easy access to goods and services at the top of their purchase criteria. Unfortunately, too few businesses deliver adequate levels of convenience, and they fail to attract and retain customers. One print and framing shop, for instance, alienated many potential customers with its abbreviated business hours—9 to 5 daily, except for Wednesday afternoons, Saturday, and Sunday when the shop was closed! Other companies make it a chore to do business with them. In an effort to defend themselves against unscrupulous customers, these businesses have created elaborate procedures for exchanges, refunds, writing checks, and other basic transactions.

Successful companies go out of their way to make it easy for customers to do business with them. *Kathleen Giordano, known as the Lady Barber, packs her scissors and clippers and makes "house" calls on her busy clients, usually in their offices, giving them the ultimate in convenience. Her customers, many of whom are entrepreneurs, work on their computers, make telephone calls, and even conduct business meetings—all while Giordano snips away!* One New York City plastic surgeon also makes office calls on his clients, showing up with a small, discreet cooler that keeps his supply of Botox injections cool. Most of his office call patients are men, whom the doctor notes prefer to keep their treatments private.[49]

Many small companies have had success by finding simple ways to make it easier for customers to do business with them. How can entrepreneurs boost the convenience levels of their businesses? By conducting a "convenience audit" from the customer's point of view to get an idea of its ETDBW ("Easy To Do Business With") index:

- Is your business located near your customers? Does it provide easy access?
- Are your business hours suitable to your customers? Should you be open evenings and weekends to serve them better?
- Would customers appreciate pickup and delivery service? The owner of a restaurant located near a major office complex installed a Web site and a fax machine to receive orders from busy office workers; a crew of employees would deliver lunches to the workers at their desks!
- Does your company make it easy for customers to make purchases on credit or with credit cards?
- Are you using technology to enhance customer convenience? nTag Interactive, a company started by Rick Borovoy and George Eberstadt, sells a unique lead retrieval system based on radio frequency identification (RFID), a topic Borovoy researched to earn his Ph.D. The wearable device uses RFID technology to allow trade show exhibitors and attendees to transfer information about themselves or their products, respond to surveys (or evaluate survey results in real time), and even identify people in the crowd with common interests or complementary needs—automatically! Users of nTag cite the device's ability to enhance the networking process conveniently as a major advantage.[50]
- Are your employees trained to handle business transactions quickly, efficiently, and politely? Waiting while rude, poorly trained employees fumble through routine transactions destroys customer goodwill.
- Do your employees use common courtesy when dealing with customers?
- Does your company offer "extras" that make customers' lives easier? With a phone call to one small gift store, customers in need of a special gift simply tell how much they want to spend, and the owner takes care of the rest—selecting the gift, wrapping it, and shipping it. All customers have to do is pay the invoice when it arrives in the mail.
- Can you adapt existing products to make them more convenient for customers? When J.M. Smucker Company began test-marketing a premade, frozen peanut butter and jelly sandwich, CEO Tim Smucker was amazed at the results. The sandwiches, called Uncrustables, generated $20 million in sales, and Smucker now sells them nationwide.[51]
- Does your company handle telephone calls quickly and efficiently? Long waits on hold, transfers from one office to another, and too many rings before answering signal customers that they are not important. Jerre Stead, CEO of Ingram Micro Inc., a distributor of computer products, expects every telephone call to the company to be answered within three seconds![52]

Company Example →

Concentration on Innovation. Innovation is the key to future success. Markets change too quickly and competitors move too fast for a small company to stand still and remain competitive. Because of their organizational and managerial flexibility, small businesses often can detect and act on new opportunities faster than large companies. Innovation is one of the greatest strengths of entrepreneurs, and it shows up in the new products, unique techniques, and unusual approaches they introduce. One study of companies with revenues less than $50 million by Coopers and Lybrand showed that nearly two-thirds of their CEOs believe their ability to develop new products represents a major competitive advantage.[53] *Victor and Janie Tsao, who launched Linksys Inc. in their garage in 1988, realized the importance of innovation early on in the life of their business. The company's unique, affordable wireless routers and hubs have become so popular among home computer users for easily and inexpensively linking home computers and peripherals that the company is the second leading manufacturer in the industry. The Tsaos' approach is simple: Study exactly what customers want networking technology to do and then roll out products rapidly to meet those needs. Linksys's size and flexibility are major competitive weapons. "We launch a new product a week," says one top manager. "By the time our competitors realize what's going on, we're already at work on the next one."[54]*

Despite financial constraints, small businesses frequently are leaders in innovation. For instance, small companies accounted for every significant breakthrough in the computer industry—including handhelds (Palm), microcomputers (Apple Computer), and minicomputers (Digital). Start-up businesses also led the way in developing each generation of computer disk drives. Even in the hotly competitive pharmaceutical industry, the dominant drugs in many markets were discovered by small companies rather than by industry giants, such as Merck or GlaxoSmithKline, with their multimillion dollar R&D budgets.

Although product and service innovation has never been more important to small companies' success, it has never been more challenging. Companies of all sizes are feeling the pressure to develop new products and get them to market faster than ever before. More intense competition, often from across the globe, as well as rapid changes in technology and improvements in communication have made innovation more crucial to business success. "Today's innovation is tomorrow's imitation is next month's commodity," says one business writer.[55] One survey of U.S. companies found that executives expected new products to account for 39 percent of profits in the next five years compared to just 25 percent in the previous five.[56] Ely Callaway, founder of Callaway Golf, the company that makes the famous Big Bertha club, claimed that innovation was his "No. 1 priority and a core value outlined in the company's mission statement. That's because Callaway Golf's long-term success depends on satisfying our customers with a constant stream of innovative new products."[57]

There is more to innovation than spending megadollars on research and development. How do small businesses manage to maintain their leadership role in innovating new products and services? They use their size to their advantage, maintaining their speed and flexibility much like a martial arts expert does against a larger opponent. Their closeness to their customers enables them to read subtle shifts in the market and to anticipate trends as they unfold. Their ability to concentrate their efforts and attention in one area also gives small businesses an edge in innovation. "Small companies have an advantage: a dedicated management team focused solely on a new product or market," says one venture capitalist.[58] *Woody Norris, holder of 43 patents and founder of American Technology Corporation in San Diego, has developed a sound technology using sonic beams that enable sound to be shaped, directed, and focused, much like light beams. The innovative technology, called Hypersonic Sound, enables sound waves beamed at one person to hear them while another person standing nearby cannot. Norris sees a multitude of applications for his invention, some already in operation. The military currently is testing the technology, and Norris*

Company Example

Company Example

is working with automakers to develop speakers that enable passengers to listen to different music without disturbing fellow passengers. Some supermarkets currently use the technology to beam recorded messages to individual shoppers based on the products they select from the store's shelves![59]

To be an effective innovator, an entrepreneur should:

- Make innovation a priority in the company by devoting management time and energy to it.
- Measure the company's innovative ability. Tracking the number of new products or services introduced and the proportion of sales products less than five years old generate can be useful measures of a company's ability to innovate.
- Set goals and objectives for innovation. Establishing targets and rewarding employees for achieving them can produce amazing results.
- Encourage new product and service ideas among employees. Workers have many incredible ideas, but they will lead to new products or services only if someone takes the time to listen to them.
- Always be on the lookout for new product and service ideas. They can come to you (or to anyone in the company) when you least expect it.
- Keep a steady stream of new products and services coming. Even before sales of her safety-handle children's toothbrush took off, Millie Thomas, founder of RGT Enterprises, had developed other children's products using the same triangular-shaped handle, including a crayon holder, paintbrushes, and fingernail brushes.[60]

Table 7.4 describes a screening device for testing the viability of new product ideas.

Dedication to Service and Customer Satisfaction. Small companies have discovered that providing superior personalized customer service can be a powerful strategic weapon against their larger rivals in whose stores customers often are ignored and have to serve themselves. Small companies that lack the financial resources of their larger rivals have

Table 7.4

Testing the Viability of a New Product Idea

Testing the viability of new product ideas in their early stages of development can help entrepreneurs avoid expensive product failures later—after they have already invested significant amounts of cash in developing and launching them. The Chester Marketing Group, Inc., of Washington Crossing, Pennsylvania, has developed the following test to determine the viability of a new product idea at each stage in the product development process. To calculate a new product idea's score, entrepreneurs simply multiply the score for each criterion by its weight and then add up the resulting weighted scores. For a product to advance to the next stage in the development process, its score should be at least 16.

Criterion	Score			Weight	Weighted Score
Extent of target market need	Below Average 1	Average 2	Above Average 3	2	
Potential profitability	Below Average 1	Average 2	Above Average 3	2	
Likely emergence of competition	Below Average 1	Average 2	Above Average 3	1	
Service life cycle	Below Average 1	Average 2	Above Average 3	1	
Compatibility with company strengths	Below Average 1	Average 2	Above Average 3	2	
				Total Weighted Score	

Source: Roberta Maynard, "Test Your Product Idea," *Nation's Business,* October 1997, p. 23.

discovered that offering exceptional customer service is one of the most effective ways to differentiate themselves and to attract and maintain a growing customer base. "It doesn't take money to [provide] good customer service," says the head of one retail company. "It takes a commitment."[61] Unfortunately, the level of service in most companies is poor. Those businesses that are not able to improve the quality of their service to customers will fail, whereas those that can create superior customer service will excel.

<table>
<tr><td>Company Example</td><td>→</td></tr>
</table>

Mark Soderstrom, founder of Southstream Seafoods, a small importer and wholesaler of frozen seafood, discovered early on that his business would have to set itself apart with superb customer service in order to thrive in an extremely competitive business. Rapid swings in fish prices can create both opportunities and problems for Southstream's customers, so Soderstrom began using a customer relationship management (CRM) software package to give customers updated information about changes in market prices so they could make good business decisions at purchase time. With the system, Southstream sends anywhere from 500 to 1,000 "customized" faxes a week with pricing information on products each customer is interested in. Customers find the information to be extremely valuable. "Knowledge is power," says Soderstrom, "and we're the people providing them with that power." Soderstrom credits his company's superior customer service as a major source of his company's success and growth, up from sales of $4 million to more than $60 million in just 10 years![62]

Successful businesses recognize that superior customer service is only an intermediate step toward the goal of customer satisfaction. These companies seek to go beyond customer satisfaction, striving for *customer astonishment*! They concentrate on providing customers with *quality, convenience,* and *service* as their customers define those terms. Certainly, the least expensive—and the most effective—way to achieve customer satisfaction is through friendly, personal service. Numerous surveys of customers in a wide diversity of industries, from manufacturing and services to banking and high technology, conclude that the most important element of service is "the personal touch." Indeed, a study conducted by market research firm NFO WorldGroup found that friendly service, not the food, is the primary reason customers return to a restaurant![63] Whatever the nature of the business, calling customers by name, making attentive, friendly contact, and truly caring about customers' needs and wants are more essential than any other factor, even convenience, quality, and speed!

How can a company achieve stellar customer service and satisfaction?

Listen to Customers. The best companies constantly listen to their customers and respond to what they hear. This allows them to keep up with customers' changing needs and expectations. The only way to find out what customers really want and value is to ask them. Businesses rely on a number of techniques including surveys, focus groups, telephone interviews, comment cards, suggestion boxes, toll-free hot lines, and regular one-on-one conversations with customers (perhaps the best technique). Starbucks founder Howard Schultz resisted using skim milk in the company's Italian lattes until he spent time working in a Starbucks outlet and listened to customers repeatedly ask for it.[64]

Define Superior Service. Based on what customers say, managers and employees must decide exactly what "superior service" means in the company. Such a statement should (1) be a strong statement of intent, (2) differentiate the company from others, and (3) have value to customers. Deluxe Corporation, a printer of personal checks, defines superior service quite simply: 48 hour turnaround, zero defects.

Set Standards and Measure Performance. To be able to deliver on its promise of superior service, a business must establish specific standards and measure overall performance against them. Satisfied customers should exhibit at least one of three behaviors: loyalty (increased customer retention rate), increased purchases (climbing sales and sales per customer), and resistance to rivals' attempts to lure them away with lower prices (market share and price tolerance).[65] Companies must track performance on these and other service standards and reward employees accordingly.

Examine Your Company's Service Cycle. What steps must a customer go through to get your product or service? Business owners often are surprised at the complexity that has seeped into their customer service systems as they have evolved over time. One of the most effective techniques is to work with employees to flowchart each component in the company's service cycle, including everything a customer has to do to get your product or service. The goal is to look for steps and procedures that are unnecessary, redundant, or unreasonable and then to eliminate them.

Hire the right employees. The key ingredient in the superior service equation is *people.* There is no substitute for friendly, courteous sales and service representatives. A customer service attitude requires hiring employees who believe in and embrace customer service. *Mike Faith, founder of Headsets.com, a San Francisco–based Internet and catalog retailer of telephone headsets, tries out each potential customer service representative before he decides whether to hire him or her. Faith looks for people who are outgoing, patient, and even-tempered during the company's four-interview process; candidates also must pass a battery of tests, including emotional profiling and IQ tests. Those who pass this phase must take a two-week training course and pass a "final exam" with a score of at least 95 before they join the company and talk to customers. Although the Headsets.com screening process is extremely rigorous and demanding—only one candidate in 30 is hired—Faith credits it with helping his company's sales climb from $3 million to $15 million in just four years!*[66]

Company Example

Train Employees to Deliver Superior Service. Successful businesses train every employee who deals directly with customers; they don't leave the art of customer service to chance. Superior service companies devote 1 to 5 percent of their employees' work hours to training, concentrating on how to meet, greet, and serve customers. "Employees need to be trained to instinctively provide good service," says John Tschol, founder of the Service Quality Institute.[67]

Empower Employees to Offer Superior Service. One of the biggest single variables determining whether employees deliver superior service is whether they perceive they have permission to do so. The goal is to push decision making down the organization to the employees who have contact with customers. This includes giving them the freedom to circumvent company policy if it means improving customer satisfaction. At Ritz-Carlton Hotels, every employee is authorized to spend up to $2,000 to resolve a customer's complaint.[68] If frontline workers don't have the power to solve disgruntled customers' problems, they quickly become frustrated and the superior service cycle breaks down. To be empowered, employees need knowledge and information, adequate resources, and managerial support.

Use Technology to Provide Improved Service. The role of technology is not to create a rigid bureaucracy but to free employees from routine clerical tasks, giving them more time and better tools to serve customers more effectively. Ideally, technology gives workers the information they need to help their customers and the time to serve them. *Mike Schapansky, owner of Pure-Chem, a pool maintenance company in Austin, Texas, equips his service technicians with handheld computers to boost customer service. Technicians use the Palm Pilots to record pool readings that are fed into a database at the end of each day. The system enables Pure-Chem to monitor customers' pools more closely and to respond to service calls more quickly.*[69]

Company Example

Reward Superior Service. What gets rewarded gets done. Companies that want employees to provide stellar service must offer rewards for doing so. One National Science Foundation study concluded that when pay is linked to performance, employees' motivation and productivity climb by as much as 63 percent.[70]

Get Top Managers' Support. The drive toward superior customer service will fall far short of its target unless top managers support it fully. Success requires more than just a verbal commitment; it calls for managers' involvement and dedication. Periodically, managers should spend time in customer service positions to maintain contact with customers, frontline employees, and the challenges of providing good service.

Emphasis on Speed. We live in a world of instantaneous expectations. Technology that produces immediate results at the click of a mouse and allows for real-time communication has altered our sense of time and space. Speed reigns. Customers now expect companies to serve them at the speed of light! In such a world, speed has become a major competitive weapon. World-class companies recognize that reducing the time it takes to develop, design, manufacture, and distribute a product reduces costs, increases quality, and boosts market share. One study by McKinsey and Company found that high-tech products that come to market on budget but six months late will earn 33 percent less profit over five years. Bringing the product out on time but 50 percent over budget cuts profits just 4 percent![71] Service companies also know that they must build speed into their business systems if they are to satisfy their impatient, time-sensitive customers.

This philosophy of speed is called **time compression management (TCM)**, and it involves three aspects: (1) speeding new products to market, (2) shortening customer response time in manufacturing and delivery, and (3) reducing the administrative time required to fill an order. Studies show plenty of room for improvement; most businesses waste 85 to 99 percent of the time it takes to produce products or services without ever realizing it![72] Although speeding up the manufacturing process is a common goal, companies using TCM have learned that manufacturing takes only 5 percent to 10 percent of the total time between taking an order and getting the product into the customer's hands. The rest is consumed by clerical and administrative tasks. The primary opportunity for TCM lies in its application to the administrative process.

Companies relying on TCM to help them turn speed into a competitive edge should:

- "Reengineer" the entire process rather than attempt to do the same things in the same way, only faster.
- Study every phase of the business process, whether it involves manufacturing, shipping, administration, or some other function, looking for small improvements that speed up the entire process.
- Create cross-functional teams of workers and give them the power to attack and solve problems. In world-class companies, product teams include engineers, manufacturers, salespeople, quality experts—even customers.
- Share information and ideas across the company. Easy access to meaningful information can speed a company's customer response time.
- Set aggressive goals for time reduction and stick to the schedule. Some companies using TCM have been able to reduce cycle time from several weeks to just a few hours!
- Instill speed in the culture. At Domino's Pizza, kitchen workers watch videos of the fastest pizza makers in the country.
- Use technology to find shortcuts wherever possible. Rather than build costly, time-consuming prototypes, many time-sensitive businesses use computer-aided design and computer-assisted manufacturing (CAD/CAM) to speed product design and testing.

Company Example →

Zara, a Spanish clothing manufacturer and retailer, uses speed to gain a competitive advantage in the fashion market, where tastes can change extremely quickly. Using a high-tech system that collects real-time sales information and funnels it to computerized manufacturing facilities, Zara is able to design and manufacture a new fashion collection in just four to five weeks. Most of its competitors require nine months to accomplish the same task. Zara can deliver current merchandise to its stores twice a week, something most competitors only dream about. The result of Zara's speed advantage is the ability to capitalize on the latest fashion trends and to avoid being stuck with large inventories of out-of-style merchandise.[73]

IN THE FOOTSTEPS OF AN ENTREPRENEUR...

Striving for Perfect Customer Service

Guests travel from all over the world to come to the Inn at Little Washington, a small village 70 miles west of Washington, D. C. and the first town to be named in honor of the first president of the United States, George Washington, who mapped out the city in 1749 when he was a surveyor. The inn has won practically every award possible in its industry. Owners Reinhardt Lynch and Patrick O'Connell take great satisfaction in knowing that *both* their hotel and their restaurant have won Mobil five-star ratings (the highest ranking achievable) an unbelievable five times! The inn's 100-seat dining room has been named the best restaurant in America, the equivalent of an Academy Award in the movie industry. The inn is a favorite among upscale guests looking for a respite from hectic schedules or a grueling travel agenda and scores an impressive number of repeat customers. Although the inn is well known for its spectacular food and cozy, quaint accommodations, its customer service is its most famous feature. *That's* really what sets the inn apart from its competition! What lessons can entrepreneurs learn from the Inn at Little Washington's approach to customer service? O'Connell offers the following suggestions for giving customers "the perfect experience."

Measure the customer's mood

When a party arrives at the dining room, the captain assigns a "mood rating" for the guests' state of mind, a number between 1 (low) and 10 (high) that indicates their level of contentment. A number of 7 or less indicates displeasure. Even though the inn had nothing to do with creating this negative mind-set, it becomes the concern of every employee. The rating is entered into the inn's computer system, where every staff member can see it. The goal? According to O'Connell, "No one should leave here below a 9." To transform guests' attitudes, staff members hold nothing back. They have been known to offer grumpy guests a tour of the kitchen, a complimentary round of champagne, a visit from one of the owners, and other "extras"—whatever it takes to make customers satisfied.

Cultivate expertise

Lynch and O'Connell demand that every employee be courteous to guests. One traveler said that arriving at the inn reminds him of visiting his grandparents, who come bursting out of the house at the first sight of their children and grandchildren with a warm greeting. They also require employees to develop an extraordinary degree of competence in their jobs, learning everything they can to become more proficient in serving customers. Everyone—from managers to waiters—gets a research project, a topic on which they must become experts. The assignment may be wild mushrooms, French Merlot wines, bread making, or some other topic, and staffers must demonstrate their expertise with presentations made to the rest of the employees.

Tolerate failure—once

Transforming guests from unhappy grumps to satisfied customers who are eager to return means that staffers have to be "on" 100 percent of the time and execute their jobs flawlessly. No one is perfect all of the time, however. When a gaffe occurs (for example, removing a guest's plate at the improper time or failing to know the answer to a question), O'Connell points out the mistake immediately, a practice he calls "instant correction." Employees do not have the opportunity to form bad habits.

Hire for attitude

When they first started their business, Lynch and O'Connell hired employees based on their technical skills and experience, which, they assumed, were the best indicators of success. They were wrong. Now they hire employees based on their attitudes. "We found that over time, nice people can be taught almost anything," says O'Connell. The practice works; employee turnover at the inn is miniscule in an industry known for incredibly high turnover rates.

Don't say "no"

The owners forbid staffers from answering a customer's question with the word "no." They want to avoid the negative connotations of the word altogether. If a customer asks, "Is this dessert sweet?" the waiter will not say "no," even if the dish is spicy. Instead, he or she will describe the dessert in detail, allowing the guest to make an informed decision. Before they are allowed to become "full cut" waiters, trainees must endure an onslaught of questions about the inn, its menu, and every detail of its operation. To help employees stay informed, Lynch and O'Connell publish an in-house monthly newsletter and a list of the 12 most frequently asked questions and how they are to be answered.

1. Do most upscale restaurants match the level of service the inn provides? Why or why not?
2. Select a local business (not necessarily a restaurant) with which you are familiar. Form a team with a few of your classmates to brainstorm ways that the company can use the principles from the Inn at Little Washington and others you develop to improve its customer service.

Sources: Adapted from D. M. Osborne, "A Recipe for Perfection," *Inc.,* July 2003, pp. 36–37; Laura Werlin, "The Inn at Little Washington," www.sallys-place.com/travel/n_america/eus_little_washington.htm.

Marketing on the World Wide Web (WWW)

5. Discuss marketing opportunities the World Wide Web offers and how entrepreneurs can take advantage of them.

Much like the telephone, the fax machine, and home shopping networks, the World Wide Web (WWW, or Web) has become a revolutionary business tool. Although most entrepreneurs have heard about the **World Wide Web**, the vast network that links computers around the globe via the Internet and opens up endless oceans of information to its users, the majority of them are still struggling to understand what it is, how it can work for them, and how they can establish a presence on it. Businesses get on the Web by using one of thousands of "electronic gateways" to set up an address (called a Universal Resource Locator, or URL). By establishing a creative, attractive Web site as the electronic storefront for a company on the Web, even the smallest companies can market their products and services to customers across the globe. With its ability to display colorful graphics, sound, animation, and video as well as text, the Web enables small companies to equal or even surpass their larger rivals' Web presence. Although small companies cannot match the marketing efforts of their larger competitors, a creative Web page can be the "great equalizer" in a small company's marketing program, giving it access to markets all across the globe. The Web gives small businesses the power to broaden their scope to unbelievable proportions. Web-based businesses are open around the clock, seven days a week and can reach customers anywhere in the world. Dean Talbert, owner of the 10,000-acre Alice L Ranch in California, now uses the Web to buy and sell cattle, which is a big change from the traditional face-to-face methods still used by most ranchers. "I'm selling to people back east, places I've never sold to before the Internet," he says.[74]

The Web has become a mainstream marketing medium, one that small business owners cannot afford to ignore, primarily because of its impressive power and reach. In 2004, 30 percent of the U.S. population made purchases online; by 2008, experts estimate that the online buying population will be 50 percent, representing a huge opportunity for businesses that are Web-savvy.[75] Online retail sales in the United States, which hit $65 billion in 2004, are expected to climb to $117 billion by 2008.[76] As impressive as the business-to-consumer (B-to-C) sales are, sales in the business-to-business (B-to-B) market dwarf them! In fact, 93 percent of all e-commerce is in the B-to-B sector. Unfortunately, most small businesses are not yet taking advantage of the Web's tremendous marketing potential; only 43 percent of small companies have Web sites.[77] Of those small businesses that do have Web sites, only 40 percent actually generate revenues from online sales. The most common reasons business owners cite for not creating a Web presence are concerns that their products and services are not suitable for online sales and the failure to see the benefit of selling online.[78] The result is a disproportionately small impact of small companies on the Web. According to Forrester Research, although small businesses make nearly 50 percent of all retail sales in the United States, they account for just 6 percent of all *online* sales![79]

Small companies that have had the greatest success selling on the Web have marketing strategies that emphasize their existing strengths and core competencies. Their Web marketing strategies reflect their "brick-and-mortar" marketing strategies, often focusing on building relationships with their customers rather than merely scouting for a sale. These companies understand their target customers and know how to reach them using the Web. They create Web sites that provide meaningful information to their customers, that customize themselves based on each customer's interests, and that make it easy for customers to find what they want. In short, their Web sites create the same sense of trust and personal attention customers get when dealing with a local small business.

Using the Web as a marketing tool allows entrepreneurs to provide both existing and potential customers with meaningful information in an interactive rather than a passive setting. Well-designed Web sites include interactive features that allow customers to access information about a company, its products and services, its history, and other features such as question-and-answer sessions with experts or the ability to conduct e-mail or online conversations with company officials. A survey by International Customer Service Association and e-Satisfy Ltd. found that just 4 percent of Web sites use live, online chats even though other studies show that the inability to talk with a salesperson is the reason that 94 percent of visitors to Web sites never buy.[80] An online chat feature on the company's Web site has allowed John Moore, owner of Spill 911 Inc., a small industrial product supplier, to reduce the number of customers abandoning their shopping carts by 60 percent. Moore says the chat feature allows customers to ask specific questions and reassures them that they are dealing with a reputable company.

The Web allows business owners to link their companies' home pages to other related Web sites, something advertisements in other media cannot offer. For instance, a company selling cookware might include hypertext links on its Web page to other pages containing recipes, cookbooks, foods, and other cooking resources. This allows small business owners to engage in cross-marketing with companies on the Web selling complementary products or services. The Web also magnifies a company's ability to provide superior customer service at minimal cost. An innovative Web site allows customers to gather information about a product or service, have their questions answered, download diagrams and photographs, or track the progress of their orders. *For more than 30 years, Peter Monticup, founder of MagicTricks.com, a Web-based e-commerce retailer of magic tricks, videos, and memorabilia located in Charlottesville, Virginia, operated brick-and-mortar magic stores that never generated more than $100,000 in annual revenues. Then in 1995 his wife Jackie, who is vice president of the business, suggested that they experiment with the World Wide Web as a marketing tool. She built a Web site and found a company to host it and another to handle the online shopping cart and inventory database functions. "The site cost us hardly anything to put up," she says. In its first year, the MagicTricks.com Web site generated 50 percent of the company's total sales. It has proved to be so effective that the Monticups decided to close their retail stores to focus exclusively on e-commerce. The site lists more than 1,400 constantly changing magic products—from card decks to the box for sawing someone in half—as well as articles on magic tricks, biographies of famous magicians, the history of magic, tips for performing magic tricks, and many other topics. The informative content "establishes our expertise and makes customers more secure about our buying recommendations," says Jackie, who spends most of her time maintaining the site and measuring its performance. Peter manages the company's inventory, and he and another professional magician provide customer service, primarily through e-mail. To boost its customer service, MagicTricks.com recently added to the site video segments in which Peter demonstrates*

Company Example

various magic tricks. The Monticups are extremely pleased with their online company's rapid growth and the flexibility it offers them as entrepreneurs. "I grew up thinking you had to have a walk-in business," says Peter. "Then I came to my senses."[81]

Just as in any marketing venture, the key to successful marketing on the World Wide Web is selling the right product or service at the right price to the right target audience. Entrepreneurs on the Web, however, also have two additional challenges: attracting Web users to their Web sites and converting them into paying customers. That requires setting up an electronic storefront that is inviting, easy to navigate, interactive, and offers more than a monotonous laundry list of items. Companies that do so are selling everything from wine and vacations to jewelry and electronics successfully on the Web. Among the top-selling items on the Web are travel services, computers and computer-related products, books, consumer electronics, clothing, and music.

We will discuss using the Web as a business tool in Chapter 13, "E-Commerce and Entrepreneurship."

The Marketing Mix

6. Discuss the "four Ps" of marketing—product, place, price, and promotion—and their role in building a successful marketing strategy.

The major elements of a marketing strategy are the "four Ps" of marketing—product, place, price, and promotion. These four elements are self-reinforcing and, when coordinated, increase the sales appeal of a product or service. Small business managers must integrate these elements to maximize the impact of their product or service on the consumer. All four Ps must reinforce the image of the product or service the company presents to the potential customer. One longtime retailer claims, "None of the modern marvels of computerized inventory control and point-of-sale telecommunications have replaced the need for the entrepreneur who understands the customer and can translate that into the appropriate merchandise mix."[82]

Product

The product itself is an essential element in marketing. Products can have form and shape, or they can be services with no physical form. Products travel through various stages of development. The **product life cycle** (see Figure 7.3) measures these stages of growth, and these measurements enable the company's management to make decisions about whether to continue selling the product and when to introduce new follow-up products.

Figure 7.3

Product Life Cycle

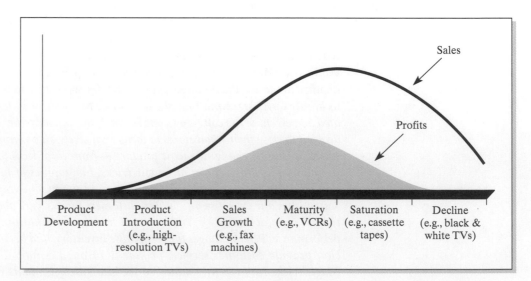

| Product Development | Product Introduction (e.g., high-resolution TVs) | Sales Growth (e.g., fax machines) | Maturity (e.g., VCRs) | Saturation (e.g., cassette tapes) | Decline (e.g., black & white TVs) |

In the *introductory stage,* marketers present their products to potential consumers. Initial high levels of acceptance are rare. Generally, new products must break into existing markets and compete with established products. Advertising and promotion help the new product be more quickly recognized. Potential customers must get information about the product and the needs it can satisfy. The cost of marketing a product at this level of the life cycle is usually high. The small company must overcome customer resistance and inertia. Thus, profits are generally low, or even negative, at the introductory stage.

After the introductory stage, the product enters the *growth and acceptance stage.* In the growth stage, consumers begin to compare the product in large enough numbers for sales to rise and profits to increase. Products that reach this stage, however, do not necessarily become successful. If in the introductory or the growth stage the product fails to meet consumer needs, it does not sell and eventually disappears from the marketplace. For successful products, sales and profit margins continue to rise through the growth stage.

In the *maturity and competition stage,* sales volume continues to rise, but profit margins peak and then begin to fall as competitors enter the market. Normally, this causes reduction in the product's selling price to meet competition and to hold its share of the market.

Sales peak in the *market saturation stage* of the product life cycle and give the marketer fair warning that it is time to begin product innovation.

The final stage of the product life cycle is the *product decline stage.* Sales continue to drop, and profit margins fall drastically. However, when a product reaches this stage of the cycle, it does not mean that it is doomed to failure. Products that have remained popular are always being revised. No firm can maintain its sales position without product innovation and change. Even the maker of Silly Putty, first introduced at the 1950 International Toy Fair (with lifetime sales of more than 300 million "eggs"), recently introduced new Day-Glo and glow-in-the-dark colors. These innovations have caused the classic toy's sales to surge by more than 60 percent.[83]

The time span of the stages in the product life cycle depends on the type of products involved. The life cycle for golf equipment has shrunk over the past decade from three or four years to less than one year today.[84] High-fashion and fad clothing has a short product life cycle, lasting for only four to six weeks. Products that are more stable may take years to complete a life cycle. Research conducted by MIT suggests that the typical product's life cycle lasts 10 to 14 years.

Understanding the product life cycle can help a business owner plan the introduction of new products to the company's product line. Too often, companies wait too late into the life cycle of one product to introduce another. The result is that they are totally unprepared when a competitor produces a " better mousetrap" and their sales decline. The ideal time to develop new products is early on in the life cycle of the current product (see Figure 7.4). Waiting until the current product is in the saturation or decline stages is like living on borrowed time.

Place

Place (or method of distribution) has grown in importance as customers expect greater service and more convenience from businesses. Because of this trend, mail-order houses, home shopping channels, home shopping parties, and the World Wide Web offering the ultimate in convenience—shop at home—have experienced booming sales in recent years. In addition, many traditionally stationary businesses have added wheels, becoming mobile animal clinics, computer repair shops, and dentist offices.

Figure 7.4

Time Between
Introduction of Products

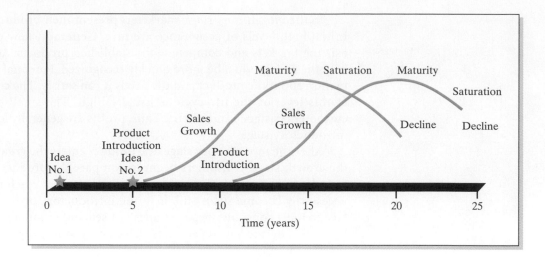

Any activity involving movement of goods to the point of consumer purchase provides place utility. Place utility is directly affected by the marketing channels of distribution, the path that goods or services and their titles take in moving from producer to consumer. Several companies, including the Pampered Chef, Southern Living, and Bill Blass, are returning to the home shopping parties pioneered by Brownie Wise at Tupperware and Mary Kay Ash at Mary Kay Cosmetics in the 1940s and 1950s. Home parties, where one enterprising sales consultant invites her friends into her home for an evening of fun, fellow-ship, and shopping, accounts for nearly $8.3 billion in sales a year.[85] Bill Blass now sells its Bill Blass New York line of women's clothing (priced from $75 to $1,000) through a network of 100 sales consultants selling from their homes and from hotel rooms, targeting women "who don't have a lot of time to shop but who want personal service," says one executive.[86]

Channels typically involve a number of intermediaries who perform specialized functions that add valuable utility to the goods or service. Specifically, these intermediaries provide time utility (making the product available when customers want to buy it) and place utility (making the product available where customers want to buy it).

For consumer goods, there are four common channels of distribution (see Figure 7.5).

1. *Manufacturer to consumer.* In some markets, producers sell their goods or services directly to consumers. Services, by nature, follow this channel of distribution. Dental care and haircuts, for example, go directly from creator to consumer.
2. *Manufacturer to retailer to consumer.* Another common channel involves a retailer as an intermediary. Many clothing items, books, shoes, and other consumer products are distributed in this manner. *Blue Bell Creameries ("We eat all we can and we sell the rest"), the third largest ice-cream retailer in the United States, currently sells its luscious line of ice cream in just 14 southern states, where second-generation owner Howard Kruse maintains tight control over distribution. The company buys its own refrigerated trucks, and only Blue Bell drivers can stock freezers in the grocery and convenience stores that account for most of the company's sales. Many customers in states outside the company's territory pay $85 to have four half-gallons of their favorite flavors packed in dry ice and shipped to them via overnight delivery.*[87]
3. *Manufacturer to wholesaler to retailer to consumer.* This is the most common channel of distribution. Prepackaged food products, hardware, toys, and other items are commonly distributed through this channel.
4. *Manufacturer to wholesaler to wholesaler to retailer to consumer.* A few consumer goods (e.g., agricultural goods and electrical components) follow this pattern of distribution.

Company Example

Figure 7.5

Channels of Distribution: Consumer Goods

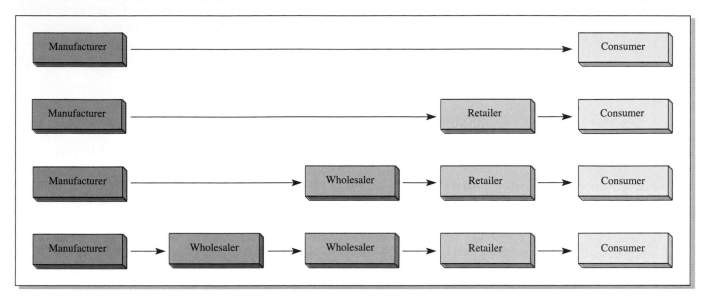

Two channels of distribution are common for industrial goods (see Figure 7.6).

1. *Manufacturer to industrial user.* The majority of industrial goods are distributed directly from manufacturers to users. In some cases, the goods or services are designed to meet the user's specifications.
2. *Manufacturer to wholesaler to industrial user.* Most expense items (paper clips, paper, rubber bands, cleaning fluids) that firms commonly use are distributed through wholesalers. For most small manufacturers, distributing goods through established wholesalers and agents is often the most effective route. With their limited resources, entrepreneurs sometimes have to rely on nontraditional distribution channels and use their creativity to get their products into customers' hands.

Price

Almost everyone agrees that the price of the product or service is a key factor in the decision to buy. Price affects both sales volume and profits, and without the right price, both sales and profits will suffer. As we will see in Chapter 10, the right price for a product or service depends on three factors: (1) a small company's cost structure, (2) an assessment

Figure 7.6

Channels of Distribution: Industrial Goods

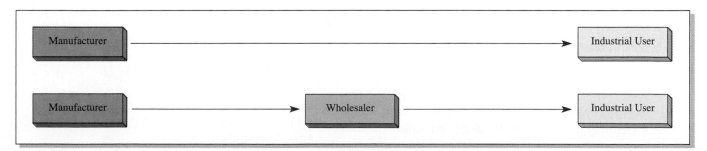

of what the market will bear, and (3) the desired image the company wants to create in its customers' minds.

For many small businesses, nonprice competition, focusing on factors other than price, is a more effective strategy than trying to beat larger competitors in a price war. Nonprice competition, such as free trial offers, free delivery, lengthy warranties, and money-back guarantees, intends to play down the product's price and stress its durability, quality, reputation, or special features.

Promotion

Promotion involves both advertising and personal selling. Advertising communicates to potential customers through some mass medium the benefits of a good or service. Personal selling involves the art of persuasive sales on a one-to-one basis.

The goals of a small company's promotional efforts are to create a brand image, to persuade customers to buy, and to develop brand loyalty. Promotion can take many forms and is put before the public through a variety of media. Entrepreneurs often must find ways to use low-cost guerrilla tactics to create promotions that get their companies noticed by both local and national media. Chapter 11, is devoted to creating an effective advertising and promotion campaign for a small company.

▌▐▐ Chapter Review

1. Describe the components of a guerrilla marketing plan and explain the benefits of preparing one.

   - A major part of the entrepreneur's business plan is the marketing plan, which focuses on a company's target customers and how best to satisfy their needs and wants. A solid marketing plan should pinpoint the specific target markets the company will serve, determine customer needs and wants through market research, analyze the firm's competitive advantages and build a marketing strategy around them, and create a marketing mix that meets customer needs and wants.

2. Explain how small businesses can pinpoint their target markets.

   - Sound market research helps the owner pinpoint his or her target market. The most successful businesses have well-defined portraits of the customers they are seeking to attract.

3. Explain how to determine customer needs through market research and outline the steps in the market research process.

   - Market research is the vehicle for gathering the information that serves as the foundation of the marketing plan. Good research does not have to be complex and expensive to be useful. The steps in conducting market research include:
     - Defining the problem: "What do you want to know?"

   - Collecting the data from either primary or secondary sources.
   - Analyzing and interpreting the data.
   - Drawing conclusions and acting on them.

4. Describe the guerrilla marketing strategies on which a small business can build a competitive edge in the marketplace.

   - When plotting a marketing strategy, owners must strive to achieve a competitive advantage, some way to make their companies different from and better than the competition. Successful small businesses rely on 11 guerrilla marketing strategies to develop a competitive edge:
   - Nichepicking
   - Entertailing
   - Building a consistent branding strategy
   - Emphasizing their uniqueness
   - Connecting with their customers
   - Focusing on customers' needs
   - Emphasizing quality
   - Paying attention to convenience
   - Concentrating on innovation
   - Dedicating themselves to service
   - Emphasizing speed

5. Discuss the marketing opportunities the World Wide Web offers and how entrepreneurs can take advantage of them.

- The Web offers small business owners tremendous marketing potential on a par with their larger rivals. Entrepreneurs are just beginning to uncover the Web's profit potential, which is growing rapidly. Successful Web sites are attractive, inviting, easy to navigate, interactive, and offer users something of value.

6. Discuss the "four Ps" of marketing—product, place, price, and promotion—and their role in building a successful marketing strategy.

- The marketing mix consists of the "four Ps":

Product. Entrepreneurs should understand where in the product life cycle their products are.

Place. The focus here is on choosing the appropriate channel of distribution and using it most efficiently.

Price. Price is an important factor in customers' purchase decisions, but many small businesses find that nonprice competition can be profitable.

Promotion. Promotion involves both advertising and personal selling.

Discussion Questions

1. What is a marketing plan? What lies at its center?
2. What objectives should a marketing plan accomplish?
3. How can market research benefit a small business owner? List some possible sources of market information.
4. Does market research have to be expensive and sophisticated to be valuable? Explain.
5. Why is it important for small business owners to define their target markets as part of their marketing strategies?
6. What is a competitive edge? How might a small company gain a competitive edge?
7. Describe how small business owners could use the following sources to a competitive advantage: niche-picking, entertailing, building a consistent branding strategy, emphasizing uniqueness, connecting with their customers, focusing on customers' needs, emphasizing quality, paying attention

to convenience, concentrating on innovation, dedicating themselves to service, and emphasizing speed.

8. What is the World Wide Web? Describe its marketing potential for small businesses.
9. Explain the concept of the marketing mix. What are the four Ps?
10. List and explain the stages in the product life cycle. How can a small firm extend its product's life?
11. With a 70 percent customer retention rate (average for most U.S. firms according to the American Management Association), every $1 million of business in 2005 will grow to more than $4 million by the year 2015. If you retain 80 percent of your customers, the $1 million will grow to a little over $6 million. If you can keep 90 percent of your customers, that $1 million will grow to more than $9.5 million. What can the typical small business do to increase its customer retention rate?

Building a Guerrilla Marketing Plan

Business PlanPro

Although entrepreneurs typically lack the large marketing budgets of their larger rivals, their marketing efforts can be just as effective, if not more effective, if these small business owners develop an innovative guerrilla marketing plan. A guerrilla marketing plan is a vital part of an entrepreneur's total marketing plan. In fact, many experts suggest that the marketing plan should occupy about one-fourth to one-third of a business plan.

In this portion of Business Plan Pro, you will complete the major components of your marketing plan. Don't expect to finish at one sitting. Building a solid marketing plan requires time and research. You must prove that a market for your products or services really does exist, and that requires *research*. This market research also forms the basis of the financial analysis you will develop for your business plan later. The companies that excel at meeting their customers' needs learn everything they can about their target customers: their characteristics, habits, preferences, demographic profiles, and other traits. Only then is it possible for entrepreneurs to create marketing strategies to reach their target customers.

Use the concepts from Chapter 7 to help you describe the goods and services you are selling. Remember to include the intangible needs that your products and/or services may meet. This portion of the plan should discuss the unique nature of the products and/or services your business provides its customer base and the factors that make your products and/or services superior to those of your competitors. You also should discuss how you will use technology to provide superior service to your customers and to gain an edge over competitors.

A key ingredient of any marketing plan is a thorough description of the customers at whom a company aims its products and services. This is where extensive market research begins to pay off. Like the financial portion of a business plan that focuses on cash flow, profits, and owner's equity, the market analysis examines numbers but analyzes them from a different perspective. Here the ultimate focus is on target customers. Be specific as you describe the segments that make up your company's target customers and estimate the growth in each market segment over a five-year time horizon. If you report exceptionally large percentage increases or decreases in any segment over the time period, be sure to explain both the causes of these changes as well as their impact on your business venture. Identifying key trends that influence the growth of each market segment also helps. The more specifically you can describe the market segment, the better your understanding of the importance of each segment to your business and which marketing strategies will reach them best. Locating a market segment is only part of the picture, however. Your marketing plan also must demonstrate the methods and techniques you will use to reach your target customers.

The Business You're In section asks you to develop an overview of the industry in which you compete and its key participants, including the economic and competitive environment of the business. If other external factors such as the political or legal/regulatory environment are relevant to understanding your business, be sure to include a description of them. This section of the plan also asks you to describe your company's distribution strategy—how you intend to get products and services into customers' hands.

Your company's sales strategy, how you plan to sell your product/services, is the focus of the Your Sales Forecast section of Business Plan Pro. Every business is unique, and the sales strategy must be tailored to the relationship between buyers' needs and wants and the key features of the products and services that you are offering. This section also addresses sales representatives' compensation and order processing.

Completing the Sales Forecast Table allows you to verify that your sales forecasts and estimates for cost of goods sold are realistic. This is the narrative that explains the numbers in the Sales Forecast Table. Be sure that you state clearly the assumptions on which you based your sales forecasts. Are the assumptions that support your sales estimates reasonable? Explain why your sales are projected to increase or decrease over time.

Defining your company's competitive edge boils down to defining those things that set your company apart from its competitors. What can you offer your customers that competitors cannot or do not?

Once you complete these sections of Business Plan Pro, you have a basic marketing plan in place. Across the next several chapters, you will fill in the missing pieces to the all-important marketing puzzle.

Chapter 8
Creating a Solid Financial Plan

> *You can't tell who's swimming naked until after the tide goes out.*
> —David Darst

> *In the wake of numerous corporate financial scandals in which managers misrepresented their companies' financial positions, one pundit offers this definition of EBIT (in reality, earnings before interest and taxes): "earnings before irregularities and tampering."*
> —Mortimer B. Zuckerman

Upon completion of this chapter, you will be able to:

1. Understand the importance of preparing a financial plan.

2. Describe how to prepare financial statements and use them to manage a small business.

3. Create projected financial statements.

4. Understand the basic financial statements through ratio analysis.

5. Explain how to interpret financial ratios.

6. Conduct a break-even analysis for a small company.

One of the most important steps in launching a new business venture is fashioning a well-designed, logical financial plan. Potential lenders and investors demand such a plan before putting their money into a start-up company. More important, a financial plan can be a vital tool that helps entrepreneurs manage their businesses more effectively, steering their way around the pitfalls that cause failures. Entrepreneurs who ignore the financial aspects of their businesses run the risk of watching their companies become just another failure statistic. One financial expert says of small companies, "Those that don't establish sound controls at the start are setting themselves up to fail."[1] Still, according to one survey, one-third of all entrepreneurs run their companies without any kind of financial plan.[2] Another study found that only 11 percent of small business owners analyzed their financial statements as part of the managerial planning and decision-making process.[3] Why is the level of financial planning and analysis so low among entrepreneurs? The primary reason is the lack of financial know-how. A survey of small business owners by Greenfield Online found that accounting was the most intimidating part of managing their businesses and that more than half had no formal financial training at all.[4] To reach profit objectives, entrepreneurs cannot afford to be intimidated by financial management and must be aware of their companies' overall financial position and the changes in financial status that occur over time.

This chapter focuses on some very practical tools that will help entrepreneurs develop workable financial plans, keep them focused on their company's financial plan, and enable them to create a plan for earning a profit. They can use these tools to anticipate changes and plot an appropriate profit strategy to meet them head on. These profit planning techniques are not difficult to master, nor are they overly time consuming. We will discuss the techniques involved in preparing projected (pro forma) financial statements, conducting ratio analysis, and performing break-even analysis.

Basic Financial Reports

Before we begin building projected financial statements, it would be helpful to review the basic financial reports that measure a company's financial position: the balance sheet, the income statement, and the statement of cash flows. Studies show that the level of financial reporting among small businesses is high; some 81 percent of the companies in one survey regularly produced summary financial information, almost all of it in the form of these traditional financial statements.[5]

The Balance Sheet

The balance sheet takes a "snapshot" of a business, providing owners with an estimate of the firm's worth on a given date. Its two major sections show the assets a business owns and the claims creditors and owners have against those assets. The balance sheet is usually prepared on the last day of the month. Figure 8.1 shows the balance sheet for Sam's Appliance Shop for the year ended December 31, 200X.

The balance sheet is built on the fundamental accounting equation: Assets = Liabilities + Owner's Equity. Any increase or decrease on one side of the equation must be offset by an equal increase or decrease on the other side; hence, the name *balance sheet*. It provides a baseline from which to measure future changes in assets, liabilities, and equity (or net worth). The first section of the balance sheet lists the firm's **assets** (valued at cost, not actual market value) and shows the total value of everything the business owns. **Current assets** consist of cash and items to be converted into cash

Figure 8.1

Balance Sheet, Sam's
Appliance Shop

ASSETS		
CURRENT ASSETS		
Cash		$ 49,855
Accounts Receivable	$179,225	
Less Allowance for Doubtful Accounts	$ 6,000	$173,225
Inventory		$455,455
Prepaid Expenses		$ 8,450
Total Current Assets		$686,985
FIXED ASSETS		
Land		$ 59,150
Buildings	$ 74,650	
Less Accumulated Depreciation	$ 7,050	$ 67,600
Equipment	$ 22,375	
Less Accumulated Depreciation	$ 1,250	$ 21,125
Furniture and Fixtures	$ 10,295	
Less Accumulated Depreciation	$ 1,000	$ 9,295
Total Fixed Assets		$157,170
Intangibles (Goodwill)		$ 3,500
Total Assets		$847,655
LIABILITIES		
CURRENT LIABILITIES		
Accounts Payable		$152,580
Notes Payable		$ 83,920
Accrued Wages/Salaries Payable		$ 38,150
Accrued Interest Payable		$ 42,380
Accrued Taxes Payable		$ 50,820
Total Current Liabilities		$367,850
LONG-TERM LIABILITIES		
Mortgage		$127,150
Note Payable		$ 85,000
Total Long-Term Liabilities		$212,150
OWNER'S EQUITY		
Sam Lloyd, Capital		$267,655
Total Liabilities and Owner's Equity		$847,655

within one year or within the normal operating cycle of the company, whichever is longer, such as accounts receivable and inventory. **Fixed assets** are those acquired for long-term use in the business. **Intangible assets** include items that, although valuable, do not have tangible value, such as goodwill, copyrights, and patents.

The second section shows the business's **liabilities**—the creditors' claims against the firm's assets. **Current liabilities** are those debts that must be paid within one year or within the normal operating cycle of the company, whichever is longer, and **long-term liabilities** are those that come due after one year. This section of the balance sheet also shows the **owner's equity**, the value of the owner's investment in the business. It is the balancing factor on the balance sheet, representing all of the owner's capital contributions to the business plus all accumulated earnings not distributed to the owner(s).

The Income Statement

The **income statement** (or profit and loss statement or "P&L") compares expenses against revenue over a certain period of time to show the firm's net income or loss. The income statement is a "moving picture" of the firm's profitability over time. The annual P&L statement reports the bottom line of the business over the fiscal or calendar year. Figure 8.2 shows the income statement for Sam's Appliance Shop for the year ended December 31, 200X.

To calculate net income or loss, the owner records sales revenue for the year, which includes all income that flows into the business from the sale of goods and services. Income from other sources (rent, investments, interest) also must be included in the

Figure 8.2

Income Statement,
Sam's Appliance Shop

Net Sales Revenue		$1,870,841
COST OF GOODS SOLD		
Beginning Inventory, 1/1/xx	$ 805,745	
+ Purchases	$ 939,827	
Goods Available for Sale	$1,745,572	
− Ending Inventory, 12/31/xx	$ 455,455	
Cost of Goods Sold		$1,290,117
Gross Profit		$ 580,724
OPERATING EXPENSES		
Advertising	$ 139,670	
Insurance	$ 46,125	
Depreciation		
Building	$ 18,700	
Equipment	$ 9,000	
Salaries	$ 224,500	
Travel	$ 4,000	
Entertainment	$ 2,500	
Total Operating Expenses		$ 444,495
GENERAL EXPENSES		
Utilities	$ 5,300	
Telephone	$ 2,500	
Postage	$ 1,200	
Payroll Taxes	$ 25,000	
Total General Expenses		$ 34,000
OTHER EXPENSES		
Interest Expense	$ 39,850	
Bad Check Expense	$ 1,750	
Total Other Expenses		$ 41,600
Total Expenses		$ 520,095
Net Income		$ 60,629

revenue section of the income statement. To determine net sales revenue, owners subtract the value of returned items and refunds from gross revenue. **Cost of goods sold** represents the total cost, including shipping, of the merchandise sold during the year. Most wholesalers and retailers calculate cost of goods sold by adding purchases to beginning inventory and subtracting ending inventory. Service companies typically have no cost of goods sold. Subtracting the cost of goods sold from net sales revenue results in a company's **gross profit**. Allowing the cost of goods sold to get out of control will whittle away its gross profit, virtually guaranteeing a net loss on the income statement. Dividing gross profit by net sales revenue produces the **gross profit margin**, a percentage that every business owner should watch closely. If a company's gross profit margin slips too low, it is likely that it will operate at a loss (negative net income).

Many business owners whose companies are losing money mistakenly believe that the problem is inadequate sales volume; therefore, they focus on pumping up sales at any cost. In many cases, however, the losses are due to an inadequate gross profit margin, and pumping up sales only deepens their losses! Repairing a poor gross profit margin requires a company to raise prices, cut manufacturing or purchasing costs, refuse orders with low profit margins, or add new products with more attractive profit margins. *Increasing sales will not resolve the problem.* One business owner admits that he fell victim to this myth of profitability. His company was losing money, and in an attempt to correct the problem, he focused his efforts on boosting sales. His efforts were successful, but the results were not. The costs he incurred to add sales produced withering gross profit margins, and by the time he deducted operating costs, the business incurred an even greater net loss! Cash flow suffered, the business could not pay its bills on time, and the owner ended up filing for Chapter 11 bankruptcy. Now a successful business owner, this entrepreneur says, "Ever since, I've tracked my gross [profit] margins like a hawk."[6] Monitoring the gross profit margin over time and comparing it to those of other companies in the same industry are important steps to maintaining a company's long-term profitability.

Operating expenses include those costs that contribute directly to the manufacture and distribution of goods. General expenses are indirect costs incurred in operating the business. "Other expenses" is a catchall category covering all other expenses that don't fit into the other two categories. Total revenue minus total expenses gives the company's **net income** (or **loss**). Reducing expenses increases a company's net income. Few companies have been as successful at cost cutting as Dell Inc., the fast-growing computer maker. In one year alone, Dell managed to trim $1.3 billion in expenses while continuing to expand. "I don't think there is ever a limit to reducing costs," says chief financial officer Jim Schneider. "If we can take out even a few cents per unit by tweaking our manufacturing processes and supply chain, the sheer magnitude of units we sell adds up to a billion dollars of savings pretty quickly."[7]

Business owners must be careful when embarking on a cost-cutting mission, however. Cutting costs in areas that are vital to operating success—such as a retail jeweler cutting its advertising expenditures—can inhibit a company's ability to succeed and can lead to failure. In other cases, entrepreneurs on cost-cutting vendettas alienate employees and sap worker morale by eliminating nit-picking costs that affect employees but retaining expensive perks for themselves. *One business owner enraged employees by cutting the budget for the company Christmas party to $5 (for the whole event) and encouraging employees not to skip lines on interoffice envelopes (which, one worker calculated, cost the company $0.0064 per skipped line). Although his reasons for cutting costs were valid, this CEO lost all credibility because employees knew that when he traveled, he stayed only at upscale, butler-serviced hotels and had a chauffeur drive him to work every day!*[8]

Company Example

Pepper . . . and Salt

THE WALL STREET JOURNAL

"I'm confident that our numbers will improve, but not before the decimal point."

The Statement of Cash Flows

The **statement of cash flows** shows the changes in a company's working capital from the beginning of the accounting period by listing the sources of funds and the uses of these funds. Many small businesses never need such a statement; instead, they rely on a cash budget, a less formal managerial tool that tracks the flow of cash into and out of a company over time. (We will discuss cash budgets in Chapter 9.) Sometimes, however, creditors, lenders, investors, or business buyers may require this information.

To prepare the statement of cash flows, owners must assemble the balance sheets and the income statements summarizing the present year's operations. They begin with the company's net income for the accounting period (from the income statement). Then they add the sources of funds—borrowed funds, owner contributions, decreases in accounts payable, decreases in inventory, depreciation, and any others. Depreciation is listed as a source of funds because it is a noncash expense that is deducted as a cost of doing business. Because the owners have already paid for the item being depreciated, its depreciation is a source of funds. Next the owners subtract the uses of these funds—plant and equipment purchases, dividends to owners, repayment of debt, increases in accounts receivable, decreases in accounts payable, increases in inventory, and so on. The difference between the total sources and the total uses of funds is the increase or decrease in working capital. By investigating the changes in the firm's working capital and the reasons for them, owners can create a more practical financial plan of action for the future of the enterprise.

These statements are more than just complex documents used only by accountants and financial officers. When used in conjunction with the analytical tools described in the following sections, they can help small business managers map their firms' financial future and actively plan for profit. Merely preparing these statement is not enough, however; entrepreneurs and their employees must *understand and use* the information contained in them to make the business more effective and efficient.

Creating Projected Financial Statements

3. Create projected financial statements.

Creating projected financial statements via the budgeting process helps the small business owner transform business goals into reality. Once developed, a budget will answer such questions as: What profit can the business expect to earn? If the owner's profit objective is *x* dollars, what sales level must the business achieve? What fixed and variable expenses can the owner expect at that level of sales? The answers to these and other questions are critical to formulating a successful financial plan for the small business.

This section focuses on creating projected income statements and balance sheets for the small business. These projected (or pro forma) statements estimate the profitability and the overall financial condition of the business for future months. They are an integral part of convincing potential lenders and investors to provide the financing needed to get the company off the ground. Also, because these statements project the firm's financial position through the end of the forecasted period, they help the owner plan the route to improved financial strength and healthy business growth.

Because an established business has a history of operating data from which to construct projected financial statements, the task is not nearly as difficult as it is for a beginning business. When creating projected financial statements for a business start-up, entrepreneurs typically rely on published statistics summarizing the operation of similar-size companies in the same industry. These statistics are available from a number of sources (described later), but this section draws on information found in *RMA Annual Statement Studies,* a compilation of financial data on thousands of companies across hundreds of industries (organized by Standard Industrial Classification [SIC] Code). Because conditions and markets change so rapidly, entrepreneurs developing financial forecasts for start-ups should focus on creating projections for two years into the future. Investors mainly want to see that entrepreneurs have realistic expectations about their income and expenses and when they can expect to start earning a profit.

Projected Statements for the Small Business

One of the most important tasks confronting the entrepreneur launching a new enterprise is to determine the funds needed to begin operation as well as those required to keep going through the initial growth period. The amount of money needed to begin a business depends on the type of operation, its location, inventory requirements, sales volume, and other factors. But every new firm must have enough capital to cover all start-up costs, including funds to rent or buy plant, equipment, and tools, as well as to pay for advertising, licenses, utilities, and other expenses. In addition, the owner must maintain a reserve of capital to carry the company until it begins to make a profit. Too often entrepreneurs are overly optimistic in their financial plans and fail to recognize that expenses initially exceed income for most small firms. This period of net losses is normal and may last from just a few months to several years. Owners must be able to meet payrolls, maintain adequate inventory, take advantage of cash discounts, grant customer credit, and meet personal obligations during this time.

The Projected Income Statement. When creating a projected income statement, an entrepreneur has two options: to develop a sales forecast and work down or set a profit target and work up. Most businesses employ the latter method—the owner targets a profit figure and then determines what sales level he or she must achieve to reach it. Of course, it is important to compare this sales target against the results of the marketing plan to determine whether it is realistic. Although they are projections, financial forecasts must be based in reality; otherwise, they are nothing more than a hopeless dream. The next step is to estimate the expenses the business will incur in securing those sales. In any small business, the annual profit must be large enough to produce a return for time the owners spend operating the business, plus a return on their investment in the business.

Entrepreneurs who earn less in their own business than they could earn working for someone else must weigh carefully the advantages and disadvantages of choosing the path of entrepreneurship. Why be exposed to all of the risks, sacrifices, and hard work of beginning and operating a small business if the rewards are less than those of remaining in the secure employment of another? Ideally, the firm's net income after taxes should be at least as much as the owner could earn by working for someone else.

An adequate profit must also include a reasonable return on the owner's total investment in the business. The owner's total investment is the amount contributed to the company at its inception plus any retained earnings (profits from previous years funneled back into the operation). If a would-be owner has $70,000 to invest and can invest it in securities and earn 10 percent, he or she should not consider investing it in a small business that would yield only 3 percent.

An entrepreneur's target income is the sum of a reasonable salary for the time spent running the business and a normal return on the amount invested in the firm. Determining how much this should be is the first step in creating the projectal income statement.

The next step is to translate this target profit into a net sales figure for the forecasted period. To calculate net sales from a target profit, the owner needs published statistics for this type of business. Suppose an entrepreneur wants to launch a small retail bookstore and has determined that his target income is $29,000 annually. Statistics gathered from *RMA Annual Statement Studies* show that the typical bookstore's net profit margin (net profit divided by net sales) is 9.3 percent. Using this information, the owner can compute the sales level required to produce a net profit of $29,000:

$$\text{Net profit margin} = \frac{\text{Net profit}}{\text{Net sales (annual)}}$$

$$9.3\% = \frac{\$29,000}{\text{Net sales (annual)}}$$

$$\text{Net sales} = \frac{\$29,000}{0.093}$$

$$= \$311,828$$

Now the entrepreneur knows that to make a net profit of $29,000 (before taxes), he must achieve annual sales of $311,828. To complete the projected income statement, he simply applies the appropriate statistics from *RMA Annual Statement Studies* to the annual sales figure. Because the statistics for each income statement item are expressed as percentages of net sales, the owner merely multiplies the proper statistic by the annual sales figure to obtain the desired value. For example, cost of goods sold usually comprises 61.4 percent of net sales for the typical small bookstore. So the owner of this new bookstore expects the cost of goods sold to be the following:

$$\text{Cost of goods sold} = \$311,828 \times 0.614 = \$191,462$$

The bookstore's complete projected income statement is shown as follows:

Net sales	(100%)	$311,828
– Cost of goods sold	(61.4%)	191,462
Gross profit margin	(38.6%)	$120,366
– Operating expenses	(29.3%)	91,366
Net income (before taxes)	(9.3%)	$ 29,000

At this point, the business appears to be a lucrative venture. But remember: This income statement represents a goal that the entrepreneur may not be able to attain. The next step is to determine whether this required sales volume is reasonable. One useful technique is to break down the required annual sales volume into daily sales figures. Assuming the store will be open six days per week for 52 weeks (312 days), the owner must average $999 per day in sales:

$$\text{Average daily sales} = \frac{\$311,828}{312 \text{ days}}$$

$$= \$999/\text{day}$$

This calculation gives the owner a better perspective of the sales required to yield an annual profit of $29,000.

To determine whether the profit expected from the business will meet or exceed the entrepreneur's target income, the prospective owner should create an income statement based on a realistic sales estimate. The previous analysis showed this entrepreneur what sales level is needed to reach the desired profit. But what happens if sales are lower or higher? To answer that question, the entrepreneur must develop a reliable sales forecast using the market research techniques described in Chapter 7.

Suppose that after conducting a marketing survey of local customers and talking with nearby business owners, the prospective bookstore owner projects first year sales for the proposed business to be only $285,000. The entrepreneur must take this expected sales figure and develop a pro forma income statement.

Net sales	(100%)	$285,000
− Cost of goods sold	(61.4%)	174,990
Gross profit margin	(38.6%)	$110,010
− Operating expenses	(29.3%)	83,505
Net income (before taxes)	(9.3%)	$ 26,505

Based on sales of $285,000, this entrepreneur should expect a net income (before taxes) of $26,505. If this amount is acceptable as a return on the investment of time and money in the business, the entrepreneur should proceed with his planning.

At this stage in developing the financial plan, the owner should create a more detailed picture of the firm's expected operating expenses. One common method is to use the operating statistics found in *Dun & Bradstreet's Cost of Doing Business* reports. These booklets document typical selected operating expenses (expressed as a percentage of net sales) for 190 different lines of businesses.

To ensure that they have overlooked no business expenses in preparing their business plans, entrepreneurs should list all of the initial expenses they will incur and have an accountant review the list. Figures 8.3 and 8.4 show two useful forms designed to help assign dollar values to anticipated expenses. Totals derived from this list of expenses should approximate the total expense figures calculated from published statistics. Naturally, an entrepreneur should be more confident of the total from his or her own list of expenses because this reflects the entrepreneur's particular set of circumstances.

Entrepreneurs who follow the top down approach to building an income statement—developing a sales forecast and working down to net income—must be careful to avoid falling into the trap of excessive optimism. Many entrepreneurs using this method overestimate their anticipated revenues and underestimate their actual expenses, and the result is disastrous. To avoid this problem, some experts advise entrepreneurs to use the rule that many venture capitalists apply when they evaluate business

Figure 8.3

Anticipated Expenses

Worksheet No. 2

Estimated Monthly Expenses	Your estimate of monthly expenses based on sales of $_____ per year.	Your estimate of how much cash you need to start your business. (See column 3.)	What to put in column 2. (These figures are typical for one kind of business. You will have to decide how many months to allow for in your business.)
ITEM	COLUMN 1	COLUMN 2	COLUMN 3
Salary of owner-manager	$	$	2 times column 1
All other salaries and wages			3 times column 1
Rent			3 times column 1
Advertising			3 times column 1
Delivery expense			3 times column 1
Supplies			3 times column 1
Telephone and telegraph			3 times column 1
Other utilities			3 times column 1
Insurance			Payment required by insurance company
Taxes, including Social Security			4 times column 1
Interest			3 times column 1
Maintenance			3 times column 1
Legal and other professional fees			3 times column 1
Miscellaneous			3 times column 1
Starting costs you have to pay only once			Leave column 2 blank
Fixtures and equipment			Fill in worksheet 3 and put the total here
Decorating and remodeling			Talk it over with a contractor
Installation of fixtures and equipment			Talk to suppliers from whom you buy these
Starting inventory			Suppliers will probably help you estimate this
Deposits with public utilities			Find out from utilities companies
Legal and professional fees			Lawyer, accountant, and so on
Licenses and permits			Find out from city offices what you have to have
Advertising and promotion for opening			Estimate what you'll use
Accounts receivable			What you need to buy more stock until credit customers pay
Cash			For unexpected expenses or losses, special purchases, etc.
Other			Make a separate list and enter total
Total Estimated Cash You Need to Start		$	Add up all the numbers in column 2

Source: U.S. Small Business Administration, *Checklist for Going into Business,* Small Marketers Aid No. 71 (Washington, D.C.: GPO, 1982), pp. 6–7.

Figure 8.4

Anticipated Expenditures for Fixtures and Equipment

Worksheet No. 3
List of Furniture, Fixtures, and Equipment

Leave out or add items to suit your business. Use separate sheets to list exactly what you need for each of the items below.	If you plan to pay cash in full, enter the full amount below and in the last column.	If you are going to pay by installments, fill out the columns below. Enter in the last column your down payment plus at least one installment.			Estimate of the cash you need for furniture, fixtures, and equipment.
		Price	Down payment	Amount of each installment	
Counters	$	$	$	$	$
Storage shelves and cabinets					
Display stands, shelves, tables					
Cash register					
Safe					
Window display fixtures					
Special lighting					
Outside sign					
Delivery equipment if needed					
Total Furniture, Fixtures, and Equipment (enter this figure also in worksheet 2 under Starting Costs You Have to Pay Only Once)					$

Source: U.S. Small Business Administration, *Checklist for Going into Business,* Small Marketers Aid No. 71 (Washington, DC.: GPO, 1982), pp. 6-7.

start-ups: Divide revenues by two, multiply expenses by two, and if the business can still make it, it's a winner!

The Projected Balance Sheet. In addition to projecting the small firm's net profit or loss, the entrepreneur must develop a pro forma balance sheet outlining the fledgling company's assets and liabilities. Most entrepreneurs' primary focus is on the potential profitability of their businesses, but the assets their businesses use to generate profits are no less important. In many cases, small companies begin life on weak financial footing because their owners fail to determine their firms' total asset requirements. To prevent this major oversight, owners should prepare a projected balance sheet listing every asset the business will need and all the claims against these assets.

Assets. Cash is one of the most useful assets the business owns; it is highly liquid and can quickly be converted into other tangible assets. But how much cash should a small business have at its inception? Obviously, there is no single dollar figure that fits the needs of every small firm. One practical rule of thumb, however, suggests that the company's cash balance should cover its operating expenses (less depreciation, a noncash expense) for one inventory turnover period. Using this rule, we can calculate the cash balance for the small bookstore as follows:

Operating expenses = $83,505 (from projected income statement)
Less: Depreciation (0.9% of annual sales) of $2,565 (a noncash expense)
Equals: Cash expenses (annual) = $80,940

$$\text{Cash requirement} = \frac{\text{Cash expenses}}{\text{Average inventory turnover}}$$

$$= \frac{\$80,940}{3.5^*}$$

$$= \$23,126$$

*From *RMA Annual Statement Studies.*

Notice the inverse relationship between a small company's average inventory turnover ratio and its cash requirements. The faster a business turns its inventory, the shorter the time its cash is tied up in inventory, and the amount of cash the company requires is smaller.

Inventory. Another decision facing the entrepreneur is how much inventory the business should carry. An estimate of the inventory needed can be calculated from the information found on the projected income statement and from published statistics:

Cost of goods sold = $174,990 (from projected income statement)

$$\text{Average inventory turnover} = \frac{\text{Cost of goods sold}}{\text{Inventory level}}$$

$$= 3.5 \text{ times/year}$$

Substituting,

$$3.5 \text{ times/year} = \frac{\$153,500}{\text{Inventory level}}$$

Solving algebraically,

Inventory level = $49,997

The entrepreneur also includes $1,800 in miscellaneous current assets. Suppose the estimate of fixed assets is as follows:

Fixtures	$17,500
Office equipment	2,850
Computers/cash register	3,125
Signs	3,200
Miscellaneous	1,500
Total	$28,175

Liabilities. To complete the projected balance sheet, the owner must record all of the small firm's liabilities, the claims against the assets. The bookstore owner was able to finance 50 percent of inventory and fixtures through suppliers. The only other major claim against the firm's assets is a note payable to the entrepreneur's father-in-law for $20,000.

The final step is to compile all of these items into a projected balance sheet, as shown in Figure 8.5.

Ratio Analysis

4. Understand the basic financial statements through ratio analysis.

Would you be willing to drive a car on an extended trip without being able to see the dashboard displays showing fuel level, engine temperature, oil pressure, battery status, or the speed at which you were traveling? Not many people would! Yet, many small business owners run their companies exactly that way. They never take the time to check the vital signs of their businesses using their "financial dashboards." The result: Their companies develop engine trouble, fail, and leave them stranded along the road to successful entrepreneurship.

Figure 8.5

Projected Balance Sheet
for a Small Bookstore

ASSETS	
CURRENT ASSETS	
Cash	$ 23,126
Inventory	49,997
Miscellaneous	1,800
Total Current Assets	$ 74,923
FIXED ASSETS	
Fixtures	$ 17,500
Office Equipment	2,850
Computers/Cash Register	3,125
Signs	3,200
Miscellaneous	1,500
Total Fixed Assets	$ 28,175
Total Assets	$103,098
LIABILITIES	
CURRENT LIABILITIES	
Accounts Payable	$ 24,998
Note Payable	3,750
Total Current Liabilities	$ 28,748
LONG-TERM LIABILITIES	
Note Payable	$ 30,000
Total Liabilities	$ 58,748
Owner's Equity	$ 44,350
Total Liabilities and Owner's Equity	$103,098

Smart entrepreneurs know that once they have their businesses up and running with the help of a solid financial plan, the next step is to keep the company moving in the right direction with the help of proper financial controls. Establishing these controls—and using them consistently—is one of the keys to keeping a business vibrant and healthy. Business owners who don't may be shocked to learn that their companies are in serious financial trouble and they never knew it.

A smoothly functioning system of financial controls is essential to achieving business success. Such a system can serve as an early warning device for underlying problems that could destroy a young business. They enable an entrepreneur to step back and see the big picture and to make adjustments in the company's direction when necessary. According to one writer:

A company's financial accounting and reporting system will provide signals, through comparative analysis, of impending trouble, such as:
- Decreasing sales and falling profit margins.
- Increasing corporate overhead.
- Growing inventories and accounts receivable.

These are all signals of declining cash flows from operations, the lifeblood of every business. As cash flows decrease, the squeeze begins.
- Payments to vendors become slower.
- Maintenance on production equipment lags.
- Raw material shortages appear.
- Equipment breakdowns occur.

All of these begin to have a negative impact on productivity. Now the downward spiral has begun in earnest. The key is hearing and focusing on the signals.[9]

What are these signals, and how does an entrepreneur go about hearing and focusing on them? One extremely helpful tool is ratio analysis. **Ratio analysis**, a method of expressing the relationships between any two accounting elements, provides a convenient technique for performing financial analysis. When analyzed properly, ratios serve as barometers of a company's financial health. These comparisons enable the small business manager to determine if the firm is carrying excessive inventory, experiencing heavy operating expenses, overextending credit, managing to pay its debts on time, and to answer other questions relating to the efficient operation of the firm. Unfortunately, few business owners actually use ratio analysis; one study discovered that just 2 percent of all entrepreneurs compute financial ratios and use them in managing their businesses![10]

Clever business owners use financial ratio analysis to identify problems in their businesses while they are still problems, not business-threatening crises. Tracking these ratios over time permits an owner to spot a variety of "red flags" that are indications of these problem areas. This is critical to business success because entrepreneurs cannot solve problems they do not know exist! Business owners also can use ratio analysis to increase the likelihood of obtaining bank loans. By analyzing financial statements with ratios, an owner can anticipate potential problems and identify important strengths in advance. When evaluating a business plan or a loan request, lenders often rely on ratio analysis to determine how well managed a company is and how solid its financial footing is.

But how many ratios should a small business manager monitor to maintain adequate financial control over the firm? The number of ratios an entrepreneur can calculate is limited only by the number of accounts recorded on the company's financial statements. However, tracking too many ratios only creates confusion and saps the meaning from an entrepreneur's financial analysis. The secret to successful ratio analysis is simplicity, focusing on just enough ratios to provide a clear picture of a company's financial standing.

12 Key Ratios

In keeping with the idea of simplicity, we will describe 12 key ratios that will enable most business owners to monitor their companies' financial position without becoming bogged down in financial details. This chapter presents explanations of these ratios and examples based on the balance sheet and the income statement for Sam's Appliance Shop shown in Figures 8.1 and 8.2. We will group them into four categories: liquidity ratios, leverage ratios, operating ratios, and profitability ratios.

Liquidity Ratios. **Liquidity ratios** tell whether a small business will be able to meet its maturing obligations as they come due. A small company with solid liquidity not only is able to pay its bills on time, but it also is in a position to take advantage of attractive business opportunities as they arise. The two most common measures of liquidity are the current ratio and the quick ratio.

1. *Current ratio.* The **current ratio** measures the small firm's solvency by indicating its ability to pay current liabilities from current assets. It is calculated in the following manner:

$$\text{Current ratio} = \frac{\text{Current assets}}{\text{Current liabilities}}$$

$$= \frac{\$686,985}{\$367,850}$$

$$= 1.87:1$$

Sam's Appliance Shop has $1.87 in current assets for every $1 it has in current liabilities. Current assets are assets that the entrepreneur expects to convert into cash in the ordinary business cycle and normally include cash, notes/accounts receivable, inventory, and any other short-term marketable securities. Current liabilities are short-term obligations that come due within one year and include notes/accounts payable, taxes payable, and accruals.

The current ratio is sometimes called the working capital ratio and is the most commonly used measure of short-term solvency. Typically, financial analysts suggest that a small business maintain a current ratio of at least 2:1 (i.e., two dollars of current assets for every one dollar of current liabilities) to maintain a comfortable cushion of working capital. Generally, the higher the firm's current ratio, the stronger its financial position; but a high current ratio does not guarantee that the company's assets are being used in the most profitable manner. For example, a business maintaining excessive balances of idle cash or overinvesting in inventory would likely have a high current ratio.

With its current ratio of 1.87:1, Sam's Appliance Shop could liquidate its current assets at 53.5% (1 ÷ 1.87 = 53.5%) of book value and still manage to pay its current creditors in full.

2. *Quick ratio.* The current ratio can sometimes be misleading because it does not show the quality of a company's current assets. For instance, a company with a large number of past-due receivables and stale inventory could boast an impressive current ratio and still be on the verge of financial collapse. The **quick ratio** (or the **acid test ratio**) is a more conservative measure of a firm's liquidity because it shows the extent to which its most liquid assets cover its current liabilities. It is calculated as follows:

$$\text{Quick ratio} = \frac{\text{Quick assets}}{\text{Current liabilities}}$$

$$= \frac{\$686,985 - \$455,455}{\$367,850}$$

$$= 0.63{:}1$$

Quick assets include cash, readily marketable securities, and notes/accounts receivables—those assets that a company can convert into cash immediately if needed. Most small firms determine quick assets by subtracting inventory from current assets because inventory cannot be converted into cash quickly. Also, inventories are the assets on which losses are most likely to occur in case of liquidation.

The quick ratio is a more specific measure of a company's ability to meet its short-term obligations and is a more rigorous test of its liquidity. It expresses capacity to repay current debts if all sales income ceased immediately. Generally, a quick ratio of 1:1 is considered satisfactory. A ratio of less than 1:1 indicates that the small firm is overly dependent on inventory and on future sales to satisfy short-term debt. A quick ratio of more than 1:1 indicates a greater degree of financial security.

Leverage Ratios. **Leverage ratios** measure the financing supplied by a company's owners against that supplied by its creditors; they serve as gauges of the depth of a company's debt. These ratios show the extent to which an entrepreneur relies on debt capital (rather than equity capital) to finance operating expenses, capital expenditures, and expansion costs. As such, it is a measure of the degree of financial risk in a company. Generally, small businesses with low leverage ratios are less affected by economic downturns, but the returns for these firms are lower during economic booms. Conversely, small firms with high leverage ratios are more vulnerable to economic slides because their debt loads demolish cash flow; however, they have greater potential for large profits. "Leverage is a double-edged sword," says one financial expert. "If it works for you, you can really build something. If you borrow too much, it can drag a business down faster than anything."[11] Companies that end up declaring bankruptcy most often take on more debt than the business can handle. For example, rumors of bankruptcy frequently swirl around real estate magnate and television celebrity Donald Trump, who borrows heavily to finance his company, Trump Hotels and Casino Resorts. Recently, Trump had to restructure a portion of the company's $1.8 billion of debt to avoid bankruptcy.[12]

The following ratios will help entrepreneurs keep their debt levels manageable.

3. *Debt ratio.* A small company's **debt ratio** measures the percentage of total assets financed by its creditors. The debt ratio is calculated as follows:

$$\text{Debt ratio} = \frac{\text{Total debt (or liabilities)}}{\text{Total assets}}$$

$$= \frac{\$367,850 - \$212,150}{847,655}$$

$$= 0.68:1$$

Total debt includes all current liabilities and any outstanding long-term notes and bonds. Total assets represent the sum of the firm's current assets, fixed assets, and intangible assets. A high debt ratio means that creditors provide a large percentage of the firm's total financing. Owners generally prefer a high leverage ratio; otherwise, business funds must come either from the owners' personal assets or from taking on new owners, which means giving up more control over the business. Also, with a greater portion of the firm's assets financed by creditors, the owner is able to generate profits with a smaller personal investment. However, creditors typically prefer moderate debt ratios because a lower debt ratio indicates a smaller chance of creditor losses in case of liquidation. To lenders and creditors, high debt ratios mean a high risk of default.

4. *Debt to net worth ratio.* A small company's **debt to net worth ratio** also expresses the relationship between the capital contributions from creditors and those from owners. This ratio compares what the business "owes" to "what it is worth." It is a measure of the small firm's ability to meet both its creditor and owner obligations in case of liquidation. The debt to net worth ratio is calculated as follows:

$$\text{Debt to net worth ratio} = \frac{\text{Total debt (or liabilities)}}{\text{Tangible net worth}}$$

$$= \frac{\$367,850 + \$212,150}{\$267,655 - \$3,500}$$

$$= 2.20:1$$

Total debt is the sum of current liabilities and long-term liabilities, and tangible net worth represents the owners' investment in the business (capital + capital stock + earned surplus + retained earnings) less any intangible assets (e.g., goodwill) the firm owns.

The higher this ratio, the lower the degree of protection afforded creditors if the business should fail. Also, a higher debt to net worth ratio means that the firm has less capacity to borrow; lenders and creditors see the firm as being "borrowed up." Plus, carrying high levels of debt limits a company's options and restricts managers' flexibility. Quite simply, there isn't much "wiggle room" with a debt-laden balance sheet. Managers of a manufacturing company whose debt to equity ratio had climbed to 6:1 discovered just how crippling such a heavy debt load can be. The company was paying so much in interest on its debt that it lacked the cash to modernize its plant and equipment and to develop new products and product innovations, which made it difficult to keep up with its competitors. As sales slipped, earnings also fell, stretching the company's ability to make its interest payments, and its financial fortunes continued on a vicious downward spiral.[13]

A low ratio typically is associated with a higher level of financial security, giving the business greater borrowing potential. As a company's debt to net worth ratio approaches 1:1, its creditors' interest in the business approaches that of the owners'. If the ratio is greater than 1:1, the creditors' claims exceed those of the owners', and the business may be undercapitalized. In other words, the owner has not supplied an adequate amount of capital, forcing the business to be overextended in terms of debt.

5. *Times interest earned ratio.* The **times interest earned ratio** is a measure of the small firm's ability to make the interest payments on its debt. It tells how many times the company's earnings cover the interest payments on the debt it is carrying. The times interest earned ratio is calculated as follows:

$$\text{Times interest earned ratio} = \frac{\text{Earnings before interest and taxes (EBIT)}}{\text{Total interest expense}}$$

$$= \frac{\$60,629 + \$39,850}{\$39,850}$$

$$= 2.52{:}1$$

EBIT is the firm's net income (earnings) *before* deducting interest expense and taxes; the denominator measures the amount the business paid in interest over the accounting period.

A high ratio suggests that the company would have little difficulty meeting the interest payments on its loans; creditors would see this as a sign of safety for future loans. Conversely, a low ratio is an indication that the company is overextended in its debts; earnings will not be able to cover its debt service if this ratio is less than 1. "I look for a [times interest earned] ratio of higher than three-to-one," says one financial analyst, "which indicates that management has considerable breathing room to make its debt payments. When the ratio drops below one-to-one, it clearly indicates management is under tremendous pressure to raise cash. The risk of default or bankruptcy is very high."[14] Many creditors look for a times interest earned ratio of at least 4:1 to 6:1 before pronouncing a company a good credit risk.

Debt is a powerful financial tool, but companies must handle it carefully—just as a demolitionist handles dynamite. And, like dynamite, too much debt can be dangerous.

Entrepreneurs who use debt financing in their businesses can magnify their ability to produce a profit, but taking on too much debt can strain companies and their founders to the breaking point.

Trouble looms on the horizon for companies whose debt loads are so heavy that they must starve critical operations such as research and development, customer service, and others just to pay interest on the debt. Because their interest payments are so large, highly leveraged companies find that they are restricted when it comes to spending cash, whether on normal operations, acquisitions, or capital expenditures. Unfortunately, some companies have gone on borrowing binges, pushing their debt loads beyond the safety barrier (see Figure 8.6) and are struggling to survive.

Some entrepreneurs are so averse to debt that they run their companies with a minimum amount of borrowing, relying instead on their business's cash flow to finance growth. Jerry Edwards, president of Chef's Expressions, a small catering company, manages to generate annual sales of $2 million with just a $20,000 line of credit. "We've always funded our growth out of cash flow," says Edwards. "I had a credit line that I didn't dip into for 10 years!"[15] Growth may be slower for these companies, but their owners do not have to contend with the dangers of debt. Managed carefully, however, debt can boost a company's performance and improve its productivity. Its treatment in the tax code also makes debt a much cheaper means of financial growth than equity. When companies with AA financial ratings borrow at 10 percent, the after-tax cost is just 7.2 percent (because interest payments to lenders are tax deductible); equity financing costs more than twice that.

Operating Ratios. **Operating ratios** help the owner evaluate a small firm's performance and indicate how effectively the business employs its resources. The more effectively its resources are used, the less capital a small business will require. These five operating ratios are designed to help entrepreneurs spot those areas they must improve if their businesses are to remain competitive.

6. *Average inventory turnover ratio.* A small company's **average inventory turnover ratio** measures the number of times its average inventory is sold out, or turned over, during the accounting period. This ratio tells owners how effectively and efficiently they are managing their companies' inventory. It tells them whether their inventory level is too low

Figure 8.6

The Right Amount of
Debt Is a Balancing Act

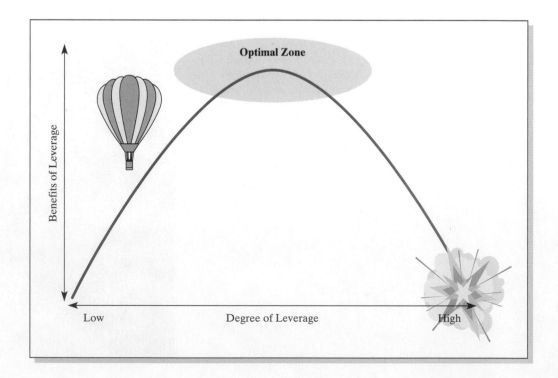

or too high and whether it is current or obsolete and priced correctly. The average inventory turnover ratio is calculated as follows:

$$\text{Average inventory turnover ratio} = \frac{\text{Cost of goods sold}}{\text{Average inventory}}$$

$$= \frac{\$1,290,117}{(\$805,745 + \$455,455) \div 2}$$

$$= 2.05 \text{ times/year}$$

Average inventory is found by adding a firm's inventory at the beginning of the accounting period to the ending inventory and dividing the result by 2.

This ratio tells an entrepreneur how fast the merchandise is moving through the business and helps to balance the company on the fine line between oversupply and undersupply. To determine the average number of days units remain in inventory, the owner can divide the average inventory turnover ratio into the number of days in the accounting period (e.g., 365 ÷ average inventory turnover ratio). The result is called **days' inventory** (or **average age of inventory**). Auto dealerships often use average age of inventory as a measure of performance,

<table>
<tr><td>

Company Example →

</td><td>

but this is an important measure of performance for other companies as well. *Dell Inc., a computer maker that has used a build-to-order strategy to become a leader in the industry, turns its inventory an astonishing 73 times a year, or every five days. The company manages its inventory and its supplier relationships so closely that Dell has no more than two hours' worth of inventory at any particular moment. Because its inventory turnover rate is so high and because it collects payments from customers before it must pay suppliers, Dell's cash flow remains strong.*[16]

</td></tr>
</table>

An above-average inventory turnover indicates that the small business has a healthy, salable, and liquid inventory and a supply of quality merchandise supported by sound pricing policies. A below-average inventory turnover suggests an illiquid inventory characterized by obsolescence, overstocking, stale merchandise, and poor purchasing procedures.

Businesses that turn their inventories more rapidly than average require a smaller inventory investment to produce a particular sales volume. That means that these companies tie up less cash in inventory that idly sits on shelves. For instance, if Sam's could turn its inventory four times each year instead of just two, the company would require an average inventory of just $322,529 instead of the current level of $630,600 to generate sales of $1,870,841.

The average inventory turnover ratio tells business owners how fast inventory is moving through their companies. Companies that turn their inventories quickly require a smaller investment in inventory than those that do not.

Increasing the number of inventory turns would free up more than $308,000 currently tied up in excess inventory! Sam's would benefit from improved cash flow and higher profits.

The inventory turnover ratio can be misleading, however. For example, an excessively high ratio could mean the firm has a shortage of inventory and is experiencing stockouts.

✦ GAINING *a* COMPETITIVE EDGE ✦

Profitability Management

Many entrepreneurs struggle to wring more profits out of their businesses, and one concept that can help them is profitability management. "Most companies have tremendous increases in cash flow and profitability available to them for free," says Jonathan Burns, a professor at MIT and an expert on profitability management. "All it takes is good management."

Profitability management is based on three simple principles:

1. Sell what you make.
2. Satisfy your customers.
3. Minimize inventory costs.

Although the principles are obvious, implementing them can be a challenge for both novice and experienced entrepreneurs. Few companies have been as successful at applying the principles of profitability management as Dell Inc., which is today the largest computer maker in the world. Founded by Michael Dell from his University of Texas dorm room, by 1994 Dell was struggling to control the consequences of his company's rapid growth— product quality, spiraling costs, and customer satisfaction. Dell's approach to profitability management played a major role in turning the company's fortunes around.

First, Dell began targeting customers that represented the best opportunity for profitability for his company: corporate customers and sophisticated individual users who replaced their computers regularly and who were less price sensitive than bargain shoppers.

Michael Dell understood that, for computer makers, controlling inventory is crucial because computer parts lose their value incredibly fast and getting stuck with six-month-old components means big losses. Dell's direct sales strategy means that the company does *not* build computers to sit on a shelf waiting for a customer to come in and buy one. Instead, Dell does not actually build a computer until a customer orders it, which reduces its investment in inventory. Still, to make profitability management work for his company, Dell had to be able to generate reliable sales forecasts and to establish a network of reliable, on-time suppliers. Managers in key areas of marketing, sales, manufacturing, and purchasing meet regularly to hone the company's sales forecasts. Dell also carefully selects its suppliers, and only those that can deliver high-quality components on short notice with generous payment terms make the cut. Today, Dell ties its suppliers into its computer database and issues orders for parts electronically to avoid the cost and time delays involved in placing paper-based orders.

The result of this strategy is an amazing industry-leading inventory turnover ratio of 73 times a year, minimal inventory carrying costs, and the ability to provide a rapid turnaround on customers' orders. Because many of its customers order online, Dell is able to collect the revenue from sales in just a few days but does not have to pay suppliers for several weeks, creating a cycle that generates positive cash flow for the company. This system enables Dell to keep customers happy by delivering customized computers to them with quick turnaround times, to keep costs low, and to build volume sales, which further enables the company to push unit costs down. "Through profitability management, companies can quickly get profitability increases of 30 to 40 percent or more," claims Byrnes.

Dell has transformed profitability management from a simple business technique into an art form and, in the process, has become the largest computer maker in the world. What can this technique do for your company?

1. Why are the principles "satisfy your customers" and "minimize inventory costs" opposing concepts at many small businesses?
2. How can a small business implement the three principles of profitability management?
3. Identify a business you believe could benefit from profitability management. Interview the owner of the company, explain the principles of profitability management, and work with him or her to develop a plan for implementing the concept in the business.

Source: Adapted from Mark Henricks, "A Tight Ship," *Entrepreneur,* December 2003, pp. 95–96.

Similarly, a low ratio could be the result of planned inventory stockpiling to meet seasonal peak demand. Another problem is that the ratio is based on an inventory balance calculated from two days out of the entire accounting period. Thus, inventory fluctuations due to seasonal demand patterns are ignored, which may bias the resulting ratio. There is no universal, ideal inventory turnover ratio. Financial analysts suggest that a favorable turnover ratio depends on the type of business, its size, its profitability, its method of inventory valuation, and other relevant factors. The most meaningful basis for comparison is other companies of similar size in the same industry (more on this later).

7. *Average collection period ratio.* A small company's **average collection period ratio** (or **days sales outstanding, DSO**) tells the average number of days it takes to collect accounts receivable. To compute the average collection period ratio, you must first calculate the firm's receivables turnover. If Sam's credit sales for the year were $1,309,589, then the receivables turnover ratio would be as follows:

$$\text{Receivables turnover ratio} = \frac{\text{Credit sales (or net sales)}}{\text{Accounts receivable}}$$

$$= \frac{\$1,309,589}{\$179,225}$$

$$= 7.31 \text{ times/year}$$

This ratio measures the number of times a company's accounts receivable turn over during the accounting period. Sam's Appliance Shop turns over its receivables 7.31 times per year. The higher a company's receivables turnover ratio, the shorter the time lag between making a sale and collecting the cash from it.

Use the following to calculate a company's average collection period ratio:

$$\text{Average collection period ratio} = \frac{\text{Days in accounting period}}{\text{Receivables turnover ratio}}$$

$$= \frac{365 \text{ days}}{7.31}$$

$$= 50.0 \text{ days}$$

Sam's Appliance Shop's accounts and notes receivable are outstanding for an average of 50 days. Typically, the higher a firm's average collection period ratio, the greater is its chance of bad debt losses. Sales don't count unless a company collects the revenue from them!

> **Company Example** → *Lee Porter, owner of Texas Auto Mart, a small used car dealership that finances its customers' purchases, operates in an industry in which one-third of its customers typically default on their auto loans. With such a low collection rate, how does Porter stay in business? First, his gross profit margin is an impressive 60 percent; he buys cars for an average of $2,000 and then sells them for an average of $5,000. Also, most of his customers make a down payment and several monthly payments even if they do default on the loan (which gives Porter the right to repossess the car and sell it again). "It's not how much you sell," says Porter. "It's how much you collect."*[17]

One of the most useful applications of the collection period ratio is to compare it to the industry average and to the firm's credit terms. Such a comparison will indicate the degree of the small company's control over its credit sales and collection techniques. One rule of thumb suggests that the firm's collection period ratio should be no more than one-third greater than its credit terms. For example, if a small company's credit terms are "net 30," its average collection period ratio should be no more than 40 days. A ratio greater than 40 days would indicate poor collection procedures, such as sloppy record keeping or failure to send invoices promptly.

> **Company Example** → *Nick Ypsilantis, CEO of AccuFile, a company that provides library staff and services to businesses, has learned the importance of sending invoices promptly. Before the company tightened its accounts receivable procedures, cash*

Table 8.1

How Lowering Your Average Collection Period Can Save You Money

Too often, entrepreneurs fail to recognize the importance of collecting their accounts receivable on time. After all, collecting accounts is not as glamorous or as much fun as generating sales. Lowering a company's average collection period ratio, however, can produce tangible—and often significant—savings. The following formula shows how to convert an improvement in a company's average collection period ratio into dollar savings:

$$\text{Annual savings} = \frac{(\text{Credit sales} \times \text{annual interest rate} \times \text{number of days average collection period is lowered})}{365}$$

where

credit sales = company's annual credit sales in $
annual interest rate = the interest rate at which the company borrows money
number of days average collection period is lowered = the difference between the previous year's average collection period ratio and the current one

Example:

Sam's Appliance Shop's average collection period ratio is 50 days. Suppose that the previous year's average collection period ratio was 56 days, a six-day improvement. The company's credit sales for the most recent year were $1,309,589. If Sam borrows money at 10.25 percent, this six-day improvement has generated savings for Sam's Appliance Shop of:

$$\text{Savings} = \frac{\$1,309,589 \times 10.25\% \times 6 \text{ days}}{365 \text{ days}} = \$2,207$$

By collecting his accounts receivable just six days faster on the average, Sam has saved his business more than $2,200! Of course, if a company's average collection period ratio rises, the same calculation will tell the owner how much that costs.

Source: "Days Saved, Thousands Earned," *Inc.,* November 1995, p. 98.

flow was a constant problem, forcing Ypsilantis to borrow money on a line of credit. By sending invoices sooner and following up promptly on past-due accounts, AccuFile has reduced its average collection period to 41 days and has not had to use its credit line at all.[18]

Just as Nick Ypsilantis has learned, slow payers represent great risk to many small businesses. Many entrepreneurs proudly point to rapidly rising sales only to find that they must borrow money to keep their companies going because credit customers are paying their bills in 45, 60, or even 90 days instead of 30. Slow receivables often lead to a cash crisis that can cripple a business. Table 8.1 shows how lowering the average collection period ratio can save a company money.

8. *Average payable period ratio.* The converse of the average collection period ratio, the **average payable period ratio**, tells the average number of days it takes a company to pay its accounts payable. Like the average collection period, it is measured in days. To compute this ratio, first calculate the payables turnover ratio. Sam's payables turnover ratio is as follows:

$$\text{Payables turnover ratio} = \frac{\text{Purchases}}{\text{Accounts payable}}$$

$$= \frac{\$939,827}{\$152,580}$$

$$= 6.16 \text{ times/year}$$

To find the average payable period ratio, use the following computation:

$$\text{Average payable period ratio} = \frac{\text{Days in accounting period}}{\text{Payables turnover ratio}}$$

$$= \frac{365 \text{ days}}{6.16}$$

$$= 59.3 \text{ days}$$

Sam's Appliance Shop takes an average of 59 days to pay its accounts with suppliers.

An excessively high average payable period ratio indicates the presence of a significant amount of past-due accounts payable. Although sound cash management calls for business owners to keep their cash as long as possible, slowing payables too drastically can severely damage a company's credit rating. Ideally, the average payable period would match (or exceed) the time it takes to convert inventory into sales and ultimately into cash. In this case, the company's vendors would be financing its inventory and its credit sales.

One of the most meaningful comparisons for this ratio is against the credit terms offered by suppliers (or an average of the credit terms offered). If the average payable period ratio slips beyond vendors' credit terms, it is an indication that the company is suffering from cash shortages or a sloppy accounts payable procedure and its credit rating is in danger. If this ratio is significantly lower than vendors' credit terms, it may be a sign that a business is not using its cash most effectively.

9. *Net sales to total assets ratio.* A small company's **net sales to total assets ratio** (also called the **total assets turnover ratio**) is a general measure of its ability to generate sales in relation to its assets. It describes how productively the firm employs its assets to produce sales revenue. The total assets turnover ratio is calculated as follows:

$$\text{Total assets turnover ratio} = \frac{\text{Net sales}}{\text{Net total assets}}$$

$$= \frac{\$1,870,841}{\$847,655}$$

$$= 2.21\!:\!1$$

The denominator of this ratio, net total assets, is the sum of all of the firm's assets (cash, inventory, land, buildings, equipment, tools, everything owned) less depreciation. This ratio is meaningful only when compared to that of similar firms in the same industry category. A total assets turnover ratio below the industry average may indicate that the small firm is not generating an adequate sales volume for its asset size.

10. *Net sales to working capital ratio.* The **net sales to working capital ratio** measures how many dollars in sales the business generates for every dollar of working capital (working capital = current assets − current liabilities). Also called the **turnover of working capital ratio**, this proportion tells the owner how efficiently working capital is being used to generate sales. It is calculated as follows:

$$\text{Net sales to working capital ratio} = \frac{\text{Net sales}}{\text{Currents assets} - \text{Current liabilities}}$$

$$= \frac{\$1,870,841}{\$686,985 - \$367,850}$$

$$= 5.86\!:\!1$$

On one hand, an excessively low net sales to working capital ratio indicates that the small firm is not employing its working capital efficiently or profitably. On the other hand, an extremely high ratio points to an inadequate level of working capital to maintain a suitable level of sales, which puts creditors in a more vulnerable position. This ratio is very helpful in maintaining sufficient working capital as the small business grows. It is critical for the small firm to keep a satisfactory level of working capital to nourish its expansion, and the net sales to working capital ratio helps define the level of working capital required to support higher sales volume.

Profitability Ratios. **Profitability ratios** indicate how efficiently a small firm is being managed. They provide the owner with information about a company's ability to generate a profit; in other words, they describe how successfully the firm is conducting business.

11. *Net profit on sales ratio.* The **net profit on sales ratio** (also called the **profit margin on sales**) measures a company's profit per dollar of sales. This ratio (which is expressed as a percentage) shows the number of cents of each sales dollar remaining after deducting all expenses and income taxes. The profit margin on sales is calculated as follows:

$$\text{Net profit on sales ratio} = \frac{\text{Net income}}{\text{Net sales}}$$

$$= \frac{\$60,629}{\$1,870,841}$$

$$= 3.24\%$$

Most small business owners believe that a high profit margin on sales is necessary for a successful business operation, but this is a myth. To evaluate this ratio properly, entrepreneurs must consider their companies' asset value, their inventory and receivables turnover ratios, and their total capitalization. For example, the typical small supermarket earns an average net profit of only one or two cents on each dollar of sales, but its inventory may turn over as many as 20 times a year. If a company's profit margin on sales is below the industry average, it may be a sign that its prices are relatively low or that its costs are excessively high, or both. *Four years after reviving the venerated Indian Motorcycle brand, Frank O'Connell, chairman and chief executive of the reincarnated company, halted production of the classic motorcycles because excessive costs made it impossible for the business to generate a profit. Sales of the motorcycles, which were priced between $17,000 and $25,000, had climbed from 1,000 to more than 3,500 in four years, but rapid cost increases had undermined Indian Motorcycle's ability to produce a profit. "Our volume continues to grow and our [dealer network] continues to grow, but the cost structure is out of line," says McConnell. "It's a stand-alone manufacturing operation that's too expensive."*[19]

Company Example

If a company's net profit on sales ratio is excessively low, the owner should check the gross profit margin (net sales minus cost of goods sold expressed as a percentage of net sales). Of course, a reasonable gross profit margin varies from industry to industry. For instance, a service company may have a gross profit margin of 75 percent, whereas a manufacturer's may be 35 percent. If this margin slips too low, it puts the company's future in immediate jeopardy.

12. *Net profit to equity ratio.* The **net profit to equity ratio** (or the **return on net worth ratio**) measures the owners' rate of return on investment. Because it reports the percentage of the owners' investment in the business that is being returned through profits annually, it is one of the most important indicators of a company's profitability or management's efficiency. The net profit to equity ratio is computed as follows:

$$\text{Net profit to equity ratio} = \frac{\text{Net income}}{\text{Owners' equity (or net worth)}}$$

$$= \frac{\$60,629}{\$267,655}$$

$$= 22.65\%$$

This ratio compares profits earned during the accounting period with the amount the owners have invested in the business during that time. If this interest rate on the owners' investment is excessively low, some of this capital might be better employed elsewhere. For instance, a business should produce a rate of return that exceeds its cost of capital. A company's cost of capital depends on the interest rates it must pay on debt capital and the return that shareholders expect on equity capital, both of which reflect the risk of providing that capital. For instance, if a small company's cost of capital is 13.5 percent and its return on equity is just 6 percent, that business has not added any economic value to its owners.

IN THE FOOTSTEPS OF AN ENTREPRENEUR...

Unraveling the Mystery of Profitability

Vickie Giannukos was puzzled. Her company, Victoria Pappas Collection, sold women's sportswear exclusively through boutiques and was generating sales of $1 million a year. Yet the company was incurring losses of $280,000. Giannukos was immersed in every aspect of her business; she designed the clothing, coordinated the manufacturing, and dealt with the sales reps that targeted key markets around the country. Giannukos recruited new boutiques to sell her sportswear line by conducting trunk shows in six cities around the country and was constantly traveling. Because she was so wrapped up in managing her company, she did not have an impartial perspective of it and its ability to produce a profit.

Only when Giannukos sat down with an experienced entrepreneur, Norm Brodsky, who asked her some basic questions and offered a different view of her company, did she finally have a revelation that set her company on the pathway to profitability. Brodsky began by asking Giannukos about the costs of each of the shows she conducted in the six cities. Two of the shows, Dallas and Atlanta, generated most of the company's sales (about $825,000) at a cost of about $90,000. The shows in the remaining four cities brought in just $175,000, yet the cost of running those shows also was $90,000. Brodsky immediately recognized that Giannukos was making a classic entrepreneurial mistake, one that he himself had made: chasing after every sale and spreading herself too thin.

When Brodsky suggested that she limit her energies to just the Dallas and Atlanta shows, Giannukos's reaction also was classic: "You don't understand. I can't skip those shows! Everyone says I have to be there to establish a presence. That's how you build a brand."

To Giannukos, dropping four shows was like taking a step backward in her business, but Brodsky knew that she was wasting money and, more important, her

valuable time on those low-performing markets. To convince her, Brodsky took her through the numbers. If she dropped those shows, her sales would decline from $1 million to $825,000, but her profits would rise. The company's gross profit margin was 38 percent; therefore, the gross profit the four low-performing shows generated was $66,500 (38 percent of their $175,000 in sales). Her cost to put on the shows in those markets was $90,000, which meant she was already incurring a loss of $23,500 (the gross profit of $66,500 minus $90,000), not counting other company expenses. By dropping these four shows, she would reduce her losses by at least $23,500!

In addition, Brodsky pointed out, dropping those four shows would enable Giannukos to devote more time to improving her results in Dallas and Atlanta, finding good sales reps in other markets, and marketing her clothing to upscale department stores. Brodsky assumed that doing so would produce a 20 percent increase in sales, pushing the company's sales revenue to $990,000 ($825,000 plus 20 percent of $825,000 equals $990,000). If her gross profit margin remained at 38 percent, this additional $165,000 in sales would produce a gross profit of $62,700 (38 percent of $165,000) with virtually no increase in costs. Brodsky predicted that in the end, Giannukos's sales would drop only $10,000 for the year ($1,000,000 minus $990,000), but she would cut her losses by $86,200 (the $23,500 loss she would avoid plus the $62,700 gross profit she would generate).

The light bulb went off as Gainnukos looked at the numbers and took her mentor's advice: She dropped the four underperforming shows to focus on Dallas and Atlanta.

Several months later, Giannukos's company was growing stronger. Just as Brodsky had projected, sales were $1 million, and Giannukos had cut her losses from $280,000 to $60,000. The following year, her forecasts called for sales of $2 million and a solid profit. Along the way, Giannukos refined her marketing and sales techniques to make them more effective, and she discovered the dangers and the extra costs of carrying excessive inventory. She continues to work on improving her sales forecasts to minimize the amount of inventory she carries at any time. Giannukos still loves owning her own business, but now she's more satisfied because she is operating it at a profit!

1. Why did Giannukos initially resist the advice to drop the four poor-performing shows?
2. What role did having accurate financial information play in Giannukos's ability to turn around her struggling business?
3. What lessons can other entrepreneurs glean from the story of Victoria Pappas Collection?

Source: Adapted from Norm Brodsky, "The Thin Red Line," *Inc.,* January 2004, pp. 49–52.

Interpreting Business Ratios

5. Explain how to interpret financial ratios.

Ratios are useful yardsticks in measuring a small company's performance and can point out potential problems before they develop into serious crises. But calculating these ratios is not enough to ensure proper financial control. In addition to knowing how to calculate these ratios, the owner must understand how to interpret them and apply them to managing the business more effectively and efficiently.

Not every business measures its success with the same ratios. In fact, key performance ratios vary dramatically across industries and even within different segments of the same industry. Entrepreneurs must know and understand which ratios are most crucial to their companies' success and focus on monitoring and controlling those. Many successful entrepreneurs identify or develop ratios that are unique to their own operations to help them achieve success. Known as **critical numbers**, these barometers of business success measure financial and operational aspects of a company's performance. When these critical numbers are headed in the right direction, a business is on track to achieve its objectives. *When Pat Croce founded Sports Physical Therapists, a business that grew into a chain of 40 sports medicine centers, he discovered that the number of new patient evaluations was the critical number he needed to track. This measure told Croce how much new business he could expect in the coming months. If the number climbed, he knew that he must begin adding staff immediately.*[20] Examples of critical numbers at other companies include:

Company Example →

- The load factor, the number of seats filled with passengers, on a luxury bus targeting business travelers with daily trips from downtown Boston to midtown Manhattan.[21]
- Sales per labor hour at a grocery store.
- Subscriber renewal rates at a magazine.
- The number of "full-season equivalent" ticket sales (or FSE, the equivalent of a 42-game season pass) for an NBA basketball team.[22]
- Percentage of rework at a photo processor. Because the percentage of rework is an important determinant of profitability, this processor graphs this critical number and posts it weekly.

Critical numbers may be different for two companies in the same industry, depending on their strategies. The key is identifying *your* company's critical numbers, monitoring them, and then driving them in the right direction. That requires communicating the importance of critical numbers to employees and giving feedback on how well the business is achieving them.

Company Example →

Over time, Norm Brodsky, owner of a highly successful records-storage business that targets law firms, accounting firms, and hospitals, discovered that his company's critical number was the number of new boxes put into storage each week, so he began tracking it closely. "Tell me how many new boxes came in during [a month]," he says, "and I can tell you our overall sales figure for [that month] within 1 or 2 percent of the actual figure." That particular critical number surprised Brodsky because new boxes account for only a small percentage of total sales; yet new-box count was the key to enabling Brodsky to forecast his company's future. Once, during a period of rapid growth (about 55 percent a year), Brodsky saw on his Monday morning report that the new-box count had fallen by 70 percent in the previous week. Alarmed, Brodsky temporarily stopped expanding the company's workforce to see if the drop was an aberration or the beginning of a business slowdown. A few weeks later, he knew that the market had changed and that sales growth indeed had slowed to 15 percent. By using his company's critical number, Brodsky avoided excessive labor costs, a nasty cash crisis, and a morale-destroying layoff and was able to keep his company on track.[23]

One of the most valuable ways to utilize ratios is to compare them with those of similar businesses in the same industry. By comparing the company's financial statistics to industry averages, the owner is able to locate problem areas and maintain adequate financial controls. "By themselves, these numbers are not that meaningful," says one financial expert of ratios, "but when you compare them to [those of] other businesses in your industry, they suddenly come alive because they put your operation in perspective."[24]

The principle behind calculating these ratios and critical numbers and then comparing them to industry norms is the same as that of most medical tests in the health care profession. Just as a healthy person's blood pressure and cholesterol levels should fall within a range of normal values, so should a financially healthy company's ratios. A company cannot deviate too far from these normal values and remain successful for long. When deviations from normal do occur (and they will), a business owner should focus on determining the cause of the deviations. In some cases, deviations are the result of sound business decisions, such as taking on inventory in preparation for the busy season, investing heavily in new technology, and others. In other instances, however, ratios that are out of the normal range for a particular type of business are indicators of what could become serious problems for a company. When comparing a company's ratios to industry standards, entrepreneurs should ask the following questions:

- Is there a significant difference in my company's ratio and the industry average?
- If so, is this a *meaningful* difference?
- Is the difference good or bad?
- What are the possible causes of this difference? What is the most likely cause?
- Does this cause require that I take action?
- What action should I take to correct the problem?

Properly used, ratio analysis can help owners identify potential problem areas in their businesses early on—*before* they become crises that threaten their very survival. Several organizations regularly compile and publish operating statistics, including key ratios, summarizing the financial performance of many businesses across a wide range of industries. The local library should subscribe to most of these publications:

Risk Management Association. The Risk Management Association publishes its *Annual Statement Studies*, showing ratios and other financial data for more than 650 different industrial, wholesale, retail, and service categories.

Dun & Bradstreet, Inc. Since 1932, Dun & Bradstreet has published *Key Business Ratios*, which covers 22 retail, 32 wholesale, and 71 industrial business categories. Dun & Bradstreet also publishes *Cost of Doing Business*, a series of operating ratios compiled from the IRS's *Statistics of Income*.

Vest Pocket Guide to Financial Ratios. This handy guide, published by Prentice Hall, gives key ratios and financial data for a wide variety of industries.

Industry trade associations. Virtually every type of business is represented by a national trade association, which publishes detailed financial data compiled from its membership. For example, owners of small supermarkets could contact the National Association of Retail Grocers or the *Progressive Grocer,* its trade publication, for financial statistics relevant to their operations.

Government agencies. Several government agencies (e.g., Federal Trade Commission, Interstate Commerce Commission, Department of Commerce, Department of Agriculture, and Securities and Exchange Commission) offer a great deal of financial operating data on a variety of industries, although the categories are more general. In addition, the IRS annually publishes *Statistics of Income,* which includes income statement and balance sheet statistics compiled from income tax returns. The IRS also publishes the *Census of Business* that gives a limited amount of ratio information.

What Do All of These Numbers Mean?

Learning to interpret financial ratios just takes a little practice! This section will show you how it's done by comparing the ratios from the operating data already computed for Sam's to those taken from *RMAs Annual Statement Studies.* (The industry median is the ratio falling exactly in the middle when sample elements are arranged in ascending or descending order.)

Sam's Appliance Shop	Industry Median

Liquidity Ratios—tell whether the small business will be able to meet its maturing obligations as they come due.

1. Current Ratio = 1.87:1   1.50:1

   Sam's Appliance Shop falls short of the rule of thumb of 2:1, but its current ratio is above the industry median by a significant amount. Sam's should have no problem meeting its short-term debts as they come due. By this measure, the company's liquidity is solid.

2. Quick Ratio = 0.63:1   0.50:1

   Again, Sam's is below the rule of thumb of 1:1, but the company passes this test of liquidity when measured against industry standards. Sam's relies on selling inventory to satisfy short-term debt (as do most appliance shops). If sales slump, the result could be liquidity problems for Sam's.

Leverage Ratios—measure the financing supplied by the company's owners against that supplied by its creditors and serve as a gauge of the depth of a company's debt.

3. Debt Ratio = 0.68:1   0.64:1

   Creditors provide 68 percent of Sam's total assets, very close to the industry median of 64 percent. Although Sam's does not appear to be overburdened with debt, the company might have difficulty borrowing additional money, especially from conservative lenders.

4. Debt to Net Worth Ratio = 2.20:1   1.90:1

   Sam's Appliance Shop owes $2.20 to creditors for every $1.00 the owners have invested in the business (compared to $1.90 in debt to every $1.00 in equity for the typical business). Although this is not an exorbitant amount of debt, many lenders and creditors will see Sam's as "borrowed up." Borrowing capacity is somewhat limited because creditors' claims against the business are more than twice those of the owners.

5. Times Interest Earned Ratio = 2.52:1   2.0:1

   Sam's earnings are high enough to cover the interest payments on its debt by a factor of 2.52, slightly better than the typical firm in the industry, whose earnings cover its interest payments just two times. Sam's Appliance Shop has a cushion (although a small one) in meeting its interest payments.

Operating Ratios—evaluate the firm's overall performance and show how effectively it is putting its resources to work.

6. Average Inventory Turnover Ratio = 2.05 times/year   4.0 times/year

    Inventory is moving through Sam's at a very slow pace, *half* that of the industry median. The company has a problem with slow-moving items in its inventory and, perhaps, too much inventory. Which items are they, and why are they slow moving? Does Sam need to drop some product lines?

7. Average Collection Period Ratio = 50.0 days   19.3 days

    Sam's Appliance Shop collects the average accounts receivable after 50 days, compared with the industry median of 19 days, more than two-and-a-half times longer. A more meaningful comparison is against Sam's credit terms; if credit terms are net 30 (or anywhere close to that), Sam's has a dangerous collection problem, one that drains cash and profits and demands *immediate* attention!

8. Average Payable Period Ratio = 59.3 days   43 days

    Sam's payables are nearly 40 percent slower than those of the typical firm in the industry. Stretching payables too far could seriously damage the company's credit rating, causing suppliers to cut off future trade credit. This could be a sign of cash flow problems or a sloppy accounts payable procedure. This problem also demands *immediate* attention.

9. Net Sales to Total Assets Ratio = 2.21:1   2.7:1

    Sam's Appliance Shop is not generating enough sales, given the size of its asset base. This could be the result of a number of factors—improper inventory, inappropriate pricing, poor location, poorly trained sales personnel, and many others. The key is to find the cause . . . *fast*!

10. Net Sales to Working Capital Ratio = 5.86:1   10.8:1

    Sam's generates just $5.86 in sales for every $1 in working capital, just over half of what the typical firm in the industry does. Given the previous ratio, the message is clear: Sam's simply is not producing an adequate level of sales. Improving the number of inventory turns will boost this ratio; otherwise, Sam's is likely to experience a working capital shortage soon.

Profitability Ratios—measure how efficiently the firm is operating and offer information about its bottom line.

11. Net Profit on Sales Ratio = 3.24%   7.6%

    After deducting all expenses, 3.24 cents of each sales dollar remains as profit for Sam's—less than half the industry median. Sam should check his company's gross profit margin and investigate its operating expenses, checking them against industry standards and looking for those that are out of balance.

12. Net Profit to Equity Ratio = 22.65%   12.6%

    Sam's Appliance Shop's owners are earning 22.65 percent on the money they have invested in the business. This yield is nearly twice that of the industry median and, given the previous ratio, is more a result of the owners' relatively low investment in the business than an indication of its superior profitability. The owners are using OPM (Other People's Money) to generate a profit.

When comparing ratios for their individual businesses to published statistics, entrepreneurs must remember that the comparison is made against averages. Owners should strive to achieve ratios that are at least as good as these average figures. The goal should be to manage the business so that its financial performance is better than the industry average. As owners compare financial performance to those covered in the published statistics, they inevitably will discern differences between them. They should note those items that are substantially out of line from the industry average. However, a ratio that varies from the average does not necessarily mean that a small business is

Figure 8.7

Trend Analysis of Ratios

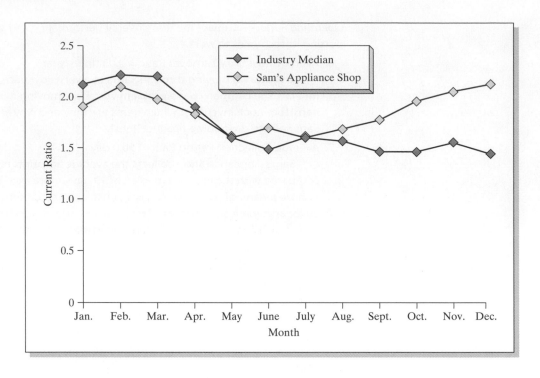

in financial jeopardy. Instead of making drastic changes in financial policy, entrepreneurs must explore why the figures are out of line. Steve Cowan, co-owner of

Professional Salon Concepts, a wholesale beauty products distributor, routinely
performs such an analysis on his company's financial statements. "I need to know whether
the variances for expenses and revenues for a certain period are similar," he says. "If
they're not, are the differences explainable? Is an expense category up just because of a
decision to spend more, or were we just sloppy?"[25]

Company Example →

In addition to comparing ratios to industry averages, owners should analyze their firms'
financial ratios over time. By themselves, these ratios are "snapshots" of the firm's finances at
a single instant; but by examining these trends over time, the owner can detect gradual shifts
that otherwise might go unnoticed until a financial crisis is looming (see Figure 8.7).

IN THE FOOTSTEPS OF AN ENTREPRENEUR...

Batting .1000 in the Auto Business

Dorian Boyland learned the value of hard work from
his mother and role model, Alice. With his mother's
help and encouragement, Boyland earned a degree
in business administration and computer science at
the University of Wisconsin while earning a name for
himself as a college All-American baseball player.
After graduation, Boyland played professional baseball, winning a World Series title with the Pittsburgh
Pirates. When he retired from baseball after eight
years, Boyland was set to begin work as a computer
systems analyst at Intel when he received a call from
Ron Tonkin, owner of one of the largest auto dealer

groups in the United States. "He told me to come
work for him for 60 days and if I liked it, I could stay,"
he recalls. "If I didn't, I still had my job at Intel."

Boyland was a natural. Within two months, he had
been promoted to assistant manager and was making
more money than he had made as a professional baseball player. "I loved the business from day one because
it was like sports," he says. "It was competitive."

A few years later, when Tonkin approached
Boyland with the idea of forming a partnership to buy
an existing Dodge dealership, Boyland jumped at the
chance. Two years later, Boyland sold his partnership

interest and bought his own Dodge dealership. As a new owner, Boyland struggled at first, mainly because he lacked a plan and a disciplined approach for implementing it. "I had a lot of inventory, so manufacturers were happy," he says. "I spent a lot on advertising, so newspapers were happy. My commission structure was high, so my salespeople were happy. But I wasn't making any money, so I wasn't happy."

Boyland spent three days at home developing a business plan that established a bottom-up formula for earning a profit by controlling expenses and monitoring cash flow. He changed the way he handled inventory, advertising, and pricing—in short, the way he managed his entire business. Boyland's plan produced results: His Dodge dealership began earning a profit and has done so every year since, not an easy accomplishment in the auto sales industry. More important, Boyland, who now does business under the name Boyland Auto, has implemented that same plan at all seven of the dealerships he now owns.

Boyland is careful about how he spends his money so he can generate a profit. He keeps advertising expenditures to less than 10 percent of gross profit. His sales team receives no salaries; their compensation is commission based. He allocates 35 percent of overhead expenses to new car sales, 30 percent to used car sales, 25 percent to service, and 10 percent to parts sales. His goal is to run his dealerships so that they produce a net profit margin of at least 3 percent of sales. "I never ask how many cars we sold," he quips. "I ask my sales managers how much profit we made." Although sales volume is important because auto makers expect

dealers to reach sales targets, Boyland focuses more on profitability. "You can be number one in terms of [sales] volume, but if you are constantly losing money, you'll be taken out of business."

Every month, Boyland sits down with the managers of all of his dealerships to review an extensive financial and operating report. The discussion is open and honest, but the real benefit comes from managers seeing the numbers their stores are generating and then exchanging ideas about how to improve them. Another important aspect of the meetings is the goal setting that takes place as managers set plans for the future.

Boyland learned early on a valuable lesson in maintaining the profitability of his auto dealerships, one he continues to improve on even now. "You have to have a passion for this business," he says. "There's a lot of money to be made and a lot of money to be lost. Whether you are selling cars or shoes, you go into business to make money. That's the bottom line."

1. Why is monitoring a company's financial performance using the techniques described in this chapter important to operating a successful business?
2. Schedule a brief interview with a car dealer in your area. Describe the 12 ratios covered in this chapter. Which of these ratios are most important to running an auto dealership successfully?
3. What other critical numbers does the dealer monitor?

Source: Adapted from Carolyn M. Brown, "Maximum Overdrive," *Black Enterprise,* June 2003, pp. 156–162.

Break-Even Analysis

6. Conduct a break-even analysis for a small company.

Another key component of every sound financial plan is a break-even analysis (or cost-volume-profit analysis). A small company's **break-even point** is the level of operation (sales dollars or production quantity) at which it neither earns a profit nor incurs a loss. At this level of activity, sales revenue equals expenses—that is, the firm "breaks even." By analyzing costs and expenses, an owner can calculate the minimum level of activity required to keep the firm in operation. These techniques can then be refined to project the sales needed to generate the desired profit. Most potential lenders and investors will require the potential owner to prepare a break-even analysis to assist them in evaluating the earning potential of the new business. In addition to its being a simple, useful screening device for financial institutions, break-even analysis can also serve as a planning device for the small business owner. It occasionally will show a poorly prepared entrepreneur just how unprofitable a proposed business venture is likely to be.

Calculating the Break-Even Point. A small business owner can calculate a firm's break-even point by using a simple mathematical formula. To begin the analysis, the owner must determine fixed costs and variable costs. **Fixed expenses** are those that do not vary with changes in the volume of sales or production (e.g., rent, depreciation expense, interest payments). **Variable expenses**, on the other hand, vary directly with changes in the volume of sales or production (e.g., raw material costs, sales commissions).

Some expenses cannot be neatly categorized as fixed or variable because they contain elements of both. These semivariable expenses change, although not proportionately, with changes in the level of sales or production (electricity would be one example). These costs remain constant up to a particular production or sales volume and then climb as that volume is exceeded. To calculate the break-even point, the owner must separate these expenses into their fixed and variable components. A number of techniques can be used (which are beyond the scope of this text), but a good cost accounting system can provide the desired results.

Here are the steps an entrepreneur must take to compute the break-even point using an example of a typical small business, the Magic Shop:

Step 1 *Determine the expenses the business can expect to incur.* With the help of a budget an entrepreneur can develop estimates of sales revenue, cost of goods sold, and expenses for the upcoming accounting period. The Magic Shop expects net sales of $950,000 in the upcoming year, with a cost of goods sold of $646,000 and total expenses of $236,500.

Step 2 *Categorize the expenses estimated in step 1 into fixed expenses and variable expenses and separate semivariable expenses into their component parts.* From the budget, the owner anticipates variable expenses (including the cost of goods sold) of $705,125 and fixed expenses of $177,375.

Step 3 *Calculate the ratio of variable expenses to net sales.* For the Magic Shop, this percentage is $705,125 ÷ $950,000 = 74 percent. So the Magic Shop uses $0.74 out of every sales dollar to cover variable expenses, leaving $0.26 as a contribution margin to cover fixed costs and make a profit.

Step 4 *Compute the break-even point by inserting this information into the following formula:*

$$\text{Break-even sales (\$)} = \frac{\text{Total fixed cost}}{\text{Contribution margin expressed as a percentage of sales}}$$

For the Magic Shop,

$$\text{Break-even sales} = \frac{\$177,375}{0.26}$$

$$= \$682,212$$

Thus, the Magic Shop will break even with sales of $682,212. At this point, sales revenue generated will just cover total fixed and variable expense. The Magic Shop will earn no profit and will incur no loss. To verify this, make the following calculations:

Sales at break-even point	$682,212
− Variable expenses (74% of sales)	−504,837
Contribution margin	177,375
− Fixed expenses	−177,375
Net income (or net loss)	$ 0

Adding in a Profit. What if the Magic Shop's owner wants to do *better* than just break even? The owner's analysis can be adjusted to consider such a possibility. Suppose the owner expects a reasonable profit (before taxes) of $80,000. What level of sales must the Magic Shop achieve to generate this? The owner can calculate this by treating the desired profit as if it were a fixed cost. In other words, the owner modifies the formula to include the desired net income:

$$\text{Sales (\$)} = \frac{\text{Total fixed expenses} + \text{Desired net income}}{\text{Contribution margin expressed as a percentage of sales}}$$

$$= \frac{\$177,375 + 80,000}{0.26}$$

$$= \$989,904$$

To achieve a net profit of $80,000 (before taxes), the Magic Shop must generate net sales of $989,904.

Break-Even Point in Units. Some small businesses may prefer to express the break-even point in units produced or sold instead of in dollars. Manufacturers often find this approach particularly useful. The following formula computes the break-even point in units:

$$\text{Break-even volume} = \frac{\text{Total fixed cost}}{\text{Sales price per unit} - \text{Variable cost per unit}}$$

For example, suppose that Trilex Manufacturing Company estimates its fixed costs for producing its line of small appliances at $390, 000. The variable costs (including materials, direct labor, and factory overhead) amount to $12.10 per unit, and the selling price per unit is $17.50. So, Trilex computes its contribution margin this way:

$$\text{Contribution margin} = \text{Price per unit} - \text{Variable cost per unit}$$

$$= \$17.50 \text{ per unit} - \$12.10 \text{ per unit}$$

$$= \$5.40 \text{ per unit}$$

So, Trilex's break-even volume is as follows:

$$\text{Break-even volume (units)} = \frac{\text{Total fixed costs}}{\text{Per-unit contribution margin}}$$

$$= \frac{\$390,000}{\$5.40 \text{ per unit}}$$

$$= 72,222 \text{ units}$$

To convert this number of units to break-even sales dollars, Trilex simply multiplies it by the selling price per unit:

$$\text{Break-even sales} = 72,222 \text{ units} \times \$17.50 = \$1,263, 889$$

Trilex could compute the sales required to produce a desired profit by treating the profit as if it were a fixed cost:

$$\text{Sales (units)} = \frac{\text{Total fixed costs} + \text{Desired net income}}{\text{Per-unit contribution margin}}$$

For example, if Trilex wanted to earn a $60,000 profit, its required sales would be:

$$\text{Sales (units)} = \frac{\$390,000 + \$60,000}{5.40} = 83,333 \text{ units}$$

Constructing a Break-Even Chart. The following outlines the procedure for constructing a graph that visually portrays the firm's break-even point (that point at which revenues equal expenses):

Step 1   *On the horizontal axis, mark a scale measuring sales volume in dollars (or in units sold or some other measure of volume).* The break-even chart for the Magic Shop, shown in Figure 8.8, uses sales volume in dollars because it applies to all types of businesses, departments, and products.

Figure 8.8

Break-Even Chart,
the Magic Shop

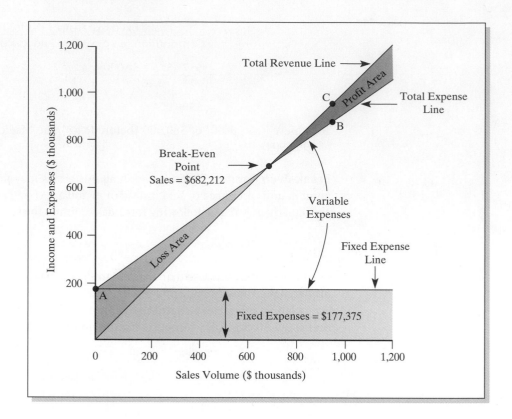

Step 2 *On the vertical axis, mark a scale measuring income and expenses in dollars.*

Step 3 *Draw a fixed expense line intersecting the vertical axis at the proper dollar level parallel to the horizontal axis.* The area between this line and the horizontal axis represents the firm's fixed expenses. On the break-even chart for the Magic Shop, shown in Figure 8.8, the fixed expense line is drawn horizontally beginning at $177,375 (point A). Because this line is parallel to the horizontal axis, it indicates that fixed expenses remain constant at all levels of activity.

Step 4 *Draw a total expense line that slopes upward beginning at the point at which the fixed cost line intersects the vertical axis.* The precise location of the total expense line is determined by plotting the total cost incurred at a particular sales volume. The total cost for a given sales level is found by the following formula:

Total expenses = Fixed expenses + Variable expenses expressed as
a percentage of sales × Sales level

Arbitrarily choosing a sales level of $950,000, the Magic Shop's total costs would be as follows:

Total expenses = $177,375 + (0.74 × $950,000)

= $880,375

Thus, the Magic Shop's total cost is $880,375 at a net sales level of $950,000 (point B). The variable cost line is drawn by connecting points A and B. The area between the total cost line and the horizontal axis measures the total costs the Magic Shop incurs at various levels of sales. For example, if the Magic Shop's sales are $850,000, its total costs will be $806,375.

Step 5 *Beginning at the graph's origin, draw a 45-degree revenue line showing where total sales volume equals total income.*

For the Magic Shop, point C shows that sales = income = $950,000.

Step 6 *Locate the break-even point by finding the intersection of the total expense line and the revenue line.* If the Magic Shop operates at a sales volume to the left of the break-even point, it will incur a loss because the expense line is higher than the revenue line over this range. This is shown by the triangular section labeled "Loss Area." On the other hand, if the firm operates at a sales volume to the right of the break-even point, it will earn a profit because the revenue line lies above the expense line over this range. This is shown by the triangular section labeled "Profit Area."

Using Break-Even Analysis. Break-even analysis is a useful planning tool for the potential small business owner, especially when approaching potential lenders and investors for funds. It provides an opportunity for integrated analysis of sales volume, expenses, income, and other relevant factors. Break-even analysis is a simple, preliminary screening device for the entrepreneur faced with the business start-up decision. It is easy to understand and use. With just a few calculations, an entrepreneur can determine the minimum level of sales needed to stay in business as well as the effects of various financial strategies on the business. It is a helpful tool for evaluating the impact of changes in investments and expenditures. *For instance, before launching LimoLiner, a company that provides luxury bus service aimed at businesspeople traveling between downtown Boston and midtown Manhattan, entrepreneur Fergus McCann calculated his venture's break-even point. Knowing that it would take a while to build a solid base of customers, McCann determined that to break even, his buses had to be only half full on each one-way trip. McCann priced a LimoLiner trip at just $69, which is $30 less than Amtrak's Acela Express and $172.50 less than a full-fare airline ticket. Satisfied that he would be able to generate at least $483 per one-way trip within a short time of opening, McCann launched LimoLiner.*[26]

Break-even analysis does have certain limitations. It is too simple to use as a final screening device because it ignores the importance of cash flows. Also, the accuracy of the analysis depends on the accuracy of the revenue and expense estimates. Finally, the assumptions pertaining to break-even analysis may not be realistic for some businesses. Break-even calculations assume the following: Fixed expenses remain constant for all levels of sales volume; variable expenses change in direct proportion to changes in sales volume; and changes in sales volume have no effect on unit sales price. Relaxing these assumptions does not render this tool useless, however. For example, the owner could employ nonlinear break-even analysis using a graphical approach.

> Company Example

▌▐ ▍ Chapter Review

1. Understand the importance of preparing a financial plan.

   - Launching a successful business requires an entrepreneur to create a solid financial plan. Not only is such a plan an important tool in raising the capital needed to get a company off the ground, but it also is an essential ingredient in managing a growing business.
   - Earning a profit does not occur by accident; it takes planning.

2. Describe how to prepare the basic financial statements and use them to manage a small business.

   - Entrepreneurs rely on three basic financial statements to understand the financial conditions of their companies:

   1. *The balance sheet.* Built on the accounting equation: Assets = Liabilities + Owner's equity (net worth), it provides an estimate of the company's value on a particular date.
   2. *The income statement.* This statement compares the firm's revenues against its expenses to determine its net income (or loss). It provides information about the company's bottom line.
   3. *The statement of cash flows.* This statement shows the change in the company's working capital over the accounting period by listing the sources and the uses of funds.

3. Create projected financial statements.

   - Projected financial statements are a basic component of a sound financial plan. They help the manager plot the company's financial future by setting operating objectives and by analyzing the reasons for variations from targeted results. Also, the small business in search of start-up funds will need these pro forma statements to present to prospective lenders and investors. They also assist in determining the amount of cash, inventory, fixtures, and other assets the business will need to begin operation.

4. Understand the basic financial statements through ratio analysis.

   ■ The 12 key ratios described in this chapter are divided into four major categories: liquidity ratios, which show the small firm's ability to meet its current obligations; leverage ratios, which tell how much of the company's financing is provided by owners and how much by creditors; operating ratios, which show how effectively the firm uses its resources; and profitability ratios, which disclose the company's profitability.

   ■ Many agencies and organizations regularly publish such statistics. If there is a discrepancy between the small firm's ratios and those of the typical business, the owner should investigate the reason

for the difference. A below-average ratio does not necessarily mean that the business is in trouble.

5. Explain how to interpret financial ratios.

   ■ To benefit from ratio analysis, the small company should compare its ratios to those of other companies in the same line of business and look for trends over time.

   ■ When business owners detect deviations in their companies' ratios from industry standards, they should determine the cause of the deviations. In some cases, such deviations are the result of sound business decisions; in other instances, however, ratios that are out of the normal range for a particular type of business are indicators of what could become serious problems for a company.

6. Conduct a break-even analysis for a small company.

   ■ Business owners should know their firm's break-even point, the level of operations at which total revenues equal total costs; it is the point at which companies neither earn a profit nor incur a loss. Although just a simple screening device, break-even analysis is a useful planning and decision-making tool.

▐ ▌ ▌ Discussion Questions

1. Why is it important for entrepreneurs to develop financial plans for their companies?

2. How should a small business manager use the ratios discussed in this chapter?

3. Outline the key points of the 12 ratios discussed in this chapter. What signals does each give a business owner?

4. Describe the method for building a projected income statement and a projected balance sheet for a beginning business.

5. Why are pro forma financial statements important to the financial planning process?

6. How can break-even analysis help an entrepreneur planning to launch a business? What information does it give an entrepreneur?

Creating a Solid Financial Plan

Business Plan Pro

Preparing the financial forecasts for their business plans intimidates some entrepreneurs, but Business Plan Pro makes this important process a snap. After you have finished studying Chapter 8, go to the section in Business Plan Pro called The Bottom Line. There you can begin building the financial forecasts for your plan by defining the assumptions on which you will base your financial statements. Then you can use the Profit and Loss Wizard to create projected income statements. Be sure to include in the Explain Projected Profit and

Loss section any explanations of the numbers in your income statements you think are significant.

Use the Benchmarks Chart and the Key Financial Indicators section of Business Plan Pro to show how your company's key ratios compare to the industry average, information you can get from *RMA Annual Statement Studies*, Dun & Bradstreet, trade associations, and other sources. This portion of your plan will help you prove that your financial forecasts are realistic.

Finally, use the Breakeven Wizard to complete a breakeven analysis for your business. You can clarify the key parts of your breakeven analysis in the Explain Breakeven Analysis section. This important calculation shows the minimum level of business activity required for your company to stay in business.

Chapter 9
Managing Cash Flow

A deficit is what you have when you haven't got as much as when you had nothing.
—Gerald F. Lieberman

Business isn't difficult—be sure the incomings are greater than the outgoings.
—A wise Vermonter

Upon completion of this chapter, you will be able to:

1. Explain the importance of cash management to the success of a small business.

2. Differentiate between cash and profits.

3. Understand the five steps in creating a cash budget and use them to build a cash budget.

4. Describe the fundamental principles involved in managing the "big three" of cash management: accounts receivable, accounts payable, and inventory.

5. Explain the techniques for avoiding a cash crunch in a small company.

Cash—a four-letter word that has become a curse for many small businesses. Lack of this valuable asset has driven countless small companies into bankruptcy. Unfortunately, many more firms will become failure statistics because their owners have neglected the principles of cash management that can spell the difference between success and failure. One small business owner compares a small company's cash to oxygen on a space trip:

> Astronauts who take off on a long space flight must take along plenty of food and water (their "healthy balance sheet"). But if they happen to run out of oxygen any time between takeoff and landing, all that food and water is of no use to them; they will perish. Cash is like oxygen to a business. When it's there, it's easily taken for granted. When it's not, death can come quickly.[1]

Developing a cash forecast is essential for new businesses because early sales levels usually do not generate sufficient cash to keep the company afloat. Too often, entrepreneurs launch their companies with insufficient cash to cover their start-up costs and the cash flow gap that results while expenses outstrip revenues. The result is business failure.

Controlling the financial aspects of a business with the profit-planning techniques described in the previous chapter is immensely important; however, by themselves, these techniques are insufficient to achieve business success. Entrepreneurs are prone to focus on their companies' income statements—particularly sales and profits. The balance sheet and the income statement, of course, show an important part of a company's financial picture, but it is just that: only part of the total picture. It is entirely possible for a business to have a solid balance sheet and to make a profit and still go out of business by *running out of cash*. Managing cash effectively requires an entrepreneur to look beyond the bottom line and focus on what it takes to keep a company going—cash.

Cash Management

1. Explain the importance of cash management to the success of a small business.

Managing cash flow is a struggle for many business owners (see Figure 9.1). **Cash management** involves forecasting, collecting, disbursing, investing, and planning for the cash a company needs to operate smoothly. Managing cash is an important task because cash is the most important yet least productive asset that a small business owns. A business must have enough cash to meet its obligations as they come due or it will experience bankruptcy. Creditors, employees, and lenders expect to be paid on time, and cash is the required medium of exchange. But some firms retain an excessive amount of cash to meet any unexpected circumstances that might arise. These dormant dollars have an income-earning potential that the owners are ignoring, and this restricts a company's growth and lowers its profitability. Proper cash management permits entrepreneurs to adequately meet the cash demands of their businesses, to avoid retaining unnecessarily large cash balances, and to stretch the profit-generating power of each dollar their companies own. Entrepreneurs must have the discipline to manage cash flow from their first day of operations. *Shortly after*

Company Example →

H. J. Heinz and two partners launched their first food business in 1875, their company's rapidly growing sales outstripped their start-up capital, and the company ran out of cash. A local newspaper called the entrepreneurs a "trio in a pickle." After the company failed, Heinz personally was liable for $20,000, a huge sum in that day. Undaunted, Heinz learned from his mistakes and launched a second food company the very next year. In this venture, he added the product that would eventually make him famous—ketchup—and with the help of careful cash management, the H. J. Heinz Company has become one of the largest food companies in the world.[2]

Although cash flow problems afflict companies of all sizes and ages, young businesses are prone to suffering cash shortages because they act like "cash sponges," soaking up every available dollar and then some. The reason is that their cash-generating "engines" have not

Figure 9.1

Causes of Cash Flow Problems Among Small Businesses

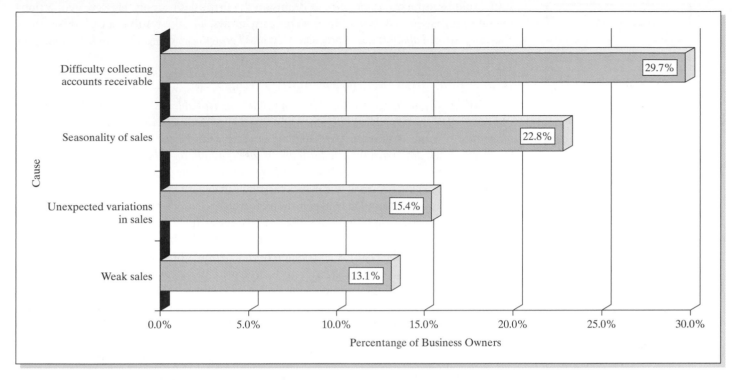

Source: © 2004 National Federation of Independent Businesses (NFIB).

had the opportunity to "rev up" to full speed and cannot generate sufficient power to produce the cash necessary to cover rapidly climbing expenses.

Owners of rapidly growing businesses also must pay particular attention to cash management. One study of successful business owners conducted by Geneva Business Bank found that the greatest potential threat to cash flow occurs when a company is experiencing

Because his first company ran out of cash, H. J. Heinz found himself "in a pickle." Like many successful entrepreneurs, however, he learned from his mistakes and went on to launch another company that would become one of the largest food companies in the world and make him famous.

Company Example →

rapid growth.[3] If a company's sales are up, the owner also must hire more employees, expand plant capacity, develop new products, increase the sales force and customer service staff, build inventory, and incur other drains on the firm's cash supply. However, collections from the increased sales often slip as a company grows, and the result is a cash crisis. *Aliza Sherman learned about the cash problems that rapid growth can bring about in her second year of business. "My partner pulled me into his office one day and announced, 'If we don't get a check in by Friday, we won't make payroll,' " she recalls. "That couldn't be possible! We had a slew of clients, a ton of work in production." Then she discovered that the company had $250,000 in accounts receivable but less than $10,000 in available cash. "Whatever money came in immediately went to paying bills that had accumulated from several months back. No matter how much revenue we generated, we could never get ahead." Fortunately for Sherman and her partner, a check did arrive in time for them to meet payroll, and the partners began focusing more on cash flow management to avoid similar problems in the future.*[4]

Unfortunately, many small business owners do not engage in cash planning. One study of 2,200 small businesses found that 68 percent performed no cash flow analysis at all![5] The result is that many successful, growing, and profitable businesses fail because they become insolvent; they do not have adequate cash to meet the needs of a growing business with a booming sales volume. The head of the National Federation of Independent Businesses says that many small business owners "wake up one day to find that the price of success is no cash on hand. They don't understand that if they're successful, inventory and receivables will increase faster than profits can fund them."[6] The resulting cash crisis may force an entrepreneur to lose equity control of the business or, ultimately, declare bankruptcy and close. Table 9.1 describes the five key cash management roles every entrepreneur must fill.

The first step in managing cash more effectively is to understand the company's **cash flow cycle**—the time lag between paying suppliers for merchandise and receiving payment from customers (see Figure 9.2). The longer this cash flow cycle, the more likely the business owner is to encounter a cash crisis. Preparing a cash forecast that recognizes this cycle, however, will help avoid a crisis.

Company Example →

John Fernsell recognizes the importance of cash management because of the length of his company's cash flow cycle. Fernsell, a former stockbroker, is the founder of Ibex Outdoor Clothing, a company that makes outdoor clothing from high- quality European wool. Ibex's

Table 9.1

Five Cash Management Roles of the Entrepreneur

Role 1: Cash Finder. This is the entrepreneur's first and foremost responsibility. You must make sure there is enough capital to pay all present (and future) bills. This is not a one-time task; it is an ongoing job.

Role 2: Cash Planner. As cash planner, an entrepreneur makes sure the company's cash is used properly and efficiently. You must keep track of its cash, make sure it is available to pay bills, and plan for its future use. Planning requires you to forecast the company's cash inflows and outflows for the months ahead with the help of a cash budget (discussed later in this chapter).

Role 3: Cash Distributor. This role requires you to control the cash needed to pay the company's bills and the priority and the timing of those payments. Forecasting cash disbursements accurately and making sure the cash is available when payments come due are essential to keeping the business solvent.

Role 4: Cash Collector. As cash collector, your job is to make sure your customers pay their bills on time. Too often, entrepreneurs focus on pumping up sales, while neglecting to collect the cash from those sales. Having someone in your company responsible for collecting accounts receivable is essential. Uncollected accounts drain a small company's pool of cash very quickly.

Role 5: Cash Conserver. This role requires you to make sure your company gets maximum value for the dollars it spends. Whether you are buying inventory to resell or computers to keep track of what you sell, it is important to get the most for your money. Avoiding unnecessary expenditures is an important part of this task. The goal is to spend cash so it will produce a return for the company.

Source: Adapted from Bruce J. Blechman, "Quick Change Artist," *Entrepreneur,* January 1994, pp. 18–21.

Figure 9.2

The Cash Flow Cycle

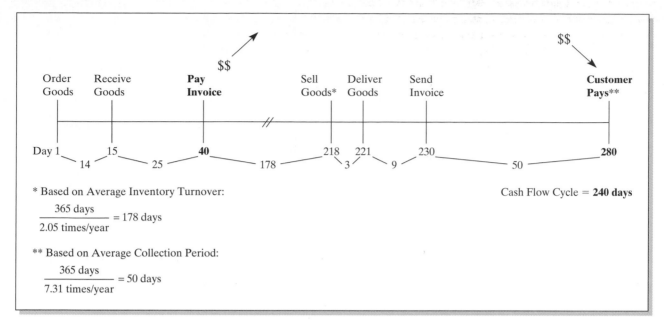

* Based on Average Inventory Turnover:

$$\frac{365 \text{ days}}{2.05 \text{ times/year}} = 178 \text{ days}$$

** Based on Average Collection Period:

$$\frac{365 \text{ days}}{7.31 \text{ times/year}} = 50 \text{ days}$$

Cash Flow Cycle = **240 days**

sales are growing rapidly, but cash is a constant problem because of its lengthy cash flow cycle. Fernsell orders wool from his European suppliers in February and pays for it in June. The wool then goes to garment makers in California, who ship finished clothing to Ibex in July and August, when Fernsell pays for the finished goods. Ibex ships the clothing to retailers in September and October but does not get paid until November, December, and sometimes January! Ibex's major cash outflows are from June to August, but its cash inflows during those months are virtually nil, making it essential for Fernsell to manage the company's cash balances carefully.[7]

The next step in effective cash management is to begin cutting down the length of the cash flow cycle. Reducing the cycle from 240 days to, say, 150 days would free up incredible amounts of cash that this company could use to finance growth and dramatically reduce its borrowing costs. What steps do you suggest the owner of the business whose cash flow cycle is illustrated in Figure 9.2 take to reduce the cycle's length?

Cash and Profits Are Not the Same

2. Differentiate between cash and profits.

When analyzing cash flow, entrepreneurs must understand that cash and profits are not the same. Profit (or net income) is the difference between a company's total revenue and its total expenses. It measures how efficiently the business is operating. Cash is the money that is readily available to use in a business. **Cash flow** measures a company's liquidity and its ability to pay its bills and other financial obligations on time by tracking the flow of cash into and out of the business over a period of time. Figure 9.3 shows the flow of cash through a typical small business. Decreases in cash occur when a business purchases, on credit or for cash, goods for inventory or materials for use in production. The resulting inventory is sold either for cash or on credit. When it takes in cash or collects accounts receivable, a company's cash balance increases. Notice that purchases for inventory and production *lead* sales; that is, these bills typically must be paid *before* sales are generated. However, collection of accounts receivable *lags* behind sales; that is, customers who purchase goods on credit may not pay until a month or more later.

Figure 9.3

Cash Flow

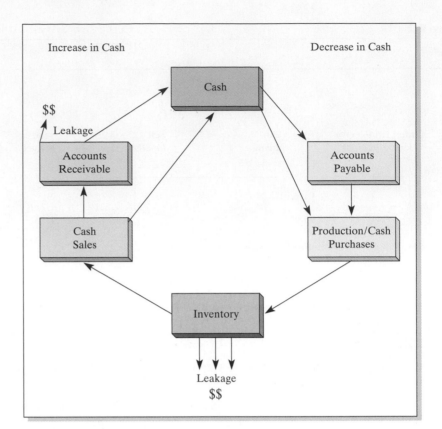

As important as earning a profit is, no business owner can pay creditors, employees, and lenders in profits; that requires *cash*! "Cash flow is more important than earnings," says Evan Betzer, a former Enron employee who now owns his own financial services firm.[8] Although profits are tied up in many forms, such as inventory, computers, or machinery, cash is the money that flows through a business in a continuous cycle without being tied up in any other asset. A company can operate in the short run with a net loss showing on its income statement, but if its cash flow becomes negative, the business is in trouble. It can no longer pay suppliers, meet payroll, pay its taxes, or any other bills. In short, the business is headed for extinction.

The Cash Budget

The need for a reliable cash forecast arises because in every business the cash flowing in is rarely "in sync" with the cash flowing out. This uneven flow of cash creates periodic cash surpluses and deficits, making it necessary for entrepreneurs to track the flow of cash through their businesses so they can project realistically the cash available throughout the year. Many owners operate their businesses without knowing the pattern of their cash flows, believing that the process is too complex or time consuming. In reality, entrepreneurs simply cannot afford to disregard the process of cash management. They must ensure that an adequate, but not excessive, supply of cash is on hand to meet their companies' operating needs.

How much cash is enough? What is suitable for one business may be totally inadequate for another, depending on each firm's size, nature, and particular situation. A business owner should prepare a **cash budget,** which is nothing more than a "cash map," showing the amount and timing of the cash receipts and the cash disbursements day by day, week by week, or month by month. It is used to predict the mount of cash the firm will need to operate smoothly over a specific period of time, and it is a valuable tool in managing a company successfully.

IN THE FOOTSTEPS OF AN ENTREPRENEUR...

A Cash Flow Dilemma

Lance Redmond stared out the window of his office and into the park along the river below. It was a beautiful fall day, and the sun reflected off the water, creating a beautiful hue of colors that magnified the brilliant reds, yellows, and oranges of the trees' leaves. One question stuck in Redmond's mind: What should he do with the check he had just received as an up-front payment from a large customer for a job the customer wanted Redmond's company to do? In light of the fact that Redmond's company, Stallion Manufacturing, a maker of industrial equipment, did not have the cash to meet a payroll due in just 20 days, the answer seemed simple: Cash the check.

The situation was much more complex than that, however. Redmond knew that his company was not capable of doing the job the customer was requesting. The scope of the job required engineering skills, equipment, and financing that Stallion Manufacturing simply did not have. Yet, here was the answer to his company's latest cash flow crisis. Redmond had never missed a payroll before, although he had come close on several occasions. He knew that if he could not give his 41 employees their paychecks on time, some of them would very likely leave the company to work elsewhere. With sales at the four-year-old company growing so fast, he could not afford to lose any of his most skilled and experienced employees.

If he cashed the check, he could use the money to meet payroll, and none of his employees would be aware that the company had narrowly escaped another cash crisis. He could even talk with managers from the company that wanted the work, pretending to consider

the opportunity to complete the job. Of course, he'd eventually have to return the $42,000 check to the customer, but this would buy him enough time to collect other accounts customers owed Stallion.

Redmond called a meeting to talk about the situation with his top managers. The chief financial officer, Sandy Camanetti, suggested they cash the check, meet with the managers from the company, and bluff, pretending to consider accepting the job.

"But we *know* we can't do the job," said Jill Sanchez, Stallion's director of marketing. "What if they find out? Do we want to risk losing a large, valuable customer that we've had for a long time?"

Later that evening at dinner, Redmond happened to see an old friend who also ran his own business and whose opinion he respected. "Got a minute?" Redmond asked his friend, pulling back a chair at the table. "I have a situation I'd like to discuss with you. I need your input."

"Sure," his friend said. "Have a seat. What's up?"

Redmond explained the scenario, pushed back from table, and said, "There you have it. What should I do?"

1. Assume the role of Lance Redmond's friend. What advice would you offer him? Explain your reasoning.
2. Explain the ethical dimensions of Redmond's situation.
3. What other recommendations can you make to Redmond for resolving this problem? Develop a list of at least three suggestions that would help Redmond manage his company's cash flow more effectively.

Preparing a Cash Budget

3. Understand the five steps in creating a cash budget and use them to build a cash budget.

Typically, a small business should prepare a projected monthly cash budget for at least one year and quarterly estimates one or two years beyond that. To be effective, a cash budget must cover all seasonal sales fluctuations. The more variable a company's sales pattern, the shorter its planning horizon should be. For example, a firm whose sales fluctuate widely over a relatively short time frame might require a weekly cash budget. The key to managing cash flow successfully is to monitor not only the amount of cash flowing into and out of a company but also the *timing* of those cash flows.

Entrepreneurs who take the time to prepare a cash budget are less likely to encounter a cash crisis and more likely to keep their companies solvent.

Regardless of the time frame selected, a cash budget must be in writing for an entrepreneur to properly visualize a company's cash position. Creating a written cash plan is not an excessively time-consuming task and can help the owner avoid unexpected cash shortages, a situation that can cause a business to fail. One financial consultant describes "a client who won't be able to make the payroll this month. His bank agreed to meet the payroll for him—but banks don't like to be surprised like that."[9] Preparing a cash budget will help business owners avoid such adverse surprises. It will also let the owner know if he is keeping excessively high amounts of cash on hand. Computer spreadsheets such as Excel and Lotus 1–2–3 make the job fast and easy to complete and allow for instant updates and "what if" analysis.

A cash budget is based on the cash method of accounting, which means that cash receipts and cash disbursements are recorded in the forecast only when the cash transaction is expected to take place. For example, credit sales to customers are not reported until the company expects to receive the cash from them. Similarly, purchases made on credit are not recorded until the owner expects to pay them. Because depreciation, bad debt expense, and other noncash items involve no cash transfers, they are omitted entirely from the cash budget.

A cash budget is nothing more than a forecast of the firm's cash inflows and outflows for a specific time period, and it will never be completely accurate. But it does give a small business owner a clear picture of a company's estimated cash balance for the period, pointing out where external cash infusions may be required or where surplus cash balances may be available for investing. Also, by comparing actual cash flows with projections, entrepreneurs can revise their forecasts so that future cash budgets will be more accurate. *Michael Koss, president and CEO of Koss Corporation, a manufacturer of stereo headphones, now emphasizes cash flow management after his company's brush with failure. In the 1980s, Koss Corporation expanded rapidly—so rapidly, in fact, that its cash flow couldn't keep pace. Debt climbed, and the company filed for reorganization under Chapter 11 bankruptcy. Emergency actions saved the business, and today Koss manages with the determination never to repeat the same mistakes. "I look at cash every single day," he says. "That is absolutely critical."*[10]

Formats for preparing a cash budget vary depending on the pattern of a company's cash flow. Table 9.2 shows a monthly cash budget for a small department store

[Company Example] →

Table 9.2

Cash Budget for Small Department Store

Assumptions:

Cash balance on December 31 = $12,000

Minimum cash balance desired = $10,000

Sales are 75% credit and 25% cash.

Credit sales are collected in the following manner:

- 60% collected in the first month after the sale.
- 30% collected in the second month after the sale.
- 5% collected in the third month after the sale.
- 5% are never collected.

SALES FORECASTS ARE AS FOLLOWS:	PESSIMISTIC	MOST LIKELY	OPTIMISTIC
October (actual)		$300,000	
November (actual)		350,000	
December (actual)		400,000	
January	$120,000	150,000	$175,000
February	160,000	200,000	250,000
March	160,000	200,000	250,000
April	250,000	300,000	340,000

The store pays 70% of sales price for merchandise purchased and pays for each month's anticipated sales in the preceding month.

Rent is $2,000 per month.

An interest payment of $7,500 is due in March.

A tax prepayment of $50,000 must be made in March.

A capital addition payment of $130,000 is due in February.

Utilities expenses amount to $850 per month.

Miscellaneous expenses are $70 per month.

Interest income of $200 will be received in February.

Wages and salaries are estimated to be

   January—$30,000

   February—$40,000

   March—$45,000

   April—$50,000

Cash Budget—Pessimistic Sales Forecast

	OCT.	NOV.	DEC.	JAN.	FEB.	MAR.	APR.
Cash Receipts:							
Sales	$300,000	$350,000	$400,000	$120,000	$160,000	$160,000	$250,000
Credit Sales	225,000	262,500	300,000	90,000	120,000	120,000	187,500
Collections:							
60%—1st month after sale				$180,000	$ 54,000	$ 72,000	$ 72,000
30%—2nd month after sale				78,750	90,000	27,000	36,000
5%—3rd month after sale				11,250	13,125	15,000	4,500
Cash Sales				30,000	40,000	40,000	62,500
Interest				0	200	0	0
Total Cash Receipts				$300,000	$197,325	$154,000	$175,000
Cash Disbursements:							
Purchases				$112,000	$112,000	$175,000	$133,000
Rent				2,000	2,000	2,000	2,000
Utilities				850	850	850	850
Interest				0	0	7,500	0

(Continued)

Table 9.2 Continued

Tax Prepayment				0	0	50,000	0
Capital Addition				0	130,000	0	0
Miscellaneous				70	70	70	70
Wages/Salaries				30,000	40,000	45,000	50,000
Total Cash Disbursements				$144,920	$284,920	$280,420	$185,920
End-of-Month Balance:							
Cash (beginning of month)				$ 12,000	$167,080	$79,485	$ 10,000
+ Cash Receipts				300,000	197,325	154,000	175,000
– Cash Disbursements				144,920	284,920	280,420	185,920
Cash (end of month)				167,080	79,485	(46,935)	(920)
Borrowing/Repayment				0	0	56,935	10,920
Cash (end of month [after borrowing])				$167,080	$ 79,485	$ 10,000	$ 10,000

Cash Budget—Most Likely Sales Forecast

	Oct.	Nov.	Dec.	Jan.	Feb.	Mar.	Apr.
Cash Receipts:							
Sales	$300,000	$350,000	$400,000	$150,000	$200,000	$200,000	$300,000
Credit Sales	225,000	262,500	300,000	112,000	150,000	150,000	225,000
Collections:							
60%—1st month after sale				$180,000	$ 67,500	$ 90,000	$ 90,000
30%—2nd month after sale				78,750	90,000	33,750	45,000
5%—3rd month after sale				11,250	13,125	15,000	5,625
Cash Sales				37,500	50,000	50,000	75,000
Interest				0	200	0	0
Total Cash Receipts				$307,500	$220,825	$188,750	$215,625
Cash Disbursements:							
Purchases				$140,000	$140,000	$210,000	$175,000
Rent				2,000	2,000	2,000	2,000
Utilities				850	850	850	850
Interest				0	0	7,500	0
Tax Prepayment				0	0	50,000	0
Capital Addition				0	130,000	0	0
Miscellaneous				70	70	70	70
Wages/Salaries				30,000	40,000	45,000	50,000
Total Cash Disbursements				$172,920	$312,920	$315,420	$227,920
End-of-Month Balance:							
Cash [beginning of month]				$ 12,000	$146,580	$ 54,485	$ 10,000
+ Cash Receipts				307,500	220,825	188,750	215,625
– Cash Disbursements				172,920	312,920	315,420	227,920
Cash (end of month)				146,580	54,485	(72,185)	(2,295)
Borrowing/Repayment				0	0	82,185	12,295
Cash (end of month [after borrowing])				$146,580	$ 54,485	$ 10,000	$ 10,000

Cash Budget—Optimistic Sales Forecast

	Oct.	Nov.	Dec.	Jan.	Feb.	Mar.	Apr.
Cash Receipts:							
Sales	$300,000	$350,000	$400,000	$175,000	$250,000	$250,000	$340,000
Credit Sales	225,000	262,500	300,000	131,250	187,500	187,500	255,000

(Continued)

Table 9.2 Continued

Collections:				
60%—1st month after sale	$180,000	$ 78,750	$112,500	$112,500
30%—2nd month after sale	78,750	90,000	39,375	56,250
5%—3rd month after sale	11,250	13,125	15,000	6,563
Cash Sales	43,750	62,500	62,500	85,000
Interest	0	200	0	0
Total Cash Receipts	$313,750	$244,575	$229,375	$260,313
Cash Disbursements:				
Purchases	$175,000	$175,000	$238,000	$217,000
Rent	2,000	2,000	2,000	2,000
Utilities	850	850	850	850
Interest	0	0	7,500	0
Tax Prepayment	0	0	50,000	0
Capital Addition	0	130,000	0	0
Miscellaneous	70	70	70	70
Wages/Salaries	30,000	40,000	45,000	50,000
Total Cash Disbursements	$207,920	$347,920	$343,420	$269,920
End-of-Month Balance:				
Cash [beginning of month]	$ 12,000	$117,830	$ 14,485	$ 10,000
+ Cash Receipts	313,750	244,575	229,375	296,125
− Cash Disbursements	207,920	317,920	343,120	269,920
Cash (end of month)	117,830	14,485	(99,560)	36,205
Borrowing/Repayment	0	0	109,560	0
Cash (end of month [after borrowing])	$117,830	$ 14,485	$ 10,000	$ 36,205

over a four-month period. Each monthly column should be divided into two sections—estimated and actual (not shown)—so that each succeeding cash forecast can be updated according to actual cash transactions. There are five steps to creating a cash budget:

1. Determining an adequate minimum cash balance.
2. Forecasting sales.
3. Forecasting cash receipts.
4. Forecasting cash disbursements.
5. Estimating the end-of-month cash balance.

Step 1: Determining an Adequate Minimum Cash Balance

What is considered an excessive cash balance for one small business may be inadequate for another, even though the two firms are in the same industry. Some suggest that a firm's cash balance should equal at least one-fourth of its current debts, but this clearly will not work for all small businesses. The most reliable method of deciding cash balance is based on past experience. Past operating records should indicate the proper cash cushion needed to cover any unexpected expenses after all normal cash outlays are deducted from the month's cash receipts. For example, past records may indicate that it is desirable to maintain a cash balance equal to five days' sales. Seasonal fluctuations may cause a company's minimum cash balance to change. For example, the desired cash balance for a retailer in December may be greater than in June.

Step 2: Forecasting Sales

The heart of the cash budget is the sales forecast. It is the central factor in creating an accurate picture of a company's cash position because sales ultimately are transformed into cash receipts and cash disbursements. For most businesses, sales constitute the major source of the cash flowing into the business. Similarly, sales of merchandise require that cash be used to replenish inventory. As a result, the cash budget is only as accurate as the sales forecast from which it is derived; an accurate sales forecast is essential to producing reliable cash flow forecast. *An overly optimistic sales forecast landed Segway LLC, the company that invented the futuristic upright motorized scooter, squarely in a cash flow bind. Known as the Segway Human Transporter, the scooter uses computer-driven gyroscopes and sensors that enable riders to stand upright and steer with simple body movements. Unveiled on live television to huge amounts of press fanfare, founder and inventor Dean Kamen projected that the company would be able to sell 50,000 to 100,000 Segways in its first year. The scooter's $4,000 price and lack of distribution outlets limited sales to just a total of 10,000 units two years after the Segway's introduction. (People simply weren't willing to spend $4,000 on something they could not test-drive!) The cash flow problems meant that Kamen had to raise $31 million to keep the company afloat in addition to the initial $100 million he raised to launch the company.*[11]

Company Example

For an established business, the sales forecast can be based on past sales, but the owner must be careful not to be excessively optimistic in projecting sales. Economic swings, increased competition, fluctuations in demand, and other factors can drastically alter sales patterns. A good cash budget must reflect the seasonality of a company's sales. Simply deriving a reasonable annual sales forecast and then dividing it by twelve does *not* produce a reliable monthly sales forecast. Most businesses have sales patterns that are "lumpy" and not evenly distributed throughout the year. For instance, 40 percent of all toy sales take place during the last six weeks of the year, and companies that make fruitcakes typically generate 50 percent to 90 percent of their sales during the holiday season.[12] *To combat a highly seasonal sales pattern and keep the Starlite Drive-In, one of only nine remaining drive-in theaters in North Carolina, in operation, owner Bob Groves has added sideline businesses to generate cash flow during the slow winter months. The rather unusual combination of businesses includes a gun shop, a shooting range, a video rental store, and a flea-market-space rental business. Groves's unique approach to boosting cash flow during months with the slowest theater ticket sales works, and the 1930s-era theater has become a landmark in the Research Triangle area.*[13]

Company Example

Several quantitative techniques, which are beyond the scope of this text (e.g., linear regression, multiple regression, time series analysis, and exponential smoothing), are available to the owner of an existing business with an established sales pattern for forecasting sales. These methods enable the small business owner to extrapolate past and present sales trends to arrive at a fairly accurate sales forecast.

The task of forecasting sales for a new firm is difficult but not impossible. For example, an entrepreneur might conduct research on similar firms and their sales patterns in the first year of operation to come up with a forecast. The local chamber of commerce and trade associations in the various industries also collect such information. Market research is another source of information that may be used to estimate annual sales for the fledgling firm. Other potential sources that may help predict sales include Census Bureau reports, newspapers, radio and television customer profiles, polls and surveys, and local government statistics. Table 9.3 gives an example of how one entrepreneur used such marketing information to derive a sales forecast for his first year of operation.

No matter what techniques small business managers employ, they must recognize that even the best sales estimate may be wrong. Many financial analysts suggest that owners create *three estimates*—an optimistic, a pessimistic, and a most likely sales estimate—and then

Table 9.3

Forecasting Sales for
a Business Start-Up

Robert Adler wants to open a repair shop for imported cars. The trade association for automotive garages estimates that the owner of an imported car spends an average of $485 per year on repairs and maintenance. The typical garage attracts its clientele from a trading zone (the area from which a business draws its customers) with a 20-mile radius. Census reports show that the families within a 20-mile radius of Robert's proposed location own 84,000 cars, of which 24 percent are imports. Based on a local market consultant's research, Robert believes he can capture 9.9 percent of the market this year. Robert's estimate of his company's first year's sales are as follows:

Number of cars in trading zone	84,000 autos
× Percent of imports	× 24%
= Number of imported cars in trading zone	20,160 imports
Number of imports in trading zone	20,160
× Average expenditure on repairs and maintenance	× $485
= Total import repair sales potential	$9,777,600
Total import repair sales potential	$9,777,600
× Estimated share of market	× 9.9%
= Sales estimate	$ 967,982

Now Robert Adler can convert this annual sales estimate of $967,982 into monthly sales estimates for use in his company's cash budget.

make a separate cash budget for each forecast (a very simple task with a computer spreadsheet). This dynamic forecast enables entrepreneurs to determine the range within which their sales and cash flows will likely be as the year progresses.

Step 3: Forecasting Cash Receipts

As noted earlier, sales constitute the major source of cash receipts. When a firm sells goods and services on credit, the cash budget must account for the delay between the sale and the actual collection of the proceeds. Remember: You cannot spend cash you haven't collected yet! For instance, proceeds for appliances sold in February might not be collected until March or April, and the cash budget must reflect this delay. To project accurately a firm's cash receipts, an entrepreneur must analyze the accounts receivable to determine the collection pattern. For example, past records may indicate that 20 percent of sales are for cash, 50 percent are paid in the month following the sale, 20 percent are paid two months after the sale, 7 percent after three months, and 3 percent are never collected. In addition to cash and credit sales, a cash budget must include any other cash the company receives such as interest income, rental income, dividends, and others.

Some small business owners never discover the hidden danger in accounts receivable until it is too late for their companies. Receivables act as cash sponges, tying up valuable dollars until an entrepreneur collects them. *When Mary and Phil Baechler started Baby Jogger Company in 1983 to make strollers that would enable parents to take their babies along on their daily runs, Mary was in charge of the financial aspects of the business and watched its cash flow closely. As the company grew, the couple created an accounting department to handle its financial affairs. Unfortunately, the financial management system could not keep up with the company's rapid growth and failed to provide the necessary information to keep its finances under control. As inventory and accounts receivable ballooned, the company headed for a cash crisis. To ensure Baby Jogger's survival, the Baechlers were forced to reduce their workforce by half. Then they turned their attention to the accounts receivable and discovered that customers owed the business almost $700,000! In addition, most of the accounts were past due. Focusing on collecting*

Company Example

Figure 9.4

Collecting Delinquent
Accounts

Source: Commercial Collection
Agency Section of the
Commercial Law League
of America.

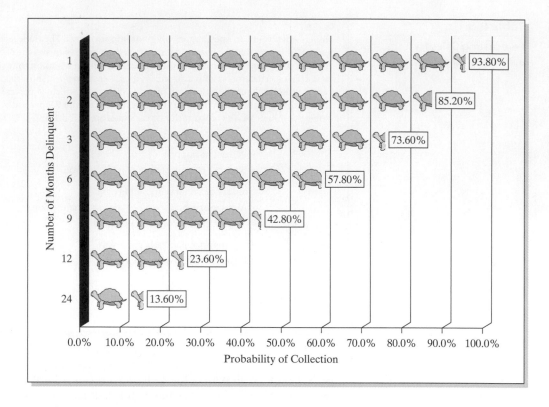

the money owed to their company, the Baechlers were able to steer clear of a cash crisis and get Baby Jogger back on track.[14]

Figure 9.4 demonstrates how vital it is to act promptly once an account becomes past due. Notice how the probability of collecting an outstanding account diminishes the longer the account is delinquent. Table 9.4 illustrates the high cost of failing to collect accounts receivable on time.

Table 9.4

Managing Accounts
Receivable

Are your customers who purchase on credit paying late? If so, these outstanding accounts receivable probably represent a significant leak in your company's profits. Regaining control of these late payers will likely improve your company's profits and cash flow.

Slow-paying customers, in effect, are borrowing money from your business interest free! They are using your money without penalty while you forgo opportunities to place it in interest-bearing investments. Exactly how much are poor credit practices costing you? The answer may surprise you.

The first step is to compute the company's average collection period ratio (see the "Operating Ratios" section in Chapter 8), which tells the number of days required to collect the typical account receivable. Then you compare this number to your company's credit terms. The following example shows how to calculate the cost of past-due receivables for a company whose credit terms are "net 30":

Average collection period	65 days
Less: credit terms	−30 days
Excess in accounts receivable	35 days
Average daily sales of $21,500 × 35 days excess*	$752,500
Normal rate of return on investment	×10%
Annual cost of excess	$ 75,250

If your business is highly seasonal, quarterly or monthly figures may be more meaningful than annual ones.

*Average daily sales $= \dfrac{\text{Annual sales}}{365} = \dfrac{\$7,487,500}{365} = \$21,500$

Step 4: Forecasting Cash Disbursements

Most owners of established businesses have a clear picture of a company's pattern of cash disbursements. In fact, many cash payments, such as rent, salaries, loan repayments, and insurance premiums, are fixed amounts due on specified dates. The key factor in forecasting disbursements for a cash budget is to *record them in the month in which they will be paid, not when the debt or obligation is incurred*. Of course, the number of cash disbursements varies with each particular business, but the following disbursement categories are standard: purchases of inventory or raw materials; wages and salaries; rent, taxes, loans and interest; selling expenses; overhead expenses; and miscellaneous expenses.

A common tendency is to underestimate cash disbursements, which can result in a cash crisis. To prevent this, wise entrepreneurs cushion their cash disbursement account, assuming it will be higher than expected. This is particularly important for entrepreneurs opening new businesses. In fact, some financial analysts recommend that new owners estimate cash disbursements as best as they can and then add on another 25 to 50 percent of the total. When setting up his company's cash budget, one entrepreneur included a line called "Murphy," an additional amount each month to account for Murphy's Law ("What can go wrong, will go wrong"). Whatever forecasting technique an entrepreneur uses, the key is to avoid underestimating cash disbursements, which may lead to severe cash shortages and possibly bankruptcy.

Sometimes business owners have difficulty developing initial forecasts of cash receipts and cash disbursements. One of the most effective techniques for overcoming the "I don't know where to begin" hurdle is to make a *daily* list of the items that generated cash (receipts) and those that consumed it (disbursements). *Susan Bowen, CEO of Champion Awards, a $9 million T-shirt screen printer, monitors cash flow by tracking the cash that flows into and out of her company every day. Focusing on keeping the process simple, Bowen sets aside a few minutes each morning to track updates from the previous day on four key numbers:*

| Company Example |

Accounts receivable: (1) What was billed yesterday? (2) How much was actually collected?

Accounts payable: (3) What invoices were received yesterday? (4) How much in total was paid out?

If Bowen observes the wrong trend—more new bills than new sales or more money going out than coming in—she makes immediate adjustments to protect her cash flow. The benefits produced (not the least of which is the peace of mind knowing no cash crisis is looming) more than outweigh the 10 minutes she invests in the process every day. "I've tried to balance my books every single day since I started my company in 1970," says Bowen.[15]

Step 5: Estimating the End-of-Month Cash Balance

To estimate a company's cash balance for each month, an entrepreneur first must determine the cash balance at the beginning of each month. The beginning cash balance includes cash on hand as well as cash in checking and savings accounts. As development of the cash budget progresses, the cash balance at the end of a month becomes the beginning balance for the following month. Next, the owner simply adds projected total cash receipts for the month and subtracts projected total cash disbursements to obtain the end-of-month balance before any borrowing takes place. A positive amount indicates that the business has a cash surplus for the month while a negative amount shows a cash shortage will occur unless the entrepreneur is able to collect or borrow additional funds.

Normally, a company's cash balance fluctuates from month to month, reflecting seasonal sales patterns. Such fluctuations are normal, but entrepreneurs must watch closely any increases and decreases in the cash balance over time. A trend of increases indicates that the small firm has ample cash that could be placed in some income-earning investment. On the other hand, a pattern of cash decreases should alert the owner that the business is approaching a cash crisis. Preparing a cash budget not only illustrates the flow of cash into and out of the small business, but it also enables a business owner to anticipate cash shortages and cash surpluses. By planning cash needs ahead of time, an entrepreneur is able to do the following:

- Increase the amount and the speed of cash flowing into the company.
- Reduce the amount and the speed of cash flowing out of the company.
- Develop a sound borrowing and repayment program.
- Impress lenders and investors with the ability to plan for and repay loans.
- Reduce borrowing costs by borrowing only when necessary.
- Take advantage of money-saving opportunities, such as economic order quantities and cash discounts.
- Make the most efficient use of the cash available.
- Finance seasonal business needs.
- Provide funds for expansion.
- Plan for investing surplus cash.

The message is simple: Managing cash flow means survival for a business. Businesses tend to succeed when their owners manage cash effectively. Those who neglect cash flow management techniques are likely to see their companies fold.

IN THE FOOTSTEPS OF AN ENTREPRENEUR...

Rowena's Cash Budget

Rowena Rowdy had been in business for slightly more than two years, but she had never taken the time to develop a cash budget for her company. Based on a series of recent events, however, she knew the time had come to start paying more attention to her company's cash flow. The business was growing fast, with sales more than tripling from the previous year, and profits were rising. However, Rowena often found it difficult to pay all of the company's bills on time. She didn't know why exactly, but she knew that the company's fast growth was requiring her to incur higher levels of expenses.

Last night, Rowena attended a workshop on managing cash flow sponsored by the local chamber of commerce. Much of what the presenter said hit home with Rowena. "This fellow must have taken a look at my company's financial records before he came here tonight," she said to a friend during a break in the presentation. On her way home from the workshop, Rowena decided that she would take the presenter's advice and develop a cash budget for her business. After all, she was planning to approach her banker about a loan for her company, and she knew that creating a cash budget would be an essential part of her loan request. She started digging for the necessary information, and this is what she came up with:

Current cash balance	$10,685
Sales pattern	63% on credit and 37% in cash
Collections of credit sales	61% in 1 to 30 days
	27% in 31 to 60 days
	8% in 61 to 90 days
	4% never collected (bad debts)

Sales forecasts:

	Pessimistic	Most Likely	Optimistic
January (actual)	—	$24,780	—
February (actual)	—	$20,900	—
March (actual)	—	$21,630	—
April	$19,100	$23,550	$25,750
May	$21,300	$24,900	$27,300
June	$23,300	$29,870	$30,000
July	$23,900	$27,500	$29,100
August	$20,500	$25,800	$28,800
September	$18,500	$21,500	$23,900

Utilities expenses	$950 per month
Rent	$2,250 per month
Truck loan	$427 per month

The company's wages and salaries (including payroll taxes) estimates are:

April	$3,550
May	$4,125
June	$5,450
July	$6,255
August	$6,060
September	$3,525

The company pays 66 percent of the sales price for the inventory it purchases, an amount that it actually pays in the following month. (Rowena has negotiated "net 30" credit terms with her suppliers.)

Other expenses include:

Insurance premiums	$1,200, payable in April and September
Office supplies	$125 per month
Maintenance	$75 per month
Uniforms/cleaning	$80 per month
Office cleaning service	$85 per month
Internet and computer service	$225 per month
Computer supplies	$75 per month
Advertising	$450 per month
Legal and accounting fees	$250 per month
Miscellaneous expenses	$95 per month

A tax payment of $3,140 is due in June. Rowena has established a minimum cash balance of $1,500. If Rowena must borrow money, she uses her line of credit at the bank, which charges interest at an annual rate of 10.25 percent. Any money that Rowena borrows must be repaid the next month.

1. Help Rowena put together a cash budget for the six months beginning in April.

2. Does it appear that Rowena's business will remain solvent, or could the company be heading for a cash crisis?

3. What suggestions can you make to help Rowena improve her company's cash flow?

The "Big Three" of Cash Management

4. Describe the fundamental principles involved in managing the "big three" of cash management: accounts receivable, accounts payable, and inventory.

It is unrealistic for business owners to expect to trace the flow of every dollar through their businesses. However, by concentrating on the three primary causes of cash flow problems, they can dramatically lower the likelihood of experiencing a devastating cash crisis. The "big three" of cash management are accounts receivable, accounts payable, and inventory. A firm should always try to accelerate its receivables and to stretch out its payables. As one company's chief financial officer states, the idea is to "get the cash in the door as fast as you can, cut costs, and pay people as late as possible."[16] Business owners also must monitor inventory carefully to avoid tying up valuable cash in an excessive stock of inventory.

Accounts Receivable

Selling merchandise and services on credit is a necessary evil for most small businesses. Many customers expect to buy on credit, so business owners extend it to avoid losing customers to competitors. However, selling to customers on credit is expensive; it requires more paperwork, more staff, and more cash to service accounts receivable. Also, because extending credit is, in essence, lending money, the risk involved is higher. Every business owner who sells on credit will encounter customers who pay late or, worst of all, who never pay at all. This revenue leakage can be the source of severe cash flow problems for a small business. Much like a leak in a water pipe, revenue leakages from undisciplined collection procedures can become significant over time and cause serious damage. One expert estimates that revenue leakages rob companies of 2 percent of their sales. Health care and Web service providers, for instance, typically lose 5 to 10 percent of their revenues each year.[17]

Selling on credit is a common practice in business. Experts estimate that 90 percent of industrial and wholesale sales are on credit and that 40 percent of retail sales are on account. One survey of small businesses across a variety of industries reported that 77 percent extend credit to their customers.[18] "Extending credit is a [double]-edged sword," says Robert Smith, president of his own public relations firm in Rockford, Illinois. "I give credit so more people can afford my publicity services. I also have people who still owe me money—and who will probably never pay."[19]

Because so many entrepreneurs sell on credit, an assertive collection program is essential to managing a company's cash flow. A credit policy that is too lenient can destroy a business's cash flow, attracting nothing but slow-paying and "deadbeat" customers. On the other hand, a carefully designed credit policy can be a powerful selling tool, attracting customers and boosting cash flow. "A sale is not a sale until you collect the money," warns the head of the National Association of Credit Management. "Receivables are the second

most important item on the balance sheet. The first is cash. If you don't turn those receivables into cash, you're not going to be in business very long."[20]

Valerie Lichman admits that when she launched her marketing and public relations firm, she was too soft on collecting accounts receivable. Her new company suffered when one client never reimbursed her for $28,000 worth of ads she had purchased for him and another failed to pay for a month's worth of work. Today a more seasoned business owner, Lichman is much more assertive at collecting accounts receivable. She always requests an up-front payment before she begins a job, and if a payment is 30 days late, she stops work completely. The system has paid off; both her company's cash balance and its profits are rising.[21]

How to Establish a Credit and Collection Policy. The first step in establishing a workable credit policy that preserves a company's cash flow is to screen customers carefully before granting credit. Unfortunately, few small businesses conduct any kind of credit investigation before selling to a new customer. According to one survey, nearly 95 percent of small firms that sell on credit sell to anyone who wants to buy.[22] If a debt becomes past due and a business owner has gathered no information about the customer, the odds of collecting the account are virtually nil.

The first line of defense against bad debt losses is a detailed credit application. Before selling to any customer on credit, a business owner should have the customer fill out a customized application designed to provide the information needed to judge the potential customer's creditworthiness. At a minimum, this credit profile should include the following information about customers:

- Name, address, social security number, and telephone number.
- Form of ownership (proprietorship, S corporation, LLC, corporation, etc.) and number of years in business.
- Credit references (e.g., other suppliers), including contact names, addresses, and telephone numbers.
- Bank and credit card references.

After collecting this information, the business owner should use it to check the potential customer's credit references! The World Wide Web is a great place to start. On the Web, entrepreneurs can gain access to potential customers' credit information at many sites including the Securities and Exchange Commission's EDGAR database of corporate information, the NASDAQ stock market, or the New York Stock Exchange. Many entrepreneurs subscribe to credit reporting services such as TransUnion, Equifax Credit Reporting, Experian, or Dun & Bradstreet so they can judge a potential customer's creditworthiness accurately and conveniently. The savings from lower bad debt expenses can more than offset the cost of using these credit reporting services. The National Association of Credit Management (NACM) is another important source of credit information because it collects information on many small businesses that other reporting services ignore. The cost to check a potential customer's credit at reporting services such as these ranges from $10 to several hundred, a small price to pay when considering selling thousands of dollars worth of goods or services to a new customer. Unfortunately, few small businesses take the time to conduct a credit check; in one study, just one-third of the businesses protected themselves by checking potential customers' credit.[23] One appliance retailer advertised, "Good credit, bad credit, no credit at all! Come see us!" His sales volume was high, but his extremely low collection rate forced him out of business.

The next step involves establishing a firm written credit policy and letting every customer know in advance the company's credit terms. The credit agreement must be in writing and should specify a customer's credit limit (which usually varies from one customer to another, depending on their credit ratings) and any deposits required (often stated as a percentage of the purchase price). It should state clearly all the terms the business will enforce if the account goes bad, including interest, late charges, attorney's fees, and others. Failure to specify these terms in the contract means they *cannot* be added later after problems arise. When will you invoice? How soon is payment due: immediately, 30 days, 60 days? Will you offer early-payment discounts? Will you add a late charge? If so, how much? The credit policies should be as tight as possible and within federal and state credit laws. According to the American Collectors Association, if a business is writing off more than 5 percent of sales as bad debts, the owner should tighten its credit and collection policy.[24]

The third step in an effective credit policy is to send invoices promptly because customers rarely pay before they receive their bills. The sooner a company sends out invoices, the sooner the customer will send payment. Manufacturers should make sure the invoice is en route to the customer as soon as the shipment goes out the door (if not before). Service companies should keep track of billable hours daily or weekly and bill as often as the contract or agreement with the client permits. Some businesses use **cycle billing,** in which a company bills a portion of its credit customers each day of the month to smooth out uneven cash receipts.

Small business owners can take several steps to encourage prompt payment of invoices:

- Ensure that all invoices are clear, accurate, and timely.
- State clearly a description of the goods or services purchased and an account number, if possible.
- Make sure that prices on invoices agree with the price quotations on purchase orders or contracts.
- Highlight the terms of sale (e.g., "net 30") on all invoices. One study by Xerox Corporation found that highlighting the "balance due" section of invoices increased the speed of collection by 30 percent.[25]
- Include a telephone number and a contact person in your organization in case the customer has a question or a dispute.
- Respond quickly and accurately to customers' questions about their bills.

Invoices that are well organized, easy to read, and enable customers to identify what is being billed are much more likely to get paid than those that are not. The key to creating "user-friendly" invoices is to design them from the customer's perspective.

> Company Example →

Bob Dempster, cofounder of American Imaging Inc., a distributor of X-ray tubes, once-handled receivables the same way most entrepreneurs do: When customers ignored the "net 30" terms on invoices, he would call them around the forty-fifth day to ask what the problem was. Payments usually would trickle in within the next two weeks, but by then 60 days had elapsed, and American Imaging's cash flow was always strained. Then Dempster decided to try a different approach. Now he makes a "customer relations call" on the twentieth day of the billing period to determine whether the customer is satisfied with the company's performance on the order. Before closing, he reminds the customer of the invoice due date and asks if there will be any problems meeting it. Dempster's proactive approach to collecting receivables has cut his company's average collection period by at least 15 days, improved cash flow, and increased customer satisfaction![26]

When an account becomes overdue, a small business owner must take immediate action. The longer an account is past due, the lower the probability is of collecting it. As soon as an account becomes overdue, many business owners send a "second notice" letter requesting immediate payment. If that fails to produce results, the next step is a telephone call. A better system is to call the customer the day after the payment is due to request payment. If the customer still refuses to pay the bill after 30 days, collection experts recommend the following:

- Send a letter from the company's attorney.
- Turn the account over to a collection agency.
- Hire a collection attorney.

Although collection agencies and attorneys will take a portion of any accounts they collect (typically around 30 percent), they are often worth the price paid. According to the American Collectors Association, only 5 percent of accounts over 90 days delinquent will be paid voluntarily.[27]

Business owners must be sure to abide by the provisions of the federal Fair Debt Collection Practices Act, which prohibits any kind of harassment when collecting debts (e.g., telephoning repeatedly, issuing threats of violence, telling third parties about the debt, or using abusive language). When collecting past-due accounts, the primary rule is, "Never lose your cool." Even if the debtor launches into an X-rated tirade when questioned about an overdue bill, the *worst* thing a collector can do is respond out of anger. Keep the call strictly business, and begin by identifying yourself, your company, and the amount of the debt. Ask the creditor what he or she intends to do about the past-due bill.

Table 9.5 describes a proactive collection system that really works.

Techniques for Accelerating Accounts Receivable. Small business owners can rely on a variety of techniques to speed cash inflow from accounts receivable:

- Speed up orders by having customers fax them to you.
- Send invoices when goods are shipped rather than a day or a week later; consider faxing or e-mailing invoices to reduce "in transit" time to a minimum.
- Indicate in conspicuous print or color the invoice due date and any late payment penalties imposed. (Check with an attorney to be sure all finance charges comply with state laws.)
- Restrict the customer's credit until past-due bills are paid. Making sure that a company's collection staff and its sales force are communicating with one another is essential. Salespeople should know which of their customers are behind in their payments. If not, they will continue to sell (most likely on credit) to those delinquent customers!
- Deposit customer checks and credit card receipts daily.
- Identify the top 20 percent of your customers (by sales volume), create a separate file system for them, and monitor them closely. Twenty percent of the typical company's customers generate 80 percent of all accounts receivable.
- Ask customers to pay a portion of the purchase price up front. Tired of chasing late payers after completing their public relations projects, Mike Clifford, founder of Clifford Public Relations, began checking potential clients' credit ratings and requiring an up-front payment of one-third of the cost of a job. Clifford also instituted a monthly billing system that tracks billable hours and related expenses. Since implementing the new system, Clifford has not experienced a single past-due account.[28]
- Watch for signs that a customer may be about to declare bankruptcy. Late payments from previously prompt payers and unreturned phone calls concerning late payments usually are the first clues that a customer may be heading for bankruptcy. If that happens, creditors typically collect only a small fraction, on average just 10 percent, of the debt owed.[29] Cynthia McKay, owner of a Le Gourmet Gift Basket franchise, lost thousands of dollars when five of her corporate clients filed for bankruptcy within a 10-month period. "That money is a weekly payroll for several employees," says McKay.[30]
- If a customer does file for bankruptcy, the bankruptcy court notifies all creditors with a "Notice of Filing" document. Upon receipt of this notice, a wise creditor creates a file to track the events surrounding the bankruptcy and takes action immediately. To have a valid claim against the debtor's assets, a creditor must file a proof-of-claim form with the bankruptcy court within a specified time, often

Table 9.5

Designing a Collection System That Really Works

A collection system that meets the business owner's cash flow requirements and deals fairly with customers can make collecting accounts receivable on time much easier. The best approach is a proactive one that seeks to avoid past-due accounts. Review your collection system and consider these questions:

- Do you perform credit checks on new customers by contacting credit rating services, analyzing their financial statements, or checking their credit references?
- Have you established a credit policy that spells out your company's expected payment terms and internal procedures for dealing with slow- or non-paying customers?
- Have you circulated that policy to all employees, especially salespeople?
- Do you routinely send a copy of your credit policy to new customers? Do you ask them to sign and return a copy of the policy?
- Have you segmented your customer base into high- and low-risk customers? Do employees know which customers fall into these categories?
- Does your policy include a mechanism for handling high- and low-risk customers differently?
- Do you and other managers in the company receive a weekly accounts receivable update that shows an aging of the company's accounts receivable?
- Do your sales and financial management staffs work together to collect past-due payments from customers?
- Do sales representatives earn commissions on sales whether the company actually receives payment?
- Does your credit policy establish clear trigger points that tell you when to turn an account over to a collection agency or attorney and when to stop doing business with delinquent customers?

Even the best collection system produces some past-due accounts. One collection expert describes four stages in the past-due debt collection process: the notification or polite reminder, the discussion, the "push" or firm demand, and the bitter end.

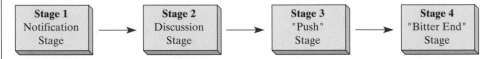

In the *notification* or *polite reminder stage,* the best approach is an upbeat, positive one. It should begin immediately after an invoice is past due. "Our records show that this bill is still unpaid. Can you check on it?"

During the *discussion stage,* the goal is to motivate the customer to pay the past due account. Generally, it is not productive to explore the reasons behind the late payment. Instead, the focus should be on the business at hand: getting the customer to make a firm commitment to pay by a specific deadline.

If the debt reaches the *push stage,* a business must take a stronger approach to collecting the outstanding debt. Experts recommend limiting this stage to no more than 10 days.

Once a debt reaches the *bitter end stage,* the company usually has few options but to turn the account over to a collection agency or attorney or to file suit in small claims court. By this stage, the relationship with the customer has soured, and the company is no longer willing to do business with that customer again.

One expert recommends persistence when dealing with past-due accounts. "Remember," she says, "it's your money, and you don't make money until you're paid."

Sources: Adapted from Jill Andresky Fraser, "Get Paid Promptly," *Inc.,* November 1996, p. 87; Jacquelyn Lynn, "You Owe It to Yourself, " *Business Start-Ups,* October 1996, pp. 54–60.

90 days. (The actual time depends on which form of bankruptcy the debtor declares.) If, after paying the debtor's secured creditors, any assets remain, the court will distribute the proceeds to unsecured creditors who have legitimate proof of claim.

- Consider using a bank's lockbox collection service (located near customers) to reduce mail time on collections. In a **lockbox** arrangement, customers send payments to a post office box the bank maintains. The bank collects the payments several times each day and deposits them immediately into the company account. The procedure sharply reduces processing and clearing times from the usual two to three days to just hours, especially if the lockboxes are located close to the firm's biggest customers' business addresses. The system can be expensive to operate (typically $55 to $100 per month plus a 30-cent to 40-cent charge for each check) and is most economical for companies with a high volume of large checks (at least 200 checks each month).

■ Track the results of the company's collection efforts. Managers and key employees (including the sales force) should receive a weekly report on the status of the company's outstanding accounts receivable.

Combining a lockbox with other cash management services from banks—such as zero balance accounts (ZBAs) and sweep accounts—can dramatically improve a small company's ability to get the most out of its available cash. A **zero balance account** is a checking account that technically never has funds in it but is tied to another master account like payroll. The company keeps the funds in the master account (where they earn interest), but it writes checks on the ZBA. At the end of each day, checks drawn on the ZBA are funded; then all activity is posted against the master account. The ZBA enables the company to keep more cash working during the float period, the time between a check being issued to its being cashed. By combining the zero balance account with a **sweep account,** which "sweeps" all funds above a predetermined minimum into an interest bearing account, the company keeps otherwise idle cash invested until it is needed to cover checks.

Accounts Payable

The second element of the "big three" of cash management is accounts payable. The timing of payables is just as crucial to proper cash management as the timing of receivables, but the objective is exactly the opposite. An entrepreneur should strive to stretch out payables as long as possible *without damaging the company's credit rating.* Paying late could cause suppliers to begin demanding prepayment or C.O.D. terms, which severely impair a company's cash flow. Small business owners should regulate their payments to vendors and suppliers to their companies' advantage. Ideally, a company will purchase an item on credit, sell it, and collect payment for it before the company must pay the supplier's invoice. In that case, the vendor's credit terms amount to an interest-free loan. That is exactly the situation that Dell Inc., the fast-growing computer maker, puts itself in. Its extremely high inventory turnover ratio of 73 times a year coupled with its ability to negotiate favorable credit terms with its suppliers and to collect customers' payments quickly means that the company enjoys an industry-leading cash conversion cycle of *negative* 37 days. On average, Dell collects payments from its customers and gets to use that cash before having to pay its suppliers 37 days later![31]

Even when the cash flow timing isn't ideal, efficient cash managers benefit by setting up a payment calendar each month that enables them to pay their bills on time and to

Company Example ➤ take advantage of cash discounts for early payment. *Nancy Dunis, CEO of Dunis & Associates, a Portland, Oregon, marketing firm, recognizes the importance of controlling accounts payable. "Our payables must be functioning just right to keep our cash flow running smoothly," says Dunis. She has set up a simple five-point accounts payable system:*[32]

1. *Set scheduling goals. Dunis strives to pay her company's bills 45 days after receiving them and to collect all her receivables within 30 days. Even though it doesn't always work that way, her goal is to make the most of her cash flow.*
2. *Keep paperwork organized. Dunis dates every invoice she receives and carefully files it according to her payment plan. "This helps us remember when to cut the check," she*

"If an invoice is due in 30 days, we pay it in 60 days. If it's due in 60 days, we pay it in 90 days. If it's due in 90 days, then they probably don't need the money anyway."

says, and, "it helps us stagger our payments over days or weeks," significantly improving the company's cash flow.

3. *Prioritize. Dunis cannot stretch out all of her company's creditors for 45 days; some demand payment sooner. Those suppliers are at the top of the accounts payable list.*

4. *Be consistent. "Companies want consistent customers," says Dunis. "With a few exceptions," she explains, "most businesses will be happy to accept 45-day payments, so long as they know you'll always pay your full obligation at that point."*

5. *Look for warning signs. Dunis sees her accounts payable as an early warning system for cash flow problems. "The first indication I get that cash flow is in trouble is when I see I'm getting low on cash and could have trouble paying my bills according to my staggered filing system," she says.*

Business owners should verify all invoices before paying them. Some unscrupulous vendors will send out invoices for goods they never shipped, knowing that many business owners will simply pay the bill without checking its authenticity. Someone in the company—for instance, the accounts payable clerk—should have the responsibility of verifying every invoice received. In a common scam targeting small businesses, the accounts payable clerk at one company caught a bogus invoice for $322 worth of copier paper and toner it never ordered nor received.[33]

Generally, it is a good idea for owners to take advantage of cash discounts vendors offer. A cash discount (e.g., "2/10, net 30"—take a 2 percent discount if you pay the invoice within 10 days; otherwise, total payment is due in 30 days) offers a price reduction if the owner pays an invoice early. The savings the discount provides usually exceeds the cost of giving up the use of a company's cash by paying early. Chris Zane, owner of Zane's Cycles, a highly successful bicycle shop in Connecticut, makes taking cash discounts a regular practice in his business. "I make my salary on the discounts we get from paying our vendors early," he says.[34]

| Company Example |

Like Zane, Jeff Schreiber, owner of Hansen Wholesale, a company that distributes home products, is in the habit of taking advantage of the cash discounts vendors offer his company. In one year alone, Schreiber, whose company generates $3.5 million in annual sales, saved $15,000. At a January trade show, he negotiated a deal with a ceiling fan vendor on a $40,000 purchase that gave him a 3 percent discount for paying before May 1 and an extra 0.75 percent discount for each month he paid before May. "Your money works better if you take advantage of the discounts," says Schreiber.[35]

Clever cash managers also negotiate the best possible credit terms with their suppliers. Almost all vendors grant their customers trade credit, and entrepreneurs should take advantage of it. However, because trade credit is so easy to get, entrepreneurs must be careful not to abuse it, putting their businesses in a precarious financial position. Favorable credit terms can make a tremendous difference in a firm's cash flow. Table 9.6 shows the most-likely cash budget from Table 9.2 with one exception: Instead of purchasing on C.O.D. terms (Table 9.2), the owner has negotiated "net 30" payment terms. Notice the drastic improvement in this small company's cash flow resulting from the improved credit terms.

If owners do find themselves financially strapped when payment to a vendor is due, they should avoid making empty promises that "the check is in the mail." Instead, they should discuss openly the situation with the vendor. Most suppliers are willing to work out payment terms for extended credit. One small business owner who was experiencing a cash crisis claims:

> One day things got so bad I just called up a supplier and said, "I need your stuff, but I'm going through a tough period and simply can't pay you right now." They said they wanted to keep me as a customer, and they asked if it was okay to bill me in three months. I was dumbfounded: They didn't even charge me interest.[36]

Table 9.6

Cash Budget,[a] Most Likely Sales Forecast

	JAN.	FEB.	MAR.	APR.
Cash Receipts:				
Sales	$150,000	$200,000	$200,000	$300,000
Credit Sales	112,500	150,000	150,000	225,000
Collections:				
60%—1st month after sale	$180,000	$ 67,500	$ 90,000	$ 90,000
30%—2nd month after sale	78,750	90,000	33,750	45,000
5%—3rd month after sale	11,250	13,125	15,000	5,625
Cash Sales	37,500	50,000	50,000	75,000
Interest	0	200	0	0
Total Cash Receipts	$307,500	$220,825	$188,750	$215,625
Cash Disbursements:				
Purchases[a]	$105,000	$140,000	$140,000	$210,000
Rent	2,000	2,000	2,000	2,000
Utilities	850	850	850	850
Interest	0	0	7,500	0
Tax Prepayment	0	0	50,000	0
Capital Addition	0	130,000	3	0
Miscellaneous	70	70	70	70
Wage/Salaries	30,000	40,000	45,000	50,000
Total Cash Disbursements[a]	$137,920	$312,920	$245,420	$262,920
End-of-Month Balance:				
Cash (beginning of month)[a]	$ 12,000	$181,580	$ 89,485	$ 32,815
+ Cash Receipts	307,500	220,825	188,750	215,625
− Cash Disbursements[a]	137,920	312,920	245,420	262,920
Cash (end of month)[a]	181,580	89,485	32,815	(14,480)
Borrowing	0	0	0	24,480
Cash (end of month [after borrowing])[a]	$181,580	$ 89,485	$ 32,815	$ 10,000

[a]After negotiating "net 30" trade credit terms.

Small business owners also can improve their firms' cash flow by scheduling controllable cash disbursements so that they do not come due at the same time. For example, paying employees every two weeks (or every month) rather than every week reduces administrative costs and gives the business more time to use its cash. Owners of fledgling businesses may be able to conserve cash by hiring part-time employees or by using freelance workers rather than full-time, permanent workers. Scheduling insurance premiums monthly or quarterly rather than annually also improves cash flow.

Inventory

Inventory is a significant investment for many small businesses and can create a severe strain on cash flow if not managed properly. Although inventory represents the largest capital investment for most businesses, few owners use any formal methods for managing it. As a result, the typical small business not only has too much inventory but also too much of the wrong kind of inventory! Because inventory is illiquid, it can quickly siphon off a company's pool of available cash. Small businesses need cash to grow and to survive, which is difficult to do if they have money tied up in excess inventory, which yields a zero rate of return. "The cost of carrying inventory is expensive," says one small business consultant. "A typical manufacturing company pays 25 percent to 30 percent of the value of the inventory for the cost of borrowed money, warehouse space, materials handling, staff, lift-truck expenses, and fixed costs. This shocks a lot of people. Once they realize it, they look at inventory differently."[37] Tracking inventory consistently enables a business owner to avoid purchasing or manufacturing goods unnecessarily. Experienced entrepreneurs often maintain different levels of inventory for different items based on how critical they are to the company's operation and on how quickly they can be replenished. For instance, the owner of one small landscape company knew that hardwood mulch was one of his best-selling items in the spring, but he refused to purchase excessive amounts of it because his primary supplier was nearby and could deliver mulch within two hours of receiving an order.

Marking down items that don't sell will keep inventory lean and allow it to turn over frequently. Even though volume discounts lower inventory costs, large purchases may tie up the company's valuable cash. Wise business owners avoid overbuying inventory, recognizing that excess inventory ties up valuable cash unproductively. In fact, only 20 percent of a typical business's inventory turns over quickly, so owners must watch constantly for stale items.[38] Carrying unsold inventory costs U.S. businesses an estimated $332 billion a year.[39]

Carrying too much inventory increases the chances that a business will run out of cash. *For example, when Tom Meredith joined Dell Inc. as its chief financial officer, he quickly discovered that excessive inventory was a major source of the cash flow problems the company was experiencing at the time. Because the company was focusing on growth, it held large inventories of costly computer components to make sure it could meet every sales opportunity. Meredith's top priority in his first few months at Dell was to cut inventory levels. "Low inventory equals high profit; high inventory equals low profit," he declares. Because the inventory that Dell carries becomes technologically obsolete so rapidly, losing 1 percent of its value each week, high inventory levels increase the likelihood of wasted cash.*[40]

Company Example →

In addition to the cost of the inventory itself, the activities required to purchase, store, and control inventory are themselves costly. Efficient cash management calls for a business to commit just enough cash to inventory to meet demand. Paring down the number of suppliers enables a business to gain more bargaining power, minimize paperwork, and perhaps earn quantity discounts. Scheduling inventory deliveries at the latest possible date will prevent premature payment of invoices. Finally, given goods of comparable quality and price, entrepreneurs should purchase goods from those suppliers who are best at making fast, frequent deliveries to keep inventory levels low.

Monitoring the big three of cash management can help every business owner avoid a cash crisis while making the best use of available cash. According to one expert, maximizing cash flow involves "getting money from customers sooner; paying bills at the last moment possible; consolidating money in a single bank account; managing accounts payable, accounts receivable, and inventory more effectively; and squeezing every penny out of your daily business."[41]

Avoiding the Cash Crunch

5. Explain the techniques for avoiding a cash crunch in a small company.

Nearly every small business has the potential to improve its cash position with little or no investment. The key is to make an objective evaluation of a company's financial policies, searching for inefficiency in its cash flow and ways to squeeze more cash out of operations. Young firms cannot afford to waste resources, especially one as vital as cash. By utilizing the following tools, the small business manager can get maximum benefit from the company's pool of cash.

Bartering

Bartering, the exchange of goods and services for other goods and services, is an effective way to conserve cash. An ancient concept, bartering began to regain popularity during recent recessions. More than 600 barter exchanges operate across the United States, catering primarily to small- and medium-sized businesses, and many of them operate on the World Wide Web. Some 475,000 companies, most of them small, engage in barter worth more than $12 billion each year.[42] Every day, entrepreneurs across the nation use bartering to buy much needed materials, equipment, and supplies—*without using cash.* The president of one barter exchange estimates that business owners can save "between $5,000 and $150,000 in yearly business costs."[43] In addition to conserving cash, companies using bartering can transform slow-moving and excess inventory into much-needed goods and services. Often business owners who join barter exchanges find new customers for the products and services they sell.

Of course, there is a cost associated with bartering, but the real benefit is that entrepreneurs "pay" for products and services at their wholesale cost of doing business and get credit in the barter exchange for the retail price. In a typical arrangement, businesses accumulate trade credits when they offer goods or services through the exchange. Then they can use their trade credits to purchase other goods and services from other members of the exchange. *When Dyana Klein needed an accountant and a computer programmer to build a custom software system for the doggie day care center she was launching, she turned to barter to conserve her young company's cash. With the help of an online barter exchange, Klein was able to exchange doggie day care for $25,000 worth of accounting and programming services. "I would not have been able to afford [the services] without [bartering]," she says. "When you're starting a new business, you have to try to save every dollar you can."*[44]

Company Example →

The typical exchange charges a $500 membership fee and a 10 percent transaction fee (5 percent from the buyer and 5 percent from the seller) on every deal. The exchange tracks the balance in each member's account and typically sends a monthly statement summarizing account activity. Rather than join a barter exchange, many enterprising entrepreneurs choose to barter on an individual basis. The place to start is with the vendors, suppliers, and customers with whom a company normally does business.

Trimming Overhead Costs

High overhead expenses can strain a small company's cash supply to the breaking point. Frugal small business owners can trim their overhead in a number of ways.

When Practical, Lease instead of Buy. Small companies acquire more productive assets through leases than through loans.[45] By leasing automobiles, computers, office equipment, machinery, and other assets rather than buying them, entrepreneurs can conserve valuable cash. The value of such assets is not in *owning* them but in *using* them. Leasing is popular among entrepreneurs because of its beneficial effects on a company's cash flow; a study by the Equipment Leasing Association found that 77 percent of small businesses use leasing as a cash management strategy.[46] Leasing also gives business owners maximum flexibility when acquiring equipment and protection against the risk of purchasing assets

Company Example

that become obsolete quickly. *Andy Fleischer, chief financial officer of Web hosting business Alabanza Corporation, recently switched from purchasing the company's servers to leasing them. Not only does leasing conserve the fast-growing company's precious cash but it also enables it to keep its technology up-to-date, a vital factor given the nature of Alabanza's business. "In the past, we bought large blocks of servers up front," explains Fleischer. Leasing, however, enables Alabanza to spread the payment terms over 36 months, freeing up sizable amounts of cash the company can use elsewhere.*[47]

Although total lease payments often are greater than those for a conventional loan, most leases offer 100 percent financing, which means the owner avoids the large capital outlays required as down payments on most loans. Also, leasing is an "off-the-balance-sheet" method of financing; the lease is considered an operating expense on the income statement, not a liability on the balance sheet. Thus, leasing conserves not only a company's cash flow but also its borrowing capacity. Leasing companies typically allow businesses to stretch payments over a longer time period than they would be able to with a conventional loan. Lease agreements also are flexible; entrepreneurs can customize their lease payments to coincide with the seasonal fluctuations in their companies' cash balances. Leasing gives entrepreneurs access to equipment even when they cannot borrow the money to buy it. After his bank rejected his loan request for a $250,000 coffee roaster for Horizon Food Group, CFO Lee Rucker decided to lease the equipment. He filled out a simple online application at Capital.com, a Web-based lease broker, and soon the roaster was in place.[48]

Entrepreneurs can choose from two basic types of leases: operating leases and capital leases. At the end of an **operating lease,** a business turns the equipment back over to the leasing company with no further obligation. Businesses often lease computer and telecommunications equipment through operating leases because it becomes obsolete so quickly. At the end of a **capital lease,** a business may exercise an option to purchase the equipment, usually for a nominal sum.

Avoid Nonessential Outlays. By forgoing costly ego indulgences such as ostentatious office equipment, first-class travel, and flashy company cars, business owners can make efficient use of a company's cash. Before putting scarce cash into an asset, every business owner should put the decision to the acid test by asking "What will this purchase add to the company's ability to compete and to become more successful?" Making across-the-board spending cuts to conserve cash is dangerous, however, because the owner runs the risk of cutting expenditures that literally drive the business. One common mistake during business slowdowns is cutting marketing and advertising expenditures. "As competitors pull back," says one adviser, "smart marketers will keep their ad budgets on an even keel, which is sufficient to bring increased attention to their products."[49] The secret to success is cutting nonessential expenditures. "If the lifeblood of your company is marketing, cut it less," advises one advertising executive. "If it is customer service, that is the last thing you want to cut back on. Cut from areas that are not essential to business growth."[50]

Negotiate Fixed Loan Payments to Coincide with Your Company's Cash Flow Cycle. Many banks allow businesses to structure loans so that they can skip specific payments when their cash flow ebbs to its lowest point. Negotiating such terms gives businesses the opportunity to customize their loan repayments to their cash flow cycles. For example, *Ted Zoli, president of Torrington Industries, a construction-materials supplier and contracting business, consistently uses "skipped payment loans" in his highly seasonal business. "Every time we buy a piece of construction machinery," he says, "we set it up so that we're making payments for eight or nine months, and then skipping three or four months during the winter."*[51]

Buy Used or Reconditioned Equipment, Especially If It Is "Behind-the-Scenes" Machinery. Many shrewd entrepreneurs purchase their office furniture at flea markets and garage sales! One restaurateur saved significant amounts of cash in the start-up phase of his business by purchasing used equipment from a restaurant equipment broker. *Mark Eshelman, cofounder of Smarte Solutions Inc., a company that markets antipiracy software, purchases the diverse array of computers he needs to test the company's software from a used PC Web site. He was so impressed with the deal he got on those systems that he purchased another 30 used computers at drastically reduced prices for his programmers and office staff to use.*[52]

Look for Simple Ways to Cut Costs. Smart entrepreneurs are always on the lookout for ways to cut the cost of operating their businesses every day. One useful technique is to sit down with employees periodically with a list of company expenses and brainstorm ways the company could conserve cash without endangering product quality or customer service. Ideas might range from installing more energy-efficient equipment to adding more fuel-efficient cars to the company fleet. *Gerry Houlihan, owner of Daniel's Restaurant in Tuckahoe, New York, recently switched from incandescent lighting to compact fluorescent lighting and installed more efficient heating and air-conditioning units to cut energy costs.*[53] *Mark Troy, CEO of Flywire, a Web-design company, went a step further and hired a financial expert to conduct an expense audit to find ways to lower the company's operating expenses. By switching law firms, shutting down equipment at night, consolidating business trips, and other simple techniques, Troy estimates that the savings to his company are between $13,450 and $17,200 per month!*[54]

Hire Part-Time Employees and Freelance Specialists Whenever Possible. Hiring part-timers and freelancers rather than full-time workers saves on both the cost of salaries and employee benefits. Robert Ross, president of Xante Corporation, a maker of laser printer products, hires local college students for telemarketing and customer support positions, keeping his recruiting, benefits, and insurance costs down.

Control Employee Advances and Loans. A manager should grant only those advances and loans that are necessary, and should keep accurate records on payments and balances.

Use Credit Cards to Make Small Purchases. Using a credit card to make small purchases from vendors who do not offer credit terms enables entrepreneurs to defer payment for up to 30 days. Entrepreneurs who use this strategy must be disciplined, however, and pay off the entire credit card balance each month. Carrying a credit card balance from month to month exposes an entrepreneur to annual interest rates of 15 percent to 25 percent—*not* a cash-conserving technique!

Company Example →

Company Example →

Company Example →

Company Example →

Establish an Internal Security and Control System. Too many owners encourage employee theft by failing to establish a system of controls. Reconciling the bank statement monthly and requiring special approval for checks over a specific amount, say $1,000, will help minimize losses. Separating record-keeping and check-writing responsibilities, rather than assigning them to a single employee, offers more protection.

Develop a System to Battle Check Fraud. Customers write about 70 billion checks a year, and merchants lose more than $13 billion in bad checks a year.[55] About 70 percent of all "bounced" checks occur because nine out of ten customers fail to keep their checkbooks balanced; the remaining 30 percent of bad checks are the result of fraud.[56] The most effective way to battle bad checks is to subscribe to an electronic check approval service. The service works at the cash register, and approval takes about a minute. The fee a small business pays to use the service depends on the volume of checks. For most small companies, charges range from a base of $25 to $100 plus a percentage of the cleared checks' value.

Change Your Shipping Terms. Changing the firm's shipping terms from "F.O.B. (free on board) buyer," in which the seller pays the cost of freight, to "F.O.B. seller," in which the buyer absorbs all shipping costs, will improve cash flow.

Switch to Zero-Based Budgeting. Zero-based budgeting (ZBB) primarily is a shift in the philosophy of budgeting. Rather than build the current year's budget on increases from the previous year's budget, ZBB starts from a budget of zero and evaluates the necessity of every item. The idea is to start the budget at zero and review all expenses, asking whether each one is necessary.

Keep Your Business Plan Current. Before approaching any potential lender or investor, a business owner must prepare a solid business plan. Smart owners keep their plans up-to-date in case an unexpected cash crisis forces them to seek emergency financing. Revising the plan annually also forces the owner to focus on managing the business more effectively.

Investing Surplus Cash

Because of the uneven flow of receipts and disbursements, a company will often temporarily have more cash than it needs—for a week, a month, a quarter, or longer. When this happens, most small business owners simply ignore the surplus because they are not sure how soon they will need it. They believe that relatively small amounts of cash sitting around for just a few days or weeks are not worth investing. However, this is not always the case. Entrepreneurs who put surplus cash to work immediately discover that the yield adds up to a significant amount over time. This money can help ease the daily cash crunch during business troughs. The goal is to identify every dollar the business does not need to pay today's bills and to invest that money to improve cash flow. However, when investing surplus cash, an entrepreneur's primary objective should not be to earn the maximum yield (which usually carries with it maximum risk); instead, the focus should be on the safety and the liquidity of the investments. The need to minimize risk and to have ready access to the cash restricts the small business owner's investment options to just a few.

Asset-management accounts, which integrate checking, borrowing, and investing services under one umbrella and were once available only to large businesses, now help small companies conserve cash. *Stanley Grossbard, president of RCDC Corporation, a diamond-cutting and wholesale business in New York City, estimates that opening an asset-management account through a brokerage firm has earned his company several*

Company Example

thousand dollars in interest and has saved $7,000 in interest paid. RCDC, with annual sales of $10 million, has a $1 million line of credit, which means the company borrows only what it needs exactly when it needs it, eliminating unnecessary interest expense. The account automatically moves the company's cash where it will earn—or save—the most money by either sweeping excess cash into interest-bearing accounts or applying it to the company's outstanding loan balance.[57]

Conclusion

Successful owners run their businesses "lean and mean." Trimming wasteful expenditures, investing surplus funds, and carefully planning and managing the company's cash flow enable them to compete effectively in a hostile market. The simple but effective techniques covered in this chapter can improve every small company's cash position. One business writer says, "In the day-to-day course of running a company, other people's capital flows past an imaginative CEO as opportunity. By looking forward and keeping an analytical eye on your cash account as events unfold (remembering that if there's no real cash there when you need it, you're history), you can generate leverage as surely as if that capital were yours to keep."[58]

▌▌▌ Chapter Review

1. Explain the importance of cash management to the success of a small business.

   ▪ Cash is the most important but least productive asset the small business has. The manager must maintain enough cash to meet the firm's normal requirements (plus a reserve for emergencies) without retaining excessively large, unproductive cash balances.

   ▪ Without adequate cash, a small business will fail.

2. Differentiate between cash and profits.

   ▪ Cash and profits are not the same. More businesses fail for lack of cash than for lack of profits.

   ▪ Profits, the difference between total revenue and total expenses, are an accounting concept. Cash flow represents the flow of actual cash (the only thing businesses can use to pay bills) through a business in a continuous cycle. A business can be earning a profit and be forced out of business because it runs out of cash.

3. Understand the five steps in creating a cash budget and use them to build a cash budget.

   ▪ The cash budgeting procedure outlined in this chapter tracks the flow of cash through the business and enables the owner to project cash surpluses and cash deficits at specific intervals.

   ▪ The five steps in creating a cash budget are as follows: forecasting sales, forecasting cash receipts, forecasting cash disbursements, and determining the end-of-month cash balance.

4. Describe the fundamental principles involved in managing the "big three" of cash management: accounts receivable, accounts payable, and inventory.

   ▪ Controlling accounts receivable requires business owners to establish clear, firm credit and collection policies and to screen customers before granting them credit. Sending invoices promptly and acting on past-due accounts quickly also improve cash flow. The goal is to collect cash from receivables as quickly as possible.

   ▪ When managing accounts payable, a manager's goal is to stretch out payables as long as possible without damaging the company's credit rating. Other techniques include: verifying invoices before paying them, taking advantage of cash discounts, and negotiating the best possible credit terms.

   ▪ Inventory frequently causes cash headaches for small business managers. Excess inventory earns a zero rate of return and ties up a company's cash unnecessarily. Owners must watch for stale merchandise.

5. Explain the techniques for avoiding a cash crunch in a small company.

   ▪ Trimming overhead costs by bartering, leasing assets, avoiding nonessential outlays, using zero-based budgeting, and implementing an internal control system boost a firm's cash flow position.

   ▪ Also, investing surplus cash maximizes the firm's earning power. The primary criteria for investing surplus cash are security and liquidity.

▌▐▌ Discussion Questions

1. Why must small business owners concentrate on effective cash flow management?
2. Explain the difference between cash and profit.
3. Outline the steps involved in developing a cash budget.
4. How can an entrepreneur launching a new business forecast sales?
5. Outline the basic principles of managing a small firm's receivables, payables, and inventory.
6. How can bartering improve a company's cash position?
7. Alan Ferguson, owner of Nupremis, Inc., a Web-based application service provider, says, "We lease our equipment and technology because our core business is deploying it, not owning it." What does he mean? Is leasing a wise cash management strategy for small businesses? Explain.
8. What steps should business owners take to conserve cash in their companies?
9. What should be a small business owner's primary concern when investing surplus cash?

Managing Cash Flow

Business PlanPro

Managing cash flow is a task that many entrepreneurs ignore—until they face a cash crisis. Cash is the resource that sustains a company, enabling it to grow and survive. Without cash, a business fails. That's why creating a cash flow forecast and using it to manage your company's cash is so important. Remember that a business's income statement can show a profit and the company can be forced to close because it runs out of cash.

Now that you have finished studying Chapter 9, go to the section in Business Plan Pro called Cash Is King.

There you can build the all-important cash flow forecasts for your company. Click on the Cash Flow Table to launch the Cash Flow Wizard that will guide you through the process of creating cash flow forecasts. The wizard will create the Cash Flow Chart automatically using the forecasts you create in the Cash Flow Table. Be sure to complete the Explain Projected Cash Flow section to explain the assumptions you made to create the cash flow projections for your business. Potential lenders and investors are as interested in your assumptions as they are in the forecasts you generate. Are your assumptions and the resulting forecasts reasonable?

Chapter 10
Pricing and Credit Strategies

> *Make a good product at a fair price—then tell the world.*
> —WILLIAM WRIGLEY JR.

> *There is hardly anything in the world that someone cannot make a little worse and sell a little cheaper, and the people who consider price alone are this man's prey.*
> —JOHN RUSKIN

Upon completion of this chapter, you will be able to:

1. Describe why pricing is both an art and a science.
2. Discuss the relationships among pricing, image, and competition.
3. Discuss effective pricing techniques for both new and existing products and services.
4. Explain the pricing techniques used by retailers.
5. Explain the pricing techniques used by manufacturers.
6. Explain the pricing techniques used by service firms.
7. Describe the impact of credit on pricing.

Pricing: The Creative Blend of Art and Science

1. Describe why pricing is both an art and a science.

If you would like to become an instant business legend, simply develop a method for pricing products or services that results in maximum net revenue. Pricing is almost always one of the entrepreneur's greatest challenges. If the price of your product or services is perceived to be too high, sales may not reach an adequate level for the business to become profitable. In the opposite extreme, pricing products or services too low may convey an image of inferior quality. Even if the products or services do sell, the lower price may not yield an adequate profit margin. A serious "side effect" of pricing too low is the reaction of customers when you attempt to adjust prices upward. Your customers will remember the initial low price and they may even feel that their loyalty is being taken advantage of. For example, when the price of gasoline rises significantly, do you believe that the price increase is due to actual availability and cost? Or do you sometimes think that the increase is due to price gouging by the supplier?

For most consumers, the price of a product or service is one of the first questions they ask. Smart entrepreneurs quickly learn the nature of their customers' sensitivity to price. Selecting and implementing an effective pricing strategy remains a challenge. However, effective pricing strategies are the result of something between an exact science based on logical factors (such as consumer feedback) and an intuitive insight based on instinct. Determining the most appropriate price for a product or service requires an entrepreneur to consider how each of the following factors will interact with one another to provide clues as to proper price level:

- The total cost associated with the product or service.
- The current and anticipated future market forces that determine both supply and demand.
- The *anticipated* pricing strategies of competitors and their *anticipated* competitive behaviors.
- The anticipated sales volume and the financial impact of production volume on unit cost.
- The existing image of the company and consumers' expectations regarding product or service quality and price.
- Any normal and predictable cycles or seasonal market variability.
- Known customer price sensitivity.
- Unique psychological factors that influence customer perceptions of price and/or quality.
- Any substitute products or services and under what conditions customers will switch.
- Traditional and expected credit terms and discount policy.
- The desired image that the seller wishes to create in customers' minds.

Notice that some of the clues are fairly concrete and others, such as "anticipated behaviors" and "desired image," are somewhat less tangible. This is where the creative blending of art and science comes into play and leads to the final pricing decision. In purely economic terms, price is the monetary value of a good or service. Price is a measure of what a customer is required to give up to obtain a good or service. For an individual, price is a reflection of value. We, as individuals, pay no more than what we believe the good or service to be worth. In the total marketplace, all potential customers evaluate the available goods and services and establish the demand for each. Value, like beauty, is in the eye of the beholder. The process of setting the price for any good or service must involve an analysis of how the market views the value of that product or service.

Entrepreneurs must develop a keen sensitivity to the psychological and economic thinking of their customers. Without being "in tune" to customers' psychological and economic motivators and their resulting most likely buying behavior, it is possible to price the good or service incorrectly. This needed customer orientation is an important nonquantitative factor in a successful pricing process. What the process achieves is seldom a single ideal price but an ideal price range. This price range can be described as the area between the **price ceiling**, which is the most the target group would be willing to pay, and the **price floor**. The price floor is established by the firm's total cost to produce the product or provide the service.

The price ceiling can only be determined by serious ongoing market research and analysis and the price floor by an equally competent understanding of the financial operations of the business. Small companies with effective pricing policies tend to have a clear picture of who their customers are and how their companies' products or services fit into their customers' perception of value. They also know with exceptional accuracy the cost associated with the production and delivery of their products or services.

The final price that business owners set depends on the desired image they want to create for their products or services: discount (bargain), middle of the road (value), or prestige (luxury). A prestige pricing strategy is not necessarily better or more effective than a no-frills, value pricing strategy. What matters most is that the company's pricing strategy enhances the image the owner wants to create for it.

| Company Example |

Some entrepreneurs compete in markets in which the cost of raw materials and supplies can fluctuate wildly due to forces beyond their control. *That's the situation Danny O'Neill, owner of The Roasterie, a wholesale coffee business that sells to upscale restaurants, coffee houses and supermarkets, found himself in when coffee prices nearly doubled in just three months.*[1] Businesses faced with rapidly rising raw materials costs should consider the following strategies:

| Company Example |

- *Communicate with customers.* Let your customers know what's happening. *The Roasterie's O'Neill was able to pass along the rising costs of his company's raw materials to customers without losing a single one. He sent his customers a six-page letter and copies of newspaper articles about the increases in coffee prices. The approach gave the Roasterie credibility and helped show customers that the necessary price increases were beyond his control.*
- *Focus on improving efficiency everywhere in the company.* Although raw materials costs may be beyond a business owner's control, other costs within the company are not. One way to dampen the effects of a rapid increase in costs is to find ways to cut costs and to improve efficiency in other areas. These improvements may not totally offset higher raw materials costs, but they can dampen their impact.
- *Consider absorbing cost increases to save accounts with long-term importance to the company.* Saving a large account might be more important than keeping pace with rising costs.
- *Emphasize the value your company provides to customers.* Unless a company reminds them, customers can forget the benefits and value its products offer. When some casinos balked at paying premium prices ($2,000 to $2,600) for his company's portable carts that dispense change to slot machine players, Russell Pike, owner of Advanced Cart Technology, emphasized to casino managers the value his carts offer. He showed them how the convenient carts would pay for themselves in a single weekend by letting casinos use them for two weeks free of charge. He then showed them how his prices compared with increased profits. "Even though our prices are high," says Pike, "they are not high for what we are doing for them."[2]
- *Anticipate rising materials costs and try to lock in prices early.* It pays to keep tabs on raw materials prices and be able to predict cycles of inflation.

Two Powerful Pricing Forces: Image and Competition

2. Discuss the relationships among pricing, image, and competition.

The art of pricing is the ability to explain the psychology behind the willingness of some market segments to pay prices that to others are ridiculous and absurd. *For example, price reflects this notion of perceived value nowhere better than in the products of the Swiss watch industry. Rolex, Cartier, Patek Philippe, Chopard, Toric, Blanepain, and Corum are legendary brands of ultrapremium handmade watches selling from $10,000 to $50,000. Owning one of these watches is a mark of financial success, yet each is less accurate at keeping time than a $10 quartz-driven Timex.*[3] *A similar example of price insensitivity can be found in fountain pens. In recent years, Renaissance Pen Company has marketed pens made from gold and platinum and encrusted with diamonds selling for as much as $230,000. One pen that contains the crystallized DNA of Abraham Lincoln sells for $1,650!*[4] Value for these examples is not found in superior technical performance but rather in their scarcity and uniqueness. Although entrepreneurs must recognize the shallow depth of the market for such ultraluxury items, the ego-satisfying ownership of limited-edition watches, pens, cars, jewelry, and so on is the psychological force supporting this pricing strategy.

Price Conveys Image

Company pricing policies offer potential customers important information about the company's overall image. For example, the prices charged by upscale men's clothing stores reflect a completely different image from those charged by factory outlets. Customers look at prices to determine what type of store they are dealing with. High prices frequently convey the idea of quality, prestige, and uniqueness. Accordingly, when developing a marketing approach to pricing, business owners must establish prices that are compatible with what their customers expect and are willing to pay. Too often, small business owners *underprice* their goods and services, believing that low prices are the only way they can achieve a competitive advantage. They fail to identify the extra value, convenience, service, and quality they can provide—all things many customers are willing to pay for. These companies fall into the trap of trying to compete solely on the basis of price when they lack the sales volume—and, hence, the lower costs—of their larger rivals. It is a recipe for failure. The consumer often equates a decline in price with a decline in quality.

Company Example → *Discounting prices on its once popular Izod polo shirts nearly cost Lacoste its entire business. Demand for the shirts, which sported a unique crocodile logo, slumped as prices fell. Discounting had eroded the company's distinctive image. Today, the company is trying to rebuild its upscale image and the cachet of its shirts by charging premium prices. Sales have been climbing.*[5]

The secret to setting prices properly is based on understanding the firm's target market, the customer groups at which the small company is aiming its goods or ser-

Company Example → vices. Target market, business image, and price are closely related. *For instance, Crème de la Crème child care centers charge a staggering $14,000 a year in tuition, compared to a national average tuition of $5,400, and parents are clamoring to enroll their children. (Some applicants have not even been conceived yet!) Despite its premium prices, Crème de la Crème had a six-month waiting list in only its first year. How did the company manage this spectacular record? The key is differentiating itself from other child care centers and marketing those differences to well-to-do parents who want only the best for their preschool children. A Crème de la Crème center features a 3,600-volume library, a math lab, television and dance studios, and a state-of-the art computer lab. The company pays 40 percent above the norm for teachers, 90 percent of whom have college degrees, compared to just 31 percent nationwide. Specialized teachers handle important subjects such as music and* *foreign languages and keep the student–teacher ratio low. Twenty security monitors ensure students' safety as they play tennis, stage plays in an open-air theater, or frolic in well-equipped playgrounds.*[6]

Consider the decision you would make if you were in a less-developed country whose water is not compatible with the digestive systems of Americans. There are two brands of bottled water, one is a world-renowned internationally marketed product priced at $2.50 per bottle, and the other selection is locally bottled water with the words "pure" and "safe" clearly stated on the bottle and priced at $1.00. Would you pay 150 percent more for the product with the international reputation? Would you equate the higher price with a guarantee of safety and quality?

IN THE FOOTSTEPS OF AN ENTREPRENEUR...

What's a Fair Price for a Product That Can Save a Life?

Tyler Thatcher, co-owner of tiny Chapman Innovations, a six-person company based in Salt Lake City, Utah, knows his company is going up against industry giant DuPont, yet he is confident in his business's ability to compete. Chapman Innovations has developed a fire-resistant fabric called CarbonX, a miracle fabric that has the potential to save the lives of firefighters, racecar drivers, soldiers, steelworkers, and others whose work or hobbies place them in the path of extreme heat or fire.

"We are not aware of any fabric that has the same protection against flame and heat," says Thatcher. "This is an entirely different approach to the problem."

He demonstrates CarbonX's miraculous properties by placing a penny on a piece of the soft black fabric he holds in his hand. He uses a small torch to heat the penny until it begins to melt, but he never drops the nearly liquid coin, and his hand is unharmed. The CarbonX fabric, which can withstand temperatures up to 2,600 degrees Fahrenheit without charring, shrinking, or catching fire, protects his hand from the intense heat.

Chapman Innovations currently sells socks, gloves, and long underwear made of CarbonX, but Thatcher sees a multitude of applications for CarbonX, ranging from oven mitts and racing suits to firefighters' clothing and airplane upholstery. The company's target markets include the military, law enforcement agencies, fire departments, motor sports teams, and companies in industries where workers are in high-risk heat environments. The major challenge Chapman Innovations faces is that industry giant DuPont controls most of the market with its market-leading fire-resistant fabric, Nomex, which the company introduced in the 1960s. Thatcher says that CarbonX is superior to Nomex in many ways, the most important of which is the level of protection against fire and extreme temperatures it offers. Although it contains strengthening fibers such as Kevlar (which, ironically, is made by DuPont), CarbonX is soft to the touch and wicks away moisture from the skin.

Recognizing that it would be impossible for a start-up company to compete with the vast resources of DuPont, Thatcher's plan for Chapman Innovations is to use a guerrilla marketing strategy that includes public relations, product demonstrations, customer testimonials, and celebrity endorsements. After seeing a demonstration that involved pouring 2,800-degree molten steel over a CarbonX balaclava that survived unharmed, managers at a steel mill began purchasing protective clothing for their workers. Two-time national drag racing champion Larry Dixon won't climb into his 8,000 horse-power dragster without his CarbonX protective suit. Thatcher has convinced Dixon to wear a CarbonX patch on his racing suit. Brian Miser, who every night sets himself on fire and then is catapulted out of a cannon for the Ringling Brothers and Barnum & Bailey Circus's "Bailey's Comet" act, also is a fan of CarbonX. "The Nomex suit lasted only one jump," he says. "I couldn't wear it again. The CarbonX suit (which cost about $1,000) lasts 100 jumps."

One dramatic example of CarbonX's protective power came during a race at the Texas Motor Speedway when Andy Hillenburg's car hit a berm and ignited. His racing suit, made of CarbonX, was saturated with fuel but did not burn, and Hillenburg escaped with only a blistered elbow.

CarbonX fabric is not cheap. Chapman Innovations currently sells it for $19 per yard, which is about 20 percent higher than DuPont's price for one yard of its Nomex fabric. Despite the premium price, sales of CarbonX have climbed rapidly, tripling in just one year, suggesting that the market is beginning to accept this innovative product.

1. What advantages does CarbonX have over existing products? How should these advantages factor into Chapman Innovations's pricing strategy?
2. What pricing strategy would you recommend to Thatcher for CarbonX? Explain.
3. Should Chapman Innovations offer to sell CarbonX at a lower price to those who risk their lives providing important public services such as fire and military protection? Explain.

Sources: Adapted from Daniel Lyons, "Hot Stuff," *Forbes,* December 22, 2003, pp. 188–190; Bob Mims, "Playing with Fire," *Salt Lake Tribune,* September 25, 2003, p. 1C; "Company Overview," Chapman Industries, www.chapmaninnovations.com/company/.

Competition and Prices

An important part of setting appropriate prices is tracking competitors' prices regularly; however, what the competition is charging is just one variable in the pricing mix. When setting prices, business owners should take into account their competitors' prices, but they should *not* automatically match or beat them. Businesses that offer customers extra quality, value, service, or convenience can charge higher prices as

Company Example ➝ long as customers recognize the "extras" they are getting. *Damon Risucci opened his first health club, when he was 24 years old. Despite tough competition from chains such as New York Sports Clubs and Equinox Fitness, he built Synergy Fitness Clubs into a successful business, with three stylish New York City locations, $7 million in revenue, and 9,500 members. But when it came to raising prices, Risucci was positively a wimp. Obsessed with being a value leader, he was determined to provide customers with a comparable experience to the chain fitness centers while charging rock-bottom prices. For almost a decade, membership fees remained at $49.99 a month—nearly half those of his rivals—despite an upscale midtown Manhattan flagship location and ever-rising rent and utility bills. "We thought our prices had to be low," Risucci says. "It was almost a core belief." Finally, after poring over his financials and holding extensive interviews with customers and staffers, Risucci built up his courage and took action. Prompted by withering margins and a hunch that his customers were willing to pay more, he raised monthly fees 16 percent for new members and the cost of personal training sessions 20 percent. The result: No one complained and not a single one of his members threatened to jump ship.*[7]

Two factors are vital to studying the effects of competition on a small firm's pricing policies: the location of the competitors and the nature of the competing goods. In most cases, unless a company can differentiate the quality and the quantity of extras it provides, it must match the prices charged by nearby competitors for identical items. For example, if a self-service station charges a nickel more for a gallon of gasoline than the self-service station across the street charges, customers will simply go across the street to buy. Without the advantage of a unique business image—quality of goods sold, value of service provided, convenient location, or favorable credit terms—a small company must match local competitors' prices or lose sales. Although the prices that distant competitors charge are not nearly as critical to the small business as are those of local competitors, it can be helpful to know them and to use them as reference points. Before matching any competitor's price change, however, the small business owner should consider the rival's motives. The competition may be establishing its price structure on the basis of a unique set of criteria and a totally different strategy.

The nature of competitors' goods also influences the small firm's pricing policies. The manager must recognize which products are substitutes for those he or she sells and then strive to keep prices in line with them. For example, the local sandwich shop should consider the hamburger restaurant, the taco shop, and the roast beef shop as competitors because they all serve fast foods. Although none of them offers the identical menu of the sandwich shop, they're all competing for the same quick-meal dollar. Of course, if a company can differentiate its product by creating a distinctive image in the consumer's mind, it may be able to set higher prices for its food. The issue in this example may hinge on how much the average customer is willing to spend. An entrepreneur may have a superior sandwich, but its price is beyond what the market is willing to spend.

In general, entrepreneurs should avoid head-to-head price competition with other firms that can more easily achieve lower prices through lower cost structures. Most locally owned drugstores cannot compete with the prices of large national drug chains. However, many local drugstores operate successfully using nonprice competition by offering more personal service, free delivery, credit sales, and other extras that the chains have eliminated. Nonprice competition can be an effective strategy for a small business in the face of larger, more powerful enterprises, especially because there are many dangers in experimenting with prices. For instance, price shifts cause fluctuations in sales volume that the small firm may not be able to tolerate. Also, frequent price changes may damage the company's image and its customer relations.

One of the deadliest games a small business can get into with competitors is a price war. Price wars can eradicate companies' profit margins and scar an entire industry for years. Price wars usually begin when one competitor believes that it can achieve a higher volume through lower price, or it believes it can exert enough pressure on competitors' profits to drive them out of business. In most cases, entrepreneurs overestimate the power of price cuts to increase sales sufficiently to improve net profitability. *McDonald's infamous "Campaign 55," in which it planned to lower to 55 cents the price of a different sandwich each month, launched another volley in an ongoing fast food price war that no company seemed to be winning. The 55-cent price was a throwback to the prices in 1955, the year McDonald's was founded. The company kicked off the campaign by selling Big Macs (which cost around 40 cents to make) for 55 cents and hoped to increase store traffic and boost sales on other menu items enough to offset the lower margin on the sandwich. Unfortunately, the increased traffic never materialized and same-store sales fell 6 percent from the year before. In less than two months, amid the complaints of its franchisees, McDonald's abandoned the promotion.*[8]

In a price war, a company may cut its prices so severely that it is impossible to achieve the volume necessary to offset the lower profit margins. If you have a 25 percent gross (profit) margin and you cut your price 10 percent, you have to roughly triple your sales volume just to break even. Even when price cuts work, their effects are often temporary. Customers lured by the lowest price usually have almost no loyalty to a business. The lesson: The best way to survive a price war is to stay out of it by emphasizing the unique features, benefits, and value your company offers its customers!

Company Example

Pricing Strategies and Tactics

3. Describe effective pricing techniques for both new and existing products and services.

There is no limit to the number of variations in pricing strategies and tactics. The wide variety of options is exactly what enables entrepreneurs to be so creative with their pricing. This section will examine some of the more commonly used tactics under a variety of conditions. Pricing always plays a critical role in a firm's overall strategy; pricing policies must be compatible with a company's total marketing plan.

New Product Pricing: Penetration, Skimming, or Sliding

Most entrepreneurs approach setting the price of a new product with a great deal of apprehension because they have no precedent on which to base their decision. If the new product's price is excessively high, it is in danger of failing because of low sales volume. However, if its price is too low, the product's sales revenue might not cover costs. When pricing any new product, an entrepreneur must satisfy three objectives:

1. *Get the price accepted.* No matter how unusual a product is, its price must be acceptable to the company's potential customers.
2. *Maintain market share as competition grows.* If a new product is successful, competitors will enter the market, and the small company must work to expand or at least maintain its market share. Continuously reappraising the product's price in conjunction with special advertising and promotion techniques helps the firm acquire and retain a satisfactory market share.
3. *Earn a profit.* Obviously, a small company must establish a price for the new product that is higher than its cost. Managers should not introduce a new product at a price below cost because it is much easier to lower the price than to increase it once the product is on the market. Pricing their products too low is a common and often fatal mistake for new businesses; entrepreneurs are tempted to underprice their products and services when they enter a new market to ensure their acceptance.

Company Example

Linda Calder, owner of Calder & Calder Promotions, a company that produces trade shows, knows how difficult it can be to raise prices. When she launched her company, Calder decided to set her price below the average price of competing trade show production companies because she thought that would give her a competitive edge. "My fee was so low . . . I sold out but did not make a profit," she says. Realizing her mistake, Calder raised prices in her second year, but her customers balked. Her sales fell by 50 percent.[9]

Entrepreneurs have three basic strategies to choose from in establishing a new product's price: penetration, skimming, and sliding down the demand curve.

Penetration. If a business introduces a product into a highly competitive market in which a large number of similar products are competing for acceptance, the product must penetrate the market to be successful. To gain quick acceptance and extensive distribution in the mass market, a company introduces the product at a low price. In other words, it sets the price just above total unit cost to develop a wedge in the market and quickly achieve a high volume of sales. The resulting low profit margins may discourage other competitors from entering the market with similar products.

In most cases, a penetration pricing strategy is used to introduce relatively low-priced goods into a market in which no elite segment and little opportunity for differentiation exist. The introduction is usually accompanied by heavy advertising and promotional techniques, special sales, and discounts. Entrepreneurs must recognize that penetration pricing is a long-range strategy; until a company achieves customer acceptance for the product, profits are likely to be small. *Daniel Gould created Synergy Investment, a design and retrofit lighting systems company, in 1994, carving out a niche for himself with few real competitors. He offered his customers what he calls "the Wal-Mart attitude: give them rock-bottom prices all the time." But at the end of the day, he says, "I didn't have much to show for it. Basically, I was giving it away." Another problem that Gould had was adjusting his fees accordingly when the job was more complex and time consuming than he had originally estimated. He was loath to do this because he both wanted to honor his commitments and feared losing valued customers. In time, he began to get a sense of the true market value of his work, which is a highly specialized combination of consulting and contracting. He realized, too late, that "I could've charged more, and people wouldn't have blinked." Gould thinks he's been "continually behind the curve for pricing compared with the market." Although he has gradually raised his prices over the past few years, he remains "the low-cost provider."*[10]

Another danger of a penetration pricing strategy is that it attracts customers who know no brand loyalty. Companies that attract customers by offering low introductory prices must wonder what will become of their customer bases if they increase their prices or if a competitor undercuts them. If a penetration pricing strategy works, however, and the product achieves mass-market penetration, sales volume increases, economies of scale result in lower unit cost, and the company earns adequate profits. The objective of the penetration strategy is to achieve quick access to the market in order to realize high sales volume as soon as possible.

Skimming. A skimming pricing strategy often is used when a company introduces a new product into a market with little or no competition. Sometimes a company uses this tactic when introducing a product into a competitive market that contains an elite group that seems willing and is able to pay a premium price. The firm sets a higher-than-normal price in an effort to quickly recover the initial developmental and promotional costs of the product. Product development or start-up costs usually are substantial, owing to intensive promotional expenses and high initial costs. The idea is to set a price well above the total unit cost and to promote the product heavily to appeal to the segment of the market that is not sensitive to price. This pricing tactic often reinforces the unique, prestigious image of a business and projects a quality picture of the product.

In cases in which development costs are extremely high, as in new high technology products, the skimming technique helps the firm recoup its research and development costs in a shorter time span. As sales volume increases with the broad acceptance of the new products, the firm can lower its price. When a company employs a skimming strategy, it always can lower the price to generate additional sales to increase the firm's total revenue.

Sliding Down the Demand Curve. One variation of the skimming pricing strategy is called sliding down the demand curve. Using this tactic, the firm introduces a product at a high price. Then technological advancements enable the firm to lower its costs quickly and to reduce the product's price sooner than its competition can. By beating other businesses in a price decline, the firm discourages competitors and, over time, becomes a high-volume producer. Computers, DVD players, and other electronic equipment are a prime example of products introduced at a high price that quickly cascaded downward as companies forged important technological advances.

Sliding is a short-term pricing strategy that assumes that competition will eventually emerge. But even if no competition arises, the firm almost always lowers the product's price to attract a larger segment of the market. Yet, the initial high price contributes to a rapid return of start-up costs and generates a pool of funds to finance expansion and technological advances.

Pricing Techniques for Established Products and Services

Each of the following pricing techniques can become part of the toolbox of pricing tactics entrepreneurs use to set prices for established goods and services.

Odd Pricing. Although studies of consumer reactions to prices are mixed and generally inconclusive, many entrepreneurs use the technique known as **odd pricing**. They set prices that end in odd numbers (frequently 5, 7, or 9) because they believe that an item selling for $12.95 appears to be much cheaper than an item selling for $13.00. Psychological techniques such as odd pricing are designed to appeal to certain customer interests, but their effectiveness remains to be proved.

Price Lining. Price lining is a technique that greatly simplifies the pricing function. Under this system, the manager stocks merchandise in several different price ranges or price lines. Each category of merchandise contains items that are similar in appearance, quality, cost, performance, or other features. For example, most music stores use price lines for their CDs to make it easier for customers to select items and to simplify stock planning. Most lined products appear in sets of three—good, better, and best—at prices designed to satisfy different market segment needs and incomes.

Leader Pricing. Leader pricing is a technique in which the smaller retailer marks down the customary price (i.e., the price consumers are accustomed to paying) of a popular item in an attempt to attract more customers. The company earns a much smaller profit on each unit because the markup is lower, but purchases of other merchandise by customers seeking the leader item often boost sales and profits. (Think low-priced turkeys at Thanksgiving.) In other words, the incidental purchases that consumers make when shopping for the leader item boost sales revenue enough to offset a lower profit margin on the leader.

Geographic Pricing. Small businesses whose pricing decisions are greatly affected by the costs of shipping merchandise to customers across a wide range of geographic regions frequently employ one of the **geographic pricing** techniques. For these companies, freight expenses constitute a substantial portion of the cost of doing business and often cut deeply into already narrow profit margins. One type of geographic pricing is **zone pricing**, in which a company sells its merchandise at different prices to customers located in different territories. For example, a manufacturer might sell at one price to customers east of the Mississippi and at another to those west of the Mississippi. The U.S. Postal Service's parcel post charges are a good example of zone pricing. The small business must be able to show a legitimate basis (e.g., difference in selling or transportation costs) for the price discrimination or risk violating Section 2 of the Clayton Act.

Another variation of geographic pricing is the **uniform delivered pricing**, a technique in which the firm charges all of its customers the same price regardless of their location, even though the cost of selling or transporting merchandise varies. The firm calculates the proper freight charges for each region and combines them into a uniform fee. The result is that local customers subsidize the firm's charge for shipping merchandise to distant customers.

A final variation of geographic pricing is **F.O.B. seller** in which the small company sells its merchandise to customers on the condition that they pay all shipping costs. In this way, the company can set a uniform price for its product and let each customer cover the freight cost.

Opportunistic Pricing. When products or services are in short supply, customers are willing to pay more for products they need. Some businesses use such circumstances to maximize short-term profits by engaging in price gouging. Many customers have little choice but to pay the higher prices. Opportunistic pricing may backfire, however, because customers know that a company that charges unreasonably high prices is exploiting them. For instance, after a major hurricane, a convenience store owner jacked up prices on virtually every item, selling packs of batteries for $10 each. Neighborhood residents had little choice but to pay the higher prices. After the incident, customers remembered the store's price gouging and began to shop elsewhere. The convenience store's sales never recovered and the store eventually went out of business.

Discounts. Many small businesses use **discounts**, or **markdowns**, reductions from normal list prices, to move stale, outdated, damaged, or slow-moving merchandise. A seasonal discount is a price reduction designed to encourage shoppers to purchase merchandise before an upcoming season. For instance, many retail clothiers offer special sales on winter coats in midsummer. Some firms grant purchase discounts to special groups of customers, such as senior citizens or students, to establish a faithful clientele and to generate repeat business. It is very common for students to find merchants located near their schools who offer student discounts on all purchases. Such a strategy can be quite successful in developing a large volume of student business. Large retailers commonly offer a percentage discount to all seniors or they have a certain day of the month set aside for senior shopping with special discounts.

Multiple Unit Pricing. Multiple pricing is a promotional technique that offers customers discounts if they purchase in quantity. Many products, especially those with a relatively low unit value, are sold using multiple pricing. For example, instead of selling an item for 50 cents, a small company might offer five for $2.

Bundling. Many small businesses have discovered the marketing benefits of **bundling**, grouping together several products or services, or both, into a package that offers customers extra value at a special price. For instance, many software manufacturers bundle several computer programs (such as a word processor, spreadsheet, database, presentation graphics, and Web browser) into "suites" that offer customers a discount over purchasing the same packages separately. The tourism industry has discovered a large market for

Company Example → travelers who want their entire vacation bundled into a one-price experience. *One company, Funjet Vacations, includes airfare, ground transportation, hotel accommodations, and discounts on local attractions all in one reasonably priced travel package.*

Optional-product pricing involves selling the base product for one price but selling the options or accessories at a much higher percentage markup. Automobiles are often sold at a base price with each option priced separately. In some cases, the car is sold with some of the options "bundled" together as explained previously.

Captive-product pricing is the granddaddy of marketing pricing tactics when the base product is not functional without the appropriate accessory. King Gillette, the founder of Gillette razors, taught the business world that the money is not in the razor (the product) but in the blades (the accessory). Today we see the same pricing strategy used by Nintendo and other electronic game manufacturers that have a low margin on the product but a substantially high margin on the game cartridges.

By-product pricing is a technique in which the revenues from the sale of by-products enable a firm to be more competitive in its pricing of the main product. For years, sawmills thought that bark chips were a nuisance. Now they are packaged and sold to gardeners who

Company Example → use the bark chips for ground cover. *The best example of by-products that were once viewed as worthless and now are valuable is zoo animal droppings. They are marketed under the clever name "Zoo Doo." Customers can even sign up for the "Dung of the Month" Club.*

Suggested Retail Prices. Many manufacturers print suggested retail prices on their products or include them on invoices or in wholesale catalogs. Small business owners frequently follow these suggested retail prices because doing so eliminates the need to make a pricing decision. Nonetheless, following prices established by a distant manufacturer may create

Many zoos have discovered that they can use by-product pricing to boost revenue by marketing animal droppings as "Zoo Doo," an organic fertilizer.

problems for the small firm. For example, a haberdasher may try to create a high-quality, exclusive image through a prestige pricing policy, but manufacturers may suggest discount outlet prices that are incompatible with the small firm's image. Another danger of accepting the manufacturer's suggested price is that it does not take into consideration the small firm's cost structure or competitive situation. A manufacturer cannot force a business to accept a suggested retail price or require a business to agree not to resell merchandise below a stated price because such practices violate the Sherman Antitrust Act and other legislation.

Follow-the-Leader Pricing. Some businesses make no effort to be price leaders in their immediate geographic areas and simply follow the prices that their competitors establish. Entrepreneurs wisely monitor their competitors' pricing policies and individual prices by reviewing their advertisements or by hiring part-time or full-time comparison shoppers. But then these entrepreneurs use this information to establish a "me too" pricing policy, which eradicates any opportunity to create a special price image for their businesses. Maintaining a follow-the-leader pricing policy may not be healthy for a small business because it robs the company of the opportunity to create a distinctive image in its customers' eyes.

Below-Market Pricing. Some small businesses choose to create a discount image in the market by offering goods at below-market prices. By setting prices below those of their competitors, these firms hope to attract a sufficient level of volume to offset the lower profit margins. Many retailers using a below-market pricing strategy eliminate most of the extra services that their above-market-pricing competitors offer. For instance, these businesses trim operating costs by cutting out services such as delivery, installation, credit granting, and sales assistance. Below-market pricing strategies can be risky for small companies because they require them to achieve high sales volume to remain competitive.

Adjustable or Dynamic Pricing. For most of the history of business, price was set through face-to-face bargaining. Merchants knew their customers and their price sensitivity and bargaining skills. The result was that the final price for identical merchandise or services could vary significantly. In the mass marketing era of the latter half of the twentieth century when individual identity became blurred, the trend became to have an established "fixed" price for the goods or service.

Figure 10.1

Pricing Strategy
Balancing Act

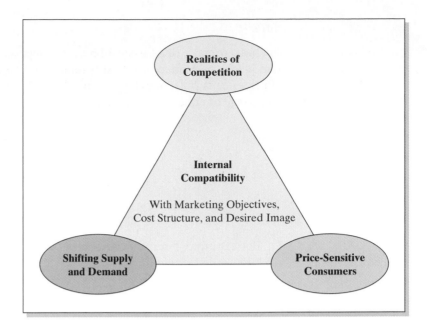

With the Internet, the marketplace is beginning to see the reemergence of adjustable or **dynamic pricing**. Computer software is blending the disciplines of microeconomics, mathematics, and psychology into programs capable of analyzing a customer's price sensitivity based on that potential customer's previous purchasing behavior. The airline and hospitality industries have been employing adjustable pricing for some time. For this reason, people on the same flight may have paid different prices for their tickets. Software firms such as ProfitLogic, Optivo, Endus.com, Zillant, and KhL Metrics all employ a blending of consumer data with sophisticated mathematical models to help retailers set prices in ways they believe will maximize profits.[11]

In summary, there is a wide variety of pricing strategies or tactics and each has a set of specific situations in which it is most appropriate. Additionally, the pricing strategy selected must be both internally and externally compatible (see Figure 10.1). Internally, the pricing strategy must be compatible with the firm's marketing objectives and the other components of the marketing mix, as well as the firm's cost structure. Externally, the pricing strategy must be consistent with the competitive realities of the market and the shifting forces of supply and demand. The forces that shape the pricing decision can change rapidly and, therefore, the pricing strategy is never completely fixed. Pricing decisions take into consideration the firm's cost, the special value the product or service creates for the buyer, as well as aggressively coping with the pricing tactics of competitors.

The underlying forces that dictate how a business prices its goods or services vary greatly among industries. In many instances, the nature of the business itself has unique factors that determine the pricing strategy. The next three sections will investigate pricing techniques used in retailing, manufacturing, and service firms.

Pricing Techniques for Retailers

4. Explain the pricing techniques used by retailers.

As retail customers have become more price conscious, retailers have changed their pricing strategies to emphasize value. This value–price relationship allows for a wide variety of highly creative pricing and marketing practices. Delivering high levels of recognized value in products and services is one key to retail customer loyalty. To justify paying a higher price than those charged by competitors, customers must perceive a company's products or services as giving them greater value.

Markup

The basic premise of a successful business operation is selling a good or service for more than it costs to produce it. The difference between the cost of a product or service and its selling price is called **markup** (or **markon**). Markup can be expressed in dollars or as a percentage of either cost or selling price:

$$\text{Dollar markup} = \text{Retail price} - \text{Cost of the merchandise}$$

$$\text{Percentage (of retail price) markup} = \frac{\text{Dollar markup}}{\text{Retail price}}$$

$$\text{Percentage (of cost) markup} = \frac{\text{Dollar markup}}{\text{Cost of unit}}$$

For example, if a man's shirt costs $15, and the manager plans to sell it for $25, markup would be as follows:

$$\text{Dollar markup} = \$25 - \$15 = \$10$$

$$\text{Percentage (of retail price) markup} = \frac{\$10}{\$25}$$

$$= 40\%$$

$$\text{Percentage (of cost) markup} = \frac{\$10}{\$15}$$

$$= 66.67\%$$

The cost of merchandise used in computing markup includes not only the wholesale price of the merchandise but also any incidental costs (e.g., selling or transportation charges) that the retailer incurs and a profit minus any discounts (e.g., quantity, cash) that the wholesaler offers.

Once business owners have a financial plan in place, including sales estimates and anticipated expenses, they can compute the firm's initial markup. The **initial markup** is the *average* markup required on all merchandise to cover the cost of the items, all incidental expenses, and a reasonable profit.

$$\text{Initial dollar markup} = \frac{\text{Operating expenses} + \text{Reductions} + \text{Profits}}{\text{Net sales} + \text{Reductions}}$$

Operating expenses are the cost of doing business, such as rent, utilities, and depreciation; reductions include employee and customer discounts, markdowns, special sales, and the cost of stockouts. For example, if a small retailer forecasts sales of $380,000, expenses of $140,000, and $24,000 in reductions, and he or she expects a profit of $38,000, the initial markup percentage will be:

$$\text{Initial markup percentage} = \frac{\$140,000 + \$24,000 + \$38,000}{\$380,000 + \$24,000}$$

$$= 50\%$$

Thus, this retailer knows that an average markup of 50 percent is required to cover costs and generate an adequate profit.

Some businesses use a standard markup on all of their merchandise. This technique, which is usually used in retail stores carrying related products, applies a standard percentage markup to all merchandise. Most stores find it much more practical to use a flexible markup, which assigns various markup percentages to different types of products. Because of the wide range of prices and types of merchandise they sell, department stores frequently rely on a flexible markup. It would be impractical for them to use a standard markup on all items because they have such a divergent cost and volume range. For instance, the markup percentage for socks is not likely to be suitable as a markup for washing machines.

Once owners determine the desired markup percentage, they can compute the appropriate retail price. Knowing that the markup of a particular item represents 40 percent of the retail price:

$$Cost = Retail\ price\ markup$$

$$= 100\% - 40\%$$

$$= 60\%\ of\ retail\ price$$

Assuming that the cost of the item is $18.00, the retailer can rearrange the percentage (of retail price) markup formula:

$$Retail\ price = \frac{Dollar\ cost}{Percentage\ cost}$$

Solving for retail price, the retailer computes the following price:

$$Retail\ price = \frac{\$18.00}{0.60} = \$30.00$$

Thus, the owner establishes a retail price of $30.00 for the item using a 40 percent markup.

Finally, retailers must verify that the computed retail price is consistent with their planned initial markup percentage. Will it cover costs and generate the desired profit? Is it congruent with the firm's overall price image? Is the final price in line with the company's strategy? Is it within an acceptable price range? How does it compare with the prices charged by competitors? Perhaps most important, are the customers willing and able to pay this price?

Pricing Techniques for Manufacturers

5. Explain the pricing techniques used by manufacturers.

For manufacturers, the pricing decision requires the support of accurate, timely accounting records. The most commonly used pricing technique for manufacturers is cost-plus pricing. Using this method, manufacturers establish a price composed of direct materials, direct labor, factory overhead, selling and administrative costs, plus the desired profit margin.

The main advantage of the cost-plus pricing method is its simplicity. Given the proper cost accounting data, computing a product's final selling price is relatively easy. Also, because it adds a profit onto the top of the firm's costs, the manufacturer is guaranteed the desired profit margin. This process, however, does not encourage the manufacturer to use its resources efficiently. Even if the company fails to use its resources in the most effective manner, it will still earn a reasonable profit, and thus, there is no motivation to conserve resources in the manufacturing process. Finally, because manufacturers' cost structures vary so greatly, cost-plus pricing fails to consider the competition sufficiently. But, despite its drawbacks, the cost-plus method of establishing prices remains prominent in many industries such as construction and printing.

Direct Costing and Price Formulation

One requisite for a successful pricing policy in manufacturing is a reliable cost accounting system that can generate timely reports to determine the costs of processing raw materials into finished goods. The traditional method of product costing is called **absorption costing** because all manufacturing and overhead costs are absorbed into the finished product's total cost. Absorption costing includes direct materials and direct labor, plus a portion of fixed and variable factory overhead costs, in each unit manufactured. Full-absorption financial statements, used in published annual reports and in tax reports, are very useful in performing financial analysis. But full-absorption statements are of little help to a manufacturer when determining prices or the impact of price changes.

A more useful technique for managerial decision making is **variable (or direct) costing**, in which the cost of the products manufactured includes only those costs that vary directly with the quantity produced. In other words, variable costing encompasses direct materials, direct labor, and factory overhead costs that vary with the level of the firm's output of finished goods. Factory overhead costs that are fixed (e.g., rent, depreciation, and insurance) are *not* included in the costs of finished items. Instead, they are considered to be expenses of the period.

A manufacturer's goal in establishing prices is to discover the cost combination of selling price and sales volume that exceeds the variable costs of producing a product and contributes enough to cover fixed costs and earn a profit. The problem with using full-absorption costing is that it clouds the true relationships among price, volume, and costs by including fixed expenses in unit cost. Using a direct-costing basis yields a constant unit cost of the product no matter what the volume of production is. The result is a clearer picture of the price–volume–cost relationship.

The starting point for establishing product prices is the direct-cost income statement. As Table 10.1 indicates, the direct-cost statement yields the same net profit as does the full-absorption income statement. The only difference between the two statements is the format. The full-absorption statement allocates costs such as advertising, rent, and utilities according to the activity that caused them, but the direct-cost income statement separates expenses into fixed and variable costs. Fixed expenses remain constant regardless of the production level, but variable expenses fluctuate according to production volume.

When variable costs are subtracted from total revenues, the result is the manufacturer's **contribution margin,** the amount remaining that contributes to covering fixed expenses and earning a profit. Expressing this contribution margin as a percentage of total revenue yields the firm's contribution percentage. Computing the contribution percentage is a critical step in establishing prices through the direct-costing method. This manufacturer's contribution percentage is 36.5 percent, which is calculated as follows:

$$\text{Contribution percentage} = 1 - \frac{\text{Variable expenses}}{\text{Revenues}}$$

$$= 1 - \frac{\$502,000}{\$790,000} = 36.5\%$$

Computing a Break-Even Selling Price

A manufacturer's contribution percentage tells what portion of total revenue remains after covering variable costs to contribute toward meeting fixed expenses and earning a profit. This manufacturer's contribution percentage is 36.5 percent, which means that variable costs absorb 63.5 percent of total revenues. In other words, variable costs

Table 10.1

A Full-Absorption Versus a Direct-Cost Income Statement

Full-Absorption Income Statement

Revenues		$790,000
Cost of goods sold:		
Materials	$250,500	
Direct labor	190,200	
Factory overhead	120,200	
Gross profit		$560,900
Operating expenses:		
General and administrative	$ 66,100	
Selling	112,000	
Other	11,000	
Total Expenses		$189,100
Net Income (before taxes)		$ 40,000

Direct-Cost Income Statement

Revenues (100%)		$790,000
Variable cost		
Materials	$250,500	
Direct labor	190,200	
Variable factory overhead	13,200	
Variable selling expenses	48,100	
Total Variable Costs (63.54%)		$502,000
Contribution Margin (36.46%)		288,000
Fixed costs		
Fixed factory overhead	$107,000	
Fixed selling expenses	63,900	
General and administrative	66,100	
Other	11,000	
Total Fixed Costs		248,000
Net Income (before taxes)		$ 40,000

represent 63.5 percent $(1.00 - 0.365 = 0.635)$ of the product's selling price. Suppose that this manufacturer's variable costs include the following:

Material	$2.08/unit
Direct labor	$4.12/unit
Variable factory overhead	$0.78/unit
Total variable cost	$6.98/unit

The minimum price at which the manufacturer would sell the item is $6.98. Any price below that would not cover variable costs. To compute the break-even selling price for this product, find the selling price using the following equation:

$$\text{Profit} = \frac{\left(\text{Selling Price} \times \text{Quantity produced}\right) + \left(\text{Variable cost per unit} \times \text{Quantity produced}\right) + \text{Total fixed cost}}{\text{Quantity produced}}$$

which becomes:

$$\text{Break-even selling price} = \frac{\text{Profit} + \left(\text{Variable cost per unit} \times \text{Quantity produced}\right) + \text{Total fixed cost}}{\text{Quantity produced}}$$

To break even, the manufacturer assumes $0 profit. Suppose that its plans are to produce 50,000 units of the product and that fixed costs will be $110,000. The break-even selling price is as follows:

$$\text{Break-even selling price} = \frac{\$0 \ + \ (\$6.98/\text{unit} \ \times \ 50{,}000 \ \text{units}) \ + \ \$110{,}000}{50{,}000 \ \text{units}}$$

$$= \frac{\$459{,}000}{50{,}000 \ \text{units}}$$

$$= \$9.18 \ \text{per unit}$$

Thus, $2.20 ($9.18/unit - $6.98/unit) of the $9.18 break-even price goes toward meeting fixed production costs. But suppose the manufacturer wants to earn a $50,000 profit. Then the required selling price is:

$$\text{Selling price} = \frac{\$50{,}000 \ + \ (6.98/\text{unit} \ \times \ 50{,}000 \ \text{units}) \ + \ \$110{,}000}{50{,}000 \ \text{units}}$$

$$= \frac{\$509{,}000}{50{,}000 \ \text{units}}$$

$$= \$10.18/\text{unit}$$

Now the manufacturer must decide whether customers will purchase 50,000 units at $10.18. If the manufacturer thinks they won't, it must decide either to produce a different, more profitable product or to lower the selling price by lowering either its cost or its profit target. Any price above $9.18 will generate some profit, although less than that desired. In the short run, the manufacturer could sell the product for less than $9.18 if competitive factors so dictate, but not below $6.98 because a price below $6.98 would not cover the variable costs of production.

Because the manufacturer's capacity in the short run is fixed, pricing decisions should be aimed at using resources most efficiently. The fixed cost of operating the plant cannot be avoided, and the variable costs can be eliminated only if the firm ceases to offer the product. Therefore, the selling price must be at least equal to the variable costs (per unit) of making the product. Any price above that amount contributes to covering fixed costs and providing a reasonable profit.

Of course, over the long run, the manufacturer cannot sell below total costs and continue to survive. So selling price must cover total product costs—both fixed and variable—and generate a reasonable profit.

IN THE FOOTSTEPS OF AN ENTREPRENEUR...

Putting a Price on Love

The oldest dating site on the Internet is Match.com, which began business in 1995. In an increasingly complex society where time is limited, Match.com had projected revenues of $313 million for 2003. The company's matching system is based on clients' responses to the firm's "personal-attraction" test. Results are analyzed through the application of sophisticated statistical models to produce a personal profile that can then be matched against those of others whose profiles indicate compatibility.

Match.com is not without competition. The following table provides a comparison of key features of Match.com and several of its major competitors:

Company	Started	Unique Visitors in May	Price	What's Special
Match.com	1995	5.1 million	$24.95/month	Personality test (related search is on its way); singles trips and events
AmericanSingles.com	1999	3.6 million	$24.95/month	Prewritten "tease" greetings for the tongue-tied; free chat rooms; only major site to show how many people are on at a given time
Spring Street Networks	1999	3.6 million	$24.95 for 25 e-mail messages	"Play" option searches for people seeking casual relationships; video chat
Yahoo Personals	1997	3.5 million	$19.95/month	"Matchmaker" option lets people post profiles of their friends; video and voice greetings on profile page
Lavalife	1997	669,000	$24.99 for 23 e-mail messages	

Competitors recognize that, excluding porn and gambling Web sites, consumers spend more on dating sites than any other form of online content for a total $228 million per year.

Will these services help you find "true love"? The jury is still out about whether the matching model generates long-term relationships, but Match.com is confident that it produces better dates. The company sees itself as a far superior alternative to single's bars and personal ads in local newspapers. The better sites tend to offer the same options for their clients: description of the client, photos, and e-mail or instant message addresses. The ability to match people is based on the client's answers to the "personal-attraction" test and the use of these data in what Match.com terms the "love algorithm."

Now the bottom-line question: If this model is successful in identifying people with whom you are compatible based on your test results, what would you pay for this service? Currently the fee is $24.95 per month, or about $300 per year. If Match.com's continually refined model increasingly improves the quality of dates, or even leads to marriage, what price would consumers be willing to pay?

1. Currently, prices charged by the top dating Web sites are fairly equal. What message would Match.com send to the market if it raised its monthly fee by $10?
2. How price sensitive do you believe this market is? Why?
3. If Match.com created a series of special niche markets, as other smaller competitors have, could the company raise the price for these services? If so, why?

Source: Adapted from Susan Orenstein, "The Love Algorithm," *Business 2.0,* August 2003, pp. 117–121.

Pricing Techniques for Service Firms

6. Explain the pricing techniques used by service firms.

Service businesses must establish their prices on the basis of the materials used to provide the service, the labor employed, an allowance for overhead, and a profit. As in a manufacturing operation, a service firm must have a reliable and accurate accounting system to keep a tally of the total costs of providing the service. Most service firms base their prices on an hourly rate, usually the actual number of hours required to perform the service. For most firms, labor and materials constitute the largest portion of the cost of the service. To establish a reasonable and profitable price for service, the small business owner must know the cost of materials, direct labor, and overhead for each unit of service. Using these basic cost data and a desired profit

Table 10.2

Direct-Cost Income
Statement, Jerry's TV
Repair Shop

Sales Revenue		$199,000
Variable Expenses:		
Labor	$ 52,000	
Materials	40,500	
Variable factory overhead	11,500	
Total Variable Expenses	$104,000	
Fixed Expenses:		
Rent	$ 2,500	
Salaries	38,500	
Fixed overhead	27,000	
Total Fixed Expenses	$ 68,000	
Total Costs		$172,000
Net Income		$ 27,000

margin, the owner of the small service firm can determine the appropriate price for the service.

Consider a simple example for pricing a common service—television repair. Jerry's TV Repair Shop uses the direct-costing method to prepare an income statement for exercising managerial control (see Table 10.2). Jerry estimates that he and his employees spend about 12,800 hours in the actual production of television repair service. So total cost per productive hour for Jerry's TV Repair Shop comes to the following:

$$\text{Total cost per hour} = \frac{\$172,000}{12,800 \text{ hours}} = \$13.44/\text{hour}$$

Now Jerry must add in an amount for his desired profit. He expects a net operating profit margin of 18 percent on sales. To compute the final price, he uses this equation:

$$\text{Price per hour} = \text{Total cost per productive hour} \times \frac{1.00}{(1.0 - \text{Net profit target as \% of sales})}$$

$$= \$13.44 \times 1.219$$

$$= \$16.38/\text{hour}$$

A price of $16.38 per hour will cover Jerry's costs and generate the desired profit. Smart service shop owners compute the cost per production hour at regular intervals throughout the year because they know that rising costs can eat into their profit margins very quickly. Rapidly rising labor costs and materials prices dictate that the service firm's price per hour be computed even more frequently. As in the case of the retailer and the manufacturer, Jerry must evaluate the pricing policies of competitors and decide whether his price is consistent with the firm's image.

Of course, the price of $16.38 per hour assumes that all jobs require the same amount of materials. If this is not a valid assumption, Jerry must recompute the price per hour without including the cost of materials.

$$\text{Cost per productive hour} = \frac{\$172,000 - 40,500}{12,800 \text{ hours}}$$

$$= \$10.27/\text{hour}$$

Adding in the desired 18 percent net operating profit on sales yields:

$$\text{Price per hour} = \$10.27/\text{hour} \times \frac{1.00}{(1.0 - 0.18)}$$

$$= \$10.27/\text{hour} \times 1.219$$

$$= \$12.52/\text{hour}$$

Under these conditions Jerry would charge $12.52 per hour plus the actual cost of materials used and any markup on the cost of materials. For instance, a repair job that takes four hours to complete would have the following price:

Cost of service (4 hours × $12.52/hour)	$50.08
Cost of materials	$21.00
Markup on materials	$ 2.10
Total price	$73.18

The Impact of Credit on Pricing

Credit Strategies

7. Describe the impact of credit on pricing.

In today's business environment, linking a company's pricing strategy to its credit strategy is essential because consumers increasingly rely on credit cards to make purchases. More than 80 percent of U.S. household have credit cards, and the average household has 17 cards! With more than 1.2 billion credit cards in circulation, customers are rapidly replacing cash with plastic for many of their transactions. The average credit line has climbed from $1,800 in 1992 to $3,500 today, and customers now make 30 percent of their personal consumption expenditures with either credit or debit cards.[12] As one might suspect, shoppers' penchant for credit cards also has led to record levels of consumer debt. This "buy now and pay later" philosophy means that U.S. consumers owe a record $2 trillion in credit card and other debt (excluding real estate–related debt), an amount that exceeds the gross domestic products of India, Russia, Poland, Australia, and South Korea combined![13] To stay competitive, small companies must recognize customers' preference for using plastic to make purchases. In fact, studies show that when stores accept credit cards, shoppers are more likely to make purchases, and the amounts of those purchases are higher than for stores that do not accept credit cards.

The convenience of credit cards is not free to business owners, however. Companies must pay to use the system—typically 1 to 6 percent of the total credit card charges—which they in turn must factor into the prices of their products or services. They also pay a transaction fee of 5 to 50 cents per charge and must purchase or lease equipment to process transactions. Given customer expectations, small businesses find it difficult to refuse major cards, even when the big card companies raise the fees that merchants must pay. Fees operate on a multistep process. On a $100 Visa or MasterCard purchase at a typical business, a processing bank buys the credit card slip from the retailer for $97.44. Then that bank sells the slip to the bank that issued the card for about $98.80. The remaining $1.20 discount is called the interchange fee, which is what the processing bank passes along to the issuing bank. Before it can accept credit cards, a business must obtain merchant status from either a bank or an independent sales organization (ISO). The accompanying "Gaining a Competitive Edge" feature on page 322 describes how a small company can obtain merchant status.

✦ GAINING *a* COMPETITIVE EDGE ✦

How to Obtain Merchant Status

Acquiring merchant status enables small businesses to accept credit-card payments for goods and services, whether they sell online or offline. Offering customers the convenience of paying with credit cards enhances a company's reputation and translates directly into higher sales. Qualifying for a merchant accounts is not easy for many small companies, however, because merchant service providers (MSPs) such as banks view granting merchant accounts in the same manner as making a loan to a business. "When we give you the ability to accept credit cards," explains one banker, "we are giving you the use of funds before we get them." Although small storefront businesses with operating histories of less than two years may have difficulty establishing merchant accounts, home-based businesses and mail-order companies or entrepreneurs doing business over the World Wide Web typically have the greatest difficulty convincing banks to set them up with credit card accounts.

For instance, when Steve and Shelly Bloom, owners of Crystal Collection, a small glass art importer, applied for merchant status, their bank denied their request because their company is home-based. The Blooms then turned to an independent sales organization (ISO) the bank recommended, and the ISO helped them get merchant status through another bank. Because their business represents a higher-than-normal risk to credit card–issuing banks, the Blooms pay higher fees than small storefront companies. Their fees include either 2.5 percent of their monthly credit card transactions or $25 (whichever is higher), a 20 cent per transaction handling fee, a $15 monthly fee, and $32 per month to rent the point-of-sale terminal to process credit card transactions.

What can business owners do to increase their chances of gaining merchant status so that they can accept customers without driving their costs sky-high? Try these tips:

- *Recognize that business start-ups and companies that have been in business less than two years face the greatest obstacles in gaining merchant status.* Entrepreneurs just starting out in business should consider applying for merchant status when they approach a bank for start-up capital. Existing companies can boost their chances of success by preparing a package to present to the bank—credit references, financial statements, business description, and an overview of the company's marketing plan, including a detailed customer profile.

- *Apply with your own bank first.* The best place to begin the application process is with your own bank; ISOs typically charge higher fees than banks. "When we look at an application," says one banker, "we consider three critical things: the principal, the product, and the process. In other words, we need to know about you, what you are selling, and how you are selling it." If your banker cannot set up a credit card account for your business, ask for a referral to an ISO that might be interested.

- *Know what information the MSP is looking for and be prepared to provide it.* Before granting merchant status, banks and ISOs want to make sure that a business is a good credit risk. Treat the application process in the same way you would an application for a loan—because, in essence, it is. In addition to the package mentioned previously, business owners should be able to estimate their companies' credit card volume and their average transaction size.

- *Make sure you understand the costs involved.* When merchants accept credit cards, they do not receive the total amount of the sale; they must pay a transaction charge to the bank. Costs typically include start-up fees ranging from $50 to $200; interchange fees of 25 cents to 70 cents per credit purchase; the discount rate, which is a percentage of the actual sales amount and usually ranges from 1 to 6 percent; monthly statement fees of $4 to $20; equipment rental or purchase costs, which can range from $250 to $1,500 or more; and miscellaneous fees. Some MSPs also hold back a percentage of a merchant's transactions to cover chargebacks, contested fees that are settled in favor of the credit card holder. Many chargebacks are the result of credit card fraud. Because the cost of accepting credit cards can be substantial, business owners must be sure that accepting them will produce valuable benefits.

- *Shop around.* Too often, business owners take the first deal offered to them, only to regret it later. "One of the problems is that merchants are forced by society to give people credit, and they get panicky if they can't take credit cards," says one expert. "So they make a pact with the devil and don't do their due diligence before signing [the merchant status agreement]."

- *Have a knowledgeable attorney look over your contract before you sign it.* Otherwise, you may not discover clauses that work a hardship on your business until it's too late.

Accepting credit cards may not be important for every business, but for those whose customers expect that convenience, acquiring merchant status can spell the difference between making a sale and losing it.

1. Use the World Wide Web to research how e-commerce companies conduct credit-card transactions. How do they secure the privacy of these transactions?

Sources: Adapted from "Merchant Accounts 101," *Small Business Computing,* July 17, 2003, www.smallbusinesscomputing.com/emarketing/article.pho/2236521; Charles Gajeway, "Finished Business," *Small Business Computing,* January 2001, pp. 58–59; Johana S. Billings, "Taking Charge," *Business Start-Ups,* November 1997, pp. 16–18; Lin Gresing-Pophal, "Let Them Use Plastic," *Business Start-Ups,* May 1996, pp. 16–18; Cynthia E. Griffin, "Charging Ahead," *Entrepreneur,* April 1997, pp. 54–57; Frances Cerra Whittelsey, "The Minefield of Merchant Status," *Nation's Business,* January 1997, pp. 38–40; Gajeway, "Finished Business," *Small Business Computing,* January 2001, pp. 58–59.

More small businesses also are equipping their stores to handle debit card transactions, which act as electronic checks, automatically deducting the purchase amount from a customer's checking account. The equipment is easy to install and to set up, and the cost to the company is negligible. The payoff can be big, however, in the form of increased sales.

Although it has become an essential element of business, credit card sales have many associated fees. Not all merchant account providers charge all of these fees, but entrepreneurs can expect to see some of these: (a) application fee (usually waived), (b) equipment fee, (c) licensing fee, (d) transaction fee, (e) holdbacks and chargebacks. Each of these fees is added to the discount rate discussed earlier.

Entrepreneurs need to price their goods and services at a level that reflects the cost associated with the use of credit cards. One advantage of making a sale via a major credit card is the fact that when the issuer of the card approves the transaction, the merchant will be paid. When a sale is paid for by personal check, no such guarantee exists.

E-Business and Credit Cards

When it comes to online business transactions, currently the most common way to make payments is via credit cards. Although credit and charge cards are the most common ways to pay for purchases online, debit cards that authorize merchants to electronically debit your bank account are also being used. Your debit card may be your automated teller machine (ATM) card and may require you to use a personal identification number (PIN). It may be a card that requires only some form of signature or other identification, or it may have a combination of these features. Although using a debit card is similar to using a credit card, there is one important difference: When you use a debit card, the money for the purchase is transferred almost immediately from your bank account to the merchant's account.

The Internet is a dynamic environment and forms of payment are rapidly evolving. So it's no wonder that a number of electronic payment systems—sometimes referred to as "electronic money"—are under development for simplifying purchases online. For example, "stored-value" cards enable consumers to transfer cash value to the card. Some stored value cards work off line (say, to buy a snack at a vending machine); others work online (to buy goods from a Web site); or they may have both features. Some stored value cards contain computer chips that make them "smart" cards: They can act like a credit card as well as a debit card and can also contain stored value.

Some Internet-based payment systems enable value to be transmitted through computers. Consumers can use them to make "micropayments." Micropayments are extremely small payments—for an item like a sheet of music or a short article. When consumers use electronic money to make a purchase, they decrease the balance on their card or computer by the amount of the purchase. Some cards can be "reloaded" with additional value, say, at a cash machine; other cards are "disposable" so you can throw them away after you use them.

Internet vendors are constantly challenged by the need to provide secure ways to transact business in a safe environment. Many potential consumers are hesitant about online transactions for reasons of security and privacy. As a result, computer encryption software is being used to protect customers from theft of their personal financial information, such as credit card numbers, as well as other personal information that would jeopardize customers' privacy. In the very near future, Internet businesses will need to subscribe to these costly encryption software services if they expect to do business. The e-commerce marketplace is virtually global in scope. To participate effectively in this market, the full array of financial and logistics electronic services must be seamless and secure.

Installment Credit

Small companies that sell big-ticket consumer durables—major appliances, cars, and boats—frequently rely on installment credit. Because very few customers can purchase such items in a single lump-sum payment, small businesses finance them over an extended time. The time horizon may range from just a few months up to 30 or more years. Most companies require the customer to make an initial down payment for the merchandise and then finance the balance for the life of the loan. The customer repays the loan principal plus interest on the loan. One advantage of installment loans for a small business is that the owner retains a security interest as collateral on the loan. If the customer defaults on the loan, the owner still holds the title to the merchandise. Because installment credit absorbs a small company's cash, many rely on financial institutions such as banks and credit unions to provide the installment credit. When a business has the financial strength to "carry its own paper," the interest income from the installment loan contract often yields more than the initial profit on the sale of the product. For some businesses, such as furniture stores, this has traditionally been a major source of income.

Trade Credit

Companies that sell small-ticket items frequently offer their customers trade credit; that is, they create customer charge accounts. The typical small business bills its credit customers each month. To speed collections, some offer cash discounts if customers pay their balances early; others impose penalties on late payers. Before deciding to use credit as a competitive weapon, the small business owner must make sure that the firm's cash position is strong enough to support that additional pressure.

For manufacturers and wholesalers, trade credit is traditional. Chapter 8 showed how the potential problems of being unable to adequately control the amount of accounts payable outstanding is a major cause of lost profitability and even total failure. In reality, trade credit is a double-edged sword. Small businesses must be willing to grant credit to purchasers to get, and keep, their business; they must work extremely hard and often be very tough with debtors who do not pay as they agreed to.

▌▐▐ Chapter Review

1. Describe why pricing is both an art and a science.
   - Pricing requires a knowledge of accounting to determine the firm's cost, strategy to understand the behavior of competitors, and psychology to understand the behavior of customers.

2. Discuss the relationships among pricing, image, and competition.
   - Company pricing policies offer potential customers important information about the firm's overall image. Accordingly, when developing a marketing

approach to pricing, business owners must establish prices that are compatible with what their customers expect and are willing to pay. Too often, small business owners *underprice* their goods and services, believing that low prices are the only way they can achieve a competitive advantage. They fail to identify the extra value, convenience, service, and quality they give their customers—all things many customers are willing to pay for.

- An important part of setting appropriate prices is tracking competitors' prices regularly; however, what the competition is charging is just one variable in the pricing mix. When setting prices, business owners should take into account their competitors' prices, but they should not automatically match or beat them. Businesses that offer customers extra quality, value, service, or convenience can charge higher prices as long as customers recognize the "extras" they are getting. Two factors are vital to studying the effects of competition on the small firm's pricing policies: the location of the competitors and the nature of the competing goods.

3. Discuss effective pricing techniques for both new and existing products and services.

- Pricing a new product is often difficult for the small business manager, but it should accomplish three objectives: getting the product accepted; maintaining market share as the competition grows; and earning a profit.
- There are three major pricing strategies generally used to introduce new products into the market: penetration, skimming, and sliding down the demand curve.
- Pricing techniques for existing products and services include odd pricing, price lining, leader pricing, geographic pricing, opportunistic pricing, discounts, multiple pricing, bundling, and suggested retail pricing.

4. Explain the pricing techniques used by retailers.

- Pricing for the retailer means pricing to move merchandise. Markup is the difference between the cost of a product or service and its selling price.
- Some retailers use age of retail price, but others put a standard markup on all their merchandise; more frequently, they use a flexible markup.

5. Explain the pricing techniques used by manufacturers.

- A manufacturer's pricing decision depends on accurate cost accounting records. The most common technique is cost-plus pricing, in which the manufacturer charges a price that covers the cost of producing a product plus a reasonable profit. Every manufacturer should calculate a product's break-even price, the price that produces neither a profit nor a loss.

6. Explain the pricing techniques used by service firms.

- Service firms often suffer from the effects of vague, unfounded pricing procedures and frequently charge the going rate without any idea of their costs. A service firm must set a price based on the cost of materials used, labor involved, overhead, and a profit. The proper price reflects the total cost of providing a unit of service.

7. Describe the impact of credit on pricing.

- Offering customer credit enhances a small company's reputation and increases the probability, speed, and magnitude of customers' purchases. Small firms offer three types of customer credit: credit cards, installment credit, and trade credit (charge accounts).

▌▌▌ Discussion Questions

1. What does the price of a good or service represent to the customer? Why is a customer orientation to pricing important?
2. How does pricing affect a small firm's image?
3. What competitive factors must the small firm consider when establishing prices?
4. Describe the strategies a small business could use in setting the price of a new product. What objectives should the strategy seek to achieve?
5. Define the following pricing techniques: odd pricing, price lining, leader pricing, geographic pricing, and discounting.
6. Why do many small businesses use the manufacturer's suggested retail price? What are the disadvantages of this technique?
7. What is markup? How is it used to determine prices?
8. What is a standard markup? A flexible markup?
9. What is follow-the-leader pricing? Why is it risky?
10. What is cost-plus pricing? Why do so many manufacturers use it? What are the disadvantages of using it?
11. Explain the difference between full-absorption costing and direct costing. How does absorption costing help a manufacturer determine a reasonable price?

12. Explain the techniques used by a small service firm setting an hourly price.
13. What is the relevant price range for a product or service?
14. What advantages and disadvantages does offering trade credit provide to a small business?
15. What are the most commonly used methods to purchase online using credit? What reasons can you give for consumer uncertainty when giving credit card information online as opposed to via the telephone?
16. What advantages does accepting credit cards provide a small business? What costs are involved?
17. What steps should a small business owner take to earn merchant status?

Pricing and Credit Strategies

Business PlanPro

Pricing is an important part of the entire marketing plan, but determining the ideal price for a product or service can be a challenge. Setting a price that is too low may generate lots of sales volume, but it strains a company's ability to earn a profit and generate positive cash flow. Setting a price that is too high sends potential customers scurrying to the competition, and sales never materialize.

Pricing involves both science and art. The first step is determining exactly what it costs your company to provide a product or service to customers. The second step involves establishing a price that covers total costs, generates a profit, and creates the desired image for your business in your customers' minds. Are your company's prices consistent with your target customers' perception of value? The exercises for Chapter 10 that accompany Business Plan Pro are designed to help you determine an acceptable price range for your company's products or services. Once you finish these exercises, you are ready to complete the Pricing Strategy section of Business Plan Pro.

Chapter 11
Integrated Marketing Communications

> *There is no such thing as national advertising. All advertising is local and personal. It's one man or woman reading one newspaper in the kitchen or watching TV in the den.*
>
> —MORRIS HITE

> *To advertise when trade is dull
> Is useless, don't you see?
> I advertise each day, and trade
> Is never dull with me.*
>
> —*PRINTER'S INK* (JANUARY 9, 1895)

Upon completion of this chapter, you will be able to:

1. Explain the value of integrated marketing communications.
2. Describe the basis of an integrated marketing communications plan.
3. Describe the elements of a marketing communications plan.
4. Describe the advantages and disadvantages of the various advertising media.
5. Discuss the four basic methods for preparing a marketing communications budget.
6. Explain practical methods for stretching a small business owner's advertising budget.

Integrated Marketing Communications

1. Explain the value of integrated marketing communications.

Integrated marketing communications is designed to maximize the value of a company's expenditures for advertising, promotion, public relations, direct marketing, and personal selling techniques by ensuring that each element delivers the same clear, consistent, and compelling message about the business and its products or services. The market receives a single powerful reinforcing message from all marketing communications sources. Customers respond best to a positive message that is delivered consistently by each source.

To achieve maximum benefit, all marketing communications must convey the same positive message about the business and its products or services. A company's brand represents the customer's perceptions and feelings about its products or services. Perceptions and feelings exist in the mind of the customer, and when these are very positive feelings, the result is customer loyalty. The strength of a brand is not limited by the size of the firm or its marketing budget, however. Many small local businesses have created a powerful bond with their customers and, consequently, have a strong market position. One goal of an integrated marketing communications strategy is to create *brand equity,* which is measured in terms of customer loyalty and the customer's willingness to pay a premium for the product or service.

Very successful brands have customers who consistently define the product in terms of one or more specific attributes or benefits. For example, Nordstrom department stores are defined by friendly customer service, Volvo automobiles are known for safety, and FedEx for guaranteed overnight delivery. A positive brand image is an intangible asset that must be protected. Consequently, all marketing communications must support and reinforce those initial attributes and benefits that distinguish and differentiate the firm's product or service. For this reason, one of the first steps is to carefully and thoughtfully define the company's *unique selling proposition.*

Branding and Communicating the Unique Selling Proposition

Entrepreneurs should build their integrated marketing communications around a **unique selling proposition (USP),** a key customer benefit or a product or service that sets it apart from its competition. To be effective, a USP must actually *be* unique—something the competition does not (or cannot) provide—as well as compelling enough to encourage customers to buy. One technique is to replace your company's name and logo with those of your top competitor. Does the ad still make sense? If so, the ad is not based on your company's unique selling proposition! Unfortunately, many business owners never define their companies' USP, and the result is an uninspiring "me-too" message that cries out "buy from us" without offering customers any compelling reason to do so.

A successful USP answers the critical question every customer asks: "What's in it for me?" A successful USP should express in no more than 10 words what a business can do for its customers. Can your product or service save your customers time or money, make their lives easier or more convenient, improve their self-esteem, or make them feel better? If so, you have the foundation for building a USP. The USP becomes the heart of your

Company Example ➔ advertising message. *For instance, the owner of a quaint New England bed and breakfast came up with a four-word USP that captures the essence of the escape her business offers guests from their busy lives: "Delicious beds, delicious breakfasts." Sheila Paterson, co-founder of Marco International, a marketing consulting firm, says her company's USP is "Creative solutions for impossible marketing problems."*[1]

The best way to identify a meaningful USP is to describe the primary benefit your product or service offers customers and then to list other secondary benefits it provides. You are unlikely to have more than three top benefits. Be sure to look beyond just the physical characteristics of your product or service. Sometimes the most powerful USP is the *intangible* or *psychological* benefit a product or service offers customers—for example,

Table 11.1

A Six-Sentence Marketing Communications Strategy

> *Does your advertising deliver the message you want to the audience you are targeting? If not, try stating your strategy in six sentences:*
>
> *Primary purpose.* What is the primary purpose of this ad? "The purpose of Rainbow Tours' ads is to get people to call or write for a free video brochure."
>
> *Primary benefit.* What USP can you offer customers? "We will stress the unique and exciting places our customers can visit."
>
> *Secondary benefits.* What other key benefits support your USP? "We will also stress the convenience and value of our tours and the skill and experience of our tour guides."
>
> *Target audience.* At whom are we aiming the ad? "We will aim our ads at adventurous male and female singles and couples, 21 to 34, who can afford our tours."
>
> *Audience reaction.* What response do you want from your target audience? "We expect our audience to call, e-mail, or write to request our video brochure."
>
> *Company personality.* What image do we want to convey in our ads? "Our ads will reflect our innovation, excitement, conscientiousness, and our warm, caring attitude toward our customers."
>
> *Source:* Adapted from Jay Conrad Levinson, "The Six-Sentence Strategy," *Communication Briefings,* December 1994, p. 4.

safety, security, acceptance, status, and others. You must be careful, however, to avoid stressing minuscule differences that are irrelevant to customers. Before developing an integrated marketing communications program, it is also important to develop a brief list of the facts that support your company's USP—for example, 24-hour service, a fully trained staff, awards won, and so on. By focusing the message on these top benefits and the facts supporting them, business owners can communicate their USPs to their target audiences in meaningful, attention-getting ways. Building a firm's marketing message around a USP spells out for customers the specific benefit they get if they buy that product or service and why they should do business with your company rather than with the competition.

Table 11.1 describes a six-sentence marketing communications strategy designed to create powerful ads that focus on a USP.

The Basis of an Integrated Marketing Communications Plan

2. Describe the basis of an integrated marketing communications plan.

Every small business needs a plan to ensure that the money invested in its marketing communications is not wasted. A well-developed plan does not guarantee success, but it does increase the likelihood of achieving positive results. Some entrepreneurs believe that because of limited budgets they cannot afford the luxury of marketing communications. This mind-set views the process as an expense they undertake only when their budgets permit—a leftover expense, something to spend money on if anything remains after paying the other bills. These owners discover, often after it is too late, that communicating with customers is not just an expense; it is an *investment* in a company's future. Advertising, promotion, and public relations can be effective means of increasing sales by informing customers of the business and its goods and services, by improving the image of the firm and its products, or by persuading customers to purchase the firm's goods or services. A megabudget is *not* a prerequisite for building an effective marketing communications campaign. With a little creativity and ingenuity, a small company can make its voice heard above the clamor of its larger competitors and it can do this within

Company Example

a limited budget. *For example, Scott Fiore, owner of The Herbal Remedy, a natural pharmacy in Littleton, Colorado, keeps his company's name in front of customers by using* *traditional advertising media, writing articles on herbal remedies for local magazines, and taking advantage of publicity. Fiore, who spends about $1,400 a month on traditional advertising media, regularly buys radio ads that run during a popular talk show on health because he knows that the show reaches many of his target customers. On several occasions, the show's host has called Fiore to ask questions about a particular herb, giving The Herbal Remedy a promotional boost that normal advertising just cannot buy. Fiore also sponsors a series of free in-store seminars on a variety of health topics, and some have drawn standing-room only crowds. One of the most effective forms of promotion for Fiore is word-of-mouth advertising from satisfied customers. Their positive experience helped Fiore's customer base to grow rapidly. Fiore's promotional efforts are not only fun for both him and his customers, but they also create interest in his store's herbal products and keep his business thriving in the face of larger competitors—and for very little money.*[2]

The first step is to define the purpose of the company's marketing communications program by creating specific, realistic, and measurable objectives. In other words, an entrepreneur must decide, "What do I want to accomplish with my messages?" For instance, some ads are designed to stimulate responses by encouraging customers to purchase a particular product in the immediate future. The object here is to trigger a purchase decision. Other ads seek to build the firm's image among its customers and the general public. These ads try to create goodwill by keeping the firm's name in the public's memory so that customers will recall the firm's name when they decide to purchase a product or service. Still other ads strive to draw new customers, build mailing lists, increase foot traffic in a store, or introduce a company or a product into a new territory.

The second step in developing a marketing communications plan is to focus on the desired target audience. An entrepreneur who does not know the characteristics of the target market cannot effectively reach that target. A marketing communications plan does not have to reach tens of thousands of people to be successful. However, it must efficiently,

Pepper . . . and Salt

THE WALL STREET JOURNAL

"Not much. Roger and I are just sitting around, letting ourselves be targeted by advertisers."

Company Example	→

effectively, and consistently reach the people who are most likely to buy a company's product or services. *In the 1990s, ThermoSpas, a maker of hot tubs, placed ads that featured scantily-clad girls frolicking in its hot tubs in men's magazines such as* Playboy *and* Penthouse. *Sales were anything but bubbly. Today, ThermoSpas targets a different audience, aging baby boomers, with a different message: "We turn water into therapy." Ads now feature silver-haired models and appear in publications such as the* Christian Science Monitor *and* Arthritis Today. *The shift in its marketing communications strategy has worked; ThermoSpas's sales climbed an impressive 20 percent in the first year of its new approach even though industry sales were stagnant.*[3]

An entrepreneur should address the following questions to focus a company's marketing communications efforts.

- What business are we in? How do our products or services create value for our customer?
- What image do we want to project?
- Who are our target customers and what are their characteristics?
- Through which media can they best be reached?
- What do our customers *really* purchase from us?
- What benefits can customers derive from our goods or services?
- How can we prove those benefits to our target customers?
- What sets our company, products, or services apart from the competition?
- How do we want to position our company in the market?
- What advertising approach do our competitors take?

As stated before, answering these questions will help entrepreneurs define their businesses and profile their customers, which will help focus a specific marketing message on the target market and deliver more for their advertising dollars. Defining these issues at the outset enables entrepreneurs to select the media that will reach their target audiences with the least amount of waste. For instance, the owner of a small photography studio specializing in portraits might know from experience that target customers are "parents, ages 25 to 45, with children under 14" and that mothers are the ones who control the buying decision.

Once business owners have defined their target audience, they can design marketing messages and choose the media for transmitting them. At this stage, the owners decide what to say and how to say it. Creativity and originality come into play as advertising, publicity, personal selling, and direct marketing are weaved together for increased marketing impact.

The Elements of a Marketing Communications Plan

3. Describe the operational elements of a marketing communications plan.

Entrepreneurs implement a marketing communications plan by ensuring that all elements of the plan (advertising, publicity, public relations, sponsorships, and personal selling) deliver a consistent message that is based on the firm's unique selling proposition. Each element supports the others and is designed to constantly reinforce the company's fundamental marketing message.

Advertising

Advertising is any sales presentation that is nonpersonal in nature and is paid for by an identified sponsor. The benefit accruing to a business from effective advertising is recognition that lasts for a long time. Effective advertising, in any medium, is constructed on a strong, positive, and well-researched product or brand positioning statement that represents a precise understanding of who the target audience is, how

Figure 11.1

Fundamentals of a
Successful Advertisement

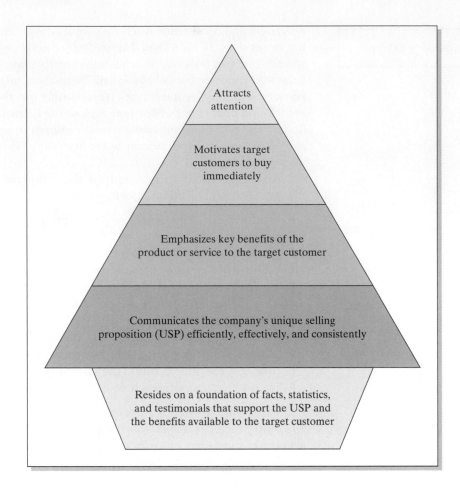

a company's product or services are capable of satisfying their needs and wants, and the message to which customers will respond most positively. Figure 11.1 illustrates the characteristics of a successful ad.

A company's target audience and the nature of its message determine the advertising media it will use. However, the process does not end with creating and broadcasting an ad. The final step involves evaluating the ad campaign's effectiveness. Did it accomplish the objectives it was designed to accomplish? Immediate-response ads can be evaluated in a number of ways. For instance, an owner can include coupons that customers redeem to get price reductions on products and services. Dated coupons identify customer responses over certain time periods. Some firms use hidden offers, which are statements hidden somewhere in an ad that offer customers special deals if they mention an ad or bring in a coupon from an ad. For example, Scott Fiore of The Herbal Remedy puts a "bring this ad in for 10 percent off" message in his print ads so he can track each ad's success rate and adjust his advertising expenditures accordingly.

Business owners can also gauge an ad's effectiveness by measuring the volume of store traffic generated. Effective advertising should increase store traffic, which boosts sales of advertised and nonadvertised items. Of course, if an advertisement promotes a particular bargain item, the owner can judge its effectiveness by comparing sales of the items to preadvertising sales levels. Remember: The ultimate test of an ad is whether or not it increases sales!

Ad tests can help determine the most effective methods of reaching potential customers. An owner can design two different ads (or use two different media or broadcast times) that are coded for identification and see which one produces more responses.

Company Example

For example, a business owner can use a split run of two different ads in a local newspaper. That is, the owner can place one ad in part of the paper's press run and another ad in the remainder of the run. Then the owner can measure the response level to each ad to compare its effectiveness. Table 11.2 offers 12 tips for creating an effective advertising campaign. *Greg Schirf is the founder of Schirf Brewing Company in Park City, Utah. Why would anyone open a brewery in Utah where 70 percent of the population are members of the Church of Latter Day Saints (Mormons), which forbids the consumption of alcohol?*

Table 11.2

Twelve Tips for Effective Advertising

1. *Plan more than one advertisement at a time.* An advertising campaign is likely to be more effective if it is developed from a comprehensive plan for a specific time period. A piecemeal approach produces ads that lack continuity and a unified theme.

2. *Set long-run advertising objectives.* One cause of inadequate planning is the failure to establish specific objectives for the advertising program. If an entrepreneur never defines what is expected from advertising, the program is likely to lack a sense of direction.

3. *Use advertisements, themes, and vehicles that appeal to diverse groups of people.* Although personal judgement influences every business decision, business owners cannot afford to let bias interfere with advertising decisions. For example, you should not use a particular radio station simply because you like it. What matters is whether the company's target customers listen to the station.

4. *View advertising expenditures as investments, not as expenses.* In an accounting sense, advertising is a business expense, but money spent on ads tends to produce sales and profits over time that might not be possible without advertising. An effective advertising program generates more sales than it costs. You must ask, "Can I afford *not* to advertise?"

5. *Use advertising that is different from your competitors' advertising.* Some managers tend to "follow the advertising crowd" because they fear being different from their competitors. "Me-too" advertising frequently is ineffective because it fails to create a unique image for the firm. Don't be afraid to be different!

6. *Choose the media vehicle that is best for your business even if it's not number one.* It is not uncommon for several media within the same geographic region to claim to be "number one." Different media offer certain advantages and disadvantages. Entrepreneurs should evaluate each according to its ability to reach their target audiences most effectively.

7. *Consider using someone else as the spokesperson on your TV and radio commercials.* Although being your own spokesperson may lend a personal touch to your ads, the commercial may be seen as nonprofessional or "homemade." The ad may detract from the company's image rather than improve it.

8. *Limit the content of each ad.* Some entrepreneurs think that to get the most for their advertising dollar, they must pack their ads full of facts and illustrations. But overcrowded ads confuse customers and are often ignored. Simple, well-designed ads that focus on your USP are much more effective.

9. *Devise ways of measuring your ads' effectiveness that don't depend on just two or three customers' responses.* Measuring the effectiveness of advertising is an elusive art at best. But the opinions of a small unrepresentative sample of customers, whose opinions may be biased, is not a reliable gauge of an ad's effectiveness. The techniques described earlier offer a more objective measurement of an ad's ability to produce results.

10. *Do not stop the ad if something does not happen immediately.* Some ads are designed to produce immediate results, but many ads require more time because of the lag effect they experience. One of advertising's rules is: It's not the size; it's the frequency. The head of one advertising agency claims, "The biggest waste of money is stop-and-start advertising." With advertising, patience is essential, and entrepreneurs must give an advertising campaign a reasonable time to produce results. One recent study concluded that sales increases are most noticeable four to six months after an advertising campaign begins. One advertising expert claims that successful advertisers "are not capricious ad-by-ad makers; they're consistent ad campaigners."

11. *Emphasize the benefits that the product or service provides to the customer.* Too often, ads emphasize only the features of the products or services a company offers without mentioning the benefits they provide customers. Customers really don't care about a product's or service's "bells and whistles"; they are much more interested in the *benefits* those features can give them! Their primary concern is "What's in it for me?"

12. *Evaluate the cost of different advertising medium.* Remember the difference between the absolute and relative cost of an ad. The medium that has a low absolute cost may actually offer a high relative cost if it does not reach your intended target audience. Evaluate the cost of different media by looking at the cost per thousand customers reached. Remember: No medium is a bargain if it fails to connect you with your intended customers.

Sources: Adapted from Sue Clayton, "Advertising," *Business Start-Ups,* December 1995, pp. 6–7; The University of Georgia Small Business Development Center, *Marketing for Small Business* (The University of Georgia Small Business Development Center: Athens, Georgia), 1992, p. 69; "Advertising Leads to Sales," *Small Business Reports,* April 1988, p. 14; Shelly Meinhardt, "Put It in Print," *Entrepreneur,* January 1989, p. 54; Danny R. Arnold and Robert H. Solomon, "Ten 'Don'ts' in Bank Advertising," *Burroughs Clearing House,* vol. 16, no. 12, September 1980, pp. 20–24, 43–43; Howard Dana Shaw, "Success with Ads," *In Business,* November/December 1991, pp. 48–49; Jan Alexander and Aimee L. Stern, "Avoid the Deadly Sins in Advertising," *Your Company,* August/September 1997, p. 22.

Greg Schirf's advertising creates great controversy in the conservative state of Utah, and the reaction of authorities to his ads generates a world of free publicity. Consider his irreverent ads, including: "The other local religion, Wasatch Beer" and "Polygamy Porter: Why have just one?" Schirf's ads have been successful in drawing attention to his products, but it is important to recognize that this style has inherent risks.[4]

Publicity and Public Relations

Publicity is any commercial news covered by the media that boosts sales but for which a small business does not pay. It is generated by allowing someone, often a newspaper or magazine writer, to tell a positive story about a business, its people, or its products or services. Publicity can be a powerful influence in how customers view a business because it is viewed as more credible and more objective than advertising.

The following tactics can help any small business owner stimulate publicity for his or her firm:

▪ *Write an article that will interest your customers or potential customers.* Business owners often overlook the fact that newspapers and magazines are almost always in search of interesting and newsworthy material that fits their readerships. One investment adviser writes a monthly column for the local newspaper on timely topics such as retirement planning, minimizing tax bills, and investment strategies. Not only do the articles help build her credibility as an expert, but they also have attracted new customers to her business.

When writing articles, remember to keep them short, with 200 to 300 words for a new product release, 500 to 1,000 words on how your products or services solved a unique problem or helped a customer, and at the most a 3,000-word feature article if addressing a relevant issue on which you or your firm is considered an authority or expert. Whenever possible, support your article with photos, charts, or diagrams that further illustrate your message and improve reader understanding.

▪ *Sponsor an offbeat event designed to attract attention.* Karen Neuburger, owner of Karen Neuburger's Sleepwear, throws pajama parties in stores across the country to promote her line of sleepwear. Local news media almost always cover the party, giving Neuburger's company lots of free exposure.[5]

▪ *Involve celebrities "on the cheap."* Few small businesses can afford to hire celebrities as spokespersons for their companies. Some companies have discovered other ways to get celebrities to promote their products, however. For instance, when Karen Neuburger learned that Oprah Winfrey is a "pajama connoisseur," she sent the talk show host a pair of her pajamas. The move paid off: Neuburger has appeared on Winfrey's popular television show on three separate occasions.[6]

▪ *Contact local TV and radio stations and offer to be interviewed.* Many local news or talk shows are looking for guests to talk about topics of interest to their audiences (especially in January and February). Even local shows can reach new customers.

▪ *Publish a newsletter.* With a personal computer and desktop publishing software, any entrepreneur can publish a professional-looking newsletter. Freelancers can offer design and editing advice. Use the newsletter to reach present and potential customers.

▪ *Contact local business and civic organizations and offer to speak to them.* A powerful, informative presentation can win new business. (Be sure your public speaking skills are up to par first! If not, consider joining Toastmasters.)

▪ *Offer or sponsor a seminar.* Teaching people about a subject you know a great deal about builds confidence and goodwill among potential customers. The owner of a landscaping service and nursery offers a short course in landscape architecture and always sees sales climb afterward.

■ *Write news releases and fax or e-mail them to the media.* The key to having a news release picked up and printed is finding a unique angle on your business or industry that would interest an editor. Keep it short, simple, and interesting. E-mail press releases should be shorter than printed ones—typically four or five paragraphs rather than one or two pages—and they should include a company's Web site address. *Steve Hoffman, cofounder of LavaMind, a CD-ROM game and Web site development company, uses e-mail press releases to generate publicity for his company. Hoffman's e-mail press releases have led to articles in the* New York Times, Wall Street Journal, Business Week, *and others as well as to television coverage on ABC, PBS, and NBC. Hoffman says that half of LavaMind's sales have come as a result of the publicity generated by his e-mail releases.*[7]

■ *Volunteer to serve on community and industry boards and committees.* You can make your town a better place to live and work and raise your company's visibility at the same time.

■ *Sponsor a community project or support a nonprofit organization or charity.* Not only will you be giving something back to the community, but you will also gain recognition, goodwill, and perhaps customers for your business. *The owner of a dry-cleaning business received the equivalent of thousands of dollars' worth of advertising from the publicity generated by a program called "Give the Gift of Warmth." Customers donated winter coats, which the company cleaned for free and then distributed to the needy.*

■ *Promote a cause.* Business owners who have a passion for a cause should act on its behalf. Socially responsible acts often turn into highly successful public relations efforts that attract valuable publicity.

Sponsorships and Special Events

Although sponsorships and special events are a relatively new promotional medium for small companies, a growing number of small businesses are finding that sponsoring special events attracts a great deal of interest and provides a lasting impression of the company in customers' minds. As customers become increasingly harder to reach through any single advertising medium, companies of all sizes are finding that sponsoring special events—from wine tastings and beach volleyball tournaments to fitness walks and car races—is an excellent way to reach their target audiences.

There is a wide range in the cost of sponsorships. Sponsoring a hole at a charitable golf outing may be as little as $100, whereas landing the name of your business or product on the hood of a car driven by a NASCAR legend may cost as much as $7 million. Sponsorships and participation in special events can be very cost effective if the entrepreneur supports events where attendees are potential customers. Local festivals and events gain the sponsor a great deal of positive public relations. Support for charity functions enhances the sponsor's community image and often attracts new customers. *For instance, the owner of one small art gallery generates thousands of dollars' worth of publicity and recognition for her company with her sponsorship of a local art show, from which the proceeds go to a local children's hospital. The gala event features a sidewalk art exhibit, a "meet the artists" luncheon, and a competition among local artists. Hundreds of potential customers flock to her gallery on the night the winners are announced. The sponsorship costs the gallery owner a few thousand dollars, but the "buzz" it generates for her company is worth many times the cost!*

Small companies do not have to rely on other organizations' events to generate advertising opportunities; they can create their own special events. Creativity and uniqueness are essential ingredients in any special event promotion, and most entrepreneurs excel at those. The following tips will help entrepreneurs get the most promotion impact from their sponsorship of an event:

- *Do not count on sponsorships for your entire advertising campaign.* Sponsorships are most effective when they are part of a coordinated advertising effort. Most sponsors spend no more than 10 percent of their advertising budgets on sponsorships.
- *Look for an event that is appropriate for your company and its products and services.* The owner of a small music store in an upscale mountain resort sponsors a local jazz festival every summer during the busy tourist season and generates lots of business among both residents and tourists. Ideally, an event's audience should match the sponsoring company's target audience. Otherwise, the sponsorship will be a waste of money.
- *Research the event and the organization hosting it before agreeing to become a sponsor.* How well attended is the event? What is the demographic profile of the event's visitors? Is it well organized?
- *Try to become a dominant (or, ideally, the only) sponsor of the event.* A small company can be easily lost in a crowd of much larger companies sponsoring the same event. If sole sponsorship is too expensive, make sure that your company is the only one from its industry sponsoring the event.
- *Clarify the costs and level of participation required for sponsorship up front.*
- *Get involved.* Do not simply write a check for the sponsorship fee and then walk away. Find an event that is meaningful to you, your company, and its employees and take an active role in it. Your sponsorship dollars will produce a higher return if you do.

In some cases the line between advertising and promotion has become blurry. In recent years, entrepreneurs have begun to explore new methods of placing their products or services before the targeted market in a more subtle fashion. *Sponsorship* of participants in sporting events or entertainment comes first to mind, such as laundry detergent manufacturers that sponsor NASCAR race teams or musical group tours. They key is to have your product or service identified with an individual, group, or sport that your target customers admire.

Company Example → The next step up the hierarchy is *product placement,* a term that broadly describes the strategy of having your product seen in successful movies or television programs. It is highly sophisticated yet subtle brand exposure. *For example, Roxy, the California clothing company that targets younger consumers with its trendy clothing styles, coproduces a television show for MTV. Throughout the show, the cast wears Roxy clothing exclusively.*[8]

Company Example → *Branded content* is the ultimate integration of advertising and entertainment. Branded content creates an entertainment product (documentary, music video, book, or even Broadway play) to reflect a brand's image or spirit. *For example, Nike's documentary, "The Road to Paris," profiles six-time Tour de France champion cyclist and Nike endorser, Lance Armstrong.*[9]

IN THE FOOTSTEPS OF AN ENTREPRENEUR...

A Minimalists Approach to Marketing

Quiksilver, a California-based company that sells sportswear aimed at aficionados of board sports, walks the fine line between aggressively promoting its brand and its products and maintaining its image as a small firm determined to preserve its brand's "cool." The company began making board shorts and wetsuits in 1970 when two avid surfers from Australia, Alan Green and John Law, developed much-improved surfing shorts designed specifically for surfing and began selling them under the

Quiksilver name. In 1976, surfers Jeff Hakman and Buzz McKnight convinced Green and Law to grant them the license to distribute Quiksilver board shorts in the United States. Hakman and McKnight began the arduous task of building name recognition for their business using word-of-mouth advertising, superior quality, excellent customer service, and their extensive list of contacts at surf shops along the coastal regions of the United States. Quiksilver's innovations in comfortable, durable, and fast-drying fabrics and its cutting-edge colors and designs made its products a hit with teen and young adult markets across the globe. Before long, the company was making clothing for skateboarders and snowboarders as well. In addition to its performance clothing, Quiksilver now offers a diverse line of consumer products, including a complete clothing collection, accessories, eyewear, watches, and wetsuits. The company's Roxy brand targets young women with a line of activewear and swimwear.

Of course, Quiksilver faces plenty of stiff competition, some of it from giant companies with huge advertising budgets such as Nike. Yet, Danny Kwock, another company co-founder, is not threatened by the high profile marketing tactics of the company's competitors. "We don't want to slap our name on everything like we're this big company," he explains. "Big is the enemy of cool."

Yet managers at Quiksilver understand the importance of advertising their brands and keeping their name in front of their target customers, who are famous for their fickle nature and lack of brand loyalty. In addition to traditional advertising methods such as magazine ads, Quiksilver's approach to advertising more often is unique and offbeat. For instance, Quiksilver produced a series of two-and-a-half minute "commercials" featuring popular figures in surfing and skateboarding. The "5-4-3-2-1" episodes portrayed the sports as hobbies that help young people cope with life's problems, but they never once mentioned Quiksilver or any of its brands. Because the spots were not considered advertisements, Fox Sports Network agreed to broadcast them at no charge. Quiksilver's goal, according to Kwock, is to "grow these sports."

Quiksilver also sponsors sports professionals such as six-time world professional surfing champion Kelly Slater and four-time women's world surfing champion Lisa Anderson. Like most of the professionals Quiksilver sponsors, Slater and Anderson are involved in developing new products for Quiksilver. The company also sponsors a number of surf teams

and snowboard teams as well as skateboarders, sailboarders, wakeboarders, and motocross riders as a way of generating publicity.

Another important element of Quiksilver's marketing communications program is the competitive events the company has created. These "Quik" events include both professional and amateur snowboarding, skateboarding, wakeboarding, and surfing competitions that give the company's brands a great deal of exposure.

In 2001, Quiksilver launched an entertainment division that has since created both print and video deals with strategic partners. The company is working with publisher HarperCollins to create a series of fictional books called Luna Bay that follow surfing themes and are aimed at girls between the ages of nine and twelve. Although the books are subtitled *A Roxy Girl Series,* none of the first four books in the series actually mentions Roxy or other Quiksilver products. Quiksilver also partnered with MTV on a reality television series called *Surf Girls* in which 14 amateur surfer girls traveled to exotic locations such as Tahiti, Hawaii, and Samoa for a chance to win a spot in the World Championship Tour of Surfing. Although many of the show's participants wore Roxy clothing, Quiksilver managers encouraged the show's producers to include competitors' clothing brands as well. They wanted to ensure that the show "didn't sell out to the surf community."

Quiksilver's approach to marketing communications may be offbeat, but it seems to be working even though it spends just 4.5 percent of revenue on marketing, compared to Nike's 11 percent. Company sales have reached the $1 billion mark and are growing rapidly. Commenting on the company's unique approach to marketing communications, Taylor Whisenand, Quiksilver's marketing director says, "We don't want to get too mainstream with our marketing."

1. Why does Quiksilver want to avoid getting "too mainstream" with its marketing communications strategy? Do you agree with their decision?
2. Quiksilver veteran Danny Kwock says, "Spending a ton of dough on marketing is the easy way out." What does he mean? What are the implications for the owners of small companies that lack large marketing communications budgets?

Sources: Adapted from "Hangin' $1 Billion," *Business 2.0,* May 2003, p. 30; Maurenn Tkacik, "Quiksilver Keeps Marketing to a Minimum," *Wall Street Journal,* August 28, 2002, p. B4; Tkacik, "Roxy Builds TV, Book Series Around Its Own Surf Wear," *Wall Street Journal,* February 19, 2003, pp. B1, B6; "Company History," Quiksilver, www.quiksilver.com/?pageID=70.

Personal Selling

Advertising and promotion often mark the beginning of a sale, but personal selling usually is required to close the sale. **Personal selling** is the personal contact between salespeople and potential customers resulting from sales efforts. Effective personal selling can give the small company a definite advantage over its larger competitors by creating a feeling of personal attention. Personal selling deals with the salesperson's ability to match customer needs to the firm's goods and services. Top salespeople have the following profile:

- They are enthusiastic and alert to opportunities. They realize that they may find the next great account through a chance social meeting rather than a scheduled sales call. Star sales representatives also demonstrate deep concentration, high energy, and drive.
- They are experts in the products or services they sell. They understand how their product lines or services can help their customers, and they are able to articulate this to customers.
- Top salespeople concentrate on select accounts. They focus on customers with the greatest sales potential.
- They plan thoroughly. On every sales call, the best representatives act with a purpose to close the sale.
- Top salespeople use a direct approach. They get right to the point with customers.
- They work from the customer's perspective. They have empathy for their customers and know their customers' businesses and their needs.
- They use past success stories. They encourage customers to express their problems and then present solutions using examples of past successes.
- They leave sales material with clients. The material gives the customer the opportunity to study the company and product literature in more detail.[10]
- Top salespeople see themselves as problem solvers, not just vendors. Their perspective is "How can I be a valuable resource for my customers?"
- They measure their success not just by sales volume but also by customer satisfaction.[11]

Effective selling is never an accident, and it is wrong to assume that anyone can be successful at personal selling. Selling requires training about the product or service. You cannot effectively sell what you do not understand. And what may be worse, an uninformed salesperson may misrepresent the firm's products or services. Hire capable individuals who display empathy for customers, are personally motivated to succeed, are patient, and possess the ability to focus on the satisfaction of the customer's buying needs.

Sales training needs to be a blend of product or service knowledge as well as the most important basic selling skills of listening to customers and closing the sale.

The Selling Process

Small business owners can improve their sales representatives' "batting averages" by following some basic guidelines.

Establish a Selling System. A successful sales call usually is the result of a systematic sales approach.

1. *Create a feeling of mutual trust and respect.* Establish a rapport with the prospect at the outset. Customers seldom buy from salespeople they dislike or distrust.
2. *Ask the prospect questions that will reveal the key criteria that must be met to obtain the sale.* Customers tend to have a few "must" criteria that will influence their

willingness to buy; identify these and then base your selling approach on meeting or exceeding these key criteria. The goal is to identify the prospect's needs, preferences, concerns, and problems.

3. *Demonstrate, explain, and show.* Make clear the features and benefits of your product or service and point out how they meet the prospect's needs or solve his or her problem.

4. *Validate.* Prove the claims about your product or service. If possible, offer the prospect names and numbers of other satisfied customers (with their permission, of course). Testimonials really work.

5. *Overcome objections.* Listen for objections from the prospect. Try to determine the *real* objection and confront it. Work to overcome it. Objections can be the salesperson's best friend; they tell you what must be "fixed" before the prospect will commit to an order. Remember to focus on the customer's buying criteria.

6. *Close.* Ask for a decision. Good sales representatives know when the prospect flashes the green light on a sale. They stop talking and ask for the order.

Be Empathetic and Stress Value. The best salespeople look at the sale from the customer's viewpoint, not their own! Doing so encourages the sales representative to stress *value* to the customer.

Set Multiple Objectives. Before making a sales call, salespeople should set three objectives:

1. *The primary objective*—the most reasonable outcome expected from the meeting. It may be to get an order or to learn more about a prospect's needs.

2. *The minimum objective*—the very least the salesperson will leave with. It may be to set another meeting or to identify the prospect's primary objectives.

3. *The visionary objective*—the most optimistic outcome of the meeting. This objective forces the salesperson to be open-minded and to shoot for the top.

Monitor Sales Efforts and Results. Selling is just like any other business activity and must be controlled. At a minimum, the business owner should know:

1. Actual sales versus projected sales.
2. Sales generated per call made.
3. Total sales costs.
4. Sales by product, salesperson, territory, customers, and so on.
5. Profit contribution by product, salesperson, territory, customer, and so on.

Selecting Advertising Media

4. Describe the advantages and disadvantages of the various advertising media.

Entrepreneurs quickly discover that there is a wide array of advertising media options, including newspapers, magazines, radio, television, direct mail, the World Wide Web, as well as many specialty media. Each of these media options has both advantages and disadvantages. The relative effectiveness of each media depends on its ability to reach, inform, and influence the customers of the desired target market.

Key Advertising Concepts

One of the most important decisions an entrepreneur must make is which media to use to disseminate the company's message. The medium used to transmit the message influences the customer's perception—and reception—of it. The right message broadcast in the wrong medium is ineffective. Before selecting the vehicle for the message, entrepreneurs should consider several important questions:

How large is my firm's trading area? How big is the geographical region from which the firm will draw its customers? The size of this area influences the choice of media.

Who are my target customers and what are their characteristics? Determining a customer profile often points to the appropriate medium to use to get the message across most effectively.

Which media are my target customers most likely to watch, listen to, or read? Until they know who their target audience is, business owners cannot select the proper advertising media to reach it.

What budget limitations do I face? Every business owner must direct the firm's advertising program within the restrictions of an operating budget. Certain advertising media cost more than others.

What media do my competitors use? It is helpful for small business managers to know the media their competitors use, although they should *not* automatically assume that those avenues are the best choice. An approach that differs from the traditional one may produce better results.

How important is repetition and continuity of my advertising message? Generally, an ad becomes effective only after it is repeated several times, and many ads must be continued for some time before they produce results. Some experts suggest that an ad must be run at least six times in most mass media before it becomes effective.

How does each medium compare with others in its audience, its reach, and its frequency? **Audience** measures the number of paid subscribers a particular medium attracts and is called *circulation* in most print media such as newspapers and magazines. **Reach** is the total number of people exposed to an ad at least once in a period of time, usually four weeks. **Frequency** is the average number of times a person is exposed to an ad in that same time period.

What does the advertising medium cost? There are two types of advertising costs the small business manager must consider: the absolute cost and the relative cost. **Absolute cost** is the actual dollar outlay a business owner must make to place an ad in a particular medium for a specific time period. An even more important measure is an ad's **relative cost,** the ad's cost per potential customer reached. Relative cost is most often expressed as **cost per thousand (CPM),** the cost of the ad per 1,000 customers reached. Suppose a manager decides to advertise his or her product in one of two newspapers in town. The *Sentinel* has a circulation of 21,000 and charges $1,200 for a quarter-page ad. The *Democrat* has a circulation of 18,000 and charges $1,300 for the same space. Reader profiles of the two papers suggest that 25 percent of *Sentinel* readers and 37 percent of *Democrat* readers are potential customers. Using this information, the manager computes the following relative costs:

	Sentinel	**Democrat**
Circulation	21,000	18,000
Percentage of readers that are potential customers (p.c.)	× 25%	× 37%
Potential customers reached	5,250	6,660
Absolute cost of ad	$1,200	$1,300

Relative cost of ad (CPM) $\frac{\$1,200}{5,250} = .22857$ or $228.57 per 1,000 potential customers

$\frac{\$1,300}{6,660} = .19520$ or $195.20 per 1,000 potential customers

Figure 11.2

Advertising Expenditures by Medium

Source: Used by permission. © Universal McCann. All rights reserved

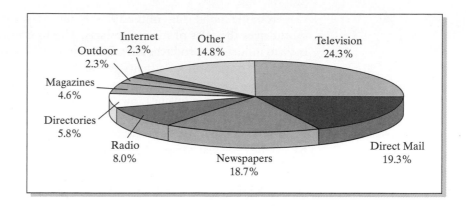

Although the *Sentinel* has a larger circulation and a lower absolute cost for running the ad, the *Democrat* will serve the small business owner better because it offers a lower cost per thousand potential customers (CPM) reached. It is important to note that this technique does not give a reliable comparison across media; it is a meaningful comparison only within a single medium. Differences among the format, presentation, and coverage of ads in different media are so vast that such comparisons are not meaningful.

Traditional Media Options

Choosing advertising media is no easy task because each has distinctive advantages, disadvantages, and cost. The "right" message in the "wrong" medium will miss its mark. Figure 11.2 gives a breakdown of U.S. business advertising expenditures by medium.

Word-of-Mouth Advertising and Endorsements. Perhaps the most effective and certainly the least expensive form of advertising is **word-of-mouth advertising** in which satisfied customers recommend a business to friends, family members, and acquaintances. Unsolicited testimonials are powerful because they carry so much weight among potential customers. The best way to generate positive word-of-mouth advertising is to provide superior quality and service. Providing that level of service and quality leads to loyal customers who become walking advertisements for the companies they believe in. Word-of-mouth advertising can make or break a business because *dissatisfied* customers also speak out against businesses that treat them poorly. To ensure that the word-of-mouth advertising a company generates is positive, business owners must actually do what they want their customers to say they do.

Company Example →

For instance, Fred Anderson, owner of Anderson's Landscape Construction, a landscape planning and design service that targets upscale homeowners, relies totally on word-of-mouth advertising for his company's sales. Anderson counts on referrals from professional architects and from satisfied customers to generate new business. If a customer is unhappy about any aspect of a project his company has done, Anderson fixes it to the customer's satisfaction at no extra charge, which surprises some people.[12]

A customer endorsement is an effective way of converting the power of word-of-mouth to an advertising message. The more recognized the person making the endorsement, the more potential customers will be influenced to buy. Of course, unpaid and unsolicited endorsements are the most valuable. In a cynical world, many potential customers are turned off by what they believe is simply a paid statement from a person who may or may not have used the product. The Holy Grail of word-of-mouth advertising is what experts call "buzz." Buzz occurs when a product is hot and everyone is talking about it.

From the mood rings of the 1970s to the redesigned Volkswagen Beetle of the 1990s, buzz drives the sales of many products. The Internet has only magnified the power of buzz to influence a product's sales. Buzz on the Web has become a powerful force in influencing the popularity of a firm's products or services. What can business owners do to start a buzz about their companies or their products or services? Sometimes buzz starts on its own, leaving a business owner struggling to keep up with the fury it creates. More often than not, however, business owners can give it a nudge by creating interest in, mystique surrounding, and curiosity in a product or service. For instance, record companies have gotten on chat rooms to anonymously hype their new CD releases.

Newspapers. Traditionally, the local newspaper has been the medium that most small companies rely on to get their messages across to customers. Although the number of newspapers in the United States has declined in recent years, the medium attracts nearly 19 percent of all advertising dollars nationwide.

Newspapers provide several *advantages* to the small business advertiser:

Selected geographical coverage. Newspapers are geared to a specific geographic region, and they reach potential customers across all demographic classes. In general, they provide extensive coverage of a company's immediate trading area.

Flexibility. Newspaper advertisements can be changed readily on very short notice. Entrepreneurs can select the size of the ad, its location in the paper, and the days on which it runs. For instance, auto repair shops often advertise their tune-up specials in the sports section on weekends; party shops display their ads in the entertainment section.

Timeliness. Papers almost always have very short closing times, the publication deadline prior to which the advertising copy must be submitted. Many newspapers allow advertisers to submit their copy as late as 24 hours before the ad runs.

Communication potential. Newspaper ads can convey a great deal of information by employing attractive graphics and copy. Properly designed, they can be very effective in attracting attention and persuading readers to buy.

Low costs. Newspapers normally offer advertising space at low absolute cost and, because of their blanket coverage of a geographic area, at low relative cost as well.

Prompt responses. Newspaper ads typically produce relatively quick customer response. A newspaper ad is likely to generate sales the very next day, and advertisers who use coupons can track the response to an ad. This advantage makes newspapers an ideal medium for promoting special events such as sales, grand openings, or the arrival of a new product.

Of course, newspaper advertisements also have *disadvantages:*

Wasted readership. Because newspapers reach such a variety of people, at least a portion of an ad's coverage will be wasted on those who are not potential customers. This nonselective coverage makes it more difficult for newspapers to reach specific target markets than ads in other media can.

Reproduction limitations. The quality of reproduction in newspapers is limited, especially when compared with that of magazines and direct mail. Recent technological advances, however, are improving the quality of reproduction in newspaper ads.

Lack of prominence. One frequently cited drawback of newspapers is that they carry so many ads that a small company's message might be lost in the crowd. The typical newspaper is 62 percent advertising. This disadvantage can be overcome by increasing the size of the ad or by adding color to it. Color can increase the reading of ads by as much as 80 percent over black-and-white ads. Studies show that two-color ads do "pull" better than black-and-white ones but only by a small margin. The *real* increase in ad recall and response comes from using full four-color ads. Bold headlines, illustrations, and photographs also increase an ad's prominence.

Proper ad placement in the newspaper can increase an ad's effectiveness. The best locations are on a right-hand page, near the right margin, above the half-page mark, or next to editorial articles. The most-read sections in the typical newspaper are the main news section and the comics!

Declining readership. Newspaper circulation as a percentage of U.S. households has dropped from 98 percent in 1970 to less than 70 percent today. Newspaper ads are more effective with older adults and those with higher education and income. They are less effective with younger adults.

Short ad life. The typical newspaper is quickly discarded and, as a result, an ad's life is extremely short. Business owners can increase the effectiveness of their ads by giving them greater continuity. Spot ads can produce results, but maintaining a steady flow of business requires some degree of continuity in advertising.

Buying Newspaper Space. Newspapers typically sell ad space by lines and columns or inches and columns. For instance, a 4-column × 100-line ad occupies four columns and 100 lines of space (14 lines are equal to 1 column inch). For this ad, the small business owner would pay the rate for 400 lines. Most papers offer discounts for bulk, long-term, and frequency contracts and for full-page ads. Advertising rates vary from one paper to another, depending on such factors as circulation and focus. Entrepreneurs would do well to investigate the circulation statements, advertising rates, and reader profiles of the various newspapers available before selecting one.

Radio. Newspapers offer blanket advertising coverage of a region, but radio permits advertisers to appeal to specific audiences over large geographic areas. By choosing the appropriate station, program, and time for an ad, a small company can reach virtually *any* target market.

Radio advertising offers several *advantages:*

Universal infiltration. The radio's nearly universal presence gives advertisements in this medium a major advantage. Virtually every home and car in the United States is equipped with a radio, which means that radio ads receive a tremendous amount of exposure in the target market. According to the Radio Advertising Bureau, radio reaches 75 percent of all customers each day and 94 percent of customers each week![13]

Market segmentation. Radio advertising is flexible and efficient because advertisers can choose stations directed toward a specific market within a broad geographic region. Radio stations design their formats to appeal to specific types of audiences. (Ever notice how the stations you listen to are not the same ones your parents listen to?) AM stations, which once ruled the airways, now specialize mainly in "talk formats" such as call-in, news, religion, sports, and automotive shows. On the FM dial, country, top 40, rap, easy listening, modem rock, rhythm and blues, Spanish, and "golden oldies" stations have listener profiles that give entrepreneurs the ability to pinpoint virtually any advertising target.

Flexibility and timeliness. Radio commercials have short closing times and can be changed quickly. Small firms dealing in seasonal merchandise or advertising special sales or events can change their ads on short notice to match changing market conditions.

Friendliness. Radio ads are more "active" than ads in printed media because they use the spoken word to influence customers. Vocal subtleties used in radio ads are

Table 11.3

Guidelines for Producing Effective Radio Copy

- *Mention the business often.* This is the single most important and inflexible rule in radio advertising. Also make sure listeners know how to find your business. If the address is complicated, use landmarks.
- *Stress the benefit to the listener.* Don't say, "Dixon's has new fall fashions." Say, "Dixon's fall fashions make you look fabulous."
- *Use attention-getters.* One key to a successful radio ad is grabbing listeners' attention and holding it. Radio gives the options of music, sound effects, and unusual voices. Crack the barrier with sound.
- *Zero in on your audience.* Know to whom you're selling. Radio's selectivity attracts the right audience. It's up to you to communicate in the right language.
- *Keep the copy simple and to the point.* Don't try to impress listeners with vocabulary. "To be or not to be" may be the best-known phrase in the language. . . and the longest word has just three letters.
- *Sell early and often.* Don't back into the selling message. At most, you've got 60 seconds. Make the most of them. Don't be subtle.
- *Write for the ear.* Write conversationally.
- *Prepare your copy.* Underline words you want to emphasize.
- *Triple space.* Type clean, legible copy. Make the announcer rehearse.
- *Use positive action words.* Use words such as *now* and *today,* particularly when you're writing copy for a sale. Radio has qualities of urgency and immediacy. Take advantage of them by including a time limit or the date the sale ends.
- *Put the listener in the picture.* Radio's theater of the mind means you don't have to talk about a new car. With sounds and music, you can put the listener behind the wheel.
- *Focus the spot on getting a response.* Make it clear what you want the listener to do. Don't try to get a mail response. Use phone numbers only, and repeat the number three times. End the spot with the phone number.
- *Don't stay with a loser.* Direct-response ads produce results right way—or not at all. Don't stick with a radio spot that is not generating sales. Change it.

Source: Radio Basics, Radio Advertising Bureau.

impossible to convey through printed media. Spoken ads can suggest emotions and urgency, and they lend a personalized tone to the message. Table 11.3 offers a guide to producing effective radio copy.

Radio advertisements also have some *disadvantages:*

Poor listening. Radio's intrusiveness into the public life almost guarantees that customers will hear ads, but they may not listen to them. Listeners are often engaged in other activities while the radio is on and may ignore the message.

Need for repetition. Listeners usually do not respond to radio ads after a single exposure to them. Radio ads must be broadcast repeatedly to be effective. Consistency in radio ads is the key to success.

Limited message. Radio ads are limited to one minute or less, so small business owners must keep their messages simple, covering only one or two points. Also, radio spots do not enable advertisers to demonstrate their products or services. Although listeners can hear the engine purr, they can't see the car; spoken messages can only describe the product or service.

Buying Radio Time. The small business owner can zero in on a specific advertising target by using the appropriate radio station. Stations follow various formats—from rap to rhapsodies—to appeal to specific audiences. Radio advertising time usually sells in 15-second, 30-second, and 60-second increments, with the latter being the most common. Fixed spots are guaranteed to be broadcast at the times specified in the owner's contract with the station. Preemptible spots are cheaper than fixed spots, but the advertiser risks being preempted by an advertiser willing to pay the fixed rate for a time slot. Floating spots are the least expensive, but the advertiser has no control over broadcast times. Many stations offer package plans, using flexible combinations of fixed, preemptible, and floating spots.

Radio rates vary depending on the time of day they are broadcast and, like television, there are prime-time slots knows as drive-time spots. Although exact hours may differ from station to station, the following classifications are common (listed in descending order of cost):

Class AA: Morning drive time—6 A.M. to 10 A.M.
Class A: Evening drive time—4 P.M. to 7 P.M.
Class B: Home worker time—10 A.M. to 4 P.M.
Class C: Evening time—7 P.M. to midnight
Class D: Nighttime—midnight to 6 A.M.

Some stations may also have different rates for weekend time slots.

Television. In advertising dollars spent, television now ranks first in popularity of all media. Although the cost of national TV ads precludes their use by most small businesses, local spots can be an extremely effective means of broadcasting a small company's message. A 30-second commercial on network television may cost more than $500,000, but a 30-second spot on local cable television, which now is in more than 75 million U.S. homes, may go for $200 or less. "Prime time spots on broadcast TV cost $2,000 to $3,000 in this area. Prime time cable spots go for $175," says Leslie Speidel, a media buyer in Raleigh, North Carolina.

Television offers a number of distinct *advantages:*

Broad coverage. Television ads provide extensive coverage of a sizeable region, and they may reach a significant portion of the population. About 98 percent of the homes in the United States have a television, and the average household spends 7 hours and 12 minutes each day tuned in to television.[14] Because many cable channels focus their broadcasting on topical areas—from home and garden or food to science or cartoons—cable television offers advertisers the ability to reach specific target markets much as they can through radio ads. Because there is an inverse relationship between time spent in television viewing and education level, television ads overall are more likely to reach people with lower educational levels.

Visual advantage. The primary benefit of television is its capacity to present the advertiser's product or service visually. With TV ads, entrepreneurs are not limited to mere descriptions of a product or service; instead, they can demonstrate its uses and show firsthand its advantages. For instance, a specialty shop selling a hydraulic log splitter can design a television commercial to show how easily the machine works. The ability to use sight, sound, and motion makes TV ads a powerful selling tool.

Flexibility. Television ads can be modified quickly to meet the rapidly changing conditions in the marketplace. Advertising on TV is a close substitute for personal selling. Like a sales representative's call, television commercials can use "hard sell" techniques, attempt to convince through logic, appeal to viewers' emotions, persuade through subtle influence, or use any number of other strategies. In addition, advertisers can choose the length of the spot (30-second ads are most common), its time slot, and even the program during which to broadcast the ad.

Design assistance. Few entrepreneurs have the skills to prepare an effective television commercial. Although professional production firms might easily charge $50,000 to produce a commercial, the television station from which a manager purchases the air time often is willing to help design and produce the ad very inexpensively.

Television advertising also has several *disadvantages:*

Brief exposure. Most television ads are on the screen for only a short time and require substantial repetition to achieve the desired effect. One of the realities is that television viewers often avoid or ignore commercial messages. The commercial is the time to get up and do whatever needs to be done before the program returns.

Clutter. The typical person sees 1,500 advertising messages a day, and more ads are on the way! With so many ads beaming across the airwaves, a small business's advertising message could easily become lost in the shuffle.

"Zapping." **Zappers,** television viewers who flash from one channel to another, especially during commercials, or those who use recording devices such as TiVo to bypass commercials, pose a real threat to TV advertisers. Remote controls invite zapping, which can cut deeply into an ad's target audience. Zapping prevents TV advertisers from reaching the audiences they hope to reach.

Fragmented audience. As the number of channels available proliferates, the question of where to advertise becomes more difficult to answer. Network television has lost audience steadily over the past 20 years to cable television. About 96 percent of cable television households receive more than 30 channels.[15]

Costs. TV commercials can be expensive to create. A 30-second ad can cost several thousand dollars to develop, even before the owner purchases airtime. Advertising agencies and professional design firms offer design assistance—sometimes at hefty prices—so many small business owners hire less expensive freelance ad designers or turn to the stations on which they buy airtime for help with their ads. Table 11.4 offers some suggestions for developing creative television commercials.

Using Television Creatively. Although television ads are not affordable for every small business, many entrepreneurs have found creative ways to use the power of television advertising without spending a fortune. Two popular methods include creating infomercials and using home shopping networks. **Infomercials** (also called direct-response television), full-length television commercials packed with information, testimonials, and a sales pitch, are popular tools for selling everything from mops to computers. Producing and airing a half-hour infomercial can be expensive, often costing $50,000 or more, but entrepreneurs can save money by doing some of the work themselves and hiring freelance professionals for a share of the profits.

| Company Example |

After he launched Smart Inventions, Jon Nokes set out across the country to promote his latest product, the SmartMop, a unique mop from Finland with a self-wringing feature. In its first year, SmartMop generated $1.8 million in sales, but Nokes knew he could do much better if only he could let customers see the benefits of the SmartMop. Nokes worked with a production company to create a 28-minute infomerical for $60,000 to demonstrate the user-friendly

Table 11.4

Guidelines for Creative TV Ads

Source: Radio Basics, Radio Advertising Bureau.

- *Keep it simple.* Stick to a simple concept to avoid confusing the viewer.
- *Have one basic idea.* The message should focus on a single, important benefit to the customer. Why should people buy from your business?
- *Make your point clear.* The customer benefit should be obvious and easy to understand.
- *Make it unique.* To be effective, a television ad must reach out and grab the viewer's attention. Take advantage of television's visual experience.
- *Get viewer attention.* Unless viewers watch the ad, its effect is lost.
- *Involve the viewer.* To be most effective, an ad should portray a situation to which the viewer can relate. Common, everyday experiences are easiest for people to identify with.
- *Use emotion.* The most effective ads evoke an emotion from the viewer—a laugh, a tear, or a pleasant memory.
- *Consider production values.* Television offers vivid sights, colors, motions, and sounds. Use them!
- *Prove the benefit.* Television enables an advertiser to prove a product's or service's customer benefit by actually demonstrating it.
- *Identify your company well and often.* Make sure your store's name, location, and product line stand out. The ad should portray your company's image.

Source: Adapted from *How to Make a Creative Television Commercial,* Television Bureau of Advertising, Inc.

mop. Consumer response to the infomercial amazed even Nokes. Whenever the infomercial aired, orders poured in so that Nokes had to invest in a larger manufacturing facility to keep up with the demand. After a year of airing the infomercial, sales of the SuperMop had climbed to $44 million.[16]

To become an infomercial star, a product should meet the following criteria:[17]

- Be unique and of good quality.
- Solve a common problem.
- Be easy to use and easy to demonstrate.
- Appeal to a mass audience.
- Have an aha! factor that makes customers think "What a great idea!"

Shopping networks such as QVC and the HSN offer entrepreneurs another route to television. Time on these networks is free, but getting a product accepted is tough. Only a small percentage of the products reviewed by QVC and HSN are featured on the show. Shopping networks look for products that offer quality, have "demonstration appeal," and are typically priced between $15 and $50 (although there are exceptions). Landing a product on one of these networks may be a challenge, but entrepreneurs who do often sell thousands of units in a matter of minutes. *After they won a QVC product search competition, Kim and Scott Holstein, founders of Kim & Scott's Gourmet Pretzels, appeared 20 times on the popular television shopping network. As a result, traffic on their Web site jumped 400 percent in just two months, and sales climbed 80 percent within one year.*[18]

> Company Example →

Magazines. Another advertising medium available to the small business owner is magazines. Today, customers have more than 18,600 magazine titles from which to choose.[19] Magazines have a wide reach; nearly 9 out of 10 adults read an average of 7 different magazines per month. The average magazine attracts 6 hours and 3 minutes of total adult reading time, and studies show that the reader is exposed to 89 percent of the ads in the average copy.[20]

Magazines offer several *advantages* for advertisers:

Long life spans. Magazines have a long reading life because readers tend to keep them longer than other printed media. Few people read an entire magazine at one sitting. Instead, most pick it up, read it at intervals, and come back to it later. The result is that each magazine ad has a good chance of being seen several times.

Multiple readership. The average magazine has a readership of 3.9 adult readers, and each reader spends about one hour and 33 minutes with each copy. Many magazines have a high "pass-along" rate; they are handed down from reader to reader. For instance, the in-flight magazines on jets reach many readers.

Target marketing. By selecting the appropriate special-interest periodical, small business owners can reach those customers with a high degree of interest in their goods or services. Once business owners define their target markets, they can select magazines whose readers most closely match their customer profiles. For instance, *House and Garden* magazine reaches a very different audience than *Rolling Stone.*

Ad quality. Magazine ads usually are of high quality. Photographs and drawings can be reproduced very effectively, and color ads are readily available. Advertisers can also choose the location of their ads in a magazine and can design creative ads that capture readers' attention.

Magazines also have several *disadvantages:*

Costs. Magazine advertising rates vary according to their circulation rates; the higher the circulation, the higher the rate. Thus, local magazines, whose rates are often comparable to newspaper rates, may be the best bargain for small businesses.

Long closing times. Another disadvantage of magazines is the relatively long closing times they require. For a weekly periodical, the closing date for an ad may be several weeks before the actual publication date, making it difficult for advertisers to respond quickly to changing market conditions.

Lack of prominence. Another disadvantage of magazine ads arises from their popularity as an advertising vehicle. The effectiveness of a single ad may be reduced because of a lack of prominence; 48.3 percent of the typical magazine content is devoted to advertising.[21] Proper ad positioning, therefore, is critical to an ad's success. Research shows that readers "tune out" right-hand pages and look mainly at left-hand pages.

Specialty Advertising. As advertisers have shifted their focus to "narrowcasting" their messages to target audiences and away from "broadcasting," specialty advertising has grown in popularity. Advertisers now spend more than $3 billion annually on specialty items. This category includes all customer gift items imprinted with the company's name, address, telephone number, and slogan. Specialty items are best used as reminder ads to supplement other forms of advertising and help to create goodwill among existing and potential customers.

Specialty advertising offers several *advantages*:

Reaching select audiences. Advertisers have the ability to reach specific audiences with well-planned specialty items.

Personalized nature. By carefully choosing a specialty item, business owners can "personalize" their advertisements. When choosing advertising specialties, a small business owner should use items that are unusual, related to the nature of the business, and meaningful to customers.

Versatility. The rich versatility of specialty advertising is limited only by the business owner's imagination. Advertisers print their logos on everything from pens and scarves to wallets and caps.

There are *disadvantages* to specialty advertising:

Potential for waste. Unless business owners choose the appropriate specialty item, they will be wasting their time and money. The options are virtually unlimited.

Costs. Some specialty items can be quite expensive. Plus, some owners have a tendency to give advertising materials to anyone—even to those who are not potential customers.

Point-of-Purchase Ads. In the last several years, in-store advertising has become more popular as a way of reaching the customer at a crucial moment—the point of purchase. Research suggests that consumers make 66 percent of all buying decisions at the point of sale.[22] Self-service stores are especially well suited for in-store ads because they remind people of the products as they walk the aisles. These in-store ads are not just simple signs or glossy photographs of the product in use. Some businesses use in-store music interspersed with household hints and, of course, ads. Another ploy involves tiny devices that sense when a customer passes by and trigger a prerecorded sales message.

Outdoor Advertising. National advertisers have long used outdoor ads. This medium is proving to be popular among small firms (especially retailers) as well. Spending on outdoor ads is growing at a rate faster than that of most other media, at nearly 10 percent a year. Very few small businesses rely solely on outdoor advertising; instead, they supplement other advertising media with billboards. With a creative outdoor campaign, a small

Company Example ⟶ company can make a big impact on a small budget. *Hamp Lindsey, owner of Wade's Restaurant, a family-style restaurant that Lindsey's father started in 1947, has achieved a high level of name recognition in his market in Spartanburg, South Carolina. After customers repeatedly told Lindsey how much they enjoyed his restaurant's home-style vegetables and meat, he decided to focus his advertising message there. Lindsey launched an outdoor ad campaign (without the help of an advertising agency) when the idea for a "Bean me up, Scottie" slogan came to him. Before he knew it, customers were recommending their own clever slogans such as "Sas-squash," "Darth-Tater," and "Spider-Ham," all of which became part of an ongoing outdoor ad campaign with whimsical illustrations.*[23]

Outdoor advertising offers certain *advantages* to a small business:

High exposure. Outdoor advertising offers a high-frequency exposure; studies suggest that the typical billboard reaches an adult 29 to 31 times each month. Most people tend to follow the same routes in their daily traveling, and billboards are there waiting for them when they pass by.

Broad reach. The nature of outdoor ads makes them effective devices for reaching a large number of potential customers within a specific area. Not only has the number of cars on the road increased, but the number of daily vehicle trips people take has also climbed. In addition, the people outdoor ads reach tend to be younger, wealthier, and better educated than the average person.

Attention-getting. The introduction of new technology such as 3-D, fiber optics, and other creative special effects to outdoor advertising has transformed billboards from flat, passive signs to innovative, attention-grabbing promotions that passers-by cannot help but notice.

Flexibility. Advertisers can buy outdoor advertising units separately or in a number of packages. Through its variety of graphics, design, and unique features, outdoor advertising enables small advertisers to match their messages to a particular audience.

Cost efficiency. Outdoor advertising offers one of the lowest costs per thousand customers reached of all advertising media. Experts estimate the cost per thousand viewers (CPM) for outdoor ads is about $2, compared to $5 for drive-time radio spots, $9 for magazine ads, and $10 to $20 for newspaper ads and prime-time television spots.[24]

Outdoor ads also have several *disadvantages*:

Brief exposure. Because billboards are immobile, the reader is exposed to the advertiser's message for only a short time—typically no more than 5 seconds. As a result, the message must be short and to the point.

Limited ad recall. Because customers often are zooming past outdoor ads at high speed, they are exposed to an advertising message very briefly, which limits their ability to retain the message.

Legal restrictions. Outdoor billboards are subject to strict regulations and to a high degree of standardization. Many cities place limitations on the number and type of signs and billboards allowed along the roadside.

Lack of prominence. A clutter of billboards and signs along a heavily traveled route tends to reduce the effectiveness of a single ad that loses its prominence among the crowd of billboards.

Using Outdoor Ads. Technology has changed the face of outdoor advertising dramatically in recent years. Computerized painting techniques render truer, crisper, and brighter colors and have improved the quality of outdoor ads significantly. Vinyl surfaces accept print-quality images and are extremely durable. Digital technology, three-dimensional effects, computerized lighting, and other advances enable companies to create animated, continuous-motion ads that really capture viewers' attention at reasonable cost. Because the outdoor ad is stationary and the viewer is in motion, small business owners must pay special attention to its design. An outdoor ad should:

- Identify the product and the company clearly and quickly.
- Use a simple background. The background should not compete with the message.

It's hard to focus on a particular ad in all of this roadside clutter—especially while driving!

- Rely on large illustrations that jump out at the viewer.
- Include clear, legible type. All lowercase or a combination of uppercase and lowercase letters works best. Very bold or very thin typefaces become illegible at a distance.
- Use black-and-white designs. Research shows that black-and-white outdoor ads are more effective than color ads. If color is important to the message, pick color combinations that contrast both hue and brightness—for example, black on yellow.
- Emphasize simplicity; short copy and short words are best. Don't try to cram too much onto a billboard. One study found that ads with fewer than eight words were most effective and those containing more than 10 words were least effective.
- Be located on the right-hand side of the highway.

One of the latest trends in outdoor advertising is "talking billboards." The text directs viewers to tune into a specific radio frequency, where they hear a short commercial. Those who tune in hear jokes, skits, and, of course, a commercial for the company and its products.

Transit Advertising. Transit advertising includes advertising signs inside and outside some 70,000 public transportation vehicles throughout the country's urban areas. The medium is likely to grow as more cities look to public transit systems to relieve transportation problems.

Transit ads offer a number of *advantages:*

Wide coverage. Transit advertising offers advertisers mass exposure to a variety of customers. The message literally goes to where the people are. This medium also reaches people with a wide variety of demographic characteristics.

Repeat exposure. Transit ads provide repeated exposure to a message. The typical transit rider averages 24 rides per month and spends 61 minutes per day riding.

Low cost. Even small business owners with limited budgets can afford transit advertising. One study shows that transit advertising costs on average only $0.30 per thousand.[25]

Flexibility. Transit ads come in a wide range of sizes, numbers, and duration. With transit ads, a business owner can select an individual market or any combination of markets across the country.

Transit ads also have several *disadvantages:*

Generality. Even though a small business can choose the specific transit routes on which to advertise, it cannot target a particular segment of the market through transit advertising. The effectiveness of transit ads depends on the routes that public vehicles travel and on the people they reach, which, unfortunately, the advertiser cannot control.

Limited appeal. Unlike many media, transit ads are not beamed into the potential customer's residence or business. The result is that customers cannot keep them for future reference. Also, these ads do not reach with great frequency the upper-income, highly educated portion of the market.

Brief message. Transit ads do not permit the small advertiser to present a detailed description or a demonstration of the product or service for sale. Although inside ads have a relatively long exposure (the average ride lasts 22.5 minutes), outside ads must be brief and to the point.

Direct Mail. Direct mail has long been a popular method of direct marketing and includes such tools as letters, postcards, catalogues, discount coupons, brochures, computer disks, and videotapes mailed to homes or businesses. The earliest known catalogues were printed by fifteenth-century printers. Today, direct-mail marketers sell virtually every kind of product imaginable from Christmas trees and lobsters to furniture and clothing (the most popular mail-order purchase). Responding to the convenience of "shopping at home," customers purchase more than $500 billion worth of goods and services through mail order each year.

Direct mail offers some distinct *advantages* to the small business owner:

Selectivity. The greatest strength of direct-mail advertising is its ability to target a specific audience to receive the message. Depending on mailing list quality, an owner can select an audience with virtually any set of characteristics. Small business owners can develop, rent, or purchase a mailing list of prospective residential, commercial, or industrial customers.

Flexibility. Another advantage of direct mail is its capacity to tailor the message to the target. The advertiser's presentation to the customer can be as simple or as elaborate as necessary. For instance, one custom tailor shop achieved a great deal of success with fliers it mailed to customers on its mailing list when it included a swatch of material from the fabric for the upcoming season's suits. With direct mail, the tone of the message can be personal, creating a positive psychological effect. In addition, the advertiser controls the timing of the campaign; he or she can send the ad when it is most appropriate.

Reader attention. With direct mail, an advertiser's message does not have to compete with other ads for the reader's attention. People enjoy getting mail, and more than half of us open and read what we receive. For at least a moment, direct mail gets the recipient's undivided attention. If the message is on the mark and sent to the right audience, direct mail ads can be a powerful advertising tool.

Rapid feedback. Direct mail advertisements produce quick results. In most cases, the ad will generate sales within three or four days after customers receive it. Business owners should know whether a mailing has produced results within a relatively short time period.

Measurable results and testable strategies. Because they control their mailing lists, direct marketers can readily measure the results their ads produce. Also, direct mail enables advertisers to test different ad layouts, designs, and strategies (often within the same "run") to see which one "pulls" the

Table 11.5

Guidelines for Creating Direct-Mail Ads That Really Work

"Mail order means trend watching, meticulous planning, and devouring news and information on the industry, your niche, technology, politics, and the world—and that's just for starters," says one observer. "You'll have to deal with the laws of a vast federal bureaucracy and 50 states (plus a couple hundred countries if you go international), the intricacies of designing and mailing a catalog, and the fickle nature of a demanding public."

You'll also have to write copy that will get results. Try these proven techniques:

- Promise readers your most important benefit in the headline or first paragraph.
- Use short "action" words and paragraphs.
- Make the copy look easy to read with lots of "white space."
- Use eye-catching words such as *free, you, save, guarantee, new, profit, benefit, improve,* and others.
- Consider using computerized "handwriting" somewhere on the page or envelope; it attracts attention.
- Forget grammatical rules; write as if you were speaking to the reader.
- Repeat the offer three or more times in various ways.
- Back up claims and statements with proof and endorsements whenever possible.
- Ask for the order or a response.
- Ask questions such as "Would you like to lower your home's energy costs?" in the copy.
- Use high-quality copy paper and envelopes (those with windows are best) because they stand a better chance of being opened and read. Brown envelopes that resemble government correspondence work well.
- Envelopes that resemble bills almost always get opened.
- Address the envelope to an individual, not "Occupant."
- Use stamps if possible. They get more letters opened than metered postage.
- Use a postscript (P.S.) always—they are the most often read part of a printed page. Make sure the P.S. contains a "hook" that will encourage the recipient to read on.
- Include a separate order form that passes the following "easy" test:

  Easy to find. Consider using brightly colored paper or a unique shape.
  Easy to understand. Make sure the offer is easy for readers to understand. Marketing expert Paul Goldberg says, "Confuse 'em and you lose 'em."
  Easy to complete. Keep the order form simple and unconfusing.
  Easy to pay. Direct mail ads should give customers the option to pay by whatever means is most convenient.
  Easy to return. Including a postage-paid return envelope (or at a minimum a return envelope) will increase the response rate.

- *Build and maintain a quality mailing list over time.* The right mailing list is the key to a successful direct mail campaign. You may have to rent lists to get started, but once you are in business, use every opportunity to capture information about your customers. Constantly focus on improving the quality of your mailing list.

Sources: Adapted from Kim T. Gorcon, "Copy Right," *Business Start-Ups,* June 1998, pp. 18–19; Paul Hughes, "Profits Due," *Entrepreneur,* February 1994, pp. 74–78; "Why They Open Direct Mail," *Communications Briefings,* December 1993, p. 5; Ten Lammers, "The Elements of Perfect Pitch," *Inc.,* March 1992, pp. 53–55; "Special Delivery," *Small Business Reports,* February 1993, p. 6; Gloria Green and James W. Peltier, "How to Develop a Direct Mail Program," *Small Business Forum,* Winter 1993/1994, pp. 30–45; Susan Headden, "The Junk Mail Deluge," *U.S. News & World Report,* December 8, 1997, pp. 40–48.

greatest response. The best direct marketers are always fine-tuning their ads to make them more effective. Table 11.5 offers guidelines for creating direct mail ads that really work.

Effectiveness. The right message targeted at the right mailing list can make direct mail one of the most efficient forms of advertising. Direct mail to the right people produces results.

Direct-mail ads also suffer from several *disadvantages:*

Inaccurate mailing lists. The key to the success of the entire mailing is the accuracy of the customer list. A poor list is a waste of money.

Clutter. The average person in the United States receives more than 600 pieces of direct mail each year. With that volume of direct mail, it can be difficult for an advertisement to get customers' attention.

High relative costs. Relative to the size of the audience reached, the cost of designing, producing, and mailing an advertisement via direct mail is high. But if the mailing is well planned and properly executed, it can produce a high percentage of returns, making direct mail one of the least expensive advertising methods in terms of results.

Rising postal rates. One of the primary causes of the high costs of direct mail ads is postage costs, which continue to rise.

High throwaway rate. Often called junk mail, direct-mail ads become "junk" when an advertiser selects the wrong audience or broadcasts the wrong message. In fact, the typical direct-mail advertising campaign can supplement its traditional direct-mail pieces with toll-free (800) numbers and carefully timed follow-up phone calls.

How to Use Direct Mail. The key to a direct mailing's success is the right mailing list. Even the best direct-mail ad will fail if sent to the "wrong" customers. Owners can develop lists themselves, using customer accounts, telephone books, city and trade directories, and other sources. Other sources for mailing lists include companies selling complementary but not competing products; professional organizations' membership lists; business or professional magazines' subscription lists; and mailing list brokers who sell lists for practically any need. Advertisers can locate list brokers through *The Direct Marketing List Source* from the Standard Rate and Data Service found in most public libraries.

"High-Tech" Direct Mail. Sending out ads on CDs is an excellent way to reach upscale households and businesses. Not only do computer-based ads give advertisers the power to create flashy, attention-grabbing designs, but they also hold the audience's attention.

Compact discs (CDs) offer advertisers the same benefits as computer disks with one extra—more space to do it in. Companies are using CDs with interactive ads to sell everything from cars to computers. The ads usually contain videos, computer games, quizzes, animation, music, graphics, and other features to engage more of their audiences' senses. In a world in which U.S. households receive *4.5 million tons* of paper each year in the form of direct-mail ads, multimedia ads can offer a distinct advantage: They get noticed.

The World Wide Web. The past decade has witnessed the World Wide Web reshape the way companies conduct business and transform e-commerce into a major economic force. Just as the Web has become a common tool for conducting business, it also has become a popular medium for advertisers. Increasingly, small businesses are turning to the World Wide Web as a valuable way to reach their customers and to build an awareness of their products and services. The Internet has proved to be the fastest-growing advertising medium in history. Using the time required for radio, television, and the Internet to reach 50 million users as a basis for comparing the three media, the Internet is the clear winner. Radio required 38 years to reach that milestone, and television took 13 years; the Internet, however, hit 50 million users in just

Company Example

five years. *One couple living in the remote town of Torrey, Utah, has figured out a way to reach their particular market through the use of a Web site. Eldon and Erika Reed are owners of the Torrey Pines Inn near Capital Reef national park in south central Utah. Capital Reef is the least visited national park, but it is the one most frequented by the citizens of Utah. Typical visitors to the park lead an active lifestyle and enjoy the remote hiking trails and campsites located throughout the more than 200,000 acres of unspoiled wilderness. Potential visitors looking to stay in more comfortable lodging can easily access www.torreypinesinn.com and find information on the various accommodations, rates, and local information. In addition, keeping in touch with former visitors through the Internet is one way to increase the odds of a return visit!*

The Web's multimedia capabilities make it an ideal medium for companies to demonstrate their products and services with full motion, color, and sound and to get customers involved in the demonstration. Businesses that normally use direct mail can bring the two-dimensional photos and product descriptions in their print catalogues to life, avoid the expense of mailing them, and attract new customers that traditional mailings might miss.

Advertisements on the Web take five basic forms: banner ads, cookies, full-page ads, "push" technology ads, and e-mail ads. **Banner ads** are small rectangular ads that reside on Web sites, much like roadside billboards, touting a company's product or service. When visitors to a site click on the banner ad, they go straight to the advertiser's home page. One measure of a banner ad's effectiveness is the number of impressions it produces. An **impression** occurs every time an ad appears on a Web page, whether or not the user clicks on the ad to explore it. Another common way of judging banner ads is the **click-through rate,** which is calculated by dividing the number of times customers actually click on the banner ad by the number of impressions for that ad. The cost of a banner ad to an advertiser depends on the number of users who actually click on it. The cost of creating a banner ad ranges from practically nothing for do-it-yourselfers to as much as $3,000 if the ad is designed by a professional and includes animation and high levels of interactivity.

Banner ads do not have to be expensive, however. Many small business owners increase the exposure their banner ads receive by joining a banner exchange program that is similar to advertising cooperatives. In a banner exchange program, member companies can post their banners on each other's sites. These programs work best for companies selling complementary products or services. For instance, a small company selling gourmet food products over the Web might exchange banner ads with a company using the Web to sell fine wines or one selling upscale kitchen tools and appliances. Two of the largest banner exchange Web sites are Microsoft bCentral and Smartclicks.

The primary disadvantage of banner ads is that Web users can easily ignore them. These ads have become such a part of the Web page landscape that frequent users may tend to ignore them. As this phenomenon expands, Web designers search for the best page placement for banner ads, as well as any "bells and whistles" that will attract browsers and encourage them to click through. One newer form of Web advertising is more difficult to ignore. Known as an **interstitial** or **pop-up,** this is a separate window of advertising that pops open spontaneously, blocking the site behind it. It is designed to grab consumers' attention for the few nanoseconds it takes them to close the window. The danger, of course, is that the attention received is not necessarily positive. These ads are often perceived as an annoying intrusion. A slight variation on this is the "pop-under" ad that immediately goes behind the active screen but stays open until the browser window is closed.

IN THE FOOTSTEPS OF AN ENTREPRENEUR...

Flowers Are Popping Up on the Web

Mike Perry considers the basement of the flower shop started by his parents in 1959 to be his strategic bunker. From there he is launching a counterattack on the company's competitors, including the flower departments of the local Home Depot and 7-Eleven, that are cutting into the sales of Perry's Florist. His weapon: the World Wide Web. When Perry first started, his tactics worked well, and the Long Island flower shop was selling flowers to customers across the United States from its Web site, which Perry promoted primarily through paid search engine listings. Soon, however, Perry found it hard to compete with the Web-based sales efforts of industry

giants such as 1–800-Flowers.com and FTD.com, whose Web sites dominated search engine listings. As more large companies began bidding for prime search engine placement, Perry found the cost of search engine placement too high for his small business.

Perry returned to his basement headquarters to rethink his online strategy and came up with another winning idea for selling flowers online: pop-up ads. Although much loathed by most Web users, pop-up ads have helped sales at Perry's Florist bloom from $1 million to more than $2.75 million in less than five years. Perry says that one-third of the company's sales come from new customers that the pop-up ads have attracted.

Skeptical about using pop-up ads when his online advertising agency first suggested them ("They're annoying to me as an Internet user," he says), Per has become a believer. He says that if done properly, pop-up ads can generate online sales. Software called adware that piggybacks on programs users download for free such as ClockSync and WeatherCast generate pop-up ads for Perry's Florist. Once installed (often without the user's knowledge), these programs track the Web sites the user visits and then generate pop-up ads related to that content. The idea is to produce a pop-up ad just when the user is most interested in the product.

Perry signed up for a test run that would cost him 36 cents every time a user clicked on one of his pop-up ads. The results were immediate and surprising. "I was blown away," says Perry. Web analytics showed that he was paying between $9 and $10 to make a sale that averaged $60. On a typical sale, Perry's Florist received $6.99 in service fees that the customer paid and a $5 rebate from the floral network such as FTD that the shop used to fulfill the order. (Most of the orders he receives online are outside the central Long Island area Perry's store serves, so he relies on floral networks to fill the orders.) Perry's Florist also receives 20 percent of the sale price from the florist who actually delivers the flowers. In all, Perry's Florist receives $24 on a typical Web-generated order. Subtracting the company's approximate $9 total cost to acquire the order leaves the florist with a profit of $15 per sale.

Perry is so pleased with the advertising technique that he now spends more than $130,000 a year on pop-up ads. Although the cost to acquire an order has crept up to $12, sales to first-time customers through pop-up ads have climbed to an impressive $750,000 a year. The company's weekly sales volume is about 800 orders, one-third more than the amount Perry was generating sales through search engine referrals. Perry's only concern is the potential for alienating customers with the pop-up ads. Still, he says, of the thousands of people who see his ads each week, he receives complaints from just two or three people. Although software that can disable pop-ups is available, few people bother to use it, which is good news for Perry's Florist. Perry is now beginning to see some of his competitors using pop-up ads as well, and he wonders how long his competitive edge will last.

1. How do you feel about pop-up ads on the Internet?
2. What ethical issues does Perry face by using pop-up ads? Should Perry continue to use pop-up ads to attract customers? Explain.
3. What other marketing techniques can you recommend that Perry consider using to attract customers to the Perry's Florist Web site?

Sources: Adapted from Josh Taylor, "Flowers That Pop," *FSB,* December 2003/January 2004, pp. 59–60; Michael Totty, "Pesky Pop-Up Internet Ads Go Mainstream, as 'Adware' Gains Acceptance," *Wall Street Journal,* June 22, 2004, pp. B1, B3; "About Us," Perry's Florist, www.perrysflorist.com/about.cfm.

Cookies are small programs that attach to users' computers when they visit certain Web sites. These programs track the locations users visit while in the site and use this electronic footprint to send pop-up ads that would be of interest to the user. For instance, a Web user who frequently visits garden sites might find ads for garden tools and seed companies popping up on the screen. Many sites that require users to register before they can enter are collecting information to create cookie files. Cookies cannot access a user's computer, read sensitive information such as a credit card numbers or passwords, or send such data back to the company that created the cookie. Nor can they alter the files on a computer's hard drive. Cookies can, however, track users' Web browsing patterns, revealing which pages they view and how often they view them. Because cookies record users' Web use and habits transparently (and usually without users' express permission), their use has become somewhat controversial. Some companies use the information they glean from cookies to make inferences about customers' interests and then target ads at them based on those inferences.

Full-page ads are those that download to Web users' screens before they can access certain Web sites. They are common on popular game sites that attract a high volume of Web traffic. **Push technology ads** appear on users' screens when they download information such as news, sports, or entertainment from another site. For instance, a Web user downloading sports information might receive an ad for athletic shoes or

T-shirts with the information. One advantage of Web advertising is its ability to track the results that an ad produces. Web technology enables advertisers to count the number of visitors to a site and to track the number of people who actually click on the ads placed there.

Nua Internet Surveys estimates that the number of individuals online currently exceeds 600 million worldwide. E-mail is the most common application on the Internet, and e-mail advertising capitalizes on that popularity. **E-mail advertising,** in which companies broadcast their message via e-mail, has expanded at an unprecedented rate. E-mail advertising takes two forms: permission e-mail and spam. As its name suggests, **permission e-mail** involves sending e-mail ads to customers with their permission; **spam** is unsolicited commercial e-mail. Because most e-mail users see spam as a nuisance, they often view companies that use it in a negative light. Entrepreneurs would be wise to exclude spam from their Web advertising plans. However, permission e-mail can be an effective and money-saving advertising tool. Permission e-mail messages often produce very high response rates.

E-mail message cost is much lower than that of direct mail. Heidi Anderson, coauthor of *Sometimes the Messenger Should Be Shot: Building a Spam-Free E-mail Marketing Program,* recently conducted a test comparing the cost of a traditional direct-mail campaign versus an e-mail campaign. To run a clean test, one company designed identical offers and selected similar target audiences. It used traditional channels on the direct mail piece and worked with Blue Ink Solutions to implement the e-mail component of the test. The company sent about 90,000 direct-mail pieces and about 93,000 e-mail messages. Anderson reports that on every metric, e-mail outperformed direct mail. For example: The e-mails were sent at a quarter of direct mail's cost, the cost per initial response of was $80 for direct mail versus $10.31 for e-mail, and the cost per lead for direct mail was $4,026.00 versus $44.80 for e-mail—an 890 percent difference![10]

For an online advertisement to be really effective, customers must want to receive the message. When customers request information, it is referred to as opt-in e-mail. The return communications should be personal and relevant and respect the reader.

Building an e-mail list simply requires attention to the basics of marketing. The goal is to have qualified potential buyers identify themselves to you by sharing their e-mail addresses. The reward may be a one-time discount, special offer, special report, entry in a sweepstakes, or drawing for a prize. Once a small company obtains potential customers' e-mail addresses, the next step is to send a message that is useful and of interest to them. The message must be geared to their interests and should highlight the unique selling proposition of the product or service.

Many companies have success with creative e-mail newsletters sent to customers.

Company Example ➞ *For example, Paul Frederick, a maker of fine men's shirts, sends a weekly e-mail newsletter to customers (with their permission) that covers everything from fashion do's and don'ts to the hottest new styles. The electronic newsletter contains links to the company's Web site, where customers can browse through the catalog, use the "Create Your Shirt" feature to design their own shirts, and take advantage of special deals for on-line customers. The combination of its e-mail advertising campaign and its user-friendly Web site gives Paul Frederick and edge over its rivals.*

Directories. Directories are an important medium for reaching those customers who have already made purchase decisions. The directory simply helps these customers locate the specific product or service they have decided to buy. Directories include telephone books, industrial or grade guides, buyer guides, annuals, catalog files, and yearbooks that list various businesses and the products they sell.

Directories offer several *advantages* to advertisers:

Prime prospects. Directory listings reach customers who are prime prospects because they have already decided to purchase an item. The directory just helps them find what they are looking for.

Long life. Directory listings usually have long lives. A typical directory may be published annually.

However, there are certain *disadvantages* to using directories:

Lack of flexibility. Listings and ads in many directories offer only a limited variety of design features. Business owners may not be as free to create unique ads as in other printed media.

Ad clutter. In many directories, ads from many companies are clustered together so closely that no single ad stands out from the rest.

Obsolescence. Because directories are commonly updated only annually, some of their listings become obsolete. This is a problem for a small firm that changes its name, location, or phone number.

When choosing a directory, the small business owner should evaluate several criteria:

- *Completeness.* Does the directory include enough listings that customers will use it?
- *Convenience.* Are the listings well organized and convenient? Are they cross-referenced?
- *Evidence of use.* To what extent do customers actually use the directory? What evidence of use does the publisher offer?
- *Age.* Is the directory well established and does it have a good reputation?
- *Circulation.* Do users pay for the directory or do they receive complimentary copies? Is there an audited circulation statement?

Trade Shows. Trade shows provide manufacturers and distributors with a unique opportunity to advertise to a preselected audience of potential customers who are inclined to buy. Literally thousands of trade shows are sponsored each year, and carefully evaluating and selecting a few shows can produce profitable results for a business owner. A study by the Center for Exhibition Industry Research found that trade show success does *not* depend on how much an exhibitor spends; instead, success is a function of planning, preparation, and follow-up.[26]

Trade shows offer the following *advantages:*

A natural market. Trade shows bring together buyers and sellers in a setting in which products can be explained, demonstrated, and handled. Comparative shopping is easy, and the buying process is more efficient.

Preselected audience. Trade exhibits attract potential customers with a specific interest in the goods or services being displayed. There is a high probability that these persons will make a purchase.

New customer market. Trade shows offer exhibitors a prime opportunity to reach new customers and to contact people who are not accessible to sales representatives.

Cost advantage. As the cost of making a field sales call continues to escalate, more companies are realizing that trade shows are an economical method for making sales contacts and presentations.

There are, however, certain *disadvantages* associated with trade shows:

Increasing costs. The cost of exhibiting at trade shows is rising quickly. Registration fees, travel and setup costs, sales salaries, and other expenditures may be a barrier to some small firms.

Wasted effort. A poorly planned exhibit ultimately costs the small business more than its benefits are worth. Too many firms enter exhibits in trade shows without proper preparation, and they end up wasting their time, energy, and money on unproductive activities.

To avoid these disadvantages, business owners should:

- Establish objectives for the show. Do you want to generate 100 new sales leads, make new product presentations to 500 potential customers, or make $5,000 in sales?
- Communicate with key potential customers *before* the show; send them invitations or invite them to stop by your booth for a special gift.
- Make your display memorable. Be sure your exhibit shows your company and its products or services in the best light.
- Have knowledgeable salespeople staffing the booth. Attendees appreciate meeting face-to-face with knowledgeable and friendly staff.
- Demonstrate your product or service; let customers see it in action.
- Learn to distinguish between serious customers and "tire-kickers."
- Distribute literature that clearly communicates the product or service sold.
- Project a professional image at all times.
- Follow up promptly on sales leads. The most common mistake trade show participants make is failing to follow up on the sales leads the show generated. If you are not going to follow up leads, why bother to attend the show in the first place?

✦ GAINING *a* COMPETITIVE EDGE ✦

The Changing Face of Advertising

Because people now have hundreds of television channels available, devices that enable them to skip commercials, and the tendency to block out ads in any medium simply because they are so prevalent, the advertiser's job has become extremely challenging. Never before have consumers been so resistant to advertising messages, and never before have companies been so intent on reaching consumers with advertising. The contest is proving to be an interesting one that is demanding creativity and innovation from advertisers. Although the 30-second television or radio ad is in no danger of disappearing anytime soon, advertisers are coming up with new ways to reach potential customers with their messages. Following are just some of the new media and techniques that companies are using to reach potential customers.

- Eric Cohen and Joyce Shulman, founders of Jump Media Ltd., a small advertising company, were eating take-out pizza at home one night when they began to look at the box. "There were 16 inches of available [advertising] space," says Shulman. Soon, Jump Media's pizza box ads were drawing national attention, and the partners began promoting other non-traditional advertising space such as coffee cups, ice bags, and a luxury coach that transports well-heeled New Yorkers to the Hamptons.

- One company promoted its new video game by hiring young people to take laptop computers into Starbucks coffee shops where they would sit and play the game for several hours. Curious observers would ask questions about the game and, before they knew it, were trying it themselves. Many handed over their e-mail addresses so they could learn more about the game.
- Burger King implemented a viral marketing campaign using a character called the Subservient Chicken. Visitors to the Web site type in commands—sit on the couch, stand on one foot, do yoga, sleep, watch television, and others—that a guy dressed in a chicken suit then follows. At the bottom of the page are links that promote Burger King's chicken sandwiches. Amazingly, Web users, whose attention spans are notoriously short, spend an average of seven minutes per visit to the site, and many e-mailed the Web site's address to their friends.
- When BMW launched its Mini Cooper sports car, it chose to do so without using television ads. Instead, the company used "on-the-street" attention-getting tactics such as mounting Minis on top of Ford Excursion sport utility vehicles, which drove around the streets of several major cities attracting lots of attention.

■ To promote its line of sport utility vehicles, Jeep commissioned a video game, "Jeep 4 x 4: Trail of Life," that the company allowed Web users to download at no charge. The stars of the game, of course, were the vehicles. Within six months, more than 250,000 potential customers had downloaded the game (and provided Jeep with their names and e-mail addresses in the process). Because the ads are (not so subtly) built into the videogames, users cannot avoid them; they become a natural part of the action and enable customers to interact with the company's products. Hoby Buppert, creator of the world's most caffeinated soft drink, Bawls Guarana, has paid to place his company's product in several video games. In one, Bawls bottle caps are used as currency, and in another, players get energy points from the company's vending machines. Bawls considers the video games to be an ideal medium for reaching his company's target audience.

■ Product placements in movies and television shows and product tie-ins with movies are popular techniques. In response to the popularity of the *Lord of the Rings* series, Middle Earth Furniture of Staffordshire, England, launched its custom-made line of furniture inspired by the movies. Customers can purchase everything from a $2,200 oak Darkness and Light chair with a carved Eye of Sauron to a round oak Ancient Ent dining room table inlaid with a bronze map of Middle Earth.

■ Cunning Stunts Communications, a marketing firm in the United Kingdom, pays students to display temporary tattoos of company logos and names on their foreheads for at least three hours in public. CI Host, a Web hosting company in Texas, paid a man $7,000 to tattoo (permanently) its logo on the back of his head. A Cleveland-based advertising agency hired young people to promote a new Dunlop tire by shaving the tire tread pattern into their hair. They became known as the "Tread Heads."

1. Suppose that a company wants to promote a new energy bar aimed at people for whom exercise is a priority. Work with a team of students to come up with innovative ways the company could advertise its product.

Sources: Adapted from Suzanne Vranica, "Ad Agency's Latest Pitch Is in the Classroom," *Wall Street Journal,* June 15, 2004, pp. B1, B10; Gwen Moran, "Get in the Game," *Entrepreneur,* March 2004, p. 24; Kevin J. Delaney, "Ads in Videogames Pose a New Threat to Media Industry," *Wall Street Journal,* July 28, 2004, pp. A1, A8; Nichole L. Torres, "Think Outside the Box," *Entrepreneur B.Y.O.B.,* February 2004, p. 108; Danielle Reed, "See the Movie, Buy the Armoire," *Wall Street Journal,* June 11, 2004, p. W10; Nicole Gull, "Logos That Turn Heads," *Inc.,* December 2003, p. 12.

Preparing a Marketing Communications Budget

5. Discuss the four basic methods for preparing a marketing communications budget.

One of the most challenging decisions confronting a small business owner is how much to invest in marketing communications. The amount the owner wants to spend and the amount the firm can afford to spend usually differ significantly. There are four methods of determining a marketing communications budget: *what is affordable, matching competitors, percentage of sales, and objective and task.*

Under the what-is-affordable method, the owner sees marketing communications as a luxury. He or she views marketing communications completely as an expense, not as an investment that produces sales and profits in the future. Therefore, as the name implies, management spends whatever it can afford. Too often, the marketing communications are allocated funds after all other budget items have been financed. The result is an inadequate marketing communications budget. This method also fails to relate the marketing communications budget to the marketing communications objective.

Another approach is to match the marketing communications expenditures of the firm's competitors, either in a flat dollar amount or as a percentage of sales. This method assumes that a firm's marketing communications needs and strategies are the same as those of its competitors. Although competitors' actions can be helpful in establishing a floor for marketing communications expenditures, relying on this technique can lead to blind imitation instead of a budget suited to the small firm's circumstances.

The most commonly used method of establishing a marketing communications budget is the simple percentage-of-sales approach. This method relates marketing communications expenditures to actual sales results. Tying marketing communications expenditure to sales is generally preferred to relating them to profits because sales tend to fluctuate less than profits.

A useful rule of thumb when establishing a marketing communications budget: 10 percent projected sales the first year of business; 7 percent the second year; and at least 5 percent each year after that. Relying totally on such broad rules can be dangerous, however. They may not be representative of a small company's marketing communications needs.

The objective-and-task method is the most difficult and least used technique for establishing a marketing communications budget. It also is the method most often recommended by marketing communications experts. With this method, an owner links marketing communications expenditures to specific objectives. Although the previous methods break down the total amount of funds allocated to marketing communications, the task method builds up the marketing communications funds by analyzing what it will cost to accomplish these objectives. For example, suppose that a manager wants to boost sales of a particular product 10 percent by attracting local college students. He may determine that a nearby rock radio station would be the best medium to use. Then he must decide on the number and frequency of the ads and estimate their costs.

A manager follows this same process for each marketing communications objective. A common problem with the method is the tendency for the manager to be overly ambitious in setting marketing communications objectives, which leads to unrealistically high

Figure 11.3

A Sample Advertising Calendar

October						
Sun	Mon	Tue	Wed	Thu	Fri	Sat
Advertising Budget for October: 9% of Sales = $2,275 Co-op Ads = $ 550 Total = $2,825		October Advertising Expenditures: $2,845 Under/(Over) Budget: $20 Remaining Balance: $6,400		**1** WPCC Radio 5 spots, $125 Billboard, $350	**2** The Chronicle 140 lines, $100	**3**
4	**5**	**6**	**7**	**8**	**9** The Chronicle 140 lines, $100	**10**
11	**12**	**13** Meet w/ Leslie re: November ad campaigns, 2 p.m.	**14**	**15** Envelope "Stuffer" in invoices: Halloween Sale, $175	**16** The Chronicle 140 lines, $100	**17** WPCC Radio, 5 spots, $100
18	**19**	**20** WPCC Radio, 5 spots, $125	**21**	**22** Direct Mail, Halloween Sale Promo "Preferred Customers," $120	**23** The Chronicle 140 lines, $100	**24** WPCC Radio, 5 spots, $100
25	**26** WPCC Radio, 5 spots, $125	**27** WPCC Radio, 5 spots, $125	**28** WPCC Radio, 5 spots, $125	**29** WPCC Radio, 5 spots, $125	**30** The Chronicle Half-page spread, Sale, $300	Halloween Sale **31** WPCC Radio, Live remote broadcast, $425

marketing communications expenditures. The manager may be forced to alter objectives, or the plans to reach them, to bring the marketing communications budget back to a reasonable level. However, the plan can still be effective.

One of the most effective tools for developing a marketing communications plan is a simple calendar. The most critical and important sales date can first be identified and then the necessary advertising can be planned in a way to maximize sales (see Figure 11.3 on page 360). The calendar enables the owner to prepare for holidays and special events, to monitor actual and budgeted expenditures, and to ensure that ads are scheduled on the appropriate media at the proper times.

How to Advertise Big on a Small Budget

6. Explain practical methods of stretching a small business owner's advertising budget.

The typical small business does not have the luxury of an unlimited marketing communications budget. Most cannot afford to hire a professional ad agency. This does not mean, however, that a small company can afford to take a second-class position when it comes to advertising. Most advertising experts say that, unless a small company spends more than $10,000 a year on advertising, it probably doesn't need an ad agency. For most, hiring freelance copywriters and artists on a per-project basis is a much better bargain. With a little creativity and a dose of ingenuity, small business owners can stretch their advertising dollars and make the most of what they spend. Three useful techniques to do this are *cooperative advertising, shared advertising,* and *publicity.*

Cooperative Advertising

In cooperative advertising, a manufacturing company shares the cost of advertising with a retailer if the retailer features its products in those ads. Both the manufacturer and the retailer get more advertising per dollar by sharing expenses. Cooperative advertising not only helps small businesses stretch their advertising budgets, but it also offers another source of savings: the free advertising packages that many manufacturers supply to retailers. These packages usually include photographs and illustrations of the product as well as professionally prepared ads to use in different media.

Shared Advertising

In **shared advertising,** a group of similar businesses forms a syndicate to produce generic ads that allow the individual businesses to dub in local information. The technique is especially useful for small businesses that sell relatively standardized products or services such as legal assistance, autos, and furniture. Because the small firms in the syndicate pool their funds, the result usually is higher-quality ads and significantly lower production costs.

Publicity

The press can be either a valuable friend or a fearsome foe to small businesses, depending on how well the owners handle they firms' publicity. Too often, entrepreneurs take the attitude, "My business is too small to be concerned about public relations." However, wise small business managers recognize that investing time and money in public relations (publicity) benefits both the community and the company. The community gains the support of a good business citizen, and the company earns a positive image in the marketplace.

Many small businesses rely on media attention to get noticed, and getting that attention takes a coordinated effort. Publicity doesn't just happen; business owners must work at getting their companies noticed by the media. Although such publicity may not be free, it definitely can lower the company's advertising expenditures and still keep its name before the public. Because small companies' advertising budgets are limited, publicity takes on significant importance.

One successful publicity technique is *cause marketing,* in which a small business sponsors and promotes fund-raising activities of nonprofit groups and charities while raising its own visibility in the community. In most cases, the cost of sponsorship is modest in comparison with the excellent exposure the business receives as participants now view the sponsoring company in a favorable fashion.

Other Ways to Save

Other cost-saving suggestions for advertising expenditures include the following:

- *Repeat ads that have been successful.* In addition to reducing the cost of ad preparation, repetition may create a consistent image in a small firm's advertising program.
- *Use identical ads in different media.* If a billboard has been an effective advertising tool, an owner should consider converting it to a newspaper or magazine ad or a direct-mail flier.
- *Hire independent copywriters, graphic designers, photographers, and other media specialists.* Many small businesses that cannot afford a full-time advertising staff buy their advertising services à la carte. They work directly with independent specialists and usually receive high-quality work that compares favorably with that of advertising agencies without paying a fee for overhead.
- *Concentrate advertising during times when customers are most likely to buy.* Some small business owners make the mistake of spreading an already small advertising budget evenly—and thinly—over a 12-month period. A better strategy is to match advertising expenditures to customers' buying habits.

▌▐▐ Chapter Review

1. Explain the value of integrated marketing communications.
   - All marketing communications messages from any medium are clear, consistent, and compelling.
   - Each communication conveys the same positive message.
   - Branding of the firm's products or services is supported by communicating the correct *unique selling proposition* (USP).
2. Describe the basis of an integrated marketing communications plan.
   - Focus on your target audience.
   - Know exactly what you want your message to achieve.
3. Describe the operational elements of a marketing communications plan.
   - Advertising
   - Publicity and public relations
   - Personal selling
4. Describe the advantages and disadvantages of the various advertising media.

   - The medium used to transmit an advertising message influences the consumer's perception—and reception—of it.
   - Media options include newspapers, radio, television, magazines, direct mail, the World Wide Web, outdoor advertising, transit advertising, directories, trade shows, special events and promotions, and point-of-purchase ads.
5. Discuss the four basic methods for preparing a marketing communications budget.

   - Four basic methods are what is affordable; matching competitors; percentage of sales; objective and task.
6. Explain practical methods for stretching a small business owner's advertising budget.

   - Despite their limited advertising budgets, small businesses do not have to take a second-class approach to advertising. Three techniques that can stretch a small company's advertising dollars are cooperative advertising, shared advertising, and publicity.

▌▌▌ Discussion Questions

1. What are the three elements of promotion? How do they support one another?
2. What factors should a small business manager consider when selecting advertising media?
3. What is a unique selling proposition? What role should it play in a company's advertising strategy?
4. Review the advantages and disadvantages of the following advertising media:

   Newspapers
   Radio
   Television
   Magazines
   Specialty advertising
   Direct mail
   Outdoor advertising
   Transit advertising
   Directories
   Trade shows

   Assume you are a small business owner who has an advertising budget of $1,500 to invest in a campaign promoting a big July 4 "blowout" sale. Where would you be most likely to invest your advertising budget if you were trying to reach customers in the 25–45 age range with higher than average disposable income who are likely to be involved in boating activities in a local resort town? Explain your answer. How would you generate free publicity to extend your advertising budget?
5. What are fixed spots, preemptible spots, and floating spots in radio advertising?
6. Describe the characteristics of an effective outdoor advertisement.
7. Briefly outline the steps in creating an advertising plan. What principles should the small business owner follow when creating an effective advertisement?
8. Describe the common methods of establishing an advertising budget. Which method is most often used? Which technique is most often recommended? Why?
9. What techniques can small business owners use to stretch their advertising budgets?

Integrated Marketing Communications

BusinessPlanPro

A coordinated, constant, and consistent advertising, promotion, and public relations effort is essential to a small company's success. Companies that fail to maintain a high profile among their target customers are soon forgotten. The exercises for Chapter 11 that accompany Business Plan Pro are designed to help you define your company's unique selling proposition (USP) and then develop an advertising and promotion plan that communicates that USP effectively to your target customers. Once you finish these exercises, you are ready to complete the Promotion Strategy section of Business Plan Pro.

Chapter 12
Global Marketing Strategies

> *It is easier to go to the moon than it is to enter the world of another civilization. Culture—not space—is the greatest distance between two people.*
>
> —Jamake Highwater

> *Knowledge, learning, information, and skilled intelligence are the raw materials of international commerce and are today spreading throughout the world as vigorously as miracle drugs, synthetic fertilizers, and blue jeans did earlier.*
>
> —from *A Nation at Risk*

Upon completion of this chapter, you will be able to:

1. Explain why "going global" has become an integral part of many small companies' strategies.

2. Describe the eight principal strategies small businesses can use to go global.

3. Explain how to build a successful export program.

4. Discuss the major barriers to international trade and their impact on the global economy.

5. Describe the trade agreements that have the greatest influence on foreign trade.

Until recently, the world of international business was much like the world of astronomy before Copernicus, who revolutionized the study of the planets and the stars with his theory of planetary motion. In the sixteenth century, his Copernican system replaced the Ptolemaic system, which held that the earth was the center of the universe with the sun and all the other planets revolving around it. The Copernican system, however, placed the sun at the center of the solar system with all of the planets, including the earth, revolving around it. Astronomy would never be the same.

In the same sense, business owners across the globe were guilty of having Ptolemaic tunnel vision when it came to viewing international business opportunities. Like their pre-Copernican counterparts, owners saw an economy that revolved around the nations that served as their home bases. Market opportunities stopped at their homeland's borders. Global trade was only for giant corporations that had the money and the management to tap foreign markets and enough resources to survive if the venture flopped.

Today, the global marketplace is as much the territory of small, upstart companies as it is that of giant multinational corporations. *For instance, Pelican Publishing Company of Gretna, Louisiana, has a staff of 35 and publishes just over 100 books a year. However, this tiny publisher has achieved a great deal of success in international markets. Five years after Milburn and Nancy Calhoun purchased the company in 1970, Pelican had its first big seller,* See You at the Top, *by motivational guru Zig Ziglar. The book, according to Milburn, is "the kind of book whose principles work well across numerous cultures." It sold 1.6 million copies and gave the Calhouns the idea of taking their small company into international markets. They started simply, selling only the rights to foreign sales in 19 languages, ranging from Bulgarian and Chinese to Russian and Slovenian. As the company's international sales and the owners' international experience grew, the Calhouns branched into other types of books, such as cooking, travel, children's literature, history, and regional, and began distributing books in foreign markets rather than merely selling foreign rights to their titles. Using the world's largest gathering of publishers, the Frankfurt Book Fair in Germany, as their springboard, the Calhouns now sell their books in the United Kingdom, New Zealand, South Africa, Canada, Singapore, Malaysia, India, and other nations. Pelican's children's books, which already sell well in Mexico, are now taking off in Japan. One lesson the Calhouns have learned is the importance of tailoring books to suit cultural preferences. The Calhouns say that although*

Company Example →

Milburn and Nancy Calhoun, owners of Pelican Publishing Company, prove that small companies can sell their products successfully in global markets.

foreign sales currently account for a small portion of their company's total sales, those sales are vital to its financial health, and they are growing fast.[1]

Just a few years ago, military might governed world relationships; today, commercial trade and economic benefit have become the forces that drive global interaction. Since World War II, the proportion of trade as a share of global income has climbed from 7 percent to 21 percent. In that same time period, world trade has increased 15-fold, compared with a sixfold increase in production. Countries at every stage of development are reaping the benefits of increased global trade. Developing countries now account for about 25 percent of world trade, up from 20 percent a decade ago. In the United States alone, international trade now accounts for 24 percent of gross domestic product. The future of international business appears to be bright. According to management consulting firm McKinsey and Company, global markets produced and consumed 20 percent of the world's $28 trillion gross domestic product in 2000; by 2027, gross domestic product will be $73 trillion, and global markets will account for 80 percent of total world output.[2]

Political, social, cultural, technological, and economic changes continue to sweep the world, creating a new world order—and a legion of both problems and opportunities for businesses of all sizes. Market economies are replacing centralized economies in countries where only decades ago private ownership of productive assets was unthinkable. Technological advances have cut the cost of long-distance communications and transactions so low that conducting business globally costs no more than doing business locally. These changes are creating instability for businesses of *any* size going global, but they also are creating tremendous opportunities for those small companies ready to capitalize on them. One report on the impact of increasing globalization concludes:

> In a world without significant geographic boundaries, the rules are going to change. The good news is that companies will have access to the world's finest resources: the most talented labor, the largest markets, the most advanced technologies, and the cheapest and best suppliers of goods and services. The bad news is that the risks will be high because every business will have to compete against the world's best, and integrating markets are volatile and uncertain.[3]

Company Example	→

Sheila Brady, president of Brady Associates Inc., a small landscape architecture firm in California, observed the rapid pace at which many Asian economies were expanding and decided that her company could benefit from that growth. A trip to Vietnam and several visits to China opened the door to international markets to Brady's 23-person business. Eventually, meetings with government officials in those countries produced contracts for urban design and environmental planning services across the Pacific Rim, where rapid, often uncontrolled growth has created a huge need for Brady's services. International business has been so good at her $2 million per year company that Brady ultimately plans to establish a small office in Asia.[4]

Expanding a business beyond its domestic borders may actually enhance a small company's performance. In recent years, studies have concluded that small companies that export earn more, grow faster, create higher-paying jobs, and are more likely to survive than their purely domestic counterparts.[5]

Why Go Global?

1. Explain why "going global" has become an integral part of many small companies' strategies.

Businesses can no longer consider themselves to be domestic companies in this hotly competitive global environment. "In the global economy, the competitor six time zones away is potentially as serious a threat as the competitor six blocks away," says one expert.[6] For companies across the world, going global is a matter of survival, not preference. No matter where a company's home base is, competitors are forcing it to think

Company Example

globally. *For example, the executives of a small Oregon company manufacturing robotic-vision systems to cut french fries discovered that a Belgian company had developed a similar competing device. "There are an awful lot of people in the rest of the world who think they are pretty good at doing your business," warns Lester Thurow.*[7] Virtually every business—large or small, global or strictly domestic—faces global competition. Companies that fail to see the world as a global marketplace risk being blindsided in their markets both at home and abroad.

Failure to cultivate global markets can be a lethal mistake for modern businesses—whatever their size. In short, to thrive in the twenty-first century, small businesses must take their place in the world market! To be successful, companies must consider themselves as businesses without borders. "If a company really is a global competitor, it is going to be shipping all over the place from all over the place," says one executive.[8]

Entrepreneurs who take the plunge into global business can reap the following benefits:

Company Example

- *Offset sales declines in the domestic market.* Markets in foreign countries may be booming when those in the United States are sagging, becoming a countercyclical balance for small companies. *Metz Tool and Die thrived from its inception in 1959 through the 1990s before the domestic tool-and-die industry suffered a prolonged slowdown that severely affected the company. For more than a year, Metz managers worked with a local U.S. Export Assistance Center to develop a global marketing plan to guide its foray into international business. The market analysis pointed Metz to Mexico, and the company soon began shipping its die-cast injection molds there. Metz's first two orders in the Mexican market represented a 25 percent increase in the small manufacturer's sales!*[9]
- *Increase sales and profits.* Two forces are working in tandem to make global business increasingly attractive for small companies: rising income levels in many nations, where demand for imported goods then rises, and the realization that 96 percent of the world's population lies outside of the United States.
- *Extend products' life cycles.* Many consumers across the world have an affinity for anything American, which has allowed some companies to take products that have reached the maturity stage of the product life cycle in the United States and sell them very successfully in foreign markets.
- *Lower manufacturing costs.* In industries characterized by high levels of fixed costs, businesses that expand into global markets can lower their manufacturing costs by spreading these fixed costs over a larger number of units.
- *Improve competitive position.* Going up against some of the toughest competition in the world forces a company to hone its competitive skills.
- *Raise quality levels.* Customers in many global markets are much tougher to satisfy than those in the United States. One reason Japanese products have done so well worldwide is who Japanese companies must build products to satisfy their customers at home, who demand extremely high quality and are sticklers for detail. Businesses that compete in global markets learn very quickly how to boost their quality levels to world-class standards. "Japan is the most demanding market in the world," says one global manager doing business there. "Japanese consumers look for quality in the tiniest details. Products that survive there have a better chance of succeeding in other markets."[10]
- *Become more customer oriented.* Delving into global markets teaches business owners about the unique tastes, customs, preferences, and habits of customers in many different cultures. Responding to these differences imbues these businesses with a degree of sensitivity toward their customers, both domestic and foreign.

Unfortunately, not enough entrepreneurs have learned to see their companies from a global perspective. Indeed, learning to *think globally* may be the first—and most threatening—obstacle an entrepreneur must overcome on the way to creating a truly global business. One British manager explains:

> If you are operating in South America, you'd better know how to operate in conditions of hyperinflation. If you're operating in Africa, you'd better know a lot about government relations and the use of local partners. If you're operating in Germany, you'd better understand the mechanics of codetermination and some of the special tax systems that one finds in that country. If you're operating in China, it's quite useful in trademark matters to know how the People's Court of Shanghai works. . . . If you're operating in Japan, you'd better understand the different trade structure.[11]

Company Example ➔ *David Montague, owner of Montague Corporation, a small manufacturer of unique folding bikes, operates his business with a global perspective. Montague designs its bikes in Cambridge, Massachusetts, manufactures them in Taiwan, and sells most of them in Europe and the United States. In addition to selling bikes in the consumer market, Montague also has developed a special tactical mountain bike for military use. Coordinating his business across three continents requires Montague to use the latest information and communication technology available. (He often gets up at 5 A.M. to talk to workers in Germany.) However, his global diversification offers a measure of security: Montague is not dependent on any single economy for his company's success.[12]*

Gaining a foothold in newly opened foreign markets or maintaining a position in an existing one is no easy task, however. Until an entrepreneur develops the attitude of operating a truly global company rather than a domestic company that happens to be doing business abroad, achieving success in international business is difficult. That attitude starts at the top with the executive's office. Success in the global economy also requires constant innovation; staying nimble enough to use speed as a competitive weapon; maintaining a high level of quality and constantly improving it; being sensitive to foreign customers' unique requirements; adopting a more respectful attitude toward foreign habits and customs; hiring motivated, multilingual employees; and retaining a desire to learn constantly about global markets. In short, the path to success requires businesses to become "insiders" rather than just "exporters."

Montague Corporation, a small manufacturer of unique folding bikes founded by David Montague, operates as a truly global company. Montague designs its bikes in the United States, manufactures them in the Far East, and sells most of them in Europe and the United States.

Before venturing into the global marketplace, an entrepreneur should consider six questions:

1. Is there a profitable market in which our company has the potential to be successful over the long run? Table 12.1 shows a country screening matrix designed to help entrepreneurs decide which countries offer the best opportunities for their products.
2. Do we have and are we willing to commit adequate resources of time, people, and capital to a global campaign?
3. Are domestic pressures forcing our company to consider global opportunities?
4. Do we understand the cultural differences, history, economics, values, opportunities, and risks of conducting business in the country(s) we are considering?
5. Is there a viable exit strategy for our company if conditions change or the new venture does not succeed?
6. Can we afford not to go global?

Table 12.1

A Country Screening Matrix

For an entrepreneur considering launching a global business venture, getting started often is the hardest step. "The world is such a big place! Where do I start?" is a typical comment from entrepreneurs considering global business. The following matrix will help you narrow down your options. Based on preliminary research, select three to five countries that you believe have the greatest market potential for your products. Then use the following factors to guide you as you conduct more detailed research into these countries and their markets. Rate each factor on a scale of 1 (lowest) to 5 (highest). Based on your ratings, which country has the highest score?

MARKET FACTOR	COUNTRY 1 RATING	COUNTRY 2 RATING	COUNTRY 3 RATING
Demographic/Physical Environment			
▪ Population size, growth, density			
▪ Urban and rural distribution			
▪ Climate and weather variations			
▪ Shipping distance			
▪ Product-significant demographics			
▪ Physical distribution and communication network			
▪ Natural resources			
Political Environment			
▪ System of government			
▪ Political stability and continuity			
▪ Ideological orientation			
▪ Government involvement in business			
▪ Attitudes toward foreign business (trade restrictions, tariffs, nontariff barriers, bilateral trade agreements)			
▪ National economic and developmental priorities			
Economic Environment			
▪ Overall level of development			
▪ Economic growth: GDP, industrial sector			
▪ Role of foreign trade in the economy			
▪ Currency: inflation rate, availability, controls, stability of exchange rate			
▪ Balance of payments			
▪ Per capita income and distribution			
▪ Disposable income and expenditure patterns			

(Continued)

Table 12.1

Continued

Market Factor	Country 1 Rating	Country 2 Rating	Country 3 Rating
Social/Cultural Environment			
▪ Literacy rate, educational level			
▪ Existence of middle class			
▪ Similarities and differences in relation to home market			
▪ Language and other cultural considerations			
Market Access			
▪ Limitations on trade: high tariff levels, quotas			
▪ Documentation and import regulations			
▪ Local standards, practices, and other non-tariff barriers			
▪ Patents and trademark protection			
▪ Preferential treaties			
▪ Legal considerations for investment, taxation, repatriation, employment, code of laws			
Product Potential			
▪ Customer needs and desires			
▪ Local production, imports, consumption			
▪ Exposure to and acceptance of product			
▪ Availability of linking products			
▪ Industry-specific key indicators of demand			
▪ Attitudes toward products of foreign origin			
▪ Competitive offerings			
Local Distribution and Production			
▪ Availability of intermediaries			
▪ Regional and local transportation facilities			
▪ Availability of manpower			
▪ Conditions for local manufacture			
Total Score			

Source: "International Business Plan," *Breaking into the Trade Game: A Small Business Guide*, U.S. Small Business Administration Office of International Trade (Washington, D.C.: 2001), www.sba.gov/oit/info/Guide-To-Exporting/trad6.html.

IN THE FOOTSTEPS OF AN ENTREPRENEUR...

Where Do We Start?

Specialty Building Supplies is a small company with $6.4 million in annual sales that manufactures and sells a line of building supply products such as foundation vents, innovative insulation materials, and fireplace blowers to building supply stores in the northeastern United States. The eight-year-old company, founded by Tad Meyers, has won several awards for its unique and innovative products and has earned a solid reputation among its supply store customers and the builders and homeowners who ultimately buy its products. Before launching the company, Meyers had been a home builder. As he

watched the price of home heating fuels climb dramatically over time, Meyers began to incorporate into the houses he built simple, inexpensive ways to help homeowners save energy. He began tinkering with existing products, looking for ways to improve them. The first product he designed (and the product that ultimately led him to launch Specialty Building Supplies) was an automatic foundation vent that was thermostatically controlled (no electricity needed). The vent would automatically open and close based on the outside temperature, keeping cold drafts from blowing under a house. Simple and inexpensive in its design, the Autovent was a big hit in newly constructed homes in the Northeast because it not only saved energy but it also avoided a major headache for homeowners in cold climates: water pipes that would freeze and burst. Before long, Meyers stopped building houses and focused on selling the Autovent. Its success prompted him to add other products to the company's line.

Specialty's sales have been lackluster for more than a year now, primarily due to a slump in new home construction in its primary market. Tad Meyers recently met with the company's top marketing managers and salespeople to talk about their options for getting Specialty's sales and profit growth back on track. "What about selling our products in international markets?" asked Dee Rada, the company's marketing manager. "I read an article just last week about small companies doing good business in other countries, and many of them were smaller than we are."

"Interesting idea," Meyers said, pondering the concept. "I've never really thought about selling anything overseas. In fact, other than my years in the military, I've never traveled overseas and don't know anything about doing business there."

"It's a big world out there. Where should we sell our products?" said Hal Milam, Specialty's sales manager. "How do we find out what the building codes are in foreign countries? Would we have to modify our designs to meet foreign standards?"

"I don't know," shrugged Meyers. "Those are some good questions."

"How would we distribute our products?" asked Rada. "We have an established network of distributors here in the United States, but how do we find foreign distributors?"

"I wonder if exporting is our only option," Meyers said. "There must be other ways to get into the global market besides exporting. What do you think? Where do we start?"

1. What advice would you offer Meyers and the other managers at Specialty Building Supplies about their prospects of going global?
2. How would you suggest these managers go about finding the answers to the questions they have posed? What other questions would you advise them to answer?
3. Outline the steps these managers should take to assemble an international marketing plan.

Going Global: Strategies for Small Businesses

2. Describe the eight principal strategies small businesses can use to go global.

A growing number of small businesses are recognizing that going global is not a strategy reserved solely for industry giants such as General Motors, IBM, Boeing, and General Electric. In fact, John Naisbitt, trend-spotting author of *The Global Paradox*, says that the increasing globalization of business actually *favors* smaller companies. "In the huge global economy, there will be smaller and smaller market niches," says Naisbitt. "In this global economy, the competitive edge is swiftness to market and innovation. Small units are much better at speed to market and innovation. As a result, they can innovate faster, not just in products but in internal operations, to take advantage of the new technologies."[13] Their agility and adaptability gives small firms the edge in today's highly interactive, fast-paced global economy. "The bigger the world economy, the more powerful its smallest players," concludes Naisbitt.[14]

Becoming a global business depends on instilling a global culture throughout the organization that permeates *everything* the company does. Entrepreneurs who routinely conduct international business have developed a global mind-set for themselves and their companies. As one business writer explains:

> The global [business] looks at the whole world as *one market*. It manufactures, conducts research, raises capital, and buys supplies wherever it can do the job best. It keeps in touch with technology and market trends around the world. National boundaries and regulations tend to be irrelevant, or a mere hindrance. [Company] headquarters might be anywhere.[15]

As cultures from around the globe become increasingly interwoven, the ability to go global will determine the relative degree of success (or lack of it!) for more and more small businesses.

Small companies pursuing a global presence have eight principal strategies available: the World Wide Web, relying on trade intermediaries, joint ventures, foreign licensing,

Figure 12.1

Eight Principal Strategies for Pursuing Global Markets

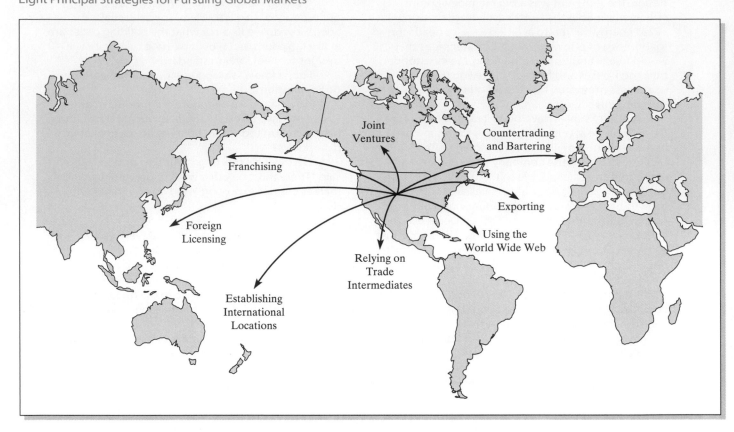

franchising, countertrading and bartering, exporting, and establishing international locations (see Figure 12.1).

The World Wide Web

Perhaps in our technology-rich environment, the simplest and least expensive way for a small business to begin conducting business globally is to establish a site on the World Wide Web. The Web gives small businesses tremendous marketing potential all across the globe without having to incur the expense of opening international locations. With a well-designed Web site, a small company can extend its reach to customers anywhere in the world—without breaking the budget! A Web site is available to anyone, anywhere in the world and provides 24-hour exposure to a company's products or services, so time differences become meaningless.

Establishing a presence on the Web is an essential ingredient in the strategies of small companies trying to reach customers outside the borders of the United States. Although Internet usage varies greatly by region of the world (see Figure 12.2), the number of potential online customers is growing extremely fast. Notice that of the estimated 760 million Internet users worldwide, 70 percent live outside of North America. By 2008, the number of Internet users is expected to double to 1.5 billion![16]

Most small companies follow a three-step evolutionary process to conducting global business on the Web:

Step 1   *Connecting to e-mail.* Even though it lacks the ability to provide the wealth of visual images and sounds available on the Web, e-mail gives entrepre-

Figure 12.2

Internet Users Worldwide by Region

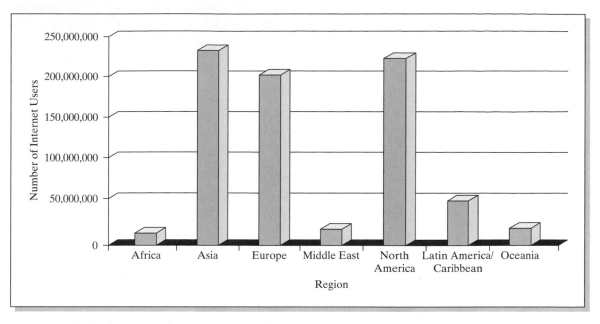

Source: Reproduced with permission from www.internetworldstats.com.

neurs the ability to communicate with customers anywhere in the world quickly and easily. E-mail correspondence is often the first step to establishing lasting relationships with international customers. Not only is e-mail less expensive than international telephone calls, but it also overcomes many of the problems associated with different time zones. *James Cantor, CEO of Eastern Avionics International, a small company that markets navigation and communication equipment to private pilots, has used e-mail to boost his company's sales in foreign markets. Because he speaks only English, Cantor relies on a Web-based translation program to help him translate the e-mail orders and inquiries he often gets from customers written in French, German, Spanish, Italian, and Portuguese into English. In just 10 weeks, Eastern Avionics international sales had climbed 60 percent.*[17]

Step 2   *Conducting international market research electronically.* Once business owners begin to see the power of the Web and its ability to attract customers across the globe, they become interested in using it as a more proactive tool to generate sales and research markets in other countries. *After experiencing initial success with her company's Web site, Sharon Doherty, owner of Vellus Products Inc., a maker of pet-grooming products in Columbus, Ohio, began using the Web to explore potential markets abroad. She spends an average of two hours a day researching markets, studying competitors, and scouting out potential customers in foreign countries. International sales now account for more than half of Vellus Products's revenues.*[18] As Doherty's experience shows, entrepreneurs have a wealth of international marketing information at their fingertips from sources on the Web.

Step 3   *Creating a globally accessible Web site.* Companies soon see the need to educate their international customers about the features and the benefits of their products and services and set up Web sites to reach them. Designed properly, a Web site can be an engaging marketing tool. *Shortly after starting his*

Company Example →

Company Example →

Company Example →

company, Greg Jackson created a Web site for his boat brokering business, Carolina Classic Boats, that specializes in buying, selling, and trading antique wooden boats made from the 1920s to the 1950s by manufacturers such as Chris Craft, Gar Wood, Hacker Craft, and Riva. Although Jackson operates from a small southern town of just 10,000 residents, his company operates globally with the help of the Web site, where customers can see photographs and read detailed descriptions of the boats they are considering. Jackson has bought, sold, and shipped classic boats all over the world from Europe to Australia.

Entrepreneurs who want to reach foreign customers should make the effort to provide alternative language options on the site's opening page. Simply by clicking on the appropriate language button, customers can shop comfortably in their native languages. Ensuring fast, reasonably priced shipping for international customers also will keep them coming back to a company's Web site. *When Barewalls.com, a small e-tailing company that sells a wide selection of posters and prints, decided to tackle international markets, it first targeted English-speaking countries such as Canada, Australia, and the United Kingdom. Its success in those markets led Barewalls.com's owners to pursue Korea, where they formed an alliance with a Korean partner, who adapted the Barewalls.com Web site to suit Korean customers. Barewalls.com's international efforts have produced a 20 percent increase in the company's sales.*[19]

| Company Example | → |

Relying on Trade Intermediaries

Another relatively easy way to break into international markets is by using a trade intermediary. Trade intermediaries serve as distributors in foreign countries for domestic companies of all sizes. They rely on their networks of contacts, their extensive knowledge of local customs and markets, and their experience in international trade to market products effectively and efficiently all across the globe. Although a broad array of trade intermediaries is available, the following are ideally suited for small businesses:

Trade intermediaries such as these are becoming increasingly popular among businesses attempting to branch out into world markets because they make that transition so much faster and so much easier. Most small businesses simply do not have the knowledge, resources, or confidence to go global alone. Intermediaries' global networks of buyers and sellers allow their small business customers to build their international sales efforts much faster and with fewer hassles and mistakes.

Export Management Companies (EMCs). Export management companies (EMCs) are an important channel of foreign distribution for small companies just getting started in international trade or for those lacking the resources to assign their own people to foreign markets. Most EMCs are merchant intermediaries, working on a buy-and-sell arrangement with domestic small companies. They provide small businesses with a low-cost, efficient, independent international marketing department, offering services ranging from market research on foreign countries and advice on patent protection to arranging financing and handling shipping. More than 1,000 EMCs operate across the United States, and many of them specialize in particular products or product lines. The chief advantage of using an export management company is that a small business's products get international exposure without having to tie up its own resources excessively.

| Company Example | → |

Hamilton Manufacturing Corporation, a small maker of machines that exchange coins for paper currency, used an export management company to break into foreign markets. James Nesmith, president of the small concern, turned to International Projects Inc., a Toledo, Ohio-based EMC, for help in selling Hamilton's newly developed machines designed to exchange foreign currency. Going global alone "was a lot more than I could handle," says Nesmith. So Hamilton signed a five-year agreement with International Projects to sell the machines abroad, and its foreign sales are climbing rapidly.

Export Trading Companies (ETCs). Another tactic for getting into international markets with a minimum of cost and effort is through an export trading company (ETC). ETCs have been an important vehicle in international trade throughout history. The Hudson's Bay Company and the East India Company were dominant powers in world trade in the sixteenth, seventeenth, and eighteenth centuries.

Export trading companies are businesses that buy and sell products in a number of countries, and they typically offer a wide range of services such as exporting, importing, shipping, storing, distributing, and others to their clients. Unlike EMCs, which tend to focus on exporting, ETCs usually perform both import and export trades across many countries' borders. However, like EMCs, ETCs lower the risk of exporting for small businesses. Some of the largest trading companies in the world are based in the United States and Japan. In fact, many businesses that have navigated successfully Japan's complex system of distribution have done so with the help of ETCs.

In 1982, Congress passed the Export Trading Company Act to allow producers of similar products to form ETC cooperatives without the fear of violating antitrust laws. The goal was to encourage U.S. companies to export more goods by allowing businesses in the same industry to band together to form export trading companies.

Manufacturer's Export Agents (MEAs). **Manufacturer's export agents (MEAs)** act as international sales representatives in a limited number of markets for various noncompeting domestic companies. Unlike the close partnering relationship formed with most EMCs, the relationship between an MEA and a small company is a short-term one in which the MEA typically operates on a commission basis.

Export Merchants. **Export merchants** are domestic wholesalers who do business in foreign markets. They buy goods from many domestic manufacturers and then market them in foreign markets. Unlike MEAs, export merchants often carry competing lines, which means they have little loyalty to suppliers. Most export merchants specialize in particular industries—office equipment, computers, industrial supplies, and others.

Resident Buying Offices. Another approach to exporting is to sell to a **resident buying office,** a government-owned or privately-owned operation established in a country for the purpose of buying goods made there. Many foreign governments and businesses have set up buying offices in the United States. Selling to them is just like selling to domestic customers because the buying office handles all the details of exporting.

Company Example →

Foreign Distributors. Some small businesses work through foreign distributors to reach international markets. Domestic small companies export their products to these distributors who handle all of the marketing, distribution, and service functions in the foreign country. *Farouk Systems, Inc., a Houston-based manufacturer of natural hair care and spa products, was experienced in international business, having taken its products successfully to more than 60 countries. When Farouk wanted to move into the unique cultures of Southeast Asia, however, it turned to the Gold Key program of the U.S. Commercial Service for help locating distributors. Managers at Farouk were particularly interested in Singapore because their preliminary research showed that women there spend far more on beauty care products than in other Southeast Asian countries. Gold Key representatives took the characteristics of the ideal distributor on Farouk's list and developed a list of the distributors that met those criteria. After interviewing the finalists to judge the "chemistry" between the potential partners, Farouk managers chose Tru-Line Beauty Consultants, a small company that has the largest beauty products sales staff in Singapore.*[20]

The key to establishing a successful relationship with a trade intermediary is conducting a thorough screening to determine what type of intermediary—and which one in particular—will serve a small company's needs best. A company looking for an intermediary should compile a list of potential candidates using some of the sources listed in Table 12.2. The 50 World Trade Centers (most of which are affiliated with the U.S. government) and the Export Assistance Centers located in more than 100 cities across the United States and in 80 countries around the world offer valuable advice and assistance to small businesses wanting to get started in conducting global business. In addition, entrepreneurs can find reliable intermediaries by using their network of contacts in foreign countries and by attending international trade shows while keeping an eye out for potential candidates.

Table 12.2

Resources for Locating a Trade Intermediary

Trade intermediaries make doing business around the world much easier for small companies, but finding the right one can be a challenge. Fortunately, several government agencies offer a wealth of information to businesses interested in reaching into global markets with the help of trade intermediaries. Entrepreneurs looking for help in breaking into global markets should contact the International Trade Administration, the U.S. Commerce Department, and the Small Business Administration first to take advantage of the following services:

- *Agent/Distributor Service (ADS).* Provides customized searches to locate interested and qualified foreign distributors for a product or service. (Search cost is $250 per country.)
- *Commercial Service International Contacts (CSIC) List.* Provides contact and product information for more than 82,000 foreign agents, distributors, and importers interested in doing business with U.S. companies.
- *Country Directories of International Contacts (CDIC) List.* Provides the same kind of information as the CSIC List but is organized by country.
- *Global Diversity Initiative (GDI).* Offered by the U.S. Commercial Service, the Global Diversity Initiative is aimed at helping minority-owned companies become exporters. Contact your local Export Assistance Center or visit www.buyusa.gov.
- *Global Trade & Technology Network (GTTN).* Founded by the U.S. Agency for International Development, this Internet-based network helps small companies spot and cultivate international business opportunities in more than 40 developing countries and emerging markets. Visit www.usgtn.net or call (202) 628–9750.
- *Industry Sector Analyses (ISAs).* Offer in-depth reports on industries in foreign countries, including information on distribution practices, end users, and top sales prospects.
- *International Market Insights (IMIs).* Include reports on specific foreign market conditions, upcoming opportunities for U.S. companies, trade contacts, trade show schedules, and other information.
- *Trade Opportunity Program (TOP).* Provides up-to-the-minute, prescreened sales leads around the world for U.S. businesses, including joint venture and licensing partners, direct sales leads, and representation offers.
- *International Company Profiles (ICPs).* Commercial specialists will investigate potential partners, agents, distributors, or customers for U.S. companies and will issue profiles on them.
- *Commercial News USA.* A government-published magazine that promotes U.S. companies' products and services to 259,000 business readers in 152 countries at a fraction of the cost of commercial advertising. Small companies can use *Commercial News USA* to reach new customers around the world for as little as $395.
- *Gold Key Service.* For a small fee, business owners wanting to target a specific country can use the Department of Commerce's Gold Key Service, in which experienced trade professionals arrange meetings with prescreened contacts whose interests match their own.
- *Matchmaker Trade Delegations Program.* Helps small U.S. companies establish business relationships in major markets abroad by introducing them to the right contacts.
- *Multi-State/Catalog Exhibition Program.* Working with state economic development offices, the Department of Commerce presents companies' product and sales literature to hundreds of interested business prospects in foreign countries.
- *International Fair Certification Program.* Promotes U.S. companies' participation in foreign trade shows that represent the best marketing opportunities for them.
- *National Trade Data Bank (NTDB).* Most of the preceding information is available on the NTDB, the U.S. government's most comprehensive database of world trade data. With the NTDB, small companies have access to information that only *Fortune* 500 companies could afford.

(Continued)

Table 12.2

Continued

> - *Economic Bulletin Board (EBB).* Provides online trade leads and valuable market research on foreign countries compiled from a variety of federal agencies.
> - *U.S. Export Assistance Centers.* The Department of Commerce has established 104 export centers (USEACs) around the country to serve as one-stop shops for entrepreneurs needing export help. Call (800) USA-TRADE.
> - *Trade Information Center.* Helps locate federal export assistance, provides export assistance, and offers a 24-hour automated fax retrieval system that gives entrepreneurs free information on export promotion programs, regional market information, and international trade agreements. Call (800) USA-TRADE.
> - *Office of International Trade.* The Small Business Administration provides a variety of export development assistance, how-to publications, and information on foreign markets.
> - *Export Hotline.* Provides no-cost trade information on more than 50 industries in 80 countries. Call (800) 872–9767.
> - *Export Opportunity Hotline.* Trade specialists have access to online databases and reports from government and private agencies concerning foreign markets. Call (202) 628–8389.

Joint Ventures

Joint ventures, both domestic and foreign, lower the risk of entering global markets for small businesses. They also give small companies more clout in foreign lands. In a **domestic joint venture,** two or more U.S. small businesses form an alliance for the purpose of exporting their goods and services abroad. For export ventures, participating companies get antitrust immunity, allowing them to cooperate freely. The businesses share the responsibility and the costs of getting export licenses and permits, and they split the venture's profits. Establishing a joint venture with the right partner has become an essential part of maintaining a competitive position in global markets for a

Company Example

growing number of industries. *Yamas Controls Inc., a small California maker of environmental control systems, formed a joint venture with Bechtel Group Inc., the giant construction and engineering company, to provide its systems to the Chinese government. Without the joint venture, Yamas most likely would not have been able to break into the Chinese market. With it, the company's annual sales have grown from $4 million to $40 million in just eight years. Not only did the joint venture lower Yamas's risk of selling in foreign markets, but it also opened the door for similar projects with several U.S., European, and Chinese firms.*[21]

In a **foreign joint venture,** a domestic small business forms an alliance with a company in the target nation. The host partner brings to the joint venture valuable knowledge of the local market and its method of operation as well as of the customs and the tastes of local customers, making it much easier to conduct business in the foreign country. Forming a joint venture with a local company often is the best way for a business to negotiate the maze of government regulations in some countries. Some foreign countries place limitations on how joint ventures operate. Some nations, for example, require host companies to own at least 51 percent of the venture. "The only way to be German in Germany, Canadian in Canada, and Japanese in Japan is through alliances," says one international manager.[22] When Subway, one of the leading franchises in the world, enters a foreign market with one of its sandwich shops, it often looks for a local company with which to form a joint venture. "Nobody knows an area like a local partner," says Don Fertman, a director of international development at Subway. "That's the number one consideration."[23]

The most important ingredient in the recipe for a successful joint venture is choosing the right partner. A productive joint venture is much like a marriage, requiring commitment and understanding. In addition to picking the right partner(s), a second key to creating a successful alliance is to establish common objectives. Defining *exactly* what each party in the joint venture hopes to accomplish at the outset will minimize the opportunity for misunderstandings and disagreements later on. One important objective should always be to use the joint venture as a learning experience, which requires a long-term view of the business relationship. Issues to address *before* entering into a joint venture include:

- What contributions will each party make?
- Who will be responsible for making which decisions?
- How much control will each party have over the joint venture's direction?
- How will the earnings from the joint venture be allocated?
- How long will the joint venture last? Under what circumstances can the parties terminate the relationship?

Unfortunately, most joint ventures fail. That makes it essential for the companies in an alliance to establish a contingency plan for getting out in case the joint venture doesn't work. Common problems leading to failure include improper selection of partners, incompatible management styles, failure to establish common goals, inability to be flexible, and failure to trust one another. What can entrepreneurs do to avoid these pitfalls in joint ventures?

- Understand their partner's reasons and objectives for joining the venture.
- Select a partner who shares their company's values and standards of conduct.
- Spell out in writing exactly how the venture will work, what each partner's responsibilities are, and where decision-making authority lies.
- Select a partner whose skills are different from but compatible with those of their own companies.
- Prepare a "prenuptial agreement" that spells out what happens in case of a "business divorce."

Foreign Licensing

Rather than sell their products or services directly to customers overseas, some small companies enter foreign markets by licensing businesses in other nations to use their patents, trademarks, copyrights, technology, processes, or products. In return for licensing its assets, a small company collects royalties from the sales of its foreign licenses. Licensing is a relatively simple way for even the most inexperienced business owners to extend their reach into global markets. Most small companies lack the capital, personnel, and experience to invest directly in foreign facilities. In addition, entering a foreign market correctly requires research and learning about the culture, the people, and their preferences—something that requires time that most entrepreneurs don't have. The alternative is to license by finding someone who is already at home in that market and can capture it for you. Licensing is ideal for companies whose value lies in unique products or services, a recognized name, or proprietary technology or processes. "You have this little treasure trove of value," says one intellectual property attorney, "and licensing is

Company Example ➞ the key to unlocking it."[24] *For example, Joe Boxer Corporation, the widely known maker of underwear, activewear, lingerie, sleepwear, bedding, towels, tablecloths, and placemats, licenses its uniquely designed collections (picture boxer shorts adorned with pink pigs or glow-in-the-dark lips) to companies across the globe. Because of Joe Boxer's licensing arrangements, even the most conservative dressers in Canada, Australia, New Zealand, the United Kingdom, Mexico, Belgium, and the Netherlands can add a splash of excitement to their wardrobes—even if it is underneath!*[25]

Although many business owners consider licensing only their products to foreign companies, the licensing potential for intangibles such as processes, technology, copyrights, and trademarks often is greater. Entrepreneurs who enter licensing agreements often find that they make more money more simply than they could from actually selling their finished products in highly competitive markets that they may not understand fully. Disney licenses its famous cartoon characters, including Mickey and Minnie Mouse, Goofy, Roger Rabbit, and others to manufacturers in countries across the world. Independent record companies in the United States frequently rely on licensing deals with record distributors in foreign lands to sell their recordings. Foreign licensing enables a small business to enter foreign markets quickly, easily, and with virtually no capital investment. Risks to the company include the potential of losing control over its manufacturing and marketing and creating a competitor if the licensee gains too much knowledge and control. Securing proper patent, trademark, and copyright protection beforehand can minimize these risks, however. *Lil Lovell, founder of the original Coyote Ugly Saloon, learned a hard lesson about foreign licensing agreements. After GQ magazine published a story about the unique saloon, written by a former Coyote Ugly bartender, Disney released a movie based on Lovell's bourbon-and-beer joint. Lovell knew she had to make the most of the publicity the movie brought her business, and she saw that her dream of creating an international chain of bars was within reach. Because she lacked the capital to expand on her own, she decided to license the Coyote Ugly trademark. Lovell quickly created licensing agreements for 14 bars in locations ranging from Cabo San Lucas, Mexico, to Boston. However, because a licensing agreement does not give the licensor the control over licensees that a franchise contract gives franchisers over its franchisees, Lovell had virtually no input into how the bars were run. Frustrated, Lovell decided to change future agreements to ensure that she had a controlling stake in all new Coyote Ugly Saloons.*[26]

Company Example →

International Franchising

Franchising has become a major export industry for the United States. Over the past decade, a growing number of franchises have been attracted to international markets to boost sales and profits as the domestic market has become increasingly saturated with outlets and much tougher to wring growth from. International franchisers sell virtually every kind of product or service imaginable—from fast food to child day care—in global markets. In some cases, the products and services sold in international markets are identical to those sold in the United States. However, most franchisers have learned that they must modify their products and services to suit local tastes and customs. In the United States, prescription drugs are the primary emphasis at locations of the Medicine Shoppe, a drugstore franchise; however, in many of the company's international locations such as India and Malaysia, the Medicine Shoppe shifts its focus to over-the-counter drugs, which are prevalent in those cultures.[27] Like the Medicine Shoppe, fast-food chains operating in other countries often must make adjustments to their menus to please locals' palates. *In Japan, McDonald's (known as "Makudonarudo") outlets sell teriyaki burgers, rice burgers, and katsu burgers (cheese wrapped in a roast pork cutlet topped with katsu sauce and shredded cabbage) in addition to their traditional American fare. In the Philippines, the McDonald's menu includes a spicy Filipino-style burger, spaghetti, and chicken with rice. In Switzerland, McDonald's reaches hungry commuters in transit. The company has commissioned two railroad dining cars, each seating about 40 people, that run on two routes—from Geneva to Basel and Geneva to Brig. In addition to Big Macs, diners have a choice of red or white wine and beer. And because Egg McMuffins don't appeal to Swiss palates, the rolling restaurants offer the more traditional Swiss breakfast of croissant, marmalade, butter, and hard cheese. In Germany, McDonald's restaurants sell beer, and in Great Britain they offer British Cadbury chocolate sticks. Domino's Pizza operates more than 2,550 restaurants in 50 countries, where local managers have developed new pizza flavors such as mayonnaise and potato (Japan), lamb and*

Company Example →

As the domestic market has become increasingly saturated, franchises are turning to international markets for growth. The key to their success: adapting their products and services to suit local tastes.

pickled ginger (India), tuna and sweet corn (England), and reindeer sausage (Iceland) to cater to customers' preferences.

Although franchise outlets span the globe, Canada is the primary market for U.S. franchisers, with Japan and Europe following. These markets are most attractive to franchisers because they are similar to the U.S. market—a large middle-class population, rising personal incomes, strong demand for consumer goods, growing service economies, and spreading urbanization. Europe also holds special interest for many U.S. franchises as trade barriers there continue to topple, opening up the largest—and one of the most affluent—markets in the world. Although large franchisers are already well established in many European nations, a new wave of smaller franchisers is seeking to establish a foothold there. Growth potential is the primary attraction. Eastern European countries that recently have thrown off the chains of Communism are turning to franchising to help them move toward a market economy. Developing nations, where 80 percent of the world's population resides, hold promise for franchising in the future, with their large populations and budding economies. The U.S. Department of Commerce predicts that 75 percent of the growth in world trade over the next two decades will come from developing nations.[28] For franchisers entering these emerging nations, many of which are still in the volatile stages of formation, patience is the key. Profits may be years in coming, but franchisers see the long-term benefits of establishing a presence in these markets early on. In 1994, the Medicine Shoppe struck a deal with a company in Taiwan to open locations in that country. Today, the Medicine Shoppe has more than 100 locations in Taiwan and has since expanded into eight other developing nations, including India and Malaysia.[29]

Countertrading and Bartering

As business becomes increasingly global, companies are discovering that attracting customers is just one part of the battle. Another problem global businesses face when selling to some countries is that their currencies are virtually worthless outside their borders, so getting paid in a valuable currency is a real challenge! Companies wanting to reach these markets must countertrade or barter. A **countertrade** is a transaction in which a company selling goods or services in a foreign country agrees to help promote investment and trade in that country. The goal of the transaction is to help offset the capital drain from the foreign country's purchases. As entrepreneurs enter more developing nations, they will discover the need to develop skill at implementing this global trading strategy.

Big businesses are accustomed to countertrading to reach certain markets, but small- and medium-sized companies usually lack the skills and the resources needed to conduct countertrades on their own. However, they can tie into deals made by large corporations. *For instance, when export giant McDonnell Douglas sold $1.5 billion worth of jets to Spain recently, it agreed to a countertrade. As part of the deal, Cornnuts, Inc., a small maker of snack foods, agreed to open an office in Spain and to introduce hybrid corn technology there. Cornnuts had been eyeing Spain as an export market but didn't know how to get started. McDonnell Douglas arranged key meetings with Spanish officials and even helped the small company write its presentation and translate it into Spanish. The countertrade has proved to be a winner for Spain, McDonnell Douglas, and Cornnuts.*[30]

> **Company Example**

Countertrading does suffer from numerous drawbacks. Countertrade transactions can be complicated, cumbersome, and time consuming. They also increase the chances that a company will get stuck with useless merchandise that it cannot move. They can lead to unpleasant surprises concerning the quantity and quality of products required in the countertrade. Still, countertrading offers one major advantage: Sometimes it's the only way to make a sale!

Entrepreneurs must weigh the advantages against the disadvantages for their companies before committing to a countertrade deal. Because of its complexity and the risks involved, countertrading is not the best choice for a novice entrepreneur looking to break into the global marketplace.

Bartering, the exchange of goods and services for other goods and services, is another way of trading with countries lacking convertible currency. In a barter exchange, a company that manufactures electronics components might trade its products for the coffee that a business in a foreign country processes, which it then sells to a third company for cash. Barter transactions require finding a business with complementary needs, but they are much simpler than countertrade transactions.

Exporting

> **3.** Explain how to build a successful export program.

For years, small businesses in the United States could afford the luxury of conducting business at home in the world's largest market, never having to venture outside its borders. With increased global competition putting pressure on domestic markets and trade agreements opening up foreign markets as never before, however, small companies increasingly are looking toward exporting as a global business strategy. Large companies still dominate exporting. Although small companies account for 97 percent of the companies involved in exporting, they generate only one-third of the nation's export sales.[31] Only about 1 percent of America's small businesses export goods and services to other countries. However, a growing number of small companies, realizing the incredible profit potential it offers, are making exporting an ever-expanding part of their marketing plans. In 1991, the average international sales of an *Inc.* 500 company were just 3 percent of its total sales; today, international sales average more than 14 percent of total sales at *Inc.* 500 companies.[32]

> **Company Example**

InterClean Equipment Inc., a small maker of automatic truck and car washing systems, recently closed a deal to install a high-tech washing system for the Abu Dhabi National Oil Company (ADNOC) to keep its trucks clean and to protect the environment. Executives at InterClean used the resources of the U.S. Export Assistance Center and the Gold Key service to explore international markets. After five years of work, ADNOC decided to install one of InterClean's systems at one of its maintenance stations because of its ability to clean oil transport trucks in an environmentally friendly manner in just two-and-a-half minutes. The system is "touchless," requires no employees, and 90 percent of the water used is recycled. The company's primary customers are local governments, school districts, and industrial companies in Singapore, Kuwait, Italy, South Africa, and East Asia. Since breaking into international markets, InterClean has grown to 35 employees, and exports now account for 20 percent of its total sales.[33]

Approximately 250,000 U.S. companies currently export; however, experts estimate that at least twice as many are capable of exporting but are not doing so.[34] The biggest barrier facing companies that have never exported is not knowing where or how to start. Paul Hsu, whose company sells ginseng across the globe, explains, "Exporting starts with a global mind-set, which unfortunately, is not all that common among owners of small- and medium-sized businesses in the United States. Most entrepreneurs in the United States envision markets only within domestic and sometimes even state borders, while Japanese and other foreign entrepreneurs look at export markets first."[35] Breaking the psychological barrier to exporting is the first—and most difficult—step in setting up a successful program. The next step to creating a successful export business is to develop a clear export strategy. In fact, a recent study of 346 small exporting companies by Pierre-André Julien and Charles Ramangahahy found that small companies with well-defined export strategies outperformed those that merely dabbled in exporting.[36] What must an entrepreneur do to create a workable export strategy?

1. *Recognize that even the tiniest companies and least experienced entrepreneurs have the potential to export.* Size is no prerequisite for a successful export program. *Ed Hernando loved to cook and made dishes for friends and family. Before he knew it, Hernando had built a small family business, Hernando Fine Foods, selling a seafood and vegetable batter mix he had developed while experimenting in the family kitchen. The company's products sold well in the United States, but Hernando had never even considered exporting them to other countries until he participated in the U.S. Department of Commerce's Global Diversity Initiative (GDI), a program designed to encourage minority-owned businesses to export. Through the GDI, Hernando saw sales opportunities in Brazil and Mexico, where he participated in trade mission trips and met with potential distributors. Within a matter of months, Hernando Fine Foods was selling its batter mixes in both countries.*[37]

   Exporting not only can boost a small company's sales, but it also can accelerate its growth rate. Studies suggest that small companies that export grow markedly faster than those that do not.

2. *Analyze your product or service.* Is it special? New? Unique? High quality? Priced favorably due to lower costs or exchange rates? Does it appeal to a particular niche? In which countries would there be sufficient demand for it? In many foreign countries, products from America are in demand because they have an air of mystery about them! Exporters quickly learn the value foreign customers place on quality. *Ron Schutte, president of Creative Bakers of Brooklyn, a company that makes presliced cheesecakes for restaurants, saw an opportunity to sell in Japan. The only modification Schutte made to his high-quality cheesecakes was reducing the portion size from 4.5 ounces to 2.25 ounces to accommodate Japanese diners' smaller appetites.*[38]

3. *Analyze your commitment.* Are you willing to devote the time and the energy to develop export markets? Does your company have the necessary resources to capitalize on market opportunities? In any international venture, patience is essential. One expert estimates that penetrating a foreign market requires at least three years.[39] Laying the groundwork for an export operation can take from six to eight months (or longer), but entering foreign markets isn't as tough as most entrepreneurs think. "One of the biggest misconceptions people have is that they can't

Company Example

Company Example

Table 12.3

Management Issues
in the Export Decision

I. Experience

1. With what countries has your company already conducted business (or from what countries have you received inquiries about your product or service)?
2. What product lines do foreign customers ask about most often?
3. Prepare a list of sale inquiries for each buyer by product and by country.
4. Is the trend of inquiries or sales increasing or decreasing?
5. Who are your primary domestic and foreign competitors?
6. What lessons has your company learned from past export experience?

II. Management and Personnel

1. Who will be responsible for the export entity's organization and staff? (Do you have an export "champion"?)
2. How much top management time
   a. should you allocate to exporting?
   b. can you afford to allocate to exporting?
3. What does management expect from its exporting efforts? What are your company's export goals and objectives?
4. What organizational structure will your company require to ensure that it can service export sales properly? (Note the political implications, if any.)
5. Who will implement the plan?

III. Production Capacity

1. To what extent is your company using its existing production capacity? Is there any excess? If so, how much?
2. Will filling export orders hurt your company's ability to make and service domestic sales?
3. What will additional production for export markets cost your company?
4. Are there seasonal or cyclical fluctuations in your company's workload? When? Why?
5. Is there a minimum quantity foreign customers must order for a sale to be profitable?
6. To what extent would your company need to modify its products, packaging, and design specifically for its export targets? Is your product quality adequate for foreign customers?
7. What pricing structure will your company use? Will prices be competitive?
8. How will your company collect payment on its export sales?

IV. Financial Capacity

1. How much capital will your company need to begin exporting? Where will it come from?
2. How will you allocate the initial costs of your company's export effort?
3. Does your company have other expansion plans that would compete with an exporting effort?
4. By what date do you expect your company's export program to pay for itself?
5. How important is establishing a global presence to your company's future success?

Source: Adapted from *A Basic Guide to Exporting* (Washington, D.C.: U.S. Department of Commerce, 1986), p. 3.

---

market overseas unless they have a big team of lawyers and specialists," says one export specialist. "That just isn't true."[40] Table 12.3 summarizes key issues managers must address in the export decision.

4. *Research markets and pick your target.* Before investing in a costly sales trip abroad, entrepreneurs should make a trip to the local library or the nearest branch of the Department of Commerce and the International Trade Administration. Exporters can choose from a multitude of guides, manuals, books, statistical reports, newsletters, videos, and other resources to help them research potential markets. Armed with research, small business owners can avoid wasting a lot of time and money on markets with limited potential for their products and can concentrate on those with the greatest promise. The World Bank projects that by 2020, the world's largest economies will be China, the United States, Japan, India, Indonesia, Germany, and Korea.

Company Example →

Managers at Ekkwill Tropical Fish Farm, a wholesale fish supplier, discovered through research that collecting fish is an even more popular hobby in Japan than in the United States. Ekkwill now flies one-third of its production—some 4 million fish—to Japan as well as to Latin America, Asia, Canada, and the West Indies. Its best-selling fish in international markets are Florida gars, red swordtails, and new world cichlids, all common breeds in North America but considered exotic in other lands.[41]

Research shows export entrepreneurs whether they need to modify their existing products and services to suit the tastes and preferences of their foreign target customers. Sometimes foreign customers' lifestyles, housing needs, body sizes, and cultures require exporters to make alterations in their product lines. *For instance, when Rodney Robbins, CEO of Robbins Industries, a maker of measuring cups and spoons, was negotiating with a distributor prior to entering the Swedish and British markets, he learned that he would have to modify his products slightly. The British use measuring utensils labeled in milliliters whereas the Swedes prefer deciliters.*[42] Such modifications can sometimes spell the difference between success and failure in the global market.

In other cases, products destined for export need little or no modification. *Before he began exporting his company's batter mixes to Brazil and Mexico, Ed Hernando conducted taste tests and discovered that foreign customers preferred the products just the way they were. "The only thing I did was change my packaging to Portuguese and Spanish languages," he says.*[43] Experts estimate that one-half of exported products require little modification; one-third require moderate modification; only a few require major changes. Table 12.4 offers questions to guide entrepreneurs conducting export research.

5. *Develop a distribution strategy.* Should you use an export intermediary or sell directly to foreign customers? Small companies just entering international markets may prefer to rely on export intermediaries to break new ground. *Lynn Cooper, president of BFW Inc., a 25-year-old medical lighting supplier, uses wholesale distributors to sell her company's products in 25 countries. Exports account for 30 percent of BFW's sales, and Cooper is happy with her method of distribution. "With distributors, the risk to us is minimal, but we still know just where the products are going," she says.*[44]

6. *Find your customer.* Small businesses can rely on a host of export specialists to help them track down foreign customers. (Refer to Table 12.2 for a list of some of the resources available from the government.) The U.S. Department of Commerce and

Company Example

Company Example

Company Example

Table 12.4

Questions to Guide International Market Research

- Is there an overseas market for your company's products or services?
- Are there specific target markets that look most promising?
- Which new markets abroad are most likely to open up or expand?
- How big is the market your company is targeting, and how fast is it growing?
- What are the major economic, political, legal, social, technological, and other environmental factors affecting this market?
- What are the demographic and cultural factors affecting this market? For example, disposable income, occupation, age, gender, opinions, activities, interests, tastes, and values.
- Who are your company's present and potential customers abroad?
- What are their needs and desires? What factors influence their buying decisions: price, credit terms, delivery terms, quality, brand name, others?
- How would they use your company's product or service? What modifications, if any, would be necessary to sell to your target customers?
- Who are your primary competitors in the foreign market?
- How do competitors distribute, sell, and promote their products? What are their prices?
- What are the best channels of distribution for your product?
- What is the best way for your company to gain exposure in this market?
- Are there any barriers such as tariffs, quotas, duties, or regulations to selling your product in this market? Are there any incentives?
- Are there any potential licensing or joint venture partners already in this market?

Source: Adapted from *A Basic Guide to Exporting* (Washington, D.C.: Department of Commerce, 1986), p. 11.

the International Trade Administration should be the first stops on an entrepreneur's agenda for going global. These agencies have market research available through the U.S. Commercial Service Market Research Library for locating the best target markets for a particular company and specific customers in those markets. Industry Sector Analyses (ISAs), International Market Insights (IMIs), and Customized Market Analyses (CMAs) are just some of the reports and services global entrepreneurs find most useful. They also have knowledgeable staff specialists experienced in the details of global trade and in the intricacies of foreign cultures. *When Phillip Kirsch, founder of IPM Tech, a small company that has developed a simple, environmentally safe, effective method of controlling pests, began to explore potential export markets for his company's products, he turned to industry sector reports for the information he needed. With the help of the reports and Commercial Service trade specialists, Kirsch determined that New Zealand, South Africa, the Netherlands, and Canada were the best markets to target initially. IPM Tech's export program is now profitable, and Kirsch says that the 14 countries to which the company now exports are just the beginning of a more comprehensive export strategy.*[45]

Other entrepreneurs search out customers on their own. *For instance, Jeff Ake, co-owner of Electronic Liquid Fillers, Inc., a small packaging equipment company, spent seven weeks calling on potential customers in the Pacific Rim. He identified his target customers with the help of foreign-based, English-language industry trade magazines. During his travels, Ake used the local English-language equivalent of the Yellow Pages to find others.*[46]

7. *Find financing.* One of the biggest barriers to small business exports is lack of financing. Access to adequate financing is a crucial ingredient in a successful export program because the cost of generating foreign sales often is higher and collection cycles are longer. The trouble is that bankers and other sources of capital don't always understand the intricacies of international sales and view financing them as highly risky ventures. Also, among major industrialized nations, the U.S. government spends the least per capita to promote exports.

Several federal, state, and private programs are operating to fill this export financing void, however. Programs such as the SBA's Export Working Capital Program (loan guarantees up to $1.5 million or 90 percent of the loan amount, whichever is less), the Export-Import Bank, the Overseas Private Investment Corporation, and a variety of state-sponsored programs offer export-minded entrepreneurs both direct loans and loan guarantees. (A list of all state foreign trade assistance offices is available on the Commerce Department's National Export Directory.) In recent years, the Export-Import Bank has emphasized loans and loan guarantees for small exporters. The Bankers Association for Foreign Trade is an association of 150 banks of all sizes from around the world that matches exporters needing foreign trade financing with interested banks. *Once Metz Tool and Die began implementing its export strategy to sell its custom-made molds in Mexico, managers at the small manufacturer turned to the Small Business Administration and the Export-Import Bank for the financing it needed to fill and ship the orders. A loan guarantee from the SBA's Export Working Capital program convinced a local bank, AMCORE Bank, to grant Metz a $500,000 loan, and the Export-Import Bank provided the financing for Metz to acquire the necessary insurance to complete its global transactions.*[47]

8. *Ship your goods.* Export novices usually rely on international freight forwarders and custom-house agents—experienced specialists in overseas shipping—for help in navigating the bureaucratic morass of packaging requirements and paperwork demanded by customs. These specialists, also known as transport architects, are to exporters what travel agents are to passengers and normally charge relatively small fees for a valuable service. They move shipments of all sizes to destinations all over

the world efficiently, saving entrepreneurs many headaches. "[A freight forwarder] is going to be sure that his client conforms with all the government regulations that apply to export cargo," explains the owner of an international freight forwarding business. "He acts as an agent of the exporter, and, in most circumstances, is like an extension of that exporter's traffic department." The Johnston Sweeper Company, a manufacturer of street sweepers, ships its 20,000-pound pieces of equipment worldwide with the help of an international freight forwarder.[48] Table 12.5 features common international shipping terms and their meaning.

Table 12.5

Common International Shipping Terms and Their Meaning

Shipping Term	Seller's Responsibility	Buyer's Responsibility	Shipping Method(s) Used
FOB ("Free on Board"), Seller	Deliver goods to carrier and provide export license and clean on-board receipt. Bear risk of loss until goods are delivered to carrier.	Pay shipping, freight, and insurance charges. Bear risk of loss while goods are in transit.	All
FOB ("Free on Board"), Buyer	Deliver goods to the buyer's place of business and provide export license and clean on-board receipt. Pay shipping, freight, and insurance charges.	Accept delivery of goods after documents are tendered.	All
FAS ("Free Along Side"), Vessel	Deliver goods alongside ship. Provide an "alongside" receipt.	Provide export license and proof of delivery of the goods to the carrier. Bear risk of loss once goods are delivered to the carrier.	Ship
CFR ("Cost and Freight")	Deliver goods to carrier, obtain export licenses, and pay export taxes. Provide buyer with clean bill of lading. Pay freight and shipping charges. Bear risk of loss until goods are delivered to buyer.	Pay insurance charges. Accept delivery of goods after documents are tendered.	Ship
CIF ("Cost, Insurance, and Freight")	Same as CFR plus pay insurance charges and provide buyer with insurance policy.	Accept delivery of goods after documents are tendered.	Ship
CPT ("Carriage Paid to . . .")	Deliver goods to carrier, obtain export license, and pay export taxes. Provide buyer with clean transportation documents. Pay shipping and freight charges.	Pay insurance charges. Accept delivery of goods after documents are tendered.	All
CIP ("Carriage and Insurance Paid to . . .")	Same as CPT plus pay insurance changes and provide buyer with insurance policy.	Accept delivery of goods after documents are tendered.	All
DDU ("Delivered Duty Unpaid")	Obtain export license, pay insurance charges, and provide buyer documents for taking delivery.	Take delivery of goods and pay import duties.	All
DDP ("Delivered Duty Paid")	Obtain export license and pay import duty, pay insurance changes, and provide buyer documents for taking delivery.	Take delivery of goods.	All

Source: Adapted from *Guide to the Finance of International Trade,* edited by Gordon Platt (HBSC Trade Services, Marine Midland Bank, and the *Journal of Commerce*), infoserv2.ita.doc.gov/efm/efm.nsf/503d177e3c63f0b48525675900112e24/6218a8703573b32985256759004c41f3/$FILE/Finance_.pdf>, pp. 6–10.

Figure 12.3

How a Letter of Credit Works

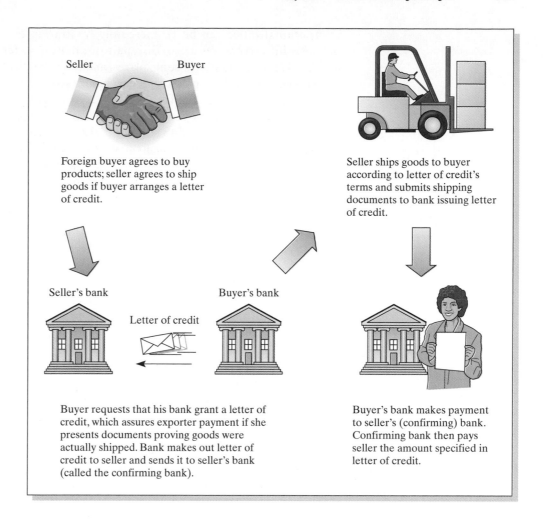

Seller   Buyer

Foreign buyer agrees to buy products; seller agrees to ship goods if buyer arranges a letter of credit.

Seller ships goods to buyer according to letter of credit's terms and submits shipping documents to bank issuing letter of credit.

Seller's bank   Buyer's bank

Letter of credit

Buyer requests that his bank grant a letter of credit, which assures exporter payment if she presents documents proving goods were actually shipped. Bank makes out letter of credit to seller and sends it to seller's bank (called the confirming bank).

Buyer's bank makes payment to seller's (confirming) bank. Confirming bank then pays seller the amount specified in letter of credit.

9. *Collect your money.* Collecting foreign accounts can be more complex than collecting domestic ones; but by picking their customers carefully and checking their credit references closely, entrepreneurs can minimize bad-debt losses. Financing foreign sales often involves special credit arrangements such as letters of credit and bank (or documentary) drafts. A **letter of credit** is an agreement between an exporter's bank and the foreign buyer's bank that guarantees payment to the exporter for a specific shipment of goods. In essence, a letter of credit reduces the financial risk for the exporter by substituting a bank's creditworthiness for that of the purchaser (see Figure 12.3). A **bank draft** is a document the seller draws on the buyer, requiring the buyer to pay the face amount (the purchase price of the goods) either on sight (a sight draft) or on a specified date (a time draft) once the goods are shipped. Rather than use letters of credit or drafts, some exporters simply require cash in advance or cash on delivery (C.O.D.). Insisting on cash payments up-front, however, may cause some foreign buyers to reject a deal. The parties to an international deal should always come to an agreement in advance on an acceptable method of payment.

Establishing International Locations

Once established in international markets, some small businesses set up permanent locations there. Establishing an office or a factory in a foreign land can require a substantial investment reaching beyond the budgets of many small companies. Plus, setting up an international office can be an incredibly frustrating experience in some countries. Business infrastructures are in disrepair or are nonexistent. Getting a telephone line installed can take months in some places, and finding reliable equipment to move goods to customers is nearly impossible. Securing necessary licenses and permits from bureaucrats often takes more than filing the necessary paperwork; in some nations, bureaucrats expect payments to "grease the wheels of justice." Finding the right person to manage an international office is crucial to success; it also is a major challenge, especially for small businesses. Small companies usually have lean management staffs and cannot afford to send key people abroad without running the risk of losing their focus.

> Company Example ⟶

Few small businesses begin their global ventures by establishing international locations, preferring, instead, to build a customer base through some of the other strategies covered earlier in this section. *For example, Domes International, a Memphis, Tennessee–based company that manufactures low-maintenance, inexpensive dome-shaped homes out of fiberglass, began its global ventures by exporting to India. The company was so successful in India that managers decided to build a manufacturing facility there to be able to serve the local market more efficiently. Locating a plant there also will allow Domes International to supply its low-cost homes, some of which resemble igloos and others that look more like marshmallows, to customers in nearby Pakistan, Afghanistan, Bangladesh, and Sri Lanka. With help from the U.S. Commercial Service, Domes International received $1.2 million in financing from the Overseas Private Investment Corporation (OPIC) to construct the manufacturing plant. "It will serve a market of 50 million people by providing affordable housing that will survive even the harshest conditions," says OPIC's president.*[49]

Small companies that establish international locations can reap significant benefits. Start-up costs are lower in some foreign countries, and lower labor costs can produce significant savings as well. In addition, by locating in a foreign country, a business learns firsthand how its culture influences business and how it can satisfy customers' demands most effectively. In essence, the business becomes a local corporate citizen.

Going global by employing one or more of these eight strategies can put tremendous strain on a small company, but the benefits of cracking international markets can be significant. Not only does going global offer attractive sales and profit possibilities, but it also strengthens the company's competitive skills and enhances its overall reputation. Pleasing tough foreign customers also keeps companies on their competitive toes.

IN THE FOOTSTEPS OF AN ENTREPRENEUR...

Mandolins from Montana to the World

In 1980, Bruce Weber, a talented musician and artist, started working at the Flatiron Mandolin and Banjo Company in Bozeman, Montana, where he learned as much as he could about lathery, the making of stringed instruments. Several years later, Gibson Guitar purchased Flatiron and moved the operation to Nashville, Tennessee. Weber and a core of experienced luthiers (stringed instrument makers) couldn't stand the idea of leaving the beauty of Montana and all that their lifestyles there offered, and they began to plan to launch their own mandolin-making business. Their reputations for integrity and quality already had created a

loyal following of customers who were begging them to go into business for themselves, and so they did.

In 1997, with a loan from First Security Bank and a development grant for creating jobs in Belgrade, Montana, Weber and his small team of skilled artisans launched Sound to Earth Ltd in Weber's backyard. Their goal was to integrate their moral values and their work ethics into a successful business. By early 2003, Sound to Earth had captured 30 percent of the U.S. mandolin market, sales were growing, and the number of employees had increased from just five to 26. When hiring new employees, Weber looks for artists, whether their specialties are painting, sculpting, pottery, or fly-tying. As long as an employee has a passion for art and craftsmanship, Weber and his colleagues can teach the skills necessary to craft the company's beautiful mandolins, which can take up to 80 hours over an eight-week period to build.

Weber soon saw an opportunity for Sound to Earth to ply the waters of global trade. Twice a year, Weber and some of his team attend a trade show sponsored by the National Association of Music Merchants, where they meet many international distributors who are interested in selling their instruments overseas. Sound to Earth's Web site is another important link in its international business strategy, especially given its location in Logan, Montana. "The Internet has played a huge part in our sales," says Weber, "because people find our products online and then go to their dealers to request them." That is just how the company landed a distribution contract with a large instrument dealer in London.

Weber has big plans for Sound to Earth's future, including the addition of guitars and fiddles to the product line and pursuing sales in other countries around the world. Although export sales currently account for only 5 percent of the company's total sales, Weber sees the appeal of the mandolin as nearly universal because "mandolin music brings people together, families together—it's happy music." The company's next target is Japan, where, surprisingly, blue grass music is becoming popular. Europe also is on the company's radar screen as a potential market. Weber plans to attend the music industry's largest trade show, the Musikmesse, in Frankfurt, Germany, to search for potential distributors there. Weber believes that Sound to Earth is just beginning to realize its potential for international sales and that the company's global strategy will prove to be a beautiful tune.

1. What advice would you offer Weber about increasing Sound to Earth's international sales?
2. Which of the eight strategies for going global discussed in this chapter would you recommend for Sound to Earth? Explain.

Sources: Adapted from Inge McNeese and Shae Wright, "Mandolins for a Global Market: Handmade in Montana," *Export America,* January 2004, pp. 6–7; Sound to Earth Ltd, www.soundtoearth.com.

Barriers to International Trade

4. Discuss the major barriers to international trade and their impact on the global economy.

Governments have always used a variety of barriers to block free trade among nations in an attempt to protect businesses within their own borders. The benefit of protecting their own companies, however, comes at the expense of foreign businesses, which face limited access to global markets. Ultimately, customers in nations that restrict free trade pay the price in the form of higher prices and smaller supplies of goods available. Numerous trade barriers—both domestic and international—restrict the freedom of businesses in global trading. Even with these barriers, international trade has grown more than 36-fold to over *$9 trillion* since the 1970s.[50]

Domestic Barriers

Sometimes the biggest barriers potential exporters face are right here at home. Three major domestic roadblocks are common: attitude, information, and financing. Perhaps the biggest barrier to small businesses exporting is the attitude: "I'm too small to export. That's just for big corporations." The first lesson of exporting is "Take nothing for granted about who can export and what you can and cannot export." The first step to building an export program is recognizing that the opportunity to export exists.

Another reason entrepreneurs neglect international markets is a lack of information about how to get started. The key to success in international markets is choosing the correct target market and designing the appropriate strategy to reach it. That requires access to information and research. Although a variety of government and private organizations make volumes of exporting and international marketing information available, many small business owners never use it. A successful global marketing strategy also recognizes that not all international markets are the same. Companies must be flexible and willing to make adjustments to their products and services, promotional campaigns, packaging, and sales techniques.

Another significant obstacle is the lack of export financing available. A common complaint among small exporters is that they lose export business simply because they cannot get the financing to support it. Many bankers that serve small companies' financial needs do not have experience in conducting international business and simply deny loans for international transactions because they see them as too risky.

International Barriers

Domestic barriers are not the only ones export-minded entrepreneurs must overcome. Trading nations also erect obstacles to free trade. Two types of international barriers are common: tariff and nontariff.

Tariff Barriers. A **tariff** is a tax, or duty, that a government imposes on goods and services imported into that country. Imposing tariffs raises the price of the imported goods—making them less attractive to consumers—and protects the makers of comparable domestic products and services. Established in the United States in 1790 by Alexander Hamilton, the tariff system generated the majority of federal revenues for about 100 years. Today, the U.S. tariff code lists duties on thousands of items, ranging from brooms and fish fillets to steel and fence posts. *Toy Biz, Inc., a subsidiary of Marvel Comics, recently won a battle (retroactively) over tariffs levied on plastic action figures of X-Men characters the company imported from China. U.S. customs officials claimed the action figures were "dolls" subject to a tariff of 12 percent, but managers at Toy Biz argued that the figures were "toys" subject to a tariff of 6.8 percent. In a 32-page decision, a judge in the Court of International Trade ruled in favor of Toy Biz, declaring that the X-Men figures indeed were toys and not dolls.*[51]

Nations across the globe rely on tariffs to protect local manufacturers of certain products. If a small company's products are subject to those tariffs, exporting to that nation becomes much more difficult because remaining price competitive with products made by local manufacturers is virtually impossible. *When the market for their boat sail manufacturing business in the United States slipped, Bob Pattison and Tim Yourieff, owners of Neil Pryde Sails International, decided to expand into international sales. The U.S. market made up 90 percent of the company's sales, and its future growth was questionable. Pattison and Yourieff, whose company makes everything from $170 sails for small boats to $20,000 custom-made sails for racing yachts, wanted to target the most prized sail market in the world: Europe. The major barrier they faced was a 14 percent tariff European countries imposed on sails from the United States, making their product much more costly than European-made sails. When they made their decision to move into Europe, currency exchange rates for a weakening dollar enabled them to more than offset the surcharge added to their sails by the tariff. By emphasizing the quality of their product, Pattison and Yourieff finally were able to break into the European sail market.*[52]

Nontariff Barriers. Many nations have lowered the tariffs they impose on products and services brought into their borders, but they rely on other nontariff structures as protectionist trade barriers.

Quotas. Rather than impose a direct tariff on certain imported products, nations often use quotas to protect their industries. A **quota** is a limit on the amount of a product imported into a country. Recently, three U.S.-based manufacturers of coat hangers asked the U.S. International Trade Commission (ITC) to impose a quota on wire hangers from China because imports of the hangers were "increasing rapidly" and threatened to cause "material injury" to the domestic hanger makers. After reviewing the evidence, the ITC voted to protect the domestic makers of wire hangers.[53] The U.S. textile industry, which

Company Example

Company Example

has lost market share to competitors in the East Asia (particularly China) that can make textiles much cheaper, is concerned about further deterioration as quotas that limit imported textiles are scheduled to expire soon.

Embargoes. An **embargo** is a total ban on imports of certain products or all products from a particular nation. The motivation for embargoes is not always economic; in fact, politics often lies at the heart of embargoes. From 1975 until 1994, the United States imposed an embargo on all goods from Vietnam as a result of the Vietnam War, and an embargo on trade with Cuba, begun in 1963, still exists today. Embargoes operate in other parts of the world as well. Traditionally, Taiwan, South Korea, and Israel have banned imports of Japanese autos.

Dumping. In an effort to grab market share quickly, some companies have been guilty of **dumping** products, selling large quantities of them in foreign countries below cost. The United States has been a dumping target for steel, televisions, shoes, and computer chips in the past. Under the U.S. Antidumping Act, a company must prove that the foreign company's prices are lower here than in the home country and that U.S. companies are directly harmed. In response to a complaint from a group of 30 U.S.-based manufacturers of wood furniture, the U.S. International Trade Commission ruled that Chinese manufacturers were dumping wooden bedroom furniture in the United States at unfairly low prices, and, as a result, were damaging the ability of domestic producers to compete. In just two years, they claimed, their sales fell 23 percent, their net income dropped 75 percent, and they were forced to cut their workforces by 28 percent. The U.S. furniture manufacturers asked the ITC to impose stiff tariffs of 440 percent on all wooden bedroom furniture from China.[54]

Political Barriers

Entrepreneurs who go global quickly discover a labyrinth of political tangles. Although many American business owners complain of excessive government regulation in the United States, they are often astounded by the complex web of governmental and legal regulations and barriers they encounter in foreign countries.

Companies doing business in politically risky lands face the very real dangers of government takeovers of private property; attempts at coups to overthrow ruling parties; kidnappings, bombings, and other violent acts against businesses and their employees; and other threatening events. Employees of several companies working to rebuild Iraq after the war there have been killed in uprisings by militants loyal to the former regime. Companies' investments of millions of dollars may evaporate overnight in the wake of a government coup or the passage of a law nationalizing an industry (giving control of an entire industry to the government).

Some nations welcome foreign business investment whereas others do everything they can to discourage competition from foreign companies. *For example, so that Japanese companies could catch up, the Japanese recently used a web of regulations to stall a California company that had developed a system for electronically mapping cities to improve ambulance, police, and fire services. The government decided that the company, Etak Inc., needed a license before it could proceed. By the time the license materialized, a Japanese competitor had erased Etak's head start and had captured most of the market.*[55]

Company Example

Business Barriers

U.S. companies doing business internationally quickly learn that business practices and regulations in foreign lands can be quite different from those in the United States. Simply duplicating the practices they have adopted (and have used successfully) in the domestic market and using them in foreign markets is not always a good idea. Perhaps the biggest shock comes in the area of human resources management, where international managers discover that practices common in the United States such as overtime, working women, and employee benefits are restricted, disfavored, or forbidden in other cultures. Business owners new to international business sometimes are shocked at the wide range of labor costs they encounter and the severe lack of skilled labor in some regions. In some countries, what appear to be "bargain" labor rates turn out to be excessively high after accounting for the quality of the labor force and the mandated benefits their governments impose—from company-sponsored housing, meals, and clothing to required profit sharing and extended vacations. For instance, in most European nations, workers are accustomed to four to six weeks of vacation compared to two weeks in the United States. One company that opened an office in Germany learned that workers expected six weeks of paid vacation, 14 paid holidays, and 14 days of sick leave; in essence, a typical employee was not working for almost three months out of the year![56] In many nations, labor unions are present in almost every company, yet they play a very different role from the unions in the United States. Although management–union relations are not as hostile as in the United States and strikes are not as common, unions can greatly complicate a company's ability to compete effectively.

Cultural Barriers

The **culture** of a nation includes the beliefs, values, views, and mores that its inhabitants share. Differences in cultures among nations create another barrier to international trade. The diversity of languages, business philosophies, practices, and traditions make international trade more complex than selling to the business down the street. Entrepreneurs wanting to do business in international markets must have a clear understanding and appreciation of the cultures in which they plan to do business. Consider the following examples:

- A U.S. entrepreneur, eager to expand into the European Community, arrives at his company's potential business partner's headquarters in France. Confidently, he strides into the meeting room, enthusiastically pumps his host's hand, slaps him on the back, and says, "Tony, I've heard a great deal about you; please, call me Bill." Eager to explain the benefits of his product, he opens his briefcase and gets right down to business. The French executive politely excuses himself and leaves the room before negotiations ever begin, shocked by the American's rudeness and ill manners. Rudeness and ill manners? Yes—from the French executive's perspective.
- Another American business owner flies to Tokyo to close a deal with a Japanese executive. He is pleased when his host invites him to play a round of golf shortly after he arrives. He plays well and manages to win by a few strokes. The Japanese executive invites him to play again the next day, and again the American wins by a few strokes. Invited to play another round the following day, the American asks, "But when are we going to start doing business?" His host, surprised by the question, says, "But we *have* been doing business."

When American businesspeople enter international markets for the first time, they often are amazed at the differences in foreign cultures' habits and customs. In the first scenario described, for instance, had the entrepreneur done his homework, he would have known that the French are very formal (backslapping is *definitely* taboo!) and do not typically use first names in business relationships (even among longtime colleagues). In the second scenario, a global manager would have known that the Japanese place a tremendous importance on developing personal relationships before committing to any business deals. Thus, he would have seen the golf games for what they really were: an integral part of building a business relationship.

Understanding and heeding these often subtle cultural differences is one of the most important keys to international business success. "There's more to business than just business," says one writer, "particularly when confronting the subtleties of deeply ingrained cultural customs, conventions, and protocols that abound in today's global marketplace."[57] Conducting a business meeting with a foreign executive in the same manner as one with an American businessperson could doom the deal from the outset. Business customs and behaviors that are acceptable—even expected—in this country may be taboo in others.

Entrepreneurs who fail to learn the differences in the habits and customs of the cultures in which they hope to do business are at a distinct disadvantage. When it comes to conducting international business, a lack of understanding of cultures and business practices can be as great a barrier to structuring and implementing a business transaction as an error in the basic assumptions of the deal. Consider, for instance, the American who was in the final stages of contract negotiations with an Indonesian company. Given the size of the contract and his distance from home, the American business executive was nervous. Sitting across from his Indonesian counterpart, the American propped his feet up. Obviously angered, the Indonesian business owner stormed out of the room, refusing to sign the contract and leaving the American executive totally bewildered. Only later did he discover that exposing the soles of one's shoes to an Indonesian is an insult. Profuse apologies and some delicate negotiations salvaged the deal.[58]

In another incident, an American went to Malaysia to close a sizeable contract. In an elaborate ceremony, he was introduced to a man he thought was named "Roger." Throughout the negotiations, he called the man "Rog," not realizing that his potential client was a "rajah," a title of nobility, not a name.[59]

On his first trip to the Middle East, an American executive was touring the city with his Arab business contact. As they strolled along the dusty streets, the host reached over, took the executive's hand in his, and the two continued to walk, the host's hand holding the executive's. Totally stunned, the American didn't even have the presence of mind to jerk his hand away—much to his good fortune. He learned later that in his host's country, taking his hand was a sign of great respect and friendship. Jerking his hand away from his host would have been considered a major insult![60]

An American business woman in London was invited to a party hosted by an advertising agency. Unsure of her ability to navigate the streets and subways of London alone, she approached a British colleague who was driving to the party and asked him, "Could I get a ride with you?" After he turned bright red from embarrassment, he regained his composure and politely said, "Lucky for you I know what you meant." Unknowingly, the young woman had requested a sexual encounter with her colleague, not a lift to the party![61]

Company Example → Inaccurate translations of documents into other languages often pose embarrassing problems for companies conducting international business. *Interactive Magic, a North Carolina software company, had introduced several computer games in Germany that had been quite successful. Executives at the small company expected that their newest release, "Capitalism," would be the best-selling game yet. After the game hit store shelves in Germany, however, managers discovered that the instructions told customers to use a nail file to get the game running on their computers. In the translation from English to German, the word file somehow lost its electronic meaning and became a beauty accessory![62]* In other cases, mistranslated ads have left foreign locals scratching their heads, wondering why a company's advertising message would say *that!* For example, when an ad for Kentucky Fried Chicken that was supposed to say "Finger lickin' good" was translated into Chinese, it came out as "Eat your fingers off." An ad for the Parker Pen Company that was supposed to say "Avoid embarrassment" in Spanish actually said "Avoid pregnancy," leaving Parker Pen executives quite embarrassed themselves.[63]

The accompanying "Gaining a Competitive Edge" feature shows the importance of learning about a nation's culture before conducting business there.

✦ GAINING *a* COMPETITIVE EDGE ✦

The Secret Language of International Business

When U.S. businesspeople enter international markets for the first time, they often are amazed at the differences in foreign cultures' habits and customs. Understanding and heeding these often subtle cultural differences is one of the most important keys to international business success. The maze of cultural variables from one country to another can be confusing, but with proper preparation and a little common sense, any manager can handle international transactions successfully. In short, before packing your bags, do your homework. In most cases, conducting international business successfully requires managers to have unlimited patience, a long-term commitment, and a thorough knowledge of the local market, business practices, and culture. The key for entrepreneurs is learning to be sensitive to the business cultures in which they operate. Consider these pointers.

- Patience is a must for doing business in Spain. Like the French, Spaniards want to get to know business associates before working with them. In the United States, business comes before pleasure, but in Spain business is conducted after dinner, when the drinks and cigars are served. "I've known American businessmen who have shocked their Spanish host by pulling out their portfolios and charts before dinner is even served," says one expert. In Spain, women should avoid crossing their legs; it is considered unladylike. Men usually cross their legs at the knees.

- Appearance and style are important to Italian businesspeople; they judge the polish and the expertise of the company's executives as well as the quality of its products and services. Italians expect presentations to be organized, clear, and exact. A stylish business wardrobe also is an asset in Italy. Physical contact is an accepted part of Italian society. Don't be surprised if an Italian businessperson uses a lingering handshake or touches you occasionally when doing business.

- In Great Britain, businesspeople consider it extremely important to conduct business "properly" with formality and reserve. Boisterous behavior such as backslapping or overindulging in alcohol and ostentatious displays of wealth are considered ill-mannered. The British do not respond to hard-sell tactics but do appreciate well-mannered executives. Politeness and impeccable manners are useful tools for conducting business successfully in Great Britain.

- In Mexico, making business appointments through a well-connected Mexican national will go a long way to assuring successful business deals. "People in Mexico do business with somebody they know, they like, or they're related to," says one expert. Because family and tradition are top priorities for Mexicans, entrepreneurs who discuss their family heritages and can talk knowledgeably about Mexican history are a step ahead. In business meetings, making extended eye contact is considered impolite.

- In China, entrepreneurs will need an ample dose of the "three Ps": patience, patience, patience. Nothing in China—especially business—happens fast! In conversations and negotiations, periods of silence are common; they are a sign of politeness and contemplation. The Chinese view personal space much differently than Americans; in normal conversation, they will stand much closer to their partners.

- American entrepreneurs doing business in the Pacific Rim should avoid hard-sell techniques, which are an immediate turnoff to Asian businesspeople. Harmony, patience, and consensus make good business companions in this region. It is also a good idea to minimize the importance of legal documents in negotiations. Although getting deals and trade agreements down in writing always is advisable, attempting to negotiate detailed contracts (as most U.S. businesspeople tend to do) would insult most Asians, who base their deals on mutual trust and benefits.

- Japanese executives conduct business much like the British: with an emphasis on formality, thoughtfulness, and respect. Don't expect to hear Japanese executives say no, even during a negotiation; they don't want to offend or to appear confrontational. Instead of saying no, the Japanese negotiator will say, "It is very difficult," "Let us think about that," or "Let us get back to you on that." Similarly, yes from a Japanese executive doesn't necessarily mean that. It could mean, "I understand," "I hear you," or "I don't understand what you mean, but I don't want to embarrass you."

- In Japan and South Korea, exchanging business cards, known in Japan as *meishi,* is an important business function (unlike Great Britain, where exchanging business cards is less popular). A Western executive who accepts a Japanese companion's card and then slips it into his pocket or scribbles notes on it has committed a major blunder. Tradition there says a business card must be treated just as its owner would be—with respect. Travelers should present their own cards using both hands with the card positioned so the recipient can read it. (The flip side should be printed in Japanese, an expected courtesy.)

- Greeting a Japanese executive properly includes a bow and a handshake—showing respect for both cultures. In many traditional Japanese businesses, exchanging gifts at the first meeting is appropriate. Also, a love of golf (the Japanese are crazy about the game) is a real plus for winning business in Japan.

1. What steps should an entrepreneur take to avoid committing cultural blunders when conducting global business?

Source: Adapted from Laura Fortunato, "Japan: Making It in the USA," *Region Focus,* Fall 1997, p. 15; David Stamps, "Welcome to America," *Training,* November 1996, p. 30; Barbara Pachter, "When in Japan, Don't Cross Your Legs," *Business Ethics,* March/April 1996, p. 50; Tom Dunkel, "A New Breed of People Gazers," *Insight,* January 13, 1992, pp. 10–14; M. Katherine Glover, "Do's and Taboos," *Business America,* August 13, 1990, pp. 2–6; Deidre Sullivan, "An American Businesswoman's Guide to Japan," *Overseas Business,* Winter 1990, pp. 50–55; Stephanie Barlow, "Let's Make a Deal," *Entrepreneur,* May 1991, p. 40; "Worldy Wise," *Entrepreneur,* March 1991, p. 40; David Altany, "Culture Clash," *Industry Week,* October 2, 1989, pp. 13–20; Edward T. Hall, "The Silent Language of Overseas Business," *Harvard Business Review,* May–June 1960, pp. 5–14; John S. McClenahen, Andrew Rosenbaum, and Michael Williams, "As Others See U.S.," *Industry Week,* January 8, 1990, pp. 80–82; James Bredin, "Japan Needs to Be Understood," *Industry Week,* April 20, 1992, pp. 24–26; David L. James, "Don't Think about Winning," *Across the Board,* April 1992, pp. 49–51; "When in Japan," *Small Business Reports,* January 1992, p. 8; Bernie Ward, "Other Climates, Other Cultures," *Sky,* March 1992, pp. 72–86; *Roger E. Axtell, Gestures: The Do's and Taboos of Body Language around the World* (New York: John Wiley and Sons, 1991); Suzanne Kreiter, "Customs Differ Widely from Those in the U.S.," *Greenville News,* September 26, 1993, p. 15D; Bradford W. Ketchum, "Going Global: East Asia-Pacific Rim," *Inc.* (Special Advertising Section), May 20, 1997; Valerie Frazee, "Getting Started in Mexico," *Global Workforce,* January 1997, pp. 16–17.

International Trade Agreements

5. Describe the agreements that have the greatest influence on foreign trade.

In an attempt to boost world trade, nations have created a variety of trade agreements over the years. Although hundreds of agreements are paving the way for free trade across the world, the following stand out with particular significance: the General Agreement on Tariffs and Trade (GATT) and the World Trade Organization (WTO) and the North American Free Trade Agreement (NAFTA).

GATT and the World Trade Organization

Created in 1947, the General Agreement on Tariffs and Trade (GATT) became the first global tariff agreement. It was designed to reduce tariffs among member nations and to facilitate trade across the globe. Originally signed by the United States and 22 other nations, GATT grew to include 124 member countries that together accounted for nearly 90 percent of world trade.

The World Trade Organization (WTO) came into being in January 1995 and replaced GATT. The WTO is an international organization designed to help exporters and importers do business by regulating the rules of trade between its member nations and by providing a forum for trade negotiations. Currently, the WTO has 147 member countries, including the newest member, China. These member countries represent more than 97 percent of world trade, and an additional 30 nations are actively seeking membership. At the heart of the WTO process, known as the multilateral trading system, are the rules and agreements that are the result of negotiations among its members. The WTO actively implements the rules established by GATT and continues to negotiate additional trade agreements. Through the agreements of the WTO, members commit themselves to nondiscriminatory trade practices. These agreements spell out the rights and obligations of member nations and guarantee that their products will be treated fairly and consistently in other member countries' markets. In addition, the WTO's intellectual property agreement, which covers patents, copyrights, and trademarks, amounts to rules for trade and investment in ideas and creativity.

In addition to the development of agreements among members, the WTO is involved in the resolution of trade disputes among members. The WTO system is designed to encourage dispute resolutions through consultation. If this approach fails, the WTO has a procedure that culminates in a ruling by a panel of experts.

NAFTA

The North American Free Trade Agreement (NAFTA) created the world's largest free trade zone among Canada, Mexico, and the United States. A **free trade zone** is an association of countries that have agreed to knock down trade barriers—both tariff and nontariff—among partner nations. Under the provisions of NAFTA, these barriers were eliminated for trade among the three countries, but each remained free to set its own tariffs on imports from nonmember nations.

NAFTA forged a unified U.S.-Canada-Mexico market of 406 million people with a total annual output of more than $11 trillion of goods and services. This important trade agreement binds together the three nations on the North American continent into a single trading unit stretching from the Yukon to the Yucatan. Today, Canada and Mexico are the largest trading partners for companies in the United States.

NAFTA's provisions have encouraged trade among the three nations, made that trade more profitable and less cumbersome, and opened up new opportunities for a wide

> [Company Example] →

assortment of companies. *For instance, Melton Truck Lines, a winner of a Presidential "E" Award for excellence in exporting, began transporting products to both Mexico and Canada in 1970. Since NAFTA's enactment, Melton has seen its shipments to Mexico and Canada double. "Export sales now make up more than 22 percent of our business," says president Robert Peterson.*[64]

Among NAFTA's provisions are:

- *Tariff reductions.* Immediate reduction and then a gradual phasing out of most tariffs on goods traded among the three countries.
- *Nontariff barriers eliminated.* Elimination of most nontariff barriers to free trade by 2008.
- *Simplified border processing.* Mexico, in particular, opens its border and interior to U.S. truckers and simplifies border processing.
- *Tougher health and safety standards.* Industrial standards involving worker health and safety become more stringent and more uniform.

Conclusion

For a rapidly growing number of small businesses, conducting business on a global basis will be the key to future success. A small company going global exposes itself to certain risks, but, if planned and executed properly, a global strategy can produce huge rewards. To remain competitive, businesses of all sizes must assume a global posture. Global effectiveness requires managers to be able to leverage workers' skills, company resources, and customer know-how across borders and throughout cultures across the world. Managers also must concentrate on maintaining competitive cost structures and a focus on the core of every business—the *customer!* Robert G. Shaw, CEO of International Jensen Inc., a global maker of home and automobile stereo speakers, explains the importance of retaining that customer focus as his company pursues its global strategy: "We want [our customers] to have the attitude of [our] being across the street. If we're going to have a global company, we have to behave in that mode—whether [the customer is] across the street—or seven miles, seven minutes, or 7,000 miles away."[65]

Few businesses can afford the luxury of basing the definition of their target market on the boundaries of their home organization's borders. The manager of one global business, who discourages the use of the word domestic among his employees, says, "Where's 'domestic' when the world is your market?"[66] Although there are no surefire rules for going global, small businesses wanting to become successful international competitors should observe these guidelines:

- Make yourself at home in all three of the world's key markets—North America, Europe, and Asia. This triad of regions is forging a new world order in trade that will dominate global markets for years to come.
- Appeal to the similarities within the various regions in which you operate but recognize the differences in their specific cultures. Although the European Union is a single trading bloc comprised of 15 countries with a combined population of 291 million people, smart entrepreneurs know that each country has its own cultural uniqueness and do not treat them as a unified market.
- Be willing to commit the necessary resources to make your global efforts successful. Going global requires an investment of time, talent, money, and patience.
- Develop new products for the world market. Make sure your products and services measure up to world-class quality standards.
- Use the many resources available, such as the Department of Commerce and the International Trade Administration, to research potential markets and to determine the ideal target markets for your products.
- Familiarize yourself with foreign customs and languages; constantly scan, clip, and build a file on other cultures—their lifestyles, values, customs, and business practices.
- Learn to understand your customers from the perspective of *their* culture, not your own. Bridge cultural gaps by being willing to adapt your business practices to suit their preferences and customs.
- "Glocalize." Make global decisions about products, markets, and management, but allow local employees to make tactical decisions about packaging, advertising, and service. Building relationships with local companies that have solid reputations in a region or a country can help overcome resistance, lower risks, and encourage residents to think of them as local companies.
- Make positive and preferably visible contributions to the local community. A company's social responsibility does not stop at the borders of its home country. Seattle-based Starbucks enhances its reputation in the Chinese communities in which it does business by donating coffee and snacks for local celebrations such as the Autumn Moon Festival. Once, when a group of protesters approached the U.S. Embassy in Beijing, they stopped at a nearby Starbucks café to buy coffee. Rather than being the object of a protest, the branch actually saw sales climb![67]
- Train employees to think globally, send them on international trips, and equip them with state-of-the-art communications technology.
- Hire local managers to staff foreign offices and branches.
- Do whatever seems best wherever it seems best, even if people at home lose jobs or responsibilities.
- Consider using partners and joint ventures to break into foreign markets you cannot penetrate on your own.

By its very nature, going global can be a frightening experience for an entrepreneur considering the jump into international markets. Most of those who have already made the jump, however, have found that the benefits outweigh the risks and that their companies are much stronger because of it.

Chapter Review

1. Explain why "going global" has become an integral part of many small companies' marketing strategies.

   - Companies that move into international business can reap many benefits, including offsetting sales declines in the domestic market, increasing sales and profits, extending their products' life cycles, lowering manufacturing costs, improving competitive position, raising quality levels, and becoming more customer oriented.

2. Describe the eight principal strategies small businesses can use to go global.

   - Perhaps the simplest and lest expensive way for a small business to begin conducting business globally is to establish a site on the World Wide Web. Companies wanting to sell goods on the Web should establish a secure ordering and payment system for on-line customers.
   - Trade intermediaries such as export management companies, export trading companies, manufacturer's export agents, export merchants, resident buying offices, and foreign distributors can serve as a small company's "export department."
   - In a domestic joint venture, two or more U.S. small companies form an alliance for the purpose of exporting their goods and services abroad. In a foreign joint venture, a domestic small business forms an alliance with a company in the target area.
   - Some small businesses enter foreign markets by licensing businesses in other nations to use their patents, trademarks, copyrights, technology, processes, or products.
   - Over the past decade, a growing number of franchises have been attracted to international markets to boost sales and profits as the domestic market has become increasingly saturated with outlets and much tougher to wring growth from. International franchisers sell virtually every kind of product or service imaginable in global markets. Most franchisers have learned that they must modify their products and services to suit local tastes and customs.
   - Some countries lack a hard currency that is convertible into other currencies, so companies doing business there must rely on countertrading or bartering. A countertrade is a transaction in which a business selling goods in a foreign country agrees to promote investment and trade in that country. Bartering involves trading goods and services for other goods and services.
   - Although small companies account for 97 percent of the companies involved in exporting, they generate only one-third of the nation's export sales. However, small companies, realizing the incredible profit potential it offers, are making exporting an ever-expanding part of their marketing plans. In 1991, the average international sales of an *Inc. 500* company were just 3 percent of its total sales; today, international sales average more than 14 percent of total sales at *Inc. 500* companies.
   - One established in international markets, some small businesses set up permanent locations thee. Although they can be very expensive to establish and maintain, international locations give businesses the opportunity to stay in close contact with their international customers.

3. Explain how to build a successful export program.

   - Building a successful export program takes patience and research. Steps include: realize that even the tiniest firms have the potential to export; analyze your product or service; analyze your commitment to exporting; research markets and pick your target; develop a distribution strategy; find your customer; find financing; ship your goods; and collect your money.

4. Discuss the major barriers to international trade and their impact on the global economy.

   - Three domestic barriers to international trade are common: the attitude that "we're too small to export," lack of information on how to get started in global trade, and a lack of available financing.
   - International barriers include tariffs, quotas, embargoes, dumping, political business, and cultural barriers.

5. Describe the trade agreements that have the greatest influence on foreign trade.

   - Created in 1947, the General Agreement on Tariffs and Trade (GATT), the first global tariff agreement, was designed to reduce tariffs among member nations and to facilitate trade across the globe.
   - The World Trade Organization (WTO) was established in 1995 and replaced GATT. The WTO has 147 member nations and represents more than 97 percent of all global trade. The WTO is the governing body that resolves trade disputes among members.
   - The North American Free Trade Agreement (NAFTA) created a free trade area among Canada, Mexico, and the United States. The agreement created an association that knocked down trade barriers, both tariff and nontariff, among these partner nations.

▌▌▌ Discussion Questions

1. Why must entrepreneurs learn to think globally?
2. What forces are driving small businesses into international markets?
3. What advantages does going global offer a small business owner? Risks?
4. Outline the seven strategies that small businesses can use to go global.
5. Describe the various types of trade intermediaries small business owners can use. Explain the functions they perform.
6. What is a domestic joint venture? A foreign joint venture? What advantages does taking on an international partner through a joint venture offer? Disadvantages?
7. What mistakes are first-time exporters most likely to make? Outline the steps a small company should take to establish a successful export program.
8. What are the benefits of establishing international locations? Disadvantages?
9. Describe the barriers businesses face when trying to conduct business internationally. How can a small business owner overcome these obstacles?
10. What is a tariff? A quota? What impact do they have on international trade?
11. Thirty furniture makers in the United States recently asked the U.S. International Trade Commission (ITC) to impose high tariffs on Chinese makers of wooden bedroom furniture for dumping their products in the U.S. market at extremely low prices. The U.S. manufacturers claimed that the Chinese imports single-handedly sent their industry into a deep tailspin. The Chinese factory owners contend that their low-cost furniture is the result of taking a labor-intensive product and building it with low-priced workers in high-tech modern factories. Identify the stakeholders in this trade dispute. What are the consequences for each stakeholder likely to be if the ITC were to impose tariffs on Chinese furniture? What impact do tariffs have on international trade? If you served on the International Trade Commission, what factors would you consider in making your decision? How would you vote in this case? Explain.
12. What impact have the WTO and NAFTA had on small companies wanting to go global? What provisions are included in these trade agreements?
13. What advice would you offer an entrepreneur interested in launching a global business effort?

Global Marketing Strategies

Business PlanPro

If you are considering conducting business internationally, go to the exercises for Chapter 12 of Business Plan Pro where you will find a series of questions that will help you assess your company's ability to go global.

After completing these exercises, you may discover that global markets present another potential target market for your company's products and services. If so, you should modify the Your Market section of Business Plan Pro to reflect your company's global marketing strategy.

Chapter 13
E-Commerce and Entrepreneurship

" *If you don't believe deeply, wholly, and viscerally that the 'Net is going to change your business, you're going to lose. And if you don't understand the advantages of starting early and learning fast, you're going to lose.*
—GARY HAMEL AND JEFF SAMPLER

In the mental geography of e-commerce, distance has been eliminated. There is only one economy and one market.
—PETER DRUCKER "

Upon completion of this chapter, you will be able to:

1. Describe the benefits of selling on the World Wide Web.
2. Understand the factors an entrepreneur should consider before launching into e-commerce.
3. Explain the 12 myths of e-commerce and how to avoid falling victim to them.
4. Explain the basic strategies entrepreneurs should follow to achieve success in their e-commerce efforts.
5. Learn the techniques of designing a killer Web site.
6. Explain how companies track the results from their Web sites.
7. Describe how e-businesses ensure the privacy and security of the information they collect and store from the Web.

As a student of business, you are fortunate to witness the emergence of an event that is reshaping the way companies of all sizes do business: e-commerce. E-commerce is creating a new economy, one that is connecting producers, sellers, and customers via technology in ways that have never been possible before. The result is a whole new set of companies built on business models that are turning traditional methods of commerce and industry on their heads. Companies that ignore the impact of the Internet on their markets run the risk of becoming as relevant to customers as rotary-dial telephones. The most successful companies are embracing the Internet, not as merely another advertising medium or marketing tool but as a mechanism for transforming their companies and changing *everything* about the way they do business. As these companies discover new, innovative ways to use the Internet, computers, and communications technology to connect with their suppliers and to serve their customers better, they are creating a new industrial order. In short, e-commerce has launched a revolution. Just as in previous revolutions in the business world, some old players are being ousted, and new leaders are emerging. The winners are discovering new business opportunities, new ways of designing work, and new ways of organizing and operating their businesses.

Perhaps the most visible changes are occurring in the world of retailing. Although e-commerce will not replace traditional retailing, no retailer, from the smallest corner store to industry giant Wal-Mart, can afford to ignore the impact of the World Wide Web on their business models. Companies can take orders at the speed of light from anywhere in the world and at any time of day. The Internet enables companies to collect more information on customers' shopping and buying habits than any other medium in history. This ability means that companies can focus their marketing efforts like never before— for instance, selling garden supplies to customers who are most likely to buy them and not wasting resources trying to sell to those who have no interest in gardening. The capacity to track customers' Web-based shopping habits allows companies to personalize their approaches to marketing and to realize the benefits of individualized (or one-to-one) marketing (refer to Chapter 7). Ironically, the same Web-based marketing approach that allows companies to get so personal with their customers also can make shopping extremely impersonal. Entrepreneurs who set up shop on the Web will likely never meet their customers face-to-face or even talk to them. Yet, those customers, who can live anywhere in the world, will visit the online store at all hours of the day or night and expect to receive individual attention. Making a Web-based marketing approach succeed requires a business to strike a balance, creating an e-commerce strategy that capitalizes on the strengths of the Web while meeting customers' expectations of convenience and service.

In the world of e-commerce, the new business models recognize the power the Internet gives customers. Pricing, for example, is no longer as simple as it once was for companies. Auction sites such as eBay and Priceline.com mean that entrepreneurs can no longer be content to take into account only local competitors when setting their own prices. With the Web, price transparency is now the rule of the day. With a few mouse clicks, customers can compare the prices of the same or similar products and services from companies across the globe. In the new wired and connected economy, the balance of power is shifting to customers, and new business models recognize this fact. Consider, for example, the challenges auto dealers face when selling to customers armed with dealer cost and pricing information gathered from any one of dozens of Web sites. J.D. Power and Associates reports that 60 percent of new car buyers in the United States use the Internet for research before they make their purchases, up from just 25 percent in 1998.[1] Because they know the dealer's wholesale cost of a new car, these informed customers are taking price out of the buying equation, causing dealers to emphasize other factors such as service or convenience to build long-term relationships.

In this fast-paced world of e-commerce, size no longer matters as much as speed and flexibility do. One of the Web's greatest strengths is its interactive nature, the ability to

© 2000 Randy Glasbergen.
www.glasbergen.com

"Our competition launched their web site, stole all
of our customers and put us out of business
while you were in the john."

provide companies with instantaneous customer feedback, giving them the opportunity to learn and to make necessary adjustments. Businesses, whatever their size, that are willing to experiment with different approaches to reaching customers and are quick to learn and adapt will grow and prosper; those that cannot will fall by the wayside. The Internet is creating a new industrial order, and companies that fail to adapt to it will soon become extinct.

E-commerce is redefining even the most traditional industries such as the retail grocery business. Despite the legacy of Webvan, an Internet grocer that proved to be one of the greatest failures of the dot-bomb era (burning through nearly $1 billion in venture capital before flaming out), several grocers are challenging the traditional industry model with Web-based ventures. *FreshDirect Inc. in New York City has 100,000 customers in Manhattan for its Web grocery service, which offers more than 8,000 types of fresh meats, vegetables, and other grocery items delivered directly to shoppers' homes for a flat $3.95 fee. Using the business model perfected by computer maker Dell Inc., FreshDirect fills online orders as customers place them and then delivers them using its fleet of trucks. Business is going so well that the company plans to begin selling gourmet foods such as caviar, fancy meats, and cheeses to customers across the company from its Web site. "We're about food,"* says cofounder and CEO Joe Fedele. *"The Internet is just a tool. The only reason we chose the Internet was that it helped us reach people at a lower transaction cost."*[2]

High-volume, low-margin commodity products are best suited for selling on the Web. Indeed, among the items purchased most often online are books, music, travel services, videos and DVDs, clothing, computer hardware and software, and consumer electronics. However, companies can—and do—sell practically anything over the Web, from antiques and pharmaceuticals to popcorn and drug-free urine. The most commonly cited reasons among owners of small and midsized companies for taking their companies to the Web are (1) to reach new customers, (2) to sell goods and services, (3) to disseminate information more quickly, (4) to keep up with competitors, and (5) to reach global markets.[3]

Companies of all sizes are establishing a presence on the Web because that's where their customers are. The number of Internet users worldwide now stands at more than 605 million, up from 147 million at the end of 1998 (see Figure 13.1).[4] Consumers have

Company Example

Figure 13.1

Internet Users by World Region

Source: Adapted from *E-Commerce and Development Report 2003,* United Nations Conference on Trade and Development (New York and Geneva: 2003), pp. 2–4.

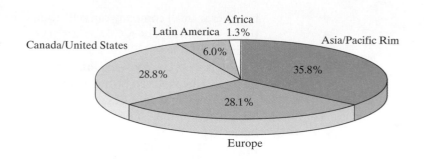

adopted the Internet much more quickly than any other major innovation in the past. It reached 50 percent penetration in the United States in just seven years, compared to 30 years for the computer, 40 years for electricity, and more than 100 years for steam power.[5] In the United States, e-commerce sales, both business-to-business (B2B) and business-to-consumer (B2C), now top $3.5 billion a year and are growing at more than 13 percent annually.[6] A report by Jupiter Research found that 30 percent of the U.S. population made purchases online in 2004 and that by 2008 half of the U.S. population will make online purchases. The report also concluded that the average annual online purchase will climb from $585 per buyer in 2004 to $780 per buyer in 2008.[7] Although this rapid rate of growth will not last indefinitely, the Web represents a tremendous opportunity that businesses simply cannot afford to ignore.

Benefits of Selling on the Web

1. Describe the benefits of selling on the World Wide Web.

According to a study by Interland, a company that provides online services for small businesses, 78 percent of small business owners whose firms have Web sites report that their businesses benefit by having a site. The major benefits they cite include enhanced credibility, improved marketing efforts, higher sales, and lower costs.[8] Although a Web-based sales strategy does not guarantee success, small companies that have established Web sites realize many benefits, including the following:

Company Example ⟶

- *The opportunity to increase revenues.* For many small businesses, launching a Web site is the equivalent of opening a new sales channel. Companies that launch e-commerce efforts soon discover that their sites are generating additional sales from new customers. *The Cheesecake Factory, a California company that operates a chain of restaurants, had been selling its specialty desserts through traditional mail order channels when managers decided in 2002 to begin offering them on the company's Web site. The boost from the Web enabled the Cheesecake Factory to double its catalog sales in less than one year, and Web-based orders now account for more than 70 percent of all catalog orders. Because the cost of placing online orders is minimal, the Cheesecake Factory earns a higher profit margin on Web orders than on traditional telephone or mail orders.*[9]
- *The ability to expand their reach into global markets.* The Web is the most efficient way for small businesses to sell their products to the millions of potential customers who live outside the borders of the United States. Tapping into these global markets through more traditional methods would be too complex and too costly for the typical small business. Yet, on the Web, a small company can sell its products efficiently to customers anywhere in the world at any time of day.
- *The ability to remain open 24 hours a day, seven days a week.* More than half of all retail sales occur after 6 P.M., when many traditional stores close. Extending the hours a brick-and-mortar store remains open can increase sales, but it also takes a toll on the business owner and the employees. With a Web site up and running,

however, a small company can sell around the clock without having to incur additional staffing expenses. Customers never have to worry about whether or not an online store is "open."

■ *The capacity to use the Web's interactive nature to enhance customer service.* Although selling on the Web can be highly impersonal because of the lack of human interaction, companies that design their sites properly can create an exciting, interactive experience for their online visitors. Customers can contact a company at any time of the day, can control the flow of information they get, and in some cases can interact with company representatives in real time. In addition, technology now allows companies to "personalize" their sites to suit the tastes and preferences of individual customers. Drawing on a database containing information customers have provided in the past, modern Web sites can customize themselves, displaying content that appeals to an individual visitor. For instance, a site selling clothing can greet a returning customer by name and ask if she is shopping for herself or for someone on her personal shopping list. Based on her response, the site can recall appropriate sizes and favorite styles and colors and can even make product recommendations.

■ *The power to educate and to inform.* Far more than most marketing media, the Web gives entrepreneurs the power to educate and to inform customers. Women and members of Generation Y, especially, crave product information before they make purchases. The Web allows business owners to provide more detailed information to visitors than practically any other medium. For instance, a travel company advertising an Alaskan tour in a newspaper or magazine might include a brief description of the tour, a list of the destinations, a telephone number, the price, and perhaps a photo or two. A Web-based promotion for the same tour could include all of the information just mentioned as well as a detailed itinerary with dozens of breathtaking photographs; descriptions and photographs of all accommodations; advice on what to pack; airline schedules, seating configurations, and availability; information on optional side trips; comments from customers who have taken this tour before; and links to other Web sites about Alaska, the weather, and fun things to do in the region.[10] Companies that provide shoppers with useful information have an edge when it comes to attracting and retaining customers.

■ *The ability to lower the cost of doing business.* The Web is one of the most efficient ways of reaching both new and existing customers. Properly promoted, a Web site can reduce a company's cost of generating sales leads, providing customer support, and distributing marketing materials. For instance, sending customers an e-mail newsletter is much less expensive than paying the printing and postage costs of sending the same newsletter by "snail mail."

Company Example →

By integrating its Web site and its inventory control system, a company also can reduce its inventory costs by shortening the sales cycle. Linking Web sales activity directly to suppliers enables a business to cut its purchasing costs. *For instance, FreshDirect, the online grocer, uses the Internet to shorten its supply chain for seafood, resulting in higher-quality products for its customers and a smaller investment inventory for the company. As boats arrive at the docks in lower Manhattan in the early evening, FreshDirect representatives place initial orders. At midnight, FreshDirect stops taking customer orders for the next day and provides exact orders and quantities to its seafood buyers. The shipments arrive around 3 A.M. at the company's 300,000 square-foot Long Island City processing center, where employees cut and package them into customers' desired orders, a process that is completed by midmorning. Customer deliveries begin at 4 P.M. that same day, often resulting in a "dock-to-door" time of less than 24 hours. FreshDirect typically has just one day's worth of seafood inventory in stock, compared to seven to nine days' worth at a traditional grocery store.*[11]

Company Example →

■ *The capacity to improve the efficiency of the purchasing process.* Transferring at least some of their purchases to the Internet can save businesses money because the cost of online transactions is much lower than regular paper-based transactions. *Tim Walters, the used car manager at Fagan Chevrolet, a small auto dealership in Janesville, Wisconsin, used to spend a great deal of time and money traveling to six regional auto auctions to purchase used cars for the dealership. Now Walters attends those auctions only occasionally, choosing instead to purchase most of the dealership's used cars online from Smart-Auction, a Web site that General Motors Acceptance Corporation operates to sell cars that are returned after their lease arrangements expire.* Online auctions now account for about 8 percent of total used car purchases made by auto dealers and are expected to account for 15 percent of sales in the future.[12]

■ *The ability to spot new business opportunities and to capitalize on them.* E-commerce companies are poised to give customers just what they want when they want it. As the number of dual-career couples rises and the amount of available leisure time shrinks, consumers are looking for ways to increase the convenience of shopping, and the Web is fast becoming the solution they seek. Increasingly, customers view shopping as an unpleasant chore that cuts into already scarce leisure time, and they are embracing anything that reduces the amount of time they must spend shopping. Entrepreneurs who tap into customers' need to buy goods more conveniently and with less hassle are winning the battle for market share. New opportunities to serve customers' changing needs and wants are constantly arising, and the Web is the birthplace of many of them.

■ *The power to track sales results.* The Web gives businesses the power to track virtually any kind of activity on their Web sites, from the number of visitors to the click-through rates on their banner ads. Because of the Web's ability to monitor traffic continuously, entrepreneurs can judge the value their sites are generating for their companies. With modern Web analytics tools, entrepreneurs can track not only the number of visitors to their sites but also how they got there, how they maneuver around the site, and what they buy. Web entrepreneurs can experiment with different designs and layouts for their sites to determine their impact on the site's **conversion rate**, the percentage of visitors to a Web site who actually make a purchase.

Company Example →

Men's clothier Jos. A. Bank is reaping many of these benefits. In 1998, the company began a market test to see whether or not customers would purchase its clothing over the Web. The company hired a third-party hosting site that took customers' orders and faxed them to Jos. A. Bank, which then shipped the merchandise. When this decidedly low-tech approach proved to be successful, Jos. A. Bank brought the operation of its Web site in-house. With the help of a local Web development company, Jos. A. Bank created a site featuring a handy search engine, an easy checkout process, and its popular customized "build-a-suit" feature. The company, which has 128 brick-and-mortar stores nationwide, says that its online store generates the largest volume of sales and accounts for 20 percent of the company's revenue![13]

Factors to Consider Before Launching into E-Commerce

2. Understand the factors an entrepreneur should consider before launching into e-commerce.

Despite the many benefits the Web offers, not every small business owner is ready to embrace e-commerce. Recent surveys by research firms IDC and AMI Partners found that just 43 percent of U.S. companies with fewer than 100 employees have Web sites and that only 40 percent of those companies actually sell merchandise online.[14] Although small companies account for more than half of all retail sales in the United States, they generate only 6 percent of online retail sales.[15] Why are so many small companies hesitant to use the Web as a business tool? For many entrepreneurs, the key barrier is not knowing where or how to start an e-commerce effort, whereas for others cost concerns are a major issue.

Other roadblocks include the fear that customers will not use the Web site and the problems associated with ensuring online security.

Whatever their size, traditional companies must realize that selling their products and services on the Web is no longer a luxury. Business owners who are not at least considering creating a Web presence or integrating the Web creatively into their operations are putting their companies at risk. One business writer says, "A company that neglects its Web site may be committing commercial suicide. A Web site is increasingly becoming the gateway to a company's brand, products, and services—even if the firm does not sell online."[16] However, before launching an e-commerce effort, business owners should consider the following important issues:

- How a company exploits the Web's interconnectivity and the opportunities it creates to transform relationships with its suppliers and vendors, its customers, and other external stakeholders is crucial to its success.
- Web success requires a company to develop a plan for integrating the Web into its overall strategy. The plan should address issues such as site design and maintenance, creating and managing a brand name, marketing and promotional strategies, sales, and customer service.
- Developing deep, lasting relationships with customers takes on even greater importance on the Web. Attracting customers on the Web costs money, and companies must be able to retain their online customers to make their Web sites profitable.
- Creating a meaningful presence on the Web requires an ongoing investment of resources—time, money, energy, and talent. Establishing an attractive Web site brimming with catchy photographs of products is only the beginning.
- Measuring the success of its Web-based sales effort is essential to remaining relevant to customers whose tastes, needs, and preferences are always changing.

Doing business on the Web takes more time and energy than many entrepreneurs think. Answering the following questions will help entrepreneurs make sure they are ready to do business on the Web and avoid unpleasant surprises in their e-commerce efforts:

- What exactly do you expect a Web site to do for your company? Will it provide information only, reach new customers, increase sales to existing customers, improve communication with customers, enhance customer service, or reduce your company's cost of operation? Will customers be able to place orders from the site, or must they call your company to buy?
- How much can you afford to invest in an e-commerce effort?
- What rate of return do you expect to earn on that investment?
- How long can you afford to wait for that return?
- How well suited are your products and services to selling on the Web?
- How will the "back office" of your Web site work? Will your site be tied into your company's inventory control system?
- How will you handle order fulfillment? Can your fulfillment system handle the increase in volume you are expecting?
- What impact, if any, will your Web site have on your company's traditional channels of distribution?
- What mechanism will your site use to ensure secure customer transactions?
- How will your company handle customer service for the site? What provisions will you make for returned items?
- How do you plan to promote the site to draw traffic to it?
- What information will you collect from the visitors to your site? How will you use it? Will you tell visitors how you intend to use this information?

■ Have you developed a privacy policy? Have you posted that policy on your company's Web site for customers?

■ Have you tested your site with real, live customers to make sure that it is easy to navigate and easy to order from?

■ How will you measure the success of your company's Web site? What objectives have you set for the site?

12 Myths of E-Commerce

3. Explain the 12 myths of e-commerce and how to avoid falling victim to them.

Although many entrepreneurs have boosted their businesses with e-commerce, setting up shop on the Web is no guarantee of success. Scores of entrepreneurs have plunged unprepared into the world of e-commerce only to discover that there is more to it than merely setting up a Web site and waiting for the orders to start pouring in. Make sure that you do not fall victim to one of the following e-commerce myths.

Myth 1. Setting up a business on the Web is easy and inexpensive. A common misconception is that setting up an effective Web site for an online business is easy and inexpensive. Although practically anyone with the right software can post a static page in just a few minutes, creating an effective, professional, and polished Web site can be an expensive, time-consuming project. Most small businesses start their online efforts by creating sites that are simple "electronic flyers," pages that post product information, a few photographs, prices, and telephone and fax numbers. Although these simple sites lack the capacity for true electronic commerce, they do provide a company with another way of reaching both new and existing customers.

The average initial investment a small company makes in setting up a Web site is $8,500.[17] Creating a genuinely transaction-capable Web site typically requires a much higher investment and a great deal of time, however. According to a study by Jupiter Communications, setting up an e-commerce site takes most companies at least six months to complete. The study also revealed that setting up the site is only the first investment required. Companies cited these follow-up investments: (1) redesign Web site, (2) buy more hardware to support Web site, (3) automate or expand warehouse to meet customer demand, (4) integrate Web site into inventory control system, and (5) increase customer call center capacity.[18]

Myth 2. If I launch a site, customers will flock to it. Some entrepreneurs think that once they set up their Web sites, their expenses end there. Not true! Without promotional support, no Web site will draw enough traffic to support a business. With more than 3.5 billion Web pages in existence and the number growing daily, getting a site noticed has become increasingly difficult. Even listing a site with popular Web search engines cannot guarantee that customers surfing the Web will find your company's site. Just like traditional retail stores seeking to attract customers, virtual companies have discovered that drawing sufficient traffic to a Web site requires promotion—and lots of it! "No one will know you're on the Web unless you tell them and motivate them to visit," explains Mark Layton, owner of a Web-based distributor of computer supplies and author of a book on e-commerce.[19]

Entrepreneurs with both physical and virtual stores must promote their Web sites at every opportunity by printing their URLs on everything related to their physical stores—on signs, in print and broadcast ads, in store windows, on shopping bags, on merchandise labels, and anywhere else their customers will see. A recent study of small companies with Web sites by Web hosting service Interland found that 88 percent included their Web addresses on business materials and 53 percent included them in their off-line advertisements.[20] Virtual shop owners should consider buying ads in traditional advertising media as well as using banner ads, banner exchange programs, and cross-marketing arrangements with companies selling complementary products on their on Web sites. Other techniques include creating some type of interactivity with customers such as a Web-based newsletter, writing articles that link to the company's site, hosting a chat room that allows customers to interact with one another and with company personnel, establishing a Web log (or "blog," a regularly updated online journal), or sponsoring a contest. For instance, Williams Nursery, an 81-year-old family business, has been successful in promoting both its Web site and its retail store with a variety of creative contests, from scarecrow building to Halloween costumes.[21]

Web logs are easy to create, but they require regular updating to attract visitors. Web logs with fresh, entertaining content can be an effective way to draw potential customers to a company's Web site. *Primal Records, a small recording company and record store in Berkeley, California, uses a blog to update customers about company news, special sales and promotions, inventory updates, and in-store events. Primal also includes a message board in its blog, enabling the company to stay in touch with its customers and their musical preferences, a vital task in its industry.*[22]

Company Example

The key to promoting a Web site successfully is networking, building relationships with customers, other companies, trade associations, online directories, and other Web sites the company's customers visit. "You need to create relationships with the businesses and people with whom you share common customers," says Barbara Ling, author of a book on e-commerce. "Then you need to create links between sites to help customers find what they are looking for."[23]

Myth 3. Making money on the Web is easy. Promoters who hawk "get-rich-quick" schemes on the Web lure many entrepreneurs with the promise that making money on the Web is easy. It isn't. One recent study by SuperPages.com reports that 55 percent of small businesses say their Web sites have either broken even or are profitable.[24] Making money on the Web is possible, but it takes time and requires an up-front investment. As hundreds of new sites spring up every day, getting a company's site noticed requires more effort and marketing muscle than ever before. One study by the Boston Consulting Group, a management consulting firm, and shop.org, an Internet retailing trade association, found that Web retailers invested 65 percent of their revenues in marketing and advertising, compared to their off-line counterparts, who invested just 4 percent.[25]

Myth 4. Privacy is not an important issue on the Web. The Web allows companies to gain access to almost unbelievable amounts of information about their customers. Many sites offer visitors "freebies" in exchange for information about themselves. Companies then use this information to learn more about their target customers and how to market to them most effectively. Concerns over the privacy of and the use of this information have become the topic of debate by many interested parties, including government agencies, consumer watchdog groups, customers, and industry trade associations.

Companies that collect information from their online customers have a responsibility to safeguard their customers' privacy, to protect that information from unauthorized use, and to use it responsibly. That means that businesses should post a privacy statement on their Web sites, explaining to customers how they intend to use the information they collect. One of the surest ways to alienate online customers is to abuse the information collected from them by selling it to third parties or by spamming customers with unwanted solicitations.

Businesses that publish privacy policies and then adhere to them build trust among their customers, an important facet of doing business on the Web. A study by Jupiter Communications found that 64 percent of Web customers distrust Web sites.[26] According to John Briggs, director of e-commerce for the Yahoo Network, customers "need to trust the brand they are buying and believe that their online purchases will be safe transactions. They need to feel comfortable that [their] personal data will not be sold and that they won't get spammed by giving their e-mail address. They need to know about shipping costs, product availability, and return policies up-front."[27] Privacy *does* matter on the Web, and businesses that respect their customers' privacy will win their customers' trust. Trust is the foundation on which companies build the long-term customer relationships that are so crucial to Web success.

Myth 5. The most important part of any e-commerce effort is technology. Although understanding the technology of e-commerce is an important part of the formula for success, it is *not* the most crucial ingredient. What matters most is the ability to understand the underlying business and to develop a workable business model that offers customers something of value at a reasonable price while producing a reasonable return for the company. The entrepreneurs who are proving to be most successful in e-commerce are those who know how their industries work inside and out and then build an e-business around that knowledge. They know that they can hire Webmasters, database experts, and fulfillment companies to design the technical aspects of their online businesses, but that nothing can substitute for a solid understanding of their industry, their target market, and the strategy needed to pull the various parts together. The key is seeing the Web for what it really is: another way to reach and serve customers with an effective business model and to minimize the cost of doing business.

> Company Example →

Dell Computer, the pioneer of the online build-to-order model, has integrated the Web into its business strategy very effectively. Dell allows shoppers to customize their PCs at Dell.com, get a delivery date, and track the status of their orders at any time. Dell also uses the Web to control one of the most challenging aspects of its business: managing inventory. Dell's component suppliers log onto a special site to get instructions about which parts to deliver, how many to ship, and where and when to deliver them. Using the Web to tie together its supply chain, Dell keeps its inventory levels so low that it turns its inventory an amazing 73 times a year![28]

The key to Dell's success on the Web is the company's knowledge of the computer industry to which it then applies the technology of the Web. Unfortunately, many entrepreneurs tackle e-commerce by focusing on technology first and then determine how that technology fits their business idea. "If you start with technology, you're likely to going to buy a solution in search of a problem," says Kip Martin, program director of META Group's Electronic Business Strategies. Instead, he suggests, "Start with the business and ask yourself what you want to happen and how you'll measure it. *Then* ask how the technology will help you achieve your goals. Remember: Business first, technology second."[29]

Myth 6. "Strategy? I don't need a strategy to sell on the Web! Just give me a Web site, and the rest will take care of itself." Building a successful e-business is no different than building a successful brick-and-mortar business, and that requires a well-thought-out strategy. Building a strategy means that an entrepreneur must first develop a clear definition of the company's target audience and a thorough understanding of those customers' needs, wants, likes, and dislikes. To be successful, a Web site must be appealing to the customers it seeks to attract just as a traditional store's design and décor must draw foot traffic. Before your Web site can become the foundation for a successful e-business, you must create it with your target audience in mind.

> Company Example →

Zappos.com bills itself as the Web's most popular shoe store. The company, founded in 1999 by Nick Swinmurn after a frustrating and fruitless trip to a local mall in search of shoes, offers online customers a huge selection of all types of shoes, including dress and athletic shoes for men and women, extra-wide shoes for hard-to-fit feet, and even "vegetarian" shoes made from materials other than leather. Swinmurn's strategy for Zappos.com is simple: offer customers the greatest variety and selection of shoes possible to gain an edge over brick-and-mortar stores that are limited in the stock they can carry. For instance, the company stocks 200 to 300 styles in a wide array of sizes of its top-selling brands. As part of Zappos.com's commitment to customer service, the company offers free expedited shipping (even on shoes customers return) and a sophisticated warehouse system that provides shoppers real-time information on the availability of any particular shoe. The strategy is working; within its first five years of operation, the company's sales have skyrocketed to $125 million![30]

Myth 7. On the Web, customer service is not as important as it is in a traditional retail store. A study conducted by Jupiter Research found that 72 percent of online buyers cite customer service as a critical factor in their online shopping satisfaction; yet, only 41 percent say they are satisfied with the service they receive from online merchants.[31] The fact is that many Web sites treat customer service as an afterthought, and this attitude costs businesses plenty. According to a study by researcher Jakob Nielsen, 56 percent of the time an online shopper is unable to complete an e-commerce transaction, costing online stores billions of dollars in lost sales due to poor customer service.[32] Sites that are difficult to navigate, slow to load, offer complex checkout systems, or confuse shoppers will turn customers away quickly, never to return. Online merchants must recognize that customer service is just as important (if not more so) on the Web as it is in traditional brick-and-mortar stores.

There is plenty of room for improvement in customer service on the Web. Research shows that 75 percent of Web shoppers who fill their online shopping carts become frustrated and abandon them without checking out.[33] The most common reasons for leaving a site without purchasing include the following: (1) shipping and handling charges were too high, (2) delivery times were too long, (3) the checkout process required too much information to make a purchase, and (4) insufficient product information was available.[34]

E-commerce entrepreneurs can reduce the likelihood that customers will leave their companies' Web sites frustrated and unlikely to return by taking the following steps:[35]

- Reduce the number of steps required to complete the checkout process. Just as in regular retail stores, online customers appreciate a quick, efficient checkout process that is as simple as possible. A convoluted checkout process is an invitation to customers to abandon their shopping carts.
- Include a progress indicator on each checkout page. Clearly numbering the steps in the process and letting customers know where they are in that process will improve customer retention rates during checkout.
- Provide a link back to the items in the customers' shopping cart. This allows customers to return to the product page to make sure they selected the correct item without losing their place in the checkout process.
- Allow customers to see whether or not an item is in stock on the product page. Customers become frustrated when they learn that an item is out of stock after having clicked through most or all of the checkout process.
- Include product photos in the shopping cart. Research shows that simply including product photos increases a company's conversion rate by as much as 10 percent.
- Make it easy for customers to change the contents of their shopping carts. The cart page should allow customers to change quantities, colors, sizes, and other options or to delete an item from the cart with just one mouse click.
- Give customers the option of calling to resolve problems they encounter during checkout. A toll-free line enables a company to track the number of problem-solving calls, which can point out flaws in the design of the Web site or the checkout process.
- Make it easy for customers to pay for their online purchases. Credit cards are a popular online payment method, but many small companies do not generate enough revenue to justify the costs of gaining credit card merchant status. If a small company's credit card sales are no more than $250 per month, the credit card company charges about 35 percent of each transaction, compared to just 3 to 5 percent for monthly credit card sales of at least $7,500 per month. Electronic payment services such as PayPal, which is now owned by eBay and is the largest online payment system, allows customers to send payments to anyone with an e-mail address through their checking accounts or their credit cards. Customers who sign up for

the free service can use their PayPal accounts to buy products online conveniently, and PayPal charges the company making the sale an average of 3.3 percent of the transaction, no matter what its monthly volume is. When a merchant signs on with PayPal it simply adds PayPal's "Web Accept" button to its site, which customers click on to pay with their PayPal accounts.

<table>
<tr><td>Company Example ➤</td><td></td></tr>
</table>

Jennifer Geronaitis, owner of Tea Time World Wide, a small online retailer of tea and gourmet food, considered establishing a merchant credit card account but instead opted to use PayPal because of its lower costs. For her company's sales volume, a merchant account would have cost $50 per month plus 2.25 percent and 25 cents per transaction. With PayPal, Geronaitis pays 2.9 percent plus 30 cents per transaction. Geronaitis calculated that until her monthly sales exceed $6,000 a month, PayPal is less expensive than a traditional merchant account.[36]

In an attempt to improve the level of service they offer, many sites provide e-mail links to encourage customer interaction. Unfortunately, e-mail takes a very low priority at many e-businesses. One study by Jupiter Communications found that 42 percent of business Web sites took longer than five days to respond to e-mail inquiries, never replied at all, or simply were not accessible by e-mail![37] The lesson for e-commerce entrepreneurs is simple: Devote time, energy, and money to developing a functional mechanism for providing superior customer service. Those who do will build a sizeable base of loyal customers who will keep coming back. Perhaps the most significant actions online companies can take to bolster their customer service efforts are providing a quick online checkout process, creating a well-staffed and well-trained customer response team, offering a simple return process, and providing an easy order-tracking process so customers can check the status of their orders at any time.

Myth 8. Flash makes a Web site better. Businesses that fall into this trap pour most of their e-commerce budgets into designing flashy Web sites with all of the "bells and whistles." The logic is that to stand out on the Web, a site really has to sparkle. That logic leads to a "more is better" mentality when designing a site. On the Web, however, "more" does *not* necessarily equate to "better." Although fancy graphics, bright colors, playful music, and spinning icons can attract attention, they also can be quite distracting and very slow to download. Sites that download slowly may never have the chance to sell because customers will click to another site. Keep the design of your site simple.

<table>
<tr><td>Company Example ➤</td><td></td></tr>
</table>

Travelocity, once the largest online travel agency, recently revamped its Web site after studies showed that it lacked distinction and overloaded customers with information that was poorly organized. "Consumers said, 'You're all cluttered, almost like a Turkish bazaar,'" says Jeff Glueck, the company's chief marketing officer. The redesigned site cuts the information on the Travelocity home page by half, organizes that information in a more intuitive manner, and uses more subdued colors. Rather than being overwhelmed with information when they arrive at the site, customers now use drop-down menus to access the travel and booking information they need.[38]

Myth 9. It's what's up front that counts. Designing an attractive Web site is important to building a successful e-business. However, designing the back office, the systems that take over once a customer places an order on a Web site, is just as important as designing the site itself. If the behind-the-scenes support is not in place or cannot handle the traffic from the Web site, a company's entire e-commerce effort will come crashing down. Although e-commerce can lower many costs of doing business, it still requires a basic infrastructure somewhere in the channel of distribution to process orders, maintain inventory, fill orders, and handle customer service. Many entrepreneurs hoping to launch virtual businesses are discovering the need for a "clicks-and-mortar" approach to provide the necessary infrastructure to serve their customers. "The companies with warehouses, supply-chain management, and solid customer service are going to be the ones that survive," says Daryl Plummer, head of the Gartner Group's Internet and new media division.[39]

To customers, a business is only as good as its last order, and many e-companies are not measuring up. One study suggests that only 30 percent of e-commerce Web sites feature real-time inventory look-up, which gives online shoppers the ability to see if an item they want to purchase is actually in stock.[40] In addition, only 7 percent of Web sites are linked to the back office.[41] These figures will increase as software to integrate Web sites with the back office becomes easier to use and more affordable, but in the meantime customers will have to endure late shipments, incorrect orders, and poor service.

Web-based entrepreneurs often discover that the greatest challenge their businesses face is not necessarily attracting customers on the Web but creating a workable order fulfillment strategy. Order fulfillment involves everything required to get goods from a warehouse into a customer's hands and includes order processing, warehousing, picking and packing, shipping, and billing. Some entrepreneurs choose to handle order fulfillment in-house with their own employees, whereas others find it more economical to hire specialized fulfillment houses to handle these functions. Virtual order fulfillment (or drop-shipping) suits many e-tailers perfectly. When a customer orders a product from its Web site, the company forwards the order to its wholesaler or distributor, which then ships the product to the customer with the online merchant's label on it. Although e-tailers avoid the major problems that managing inventory present, they lose control over delivery times and service quality. Also, finding a fulfillment house willing to handle a relatively small volume of orders at a reasonable price can be difficult for some small businesses. Major fulfillment providers include Federal Express, UPS, NewRoads, and NFI Interactive.

Myth 10. E-commerce will cause brick-and-mortar retail stores to disappear. The rapid growth of e-commerce does pose a serious threat to some traditional retailers, especially those that fail to find ways to capitalize on the opportunities the Web offers them. A study by UCLA found that 66 percent of Internet purchasers say that online buying has reduced the number of visits they make to retail stores.[42] However, it is unlikely that Web-based shopping will replace completely customers' need and desire to visit real stores selling real merchandise that they can see, touch, and try on. That's one reason that online retail sales in the United States account for just 1.6 percent of total retail sales, although online sales are growing much faster than are off-line sales.[43]

Some products simply lend themselves to selling in real stores more naturally than in online shops. For instance, furniture stores and supermarkets have struggled for success online. On the other hand, other items, particularly standard commodity products for which customers have little loyalty, are ideally suited for online sales. Virtual stores have and will continue to drive out of existence some traditional companies that resist creating new business models or are too slow to change. Shoppers have become so comfortable with online shopping that they see no great differences between shopping in a store and shopping online. To remain competitive, traditional brick-and-mortar stores must find ways to transform themselves into flexible click-and-mortar operations that can make the convenience, the reach, and the low transaction costs of the Web work for them.

Company Example ⟶ *REI, Inc., a retailer of outdoor gear and apparel with 60 stores, integrates its Web presence into its retail outlets using in-store kiosks that give customers access to more than 178,000 items from its Web site. Both online and in-store customers can access more than 400 how-to articles and clinics to help them evaluate and select the right product for their needs. REI.com's "Learn and Share" section gives (and takes) valuable advice on a variety of topics ranging from rock climbing to fly fishing. Customers' response to in-store Web access has been phenomenal. REI says that the revenue generated by its in-store kiosks is equivalent to that generated by a 25,000-square-foot store!*[44]

Myth 11. The greatest opportunities for e-commerce lie in the retail sector. As impressive as the growth rate and total volume for online retail sales are, they are dwarfed by those in the online business-to-business (B2B) sector, where businesses sell to one

REI, a popular retailer of outdoor gear, incorporates its Web strategy into its retail locations using kiosks that give in-store shoppers access to all of the information and products that online shoppers have. The strategy works; the kiosks generate sales revenue equivalent to that of a 25,000 square-foot store.

another rather than to retail customers. In fact, B2B sales account for about 83 percent of all e-commerce transactions.[45] Entrepreneurs who are looking to sell goods to other businesses on the Web will find plenty of opportunities available in a multitude of industries.

Business-to-business e-commerce is growing so rapidly because of its potential to boost productivity, slash costs, and increase profits. This brand of e-commerce is transforming the way companies design and purchase parts, supplies, and materials as well as the way they manage inventory and process transactions. The Web's power to increase the speed and the efficiency of the purchasing function represents a fundamental departure from the past. Experts estimate that transferring purchasing to the Web can cut total procurement costs by 10 percent and transaction costs by as much as 90 percent.[46] For instance, Chris Cogan, CEO of GoCo-op, an Internet purchasing site for hotels, restaurants, and health care companies, explains, "We estimate [that] the average cost of executing a paper purchase order is $115." Businesses using his company's Web-based purchasing system "get that cost down to $10," he says.[47]

Business-to-business e-commerce is growing because of the natural link that exists with business-to-consumer e-commerce. As we have seen, one of the greatest challenges Web-based retailers face is obtaining and delivering the goods their customers order fast enough to satisfy customers' expectations. Increasingly, Web-based retailers are connecting their front office sales systems and their back office purchasing and order fulfillment systems with those of their suppliers. The result is a faster, more efficient method of filling customer orders. So far the most successful online business-to-business companies are those that have discovered ways of tying their front offices, their back offices, their suppliers, and their customers together into a single, smoothly functioning, Web-based network. *Cisco Systems, a maker of computer routers, switches, and other hardware, provides a good example of a fully integrated B2B company. Customers go to the Cisco Web site to check out product specifications and to place orders. Cisco then uses the Internet to transfer those orders directly to its suppliers, which then ship the necessary raw materials to Cisco, or, in many cases, ship products directly to customers. (About 65 percent of Cisco's orders go directly from the supplier to the customer without Cisco ever handling them!) The efficiency*

Company Example

of this system minimizes the amount of raw materials inventory that Cisco must carry and allows customers to check on the status of their orders over the Web as well. Cisco keeps its costs low and its customers happy with its innovative Web-based strategy.[48]

Myth 12. It's too late to get on the Web. A common myth, especially among small companies, is that those businesses that have not yet moved onto the Web have missed a golden opportunity. The reality is that the Internet is still in its infancy, and companies are still figuring out how to succeed on the Web. Recall that just over half of small companies' Web sites are profitable. For every e-commerce site that exists, many others have failed. An abundance of business opportunities exists for those entrepreneurs insightful enough to spot them and clever enough to capitalize on them.

One fact of e-commerce that has emerged is the importance of speed. Companies doing business on the Web have discovered that those who reach customers first often have a significant advantage over their slower rivals. "The lesson of the Web is not how the big eat the small, but how the fast eat the slow," says a manager at a venture capital firm specializing in Web-based companies.[49]

Succumbing to this myth often leads entrepreneurs to make a fundamental mistake once they finally decide to go online: They believe they have to have a "perfect" site before they can launch it. Few businesses get their sites "right" the first time. In fact, the most successful e-commerce sites are constantly changing, removing what does not work and adding new features to see what does. Successful Web sites are much like a well-designed flower garden, constantly growing and improving, yet changing to reflect the climate of each season. Their creators worry less about creating the perfect site at the outset than about getting a site online and then fixing it, tweaking it, and updating it to meet changing customer demands.

IN THE FOOTSTEPS OF AN ENTREPRENEUR...

Rafting the Web to Success

Your trip down California's Stanislaus River offers panoramic views of the beautifully rugged Sequoia country, scenic stair-step waterfalls, and exhilarating stretches of white water. Yet you manage to remain completely dry because you are not actually there! You are taking a virtual 3-D tour of the river over the Web from the All-Outdoors Whitewater Rafting Company's site. AO Rafting is a second-generation family business founded in 1961 by George Armstrong, then a public school teacher in Concord, California. Armstrong formed an outdoor activities club and, using borrowed equipment, began taking his students to nearby rivers. The kids loved it, and soon Armstrong's whole family was involved in guiding various groups on white-water river trips.

The company grew slowly throughout the 1970s, mostly by word of mouth. As AO Rafting's customer base grew and repeat customers returned, revenues climbed, reaching $750,000 in the 1980s. When the company's sales crossed the $1 million mark, George's sons, Gregg and Scott, were running the business on

a daily basis. The Armstrongs were spending about $150,000 a year on their marketing effort, which consisted of glossy print catalogs, Yellow Pages ads, direct-mail campaigns, and discount programs for corporate groups. The brothers were overwhelmed by the time and energy required to coordinate the multiple marketing efforts and run the remainder of the business. "I was managing a whole train of marketing programs," says Gregg. "Instead of 10 avenues, I wished there was one way to reach everyone."

Having made a decision to focus on growing their company, the Armstrongs began to explore the World Wide Web, which at the time was just emerging as a business tool. They approached Jamie Low, one of their guides who had studied marketing in college and had worked as a graphic designer, with an offer: "Our future is on the Internet, and you're the guy who is going to take us there." Low accepted the challenge. AO Rafting immediately registered its URL and gave Low the go-ahead to set up a Web site. "The Internet could express everything we were trying to pack into all of the other marketing materials," says Gregg. "The Internet was much easier to update [than our print brochures]. It could replace this marketing monster we had built."

The company's basic approach to designing its Web site was one of simplicity—easy to find, easy to navigate, and easy to book trips. Because they understood the importance of search engines to the typical Web browser, the Armstrongs made sure they registered the site on every major search engine and received good placement. That proved to be a wise decision because 70 percent of the company's new business comes from customers using search engines to locate their site.

AO Rafting has been through several revisions of its site, but the basic architecture of its current site was launched in 1997. The payoff was almost immediate. In just a few months, 55 percent of the company's revenue was coming through its Web site! The Web site also lowered AO Rafting's marketing costs. "We had been spending 20 to 25 percent of our revenues on marketing," says Gregg. "With the Web it's now about 5 to 10 percent," adds Scott. In addition to lowering the company's marketing costs, the Web site also produces results that are much easier to track. Today, the Armstrongs generate reports that provide details on how customers found the AO Rafting site and what they are looking for once they get there. Today, 84 percent of the company's business comes through its Web site, and sales have grown to more than $2 million. "It's well worth the investment of resources [we made]," says Gregg. "It's the best investment AO has ever made."

1. What benefits has AO Rafting gained from its Web site?
2. The Armstrongs developed their company's Web site internally, using one of their own employees. What are the advantages and the disadvantages of this approach? What other options do small companies have for developing a Web site?
3. What steps can AO Rafting take to promote its Web site to attract new customers and generate more business?

Source: Adapted from Michael Warshaw, "A Web Strategy Runs Through It," *Inc.,* November 2001, pp. 134–138.

Strategies for E-Success

4. Explain the basic strategies entrepreneurs should follow to achieve success in their e-commerce efforts.

The average Web user spends an average of seven hours online each week.[50] Teenagers and young men now spend more time online than they do watching television.[51] Across a lifetime, the average baby boomer will spend 5 years and 6 months online; the average Generation Xer will spend 9 years and 11 months online; and the average Generation Y user will spend 23 years and 2 months on line, almost one-third of their lives![52] However, converting these Web surfers into online customers requires a business to do more than merely set up a Web site and wait for the hits to start rolling up. Doing business from a Web site is like setting up shop on a dead-end street or a back alley. You may be ready to sell, but no one knows you are there! Building sufficient volume for a site takes energy, time, money, creativity, and, perhaps most importantly, a well-defined strategy. Many entrepreneurs choose to start their e-commerce efforts small and simply and then expand them as sales grow and their needs become more sophisticated. Others make major investments in creating full-blown, interconnected sites at the outset. The cost of setting up a Web site varies significantly, depending on which options an entrepreneur chooses.

Although the Web is a unique medium for creating a company, launching an e-business is not much different from launching a traditional off-line company. The basic drivers of a successful business are the same on the Web as they are on Main Street. To be successful, both off-line and online companies require solid planning and a well-formulated strategy that emphasizes customer service. The goals of e-commerce are no different from traditional off-line businesses—to increase sales, improve efficiency, and boost profits. Yet, the Web has the power to transform businesses, industries, and commerce itself. How a company integrates the Web into its overall business strategy determines how successful it ultimately will become. Following are some guidelines for building a successful Web strategy for a small e-company.

Focus on a Niche in the Market

Like Curly, the crusty old trail boss in the movie *City Slickers,* who said that the secret to happiness was "one thing," many small businesses are finding success on the Web by focusing on one thing. Rather than try to compete head-to-head with the dominant players on the Web who have the resources and the recognition to squash smaller competitors, smart entrepreneurs focus on serving market niches. Smaller companies' limited resources usually are better spent serving niche markets than trying to be everything to everyone (recall the discussion of the focus strategy in Chapter 2). The idea is to concentrate on serving a small corner of the market the giants have overlooked. Niches exist in every industry and can be highly profitable, given the right strategy for serving them. A niche can be defined in many ways, including by geography, by customer profile, by product, by product usage, and many others. *As its name implies, the Garlic Store, located in Fort Collins, Colorado, sells everything garlic to customers across the globe. The company's inventory includes everything from fresh garlic (of course!) and garlic sauces to garlic jams and books on garlic. The site even boasts a "garlic cam" so visitors can "watch" a crop of garlic grow!* Recall from Chapter 2 that one disadvantage of a focus strategy is being so narrowly focused that attracting a large enough customer base can be a challenge. Without the power of the Web, it is unlikely that the Garlic Store would be able to survive from its single location on Weld County Road 13 in Fort Collins![53] Because of its broad reach, the Web is the ideal mechanism for implementing a focus strategy because small companies can reach large numbers of customers with a common interest.

Develop a Community

On the Web, competitors are just a mouse click away. To attract customers and keep them coming back, e-companies have discovered the need to offer more than just quality products and excellent customer service. Many seek to develop a community of customers with similar interests, the nucleus of which is their Web site. The idea is to increase customer loyalty by giving customers the chance to interact with other like-minded visitors or with experts to discuss and learn more about topics they are passionate about. E-mail lists, chat rooms, customer polls ("What is your favorite sports drink?"), Web logs, guest books, and message boards are powerful tools for building a community of visitors at a site because they give visitors the opportunity to have conversations about products, services, and topics that interest them. *Jim Coudal, founder of Coudal Partners Inc., a Chicago-based advertising agency, has relied on a Web log to attract customers from around the globe and to build a stellar reputation for creative ads since 1999. In addition to interesting text, Coudal's blog includes eye-catching photographs, links to articles on everything from advertising history to famous film directors, and information about the latest trends in advertising. Updated twice a day by one of the company's eight employees, the blog attracts 12,000 visitors to the site each*

Company Example

Company Example

week—and the company has never had to purchase an ad![54] Like Coudal Partners, companies that successfully create a community around their Web sites turn mere customers into loyal fans who keep coming back and, better yet, invite others to join them.

Attract Visitors by Giving Away "Freebies"

One of the most important words on the Internet is "free." Many successful e-merchants have discovered the ability to attract visitors to their site by giving away something free and then selling them something else. One e-commerce consultant calls this cycle of giving something away and then selling something "the rhythm of the Web."[55] The "freebie" must be something customers value, but it does *not* have to be expensive nor does it have to be a product. In fact, one of the most common giveaways on the Web is *information*. (After all, that's what most people on the Web are after!) Creating a free online or e-mail newsletter with links to your company's site, of course, and to others of interest is one of the most effective ways of drawing potential customers to a site. Meaningful content presented in a clear, professional fashion is a must. Experts advise keeping online newsletters short—no more than about 600 words. *Poor Richard's E-Mail Publishing* by Chris Pirillo (Top Floor Publishing) offers much useful advice on creating online newsletters.

> **Company Example** →

Tom Natoci and Putnam Weekly of Cloverleaf Wine and Spirits in Southfield, Michigan, decided to launch a weekly e-mail newsletter that would help the company connect with its customers. One of the store's regular customers helped create a template for the newsletter, and Weekly attracted subscribers by putting a stack of registration forms next to the cash register. The first edition of the newsletter went out to just 30 people, and it featured only the shop's most popular wines and a few well-known spirits. Within a year and a half, Cloverleaf was sending the newsletter, which by then included features on unique wine offerings, invitations to wine tastings and other events, and announcements of special shipments and sales, to more than 900 people. Natoci and Weekly say that the newsletter, which costs almost nothing to produce and mail, has boosted sales for Cloverleaf by 12 percent. "It's uncanny," says Weekly, "but I no sooner hit the 'send' key on the newsletter and the phone starts ringing with orders."[56]

Make Creative Use of E-Mail, but Avoid Becoming a "Spammer"

Used properly and creatively, e-mail can be an effective way to build traffic on a Web site. Just as with any newsletter, the e-mail's content should offer something of value to recipients. Supported by online newsletters or chat rooms, customers welcome well-constructed permission e-mail that directs them to a company's site for information or special deals, unlike unsolicited and universally despised e-mails known as *spam*.

Companies often collect visitors' e-mail addresses when they register to receive a freebie. To be successful at collecting a sufficient number of e-mail addresses, a company must make clear to customers that they will receive messages that are meaningful to them and that the company will not sell e-mail addresses to others (which should be part of its posted privacy policy). Once a company has a customer's permission to send information in additional e-mail messages, it has a meaningful marketing opportunity to create a long-term customer relationship.

Make Sure Your Web Site Says "Credibility"

A joint study by Shop.org and the Boston Consulting Group concluded that trust and security issues are the leading inhibitors of online shopping.[57] Unless a company can build among customers *trust* in its Web site, selling is virtually impossible. Visitors begin to evaluate the credibility of a site as soon as they arrive. Does the site look professional? Are there misspelled words and typographical errors? If the site provides information, does it note the sources of that information? If so, are those sources legitimate? Are they trustworthy? Is the presentation of the information fair and objective, or is it biased? Does the company include a privacy policy posted in an obvious place?

One of the simplest ways to establish credibility with customers is to use brand names they know and trust. Whether a company sells nationally recognized brands or its own well-known private brand, using those names on its site creates a sense of legitimacy. People buy brand names they trust, and online companies can use that to their advantage. Another effective way to build customer confidence is by joining an online seal program such as TRUSTe or BBBOnLine. The online equivalent of the Underwriter Laboratories stamp or the Good Housekeeping Seal of Approval, these seals mean that a company meets certain standards concerning the privacy of customers' information and the resolution of customer complaints. Finally, providing a street address, an e-mail address, and a toll-free telephone number sends a subtle message to shoppers that a legitimate business is behind a Web site. Many small companies include photographs of their brick-and-mortar stores and of their employees to combat the Web's anonymity and to give shoppers the feeling that they are supporting a friendly small business.

Consider Forming Strategic Alliances

Most small companies seeking e-commerce success lack the brand and name recognition that larger, more established companies have. Creating that sort of recognition on the Web requires a significant investment of both time and money, two things that most small companies find scarce. If building name recognition is one of the keys to success on the Web, how can small companies with their limited resources hope to compete? One option is to form strategic alliances with bigger companies that can help a small business achieve what it could not accomplish alone. One expert says, "The question is no longer, 'Should I consider an alliance?' Now the questions are 'What form should the alliance take?' and 'How do I find the right partner?' "[58]

One of the easiest ways to begin forging alliances online is through an affiliate marketing program. Also known as referral or associate marketing, this technique involves an online merchant paying a commission to another online business (the affiliate) for directing customers to the merchant's Web site. A study by Forrester Research found that more than half of all online retailers used an affiliate program and 99 percent of them reported that it was an effective method of driving sales. When coordinated properly with the right affiliates, a referral marketing program can generate 10 percent to 40 percent of a company's online sales.[59]

Company Example →

Delightful Deliveries, an online store based in Syosset, New York, that sells more than 1,000 products, including gourmet food items, gift baskets, and sumptuous desserts, is built on a network of successful alliances with other companies. Founder Eric Lituchy accepts orders through Delightful Deliveries' Web site and then forwards those orders to the company's 25 partners, including Mrs. Fields Cookies, Omaha Steaks, Ghirardelli Chocolates, and others. Delightful Deliveries' sales are approaching $4 million a year, yet the company does not carry inventory! Lituchy simply markets his company's product offerings online and then lets his strategic partners ship the items directly to his customers.[60]

Before plunging into a strategic alliance with a larger partner, however, entrepreneurs must understand their dark side. Research shows that the success rate of Internet strategic alliances is just 55 percent.[61] The most common reasons for splitting up? One study found the following causes: incompatible corporate cultures (75 percent), incompatible management personalities (63 percent), and differences in strategic priorities (58 percent).[62]

Make the Most of the Web's Global Reach

The Internet has reduced dramatically the cost of launching a global business initiative; even the tiniest of businesses can engage in international business with a well-designed Web site. Still, despite the Web's reputation as an international marketplace, many Web entrepreneurs fail to utilize fully its global reach. Although 85 percent of the Web's pages are in English, only 43 percent of Web users speak English (and that percentage is declining).[63] It does not make sense for entrepreneurs to limit their Web sites to less than half the world because of a language barrier. A top manager at Travelocity, a travel planning Web site, says that whenever his company adds country-specific features to its site, sales in that country typically double.[64]

E-companies wanting to draw significant sales from foreign markets must design their sites with customers from other lands and cultures in mind. A common mechanism is to include several "language buttons" on the opening page of a site that take customers to pages in the language of their choice. Virtual companies trying to establish a foothold in foreign markets by setting up Web sites dedicated to them run the same risk that actual companies do: offending international visitors by using the business conventions and standards they are accustomed to using in the United States. Business practices, even those used on the Web that are acceptable, even expected, in the United States, may be taboo in other countries. A little research into the subtleties of a target country's culture and business practices can save a great deal of embarrassment and money. Creating secure, simple, and reliable payment methods for foreign customers also will boost sales.

When translating the content of their Web pages into other languages, e-companies must use extreme caution. This is *not* the time to pull out their notes from an introductory Spanish course and begin their own translations. Hiring professional translation and localization services to convert a company's Web content into other languages minimizes the likelihood of a company unintentionally offending foreign customers.

Promote Your Web Site Online and Off-Line

E-commerce entrepreneurs have to use every means available—both online and off-line—to promote their Web sites and to drive traffic to it. In addition to using traditional online techniques such as registering with search engines, creating banner ads, and joining banner exchange programs, Web entrepreneurs must promote their sites off-line as well. Ads in other media such as direct mail or newspapers that mention a site's URL will bring customers to it. It is also a good idea to put the company's Web address on *everything* a company publishes, from its advertisements and letterhead to shopping bags and business cards. A passive approach to generating Web site traffic is a recipe for failure. On the other hand, entrepreneurs who are as innovative at promoting their e-businesses as they are at creating them can attract impressive numbers of visitors to their sites.

Develop an Effective Search Marketing Strategy

Because of the growing popularity of search engines among Internet shoppers, Web search strategies have become an essential part of online companies' promotion strategies. A recent survey by the Kelsey Group reported that 64 percent of online shoppers said that a search engine was the main way to find something on the Internet.[65] Recognizing that the sheer number of Web pages is overwhelming, it is no surprise that Internet shoppers use search engines extensively. Studies by Jupiter Media Metrix show that 77 percent of Internet shoppers go straight to a search engine to find the products and services they want. Unfortunately, business owners invest less than 1 percent of their marketing budget in landing highly placed spots on popular search engines.[66] For a company engaged in e-commerce, a well-defined search marketing strategy should be part of its overall marketing strategy.

One of the biggest challenges facing e-commerce entrepreneurs is maintaining the effectiveness of their search engine marketing strategies. Because the most popular search engines are constantly updating and refining their algorithms, the secretive formulas and methodology search engines use to find and rank the results of Web searches, Web entrepreneurs also must evaluate and refine constantly their search strategies. A company's Web search strategy must recognize the three basic types of search engine results: natural or organic listings, paid or sponsored listings, and paid inclusion. **Natural listings** often arise as a result of "spiders," powerful programs search engines use to crawl around the Web, analyzing sites for keywords, links, and other data. Based on what they find, spiders index Web sites so that a search engine can display a listing of relevant Web sites when a person enters a keyword in the engine to start a search. Some search engines use people-powered searches rather than spider-powered ones to assemble their indexes. With natural listings, an entrepreneur's goal is to get his or her Web site displayed at or near the top of the list of search results, a technique known as search engine optimization. Companies can use the following tips to improve their search placement results:

- Conduct brainstorming sessions to develop a list of keywords and phrases that searchers are likely to use when using a search engine to locate a company's products and services and then use those words and phrases on your Web pages. Usually, simple terms are better than industry jargon.
- Visit competitors' sites for keyword ideas, but avoid using the exact phrases. Simply right-clicking on a competitor's Web page and choosing "View Source" will display the keywords used on the site.
- Consider using less obvious keywords and brand names. For instance, rather than use just "bicycles," a small bicycle retailer should consider keywords such as "racing bikes" or "LeMond."
- Ask customers which words and phrases they use when searching for the products and services the company sells.
- Use data analysis tools to review Web logs to find which words and phrases (and which search engines) brought visitors to the company's Web site.
- Hire services such as Wordtracker that monitor and analyze Web users' search engine tendencies.

Company Example →

Aubuchon Hardware, a family-owned chain of 135 hardware stores based in Westminster, Massachusetts, was getting solid results from its Web site by paying for more than 4,000 words in paid listings. However, managers wanted to expand their online product listings without incurring the additional expense of paid listings, so they hired iProspect.com to optimize their Web site to make the most of natural listings. Aubuchon modified its Web site to include features on specific products such as cordless drills. Within two months of making the changes to its site, Aubuchon saw its online sales volume more than double![67]

Paid or sponsored listings are short text advertisements with links to the sponsoring company's Web site that appear on the results pages of a search engine when a user types in a keyword or phrase. Google, the most popular search engine, displays paid listings as "sponsored links" at the top and down the side of each results page, and Yahoo! shows "sponsored results" at the top and the bottom of its results pages. Advertisers bid on keywords to determine their placement on a search engine's results page. The highest bidder for a keyword gets the most prominent placement (at the top) on the search engine's results page when a user types in that keyword on the search engine. The advertiser pays only when a shopper clicks through to its Web site from the search engine. For this reason, paid listings also are called pay for placement, pay per click, and pay for performance ads.

At one popular search engine, the average bid for keywords in its paid listings is 40 cents, but some words can bring as much as $100! Although it can be expensive, one advantage of paid listings is the ability of the advertiser to evaluate the effectiveness of the listing.

| Company Example | → | *Mark Kini, owner of Boston Chauffeur, recognized the importance of search engine listings to his 18-person limousine service and began purchasing keywords and placement on major search engines such as Google and Yahoo! His search marketing strategy was a success, placing his company at the top of Google's result list, enabling Kini to land several Fortune 500 companies as clients. As search marketing strategies have become more popular among advertisers, however, Kini has watched the cost of marketing his company this way climb from $60,000 his first year to $100,000. Kini also devotes about an hour a day to comparing the results of his keywords to those used by his rivals.*[68] |

As Mark Kini learned, paid listings can strain a small company's marketing budget. For increasing a Web site's visibility, one popular alternative to paid listings is a tool known as paid inclusion. In **paid inclusion**, a company pays a search engine for the right to submit either selected pages or the content of its entire Web site. To keep their natural listings current, search engines regularly crawl through the Internet in the hunt for new and updated Web sites and material to include in their databases, but searching through the huge volume of pages on the Web means that it may take weeks or even months to locate a company's Web site. Because a company pays to submit its Web content into the search engine's database, a paid inclusion eliminates the necessity of waiting for a search engine to find its site. Not every search engine accepts paid inclusions, however.

| Company Example | → | *Lippincott Williams & Wilkins, a Philadelphia publisher of medical information, offered such a wide variety of products that describing them with a reasonable number of keywords was impractical. Heather Walls, the company's Internet content specialist, decided to try paid inclusions instead, which allowed the search engines to draw on the entire content of the company's site. Since Walls began using paid inclusions, traffic to the publisher's Web site has risen 15 percent. Plus, she discovered that visitors who come to the site by way of the search engines are twice as likely to make a purchase as those the company reaches through other media.*[69] |

Designing a Killer Web Site

5. Learn the techniques of designing a killer Web site.

World Wide Web users are not a patient lot. They sit before their computers, surfing the Internet, their fingers poised on their mouse buttons, daring any Web site to delay them with files that take a long time to load (according to one study, that's anything more than 8 seconds).[70] Slow-loading sites or sites that don't deliver on their promises will cause a Web user to move on faster than a bolt of lightning can strike. With more than 4 million Web sites online, how can an entrepreneur design a Web site that will capture and hold potential customers' attention long enough to make a sale? What can they do to keep customers coming back on a regular basis? There is no surefire formula for stopping surfers in their tracks, but the following suggestions will help.

Start with Your Target Customer

Before launching into the design of their Web sites, entrepreneurs must paint a clear picture of their target customers. Only then are they ready to design a site that will appeal to their customers. The goal is create a design in which customers see themselves when they visit. Creating a site in which customers find a comfortable fit requires a careful blend of market research, sales know-how, and aesthetics. The challenge for a business on the Web is to create the same image, style, and ambiance in its online presence as in its off-line stores.

Select the Right Domain Name

Choose a domain name that is consistent with the image you want to create for your company and register it. Entrepreneurs should never underestimate the power of the right domain name or universal resource locator (URL), which is a company's address on the Internet. It not only tells Web surfers where to find a company, but it also should suggest something about the company and what it does. Even the casual Web surfer could guess that the "toys.com" name belongs to a company selling children's toys. (It does; it belongs to eToys Inc., which also owns "etoys.com," "e-toys.com," and several other variations of its name.) The ideal domain name should be:

- *Short.* Short names are easy for people to remember, so the shorter a company's URL is, the more likely potential customers are to recall it.
- *Memorable.* Not every short domain name is necessarily memorable. Some business owners use their companies' initials as their domain name (for example, www.sbfo.com for Stanley Brothers Furniture Outlet). The problem with using initials for a domain name is that customers rarely associate the two, which makes a company virtually invisible on the Web.
- *Indicative of a company's business or business name.* Perhaps the best domain name for a company is one that customers can guess easily if they know the company's name. For instance, mail-order catalogue company L.L. Bean's URL is www.llbean.com, and New Pig, a maker of absorbent materials for a variety of industrial applications, uses www.newpig.com as its domain name. (The company carries this concept over to its toll-free number, which is 1–800-HOT-HOGS.)
- *Easy to spell.* Even though a company's domain name may be easy to spell, it is usually wise to buy several variations of the correct spelling simply because some customers are not likely to be good spellers!

Just because entrepreneurs come up with the perfect URL for their company's Web sites does not necessarily mean that they can use it. Domain names are given on a first-come, first-served basis. Before business owners can use a domain name, they must ensure that someone else has not already taken it. The simplest way to do that is to go to a domain name registration service such as Network Solutions at www.networksolutions.com or NetNames at www.netnames.com to conduct a name search. Entrepreneurs who find the domain name they have selected already registered to someone else have two choices: They can select another name, or they can try to buy the name from the original registrant. Some entrepreneurs buy the rights to their name relatively cheaply, but not every Web start-up is as fortunate. Business incubator eCompanies purchased the rights to the domain name "business.com" from an individual for $7.5 million![71]

Finding unregistered domain names can be a challenge, but several new top-level domain names recently became available: .aero (airlines), .biz (any business site), .coop (business cooperatives), .info (any site), .museum (museums), .name (individuals' sites), and .pro (professionals' sites). Once an entrepreneur finds an unused name that is suitable, he or she must register it (plus any variations of it)—and the sooner, the better! Finding unregistered domain names is becoming more difficult; 98 percent of the words in *Webster's English Dictionary* have been registered as Internet domain names![72] Registering is quite easy: Simply use one of the registration services listed earlier to fill out a form and pay $98, which registers the name for two years. The registration renewal fee is $49 per year, but discounts for multiple-year registrations apply. Although not required, registering the domain name with the U.S. Patent and Trademark Office (USPTO) at a cost of $245 provides maximum protection for a company's domain name. The USPTO's Web site (www.uspto.gov) not only allows users to register a trademark online, but it also offers useful information on trademarks and the protection they offer.

Give Customers What They Want

Although Web shoppers are price conscious, they rank fast, reliable delivery high on their list of criteria in their purchase decisions. Studies also show that surfers look for a large selection of merchandise available to them immediately. Remember that the essence of the selling on the Web is providing *convenience* to customers. Sites that allow them to shop whenever they want, to find what they are looking for easily, and to pay for it conveniently and securely will keep customers coming back. Furniture maker Herman Miller's Web site not only makes it easy for shoppers to browse and to buy its products, but the site also offers research on the benefits of ergonomic designs and allows visitors to try various furniture layouts in rooms created with a special 3-D design tool.[73] One of the reasons Amazon.com has become the largest online retailer is that its five-point strategy is designed to give online shoppers exactly what they want: low prices, wide selection, product availability, shopping convenience, and extensive information about the products it sells.[74]

Figure 13.2 shows the features that make shoppers in the United States most likely to buy from a Web site.

Establish Hyperlinks

Establish hyperlinks with other businesses, preferably those selling products or services that complement yours. Listing the Web addresses of complementary businesses

Figure 13.2

Features That Make U.S. Shoppers More Likely to Buy from a Web Site

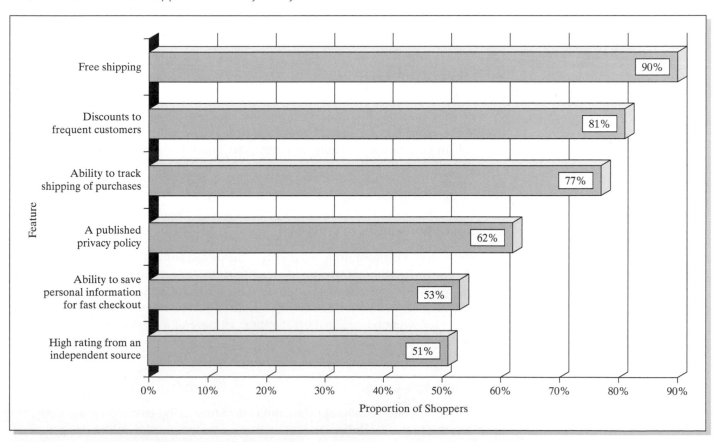

on a company's site and having them list your address on their sites offers customers more value and can bring traffic to your site that you otherwise would have missed. For instance, the owner of a site selling upscale kitchen gadgets should consider a cross-listing arrangement with sites that feature gourmet recipes, wines, and kitchen appliances.

Include E-Mail Options

Include an e-mail option, an address, and a telephone number in your site. Customers appreciate the opportunity to communicate with your company. If you include e-mail access on your site, however, be sure to respond to it promptly. Nothing alienates cyber-customers faster than a company that is slow to respond or fails to respond to their e-mail messages. Also be sure to include an address and a toll-free telephone number for customers who prefer to write or call with their questions. Unfortunately, many companies either fail to include their telephone numbers on their sites or bury them so deeply within the sites' pages that customers never find them.

Offer Online Order Tracking

Give shoppers the ability to track their orders online. Many customers who order items online want to track the progress of their orders. One of the most effective ways to keep a customer happy is to send an e-mail confirmation that your company received the order and another e-mail notification when you ship the order. The shipment notice should include the shipper's tracking number and instructions on how to track the order from the shipper's site. Order and shipping confirmations instill confidence in even the most Web-wary shoppers.

Offer Web Specials

Give Web customers a special deal that you don't offer in any other advertising piece. Change your specials often (weekly, if possible) and use clever "teasers" to draw attention to the offer. Regular special offers available only on the Web give customers an incentive to keep visiting a company's site. Also provide product prices and shipping charges early in the transaction. Customers do not like to be surprised by high charges at checkout.

Look for Opportunities to Cross-Sell

Sales clerks in brick-and-mortar retail stores quickly learn the art of cross-selling, offering, for example, a customer who purchases a shirt the opportunity to purchase a matching tie as well. Online merchants can use the same tactic. Amazon.com employs this sales strategy extremely well with its display that reads "Others who purchased this book also bought the following books," making it appear as more of a service to shoppers than a clever selling tactic.

Follow a Simple Design

Catchy graphics and photographs are important to snaring customers, but designers must choose them carefully. Designs that are overly complex take a long time to download, and customers are likely to move on before they appear. Web Site Garage (http://websitegarage.netscape.com), a Web site maintenance company, offers companies a free evaluation of how their sites measure up in terms of speed.

Specific design tips include:

- Avoid clutter. The best designs are simple and elegant with a balance of both text and graphics.
- Avoid huge graphic headers that must download first, prohibiting customers from seeing anything else on your site as they wait (or, more likely, *don't* wait). Use graphics judiciously so that the site loads quickly. Research suggests that if a Web page takes longer than 8 seconds to load, one-third of potential visitors abandon the site.[75]
- Include a menu bar at the top of the page that makes it easy for customers to find their way around your site.
- Make the site easy to navigate by including easy-to-follow navigation buttons at the bottom of pages that enable customers to return to the top of the page or to the menu bar. This avoids "the pogo effect," where visitors bounce from page to page in a Web site looking for what they need. Without navigation buttons or a site map page, a company runs the risk of customers getting lost in its site and leaving. Organizing a Web site into logical categories also helps.
- Minimize the number of clicks required for a customer to get to any particular page in the site. Long paths increase the likelihood of customers bailing out before they reach their intended destination.
- Incorporate meaningful content in the site that is useful to visitors, well organized, easy to read, and current. The content should be consistent with the message a company sends in the other advertising media it uses. Although a Web site should be designed to sell, providing useful, current information attracts visitors, keeps them coming back, and establishes a company's reputation as an expert in the field.
- Include a "frequently asked questions (FAQ)" section. Adding this section to a page can reduce dramatically the number of telephone calls and e-mails customer service representatives must handle. FAQ sections typically span a wide range of issues—from how to place an order to how to return merchandise—and cover whatever topics customers most often want to know about.
- Be sure to include privacy and return policies as well as product guarantees the company offers.
- Avoid fancy typefaces and small fonts because they are too hard to read.
- Be vigilant for misspelled words, typographical errors, and formatting mistakes; they destroy a site's credibility in no time and send customers fleeing to competitors' sites.
- Don't put small fonts on "busy" backgrounds; no one will read them!
- Use contrasting colors of text and graphics. For instance, blue text on a green background is nearly impossible to read.
- Be careful with frames. Using frames that are so thick that they crowd out text makes for a poor design.
- Test the site on different Web browsers and on different size monitors. A Web site may look exactly the way it was designed to look on one Web browser and be a garbled mess on another. Sites designed to display correctly on large monitors may not view well on small ones. *Jeff Bjorck, a composer who sells musical CDs on his Web site, Purepiano.com, discovered that on one Web browser the site looked exactly the way he had designed it; on other browsers, however, line spacing, fonts, and item positioning were quite different. Bjorck purchased an inexpensive software package, Keynote Mechanic, that adapted the original HTML code so that the site looked uniform across all browsers. The program also helped Bjorck optimize the use of graphic images so that the site loaded much faster.*[76]
- Use your Web site to collect information from visitors, but don't tie up visitors immediately with a tedious registration process. Most will simply leave the site

Company Example →

never to return. Offers for a free e-mail newsletter or a contest giveaway can give visitors enough incentive to register with a site.

- Incorporate a search function that allows shoppers to type in the items they want to purchase. Unlike in-store shoppers, who might browse until they find the item, online shoppers usually want to go straight to the products they seek. Ideally, the search function acknowledges common misspellings of key terms, avoiding the dreaded "No Results Found" message.
- Include company contact information and an easy-to-find customer service telephone number.
- Avoid automated music that plays continuously and cannot be cut off.
- Make sure the overall look of the page is appealing. "When a site is poorly designed, lacks information, or cannot support customer needs, that [company's] reputation is seriously jeopardized," says one expert.[77]
- Remember: Simpler usually is better.

Assure Customers That Online Transactions Are Secure

If you are serious about doing business on the Web, make sure that your site includes the proper security software and encryption devices. Computer-savvy customers are not willing to divulge their credit card numbers on sites that are not secure.

Confirm Online Transactions

Order-confirmation e-mails, which a company can generate automatically, let a customer know that the company received the online order and can be an important first line of defense against online fraud. If the customer claims not to have placed the order, the company can cancel it and report the credit card information as suspicious.

Keep Your Site Updated

Customers want to see something new when they visit stores, and they expect the same when they visit virtual stores as well. Delete any hyperlinks that have disappeared and keep the information on your Web site current. One sure way to run off customers on the Web is to continue to advertise your company's "Christmas Special" in August! On the other hand, fresh information and new specials keep customers coming back.

Test Your Site Often

Smart e-commerce entrepreneurs check their sites frequently to make sure they are running smoothly and are not causing customers unexpected problems. A good rule of thumb is to check your site at least monthly—or weekly if its content changes frequently.

Consider Hiring a Professional Designer

Pros can do it a lot faster and better than you can. However, don't give designers free rein to do whatever they want to with your site. Make sure it meets your criteria for an effective site that can sell.

Entrepreneurs must remember that on the World Wide Web every company, no matter how big or small it is, has the exact same screen size for its site. What matters most is not the size of your company but how you put that screen size to use.

✦ GAINING *a* COMPETITIVE EDGE ✦

Hitching a Ride on eBay

Marsha and William Pater, owners of Pater Tool Supply near Chicago, were looking for a way to expand their business, so they decided to give eBay, the giant Web-based auction site, a try. They began by listing a few basic items such as drill bits, hand tools, and a few overstocked items that had been sitting in their retail store far too long. To their surprise, the items sold quickly, and the Paters knew they had discovered a new sales channel for their small company. Today, the Paters list more than 500 items on eBay, and the sales of those items add on average $10,000 to the company's monthly sales revenue.

Pater Tool Supply is just one of about 450,000 small businesses that tap into eBay to sell merchandise online whether or not they have their own Web sites. On a typical day, some 12 million items are available, 1.7 million new listings are posted, and sales totaling $66 million take place—much of them from entrepreneurs operating their own eBay businesses. Sales of clothing and accessories alone on eBay exceed $1 billion a year! However, shoppers can find almost anything on eBay—from antique duck decoys and jewelry to Lear jets and cars. Indeed, used cars and parts now make up eBay's biggest single category of sales. Describing the uniqueness of the company, CEO Meg Whitman says that eBay is "one part company, one part town-hall meeting, and one part entertainment."

Founded in 1995 by Pierre Omidyar using a computer in his spare bedroom, eBay is one of the fastest-growing businesses in the world and has been profitable since it first opened for business. In addition to its auction listings, eBay operates virtual stores for 150,000 entrepreneurs worldwide. Steve Weinberg started selling new and refurbished consumer electronics such as digital cameras, DVD players, and other items as a hobby in 1999. Today, Weinberg's eBay store is his full-time job, and his monthly sales, which now exceed $25,000 a month, qualify him for additional benefits as an eBay power seller. Like Weinberg, entrepreneurs hitching a ride on eBay are able to exploit the Web's global reach at very little expense. With more than 100 million registered users worldwide, half of eBay's sales come from outside the United States.

How does an entrepreneur go about setting up an eBay business? The process is quite simple. All buyers and sellers have to be registered with eBay before they can participate in an online auction. Once registered, a seller writes a description of the items to be sold, being careful not to overpromise and end up with poor customer satisfaction ratings from buyers. Experienced eBay sellers say that the keys to sales success are writing clear, interesting descriptions of items, providing detailed photographs, setting competitive prices, and being available to answer potential buyers' questions.

The seller then includes a digital photograph of the item to be posted on eBay with the product description. The seller sets a minimum opening price (and, if desired, a reserve price, the minimum price the bids must reach before he or she will actually sell the item) and the length of time the auction will run (usually seven days), sits back, and waits for the bidding to begin. Only the seller sees the details of all of the bids submitted for an item, and sellers have the ability to check the reputations of the bidders and can reject a potential buyer's bid if necessary. Once the auction ends, the seller contacts the buyer to work out payment, which typically includes checks, money orders, or electronic payment systems such as PayPal (which eBay purchased for $1.5 billion in 2002). Sellers pay a small fee to list an item for auction, and they pay eBay a commission once the item sells.

David Schultz is a satisfied eBay entrepreneur. He began learning about eBay when his former boss asked him to explore ways to sell merchandise online. Based on what he learned about the online auction company, Schultz decided to start his own business, ITEPVisions in Orlando, Florida, to sell baby and children's furniture through eBay. Annual sales are $2.5 million, making Schultz quite happy to hitch his business onto the eBay star.

1. What advantages and disadvantages does selling on eBay offer entrepreneurs?
2. Form a team with several of your classmates. Working together, choose a product category you think would sell well on eBay and develop a strategy for selling it. Write a sample description of a sample product. What type of photograph would you provide? What introductory price would you set?

Source: Adapted from Jacquelyn Lynn, "Let the Bidding Begin," *Entrepreneur B.Y.O.B,* September 2003, pp. 96–102; Patricia Fusco, "Small Businesses Growing with eBay," *Small Business Computing,* February 26, 2004, www.smallbusinesscomputing.com/emarketing/article.php/3317831; "At the Drop of a Hammer," *The Economist,* May 15, 2004, pp. 12–14; Nick Wingfield, "Hitching a Ride on eBay," *Wall Street Journal,* October 20, 2003, pp. R4–R5.

Tracking Web Results

Software Solutions

6. Explain how companies track the results from their Web sites.

Company Example

As they develop their Web sites, entrepreneurs seek to create sites that generate sales, improve customer relationships, or lower costs. How can entrepreneurs determine the effectiveness of their sites? A common thread running through commercially successful Web sites is the ability to analyze how customers are using the sites and then fine-tuning the sites to enhance their value to customers. **Web analytics**, tools that measure a Web site's ability to attract customers, generate sales, and keep customers coming back, help entrepreneurs know what works—and what doesn't—on the Web. *Jason MacMurray, director of marketing for BodyTrends.com, an online health and fitness store, uses an off-the-shelf Web analytics program to learn everything he can about how visitors interact with the company's Web site. MacMurray can monitor how many people visit the site, how they got there, which keywords they used if they arrived by a search engine, which pages they visited, how long they stayed on each page, how many visitors actually made purchases, and many other useful characteristics. The software also routinely checks to make sure that all of the 3,000-plus pages on BodyTrend's Web site are functioning properly. "The better information we have about our site," says MacMurray, "the better we can run our business."*[78]

In the early days of e-commerce, entrepreneurs tried to create sites that were both "sticky" and "viral." A **sticky site** is one that acts like electronic flypaper, capturing visitors' attention and offering them useful, interesting information that makes them stay at the site. The premise of stickiness is that the longer customers stay in a site, the more likely they are to actually purchase something and to come back to it. A **viral site** is one that visitors are willing to share with their friends. This "word-of-mouse" advertising is one of the most effective ways of generating traffic to a company's site. As the Web has matured as a marketing channel, however, the shortcomings of these simple measures have become apparent, and other e-metrics continue to emerge. E-businesses now focus on **recency**, the length of time between a customer's visits to a Web site. The more frequently customers visit a site, the more likely they are to become loyal customers. Another important measure of Web success is the **conversion** (or **browse-to-buy**) **ratio**, which measures the proportion of visitors to a site that actually make a purchase.

How can online entrepreneurs know if their sites are successful? Answering that question means that entrepreneurs must track visitors to their sites, the paths within the site, and the activity they generate while there. A variety of methods for tracking Web results are available, but the most commonly used ones include counters and log-analysis software. The simplest technique is a **counter**, which records the number of "hits" a Web site receives. Although counters measure activity on a site, they do so only at the broadest level. If a counter records 10 hits, for instance, there is no way to know if those hits came as a result of 10 different visitors or as a result of just one person making 10 visits. Plus, counters cannot tell Web entrepreneurs where visitors to their sites come from or which pages they look at on the site.

A more meaningful way to track activity on a Web site is through **log-analysis software**, which has the goal of helping entrepreneurs understand visitors' online behavior. Server logs record every page, graphic, audio clip, or photograph that visitors to a site access, and log-analysis software analyzes these logs and generates reports describing how visitors behave when they get to a site. With this software, entrepreneurs can determine how many unique visitors come to their site and how often repeat visitors return. Owners of e-stores can discover which FAQ customers click on most often, which part of a site they stayed in the longest, which site they came from, and how the volume of traffic at the site affected the server's speed of operation. **Click-stream analysis** allows entrepreneurs to determine the paths visitors take while on a site and to pinpoint the areas in which they spend the most—and the least—time. These Web analytics tools give e-commerce entrepreneurs the ability to infer what visitors think about a Web site, its products, its content, its design, and other features. Feedback from log-analysis software helps entrepreneurs redesign their sites to eliminate confusing navigation, unnecessary graphics, meaningless content, incomplete information, and other problems that can cause visitors to leave.

Other tracking methods available to owners of e-businesses include:

- *Clustering.* This software observes visitors to a Web site, analyzes their behavior, and then groups them into narrow categories. Companies then target each category of shoppers with products, specials, and offers designed to appeal to them.
- *Collaborative filtering.* This software uses sophisticated algorithms to determine visitors' interests by comparing them to other shoppers with similar tastes. Companies then use this information to suggest products an individual customer would most likely be interested in, given his or her profile.
- *Profiling systems.* These programs tag individual customers on a site and note their responses to the various pages in the site. Based on the areas a customer visits most, the software develops a psychographic profile of the shopper. For instance, a visitor who reads an article on massage techniques might receive an offer for a book on alternative medicine or a magazine focusing on environmental issues.
- *Artificial intelligence (AI).* This software, sometimes called neural networking, is the most sophisticated of the group because it actually learns from users' behavior. The more these programs interact with customers, the "smarter" they become. Over time, they can help online marketers know which special offers work best with which customers, when customers are most likely to respond, and how to present the offer.

Return on Investment

Just like traditional businesses, e-businesses must earn a reasonable return on an entrepreneur's investment. The difficulty, however, is that much of the total investment required to build, launch, maintain, and market a Web site is not always obvious. Plus, the payoffs of a successful site are not easy to measure and do not always fit neatly into traditional financial models that calculate return on investment (ROI). For instance, how can a business with both a clicks-and-bricks presence determine exactly how many customers come into its retail store as a result of having visited its Web site? Can it quantify the increase in customer loyalty as a result of its e-commerce efforts? Many companies have discovered that the payoff from their online sales efforts are long term and sometimes intangible.

Owners of e-businesses are developing new models to evaluate the performances of their companies. In addition to calculating ROI, many online businesses compute **cost per action (CPA)**, the amount it costs to produce a particular customer action such as registering for a newsletter, requesting information, downloading an article, and others. The actions a company uses should correlate to future sales. **Cost per order (CPO)** is a common measurement for online retailers. It measures the cost a company incurs to generate a customer order and can be calculated across all product lines or for a specific product. Ipswitch Inc., a software development company, examines its Web site from three perspectives: what it costs, what it generates in revenues, and what savings it produces for the company. Managers have determined that for every dollar they spend on their Web site, Ipswitch generates $22 in online sales. They also know that if they had produced those sales through sales representatives, the company would have incurred an additional $2.3 million in costs![79]

Ensuring Web Privacy and Security

Privacy

7. Describe how e-businesses ensure the privacy and security of the information they collect and store from the Web.

The Web's ability to track customers' every move naturally raises concerns over the privacy of the information companies collect. E-commerce gives businesses access to tremendous volumes of information about their customers, creating a responsibility to protect that information and to use it wisely. A recent survey by Forrester Research discovered that just 6 percent of online customers trust Web sites with their personal information.[80] Yet, the Federal Trade Commission estimates that 97 percent of commercial Web sites collect personal information from their customers.[81] The potential for breaching customers' privacy is present in any e-business. To make sure they are using the information they collect from visitors to their Web sites legally and ethically and safeguarding it adequately, companies should take the following steps:

Take an Inventory of the Customer Data Collected. The first step to ensuring proper data handling is to assess exactly the type of data the company is collecting and storing. How are you collecting the information? Why are you collecting it? How are you using it? Do visitors know how you are using the data? Do you need to get their permission to use the data in this way? Do you use all of the data you are collecting?

Develop a Company Privacy Policy for the Information You Collect. A **privacy policy** is a statement explaining the nature of the information a company collects online, what it does with that information, and the recourse customers have if they believe the company is misusing the information. *Every* online company should have a privacy policy, but research firm Computer Economics estimates that only half of online U.S. businesses have developed one.[82] Several online privacy firms, such as TRUSTe (www.truste.org), BBBOnline (www.bbbonline.com), and BetterWeb (www.betterweb.com), offer Web "seal programs," the equivalent of a Good Housekeeping seal of privacy approval. To earn a privacy seal of approval, a company must adopt a privacy policy, implement it, and monitor its effectiveness. Many of these privacy sites also provide online policy wizards, automated questionnaires that help e-business owners create comprehensive privacy statements.

Post Your Company's Privacy Policy Prominently on Your Web Site and Follow It. Creating a privacy policy is not sufficient; posting it in a prominent place on the Web site (accessible from every page on the site) and then abiding by it make a policy meaningful. Whether or not a company has a privacy policy posted prominently often determines whether or not a customer will do online business with it. One of the worst mistakes a company can make is to publish its privacy policy online and then fail to follow it. Not only is this unethical, but it also can lead to serious damage awards if customers take legal action against the company.

Company Example →

KBKids.com, an online retailer of children's toys, games, and videos, post its privacy policy in a highly prominent position on its site using a large tab that links to a separate page. The page provides a comprehensive description of its policy, the way it collects information, how customers can view the information the company collects, and its affiliation with BBBOnLine. "We established a security and privacy policy to assure our customers that we respect the information they provide to us and that its only use is to help us serve them better," says KBKids.com's marketing vice president.[83]

Security

Concerns about security and fraud present the greatest obstacles to the growth of e-commerce. A company doing business on the Web faces two conflicting goals: to establish a presence on the Web so that customers from across the globe can have access to its site and the information maintained there and to preserve a high level of security so that the business, its site, and the information it collects from customers are safe from hackers and intruders intent on doing harm. Companies have a number of safeguards available to them, but hackers with enough time, talent, and determination usually can beat even the most sophisticated safety measures. If hackers manage to break into a system, they can do irreparable damage, stealing programs and data, modifying or deleting valuable information, changing the look and content of sites, or crashing sites altogether. For instance, hackers recently broke into one company's e-commerce site, stealing information on more than 15,000 customers' credit card accounts, including their credit card numbers. Other hackers flooded Amazon.com's Web site with so many hits that legitimate users were locked out (a denial of service attack), costing the company an estimated $244,000 in lost sales every hour it was out of service.[84]

One of the most dangerous scams on the Internet is **phishing** (as in luring prey with an attractive bait), a scheme in which a thief dupes computer users into revealing, sometimes unknowingly, their user names, passwords, and other private information. One recent phishing scam involved a hidden program that took screen captures as customers logged onto their secure banking Web sites that were then e-mailed to the criminals. Another thief using the cyber-name Robotector sent an e-mail with the subject line "I still love you" to 3 million people. The message contained a virus that recorded victims' user names and passwords whenever they visited more than 30 online banks or financial sites worldwide and then e-mailed the results back to Robotector. "The Internet is a great thing," says Robotector who refuses to reveal just how much money he has stolen with the scam and who has not yet been caught. The real danger is that scams such as these could erode customers' confidence in e-commerce, causing its growth to slow dramatically and posing real threats to online entrepreneurs.[85]

Security threats are real for companies of all sizes, and entrepreneurs must contend with that reality. The *Internet Security Threat Report* found that an average of seven new software security flaws, "chinks in the armor" of a software package that make it vulnerable to hackers, are discovered each day. The implications of these flaws can be devastating to businesses. During one recent 12-day period, for instance, four viruses infiltrated the Internet, causing an estimated $2 billion in damages.[86] To date, nearly 63,000 viruses (including Mydoom, the fastest-spreading virus yet) have infected the Internet, causing an estimated $65 billion in damages to those affected by the malicious programs.[87] To minimize the likelihood of invasion by hackers and viruses, e-companies rely on several tools, including virus detection software, intrusion detection software, and firewalls. Perhaps the most basic level of protection, **virus detection software** scans computer drives for viruses, nasty programs written by devious hackers and designed to harm computers and the information they contain. The severity of viruses ranges widely, from relatively harmless programs that put humorous messages on a user's screen to those that erase a computer's hard drive or cause the entire system to crash. Because hackers are *always* writing new viruses to attack computer systems, entrepreneurs must keep their virus detection software up-to-date and must run it often. An attack by one virus can bring a company's entire e-commerce platform to a screeching halt in no time! The "I love you" virus infected computer systems across the globe, leaving companies with an estimated $15 billion in damages and downtime.

Intrusion detection software is essential for any company doing business on the Web. These packages constantly monitor the activity on a company's network server and sound an alert if they detect someone breaking into the company's computer system or if they detect unusual network activity. Intrusion detection software not only can detect attempts by unauthorized users to break into a computer system while they are happening, but it also can trace the hacker's location. Most packages also have the ability to preserve a record of the attempted break-in that will stand up in court so that companies can take legal action against cyber-intruders.

A **firewall** is a combination of hardware and software operating between the Internet and a company's computer network that allows authorized employees to have access to the Internet but keeps unauthorized users from entering a company's network and the programs and data it contains. Establishing a firewall is essential for any company operating on the Web, but entrepreneurs must make sure that their firewalls are set up properly. Otherwise, they are useless! One recent study of more than 2,000 Web sites by ICSA.net, a security consulting firm, found that even though every site had a firewall in place, more than 80 percent were vulnerable to attack with commonly available software because the firewalls were not properly designed.[88] Even with all of these security measures in place, it is best for a company to run its Web page on a separate server from the network that runs the business. If hackers break into the Web site, they still do not have access to the company's sensitive data and programs.

The Computer Security Institute (www.gocsi.com) offers articles, information, and seminars to help business owners maintain computer security. The *Business Security e-Journal* (www.lubrinco.com) is a free monthly newsletter on computer security, and *Information Security Magazine* (www.infosecuritymag.com), published by the International Computer Security Association (www.icsa.net), also offers helpful advice on maintaining computer security. For entrepreneurs who want to test their sites' security, the ICSA offers its Security Snapshot system (free of charge) that runs various security tests on a site and then e-mails a "Risk Index" score in six different categories, including the site's risk of hacker intrusion.

In e-commerce just as in traditional retailing, sales do not matter unless a company gets paid! On the Web customers demand transactions they can complete with ease and convenience, and the simplest way to allow customers to pay for e-commerce transactions is with credit cards. From a Web customer's perspective, however, one of the most important security issues is the security of his or her credit card information. To ensure the security of their customers' credit card information, online retailers typically use **secure sockets layer (SSL) technology** to encrypt customers' transaction information as it travels across the Internet. By using secure shopping cart features from storefront-building services or Internet service providers, even the smallest e-commerce stores can offer their customers secure online transactions.

Processing credit card transactions requires a company to obtain an Internet merchant account from a bank or financial intermediary. Setup fees for an Internet merchant account typically range from $500 to $1,000, but companies also pay monthly access and statement fees of between $40 and $80 plus a transaction fee of 10 to 60 cents per transaction. Once an online company has a merchant account, it can accept credit cards from online customers.

Online credit card transactions also pose a risk for merchants; online companies lose an estimated $1 billion a year to online payment fraud each year.[89] The most common problem is **chargebacks**, online transactions that customers dispute. Unlike credit card transactions in a retail store, those made online involve no signatures, and Internet merchants incur the loss when a customer disputes an online credit card transaction. Experts estimate that payment fraud online is 5 to 10 times greater than in brick-and-mortar stores.[90] A thief in Romania recently tried to use a stolen credit card to purchase eight handbags from Velma Handbags, a small company founded by Margaret Cobbs, but the company that handles her credit card transactions discovered the attempt and stopped the $380 transaction.[91] Raymond Attipa wasn't as lucky. Founder of topautoparts.com, a Web-based seller of aftermarket automotive parts, Attipa folded his online business after incurring $35,000—one-fourth of the company's annual sales—in fraudulent credit card charges in a single year.[92]

One way to prevent fraud is to ask customers for their card verification value (CVV, CID, or CVV2), the three-digit number above the signature panel on the back of the credit card, as well as their card number and expiration date. Online merchants also can subscribe to a real-time credit card processing service that authorizes credit card transactions, but the fees can be high. Also, using a shipper that provides the ability to track shipments so online merchants can prove that the customer actually received the merchandise helps minimize the threat of payment fraud.

▌▐ ▌ Chapter Review

1. Describe the benefits of selling on the World Wide Web. Although a Web-based sales strategy does not guarantee success, the companies that have pioneered Web-based selling have realized many benefits, including the following:

   - The opportunity to increase revenues.
   - The ability to expand their reach into global markets.
   - The ability to remain open 24 hours a day, seven days a week.
   - The capacity to use the Web's interactive nature to enhance customer service.
   - The power to educate and to inform.
   - The ability to lower the cost of doing business.
   - The ability to spot new business opportunities and to capitalize on them.
   - The power to track sales results.

2. Understand the factors an entrepreneur should consider before launching into e-commerce. Before launching an e-commerce effort, business owners should consider the following important issues:

   - How a company exploits the Web's interconnectivity and the opportunities it creates to transform relationships with its suppliers and vendors, its customers, and other external stakeholders is crucial to its success.
   - Web success requires a company to develop a plan for integrating the Web into its overall strategy. The plan should address issues such as site design and maintenance, creating and managing a brand name, marketing and promotional strategies, sales, and customer service.
   - Developing deep, lasting relationships with customers takes on even greater importance on the Web. Attracting customers on the Web costs money, and companies must be able to retain their online customers to make their Web sites profitable.
   - Creating a meaningful presence on the Web requires an ongoing investment of resources—time, money, energy, and talent. Establishing an attractive Web site brimming with catchy photographs of products is only the beginning.
   - Measuring the success of Web-based sales efforts is essential to remaining relevant to customers whose tastes, needs, and preferences are always changing.

3. Explain the 12 myths of e-commerce and how to avoid falling victim to them. The 12 myths of ecommerce are:

   Myth 1. Setting up a business on the Web is easy and inexpensive.
   Myth 2. If I launch a site, customers will flock to it.
   Myth 3. Making money on the Web is easy.
   Myth 4. Privacy is not an important issue on the Web.
   Myth 5. The most important part of any e-commerce effort is technology.
   Myth 6. "Strategy? I don't need a strategy to sell on the Web! Just give me a Web site, and the rest will take care of itself."
   Myth 7. On the Web, customer service is not as important as it is in a traditional retail store.
   Myth 8. Flash makes a Web site better.
   Myth 9. It's what's up front that counts.
   Myth 10. E-commerce will cause brick-and-mortar retail stores to disappear.
   Myth 11. The greatest opportunities for e-commerce lie in the retail sector.
   Myth 12. It's too late to get on the Web.

4. Explain the basic strategies entrepreneurs should follow to achieve success in their e-commerce efforts. Following are some guidelines for building a successful Web strategy for a small e-company:

   - Consider focusing on a niche in the market.
   - Develop a community of online customers.
   - Attract visitors by giving away "freebies."
   - Make creative use of e-mail, but avoid becoming a "spammer."
   - Make sure your Web site says "credibility."
   - Consider forming strategic alliances with larger, more established companies.
   - Make the most of the Web's global reach.
   - Promote your Web site online and off-line.

5. Learn the techniques of designing a killer Web site. There is no surefire formula for stopping surfers in their tracks, but the following suggestions will help:

   - Select a domain name that is consistent with the image you want to create for your company and register it.
   - Be easy to find.
   - Give customers want they want.
   - Establish hyperlinks with other businesses, preferably those selling products or services that complement yours.

- Include an e-mail option and a telephone number in your site.
- Give shoppers the ability to track their orders online.
- Offer Web shoppers a special all their own.
- Follow a simple design for your Web page.
- Assure customers that their online transactions are secure.
- Keep your site updated.
- Consider hiring a professional to design your site.

6. Explain how companies track the results from their Web sites.

- The simplest technique for tracking the results of a Web site is a counter, which records the number of "hits" a Web site receives. Another option for tracking Web activity is through log-analysis software. Server logs record every page, graphic, audio clip, or photograph that visitors to a site access, and log-analysis software analyzes these logs and generates reports describing how visitors behave when they get to a site.

7. Describe how e-businesses ensure the privacy and security of the information they collect and store from the Web. To make sure they are using the information they collect from visitors to their Web sites legally and ethically, companies should take the following steps:

- Take an inventory of the customer data collected.
- Develop a company privacy policy for the information you collect.
- Post your company's privacy policy prominently on your Web site and follow it.
- Ensure the security of information companies collect and store from Web transactions by relying on virus and intrusion detection software and firewalls to ward off attacks from hackers.

▌▌▌ Discussion Questions

1. How have the Internet and e-commerce changed the ways companies do business?
2. Explain the benefits a company earns by selling on the Web.
3. Discuss the factors entrepreneurs should consider before launching an e-commerce site.
4. What are the 12 myths of e-commerce? What can an entrepreneur do to avoid them?
5. Explain the five basic approaches available to entrepreneurs for launching an e-commerce effort. What are the advantages, the disadvantages, and the costs associated with each one?
6. What strategic advice would you offer an entrepreneur about to start an e-company?

7. What design characteristics make for a successful Web page?
8. Explain the characteristics of an ideal domain name.
9. Describe the techniques that are available to e-companies for tracking results from their Web sites. What advantages does each offer?
10. What steps should e-businesses take to ensure the privacy of the information they collect and store from the Web?
11. What techniques can e-companies use to protect their banks of information and their customers' transaction data from hackers?
12. Why does evaluating the effectiveness of a Web site pose a problem for online entrepreneurs?

E-Commerce and Entrepreneurship

Business PlanPro

The Internet is transforming the ways that many small companies operate, giving them the ability to sell their goods and services around the clock, reach customers across the globe, connect with suppliers more effectively, provide unprecedented levels of customer service, understand and respond to customers' preferences, and create new and innovative methods of conducting business. In the world of e-commerce, companies have learned that size matters far less than speed and flexibility.

The exercises for Chapter 13 that accompany Business Plan Pro are designed to help you define your company's Web strategy, assess your company's readiness to engage in e-commerce, and evaluate the quality of your company's Web site. Once you finish these exercises, you are ready to complete the section of Business Plan Pro called Your Web Plan.

Chapter 14
Sources of Equity Financing

> *Rule # 1: You can never have too much equity. Rule # 2: You can never have too much capital. Rule # 3: When Rules 1 and 2 conflict, choose Rule #2.*
> —PEG WYANT, VENTURE CAPITALIST

> *If you don't know who the fool is in a deal, it's you.*
> —MICHAEL WOLFF

Upon completion of this chapter, you will be able to:

1. Explain the differences in the three types of capital small businesses require: fixed, working, and growth.

2. Describe the various sources of equity capital available to entrepreneurs, including personal savings, friends and relatives, angels, partners, corporations, venture capital, and public stock offerings.

3. Describe the process of "going public," as well as its advantages and disadvantages and the various simplified registrations and exemptions from registration available to small businesses.

4. Explain the various simplified registrations, exemptions from registration, and other alternatives available to entrepreneurs wanting to sell shares of equity to investors.

Raising the money to launch a new business venture has always been a challenge for entrepreneurs. Capital markets rise and fall with the stock market, overall economic conditions, and investors' fortunes. These swells and troughs in the availability of capital make the search for financing look like a wild roller-coaster ride. Entrepreneurs, especially those in less glamorous industries or those just starting out, soon discover the difficulty of finding outside sources of financing. Many banks shy away from making loans to start-ups, venture capitalists are looking for ever-larger deals, private investors have grown cautious, and making a public stock offering remains a viable option for only a handful of promising companies with good track records and fast-growth futures. The result has been a credit crunch for entrepreneurs looking for small to moderate amounts of start-up capital. Entrepreneurs and business owners needing between $100,000 and $3 million are especially hard hit because of the vacuum that exists at that level of financing.

In the face of this capital crunch, business's need for capital has never been greater. Experts estimate the small business financing market to be $170 billion a year; yet, that still is not enough to satisfy the capital appetites of entrepreneurs and their cash-hungry businesses.[1] When searching for the capital to launch their companies, entrepreneurs must remember the following "secrets" to successful financing:

| Company Example |

- *Choosing the right sources of capital for a business can be just as important as choosing the right form of ownership or the right location.* It is a decision that will influence a company for a lifetime, so entrepreneurs must weigh their options carefully and understand the consequences of the deal before committing to a particular funding source. *When he launched his technology company, one entrepreneur convinced 10 of his former college buddies to make an equity investment of $150,000 in the business. Unfortunately, the entrepreneur failed to realize that he had given up control over future financing arrangements that would affect the original investors' shares. Later, when a venture capital firm wanted to invest $5 million in the fast-growing business, the 10 investors vetoed the deal. "They thought that VCs (venture capitalists) were vampires, trying to steal their money," says the entrepreneur. Ultimately, the entrepreneur and the 10 investors agreed to restructure the company's financing. The business survived, but their friendships did not.*[2]
- *The money is out there; the key is knowing where to look.* Entrepreneurs must do their homework *before* they set out to raise money for their ventures. Understanding which sources of funding are best suited to the various stages of a company's growth and then taking the time to learn how those sources work are essential to success.
- *Creativity counts.* To find the financing their businesses demand, entrepreneurs must use as much creativity in attracting financing as they did in generating the ideas for their products and services.
- *The World Wide Web puts at entrepreneurs' fingertips vast resources of information that can lead to financing.* The Web often offers entrepreneurs, especially those looking for relatively small amounts of money, the opportunity to discover sources of funds that they otherwise might miss. The Web site created for this book (www.prenhall.com/scarborough) provides links to many useful sites related to raising both start-up and growth capital. The Web also provides a low-cost, convenient way for entrepreneurs to get their business plans into potential investors' hands anywhere in the world. When searching for sources of capital, entrepreneurs must not overlook this valuable tool!
- *Be thoroughly prepared before approaching potential lenders and investors.* In the hunt for capital, tracking down leads is tough enough; don't blow a potential deal by failing to be ready to present your business idea to potential lenders and investors in a clear, concise, convincing way. That, of course, requires a solid business plan.

■ *Entrepreneurs cannot overestimate the importance of making sure that the "chemistry" among themselves, their companies, and their funding sources is a good one.* Too many entrepreneurs get into financial deals because they needed the money to keep their businesses growing only to discover that their plans do not match those of their financial partners. *When his bank called the loans of two $500,000 homes he had under construction, Bob Shellenberger, owner of Highland Homes of Saint Louis, a company that builds upscale speculation houses, immediately turned to a casual acquaintance who previously had expressed an interest in investing in the business. "We shook hands," says Shellenberger, acknowledging his mistakes. "But did we have a written agreement? No. Did we research his background? No." Shellenberger soon learned that his newfound investor expected to be consulted on every detail of the houses the company was building, which stretched their completion times from the expected five months to 10 months. Although frustrated with his first experience with an outside investor, Shellenberger used it as a learning experience. Periodically, he invites an investor to participate in a building project, but now he is much more selective in his choices, and he conducts extensive background searches on every potential investor.*

> Company Example

Rather than rely primarily on a single source of funds as they have in the past, entrepreneurs must piece together capital from multiple sources, a method known as **layered financing**. They have discovered that raising capital successfully requires them to cast a wide net to capture the financing they need to launch their businesses. *While earning his M.B.A. at Carnegie Mellon University, Cormac Kinney came up with an idea for software that would enable stock traders to track stocks at a glance using color squares of different hues and intensities that appear on their computer monitors. Kinney convinced Marc Graham, a research scientist at the university, to create the software in exchange for part ownership in the company, NeoVision Hypersystems. To get the business up and running, both Kinney and Graham invested thousands of dollars of their own money, but they needed more. With business plan in hand, they turned to family and friends for $100,000 and convinced one of Kinney's former bosses to put in another $100,000. Then, using a network of connections, Kinney and Graham found three private investors who put up an additional $800,000 and helped the young company acquire a bank loan. One of the private investors introduced the entrepreneurs to a partner in a venture capital firm that ultimately invested $2 million in NeoVision. The company continues to grow, and the cofounders are considering another round of venture capital and perhaps making an initial public offering to meet NeoVision's appetite for capital.*[3]

> Company Example

This chapter and the next will guide you through the myriad of financing options available to entrepreneurs, focusing on both sources of equity (ownership) and debt (borrowed) financing.

Planning for Capital Needs

1. Explain the differences in the three types of capital small businesses require: fixed, working, and growth.

Becoming a successful entrepreneur requires one to become a skilled fund-raiser, a job that usually requires more time and energy than most business founders anticipate. In start-up companies, raising capital can easily consume as much as one-half of the entrepreneur's time and can take many months to complete. Most entrepreneurs are seeking less than $1 million (indeed, most need less than $100,000), which may be the toughest money to secure. Where to find this seed money depends, in part, on the nature of the proposed business and on the amount of money required. For example, the creator of a computer software firm would have different capital requirements than the founder of a coal mining operation. Although both entrepreneurs might approach some of the same types of lenders or investors, each would be more successful targeting specific sources of funds best suited to their particular financial needs.

Capital is any form of wealth employed to produce more wealth. It exists in many forms in a typical business, including cash, inventory, plant, and equipment. Entrepreneurs need three different types of capital:

Fixed Capital

Fixed capital is needed to purchase a business's permanent or fixed assets such as buildings, land, computers, and equipment. Money invested in these fixed assets tends to be frozen because it cannot be used for any other purpose. Typically, large sums of money are involved in purchasing fixed assets, and credit terms usually are lengthy. Lenders of fixed capital expect the assets purchased to improve the efficiency and, thus, the profitability of the business, and to create improved cash flows that ensure repayment.

Working Capital

Working capital represents a business's temporary funds; it is the capital used to support a company's normal short-term operations. Accountants define working capital as current assets minus current liabilities. The need for working capital arises because of the uneven flow of cash into and out of the business due to normal seasonal fluctuations. Credit sales, seasonal sales swings, or unforeseeable changes in demand will create fluctuations in *any* small company's cash flow. Working capital normally is used to buy inventory, pay bills, finance credit sales, pay wages and salaries, and take care of any unexpected emergencies. Lenders of working capital expect it to produce higher cash flows to ensure repayment at the end of the production/sales cycle.

Growth Capital

Growth capital, unlike working capital, is not related to the seasonal fluctuations of a small business. Instead, growth capital requirements surface when an existing business is expanding or changing its primary direction. For example, a small manufacturer of silicon microchips for computers saw his business skyrocket in a short time period. With orders for chips rushing in, the growing business needed a sizable cash infusion to increase plant size, expand its sales and production workforce, and buy more equipment. During times of such rapid expansion, a growing company's capital requirements are similar to those of a business start-up. Like lenders of fixed capital, growth capital lenders expect the funds to improve a company's profitability and cash flow position, thus ensuring repayment.

Although these three types of capital are interdependent, each has certain sources, characteristics, and effects on the business and its long-term growth that entrepreneurs must recognize. Table 14.1 shows the various stages of a company's growth and the sources of capital most suitable in each stage.

Sources of Equity Financing

2. Describe the various sources of equity financing available to entrepreneurs.

Equity capital represents the personal investment of the owner (or owners) in a business and is sometimes called *risk* capital because these investors assume the primary risk of losing their funds if the business fails. *For instance, private investor Victor Lombardi lost the $3.5 million he invested in a start-up called NetFax, a company that was developing the technology to send faxes over the Internet. When NetFax's patent application stalled, the company foundered. Just three years after its launch, NetFax ceased operations, leaving Lombardi's investment worthless.*[4]

Table 14.1

Equity Capital Sources
at Various Stages of
Company Growth

Characteristics	START-UP	EARLY	EXPANSION	PROFITABILITY
	Business is in conceptual phase and exists only on paper.	Business is developing one or more products or services but is not yet generating sales.	Business is selling products or services and is generating revenue and is beginning to establish a customer base.	Company has established a customer base and is profitable.
POSSIBLE SOURCES OF FUNDING	LIKELIHOOD OF USING EACH SOURCE: H = HIGHLY LIKELY; P = POSSIBLE; U = UNLIKELY			
Personal savings	H	H	H	H
Retained earnings	U	U	U	H
Friends and relatives	H	H	P	P
Angel investors	H	H	P	U
Partners	H	H	P	U
Corporate venture capital	P	H	H	H
Venture capital	U	P	H	H
Initial public offering (IPO)	U	U	P	H
Regulation S-B offering	U	U	P	H
Small Company Offering Registration (SCOR)	U	P	P	H
Private placements	U	P	P	H
Intrastate offerings (Rule 147)	U	P	P	H
Regulation A	U	P	P	H

If a venture succeeds, however, founders and investors share in the benefits, which can be quite substantial. The founders of and early investors in Yahoo!, Sun Microsystems, FedEx, Intel, and Microsoft became multimillionaires when the companies went public and their equity investments finally paid off. To entrepreneurs, the primary advantage of equity capital is that it does not have to be repaid like a loan does. Equity investors are entitled to share in the company's earnings (if there are any) and usually to have a voice in the company's future direction.

The primary disadvantage of equity capital is that the entrepreneur must give up some—perhaps *most*—of the ownership in the business to outsiders. Although 50 percent of something is better than 100 percent of nothing, giving up control of your company can be disconcerting and dangerous. Many entrepreneurs who give up majority ownership in their companies in exchange for equity capital find themselves forced out of the businesses they started! Entrepreneurs are most likely to give up more equity in their businesses in the start-up phase than in any other.

We now turn our attention to nine common sources of equity capital.

Personal Savings

The *first* place entrepreneurs should look for start-up money is in their own pockets. It's the least expensive source of funds available! Entrepreneurs apparently see the benefits of

Company Example ➤ self-sufficiency; the most common source of equity funds used to start a small business is the entrepreneur's pool of personal savings. *Before David and Robin Penn launched their preschool, The Learning Center, their business plan helped them determine that they would need $125,000. The Penns invested everything they could into the business—$13,000—before raising $12,000 from family and friends. The couple also managed to secure a bank loan of $100,000 guaranteed by the Small Business Administration to fulfill their company's capital requirements.*[5]

Lenders and investors *expect* entrepreneurs to put their own money into a business start-up. If entrepreneurs are not willing to risk their own money, potential investors are not likely to risk their money in the business either. Furthermore, failing to put up sufficient capital of their own means that entrepreneurs must either borrow an excessive amount of capital or give up a significant portion of ownership to outsiders to fund the business properly. Excessive borrowing in the early days of a business puts intense pressure on its cash flow, and becoming a minority shareholder may dampen a founder's enthusiasm for making a business successful. Neither outcome presents a bright future for the company involved.

Friends and Family Members

Company Example ➤ Although most entrepreneurs look to their own bank accounts first to finance a business, few have sufficient resources to launch their businesses alone. In fact, three out of four people who start businesses do so with capital from outside sources.[6] After emptying their own pockets, entrepreneurs should look to friends and family members who might be willing to invest in a business venture. Because of their relationships with the founder, these people are most likely to invest. *While Jill Crawley and her husband were building a business plan to launch a restaurant in Sharon, Massachusetts, they talked with family members and friends about putting up part of the start-up costs. In addition to the money they invested, the Crawleys raised $75,000 from their parents, a few other family members, and some close family friends before successfully launching Coriander. Citing the advantages of financing from family and friends, Crawley says, "These are people who sincerely want to see us realize our dreams. They are not going to be hanging over our shoulders."*[7]

The Global Entrepreneurship Monitor, a study of entrepreneurial trends across the globe, found that family members and friends are the biggest source of external capital used to launch new businesses. Investments from family and friends account for more than 70 percent of all venture dollars at start-up, but the amounts invested typically are small. The study shows that 75 percent of these informal investors put up no more than $5,000.[8] Often family members and friends are more patient than other outside investors and are less meddlesome in a business's affairs than many other types of investors. Investments from family and friends are an excellent source of seed capital and bridge financing, the money that gets a young business far enough along to attract money from private investors or venture capital companies. Inherent dangers lurk in family business investments, however. Unrealistic expectations or misunderstood risks have destroyed many friendships and have ruined many family reunions. To avoid this problem, an entrepreneur must honestly present the investment opportunity and the nature of the risks involved to avoid alienating friends and family members if the business fails. On the other hand, some investments return more than friends and family members ever could have imagined. In 1995, Mike and Jackie Bezos invested $300,000 into their son Jeff's start-up business, Amazon.com. Today, Mike and Jackie own 6 percent of Amazon.com's stock, and their shares are worth billions of dollars![9]

Table 14.2 offers suggestions for structuring family and friendship financing deals.

Table 14.2

Suggestions for Structuring Family and Friendship Financing Deals

Tapping family members and friends for start-up capital, whether in the form of equity or debt financing, is a popular method of financing business ideas. In a typical year, some 6 million individuals in the United States invest about $100 billion in entrepreneurial ventures. Unfortunately, these deals don't always work to the satisfaction of both parties. For instance, when actor Don Johnson needed seed capital to launch DJ Racing, a company that designs and races speedboats, he approached a wealthy Miami friend who made a $300,000 interest-free loan on nothing but a handshake. Within a year, a dispute arose over when Johnson was to pay back the loan. A lawsuit followed, which the two now former friends settled out of court. The following suggestions can help entrepreneurs avoid needlessly destroying family relationships and friendships:

- *Consider the impact of the investment on everyone involved.* Will it work a hardship on anyone? Are investors putting up the money because they want to or because they feel obligated to? Can all parties afford the loan if the business folds? Lynn McPhee used $250,000 from family members to launch Xuny, a Web-based clothing store. "Our basic rule of thumb was if [the investment is] going to strap someone, we won't take it," she says.
- *Keep the arrangement strictly business.* The parties should treat all loans and investments in a business-like manner, no matter how close the friendship or family relationship, to avoid problems down the line. If the transaction is a loan exceeding $10,000, it must carry a rate of interest at least as high as the market rate; otherwise the IRS may consider the loan a gift and penalize the lender.
- *Settle the details up front.* Before any money changes hands, the parties must agree on the details of the deal. How much money is involved? Is it a loan or an investment? How will investors cash out? How will the loan be paid off? What happens if the business fails?
- *Never accept more than investors can afford to lose.* No matter how much capital you may need, accepting more than family members or friends can afford to lose is a recipe for disaster—and perhaps bankruptcy for the investors.
- *Create a written contract.* Don't make the mistake of closing a financial deal with just a handshake. The probability of misunderstandings skyrockets! Putting an agreement in writing demonstrates the parties' commitment to the deal and minimizes the chances of disputes from faulty memories and misunderstandings.
- *Treat the money as "bridge financing."* Although family and friends can help you launch your business, it is unlikely that they can provide enough capital to sustain it over the long term. Sooner or later, you will need to establish a relationship with other sources of credit if your company is to survive and thrive. Consider money from family and friends as a bridge to take your company to the next level of financing.
- *Develop a payment schedule that suits both the entrepreneur and the lenders or investors.* Although lenders and investors may want to get their money back as quickly as possible, a rapid repayment or cash-out schedule can jeopardize a fledgling company's survival. Establish a realistic repayment plan that works for the parties without putting excessive strain on the young company's cash flow.
- *Have an exit plan.* Every deal should define exactly how investors will "cash out" their investments.

Sources: Adapted from Andrea Coombes, "Retirees as Venture Capitalists," CBS.MarketWatch.com, November 2, 2003, http://netscape.marketwatch.com/news/story.asp?dist=feed&siteid=netscape&guid={1E1267CD-32A4–4558–9F7E-40E4B7892D01}; Paul Kvinta, "Frogskins, Shekels, Bucks, Moolah, Cash, Simoleans, Dough, Dinero: Everybody Wants It. Your Business Needs It. Here's How to Get It," *Smart Business*, August 2000, pp. 74–89; Alex Markels, "A Little Help from Their Friends," *Wall Street Journal*, May 22, 1995, p. R10; Heather Chaplin, "Friends and Family," *Your Company*, September 1999, p. 26.

Angels

After dipping into their own pockets and convincing friends and relatives to invest in their business ventures, many entrepreneurs still find themselves short of the seed capital they need. Frequently, the next stop on the road to business financing is private investors. These **private investors** (or **angels**) are wealthy individuals, often entrepreneurs themselves, who invest in business start-ups in exchange for equity stakes in the companies. Alexander Graham Bell, inventor of the telephone, used angel capital to start Bell Telephone in 1877.

In many cases, angels invest in businesses for more than purely economic reasons (often because they have experience and a personal interest in the industry), and they are willing to put money into companies in the earliest stages, long before venture capital firms and institutional investors jump in. Angel financing, the fastest-growing segment of the small business capital market, is ideal for companies that have outgrown the capacity of investments from friends and family but are still too small to attract the interest of venture capital companies. For instance, after raising the money to launch Amazon.com from family and friends, Jeff Bezos turned to angels because venture capital firms were not interested in a business start-up. Bezos attracted $1.2 million from a dozen angels before landing $8 million from venture capital firms a year later.[10]

IN THE FOOTSTEPS OF AN ENTREPRENEUR...

The Dangers of Family Money

Chris Baggott longed to start his own business, so he quit his job at a marketing firm and purchased Sanders Dry Cleaning, a local business that he eventually built into a chain with seven locations. However, Baggott did not realize his dream of owning a business alone. Because he lacked the money he needed to purchase the dry cleaning operation, Baggott borrowed $45,000 from James Anderson, his father-in-law, who also agreed to cosign a $600,000 bank loan. With his business plan in hand and the financing and loan guarantees in place, the deal went through.

Shortly after he took over the dry cleaning operation, however, Baggott noticed that his sales were slipping. "The business casual trend was catching fire," he recalls. "People just stopped wearing suits." Monthly sales revenue fell to $60,000, far below the projections of $110,000 a month in his business plan and not enough to cover regular business expenses and the monthly loan payment to the bank of $14,000. He tried to cover the expenses with high-interest credit cards but soon began falling behind in his payments to the bank. That resulted in some very difficult telephone calls to Anderson, his father-in-law, who was aware of the company's problems because the bank loan officer was already calling Anderson to make up the missed loan payments. "He'd call and say, 'What the heck is going on here?' And then he'd have to write a check to cover it from his own funds," recalls Baggott.

Before long, Baggott sold the business, paid his debts, and got on with his life. One debt Baggott was unable to repay was the one he owed his father-in-law, Anderson, who ultimately lost tens of thousands of dollars as a result of the deal. "It was painful," says Baggott. Anderson is unbothered by the incident. "You win some, lose some," he says philosophically. Still,

Baggott says the deal-gone-bad strained their personal relationship.

A few years later, Baggott launched another business, ExactTarget, an e-mail marketing company. To raise the capital he needed for the start-up, he once again turned to family and friends, but this time he emphasized to each potential investor the risks involved in the venture. "I said, 'Here's our business plan, but this is just a plan, and the chances are good you'll never see this money again.'" In the end, he raised more than $1 million from family and friends, and the business is successful. ExactTarget has grown from just two to 70 employees, and sales are growing rapidly.

Among Baggott's investors in ExactTarget is James Anderson, his father-in-law. How did he muster the courage to approach Anderson as an investor after the first venture had gone so wrong? "I knew I had a great idea," says Baggott, "and I felt obligated to let him in. Had I not let him in, and then I made money in this business, how much would that have strained our relationship?"

1. Professor David Deeds of Case Western University says of investments in business start-ups from family members and friends, "It's the highest-risk money you'll ever get. The venture may succeed or fail, but either way, you still have to go to Thanksgiving dinner." What does he mean?
2. What should Chris Baggott have done differently when he approached his father-in-law about investing in his initial business, the dry cleaning shop?
3. What advice would you offer to an entrepreneur seeking capital from family members and friends to launch a business?

Source: Adapted from Alison Stein Wellner, "Blood Money," *Inc.,* December 2003, pp. 48–50.

Angels are a primary source of start-up capital for companies in the embryonic stage through the growth stage, and their role in financing small businesses is significant. Experts estimate that 400,000 angels invest $50 billion a year in 50,000 small companies, most of them in the start-up phase.[11] Angels invest two to five times as much money in 20 to 30 times as many small companies as institutional venture capital firms. Former Beatle Paul McCartney has joined the ranks of angel investors, putting an undisclosed amount of money into Magex, a company that encrypts digital material on the World Wide Web.[12] Because the angel market is so fragmented, we may never get a completely accurate estimate of its investment in business start-ups. However, experts concur on one fact: Angels are a vital source of external equity capital for small businesses.

Pepper . . . and Salt

THE WALL STREET JOURNAL

"Great concept and I'd love to invest, I'm just avoiding the high tech sector, right now."

Angels fill a significant gap in the seed capital market. They are most likely to finance start-ups with capital requirements in the $10,000 to $2 million range, well below the $3 million to $10 million minimum investments most professional venture capitalists prefer. Because a $500,000 deal requires about as much of a venture capitalist's time to research and evaluate as a $5 million deal does, venture capitalists tend to focus on big deals, where their returns are bigger. Angels also tolerate risk levels that would make venture capitalists shudder; as many as 90 percent of angel-backed companies fail.[13] One angel investor, a former executive at Oracle Corporation, says that of the 10 companies he has invested in, seven have flopped. Three of the start-ups, however, have produced fifty-fold returns![14] Because of the inherent risks in start-up companies, many venture capitalists have shifted their investment portfolios away from start-ups toward more established firms. That's why angel financing is so important: Angels often finance deals that no venture capitalist will consider. *While working as a server in a restaurant, Stacey Belkin met Scott Adams, creator of the Dilbert cartoon, who was a regular customer at the California eatery. Belkin casually mentioned that one day she wanted to start her own restaurant, and Adams said that if she put together a business plan, he would consider making an investment in her business. "She followed up the next day," recalls Adams. Before long, Belkin was launching Stacey's Café in Pleasanton, California, with financing provided by angel investor Scott Adams. The restaurant was so successful that, with Adams's support, Belkin has opened a second location in Dublin, California. One benefit of having a famous cartoonist as an investor is that both restaurants sell personalized Dilbert products signed by the author![15]*

Because angels prefer to maintain a low profile, the real challenge lies in *finding* them. Most angels have substantial business and financial experience, and many of them are entrepreneurs or former entrepreneurs. The typical angel invests in companies at the start-up or infant growth stage and accepts 30 percent of the investment opportunities presented, makes an average of two investments every three years, and has invested an average of $150,000 of equity in 3.5 firms.[16] When evaluating a proposal, angels look for a qualified management team ("We invest in people," says one angel), a business with a clearly defined niche, the potential to dominate the market, and a competitive advantage. They also want to see market research that proves the existence of a sizable and profitable customer base.

Company Example →

Scott Adams, creator of the famous Dilbert cartoon, became a private investor in Stacey Belkin's restaurant, Stacey's Cafe, in Pleasanton, California. The restaurant was so successful that Stacey has opened a second location in which Adams also invested.

Because angels frown on "cold calls" from entrepreneurs they don't know, locating them boils down to making the right contacts. Asking friends, attorneys, bankers, stockbrokers, accountants, other business owners, and consultants for suggestions and introductions is a good way to start. Networking is the key. One entrepreneur who has successfully raised an average of $120,000 a month for his growing business has developed a list of more than 100 potential angels through an extensive network of contacts in the industry.[17] Angels almost always invest their money locally, so entrepreneurs should look close to home for them—typically within a 50- to 100-mile radius. Angels also look for businesses they know something about and most expect to invest their knowledge, experience, and energy as well as their money in a company. In fact, the advice and the network of contacts that angels bring to a deal can sometimes be as valuable as their money! *Jordan Warshafsky, CEO of TyRx Pharma Inc., a fast-growing biotech company, found the contacts and the advice angel investors brought to his company to be invaluable. When Warshafsky, a veteran pharmaceutical executive, stepped in to manage the company, he saw the potential its products offered but knew he had to raise money fast because the company's cash balance was falling dangerously low. After several meetings with representatives from the Common Angels, a Boston-based group of 18 angel investors, Warshafsky closed a deal for a $300,000 investment and has since been contacted by venture capital firms wanting to invest in the company. Warshafsky says that whenever he encounters a difficult problem, he can call on any of the 18 angel investors, who can offer advice or refer him to an experienced professional in the industry—a benefit he considers to be priceless.[18]*

[Company Example] →

[Company Example] →

As Warshafsky's experience proves, angels often invest in clusters, many of them through one of the nation's 170 angel capital networks. With the right approach, an entrepreneur can attract more money from an angel capital group than from an individual investor. *In 1995, Hans Severiens, a professional investor, created the Band of Angels, a group of about 150 angels (mostly Silicon Valley millionaires) who meet monthly in Portola Valley, California, to listen to entrepreneurs pitch their business plans. The Band of Angels reviews about 30 proposals each month before inviting a handful of entrepreneurs to make brief presentations at its monthly meeting. Interested members often team up with one another to invest in the businesses they consider most promising. The Band of Angels' average investment is $600,000, which usually nets the investors between 15 percent and 20 percent of* *a company's stock. Since its inception, the Band of Angels has invested more than $90 million in promising young companies.*[19]

The Internet has expanded greatly the ability of entrepreneurs in search of capital and angels in search of businesses to find one another. Dozens of angel networks have opened on the World Wide Web, including AngelMoney.com, Business Angels International, Garage Technology Ventures, CommonAngels.com, The Capital Network, WomenAngels.net, and many others. The Small Business Administration's Access to Capital Electronic Network, ACE-Net, is a Web-based listing service that provides a marketplace for entrepreneurs seeking between $250,000 and $5 million in capital and angels looking to invest in promising businesses. Entrepreneurs pay $450 a year to list information about their companies on the site, which potential angels can access at any time.

Angels are an excellent source of "patient money," often willing to wait five to seven years or longer to cash out their investments. They earn their returns through the increased value of the business, not through dividends and interest. For example, more than 1,000 early investors in Microsoft Inc. are now millionaires, and the original investors in Genentech Inc. (a genetic engineering company) have seen their investments increase more than 500 times.[20] Angels' return-on-investment targets tend to be lower than those of professional venture capitalists. Although venture capitalists shoot for 60 percent to 75 percent returns annually, private investors usually settle for 20 percent to 50 percent (depending on the level of risk involved in the venture). The average rate of return for angels is 30 percent a year.[21] Private investors typically take less than 50 percent ownership, leaving the majority ownership to the company founder(s). The lesson: If an entrepreneur needs relatively small amounts of money to launch a company, angels are a primary source.

Table 14.3 offers useful tips for attracting angel capital.

Partners

Company Example →

As we saw in Chapter 3, entrepreneurs can take on partners to expand the capital base of a business. *When Lou Bucelli and Tim Crouse were searching for the money to launch CME Conference Video, a company that produces and distributes videotapes of educational conferences for physicians, they found an angel willing to put up $250,000 for 40 percent of the business. Unfortunately, their investor backed out when some of his real estate investments went bad, leaving the partners with commitments for several conferences but no cash to produce and distribute the videos. With little time to spare, Bucelli and Crouse decided to form a series of limited partnerships with people they knew, one for each videotape they would produce. Six limited partnerships produced $400,000 in financing, and the tapes generated $9.1 million in sales for the year. As the general partners, Bucelli and Crouse retained 80 percent of each partnership. The limited partners earned returns of up to 80 percent in just six months. Within two years, their company was so successful that venture capitalists started calling. To finance their next round of growth, Bucelli and Crouse sold 35 percent of their company to a venture capital firm for $1.3 million.*[22]

Before entering into any partnership arrangement, however, entrepreneurs must consider the impact of giving up some personal control over operations and of sharing profits with others. Whenever entrepreneurs give up equity in their businesses (through whatever mechanism), they run the risk of losing control over it. As the founder's ownership in a company becomes increasingly diluted, the probability of losing control of its future direction and the entire decision-making process increases.

Corporate Venture Capital

Large corporations have gotten into the business of financing small companies. Today 20 percent of all venture capital invested comes from corporations.[23] Approximately

Table 14.3

Tips for Attracting Angel Financing

Although they are an important source of small business financing, angels can be extremely difficult to locate. You won't find them listed under "Angels" in the Yellow Pages of the telephone directory. Patience and persistence—and connections—pay off in the search for angel financing, however. How does an entrepreneur needing financing find an angel to help launch or expand a company and make the deal work?

- *Start early.* Finding private investors takes a lot longer than most entrepreneurs think.
- *Have a business plan ready.* Once you find potential private investors, don't risk them losing interest while you put together a business plan. Have the plan ready to go *before* you begin your search.
- *Look close to home.* Most angels prefer to invest their money locally, so conduct a thorough search for potential angels within a 50- to 100-mile radius of your business.
- *Canvass your industry.* Angels tend to specialize in particular industries, usually ones they know a lot about.
- *Recognize that, in addition to the money they invest, angels also want to provide their knowledge and expertise.* Indeed, angels' experience and knowledge can be just as valuable as their money *if* entrepreneurs are willing to accept it.
- *Remember that angels invest for more than just financial reasons.* Angels want to earn a good return on the money they invest in businesses, but there's usually more to it than that. Angels often invest in companies for personal reasons.
- *Join local philanthropic organizations, chambers of commerce, nonprofit organizations, and advisory boards.* Potential investors often are involved in such organizations.
- *Ask business professionals such as bankers, lawyers, stockbrokers, accountants, and others for names of potential angels.* They know people who have the money and the desire to invest in business ventures.
- *Network, network, network.* Finding angel financing initially is a game of contacts—getting an introduction to the right person from the right person.
- *Investigate the investors and their past deals.* Never get involved in a deal with an angel you don't know or trust. Be sure you and your investors have a common vision of the business and the deal.
- *Summarize the details of the deal in a letter of intent.* Although a letter of intent is not a legal document, it outlines the basic structure of the deal and exposes the most sensitive areas being negotiated so that there are no surprises. What role, if any, will the angel play in running the business? Angels can be a source of valuable help, but some entrepreneurs complain of angels' meddling.
- *Keep the deal simple.* The simpler the deal is, the easier it will be to sell to potential investors. Probably the simplest way to involve angels is to sell them common stock.
- *Nail down the angels' exit path.* Angels make their money when they sell their ownership interests. Ideally, the exit path should be part of structuring the deal. Will the company buy back the angels' shares? Will the company go public so the angels can sell their shares on the market? Will the owners sell out to a larger company? What is the time frame for doing so?
- *Avoid intimidating potential investors.* Most angels are turned off by entrepreneurs with an attitude of "I have someone else who will do the deal if you don't." In the face of such coercion, many private investors simply walk away from the deal.
- *Always be truthful.* Overpromising and underdelivering will kill a deal and spoil future financing arrangements.
- *Develop alternative financing arrangements.* Never back an angel into a corner with "take this deal or leave it." Have alternative plans prepared in case the investor balks at the outset.
- *Don't take the money and run.* Investors appreciate entrepreneurs who keep them informed—about how their money is being spent and the results it shows. Prepare periodic reports for them.
- *Stick to the deal.* It's tempting to spend the money where it's most needed once it is in hand. Resist! If you promised to use the funds for specific purposes, do it. Nothing undermines an angel's trust as quickly as violating the original plan.

300 large corporations across the globe, including Intel, Motorola, Cisco Systems, Nokia, UPS, Radio Shack, and General Electric, invest in start-up companies, most often those in the product development and sales growth stages. Young companies not only get a boost from the capital injections large companies give them, but they also stand to gain many other benefits from the relationship. The right corporate partner may share technical expertise, distribution channels, marketing know-how, and provide introductions to important customers and suppliers. Another intangible yet highly important advantage an investment from a large corporate partner gives a start-up is credibility, often referred to as "market validation." Doors that otherwise would be closed to a small company magically open when the right corporation becomes a strategic partner.

Foreign corporations also are interested in investing in small U.S. businesses. Often these corporations are seeking strategic partnerships to gain access to new technology, new products, or access to lucrative U.S. markets. In return, the small companies they invest in benefit from the capital infusion as well as from their partners' international experience and connections. Some small companies are turning to their customers for the resources they need to fuel their rapid growth. Recognizing how interwoven their success is with that of their suppliers, corporate giants such as AT&T, JCPenney, and Ford now offer financial support to many of the small businesses from which they buy.

Company Example ➞ *When John Glossner and David Routenburg, founders of Sandbridge Technologies, needed capital to launch the wireless handset technology they had developed, they turned to multinational giant Siemens AG. Glossner and Routenburg already had identified Siemens as a potential customer for Sandbridge Technologies' products, and they also knew that Siemens was a potential source of venture capital. After several rounds of negotiations, Sandbridge received a multimillion dollar investment and, of course, market validation, from the $80 billion giant that opened doors for the small company. "[Corporate venture capital] has a magnetic effect," says Routenburg. "That magnetism attracts customers, partners, and investors, who see the corporate investments as a stamp of approval by industry giants. It's a real differentiator over others that don't have this kind of connection."*[24]

Venture Capital Companies

Venture capital companies are private, for-profit organizations that purchase equity positions in young businesses they believe have high-growth and high-profit potential, producing annual returns of 300 to 500 percent over five to seven years. More than 3,000 venture capital firms operate across the United States today, investing in promising small companies in a wide variety of industries (see Figure 14.1). Many colleges and universities across the nation now

Figure 14.1

Venture Capital Financing

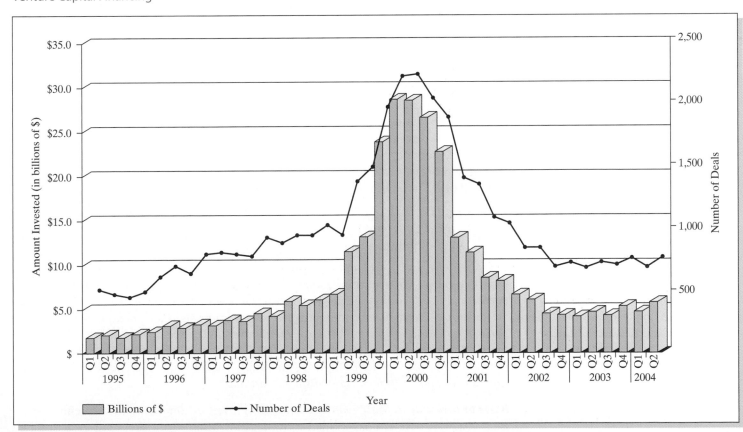

Source: PriceWaterhouse Coopers Moneytree Report, http://www.pwc.moneytree.com.

have venture funds designated to invest in promising businesses started by their students, alumni, and faculty. Even government entities such as the Central Intelligence Agency (CIA), the U.S. Army, the Defense Advanced Research Project Agency (DARPA), and the National Security Agency (NSA) have launched venture capital firms to invest in promising small businesses that are creating technologies to fight the war on terrorism. For instance, DARPA has invested in a company that has developed strength-enhancing body armor, a mechanically powered exoskeleton (remember RoboCop?) that enables people to carry heavy objects and travel great distances with ease.[25] *Since its founding in 1999, the CIA's venture fund, In-Q-Tel, has invested in several small companies including Sourcefire Network Security, a computer network security firm that has developed products designed to protect computer networks from attacks by cyber-terrorists. The boost from In-Q-Tel's investments has enabled Sourcefire to raise $18 million from other venture capital firms.*[26]

Venture capital firms, which provide about 7 percent of all funding for private companies, have invested billions of dollars in high-potential small companies over the years, including such notable businesses as Apple Computer, Microsoft Inc., Intel, and Outback Steakhouse. Although companies in high-tech industries such as the Internet, communications, computer hardware and software, medical care, and biotechnology are the most popular targets of venture capital, a company with extraordinary growth prospects has the potential to attract venture capital, whatever its industry. Table 14.4 offers a humorous look at how venture capitalists decipher the language of sometimes overly optimistic entrepreneurs.

Policies and Investment Strategies. Venture capital firms usually establish stringent policies to govern their overall investment strategies.

Investment Size and Screening. Depending on the size of the venture capital corporation and its cost structure, minimum investments range from $50,000 to $5 million. Investment ceilings, in effect, do not exist. Most firms seek investments in the $3 million to $10 million range to justify the cost of investigating the large number of proposals they receive.

The venture capital screening process is *extremely* rigorous. The typical venture capital company invests in less than 1 percent of the applications it receives! For example, the average venture capital firm screens about 1,200 proposals a year, but more than 90 percent are rejected immediately because they do not match the firm's investment criteria. The remaining 10 percent are investigated more thoroughly at a cost ranging from $2,000 to $3,000 per proposal. At this time, approximately 10 to 15 proposals will have passed the screening process, and these are subjected to comprehensive review. The venture capital firm will invest in three to six of these remaining proposals.

Ownership. Most venture capitalists prefer to purchase ownership in a small business through common stock or convertible preferred stock. Typically, a venture capital company seeks to purchase 15 percent to 40 percent of a business, but in some cases, a venture capitalist may buy 70 percent or more of a company's stock, leaving its founders with a minority share of ownership. Entrepreneurs must weigh the positive aspects of receiving needed financing against the negative features of owning a smaller share of the business. *When Form + Function, an information technology firm, was looking to expand, founder Bob Bernard and his management team convinced a venture capital firm, Wheatley Partners, to invest $8.5 million in the company in exchange for 27 percent of its stock. Two years later, the company acquired another consulting firm for $6 million using a second round of venture capital and changed its name to Whittman-Hart Inc.*[27]

Stage of Investment. Most venture capital firms invest in companies that are either in the early stages of development (called early stage investing) or in the rapid-growth phase (called expansion stage investing); few invest in businesses that are only in the start-up

Table 14.4

Deciphering the Language of the Venture Capital Industry

By nature, entrepreneurs tend to be optimistic. When screening business plans, venture capitalists must make an allowance for entrepreneurial enthusiasm. Here's a dictionary of phrases commonly found in business plans and their accompanying venture capital translations.

Exploring an acquisition strategy—Our current products have no market.

We're on a clear P2P (pathway to profitability)—We're still years away from earning a profit.

Basically on plan—We're expecting a revenue shortfall of 25 percent.

Internet business model—Potentially bigger fools have been identified.

A challenging year—Competitors are eating our lunch.

Considerably ahead of plan—Hit our plan in one of the last three months.

Company's underlying strength and resilience—We still lost money, but look how we cut our losses.

Core business—Our product line is obsolete.

Currently revising budget—The financial plan is in total chaos.

Cyclical industry—We posted a huge loss last year.

Entrepreneurial CEO—He or she is totally uncontrollable, bordering on maniacal.

Facing challenges—Our sales continue to slide, and we have no idea why.

Facing unprecedented economic, political, and structural shifts—It's a tough world out there, but we're coping the best we can.

Highly leverageable network—No longer works but has friends who do.

Ingredients are there—Given two years, we might find a workable strategy.

Investing heavily in R&D—We're trying desperately to catch the competition.

Limited downside—Things can't get much worse.

Long sales cycle—Yet to find a customer who likes the product enough to buy it.

Major opportunity—It's our last chance.

Niche strategy—A small-time player.

On a manufacturing learning curve—We can't make the product with positive margins.

Passive investor—Someone who phones once a year to see if we're still in business.

Positive results—Our losses were less than last year.

Refocus our efforts—We've blown our chance, and now we have to fire most of our employees.

Repositioning the business—We've recently written off a multimillion-dollar investment.

Selective investment strategy—The board is spending more time on yachts than on planes.

Solid operating performance in a difficult year—Yes, we lost money and market share, but look how hard we tried.

Somewhat below plan—We expect a revenue shortfall of 75 percent.

Expenses were unexpectedly high—We grossly overestimated our profit margins.

Strategic investor—One who will pay a preposterous price for an equity share in the business.

Strongest fourth quarter ever—Don't quibble over the losses in the first three quarters.

Sufficient opportunity to market this product no longer exists—Nobody will buy the thing.

Too early to tell—Results to date have been grim.

A team of skilled, motivated, and dedicated people—We've laid off most of our staff, and those who are left should be glad they still have jobs.

Turnaround opportunity—It's a lost cause.

Unique—We have no more than six strong competitors.

Volume sensitive—Our company has massive fixed costs.

Window of opportunity—Without more money fast, this company is dead.

Work closely with the management—We talk to them on the phone once a month.

A year in which we confronted challenges—At least we know the questions even if we haven't got the answers.

Sources: Adapted from Scott Herhold, "When CEOs Blow Smoke," *e-company*, May 2001, pp. 125–127; Suzanne McGee, "A Devil's Dictionary of Financing," *Wall Street Journal*, June 12, 2000, p. C13; John F. Budd Jr., "Cracking the CEO's Code," *Wall Street Journal*, March 27, 1995, p. A20; "Venture-Speak Defined," *Teleconnect*, October 1990, p. 42; Cynthia E. Griffin, "Figuratively Speaking," *Entrepreneur*, August 1999, p. 26.

phase (see Figure 14.2). According to the Global Entrepreneurship Monitor, only one in 10,000 entrepreneurs worldwide receives venture capital funding at start-up.[28] Some venture capital firms specialize in acquisitions, providing the financing for managers and employees of a business to buy it out. About 98 percent of all venture capital goes to businesses in the early, expansion, and later stages, although some venture capital firms are showing more interest in companies in the start-up phase because of the tremendous returns that are possible by investing then.[29] Most venture capital firms do not make just a single investment in a company. Instead, they invest in a company over time across several stages, and their investments often total $10 to $15 million.

Figure 14.2

Venture Capital Funding by Stage

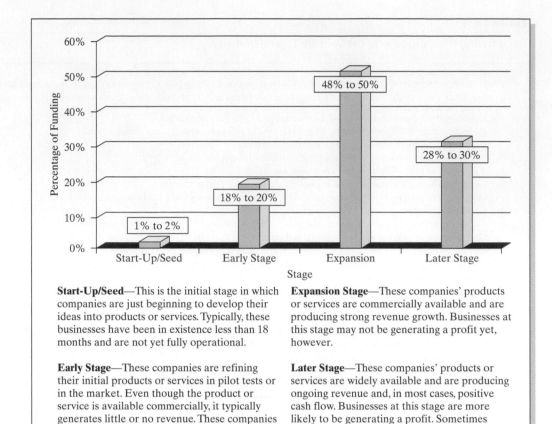

Start-Up/Seed—This is the initial stage in which companies are just beginning to develop their ideas into products or services. Typically, these businesses have been in existence less than 18 months and are not yet fully operational.

Early Stage—These companies are refining their initial products or services in pilot tests or in the market. Even though the product or service is available commercially, it typically generates little or no revenue. These companies have been in business less than three years.

Expansion Stage—These companies' products or services are commercially available and are producing strong revenue growth. Businesses at this stage may not be generating a profit yet, however.

Later Stage—These companies' products or services are widely available and are producing ongoing revenue and, in most cases, positive cash flow. Businesses at this stage are more likely to be generating a profit. Sometimes these businesses are spin-offs of already established successful private companies.

Control. In exchange for the financing they receive from venture capitalists, entrepreneurs must give up a portion of their businesses, sometimes surrendering a majority interest and control of its operations. Most venture capitalists prefer to let the founding team of managers employ its skills to operate a business *if* they are capable of managing its growth. However, it is quite common for venture capitalists to join the boards of directors of the companies they invest in or to send in new managers or a new management team to protect their investments. In other words, venture capitalists are *not* passive investors! Some serve only as financial and managerial advisers, whereas others take an active role managing the company—recruiting employees, providing sales leads, choosing attorneys and advertising agencies, and making daily decisions. The majority of these active venture capitalists say they are forced to step in because the existing management team lacked the talent and experience to achieve growth targets. *Joan Lyman, cofounder of SecureWorks, Inc., was CEO of the Internet security company when she decided to relinquish control of the business in exchange for a $30 million capital infusion from venture capital firms. Two years later, she came to regret her decision when the investors replaced her as CEO. Having learned a valuable lesson, Lyman has since launched another technology company with her own money, and this time, she says she will not give up a majority interest in her company.*[30]

A study by the Stanford Business School found that entrepreneurs who financed their businesses with venture capital were more than twice as likely to be replaced as CEO than those who relied on other forms of financing.[31] One cautionary note for every entrepreneur seeking venture capital is to find out before the deal is done *exactly* how much control and "hands-on" management investors plan to assume.

Company Example

Investment Preferences. The venture capital industry has undergone important changes over the past two decades. Venture capital funds are larger, more numerous, more professional, and more specialized. As the industry grows, more venture capital funds are focusing their investments in niches—everything from low-calorie custards to the Internet. Some will invest in almost any industry but prefer companies in particular stages, including the start-up phase. Traditionally, however, only about 2 percent of the companies receiving venture capital financing are in the start-up (seed) stage when entrepreneurs are forming a company or developing a product or service. Most of the start-up businesses that attract venture capital today are technology companies and life science companies (e.g., biotechnology firms and medical device makers).

What Venture Capitalists Look For. Entrepreneurs must realize that it is very difficult for any small business, especially start-ups, to pass the intense screening process of a venture capital company and qualify for an investment. Venture capital firms finance an average of about 3,500 deals in a typical year.[32] Two factors make a deal attractive to venture capitalists: high returns and a convenient (and profitable) exit strategy. When evaluating potential investments, venture capitalists look for the following features:

Competent Management. Venture capitalist firms believe in the adage "Money follows management." To them, the most important ingredient in the success of any business is the ability of the management team. From a venture capitalist's perspective, the ideal management team has experience, managerial skills, commitment, and the ability to build teams. When the managers at the venture capital firm Wheatley Partners decided to invest in Form + Function, they cited the quality of the management team as a major factor in their decision.[33]

Competitive Edge. Investors are searching for some factor that will enable a small business to set itself apart from its competitors. This distinctive competence may range from an innovative product or service that satisfies unmet customer needs to a unique marketing or R&D approach. It must be something with the potential to make the business a leader in its field. A study by Global Insight shows how dominant venture-funded businesses are in their industries. Companies that received venture funding between 1980 and 2000 generated 11 percent of the entire U.S. gross domestic product in 2000! The report cited the importance of these companies in terms of their total sales, exports, investments in R&D, and contributions to the tax base.[34]

Growth Industry. Hot industries attract profits—and venture capital. Most venture capital funds focus their searches for prospects in rapidly expanding fields because they believe the profit potential is greater in these areas. Venture capital firms are most interested in young companies that have enough growth potential to become at least $100 million businesses within three to five years. Venture capitalists know that most of the businesses they invest in will flop, so their winners have to be *big* winners.

Viable Exit Strategy. Venture capitalists not only look for promising companies with the ability to dominate a market, but they also want to see a plan for a feasible exit strategy, typically to be executed within three to five years. Venture capital firms realize the return on their investments when the companies they invest in either make an initial public offering or sell out to another business. The exit strategy Wheatley Partners defined for its investment in Form + Function was for the company to make an initial public offering of its stock within five years.[35]

Intangible Factors. Some other important factors considered in the screening process are not easily measured; they are the intuitive, intangible factors the venture capitalist detects by gut feeling. This feeling might be the result of the small firm's solid sense of direction,

> Company Example →

its strategic planning process, the chemistry of its management team, or a number of other factors.

Rick Holt and David Grano, cofounders of APTUS Financial LLC, a company on the cutting edge of technology designed for wireless banking transactions, parlayed their experience in both the banking and high-tech industries into venture capital to fuel the growth of their business. The pair had launched APTUS Financial with their own money and had developed a leading position with their unique products, but they needed growth capital to retain that edge. With sales of $4.2 million, the company had a successful track record, and both entrepreneurs had relevant management experience. Holt says that the credibility that their experience and the investment of their own capital provided was key to their ability to raise $1.5 million in venture capital.[36]

Despite its many benefits, venture capital is not suitable for every entrepreneur. "VC money comes at a price," warns one entrepreneur. "Before boarding a one-way money train, ask yourself if this is the best route for your business and personal desires, because investors are like department stores the day after Christmas—they expect a lot of returns in a short period of time."[37]

IN THE FOOTSTEPS OF AN ENTREPRENEUR...

eBridge Technologies

After serving nine years in the military, Brad Cunningham decided to change his career path and start a business. The discipline and the planning skills he acquired in the military paid off, and eBridge Technologies, which designs software and provides information technology services, is growing steadily at a rate of 20 to 25 percent a year. The company generates sales of $700,000 a year and has won numerous awards for its software products that help customers of all sizes manage key operations such as manufacturing, quality assurance, and supply chain management. eBridge Technologies' customer list includes notable names such as Fuji and Liz Claiborne, both companies whose operations span the globe.

One of eBridge Technologies' major strengths is its solid customer base; some 80 percent of the company's revenue comes from its existing client base. Underlying that strength, however, is a weakness that concerns Cunningham: Only 20 percent of sales comes from new clients, the lifeblood of a company's future. The problem is that the small company's nine employees are caught in a vicious cycle: They are so involved in developing new software, improving existing products, and handling customer service that they have very little time to devote to developing new clients and boosting sales.

Cunningham's goal is to raise enough growth capital for the company to hire a small force of sales and marketing representatives, including a business development manager, a senior sales and marketing manager,

salespeople, and administrative staff to support them. None of that comes cheaply, however. Cunningham estimates that the total cost for his growth plan is $1.5 million. Business advisors estimate that eBridge currently is worth about $3.5 million. They also suggest that if Cunningham decides to rely on equity financing for growth capital, he should plan on giving up 30 percent to 35 percent of the company's stock.

eBridge Technologies is located in Greenville, South Carolina, and that's where Cunningham began his search for capital. He worked with local experts to develop a list of prospects and then made his pitch to potential investors. None of the local leads panned out, and, after 100 pitches, Cunningham is left wondering where the capital to fuel his company's growth is going to come from. "We've been blown away by how positive people are about our business model, our customers, and our products," he says. "But nobody's opened a checkbook. We're watching some of our market opportunity go by."

1. Assume the role of financial consultant to Cunningham. Where would you recommend he search for the capital to accomplish the goals he has established for eBridge Technologies? Explain your reasoning.
2. Would you recommend that Cunningham avoid certain sources of equity capital in his search? Explain.

Source: Adapted from David Worrell, "Growing Up Is Hard to Do," *Entrepreneur,* April 2004, pp. 74–75.

Public Stock Sale ("Going Public")

In some cases, entrepreneurs can "go public" by selling shares of stock in their corporations to outside investors. In an **initial public offering (IPO)**, a company raises capital by selling shares of its stock to the general public for the first time. A public offering is an effective method of raising large amounts of capital, but it can be an expensive and time-consuming process filled with regulatory nightmares. "An IPO can be a wonderful thing," says one investment banker, "but it's not all sweetness and light."[38] Once a company makes an initial public offering, *nothing* will ever be the same again. Managers must consider the impact of their decisions not only on the company and its employees but also on shareholders and the value of their stock.

Going public isn't for every business. In fact, most small companies do not meet the criteria for making a successful public stock offering. In a typical year, only about 550 companies manage to make initial public offerings of their stock, and only 20,000 companies in the United States—less than 1 percent of the total—are publicly held. Few companies with less than $10 million in annual sales manage to go public successfully. It is extremely difficult for a start-up company with no track record of success to raise money with a public offering. Instead, investment bankers who underwrite public stock offerings typically look for established companies with the following characteristics:

- Consistently high growth rates (usually at least 20 percent a year).
- Strong record of earnings.
- Three to five years of audited financial statements.
- A solid position in rapidly growing markets.
- A sound management team and a strong board of directors.

Figure 14.3 shows the number of IPOs since 1981, along with the amount of capital raised during that time.

Entrepreneurs who are considering taking their companies public should first consider carefully the advantages and the disadvantages of an IPO. The *advantages* include the following:

Ability to Raise Large Amounts of Capital. The biggest benefit of a public offering is the capital infusion the company receives. After going public, the corporation has the cash to fund R&D projects, expand plants and facilities, repay debt, or boost working capital balances without incurring the interest expense and the obligation to repay associated with debt financing. *For instance, when Vince and Linda McMahon's World Wrestling Entertainment went public, the sale of 10 million shares at $17 per share generated more than $170 million for the company (before subtracting the expenses of making the offering).*[39]

Improved Corporate Image. All of the media attention a company receives during the registration process makes it more visible. Plus, becoming a public company in some industries improves its prestige and enhances its competitive position, one of the most widely recognized, intangible benefits of going public.

Improved Access to Future Financing. Going public boosts a company's net worth and broadens its equity base. Its improved stature and financial strength make it easier for the firm to attract more capital—both debt and equity—and to grow.

Attracting and Retaining Key Employees. Public companies often use stock-based compensation plans to attract and retain quality employees. Stock options and bonuses are excellent methods for winning employees' loyalty and for instilling a healthy ownership attitude among them. Employee stock ownership plans (ESOPs) and stock purchase plans are popular recruiting and motivational tools in many small corporations, enabling them to hire top-flight talent they otherwise would not be able to afford.

---

3. Describe the process of "going public," as well as its advantages and disadvantages and the various simplified registrations and exemptions from registration available to small businesses.

Company Example →

Figure 14.3

Initial Public Offerings (IPOs)

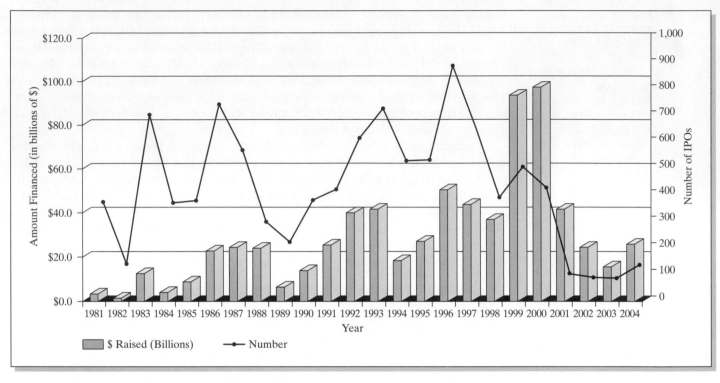

Source: Thomson Financial Securities Data and Renaissance Capital, Greenwich, CT, www.ipohome.com, 2004.

Using Stock for Acquisitions. A company whose stock is publicly traded can acquire other businesses by offering its own shares rather than cash. Acquiring other companies with shares of stock eliminates the need to incur additional debt.

Listing on a Stock Exchange. Being listed on an organized stock exchange, even a small regional one, improves the marketability of a company's shares and enhances its image. World Wrestling Entertainment's stock trades on the New York Stock Exchange, giving it more clout in its market. Most small companies' stocks, however, do not qualify for listing on the nation's largest exchanges—the New York Stock Exchange (NYSE) and the American Stock Exchange (AMEX). However, the AMEX offers a market for small-company stocks, The Emerging Company Marketplace. Most small companies' stocks are traded on either the National Association of Securities Dealers Automated Quotation (NASDAQ) system's National Market System (NMS) and its emerging small-capitalization exchange or one of the nation's regional stock exchanges. The most popular regional exchanges include the Midwest (MSE), Philadelphia (PHLX), Boston (BSE), and Pacific (PSE).

Despite these advantages, many factors can spoil a company's attempted IPO. In fact, only 5 percent of the companies that attempt to go public ever complete the process.[40]

The *disadvantages* of going public include the following:

Dilution of Founder's Ownership. Whenever entrepreneurs sell stock to the public, they automatically dilute their ownership in their businesses. Most owners retain a majority interest in the business, but they may still run the risk of unfriendly takeovers years later after selling more stock.

Loss of Control. If enough shares are sold in a public offering, the company founder risks losing control of the company. If a large block of shares falls into the hands of dissident stockholders, they could vote the existing management team (including the founder) out.

Loss of Privacy. Taking their companies public can be a big ego boost for owners, but they must realize that their companies are no longer solely theirs. Information that was once private must be available for public scrutiny. The initial prospectus and the continuous reports filed with the Securities and Exchange Commission (SEC) disclose a variety of information about the company and its operations—from financial data and raw material sources to legal matters and patents—to *anyone*, including competitors. One study found that loss of privacy and loss of control were most commonly cited as the reasons that CEOs choose not to attempt IPOs.[41]

Regulatory Requirements and Reporting to the SEC. Operating as a publicly held company is expensive. Complying with the provisions of the Sarbanes-Oxley Act, which was passed in 2002 to protect shareholders of publicly held companies from unethical and illegal acts of managers and directors, has led to significant cost increases for public companies. Created in response to several high-profile accounting scandals at major corporations, the act shields investors from abuses by corporate managers and board members by establishing requirements that improve the accuracy and the reliability of the information a corporation dis-

Company Example

closes. *The founder and the chief operating officer of Landair Transport Inc., a transportation company based in Greenville, Tennessee, recently purchased all of the shares of the company's stock, transforming it from a publicly held entity once traded on the NASDAQ to a privately held one. They cited the increased cost of complying with Sarbanes-Oxley and other regulations as the primary reason for their decision to take the company private.*[42]

Publicly held companies also incur additional costs because they must file periodic reports with the SEC, which often requires a more powerful accounting system, a larger accounting staff, and greater use of attorneys and other professionals. Complying with the SEC's accounting and filing requirements alone can cost $150,000 a year or more.

Filing Expenses. A public stock offering usually is an expensive way to generate funds to finance a company's growth. For the typical small company, the cost of a public offering is about 15 percent of the capital raised. On small offerings, costs can eat up as much as 40 percent of the capital raised, whereas on larger offerings, those above $25 million, only 10 to 12 percent will go to cover expenses. Once an offering exceeds $15 million, its relative issuing costs drop. The largest cost is the underwriter's commission, which is typically 7 percent of the proceeds of the offering. Figure 14.4 shows a breakdown of the costs associated with a typical IPO.

Figure 14.4

The Cost of Going Public: Typical Costs of a $20 Million IPO

Source: Jill Andresky Fraser, "The Road to Wall Street," *Inc.*, June 2002, p. 86.

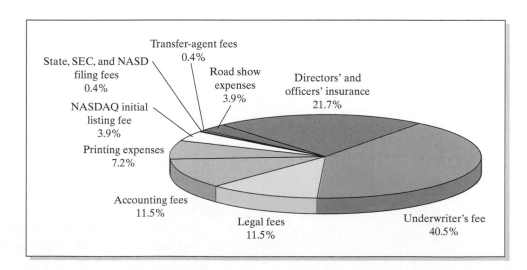

Accountability to Shareholders. The capital that entrepreneurs manage and risk is no longer just their own. The managers of a publicly held firm are accountable to the company's shareholders. Indeed, the law requires that managers recognize and abide by a relationship built on trust. Profit and return on investment become the primary concerns for investors. If the stock price of a newly public company falls, shareholder lawsuits are inevitable. Investors whose shares decline in value often sue the company's managers for fraud and the failure to disclose the potential risks to which their investment exposes them. After the technology company he purchased stock in failed, one investor, rather than filing a lawsuit, turned his now worthless stock certificates (that at one point were worth $8.5 million) into placemats for his kitchen table![43]

Pressure for Short-Term Performance. In privately held companies, entrepreneurs are free to follow their strategies for success, even if those strategies take years to produce results. When a company goes public, however, entrepreneurs quickly learn that shareholders are impatient and expect results immediately. Founders are under constant pressure to produce growth in profits and in market share, which requires them to maintain a delicate balance between short-term results and long-term strategy. David Klock, who took his company Comp Benefits private in 1999, says, "I am glad we're private because [it gives us] the ability to make investments that may take two or three quarters to give a good return. That's difficult to do as a public company."[44]

Loss of Focus. As impatient as they can be, entrepreneurs often find the time demands of an initial public offering frustrating and distracting. Managing the IPO takes time away from managing the company. Working on an IPO can consume as much as 75 percent of top managers' time, robbing top managers of their ability to manage the business effectively.

Timing. While it prepares its offering, a company also runs the risk that the market for IPOs or for a particular issue may go sour. Factors beyond managers' control, such as declines in the stock market and potential investors' jitters, can quickly slam shut a company's "window of opportunity" for an IPO even after top managers have spent months and many thousands of dollars working on the offering. *For instance, Netgear Inc., a manufacturer of networking hardware, filed for an IPO just before the market for high-tech stocks soured. Three years later, after the stock market and the economy recovered, Netgear managed to complete its IPO, selling 7 million shares of stock at $7 per share and raising $98 million. Netgear was fortunate in some respects; many companies planning IPOs were forced to withdraw their proposed stock offerings altogether.*[45]

The Registration Process. Taking a company public is a complicated, bureaucratic process that usually takes several months to complete. Many experts compare the IPO process to running a corporate marathon, and both the company and its management team must be in shape and up to the grueling task. The typical entrepreneur *cannot* take his or her company public alone. It requires a coordinated effort from a team of professionals, including company executives, an accountant, a securities attorney, a financial printer, and at least one underwriter. The key steps in taking a company public follow.

Choose the Underwriter. The single most important ingredient in making a successful IPO is selecting a capable **underwriter** (or **investment banker**). The underwriter serves two primary roles: helping to prepare the registration statement for the issue and promoting the company's stock to potential investors. The underwriter works with company managers as an adviser in preparing the registration statement that must be filed with the SEC, promoting the issue in a road show, pricing the stock, and providing after-market support. Once the registration statement is finished, the

Company Example

In 1961, Dick Cabela (right) started a business by offering a set of hand-tied fishing flies for $1. In 1963, Dick's brother Jim joined the business to help manage operations. Today, Cabela's, which recently completed a $150 million initial public offering, carries more than 235,000 products that it sells to outdoor enthusiasts in more than 100 countries around the world.

underwriter's primary job is selling the company's stock through an underwriting syndicate of other investment bankers it develops.

Company Example →

Cabela's, a company founded in 1961 that sells hunting, fishing, and outdoor equipment online, through catalogs, and from nine retail stores, recently filed for an initial public offering. The company selected Credit Suisse First Boston as its underwriter to manage the offering of 9.375 million shares that generated $150 million in capital for the company that has been privately held by the Cabela family for four decades.[46]

Negotiate a Letter of Intent. To begin an offering, the entrepreneur and the underwriter must negotiate a **letter of intent,** which outlines the details of the deal. The letter of intent covers a variety of important issues, including the type of underwriting, its size and price range, the underwriter's commission, and any warrants and options included. It almost always states that the underwriter is not bound to the offering until it is executed—usually the day before or the day of the offering. However, the letter usually creates a binding obligation for the company to pay any direct expenses the underwriter incurs relating to the offer.

There are two types of underwriting agreements: firm commitment and best effort. In a **firm commitment agreement,** the underwriter agrees to purchase all of the shares in the offering and then resells them to investors. This agreement *guarantees* that the company will receive the required funds, and most large underwriters use it. In a **best efforts agreement,** the underwriter merely agrees to use its best efforts to sell the company's shares and does not guarantee the company will receive the needed financing. The managing underwriter acts as an agent, selling as many shares as possible through the syndicate. Some best efforts contracts are all or nothing—if the underwriter cannot sell all of the shares, the offering is withdrawn. Another version of the best efforts agreement is to set a minimum number of shares that must be sold for the issue to be completed. These methods are riskier because the company has no guarantee of raising the required capital.

The company and the underwriter must decide on the size of the offering and the price of the shares. To keep the stock active in the aftermarket, most underwriters prefer to offer a *minimum* of 400,000 to 500,000 shares. A smaller number of shares inhibits sufficiently broad distribution. Most underwriters recommend selling 25 percent to 40 percent of the company in the IPO. They also strive to price the issue so that the total value of the offering is at least $8 to $15 million. (Although there are exceptions, some underwriters, especially regional ones, are interested in doing IPOs in the $2 to $5 million range.) To meet these criteria and to keep interest in the issue high, the underwriter usually recommends an initial price between $10 and $20 per share.

Most letters of intent include a **lock-up agreement** that prevents the sale of insider shares, those owned by directors, managers, founders, employees, and other insiders, for 12 to 36 months. The sale of these shares early in a company's public life could send negative signals to investors, eroding their confidence in the stock and pushing its price downward.

Prepare the Registration Statement. After a company signs the letter of intent, the next task is to prepare the **registration statement** to be filed with the Securities and Exchange Commission (SEC). This document describes both the company and the stock offering and discloses information about the risks of investing. It includes information on the use of the proceeds, the company's history, its financial position, its capital structure, any risks it faces, its managers, and many other details. The statement is extremely comprehensive and may take months to develop. To prepare the statement, entrepreneurs must rely on their team of professionals.

File with the SEC. When the registration statement is finished (with the exception of pricing the shares, proceeds, and commissions, which cannot be determined until just before the issue goes to market), the company officially files the statement with the SEC and awaits the review by the Division of Corporate Finance. The division sends notice of any deficiencies in the registration statement to the company's attorney in a comment letter. The company and its team of professionals must cure all of the deficiencies in the statement noted in the comment letter. Finally, the company files the revised registration statement, along with a pricing amendment (giving the price of the shares, the proceeds, and the commissions).

Wait to Go Effective. While waiting for the SEC's approval, the managers and the underwriters are busy. The underwriters are building a syndicate of other underwriters who will market the company's stock. (No sales can be made prior to the effective date of the offering, however.) The SEC also limits the publicity and information a company may release during this quiet period (which officially starts when the company reaches a preliminary agreement with the managing underwriter and ends 90 days after the effective date).

Securities laws do permit a **road show,** a gathering of potential syndicate members sponsored by the managing underwriter. Its purpose is to promote interest among potential underwriters in the IPO by featuring the company, its management, and the proposed deal. The managing underwriter and key company officials barnstorm major financial centers at

> **Company Example** → a grueling pace. *During the road show for Ashford.com, an online retailer of luxury goods that raised $75 million in its IPO, top managers courted potential investors on two continents, hitting 24 cities in just 14 days! "In one day, we had a breakfast meeting in Frankfurt, flew to Paris for lunch meetings, then to New York, and finally to Baltimore," says David Gow, Ashford's chief financial officer. "We kept gaining hours. It was the never-ending day."*[47]

On the last day before the registration statement becomes effective, the company signs the formal underwriting agreement. The final settlement, or closing, takes place a few days after the effective date for the issue. At this meeting the underwriters receive their shares to sell and the company receives the proceeds of the offering.

Typically, the entire process of going public takes from 60 to 180 days, but it can take much longer if the issuing company is not properly prepared for the process.

Meet State Requirements. In addition to satisfying the SEC's requirements, a company also must meet the securities laws in all states in which the issue is sold. These state laws (or "blue sky" laws) vary drastically from one state to another, and the company must comply with them.

IN THE FOOTSTEPS OF AN ENTREPRENEUR...

In Search of Capital

In 1991, Lori Bonn Gallagher launched her jewelry design and manufacturing business, Lori Bonn Designs, in Oakland, California, with $1,000 from her personal savings. Her company's midpriced to upper-priced jewelry has found a market, and sales have climbed to more than $3 million a year. The company has been profitable since its first year of operation. As her company grew, Gallagher used a variety of funding sources, including the retained earnings of the company and bank loans. Once she landed a few major retailers such as Nordstrom and Sak's Fifth Avenue, she started factoring the company's accounts receivable. Currently, Gallagher has a six-figure line of credit at a bank that she draws on primarily for working capital.

The line of credit and the other sources of capital that Lori Bonn Designs has relied on in the past are not enough to fuel the growth Gallagher sees for her company, however. "My product is selling really, really well right now," she says. "I can't produce enough to meet the demand from my customers. There's so much opportunity. We could get to [$10 million in annual sales] much faster, but

to do that I need significantly more capital than I've gotten so far."

Gallagher wants to hire someone to manage the financial aspects of the business, freeing her to focus on what she does best: jewelry design and marketing. She also wants to launch an aggressive national marketing campaign, to expand into international markets, and to improve the company's inventory control procedures. "What I really need is a couple million dollars and a smart person or two to serve on my board," quips Gallagher. She still owns 100 percent of the company's stock, and she would prefer not to give up a large stake in the company to outsiders.

1. Assume the role of financial consultant to Gallagher. What steps should she take to prepare her company before she begins her search for capital?
2. Where would you recommend she search for the capital to accomplish the goals she has established for her business? Explain your reasoning.

Source: Adapted from Jill Andresky Fraser, "Money Hunt: Plans for Growth," *Inc.*, March 2001, pp. 56–57.

Simplified Registrations and Exemptions

4. Explain the various simplified registrations, exemptions from registration, and other alternative available to entrepreneurs wanting to sell shares of equity to investors.

The IPO process described previously (called an S-1 filing) requires maximum disclosure in the initial filing and discourages most small businesses from using it. Fortunately, the SEC allows several exemptions from this full-disclosure process for small businesses. Many small businesses that go public choose one of these simplified options the SEC has designed for small companies. The SEC has established the following simplified registration statements and exemptions from the registration process.

Regulation S-B. Regulation S-B is a simplified registration process for small companies seeking to make initial or subsequent public offerings. Not only does this regulation simplify the initial filing requirements with the SEC, but it also reduces the ongoing disclosure and filings required of companies. Its primary goals are to open the doors to capital markets to smaller companies by cutting the paperwork and the costs of raising capital. Companies using the simplified registration process have two options: Form SB-1, a "transitional" registration statement for companies issuing less than $10 million worth of securities over a 12-month period and Form SB-2, reserved for small companies seeking more than $10 million in a 12-month period.

To be eligible for the simplified registration process under Regulation S-B, a company must:

- Be based in the United States or Canada.
- Have revenues of less than $25 million.

- Have outstanding publicly held stock worth no more than $25 million.
- Not be an investment company.
- Provide audited financial statements for two fiscal years.

The goal of Regulation S-B's simplified registration requirements is to enable smaller companies to go public without incurring the expense of a full-blown registration. Total costs for a Regulation S-B offering are approximately $35,000.

Regulation D (Rule 504): Small Company Offering Registration (SCOR). Created in the late 1980s, the Small Company Offering Registration (also known as the Uniform Limited Offering Registration, ULOR) now is available in all 50 states and the District of Columbia. A little known tool, SCOR is designed to make it easier and less expensive for small companies to sell their stock to the public by eliminating the requirement for registering the offering with the SEC. The whole process typically costs less than half of what a traditional public offering costs. Entrepreneurs using SCOR will need an attorney and an accountant to help them with the issue, but many can get by without a securities lawyer, which can save tens of thousands of dollars. Many entrepreneurs even choose to market their companies' securities themselves (for example, to customers), saving the expense of hiring a broker. However, selling an issue is both time- and energy-consuming, and most SCOR experts recommend hiring a professional securities or brokerage firm to sell the company's shares. The SEC's objective in creating SCOR was to give small companies the same access to equity financing that large companies have via the stock market while bypassing many of the same costs and filing requirements.

The capital ceiling on a SCOR issue is $1 million, and the price of each share must be at least $5. That means that a company can sell no more than 200,000 shares (making the stock less attractive to stock manipulators). A SCOR offering requires only minimal notification to the SEC. The company must file a standardized disclosure statement, the U-7, which follows a simple question-and-answer format that closely resembles a standard business plan. The form, which asks for information such as how much money the company needs, what the money will be used for, what investors receive, how investors can sell their investments, and other pertinent questions, also serves as a business plan, a state securities offering registration, a disclosure document, and a prospectus. Entrepreneurs using SCOR may advertise their companies' offerings and can sell them directly to any investor with no restrictions and no minimums. An entrepreneur can sell practically any kind of security through a SCOR, including common stock, preferred stock, convertible preferred stock, stock options, stock warrants, and others.

Company Example →

Dwayne Fosseen, founder of Mirenco, Inc., a company that has developed patented technology to improve the fuel economy, reduce the emissions, and lower the maintenance costs associated with cars and trucks, relied on a SCOR offering to secure an early round of outside capital for his business. After launching Mirenco with his own funds, Fosseen obtained patents for his technology and then landed a grant from the Department of Energy. Needing more capital for expansion, Mirenco raised money through both SB-2 and SCOR offerings. Based in tiny Radcliffe, Iowa, Mirenco, whose shares trade on the OTC Bulletin Board, used the proceeds of its offerings to build a new headquarters, to fund more research and development, and to expand the market for its innovative products.[48]

A SCOR offering offers entrepreneurs needing equity financing several *advantages*:

- Access to a sizable pool of equity funds (up to $1 million in a year) without the expense of full registration with the SEC. Companies often can complete a SCOR offering for less than $25,000.
- Few restrictions on the securities to be sold and on the investors to whom they can be sold.
- The ability to market the offering through advertisements to the public.

- Young or start-up companies can qualify.
- No requirement of audited financial statements for offerings less than $500,000.
- Faster approval of the issue from regulatory agencies.
- The ability to make the offering in several states at once.

There are, of course, some *disadvantages* to using SCOR to raise needed funds:

- Partnerships cannot make SCOR offerings.
- A company can raise no more than $1 million in a 12-month period.
- An entrepreneur must register the offering in every state in which shares of stock will be sold, although current regulations allow simultaneous registration in multiple states.
- The process can be time-consuming, distracting an entrepreneur from the daily routine of running the company. A limited secondary market for the securities may limit investors' interest. Currently, SCOR shares must be traded through brokerage firms that make small markets in specific stocks. However, the Pacific Stock Exchange and the NASDAQ's electronic bulletin board recently began listing SCOR stocks, so the secondary market for them has broadened.

Regulation D (Rules 505 and 506): Private Placements. Rules 505 and 506 are exemptions from federal registration requirements that give emerging companies the opportunity to sell stock through private placements without actually going public. In a private placement, the company sells its shares directly to private investors without having

Company Example ➤ to register them with the SEC. *For example, tiny Eximias Pharmaceutical Corporation, which has developed promising drugs for treating liver cancer, recently used Regulation D to make a $63.5 million private placement of its stock. Eximias used the money to complete the extensive rounds of clinical trials required for approval of Thymitaq from the Food and Drug Administration and to develop other drugs as well.*[49]

A *Rule 505* offering has a higher capital ceiling than a SCOR offering ($5 million) in a 12-month period but imposes more restrictions (no more than 35 nonaccredited investors, no advertising of the offer, and more stringent disclosure requirements).

Rule 506 imposes no ceiling on the amount that can be raised, but, like a Rule 505 offering, it limits the issue to 35 nonaccredited investors and prohibits advertising the offer to the public. There is no limit on the number of accredited investors, however. Rule 506 also requires detailed disclosure of relevant information, but the extent depends on the size of the offering.

These Regulation D rules minimize the expense and the time required to raise equity capital for small businesses. Fees for private placements typically range from 1 to 5 percent rather than the 7 to 13 percent underwriters normally charge for managing a public offering. Offerings made under Regulation D do impose limitations and demand certain disclosures, but they only require a company to file a simple form (Form D) with the SEC within 15 days of the first sale of stock.

Section 4(6). Section 4(6) covers private placements and is similar to Regulation D, Rules 505 and 506. It does not require registration on offers up to $5 million if they are made only to accredited investors.

Intrastate Offerings (Rule 147). Rule 147 governs intrastate offerings, those sold only to investors in a single state by a company doing business in that state. To qualify, a company must be incorporated in the state, maintain its executive offices there, have 80 percent of its assets there, derive 80 percent of its revenues from the state, and use 80 percent of the offering proceeds for business in the state. There is no ceiling on the amount of the offering.

Company Example ➤ The goal of intrastate offerings is to enhance the local financing of local businesses. *Gary Hoover put up just $5,000 of his own money and convinced several private investors to pur-*

chase $850,000 worth of preferred stock to launch TravelFest, a retail store that caters to travelers. As the company grew, Hoover decided to make an intrastate offering under Rule 147 to raise the money he needed for expansion. He registered the offering in TravelFest's home state of Texas, where resident investors purchased $5.6 million in convertible preferred stock.[50]

Regulation A. Regulation A, although currently not used often, allows an exemption for offerings up to $5 million over a 12-month period. Regulation A imposes few restrictions, but it is more costly than the other types of exempted offerings, usually running between $80,000 and $120,000. The primary difference between a SCOR offering and a Regulation A offering is that a company must register its SCOR offering only in the states where it will sell its stock; in a Regulation A offering, the company also must file an offering statement with the SEC. Like a SCOR offering, a Regulation A offering allows a company to sell its shares directly to investors.

Direct Stock Offerings. Many of the simplified registrations and exemptions discussed previously give entrepreneurs the power to sidestep investment bankers and sell their companies' stock offerings directly to investors and, in the process, save themselves thousands of dollars in underwriting fees. By going straight to Main Street rather than through underwriters on Wall Street, entrepreneurs cut out the underwriter's commission, many legal expenses, and most registration fees. Entrepreneurs willing to handle the paperwork requirements and to market their own shares can make direct public offerings (DPOs) for about 6 percent of the total amount of the issue, compared with 15 percent for a traditional stock offering. *Thanksgiving Coffee Company, a business that sells organically grown coffee and related products, recently engineered a successful direct public offering. Founders Paul and Joan Katzeff targeted their base of loyal customers and those who supported their company's focus on social responsibility. In addition to a notice of the offering on Thanksgiving Coffee's Web site, the company included announcements in customers' orders, in strategic locations throughout the store, and in some magazines and newspapers. Within a few months, Thanksgiving Coffee had sold all of the shares in its offering.[51]*

Company Example →

The World Wide Web (WWW) has opened a new avenue for direct public offerings and is one the fastest-growing sources of capital for small businesses. Much of the Web's appeal as a fund-raising tool stems from its ability to reach large numbers of prospective investors very quickly and at a low cost. The Web enables a small company to make its investment prospectus available to the world at a minimal cost. Companies making direct stock offerings on the Web most often make them under either Regulation A or Regulation D and usually generate between $300,000 and $4 million for the company.

Direct public offerings work best for companies that have a single product or related product lines, a base of customers who are loyal to the company, good name recognition, and annual sales between $3 million and $25 million. The first company to make a successful DPO over the Internet was Spring Street Brewing, a microbrewery founded by Andy Klein. Klein raised $1.6 million in a Regulation A offering in 1996. Companies that make successful direct public offerings of their stock over the Web must meet the same standards as companies making stock offerings using more traditional methods. Experts caution Web-based fund seekers to make sure their electronic prospectuses meet SEC and state requirements. Table 14.5 provides a brief quiz to help entrepreneurs determine whether or not their companies would be good candidates for a DPO.

Foreign Stock Markets

Sometimes foreign stock markets offer entrepreneurs access to equity funds more readily than U.S. markets. The United Kingdom's Unlisted Securities Market and the OFEX as well as the Vancouver Stock exchange are especially attractive to small companies. Both

Table 14.5

Is a Direct Public Offering for You?

Drew Field, an expert in direct public offerings (DPO), has developed the following 10-question quiz to help entrepreneurs decide whether or not their companies are good candidates for a DPO.

1. Does your company have a history of consistently profitable operations under the present management?
2. Is your company's present management team honest, socially responsible, and competent?
3. In 10 words or fewer, can you explain the nature of your business to laypeople new to investing?
4. Would your company excite prospective investors, making them want to share in its future?
5. Does your company have natural affinity groups, such as customers with strong emotional loyalty?
6. Do members of your natural affinity groups have discretionary cash to risk for long-term gains?
7. Would your company's natural affinity groups recognize your company's name and consider your offering materials?
8. Can you get the names, addresses, and telephone numbers of affinity group members, as well as some demographic information about them?
9. Can a high-level company employee spend half-time for six months as a DPO project manager?
10. Does your company have—or can you obtain—audited financial statements for at least the last two fiscal years?

Sources: Drew Field Direct Public Offers, Screen Test for a Direct Public Offering, www.dfdpo.com/screen.htm; Stephanie Gruner, "Could You Do a DPO?" *Inc.*, December 1996, p. 70.

Company Example →

encourage equity listings of small companies, and the costs of offerings are usually lower than in the United States. *Thomas Burnham, founder of South Beach Cafe, turned to OFEX to raise the $700,000 he needed to open his third café in London. After opening two successful locations in Michigan, Burnham decided to take his gourmet café concept international and to use foreign capital to finance the expansion. After submitting a business plan and a fairly simple prospectus, he made a successful public offering on OFEX, raising $750,000. Five months after the offering, the first South Beach Cafe in London opened its doors. Burnham's first foreign offering proved so successful that he returned a year later and raised $3 million to fuel the company's expansion into Europe.*[52]

Securing capital to launch or to expand a small business is no easy task. However, entrepreneurs who understand the equity funding options that are available and are prepared to go after them stand a much better chance of getting the financing they seek than those who don't.

Chapter Review

1. Explain the differences in the three types of capital small businesses require: fixed, working, and growth.

   - Capital is any form of wealth employed to produce more wealth. Three forms of capital are commonly identified: fixed capital, working capital, and growth capital.
   - Fixed capital is used to purchase a company's permanent or fixed assets; working capital represents the business's temporary funds and is used to support the business's normal short-term operations; growth capital requirements surface when an existing business is expanding or changing its primary direction.

2. Describe the various sources of equity capital available to entrepreneurs, including personal savings, friends and relatives, angels, partners, corporations, venture capital, and public stock offerings.

   - The most common source of financing a business is the owner's personal savings. After emptying their own pockets, the next place entrepreneurs turn for capital is family members and friends. Angels are private investors who not only invest their money in small companies, but they also offer valuable advice and counsel to them. Some business owners have success financing their companies by taking on limited partners as investors or by forming an alliance with a corporation, often a customer or a supplier. Venture capital companies are for-profit, professional investors looking for fast-growing companies in "hot" industries. When screening prospects, venture capital firms look for competent management, a competitive edge, a growth industry, and important intangibles that will make a business successful. Some owners choose to attract capital by taking their companies public, which requires registering the public offering with the SEC.

3. Describe the process of "going public," as well as its advantages and disadvantages and the various simplified registrations and exemptions from registration available to small businesses.

   ■ Going public involves (1) choosing the underwriter, (2) negotiating a letter of intent, (3) preparing the registration statement, (4) filing with the SEC, and (5) meeting state requirements.

   ■ Going public offers the advantages of raising large amounts of capital, improved access to future financing, improved corporate image, and gaining listing on a stock exchange. The disadvantages

include dilution of the founder's ownership, loss of privacy, reporting to the SEC, filing expenses, and accountability to shareholders.

4. Explain the various simplified registrations, exemptions from registration, and other alternatives available to entrepreneurs wanting to sell shares of equity to investors.

   ■ Rather than go through the complete registration process, some companies use one of the simplified registration options and exemptions available to small companies: Regulation S-B, Regulation D (Rule 504) Small Company Offering Registration (SCOR), Regulation D (Rule 505 and Rule 506) Private Placements, Section 4(6), Rule 147, Regulation A, direct stock offerings, and foreign stock markets.

▌▌▌ Discussion Questions

1. Why is it so difficult for most small business owners to raise the capital needed to start, operate, or expand their ventures?

2. What is capital? List and describe the three types of capital a small business needs for its operations.

3. Define equity financing. What advantage does it offer over debt financing?

4. What is the most common source of equity funds in a typical small business? If an owner lacks sufficient equity capital to invest in the firm, what options are available for raising it?

5. What guidelines should entrepreneurs follow if friends and relatives choose to invest in their businesses?

6. What is an angel investor? Assemble a brief profile of the typical private investor. How can

entrepreneurs locate potential angels to invest in their businesses?

7. What advice would you offer an entrepreneur on how to strike a deal with a private investor and avoid problems?

8. What types of businesses are most likely to attract venture capital? What investment criteria do venture capitalists use when screening potential businesses? How do these compare to the typical angel's criteria?

9. How do venture capital firms operate? Describe their procedure for screening investment proposals.

10. Summarize the major exemptions and simplified registrations available to small companies wanting to make public offerings of their stock.

Sources of Equity Financing

Business PlanPro

In addition to serving as a tool for managing a business, a business plan is an important instrument in the search for capital. Many entrepreneurs turn to outside sources for financing their businesses for either equity capital, which represents ownership in a business, or debt capital, which involves borrowed funds the business must repay at some point.

Now that you have finished studying Chapter 14, return to the section in Business Plan Pro called Financial Plan. There you can describe the amount and the type of equity

investment you are seeking. Click the Investment Offering Table to launch the Investment Offering Wizard that will guide you through the process of defining the equity investment you are seeking for your business. Be sure to complete the Explain Investment Offering section to explain the details of your investment offering. Which of the following sources do you plan to approach for equity capital?

■ Friends and family members
■ Private investors ("angels")
■ Partners
■ Corporate venture capital
■ Venture capital companies
■ Public stock sale
■ Simplified registrations and exemptions

Chapter 15
Sources of Debt Financing

Always borrow from pessimists. They never expect to get it back.
—Anonymous

Don't ever borrow a little bit of money because when you borrow a little bit of money, you have a serious creditor if you run short. And, if you borrow a lot of money, you have a partner when you get into trouble.
—Fred Smith, founder, FedEx

Upon completion of this chapter, you will be able to:

1. Describe the various sources of debt capital and the advantages and disadvantages of each.

2. Explain the types of financing available from nonbank sources of credit.

3. Identify the sources of government financial assistance and the loan programs these agencies offer.

4. Describe the various loan programs available from the Small Business Administration.

5. Discuss state and local loan programs.

6. Discuss valuable methods of financing growth and expansion internally with bootstrap financing.

7. Explain how to avoid becoming a victim of a loan scam.

Debt financing involves the funds that the small business owner borrows and must repay with interest. Lenders of capital are more numerous than investors, although small business loans can be just as difficult (if not more difficult) to obtain. Although borrowed capital enables entrepreneurs to maintain complete ownership of their businesses, it must be carried as a liability on the balance sheet as well as be repaid with interest at some point in the future. In addition, because small businesses are considered to be greater risks than bigger corporate customers, they must pay higher interest rates because of the risk–return trade-off—the higher the risk, the greater the return demanded. Most small firms pay the **prime rate,** the interest rate banks charge their most creditworthy customers, *plus* two or more percentage points. Still, the cost of debt financing often is lower than that of equity financing. Because of the higher risks associated with providing equity capital to small companies, investors demand greater returns than lenders. Also, unlike equity financing, debt financing does not require entrepreneurs to dilute their ownership interest in the company.

The need for debt capital can arise from a number of sources, but financial experts identify the following reasons business owners should consider borrowing money:[1]

- *Increasing the company's workforce and/or inventory to boost sales.* Sufficient working capital is the fuel that feeds a company's growth.
- *Gaining market share.* Businesses often need extra capital as their customer bases expand and they incur the added expense of extending credit to customers.
- *Purchasing new equipment.* Financing new equipment that can improve productivity, increase quality, and lower operating expenses often takes more capital than a growing company can generate internally.
- *Refinancing existing debt.* As companies become more established, they can negotiate more favorable borrowing terms compared to their start-up days, when entrepreneurs take whatever money they can get at whatever rate they can get. Replacing high-interest loans with loans carrying lower interest rates can improve cash flow significantly.
- *Taking advantage of cash discounts.* Suppliers sometimes offer discounts to customers who pay their invoices early. As you will learn in Chapter 17, business owners should take advantage of cash discounts in most cases.
- *Buying the building in which the business is located.* Many entrepreneurs start out renting the buildings that house their businesses; however, if location is crucial to their success, it may be wise to purchase the location.
- *Establishing a relationship with a lender.* If a business has never borrowed money, taking out a loan and developing a good repayment and credit history can pave the way for future financing. Smart business owners know that bankers who understand their businesses play an integral role in their companies' ultimate success.
- *Retiring debt held by a "nonrelationship" creditor.* Entrepreneurs find that lenders who have no real interest in their companies' long-term success or do not understand their businesses can be extremely difficult to work with. They prefer to borrow money from lenders who are willing to help them achieve their business mission and goals.
- *Foreseeing a downturn in business.* Establishing access to financing before a business slowdown hits insulates a company from a serious cash crisis and protects it from failure.

Entrepreneurs seeking debt capital are quickly confronted with an astounding range of credit options varying greatly in complexity, availability, and flexibility. Not all of these sources of debt capital are equally favorable, however. By understanding the various sources of capital—both commercial and government lenders—and their characteristics, entrepreneurs can greatly increase the chances of obtaining a loan.

We now turn to the various sources of debt capital.

Sources of Debt Capital

Commercial Banks

Commercial banks are the very heart of the financial market, providing the greatest number and variety of loans to small businesses. One study by the Federal Reserve concluded that commercial banks provide 57 percent of the traditional financing available to small businesses and that 80 percent of all loans to existing businesses come from banks![2] For small business owners, banks are lenders of *first* resort, especially as their companies grow. Most small business bank loans are for less than $100,000 (see Figure 15.1).

Banks tend to be conservative in their lending practices and prefer to make loans to established small businesses rather than to high-risk start-ups. One expert estimates that only 5 to 8 percent of business start-ups get bank financing.[3] Bankers want to see evidence of a company's successful track record before committing to a loan. They are concerned with a small company's operating past and will scrutinize its records to project its position in the immediate future. They also want proof of a company's stability and its ability to generate adequate cash flows that ensure repayment of the loan. If they do make loans to a start-up venture, banks like to see significant investment from the owner, sufficient cash flows to repay the loan, ample collateral to secure it, or a Small Business Administration (SBA) guarantee to insure it. Studies suggest that small banks (those with less than $300 million in assets) are most likely to lend money to small businesses.[4]

Company Example →

After banks refused to lend him $500,000 to purchase the rights to five Blimpie franchises in Michigan because of the risk involved, Todd Recknagel developed a plan to give bankers exactly what they wanted. He convinced four wealthy friends to guarantee the bank loan in exchange for 32 percent of his company's stock. A bank accepted his loan proposal, lending the money at just 0.5 percent above the prime rate and paving the way for Recknagel's success. He now owns eight Blimpie franchises, has repaid the original loan, repurchased the investors' stock, and has an SBA-guaranteed fixed-rate loan to finance growth.[5]

When evaluating a loan application, banks focus on a company's capacity to create positive cash flow because they know that's where the money to repay their loans will come from.

Figure 15.1

Small Business Loans by Size of Loan

Source: Small Business and Micro Business Lending in the United States 2002, Small Business Administration Office of Advocacy (Washington, D.C.), December 2003, p. 4, www.sba.gov/advo/stats/lending/2002/sbl_study.pdf.

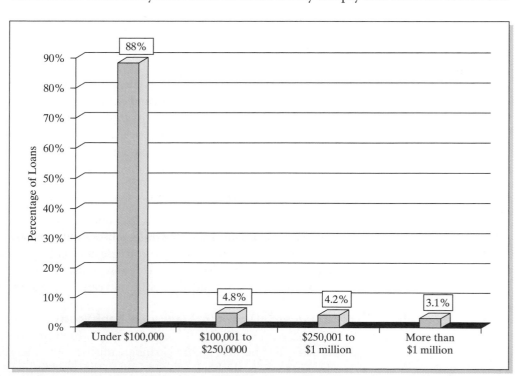

"Beg."

The first question in most bankers' minds when reviewing an entrepreneur's business plan is "Can this business generate sufficient cash to repay the loan?" Even though they rely on collateral to secure their loans, the last thing banks want is for a borrower to default, forcing them to sell the collateral (often at "fire sale" prices) and use the proceeds to pay off the loan. *That's* why bankers stress cash flow when analyzing a loan request, especially for a business start-up. "Cash is more important than your mother," jokes one experienced borrower.[6]

For any loan they make to small businesses, banks, as well as many other lenders, also require that entrepreneurs sign a personal guarantee. By making a personal loan guarantee, an entrepreneur is pledging that he or she will be personally liable for repaying the loan in the event that the business itself cannot repay the loan. Recall from Chapter 3 that in the eyes of the law a sole proprietor or a general partner and the business are one and the same; therefore, for them, personal loan guarantees are redundant. However, because the owners of S corporations, corporations, and LLCs are separate from their businesses, they are not automatically responsible for the company's debts. Once the owners of these businesses sign a personal loan guarantee, however, they become liable for their companies' loans. (It is as if these individuals have "cosigned" the loan with the business.)

Short-Term Loans

Short-term loans, extended for less than one year, are the most common type of commercial loan banks make to small companies. These funds typically are used to replenish the working capital account to finance the purchase of inventory, boost output, finance credit sales to customers, or take advantage of cash discounts. As a result, an owner repays the loan after converting inventory and receivables into cash. There are several types of short-term loans.

Commercial Loans (or Traditional Bank Loans). The basic short-term loan is the commercial bank's specialty. It is usually repaid as a lump sum within three to six months and is unsecured because secured loans are much more expensive to administer and maintain. In other words, the bank grants a loan to the small business owner without requiring him or her to pledge any specific collateral to support the loan in case of default. The owner is expected to repay the total amount of the loan at maturity. Sometimes the interest due on the loan is prepaid—deducted from the total amount borrowed. Until a small business is able to prove its financial strength and liquidity (cash flow) to the bank's satisfaction, it will probably not qualify for this kind of commercial loan.

Lines of Credit. One of the most common requests entrepreneurs make of banks is to establish a **line of credit,** a short-term loan with a preset limit that provides much needed cash flow for day-to-day operations. With an approved line of credit, business owners can borrow up to the predetermined ceiling at any time during the year quickly and conveniently by writing themselves a loan. Banks usually limit the open line of credit to 40 to 50 percent of the company's present working capital, although they will lend more for highly seasonal businesses. It is usually extended for one year (or more) and is secured by collateral, although some banks offer unsecured lines of credit to small companies with solid financial track records. A business typically pays a small handling fee (1 to 2 percent of the maximum amount of credit) plus interest on the amount borrowed—usually prime plus three points or more. One study of small businesses with lines of credit found that 76 percent used them; the remaining 24 percent have established their lines as a safety net but had not activated them.[7]

Company Example	→

Rich McElaney, CEO of Micromarketing, a company that helps retailers prepare targeted direct-mail campaigns, recently landed his company's first bank line of credit to finance its rapid growth and to diversify its customer base. Because of Micromarketing's track record of success and its solid cash flow, McElaney had no trouble securing the $3 million line of credit.[8]

Table 15.1 shows one method for determining how large a line of credit a small company should seek.

Table 15.1

How Large Should Your Line of Credit Be?

Determining how large a small company's line of credit should be is an important step for a growing business. As a company's sales grow, so will its inventory and accounts receivable balances, both of which tie up valuable cash. To avoid experiencing a cash crisis, many growing companies rely on a line of credit. How large should that line of credit be? The following formula will help you answer that question:

Average collection period ratio + Average inventory turnover ratio − Average payable period ratio = Cash flow cycle

Cash flow cycle × Average daily sales − Forecasted annual profit = Line of credit requirement

Example:

Suppose that Laramie Corporation has an average collection period ratio of 49 days and an average inventory turnover ratio of 53 days. The company's average payable period is 39 days, its annual sales are $5,800,000, and its net profit margin is 6.5 percent. What size line of credit should Laramie seek?

Average collection period ratio	49 days
Plus average inventory turnover ratio	53 days
Total	102 days
Minus average payable period ratio	<u>39 days</u>
Cash flow cycle	63 days
Annual sales	$5,800,000
Average daily sales (Annual sales ÷ 365 days)	$15,890
Cash flow cycle	63 days
Times average daily sales	<u>$15,890</u>
Equals	$1,001,096
Minus forecasted profit (annual sales × net profit margin)	<u>$377,000</u>
Equals line of credit requirement	$624,096

Laramie Corporation should seek a line of credit of $624,000.

Source: Adapted from George M. Dawson, "It Figures," *Entrepreneur Start-Ups*, December 2000, p. 27.

Floor Planning. Floor planning is a form of financing frequently employed by retailers of big-ticket items that are easily distinguishable from one another (usually by serial number), such as automobiles, boats, and major appliances. For example, a commercial bank finances Auto City's purchase of its inventory of automobiles and maintains a security interest in each car in the order by holding its title as collateral. Auto City pays interest on the loan monthly and repays the principal as the cars are sold. The longer a floor-planned item sits in inventory, the more it costs the business owner in interest expense. Banks and other floor planners often discourage retailers from using their money without authorization by performing spot checks to verify prompt repayment of the principal as items are sold.

Intermediate and Long-Term Loans

Banks primarily are lenders of short-term capital to small businesses, although they will make certain intermediate and long-term loans. Intermediate and long-term loans are extended for one year or longer and are normally used to increase fixed- and growth-capital balances. Commercial banks grant these loans for starting a business, constructing a plant, purchasing real estate and equipment, and other long-term investments. Loan repayments are normally made monthly or quarterly.

Term Loans. Another common type of loan banks make to small businesses is a **term loan**. Typically unsecured, banks grant these loans to businesses whose past operating history suggests a high probability of repayment. Some banks make only secured term loans, however. Term loans impose restrictions (called **covenants**) on the business decisions an entrepreneur makes concerning the company's operations. For instance, a term loan may set limits on owners' salaries, prohibit further borrowing without the bank's approval, or require that the company submit financial reports and analyses on a particular schedule. Other term loans require a business to maintain certain financial ratios pertaining to debt and working capital. An entrepreneur must understand all of the terms attached to a loan before accepting it.

Installment Loans. These loans are made to small firms for purchasing equipment, facilities, real estate, and other fixed assets. When financing equipment, a bank usually lends the small business from 60 to 80 percent of the equipment's value in return for a security interest in the equipment. The loan's amortization schedule typically coincides with the length of the equipment's usable life. When financing real estate (commercial mortgages), banks typically will lend up to 75 to 80 percent of the property's value and will allow a lengthier repayment schedule of 10 to 30 years.

Discounted Installment Contracts. Banks will also extend loans to small businesses when the owner pledges installment contracts as collateral. The process operates in the same manner as discounting accounts receivable (discussed later). For example, Acme Equipment Company sells several pieces of heavy equipment to General Contractors Inc. on an installment basis. To obtain a loan, Acme pledges the installment contract as collateral and receives a percentage of the contract's value from the bank. As Acme receives installment payments from General Contractors, it transfers the proceeds to the bank to satisfy the loan. If the installment contract is with an established, reliable business, the bank may lend the small company 100 percent of the contract's value.

Character Loans. Banking regulatory changes intended to create jobs by increasing the credit available to small- and medium-sized companies now allow banks to make **character loans.** Rather than requiring entrepreneurs to prove their creditworthiness with financial statements, evaluations, appraisals, and tax returns, banks making character loans base their lending decisions on the borrower's reputation and reliability (i.e., "character"). Two entrepreneurs who cofounded a river touring business received a character loan from a small local bank. Because of their solid reputations in the community and their overall business experience, they were able to borrow $20,000 to purchase canoes, supplies, and safety equipment and to hire guides without even pledging any collateral. "We simply signed our names on the loan agreement and got the money to launch the company," says one of the partners.

The accompanying "Gaining a Competitive Edge" feature describes how small business owners can maintain positive relationships with their bankers.

✦ GAINING *a* COMPETITIVE EDGE ✦

Maintaining a Positive Relationship with Your Banker

Too often, entrepreneurs communicate with their bankers only when they find themselves in a tight spot and needing money. Unfortunately, that's not the best way to manage a working relationship with a bank. "Businesspeople have a responsibility to train their bankers in their businesses," says one lending adviser. "A good banker will stay close to the business, and a good business will stay close to the banker." A good banking relationship has the power to influence in a significant way the success of a small business.

How can business owners develop and maintain a positive relationship with their bankers? The first step is picking the right bank and the right banker. Some banks are not terribly enthusiastic about making small business loans, and others target small businesses as their primary customers. It's a good idea to visit several banks—both small community banks and large national banks—and talk with a commercial loan officer about your banking needs and the bank's products and services. After finding the right banker, an entrepreneur must focus on maintaining effective *communication.* The best strategy is to keep bankers informed—*of both good news and bad.*

Tim Chen, owner of Keys Fitness Products, knows that's the secret to keeping bankers in his company's corner. He is always finding ways to show his bank that his company has proper financial controls in place. The former financial analyst makes it a point to send his bankers regular financial reports. He calls them twice each month to discuss "our supply sources, our pricing strategy, our marketing channels. We want them to be confident about our long-term growth prospects as well as our short-term results," says Chen. That means he also lets them know when problems arise in his wholesale exercise equipment business.

Chen's approach has impressed his bankers so much that they have raised his firm's line of credit from $50,000 to $4 million! What else can entrepreneurs do to manage their banking relationships?

Understand the factors that influence a banker's decision to lend money. Bankers *want* to lend money to businesses; that's how they generate a profit. However, they want to lend money to businesses they believe offer a very high probability of repaying their loans on time. Bankers look for companies that are good credit risks and have clear plans for success.

Invite the banker to visit your company. An on-site visit gives the banker the chance to see exactly what a company does and how it does it. It's also a great opportunity to show the bank where and how its money is put to use.

Make a good impression. A company's physical appearance can go a long way toward making either a positive (or a negative) impression on a banker. Lenders appreciate clean, safe, orderly work environments and view sloppily maintained facilities (such as spills, leaks, and unnecessary clutter) as negatives.

Send customer mailings to the banker as well. "Besides the numbers, we try to give our bankers a sense of our vision for the business," says Mitchell Goldstone, president of Thirty-Minute Photos Etc. Goldstone sends customer mailings to his bankers "so they know we're thinking about opportunities to generate money."

Send the banker samples of new products. "I try to make my banker feel as if he's a partner," says Drew Santin, president of a product-development company. "Whenever we get a new machine, I go out of my way to show the banker what it does."

Show off your employees. Bankers know that one of the most important components of building a successful company is a dedicated team of capable employees. Giving bankers the opportunity to visit with employees and ask them questions while touring a company can help alleviate fears that they are pumping their money into a high-risk "one-person show."

Know your company's assets. Almost always interested in collateral, bankers will want to judge the quality of your company's assets—property, equipment, inventory, accounts receivable, and others. Be sure to point them out. "As you walk the lender through your business," says one experienced banker, "it's always a good idea to identify assets the banker might not think of."

Be prepared to personally guarantee any loans the bank makes to your business. Even though many business owners choose the corporate form of ownership for its limited liability benefits, some are surprised when a banker asks them to make personal guarantees on business loans. It's a common practice, especially on small business loans.

Keep your business plan up-to-date and make sure your banker gets a copy of it. Bankers lend money to companies that can demonstrate that they will use the money wisely and productively. They also want to make sure that the company offers a high probability of repayment. The best way to provide bankers with that assurance is with a solid business plan.

Know how much money you need and how you will repay it. When a banker asks "How much money do you need?" the correct answer is not "How much can I get?"

1. What advantages do entrepreneurs gain by communicating openly with their bankers?
2. Why do so few entrepreneurs follow Tim Chen's example when dealing with their bankers?
3. What are the consequences of an entrepreneur failing to communicate effectively with a banker?

Sources: Adapted from Keith Lowe, "Keep Your Banker Informed," *Entrepreneur,* April 1, 2002, www.entrepreneur.com/article/0,4621, 298380,00.html; David Worrell, "Attacking a Loan," *Entrepreneur,* July 2002, www.entrepreneur.com/article/0,4621,300734,00.html; Maggie Overfelt, "How to Raise Cash During Crunch Time," *FSB,* March 2001, pp. 35–36; Jenny McCune, "Getting Banks to Say 'Yes,'" Bankrate.com, March 19, 2001, www.bankrate.com /brm/news/biz/Capital_borrowing/200010319a.asp; Joan Pryde, "Lending a Hand with Financing," *Nation's Business,* January 1998, pp. 53–59; Joseph W. May, "Be Frank with Your Bank," *Profit,* November/December 1996, pp. 54–55; "They'll Up Your Credit If. . . ," *Inc.,* April 1994, p. 99; Jane Easter Bahls, "Borrower Beware," *Entrepreneur,* April 1994, p. 97; Jacquelyn Lynn, "You Can Bank on It," *Business Start-Ups,* August 1996, pp. 56–61; Stephanie Barlow, "Buddy System," *Entrepreneur,* March 1997, pp. 121–125; Carlye Adler, "Secrets from the Vault," *FSB,* June 2001, p. 33.

Nonbank Sources of Debt Capital

2. Explain the types of financing available from nonbank sources of credit.

Although they are usually the first stop for entrepreneurs in search of debt capital, banks are not the only lending game in town. We now turn our attention to other sources of debt capital that entrepreneurs can tap to feed their cash-hungry companies.

Asset-Based Lenders

Asset-based lenders, which are usually smaller commercial banks, commercial finance companies, or specialty lenders, allow small businesses to borrow money by pledging otherwise idle assets such as accounts receivable, inventory, or purchase orders as collateral. This form of financing works especially well for manufacturers, wholesalers, distributors, and other companies with significant stocks of inventory, accounts receivable, equipment, real estate, or other assets. Even unprofitable companies whose income statements could not convince loan officers to make traditional loans can get asset-based loans. These cash-poor but asset-rich companies can use normally unproductive assets—accounts receivable, inventory, equipment, and purchase orders—to finance rapid growth and the cash crises that often accompany it. Even large companies such as Levi Strauss, Goodyear, and RiteAid rely on asset-based loans.[9]

Although asset-based lenders consider a company's cash flow, they are much more interested in the quality of the assets pledged as collateral. The amount a small business can borrow through asset-based lending depends on the **advance rate,** the percentage of an asset's value that a lender will lend. For example, a company pledging $100,000 of accounts receivable might negotiate a 70 percent advance rate and qualify for a $70,000 asset-based loan. Advance rates can vary dramatically depending on the quality of the assets pledged and the lender. Because inventory is an illiquid asset (i.e., hard to sell), the advance rate on inventory-based loans is quite low, usually 10 percent to 50 percent. Steven Melick, CEO of the Sycamore Group, an e-business software developer, gets an 85 percent advance rate on his company's loans from GE Capital by pledging high-quality accounts receivable as collateral.[10] The most common types of asset-based financing are discounting accounts receivable and inventory financing.

Discounting Accounts Receivable. The most common form of secured credit is accounts receivable financing. Under this arrangement, a small business pledges its accounts receivable as collateral; in return, the lender advances a loan against the value of approved accounts receivable. The amount of the loan tendered is not equal to the face value of the accounts receivable, however. Even though the lender screens the firm's accounts and accepts only qualified receivables, it makes an allowance for the risk involved because some will be written off as uncollectible. A small business usually can borrow an amount equal to 55 to 80 percent of its receivables, depending on their quality. Generally, lenders will not accept receivables that are past due.

Company Example → Many commercial finance companies engage in accounts receivable financing. *Kyle Jodice, founder of Milnucorp, a small distributor of products ranging from hula hoops to tank parts, uses accounts receivable financing from Action Capital, a commercial finance company in Atlanta, to get the cash he needs to purchase inventory. Action Capital advances money based on Milnucorp's accounts receivable. After Action Capital collects payment from Milnucorp's customers, typically within 40 to 60 days, the commercial finance company remits the payments to Jodice after subtracting the amount of the loan and the interest it charges.*[11]

Inventory Financing. Here, a small business loan is secured by a company's inventory of raw materials, work in process, and finished goods. If an owner defaults on the loan, the lender can claim the firm's inventory, sell it, and use the proceeds to satisfy the loan (assuming the bank's claim is superior to the claims of other creditors). Because inventory usually is not a highly liquid asset and its value can be difficult to determine, lenders are willing to lend only a portion of its worth, usually no more than 50 percent of the inventory's value. Most asset-based lenders avoid inventory-only deals; they prefer to make loans backed by inventory *and* more secure accounts receivable.

Company Example → *Jeffrey Martinez-Malo, president of Ocean World Fisheries USA, a company that imports shrimp and crab from Latin America to the United States, uses inventory financing from Gerber Trade Finance to avoid cash flow problems. Ocean World Fisheries' suppliers demand payment as soon as they ship an order of seafood. However, because the company's customers are scattered across the country, collecting its accounts takes time. Martinez-Malo now has a $600,000 line of credit secured by the company's inventory at 2 percent above the prime rate.*[12]

Asset-based financing is a powerful tool. A small business that could obtain a $1 million line of credit with a bank would be able to borrow as much as $3 million by using accounts receivable as collateral. It is also an efficient method of borrowing because a small business owner has the money he needs when he needs it. In other words, the business pays only for the capital it actually needs and uses.

However, asset-based loans are more expensive than traditional bank loans because of the cost of originating and maintaining them and the higher risk involved. To ensure the quality of the assets supporting the loans they make, lenders must monitor borrowers' assets, perhaps as often as weekly, making paperwork requirements on these loans intimidating, especially to first-time borrowers. Rates usually run from two to eight percentage points (or more) above the prime rate. Because of this rate differential, small business owners should not use asset-based loans over the long term; their goal should be to establish their credit through asset-based financing and then to move up to a line of credit. Figure 15.2 shows the upward trend in asset-based borrowing since 1980.

Figure 15.2

Asset-Based Loans

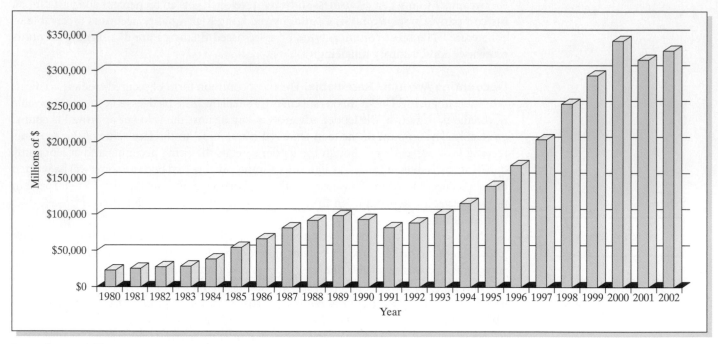

Source: Commercial Finance Association.

Trade Credit

Because of its ready availability, trade credit is an extremely important source of financing to most entrepreneurs. When banks refuse to lend money to a start-up business because they see it as a bad credit risk, an entrepreneur may be able to turn to trade credit for capital. Getting vendors to extend credit in the form of delayed payments (e.g., "net 30" credit terms) usually is much easier for small businesses than obtaining bank financing. Essentially, a company receiving trade credit from a supplier is getting a short-term, interest-free loan for the amount of the goods purchased.

It is no surprise that businesses receive three dollars of credit from suppliers for every two dollars they receive from banks as loans.[13] Vendors and suppliers usually are willing to finance a small business owner's purchase of goods from 30 to 90 days, interest free.

Company Example →
For instance, Gus Walboldt, owner of AMCAL, a fine-art publishing company, uses supplier financing as an integral part of his company's 20-year growth plan. Because calendars represent a large portion of AMCAL's sales, its business is highly seasonal, which creates significant cash flow problems. "We would spend half the year flush with cash [and the other half] cash poor," says Walboldt. Walboldt worked out a financing arrangement with the companies that print the calendars. AMCAL pays the printers' labor and material costs when the calendars are printed during the summer months and then covers their profit margins when its cash flow swells in the fall.[14] The key to maintaining trade credit as a source of funds is establishing a consistent and reliable payment history with every vendor.

Equipment Suppliers

Most equipment vendors offer to finance the purchase to encourage business owners to purchase equipment. This method of financing is similar to trade credit but with slightly different terms. Usually, equipment vendors offer reasonable credit terms with only a modest down payment with the balance financed over the life of the equipment (often several years). In some cases, the vendor will repurchase equipment for salvage value at the end of its useful life and offer the business owner another credit agreement on new equipment. Start-up companies often use trade credit from equipment suppliers to purchase equipment and fixtures such as counters, display cases, refrigeration units, machinery, and the like. It pays to scrutinize vendors' credit terms, however; they may be less attractive than those of other lenders.

Commercial Finance Companies

When denied a bank loan, small business owners often look to commercial finance companies for the same type of loan. Commercial finance companies are second only to banks in making loans to small businesses and, unlike their conservative counterparts, are willing to tolerate more risk in their loan portfolios.[15] For instance, Chris Lehnes, a top manager at CIT Small Business Lending, says that his company regularly makes loans to small businesses with debt to equity ratios of 10:1 (10 times as much debt as equity), a situation that would send most bankers scurrying back to their vaults. Of course, like banks, finance companies' primary consideration is collecting their loans, but finance companies tend to rely more on obtaining a security interest in some type of collateral, given the higher-risk loans that make up their portfolios. Because commercial finance companies depend on collateral to recover most of their losses, they do not always require a complete set of financial projections of future operations as most banks do. However, this does *not* mean that they neglect carefully evaluating a company's financial position, especially its cash balance, before making a loan. "We're looking at the projected cash flow—the ability of the business to repay us," says CIT's Lehnes. "We put a lot of weight on what the business has done in the past couple of years."[16]

Approximately 150 large commercial finance companies such as AT&T Small Business Lending, UPS Capital, GE Capital, CIT Small Business Lending, and others make a variety of loans to small companies, ranging from asset-based loans and business leases to construction and Small Business Administration loans. Dubbed "the Wal-Marts of finance," commercial finance companies usually offer many of the same credit options as commercial banks do, including intermediate and long-term loans for real estate and fixed assets as well as short-term loans and lines of credit. However, because their loans are subject to more risks, finance companies charge higher interest rates than commercial banks (usually at least prime plus 2 percent). Their most common methods of providing credit to small businesses are asset based–accounts receivable financing and inventory loans. Specific rates on these loans vary but can be as high as 20 to 30 percent (including fees), depending on the risk a particular business presents and the quality of the assets involved. Entrepreneurs whose companies bankers shun because of their short track records, less than perfect credit ratings, or fluctuating earnings often find the loans they need at commercial finance companies.

Company Example

The Atlanta Bread Company, a restaurant and bakery franchiser, recently borrowed $1.8 million from the finance arm of UPS, UPS Capital, to purchase new, more efficient processing equipment at its Atlanta commissary, which serves more than 160 franchised locations in 24 states. Company officials say that the financing from UPS Capital is essential to the Atlanta Bread Company's growth plans.[17]

Savings and Loan Associations

Savings and loan associations (S&Ls) specialize in loans for real property. In addition to their traditional role of providing mortgages for personal residences, savings and loan associations offer financing on commercial and industrial property. In the typical commercial or industrial loan, the S&L will lend up to 80 percent of the property's value with a repayment schedule of up to 30 years. Minimum loan amounts are typically $50,000, but most S&Ls hesitate to lend money for buildings specially designed for a particular customer's needs. S&Ls expect the mortgage to be repaid from the firm's future profits.

Stock Brokerage Houses

Stockbrokers are getting into the lending business, too, and many of them offer loans to their customers at lower interest rates than banks. These **margin loans** carry lower rates because the collateral supporting them—the stocks and bonds in the customer's portfolio—is of high quality and is highly liquid. Moreover, brokerage firms make it easy to borrow. Usually, brokers set up a line of credit for their customers when they open a brokerage account. To tap that line of credit, a customer simply writes a check or uses a debit card. Typically, there is no fixed repayment schedule for a margin loan; the debt can remain outstanding indefinitely, as long as the market value of the borrower's portfolio of collateral meets minimum requirements. Aspiring entrepreneurs can borrow up to 50 percent of the value of their stock portfolios, up to 70 percent of their bond portfolios, and up to 90 percent of the value of their government securities. For example, one woman borrowed $60,000 to buy equipment for her New York health club, and a St. Louis doctor borrowed $1 million against his brokerage account to help finance a medical clinic.[18]

There is risk involved in using stocks and bonds as collateral on a loan. Brokers typically require a 30 percent cushion on margin loans. If the value of the borrower's portfolio drops, the broker can make a **margin call**—that is, the broker can call the loan in and require the borrower to provide more cash and securities as collateral. Recent swings in the stock market have translated into margin calls for many entrepreneurs, requiring them to repay a significant portion of their loan balances within a matter of days—or hours. If an account lacks adequate collateral, the broker can sell off the customer's portfolio to pay off the loan.

Insurance Companies

For many small businesses, life insurance companies can be an important source of business capital. Insurance companies offer two basic types of loans: policy loans and mortgage loans. **Policy loans** are extended on the basis of the amount of money paid through premiums into the insurance policy; with a policy loan, a business owner is becoming his or her own bank, borrowing against the money accumulated in an insurance policy. It usually takes about two years for an insurance policy to accumulate enough cash surrender value to justify a loan against it. Once he or she accumulates cash value in a policy, an entrepreneur may borrow up to 95 percent of that value for any length of time. Interest is levied annually, but the entrepreneur determines the repayment rate, or repayment may be deferred indefinitely. However, the amount of insurance coverage is reduced by the amount of the loan. Policy loans typically offer very favorable interest rates, sometimes below the prime rate. Only insurance policies that build cash value—that is, combine a savings plan with insurance coverage—offer the option of borrowing. These include whole life (permanent insurance), variable life, universal life, and many corporate-owned life insurance policies. Term life insurance, which offers only pure insurance coverage, has no borrowing capacity.

Insurance companies make **mortgage loans** on a long-term basis on real property worth a minimum of $500,000. They are based primarily on the value of the real property being purchased. The insurance company will extend a loan of up to 75 or 80 percent of the real estate's value and will allow a lengthy repayment schedule over 25 or 30 years so that payments do not strain the firm's cash flows excessively. Many large real estate developments such as shopping malls, office buildings, and theme parks rely on mortgage loans from insurance companies.

Credit Unions

Credit unions, nonprofit financial cooperatives that promote saving and provide loans to their members, are best known for making consumer and car loans. However, many are also willing to lend money to their members to launch businesses, especially since many banks have restricted loans to higher-risk start-ups. Of the 10,000 federally and state-chartered credit unions operating in the United States, about 1,600 are actively making business loans, many of them in amounts smaller than most banks typically make. In fact, the average credit union loan is $88,000, but some credit unions have made business loans in the millions of dollars.[19] Credit unions have more than $7.5 billion in small business loans outstanding.[20]

Credit unions don't make loans to just anyone; in most cases, to qualify for a loan, an entrepreneur must be a member. Lending practices at credit unions are very much like those at banks, but they are subject to restraints that banks are not. For instance, credit unions are prohibited from making business loans that total more than 12.25 percent of their assets. Recent changes in legislation, however, exempt certain business loans from that limitation. In another move favoring entrepreneurs, the U.S. Small Business Administration recently opened its loan programs to credit unions, providing even more avenues for entrepreneurs seeking financing.

Increasingly, entrepreneurs are turning to credit unions to finance their businesses' capital needs. *Curcio Printing, a family-owned commercial printer in Vestal, New York, needed to borrow $1 million to purchase a new printing press, but the Curcios sensed that their bankers were balking at making the loan, despite the company's stellar credit rating. The family applied for the loan at the Visions Credit Union in nearby Endicott, New York, and was elated not only to get the loan approved but also to receive better loan terms than they could have gotten from the bank. Plus, the credit union approved their application much faster than their bank had on their previous loans. "Not only did we get the best rate, [but] we got service, like banking used to be," says Gina Curcio, whose parents founded the company in 1984.[21]*

Company Example

Bonds

Bonds, which are corporate IOUs, have always been a popular source of debt financing for large companies, but few small business owners realize that they can also tap this valuable source of capital. Although the smallest businesses are not viable candidates for issuing bonds, a growing number of small companies are finding the funding they need through bonds when banks and other lenders say no. Because of the costs involved, issuing bonds usually is best suited for companies generating annual sales between $5 million and $30 million and have capital requirements between $1.5 million and $10 million. Although they can help small companies raise much needed capital, bonds have certain disadvantages. The issuing company must follow the same regulations that govern businesses selling stock to public investors. Even if the bond issue is private, the company must register the offering and file periodic reports with the SEC.

Convertible bonds, bonds that give the buyer the option of converting the debt to equity by purchasing the company's stock at a fixed price in the future, have become more popular for small companies. In exchange for offering the option to convert the bond into stock, the small company issuing the convertible bonds gets the benefit of paying a lower interest rate on the bond than on a traditional bond.

Small manufacturers needing money for fixed assets with long repayment schedules have access to an attractive, relatively inexpensive source of funds in **industrial development bonds (IDBs).** A company wanting to issue IDBs must get authorization from the appropriate municipality and the state before proceeding. Typically, the amount of money small companies issuing IDBs seek to raise is at least $1 million, but some small manufacturers have raised as little as $500,000 using a mini-bond program created in 1999 that offers a simple application process and short closing times. Companies raising money through mini-bonds typically work with a local or state economic development agency to win approval for a bond issue. Each state has its own criteria, such as job creation, expansion of the tax base, and others, that companies must meet to be eligible to issue mini-bonds. *Ned Golterman used mini-bonds to finance the expansion of his building materials company in St. Louis, Missouri. Working with the St. Louis County Economic Authority, Golterman was able to close the deal in about the same time it would have taken to close a bank loan, and he was able to borrow money at 2 percent below the bank's best interest rate! "My mini-bond [issue] gave me the money I needed for expansion, [and] it allowed me to pay over a much longer period than any commercial bank would allow," says Golterman.*[22]

> Company Example

To open IDBs up to even smaller companies, some states pool the industrial bonds of several small companies too small to make an issue alone. By joining together to issue composite industrial bonds, companies can reduce their issuing fees and attract a greater number of investors. The issuing companies typically pay lower interest rates than they would on conventional bank loans, often below the prime interest rate.

Private Placements

In the previous chapter, we saw how companies can raise capital by making private placements of their stock (equity). Private placements are also available for debt instruments. A private placement involves selling debt to one or a small number of investors, usually insurance companies or pension funds. Private placement debt is a hybrid between a conventional loan and a bond. At its heart, it is a bond, but its terms are tailored to the borrower's individual needs, as a loan would be.

Privately placed securities offer several advantages over standard bank loans. First, they usually carry fixed interest rates, rather than the variable rates banks often charge. Second, the maturity of private placements is longer than most bank loans: 15 years rather than five. Private placements do not require hiring expensive investment bankers. Finally, because private investors can afford to take greater risks than banks, they are willing to finance deals for fledgling small companies. *For example, Longview Fibre, a timber company and paper-products maker, has tapped the private placement market repeatedly over the years, borrowing to buy everything from timberland to pulp machines. The company cites the speed and ease of getting the financing it needs as major advantages.*[23]

> Company Example

Small Business Investment Companies (SBICs)

The Small Business Investment Company program was started after Russia's successful launch of the first space satellite, Sputnik, in 1958. Its goal was to accelerate the United States' position in the space race by funding high-technology start-ups. Created by the 1958 Small Business Investment Act, **small business investment companies (SBICs)** are privately owned financial institutions that are licensed and regulated by the SBA. The 400-plus SBICs operating across the United States use a combination of private capital and federally guaranteed debt to provide long-term venture capital to small businesses. In other words, SBICs operate like any other venture capital fund, but, unlike traditional venture capital funds, they use private capital and borrowed government funds to provide both debt and equity financing to small businesses. There are two types of SBICs: regular SBICs and Specialized SBICs (SSBICs). More than 100 SSBICs provide credit and capital to small businesses that are at least 51 percent owned by minorities and socially or economically disadvantaged people. Since their inception in 1969, SSBICs have helped finance more than 25,000 minority-owned companies with investments totaling $2.34 billion.

Since 1960, SBICs have provided more than $36.5 billion in long-term debt and equity financing to more than 109,000 small businesses, adding many thousands of jobs to the U.S. economy.[24] Most SBICs prefer later-round financing and leveraged buyouts (LBOs) over funding raw start-ups. Because of changes in their financial structure made a few years ago, however, SBICs now are better equipped to invest in start-up companies. In fact, 43 percent of SBIC investments go to companies that are no more than three years old.[25] Funding from SBICs helped launch companies such as Apple Computer, FedEx, America Online, Sun Microsystems, and Outback Steakhouse.

Both SBICs and SSBICs must be capitalized privately with a minimum of $5 million to $10 million, at which point they qualify for up to four dollars in long-term SBA loans for every dollar of private capital invested in small businesses. As a general rule, both SBICs and SSBICs may provide financial assistance only to small businesses with a net worth of less than $18 million and average after-tax earnings of $6 million during their past two years. However, employment and total annual sales standards vary from industry to industry. SBICs are limited to a maximum investment or loan amount of 20 percent of their private capital to a single client, but SSBICs may lend or invest up to 30 percent of their private capital in a single small business.

Operating as government-backed venture capitalists, SBICs provide both debt and equity financing to small businesses. Currently, the average amount of SBIC financing in a company is $556,100.[26] Because of SBA regulations affecting the financing arrangements an SBIC can offer, many SBICs extend their investments as loans with an option to convert the debt instrument into an equity interest later. Most SBIC loans are between $100,000 and $5 million, and the loan term is longer than most banks allow. When they make equity investments, SBICs are prohibited from obtaining a controlling interest in the companies in which they invest (no more than 49 percent ownership). The most common forms of SBIC financing (in order of their frequency) are straight debt instruments (46.0%), debt instruments combined with equity investments (28.2%), and equity-only investments (25.8%).[27]

| Company Example | → |

After spending 40 hours on a basic market research project, Mahendra Vora and Sundar Kadayam recognized the need for more advanced tools for searching the Internet and Web-based databases of public information. The pair decided to launch Intelliseek, a company that would provide software to capture, track, and analyze information companies need for market research, strategic planning, and product development. Vora had already launched and sold three successful businesses, which enabled him to invest a few million dollars of his own money in the start-up, which was enough to get Intelliseek through two product launches. The company (whose slogan is "Make Money, Have Fun") grew quickly, reaching $10 million in annual sales within six years, and needed a capital infusion to sustain its growth rate. Vora turned to River Cities Capital Fund, a Cincinnati-based SBIC, which provided much needed capital to the promising young company. The commitment from River Cities Capital opened the door to $6 million in other financing deals from traditional venture capital funds. "Once you get a VC (venture capitalist) like River Cities," says Vora, "it is much easier to get access to bigger VCs."[28]

Small Business Lending Companies (SBLCs)

Small Business Lending Companies (SBLCs) make only intermediate and long-term SBA-guaranteed loans. They specialize in loans that many banks would not consider and operate on a nationwide basis. For instance, most SBLC loans have terms extending for

Mahendra Vora and Sundar Kadayam used SBIC financing to launch their software company, Intelliseek (slogan: "Make Money, Have Fun"). The investment from the River Cities Capital Fund opened the door to financing from traditional venture capital firms.

at least 10 years. The maximum interest rate for loans of seven years or longer is 2.75 percent above the prime rate; for shorter-term loans, the ceiling is 2.25 percent above prime. Another feature of SBLC loans is the expertise the SBLC offers borrowing companies in critical areas.

SBLCs also screen potential investors carefully, and most of them specialize in particular industries. The result is a low loan default rate of roughly 4 percent. Corporations own most of the nation's SBLCs, giving them a solid capital base.

IN THE FOOTSTEPS OF AN ENTREPRENEUR...

The Dangers of Debt

During their college breaks, brothers Josh and Seth Frey, both in their early twenties, launched a business selling ice cream and desserts from a converted truck they had bought from the U.S. Postal Service. Seth graduated and went to work as an account manager for a commercial security company. Josh, who was still in college, came up with the idea for a business marketing "care packages" to parents of college students. He purchased a mailing list of 8,000 names from the University of Wisconsin at Madison, and started selling his care packages, which he named "Granny's Goodies" in honor of his 89-year-old grandmother, to parents of college students for $10 each. He earned $2,500 during his senior year, and after graduation, set up shop in his parents' basement to operate the business full-time and convinced his brother to return to the business as well. "I left a $30,000-a-year job to make zero," recalls Seth. Within two years, Granny's Goodies was generating sales of $300,000, but sales were highly seasonal, peaking at the beginning of the school year and at the end of each semester around exams. In the summer, sales were sparse.

The Freys decided to target new markets to boost sales and smooth out the seasonal nature of their business. Their big break came when the *Washington Times* did a story about their business, and companies began ordering care packages for customers, employees, and others. The Freys received an SBA-guaranteed loan from a bank and moved their operation into a renovated warehouse. Within a few years, sales had climbed to $1.5 million as the brothers settled in to the mail-order business and began to focus on selling to recruiting, legal, accounting, real estate, and mortgage companies. As sales increased, so did the level of the company's borrowing. Total debt reached

$250,000, and the Frey brothers were making personal guarantees on every loan. "It got to the point where we were trying to manage the business and the debt, and we lost focus on sales," says Seth.

Granny's Goodies took on debt without the Freys knowing exactly how they would use the money and what type of return it would generate. As a result, Granny's Goodies grew fast, but its debt load grew faster. "We didn't have the systems and processes in place to maintain control," admits Seth, "which led to a litany of issues between my brother and me. Unfortunately, the debt brought the business down. We weren't using it for the right purposes."

Despite an avalanche of problems because of the debt, Granny's Goodies managed to survive, but the brothers' partnership did not. Seth and Josh decided to split the customer lists, the assets, and the debt and go their separate ways. Josh continues to operate Granny's Goodies, and Seth now runs Big Frey Promotional Products in Chicago. Reflecting on his experience, Seth says, "Debt is challenging. You have to be smart about using the money you receive and have a plan for using it or you'll just dig yourself into a hole."

1. Under what circumstances should a small business consider borrowing money?
2. Assume the role of financial consultant to the Freys. What should they have done differently as Granny's Goodies grew? What role should debt and equity financing have played in financing the growth of their business? Explain your reasoning.
3. What other sources of funding should the Freys have considered as their business grew?

Sources: Adapted from Geoff Williams, "Staying Power," *Entrepreneur*, June 1998, www.entrepreneur.com/article/0,4621,228755,00.html; David Worrell, "Debt End Ahead," *Entrepreneur*, July 2004, pp. 53–54; "About Us," Granny's Goodies, www.grannysgoodies.com.

Federally Sponsored Programs

3. Identify the sources of government financial assistance and the loan programs these agencies offer.

Federally sponsored lending programs have suffered from budget reductions in the past several years. Current trends suggest that the federal government is reducing its involvement in the lending business, but many programs are still quite active and some are actually growing.

Economic Development Administration (EDA)

The Economic Development Administration, a branch of the Commerce Department, offers loan guarantees to create new businesses and to expand existing businesses in areas with below-average income and high unemployment. Focusing on economically distressed communities, the EDA finances long-term investment projects needed to stimulate economic growth and to create jobs by making loan guarantees. The EDA guarantees loans up to 80 percent of business loans between $750,000 and $10 million. Entrepreneurs apply for loans through private lenders, for whom an EDA loan guarantee significantly reduces the risk of lending. Start-up companies must supply 15 percent of the guaranteed amount in the form of equity, and established businesses must make equity investments of at least 15 percent of the guaranteed amount. Small businesses can use the loan proceeds in a variety of ways, including supplementing working capital, purchasing equipment, buying land, and renovating buildings.

EDA business loans are designed to help replenish economically distressed areas by creating or expanding small businesses that provide employment opportunities in local communities. To qualify for a loan the business must be located in a disadvantaged area, and its presence must directly benefit local residents. Some communities experiencing high unemployment or suffering from the effects of devastating natural disasters have received EDA Revolving Loan Fund (RLF) grants to create loan pools for local small businesses. Since 1972, the EDA has funded more than 600 Revolving Loan Funds that have, in turn, made loans totaling $700 million to more than 15,000 private businesses. The typical RLF loan is $56,600, and most loans are for business expansion.[29]

Department of Housing and Urban Development (HUD)

HUD sponsors several loan programs to assist qualified entrepreneurs in raising needed capital. The Community Development Block Grants (CDBGs) are extended to cities and towns that, in turn, lend or grant money to entrepreneurs to start small businesses that will strengthen the local economy. Grants are aimed at cities and towns in need of revitalization and economic stimulation. Some grants are used to construct buildings and plants to be leased to entrepreneurs, sometimes with an option to buy. Others are earmarked for revitalizing a crime-ridden area or making start-up loans to entrepreneurs or expansion loans to existing business owners. No ceilings or geographic limitations are placed on CDBG loans and grants, but projects must benefit low- and moderate-income families.

The EDA also makes loan guarantees through its Section 108 provision of the Community Block Development Grant program. The agency has funded more than 1,200 projects since its inception in 1978. These loan guarantees allow a community to transform a portion of CDBG funds into federally guaranteed loans large enough to pursue economic revitalization projects that can lead to the renewal of entire towns. For instance, the city of Greenville, South Carolina, used Section 108 funds to renovate a public market designed to serve as an anchor in its West End section that was targeted for revitalization. Since its construction, 16 small businesses have located in the market, creating new jobs and stimulating economic growth in the area.[30]

U.S. Department of Agriculture's Rural Business-Cooperative Service

The U.S. Department of Agriculture provides financial assistance to certain small businesses through the Rural Business-Cooperative Service (RBS). The RBS program is open to all types of businesses (not just farms) and is designed to create nonfarm employment opportunities in rural areas—those with populations below 50,000 and not adjacent to a city where densities exceed 100 people per square mile. Entrepreneurs in many small towns, especially those with populations below 25,000, are eligible to apply for loans

Company Example

through the RBS program, which makes $900 million in loan guarantees each year. *Frederick James and Sanco Rembert received financing from the RBS to expand and improve their church furnishings business, Church Manufacturing Corporation. The company, which builds and installs pews, pulpits, and other furnishings in churches across the country, used the funding to earn ISO 9000 certification and to upgrade its equipment and facilities.*[31]

The RBS does make a limited number of direct loans to small businesses, but the majority of its activity is in loan guarantees. Through its Business and Industry Guaranteed Loan Program, the RBS will guarantee as much as 80 percent of loans up to $25 million (although actual guarantee amounts are almost always far less) for qualified applicants. Entrepreneurs apply for loans through private lenders, who view applicants with loan guarantees much more favorably than those without such guarantees. The RBS guarantee reduces the lender's risk dramatically because the guarantee means that the government agency would pay off the loan balance (up to the ceiling) if the entrepreneur defaults on the loan.

To make a loan guarantee, the RBS requires much of the same documentation as most banks and most other loan guarantee programs. Because of its emphasis on developing employment in rural areas, the RBS requires an environmental-impact statement describing the jobs created and the effect the business has on the area. The Rural Business-Cooperative Service also makes grants available through several other programs to businesses and communities for the purpose of encouraging small business development and growth.

Small Business Innovation Research (SBIR) Program

Started as a pilot program by the National Science Foundation in the 1970s, the SBIR program has expanded to 10 federal agencies, ranging from NASA and the Department of Defense to the Department of Agriculture and the Department of Energy, and has an annual budget of about $1 billion. These agencies award cash grants or long-term contracts to small companies wanting to initiate or to expand their research and development (R&D) efforts. About 43 percent of the small companies that participate in the SBIR program have fewer than 10 employees. SBIR grants give innovative small companies the opportunity to attract early-stage capital investments *without* having to give up significant equity stakes or taking on burdensome levels of debt.

The SBIR process includes three phases. Phase I (project feasibility) grants, which determine the feasibility and commercial potential of a technology or product, last for up to six months and have a ceiling of $100,000. Phase II (prototype development) grants, designed to develop the concept into a specific technology or product, run for up to 24 months with a ceiling of $750,000. Approximately 40 percent of all Phase II applicants receive funding. Phase III is the commercialization phase, in which the company pursues commercial applications of the research and development conducted in phases I and II and must use private or non-SBIR federal funding to bring a product to market. Competition for SBIR funding is intense; only 12 percent of the small companies that apply receive funding. So far, more than 36,000 SBIR awards totaling in excess of $10 billion have gone to small companies that traditionally have had difficulty competing with big corporations for federal R&D dollars. The government's dollars have been well invested. About one in four small businesses receiving SBIR awards have achieved commercial success for their products.[32]

Company Example

When Rob Reis's 2-year-old son wandered off during a visit to a local grocery store, the entrepreneur came up with the idea for a radio frequency identification (RFID) tag designed to track lost children. He and friend Vic Verma launched Savi Technology to manufacture and market the device, which they named Tagalong. While they worked on refining the device, Reis and Verma saw an opportunity for a similar device designed for the military. When attached to cargo containers and crates, the Savitag, a radio transceiver with an embedded microcomputer, *enables military planners to track the shipment of materials anywhere in the world on a real-time basis. (Before Savitag, tracking containers presented a huge problem for the military; in Desert Storm, the contents of more than half of the 40,000 containers shipped to the Middle East went unused because no one knew where they were or what was in them.) To develop the technology for Savitag, Savi Technology applied for and received an SBIR grant from the Defense Advanced Research Projects Agency (DARPA). The company also won Phase II and Phase III SBIR awards totaling $2.5 million. Savi Technology, which holds 33 patents in RFID technology, used the Phase III grant and private venture capital funding to market Savitag technology for commercial uses in the trucking, shipping, and rail industries.*[33]

The Small Business Technology Transfer Program

The Small Business Technology Transfer (STTR) program complements the Small Business Innovation Research (SBIR) program. Whereas the SBIR focuses on commercially promising ideas that originate in small businesses, the STTR uses companies to exploit the vast reservoir of commercially promising ideas that originate in universities, federally funded R&D centers, and nonprofit research institutions. Researchers at these institutions can join forces with small businesses and can spin off commercially promising ideas while remaining employed at their research institutions. Five federal agencies award grants in two of three phases (up to $100,000 in Phase I and up to $750,000 in Phase II) to these research partnerships. The STTR's annual budget is approximately $1.5 billion.

Small Business Administration (SBA)

4. Describe the various loan programs available from the Small Business Administration.

The Small Business Administration (SBA) has several programs designed to help finance both start-up and existing small companies that cannot qualify for traditional loans because of their thin asset base and their high risk of failure. In its 50-plus years of operation, the SBA has helped 20 million companies through a multitude of programs get the financing they need for start-up or for growth. The SBA's $45 billion loan portfolio makes it the largest single financial backer of small businesses in the nation.[34] To be eligible for SBA funds, a business must be within the SBA's criteria for defining a small business. Also, some types of businesses, such as those engaged in gambling, pyramid sales schemes, or real estate investment, among others, are ineligible for SBA loans.

The loan application process can take from between three days to many months, depending on how well prepared the entrepreneur is and which bank is involved. To speed up processing times, the SBA has established a Certified Lender Program (CLP) and a Preferred Lender Program (PLP). About 850 lenders across the United States are certified lenders, and another 500 qualify as preferred lenders.[35] Both programs are designed to encourage banks and other lenders to become frequent SBA lenders. When a lender makes enough good loans to qualify as a **certified lender**, the SBA promises a fast turnaround time for the loan decision—typically three to ten business days. When a lender becomes a **preferred lender**, it makes the final lending decision itself, subject to SBA review. In essence, the SBA delegates the application process, the lending decision, and other details to the preferred lender. The SBA guarantees up to 75 percent of PLP loans in case the borrower fails and defaults on the loan. The minimum PLP loan guarantee is $100,000, whereas the maximum is $500,000. Using certified or preferred lenders can reduce the processing time for an SBA loan considerably.

To further reduce the paperwork requirements involved in its loans, the SBA recently instituted the **Low Doc** (for "low documentation") **Loan Program**, which allows small businesses to use a simple one-page application for all loan applications. Before the

Low Doc Program, a typical SBA loan application required an entrepreneur to complete at least 10 forms, and the SBA often took 45 to 90 days to make a decision about an application. Under the Low Doc Program, response time is just 36 hours.

To qualify for a Low Doc loan, a company must have average sales below $5 million during the previous three years and employ fewer than 100 people. The maximum loan amount is $150,000, and businesses can use Low Doc loans for working capital, machinery, equipment, and real estate. The SBA guarantees a maximum of 85 percent of the loan amount. Borrowers must be willing to provide a personal guarantee for repayment of the loan principal. Interest rates are prime-plus-2.75 percent on loans of seven years or longer and prime-plus-2.25 percent on loans of less than seven years. The average Low Doc loan is $79,500.

Company Example

Richard Smith, owner of a white-water rafting business, needed money to expand his 20-year-old company and to buy new equipment. Smith, however, was hesitant to approach the SBA because he wanted to avoid "myriads of paperwork." At his banker's urging, Smith decided to try the Low Doc Program, and within days of submitting his application, he received a $100,000 loan.[36]

Another program designed to streamline the application process for SBA loan guarantees is the **SBA*Express* Program**, in which participating lenders use their own loan procedures and applications to make loans of up to $2 million to small businesses. Because the SBA guarantees up to 50 percent of the loan, banks are often more willing to make smaller loans to entrepreneurs who might otherwise have difficulty meeting lenders' standards. Lenders can charge up to 6.5 percent above the prime interest rate on SBA*Express* loans below $50,000 and up to 4.5 percent above prime on loans above $50,000. The average SBA*Express* loan is $44,440, and loan maturities on these loans typically are seven

Company Example

years but can go as long as 25 years.[37] *Mike Robillard, president of San Antonio Clippers in San Antonio, Texas, used an SBAExpress loan to add two locations to his Sports Clips hair salon franchise operation. Robillard needed growth capital quickly to secure the best locations, a key to success in his industry. "We had to start laying out money quickly to lock down those locations," he says.*[38]

SBA Loan Programs

7(a) Loan Guaranty Program. The SBA works with local lenders (both bank and nonbank) to offer a variety of loan programs all designed to help entrepreneurs who cannot get capital from traditional sources gain access to the financing they need to launch and grow their businesses. By far, the most popular SBA loan program is the **7(a) loan guaranty program** (see Figure 15.3), which makes loans up to $2 million to small businesses. Private lenders actually extend these loans to companies, but the SBA guarantees them (85 percent of loans up to $150,000; 75 percent of loans above $150,000 up to the loan guarantee ceiling of $1,500,000). In other words, the SBA does not actually lend any money; it merely acts as an insurer, guaranteeing the lender a certain repayment in case the borrower defaults on the loan. Because the SBA assumes most of the credit risk, lenders are more willing to consider riskier deals that they normally would refuse. In a typical year, the SBA guarantees loans to about 43,000 small businesses that would have difficulty getting loans

Company Example

without the help of the SBA guarantee. *In 1964, Fred Ruiz and his father, Louis, launched a frozen Mexican food company, and soon demand for their El Monterey® brand burritos, enchiladas, and tamales was growing rapidly. Then federal regulations required the young company to renovate its 2,200-square-foot plant or reduce its production drastically. Ruiz went to every bank in Tulare, California, but "they all turned me down," he recalls. A new bank that handled SBA loans suggested that Ruiz apply for an SBA 7(a) loan. Less than one week after presenting his business plan to the bank, Ruiz received approval for a $50,000 SBA loan, which the company used to meet federal regulations. Two years later, when faced with the*

Figure 15.3

SBA 7(A) Guaranteed Loans

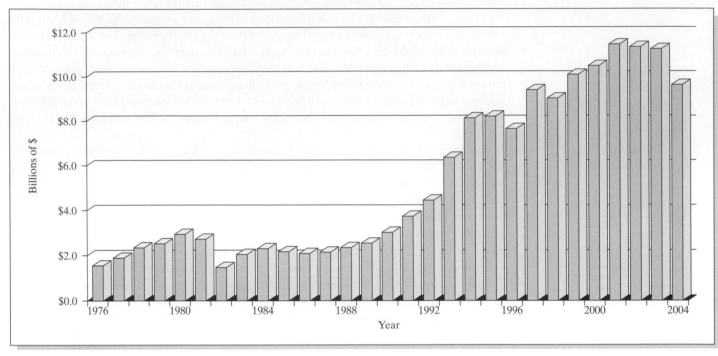

Source: U.S. Small Business Administration.

opportunity to double the company's sales, Ruiz once again turned to the SBA and received a $250,000 loan the company used to build a new 5,000-square-foot warehouse. Today, Ruiz Foods is the largest manufacturer of frozen Mexican food in the United States with 1,800 employees and product distribution in the United States, Canada, Mexico, and Central America. "We wouldn't have survived without the SBA," says Ruiz.[39]

Fred Ruiz and his father used a loan guarantee from the Small Business Administration (SBA) to build their family business into the largest manufacturer of frozen Mexican food in the United States.

Qualifying for an SBA loan guarantee requires cooperation among the entrepreneur, the participating bank, and the SBA. The participating bank determines the loan's terms and sets the interest rate within SBA limits. Contrary to popular belief, SBA guaranteed loans do *not* carry special deals on interest rates. Typically, rates are negotiated with the participating bank, with a ceiling of prime-plus-2.25 percent on loans of less than seven years and prime-plus-2.75 percent on loans of seven to 25 years. Interest rates on loans of less than $25,000 can run up to prime-plus-4.75 percent. The average interest rate on SBA-guaranteed loans is prime-plus-2 percent (compared to prime-plus-1 percent on conventional bank loans). The SBA also assesses a one-time guaranty fee of between 2.5 percent and 3.5 percent for all loan guarantees, depending on the loan amount.

The average loan through the 7(a) guaranty program has dropped from $232,500 in 2002 to $162,500, and the average duration of an SBA loan is 12 years—longer than the average commercial small business loan. In fact, longer loan terms are a distinct advantage of SBA loans. At least half of all bank business loans are for less than one year. By contrast, SBA real estate loans can extend for up to 25 years (compared to just 10 to 15 years for a conventional loan), and working capital loans have maturities of seven years (compared with two to five years at most banks). These longer terms translate into lower payments, which are better suited for young, fast-growing, cash-strapped companies.

The CAPLine Program. In addition to its basic 7(a) loan guarantee program (through which the SBA makes about 85 percent of its loans), the SBA provides guarantees on small business loans for start-up, real estate, machinery and equipment, fixtures, working capital, exporting, and restructuring debt through several other methods. About two-thirds of all SBA's loan guarantees are for machinery and equipment or working capital. The **CAPLine Program** offers short-term capital to growing companies needing to finance seasonal buildups in inventory or accounts receivable under five separate programs, each with maturities up to five years: seasonal line of credit (provides advances against inventory and accounts receivable to help businesses weather seasonal sales fluctuations), contract line of credit (finances the cost of direct labor and materials costs associated with performing contracts), builder's line of credit (helps small contractors and builders finance labor and materials costs), standard asset-based line of credit (an asset-based revolving line of credit for financing short-term needs), and small asset-based line of credit (an asset-based revolving line of credit). CAPLine is aimed at helping cash-hungry small businesses by giving them a credit line to draw on when they need it. These loans built around lines of credit are what small companies need most because they are so flexible, efficient, and, unfortunately, so hard for small businesses to get from traditional lenders.

Loans Involving International Trade. For small businesses going global, the SBA has the **Export Working Capital (EWC) Program**, which is designed to provide working capital to small exporters by providing loan guarantees of 90 percent of the loan amount up to $1.5 million. The SBA works in conjunction with the Export-Import Bank to administer this loan guarantee program. Applicants file a one-page loan application, and the response time normally is 10 days or less. Loan proceeds must be used to finance small business exports. *Crown Products Inc., a small company generating more than $16 million in annual sales by exporting grocery products to more than 70 countries, typifies the small companies that benefit most from the EWC program. In its early years, Crown's retained earnings and its owners financed the company's growth. But as its growth accelerated, the company's cash needs began to outstrip its internal funding sources. With the help of the Hibernia National Bank, owners Kee Lee, Sun Kim, and Jeffrey Teague were able to land a $750,000 line of credit that fueled the company's international growth.*[40]

Company Example

The **International Trade Program** is for small businesses that are engaging in international trade or are adversely affected by competition from imports. The SBA allows global entrepreneurs to combine loans from the Export Working Capital Program with those from the International Trade Program for a maximum guarantee of $1.25 million. Loan maturities range from one to 25 years.

Section 504 Certified Development Company Program. Established in 1980, the SBA's Section 504 program is designed to encourage small businesses to expand their facilities and to create jobs. Section 504 loans provide long-term, fixed-asset financing to small companies to purchase land, buildings, or equipment. Because they are designated for fixed-asset purchases that provide basic business infrastructure to small companies that otherwise might not qualify, 504 loans are intended to serve as a catalyst for economic development. Three lenders play a role in every 504 loan: a bank, the SBA, and a **certified development company (CDC).** A CDC is a nonprofit organization licensed by the SBA and designed to promote economic growth in local communities. Some 268 CDCs now operate across the United States. An entrepreneur generally is required to make a down payment of just 10 percent of the total project cost. The CDC puts up 40 percent at a low, long-term, fixed rate, supported by an SBA loan guarantee in case the entrepreneur defaults. The bank provides at market rates long-term financing for the remaining 50 percent, which also is supported by an SBA guarantee. The major advantages of Section 504 loans are their fixed rates and terms, their 10 to 20 year maturities, and the low down payment required.

Company Example →

Joe Bert, owner of Certified Financial Group (CFG) in Long Beach, California, found the ideal building to house his growing personal finance consulting firm. The location was next to bustling Interstate 4, and with interest rates at record low levels, Bert was ready to purchase the vacant 8,000-square-foot building. Bert was paying $10,000 a month to rent CFG's existing building, and he saw the chance to lower his monthly expenses and own the company's location. Unfortunately, when he began shopping for a loan, the commercial banks expected a down payment on the new location of 20 to 25 percent, something Bert knew his company could not do and still have enough cash to purchase the computers, equipment, and marketing campaigns that kept his business growing. Then Bert discovered a lender in the SBA's 504 program offering attractive interest rates, long loan amortization schedules, and only a 10 percent down payment requirement. Within months of his application, Bert closed the deal on the new property and, in doing so, cut his company's monthly payments to $6,500 a month. "It was ideal for a real estate loan," says Bert. "But I never knew it existed."[41]

As attractive as they are, 504 loans are not for every business owner. The SBA imposes several restrictions on 504 loans:

- For every $35,000 the CDC loans, the project must create at least one new job or achieve a public policy goal such as rural development, expansion of exports, minority business development, and others.
- Machinery and equipment financed must have a useful life of at least 10 years.
- The borrower must occupy at least two-thirds of a building constructed with the loan, or the borrower must occupy at least half of a building purchased or remodeled with the loan.
- The borrower must qualify as a small business under the SBA's definition and must not have a tangible net worth in excess of $7 million nor an average net income in excess of $2.5 million after taxes for the preceding two years.

Because of strict equity requirements, existing small businesses usually find it easier to qualify for 504 loans than do start-ups.

Microloan Program. Recall from the previous chapter that about three-fourths of all entrepreneurs need less than $100,000 to launch their businesses. Indeed, research suggests that most entrepreneurs require less than $50,000 to start their companies. Unfortunately, loans of that amount can be the most difficult to get. Lending these relatively small amounts to entrepreneurs starting businesses is the purpose of the SBA's microloan program. Called **microloans** because they range from just a hundred dollars to as much as $35,000, these loans have helped thousands of people take their first steps toward entrepreneurship. Banks typically have shunned loans in such small amounts because they considered them to be unprofitable. In 1992, the SBA began funding microloan programs at 96 private nonprofit lenders in 44 states in an attempt to "fill the void" in small loans to start-up companies, and the program has expanded from there. Since its inception, the microloan program has made loans totaling more than $110 million! The average microloan is $10,500 with a maturity of 37 months (the maximum term is six years), and lenders' standards are less demanding than those on conventional loans. The typical microloan recipient is a small company with five or fewer employees and collateral that bankers shun for traditional loans: (e.g., earthworms from a fish bait farmer in Ohio and a Minnesota grocery store's frozen fish inventory).[42] All microloans are made through 170 nonprofit intermediaries approved by the SBA such as Trickle Up and ACCION International. Although microloans are available to anyone, the SBA hopes to target those entrepreneurs who have the greatest difficulty getting start-up and expansion capital: women, minorities, and people with low incomes.

Company Example →

After suffering health problems as a result of his intense schedule in the corporate world, Kevin Dungan decided to change careers and launch his own business, a mosquito-spraying service called Skeeter Beeters in Hibbing, Minnesota. When Dungan took his business plan to local banks and requested a traditional bank loan, the bankers turned him down. Finally, Dungan found the Northeast Entrepreneur Fund, a lender in the SBA's microloan program. Working with an advisor from the lender, he polished his business plan and received a $24,000 microloan from the Northeast Entrepreneur Fund as well as a $21,000 loan from a bank that had previously rejected his loan application.[43]

Prequalification Loan Program. The **Prequalification Loan Program** is designed to help disadvantaged entrepreneurs, such as those in rural areas, minorities, women, the disabled, those with low incomes, veterans, and others, prepare loan applications and "prequalify" for SBA loan guarantees before approaching banks and lending institutions for business loans. Because lenders are much more likely to approve loans that the SBA has prequalified, these entrepreneurs have greater access to the capital they need. The maximum loan guaranteed under this program is $250,000, and loan maturities range from seven to 25 years. A local Small Business Development Center usually helps entrepreneurs prepare their loan applications at no charge.

Company Example →

Lola Howerton, owner of a small funeral home in Virginia, had to turn down several large funerals because she did not have the facilities to accommodate them. When she approached two banks for a $225,000 loan to expand her business, both rejected her application. Then Howerton learned about the SBA's prequalification program. She met with a representative from a local Small Business Development Center who helped her prepare a business plan and then received a letter from the SBA prequalifying her for a loan guarantee. With her business plan and the prequalifying letter, Howerton found banks very receptive to her loan request. Four banks offered to lend her the money she needed, and the terms were better than Howerton expected.[44]

Disaster Loans. As their name implies, **disaster loans** are made to small businesses devastated by financial or physical losses from hurricanes, floods, tornadoes, and other disasters. Business physical disaster loans are designed to help companies repair or replace damage to physical property (buildings, equipment, inventory, etc.) caused by the disaster, and economic injury loans provide working capital for businesses throughout the disaster period. The maximum disaster loan usually is $500,000, but Congress often raises that ceiling when circumstances warrant. Disaster loans carry below-market interest rates and long payback periods. Loans for physical damage above $10,000 and financial damage of more than $5,000 require the entrepreneur to pledge some kind of collateral, usually a lien on the business property. In the aftermath of the terrorist attacks on September 11, 2001, that destroyed, damaged, or disrupted an estimated 14,000 businesses in lower Manhattan alone, the SBA approved more than $200 million in disaster loans.[45]

SBA's 8(a) Program. The SBA's 8(a) business development program is designed to help minority-owned businesses become more competitive and get a fair share of federal government contracts. Through this program, the SBA directs about $4.5 million each year to small businesses with "socially and economically disadvantaged" owners. Once a small business convinces the SBA that it meets the program's criteria, it finds a government agency needing work done. The SBA then approaches the federal agency that needs the work done and arranges for a contract to go to the SBA. The agency then subcontracts the work to the small business. Government agencies cooperate with the SBA in its 8(a) program because the law requires them to set aside a portion of their work for minority-owned firms. *Through the SBA's 8(a) program, Paul Hsu's company, Manufacturing Technologies Inc. (MTI), won its first government contract, a contract to build an underwater sonar testing device for the U.S. Navy, but the small business lacked the capital to perform the work. With the help of an SBA loan, Hsu managed to complete the contract and landed several other contracts under the 8(a) business development program. Today MTI, based in Fort Walton Beach, Florida, is a diversified electronics company with 460 employees and sales of $42 million.*[46]

> Company Example →

State and Local Loan Development Programs

> 5. Discuss state and local loan programs.

> Company Example →

Just when many federally funded programs are facing cutbacks, state-sponsored loan and development programs are becoming more active in providing funds for business start-ups and expansions. Many states have decided that their funds are better spent encouraging small business growth rather than "chasing smokestacks"—trying to entice large businesses to locate in their boundaries. These programs come in many forms, but they all tend to focus on developing small businesses that create the greatest number of jobs and economic benefits. *For example, when Sandy and Tom Hood were looking for a bigger and better location for their commercial door and hardware distribution business, HC HoodCo, in Bellefonte, Pennsylvania, they were surprised to learn that the state offered commercial loans for established small companies that were expanding and creating jobs. After the Hoods found the ideal location for their $4-million-a-year business in an industrial park, they applied for a loan from Pennsylvania's Small Business First Fund. The state fund approved a loan for $200,000, half of the cost of the new location, which enabled the entrepreneurial couple to convince a private lender to provide the balance. The only requirement for the loan from the Small Business First Fund was that HC HoodCo create one new job for every $25,000 it received.*[47] Like the Hoods, entrepreneurs who apply for state and local funding must have patience and must be willing to slog through some paperwork. The Hoods began their application process in March and received their loan in August. One advantage, however, was the lower down payment required. Any bank would require a 20 to 25 percent down payment on a project like the one the Hoods had in mind, but the state required only a 10 percent down payment.

Although each state's approach to economic development and job growth is unique, one common element is some kind of small business financing program: loans, loan guarantees, development grants, venture capital pools, and others. One approach many states have had success with is **Capital Access Programs (CAPs).** First introduced in 1986 in Michigan, 22 states now offer CAPs that are designed to encourage lending institutions to make loans to businesses that do not qualify for traditional financing. Under a CAP, a bank and a borrower each pay an up-front fee (a portion of the loan amount) into a loan-loss reserve fund at the participating bank, and the state matches this amount. The reserve fund, which normally ranges from 6 to 14 percent of the loan amount, acts as an insurance policy against the potential loss a bank might experience on a loan and frees the bank to make loans that it otherwise might refuse. One study of CAPs found that 55 percent of the entrepreneurs who received loans under a CAP would not have been granted loans without the backing of the program.[48]

Even cities and small towns have joined in the effort to develop small businesses and help them grow. More than 7,500 communities across the United States operate **revolving loan funds (RLFs)** that combine private and public funds to make loans to small businesses, often at below-market interest rates. As money is repaid into the funds, it is loaned back out to other entrepreneurs. A study by the Corporation for Enterprise Development of RLFs in seven states found that the median RLF loan was $40,000 with a maturity of five years.[49] *Arlis Hanson, owner of Ag Services, a soybean-processing business in Huffton, South Dakota, received a $150,000 loan from a revolving loan fund, Rural Electric Economic Development Inc. (REED). Hanson used the loan to purchase new equipment and inventory and to increase his company's production of soybean oil.*[50]

Company Example

Internal Methods of Financing

6. Discuss valuable methods of financing growth and expansion internally with bootstrap financing.

Small business owners do not have to rely solely on financial institutions and government agencies for capital. Instead, the business itself has the capacity to generate capital. This type of financing, called **bootstrap financing**, is available to virtually every small business and encompasses factoring, leasing rather than purchasing equipment, using credit cards, and managing the business frugally.

Factoring Accounts Receivable

Instead of carrying credit sales on its own books (some of which may never be collected), a small business can sell outright its accounts receivable to a factor. A **factor** buys a company's accounts receivable and pays for them in two parts. The first payment, which the factor makes immediately, is for 50 to 80 percent of the accounts' agreed-upon value, which is typically discounted at a rate of 3 to 5 percent of the value of the invoice. The factor makes the second payment of 15 to 18 percent, which makes up the balance less the factor's service fees, when the original customer pays the invoice. Because factoring is a more expensive type of financing than loans from either banks or commercial finance companies, many entrepreneurs view factors as lenders of last resort. However, for businesses that cannot qualify for those loans, factoring may be the only choice!

Begun by American colonists to finance their cotton trade with England, factoring has become an important source of capital for many small businesses that depend on fast billing turnaround across a multitude of industries ranging from hardware stores and pharmacies to pest control firms and hiring agencies (see Figure 15.4). Factoring deals are either with recourse or without recourse. Under deals arranged with recourse, a small business owner retains the responsibility for customers who fail to pay their accounts.

Figure 15.4

Factoring Volume

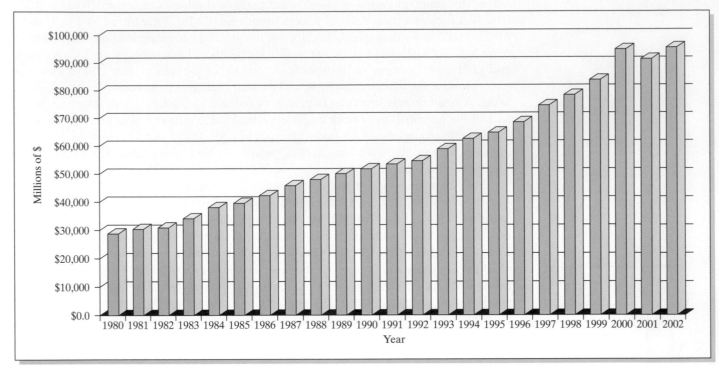

The business owner must take back these uncollectible invoices. Under deals arranged without recourse, however, the owner is relieved of the responsibility of collecting them. If customers fail to pay their accounts, the factor bears the loss. Because the factoring company assumes the risk of collecting the accounts, it normally screens the firm's credit customers, accepts those judged to be creditworthy, and advances the small business owner a portion of the value of the accounts receivable. Factors will discount anywhere from 2 to 40 percent of the face value of a company's accounts receivable, depending on a small company's:

- Customers' financial strength, credit ratings, and their ability to pay their invoices on time.
- Industry and its customers' industries because some industries have a reputation for slow payments.
- History and financial strength, especially in deals arranged with recourse.
- Credit policies.

The discount rate on deals without recourse usually is higher than on those with recourse because of the higher level of risk they carry for the factor.

Although factoring is more expensive than traditional bank loans (a 2 percent discount from the face value of an invoice due in 30 days amounts to an annual interest rate of 24.5 percent), it is a source of quick cash and is ideally suited for fast-growing companies, especially start-ups that cannot qualify for bank loans. "Factoring provides a business with immediate cash for accounts receivable because a business can sell receivables as soon as they are generated," explains the head of one factoring operation.[51] Small companies that sell to government agencies and large corporations, both famous for stretching out their payments for 60 to 90 days or more, also find factoring

Company Example

attractive because they collect the money from the sale (less the factor's discount) much faster. *For example, when the U.S. government needed to ship a massive amount of equipment including generators, road repair machinery, and water purifiers to Afghanistan, it hired IAP Worldwide Services, a small company specializing in logistics, to perform much of the work. To fulfill the government contract, IAP had to purchase the goods and deliver them to various sites in Afghanistan, which required a sizable cash outlay. An experienced government contractor, IAP managers also knew that it would most likely be months before they collected payments from the government. To maintain the company's cash flow, managers turned to Rockland Credit Finance, a factor, for faster payment of the government invoices.*[52]

Leasing

Leasing is another common bootstrap financing technique. Today, small businesses can lease virtually any kind of asset—from office space and telephones to computers and heavy equipment. By leasing expensive assets, a small business owner is able to use them without tying up valuable capital for an extended period of time. In other words, entrepreneurs can reduce the long-term capital requirements of their businesses by leasing equipment and facilities, and they are not investing their capital in depreciating assets. Also, because no down payment is required and because the cost of the asset is spread over a longer time (lowering monthly payments), the company's cash flow improves.

Credit Cards

Unable to find financing elsewhere, some entrepreneurs have launched their companies using the fastest and most convenient source of debt capital available: credit cards! A survey by Arthur Andersen and National Small Business United found that 50 percent of the owners of small and medium-sized businesses used credit cards as a source of funds.[53] Putting business start-up costs on credit cards charging 21 percent or more in annual interest is expensive, risky, and can lead to severe financial woes, but some determined

Although it can be a risky strategy, using credit cards is a popular method of financing among entrepreneurs. Diana Frederick and Kevin Steele used credit cards to purchase inventory and supplies when they launched their karaoke-based retail store, Karaoke Star Store & Stage.

Company Example →

entrepreneurs have no other choice. Credit cards are a ready source of temporary financing that can carry a company through the start-up phase until it begins generating positive cash flow. *When Diana Frederick decided to launch a party hosting and planning business with a karaoke theme, no bank would lend her the money she needed. As a typical resourceful entrepreneur would do, Frederick turned to the only available source of funding she had: credit cards. She charged a $5,000 customized portable karaoke system and a diverse collection of music and began hosting parties. Three years later, when she teamed with Kevin Steele to open a karaoke-based retail store, Karaoke Star Store & Stage, Frederick once again used credit cards to purchase inventory and supplies. "Credit cards are the easiest way to get money," she says. Her financing decision paid off. Today, Karaoke Star Store & Stage is thriving, employing 14 workers and ringing up annual sales of more than $2 million.*[54]

Entrepreneurs who do finance their companies with credit cards should use different cards for business and personal expenses.

Where *Not* to Seek Funds

7. Explain how to avoid becoming a victim of a loan scam.

Entrepreneurs searching for capital must be wary of con artists whose targets frequently include financially strapped small businesses. The swindle usually begins when the con artist scours an area for "DEs"—Desperate Entrepreneurs—in search of quick cash injections to keep their businesses going. Usually, the small business scheme follows one of two patterns (although a number of variations exist). Under one scheme, the small business owner is guaranteed a loan for whatever amount he or she needs from a nonexistent bank with false credentials. The con artist tells the owner that loan processing will take time and that in the meantime the owner must pay a percentage of the loan amount as an advance fee. Of course, the loan never materializes, and the small business owner loses the deposit, sometimes several hundred thousand dollars. *Richard Gould, owner of a small chain of drive-through restaurants, believed that his business was an ideal candidate for franchising, but he needed the money to finance the expansion. He answered an ad in an industry trade journal from a company claiming to have capital to invest in growing businesses. When the company officials told Gould that he would have to pay a $60,000 fee up front, he refused. Ultimately, however, he paid the company $18,000 for the promise of attracting as much as $3 million from investors it supposedly represented. Gould never received a dime in investments from the company.*[55]

Company Example →

Another common scam begins with a con artist who claims to be a representative of the Small Business Administration and promises the cash-hungry small business owner an SBA loan if the owner pays a small processing fee. Again, the loan never appears, and the small business owner loses his or her deposit.

Unfortunately, scams by con artists preying on unsuspecting business owners in need of capital are more common than ever. The World Wide Web has made crooks' jobs easier. On the Web, they can establish a legitimate-looking presence, approach their targets anonymously, and vanish instantly—all while avoiding mail fraud charges if they happen to get caught. These con artists move fast, cover their trails well, and are extremely smooth. The best protection against such scams is common sense and remembering "If it sounds too good to be true, it probably is." Experts offer the following advice to business owners:

- Be suspicious of anyone who approaches you—unsolicited—with an offer for "guaranteed financing."
- Watch out for red flags that indicate a scam: "guaranteed" loans, credit or investments; up-front fees; pitches over the World Wide Web; Nigerian-letter scams (promises to cut you in for a share if you help transfer large amounts of money from

distant locations, such as Nigeria. Of course, the con artists will need the numbers for your account, which they promptly clean out.)

- Conduct a thorough background check on any lenders, brokers, or financiers you intend to do business with. Does the company have a listing in the telephone book? Does the Better Business Bureau have a record of complaints against the company? Does the company have a physical location? If so, visit it.

- Ask the lender or broker about specific sources of financing. Then call to verify the information.

- Make sure you have an attorney review all loan agreements before you sign them.

- *Never* pay advance fees for financing, especially on the World Wide Web, unless you have verified the lender's credibility.

▌▌▌ Chapter Review

1. Describe the various sources of debt capital and the advantages and disadvantages of each.

   - Commercial banks offer the greatest variety of loans, although they are conservative lenders. Typical short-term bank loans include commercial loans, lines of credit, discounting accounts receivable, inventory financing, floor planning, and character loans.

2. Explain the types of financing available from non-bank sources of credit.

   - Asset-based lenders allow small businesses to borrow money by pledging otherwise idle assets such as accounts receivable, inventory, or purchase orders as collateral.

   - Trade credit is used extensively by small businesses as a source of financing. Vendors and suppliers commonly finance sales to businesses for 30, 60, or even 90 days.

   - Equipment suppliers offer small businesses financing similar to trade credit but with slightly different terms.

   - Commercial finance companies offer many of the same types of loans that banks do, but they are more risk oriented in their lending practices. They emphasize accounts receivable financing and inventory loans.

   - Savings and loan associations specialize in loans to purchase real property—commercial and industrial mortgages—for up to 30 years.

   - Stockbrokerage houses offer loans to prospective entrepreneurs at lower interest rates than banks because they have high-quality, liquid collateral—stocks and bonds in the borrower's portfolio.

   - Insurance companies provide financing through policy loans and mortgage loans. Policy loans are extended to the owner against the cash surrender value of insurance policies. Mortgage loans are made for large amounts and are based on the value of the land being purchased.

   - Small Business Investment Companies are privately owned companies licensed and regulated by the SBA that qualify for SBA loans to be invested in or loaned to small businesses.

   - Small Business Lending Companies make only intermediate and long-term loans that are guaranteed by the SBA.

3. Identify the sources of government financial assistance and the loan programs these agencies offer.

   - The Economic Development Administration, a branch of the Commerce Department, makes loan guarantees to create and expand small businesses in economically depressed areas.

   - The Department of Housing and Urban Development extends grants (such as Community Development Block Grants) to cities that, in turn, lend and grant money to small businesses in an attempt to strengthen the local economy.

   - The Department of Agriculture's Rural Business-Cooperative Service loan program is designed to create nonfarm employment opportunities in rural areas through loans and loan guarantees.

   - The Small Business Innovation Research Program involves 10 federal agencies that award cash grants or long-term contracts to small companies wanting to initiate or to expand their research and development (R&D) efforts.

   - The Small Business Technology Transfer Program allows researchers at universities, federally funded R&D centers, and nonprofit research institutions to join forces with small businesses and develop commercially promising ideas.

4. Describe the various loan programs available from the Small Business Administration.

- Almost all SBA loan activity is in the form of loan guarantees rather than direct loans. Popular SBA programs include the Low Doc Program, the SBA*Express* Program, the 7(a) loan guaranty program, the CAPLine Program, the Export Working Capital Program, the Section 504 Certified Development Company program, the microloan program, the Prequalification Loan Program, the disaster loan program, and the 8(a) program.
- Many state and local loan and development programs, such as Capital Access Programs and Revolving Loan Funds, complement those sponsored by federal agencies.

5. Discuss state and local economic development programs.

- In an attempt to develop businesses that create jobs and economic growth, most states offer small business financing programs, usually in the form of loans, loan guarantees, and venture capital pools.

6. Discuss valuable methods of financing growth and expansion internally with bootstrap financing.

- Small business owners may also look inside their firms for capital. By factoring accounts receivable, leasing equipment instead of buying it, by minimizing costs and using credit cards, owners can stretch their supplies of capital.

7. Explain how to avoid becoming a victim of a loan scam.

- Entrepreneurs hungry for capital for their growing businesses can be easy targets for con artists running loan scams. Entrepreneurs should watch out for promises of "guaranteed" loans, up-front fees, pitches over the World Wide Web, and Nigerian-letter scams.

▌▐ ▐ Discussion Questions

1. What role do commercial banks play in providing debt financing to small businesses? Outline and briefly describe the major types of short-term, intermediate, and long-term loans commercial banks offer.
2. What is trade credit? How important is it as a source of debt financing to small firms?
3. Explain how asset-based financing works. What is the most common method of asset-based financing? What are the advantages and disadvantages of using this method of financing?
4. What function do SBICs serve? How does an SBIC operate? What methods of financing do SBICs rely on most heavily?
5. Briefly describe the loan programs offered by the following:
   A. Economic Development Administration.
   B. Department of Housing and Urban Development.
   C. Department of Agriculture.
   D. local development companies.
6. Explain the purpose and the methods of operation of the Small Business Innovation Research Program and the Small Business Technology Transfer Program.
7. Which of the Small Business Administration's loan programs accounts for the majority of its loan activity? How does the program work?
8. Explain the purpose and the operation of the SBA's microloan program.
9. How can a firm employ bootstrap financing to stretch its current capital supply?
10. What is a factor? How does the typical factor operate? Explain the advantages and the disadvantages of factoring. What kinds of businesses typically use factors?

Sources of Debt Financing

Business PlanPro

Many entrepreneurs are reluctant to give up shares of ownership in their companies that equity capital requires and turn instead to debt capital as a source of funds. Although entrepreneurs who use debt capital retain ownership of their companies, they must carry the debt load as a liability on their companies' balance sheets and must repay the debt with interest at a later date.

Now that you have read about sources of debt financing, go to the exercises that accompany Chapter 15 of Business Plan Pro where you will find a series of questions that will help you assess your company's potential for attracting debt financing. After completing these exercises, you may discover that debt financing is suitable for your business. If so, the exercises will help you identify the sources of debt capital you should consider approaching. When you have completed the exercises, you may need to update the Startup Funding portion of the section called The Bottom Line in Business Plan Pro to reflect the use of debt capital in your company's financial plan.

Chapter 16

Location, Layout, and Physical Facilities

> *The world is round, and the place which may seem like the end may also be only the beginning.*
> —IVY BAKER PRIEST

> *There's a lot more business out there in small town America than I ever dreamed of.*
> —SAM WALTON

Upon completion of this chapter, you will be able to:

1. Explain the stages in the location decision.

2. Describe the location criteria for retail and service businesses.

3. Outline the basic location options for retail and service businesses.

4. Explain the site selection process for manufacturers.

5. Discuss the benefits of locating a start-up company in a business incubator.

6. Describe the criteria used to analyze the layout and design considerations of a building, including the Americans with Disabilities Act.

7. Explain the principles of effective layouts for retailers, service businesses, and manufacturers.

8. Evaluate the advantages and disadvantages of building, buying, and leasing a building.

Few decisions entrepreneurs make have as lasting and as dramatic an impact on their businesses as the choice of a location. Selecting the right location increases the chances that a company will prosper, but choosing the wrong location puts a business at a distinct disadvantage from the start. Entrepreneurs must look beyond their "comfort zones" to discover the locations that are best suited to the new venture. Today's electronic search tools enable entrepreneurs to step outside of their comfort zones and conduct a search for the best location for the business. The hundreds of hours that one may spend collecting and analyzing the data that is relevant to choosing a location for a specific type of business will pay off in ample customer traffic and high sales. The data available from a variety of sources, much of it at no cost, represents an amazing resource when it comes to making critical decisions such as where to locate a business. The key is to find that data and use it to make an informed location decision.

The first step is to list the information needed to conduct a comparison of locations. What data might provide real insight into the buying behaviors of your potential target audience? Which information will be useful in determining the basic demographic, competitive, and regulatory environment of potential locations? When searching for demographic, market, and regulatory information entrepreneurs must act much like the prospectors in the days of the Gold Rush, searching for the nuggets of information they need among the piles of rubble.

Always keep in mind that a business must locate where its customers are, unless the company is a destination retailer. In that case, the customer comes to the company. A retailer such as Bass Pro Shops in Springfield, Missouri, draws customers from all over the United States and abroad. However, customers may not search for a new business trying to establish itself in a market. Ask yourself: Where is the strongest concentration of potential customers who fit the profile of the target market? Among these various potential locations, where are the competitors weakest? What, if any, are the physical or psychological barriers to operating in the potential locations? The answers to these questions come only from doing the research.

The best location for your business can become a competitive advantage through conducting the research and subsequently making a good decision. The choice of location can make or break any business venture. *One entrepreneur decided to fulfill a lifelong dream when he was "downsized" from his corporate position. The entrepreneur had all of the skills and education necessary to make a success of his auto parts store. His all-consuming love of automobiles—especially muscle cars—his expertise in sales, a background in bookkeeping, and his excellent reputation for honesty and fair treatment seemed like more than enough to guarantee success. He positioned his business to compete with the larger chain parts stores by offering hard-to-find parts and delivery service. What could be wrong with this picture? What finally forced the business into bankruptcy? Location! The entrepreneur located his store in an economically depressed city on a blind curve. It was virtually impossible to see the business in one direction until well past the store, and only at risk to life and limb could anyone maneuver in or out of the small parking area.* Sadly, this is a familiar scenario that leads to the failure of many a small business. The first section of this chapter serves as a guide to help entrepreneurs qualify their choices among various location alternatives.

> Company Example

The Logic of Location: From Region to State to City to Site

1. Explain the stages in the location decision.

An entrepreneur's ultimate goal is to locate the company at a site that will maximize the likelihood of success. The more entrepreneurs invest in researching potential locations, the higher is the probability that they will find the spot that is best suited for their businesses. The trick is to keep an open mind about where the best location might be. Just as with most decisions affecting a business, the customer drives the choice of the "best" location for a business. Choosing an appropriate location is essentially a matter of selecting a site that best serves the needs of the business's target market. Is there a location where the new business will have the greatest number of customers that need, want, and can afford the products or services your business provides? The better entrepreneurs know and understand their target customers' characteristics, demographic profiles, and buying behavior, the greater are their chances of identifying the right location from which to serve them.

The search for the ideal location involves research that entrepreneurs can conduct in libraries, by telephone, in person, and on the World Wide Web. The logic of location selection is to begin with a broad regional search and then to systematically narrow the focus of the site selection process (see Figure 16.1).

Selecting the Region

The first step in selecting the best location is to focus at the regional level. Which region of the country has the characteristics necessary for your business to succeed? Common requirements include rapid growth in the population of a certain age group,

Figure 16.1

Logic of Choosing a Location

Source: From Dale M. Lewison and M. Wayne DeLozier, *Retailing* (Columbus, OH: Merrill/Macmillan Publishing, 1984), p. 341.

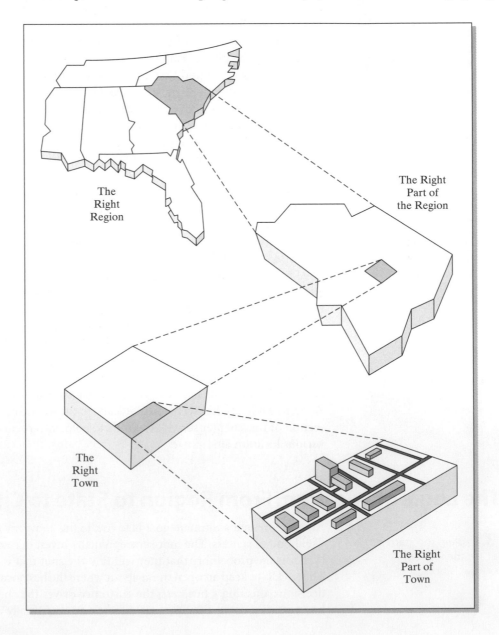

rising disposable incomes, the existence of specific infrastructure, a pool of skilled workers, and low operating costs. Each of these factors impacts revenues and cost.

At the broadest level of the location decision, entrepreneurs usually identify regions of the country that are experiencing substantial growth. Every year, many popular business publications prepare reports on which regions of the nation are growing, which are stagnant, and which are declining. Studying shifts in population and industrial growth will give an entrepreneur an idea of where the action is—and isn't. For example, how large is the population? How fast is it growing? What is the demographic makeup of the overall population? Which segments are growing fastest? Which are growing the slowest? What is the population's income? Is it increasing or decreasing? Are other businesses moving into the region? If so, what kind of businesses? In general, owners want to avoid dying regions; these regions simply may not be able to provide a broad base of potential customers. A firm's customers will be people, businesses, and government, and if it is to be successful, the business must locate in a place that is convenient to them.

One of the first electronic stops entrepreneurs should make when conducting a regional evaluation is the U.S. Census Bureau, which offers the equivalent of a gold mine of important demographic and economic information. The Census Bureau makes most of the information contained in its valuable data banks available to entrepreneurs through its easy-to-use Web site (www.census.gov). There entrepreneurs can view summary tables and handy maps for practically any of the bureau's available data at many levels of detail, ranging from the nation as a whole to individual states, counties, census tracts, and even city blocks. For many entrepreneurs, reports based on the well-known decennial census are some of the most useful tools for selecting a location. This database contains both demographic and economic information about the residents of a particular area, including age, gender, ancestry, marital status, language spoken, education level, occupation, travel time to work, income level, and other population characteristics. This census also includes a housing report that contains information on the number of rooms (and the number of bedrooms) in a home, the age of the home, the utility costs of operating the home, the home's value, the number of cars at the home, and other characteristics.

In addition to the decennial census that the bureau conducts of every household in the United States every 10 years, the bureau takes nearly 100 other surveys and censuses that entrepreneurs can use to find the ideal location for their businesses. For instance, in an effort to provide reliable annual updates to the decennial census, the Census Bureau conducts the American Community Survey (ACS), which includes about 3 million households. Using the ACS, entrepreneurs can judge how rapidly an area is growing and how quickly its population makeup is changing.

The Census Bureau also conducts the Economic Census every five years (in years that end in 2 and 7), which provides a portrait of businesses in local communities across the nation. The Economic Census is helpful to entrepreneurs developing business plans for start-up ventures, existing business owners who want to learn about their competitors and their potential business customers, or those in search of a location near potential customers or away from competitors. The data are organized using the popular North American Industry Classification System (NAICS) and include information such as the number of establishments in an industry, their sales, shipments, number of employees, and annual payroll. The Annual Survey of Manufactures (ASM) provides similar information for makers of more than 1,800 classes of products

These Web resources give entrepreneurs instant access to important site location information that only a few years ago would have taken many hours of intense research to compile. *American Demographics* magazine (www.demographics.com) is another exceptional source of information on current demographic trends that impact our society. This publication provides in-depth articles that enable the entrepreneur to gain valuable insights into the changes in our society that produce valuable business opportunities. Access to most of the articles requires a subscription to *American Demographics.* AmeriStat (www.ameristat.org) provides a detailed breakdown of the most relevant data collected from the most recent census. The site also includes helpful articles that discuss the implications of the changing demographic and economic profile of the nation's population, such as the impact of aging baby boomers on business and the composition of the U.S. workforce. STAT-USA (www.statusa.gov) is a service of the United States Department of Commerce that offers both financial and economic data about the United States as well as trade data for the nation and for Europe. Here entrepreneurs can locate everything from the latest consumer price index and the number of housing starts to leads for global trading partners and tips on conducting business in practically any country in the world.

Other helpful resources merit mention as well. *Demographics USA* is a three-edition series covering the United States, its counties, and zip code areas. This useful publication provides market surveys on various segments of U.S. demographics, including purchasing power, retail sales by type of merchandise, employment and payroll data, and forecasts of economic conditions down to the county level. Entrepreneurs can use *Demographics USA* to analyze the level of competition in a particular area, assess the sales potential of a particular location, compare consumers' buying power across a dozen categories, and more. *Lifestyle Market Analyst,* an annual publication, matches population demographics with lifestyle interests. Section 1 gives demographics and lifestyle information by "Areas of Dominant Influence." Section 2 gives demographic and geographic information according to 57 lifestyle interests. Section 3 lists areas of dominant influence and lifestyles according to 42 demographic segments. It is wise to consult the introductory material on how to use this source. Entrepreneurs can use *Lifestyle Market Analyst* to determine, for example, how likely members of a particular market segment are to own a dog, collect antiques, play golf, own a vacation home, fly frequently, invest in stocks or bonds, or participate in a host of other activities.

Markets of the U.S. for Business Planners provides current and historical profiles of 183 U.S. urban economies by major section and industry. It includes regional maps, graphics, and economic commentary. *Rand McNally Commercial Atlas & Marketing Guide* is an annual publication that features maps, transportation, communication, and population data as well as a variety of economic data. Rand McNally also offers this guide in an online, interactive version on its Web site. The *Commercial Atlas & Marketing Guide* includes population, income, buying power, and sales data by store type for most areas in the United States, including small towns not covered in detail by the U.S. Census data. It also lists the largest U.S. firms in a variety of industries. Each state map includes an analysis of businesses and manufacturers by county, and a list of banking facilities. The *Sourcebook of County Demographics* is another annual publication that provides up-to-date estimates for more than 80 economic and demographic characteristics such as age distribution, population, education, employment, housing, income distribution, race, household income, and others as well as consumer spending indexes for 20 product and service categories. The *Community Sourcebook of Zip Code Demographics* provides similar types of information as the *Sourcebook of County Demographics* but does so by zip code. This publication also provides lifestyle descriptions of consumers living in particular zip code areas.

Sales and Marketing Management's *Survey of Buying Power,* published annually, provides statistics, rankings, and projections for every county and media market in the

United States with demographics segmented by age, race, city, county, and state. This publication also includes current information on retail spending and forecasts for each category. The data are divided into 323 metro markets as defined by the Census Bureau and 210 media markets, which are television or broadcast markets defined by Nielsen Media Research. The *Survey* also includes several unique statistics. Effective buying income (EBI) is a measure of disposable income, and the buying power index (BPI), for which the *Survey* is best known, is a unique measure of spending power that takes population, EBI, and retail sales into account to determine a market's ability to buy goods and services. The *Editor and Publisher Market Guide* is similar to the *Survey of Buying Power,* but provides additional information on markets. This guide includes detailed information on key cities.

Finally, the Small Business Administration's Small Business Development center (SBDC) program also offers location analysis assistance to entrepreneurs. Some 600 centers nationwide provide training, counseling, research, and other specialized assistance to entrepreneurs and existing business owners on a wide variety of subjects—all at no charge. To locate the SBDC nearest you, contact the SBA office in your state or go the to SBA's Small Business Development Center home page at www.sba.gov/sbdc/.

The task of analyzing potential locations—gathering and synthesizing data on a wide variety of demographic and geographic variables—is one ideally suited for a computer. In fact, a growing number of entrepreneurs are relying on geographic information systems (GISs), powerful software programs that combine map drawing with database management capability, to pinpoint the ideal location for their business. *One such product called iSite helps companies evaluate locations and make informed decisions. According to Jim Stone, CEO of geoVue, developer of iSite, "We deliver a software solution that integrates maps and market data to support decisions involving location." One customer, World Savings Bank, uses the product to evaluate specific opportunities in a trade area, understand the demographic profile of customers in that area, determine how many branches a specific area can sustain, decide where to locate them, and estimate what the performance of a branch would be in any given location. iSite is available both as a Windows-based and a Web-based application, and the program contains locations throughout the United States, as well as some international locations. Enter an address, and the software automatically finds that location on a map along with information about the vicinity, such as the location of nearby shopping centers, retail businesses, and other employers.*[1] The visual displays of software such as iSite highlight what otherwise would be indiscernible business trends. The days when managers stuck colored pins into maps taped on a wall to analyze population characteristics are gone!

Using a GIS program, entrepreneurs can plot an existing customer base on a map, with various colors representing the different population densities. Then they can zoom in on the areas with the greatest concentration of customers, mapping a detailed view of zip code borders or even city streets. Geographic information system street files originate in the U.S. Census Bureau's TIGER (Topological Integrated Geographic Encoding Referencing) file, which contains map information broken down for every street in the country and detailed block statistics for the 345 largest urban areas. In essence, TIGER is a computerized map of the entire United States and, when linked with a database, gives small business owners incredible power to pinpoint existing and potential customers as well as competitors. This digital map can be downloaded at no cost and be tailored to reflect census tracts, railroads, highways, waterways, and other physical attributes of any area in the United States, but the user must have either mapping or GIS software to access and use the TIGER files. Many private vendors offer GIS software packages with additional enhancements that are based on TIGER files.

Company Example

IN THE FOOTSTEPS OF AN ENTREPRENEUR...

Solving the Location Puzzle

Technology has made finding the right location for a business much easier. Modern software uses a combination of neural network analysis, demographic data mining, and mapping tools to help entrepreneurs find sites that are close to high concentrations of their target customers but are far enough away from direct competitors. Existing companies can merge information from their own customer databases with data from the U.S. Census Bureau and other sources to determine, for instance, how far customers will travel to shop for shoes or computers. MapInfo, one company that offers this type of software, says that it can determine not only which areas of a city offer the greatest sales potential but also which intersections will attract the greatest number of customers. Using a technique called predictive analysis, MapInfo software can forecast the sales volume a particular store located at a specific location will generate and can produce color-coded maps showing other prime locations.

For years, Home Depot had considered locating a store in New York City, but residents there did not fit the profile of the company's target customers, who typically live in suburban areas and own big homes. However, when a site became available in Queens, Home Depot managers worked with MapInfo to analyze the home products sales potential of the location. The forecasts amazed Home Depot managers, who decided to take a chance and open a store in an area saturated with small row houses and apartments rather than stately homes with large yards. The forecasts were accurate: The Queens Home Depot store is now one of the highest volume locations in the entire company. Although the average amount customers spend there is well below what the typical suburban customer spends, the sheer volume of customers (some 800,000 households make up the borough) in the surrounding area more than make up for it.

Managers at Home Depot thought that their locations in the company's hometown, Atlanta, Georgia, had saturated that market as early as 1979. However, using MapInfo to analyze the growth in the Atlanta

area over the past two decades showed that there was room for the company to expand. Home Depot now has 40 stores in the Atlanta metro area.

For fast-food restaurants, location is one of the key factors for success. Because diners typically are willing to drive only five minutes for fast food, these restaurants often locate in clusters to give customers the array of choices they seek. Using MapInfo's software, Arby's discovered that diners were willing to travel 20 percent farther for one of the company's roast beef sandwiches than for one of its chicken sandwiches. The study showed that customers could get chicken products at any number of fast food locations but saw Arby's roast beef sandwiches as "destination" products.

By 2001, fabric and crafts retailer Jo-Ann Stores had dozens of standard retail stores and 70 superstores across the United States, but managers were concerned that the superstores might not be generating sufficient profits to justify the extra cost of building them. MapInfo took a sample of Jo-Ann Stores' customers and used the data to develop an ideal customer profile, which it then mapped against demographic statistics. The study showed that Jo-Ann Stores could build as many as 700 superstores! It also proved that the superstores were paying their way, generating $150 in sales per square foot, compared to just $105 per square foot for the smaller stores. Commenting on the power of the company's new method of location analysis, one vice-president says, "We have moved from intuition, gut-feel, and deal-making into science."

1. Why would it be difficult for businesses to conduct location analyses such as the ones described here without the benefit of technology?
2. What benefits does a scientifically based approach to location analysis offer over one based on intuition? Is there a place for intuition in selecting a location? Explain.

Source: Adapted from Amy Cortese, "Is Your Business in the Right Spot?" *Business 2.0,* May 2004, pp. 76–77.

Selecting the State

Every state has a business development office to recruit new businesses to that state. Even though the publications produced by these offices will be biased in favor of locating in that state, they still are an excellent source of facts and can help entrepreneurs assess the business climate in each state. Some of the key issues to explore include the laws, regulations, and taxes that govern businesses and any incentives or investment credits the state may offer to businesses locating there. Other factors to consider include proximity to markets, proximity to raw materials, wage rates, quantity and quality of the labor supply, general business climate, and tax rates.

Proximity to Markets. Locating close to markets they plan to serve is extremely critical to manufacturers, especially when the cost of transporting finished goods is high relative to their value. Locating near customers is necessary to remain competitive. Service firms often find that proximity to their clients is essential. If a business is involved in repairing equipment used in a specific industry, it should be located where that industry is concentrated. The more specialized a business, or the greater the relative cost of transporting the product to the customer, the more likely it is that proximity to the market will be of critical importance in the location decision. *After German automaker BMW chose upstate South Carolina as the site for its first assembly plant in North America, the counties near the plant immediately became the locations of choice for many BMW suppliers. Because BMW wanted quick deliveries with minimal inventory investment, many of its suppliers decided to set up plants close to the assembly operation. Since BMW located in upstate South Carolina, more than 100 new automotive suppliers have located there as well.*

Proximity to Needed Raw Materials. A business that requires raw materials that are difficult or expensive to transport may need a location near the source of those raw materials. For example, fish-process plants are almost always located close to ports. Some companies locate close to the source of raw materials because of the cost of transporting heavy low-value materials over long distances. *For instance, the owner of a small company making kitty litter chose a location near a large vein of kaolin, highly absorbent clay and the basic raw material in his finished product. Transporting the heavy, low-value material over long distances would be impractical and unprofitable.* In situations in which bulk or weight is not a factor, locating close to suppliers can facilitate quick deliveries and reduce inventory holding costs. The value of products and materials, their cost of transportation, and their unique functions all interact in determining how close a business needs to be to its sources of supply.

Labor Supply. Two distinct factors are important for entrepreneurs analyzing the labor supply in a potential location: the number of workers available in the area and their level of education, training, and experience. Business owners want to know how many qualified people are available in the area to do the work required in the business. The size of the local labor pool determines a company's ability to fill jobs at reasonable wages. However, employment and labor cost statistics can be misleading if a company needs people with specific qualifications. Some states have attempted to attract industry with the promise of cheap labor. Unfortunately, businesses locating in those states found exactly what the term implied: unskilled, low-wage labor. Unskilled laborers can be difficult to train.

Knowing the exact nature of the labor needed and preparing job descriptions and job specifications in advance will help business owners determine whether there is a good match between their company and the available labor pool. Checking educational statistics in the state to determine the number of graduates in relevant fields of study will provide an idea of the local supply of qualified workers. Such planning will result in choosing a location with a steady source of quality workers.

For instance, North Carolina's Research Triangle, an area defined by the surrounding communities of Raleigh, Durham, and Chapel Hill, has become a mecca for companies in high-tech industries, such as computer software, semiconductors, communications, pharmaceuticals, and biotech, because of the area's pool of highly skilled labor. Major colleges such as Duke University, the University of North Carolina, and North Carolina

NC State's *Centennial Campus* 12 building complex forms a "technopolis" of university, corporate, and government R&D facilities and business incubators. Centennial Campus is proving to be the logical choice for businesses and government agencies requiring R&D facilities near research faculty and graduate students who can supplement project teams on a just-in-time basis.

State University funnel talented graduates trained in fields such as virtual reality and market research into local companies. For example *Centennial Campus* is NC State's vision of the campus of the future. The 12 building complex (with 13 additional buildings in design or construction) forms a "technopolis" of university, corporate, and government R&D facilities and business incubators. In addition, the master plan for the campus features a hotel/conference center complex and a town center on Lake Raleigh, a golf course, and residential neighborhoods. This facility exemplifies a national trend in which universities are redesigning education and research efforts to include faculty spin-off companies, real-world experience for students, and closer ties to the industries that translate into quality-of-life improvements for the public.[2]

As the preceding example suggests, what occurs over time is the creation of "clusters" of companies and a pool of highly trained employees. It is very common to find new entrepreneurial ventures among these industry or technology clusters because of this pool of highly qualified employees. It is possible, with some basic demographic research, to map these clusters of technology and identify the depth of the pool of skilled employees.

Wage Rates. Wage rates provide another measure for comparison among states. Entrepreneurs should determine the wage rates for jobs that are related to their particular industry or company. In addition to published government surveys, local newspapers will give entrepreneurs an idea of the wages local companies must pay to attract workers. What trends have emerged in wage rates over time? How does the rate of increase in wage rates compare among states? Another factor influencing wage rates is the level of union activity in a state. How much union organizing activity has the state seen within the past two years? Is it increasing or decreasing? Which industries have unions targeted in the recent past?

The issue becomes the nature of the employee that the business needs, the availability of workers with those skills and the current and anticipated future wage rates for the specific skills needed. Additionally, the issue of availability of skilled employees in the case of rapid growth should be considered. Is the depth of the workforce sufficient to supply the needs of the business under the condition of rapid expansion without resulting in an unacceptable increase in wages?

Business Climate. What is the state's overall attitude toward your kind of business? Has it passed laws that impose restrictions on the way a company can operate? Does the state impose a corporate income tax? Is there an inventory tax? Are there "blue laws" that prohibit certain business activity on Sundays? Does the state offer small business support programs or financial assistance to entrepreneurs? Some states are more "small business friendly" than others.

Several business publications have named Austin, Texas, as one of the best areas for small businesses, citing its positive attitude toward growing and developing small companies as a major asset. Many factors make Austin a desirable location for start-up companies, including its diversified economic base; a strong core of *Fortune* 500 companies, including Dell, Motorola, and IBM; a significant population of private investors ready to invest in promising small companies; and several state and local government support systems offering entrepreneurial assistance and advice. The University of Texas system supplies companies with a steady crop of highly creative college graduates. Business incubators and a large pool of retired executives ready to offer business advice also provide important pieces of business infrastructure. "Austin has a strong venture capital community, the legal and accounting systems to support start-ups, a good university with technologies coming out of it, and a nice quality of life," says Carolyn Stark, head of the Austin Technology Council. It is no surprise that Austin is home to more than 1,800 technology companies, 1,100 of which are small businesses.[3]

Table 16.1 provides an abbreviated example of an evaluation matrix that can be constructed by an entrepreneur to assist in the state-to-state evaluation process. Because of the unique nature of each business venture, an entrepreneur should modify the table to include location criteria that are relevant to the specific business and then weigh each criterion in the appropriate manner. This simple evaluation tool allows entrepreneurs to transform a location decision based solely on subjective feelings into one based on objective criteria.

Tax Rates. Another important factor entrepreneurs must consider when screening states for potential locations is the tax burden they impose on businesses and individuals. Income taxes may be the most obvious tax states impose on both business and individual residents,

Table 16.1
State Evaluation Matrix

LOCATION CRITERION	WEIGHT 10-HIGH 1-LOW	SCORE 5-HIGH 1-LOW	STATE WEIGHTED SCORE (WEIGHT × SCORE) FLORIDA	GEORGIA	SOUTH CAROLINA
Quality of labor force		1 2 3 4 5			
Wage rates		1 2 3 4 5			
Union activity		1 2 3 4 5			
Energy costs		1 2 3 4 5			
Tax burden		1 2 3 4 5			
Educational/training assistance		1 2 3 4 5			
Start-up incentives		1 2 3 4 5			
Quality of life		1 2 3 4 5			
Availability of raw materials		1 2 3 4 5			
Other		1 2 3 4 5			
Other		1 2 3 4 5			
Total Score					

Assign to each location criterion a weight that reflects its relative importance (10 high to 1 low). Then score each state on a scale of 1 (low) to 5 (high). Calculate the weighted score (weight × score) for each state. Finally, add up the total weighted score for each state. The state with the highest total weighted score is the best location for your business.

but entrepreneurs also must evaluate the impact of payroll taxes, sales taxes, property taxes, and specialized taxes on the cost of their operations. Currently, seven states impose no income tax on their residents, but state governments always impose taxes of some sort on businesses and individuals. In some cases, states offer special tax rates or are willing to negotiate fees in lieu of taxes for companies that will create jobs and stimulate the local economy.

Internet Access. Speedy and reliable Internet access is an increasingly important factor in the location decision. Fast Internet access through cable, DSL, or T1 lines is essential for high-tech companies and those engaging in e-commerce. Even those companies that may not do business over the Web currently are finding it nearly certain that they will use the Web as a business tool. Companies that fall behind in high-tech communications will find

> [Company Example] →

themselves at a severe competitive disadvantage. *When Darryl Lyons, a third-generation rancher, began raising Angus cattle to sell from his ranch in Okmulgee, Oklahoma, he made all of his first-year sales of $140,000 to customers located within a 100-mile radius. Then Lyons began using the Web as a marketing tool, and sales climbed to $600,000. Now reaching customers across the globe, Lyons expects sales to reach more than $1.5 million! One problem Lyons faces in his remote location, however, is fast, reliable Internet service. Bad weather interrupts his telephone and Internet service about a dozen times a year, costing him an estimated $3,000 to $4,000 in lost sales each day it is out.*[4]

Most entrepreneurs are amazed at the amount of helpful information that exists about each state if they search the right places and ask the right questions. When entrepreneurs ask questions about the feasibility of opening a new business in any state, they will find professional staffers whose job it is to provide the requested information in a timely fashion. Their job is to help you locate your business in their state. Obtaining and analyzing the information about a region and the states in it provide entrepreneurs with a clear picture of the most favorable locations. The next phase of the location selection process concentrates on selecting the best city.

Selecting the City

The final stage in the location process involves greater hands-on, or maybe "feet-on," activities. The numbers will provide the entrepreneur with leads as to potential locations, but the locations need to be investigated close up and in person. This investigation needs to be done thoroughly and on several occasions at different times of the day and night. Get to know your potential neighbors. Once you've signed the lease, it's too late to find out that a local biker gang known as "Nobody's Angels" uses the vacant building next door as an after-hours gathering place. In addition, entrepreneurs must factor into their decisions population density and growth trends, the nature of competition, the location's potential to attract customers, the cost of the location, and many other factors.

Population Trends and Density. An entrepreneur should know more about a city and its various neighborhoods than do the people who live there. By analyzing population and other demographic data, an entrepreneur can examine a city in detail, and the location decision becomes more than "a shot in the dark." Studying the characteristics of a city's residents, including population sizes and density, growth trends, family size, age breakdowns, education, income levels, job categories, gender, religion, race, and nationality, gives entrepreneurs the facts they need to make an informed location decision. In fact, using only basic census data, entrepreneurs can determine the value of the homes in an area, how many rooms they contain, how many bedrooms they contain, what percentage of the population owns their homes, and how much residents' monthly rental or mortgage payments are. Imagine how useful such information would be to someone about to launch a home accessories store!

A firm's location should match the market for its products or services, and assembling a demographic profile will tell entrepreneurs how well a particular site measures up to their target market's profile. For instance, an entrepreneur planning to open a fine china shop would likely want specific information on family income, size, age, and education. Such a shop would need to be in an area where people appreciate the product and have the discretionary income to purchase it.

Trends or shifts in population components may have more meaning than total population trends. For example, if a city's population is aging, its disposable income may be decreasing and the city may be gradually dying. On the other hand, a city may be experiencing rapid growth in the population of high-income, professional young people. For example, Atlanta, where the average age of inhabitants is 29, has seen an explosion of businesses aimed at young people with rising incomes and hearty appetites for consumption. Las Vegas, Nevada, has been a city exploding in growth due to both retirees enjoying no state income tax and a rapidly expanding business community.

Population density can be another important factor in determining the optimal business location. In many of the older cities in the eastern United States, people live or work in very high-density areas. Businesses that need high traffic volume would benefit by locating in a high-density area, and the entrepreneur can benefit from an understanding of daily ebbs and flows of population movement within the selected area.

Knowing the population density within a few miles of a potential location can give entrepreneurs a clear picture of whether the city can support their businesses and can even help them develop the appropriate marketing strategies to draw customers. Fitness club owners have discovered that population density is one of the most important factors in selecting a suitable location. Experience has taught them that customers are willing to drive or walk only so far to visit a fitness club. Information on population density and other important demographic characteristics is available from the publications mentioned earlier in this chapter and from market research companies.

Competition. For some retailers, locating near competitors makes sense because having similar businesses located near one another may increase traffic flow. **Clustering,** as this location strategy is known, works well for products for which customers are most likely to comparison shop. Most of us are familiar with auto dealers who locate next to one another in a "motor mile" in an effort to create a shopping magnet for customers. The convenience of being able to shop for dozens of brands of cars, all within a few hundred yards of one another, draws customers from a sizable trading area.

Of course, this strategy has limits. An area that is saturated with businesses of the same type can create an undesirable impact on the profitability of all competing firms. That's why

Company Example →

most business owners prefer to locate where little or no competition exists. *Applebee's International, the popular casual dining restaurant with more than 1,600 locations (most of which are franchised), has become the dominant player in this fast-growing segment of the restaurant industry by locating its outlets in small towns, where its competitors are not. For example, the Applebee's in Hays, Kansas (population 21,000) is the only brand name casual dining restaurant in town. By avoiding direct competition with other chains such as Bennigan's, Chili's, and Houlihan's, Applebee's rural location strategy is proving to be so successful that the company plans to open 25 percent of its new restaurants in counties where the number of households is 50,000 or fewer. Although average sales in the units located in rural areas are about 10 percent below those of suburban and urban Applebee's restaurants, the lower real estate and operating costs keep profit margins intact.*[5]

Studying the size of the market for a product or service and the number of existing competitors will help entrepreneurs determine whether they can capture a sufficiently large market share to earn a profit. Again, Census Bureau reports can be a valuable source of information. The bureau's *County Business Patterns Economic Profile* shows the breakdown of businesses in manufacturing, wholesale, retail, and service categories and estimates companies' annual payrolls and number of employees. The *Economic Census*, which covers 15 million businesses and is published in years that end in 2 and 7, gives an overview of the businesses in an area including their sales (or other measure of output), employment, payroll, and form of organization. It covers eight industry categories including retail, wholesale, service, manufacturing, and construction and gives statistics at not only the national level but also by state, metropolitan statistical area (MSA), county, places with 2,500 or more inhabitants, and zip code. The *Economic Census* is a useful tool for helping entrepreneurs determine whether the areas they are considering as a location are already saturated with competitors.

Entrepreneurs can gain a great deal of insight about potential locations via the Internet. Countries, states, and even cities have Web sites whose primary objective is to sell potential business owners on the benefits of their location. *Examples of this would include groups such as the Downtown Denver Partnership, Inc, which is a nonprofit business organization that represents businesses, commercial property owners, and employees of firms that are located in, of course, downtown Denver, Colorado. In this role, they maintain extensive databases and information on the downtown Denver business market, including detailed maps, demographics, market data, transportation studies, and other relevant trends that influence business in downtown Denver. A review of the data that this nonprofit generates enables a fast but thorough overview of the business complexion of the area, as well as facts and figures on the location.*

The amount of available data on the population of any city or town is staggering. These statistics enable a potential business owner to compare a wide variety of cities or towns and to narrow the choices to those few that warrant further investigation. The mass of data may make it possible to screen out undesirable locations, but it does not make a decision for an entrepreneur. Still, entrepreneurs need to see potential locations firsthand. Only by personal investigation will an entrepreneur be able to add that intangible factor of intuition into the decision-making process. Spending time at a potential location will tell an entrepreneur not only how many people frequent it but also what they are like, how long they stay, and what they buy. Walking or driving around the area will give an entrepreneur clues abut the people who live and work there. What are their houses like? What kinds of cars do they drive? What stage of life are they in? Do they have children? Is the area on the rise or is it past its prime?

The Index of Retail Saturation and Reilly's Law of Retail Gravitation. The **index of retail saturation (IRS)** is a measure of the potential sales per square foot of store space for a given product within a specific trading area. This measure combines the number of customers in a trading area, their purchasing power, and the level of competition. The index is the ratio of a trading area's sales potential for a particular product or service to its sales capacity:

$$IRS = \frac{C \times RE}{RF}$$

where:

    C = Number of customers in the trading area
    RE = Retail expenditures (the average expenditure per person ($) for the product
        in the trading area)
    RF = Retail facilities (the total square feet of selling space allocated to the product
        in the trading area)

This computation is an important one for any retailer to make. Locating in an area already saturated with competitors results in dismal sales volume and often leads to failure.

Company Example

To illustrate the index of retail saturation, let's suppose that an entrepreneur looking at two sites for a shoe store finds that he needs sales of $175 per square foot to be profitable. Site 1 has a trading area with 25,875 potential customers, each of whom spends an average of $42 on shoes annually; the only competitor in the trading area has 6,000 square feet of selling space. Site 2 has 27,750 potential customers spending an average of $43.50 on shoes annually; two competitors occupy a total of 8,400 square feet of space. The IRS of site 1 is:

$$IRS = \frac{25,875 \times 42}{6,000}$$

$$= \$181.12 \text{ sales potential per square foot}$$

The IRS of site 2 is:

$$IRS = \frac{25,750 \times 43.50}{8,400}$$

$$= \$143.71 \text{ sales potential per square foot}$$

Although site 2 appears to be more favorable on the surface, site 1 is supported by the index; site 2 fails to meet the minimum standard of $175 per square foot.

Reilly's Law of Retail Gravitation, a classic work in market analysis published in 1931 by William J. Reilly, uses the analogy of gravity to estimate the attractiveness of a particular business to potential customers. A business's ability to draw customers is directly related to the extent to which customers see it as a "destination" and is inversely related to the distance customers must travel to reach the business. Reilly's model also provides a way to estimate the trade boundary between two market areas by calculating the "break point" between them. The break point between two primary market areas is the boundary between the two where customers become indifferent about shopping at one or the other. The key factor in determining this point of indifference is the size of the communities. If two nearby cities have the same population sizes, then the break point lies halfway between them. The following is the equation for Reilly's Law:[6]

$$BP = \frac{d}{1 + \sqrt{\frac{P_b}{P_a}}}$$

where:

 BP = Distance in miles from location A to the break point
  d = Distance in miles between locations A and B
 P_a = Population surrounding location A
 P_b = Population surrounding location B

For example, if city A and city B are 22 miles apart, and city A has a population of 22,500 and city B has a population of 42,900, the break point according to Reilly's law is:

$$BP = \frac{22}{1 + \sqrt{\frac{42,900}{22,500}}} = 9.2 \text{ miles}$$

The outer edge of city A's trading area lies about nine miles between city A and city B. Although only a rough estimate, this simple calculation using readily available data can be useful for screening potential locations.

Company Example

Costs. For many businesses, the cost of locating and operating is always critical to success. Some entrepreneurs search for locations that possess a spirit of revitalization and locate when the entry cost is very low. Consider two examples: *Sabra and Bill Nickas located their gourmet restaurant near downtown Anderson, South Carolina. The past few decades had been hard on their textile-dependent community, yet the owners saw opportunity where others did not. They purchased the century-old Sullivan Hardware building at a bargain price and opened Sullivan's Metropolitan Grill. Across the country in the busy city of Los Angeles, entrepreneurs took a risk on what was a rapidly declining section of the city to open shops, which are now becoming a West Coast fashion center.* In both examples, entrepreneurs saw opportunities where others did not and located their businesses at the "right place at the right time" and at dramatically lower cost.[7]

A growing number of small cities are establishing special technology zones that offer tax exemptions and reduced fees and licensing costs in an attempt to attract high-tech businesses. Such efforts are a positive incentive for new ventures because they may be able to negotiate excellent terms and conditions for space at below market rates. It should be noted that these opportunities may have limits for technology-oriented firms if the location is lacking a qualified, technologically trained workforce.

Local Laws and Regulations. Before selecting a particular site within a city, small business owners must explore the local zoning laws to determine if there are any ordinances that would place restrictions on business activity or that would prohibit establishing a business altogether. **Zoning** is a system that divides a city or county into small cells or districts to control the use of land, buildings, and sites. Its purpose is to contain similar activities in suitable locations. For instance, one section of a city may be zoned industrial to house manufacturing operations, whereas another section may be zoned commercial for retail businesses. Before choosing a site, an entrepreneur must explore the zoning regulations to make sure it is not out of bounds. In addition to limiting the activities that can take place at a site, zoning also may control the hours of operation, parking requirements, noise limitations, and size of the businesses located there. In some cases, an entrepreneur may appeal to the local zoning commission to rezone a site or to grant a **variance** (a special exception to a zoning ordinance), but this tactic is risky and could be devastating if the board disallows the variance.

Compatibility with the Community. One of the intangibles that an entrepreneur can determine only by visiting a particular city is the degree of compatibility a business has with the surrounding community. In other words, a company's image must fit in with the character of the town and the needs and wants of its residents. Consider the costs associated with opening a retail business in an upscale, high-income community. To succeed, the business would have to match the flavor of the surrounding businesses and create an image that would appeal to upscale customers. Rents, along with fixtures and other decor items, would likely be expensive. Is there an adequate markup in your merchandise to justify such costs?

Quality of Life. One of the most important, yet most difficult to measure, criteria for a city is the quality of life it offers. Entrepreneurs have the freedom and the flexibility to locate their companies in cities that suit not only their business needs but also their personal preferences. When choosing locations for their companies, entrepreneurs often consider factors such as cultural events, outdoor activities, entertainment opportunities, safety, and the city's "personality." A city that offers a high quality of life away from the workplace enables businesses to attract and retain a quality workforce. For instance, San Diego, California, has become a hub for the biotech industry as companies of all sizes have clustered there. Capitalizing on the proximity of several key biotech research institutes such as the Salk Institute and the Scripps Research Institute, and the pool of talent at the University of California, these businesses also cite San Diego's quality of life as a key reason for their location choice. The nearby ocean, mild temperatures, and diverse opportunities for entertainment make San Diego an easy place for recruiting top-notch talent. "We have almost as many bookstores as surf shops," quips one business owner.[8]

Transportation Networks. Manufacturers and wholesalers in particular must investigate the quality of local transportation systems. If a company receives raw materials or ships finished goods by rail, is a location with rail access available in the city under consideration? What kind of highway access is available and are there any plans in the future for major construction that might impact the desired location? Will transportation costs be reasonable and does the transportation infrastructure allow for efficient distribution? For retailers, the availability of loading and unloading zones is an important feature for a suitable location.

Police and Fire Protection. Does the community in which you plan to locate offer adequate police and fire protection? An absence of adequate police and fire protection will reflect in higher insurance costs and increased risks for the owner.

Public Services. Some entity that provides water and sewer services, trash collection, and other utilities should serve the location. Streets should be in good repair with adequate drainage. Not having these services in place translates into higher costs for a business over time.

The Location's Reputation. Like people, a city or parts of a city can have a bad reputation. In some cases, the reputation of the previous business will lower the value of the location. Sites where businesses have failed repeatedly create negative impressions in customers' minds. These negative impressions are hard to overcome and may prevent customers from giving the new business a try.

IN THE FOOTSTEPS OF AN ENTREPRENEUR...

A Workspace Designed for Creativity

When Dan Wieden realized that the advertising agency he had co-founded in 1983 had outgrown the building in downtown Portland, Oregon, that had always been its home, he saw an opportunity not only to find a new location that would accommodate the company's rapid growth but also to transform the entire work environment. "For us, this wasn't about the riddle of figuring out the cubicles or making the office space different from the next guy's," says Wieden, CEO of Wieden+Kennedy, the ad agency that handles much of the advertising for Nike. "The job was figuring out how we can help people live creative lives."

In an age in which innovation often determines business success, Wieden knows that creativity is the soul of his agency and a crucial ingredient to main-

taining his company's competitive edge. That's why he set out to find a location and to create a work space that would inspire employees to be more creative. First, he studied the demographic trends in Portland and confirmed what he had suspected: The Pearl District, a rapidly changing, mixed-use neighborhood much like New York's SoHo district or San Francisco's South of Market area, was the location of preference. It would be a place where creative people would enjoy working, living, and entertaining themselves.

Wieden then found the ideal building, a 90-year-old structure with lots of character and possibilities. After working closely with Weiden and his staff to determine the type of space the company needed, the architect for the project recommended tearing out the core of the building and installing a six-story atrium designed to attract people and to provide them a comfortable place to meet informally to discuss ideas or to solve problems. Long-time employees wistfully recalled the days when the agency was small enough that everyone could gather together on a moment's notice to work on a problem. Now that the Wieden+Kennedy had 250 employees, that was impractical in the old location. The new building was designed to combat the bureaucratic tendencies every company encounters as it grows. "What we wanted was a space divided into quads or 'mini-agencies' that sat around a plaza—a general meeting place for us to have our big community together," says Wieden.

The design of employees' work spaces depends not so much on what their titles are or where they sit in the organizational chart but on what they actually do. Members of the creative team, such as writers, have interior offices with glass walls with doors but no exterior windows. Other employees have offices on the exterior walls with lots of glass, giving them commanding views of the beautiful Williamette River, Mount Hood, Mount St. Helens, and downtown Portland. Although much of the work space is open, employees who need privacy can reserve one of five closed workrooms scattered throughout the six-story building. Rather than use traditional desks, employees work on 10-foot-long tables, and the quad areas on several floors include comfortable couches (some even look as though they were rescued from someone's den) that encourage lounging. Three "kegorators," beer dispensers, see plenty of use at certain times of the day,

and so does the hammock on the rooftop deck. Some workspaces overlook the company gymnasium.

One of Wieden's boldest creative moves was to invite the Portland Institute for Contemporary Art (PICA), an organization whose mission is to promote the works of up-and-coming contemporary artists, to share the agency's workspace. The idea is that having artists roam about the building might enhance the creativity of the agency's employees. The artwork that decorates the space includes unusually shaped clay pots and a six-foot wooden beaver. "Companies like ours need to do whatever it takes to establish and maintain a strong cultural core that's based on creativity," Wieden says. "The bet is that there will be concrete and spiritual rewards for us and for our clients."

Creativity usually is a noisy, somewhat chaotic process, and Wieden+Kennedy's headquarters reflects that. Wieden enjoys seeing groups of employees sitting around the central plaza or on the couches in the quad areas discussing ideas and having fun. "If you can get people to stop thinking about making ads and start thinking about making pieces of communication, then something fresh is apt to arrive," he says.

1. Can a work environment enhance or limit employees' ability to do their jobs? Explain and describe an example.
2. How do Wieden+Kennedy's location and layout contribute to the company's ability to satisfy its clients and maintain a competitive edge?

Source: Adapted from Ron Lieber, "Creative Space," *Fast Company*, January 2001, pp. 136–146.

The Final Site Selection

Successful entrepreneurs develop a site evaluation system that is both detailed and methodical. Each type of business has different evaluation criteria and experience has taught successful entrepreneurs to analyze the facts and figures behind each potential location in search of the best possible site. A manufacturer may need to consider access to customers, raw material, suppliers, labor, and suitable transportation. Service firms need access to customers but can generally survive in lower-rent areas, whereas a retailer's prime consideration is customer traffic. The one element common to all three is the need to locate where customers want to do business.

Site location draws on the most precise information available on the makeup of the area. By using the published statistics mentioned earlier in this chapter, an owner can develop valuable insights regarding the characteristics of people and businesses in the immediate community. Two additional Census Bureau reports entrepreneurs find especially useful when choosing locations are *Summary Population,* which provides a broad demographic look at an area, and *Housing Characteristics,* which offers a detailed breakdown of areas as small as city blocks. The data are available on CD-ROM and on the Web at the Census Bureau's home page. Any small business owner with a properly equipped personal computer can access this incredible wealth of data with a few clicks of the mouse.

Location Criteria for Retail and Service Businesses

2. Describe the location criteria for retail and service businesses.

Few decisions are as important for retailers and service firms as the choice of a location. Because their success depends on a steady flow of customers, retail and service businesses must locate with their target customers' convenience and preferences in mind. The following are important considerations.

Trade Area Size

Every retail business should determine the extent of its trading area: the region from which a business can expect to draw customers over a reasonable time span. The primary variables that influence the scope of a trading area are the type and size of the operation. If a retailer is a specialist with a wide assortment of products, he or she may draw customers from a great distance. In contrast, a convenience store with a general line of merchandise may have a small trading area because it is unlikely that customers would drive across town to purchase what is available within blocks of their homes or businesses. Generally speaking, the larger the store and the greater its selection of merchandise, the broader is its trading area.

Here again is the time to return to the *Survey of Buying Power* published annually by Sales and Marketing Management to conduct a side-by-side evaluation of the retail trading areas under consideration. Two key statistics that are traditionally used are *effective buying power*, which is equivalent to disposable personal income, and the *buying power index*. The buying power index is a weighted measure that combines effective buying income, retail sales, and population size into a single economic indicator of an area's sales potential as compared with total U.S. sales. The higher the buying power index, the greater is the proven positive purchasing behavior.

The following environmental factors influence the retail trading area size.

Company Example →

- *Retail compatibility.* Shoppers tend to be drawn to clusters of related businesses. That's one reason shopping malls and outlet shopping centers are popular destinations for shoppers and are attractive locations for retailers. The concentration of businesses pulls customers from a larger trading area than a single free-standing business does. **Retail compatibility** describes the benefits a company receives by locating near other businesses selling complementary products and services. *The typical movie theater draws its customers from an area of five to seven miles; however, the AMC Grand, a collection of 24 screens under one roof, in Dallas, Texas, draws customers from as far as 25 miles away. The megaplex draws an impressive 3 million moviegoers a year. Not long after the AMC Grand megaplex opened, seven new restaurants popped up within easy walking distance of the theaters.*[9] Clever retailers choose their locations with an eye on the surrounding mix of businesses.

- *Degree of competition.* The size, location, and activity of competing businesses also influence the size of the trading area. If a business will be the first of its kind in a location, its trading area might be extensive. However, if the area already has eight or nine nearby stores that directly compete with a business, its trading area might be very small. How does the size of your planned operation compare with those that presently exist? Your business may be significantly larger and have more drawing power, giving it a competitive advantage.

- *Transportation network.* The transportation networks are the highways, roads, and public service routes that presently exist or are planned. An inconvenient location reduces the business's trading area. Entrepreneurs should check to see if the transportation system works smoothly and is free of barriers that might prevent customers from reaching their stores. Is it easy for customers traveling in the opposite direction to cross traffic? Do signs and lights allow traffic to flow smoothly?

- *Physical, cultural, or emotional barriers.* Physical barriers may be parks, rivers, lakes, or any other obstruction that hinders customers' access to the area. Locating on one side of a large park may reduce the number of customers who will drive around it to get to a store. In urban areas, new immigrants tend to cluster together, sharing a common culture and language. These trading areas are defined by cultural barriers, where inhabitants patronize only the businesses in their neighborhoods. The Little Havana section of Miami or the Chinatown sections of San Francisco, New York, and Los Angeles are examples. One powerful emotional barrier is fear. If high-crime areas exist around a site, most of a company's potential customers will not travel through those neighborhoods to reach the business. The mayors of many large cities in the United States have recognized that economic viability depends on the attitudes of both entrepreneurs and customers. The leaders of these cities are focusing their efforts on reducing crime and eliminating barriers to potential shoppers.

- *Political barriers and creations of law.* Federal, state, county, or city boundaries—and the laws within those boundaries—can influence the size of a company's trading area. State laws also created conditions where customers cross over to the next state to save money. For instance, North Carolina imposes a very low cigarette tax, and shops located on its borders do a brisk business in the product.

Entrepreneurs should evaluate the characteristics of a retail trading area thoroughly, and Table 16.2 is a helpful tool for conducting such an analysis. Once entrepreneurs rank each characteristic from 1–10 in relative importance and assign a trading area score on the 1 to 5 scale, they simply multiply the two values to get a score for each characteristic. Adding up the scores produces a total score. (Higher is better.)

Table 16.2

Retail Trading Area Analysis

Characteristics	Relative Importance 1 = Low, 10 = High	Trading Area Score 1 = Negative, 5 = Positive	Area A	Area B
	1 2 3 4 5 6 7 8 9 10	1 2 3 4 5		
Population Size and Density				
Per Capita Disposable Income				
Total Disposable Income				
Educational Levels of the Population				
Age Distribution				
Number and Size of Existing Competitors				
Existing Competitors' Strength				
Level of Market Saturation				
Population Growth Projections				
Ease of Access				
Other:				
Total Score				

Customer Traffic

Perhaps the most important screening criteria for a potential retail (and often for a service) location is the number of potential customers passing by the site during business hours. To be successful, a business must be able to generate sufficient sales to surpass its break-even point, and doing that requires an ample volume of traffic. One of the key success factors for a convenience store, for instance, is a high-traffic location with easy accessibility. Entrepreneurs should know the traffic counts (pedestrian and auto) at the sites they are considering. Shoeshine stands and kiosks in airports are examples of service businesses where the customer comes directly to the entrepreneur. The high volume of people traveling on business is a prime customer base.

Adequate Parking

If customers cannot find convenient and safe parking, they are not likely to stop in the area. Many downtown areas have lost customers because of inadequate parking. Although shopping malls typically average five parking spaces per 1,000 square feet of shopping space, many central business districts get by with 3.5 spaces per 1,000 square feet. Customers generally will not pay to park if parking is free at shopping centers or in front of competing stores. Even when a business provides free parking, some potential customers may not feel safe on the streets, especially after dark. Many large city business districts become virtual ghost towns at the end of the business day. A location where traffic vanishes after 6 P.M. may not be as valuable as mall and shopping center locations that mark the beginning of the prime sales at 6 P.M.

Room for Expansion

A location should be flexible enough to provide for expansion if success warrants it. Failure to consider this factor can force a successful business to open a second store when it would have been better to expand in its original location.

Visibility

No matter what a retailer sells or how well it serves customers' needs, it cannot survive without visibility. Highly visible locations simply make it easy for customers to make purchases. A site lacking visibility puts a company at a major disadvantage before it even opens its doors. In a competitive marketplace, customers seldom are willing to search for a business when equally attractive alternatives are easy to locate.

Some service businesses, however, can select sites with less visibility if the majority of their customer contacts are by telephone, fax, or the Internet. For example, customers usually contact plumbers by telephone; so rather than locating close to their customer bases, plumbers have flexibility in choosing their locations. Similarly, businesses that work at their customers' homes, such as swimming pool services, can operate from their homes and service vans.

Location Options for Retail and Service Businesses

3. Outline the basic location options for retail and service businesses.

There are six basic areas where retail and service business owners can locate: the central business district (CBD), neighborhoods, shopping centers and malls, near competitors, outlying areas, and at home. According to the International Council of Shopping Centers, the average cost to lease space in a shopping center is about $15 per square foot. At a regional mall, rental rates run from $20 to $40 per square foot, and in central business locations, the average cost is $43 per square foot (although rental rates can vary significantly in either direction of that average, depending on the city).[9] Of course, cost is just one factor a business owner must consider when choosing a location.

Central Business District

The central business district (CBD) is the traditional center of town—the downtown concentration of businesses established early in the development of most towns and cities. Entrepreneurs derive several advantages from a downtown location. Because businesses are centrally located, they attract customers from the entire trading area of the city. Also, small businesses benefit from the traffic generated by other stores clustered in the downtown district. However, locating in a CBD does have certain disadvantages. Intense competition, high rental rates, traffic congestion, and inadequate parking facilities characterize some CBDs. In addition, many cities have experienced difficulty in preventing the decay of their older downtown business districts. Many downtown districts withered as residents moved to the suburbs and began shopping at newer, more convenient shopping centers and malls.

Today, many cities are working to restore the unique atmosphere of their traditional downtown shopping districts. Customers find irresistible the charming atmosphere that central business districts offer, with their rich mix of shops, their unique architecture and streetscapes, and their historic character. Cities across the United States have begun to reverse the urban decay of their downtown business districts through proactive revitalization programs designed to attract visitors and residents alike to cultural events by locating major theaters and museums in the downtown area. In addition, many cities are providing economic incentives to real estate developers to build apartment and condominium complexes in the heart of the downtown area. Vitality is returning as residents live and shop in the once nearly abandoned downtown areas. The "ghost-town" image is being replaced by both young and old residents who love the convenience and excitement of life at the center of the city.

Company Example →

As residents have become more interested in preserving their downtown districts, retailers have returned to Main Street. *Borders Group recently opened a Borders Bookstore in downtown Detroit on the ground floor of Compuware Corporation's world headquarters building. Although shuttered storefronts and empty buildings are scattered throughout the area, the bookstore draws many of its customers from the more than 4,000 employees who work at Compuware and from other downtown workers. Of Borders' 480 bookstores nationwide, 50 are located in downtown settings. In other cities, large retailers such as Talbots, Gap, J. Crew, Williams-Sonoma, Eddie Bauer and Starbucks are opening stores in traditional CBDs, locations they typically have shunned in the past.*[10]

Neighborhood Locations

Small businesses that locate near residential areas rely heavily on the local trading areas for business. For example, many grocers and convenience stores located just outside residential subdivisions count on local clients for successful operation. One study of food stores found that the majority of the typical grocers' customers live within a five-mile radius. The primary advantages of a neighborhood location include relatively low operating costs and rents and close contact with customers.

Shopping Centers and Malls

Shopping centers and malls have become part of the fabric of life in the United States and more than 47,000 of them now dot the nation's landscape, occupying 5.9 billion square feet of retail space. According to the International Council of Shopping Centers, more than 203 million adults shop in shopping centers and malls each month.[11] Few malls are as upscale as the Forum Shops of Caesars Palace in Las Vegas, Nevada, where stores ring up an amazing average of $1,300 in sales per square foot.[12] Put another way, at this level of sales per square foot, a single 15,000 square foot store would produce revenues of $19.5 million! The largest mall in the United States is the Mall of America in Bloomington, Minnesota, which is home to more than 520 stores. It truly is a destination location, drawing 250,000 shoppers on a typical weekend, 40 percent of whom live more than 150 miles away.[13]

Because many different types of stores exist under one roof, malls give meaning to the term "one-stop shopping." The following are four types of shopping centers and malls:

- *Neighborhood or lifestyle shopping centers.* The typical neighborhood shopping center is relatively small, containing from 3 to 12 stores and serving a population of up to 40,000 people who are within a 10-minute drive. The anchor store in these centers is usually a supermarket or a drugstore.
- *Community shopping centers.* The community shopping center contains from 12 to 50 stores and serves a population ranging from 40,000 to 150,000 people. The leading tenant is a department or variety store.
- *Regional shopping malls.* The regional shopping mall serves a much larger trading area, usually from 10 to 15 miles or more in all directions. It contains from 50 to 100 stores and serves a population in excess of 150,000 people living within a 20- to 40-minute drive. The anchor is typically one or more major department stores.
- *Power centers.* A power center combines the drawing strength of a large regional mall with the convenience of a neighborhood shopping center. Anchored by large specialty retailers, these centers target older, wealthier baby boomers who want selection and convenience. Anchor stores usually account for 80 percent of power center space, compared with 50 percent in the typical strip shopping center. Small companies must be careful in choosing power center locations to avoid being overshadowed by their larger neighbors. Spillover traffic from the anchor stores, although not guaranteed, is the primary benefit to small businesses locating in power centers.

Because the cost of locating in a shopping center or mall can be quite high, it is important for an entrepreneur to consider these questions:

- Is there a good fit with other products and brands sold in the mall or center?
- Who are the other tenants? Which stores are the anchors that will bring people into the mall or center?
- Demographically, is the center a good fit for your products or services? What are its customer demographics?
- How much foot traffic does the mall or center generate? How much traffic passes the specific site you are considering?
- How much vehicle traffic does the mall or center generate? Check its proximity to major population centers, the volume of tourists it draws, and the volume of drive-by freeway traffic. A mall or center that scores well on all three is probably a winner.
- What is the vacancy rate? The turnover rate?
- Is the mall or center successful? How many dollars in sales does it generate per square foot? Compare its record against the industry average.

Although malls still account for the majority of retail sales, they have waned in popularity within the past 20 years. A mall location is no longer a guarantee of success. Malls have been under pressure lately, and many weaker ones have closed. Part of the problem is the bland sameness that malls exhibit in their designs and in the stores they offer. Also, the demographic makeup of malls' shoppers has changed over time, and many traditional mall shoppers are unhappy with the traffic congestion and sprawling parking lots that characterize some mall shopping experiences. Other malls have undergone extensive renovations, adding entertainment features to their existing retail space in an attempt to generate more traffic. At the Mall of America, for instance, visitors can take a break from shopping at Camp Snoopy, a seven-acre indoor amusement park, or at Underwater Adventures, an aquarium with more than 3,000 types of marine creatures.[14]

Near Competitors

One of the most important factors in choosing a retail or service location is the compatibility of nearby stores with the retail or service customer. For example, stores selling high-priced goods such as cars or merchandise that requires comparisons, such as antiques, find it advantageous to locate near competitors to facilitate comparison shopping. Locating near competitors might be a key factor for success in businesses that sell goods that customers compare on the basis of price, quality, color, and other factors.

Although some small business owners seek to avoid locations near direct competitors, others want to locate near rivals. For instance, restaurateurs know that restaurants attract other restaurants, which, in turn, attract more customers. That's why in many cities, at least one "restaurant row" develops; each restaurant feeds the others.

There are limits to locating near competitors, however. Clustering too many businesses of a single type into a small area ultimately will erode their sales once the market reaches the saturation point. As the number of gourmet coffee shops has exploded in recent years, many have struggled to remain profitable, often competing with three or four similar shops, all within easy walking distance of one another. When an area becomes saturated with competitors, the stores cannibalize sales from one another, making it difficult for all of them to survive.

Outlying Areas

In general, it is not advisable for a small business to locate in a remote area because accessibility and traffic flow are vital to retail and service success, but there are exceptions.

Some small firms have turned their remote locations into trademarks. One small gun shop was able to use an extremely remote location to its advantage by incorporating this into its advertising to distinguish itself from its competitors.

Outlying locations become a distinct disadvantage if potential customers cannot find your location, if they believe that there is no overriding reason to travel to your location, or if they fear for their safety either at your location or on the way to and from your location.

Home-Based Businesses

For more than 27 million people, home is where the business is, and their numbers are swelling. According to the Department of Commerce, home-based businesses represent the fastest-growing segment of the U.S. economy.[15] One recent study found that 52 percent of all small companies are home based.[16]

Although a home-based retail business is usually not feasible, locating a service business at home is quite popular. Many service companies do not have customers come to their places of business, so an expensive office location is unnecessary. For instance, customers typically contact plumbers or exterminators by telephone, and the work is performed in customers' homes.

Company Example

Entrepreneurs locating their businesses at home reap several benefits. Perhaps the biggest benefit is the low cost of setting up the business. Most often, home-based entrepreneurs set up shop in a spare bedroom or basement, avoiding the cost of renting, leasing, or buying a building. With a few basic pieces of office equipment—a computer, printer, fax machine, copier, telephone answering system, and scanner—a lone entrepreneur can perform just like a major corporation. *For instance, David Gans runs Truth and Fun, Inc., a state-of-the-art production studio, from a spare bedroom in his Oakland, California, home. From his high-tech, in-home studio, Gans produces a weekly radio show, the Grateful Dead Hour, that he beams by satellite to 90 radio stations across the country. "The equipment has gotten so powerful and inexpensive that one human being working from home can produce the exact same-quality program as National Public Radio," says Gans.*[17]

Choosing a home location has certain disadvantages, however. Interruptions are more frequent, the refrigerator is all too handy, work is always just a few steps away, and isolation can be a problem. Another difficulty facing some home-based entrepreneurs involves zoning laws. As their businesses grow and become more successful, entrepreneurs' neighbors often begin to complain about the increased traffic, noise and disruptions from deliveries, employees, and customers who drive through their residential neighborhoods to conduct business. Many communities now face the challenge of passing updated zoning laws that reflect the reality of today's home-based businesses while protecting the interests of residential homeowners.

The Location Decision for Manufacturers

4. Explain the site selection process for manufacturers.

The criteria for the location decision for manufacturers are very different from those of retailers and service businesses; however, the decision can have just as much impact on the company's success. In some cases, a manufacturer has special needs that influence the choice of location. In other cases the decision is influenced by municipal regulations.

Labor productivity is a critical factor for manufacturers when labor cost is a significant component of a product's total cost. Labor productivity in cost per unit of production is a simple calculation:

$$\text{Cost per unit} = \frac{\text{Labor cost per day}}{\text{Productivity (in units/day)}}$$

Company Example	→

Areas with lower labor costs may seem at first glance to be a good choice, but the lower levels of productivity associated with less trained or poorly motivated workers may result in higher cost per unit of production. *Hutchinson Technology, a company that makes the tiny suspension systems that are used in computer disk drives, maintains all four of its manufacturing plants within a 200-mile radius of tiny Hutchinson, Minnesota, despite the fact that all of its competitors manufacture their products in East Asia to take advantage of cheaper labor costs. Hutchinson's manufacturing process, which is highly automated, relies on high-quality, skilled workers to produce the tiny stainless steel strips that hold the head of computer disk drives just 8 nanometers above the surface of the spinning disk. In the face of intense competition, Hutchinson maintains 55 percent market share and ships 98 percent of its output to computer makers that are located in East Asia. Because the company has invested so heavily in automation, its labor costs are less than 15 percent of its cost of goods sold, even though wage rates for its workers in the United States are many times those of workers in East Asia. Also, because the finished product is so small, shipping costs are minimal. "Our location is one of our competitive advantages," says CEO Wayne Fortun.*[18]

Local zoning ordinances will limit a manufacturer's choice of location. If the manufacturing process creates offensive odors or noise, the business may be even further restricted in its choices. City and county planners will be able to show potential manufacturers the area of the city or county set aside for industrial development. Some cities have developed industrial parks in cooperation with private industry. These industrial parks typically are equipped with sewage and electrical power sufficient for manufacturing. Many locations are not so equipped, and it can be extremely expensive for a small manufacturer to have such utilities brought to an existing site.

The type of transportation facilities required can dictate location of the plant. Some manufacturers may need to locate on railroad siding; others may only need reliable trucking service. If raw materials are purchased by the carload for economies of scale, the location must be convenient to a railroad siding. Bulk materials are sometimes shipped by barge and, consequently, require a facility convenient to a navigable river or lake. The added cost of using multiple shipping (e.g., rail-to-truck or barge-to-truck) can significantly increase shipping costs and make a location unfeasible for a manufacturer.

In some cases the perishability of the product dictates location. Vegetables and fruits must be canned near the fields in which they are harvested. Fish must be processed and canned at the water's edge. Location is determined by quick and easy access to the perishable products. Needed utilities, zoning, transportation, and special requirements may also work together to limit the number of locations that are suitable for a manufacturer.

Foreign Trade Zones

Foreign trade zones can be attractive locations for many small manufacturers that are engaged in global trade and are looking to lower the tariffs they pay on the materials and parts they import and on the goods they export. A **foreign trade zone** is a specially designated area that allows resident companies to import materials and components from foreign countries; assemble, process, package, or manufacture them; and then ship finished products out while incurring low tariffs and duties or, in some cases, paying no tariffs or duties at all. For instance, a bicycle maker might import parts and components from around the world and assemble them onto frames made in the United States. If located in a foreign trade zone, the manufacturer pays no duties on the parts it imports or on the finished bicycles it exports. The only duty the manufacturer would pay is on bicycles it sells in the United States (see Figure 16.2).

Figure 16.2

How a Foreign Trade Zone (FTZ) Works

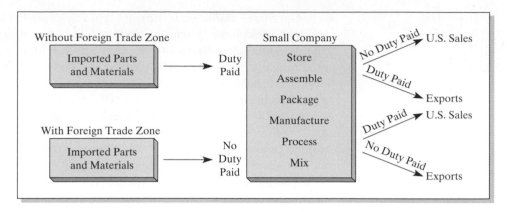

Empowerment Zones

Originally created to encourage companies to locate in economically blighted areas, **empowerment zones** offer entrepreneurs tax breaks on investments they make within zone boundaries. Companies can get federal tax credits for hiring workers living in empowerment zones and for investments they make in plant and equipment in the zones. Before becoming an empowerment zone, downtown Detroit had become a virtual ghost town, littered with crumbling buildings and unsightly vacant lots. With the tax incentives available through the empowerment zone, businesses came back to the downtown, investing more than $2 billion in 80 new projects in just the first two years. Projects ranged from a Chrysler engine factory and retail stores to housing developments and an art museum.[19]

Business Incubators

5. Discuss the benefits of locating a start-up company in a business incubator.

Business incubators have been around for four decades and have spawned more than 20,000 successful businesses. For many start-up companies, an incubator may make the ideal initial location. A **business incubator** is an organization that combines low-cost, flexible rental space with a multitude of support services for its small business residents. The overwhelming reasons for establishing an incubator are to enhance economic development in an area and to diversify the local economy. Common sponsors of incubators include government agencies; colleges and universities; partnerships among government agencies, nonprofit agencies, and private developers; and private investment groups. Business and technical incubators vary to some degree as to the types of clients they attempt to attract, but most incubator residents are engaged in light manufacturing, service businesses, and technology or research-related fields (see Figure 16.3).[20]

Figure 16.3

Incubator Clients by Type

Source: © Copyright 2004 by NBIA. All Rights Reserved Worldwide.

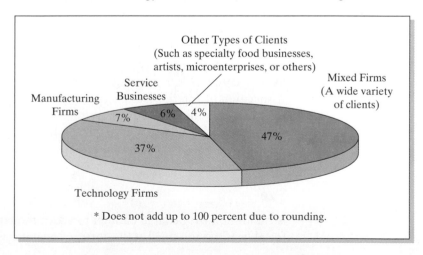

* Does not add up to 100 percent due to rounding.

The shared resources incubators typically provide their tenants include secretarial services, a telephone system, a computer and software, fax machines, meeting facilities, and, sometimes, management consulting services. An incubator will normally have entry requirements that are tied to its purpose and that detail the nature and scope of the business activities to be conducted. Incubators also have criteria that establish the conditions a business must meet to remain in the facility as well as the expectations for "graduation."

In addition to shared services, incubators offer their fledgling tenants reduced rents and another valuable resource: access to the early-stage capital that young companies need to grow. A recent survey by the National Business Incubation Association found that 83 percent of incubators provide some kind of access to seed capital, ranging from help with obtaining federal grants to making connections with angel investors.[21] Some incubators also provide assistance to resident businesses interested in exporting.

More than 950 incubators operate across the United States, and a new incubator opens, on average, every week. Most receive some type of financial assistance from their sponsors to continue operations. The investment that supports the incubator is generally a wise one because firms that graduate from incubators have only a 13 percent failure rate.

| Company Example | → |

When the biotech company that he ran from a spare bedroom in his home acquired the exclusive license to a breakthrough system that delivers medicine straight to the heart, James Grabek knew it was time to take his company, Comedicus, Inc., to the next level. Fearful of losing control of his business, Grabek ultimately turned to Genesis Business Centers, a business incubator in Minneapolis, Minnesota. Harlon T. Jacobs, president of Genesis, offered Grabek access to $50,000 in financing, free office space, and management assistance in exchange for just 5 percent of the company's stock. Grabek decided to nurture his business in the incubator and quickly accepted the offer. Within 15 months, Genesis had helped Comedicus raise $1 million in a private placement and land $4 million in licensing agreements with major pharmaceutical companies. "It was a turning point that catapulted us into the corporate world," Grabek says of his decision to move into the incubator.[22]

Layout Considerations

6. Describe the criteria used to analyze the layout and design considerations of a building, including the Americans with Disabilities Act.

Once an entrepreneur finds the right location for his or her business, the next question deals with designing proper layout for the building to maximize sales (retail) or productivity (manufacturing or service). **Layout** is the logical arrangement of the physical facilities in a business that contributes to efficient operations, increased productivity, lower energy usage, and higher sales. Planning for the most effective and efficient layout in a business can produce dramatic improvements in a company's operating effectiveness and efficiency. Similarly, poor layout can limit sales by frustrating and confusing customers as they shop and can impede employees from working at peak performance. A study by the American Society of Interior Designers found that 57 percent of office employees were dissatisfied with the layout of their work environments, saying it had a negative impact on communication, interaction, efficiency, and comfort. [23] An attractive, effective layout can help a company's recruiting efforts. Another study conducted by the American Association of Interior Designers found that employees rated the look and feel of their workspaces as the third most important consideration (after salary and benefits) when deciding whether to accept or to quit a job.[24]

The following factors have a significant impact on a building's layout and design.

Size

A building must be large enough to accommodate a business's daily operations comfortably. If it is too small at the outset of operations, efficiency will suffer. There must be room enough for customers' movement, inventory, displays, storage, work areas, offices, and restrooms. Haphazard layouts undermine employee productivity and create organizational chaos. Too many small business owners start their operations in locations that are already overcrowded and lack room for expansion. The result is that the owner is forced to make a costly move to a new location within the first few years of operation. *Dan Wieden, founder and CEO of Portland, Oregon–based advertising agency Wieden+Kennedy (W+K), wanted to avoid that mistake. Wieden knew it was time to move to a new location when the agency had 250 employees and had outgrown the building that had housed it for 18 years. The new building, which was designed to stimulate creativity and collaboration among its residents, has plenty of room to accommodate the growing agency. "Right now, we have 250 people working here," says Chris Riley, W+K's chief strategic officer, "but the building could easily hold 500."*[25]

If an owner plans any kind of expansion, will the building accommodate it? Will hiring new employees, purchasing new equipment, expanding production areas, or increasing service areas require a new location? How fast is the company expected to grow over the next three to five years? Inadequate room may become a limitation on the growth of the business. Most small businesses wait too long before moving into larger quarters, and they fail to plan the new space arrangements properly. Some experts recommend that, to avoid such problems, new businesses should plan their space requirements one to two years ahead and update the estimates every six months. When preparing the plan, managers should include the expected growth in the number and location of branches to be opened.

Construction and External Appearance

Is the construction of the building sound? It pays to have an expert look it over before buying or leasing the property. Beyond the soundness of construction, does the building have an attractive external and internal appearance? The physical appearance of the building provides customers with their first impression of a business and contributes significantly to establishing its identity in the customer's mind. This is especially true in retail businesses. Is the building's appearance consistent with the entrepreneur's desired image for the business? Small retailers must recognize the importance of creating the proper image for their store and how their shop's layout and physical facility influence this image. In many ways the building's appearance sets the tone for what the customer can expect in the way of quality and service. The appearance should, therefore, reflect the business's "personality." Should the building project an exclusive image or an economical one? Is the atmosphere informal and relaxed or formal and businesslike? Externally, the storefront, its architectural style and color, signs, entrances, and general appearance give important clues to customers about a business's image.

A glass front enables a retail business to display merchandise easily and to attract potential customers' attention. Passersby can look in and see attractive merchandise displays or, in some cases, employees busily working. *Krispy Kreme, a chain of doughnut shops along the Atlantic seaboard, attracts attention—and customers—by prominently displaying its doughnut-making equipment behind a glass wall. Most customers are mesmerized as they watch the machine turn out a batch of those tasty golden circles, which it then coats with molten icing. After watching the machine go through its doughnut-making cycle, viewers can hardly resist buying a doughnut. The smell of fresh-baked doughnuts wafting through the air doesn't hurt business either!*

Communicating the right signals through layout and physical facilities is an important step in attracting a steady stream of customers. Retail consultant Paco Underhill advises merchants to "seduce" passersby with their storefronts. "The seduction process should start a minimum of 10 paces away," he says. "A store's interior architecture is

Company Example	→

fundamental to the customer's experience—the stage upon which a retail company functions."[26] *For instance, Williams-Sonoma, an upscale retailer of kitchenware ranging from Cuisinart food processors and praline sauce to wooden spoons and dishtowels, seduces passersby with window displays that look more like someone's kitchen than a retail shop. Stores in the chain change their eye-catching displays frequently to reflect the foods of the season. The goal is not only to sell but also to make customers feel welcome and to put them in a positive frame of mind. "If you have a positive feeling," says Julie Irwin, a marketing professor at the University of Texas at Austin, "you're going to associate it with everything you see." Once inside a Williams-Sonoma store, a wonderful array of aromas rising from freshly-baked foods or hot beverages also lures customers and encourages them to stay, which increases the probability that they will buy something.*[27]

The following tips help entrepreneurs create displays that will sell:

- *Keep displays simple.* Simple, uncluttered arrangements of merchandise will draw the most attention and will have the greatest impact on potential customers. Avoid taping posters on display windows; it cheapens a store's look.
- *Keep displays clean and up to date.* Dusty, dingy displays or designs that are outdated send the wrong message to customers.
- *Promote local events.* Small companies can show their support of the community by devoting part of the display window to the promotion of local events.
- *Change displays frequently.* Customers don't want to see the same merchandise every time they visit a store. Experts recommend changing window displays at least quarterly. Businesses that sell fashionable items, however, should change their displays at least twice a month, if not weekly.
- *Get expert help, if necessary.* Some business owners have no aptitude for design! In that case, their best bet is to hire a professional to design window and in-store displays. If a company cannot afford a professional designer's fees, the entrepreneur should check with the design departments at local colleges and universities. There might be a faculty member or a talented student willing to work on a freelance basis.
- *Appeal to all of a customer's senses.* Effective displays engage more than one of a customer's senses. Who can pass up a bakery case of freshly baked, gooey cinnamon buns with their mouth-watering aroma wafting up to greet passersby?
- Contact the companies whose products you sell to see if they offer design props and assistance.

Entrances

All entrances to a business should invite customers in. Wide entryways and attractive merchandise displays that are set back from the doorway can draw customers into a business. Retailers with heavy traffic flows such as supermarkets or drugstores often install automatic doors to ensure a smooth traffic flow into and out of their stores. Retailers should remove any barriers that interfere with customers' easy access to the storefront. Broken sidewalks, sagging steps, mud puddles, and sticking or heavy doors not only create obstacles that might discourage potential customers, but they also create legal hazards for a business if they cause customers to be injured. Entrances should be lighted to create a friendly atmosphere that invites customers to enter a business.

The Americans with Disabilities Act

The **Americans with Disabilities Act (ADA),** passed in July 1990, requires practically all businesses to make their facilities available to physically challenged customers and employees. In addition, the law requires businesses with 15 or more employees to accommodate physically challenged candidates in their hiring practices. The rules of the ADA's Title III are designed to ensure that mentally and physically challenged customers have equal access to a firm's goods or services. For instance, the act requires business owners to remove architectural and communication barriers when "readily achievable." The ADA allows flexibility in how a business achieves this equal access, however. For example, a restaurant could either provide menus in braille or offer to have a staff member read the menu to blind customers. Or a small dry cleaner might not be able to add a wheelchair ramp to its storefront without incurring significant expense, but the owner could comply with the ADA by offering curbside pickup and delivery services for customers with disabilities at no extra charge.

Although the law allows a good deal of flexibility in retrofitting existing structures, buildings that were occupied after January 25, 1993, must be designed to comply with all aspects of the law. For example, buildings with three stories or more must have elevators; anywhere the floor level changes by more than one-half inch, an access ramp must be in place. In retail stores, checkout aisles must be wide enough—at least 36 inches—to accommodate wheelchairs. Restaurants must have 5 percent of their tables accessible to wheelchair-bound patrons.

Complying with the ADA does not necessarily require businesses to spend large amounts of money. Companies with $1 million or less in annual sales or with 30 or fewer full-time employees that invest in making their locations more accessible to all qualify for a tax credit. The credit is 50 percent of their expenses between $250 and $10,500. Businesses that remove physical structures or transportation barriers for employees and customers with disabilities also qualify for up to $15,000 in tax deductions.

The Americans with Disabilities Act also prohibits any kind of employment discrimination against anyone with a physical or mental disability. A physically challenged person is considered to be "qualified" if he or she can perform the essential functions of the job. The employer must make "reasonable accommodation" for a physically challenged candidate or employee without causing "undue hardship" to the business. Following are some of the specific provisions of Title III of the act:

- Restaurants, hotels, theaters, shopping centers and malls, retail stores, museums, libraries, parks, private schools, day care centers, and other similar places of public accommodation may not discriminate on the basis of disability.
- Physical barriers in existing places of public accommodation must be removed if readily achievable (i.e., easily accomplished and able to be carried out without much difficulty or expense). If not, alternative methods of providing services must be offered, if those methods are readily achievable.
- New construction of places of public accommodation and commercial facilities (nonresidential facilities affecting commerce) must be accessible.
- Alterations to existing places of public accommodation and commercial facilities must be done in an accessible manner. When alterations affect the utility of or access to a "primary function" area of a facility, an accessible path of travel must be provided to the altered areas, and the restrooms, telephones, and drinking fountains serving the altered areas must also be accessible, to the extent that the cost of making these features accessible does not exceed 20 percent of the cost of the planned alterations. The additional accessibility requirements for alterations to primary function areas do not apply to measures taken solely to comply with readily achievable barrier removal.
- Elevators are not required in newly constructed or altered buildings under three stories or with less than 3,000 square feet per floor, unless the building is a shopping center; shopping mall; professional office of a health care provider; terminal; depot; or station used for public transportation; or an airport passenger terminal.

Most businesses have found that making these reasonable accommodations for customers and employees have proven to create a more pleasant environment and have attracted new customers as well as qualified employees.

The Americans with Disabilities Act has affected, in a positive way, how businesses deal with this segment of its customers and employees. The Department of Justice offers a program that provides business owners with free information and technical assistance concerning the ADA.

Signs

One of the lowest-cost and most effective methods of communicating with customers is a business sign. Signs tell potential customers what a business does, where it is, and what it is selling. America is a very mobile society, and a well-designed, well-placed sign can be a powerful tool for reaching potential customers.

A sign should be large enough for passersby to read from a distance, taking into consideration the location and speed of surrounding traffic arteries. To be most effective, the message should be short, simple, and clear. A sign should be legible both in daylight and at night; proper illumination is a must. Contrasting colors and simple typefaces are best. Because signs become part of the surrounding scenery over time, business owners should consider changing their features to retain their effectiveness. Animated parts and unusual shapes can attract interest.

The most common problems with business signs are that they are illegible, poorly designed, improperly located, poorly maintained, and have color schemes that are unattractive or are hard to read. Most communities have sign ordinances. Before investing in a sign, an entrepreneur should investigate the local community's ordinance. In some cities and towns, local regulations impose restrictions on the size, location, height, and construction materials used in business signs.

IN THE FOOTSTEPS OF AN ENTREPRENEUR...

A New Image for Victoria's Secret Stores

Store layout and the merchandising of products must match the image of a retailer. Victoria's Secret flagship store in New York City has received a major "new look" and, based on the resulting spike in sales, the "look" will become national. As one expert says, "Victoria's Secret stores have often felt like a journey back to the Victorian era—more innocent cherub than sexpot angel."

In the past few years, Victoria's Secret has enhanced its global image through the use of supermodels such as Tyra Banks and Gisele Biindchen. The new store layout will attract customers through enticing entryways, attractive color schemes, and putting the merchandise featured in its catalogue on prominent display. The Victoria's Secret brand has been defined by its "cutting-edge" catalogues and televised fashion show. Now the firm's 1,100 stores will reflect this powerful brand image. CEO Leslie Wexner was the driving force behind the new store

image and its completely revised layout. His goal is to make Victoria's Secret "a more upscale brand in customers' minds; the goal is to boost the racy factor without cheapening the store's image." Wexner brought in the design firm Yabu Pushelberg to produce changes that will increase store traffic and sales. Kathleen Balwin, vice president of store design for Victoria's Secret, described the original stores as "soft, feminine environments." Now the redesigned stores feature what could only be described as theatrical lighting blended with classical background music.

The key idea: Store design and layout must support the brand image.

1. How would you evaluate the proper balance between selling the brand image and community "good taste"?

Source: Adapted from Monica Knemsurov, "Sexing up Victoria's Secret," *Business 2.0,* April 2004, pp. 54–55.

Interiors

Company Example

Like exterior considerations, the functional aspects of building interiors require careful evaluation and planning. Designing a functional, efficient interior is not as easy as it may seem. Technology has drastically changed the way employees, customers, and the environment interact with one another. The key is flexibility. *When managers at Breakaway Solutions, an applications service provider in New York City, realized the limitations that the cramped, dark, poorly planned workspace had on employees, they gutted the office and started over. The goal was to create a highly collaborative environment that reflects the nature of employees' work and encourages communication and interaction. The office now has a much more open, airy look and feel. Skylights in the attractive common area where software engineers often gather to solve problems (exactly the plan!) let in natural light. Perimeter walls at Breakaway are made of whiteboard material, and software engineers are constantly scribbling on them throughout the course of the workday. Movable walls enable employees to transform workspaces to meet the changing demands of the tasks they must perform during a typical day. "This building has to be about our culture," says Ari Shamash, an engineering designer at Breakaway. "High-tech companies have to be flexible, and we needed an office that was flexible."*[28]

Piecing together an effective layout is not a haphazard process. Vivian Loftness, a researcher at the Center for Building Performance, says that a building's design should provide employees with certain basic requirements, including fresh air, personal temperature and lighting control; natural light; a pleasant view; easy access to privacy and "working quiet"; readily accessible network, power, and voice connections; and ergonomically designed furniture.[29] **Ergonomics,** the science of adapting work and the work environment to complement employees' strengths and to suit customers' needs, is an integral part of a successful design. For example, chairs, desks, and table heights that enable people to work comfortably can help employees perform their job faster and more easily. Design experts claim that improved lighting, better acoustics, and proper climate control benefit the company as well as employees. An ergonomically designed workplace can improve workers' productivity significantly and lower days lost due to injuries and accidents. Unfortunately, many businesses fail to incorporate ergonomic design principles into their layouts, and the result is costly. The most frequent and most expensive workplace injuries are musculoskeletal disorders (MSDs), which cost U.S. businesses $20 billion in workers' compensation claims each year. According to the Occupational Safety and Health Administration (OSHA), MSDs account for 34 percent of all lost work–day injuries and illnesses and one-third of all workers compensation claims.[30] Workers who spend their days staring at computer monitors (a significant and growing proportion of the workforce) often are victims of MSDs.

The most common MSD is carpal tunnel syndrome (CTS), which occurs when repetitive motion causes swelling in the wrist that pinches the nerves in the arm and hand. Studies by the Bureau of Labor Statistics show that more than 42 percent of carpal tunnel syndrome cases require more than 30 days away from work.[31] The good news for employers, however, is that preventing injuries, accidents, and lost days does *not* require spending thousands of dollars on ergonomically correct solutions. Most of the solutions to MSDs are actually quite simple and inexpensive. *Sequins International, a maker of sequined fabrics and trimmings in Woodside, New York, uses adjustable chairs and machinery as well as automatic spooling devices to reduce workers' repetitive motions and taxing physical demands. These simple changes eliminated carpal tunnel syndrome and cut worker's compensation costs to just $800, down from $98,000 in 1994.*[32]

Other solutions are decidedly low tech. *For instance, when Designer Checks, a maker of custom checks based in Anniston, Alabama, consulted with an occupational therapist, owner Grady Burrow learned that one of the best ways to fight MSDs among its computer-dependent workforce is simply to take frequent breaks and to move around. Department heads began scheduling regular exercise breaks designed to stretch employees' necks, shoulders, and hands. Before long, many managers began livening up their exercise breaks with music and dancing! Visitors to Designer Checks' plant are likely to see managers and employees take to the production floor for a rousing rendition of the macarena or the hokey pokey.*[33]

When planning store, office, or plant layouts, business owners usually focus on minimizing costs. Although staying within a budget is important, minimizing injuries and enhancing employees' productivity with an effective layout should be the overriding issues. Many exhaustive studies have concluded that changes in office design have a direct impact on workers' performance, job satisfaction, and ease of communication. In a reversal of the trend toward open offices separated by nothing more than cubicles, businesses are once again creating private offices in their workspaces. Many businesses embraced open designs, hoping that they would lead to greater interaction among workers. Many companies, however, have discovered that most office workers need privacy and quiet surroundings to be productive. Michael Brill, an office space consultant, studied 11,000 workers to determine the factors that most affect their productivity and found that the ability to do distraction-free work topped the list.[34] Rather than encourage teamwork, open offices leave workers distracted, frustrated, and less productive—just like the characters in the Dilbert cartoon strip.

When evaluating an existing building's interior, an entrepreneur must be sure to determine the integrity of its structural components. Are the building's floors sufficiently strong to hold the business's equipment, inventories, and personnel? Strength is an especially critical factor for manufacturing firms that use heavy equipment. When multiple floors exist, are the upper floors anchored as solidly as the primary floor? Can inventory be moved safely and easily from one area of the plant to another? Is the floor space adequate for safe and efficient movement of goods and people? Consider the cost of maintaining the floors. Hardwood floors may be extremely attractive but require expensive and time-consuming maintenance. Carpeted floors may be extremely attractive in a retail business but may be totally impractical for a manufacturing firm. Entrepreneurs must consider both the utility and durability and maintenance requirements, attractiveness, and, if important, effectiveness in reducing noise.

Like floors, walls and ceilings must be both functional and attractive. On the functional side, walls and ceilings should be fireproof and soundproof. Are the colors of walls and ceilings compatible, and do they create an attractive atmosphere for customers and employees? For instance, many Web-related companies use bright, bold colors in their designs to appeal to their young employees. On the other hand, more conservative firms such as accounting firms and law offices decorate with more subtle, subdued tones to convey an image of trustworthiness and honesty. Upscale restaurants that want their patrons to linger over dinner use deep, luxurious tones and soft lighting to create the proper ambiance. Fast-food restaurants, on the other hand, use strong, vibrant colors and bright lighting to encourage customers to get in and out quickly, ensuring the fast table turnover they require to be successful. In most cases, ceilings should be done in light colors to reflect the store's lighting.

Lighting

Good lighting enables employees to work at maximum efficiency. Proper lighting is measured by what is ideal for the job being done. Proper lighting in a factory may be quite different from that required in an office or a retail shop. Retailers often use creative lighting to attract customers to a specific display. Jewelry stores provide excellent examples of how lighting can be used to display merchandise effectively.

Modern advances in lighting technology give small businesses more options for lighting their stores, factories, and offices. New lighting systems offer greater flexibility, increased efficiency, and lower energy consumption, and architects are designing modern buildings to maximize the use of natural lighting. One office complex that is designed to use natural light cut its energy consumption by 40 percent by installing sensors tied to a software-controlled system that automatically adjust interior lights based on the weather outside and the time of day.[35] In one study, the U.S. Department of Energy found that simply locating workers near windows had a significant impact on their health. The study reported that workers who sat near windows had 20 percent fewer symptoms that are common to workers in "sick buildings," including headaches, fatigue, stress, and carpal tunnel syndrome.[36] Other studies show that natural light increases sales in retail stores by as much as 40 percent; increases productivity in office, service, and manufacturing operations; and enhances learning in the classroom.[37]

Lighting is often an inexpensive investment when one considers its impact on the overall appearance of the business. Few people seek out businesses that are dimly lit because they convey an image of untrustworthiness. The use of natural and artificial light in combination can give a business an open and cheerful look. Many restaurant chains have added greenhouse glass additions to accomplish this.

Layout: Maximizing Revenues, Increasing Efficiency, and Reducing Costs

7. Explain the principles of effective layouts for retailers, service businesses, and manufacturers.

Layout is a business's arrangement of the physical facilities and its method of display. The ideal layout contributes to efficient operations, increased productivity, and higher sales. What is ideal depends on the type of business and on the entrepreneur's strategy for gaining a competitive edge. Retailers design their layouts with the goal of maximizing sales revenue; manufacturers design theirs to increase efficiency and productivity and to lower costs.

Layout for Retailers

Retail layout is the arrangement of merchandise in a store. A retailer's success depends, in part, on a well-designed floor display. It should pull customers into the store and make it easy for them to locate merchandise; compare price, quality, and features; and ultimately to make a purchase. Paco Underhill, retail consultant and author of *Why We Buy: The Science of Shopping*, calls a store's interior design "the stage on which a retail company functions." Unfortunately, according to Underhill, most retailers tend to set that stage with more focus on their self-serving need for convenience than on creating a satisfying shopping experience for customers. *Based on research showing that customers purchase 40 percent of all the wine sold in the United States in discount retailers and supermarkets, managers at Target decided to devote part of their SuperTarget stores' retail space to attractive wine displays. Aimed at the company's core customers, women of the Baby Boom generation, the large display cases are well organized and hold more than 100 different types of wine. The centerpiece of the displays is a series of giant posters that take those who may not be familiar with the nuances of purchasing wine through a four-step process for selecting just the right wine. The displays include easy-to-understand text with graphics that explain the terms commonly used to describe wines' tastes. There is even a "wine wheel" that helps shoppers match a wine with everyday meals such as canned soup or macaroni and cheese. Because of the effective design of the wine display, Target's wine sales have exceeded the company's expectations.*[38]

A well-designed floor plan takes customers past plenty of displays of items that they may buy on impulse. Between 65 and 70 percent of all buying decisions are made once a customer enters a store, which means that the right layout can boost sales significantly. One study found that 68 percent of the items bought on major shopping trips (and 54 percent on smaller trips) were impulse purchases. Shoppers in this study were heavily influenced by in-store displays, especially those at the ends of aisles (called end-cap displays).[39]

Smart retailers recognize that some locations within a store are superior to others. Customers' traffic patterns give the owner a clue to the best location for the items with the highest gross margin. Merchandise purchased on impulse and convenience goods should be located near the front of the store. Items people shop around for before buying and specialty goods will attract their own customers and should not be placed in prime space. Prime selling space should be reserved for products that carry the highest markups. Table 16.3 offers suggestions for locating merchandise in a small retail store.

Layout in a retail store evolves from a clear understanding of customers' buying habits. If customers come into the store for specific products and have a tendency to walk directly to those items, it will benefit retailers to place complementary products in shoppers' path. Observing customer behavior can help the owner identify the "hot spots" where merchandise sells briskly and the "cold spots" where it may sit indefinitely. By experimenting with factors such as traffic flow, lighting, aisle size, display location, sounds, signs, and colors, an owner can discover the most productive store layout.

Retailers have three basic layout patterns to choose from: the grid, the free-form layout, and the boutique. The **grid layout** arranges displays in rectangular fashion so that aisles are parallel. It is a formal layout that controls the traffic flow through the store. Most

Table 16.3

Classification and Arrangement of Merchandise in a Small Retail Store

MERCHANDISE TYPE	HOW OR WHY BOUGHT	PLACEMENT IN STORE
Impulse goods	As result of attractive visual merchandising displays	Small store: near entrance Larger store: on main aisle
Convenience goods	With frequency in small quantities	Easily accessible feature locations along main aisle
Necessities or staple goods	Because of need	Rear of one-level stores, upper floors of multilevel stores (not a hard-and-fast rule)
Utility goods	For home use: brooms, dustpans, similar items	As impulse items, up front or along main aisle
Luxury and major expense items	After careful planning and considerable "shopping around"	Some distance from entrance

Source: U.S. Small Business Administration, "Small Business Location and Layout," *Administrative Management Course Program, Topic 13* (Washington, D.C.: SBA, 1980), p. 6.

Figure 16.4

The Grid Layout

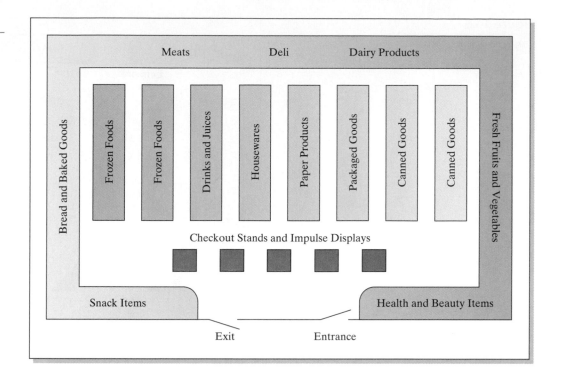

supermarkets and many discount stores use the grid layout because it is well suited to self-service stores. This layout uses the available selling space efficiently, creates a neat and organized environment, and facilitates shopping by standardizing the location of items. Figure 16.4 shows a typical grid layout.

Unlike the grid layout, the **free-form layout** is informal, using displays of various shapes and sizes. Its primary advantage is the relaxed, friendly shopping atmosphere it creates, which encourages customers to shop longer and increases the number of impulse purchases they make. Still, the free-form layout is not as efficient as the grid layout in using selling space, and it can create security problems if not properly planned. Figure 16.5 illustrates a free-form layout.

The **boutique layout** divides the store into a series of individual shopping areas, each with its own theme. It is like building a series of specialty shops into a single store. The boutique layout is informal and can create a unique shopping environment for the customer. Small department stores sometimes use this layout to create a distinctive image. Figure 16.6 shows a boutique layout for a small department store.

Business owners should display merchandise as attractively as their budgets will allow. Customers' eyes focus on displays, which tell them the type of merchandise the business sells. It is easier for customers to relate to one display than to a rack or shelf of merchandise. Open displays of merchandise can surround the focal display, creating an attractive selling area. Retailers can boost sales by displaying together items that complement each other. For example, displaying ties near dress shirts or handbags next to shoes often leads to multiple sales.

Spacious displays provide shoppers an open view of merchandise and reduce the likelihood of shoplifting. An open, spacious image is preferable to a cluttered appearance. Display height is also important because customers won't buy what they cannot see or reach. When planning in-store displays, retailers should remember the following:

■ The average man is 68.8 inches tall, and the average woman is 63.6 inches tall. The average person's normal reach is 16 inches, and the extended reach is 24 inches. Placing merchandise on high shelves discourages customers from making purchases.

Figure 16.5

The Free-Form Layout

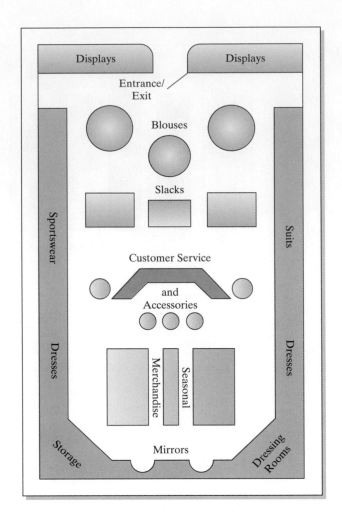

Figure 16.6

The Boutlque Layout

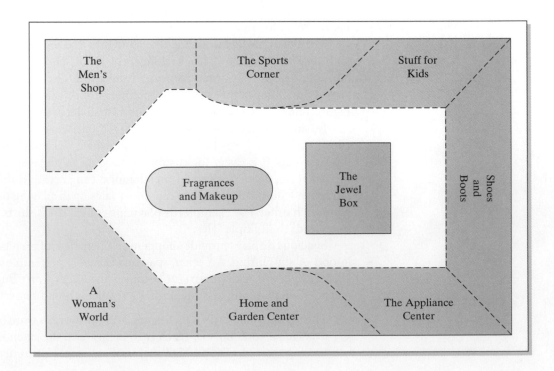

For example, putting hearing aid batteries on bottom shelves where the elderly have trouble getting to them or placing popular children's toys on top shelves where little ones cannot reach them can hurt sales. Keep items within easy reach of shoppers.

■ The average man's standing eye level is 62 inches from the floor, and the average woman's standing eye level is 57 inches from the floor.[40]

■ One study found that shoppers, especially women, are reluctant to enter narrow aisles in a store. Narrow aisles force customers to jostle past one another (experts call this the "butt-brush factor"), which makes them extremely nervous.

■ Placing shopping baskets in several areas around a store can increase sales. Seventy-five percent of shoppers who pick up a basket buy something, compared to just 34 percent of customers who do not pick up a basket.[41] Smart retailers make shopping baskets available to customers throughout the store, not just at the entrance.

■ Making shoppers hunt for the items they want to buy lowers the probability that they will purchase an item and that they will return to a particular store. Easy-to-read signs, clearly marked aisles, and displays of popular items located near the entrance make it easy for shoppers to find their way around a store.

■ Whenever possible, allow customers to touch the merchandise; they are much more likely to buy items if they can pick them up. The probability that customers shopping for clothing will make a purchase increases if they try on the garments. It pays to have friendly clerks who offer to "start a dressing room" for customers who pick up an article of clothing.[42]

Company Example →

In an effort to boost sales, Radio Shack recently unveiled a new design for its 7,200 stores across the United States. In addition to increasing the size of the stores to create wider aisles and more open space, the new layout moves the checkout counter into the center of the store, where it is more visible. Display cases near the checkout counter feature impulse items, and movable display racks make it easier for employees to organize items and to change the entire store layout in just a matter of hours. Vibrant colors and bold in-store graphics designed to attract a younger and more female audience have replaced the bland gray color scheme that dominated Radio Shack stores in the past. In the prototype stores that have implemented these layout changes, sales have doubled![43]

Even background music can be a merchandising tool if the type of music playing in a store matches the demographics of its target customers. Research shows that music is a stimulant to sales because it reduces resistance; warps the sense of time, allowing shoppers to stay longer in the store; and helps to produce a positive mental association between the music and the intended image of the store.[44] Classical music, in particular, makes shoppers feel affluent and boosts sales more than other types of music.[45]

Retailers must remember to separate the selling and nonselling areas of a store. They should never waste prime selling space with nonselling functions (storage, office, dressing area, and others). Although nonselling activities are necessary for a successful retail operation, they should not take precedence and occupy valuable selling space. Many retailers place their nonselling departments in the rear of the building, recognizing the value of each foot of space in a retail store and locating their most profitable items in the best-selling areas.

The various areas within a small store's interior space are not equal in generating sales revenue. Certain areas contribute more to revenue than others. The value of store space depends on floor location in a multistory building, location with respect to aisles and walkways, and proximity to entrances. Space values decrease as distance from the main entry-level floor increases. Selling areas on the main level contribute a greater portion to sales than do those on other floors because they offer greater exposure to customers than either basement or higher-level locations. Therefore, main-level locations carry a greater share of rent than other levels. Figure 16.7 offers one example of how rent and sales could be allocated by floors.

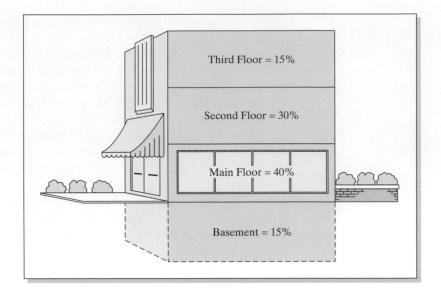

The layout of aisles in the store has a major impact on the customer exposure that merchandise receives. Items located on primary walkways should be assigned a higher share of rental costs and should contribute a greater portion to sales revenue than those displayed along secondary aisles. Figure 16.8 shows that high-value areas are exposed to two primary aisles.

Space values also depend on the spaces' relative position to the store entrance. Typically, the farther away an area is from the entrance, the lower its value. Another consideration is that most shoppers turn to the right when entering a store and will move around it counterclockwise. Finally, only about one-fourth of a store's customers will go more than halfway into the store. Using these characteristics, Figure 16.9 illustrates space values for a typical small-store layout.

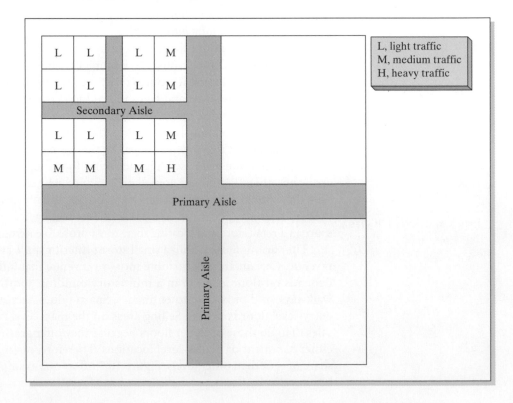

Figure 16.9

Space Values for a Small Store

Source: Used by permission of Dr. Dale M. Lewison. The University of Akron. All Rights Reserved.

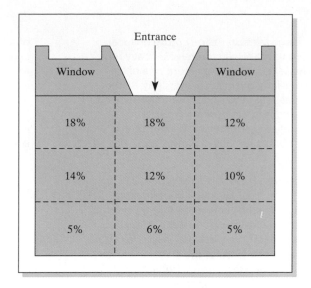

Understanding the value of store space ensures proper placement of merchandise. The items placed in the high-rent areas of the store should generate adequate sales and contribute enough profit to justify their high-value locations. The decline in value of store space from front to back of the shop is expressed in the 40–30–20–10 rule. This rule assigns 40 percent of a store's rental cost to the front quarter of the shop, 30 percent to the second quarter, 20 percent to the third quarter, and 10 percent to the final quarter. Similarly, each quarter of the store should contribute the same percentages of sales revenue.

For example, suppose that the owner of a small department store anticipates $120,000 in sales this year. Each quarter of the store should generate the following sales volume:

Front quarter	$120,000 × 0.40 = $48,000
Second quarter	$120,000 × 0.30 = $36,000
Third quarter	$120,000 × 0.20 = $24,000
Fourth quarter	$120,000 × 0.10 = $12,000
Total	$120,000

✦ GAINING *a* COMPETITIVE EDGE ✦

How to Get the Best Deal on a Lease

The Lion's Head, a popular Greenwich Village restaurant and bar, recently closed its doors after three decades as the favorite gathering place of writers, artists, and actors. "It was a great place to meet and talk," says Mike Reardon, who once owned the Lion's Head. The restaurant and bar had its ups and downs over the years, but its base of loyal customers kept it going. Then a series of steep increases in the Lion's Head's lease payments put the restaurant in a precarious financial situation. A five-year lease negotiated in 1989 raised the company's monthly rent from $5,000 to $8,000. Severe cash flow problems, due in part to the higher lease payments, forced the Lion's Head into

Chapter 11 bankruptcy. Reardon and two partners bought the business and reorganized it. When the lease came up for renewal in 1994, however, the monthly rent jumped up to $10,000. The Lion's Head's monthly overhead costs skyrocketed to $40,000, making it extremely difficult for the company to break even. Reardon began looking for a new location, but before he could find one, fate struck another blow: The neighboring Circle Repertory Theater moved, taking with it a steady stream of theater customers. Shortly thereafter, the Lion's Head closed. "New Yorkers go to the newest, hottest areas, and right now those are the Upper East Side and Soho," says one restaurateur.

"(Greenwich) Village restaurants rely more on local clientele. It's hard to make it if you have a heavy rent."

Rent and lease payments represent one of the largest expenses many business owners pay. As the Lion's Head proves, failing to negotiate a satisfactory lease can push a company's operating expenses so high that ultimately the company fails. What can a business owner do to avoid lease nightmares? The following tips will help.

- *Read the lease agreement before you sign it.* Amazingly, some small business owners simply sign their leases without even reading them, often because they fear losing out on a great location. One attorney specializing in leases says, "Take your time and read every word of the lease, no matter how many would-be tenants are behind you."
- *Ask an experienced attorney to review the lease before you sign it.* At one time, leases were relatively simple contracts. Today, however, it is not uncommon for a lease to be a "40-to-60-page document filled with very complex issues many tenants are not always equipped to deal with on their own," says a real estate broker.
- *Incorporate (or form an LLC) before you sign a lease.* Otherwise, if the business cannot make the lease payments, the landlord has the right to make the business owner personally responsible for them.
- *Try to negotiate a lease term that is as short as possible at the outset.* Many landlords ask business owners to personally guarantee lease payments. To reduce the risk of getting stuck with long-term payments, try to get a short-term lease that you can renew rather than agreeing to a 5- or 10-year term.
- *Deal only with a reputable leasing company.* Check the company's references.
- *Demand full disclosure of all financial aspects of the deal.*
- *Have your attorney and/or accountant review all the documents prior to signing.*
- *Get everything in writing.* Under the statute of frauds, courts require all contracts that transfer interest in land (such as a lease) to be in writing and be enforceable. Oral promises from a landlord don't mean a thing if a dispute arises. The owners

of a small medical consulting firm learned this lesson the hard way when they relied on their landlord's verbal promises to renew the company's lease. Within a few months, they were looking for a new location.

- *Pay close attention to the details.* Make sure the lease agreement doesn't contain any unpleasant surprises. The owner of a small flower shop was amazed when his landlord told him he would be responsible for the damage a broken pipe in his part of the building had caused in other businesses. "If you're moving into (an older) building, you could be partially liable for large future repair bills for items such as the air-conditioning system or roof if you don't structure your lease carefully," says one expert.
- *Make sure you have good insurance to cover any damage to property.* Renter's insurance is usually very inexpensive and can be a company's salvation if something goes wrong.
- *Verify that the lease's provisions on issues such as parking spaces, improvements, operating hours, air conditioning and heating, cleaning and other services, and maintenance suit your business and its financial situation.* Too often, business owners overlook these small but important matters.
- *Ask for the availability to sublease (with the landlord's approval, of course).* Otherwise, if your company folds, you may be committed to making large lease payments for many years out of your own pocket.
- *Retailers who lease spaces in shopping centers should try to include a clause that guarantees the landlord will not lease to another competing business (called an "exclusive").* They should also include an *occupancy clause*, which states that they do not pay rent until the center has a specific level of occupancy.

Sources: Adapted from Paul DeCeglie, "Beauty and the Lease," *Business Start-Ups,* November 2000, p. 32; Jan Norman, "How to: Negotiate a Lease," *Business Start-Ups,* March 1998, pp. 48–52; Kitty Barnes, "Rising Costs, Changing Tastes Lead to Last Call at Legendary Tavern," *Inc.,* March 1997, p. 26; Barbara Etchieson, "Shutting the Door on Lease Problems," *Nation's Business,* March 1996, pp. 24–25; Susan Hodges, "Getting a Grip on Your Lease," *Nation's Business,* December 1997, pp. 48–49.

Layout for Manufacturers

Manufacturing layout decisions take into consideration the arrangement of departments, workstations, machines, and stock-holding points within a production facility. The general objective is to arrange these elements to ensure a smooth work flow (in a production area) or a particular traffic pattern (in a service area).

Manufacturing facilities have come under increased scrutiny as firms attempt to improve quality, decrease inventories, and increase productivity through facilities that are integrated, flexible, and controlled. Facility layout has a dramatic effect on product mix, product processing, materials handling, storage, control, and production volume and quality. Some manufacturers are using 3-D simulation software (based on the same technology as the 3-D video games people play) to test the layout of their factory and its impact on employees and their productivity *before* they ever build them. The highly realistic simulations tell designers how well a particular combination of people, machinery, and environment interacts with one another. The software can identify potential problem areas, such as layouts that force workers into awkward positions that would cause injuries, equipment designs that cause workers to reach too far for materials, and layouts that unnecessarily add extra time to the manufacturing process by requiring extra materials handling or unneeded steps.[46]

Factors in Manufacturing Layout. The ideal layout for a manufacturing operation depends on several factors, including the following:

- *Type of product.* Product design and quality standards, whether the product is produced for inventory or for order, and physical properties such as the size of materials and products' special handling requirements, susceptibility to damage, and perishability.
- *Type of production process.* Technology used, types of materials handled, means of providing a service, and processing requirements in terms of number of operations involved and amount of interaction between departments and work centers.
- *Ergonomic considerations.* To ensure worker safety, to avoid unnecessary injuries and accidents, and to increase productivity.
- *Economic considerations.* Volume of production; costs of materials, machines, workstations, and labor; pattern and variability of demand; and length of permissible delays.
- *Space availability within facility itself.*

Types of Manufacturing Layouts. Manufacturing layouts are categorized either by the work flow in a plant or by the production system's function. There are three basic types of layouts that manufacturers can use separately or in combination—product, process, and fixed position—and they differ in their applicability of different levels of manufacturing volume.

In a **product** (or **line**) **layout,** a manufacturer arranges workers and equipment according to the sequence of operations performed on the product (see Figure 16.10). Conceptually, the flow is an unbroken line from raw materials input to finished goods. This type of layout is applicable to rigid-flow, high-volume, continuous or mass-production

Figure 16.10

Product Layout

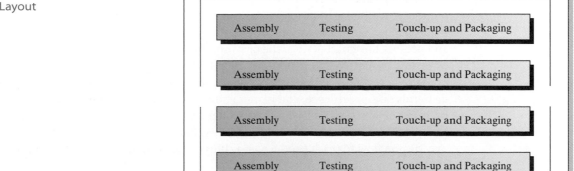

Figure 16.11

Process Layout

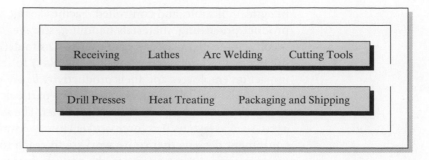

operations or when the product is highly standardized. Automobile assembly plants, paper mills, and oil refineries are examples of product layouts.

Product layouts offer the advantages of lower materials handling costs; simplified tasks that can be done with low-cost, lower-skilled labor; reduced amounts of work-in-process inventory; and relatively simplified production control activities. All units are routed along the same fixed path, and scheduling consists primarily of setting a production rate.

Disadvantages of product layouts include their inflexibility, monotony of job tasks, high fixed investment in specialized equipment, and heavy interdependence of all operations. A breakdown in one machine or at one workstation can idle the entire line. Such a layout also requires the owner to duplicate many pieces of equipment in the manufacturing facility; duplication can be cost prohibitive for a small firm.

In a **process layout,** a manufacturer groups workers and equipment according to the general function they perform, without regard to any particular product (see Figure 16.11).Process layouts are appropriate when production runs are short, when demand shows considerable variation and the costs of holding finished goods inventory are high, or when the product is customized.

Process layouts have the advantages of being flexible for doing customer work and promoting job satisfaction by offering employees diverse and challenging tasks. Their disadvantages are the higher costs of materials handling, more skilled labor, lower productivity, and more complex production control. Because the work flow is intermittent, each job must be individually routed through the system and scheduled at the various work centers, and its status must be monitored individually.

In **fixed-position layouts,** materials do not move down a line as in a product layout; because of the bulk or weight of the final product, materials are assembled in one spot. In other words, workers and equipment go to the materials rather than having the materials flow down a line to them. Aircraft assembly shops and shipyards typify this kind of layout.

Designing Layouts. The starting point in layout design is determining how and in what sequence product parts or service tasks flow together. One of the most effective techniques is to create an overall picture of the manufacturing process using assembly charts and process flowcharts. Given the tasks and their sequence, plus knowledge of the volume of products that can be produced, an entrepreneur can analyze space and equipment needs to get an idea of the facility's demand. When a product layout is being used, these demands take precedence, and manufacturers must arrange equipment and workstations to fit the production tasks and their sequence. If a process layout is used, different products place different demands on the facility. Rather than having a single best flow, there may be one flow for each product, and compromises will be necessary. As a result, any one product may not get the ideal layout.

Analyzing Production Layouts. Although there is no general procedure for analyzing the numerous interdependent factors that enter into layout design, specific layout problems lend themselves to detailed analysis. Two important criteria for selecting and designing a layout are worker effectiveness and materials handling costs.

Designing layouts ergonomically so that they maximize workers' strengths is especially important for manufacturers. Creating an environment that is comfortable and pleasant for workers will pay big benefits over time in the form of higher productivity, lower absenteeism and tardiness, and fewer injuries. Designers must be sure that they match the environment they create to workers' needs rather than trying to force workers to adapt to the environment.

Manufacturers can lower materials handling costs by using layouts designed to automate product flow whenever possible and to minimize flow distances and times. The extent of automation depends on the level of technology and amount of capital available, as well as behavioral considerations of employees. Flow distances and times are usually minimized by locating sequential processing activities or interrelated departments in adjacent areas. The following features are important to a good manufacturing layout:

1. Planned materials flow pattern
2. Straight-line layout where possible
3. Straight, clearly marked aisles
4. Backtracking kept to a minimum
5. Related operations close together
6. Minimum of in-process inventory
7. Easy adjustment to changing conditions
8. Minimum materials handling distances
9. Minimum of manual handling
10. No unnecessary rehandling of material
11. Minimum handling between operations
12. Materials delivered to production employees quickly
13. Use of gravity to move materials whenever possible
14. Materials efficiently removed from the work area
15. Materials handling done by indirect labor
16. Orderly materials handling and storage
17. Good housekeeping

Build, Buy, or Lease?

8. Evaluate the advantages and disadvantages of building, buying, and leasing a building.

Another import decision business owners must make involves the ownership of the building. The ability to obtain the best possible physical facilities given the cash the owner has available may depend largely on whether the entrepreneur decides to build, buy, or lease a building.

The Decision to Build

If a business had unlimited funds, the owner could design and build a perfect facility. However, few new business owners have this luxury. Constructing a new facility can project a positive image to potential customers. The business looks new and, consequently, creates an image of being modern and efficient and of top quality. A new building can incorporate the most modern features during construction, which can significantly lower operating costs. In addition, by constructing a new building, a business owner can incorporate into the layout features that meet the business's unique design needs such as loading docks, laboratories, or refrigeration units. Building a new facility can also improve a company's long-term productivity and efficiency.

In some rapidly growing areas, there are only a few or sometimes no existing buildings to buy or lease that match an entrepreneur's requirements. In these situations, a business owner must consider the cost of constructing a building as a significant factor in initial estimates of capital needs and break-even point. Constructing a building imposes a high initial fixed cost that an owner must weigh against the facility's ability to generate revenue and to reduce operating expenses. Building a new structure also requires more time than either buying or leasing an existing one.

The Decision to Buy

In many cases, there may be an ideal building in the area where an entrepreneur wants to locate. Buying the facility allows the entrepreneur to remodel it without seeking permission from anyone else. As with building, buying can put a drain on the business's financial resources, but the owner knows exactly what the monthly payments will be. Under a lease, rental rates can (and usually do) increase over time. If an owner believes that the property will actually appreciate in value, a decision to purchase may prove to be wise. In addition, the owner can depreciate the building each year, and both depreciation and interest are tax-deductible business expenses.

When considering the purchase of a building, the owner should use the same outline of facilities requirements developed for the building option to ensure that this property will not be excessively expensive to modify for his or her use. Remodeling can add a significant initial expense. The layout of the building may be suitable in many ways, but it may not be ideal for a particular business. Even if a building houses the same kind of business, its existing layout may be completely unsuitable for the way the new owner plans to operate.

Building or buying a building greatly limits an entrepreneur's mobility, however. Some business owners prefer to stay out of the real estate business to retain maximum flexibility and mobility. Plus, not all real estate appreciates in value. Surrounding property can become run-down and, consequently, can lower a property's value despite the owner's efforts to keep it in excellent condition. Many downtown locations have suffered from this problem.

The Decision to Lease

The major advantage of leasing is that it requires no large initial cash outlay, so the business's funds are available for purchasing inventory or for supporting current operations. Also, lease expenses are tax deductible. Firms that are short on cash usually end up leasing their facilities. Because leasing is usually the least expensive option, most start-up businesses lease their buildings.

Additional advantages of leasing include:

- The value of maintenance and repair provided by the lessor.
- The ability to upgrade equipment to meet your changing needs.
- The improved appearance of your balance sheet (if leased assets are excluded).
- No restrictions on your ability to borrow additional funds.

Then there's the other side of the leasing coin (even beyond the higher costs that a thorough cash analysis will reveal):

- You have no equity in leased equipment—although you might consider negotiating a purchase option, crediting part of the lease payments toward the purchase price.
- You probably can't cancel the agreement, so you're committed to making payments for the entire period, whether you use the equipment or not.
- While you may write off payments, you can't deduct the depreciation.

Bottom line: Leasing is more expensive over the life of the asset, but you have immediate access to equipment with little up-front investment, thereby freeing up cash for other expenses and investments. Carefully weigh the benefits and the drawbacks before signing that lease.

One major disadvantage of leasing is that the property owner might choose not to renew the lease. A successful business might be forced to move to a new location, and relocation can be extremely costly and could result in a significant loss of established customers. In many cases, it is almost like starting the business again. Also, if a business is successful, the property owner may ask for a significant increase in rent when the lease renewal is negotiated. The owner of the building is well aware of the costs associated with moving and has the upper hand in the negotiations. In some lease arrangements, the owner is compensated, in addition to a monthly rental fee, by a percentage of the tenant's gross sales. This practice is common in shopping centers.

Still another disadvantage to leasing is the limitation on remodeling. A building owner who believes that modifications will reduce the future rental value of the property will likely require a long-term lease at a higher rent or might not allow the modifications to be made. In addition, all permanent modifications of the structure become the property of the building owner.

Chapter Review

1. Explain the stages in the location decision.
   - The location decision is one of the most important decisions an entrepreneur will make, given its long-term effects on the company. An entrepreneur should look at the choice as a series of increasingly narrow decisions: Which region of the country? Which state? Which city? Which site?
   - Demographic statistics are available from a wide variety of sources, but government agencies such as the Census Bureau have a wealth of detailed data that can guide an entrepreneur in his or her location decision.

2. Describe the location criteria for retail and service businesses.
   - For retailers and many service businesses, the location decision is especially crucial. They must consider the size of the trade area, the volume of customer traffic, number of parking spots, availability of room for expansion, and the visibility of a site.

3. Outline the basic location options for retail and service businesses.
   - Retail and service businesses have six basic location options: central business districts (CBDs), neighborhoods, shopping centers and malls, near competitors, outlying areas, and at home.

4. Explain the site selection process for manufacturers.
   - A manufacturer's location decision is strongly influenced by local zoning ordinances. Some areas offer industrial parks designed specifically to attract manufacturers. Two crucial factors for most manufacturers are the accessibility to (and the cost of transporting) raw materials and the quality and quantity of available labor.

5. Discuss the benefits of locating a start-up company in a business incubator.
   - Business incubators are locations that offer flexible, low-cost rental space to their tenants as well as business and consulting services. Their goal is to nurture small companies until they are ready to "graduate" into the larger business community. Many government agencies and universities offer incubator locations.

6. Describe the criteria used to analyze the layout and design considerations of a building, including the Americans with Disabilities Act.
   - When evaluating the suitability of a particular building, an entrepreneur should consider several factors: size (is it large enough to accommodate the business with some room for growth?); construction and external appearance (is the building structurally sound, and does it create the right impression for the business?); entrances (are they inviting?); legal issues (does the building comply with the Americans with Disabilities Act, and if not, how much will it cost to bring it up to standard?); signs (are they legible, well located, and easy to see?); interior (does the interior design

contribute to your ability to make sales and is it ergonomically designed?); and lights and fixtures (is the lighting adequate to the tasks workers will be performing, and what is the estimated cost of lighting?).

7. Explain the principles of effective layout for retailers, service businesses, and manufacturers.

- Layout for retail store and service businesses depends on the owner's understanding of customers' buying habits. Retailers have three basic layout options from which to choose: grid, free-form, and boutique layouts. Some areas of a retail store generate more sales per square foot and are, therefore, more valuable than others.

- The goal of a manufacturer's layout is to create a smooth, efficient workflow. Three basic options

exist: product layout, process layout, and fixed-position layout. Two key considerations are worker productivity and materials handling costs.

8. Evaluate the advantages and disadvantages of building, buying, and leasing a building.

- Building a new building gives entrepreneurs the opportunity to design exactly what they want in a brand-new facility; however, not every small business owner can afford to tie up significant amounts of cash in fixed assets. Buying an existing building gives business owners the freedom to renovate as needed, but this can be an expensive alternative. Leasing a location is a common choice because it is economical, but business owners face the uncertainty of lease renewals, rising rents, and renovation problems.

▌▌▌ Discussion Questions

1. How do most small business owners choose a location? Is this wise?
2. What factors should a owner consider when evaluating a region in which to locate a business? Where are such data available?
3. Outline the factors entrepreneurs should consider when selecting a state in which to locate a business.
4. What factors should a seafood-processing plant, a beauty shop, and an exclusive jewelry store consider in choosing a location? List factors for each type of business.
5. What intangible factors might enter into the entrepreneur's location decision?
6. What are zoning laws? How do they affect the location decision?

7. What is the trade area for a small business? What determines a small retailer's trade area?
8. Why is it important to discover more than just the number of passersby in a traffic count?
9. What types of information can an entrepreneur collect from census data?
10. Why may a cheap location not be the best location?
11. What function does a small firm's sign serve? What are the characteristics of an effective business sign?
12. Explain the statement: "The portions of a small store's interior space are not of equal value in generating sales revenue." What areas are most valuable?
13. What are some of the major features that are important to a good manufacturing layout?
14. Summarize the advantages and disadvantages of building, buying, and leasing a building.

Location, Layout, and Physical Facilities

Business Plan Pro

Choosing the right location for a small company can give it a huge boost in generating sales and profits, but selecting the wrong location puts a business at a disadvantage from the start. Taking the time to collect information about potential sites and analyze it makes

the important location decision much easier and produces a superior location choice.

The exercises for Chapter 16 that accompany Business Plan Pro are designed to help you define the key factors that make a location ideal for your business, rate your proposed location on those factors, and evaluate the characteristics of an efficient and effective plan for the layout of your company's physical facilities. Once you finish these exercises, you are ready to complete the Company Locations and Facilities section under the category called Your Company in Business Plan Pro.

Chapter 17

Purchasing, Quality Management, and Vendor Analysis

Without the right goods, sales are impossible.
—Anonymous

Quality is never an accident; it is always the result of high intention, sincere effort, intelligent direction, and skillful execution; it represents the wise choice of many alternatives.
—William A. Foster

Upon completion of this chapter, you will be able to:

1. Understand the components of a purchasing plan.
2. Explain the principles of total quality management (TQM) and their impact on quality.
3. Conduct economic order quantity (EOQ) analysis to determine the proper level of inventory.
4. Differentiate among the three types of purchase discounts that vendors offer.
5. Calculate a company's reorder point.
6. Develop a vendor rating scale.
7. Describe the legal implications of the purchasing function.

This chapter introduces the topics of purchasing, quality management, and vendor analysis, none of which are the most glamorous or exciting jobs an entrepreneur undertakes. However, when entrepreneurs begin producing products or providing services, they quickly learn how much their products or services are dependent on the quality of the components and services they purchase from their suppliers. In many instances, the quality of a company's supply chain determines its ability to satisfy its customers and to compete effectively. "Competition is not really company versus company," says one expert, "but supply chain versus supply chain."[1]

Selecting the right vendors and designing a fast and efficient supply chain affects a small company's ability to produce and sell quality products and services at competitive prices. These decisions have far-reaching effects for a business as well as a significant impact on its "bottom line." Depending on the type of business involved, the purchasing function can consume anywhere from 25 percent to 85 percent of each dollar of sales. By shaving just 2 percent off of its cost of goods sold, a typical small company can increase its net income by as much as 28 percent! For this reason, entrepreneurs must create a purchasing plan, establish well-defined measures of product or service quality, and select vendors and suppliers based on objectively determined criteria. *A few years ago, Peter Nygard, founder of Nygard International, a women's clothing manufacturer in Toronto, Ontario, was concerned about the high and increasing level of inventory in his warehouse. The company's inventory had ballooned to its highest level ever, and what concerned Nygard even more than the amount of stock was the imbalance of the inventory. Nygard was overstocked with out-of-style fashions but was running short of items that were popular. To solve the inventory problem, Nygard developed a purchasing plan designed to create a more efficient flow of goods from "the sheep and the silkworms to the consumer," he says. Nygard invested in software that tracked both actual and forecasted sales of specific products, and he shifted the company's ordering, manufacturing, shipping, and selling operations online. The company cut its manufacturing costs by one-third and reduced the time required to fill a customer's order from three weeks to just one day! Nygard estimates that making these changes in the company's supply chain has added about $10 million a year to his company's bottom line. In addition, he says, "We can gather information and make decisions based on what is actually selling with the snap of a finger as opposed to philosophizing or assuming."[2]*

Company Example

The Purchasing Plan

1. Understand the components of a purchasing plan.

Purchasing involves the acquisition of needed materials, supplies, services, and equipment of the right quality, in the proper quantities, for reasonable prices, at the appropriate time, and from the right vendor. A major objective of purchasing is to acquire enough (but not too much) stock to ensure smooth, uninterrupted production or sales and to see that the merchandise is delivered on time. Companies large and small are purchasing goods and supplies from all across the globe. Coordinating the pieces of the global puzzle requires a comprehensive purchasing plan. The plan must identify a company's quality requirements, its cost targets, and the criteria for determining the best supplier, considering such factors as reliability, service, delivery, and cooperation.

The purchasing plan is closely linked to the other functional areas of managing a small business: production, marketing, sales, engineering, accounting, finance, and others. A purchasing plan should recognize this interaction and help integrate the purchasing function into the total organization. A small company's purchasing plan should focus on the five key elements of purchasing: quality, quantity, price, timing, and vendor selection (see Figure 17.1).

Figure 17.1

Key Components of a
Purchasing Plan

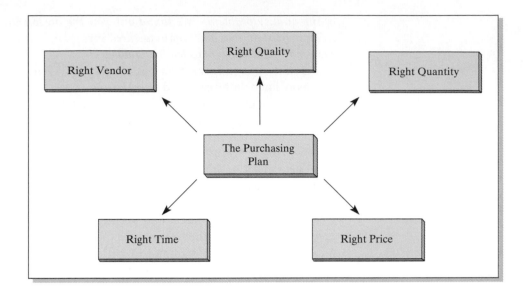

Quality

2. Explain the principles of total quality management (TQM) and their impact on quality.

Company Example

Not long ago businesses saw quality products and services as luxuries for customers who could afford them. Many companies mistakenly believed that producing or purchasing high-quality products and services was too costly. The last few decades have taught every businessperson that quality goods and services are absolutely *essential* to staying competitive. The benefits companies earn by pursuing quality products, services, and processes come not only in the form of fewer defects but also in lower costs, higher productivity, and higher customer retention rates. W. Edwards Deming, one of the founding fathers of the modern quality movement, always claimed that higher quality resulted in lower cost. Internally, companies with a quality focus report significant improvements in work-related factors such as increased employee morale, lower employee turnover, and enhanced quality of work life. Benefits such as these can result in earning a significant competitive advantage over rivals of *any* size.

Total quality companies believe in and manage with the attitude of continuous improvement, a concept the Japanese call *kaizen*. The *kaizen* philosophy holds that small improvements made continuously over time accumulate into a radically reshaped and improved process. Many companies that failed to respond to the challenge to improve the quality of their products did not survive. In our market-driven, competitive environment, consumers have made their preferences clear and quality products and competitive prices are essential to survival. *Numonics Corporation, a small manufacturer of computerized whiteboards and accessories based in Montgomeryville, Pennsylvania, used kaizen to make dramatic improvements in the production process of one of its new products, an electronic pen. Although the pen's design was superior to its predecessor, Numonics was struggling with long manufacturing times and dismal product quality. Managers brought in consultants from the Manufacturing Extension Partnership, a program designed to strengthen small manufacturing companies, to conduct a "kaizen blitz." Guided by the consultants, employees from the factory floor analyzed the manufacturing process, breaking it down into distinct components, and redesigning it into more logical "cells." Within three months, the manufacturing cells were operating, and the results astonished everyone in the company. The time required to manufacture a pen dropped from 50 minutes to just 17 minutes, and defective rates plummeted from 45 percent to 1.2 percent. Analyzing the manufacturing process one step at a time and implementing small improvements throughout allowed the employee teams to discover the primary source of the quality problem. "We found out that the biggest failures were due to PC boards, a component that we don't manufacture," says plant manager Pat Burns. "We went back to the vendor, and they corrected the problem."*[3]

Quality has an impact on both costs and revenues. Improved quality lowers the cost associated with scrap and rework time, lower warranty cost, and increased worker productivity. On the revenue side of the equation, quality improves a firm's reputation, attracts customers, and often gives a firm the opportunity to charge higher prices. The bottom-line impact of quality is increased profitability resulting from the factors listed previously.

The American Society for Quality defines quality as "the totality of features and characteristics of a product or service that bears on its ability to satisfy stated or implied needs."[4] There are at least three general, yet overlapping, categories of quality: user based, manufacturing based, and product based. The user-based category focuses on meeting or exceeding the needs and expectations of customers. Manufacturing-based quality focuses on conforming to rigid production standards, such as Motorola's six sigma program. Product-based quality focuses on the final product's ability to meet or exceed precise and quantifiable measures that define product quality. In reality, all of these categories integrate into the quality process, which results in the achievement of all measures of quality.[5]

Total Quality Management

Under the total quality management (TQM) philosophy, companies define a quality product as one that conforms to predetermined standards that satisfy customers' demands. That means getting *everything* from delivery and invoicing to installation and follow-up right the first time. Although these companies know that they may never reach their targets of perfect quality, they never stop striving for perfection, recognizing that even a 99.9 percent level of quality is not good enough (see Table 17.1).

Table 17.1

Why 99.9 Percent Quality Isn't Good Enough

Most companies willingly accept a certain percentage of errors and defects. Usually the range is 1 to 5 percent. In some companies, it is regarded as a routine part of daily operations.

However, quality consultants say that even 99.9 percent isn't good enough.
- To improve quality, many companies are relying on a single supplier for their raw materials and components.
- Partnering between suppliers and customers in such a close relationship means that those sole-source suppliers have to shoot for 100 percent quality and performance.

What would be the result if some things were done right only 99.9 percent of the time? Consider the implications:
- Two unsafe landings at Chicago's O'Hare Airport.
- 16,000 lost pieces of mail per hour.
- 200,000 incorrectly filled drug prescriptions per year.
- 5,000 incorrect surgical procedures performed each week.
- 22,000 checks deducted from the wrong accounts every hour.
- 1,314 telephone calls misdirected every minute.
- 14 babies delivered to the wrong parents each day.
- 2,488,200 magazines published with the wrong covers every year.

If you are in the unlucky one-tenth of 1 percent, the error affects you 100 percent. Plus, unless a company strives for 100 percent product or service quality, there is little chance that it will ever achieve 99.9 percent quality.

Sources: Adapted from Lieca Brown, "Sigma Management," *Point of Beginning,* August 2001, p. 6; *On the Job Performance,* (Chicago: Dartnell Corporation 1997), p. 3; Sal Marino, "Is 'Good Enough' Good Enough?" *Industry Week,* February 3, 1997, p. 22.

The businesses that have effectively implemented these programs understand that the process involves a total commitment from strategy to practice and from the top of the organization to the bottom.

Rather than trying to inspect quality into products and services after they are completed, TQM instills the philosophy of doing the job right the first time. Although the concept is simple, implementing such a process is a challenge that requires a very different kind of thinking and very different culture than most organizations are comfortable with. Because the changes TQM requires are so significant, patience is a must for companies adopting the philosophy. Consistent quality improvements rarely occur overnight. Yet, too many small business managers think, "We'll implement TQM today and tomorrow our quality will soar." TQM is *not* a "quick-fix," short-term program that can magically push a company to world-class-quality status overnight. Because it requires such fundamental, often drastic, changes in the way a company does business, TQM takes time both to implement and to produce results. Patience is a must. Although some small businesses that use TQM begin to see some improvements within just a matter of weeks, the *real* benefits take longer to realize. It takes at least three or four years before TQM principles gain acceptance among employees, and as many as eight years are necessary to fully implement TQM in a company.

To implement TQM successfully, a small business owner must rely on these fundamental principles:

- *Employ a technique called benchmarking to achieve quality outcomes.* **Benchmarking** is the process of identifying world-class processes or procedures other companies (often in other industries) currently are using and building higher-quality standards around these for your firm. This search for *best practices* is ongoing.
- *Shift from a management-driven culture to a participative, team-based one.* Two basic tenets of TQM are employee involvement and teamwork. Business owners must be willing to push decision-making authority down the organization to where the real experts are. Teams of employees working together to identify and solve problems can be a powerful force in an organization of any size. Experience with TQM has taught entrepreneurs that the combined knowledge and experience of workers are much greater than that of only one person. Tapping into the problem-solving capabilities of the team produces profitable results.
- *Modify the reward system to encourage teamwork and innovation.* Because the team, not the individual, is the building block of TQM, companies often have to modify their compensation systems to reflect team performance. Traditional compensation methods pit one employee against another, undermining any sense of cooperation. Often they are based on seniority rather than on how much an employee contributes to the company. Compensation systems under TQM usually rely on incentives, linking pay to performance. However, rather than tying pay to individual performance, these systems focus on team-based incentives. Each person's pay depends on whether the entire team (or, sometimes, the entire company) meets a clearly defined, measurable set of performance objectives.
- *Train workers constantly to give them the tools they need to produce quality and to upgrade the company's knowledge base.* One of the most important factors in making long-term, constant improvements in a company's processes is teaching workers the philosophy and the tools of TQM. Admonishing employees to "produce quality" or offering them rewards for high quality is futile unless a company gives them the tools and know-how to achieve that end. Managers must be dedicated to making their companies "learning organizations" that encourage people to upgrade their skills and give them the opportunities and incentives to do so. The most successful companies spend anywhere from 1 to 5 percent of their employees' time on training,

most of it invested in workers, not managers. To give employees a sense of how the quality of their job fits into the big picture, many TQM companies engage in **cross-training,** teaching workers to do other jobs in the company.

■ *Train employees to measure quality with the tools of statistical process control (SPC).* The only way to ensure gains in quality is to measure results objectively and to trace the company's progress toward its quality objectives. That requires teaching employees how to use statistical process control techniques such as fishbone charts, Pareto charts, control charts, and measures of process capability. Without knowledgeable workers using these quantitative tools, TQM cannot produce the intended results.

■ *Use Pareto's Law to focus TQM efforts.* One of the toughest questions managers face in companies embarking on TQM for the first time is, "Where do we start?" The best way to answer that fundamental question is to use Pareto's law (also called the 80/20 rule), which states that 80 percent of a company's quality problems arise from just 20 percent of all causes. By identifying this small percentage of causes and focusing quality improvement efforts on them, a company gets maximum return for minimum effort. This simple yet powerful rule forces workers to concentrate resources on the most significant problems first, where payoffs are likely to be biggest, and helps build momentum for successful TQM effort.

■ *Share information with everyone in the organization.* Asking employees to make decisions and to assume responsibility for creating quality necessitates that the owner share information with them. Employees cannot make sound decisions consistent with the company's initiative if owners are unwilling to give them the information they need to make those decisions.

■ *Focus quality improvements on astonishing the customer.* The heart of TQM is customer satisfaction—better yet, customer astonishment. Unfortunately, some companies focus their quality improvement efforts on areas that never benefit the customer. Quality improvements with no customer focus (either internal or external customers) are wasted.

■ *Don't rely on inspection to produce quality products and services.* The traditional approach to achieving quality was to create a product or service and then to rely on an army of inspectors to "weed out" all of the defects. Not only is such a system a terrible waste of resources (consider the cost of scrap, rework, and no-value-added inspections), but it gives managers no opportunity for continuous improvement. The only way to improve a process is to discover the cause of poor quality, fix it (the sooner, the better), and learn from it so that workers can *avoid* the problem in the future. Using the statistical tools of the TQM approach allows a company to learn from its mistakes with a consistent approach to constantly improving quality.

■ *Avoid using TQM to place blame on those who make mistakes.* In many firms, the only reason managers seek out mistakes is to find someone to blame for them. The result is a culture based on fear and the unwillingness of workers to take chances to innovate. The goal of TQM is to improve the processes in which people work, *not* to lay blame on workers. Searching out "the guilty party" doesn't solve the problem. The TQM philosophy sees each problem that arises as an opportunity for improving the company's system.

■ *Strive for continuous improvement in processes as well as in products and services.* There is no finish line in the race for quality. A company's goal must be to improve the quality of its processes, products, and services constantly, no matter how high it currently stands.

Many of these principles are evident in quality guru W. Edwards Deming's 14 points, a capsulized version of how to build a successful TQM approach (see Table 17.2).

Implementing a TQM program successfully begins at the top. If the owner or chief executive of a company doesn't actively and visibly support the initiative, the employees who must make it happen will never accept it. TQM requires change: change in the way

Table 17.2

Deming's 14 Points

Total quality management cannot succeed as a piecemeal program or without true commitment to its philosophy. W. Edwards Deming, the man most visibly connected to TQM, drove home these concepts with his 14 points, the essential elements for integrating TQM successfully into a company. Deming's message was straightforward. Companies must transform themselves into customer-oriented, quality-focused organizations in which teams of employees have the training, the resources, and the freedom to pursue quality on a daily basis. The goal is to track the performance of a process, whether manufacturing a clock or serving a bank customer, and to develop ways to minimize variation in the system, eliminate defects, and spur innovation. The 14 points are:

1. *Constantly strive to improve products and services.* This requires total dedication to improving quality, productivity, and service—*continuously.*
2. *Adopt a total quality philosophy.* There are no shortcuts to quality improvement; it requires a completely new way of thinking and managing.
3. *Correct defects as they happen* rather than relying on mass inspection of end products. Real quality comes from improving the process, not from inspecting finished products and services. At that point, it's too late. Statistical process control charts can help workers detect when a process is producing poor-quality goods or services. Then they can stop it, make corrections, and get the process back on target.
4. *Don't award business on price alone.* Rather than choosing the lowest-cost vendor, businesses should work toward establishing close relationships with the vendors who offer the highest quality.
5. *Constantly improve the system of production and service.* Managers must focus the entire company on customer satisfaction, must measure results, and must make adjustments as necessary.
6. *Institute training.* Workers cannot improve quality and lower costs without proper training to erase old ways of doing things.
7. *Institute leadership.* The supervisor's job is not to boss workers around; it is to lead. The nature of the work is more like coaching than controlling.
8. *Drive out fear.* People often are afraid to point out problems because they fear the repercussions. Managers must encourage and reward employee suggestions.
9. *Break down barriers among staff areas.* Departments within organizations often erect needless barriers to protect their own turf. Total quality requires a spirit of teamwork and cooperation across the entire organization.
10. *Eliminate superficial slogans and goals.* These only offend employees because they imply that workers could do a better job if they would only try.
11. *Eliminate standard quotas.* They emphasize quantity over quality. Not everyone can move at the same rate and still produce quality.
12. *Remove barriers to pride of workmanship.* Most workers want to do quality work. Eliminating "demotivators" frees them to achieve quality results.
13. *Institute vigorous education and retraining.* Managers must teach employees the new methods of continuous improvement, including statistical process control techniques.
14. *Take demonstrated management action to achieve the transformation.* Although success requires involvement of all levels of the organization, the impetus for change must come from the top.

These 14 interrelated elements contribute to a chain reaction effect. As a company improves its quality, costs decline, productivity increases, the company gains additional market share due to its ability to provide high-quality products at competitive prices, and the company and its employees prosper.

Source: The W. Edward Dewing Institute ©2004. Used by permission of the *MIT Press.* All rights reserved.

a company defines quality, in the way it sees its customers, in the way it treats employees, and in the way it sees itself. Successful implementation involves modification in the organization's culture as much as in the work processes.

The past few years have been trying times for the U.S. economy and its manufacturers. Nonetheless, many plants cite improved operations metrics in spite of the economy. The Census of Manufacturers data show more widespread plant improvements, including manufacturing cost reductions, when improvement strategies such as TQM are factored in. Refer to Table 17.3 for a breakdown of the quality improvement methodologies currently being utilized by U.S. manufacturers. Table 17.4 reports the outcome of these quality improvement efforts on various performance indicators.

Table 17.3

Quality Improvement
Methodologies Census of
Manufacturers Survey

PRIMARY METHODOLOGY	% OF PLANTS
Agile manufacturing	4.6%
Lean manufacturing	35.7%
Six sigma	3.3%
Lean and six sigma	7.7%
Theory of constraints (TOC)	4.9%
Total quality management	14.1%
Toyota production system	1.4%
No methodology	21.0%
Other	7.2%
Total	100.0%

Source: Used by permission. The Manufacturing Performance Institute. All rights reserved.

World-class organizations in the twenty-first century have continuous improvement as a fundamental element in all their competitive strategic initiatives. International standards for quality have emerged in the form of ISO 9000 or AMSI IASQ Q9000 standards that establish quality management procedures, detailed documentation, work instruction, and record keeping. The ISO standards were revised in December 2000 into more of a quality management system (ISO 9000:2000). The International Standards Organization has also put forth ISO 14000 as environmental management standards that are becoming accepted worldwide.

Table 17.4

Quality Improvement
Methodologies' Impact
on Median Performance
Measures

3-YEAR IMPROVEMENTS (% OF PLANTS)	TOC	TQM	OTHER	NO METHOD
Increased total inventory turns	51.2%	48.2%	43.1%	29.4%
Decreased manufacturing cycle time	78.5%	61.0%	71.6%	54.7%
Decreased manufacturing costs	59.5%	39.7%	47.6%	30.4%
Median Performance				
Annual savings due to methodology	10.0%	6.0%	5.5%	3.0%
Scrap/rework costs as % of sales	2.0%	2.0%	2.0%	2.0%
Total inventory turn rate	6.2	8.0	10.0	6.0
ROIC	10.0%	11.0%	14.5%	10.1%
Machine availability	88.0%	90.0%	85.0%	85.0%
OEE	70.0%	80.0%	83.0%	75.0%
Sales per employee	$128,000	$150,000	$163,000	$127,500

Source: Used by permission. The Manufacturing Performance Institute. All rights reserved.

IN THE FOOTSTEPS OF AN ENTREPRENEUR...

Fewer Surprises Are a Good Thing

Tom Thornbury, CEO of Softub, a $15 million maker of hot tubs, understands just how important the right vendors can be to a small company's success. In fact, he learned the hard way that one bad supplier can threaten the health of a growing business. Several years ago, Softub purchased from an outside supplier the motor, pump, and assembly unit that provides the jet action in its hot tubs. Thornbury met with the company's owner and heard other customers rave about its quality. "That was back when I was the purchasing department," says Thornbury. "That might have been the problem." Before long, defective jet assemblies turned up in Softub's factory and in customers' homes. Then the supplier went out of business. Thornbury scrambled to repair all of the faulty assemblies and tried to keep his network of distributors from defecting. He estimates the entire episode cost his company about $500,000. "If we had done a better job of surveying our suppliers," he says, "this might not have happened."

The odds of it happening again are slim. Because two-thirds of Softub's product cost is in materials—from sheet metal to nuts and bolts—that the company purchases from outside suppliers, managers saw the need to evaluate vendors more thoroughly before inviting them to become a crucial link in its production process. Under the direction of Gary Anderson, Softub's purchasing agent, cross-functional teams of 10 employees visit potential vendors on site and use a checklist Anderson developed to evaluate them. The checklist covers everything from safety devices and cleanliness to preventive maintenance and quality processes. "(The checklist) forces the team to focus on specific areas so we don't forget anything when we're on a visit," says Anderson. Team visits may take as little as two hours or as long as two days, and team members delve into every aspect of the prospective supplier's business. They interview everyone from the president to the factory workers and ask lots of questions. Before going on site, every team member receives a packet of information about the company, including any articles about it from trade journals.

Back in Softub's offices, the checklist generates a great deal of discussion about critical issues such as quality and on-time delivery. Anderson also verifies the accuracy of every potential vendor's claims by contacting at least three of its customers. When all the information is in, the team makes its recommendation to the management team, which selects one vendor. "The payoff is that we're recruiting a better breed of supplier," says Thornbury. Since beginning to use the forms, Softub is getting fewer defective products from its suppliers, and its vendor turnover rate has been cut in half. Plus, Softub has discovered one more unexpected benefit: closer relationships with quality suppliers. On several occasions, employees at Softub have given suppliers ideas and suggestions on how to solve production problems. "We're developing partnerships in which we have a pretty free exchange of information," says Thornbury. "Also, as we've gotten to know our vendors better, there are fewer surprises. In the manufacturing operation, surprises can be lethal."

1. Why is using a vendor evaluation scale important to companies such as Softub?
2. What benefits can companies that conduct vendor audits expect to gain?

Source: Adapted from Stephanie Gruner, "The Smart Vendor-Audit Checklist," Inc., April 1995, pp. 92–95.

Quantity: The Economic Order Quantity (EOQ)

3. Conduct economic order quantity (EOQ) analysis to determine the proper level of inventory.

The typical small business has its largest investment in inventory. But an investment in inventory is not profitable because dollars spent return nothing until the inventory is sold. In a sense, the small firm's inventory is its largest non-interest-bearing "account." Entrepreneurs must focus on controlling this investment and on maintaining proper inventory levels. Apparently, U.S. business is succeeding in its quest to run lean. U.S. Department of Commerce figures show that from 1981 to 2000, inventory as a percentage of gross domestic product (GDP) fell 46 percent, from 8.3 percent to 3.8 percent. During that same period, the total GDP more than tripled (from $3.1 trillion to $9.9 trillion), although the total amount tied up in inventory didn't even double, rising from $747 billion to $1.48 trillion.[6]

A primary objective of this portion of the purchasing plan is to generate an adequate turnover of merchandise by purchasing proper quantities. Tying up capital in extra inventory limits a company's working capital and exerts pressure on its cash flows. Also, a business risks the danger of being stuck with spoiled or obsolete merchandise, an extremely serious problem for many small businesses. Excess inventory also takes up valuable store or selling space that could be used for items with higher turnover rates and more profit potential. On the other hand, maintaining too little inventory can be extremely costly. An owner may be forced to reorder merchandise too frequently, escalating total inventory costs. Also, inventory stockouts will occur when customer demand exceeds the firm's supply of merchandise, causing customer ill will. Persistent stockouts are inconvenient for customers, and many customers will eventually choose to shop elsewhere. Manufacturers that run out of inventory will be forced to shut down temporarily. For instance, Mitsubishi Motors recently suspended production of its Eclipse convertibles and Galant sedans at its Normal, Illinois plant when the company ran out of the engines and transmissions it imports from Japan.[7] Carrying either too much or too little inventory both are expensive mistakes that lead to serious problems in other areas of the business.

The goal is to maintain enough inventory to meet customer orders and to satisfy production needs but not so much that storage costs and inventory investments are excessive. The analytical techniques used to determine **economic order quantities (EOQs)** will help the manager compute the amount of stock to purchase with an order or to produce with each production run to minimize total inventory costs. To compute the proper amount of stock to order or to produce, a small business owner must first determine the three principal elements of total inventory costs: the cost of the units, the holding (or carrying) cost, and the setup (or ordering) cost.

Cost of Units

The cost of the units is simply the number of units demanded for a particular time period multiplied by the cost per unit. Suppose that a small manufacturer of lawnmowers forecasts demand for the upcoming year to be 100,000 mowers. He needs to order enough wheels at $1.55 each to supply the production department.

$$\text{Total annual cost of units} = D \times C$$

where:

D = Annual demand (in units)
C = Cost of a single unit ($)

In this example,

D = 100,000 mowers $\times$ 4 wheels per mower = 400,000 wheels
C = $1.55/wheel

$$\text{Total annual cost of units} = D \times C$$
$$= 400,000 \text{ wheels} \times \$1.55$$
$$= \$620,000$$

Holding (Carrying) Costs

The typical costs of holding inventory include the costs of storage, insurance, taxes, interest, depreciation, spoilage, obsolescence, and pilferage. The expense involved in physically storing the items in inventory is usually substantial, especially if the inventories are large. The owner may have to rent or build additional warehousing facilities, pushing the cost of storing the inventory even higher. The firm may also incur expenses in transferring items into and out of inventory. The cost of storage also includes the expense of operating the facility (e.g., heating, lighting, refrigeration), as well as the depreciation, taxes, and interest on the building. Most small business owners purchase insurance on their inventories to shift the risk of fire, theft, flood, and other disasters to the insurer. The premiums paid for this coverage are also included in the cost of holding inventory. In general, the larger the firm's average inventory, the greater its holding cost.

Many small business owners fail to recognize the interest expense associated with carrying large inventories. In many cases the interest expense is evident when the firm borrows money to purchase inventory. But a less obvious interest expense is the opportunity cost associated with investing in inventory. In other words, the owner could have used the money invested in inventory (a non-interest-bearing investment) for some other purpose, such as plant expansion, research and development, or reducing debt. Thus, the cost of independently financing inventory is the cost of forgoing the opportunity to use those funds elsewhere. A substantial inventory investment ties up a large amount of money unproductively.

Depreciation costs represent the reduced value of inventory over time. Some businesses are strongly influenced by the depreciation of inventory. For example, a small auto dealer's inventory is subject to depreciation because he must sell models left over from one year at reduced prices.

Spoilage, obsolescence, and pilferage also add to the costs of holding inventory. Some small firms, especially those that deal in fad merchandise, assume an extremely high risk of obsolescence. For example, a fashion merchandiser with a large inventory of the latest styles may be left with worthless merchandise when styles suddenly change. Small companies selling perishables must always be aware of the danger of spoilage. For example, the owner of a small fish market must plan purchases carefully to ensure a fresh inventory. Unless the owner establishes sound inventory control procedures, the business will suffer losses from employee theft and shoplifting.

The following formula calculates total inventory holding costs:

$$\text{Total annual holding (carrying) costs} = \frac{Q}{2} \times H$$

where:

Q = Quantity of inventory ordered
H = Holding cost per unit per year

The greater the quantity ordered, the greater the inventory carrying costs. This relationship is shown in Table 17.5, assuming that the cost of carrying a single unit of inventory for the lawn mower manufacturer for one year is $1.25.

Setup (Ordering) Costs

The various expenses incurred in actually ordering materials and inventory or in setting up the production line to manufacture them determine the level of setup or ordering costs of a product. The costs of obtaining materials and inventory typically include preparing purchase

Table 17.5

Carrying Costs

If Q Is...	$Q/2$, Average Inventory, Is...	$Q/2 \times H$, Carrying Cost, Is...
500	250	$ 312.50
1,000	500	625.00
2,000	1,000	1,250.00
3,000	1,500	1,875.00
4,000	2,000	2,500.00
5,000	2,500	3,125.00
6,000	3,000	3,750.00
7,000	3,500	4,375.00
8,000	4,000	5,000.00
9,000	4,500	5,625.00
10,000	5,000	6,250.00

Table 17.6

Setup Cost

If Q Is...	D/Q, Number of Orders per Year, Is...	$D/Q \times S$, Ordering (Setup) Cost, Is...
500	800	$7,200.00
1,000	400	3,600.00
5,000	80	720.00
10,000	40	360.00

orders; analyzing and choosing vendors; processing, handling, and expediting orders; receiving and inspecting items; and performing all the required accounting and clerical functions. Even if the small company produces its own supply of goods, it encounters most of these same expenses. Ordering costs are usually relatively fixed, regardless of the quantity ordered.

Total setup or ordering costs are found by multiplying the number of orders made in a year (or the number of production runs in a year) by the cost of placing a single order (or the cost of setting up a single production run). In the lawnmower manufacturing example, the annual requirement is 400,000 wheels per year and the cost to place an order is $9.00, so the ordering costs are as follows:

$$\text{Total annual setup (ordering) costs} = \frac{D}{Q} \times S$$

where:

D = Annual demand
Q = Quantity of inventory ordered
S = Setup (ordering) costs for a single run (or order)

The greater the quantity ordered, the smaller the number of orders placed. This relationship is shown in Table 17.6, assuming an ordering cost of $9.00 per order.

Solving for EOQ

If carrying costs were the only expense involved in obtaining inventory, the small business manager would purchase the smallest number of units possible in each order to minimize the cost of holding the inventory. For example, if the lawnmower manufacturer purchased four wheels per order, carrying cost would be minimized:

$$\text{Carrying cost} = \frac{Q}{2} \times H$$

$$= \frac{4}{2} \times \$1.25$$

$$= \$2.50$$

but ordering cost would be outrageous:

$$\text{Ordering cost} = \frac{D}{Q} \times S$$

$$= \frac{400,000}{4} \times \$9$$

$$= \$900,000$$

Obviously this is not the small manufacturer's ideal inventory solution.

Similarly, if ordering costs were the only expense involved in procuring inventory, the small business manager would purchase the largest number of units possible in order to minimize the ordering cost. In our example, if the lawnmower manufacturer purchased 400,000 wheels per order, ordering cost would be minimized:

$$\text{Ordering cost} = \frac{D}{Q} \times S$$

$$= \frac{400,000}{400,000} \times \$9$$

$$= \$9$$

but his carrying cost would be tremendously high:

$$\text{Carrying cost} = \frac{Q}{2} \times H$$

$$= \frac{400,000}{2} \times \$1.25$$

$$= \$250,000$$

A quick inspection shows that neither of those solutions minimizes the total cost of the manufacturer's inventory. Total cost is composed of the cost of the units, carrying costs, and ordering costs:

$$\text{Total cost} = (D \times C) + \left(\frac{Q}{2} \times H\right) + \left(\frac{D}{Q} \times S\right)$$

These costs are graphed in Figure 17.2. Notice that as the quantity ordered increases, the ordering costs decrease and the carrying costs increase.

The EOQ formula simply balances the ordering cost and the carrying cost of the small business owner's inventory so that total costs are minimized. Table 17.7 summarizes the total costs for various values of Q for our lawnmower manufacturer.

As Table 17.7 and Figure 17.2 illustrate, the EOQ formula locates the minimum point on the total cost curve, which occurs where the cost of carrying inventory ($Q/2 \times H$) equals the cost of ordering inventory ($D/Q \times S$). If the small business places the smallest number of orders possible each year, its ordering cost is minimized but its carrying cost is

Figure 17.2

Inventory Costs

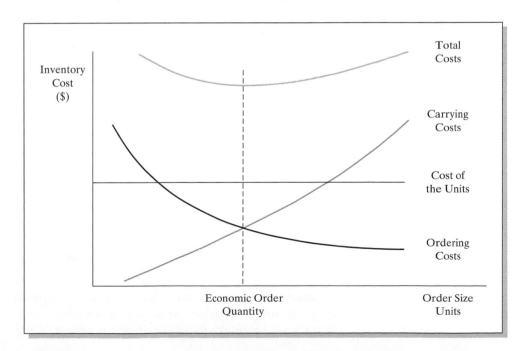

Table 17.7

Economic Order Quantity and Total Cost

If Q Is...	$D \times C$, Cost of Units, Is...	$Q/2 \times H$, Carrying Cost, Is...	$D/Q \times S$, Ordering Cost, Is...	TC, Total Cost, Is...
500	$620,000	$ 312.00	$7,200.00	$627,512.00
1,000	$620,000	$ 625.00	$3,600.00	$624,225.00
2,400	**$620,000**	**$1,500.00**	**$1,500.00**	**$623,000.00**
5,000	$620,000	$3,125.00	$ 720.00	$623,845.00
10,000	$620,000	$6,250.00	$ 360.00	$626,610.00

maximized. Conversely, if the firm orders the smallest number of units possible in each order, its carrying cost is minimized, but its ordering cost is maximized. Total inventory cost is minimized when carrying cost and ordering costs are balanced.

Let us return to our lawnmower manufacturer and compute its economic order quantity, EOQ, using the following formula:

$$S = \$9.00 \text{ per order}$$

$$C = \$1.55 \text{ per wheel}$$

$$EOQ = \sqrt{\frac{2 \times D \times S}{H}}$$

$$= \sqrt{\frac{2 \times 400,000 \times 9.00}{1.25}}$$

$$= 2,400 \text{ wheels}$$

To minimize total inventory cost, the lawnmower manufacturer should order 2,400 wheels at a time. Furthermore,

$$\text{Number of orders per year} = \frac{D}{Q}$$

$$= \frac{400,000}{2,400}$$

$$= 166.67 \text{ orders}$$

This manufacturer will place approximately 167 orders this year at a minimum total cost of $623,000, computed as follows:

$$\text{Total cost} = (D \times C) + \left(\frac{Q}{2} \times H\right) + \left(\frac{D}{Q} \times S\right)$$

$$= (400,000 \times 1.55) + \left(\frac{2,400}{2} \times 1.25\right) + \left(\frac{400,000}{2,400} \times 9.00\right)$$

$$= \$620,000 + \$1,500 + \$1,500$$

$$= \$623,000$$

Economic Order Quantity (EOQ) with Usage

The preceding EOQ model assumes that orders are filled instantaneously; that is, fresh inventory arrives all at once. Because that assumption does not hold true for many small manufacturers, it is necessary to consider a variation of the basic EOQ model that allows inventory to be added over a period of time rather than instantaneously.

In addition, a manufacturer is likely to be taking items from inventory for use in the assembly process over the same time period. For example, the lawn mower manufacturer may be producing blades to replenish his supply, but, at the same time, assembly workers are reducing the supply of blades to make finished mowers. The key feature of this version of the EOQ model is that inventories are used while inventories are being added.

Using the lawnmower manufacturer as an example, we can compute the EOQ for the blades. To make the calculation, we need two additional pieces of information: the usage rate for the blades, U, and the plant's capacity to manufacture the blades, P. Suppose that the maximum number of lawnmower blades the company can manufacture is 480 per day. We know from the previous illustration that annual demand for mowers is 100,000 units (therefore, 100,000 blades). If the plant operates 5 days per week for 50 weeks (250 days), its usage rate is:

$$U = \frac{100{,}000 \text{ units per year}}{250 \text{ days}} = 400 \text{ units per day}$$

It costs \$325 to set up the blade manufacturing line and \$8.71 to store one blade for one year. The cost of producing a blade is \$4.85. To compute EOQ we modify the basic formula to get:

$$EOQ = \sqrt{\frac{2 \times D \times S}{H \times \left(1 - \dfrac{U}{P}\right)}}$$

For the lawnmower manufacturer,

$$D = 100{,}000 \text{ blades}$$

$$S = \$325 \text{ per production run}$$

$$H = \$8.71 \text{ per blade per year}$$

$$U = 400 \text{ blades per day}$$

$$P = 480 \text{ blades per day}$$

$$EOQ = \sqrt{\frac{2 \times 100{,}000 \times 325}{8.71 \times \left(1 - \dfrac{400}{480}\right)}}$$

$$= 6{,}691.50 \text{ blades} \approx 6{,}692 \text{ blades}$$

Therefore, to minimize total inventory cost, the lawnmower manufacturer should produce 6,692 blades per production run. Also,

$$\text{Number of production runs per year} = \frac{D}{Q}$$

$$= \frac{100{,}000 \text{ blades}}{6{,}692 \text{ blades/run}}$$

$$= 14.9 = 15 \text{ runs}$$

The manufacturer will make 15 production runs during the year at a total cost of:

$$\text{Total cost} = (D \times C) + \left[\frac{(1 - U/P) \times Q \times H}{2}\right] + \left(\frac{D}{Q} \times S\right)$$

$$= (100,000 \times \$4.85) + \left(\frac{(1 - 400/480) \times 6,692}{2} \times \$8.71 \right) + \left(\frac{100,000}{6,692} \times \$325 \right)$$

$$= \$485,000 + \$4,857 + \$4,857$$

$$= \$494,714$$

Small business managers must remember that the EOQ analysis is based on estimations of cost and demand. The final result is only as accurate as the input used. Consequently, this analytical tool serves only as a guideline for decision making. The final answer may not be the ideal solution because of intervening factors, such as opportunity costs or seasonal fluctuations. Knowledgeable entrepreneurs use EOQ analysis as a starting point in making a decision and then use managerial judgment and experience to produce a final ruling.

Price

For the typical small business owner, price is always a substantial factor when purchasing inventory and supplies. In many cases, an entrepreneur can negotiate price with potential suppliers on large orders of frequently purchased items. In other instances, perhaps when small quantities of items are purchased infrequently, the small business owner must pay list price.

The typical small business owner shops around and then orders from the supplier offering the best price. Still, this does not mean the small business manager should always purchase inventory and supplies at the lowest price available. The best purchase price is the lowest price at which the owner can obtain goods and services *of acceptable quality*. This guideline usually yields the best value more often than simply purchasing the lowest-priced goods.

Recall that one of Deming's 14 points is "Don't award business on price alone." Without proof of quality, an item with the lowest initial price may produce the highest total cost. Deming condemned the practice of constantly switching suppliers in search of the lowest initial price because it increases the variability of a process and lowers its quality. Instead he recommended that businesses establish long-term relationships built on mutual trust and cooperation with a single supplier.

Supply chain management includes all the activities that produce goods and services and deliver them to the customer. The next chapter will focus more extensively on the inventory management process. Studies of the factors the entrepreneurs consider when attempting to optimize the supply chain reveal that initial price for goods and services is often less important than other factors.

When evaluating a supplier's price, small business owners must consider not only the actual price of goods and services, but also the selling terms accompanying them. In some cases, the selling terms can be more important than the price itself. Sometimes a vendor's terms might include some type of purchase discount. Vendors typically offer three types of discounts: trade discounts, quantity discounts, and cash discounts.

4. Differentiate among the three types of purchase discounts that vendors offer.

Trade Discounts

Trade discounts are established on a graduated scale and depend on a small firm's position in the channel of distribution. In other words, trade discounts recognize the fact that manufacturers, wholesalers, and retailers perform a variety of vital functions at various

Figure 17.3

Trade Discount Structure

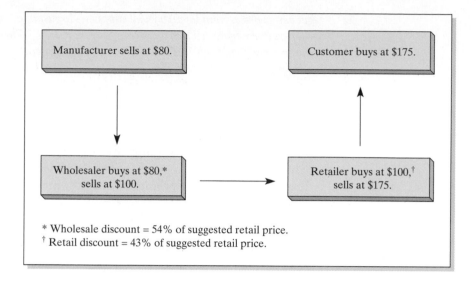

Manufacturer sells at $80.

Customer buys at $175.

Wholesaler buys at $80,*
sells at $100.

Retailer buys at $100,†
sells at $175.

* Wholesale discount = 54% of suggested retail price.
† Retail discount = 43% of suggested retail price.

stages in the channel of distribution and compensate them for providing these needed activities. Figure 17.3 illustrates a typical trade discount structure.

Quantity Discounts

Quantity discounts are designed to encourage businesses to order large quantities of merchandise and supplies. Vendors are able to offer lower prices on bulk purchases because the cost per unit is lower than for handling small orders. Quantity discounts normally exist in two forms: noncumulative and cumulative. Noncumulative quantity discounts are granted only if a certain volume of merchandise is purchased in a single order. For example, a wholesaler may offer small retailers a 3 percent discount only if they purchase 10 gross of Halloween masks in a single order. Table 17.8 shows a typical noncumulative quantity discount structure.

Cumulative quantity discounts are offered if a firm's purchases from a particular vendor exceed a specified quantity or dollar value over a predetermined time period. The time frame varies, but a yearly basis is most common. For example, a manufacturer of appliances may offer a small firm a 3 percent discount on subsequent orders if its purchases exceed $10,000 per year.

Some small business owners who normally buy in small quantities and are unable to qualify for quantity discounts can earn such discounts by joining buying groups, purchasing pools, or buying cooperatives. According to the National Cooperative Business Association, more than 50,000 small companies have joined cooperatives since 1992. *Jay DeFoor, CEO of DeFoor Drywall & Acoustical Supply Inc., in Macon, Georgia, joined Amarok, a drywall buying cooperative with more than 150 members, so his company could*

Company Example

Table 17.8

Noncumulative Quantity
Discount Structure

Order Size	Price
1–1,000 units	List price
1,001–5,000 units	List price − 2%
5,001–10,000 units	List price − 4%
10,001 units and above	List price − 6%

get better prices from large drywall suppliers. In just one year, DeFoor says the lower prices the cooperative negotiated saved his company $250,000. "There's no way I could have negotiated that on my own," says DeFoor, whose company generates annual sales of $20 million. "That's a huge part of our bottom line."[8]

Cash Discounts

Cash discounts are offered to customers as an incentive to pay for merchandise promptly. Many vendors grant cash discounts to avoid being used as an interest-free bank by customers who purchase merchandise and then neglect to pay by the invoice due date. To encourage prompt payment of invoices, many vendors allow customers to deduct a percentage of the purchase amount if payment is remitted within a specified time. Cash discount terms "2/10, net 30" are common in many industries. This notation means that the total amount of the invoice is due 30 days after its date, but if the bill is paid within 10 days, the buyer may deduct 2 percent from the total. A discount offering "2/10, EOM" (EOM means "end of month") indicates that the buyer may deduct 2 percent if the bill is paid by the end of the month after purchase.

In general, it is sound business practice to take advantage of cash discounts. The money saved by paying invoices promptly is freed up for use elsewhere. Conversely, there is an implicit (opportunity) cost of forgoing a cash discount. By forgoing a cash discount, a business owner is, in effect, paying an annual interest rate to retain the use of the discounted amount for the remainder of the credit period. For example, suppose the Print Shop receives an invoice for $1,000 from a vendor offering a cash discount of 2/10, net 30. Figure 17.4 illustrates this situation and shows how to compute the cost of forgoing the cash discount.

Actually, it cost the Print Shop $20 to retain the use of its $980 for an extra 20 days. Translate this into an annual interest rate:

$$I = P \times R \times T$$

where

I = Interest ($)
P = Principle ($)
R = Rate of interest (%)
T = Time (number of days/360)

So, to compute R, the annual interest rate,

$$R = \frac{I}{P \times T}$$

Figure 17.4

A Cash Discount

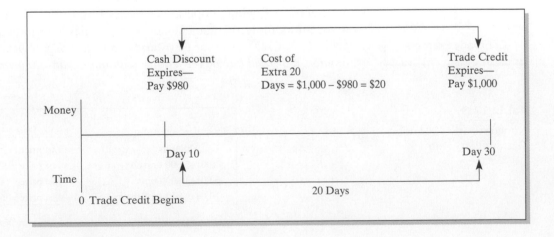

Table 17.9

Cost of Forgoing Cash
Discounts

Cash Discount Terms	Cost of Forgoing Cash Discounts (Annually)
2/10, net 30	36.735%
2/30, net 60	34.490%
2/10, net 60	13.693%
3/10, net 30	55.670%
3/10, net 60	22.268%

In our example,

$$R = \frac{\$20}{980 \times \frac{20}{360}}$$

$$= 36.735\%$$

The cost to the Print Shop of forgoing the cash discount is 36.735 percent per year! If there is $980 available on day 10 of the trade credit period, the owner should pay the invoice unless he is able to return greater than 36.735 percent on it. If the owner does not have $980 on day 10 but can borrow it at less than 36.735 percent, he should do so to take advantage of the cash discount. Table 17.9 summarizes the cost of forgoing cash discounts offering various terms.

Although it is a good idea for business owners to take advantage of cash discounts, it is not a wise practice to stretch accounts payable to suppliers beyond the payment terms specified on the invoice. Letting payments become past due can destroy the

> Company Example

trusting relationship a small company has built with its vendors. *When David Brent took over the Nutty Bavarian, a small company that sells cinnamon-glazed almonds and pecans from kiosks, the company was growing rapidly and was experiencing cash flow problems. Brent soon discovered that the company owed more than $100,000 to its nut suppliers, almost all of it past due. To make matters worse, the previous managers had ignored past-due notices and telephone calls from suppliers seeking payment. Brent took an honest, straightforward approach to solving the problem. "I went to my suppliers to ask for longer credit terms and worked out a payment plan that we could meet," he says. Although it took more than a year, Brent eventually paid off all of the company's past-due bills. "Instead of lying and saying the check's in the mail, tell suppliers what's happening and what you propose to do about it." he advises. "If you owe them, suppliers are eager to find a way to work with you." Thanks to his forthright approach with the Nutty Bavarian's suppliers, Brent has maintained close partnerships with all of the company's suppliers.*[9]

Timing—When to Order

> **5.** Calculate a company's reorder point.

Timing the purchase of merchandise and supplies is also a critical element of any purchasing plan. An entrepreneur must schedule delivery dates so that the company does not lose customer goodwill from stockouts. Also, the owner must concentrate on maintaining proper control over the firm's inventory investment without tying up an excessive amount of working capital. There is a trade-off between the cost of running out of stock and the cost of carrying additional inventory.

When planning delivery schedules for inventory and supplies, owners must consider the lead time for an order, the time gap between placing an order and receiving it.

In general, business owners cannot expect instantaneous delivery of merchandise. As a result, managers must plan reorder points for inventory items with lead times in mind. To determine when to order merchandise for inventory, a small business manager must calculate the reorder point for key inventory items. Developing a reorder point model involves determining the lead time for an order, the usage rate for the item, the minimum level of stock allowable, and the economic order quantity (EOQ). The **lead time** for an order is the time gap between placing an order with a vendor and actually receiving the goods. It may be as little as a few hours or as long as several weeks to process purchase requisitions and orders, contact the supplier, receive the goods, and sort them into the inventory. Obviously, owners who purchase from local vendors encounter shorter lead times than those who rely on distant suppliers.

The usage rate for a particular product can be determined from past inventory and accounting records. A small business owner must estimate the speed at which the supply of merchandise will be depleted over a given time. The anticipated usage rate for a product determines how long the supply will last. For example, if an owner projects that she will use 900 units in the next six months, the usage rate is five units per day (900 units/180 days). The simplest reorder point model assumes that the firm experiences a linear usage rate; that is, depletion of the firm's stock continues at a constant rate over time.

Business owners must determine the minimum level of stock allowable. If a firm runs out of a particular item (i.e., incurs stockouts), customers may lose faith in the business and may shop elsewhere. To avoid stockouts, many firms establish a minimum level of inventory greater than zero. In other words, they build a cushion, called **safety stock,** into their inventories in case demand runs ahead of the anticipated usage rate. In such cases, the owner can dip into the safety stock to fill customer orders until the stock is replenished.

To compute the reorder point for an item, the owner must combine this inventory information with the product's EOQ. The following example will illustrate the reorder point technique:

$$L = \text{Lead time for an order} = 5 \text{ days}$$

$$U = \text{Usage rate} = 18 \text{ units/ day}$$

$$S = \text{Safety stock (minimum level)} = 75 \text{ units}$$

$$\text{EOQ} = 540 \text{ units}$$

The formula for computing the reorder point is:

$$\text{Reorder point} = (L \times U) + S$$

In this example,

$$\text{Reorder point} = (5 \text{ days} \times 18 \text{ units/day}) + 75 \text{ units}$$

$$= 165 \text{ units}$$

Thus, this owner should order 540 more units when inventory drops to 165 units. Figure 17.5 illustrates the reorder point situation for this small business.

The simple reorder technique makes certain assumptions that may not be valid in particular situations. First, the model assumes that the firm's usage rate is constant, when in fact for most small businesses demand varies daily. Second, the model assumes that lead time for an order is constant when, in fact, few vendors deliver precisely within lead time estimates. Third, in this sample model, the owner never taps safety stock; however, late deliveries or accelerated demand may force the owner to dip into this

Figure 17.5

Reorder Point Model

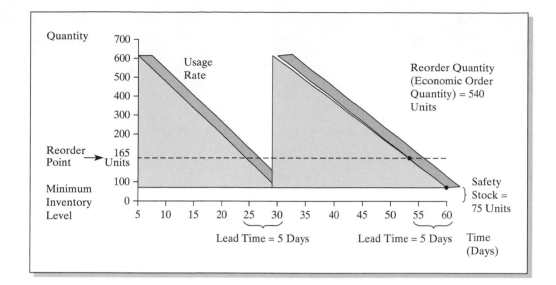

inventory reserve. More advanced models relax some of these assumptions, but the simple model can be a useful inventory guideline for making inventory decisions in a small company.

Another popular reorder point model assumes that the demand for a product during its lead time is normally distributed (see Figure 17.6). The area under the normal curve at any given point represents the probability that a particular demand level will occur. Figure 17.7 illustrates the application of this normal distribution to the reorder point model *without* safety stock. The model recognizes that three different demand patterns can occur during a product's lead time. Demand pattern 1 is an example of below-average demand during lead time; demand pattern 2 is an example of average demand during lead time; and demand pattern 3 is an example of above-average demand during lead time.

If the reorder point for this item is the average demand for the product during lead time, 50 percent of the time demand will be below average (note that 50 percent of the area under the normal curve lies below average). Similarly, 50 percent of the time, demand during lead time will exceed the average, and the firm will experience stockouts (note that 50 percent of the area under the normal curve lies above average).

To reduce the probability of inventory shortage, the small business owner can increase the reorder point above $\bar{D}_L$ (average demand during lead time). But how much should the owner increase the reorder point? Rather than attempt to define the actual

Figure 17.6

Demand During Leading

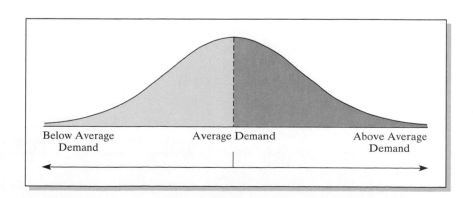

Figure 17.7

Reorder Point Without
Safety Stock

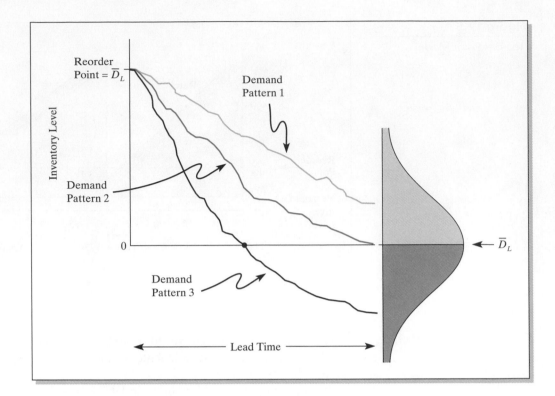

costs of carrying extra inventory versus the costs of stockouts (remember the trade-off described earlier), this model allows the small business owner to determine the appropriate reorder point by setting a desired customer level. For example, the owner may wish to satisfy 95 percent of customer demand for a product during lead time. This service level determines the amount of increase in the reorder point. In effect, these additional items serve as a safety stock:

$$\text{Safety stock} = SLF \times SD_L$$

where:

    SLF = Service level factor (the appropriate Z score)
    SD_L = Standard deviation of demand during lead time

Table 17.10 shows the appropriate service level factor (Z score) for some of the most popular target customer service levels.

Table 17.10

Service Level Factors
and Z Scores

TARGET CUSTOMER SERVICE LEVEL	Z SCORE*
99%	2.330
97.5%	1.960
95%	1.645
90%	1.275
80%	0.845
75%	0.675

*Any basic statistics book will provide a table of areas under the normal curve, which will give the appropriate Z score for any service level factor.

Figure 17.8

Reorder Point with
Safety Stock

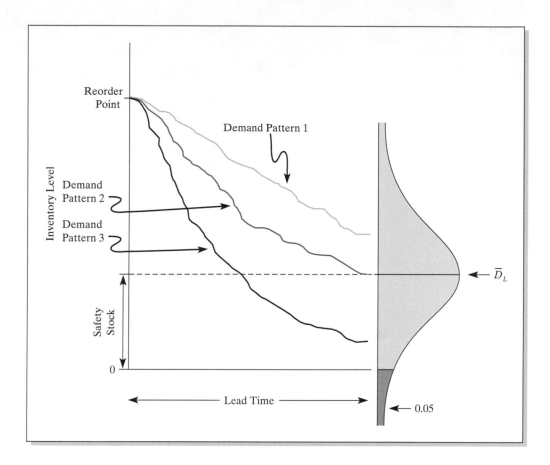

Figure 17.8 shows the shift to a normally distributed reorder point model with safety stock. In this case the manager has set a 95 percent customer service level; that is, the manager wants to meet 95 percent of the demand during lead time. The normal curve in the model without safety stock (from Figure 17.7) is shifted up so that 95 percent of the area under the curve lies above the zero inventory level. The result is a reorder point that is higher than the original reorder point by the amount of the safety stock:

$$\text{Reorder point} = \bar{D}_L + (SLF \times SD_L)$$

where:

$\bar{D}_L$ = Average demand during lead time (original reorder point)
SLF = Service level factor (the appropriate Z score)
SD_L = Standard deviation of demand during lead time

To illustrate, suppose that the average demand for a product during its lead time (one week) is 325 units with a standard deviation of 110 units. If the service level is 95 percent, the service level factor (from Table 17.10) would be 1.645. The reorder point would be:

$$R = 325 + (1.645 \times 110) = 325 + 181 = 506 \text{ units}$$

Figure 17.9 illustrates the shift from a system without safety stock to one with safety stock for this example. With a reorder point of 325 units ($\bar{D}_L$), this small business owner will experience inventory shortages during lead time 50 percent of the time. With a reorder point of 506 units (i.e., a safety stock of 181 units), the business owner will experience inventory stockouts during lead time only 5 percent of the time.

Figure 17.9

Shift from a No-Safety
Stock System to a Safety
Stock System

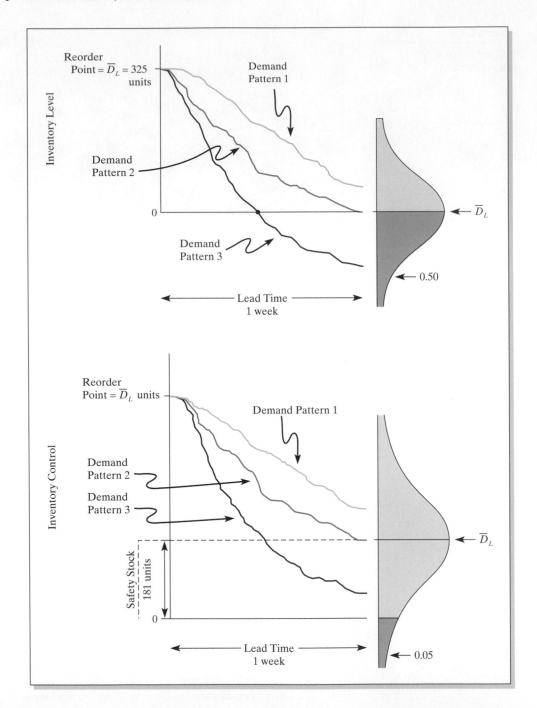

Is This a Factory or a NASCAR Pit Stop?

Most entrepreneurs know that inventory that sits on the shelf for an extended period of time costs money. Many high-tech products lose their value extremely quickly, but few companies face the problem that confronts Theragenics if it fails to mesh its purchasing plan and manufacturing operations and ends up with inventory sitting in stock. Theragenics, a Buford, Georgia, company, manufactures the radioactive seeds that are implanted to treat prostate cancer in patients. Made from the isotope palladium-103, the seeds, which are designed to deliver a precise dose of radioactivity to the targeted area, begin a rapid decline in performance the minute they are manufactured, losing 4 percent of their potency each day they exist. Therefore, if the Theragenics manufacturing process fails to meet its high-quality standards or if the company fails to deliver the seeds exactly when they are needed, it loses the entire cost of the order, which can be as much as $7,500. "We are slaves to the clock," says CEO Christine Jacobs. As a result, purchasing, manufacturing, and quality management processes at Theragenics resemble a pit stop in a NASCAR race more than they do an industrial operation. How does Theragenics manage its supply chain and manufacturing process?

Computerized logistics management. Because prostate surgery is a scheduled procedure, Theragenics knows exactly how many seeds it must produce and when it must deliver them. When the company receives an order, a customized logistics software package checks the surgery date and then works backwards to calculate a 28-step manufacturing schedule, taking into account the 4 percent decay rate of the seeds' effectiveness. The schedule determines the exact timing of each order's production schedule.

Precision manufacturing. To produce the palladium-103 isotope, Theragenics starts with the raw material rhodium, a valuable metal that sells for $500 per troy ounce. Because the quality of rhodium varies drastically, staff physicists must recalibrate each of the company's cyclotrons, miniature particle accelerators, to ensure that each batch is bombarded by a precise number of protons. Theragenics keeps cots near the scientists' work area in case they must work more than one shift to produce the proper amount of palladium-103 to meet the production schedule.

Extreme quality control. Unlike most companies, Theragenics does not count on sampling techniques to determine the quality of its manufacturing process. Because human lives are involved, the company submits every radioactive seed it produces, each one about the size of a grain of rice, to 28 different quality tests. One of the most important tests verifies the exact amount of radiation each seed gives off.

Once the seeds are tested, employees pack them into lead containers called "pigs" and ship them via FedEx to hospitals across the world.

1. What risks do small companies face when the products they make or buy sit on a shelf in a store or a warehouse for an extended period of time?
2. What lessons can other companies learn about supply chain management and quality control from Theragenics?

Source: Adapted from Justin Martin, "A Do-or-Die Supply Chain," *Business 2.0*, January/February 2004, p. 50.

Managing the Supply Chain: Vendor Analysis and Selection

6. Develop a vendor rating scale.

Businesses have discovered that managing their supply chains for maximum effectiveness and efficiency not only can increase their profitability but it also can provide them with an important competitive advantage in the marketplace. Proper **supply chain management (SCM)** enables companies to reduce their inventories, get products to market much faster, and improve customer satisfaction. SCM requires businesses to forge long-term partnerships with reliable suppliers rather than to see vendors merely as "someone trying to sell me something."

Companies are learning that, to make SCM work, they must share information with their suppliers and make their supply chains transparent to everyone involved in them. In the early days, that meant linking suppliers and companies as if they were part of one business on private data networks using electronic data interchange (EDI), which enabled companies and vendors to exchange orders and invoices electronically. The Internet takes EDI a step further. Web-based supply chain management now enables companies to share information concerning production plans, shipment schedules, inventory levels, sales forecasts, and actual sales on a real-time basis with their vendors, enabling the companies to make instant adjustments to their orders and delivery schedules. Many companies are connected via the Web to their customers and their suppliers, which enables them to respond rapidly to buyer preferences by modifying in real time the inventory they purchase. In turn, suppliers can make the fast adjustments in production scheduling to produce what the customers actually are buying. Time compression and seamless integration of the purchasing process that filters up the supply chain from the consumer to the retailer to the supplier cut the cost of producing and carrying unwanted and unsold merchandise. One consulting firm that specializes in setting up these supply chain management systems says that its clients have seen their inventory levels decline as much as 60 percent, saving those companies vast amounts of money.[10] With these systems, valuable information flows from the small business selling suits to customers up the supply chain all the way to the sheep shearer harvesting wool!

A Web-based SCM process works like this: Software at a retail store captures data from sales as they happen and looks for underlying trends for use in calculating quantities of which products to purchase in the future. For instance, SCM software at a retail store may notice that black low-rise jeans are selling more briskly than anticipated and then forecast the quantity of jeans the store should order. That information then goes up the supply chain to the jeans maker. Taking into account delivery times and manufacturing speed, the software helps the jeans maker create a detailed production plan for cutting, sewing, and shipping the garments on time. Then, the software determines how much fabric the jeans maker must have to produce the required number of black low-rise jeans and orders it from the textile producer. The software can track everything from the location of the raw materials in the production process to the quality of the finished product for everyone in the supply chain.[11] "Supply chain analytics can boost the bottom line because they produce greater efficiency, less scrap, better quality, and lower production costs and can improve the top line through greater customer satisfaction," says a top manager at IDC, a research company that has studied the impact of SCM on companies' performance. "This is basic business made better."

Company Example →

North Face, a maker of outdoor apparel whose logo is well known among college students, was generating sales of $238 million but was incurring losses of $100 million because of serious problems with its supply chain. "North Face was producing too much inventory and could not match this inventory to orders or even ship effectively," says one manager. "The company didn't know what its orders were or where its purchases were logistically. Everything had come unglued from an information and service standpoint." On-time delivery to retailers had slipped below 50 percent, which is bad for any business but particularly bad for North Face because its products were in high demand. The company was in crisis mode because its supply chain was broken. VF, a large apparel company, saw potential in North Face and purchased the company. VF's first priority was to fix the supply chain. Managers replaced the antiquated manual system that North Face had been using in a vain attempt at managing it supply chain with a more sophisticated automated system based on business intelligence software. The software compares sales for each of the company's products with inventory records to determine how many of each item North Face should order from its suppliers. It also specifies the timing of orders to meet or precede customers' requested delivery dates. The resulting reports are sent to key decision makers at North Face via e-mail. Since implementing the new system, inventory at North Face has fallen by more than 65 percent, freeing untold millions of dollars in cash flow. Lower costs have improved the company's profit margin to an impressive 14 percent of sales.[12]

Experienced business owners realize that a key link in supply chain management is finding reliable vendors that can supply them with quality merchandise, equipment, supplies, and services at reasonable prices in a timely manner. Selecting the right vendors or suppliers for a business can have an impact well beyond simply obtaining goods and services at the lowest costs. Although searching for the best price will always be an important factor, successful small business owners must always consider other factors in vendor selection such as reliability, reputation, quality, support services, speed, and proximity.

✦ GAINING *a* COMPETITIVE EDGE ✦

A Funny Thing Happened on the Way to Your Business

Every year, U.S. companies spend an amount equivalent to 10.5 percent of the nation's GDP—more than $700 billion—just to package and transport goods from one place to another. With so much at stake, it is little wonder that distribution, or logistics, has become an important part of companies' competitive strategies. "You have far more opportunities to get cost out of the supply chain than you do out of manufacturing," says one CEO. Streamlining a company's ordering and distribution process can reduce delivery times and the investments in inventory—as well as cut costs and avoid costly mistakes. Consider, for example, the following (true) distribution horror stories.

The shipping manager at a plant in China is struggling to ready a rush order of men's and women's athletic shoes for shipment to a retailer in the United States. He runs into a snag when trying to load the cartons containing the shoes into 40-foot shipping containers. He places a call to the retailer's logistics manager to ask how many shoes to put in each container. "As many as you can fit," was the reply. "Please don't bother me with such silly questions."

The Chinese shipping manager complies with the customer's request. He has workers take the shoes out of the cartons, remove them from their individual shoeboxes, and put them into the shipping containers. When the shipment arrives in the United States, the retailer's warehouse manager gets an even bigger surprise. The Chinese workers didn't even tie the shoes in pairs. The containers are filled with thousands of pairs of shoes—all floating around loose! The retailer has already advertised a big sale on these shoes and quickly arranges for workers to go to the warehouse, where they match and box thousands of pairs of shoes. The company incurs thousands of dollars of unplanned labor expenses and eventually sells the shoes at close to cost.

A dockworker is handling a shipment of margarine traveling from Denmark to Tacoma, Washington, when he notices a leak in one of the shipping containers. The cargo is loaded onto a truck headed for a warehouse, but as the driver rolls down the highway, he looks in his rearview mirror and notices yellow blobs flying from the back of his truck. At the warehouse, workers open the containers to find 2,000 cartons of margarine that have experienced a complete meltdown. "Anyone got any popcorn?" asks one worker. The shipping document from the company in Denmark failed to specify a temperature setting for the cargo.

One freight company that has contracts with two movie studios mistakenly switches their shipments. Of course, one shipment contains X-rated films, and the other contains family films. The manager at the adult video store is sorely disappointed in the mild films he receives, and the nuns at the convent expecting to watch *The Sound of Music* really get a surprise!

How can business owners avoid shipping problems such as these? Although some shipping mistakes are inevitable, the following tips can help minimize them:

- Communicate clearly with vendors, suppliers, and shipping companies. Never assume that the other party will do what you expect.
- Specify special shipping instructions when required.
- Make sure all shipping labels and instructions are legible and firmly attached to the package.
- Use pressure-sensitive packing tape to seal packages. Masking tape and cellophane tape are not strong enough to do the job.
- Try to use single shipments rather than multiple shipments. Items sent at different times or in multiple containers are more likely to go astray.
- On international shipments, verify that the shipper is familiar with the customs regulations of the destination country and knows how to negotiate them. Otherwise, your shipment could be detained indefinitely in customs.
- When in doubt about a shipment, contact a shipping professional for advice.

Source: Adapted from Steve Bates, "The Dog Ate My Shipment," *Nation's Business,* December 1997, pp. 36–37.

Vendor Certification

To add objectivity to the selection process, many firms are establishing vendor certification programs: agreements to give one supplier the majority of their business once that supplier meets rigorous quality and performance standards. Today, businesses of all sizes and types are establishing long-term "partnering" arrangements with vendors that meet their certification standards. When creating a vendor certification program, a business owner should remember the three Cs: *commitment, communication,* and *control. Commitment* to consistently meeting the quality standards of the company must be paramount. No company can afford to do business with vendors that cannot meet its quality targets. Second, a company must establish two-way *communication* with vendors. Communication implies trust, and trust creates working relationships that are long term and mutually beneficial. Treating suppliers like partners can reveal ways to boost quality and lower costs for both parties. Finally, a company must make sure that its vendors and suppliers have in place the *controls* that enable them to produce quality results and to achieve continuous improvements in their processes. In today's competitive marketplace, an entrepreneur should expect all vendors to demonstrate that they operate a continuous improvement process, which has proven to be proactive in assessing product quality.

Creating a vendor certification program requires an entrepreneur to develop a vendor rating scale that enables the company to evaluate the various advantages and disadvantages of each potential vendor. The scale enables managers to score each vendor on some measure of those purchasing criteria that are most important to their company's success. The first step in developing a scale is to determine which criteria are most important in selecting a vendor (e.g., price, quality, prompt delivery). The next step is to assign weights to each criterion to reflect its relative importance. The third step involves developing a grading scale for comparing vendors on the criteria. Developing a usable scale requires that the owner maintain proper records of past vendor performances. Finally, the owner must compute a weighted total score for each vendor and select the vendor that scores the highest on the set of criteria. Consider the following example. Bravo Bass Boats, Inc. is faced with choosing from among several suppliers of a critical raw material. The company's owner has decided to employ a vendor rating scale to select the best vendor using the following procedure.

Step 1   *Determine important criteria.* The owner of Bravo has selected the following criteria:

Quality
Price
Prompt delivery
Service
Assistance

Step 2   *Assign weights to each criterion to reflect its relative importance.*

Criterion	Weight
Quality	35
Price	30
Prompt delivery	20
Service	10
Assistance	5
Total	100

Step 3 *Develop a grading scale for each criterion.*

Criterion	Grading Scale
Quality	$\dfrac{\text{Quality Number of acceptable lots from Vendor X}}{\text{Total number of lots from Vendor X}}$
Price	$\dfrac{\text{Price Lowest quoted price of all vendors}}{\text{Price offered by Vendor X}}$
Prompt delivery	$\dfrac{\text{Prompt delivery Number of on-time deliveries from Vendor X}}{\text{Total number of deliveries from Vendor X}}$
Service	A subjective evaluation of the variety of service offered by Vendor X
Assistance	A subjective evaluation of the advice and assistance provided by Vendor X

Step 4 *Compute a weighted score for each vendor.*

Criterion	Weight	Grade	Weighted Score (weight × grade)
Vendor 1			
Quality	35	9/10	31.5
Price	30	12.5/13.5	30.0
Prompt delivery	20	10/10	20.0
Service	10	8/10	8.0
Assistance	5	4/5	5.0
Total weighted score			94.5
Vendor 2			
Quality	35	8/10	28.0
Price	30	12.5/13.5	27.8
Prompt delivery	20	8/10	16.0
Service	10	8/10	8.0
Assistance	5	4/5	4.0
Total weighted score			83.8
Vendor 3			
Quality	35	7/10	24.5
Price	30	12.5/12.5	30.0
Prompt delivery	20	6/10	12.0
Service	10	7/10	7.0
Assistance	5	1/5	1.0
Total weighted score			74.5

On the basis of this analysis of the three suppliers, Bravo should purchase the majority of this raw material from Vendor 1.

This vendor analysis procedure assumes that business owners have a detailed working knowledge of the suppliers' network. Start-up companies seldom will. Owners of start-up companies must focus on finding suppliers and then gathering data to conduct the vendor analysis. One of the best ways to do that is to ask potential vendors for references. If the references provided by the potential vendor are not potential competitors, they may be willing to verify the claims of the vendor.

In some cases, the industry trade association will have knowledge regarding the integrity of suppliers or vendors. Start-up companies can be vulnerable to scams by unethical vendors. Research about the history of every potential vendor may reduce the likelihood of being victimized by the handful of unethical vendors who prey on inexperienced entrepreneurs. New entrepreneurs may have difficulty locating ethical suppliers of inventory and materials to start their businesses. One obvious way for entrepreneurs to find vendors for their products is to approach established businesses selling similar lines and interview their managers. Although local businesses are not likely to be very cooperative with new competitors, beginning entrepreneurs can get the necessary information from businesses outside the immediate trading area.

Other sources for information on vendors include trade associations, trade shows, the local chamber of commerce, and certain publications. These publications include library reference books that list national distributors and their product lines and publications such as *McRae's Blue Book* and the *Thomas Register of American Manufacturers* (www.thomasregister.com). Both of these sources provide lists of products and services along with names, addresses, telephone numbers, and ratings of manufacturers.[13]

The *U.S. Industrial Directory* is similar to the *Thomas Register*, although its coverage is not as broad. Business owners also should consult the U.S. Chamber of Commerce publication *Sources of State Information and State Industrial Directories*, which lists state directories of manufacturers. Entrepreneurs whose product lines have an international flair may look to *Kelly's Manufacturers and Merchants Directory*, *Marcon's International Register*, or *Trade Directories of the World* for information on companies throughout the world dealing in practically every type of product or service.

The World Wide Web is another rich source of information on potential suppliers. Purchasing agents in companies of all sizes are stepping up their use of the Internet as a tool for locating and buying merchandise, equipment, and supplies. The volume of Web-based purchasing activity will continue to grow in the future as more business owners discover its power to reduce the cost of placing an order and the time required to get it delivered.

✦ GAINING *a* COMPETITIVE EDGE ✦

How to Build a Base of Competent Suppliers

Many small firms pay prices for goods and services that are too high, and they find that their options are limited by the lack of a base of competent suppliers. The broader the base of potential suppliers a business has, the stronger the likelihood they will have greater options and find the best quality and prices. The following steps in the process of scanning potential vendors are never ending:

1. *Establish your company's critical criteria for selecting a vendor.* What characteristics would the ideal vendor have? You must know up front what you are looking for in a vendor.
2. *Interview prospective vendors with the same level of intensity that you interview prospective employees.*

Both relationships influence how successful a company is at achieving quality objectives. "It's not easy to put aside the time," says James Walker, president of Octagon Research Solutions, a 60-person software company, "but for us, it's all about whether we can have a good relationship with [our vendors]." Use the criteria you established in Step 1 to establish a list of questions to ask potential vendors.

3. *Be assertive.* Ask tough questions and be a knowledgeable buyer. Don't allow suppliers to do their typical "sales pitches" before you have time to ask your questions.

4. *Get referrals.* Demand that all potential vendors supply a list of referrals of businesses that they have served over the past five years or more. Then make the necessary contacts.

5. *Visit potential vendors' businesses.* The best way to judge a vendor's ability to meet your company's needs is to see the operation firsthand. Nancy Connolly, president of Lasertone Corporation, a maker of copier and laser toner, insists on "a personal meeting between me and the president of the company," she says, before establishing a relationship with a vendor. The goal is to judge the level of the potential vendor's commitment to meeting Lasertone's needs.

6. *Don't fixate on price.* Look for value in what they sell. If your only concern is lowest price, vendors will push their lowest priced (and often lowest quality) product lines.

7. *Ask "What if?"* The real test of a strong vendor-customer relationship occurs when problems arise. Smart entrepreneurs ask vendors how they will handle particular types of problems when they arise. James Walker of Octagon Research Solutions says that Dell Computer won his company's loyalty after he purchased five laptops from the computer maker. Two of the computers were defective, but a technician quickly analyzed the problem and offered to replace the motherboards on the defective machines. When Walker asked the technician to replace the motherboards of the three other computers, he agreed to do so even though they showed no signs of the problem.

8. *Attend trade shows.* Work the room. A visit to a trade show is not a vacation; it's pure business. Find out if the next booth has a valuable new vendor who has the potential to increase your company's profits!

9. *Don't forget about local vendors.* Because of their proximity, local vendors can sometimes provide the fastest service. Solving problems often is easier because local vendors can make on-site service calls.

10. *Test a vendor before committing completely.* Susan Gilbert, owner of Café in the Park, a restaurant in San Diego, says, "Inventory is cash flow. When I'm dealing with a vendor, I need to know how quickly they can deliver, how quickly I can turn over the inventory, and keep it all tight." Rather than place an order for 100 Danish pastries with a new vendor, for instance, Gilbert starts with an order of several dozen pastries to judge the vendor's performance.

11. *Work with the vendors.* Tell your suppliers what you like and don't like about their products and service. In many cases, they can resolve your concerns. Most vendors want to build long-term relationships with their customers. Give them a chance to do so.

12. *Do unto others.* Treat your vendors well. Be selective but pay on time and treat them with respect.

1. Why do so many firms focus solely on selecting vendors that offer the lowest prices? What are the dangers of doing so?

2. Develop a list of ten questions you would ask a potential vendor of a product you select.

Sources: Adapted from Allison Stein Wellner, "Finding the Right Vendor," *Inc.*, July 2003, pp. 88–95; Jan Norman, "How to Find Suppliers," *Business Start-Ups*, October 1998, pp. 44–47.

The Final Decision

Once business owners identify potential vendors and suppliers, they must decide which one (or ones) to do business with. Entrepreneurs should consider the following factors before making the final decision about the right supplier.

Number of Suppliers. One important question the small business owner faces is "Should I buy from a single supplier or from several different sources?" Concentrating purchases at a single supplier gives the buyer individual attention from the sole supplier, especially if orders are substantial. Second, the firm may receive quantity discounts if its orders are large enough. Finally, the firm is able to cultivate a closer, more cooperative relationship with the supplier. Suppliers are more willing to assist companies they consider to be loyal customers. The result of such a partnership can be better-quality goods and services.

However, using a single vendor also has disadvantages. The small firm may experience shortages of critical materials if its only supplier suffers a catastrophe, such as a fire, strike, or bankruptcy. For instance, one small clothing maker experienced an interruption in its supply of fabric when its primary supplier's textile factory was damaged by a tornado. The textile manufacturer resumed production one month later, but the clothing maker's output suffered because it was unable to purchase material in sufficient quantities from other suppliers on such short notice.

The advantages of developing close, cooperative relationships with a single supplier outweigh the risks of sole sourcing in most cases. Business owners must exercise great caution in choosing a supplier to make sure they pick the right one, however. Otherwise, the outcome could be disastrous. *Chico's, a fast-growing women's clothing and apparel business, is constantly looking for ways to mitigate risk. Growing in excess of 35 percent annually, the company can't afford to make major operational mistakes, which only become exaggerated later. According to Ajit Patel, CIO and vice president at Chico's, "We've found that working with established and stable vendors and their partners is critical." Patel goes on to say, "As our company evolves, our vendor requirements constantly change. For example, we like to work with established, innovative, and financially viable vendors so we can mitigate our risk. When we were a younger, smaller company, price was much more important to us, and we might have taken risks to save a few bucks."*[14]

Reliability. Business owners must evaluate a potential vendor's ability to deliver adequate quantities of quality merchandise when it is needed. One common complaint small businesses have against suppliers is late delivery. Late deliveries or shortages cause lost sales and create customer ill will. If you are a small customer, sometimes you are the last to be served.

Proximity. The small firm's physical proximity is an important factor in choosing a vendor. Costs for transporting merchandise can substantially increase the cost of merchandise to the buyer. For example, one East Coast glass manufacturer found that to obtain proper-quality sand for its production operation it had to make its purchases from a midwestern supplier. The cost of transporting the sand was greater than the cost of the sand itself. Also, some vendors offer better service to local small businesses because they know the owners. In addition, a small business owner is better able to solve coordination problems with nearby vendors than with distant vendors.

Services. The small business owner must evaluate the range of services vendors offer. Do salespeople make regular calls on the firm, and are they knowledgeable about their product line? Will the sales representatives assist in planning store layout and in creating attractive displays? Will the vendor make convenient deliveries on time? Is the supplier reasonable in making repairs on equipment after installation and in handling returned merchandise? Are sales representatives able to offer useful advice on purchasing and other managerial functions? Before choosing a vendor, the small business owner should answer these and other relevant questions about suppliers.

Price Negotiations. Smaller firms usually must pay market or list price for items that are of lower value and purchased infrequently. This is not the case for goods purchased on a regular basis and that are essential components or supplies. An entrepreneur should have no compulsion about attempting to purchase the critical goods or services it needs at the best price and terms of sale. The terms of sale, as mentioned previously, can be a significant factor in the final price that the entrepreneur pays.

| Company Example |

Legal Issues Affecting Purchasing

7. Describe the legal implications of the purchasing function.

When a small business purchases goods from a supplier, ownership passes from seller to buyer. But when do title and risk of loss to the goods pass from one party to the other? The answer is important because any number of things could happen to the merchandise after it has been ordered but before it has been delivered. When they order merchandise and supplies from their vendors, small business owners should know when the ownership of the merchandise—and the risk associated with it—shifts from supplier to buyer.

Title

Before the Uniform Commercial Code (UCC) was enacted, the concept of title—the right to ownership of goods—determined where responsibility for merchandise fell. Today, however, the UCC has replaced the concept of title with three other concepts: identification, risk of loss, and insurable interest.

Identification. Identification is the first requirement that must be met. Before title can pass to the buyer, the goods must already be in existence and must be identifiable from all other similar goods. Specific goods already in existence are identified at the time the sales contract is made. For example, if Graphtech, Inc., orders a Model 477-X computer and a plotter, the goods are identified at the time the contract (oral or written) is made. Generic goods are identified when they are marked, shipped, or otherwise designated as the goods in the contract. For example, an order of fuel oil may not be identified until it is loaded into a transfer truck for shipment.

Risk of Loss. **Risk of loss** determines which party incurs the financial risk if the goods are damaged, destroyed, or lost before they are transferred. Risk of loss does *not* always pass with title. Three particular rules govern the passage of title and the transfer of risk or loss.

> *Rule 1: Agreement.* A supplier and a small business owner can agree to the terms under which title passes. Similarly, the two parties can agree (preferably in writing) to shift the risk of loss at any time during the transaction. In other words, any explicit agreement between buyer and seller determines when title and risk of loss will pass. Without an agreement, title and risk of loss pass when the seller delivers the goods under the contract.
>
> *Rule 2: F.O.B. Seller.* Under a sales contract designated F.O.B. (free on board) seller, title passes to the buyer as soon as the seller delivers the goods into the care of a carrier or shipper. Similarly, risk of loss is transferred to the small business owner when the supplier delivers the goods to the carrier. In addition, an **F.O.B. seller contract** (also a **shipment contract**) requires that the buyer pay all shipping and transportation costs. For example, a North Carolina manufacturer sells 100,000 capacitors to a buyer in Ohio with terms "F.O.B. North Carolina." Under this contract the Ohio firm pays all shipping costs, and title and risk of loss pass from the manufacturer as soon as the carrier takes possession of the shipment. If the goods are lost or damaged in transit, the buyer suffers the loss. Of course, the buyer has legal recourse against the carrier.
>
> *Rule 3: F.O.B. Buyer.* A sales contract designated F.O.B. buyer requires that the seller deliver the goods to the buyer's place of business (or to an agent of the buyer).

Title and risk of loss are transferred to the small business when the goods are delivered there or to another designated destination. Also, an **F.O.B. buyer contract** (also called a **destination contract**) requires the seller to pay all shipping and transportation costs. In the preceding example, if the contract were "F.O.B. Ohio," the North Carolina manufacturer would pay the cost of shipping the order, and title and risk of loss would pass to the Ohio company when the shipment was delivered to its place of business. In this case losses due to goods lost or damaged in transit are borne by the seller.

Insurable Interest. Insurable interest ensures the right of either party to the sales contract to obtain insurance to protect against lost, damaged, or destroyed merchandise as long as that party has "sufficient interest" in the goods. In general, if goods are identified, the buyer has an insurable interest in them. The seller has a sufficient interest as long as the seller retains title to the goods. However, under certain circumstances both the buyer and the seller have insurable interests even after title has passed to the buyer.

Receiving Merchandise

Once the merchandise is received, the buyer must verify its identity and condition. When the goods are delivered, the owner should check the number of cartons unloaded against the carrier's delivery receipt so that none are overlooked. It is also a good idea to examine the boxes for damage; if shipping cartons are damaged, the carrier should note this on the delivery receipt. The owner should open all cartons immediately after delivery and inspect the merchandise for quality and condition and also check it against the invoices to eliminate discrepancies. If merchandise is damaged or incorrect, the buyer should contact the supplier immediately and follow up with a written report. The owner should never destroy or dispose of tainted or unwanted merchandise unless the supplier specifically authorizes it. Proper control techniques in receiving merchandise prevent the small business owner from paying for suppliers' and shippers' mistakes.

Selling on Consignment

Small business owners who lack the necessary capital to invest or are unwilling to assume the risk of investing in inventory may be able to sell goods on consignment. Selling on **consignment** means that the small business owner does not purchase the merchandise carried from the supplier (called the consignor); instead, the owner pays the consignor only for the merchandise actually sold. For providing the supplier with a market for its goods, the small business owner normally receives a portion of the revenue on each item sold. The business owner (called the consignee) may return any unsold merchandise to the supplier without obligation. Under a consignment agreement, title and risk of loss do not pass to the consignee unless the contract specifies such terms. In other words, the supplier (consignor) bears the financial costs of lost, damaged, or stolen merchandise. The small business owner who sells merchandise on a consignment basis realizes the following advantages:

- The owner does not have to invest money in these inventory items, but the merchandise on hand is available for sale.
- The owner does not make payment to the consignor until the item is sold.

- Because the consignment relationship is founded on the law of agency, the consignee never takes title to the merchandise and does not bear the risk of loss for the goods.
- The supplier normally plans and sets up displays for the merchandise and is responsible for maintaining them.

Before selling items on consignment, the small business owner and the supplier should create a workable written contract, which should include the following items:

- A list of items to be sold and their quantities
- Prices to be charged
- Location of merchandise in store
- Duration of contract
- Commission charged by the consignee
- Policy on defective items and rejects
- Schedule for payments to consignor
- Delivery terms and merchandise storage requirements
- Responsibility for items lost to pilferage and shoplifting
- Provision for terminating consignment contract

If managed properly, selling goods on consignment can be beneficial to both the consignor and the consignee.

▌▌▌ Chapter Review

1. Understand the components of a purchasing plan.
   - The purchasing function is vital to every small business's success because it influences a company's ability to sell quality goods and services at reasonable prices. Purchasing is the acquisition of needed materials, supplies, services, and equipment of the right quality, in the proper quantities, for reasonable prices, at the appropriate time, and from the right suppliers.

2. Explain the principles of total quality management (TQM) and their impact on quality.
   - Under the total quality management (TQM) philosophy, companies define a quality product as one that conforms to predetermined standards that satisfy customers' demands. The goal is to get delivery and invoicing to installation and follow-up right the first time.
   - To implement TQM successfully, a small business owner must rely on 10 fundamental principles: Shift from a management-driven culture to a participative, team-based one; modify the reward system to encourage teamwork and innovation; train workers constantly to give them the tools they need to produce quality and to upgrade the company's knowledge base; train employees to measure quality with the tools of statistical process control (SPC); use Pareto's law to focus TQM efforts; share information with everyone in the organization; focus quality improvements on

   astonishing the customer; don't rely on inspection to produce quality products and services; avoid using TQM to place blame on those who make mistakes; and strive for continuous improvement in processes as well as in products and services.

3. Conduct economic order quantity (EOQ) analysis to determine the proper level of inventory.
   - A major goal of the small business is to generate adequate inventory turnover by purchasing proper quantities of merchandise. A useful device for computing the proper quantity is economic order quantity (EOQ) analysis, which yields the ideal order quantity: the amount that minimizes total inventory costs. Total inventory costs consist of the cost of the units, holding (carrying) costs, and ordering (setup) costs. The EOQ balances the costs of ordering and of carrying merchandise to yield minimum total inventory cost.

4. Differentiate among the three types of purchase discounts that vendors offer.
   - Trade discounts are established on a graduated scale and depend on a small firm's position in the channel of distribution.
   - Quantity discounts are designed to encourage businesses to order large quantities of merchandise and supplies.
   - Cash discounts are offered to customers as an incentive to pay for merchandise promptly.

5. Calculate a company's reorder point. Develop a vendor rating scale.
   - There is a time gap between placing an order and actual receiving of the goods. The reorder point model tells the owner when to place an order to replenish the company's inventory.
   - Creating a vendor analysis model involves four steps: Determine the important criteria (e.g., price, quality, prompt delivery, service, etc.); assign a weight to each criterion to reflect its relative importance; develop a grading scale for each criterion; compute a weighted score for each vendor.

6. Describe the legal implications of the purchasing function.
   - Important legal issues involving purchasing goods involve title, or ownership of the goods; identification of the goods; risk of loss and when it shifts from seller to buyer; and insurable interests in the goods. Buyer and seller can have an insurable interest in the same goods at the same time.

▌▌▌ Discussion Questions

1. What is purchasing? Why is it important for the small business owner to develop a purchasing plan?
2. What is TQM? How can it help small business owners achieve the quality goods and services they require?
3. One top manager claims that to implement total quality management successfully, "You have to change your company culture as much as your processes." Do you agree? Explain.
4. List and briefly describe the three components of total inventory costs.
5. What is the economic order quantity? How does it minimize total inventory costs?
6. Should a small business owner always purchase the products with the lowest prices? Why or why not?
7. Briefly outline the three types of purchase discounts. Under what circumstances is each the best choice?

8. What is lead time? Outline the procedure for determining a product's reorder point.
9. Explain how an entrepreneur launching a company could locate suppliers and vendors.
10. What factors are commonly used to evaluate suppliers?
11. Explain the procedure for developing a vendor rating scale.
12. Explain briefly the three concepts that have replaced the concept of title. When do title and risk of loss shift under an F.O.B. seller contract and under an F.O.B. buyer contract?
13. What should a small business owner do when merchandise is received?
14. Explain how a small business would sell goods on consignment. What should be included in a consignment contract?

Purchasing, Quality Management, and Vendor Analysis

Business PlanPro

By managing their companies' supply chains effectively, entrepreneurs can improve the quality of the products and services they offer, control the cost of purchasing or producing those products and services, and enhance the level of service they provide their customers. The issues of purchasing, quality management, and vendor analysis cut across all of the functions of an organization and, in many cases, play a significant role in determining a company's ability to compete successfully.

The exercises for Chapter 17 that accompany Business Plan Pro are designed to help you describe supply chain management strategy and the key elements of your company's purchasing plan, including quality, quantity, price, timing, and vendor analysis. Once you finish these exercises, you are ready to complete the Fulfillment component of the What You're Selling section in Business Plan Pro.

Chapter 18
Managing Inventory

> *If a product isn't selling, I want to get it out of there because it's taking up space that can be devoted to another part of my line that moves. Besides, having a product languish on the shelves doesn't do much for our image.*
> —Norman Melnick

> *Opportunity makes a thief.*
> —Francis Bacon

Upon completion of this chapter, you will be able to:

1. Explain the various inventory control systems and the advantages and disadvantages of each.
2. Describe how just-in-time (JIT) and JIT II inventory control techniques work.
3. Describe methods for reducing losses from slow-moving inventory.
4. Discuss employee theft and shoplifting and how to prevent them.

S upply chain management and inventory control are closely linked. The previous chapter focused on managing a company's supply chain—purchasing the correct materials, of the proper quality, in the correct quantity, at the best price, from the best vendors. This chapter will continue that process by discussing various inventory control methods, how to move "slow" inventory items, and how to protect inventory from theft. In today's competitive environment, the goal is to maximize the value of a company's inventory while reducing both the cost and risks of owning inventory. The issue is significant; the largest expenditure for many small businesses is for inventory: raw materials, work-in-process, or finished goods.

Business owners now understand the dangers of carrying excess inventory. For years, businesses maintained high levels of inventory so that the manufacturing or sales processes ran smoothly. Now managers realize that excess inventory simply masks other problems that a company may have such as poor quality, sloppy supply chain management, outdated equipment, inefficient layout, low productivity, and others. Reducing the amount of inventory a company carries exposes these otherwise hidden problems; only then can managers and employees solve them.

Another reason business owners are lowering inventory levels is the high cost of carrying excess inventory. Holding inventory requires renting or purchasing additional warehouse space, increasing labor costs, boosting borrowing, and tying up a company's valuable cash unnecessarily. Companies with lean inventory levels lower their costs of operation, and those savings go straight to the bottom line. The potential payoff for managing inventory efficiently is huge; companies that switch to lean inventory systems can increase their profitability 20 to 50 percent.

The information age has made techniques such as just-in-time (JIT) inventory systems available to small businesses. Electronic networks that connect a business seamlessly with its suppliers have dramatically reduced the time for needed parts or material to arrive and the need to hold inventory. At the other end of the pipeline, a company's customers expect to have what they need when they need it. In today's competitive market, few customers will wait an unreasonable time for items they want. Inventory management is an important aspect of controlling costs and responding quickly to changing customer demands.

Managing inventory effectively requires an entrepreneur to implement the following seven interrelated steps:

1. *Develop an accurate sales forecast.* The proper inventory levels for each item are directly related to the demand for that item. A business can't sell what it does not have and, conversely, an owner does not want to carry what will not sell.

2. *Develop a plan to make inventory available when and where customers want it.* Inventory will not sell if customers have a difficult time finding it. If a company is constantly running out of items customers expect to find, its customer base will dwindle over time as shoppers look elsewhere for those items. An important component of superior customer service is making sure adequate quantities of items are available when customers want them. Two ways of measuring this aspect of customer service include calculating the percentage of customer orders that a company ships on time and the percentage of the dollar volume of orders it ships on time. Tracking these numbers over time gives business owners sound feedback on how well they are managing their inventory levels from the customer's perspective.

3. *Build relationships with your most critical suppliers to ensure that you can get the merchandise you need when you need it.* Business owners must keep suppliers and vendors aware of how their merchandise is selling and communicate their needs to

them. Vendors and suppliers can be an entrepreneur's greatest allies in managing inventory. Increasingly, the word that describes the relationship between world-class companies and their suppliers is *partnership*.

4. *Set realistic inventory turnover objectives.* Keeping in touch with their customers' likes and dislikes and monitoring their inventory enable owners to estimate the most likely buying patterns for different types of merchandise. As we learned in Chapters 8 and 9, one of the factors having the greatest impact on a company's sales, cash flow, and ultimate success is its inventory turnover ratio.

5. *Compute the actual cost of carrying inventory.* Holding inventory in stock is expensive. Experts estimate that carrying unsold inventory costs U.S. businesses $332 billion a year![1] Without an accurate cost of carrying inventory, it is impossible to determine an optimal inventory level. Carrying costs include items such as interest on borrowed money, insurance expenses associated with the inventory, inventory-related personnel expenses, and all other related operating costs. When new product introductions make existing products obsolete, companies must hold inventory to an absolute minimum. For instance, in the computer industry, the onrush of new technology causes the value of a personal computer held in inventory to decline 1 percent each week! This gives computer makers big incentives to keep their inventories as lean as possible.

6. *Use the most timely and accurate information system the business can afford to provide the facts and figures necessary to make critical inventory decisions.* Computers and modern point-of-sale terminals that are linked to a company's inventory records enable business owners to know exactly which items are selling and which ones are not. *For example, the owner of a chain of baby products stores uses a computer network to link all of his stores to the computer at central headquarters. Every night, after the stores close, the point-of-sale terminals in each store download the day's sales to the central computer, which compiles an extensive sales and inventory report. When he walks into his office every morning, the owner reviews the report and can tell exactly which items are moving the fastest, which are moving the slowest, and which are not selling at all. He credits the system with the company's above-average inventory turnover ratio—and much of his chain's success.*

7. *Teach employees how inventory control systems work so that they can contribute to managing the firm's inventory on a daily basis.* All too often, the employees on the floor have no idea of how the various information systems and inventory control techniques operate or interact with one another. Consequently, the people closest to the inventory contribute little to controlling it. Well-trained employees armed with information can be one of an entrepreneur's greatest weapons in the battle to control inventory.

Company Example →

The goal is to find and maintain the proper balance between the cost of holding inventory and the requirement to have merchandise on hand when customers demand it. Either extreme can be costly. If entrepreneurs focus solely on minimizing cost, they will undoubtedly incur stockouts, lost sales, and customer ill will because they cannot satisfy their customers' needs. For instance, researchers studying inventory control systems at Bulgari, a jewelry manufacturer headquartered in Rome, Italy, discovered that stockouts of just one popular item had lowered the company's profits by 5 percent of sales.[2] At the other extreme, entrepreneurs who attempt to hold enough inventory to meet every peak customer demand will find that high inventory costs diminish their chances of remaining profitable. Walking this inventory tightrope is never easy, but the following inventory control systems can help business owners strike a reasonable balance between the two extremes.

Inventory Control Systems

1. Explain the various inventory control systems and the advantages and disadvantages of each.

Regardless of the type of inventory control system business owners choose, they must recognize the importance of **Pareto's Law** (or the **80/20 rule**), which holds that about 80 percent of the value of the firm's sales revenue is generated by 20 percent of the items kept in stock. Some of the firm's items are high-dollar volume goods, whereas others account for only a small portion of sales volume. Because most sales are generated by a small percentage of items, owners should focus the majority of their inventory control efforts on this 20 percent. Observing this simple principle ensures that entrepreneurs will spend time controlling only the most productive—and, therefore, most valuable—inventory items. With this technique in mind, we now examine three basic types of inventory control systems: perpetual, visual, and partial.

Perpetual Inventory Systems

Perpetual inventory systems are designed to maintain a running count of the items in inventory. Although a number of different perpetual inventory systems exist, they all have a common element: They all keep a continuous tally of each item added to or subtracted from the firm's stock of merchandise. The basic perpetual inventory system uses a perpetual inventory sheet that includes fundamental product information such as the item's name, stock number, description, economic order quantity (EOQ), and reorder point.

These perpetual inventory sheets are usually placed next to the merchandise in the warehouse or storage facility. Whenever a shipment is received from a vendor, the quantity is entered in the receipt column and added to the total. When the item is sold and taken from inventory, it is simply deducted from the total. As long as this procedure is followed consistently, an owner can quickly determine the number of each item on hand. Bar-coding of inventory allows the process to be done by a handheld scanner tied directly to a computer. Automating the perpetual inventory system makes it more accurate and reliable, and when inventory levels drop to the reorder trigger-point, the system generates purchase orders to replenish the supply.

Although consistent use of the system yields accurate inventory counts at any moment, sporadic use creates problems. If managers or employees take items out of stock or place them in inventory without recording them, the perpetual inventory system will yield incorrect totals and can foul up the entire inventory control system. Another disadvantage of this system is the cost of maintaining it. If not computerized, keeping such records for a large number of items and ensuring the accuracy of the system can be excessively expensive. Therefore, these systems are used most frequently and most successfully in controlling high dollar volume items that require strict monitoring. Management must watch these items closely and ensure that inventory records are accurate.

Technical advances in computerized cash registers have overcome many of the disadvantages of using the basic perpetual inventory system. Small businesses now are able to afford computerized **point of sale (POS) systems** that perform all of the functions of a traditional cash register and maintain an up-to-the-minute inventory count. Although POS systems are not new (major retailers have been using them for more than 30 years), their affordable prices are. Not so long ago, most systems required mini- or mainframe computers and cost $20,000 or more. Today, small business owners can set up POS systems on personal computers for less than $1,000. Combining a POS system with Universal Product Code (bar code) labels and high-speed scanners gives a small business a state-of-the-art checkout system that feeds vital information into its inventory control system. These systems rely on an inventory database; as items are rung up on the register, product information is recorded and inventory balances are adjusted. Using the system, business owners can tell how quickly each item is selling and how many items are in stock at any time. Plus, their inventory records are accurate and always current. They also can generate instantly a variety of reports to aid in making purchasing decisions. The system can be programmed to alert owners when the supply of a particular item drops below a predetermined reorder point or even to print automatically a purchase order to the EOQ indicated. Computerized systems such as these make it possible for the owner to use a basic perpetual inventory system for a large number of items—a task that, if performed manually, would be virtually impossible.

Specific Perpetual Inventory Control Systems. Perpetual inventory systems operate in a number of ways, but three basic variations are particularly common: the sales ticket method, the sales stub method, and the floor sample method.

- *The sales ticket method.* Most small businesses use sales tickets to summarize individual customers' transactions. These tickets serve two major purposes: They provide the customer with a sales receipt for the merchandise purchased, and they provide the owner with a daily record of the number of specific inventory items sold. The **sales ticket method** operates by gathering all the sales tickets at the end of each day and transcribing the data onto the appropriate perpetual inventory sheet. By posting inventory deductions to the perpetual inventory system from sales tickets, the small business manager can monitor sales patterns and keep close control on inventory. The primary disadvantage of using such a system is the time required to make it function properly. Most managers find it difficult to squeeze in the time needed to post sales tickets to the perpetual inventory system.

- *The sales stub method.* The principle behind the **sales stub method** of inventory control is the same as the sales ticket method, but its mechanics are slightly different. Retail stores often attach a ticket with two or more parts containing relevant product information to each inventory item in stock. When an employee sells an item, he or she removes a portion of the stub and places it in a container. At the end of the day, the owner posts the inventory deductions recorded by the stubs to the proper perpetual inventory sheet.

- *The floor sample method.* The **floor sample method** of controlling inventory is commonly used by businesses selling big-ticket items with high unit cost. In many cases, these items are somewhat bulky and are difficult to display in large numbers. For example, the owner of a small furniture store might receive a shipment of 15 rolltop desks in a particular style. A simple technique for maintaining control of these items is to attach a small pad to the display desk with sheets numbered in descending order from 15 to 1. Whenever an employee sells a rolltop desk, he or she removes a sheet from the pad. As long as the system is followed consistently, the owner is able to determine accurate inventory levels with a quick pass around the sales floor. When the supply of a particular item dwindles, the owner simply calls the vendor to replenish the inventory. The procedure is simple and serves its purpose.

IN THE FOOTSTEPS OF AN ENTREPRENEUR...

Zipping Fashions to Market

Zara, the flagship brand of private textile company Inditex, is the fastest-growing fashion retailer in the world; yet the company spends almost nothing on advertising. Founded in 1963 by then-24-year-old Amancio Ortega Gaona with just 5,000 pesetas (the equivalent of $25 today), Zara has become a powerhouse in the world of fashion, offering customers stylish, inexpensive clothing in its nearly 700 stores located in 29 countries. From its headquarters in La Coruña, situated on the northwest coast of Spain, Zara coordinates a lightening fast supply chain that makes competitors look as if they are moving in slow motion.

The company's innovative use of information, technology, and inventory control give it a significant competitive advantage in a market driven by rapidly changing fashions. Competitors such as Gap and Hennes & Mauritz (H&M) require about five months to get merchandise from the design stage to store shelves, something Zara manages to accomplish in just three weeks, even though it produces more than 10,000 different styles in a typical year! None of Zara's styles lasts for more than four weeks, which is ideal for an industry in which customers' fashion tastes change almost as frequently as the direction of the wind.

All of Zara's stores are linked electronically to headquarters, where designers are constantly monitoring sales patterns to discern which styles are selling and which ones are not. Store managers transmit customer requests to designers, and a team of fashion scouts canvass the globe looking for the hottest new fashion trends. All of this real-time information feeds into Zara's headquarters, where designers, managers, and others work together to specify fabrics, cuts, features, and price points of the flurry of new designs that the company is constantly turning out.

Another key feature of Zara's competitive advantage is its manufacturing strategy. Most retailers outsource their manufacturing to textile makers, many of which are located in East Asia. Because Zara is a retail division of textile maker Inditex, the company has 60 percent of its garments made in-house, which also saves a significant amount of time in getting products

onto store shelves. The company's high-tech factory in Spain cuts and colors fabrics, which are then cut and sewn into finished garments by Inditex. The combination of real-time information sharing among retail stores, designers, and factories and the in-house production of garments means that Zara keeps very little inventory in stock. The company's inventory is just 7 percent of annual revenues compared to 13 percent at rival retailer H&M. A single distribution center in La Coruña sorts every garment and ships them out in pre-programmed lots based on what is selling best in a particular location. Zara ships fresh, stylish merchandise to its stores twice a week, far more frequently than the one shipment every six weeks that competitors can deliver. What drives Zara's sizzling growth rate is the company's ability to get new reasonably-priced, glamorous fashions in front of style-conscious customers faster than anyone else, and it all starts with a less-than-glamorous supply chain strategy that works.

1. How does Zara's approach to supply chain management and inventory control give the company a competitive advantage?
2. What advantages does Zara reap by managing its inventory so carefully?

Sources: Adapted from Richard Heller, "Galician Beauty," *Forbes,* May 28, 2001, www.forbes.com/forbes/2001/0528/098; Jane M. Folpe, "Fashion Industrial Complex," *Fortune,* September 4, 2000, www.fortune.com/fortune/articles/0,15114,367627,00.html; Geoffrey Colvin, "Inside Business: Zara," *Fortune,* September 12, 2000, www.fortune.com/fortune/insidebusiness/0,15704,372095,00.html; "Who We Are," Inditex, www.inditex.com/en/who_we_are/our_group.

Visual Inventory Control Systems

The most common method of controlling inventory in a small business is the **visual control system,** in which managers simply conduct periodic visual inspections to determine the quantity of various items they should order. As mentioned earlier, manual perpetual inventory systems can be excessively costly and time-consuming. These systems are impractical when the business stocks a large number of low-value items with low dollar volume. Therefore, many owners rely on the simplest, quickest inventory control method: the visual system. Unfortunately, this method is also the least effective for ensuring accuracy and reliability. Oversights of key items often lead to stockouts and resulting lost sales. The biggest disadvantage of the visual control system is its inability to detect and to foresee shortages of inventory items.

In general, a visual inventory control system works best in firms in which daily sales are relatively consistent, the owner is closely involved with the inventory, the variety of merchandise is small, and items can be obtained quickly from vendors. For example, small firms dealing in perishable goods use visual control systems very successfully, and rarely, if ever, rely on analytical inventory control tools. For these firms, shortages are not likely to occur under a visual system; when they do occur, they are not likely to create major problems. Still, the manager who uses a visual inventory control system should leave reminders to make regular inspections and should be alert to shifts in customer buying patterns that alter required inventory levels.

Partial Inventory Control Systems

For small business owners with limited time and money, the most viable option for inventory management is a partial inventory control system. These systems rely on the validity of the 80/20 rule. For example, if a small business carries 5,000 different items in stock, roughly 1,000 of them account for about 80 percent of the firm's sales volume. Experienced business owners focus their inventory control efforts on those 1,000 items. Still, many managers seek to maintain tight control over the remaining 4,000 items, a frustrating and wasteful practice. Smart small business owners design their inventory control systems with this principle in mind. One of the most popular partial inventory control systems is the ABC system.

The ABC Method of Inventory Control. Too many managers apply perpetual inventory control systems universally when a partial control system would be much more practical. Partial inventory systems minimize the expense involved in analyzing, processing, and maintaining records, a substantial cost of any inventory control system. The ABC method is one such approach, focusing control efforts on that small percentage of items that accounts for the majority of the firm's sales. The typical **ABC system** divides a firm's inventory into three major categories:

> *A items* account for a high dollar usage volume.
> *B items* account for a moderate dollar usage volume.
> *C items* account for low dollar usage volume.

The **dollar usage volume** of an item measures the relative importance of that item in the firm's inventory. Note that value is not necessarily synonymous with high unit cost. In some instances, a high-cost item that generates only a small dollar volume can be classified as an A item. But, more frequently, A items are those that are low to moderate in cost and high volume by nature.

The initial step in establishing an ABC classification system is to compute the annual dollar usage volume for each product (or product category). **Annual dollar usage volume** is simply the cost per unit of an item multiplied by the annual quantity used. For instance, the owner of a stereo shop may find that she sold 190 pairs of a popular brand of speakers during the previous year. If the speakers cost her $75 per unit, their annual dollar usage volume would be as follows:

$$190 \times \$75 = \$14{,}250$$

The next step is to arrange the products in descending order on the basis of the computed annual dollar usage volume. Once so arranged, they can be divided into appropriate classes by applying the following rule:

> *A items*: roughly the top 15 percent of the items listed
> *B items*: roughly the next 35 percent
> *C items*: roughly the remaining 50 percent

For example, Florentina's small retail shop is interested in establishing an ABC inventory control system to lower losses from stockouts, theft, or other hazards. Florentina has computed the annual dollar usage volume for the store's merchandise inventory as shown in Table 18.1. (For simplicity, we show only 12 inventory items.)

The ABC inventory control method divides the firm's inventory items into three classes depending on the items' value. Figure 18.1 graphically portrays the segmentation of the items listed in Table 18.1.

Table 18.1

Calculating Annual Dollar Usage Volume and an ABC Inventory Analysis of Florentina's

ITEM	ANNUAL DOLLAR USAGE VOLUME	% OF ANNUAL DOLLAR USAGE
Paragon	$374,100	42.00
Excelsior	294,805	33.10
Avery	68,580	7.70
Bardeen	54,330	6.10
Berkeley	27,610	3.10
Tara	24,940	2.80
Cattell	11,578	1.30
Faraday	9,797	1.10
Humboldt	8,016	0.90
Mandel	7,125	0.08
Sabot	5,344	0.06
Wister	4,453	0.05
Total	$890,678	100.00%

CLASSIFICATION	ITEMS	ANNUAL DOLLAR USAGE	% OF TOTAL
A	Paragon, Excelsior	$668,905	75.10
B	Avery, Bardeen, Berkeley, Tara	175,460	19.70
C	Cattell, Faraday, Humboldt, Mandel, Sabot, Wister	46,313	5.20
Total		$890,678	100.00%

Figure 18.1

ABC Inventory Control

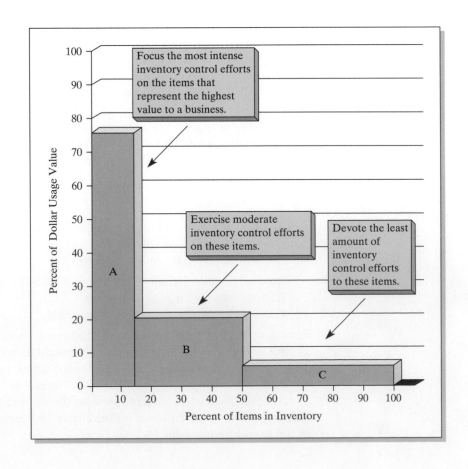

The purpose of classifying items according to their annual dollar usage volume is to establish the proper degree of control over each item held in inventory. Clearly, it is wasteful and inefficient to exercise the same level of control over C items and A items. Items in the A classification should be controlled under a perpetual inventory system with as much detail as necessary. Analytical tools and frequent counts may be required to ensure accuracy, but the extra cost of tight control for these valuable items is usually justified. Managers should not retain a large supply of reserve or safety stock because doing so ties up excessive amounts of money in inventory, but they must monitor the stock closely to avoid stockouts and lost sales.

Control of B items should rely more on periodic control systems and basic analytical tools such as EOQ and reorder point analysis (discussed in Chapter 17). Managers can maintain moderate levels of safety stock for these items to guard against shortages and can afford monthly or even bimonthly merchandise inspections. Because B items are not as valuable to the business as A items, less rigorous control systems are required.

C items typically constitute a minor proportion of the small firm's inventory value and, as a result, require the least effort and expense to control. These items are usually large in number and small in total value. The most practical way to control them is to use uncomplicated records and procedures. Large levels of safety stock for these items are acceptable because the cost of carrying them is usually minimal. Substantial order sizes often enable the business to take advantage of quantity discounts without having to place frequent orders. The cost involved in using detailed record keeping and inventory control procedures greatly outweighs the advantages gleaned from strict control of C items.

One practical technique for maintaining C items is the **two-bin system,** which keeps two separate bins full of material. The first bin is used to fill customer orders, and the second bin is filled with enough safety stock to meet customer demand during the lead time. When the first bin is empty, the owner places an order with the vendor large enough to refill both bins. During the lead-time for the order, the manager uses the safety stock in the second bin to fill customer demand.

When storage space or the type of item does not suit the two-bin system, the owner can use a **tag system.** Based on the same principles as the two-bin system, which is suitable for many manufacturers, the tag system applies to most retail, wholesale, and service firms. Instead of placing enough inventory to meet customer demand during lead time into a separate bin, the owner marks this inventory level with a brightly colored tag. When the supply is drawn down to the tagged level, the owner reorders the merchandise. Figure 18.2 illustrates the two-bin and tag systems of controlling C items.

In summary, business owners minimize total inventory costs when they spend time and effort controlling items that represent the greatest inventory value. Some inventory items require strict, detailed control techniques; others cannot justify the cost of such systems. Because of its practicality, the ABC inventory system is commonly used in industry. In addition, the technique is easily computerized, speeding up the analysis and lowering its cost. Table 18.2 summarizes the use of the ABC control system.

Physical Inventory Count

Regardless of the type of inventory control system used, every small business owner must conduct a periodic physical inventory count. Even when a company uses a perpetual inventory system, the owner must still count the actual number of items on hand because of the possibility of human error. A physical inventory count allows owners to reconcile the actual amount of inventory in stock with the amount reported through the inventory control system. These counts give managers a fresh start in determining the actual number of items on hand and enable them to evaluate the effectiveness and the accuracy of their inventory control systems.

Figure 18.2

The Two-Bin and Tag
Systems of Inventory
Control

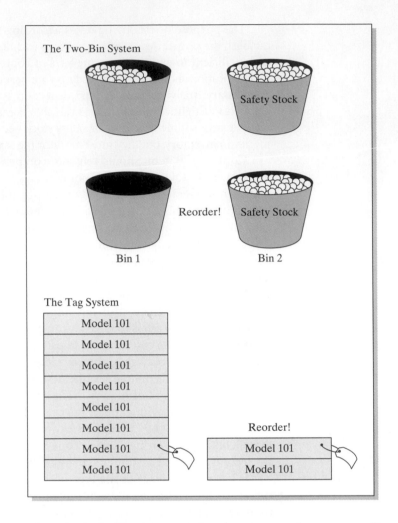

The typical method of taking inventory involves two employees; one calls out the relevant information for each inventory item, and the other records the count on a tally sheet. There are two basic methods of conducting a physical inventory count. One alternative is to take inventory at regular intervals. Many businesses take inventory at the end of the year. In an attempt to minimize counting, many managers run special year-end inventory reduction sales. This **periodic count** generates the most accurate measurement

Table 18.2

ABC Inventory Control Features

FEATURE	A ITEMS	B ITEMS	C ITEMS
Level of control	Monitor closely and maintain tight control	Maintain moderate control	Maintain loose control
Reorder point	Based on forecasted requirements	Based on EOQ calculations and past experience	When level gets low, reorder
Record keeping	Keep detailed records of receipts and disbursements	Use periodic inspections and control procedures	No records required
Safety stock	Keep low levels of safety stock	Keep moderate levels of safety stock	Keep high levels of safety stock
Inspection frequency	Monitor schedule changes frequently	Check on changes in requirements periodically	Make few checks on requirements

of inventory. The other method of taking inventory, called **cycle counting,** involves counting a number of items on a continuous basis. Instead of waiting until year-end to tally the entire inventory of items, the manager counts a few types of items each day or each week and checks the numbers against the inventory control system. Performing a series of "mini-counts" each day or each week allows for continuous correction of mistakes in inventory control systems and detects inventory problems sooner than an annual count would.

Once again, technology can make the job of taking inventory much easier for small business owners. Electronic data interchange (EDI) systems enable business owners to track their inventories and to place orders with vendors quickly and with few errors by linking them to their vendors electronically. These systems often rely on handheld computer terminals equipped with a scanning wand. An employee runs the wand across a bar-code label on the shelf that identifies the inventory item; then the employee counts the items on the shelf and enters that number using the number pad on the terminal. Then, by linking the handheld terminal to a personal computer, the employee can download the physical inventory count into the company's inventory control software in seconds.

In the past, suppliers simply manufactured a product, shipped it, and then sent the customer an invoice. To place an order, employees or managers periodically would estimate how much of a particular item they would need and when they would need it. Today, however, in many EDI or Web-based supply chain management systems, the vendor is tied directly into a company's POS (point-of-sale) system, monitoring it constantly; when the company's supply of a particular item drops to a preset level, the vendor automatically sends a shipment to replenish stock to an established level. Information that once traveled by mail (or was never shared at all), such as shipping information, invoices, inventory balances, sales, even funds, now travels instantly between businesses and their suppliers. The result is a much more efficient system of purchasing, distribution, and inventory control. *For example, when one of Ideal Supply Company's top customers asked the small supplier of industrial pipes and valves to set up an EDI system in 1990, general manager Michael Fidenza decided that doing so would give his company an edge over its rivals. "Our industry is old-fashioned," says Fidenza. "We tend to lag behind the times." Ideal Supply not only forged an even closer relationship with its big customer, but it also reaped benefits from its suppliers. Because Ideal Supply was one of the few companies in the industry with EDI capability, Fidenza was able to negotiate higher discounts from its suppliers because of increased efficiencies in the purchasing process. "One of our vendors offered us an extra 5 percent in discounts," he says. "Another plugs in an extra $10,000 worth of product with every $50,000 purchase—just because we're EDI." Ideal Supply has earned an impressive return on its original investment of $5,000 for EDI hardware and software. Today, 80 percent of the company's purchases and 15 percent of its sales are processed through its EDI system.*[3]

> Company Example

Radio Frequency Identification Tags (RFID)

Inventory control systems that use bar codes to track the movement of inventory through the supply chain have been around for years. Increasingly, businesses are replacing their bar code systems with more flexible systems based on **radio frequency identification (RFID)** tags that are attached to individual items or to shipments and that transmit data to a company's inventory management system. Each tag, which is about the size of a grain of sand, contains a tiny microchip that stores a unique electronic product code (EPC) and a tiny antenna. Because the tags use short-range radio frequencies, they can transmit information under almost any condition, avoiding the line-of-sight restrictions bar code systems experience. Once activated, the tags perform like talking bar codes and enable business owners to identify, count, and track the inventory items to which they are attached, providing highly accurate, real-time information constantly. When a shipment arrives at a warehouse or retail store, the RFID tags signal an inventory system reader, an object about the size of a coin that records the identity, the quantity, and characteristics of each item now in stock. The reader relays the information to a central inventory control system so that business owners can have access to all of this information online. Some stores have installed "smart" shelves equipped with readers that detect the identity and quantity of the items placed on them. When a customer makes a purchase, the smart shelf sends a message to the inventory control system, telling it to reduce the number on hand by the number of items the customer buys. In essence, RFID technology allows business owners to locate and track an item at any point in the supply chain—from the raw material stage to the finished product.

One winery attaches RFID tags equipped with sensors to the bottles of wine it ships to restaurants and retail stores. Not only can the winery use the Internet to track each wine bottle during shipment, but it also can detect whether or not the temperature of those bottles reaches a point that could compromise their quality by sitting, for example, on a hot loading dock.[4] The impact of RFID technology, which actually dates back to World War II, on inventory control is enormous. "This is an innovative technology similar to the Internet," says Mark Roberti, editor of *RFID Journal*. "You can now make any object smart."[5] International consulting firm McKinsey and Company estimates that once in use, RFID technology has the ability to increase companies' revenues by as much as 6 percent by reducing the time and energy staff spend finding merchandise.[6]

Just-In-Time Inventory Control Techniques

2. Describe how just-in-time (JIT) and JIT II inventory control techniques work.

Many U.S. manufacturers have turned to a popular inventory control technique called **just-in-time (JIT)** to reduce costly inventories and turn around their financial fortunes. Until recently these firms had accepted and practiced without question the following long-standing principles of manufacturing: Long production runs of standard items are ideal; machines should be up and running as much as possible; machines must produce a large number of items to justify long setup times and high costs; similar processes should be consolidated into single departments; tasks should be highly specialized and simplified; and inventories (raw materials, work-in-process, and finished goods) should be large enough to avoid emergencies such as supply interruptions, strikes, and breakdowns.

The just-in-time philosophy, however, views excess inventory as a blanket that masks problems and as a source of unnecessary costs that inhibit a firm's competitive position. Under a JIT system, materials and inventory flow smoothly through the production process without stopping. They arrive at the appropriate location just in time instead of becoming part of a costly inventory stockpile. Just-in-time is an operational philosophy that seeks to improve a company's efficiency. The key measure of manufacturing efficiency is the level of inventory maintained; the lower the level of inventory, the more efficient the production system.

The heart of the JIT philosophy is eliminating waste in whatever form it may take—time wasted moving work in process from one part of a factory to another, money wasted when employees must scrap or rework an item because of poor quality, cash tied up unnecessarily in excess inventory because of a poorly designed process, and many others. Companies using JIT successfully embrace a broader philosophy of continuous improvement (*kaizen*), which we discussed in the previous chapter. These companies encourage employees to find ways to improve processes by simplifying them, making them more efficient, and redesigning them to make them more flexible. A cornerstone of the JIT philosophy is making waste in a company visible. The idea is that hidden waste is easy to ignore; visible waste gives everyone an incentive to eliminate it. *Managers at a small company that manufactures fabrics for use in the paper making industry set off an area in the middle of the production floor and put all of the wasted fabrics there on display. The not-so-subtle message was "help us find ways to reduce this waste." Within a matter of months, with the help of suggestions from both individuals and teams of employees, the pile of waste shrank dramatically.*

In the past, only large companies could reap the benefits of computerized JIT and inventory control software, but now a proliferation of inexpensive programs designed for personal computers gives small companies that ability. The most effective businesses know that what is required is not simply the technology but the critical strategic alliances with suppliers who are themselves technologically sophisticated enough to act on a real-time basis to deliver what is needed when it is needed. The ultimate goal is to drive the inventory level as close to zero as possible.

Today, entrepreneurs recognize that extremely high quality and absolutely on-time delivery are essential elements of remaining competitive. Just-in-time systems work because suppliers recognize that if they are unable to meet the demands their customers set forth, some other company surely will. *For American Leather, a high-end custom leather furniture manufacturer, offering 30-day delivery on any product is just one of the benefits of implementing automated and just-in-time (JIT) systems. In addition, the Dallas-based company's revenues have consistently grown since its start-up in 1990, and its workforce has climbed to 300. Company founders Sanjay Chandra and Bob Duncan, both former manufacturing consultants, recognized an opportunity to use JIT methods to offer quick turnaround (two-week shipment) in an industry characterized by archaic inventory control and production methods—and the resulting long delivery times. The result was a mix of technology and software—some of it purchased off the shelf and others developed by American Leather—that enabled the company to mass produce high-quality custom leather furniture. For American Leather, automation was a natural fit to keep the company's 95 percent on-time delivery rate stable and work-in-progress inventory down to less than three days' stock.[7]*

Advocates claim that when JIT is successfully implemented, companies experience five positive results:

1. Lower investment in inventory.
2. Reduced inventory carrying and handling costs.
3. Reduced cost from obsolescence of inventory.
4. Lower investment in space for inventories and production.
5. Reduced total manufacturing costs from the better coordination needed between departments to operate at lower inventory levels.

For JIT systems to be most productive, small business owners must consider the human components of the equation as well:

1. *Mutual trust and teamwork.* Managers and employees view each other as equals, have a commitment to the organization and its long-term effectiveness, and are willing to work as a team to find and solve problems.
2. *Empowerment.* Effective organizations provide their employees with the authority to take action to solve problems. The objective is to have the problems dealt with at the lowest level and as quickly as possible.

At a technical level, JIT is most effective in repetitive manufacturing operations where there are significant inventory levels, where production requirements can be forecast accurately, and where suppliers are an integral part of the system. Experience shows that companies with the following characteristics have the greatest success with JIT:

- Reliable deliveries of all parts and supplies
- Short distance between clients and vendors
- Consistently high quality of vendors' products
- Stable and predictable product demand that allows for accurate production schedules

Just-In-Time II Techniques

In the past, some companies that adopted JIT techniques discovered an unwanted side effect: increased hostility resulting from the increased pressure they put on their suppliers to meet tight and often challenging schedules. To resolve that conflict, many businesses have turned to an extension of JIT, **just-in-time II (JIT II),** which focuses on creating a close, harmonious relationship with a company's suppliers so that both parties benefit from increased efficiency. Lance Dixon, who created the JIT II concept when he was a manager at Bose Corporation, a manufacturer of audio equipment, sought to create a working environment that empowered the supplier within the customer's organization. To work successfully, JIT II requires suppliers and their customers to share what was once closely guarded information in an environment of trust and cooperation. Under JIT II, customers and suppliers work hand in hand, acting more like partners than mere buyers and sellers.

In many businesses practicing JIT II, suppliers' employees work on site at the customer's plant, factory, or warehouse almost as if they were employees of the customer. These on-site workers are responsible for monitoring, controlling, and ordering inventory from their own companies. While at Bose, Dixon decided to try JIT II because it offered the potential to reduce sharply the company's inventories of materials and components, to cut purchasing costs, and to generate cost-cutting design and production tips from suppliers who understood Bose's process. This new alliance between suppliers and their customers would form a new supply chain that would lower costs at every one of its links. To protect against leakage of confidential information, Dixon had all of the employees from Bose's suppliers who would work in its plant sign confidentiality agreements. Dixon also put a ceiling on the amount each supplier's employee could order without previous authorization from Bose.

Company Example → Growing numbers of small companies are forging JIT II relationships with their suppliers and customers. *For instance, Northern Polymer Corporation, a seven-person plastics maker, sells plastic resin to G & F Industries, a 170-employee injection molding company in Sturbridge, Massachusetts, under a JIT II arrangement. Northern employees visit G & F's plant several times each month to check its inventory and consumption levels. Northern has set up a resin storage facility near G & F's plant so that it can restock its resin supply within just a few hours, if necessary. The arrangement "secures that piece of business for a long period," says Northern's founder, Joseph St. Martin.* As Northern Polymer's experience with G & F Industries indicates, an EDI system such as those mentioned earlier in this chapter enables many companies to operate JIT II systems without having an employee from the supplier in-house. G & F Industries, in turn, has a JIT II relationship with one of its biggest customers, Bose Corporation, and G & F does keep an employee in Bose's plant on a full-time basis.[8]

Manufacturers are not the only companies benefiting from JIT II. In a retail environment, the concept is more commonly known as **efficient consumer response (ECR),** but the principles are the same. Rather than build inventories of merchandise that might sit for months before selling (or worse, never sell at all), retailers that use ECR replenish their inventories constantly on an as-needed basis. Because vendors are linked electronically to the retailer's point-of-sale system, they can monitor the company's inventory and keep it stocked with the right merchandise mix in the right quantities. Both parties reduce the inventories they must carry and experience significant reductions in paperwork and ordering costs. Just-in-time II works best when two companies transact a significant amount of business that involves many different parts or products. Still, maintaining trust is the biggest barrier the companies must overcome.

IN THE FOOTSTEPS OF AN ENTREPRENEUR...

Getting a Good Night's Sleep

According to interviews conducted as part of a study commissioned by Unisys Corporation, the security issue most responsible for disrupting the sleep of top IT security executives is employee negligence or abuse of data warehouses or systems (97 percent). Insufficient resources to get the job done right (90 percent) is a close second.

Outsourcing IT and data management activities to reduce costs created additional information security risks that were not being managed adequately according to about 80 percent of respondents. About 70 percent of respondents indicated that a catastrophic attack on IT infrastructure, including sophisticated viruses and expert hacker penetration, was of most concern.

Table 1 provides a ranking of the top five concerns of today's security professionals.

TABLE 1: SECURITY ISSUES OF MOST CONCERN

Employee negligence or abuse	97%
Insufficient resources to get the job done right	90%
Proliferation of outsourced IT and data management	80%
Open patches and holes in application software	73%
Catastrophic attack on IT infrastructure	70%

"One of the most salient findings is that IT professionals must manage complex privacy and data protection issues with tighter budgets and fewer resources," says Janice Burg-Levi, global strategic marketing vice president for Unisys.

Table 2 summarizes the five most frequently cited measures taken to improve the information security function or to reduce data protection risk. Because employee negligence or abuse was by far the greatest concern, the vast majority of experts have implemented or revised security policies and standard operating procedures. In fact, a large group of respondents has implemented information security training programs for key personnel (i.e., those who handle, use, or secure confidential, sensitive, or private information).

Many of the information security professionals interviewed (67 percent) have conducted company-wide vulnerability assessments to identify gap areas and to set priorities for managing risk.

TABLE 2: HOW COMPANIES ARE MANAGING RISK

Revised security policies and procedures (SOPs)	93%
Training program for key personnel	83%
Conducted vulnerability and penetration assessments	67%
Improved access and authentication controls	57%
Appointment of high-level information security officer	53%

The interviews revealed frustration with the lack of funds for preventative security measures. In fact, some commented that the lack of resources is causing them to make tough allocation decisions that may leave the company's critical infrastructure vulnerable.

Some of the greatest strains to the budget include hiring and keeping the most talented staff, conducting training and awareness programs for key personnel, keeping up with the plethora of new tools that might enhance security controls, and implementing systems that help manage customer or employee preferences for privacy.

The security professionals interviewed shared what they believed to be good information security practices. These best practices include the following:

- *Integrate information security management with other corporate compliance initiatives.* It is important to combine key functions or activities with the company's privacy, corporate compliance, and internal audit initiatives.
- *Information security must be owned from the top.* The person responsible for IT security should report directly to senior management or, in the case of a small business venture, directly to the owner.
- *Introduce enabling technologies that help prevent common threats to data security and privacy.* New technologies in perimeter control, connectivity, and authentication can be of enormous value in mitigating security risks.
- *Empower information security managers.* Someone must own responsibility for information security management and be empowered to make decisions.

■ *Create the best possible training program.* As previously noted, internal employee negligence is a major cause for serious security breaches. There is a real need for teaching employees the "dos and don'ts" of information security.

■ *Conduct vigorous internal monitoring of information security processes and controls.* Many of the security professionals in this study reported very positive experiences that resulted from third-party audits, including the early identification of

serious security holes and potential regulatory compliance breaches.

1. The largest companies in financial, public, transportation, and general commercial industries are represented in this study. What steps can a small business owner take to protect the information security function or to reduce data protection risk?

Turning Slow-Moving Inventory Into Cash

3. Describe methods for reducing losses from slow-moving inventory.

Managing inventory effectively requires a business owner to monitor the company's inventory turnover ratio and to compare it with that of other firms of similar size in the same industry. As you recall, the inventory turnover ratio is computed by dividing the firm's cost of goods sold by its average inventory. This ratio expresses the number of times per year the business turns over its inventory. In most cases, the higher the inventory turnover ratio, the better the small firm's financial position will be. A very low inventory turnover ratio indicates that much of the inventory may be stale and obsolete or that inventory investment is too large.

Slow-moving items carry a good chance of loss resulting from spoilage or obsolescence. Firms dealing in trendy fashion merchandise or highly seasonal items often experience losses as a result of being stuck with unsold inventory for long periods of time. Some small business owners are reluctant to sell these slow-moving items by cutting prices, but it is much more profitable to dispose of this merchandise as quickly as possible than to hold it in stock at the regular prices. The owner who postpones marking down stale merchandise, fearing it would reduce profit and hoping that the goods will sell eventually at the regular price, is making a huge mistake. The longer the merchandise sits, the dimmer the prospects of ever selling it, much less selling it at a profit. Pricing these items below regular price or even below cost is difficult, but it is much better than having valuable working capital tied up in unproductive assets.

The most common technique for liquidating slow-moving merchandise is the markdown. Not only is the markdown effective in eliminating slow-moving goods, but it also is a successful promotional tool. Advertising special prices on such merchandise helps the small business garner a larger clientele and contributes to establishing a favorable business image. Using special sales to promote slow-moving items helps create a functional program for turning over inventory more quickly. To get rid of a large supply of out-of-style neckties, one small business offered a "one-cent sale" to customers purchasing neckwear at the regular price. One retailer of stereos and sound equipment chooses an unusual holiday—President's Day—to sponsor an all-out blitz, including special sales, prices, and promotions, to reduce its inventory. Other techniques that help eliminate slow-moving merchandise include the following:

■ Middle-of-the-aisle display islands that attract customer attention
■ One-day-only sales
■ Quantity discounts for volume purchases

- Bargain tables with a variety of merchandise for customers to explore
- Eye-catching lights and tickets marking sale merchandise

As inventory control techniques become increasingly sophisticated and accurate, slow-moving inventory will never be "lost" in the supply chain. Aggressive methods of selling slower-moving inventory enable business owners to convert inventory into cash and to produce an acceptable inventory turnover ratio. The inventory management tools described in this chapter also play an important role in avoiding slow-moving merchandise: They highlight those items that are slow-moving, enabling business owners to avoid the mistake of ordering them again. In effect, this information on what *doesn't* sell shapes entrepreneurs' decisions concerning the merchandise they order in the future. The ability to avoid slow-moving items in the first place means that business owners can invest their working capital more effectively and produce faster inventory turnover ratios, lower costs, and higher profits.

Protecting Inventory from Theft

4. Discuss employee theft and shoplifting and how to prevent them.

Small companies are a big target for crime. Security experts estimate that businesses lose $400 billion annually to criminals, although the actual loss may be even greater because so many business crimes go unreported. Whatever the actual loss is, its effect is staggering, especially on small companies. Smaller companies often lack the sophistication to identify early on the illegal actions of employees or professional thieves. When the losses are detected, it often delivers a crippling blow to a business venture that may be battling cash flow problems. When a firm has fewer assets to operate with, a loss from theft can become a major setback.

Many entrepreneurs believe that the primary sources of theft originate outside the business. In reality, most firms are victimized by their own employees.

Employee Theft

Ironically, the greatest criminal threat to small businesses comes from inside. Employee theft accounts for the greatest proportion of the criminal losses businesses suffer. One U.S. Justice Department study reports that approximately 30 percent of all employees are "hard-core pilferers." The study also estimates that without preventive security measures in place, 80 percent of employees will become involved in theft.[9] Employee theft is more prevalent than ever. Tim Dimoff, president of Mogadore, Ohio-based SACS Consulting & Investigative Services Inc., gives one reason for the increased prevalence. "I call the attitude employees take in the workplace 'entitlement,'" he says. "They justify in their minds that they are entitled to take things because they worked so hard." Dimoff adds that businesses are just as responsible as the employees are. Why? It is rare for a company to file criminal charges. Many businesses don't want the publicity or they worry about the cost to the company to prosecute, how the time away from management will affect the organization, and what it will do to employee morale. Often it may seem easier to just let the employees leave.[10]

Many times, employees steal from the companies that employ them simply because the opportunity presents itself. Often thefts by employees involve "nickel-and-dime" items (nails for a home repair job, a box of pencils for personal use), but a significant number of them involve large sums of money.

How can thefts go undetected? Most thefts occur when employees take advantage of the opportunities to steal that small business owners unwittingly give them. Typically, small business owners are so busy building their companies that they rarely even consider the possibility of employee theft—until disaster strikes. Also, many small companies do not have adequate financial, audit, and security procedures in place. Add to that mix the high degree of trust most small business owners place in their employees, and you have a perfect recipe for employee theft. Experts estimate that 95 percent of all U.S. businesses experience employee theft at an annual cost of more than $50 billion a year. The U.S. Department of Commerce states that employee theft is the cause for nearly one-third of the business bankruptcies in the country.[11] Retail security managers attribute more than 48.5 percent of their losses to employee theft, and internal theft by employees costs retailers $15 billion a year. According to University of Florida criminologist Richard C. Hollinger, Ph.D., who directs the National Retail Security Survey, "An average family of four will spend more than $440 a year in higher prices because of inventory theft. Thieves also generally target hot-selling items, which means those must-have toys on your child's holiday wish list are less likely to be available on the store shelves."[12]

What Causes Employee Theft? Employees steal from their companies for any number of reasons. Some may have a grudge against the company; others may have a drug, alcohol, or gambling addiction to support. A business owner can minimize the last two reasons. To minimize their losses to employee theft, business owners must understand how both the temptation and the opportunity to steal creep into their companies. The following are conditions that lead to major security gaps in small companies.

The Trusted Employee. The fact is that any employee could be a thief, although most are not. Studies show that younger, less devoted employees steal from their companies most often, but longtime employees can cause more damage. It is very easy in a small family business to view longtime employees almost as partners. Such a feeling, although not undesirable, can develop into a security breach. Many owners refuse to believe that their most trusted employees present the greatest security threat, but these workers have the greatest accessibility to keys, cash registers, records, and even safe combinations. Because of their seniority, these employees hold key positions and are quite familiar with operations, so they know where weaknesses in control and security procedures lie.

Small business owners should also be wary of "workaholic" employees. Is this worker really dedicated to the company, or is he or she working so hard to cover up theft? Employee thieves are unwilling to take extended breaks from their jobs for fear of being detected. As long as the dishonest employee remains on the job, he or she can cover up theft. As a security precaution, business owners should require every employee to take vacations long enough so that someone else has to take over their responsibilities (at least five consecutive business days). Most schemes are relatively simple and require day-to-day maintenance to keep them going. Business failure records are filled with stories of firms in which the "ideal" employee turned out to be a thief. "In 90 percent of the cases in which people steal from their companies, the employer would probably have described this person, right up to the time the crime was discovered, as a trusted employee," says one expert.[13]

Disgruntled Employees. Small business managers must also monitor the performance of disgruntled employees. Employees are more likely to steal if they believe that their company treats employees unfairly, and the probability of their stealing goes even higher if they believe they themselves have been treated unfairly. Employees dissatisfied with their pay or their promotions may retaliate against an employer by stealing. Dishonest employees will make up the difference between what they are paid and what they believe they are worth by stealing. Many believe pilfering is a well-deserved "perk."

Organizational Atmosphere. Many entrepreneurs unintentionally create an atmosphere that encourages employee dishonesty. Failing to establish formal controls and procedures invites theft. Nothing encourages dishonest employees to steal more than knowing they are unlikely to be caught. Four factors encourage employee theft:

1. The need or desire to steal (e.g., to support a habit or to cope with a sudden financial crisis)
2. A rationalization for the act (e.g., "They owe me this.")
3. The opportunity to steal (e.g., access to merchandise, complete control of financial functions)
4. The perception that there is a low probability of being caught (e.g., "Nobody will ever know.")

Owners must recognize that they set the example for security and honesty in the business. Employees place more emphasis on what owners do than on what they say. Business owners who install a complete system of inventory control and then ignore it are telling employees that security is unimportant. No one should remove merchandise, materials, or supplies from inventory without recording them properly. There should be no exceptions to the rules, even for bosses and their relatives. Managers should develop clear control procedures and establish penalties for violations. The single biggest deterrent to employee theft is a strong, top-down policy that is well communicated to all employees that theft will not be tolerated and that anyone caught stealing will be prosecuted—*no exceptions.*

Managers must constantly emphasize the importance of security. Small business owners must use every available opportunity to lower the temptation to steal. One business owner relies on payroll inserts to emphasize to employees how theft reduces the funds available for growth, expansion, and higher wages. Another has established a written code of ethics, spelling out penalties for violations. Workers must know that security is a team effort. Security rules and procedures must be reasonable, and the owner must treat workers equitably. Unreasonable rules are not more effective—and may even be more harmful—than poorly enforced procedures. A work environment that fosters honesty at every turn serves as an effective deterrent to employee theft.

Physical Breakdowns. Another major factor contributing to employee theft is weak physical security. The owner who pays little attention to the distribution of keys, safe combination(s), and other entry devices is inviting theft. Also, owners who fail to lock doors and windows or to install reliable alarm systems are literally leaving their businesses open to thieves both inside and outside the organization.

Open windows give dishonest employees a prime opportunity to slip stolen merchandise out of the plant or store. A manufacturer of small appliances discovered that several employees were dropping crates of finished products out of an unlocked window, picking them up after work, and reselling them. By the time the perpetrators were detected, the owner had lost nearly $10,000 worth of merchandise and supplies.

Unlocked or unmonitored doors represent another security leak for many small businesses. The greater the number of doors in a plant or store, the greater the chance of employee theft. Every unnecessary door should be locked (while still conforming to fire regulations), and all regularly used doors should be monitored. Many thefts occur as workers load and unload merchandise. If the owner allows the same employee who prepares purchase orders and handles invoices to check shipments in or out, the temptation to alter documents and steal merchandise may be too great.

Many businesses find that their profits go out with the trash, literally. When collecting trash, a dishonest employee may stash valuable merchandise in with the refuse and dump it in the receptacle. After the store closes, the thief returns to collect the loot. One drugstore owner lost more than $7,000 in merchandise in just six months through trash thefts.

Improper Cash Control. Many small business owners encourage employee theft by failing to implement proper cash control procedures. Without a system of logical, practical audit controls on cash, a firm will likely suffer internal theft. Dishonest employees quickly discover there is a low probability of detection and steal cash with impunity.

Cashiers clearly have the greatest accessibility to the firm's cash and, consequently, experience the greatest temptation to steal. The following scenario is all too common: A customer makes a purchase with the exact amount of cash and leaves quickly. The cashier fails to ring up the purchase and pockets the cash without anyone's knowledge. Some small business owners create a cash security problem by allowing too many employees to operate cash registers and handle customer payments. If a cash shortage develops, the manager is unable to trace responsibility.

A daily inspection of cash register transactions can point out potential employee theft problems. When transactions indicate an excessive amount of voided transactions or no-sale transactions, the owner should investigate. A no-sale transaction could mean the register was opened to give a customer change or to steal cash. A large number of incorrect register transactions also are a potential sign of foul play. Clerks may be camouflaging cash thefts by voiding transactions or by under-ringing sales amounts. *To cut its losses to shrinkage, Famous Footwear, a chain of retail shoe stores, recently installed a cash register monitoring system in every store. The system records every cash register transaction and looks for suspicious patterns. Within a short time, the monitoring system cut the company's unexplained inventory losses in half. When she learned about the new system, one store manager, convinced that she would soon be caught, admitted to stealing more than $2,000 in cash.*[14]

Cash shortages and overages are also clues that alert managers to possible theft. All small business owners are alarmed by cash shortages, but few are disturbed by cash overages. However, cash discrepancies in either direction are an indication of inept cashiering or of poor cash controls. The manager who investigates all cash discrepancies can greatly reduce the opportunity for cashiers to steal.

Preventing Employee Theft. Many incidents of employee theft go undetected, and of those employees who are caught stealing only a small percentage is prosecuted. The burden of dealing with employee theft falls squarely on the owner's shoulders. Although business owners cannot eliminate the possibility of employee theft, they can reduce its likelihood by using some relatively simple procedures and policies that are cost-effective to implement.

Screen Employees Carefully. Perhaps a business owner's greatest weapon against crime is a thorough pre-employment screening process. The best time to weed out prospective criminals is before hiring them! Although state and federal regulations prohibit employers from invading job applicants' privacy and from using discriminatory devices in the selection process, employers have a legitimate right to determine job candidates' integrity and qualifications. A comprehensive selection process and reliable screening devices greatly reduce the chances that an entrepreneur will hire a thief. Smart entrepreneurs verify the information applicants provide on their résumés because they know that some of them will either exaggerate or misrepresent their qualifications. A thorough background check with references and previous employers also is essential. (One question that sheds light on a former employer's feelings toward a former employee is "Would you hire this person again?")

Some security experts recommend the use of integrity tests, paper-and-pencil tests that offer valuable insight into job applicants' level of honesty. Business owners can buy integrity tests for $20 or less that are already validated (to avoid charges of discrimination) and that they can score on their own. Because drug addictions drive many employees to

---

Company Example →

steal, employers also should administer drug tests consistently to all job applicants. The most reliable drug tests cost the company from $35 to $50 each, a small price to pay given the potential losses that can result from hiring an employee with a drug habit. Use the permission granted to you on the employment application to conduct a check of the candidate's criminal background.

Create an Environment of Honesty. Creating an environment of honesty and integrity starts at the top. This requires business owners to set an impeccable example for everyone else in the company. In addition to creating a standard of ethical behavior, business owners should strive to establish high morale among workers. A positive work environment in which employees see themselves as an important part of the team is an effective deterrent to employee theft. Establishing a written code of ethics and having new employees sign "honesty clauses" offer tangible evidence of a company's commitment to honesty and integrity.

Establish a System of Internal Controls. The basis for maintaining internal security on the job is establishing a set of reasonable internal controls designed to prevent employee theft. An effective system of checks and balances goes a long way toward deterring internal crime; weak or inconsistently enforced controls are an open invitation for theft. The most basic rule is to separate among several employees related duties that might cause a security breach if assigned to a single worker. For instance, owners should avoid letting the employee who issues checks reconcile the company's bank statement. Similarly, the person who orders merchandise and supplies should not be the one who also approves those invoices for payment. Spreading these tasks among a number of employees makes organizing a theft more difficult. The owner of a small retail art shop learned this lesson the hard way. After conducting an inventory audit, he discovered that more than $25,000 worth of art supplies were missing. The owner finally traced the theft to the company bookkeeper, who was creating fictional invoices and then issuing checks to herself for the same amount.

Business owners should insist that all company records be kept up-to-date. Sloppy record keeping makes theft difficult to detect. All internal documents—shipping, ordering, billing, and collecting—should be numbered. Missing numbers should arouse suspicion. One subtle way to test employees' honesty is to commit deliberate errors occasionally to see if employees detect them. If you send an extra case of merchandise to the loading dock for shipment, does the supervisor catch it, or does it disappear?

Finally, business owners should demonstrate zero tolerance for theft. They must adhere strictly to company policy when dealing with employees who violate the company's trust. When business owners catch an employee thief, the best course of action is to fire the perpetrator and to prosecute. Too often, owners take the attitude: "Resign, return the money, and we'll forget it." Letting thieves off, however, only encourages them to move on to other businesses where they will steal again. Prosecuting a former employee for theft is never easy, but it does send a clear signal about how the company views employee crime.

The written policies and management pep talks about honesty and integrity have a great deal more meaning when employees know from past experience that the owner will prosecute. Think about what the casino owners in Las Vegas do. They share information among themselves on problem employees. They have strict policies regarding theft. They have constant surveillance of employees while at work, and they prosecute when theft occurs. Despite these efforts, employees still try to steal. If the owners of these casinos are willing to invest as much as they do in security, entrepreneurs should question what steps they are taking to protect the assets of their businesses. For a closer look at where inventory shrinkage happens, refer to Figure 18.3.

Figure 18.3

Causes of Inventory Shrinkage

Source: Used with permission. All rights reserved.

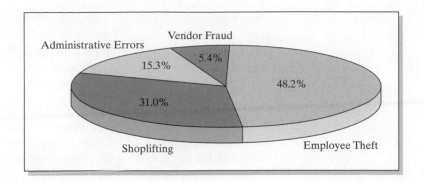

IN THE FOOTSTEPS OF AN ENTREPRENEUR . . .

Confessions of an Embezzler

Studies show that because small companies often lack proper internal controls and security measures, they are more likely to be victims of business crimes such as employee theft, shoplifting, and embezzlement. In addition to being more susceptible to crime, small companies are less able to tolerate it than their larger counterparts. Although a $100,000 loss can harm a large business, that same loss often drives a small company out of business. Bill and Linda Carey, founders of Hollow Metal Door Company (HMDC), a nine-employee business that sells, installs, and services a variety of doors, were victims of embezzlement by a trusted employee over the course of several years. Although they have managed to keep their business going, they are struggling because of the financial hardship the theft imposed on the company, which generates annual revenues of $2 million to $3 million. "I've worked 10 to 14 hour days for 30 years," says Bill with a touch of bitterness. "She wiped out years of my hard work."

In many ways, Hollow Metal Door's story is typical. Sandra (not her real name) was the company's bookkeeper. She came to work for the Careys in 1987, answering phones and helping with the company's bookkeeping. Sandra, who fit the girl-next-door stereotype, including being a high school cheerleader, was one of the first non-family member hired at HMDC. Before long, the Careys were treating Sandra like a daughter, taking an interest in her life away from the office. "They saw me get married, have kids, and grow up," Sandra says. "They were very good to me."

Unfortunately, Sandra was not good to the Careys. In 1992, Sandra, now married to her high school sweetheart, was a working mother trying to raise two sons. The family budget was always tight, and there never seemed to be enough money left at the end of the month. Sandra handled the family's finances, and she had resorted to charging regular living expenses on

high interest rate credit cards. The debt was climbing, and she had not been able to make a payment on the credit card balances in months. "I panicked," she recalls.

For the previous five years, Sandra had written checks for HMDC almost every day, and one day she decided to write a company check to pay off the family's credit card balance. The total amount was just $672. "I thought, 'Just this one time—just to get back on my feet. No one will know,'" she recalls. She knew, however, that what she had done was wrong, so she covered the theft by entering the check as if she had written it as payment to a company vendor. She carried the check in her purse for a week, trying to come up with another solution to her financial woes. The credit card company kept calling, however, and, feeling trapped, she finally mailed the check. "I can't believe I did it," she says, calling it "the stupidest idea" she ever had.

The check cleared, and no one at HMDC suspected that anything was wrong. After all, Sandra was a long-time, trusted employee, and the check was for such a small amount. Had it all stopped there, Sandra's theft might never have been discovered. Instead of "just one time" though, Sandra wrote another check, and then another ... She learned to cover her tracks by disguising the checks as payments to phony vendors that she had concocted. Sandra never used the money she stole foolishly—gambling or supporting a drug habit. She used it to pay for the family's living expenses. "Maybe we ate a little better," she says.

For seven years, Sandra told no one, not even her husband, what she was doing. Whenever HMDC's bank called, Sandra panicked, worried that the bank had detected her embezzling. "I just knew it was going to be about a check," she says, "but it never was." Sandra made sure that she was in the office the first week of every month because that's when

HMDC's bank statement arrived. She had to get to the statement first to hide her cancelled checks. "It was so easy after a while," she says. "It had gotten to the point where it didn't truly feel like I was doing anything wrong."

But she was.

After seven years of embezzling, Sandra's theft was finally uncovered while she was on a family vacation at the beach. One of her old cancelled checks turned up, and Bill Carey could not believe what he was seeing. When she returned, he met her at the door with the cancelled check in his hand. "He asked me if I did this, and all I could say was 'Yeah,'" she recalls. Carey fired Sandra on the spot, and the mild-mannered business owner watched as she cleared out her desk. Sandra realized for the first time that she might go to jail. Still, not even Sandra realized just how much she had stolen from HMDC over the seven years. The subsequent investigation showed that she had embezzled $248,383 to pay her credit card bills. "We

just lived," she recalls tearfully. "We used that money to just live." Although faced with a possible sentence of 16 years in jail, a judge sentenced Sandra to the minimum sentence, 18 months, so she could begin paying restitution to the Careys. Today, she has a menial job running errands for a business and pays $100 a month to HMDC, an amount that obviously cannot repay all that she stole. "I'm not a bad person," she says. "But I did a really bad thing."

1. Why are small companies more likely than large businesses to become victims of business crime?
2. What conditions make a small company ripe for employee theft?
3. What steps could the Careys have taken at Hollow Metal Door Company to avoid Sandra's embezzlement?

Sources: Adapted from David G. Propson, "Inside Job," *Small Business Computing,* November 2001, pp. 27–30; Cora Daniels, "Confessions of an Embezzler," *FSB,* May 2002, pp. 48–51.

Shoplifting

The most frequent business crime is shoplifting. Businesses lose an estimated $17 billion to $20 billion to shoplifters each year, and small businesses, especially retailers, suffer a significant share of those losses. Shoplifting takes an especially heavy toll on small businesses because they usually have the weakest lines of defense against shoplifters. Shoplifting losses, which ultimately are passed on to the consumer, account for approximately 3 to 4 percent of the average price tag.

Types of Shoplifters. Anyone who takes merchandise from a store without paying for it, no matter what the justification, is a shoplifter. Shoplifters look exactly like other customers. They can be young children in search of a new toy or elderly people who are short of money. Anyone can be a shoplifter, given the opportunity, the ability, and the desire to steal. For instance, in 2002 Winona Ryder was found guilty of stealing more than $5,500 worth of merchandise from a Beverly Hills Saks Fifth Avenue store. As a successful actress worth millions, Ryder certainly does not fit the image many may have of a shoplifter.

Fortunately for small business owners, most shoplifters are amateurs who steal because the opportunity presents itself. Many steal on impulse, and the theft is their first criminal act. Many of those caught have the money to pay for their "five-finger discounts." Observant business owners supported by trained store personnel can spot potential shoplifters and deter many shoplifting incidents; however, they must understand the shoplifter's profile. Experts identify five types of shoplifters.

Juveniles. Juveniles account for approximately one-half of all shoplifters. Many juveniles steal as a result of peer pressure. Most have little fear of prosecution, assuming they can hide behind their youth. When owners detect juvenile shoplifters, they must not let sympathy stand in the way of good judgment. Many hard-core criminals began their careers as shoplifters, and small business owners who fail to prosecute the youthful offender do nothing to discourage a life of crime. Juvenile offenders should be prosecuted through proper legal procedures just as any adult shoplifter would be.

Some individuals have a compulsive need to steal even though they have little, if any, need for the items they shoplift. In many cases, these shoplifters could afford to purchase the merchandise they steal.

Impulse Shoplifters. Impulse shoplifters steal on the spur of the moment when they succumb to temptation. These shoplifters do not plan their thefts, but when a prime opportunity to shoplift arises, they take advantage of it. For example, a salesperson may be showing a customer several pieces of jewelry. If the salesperson is called away, the customer might pocket an expensive ring and leave the store before the employee returns.

Many well-respected individuals are impulse shoplifters. The perpetrator might even be a regular customer. Impatient customers, after a hectic shopping day, might be unwilling to wait to pay for merchandise, or a disgruntled customer may be seeking revenge against a company; whatever the case, shoplifting is the result.

The most effective method of fighting impulse shoplifting is prevention. To minimize losses, the owner should remove the opportunity to steal by implementing proper security procedures and devices.

Shoplifters Supporting Other Criminal Behaviors. Shoplifters motivated to steal to support a drug or alcohol habit often are easy to detect because their behavior is usually unstable and erratic. One shoplifter recently apprehended was supporting a $100-a-day heroin habit by stealing small items from local retailers and then returning the merchandise for refunds. (The stores almost never asked for sales receipts.) Small business owners should exercise great caution in handling these shoplifters because they can easily become violent. Criminals deranged by drugs or alcohol might be armed and could endanger the lives of customers and employees if they are detained. It is best to let the police apprehend these shoplifters.

Kleptomaniacs. Kleptomaniacs have a compulsive need to steal even though they have little, if any, need for the items they shoplift. In many cases, these shoplifters could afford to purchase the merchandise they steal. Kleptomaniacs account for less than 5 percent of shoplifters, but their "disease" costs business owners a great deal. They need professional psychological counseling, and the owner only helps them by seeing that they are apprehended.

Professionals. Although only about 3 percent of shoplifters are professionals they are responsible for 10 percent of the total dollar losses. Because the professional shoplifter's business is theft, he or she is very difficult to detect and deter. Career shoplifters tend to focus on expensive merchandise they can sell quickly to their "fences," such as stereo equipment, appliances, guns, or jewelry. Usually the fences don't keep the stolen goods long, often selling them at a fraction of their value. Thus, apprehending and prosecuting professional shoplifters is quite difficult. Police have apprehended professional shoplifters with detailed maps of a city's shopping districts, showing target stores and the best times to make a "hit." Furthermore, many professional shoplifters are affiliated with organized crime, and they are able to rely on their associates to avoid detection and prosecution. When professional shoplifter sell stolen merchandise to a fence, the fence pays only 10 to 20 percent of the value of the merchandise.[15] Consequently, to net $300 per day when the fence pays only 20 percent, a shoplifter would need to steal $1,500 in merchandise (at 10 percent, he or she must steal $3,000 in merchandise). Refer to Table 18.3 for more information on shoplifting.

Table 18.3

Shoplifting Facts

- More than $10 billion worth of goods are stolen from retailers each year. That's more than $25 million per day.
- There are approximately 23 million shoplifters (or 1 in 11 people) in our nation. More than 10 million people have been caught shoplifting in the last five years.
- Shoplifting affects more than the offender. It overburdens the police and the courts, adds to a store's security expenses, costs consumers more for goods, costs communities lost dollars in sales tax, and hurts children and families.
- Shoplifters steal from all types of stores including department stores, specialty shops, supermarkets, drugstores, discounters, music stores, convenience stores, and thrift shops.
- There is no profile of a typical shoplifter. Men and women shoplift about equally as often.
- Approximately 25 percent of shoplifters are kids and 75 percent are Fifty-five percent of adult shoplifters say they started shoplifting in their teens.
- Many shoplifters buy and steal merchandise in the same visit. Shoplifters commonly steal from $2 to $200 per incident depending on the type of store and item(s) chosen.
- Shoplifting is often not a premeditated crime: 73 percent of adult and 72 percent of juvenile shoplifters don't plan to steal in advance.
- Eighty-six percent of kids say they know other kids who shoplift, and 66 percent say they hang out with those kids.
- Shoplifters say they are caught an average of only once in every 48 times they steal. They are turned over to the police 50 percent of the time.
- Approximately 3 percent of shoplifters are "professionals" who steal solely for resale or profit as a business. These include drug addicts who steal to support their habit, hardened professionals who steal as a lifestyle, and international shoplifting gangs who steal for profit as a business. "Professional" shoplifters are responsible for 10 percent of the total dollar losses.
- The majority of shoplifters are "nonprofessionals" who steal, not out of financial need or greed, but as a response to social and personal pressures in their lives.
- The excitement generated from "getting away with it" produces a chemical reaction resulting in what shoplifters describe as an incredible "rush" or "high" feeling. Many shoplifters will tell you that this high is their "true reward," rather than the merchandise itself.
- Drug addicts, who have become addicted to shoplifting, describe shoplifting as equally addicting as drugs.
- Even after getting caught, 57 percent of adults and 33 percent of juveniles say it is hard for them to stop shoplifting.
- Most nonprofessional shoplifters don't commit other types of crimes. They'll never steal an ashtray from your house and will return to you a $20 bill you may have dropped. Their criminal activity is restricted to shoplifting and, therefore, any rehabilitation program should be "offense specific" for this crime.

Source: Used with permission. All rights reserved.

Detecting Shoplifters. Although shoplifters can be difficult to detect, small business owners who know what to look for can spot them in action. They must always be on the lookout for shoplifters, but merchants should be especially vigilant on Saturdays and around Christmas, when shoplifters can hide their thefts more easily in the frenzy of a busy shopping day.

Shoplifters can work alone or in groups. In general, impulse shoplifters prefer solitary thefts, whereas juveniles and professionals operate in groups. A common tactic for group shoplifters is for one member of the gang to create some type of distraction while other members steal the merchandise. Business owners should be wary of loud, disruptive groups that enter their stores.

Solitary shoplifters are usually quite nervous. They avoid crowds and shy away from store personnel, preferring privacy to ply their trade. To make sure they avoid detection, they constantly scan the store for customers and employees. These shoplifters spend more time nervously looking around the store than examining merchandise. Also, they shop when the store is most likely to be understaffed, during early morning, lunch, or late evening hours. Shoplifters frequently linger in the same area for an extended time without purchasing anything. Customers who refuse the help of sales personnel or bring in large bags and packages (especially empty ones) also arouse suspicion.

Shoplifters have their own arsenal of tools to assist them in plying their trade. They often shop with booster boxes, shopping bags, umbrellas, bulky jackets, baby strollers, or containers disguised as gifts. These props often have hidden compartments that can be tripped easily, allowing the shoplifter to fill them with merchandise quickly.

Some shoplifters use specially designed coats with hidden pockets and compartments that can hold even large items. Small business owners should be suspicious of customers wearing out-of-season clothing (e.g., heavy coats in warm weather, rain gear on clear days) that could conceal stolen goods. Hooked belts also are used to enable the shoplifter to suspend items from hangers without being detected.

Another common tactic is "ticket switching" in which the shoplifter exchanges price tickets on items and then pays a very low price for an expensive item. An inexperienced or unobservant cashier may charge $9.95 for a $30.00 item that the shoplifter remarked while no one was looking.

One variation of traditional shoplifting techniques is the "grab-and-run" in which a shoplifter grabs an armload of merchandise located near an exit and then dashes out the door into a waiting getaway car. The element of surprise gives these thieves an advantage, and they are often gone before anyone in the store realizes what has happened.

Deterring Shoplifters. The problem of shoplifting is worsening. Every year, business losses due to customer theft increase, and many companies are declaring war on shoplifting. Funds allocated for fighting shoplifting losses are best spent on *prevention*. By focusing on preventing shoplifting rather than on prosecuting violators after the fact, business owners take a strong stand in protecting their firms' merchandise. Of course, no prevention plan is perfect. When violations occur, owners must prosecute; otherwise the business becomes known as an easy target. Merchants say that when a store gets a reputation for being tough on shoplifters, thefts drop off.

Knowing what to look for dramatically improves a business owner's odds in combating shoplifting:

- *Watch the eyes.* Amateurs spend excessive time looking at the merchandise they're about to steal. Their eyes, however, are usually checking to see who (if anyone) is watching them.
- *Watch the hands.* Experienced shoplifters, like good magicians, rely on sleight of hand.

- *Watch the body.* Amateurs' body movements reflect their nervousness; they appear to be unnatural.
- *Watch the clothing.* Loose, bulky clothing is the uniform of the typical shoplifter.
- *Watch for devices.* Anything a customer carries is a potential concealing device.
- *Watch for loiterers.* Many amateurs must work up the nerve to steal.
- *Watch for switches.* Working in pairs, shoplifters will split duties; one will lift the merchandise, and, after a switch, the other will take it out of the store.

Store owners can take other steps to discourage shoplifting, which are discussed next.

Train Employees to Spot Shoplifters. One of the best ways to prevent shoplifting is to train store personnel to be aware of shoplifters' habits and to be alert for possible theft. In fact, most security experts agree that alert employees are the best defense against shoplifters. Employees should look for nervous, unusual customers and monitor them closely. Shoplifters prefer to avoid sales personnel and other customers, and when employees approach them, shoplifters know they are being watched. Even when all salespeople are busy, an alert employee should approach the customer and mention, "I'll be with you in a moment." Honest customers appreciate the clerk's politeness, and shoplifters are put off by the implied surveillance.

All employees should watch for suspicious people, especially those carrying the props of concealment. Employees in clothing stores must keep a tally of the items being taken into and out of dressing rooms. Some clothing retailers prevent unauthorized use of dressing rooms by locking them. Customers who want to try on garments must check with a store employee first.

An alert cashier can be a tremendous boom to the store owner attempting to minimize shoplifting losses. A cashier who knows the store's general pricing policy and is familiar with the prices of many specific items is the best insurance against the ticket-switching shoplifter. A good cashier also should inspect all containers being sold; tool boxes, purses, briefcases, and other containers could conceal stolen merchandise.

Employees should be trained to watch for group shoplifting tactics. A group of shoppers that enters the store and then disperses in all directions may be attempting to distract employees so that some gang members can steal merchandise. Sales personnel should watch closely the customer who lingers in one area for an extended time, especially one who examines a lot of merchandise but never purchases anything.

The sales staff should watch for those individuals who consistently shop during the hours when most personnel are on breaks. Managers can help eliminate this cause of shoplifting by ensuring that their stores are well staffed at all times. Coordinating work schedules to ensure adequate coverage is a simple but effective method of discouraging shoplifting.

The cost of training employees to be alert to shoplifting "gimmicks" can be recouped many times over by preventing losses from retail theft. The local police department or chamber of commerce may be able to conduct training seminars for local small business owners and their employees, or security consulting firms might sponsor a training course on shoplifting techniques and protective methods. Refresher courses every few months can help keep employees sharp in spotting shoplifters.

Pay Attention to the Store Layout. A well-planned store layout also can be an effective obstacle in preventing shoplifting losses. Proper lighting throughout the store makes it easier for employees to monitor shoppers, whereas dimly lit areas give dishonest customers a prime opportunity to steal without detection. Also, display cases should be kept low, no more than three or four feet high, so store personnel can have a clear view of the entire store. Display counters should have spaces between them; continuous displays create a barrier between customers and employees.

Business owners should keep small expensive items such as jewelry, silver, and consumer electronic devices behind display counters or in locked cases with a sales clerk nearby. Valuable or breakable items also should be kept out of customer reach and should not be displayed near exits, where shoplifters can pick them up and quickly step outside. All merchandise displays should be neat and organized so that it will be noticeable if an item is missing.

Cash registers should be located so that cashiers have an unobstructed view of the entire store. Other protective measures include prominently posting antishoplifting signs describing the penalties involved and keeping unattended doors locked (within fire regulations). Exits that cannot be locked because of fire regulations should be equipped with noise alarms to detect any attempts at unauthorized exit.

Install Mechanical Devices. Another option a small business owner has in the attempt to reduce shoplifting losses is to install mechanical devices. A complete deterrence system can be expensive, but failure to implement one is usually more expensive. Tools such as two-way mirrors allow employees at one end of the store to monitor a customer at the other end, and one-way viewing windows enable employees to watch the entire store without being seen.

Other mechanical devices, such as closed-circuit TV cameras, convex wall mirrors, and peepholes, also help the owner protect the store from shoplifters. Not every small business can afford to install a closed-circuit camera system, but one clever entrepreneur got the benefit of such a system without the high cost. He installed one "live" camera and several "dummy" cameras that did not work. The cameras worked because potential shoplifters thought they were all live. Another high-tech weapon used against shoplifters is a mannequin named Anne Droid, which is equipped with a tiny camera behind one eye and a microphone in her nose!

An owner can deter ticket-switching shoplifters by using tamper-proof price tickets: perforated gummed labels that tear away if a customer tries to remove them or price tags attached to merchandise by hard-to-break plastic strips. Some owners use multiple price tags concealed on items to deter ticket switchers. One of the most effective weapons for combating shoplifting is the electronic article surveillance system, small tags that are equipped with electronic sensors that set off sound and light alarms if customers take them past a store exit. These tags are attached to the merchandise and can be removed only by employees with special shears. Owners using these electronic tags must make sure that all cashiers are consistent in removing them from items purchased legitimately; otherwise, they may be liable for false arrest or, at the very least, may cause customers embarrassment.

Apprehending Shoplifters. Despite all of the weapons business owners use to curtail shoplifting, the sad reality is that most of the time shoplifters are successful at plying their trade. Shoplifters say they are caught an average of only once in every 48 times they steal and that they are turned over to the police 50 percent of the time. Of those shoplifters who do get caught, less than half are prosecuted. The chance that any shoplifter will actually go before a judge is about one in 100![16] Building a strong case against a shoplifter is essential; therefore, small business owners must determine beforehand the procedures to follow once they detect a shoplifter. The store owner has to be certain that the shoplifter has taken or concealed the merchandise and has left the store with it. Although state laws vary, owners must do the following to make the charges stick:

1. *See* the person take or conceal the merchandise.
2. *Identify* the merchandise as belonging to the store.
3. *Testify* that it was taken with the intent to steal.
4. *Prove* that the merchandise was not paid for.

Most security experts agree that a business owner should never apprehend the shoplifter if he or she has lost sight of the suspect even for an instant. In that time, the person may have dumped the merchandise.

Another primary consideration in apprehending shoplifters is the safety of store employees. In general, employees should never directly accuse a customer of shoplifting and should never try to apprehend the suspect. The wisest course of action when a shoplifter is detected is to alert the police or store security personnel and let them apprehend the suspect. Apprehension *outside* the store is safest. This tactic strengthens the owner's case and eliminates unpleasant in-store scenes that upset other customers or that might be dangerous. Of course, if the stolen merchandise is very valuable, or if the criminal is likely to escape once outside, the owner may have no choice but to apprehend the shoplifter in the store.

Once business owners detect and apprehend a shoplifter, they must decide whether to prosecute. Many small business owners fail to prosecute because they fear legal entanglements or negative publicity. However, failure to prosecute encourages shoplifters to try again and gives the business the image of being an easy target. Of course, each case is an individual matter. For example, the owner may choose not to prosecute elderly or senile shoplifters or those who are mentally incompetent. But in most cases, prosecuting the shoplifter is the best option, especially for juveniles and first-time offenders. The business owner who prosecutes shoplifters consistently soon develops a reputation for toughness that most shoplifters hesitate to test. It is in the interest of every business owner to have that reputation.

Conclusion

Inventory control is one of those less-than-glamorous activities that business owners must perform if their businesses are to succeed. Although it doesn't offer the flash of marketing or the visibility of customer service, inventory control is no less important. In fact, business owners who invest the time and the resources to exercise the proper degree of control over their inventory soon discover that the payoff is huge!

Chapter Review

1. Explain the various inventory control systems and the advantages and disadvantages of each.

   - Inventory represents the largest investment for the typical small business. Unless properly managed, the cost of inventory will strain the firm's budget and cut into its profitability. The goal of inventory control is to balance the cost of holding and maintaining inventory with meeting customer demand.

   - Regardless of the inventory control system selected, business owners must recognize the relevance of the 80/20 rule, which states that roughly 80 percent of the value of the firm's inventory is in about 20 percent of the items in stock. Because only a small percentage of items account for the majority of the value of the firm's inventory, managers should focus control on those items.

   - Three basic types of inventory control systems are available to the small business owner: perpetual, visual, and partial. Perpetual inventory control systems are designed to maintain a running count of the items in inventory. Although they can be expensive and cumbersome to operate by hand, affordable computerized point-of-sale (POS) terminals that deduct items sold from inventory on hand make perpetual systems feasible for small companies. The visual inventory system is the most common method of controlling merchandise in a small business. This system works best when shortages are not likely to cause major problems. Partial inventory control systems are most effective for small businesses with limited time and money. These systems operate on the basis of the 80/20 rule.

   - The ABC system is a partial system that divides a firm's inventory into three categories depending on each item's dollar usage volume (cost per unit multiplied by quantity used per time period). The purpose of classifying items according to their value is to establish the proper degree of control over them. A items are most closely controlled by perpetual inventory control systems; B items use basic analytical tools; and C items are controlled by very simple techniques such as the two-bin system, the level control method, or the tag system.

2. Describe how just-in-time (JIT) and JIT II inventory control techniques work.

   ▪ The just-in-time system of inventory control sees excess inventory as a blanket that masks production problems and adds unnecessary costs to the production operation. Under a JIT philosophy, the level of inventory maintained is the measure of efficiency. Materials and parts should not build up as costly inventory. They should flow through the production process without stopping, arriving at the appropriate location just in time.

   ▪ JIT II techniques focus on creating a close, harmonious relationship with a company's suppliers so that both parties benefit from increased efficiency. To work successfully, JIT II requires suppliers and their customers to share what was once closely guarded information in an environment of trust and cooperation. Under JIT II, customers and suppliers work hand in hand, acting more like partners than mere buyers and sellers.

3. Describe methods for reducing losses from slow-moving inventory.

   ▪ Managing inventory requires monitoring the company's inventory turnover ratio; slow-moving items result in losses from spoilage or obsolescence.

   ▪ Slow-moving items can be liquidated by markdowns, eye-catching displays, or quantity discounts.

4. Discuss employee theft and shoplifting and how to prevent them.

   ▪ Employee theft accounts for the majority of business losses due to theft. Most small business

owners are so busy managing their companies' daily affairs that they fail to develop reliable security systems. Thus, they provide their employees with prime opportunities to steal.

   ▪ The organizational atmosphere may encourage employee theft. The owner sets the organizational tone for security. A complete set of security controls, procedures, and penalties should be developed and enforced. Physical breakdowns in security invite employee theft. Open doors and windows, poor key control, and improper cash controls are major contributors to the problem of employee theft. Employers can build security into their businesses by screening and selecting employees carefully. Orientation programs also help the employee to get started in the right direction. Internal controls, such as division of responsibility, spot checks, and audit procedures, are useful in preventing employee theft.

   ▪ Shoplifting is the most common business crime. Fortunately, most shoplifters are amateurs. Juveniles often steal to impress their friends, but prosecution can halt their criminal ways early on. Impulse shoplifters steal because the opportunity suddenly arises. Simple prevention is the best defense against these shoplifters. Alcoholics and drug addicts steal to supply some need and are usually easiest to detect. Kleptomaniacs have a compelling need to steal. Professionals are in the business of theft and can be very difficult to detect and quite dangerous.

   ▪ Three strategies are most useful in deterring shoplifters. First, employees should be trained to look for signs of shoplifting. Second, store layout should be designed with theft deterrence in mind. Finally, antitheft devices should be installed in the store.

▌▌▌ Discussion Questions

1. Describe some of the small business owner's incidental costs in carrying and maintaining inventory.
2. What is a perpetual inventory system? How does it operate? What are the advantages and disadvantages of using such a system?
3. List and describe briefly the four versions of a perpetual inventory system.
4. Give examples of small businesses that would find it practical to implement the four systems described in question 3.
5. What advantages and disadvantages does a visual inventory control system have over other methods?
6. For what type of business product line is a visual control system most effective?
7. What is the 80/20 rule, and why is it important in controlling inventory?
8. Outline the ABC inventory control procedure. What is the purpose of classifying inventory items using this procedure?

9. Briefly describe the types of control techniques that should be used for A, B, and C items.

10. What is the basis for the JIT philosophy? Under what condition does a JIT system work best?

11. What is JIT II? What is its underlying philosophy? What risks does it present to businesses?

12. Outline the two methods of taking a physical inventory count. Why is it necessary for every small business manager to take inventory?

13. Why are slow-moving items dangerous to the small business? What can be done to liquidate them from inventory?

14. Why are small companies more susceptible to business crime than large companies?

15. Why is employee theft a problem for many small businesses? Briefly describe the reasons for employee theft.

16. Construct a profile of the employee most likely to steal goods or money from an employer. What four elements must be present for employee theft to occur?

17. Briefly outline a program that could help the typical small business owner minimize losses due to employee theft.

18. List and briefly describe the major types of shoplifters.

19. Outline the characteristics of a typical shoplifter that should arouse a small business manager's suspicions. What tools and tactics is a shoplifter likely to use?

20. Describe the major elements of a program designed to deter shoplifters.

21. How can proper planning of store layout reduce shoplifting losses?

22. What must an owner do to have a good case against a shoplifter? How should a suspected shoplifter be apprehended?

Managing Inventory

Business Plan Pro

For many small businesses, inventory represents a major investment. Unfortunately, many small business owners fail to manage their inventory investments carefully, a situation that often leads to serious financial, managerial, and customer service problems. Fortunately, small companies now can afford to purchase inventory control systems that once were available only to large businesses. Technological solutions supported by a sound inventory control system enable even the smallest companies to reap the benefits of maintaining proper inventory control.

The exercises for Chapter 18 that accompany Business Plan Pro are designed to help you describe your company's inventory control strategy. If inventory represents a significant investment for your business, you should complete these exercises. Once you finish them, you may want to update the Fulfillment component of the What You're Selling section in Business Plan Pro.

Chapter 19

Staffing and Leading a Growing Company

> *Anyone can steer the ship when the sea is calm.*
> —PUBILIUS SYRUS

> *Many individuals have, like uncut diamonds, shining qualities beneath a rough exterior.*
> —DECIMUS JUNIUS JUVENALIS

Upon completion of this chapter, you will be able to:

1. Explain the challenges involved in the entrepreneur's role as leader and what it takes to be a successful leader.

2. Describe the importance of hiring the right employees and how to avoid making hiring mistakes.

3. Explain how to build the kind of company culture and structure to support the entrepreneur's mission and goals and to motivate employees to achieve them.

4. Understand the potential barriers to effective communication and describe how to overcome them.

5. Discuss the ways in which entrepreneurs can motivate their employees to achieve higher levels of performance.

The Entrepreneur's Role as Leader

1. Explain the challenges involved in the entrepreneur's role as leader and what it takes to be a successful leader.

Once a business begins to grow and the entrepreneur becomes dependent on the productive energies of others to achieve results, leadership becomes the critical variable that fuels success. **Leadership** is the process of influencing and inspiring others to work to achieve a common goal and then giving them the power and the freedom to achieve it. Without leadership ability, entrepreneurs—and their companies—never achieve the full potential of the organization or that of the employees. There is no simple formula for leadership. In today's rapidly changing business environment, entrepreneurs need to modify their leadership skills as employees change. People of multiple generations and various ethnic and cultural backgrounds have differing personal and professional needs, as well as expectations regarding the style and behavior of those whom they accept as leaders. Knowledge workers in a high-tech firm who are in their twenties and thirties can be expected to define effective leadership on a few dimensions differently than 50- and 60-year-olds from traditional manufacturing industries. Effective leadership requires the entrepreneur to know each person as an individual, as well as the unique conditions that impact the employees and the firm. Becoming and remaining an effective leader requires a willingness to remain open to the changes in both people and "things," a deep commitment to the long-term well-being of employees, and to their needs, and a high level of sensitivity. Leaders are always "on stage" in the sense that employees continually judge their actions, as well as their words.

In the recent past, some compared the leader's job to that of a symphony orchestra conductor. Like the symphony leader, a manager made sure that everyone was playing the same score, coordinated individual efforts to produce harmony, and directed the members as they played. The conductor (manager) retained virtually all of the power and made all of the decisions about how the orchestra would play the music without any input from the musicians themselves. Today's successful leader, however, is more like the leader of a jazz band, which is known for its improvisation, innovation, and creativity. Max DePree, former CEO of Herman Miller, a highly successful furniture manufacturer, explains the connection this way:

> Jazz band leaders choose the music, find the musicians, and perform—in public. But the effect of the performance depends on so many things—the environment, the volunteers playing in the band, the need for everybody to perform as individuals and as a group, the absolute dependence of the leader on the members of the band, the need for the followers to play well...The leader of the jazz band has the beautiful opportunity to draw the best out of the other musicians. We have much to learn from jazz bandleaders, for jazz, like leadership, combines the unpredictability of the future with the gifts of individuals.[1]

Management and leadership are not the same; yet both are essential to a small company's success. Leadership without management is unbridled; management without leadership is uninspired. Leadership gets a small business going; management keeps it going. Stephen Covey, author of *Principle-Centered Leadership*, explains the difference between management and leadership this way:

> Leadership deals with people; management deals with things. You manage things; you lead people. Leadership deals with vision; management deals with logistics toward that vision. Leadership deals with doing the right things; management focuses on doing things right. Leadership deals with

examining the paradigms on which you are operating; management operates within those paradigms. Leadership comes first, then management, but both are necessary.[2]

Leadership and management are intertwined; a small business that has one but not the other will go nowhere. Effective leaders consistently:

■ *Create a set of values and beliefs for employees and passionately pursue them.* Employees look to their leaders for guidance in making decisions. True leaders focus attention on the principles, values, and beliefs on which they founded their companies.

■ *Respect and support their employees.* To gain the respect of their employees, leaders must first respect those who work for them.

■ *Set the example for their employees.* Leaders' words ring hollow if they fail to "practice what they preach." Few signals are transmitted to workers faster than the hypocrisy of leaders who sell employees on one set of values and principles and then act according to a different set.

■ *Focus employees' efforts on challenging goals and keep them driving toward those goals.* Effective leaders have a clear vision of where they want their companies to go, and they are able to communicate their vision to those around them. Leaders must repeatedly reinforce the goals they set for their companies.

■ *Provide the resources employees need to achieve their goals.* Effective leaders know that workers cannot do their jobs well unless they have the tools they need. They provide workers with not only the physical resources they need to excel but also the necessary intangible resources such as training, coaching, and mentoring.

■ *Communicate with their employees.* Leaders recognize that helping workers see the company's overarching goal is just one part of effective communication; encouraging employee feedback and then listening is just as vital. In other words, they know that communication is a two-way street.

■ *Value the diversity of their workers.* Smart business leaders recognize the value of their workers' varied skills, abilities, backgrounds, and interests. When channeled in the right direction, such diversity can be a powerful weapon in achieving innovation and maintaining a competitive edge.

■ *Celebrate their workers' successes.* Effective leaders recognize that workers want to be winners and do everything they can to encourage top performance among their people. The rewards they give are not always financial; in many cases, a reward may be as simple as a hand-written congratulatory note.

■ *Value risk-taking.* Effective leaders recognize that in a rapidly changing competitive environment, they must make decisions with incomplete information and must be willing to take risks to succeed.

■ *Understand that leadership is multidimensional.* Smart leaders know that there is no one "best" style of leadership. The dimensions of leadership change depending on the people involved, the conditions and circumstances of the situation, and the desired outcome. Leading a company into the face of a serious crisis with intense time pressure demands a different style of leadership than leading that same business as it executes a carefully planed expansion into a new market.

■ *Value new ideas from employees.* Successful leaders know that because employees work every day on the front lines of the business, they see ways to improve quality, customer service, and business systems.

■ *Understand that success really is a team effort.* Small companies typically depend more on their founding entrepreneurs than on anyone else. After all, someone has to take responsibility for the toughest decisions. However, effective leaders understand that their roles are only a small piece of the entire company puzzle. *Now Who's Boss*, a six-part TLC television series, filmed six CEOs who took jobs on the front lines of their companies, where the "real work" is performed. The co-founders of the California Pizza Kitchen, for example, worked as dish washers, pizza makers, and food servers. In addition to seeing firsthand just how difficult many jobs can be, all of the CEOs had a superb refresher course in how important every worker's role is in the success of a company.[3]

- *Encourage creativity among their workers.* Rather than punish workers who take risks and fail, effective leaders are willing to accept failure as a natural part of innovation and creativity. They know that innovative behavior is the key to future success and do everything they can to encourage it among workers.
- *Maintain a sense of humor.* One of the most important tools a leader can have is a sense of humor. Without it, work can become dull and unexciting for everyone.
- *Behave with integrity at all times.* Real leaders know that they set the ethical tone in the organization. Even small lapses in a leader's ethical standards can have a significant impact on a company's ethical climate. Workers know they can trust leaders whose actions support their words. Similarly, they quickly learn not to trust leaders whose day-to-day dealings belie the principles they preach.
- *Keep their eyes on the horizon.* Effective leaders are never satisfied with what they and their employees accomplished yesterday. They know that yesterday's successes are not enough to sustain their companies indefinitely. They see the importance of building and maintaining sufficient momentum to carry their companies to the next level.

Entrepreneurs cannot bestow the mantle of "leader" on themselves. Managers may inherit their subordinates, but leaders have to earn their followers. A business owner's employees—the followers—are the ones who determine if he or she is worthy of leadership. *Without followers, there are no leaders.* Astute leaders know that their success depends on their employees' success. After all, it is the employees who will actually do the work, implement the strategies, and produce the results. To be effective, leaders must establish for their workers an environment in which they can achieve success. One expert identifies six conditions that leaders must create for their followers if a company is to succeed. Followers must (1) know what to do, (2) know how to do it, (3) understand why they are doing it, (4) want to do it, (5) have the right resources to do it, and (6) believe they have the proper leadership to guide them.[4] Great leaders do everything in their power to make these conditions thrive in their companies.

Many executives believe that their leadership styles are the product of some major life

Company Example ⟶ experience. *Jack Kahl, founder of MANCO, a small manufacturer of duct tape, says that his mother's leadership when he was seven and his father was diagnosed with tuberculosis formed the model he follows in business. His mother pulled the children together into a team to cope with the family's financial difficulties. All of the children worked to support the family. Jack Kahl learned consensual leadership from his mother and built a successful business based on its application.*[5]

To be effective, small business leaders must perform four vital tasks:

- Hire the right employees and constantly improve their skills
- Build an organizational culture and structure that allows both workers and the company to reach their potential
- Communicate the vision and the values of the company effectively and create an environment of trust among workers
- Motivate workers to higher levels of performance

Hiring the Right Employees: The Company's Future Depends on It

2. Describe the importance of hiring the right employees and how to avoid making hiring mistakes.

The decision to hire a new employee is an important one for every business, but its impact is magnified many times in a small company. Every "new hire" a business owner makes determines the heights to which the company can climb—or the depths to which it will plunge. "Bad hires" are incredibly expensive, and no organization, especially a small one, can afford too many of them. One study concluded that an employee hired into a typical entry-level position who quits after six months costs a company about $17,000 in salary, benefits, and training. In addition, the intangible costs—time invested in the new employee, lost opportunities, reduced morale among coworkers, and business setbacks— are seven times the direct costs of a bad hire. In other words, the total price tag for this bad hire is about $136,000![6]

For many companies, attracting and retaining qualified employees remains a challenge, but the problem is especially acute among rapidly growing small businesses. A comprehensive study of companies' hiring practices conducted by Staffing.org reports that:

- Staffing costs are rising overall, despite increased use of the Internet.
- New-hire quality is the top staffing priority for 70 percent of the companies surveyed.
- Companies have not traditionally differentiated between employees they want to retain and those they don't.
- The workforce shortage will get worse. Between 2000 and 2020, an estimated 76 million baby boomers will retire from the workforce, and only 45 million Generation Xers are in the pipeline to replace them.[7]

As crucial as finding good employees is to a small company's future, it is no easy task. One expert says that of every three employees a business hires, one makes a solid contribution, one is a marginal worker, and one is a hiring mistake.[8] For instance, the owner of two fast-food restaurants who copes with an annual employee turnover rate of 150 percent or more admits, "Sometimes we have to hire people, knowing that they aren't going to work out in the long term." Because employees' roles in a small company's success are magnified by the company's size, entrepreneurs can *least* afford to make hiring mistakes. Most often, those hiring mistakes come about because entrepreneurs rush into a hiring decision or they neglect to investigate thoroughly a candidate's qualifications and suitability for a job. Some small businesses spend more time and effort deciding which photocopier to lease than selecting an employee to fill a $40,000 a year job.

Although the importance of hiring decisions is magnified in small companies, small businesses are most likely to make hiring mistakes because they lack the human resources experts and the disciplined hiring procedures large companies have. In the early days of a company, entrepreneurs rarely take the time to create job descriptions and job specifications. Instead, they usually hire people because they know and trust them rather than for their job skills. As the company grows, business owners hire people to fit in around existing employees, often creating an unusual, inefficient organizational structure built around jobs that are poorly planned and designed.

The following guidelines can help small business managers avoid making costly hiring mistakes.

Create Practical Job Descriptions and Job Specifications

Small business owners must recognize that what they do *before* they ever start interviewing candidates for a position determines to a great extent how successful they will be at hiring winners. The first step is to perform a **job analysis,** the process by which a company

Table 19.1

Sample Job Description from the *Dictionary of Occupational Titles*

Worm picker: Gathers worms to be used as fish bait; walks about grassy areas, such as gardens, parks, and golf courses, and picks up earthworms (commonly called dew worms and night crawlers). Sprinkles chlorinated water on lawn to cause worms to come to the surface and locates worms by use of lantern or flashlight. Counts worms, sorts them, and packs them into containers for shipment.

determines the duties and nature of the jobs to be filled and the skills and experience required of the people who are to fill them. The first objective of a job analysis is to develop a job description, a written statement of the duties, responsibilities, reporting relationships, working conditions, and materials and equipment used in a job. A results-oriented **job description** explains what a job entails and the duties the person filling it is expected to perform. One business owner uses the following "recipe" for writing job descriptions in his company: job title, job summary, duties to be performed, nature of supervision, job's relationship to others in the company, working conditions, definitions of job-specific terms, and general comments needed to clarify any of these items.[9]

Preparing job descriptions may be one of the most important parts of the hiring process because it creates a "blueprint" for the job. Without this blueprint, managers tend to hire the person with experience whom they like the best. Useful sources of information for writing job descriptions include the manager's knowledge of the job, the workers currently holding the job, and the *Dictionary of Occupational Titles (DOT)*, available at most libraries. The *Dictionary of Occupational Titles*, published by the Department of Labor, lists more than 20,000 job titles and descriptions and serves as a useful tool for getting a small business owner started when writing job descriptions. Table 19.1 provides an example of a description drawn from the *DOT* for an unusual job.

The second objective of a job analysis is to create a **job specification,** a written statement of the qualifications and characteristics needed for a job stated in such terms as education, skills, and experience. A job specification shows the small business manager what kind of person to recruit and establishes the standards an applicant must meet to be hired. When writing job specifications, some managers define the traits a candidate needs to do a job well. Does the person have to be a good listener, empathetic, well organized, decisive, or a self-starter? A business owner about to hire a new employee who will be telecommuting from home, for instance, would look for someone with excellent communication skills, problem-solving ability, a strong work ethic, and the ability to use technology comfortably. Table 19.2 provides an example that links the tasks for a sales representative's job (drawn from a job description) to the traits or characteristics a small business owner identified as necessary to succeed in that job.

Table 19.2

Linking Tasks from the Job Description to the Traits Needed to Perform the Job

JOB TASK	TRAIT OR CHARACTERISTIC
Generate new leads and close new sales	Outgoing, persuasive, friendly
Make 15 "cold calls" per week	A self-starter, determined, optimistic, independent, confident
Analyze customer needs and recommend proper equipment	Good listener, patient, empathetic
Counsel customers about options and features required	Organized, polished speaker, "other" oriented
Prepare and explain financing methods; negotiate finance contracts	Honest, mathematically oriented, comfortable with numbers, understands basics of finance, computer literate
Retain existing customers	Relationship builder, customer focused

✦ GAINING *a* COMPETITIVE EDGE ✦

Hiring Character

It's easy enough to hire for capability. Experience and credentials are tangible, and we can verify them. We can test skills and measure them against a preset standard. That being said, what if you need to hire someone of high moral character? Most companies want leaders who *naturally* strive to do what's right. They need leaders whom employees and customers can trust. In today's environment of corporate scandals, hiring procedures still rarely attempt to gauge that side of a candidate.

One entrepreneur, Chuck Pappalardo, managing director of Trilogy Venture Search in Burlingame, California, is working on that. With the help of an ethicist, he has developed a method to guide the search for character.

1. *Conduct an internal audit to assess your company's values.* Does corporate culture allow and encourage people to do the right thing? Is character discussed among top policy makers? The point here is to determine how persons of character would fit in if they were hired.
2. *Profile the behaviors that your organization associates with character.* These fall under three categories: integrity, inspiring others, and humility. For integrity, a behavior might be "creates and sustains trust." Then develop interview questions that explore these behaviors. Many times, activities away from the corporate realm can say a lot about character. For example, the fact that the candidate

has held several responsible positions in volunteer agencies over a long period of time should not be overlooked when exploring character.

3. *To evaluate integrity, probe how a candidate confronts problems.* A Pappalardo question: "Tell me about a time you faced a grave financial dilemma or a difficult personal situation." The questions should be open-ended, forcing the candidate to say more than a sentence.
4. *To judge a person's ability to inspire, find out how that person deals with bad news and whether he or she is a consensus builder.* One good question is, "Tell me about a time you crafted a process or methodology to get a new result." Or ask about the last team the applicant built. What worked and what was least successful? Why?
5. *Gauge the individual's humility, or lack thereof.* Listen for unsubstantiated claims of accomplishment. Test the person's self-awareness. Ask, "What's the biggest misperception of you?" Says Pappalardo, "That's one of my favorites, because there are no misperceptions."

1. If you had to place a value on character and you were asked to rate it against all other factors in hiring, what percentage of 100 percent would you allocate to character? Why?

Source: Adapted from Keith H. Hammonds, "Test of Character: Developing a Method to Guide the Search for Character," *Fast Company,* November 2003, p. 40.

Plan an Effective Interview

Once managers know what they must look for in a job candidate, they can develop a plan for conducting an informative job interview. Too often, small business owners go into an interview unprepared, and, as a result, they fail to get the information they need to judge the candidate's qualifications, qualities, and suitability for the job. Conducting an effective interview requires small business owners to know what they want to get out of the interview in the first place and to develop a series of questions to extract that information. The following guidelines will help owners develop interview questions that will give them meaningful insight into an applicant's qualifications, personality, and character.

- *Develop a series of core questions and ask them of every candidate.* To give the screening process consistency, smart business owners rely on a set of relevant questions they ask in every interview. Of course, they also customize each interview using impromptu questions based on an individual's responses.
- *Ask open-ended questions rather than questions calling for "yes or no" answers.* Open-ended questions are most effective because they encourage candidates to talk about

their work experience in a way that will disclose the presence or the absence of the traits and characteristics business owners are seeking.

- *Create hypothetical situations candidates would be likely to encounter on the job and ask how they would handle them.* Building the interview around such questions gives owners a preview of the candidate's work habits and attitudes. Rather than telling interviewers about what candidates might do, these scenarios give them an idea of what candidates would do (or have done) in a job-related situation.
- *Probe for specific examples in the candidate's work experience that demonstrate the necessary traits and characteristics.* A common mistake interviewers make is failing to get candidates to provide the details they need to make an informed decision.
- *Ask candidates to describe a recent success and a recent failure and how they dealt with them.* Smart entrepreneurs look for candidates who describe both situations with equal enthusiasm because they know that peak performers put as much into their failures as they do their successes and usually learn something valuable from their failures.
- *Arrange a "noninterview" setting that allows several employees to observe the candidate in an informal setting.* Taking candidates on a plant tour or setting up a coffee break gives everyone a chance to judge a candidate's interpersonal skills and personality outside the formal interview process. These informal settings can be very revealing. One business owner was ready to extend a job offer to a candidate for a managerial position until he saw how the man mistreated a waitress who had made a mistake in his lunch order.

Table 19.3 shows an example of interview questions one manager uses to uncover the traits and characteristics he seeks in a top-performing sales representative.

Table 19.3

Interview Questions for Candidates for a Sales Representative Position

Trait or Characteristic	Question
Outgoing, persuasive, friendly, a self-starter, determined, optimistic, independent, confident	How do you persuade reluctant prospects to buy? Can you give an example?
Good listener, patient, empathetic, organized, polished speaker, "other" oriented	What would you say to a fellow salesperson who was getting more than her share of rejections and was having difficulty getting appointments?
Honest, customer oriented, relationship builder	How do you feel when someone questions the truth of what you say? Can you give an example of successfully overcoming this situation?

Other questions:

If you owned a company, why would you hire yourself?

If you were head of your department, what would you do differently? Why?

How do you acknowledge the contributions of others in your department?

IN THE FOOTSTEPS OF AN ENTREPRENEUR . . .

How Would You Answer?

Inc. magazine asked a number of entrepreneurs about the most innovative questions that they use during employee interviews and why they ask the questions. Following are a few of the questions and the entrepreneurs' reasons for asking them.

1. Jim Sheward (Fiberlink, Blue Bell, Pennsylvania)

Question: "What's the biggest career mistake you've made so far?"

Reason: "I've found that those who can't think of anything either don't take risks or aren't telling me the truth."

2. John Discerni (Physicians Formulation International, Phoenix, Arizona)

Question: "What's the last book you've read?"
Reason: "It's not what they read so much as the amount of time it takes them to answer the question: If you have to think a long time, they probably aren't that well read."

3. Tony Petrucciani (Single Source Systems, Fisher, Indiana)

Question: "Why do they make manhole covers round?"
Reason: "We ask this of potential developers to see if they get flustered, and how they think on their feet."

4. Robert Baden (Rochester Software Associates, Rochester, New York)

Question: "If I stood you next to a sky-scraper and gave you a barometer, how could you figure out how tall the building was?"
Reason: The answer: Well, there really isn't one. Baden just wants to see how creative people are.

5. Doug Chapiensky (Center Point Solutions, Denver, Colorado)

Question: "If you had your own company, what would it do?"
Reason: "I want to see if they've got that certain entrepreneurial spirit it takes to succeed in a small software company."

Source: Adapted from "101 Great Ideas for Managing People from America's Most Innovative Small Companies," *Inc.*, October 21, 1999, www.inc.com/articles/1999/10/19238.html.

Conduct the Interview

An effective interview contains three phases: breaking the ice, asking questions, and selling the candidate on the company.

Breaking the Ice. In the opening phase of the interview the manager's primary job is to diffuse the tension that exists because of the nervousness of both parties. Many skilled interviewers use the job description to explain the nature of the job and the company's

"Having spent the last six years of my life reading, writing and studying, I'd like to find an executive position that doesn't require any mental activity."

culture to the applicant. Then they use icebreakers—questions about a hobby or special interest—to get the candidate to relax. In most cases these "icebreaker" questions allow the interviewer an opportunity to gain valuable insight into the person. These are questions that generate little or no pressure and the interviewee can feel free to expound on

Company Example →

something he or she knows a great deal about. *For instance, to loosen up one very nervous but promising candidate, one entrepreneur asked about the candidate's hobby, military history. "He launched into a description of the Battle of Midway that was so enthralling, I told him, 'Since you come across like this, I'm going to give you a shot,' " recalls the business owner. "He went on to become a star salesman."*[10]

Asking Questions. During the second phase of the interview, employers ask the questions from their question bank to determine the applicant's suitability for the job. Employers' primary job at this point is to *listen.* Effective interviewers spend about 25 percent of the interview talking and about 75 percent listening. They also take notes during the interview to help them ask follow-up questions based on a candidate's comments and to evaluate a candidate after the interview is over. Experienced interviewers also pay close attention to a candidate's nonverbal clues, or body language, during the interview. They know that candidates may be able to say exactly what they want with their words but that the candidate's body language does not lie!

Some of the most valuable interview questions attempt to gain insight into the candidate's ability to reason, be logical, and to be creative. Known as **puzzle interviews,** the goal is to determine how job candidates think by asking them offbeat, unexpected questions such as, "How would you weigh an airplane without scales?", "Why are manhole covers round?", or "How would you determine the height of a building using only a barometer?" Usually, the logic and creativity a candidate uses to derive an answer is

Company Example →

much more important than the answer itself. *Todd Eberhardt, founder of Comm-Works, a small voice and data technology company in Minneapolis, Minnesota, uses puzzle interviews as part of his company's selection process. "I look at it as a part of the overall solution when you're evaluating talent," he says. "You can really get some insight into a person's thought pattern."*[11]

Another type of interview that is becoming more popular is the **situational interview,** in which the interviewer gives candidates a typical job-related situation (sometimes in the form of a role-playing exercise) to see how they respond to it. One entrepreneur had a candidate deal with an "angry customer," who was played by a fellow interviewer.

Company Example →

Kim Lopez, owner of Remedy Interactive Inc., an ergonomics software company, began using situational interviews after she made several consecutive hiring mistakes. Combining the technique with traditional interview techniques and thorough reference checks, Lopez says her company's hiring process is much improved. Recently, she asked a candidate to lead her staff in a brainstorming session. The candidate prepared an impressive presentation and handled the session so well that he got the job. Studies show that situational interviews have a 54 percent accuracy rate in predicting future job performance, much higher than the 7 percent accuracy rate of the traditional interview.[12]

Entrepreneurs must be careful to make sure they avoid asking candidates illegal questions. At one time, interviewers could ask wide-ranging questions covering just about every area of an applicant's background. Today, interviewing is a veritable minefield of legal liabilities waiting to explode in the unsuspecting interviewer's face. Companies are more vulnerable to job discrimination lawsuits now than ever before. Although the Equal Employment Opportunity Commission (EEOC), the government agency responsible for enforcing employment laws, does not outlaw specific interview questions, it does recognize that some questions can result in employment discrimination. If a candidate files charges of discrimination against a company, the burden of proof shifts to the employer

Table 19.4

Is It Legal?

Some interview questions can lead an employer into a lawsuit. Review the following questions and then decide if they are legal or illegal.

LEGAL	ILLEGAL	INTERVIEW QUESTION
❏	❏	Are you currently using illegal drugs?
❏	❏	Have you ever been arrested?
❏	❏	Do you have any children or do you plan to have children?
❏	❏	When and where were you born?
❏	❏	Is there any limit on your ability to work overtime or travel?
❏	❏	How tall are you? How much do you weigh?
❏	❏	Do you drink alcohol?
❏	❏	How much alcohol do you drink each week?
❏	❏	Would your religious beliefs interfere with your ability to do the job?
❏	❏	What contraceptive practices do you use?
❏	❏	Are you HIV positive?
❏	❏	Have you ever filed a lawsuit or worker's comp claim on a former employer?
❏	❏	Do you have physical/mental disabilities that would interfere with doing your job?
❏	❏	Are you a U.S. citizen?

Answers: 1. Legal. 2. Illegal. Employers cannot ask about an applicant's arrest record, but they can ask if a candidate has ever been *convicted* of a crime. 3. Illegal. Employers cannot ask questions that could lead to discrimination against a particular group (e.g., women, physically challenged, etc.). 4. Illegal. The Civil Rights Act of 1964 bans discrimination on the basis of race, color, sex, religion, or national origin. 5. Legal. 6. Illegal. Unless a person's physical characteristics are necessary for job performance (e.g., lifting 100-pound sacks of mulch), employers cannot ask candidates such questions. 7. Legal. 8. Illegal. Notice the fine line between question 7 and question 8; this is what makes interviewing challenging. 9. Illegal. This question would violate the Civil Rights Act of 1964. 10. Illegal. What relevance would this have to an employee's job performance? 11. Illegal. Under the Americans with Disabilities Act, which prohibits discrimination against people with disabilities, people that are HIV positive or have AIDS are considered "disabled." 12. Illegal. Workers who file such suits are protected from retribution by a variety of federal and state laws. 13. Illegal. This question also would violate the Americans with Disabilities Act. 14. Illegal. This question violates the Civil Rights Act of 1964.

to prove that all preemployment questions were job related and nondiscriminatory. In addition, many states have passed laws that forbid the use of certain questions or screening tools in interviews. To avoid trouble, business owners should keep in mind why they are asking a particular question. The goal is to find someone who is qualified to do the job well. By steering clear of questions about subjects that are peripheral to the job itself, employers are less likely to ask questions that will land them in court. Wise business owners ask their attorneys to review their bank of questions before using them in an interview. Table 19.4 offers a quiz to help you understand which kinds of questions are most likely to create charges of discrimination, and Table 19.5 describes a simple test for determining whether an interview question might be considered discriminatory.

Table 19.5

A Guide for Interview Questions

Small business owners can use the "OUCH" test as a guide for determining whether an interview question might be considered discriminatory:

■ Does the question **O**mit references to race, religion, color, sex, or national origin?
■ Does the question **U**nfairly screen out a particular class of people?
■ Can you **C**onsistently apply the question to every applicant?
■ Does the question **H**ave job-relatedness and business necessity?

Selling the Candidate on the Company. In the final phase of the interview, when employers have a "high-potential" candidate, they should try to sell the benefits of working for the company. This phase begins by allowing the candidate to ask questions about the company, the job, or other issues. Again, experienced interviewers note the nature of these questions and the insights they give into the candidate's personality. This part of the interview offers employers a prime opportunity to explain to the candidate why their company is an attractive place to work. The best candidates will have other offers, and it's up to you to make sure they leave the interview wanting to work for your company. Finally, before closing the interview, employers should thank the candidates and tell them what happens next (e.g., "We'll be contacting you about our decision within two weeks").

Check References

Small business owners should take the time to check *every* applicant's references. Although many business owners see checking references as a formality and pay little attention to it, others realize the need to protect themselves (and their customers) from hiring unscrupulous workers. Is a reference check really necessary? Absolutely! A survey conducted by an executive search firm found that more than 10 percent of candidates lie on their résumés.[13] Checking references thoroughly can help an employer uncover false or exaggerated information. Failing to do so can be costly.

Company Example → *One small company became the subject of an expensive lawsuit when the owner failed to check the references of a newly hired sales representative. While driving to a sales call, the employee, who was intoxicated, caused an accident that severely injured another person. The lawsuit came about when the injured party discovered that the sales representative had been fired from his three previous jobs for drunkenness, something a reference check would have revealed.*[14] Rather than rely only on the references candidates list on their résumés, experienced employers call an applicant's previous employers and talk to their immediate supervisors to get a clear picture of the applicant's job performance, character, and work habits.

Conduct Employment Tests

Although various state and federal laws have made using employment tests as screening devices more difficult in recent years, many companies find them quite useful. To avoid charges of discrimination, business owners must be able to prove that the employment tests they use are both valid and reliable. A **valid test** is one that measures what it is intended to measure: for example, aptitude for selling, creativity, integrity. A **reliable test** is one that measures consistently over time. Employers must also be sure that the tests they use measure aptitudes and factors that are job related. Many testing organizations offer ready-made tests that have been proved to be both valid and reliable, and business owners can use these tests safely. In today's environment, if a test has not been validated and proven to be reliable or is not job related, it's best not to use it.

Experienced small business owners don't rely on any one element in the employee selection process. They look at the total picture painted by each part of a candidate's portfolio. They know that the hiring process provides them with one of the most valuable raw materials their companies count on for success—capable, hardworking people. They also recognize that hiring an employee is not a single event but the beginning of a long-term relationship.

IN THE FOOTSTEPS OF AN ENTREPRENEUR...

Will the Last One Out Please Lock the Door?

Imagine working for a company in which there are no policies governing working hours, time off, sick leave, personal days, or vacation time. Sounds like a recipe for chaos, mayhem, and organizational inefficiency? As anarchical as it sounds, Greg Strakosch, CEO of TechTarget in Needham, Massachusetts, makes it work for the 210 employees at the interactive media company he founded in 2000. Employees are free to come and go as they please. "I detest bureaucracy and silly policies," says Strakosch. "A set number of sick days strikes me as arbitrary and dumb."

Shoshana Zuboff, a professor of business administration at Harvard University, hails TechTarget's approach to organizational structure, job design, and human resource management. Because TechTarget's highly skilled, intellectual workforce is one of its primary strengths, Zuboff says it makes no sense for the company to treat workers using the command and control philosophy of the industrial age. "We should be beyond trusting employees to do good work but not trusting them to be honest and upright about managing their time," she says.

Just because Strakosch gives workers the freedom to determine their work schedules, however, does not mean that he does not set high standards for performance. To the contrary, TechTarget is "an entirely results-oriented business," says Strakosch. "The open leave policy is a competitive weapon." The policy is one of the main reasons the company's sales have climbed 30 percent in just two years, exceeding $35 million a year. TechTarget's goal is to attract the best, most capable knowledge workers, and the open leave policy enables Strakosch to do just that. He believes that providing employees the freedom and the autonomy to do their jobs well is instrumental in maintaining the quality of the services TechTarget provides its clients. Naming TechTarget to the Boston area's "Best Places to Work" list, *Boston Business Journal* publisher Mike Olivieri says, "Accommodating employees' personal needs pays back dividends of loyalty and productivity."

Employees work closely with managers to set quarterly goals, objectives, and timetables for performance but have plenty of independence to achieve them. Strakosch and his managers set the performance bar high, however. "This is not a country club," he states. Most employees work 50 hours—sometimes more—a week, and when they are away from the office, they must remain accessible via cell phone, e-mail, or instant-messaging, all of which are technology tools that make the company's open leave policy possible in the first place. Mary Beth Cadwell, TechTarget's art director and a serious triathlete, enjoys the flexibility her job provides so much that she would not consider working at another company. "I couldn't work somewhere where I wasn't allowed to take an afternoon off for a bike ride," she says. Mothers with young children, who make up more than 10 percent of TechTarget's workforce, appreciate the flexibility the open leave policy provides them. "I never worry about choosing between being a good mother and a good employee," says one.

Strakosch admits that the policy does not suit some employees. TechTarget uses an exhaustive screening process to find workers who are responsible self-starters who enjoy autonomy, but some employees have abused the policy and were fired. Strakosch dismissed others simply because they could not produce the results the company demands in an unstructured work environment. Strakosch plans to stick with the open leave policy, however. He sees it as a key part of his company's competitive strategy, it works, and it allows him to coach his three kids' sports teams during the day!

1. What advantages does TechTarget's open leave policy give the company and its employees? What are the risks associated with such a policy?
2. Work with a small team of your classmates to develop a series of interview questions that would help TechTarget managers identify candidates who would best fit the company's culture.
3. Would an open leave policy such as the one TechTarget uses work for other small companies? Explain.

Sources: Adapted from Patrick J. Sauer, "Open-Door Management," *Inc.,* June 2003, p. 44; "Comcast Corporation Tops *Boston Business Journal*'s Second Annual 'Best Places to Work,' " *Boston Business Journal,* May 27, 2004, boston.bizjournals.com/boston/stories/2004/05/24/daily38.html; "In the News," TechTarget, www.techtarget.com/html/printhenews.htm.

Building the Right Culture and Organizational Structure

Culture

3. Explain how to build the kind of company culture and structure to support the entrepreneur's mission and goals and to motivate employees to achieve them.

Company culture is the distinctive, unwritten code of conduct that governs the behavior, attitudes, relationships, and style of an organization. It is the essence of "the way we do things around here." In many small companies, culture plays as important a part in gaining a competitive edge as strategy does. A company's culture has a powerful impact on the way people work together in a business, how they do their jobs, and how they treat their customers. Company culture manifests itself in many ways—from how workers dress and act to the language they use. At some companies, the unspoken dress code requires workers to wear suits and ties, but at many high technology companies, employees routinely show up in jeans, T-shirts, and flip-flops. At one such company, an employee says, "If someone shows up for work in a suit, everyone immediately assumes that he is interviewing for another job."

In many companies, the culture creates its own language. At Disney theme parks workers are not "employees;" they are "cast members." They don't merely go to work; their jobs are "parts in a performance." Customers are referred to as "guests." When a cast member treats someone to lunch, it's "on the mouse." Anything negative—such as a cigarette butt on a walkway—is "a bad Mickey," and anything positive is "a good Mickey."

The culture of the organization reflects the deep-seated philosophy of the founder or executives on how the people in the organization should behave toward the customers as well as toward each other. A company's culture arises from an entrepreneur's consistent and relentless pursuit of a set of core values that everyone in the company can believe in. *For instance, Amy Miller, founder of Amy's Ice Creams, a small chain of gourmet ice cream shops, knows her company's competitive edge comes not only from selling quality products and friendly service but also from selling entertainment. Miller hires employees who enjoy performing for customers. They juggle their serving spades, toss scoops of ice cream to one another behind the counter, and dance on top of the freezer. Walking into an Amy's Ice Cream Shop, customers might see employees wearing pajamas (on Sleepover Night), or have candles (on Romance Night), or strobe lights (on Disco Night) decorating the store. Because of the culture Miller has created, employees know that part of their jobs is to create fun and entertainment for their customers; that's one reason they keep coming back!*[15]

Nurturing the right culture in a company can enhance a company's competitive position by improving its ability to attract and retain quality workers and by creating an environment in which workers can grow and develop. In fact, as a younger generation of employees enters the workforce, companies are finding that offering a more open and relaxed culture gives them an edge in attracting the best workers. Like Amy's Ice Creams, these companies embrace nontraditional, relaxed, fun cultures that incorporate concepts such as casual dress, virtual teams, telecommuting, flexible work schedules, on-site massages, cappuccinos in company cafeterias, and other cutting-edge concepts. Today's organizational culture relies on several principles that are fundamental to creating a productive, fun workplace. These are:

▪ *Respect for the quality of work and a balance between work life and home life.* Modern companies must recognize that their employees have lives away from work. These businesses offer flexible work schedules, part-time work, job sharing, telecommuting, sabbaticals, and conveniences such as on-site day care or concierge services that handle employees' errands. Work/life balance issues are becoming more important to employees, and companies that address them have an edge when it comes to recruiting and retaining a quality workforce. "Employers realize that by offering

Company Example →

Company Example →

work/life programs, they are getting a lot in return in terms of productivity and commitment to the organization," says one consultant.[16]

After sacrificing most of his time and his life to his first start-up, Jeff Soderberg, founder of Software Technology Group (STG), a company that provides IT consultants to other businesses, decided that there was more to life than just work, and he built STG's culture around that philosophy. Soderberg typically leaves his Salt Lake City office at 5 P.M. to enjoy his hobby of rock climbing, and he encourages all of his employees to work no more than 40 hours a week and to take time to pursue their interests. Vice-president Lynn Labarge enjoys her passion–fly fishing–and account manager Jim Crouch, an avid skier and bicyclist, keeps his bike parked near his desk. "We have to make sure our consultants don't burn out," says Solderberg. "We have to think long-term in a business where everyone else is thinking short-term."[17]

- *A sense of purpose.* These companies rely on a strong sense of purpose to connect employees to the company's mission. At motorcycle legend Harley-Davidson, employees are so in tune with the company's mission that some of them have tattooed the company's name on their bodies!

- *Diversity.* Companies with appealing cultures not only accept cultural diversity in their workforces, they embrace it, actively seeking out workers with different backgrounds. They recognize that a workforce that has a rich mix of cultural diversity gives their companies more talent, skills, and abilities from which to draw. Because the entire world is now a potential market for many small companies, entrepreneurs realize that having their workforces look, act, and think like their customers, with all of their ethnic, racial, religious, and behavioral variety, is a strength. Experts estimate that by 2040, 70 percent of workers in the United States will be members of what are considered to be minorities.[18]

- *Integrity.* Employees want to work for a company that stands for honesty and integrity. They do not want to have to check their personal value systems at the door when they report to work. Indeed, many workers take pride in the fact they work for a company that is ethical and socially responsible. We will discuss the issues of ethics, integrity, and social responsibility in more detail in Chapter 21.

- *Participative management.* Modern managers recognize that employees expect a participative management style to be part of a company's culture. Today's workforce does not respond well to the autocratic management styles of yesteryear. To maximize productivity and encourage commitment to accomplishing the company's mission, entrepreneurs must trust and empower employees at all levels of the organization to make decisions and to take the actions they must to do their jobs well.

- *Learning environment.* Progressive companies encourage and support lifelong learning among their employees. They are willing to invest in their employees, improving their skills and helping them to reach their full potential. That attitude is a strong magnet for the best and brightest workers, who know that to stay at the top of their fields, they must always be learning. *At Stellar Solutions, an aerospace engineering services firm founded by Celeste Volz Ford in 1995, employees receive a generous benefit package, including a variety of insurance coverage and a company-sponsored flexible spending account they can use for extra medical expenses, child care, or vacation. In addition to the six weeks of vacation they receive, employees can spend another week at training sessions or conferences. In fact, if they fail to use their allotted time for training, employees cannot qualify for their full bonuses.[19]*

Company Example →

Companies that build their cultures on these principles have an edge when it comes to attracting, retaining, and motivating workers. In other words, creating the right culture helps a small company compete more effectively.

Managing Growth and a Changing Culture. As companies grow from seedling businesses into leggy saplings and beyond (perhaps into giants in the business forest), they often experience dramatic changes in their culture. Procedures become more formal, operations grow more widespread, jobs take on more structure, communication becomes more difficult, and the company's personality begins to change. As more workers come on board, employees find it more difficult to know everyone in the company and what their jobs are. Unless entrepreneurs work hard to maintain their company's unique culture, they may wake up one day to find that they have sacrificed that culture—and the competitive edge that went with it—in the name of growth.

Ironically, growth can sometimes be a small company's biggest enemy, causing a once successful business to spiral out of control into oblivion. The problem stems from the fact that the organizational structure (or lack of it!) and the style of management that makes an entrepreneurial start-up so successful often cannot support the business as it grows into adolescence and maturity. As a company grows, not only does its culture tend to change but so does the need for a management infrastructure capable of supporting that growth. Compounding the problem is the entrepreneur's tendency to see all growth as good. After all, who wouldn't want to be the founder of a small company whose rapid growth makes it destined to become the next rising star in the industry? Yet, achieving rapid growth and managing it are two distinct challenges. Entrepreneurs must be aware of the challenges rapid growth brings with it; otherwise, they may find their companies crumbling around them as they reach warp speed. *Gary Erickson, founder of Clif-Bar, the maker of one of the top-selling brands of energy bars, has seen his company grow from a tiny start-up in 1992 to a company with 130 employees and more than $100 million in sales today. For the past five years, sales have been climbing at 30 percent a year, a rate that has strained both the company's unique culture and its management structure. "We're at a point where we have to find a way to maintain this open culture while getting bigger," says Erickson. "It's a balancing act."*[20]

> Company Example

In many cases, small companies achieve impressive growth because they bypass the traditional organizational structures, forgo rigid policies and procedures, and maintain maximum flexibility. Small companies often have the edge over their larger rivals because they are naturally quick to respond, they concentrate on creating new product and service lines, and they are willing to take the risks necessary to conquer new markets.

Growth brings with it change: changes in management style, organizational strategy, and methods of operation. Growth introduces organizational complexity. In this period of transition, an entrepreneur's challenge is to walk a fine line between retaining the small company traits that are the seeds of the company's success and incorporating the elements of infrastructure that are essential to supporting and sustaining the company's growth.

IN THE FOOTSTEPS OF AN ENTREPRENEUR...

What's *Your* Company's Personality?

Every business has its own unique culture and personality, but research shows that the perceptions that owners have of their companies' personalities often are quite different from customers' and employees' perceptions. Which perception is most accurate? Thanks to entrepreneur Sandra Feteke, business owners can find out. While working as a marketing consultant, Feteke noticed that the characteristics the companies' top executives described to her over the phone or in e-mails did not reflect the actual characteristics of those same companies when she walked on site and began talking to employees and customers. This strange disconnect between perception and reality occurred so frequently that Feteke developed a theory that as they grow, companies take on a life of their own, developing personality traits and quirks that sometimes are radically different from the personalities of the founder and the staff.

To test her theory, Feteke launched her own company, Feteke + Co., which she built around CAP2, a personality test for businesses based on the popular Myers-Briggs personality inventory used by colleges, companies, and others to evaluate the personality traits of individuals. When Feteke submitted her own company to the personality profile, she found that her business was typical: Its personality did not match her personality or that of any of her staff, but the test did describe the organization accurately. "Our company had a bull-headed personality," she recalls, "a type that was convinced it was right and took exception to being questioned." Based on the results of the personality profile, Feteke set out to change her company's personality to better align it with her goals. Rather than meeting with a client about a marketing project and then working independently to create a marketing campaign, Feteke added making client contacts to her to-do list and to those of her staff. She also instituted a quarterly "meeting of the minds" with every client to discuss marketing strategies face to face. Surveys show that clients now see the company as more responsive to their needs, and Feteke has landed many new accounts based on recommendations of satisfied clients.

Like the Myers-Briggs test, Feteke's company personality test defines 16 different organizational types. One of the most common organizational profiles is "Playing by the Rules," which describes those companies in which dependability is a hallmark, quality and customer service rein supreme, but innovation is not a strength. At the other end of the spectrum is the "Fun to Do Good Work" profile, which describes companies that are flexible and fast-moving and where innovation is a key characteristic. In her book that describes her work, *Companies Are People Too*, Feteke says that entrepreneurs who take the time to understand their companies' personality profiles can more readily build on their businesses' strengths, improve on weaknesses, and improve the focus on core values.

Bob Rothschild, CEO of gourmet food manufacturer Robert Rothschild Berry Farm in Urbana, Ohio,

did just that. Rothschild was disappointed to learn that his company fit the "Playing by the Rules" profile because he considered the ability to innovate to be a key success factor in his industry. His strategy was to emphasize the company's existing strengths in its marketing strategy and its customer relationships while creating an in-house "think tank" to enhance innovation. For instance, twice each month, employees get together in cross-departmental brainstorming sessions to generate new ideas for the company. Revenues have climbed 25 percent, most of which Rothschild attributes to the changes made as a result of the personality profile.

After profiling his advertising agency, Mike Schwabl, owner of Dixon Schwabl, which is based in Victor, New York, also saw the need for more innovation in the company. "We were always known as a company that could crank things out and give our customers a quick turnaround," says Schwabl. Meeting tight deadlines, however, was limiting the creativity of his staff, so Schwabl decided to make some organizational changes. He approached Dixon Schwabl clients and explained that producing quality work takes more time, removing the intense deadlines the staff was used to dealing with. He also created a more playful work environment, giving everyone in the company a water gun and installing a slide employees can take to get from the second floor to the first. Schwabl instituted weekly team creative lunches and staff outings and gave employees more responsibility and autonomy to do their jobs. A year after making the changes, Schwabl tested the agency's personality again, and this time it fit the "Fun to Do Good Work" profile—a spontaneous, innovative, energetic place to work. "Our employees are more motivated to do great work," he says, "and it's become easier to attract new clients."

1. What can entrepreneurs learn by submitting their companies to a personality profile test such as the one Feteke has developed?
2. How can entrepreneurs use the results of a company personality profile to improve their companies?

Sources: Adapted from Bobbie Gossage, "Mom & Pop Psychology," *Inc.,* December 2003, pp. 38–40; Eric Schoeniger, "Up With Companies (Including Yours)," *Unisys Exec Online,* October 2003, www.unisys.com/execmag/strategy/internal/leadership/2003_10_dialog1.htm; Sarah Reicks, "Author to Discuss the Importance of a Company's 'Personality'," *Quad City Business Journal,* August 31, 2004, www.unisys.com/execmag/strategy/internal/leadership/2003_10_dialog1.htm.

Organizational Evolution

When the opportunity to grow presents itself and the organization's resources and capabilities support expansion, the initial component of success may lie in the founder's willingness to evolve the firm from a top-down, single-leader structure to one that is more team based. The founder must accept that size and complexity create situations that require delegating authority and empowering employees. Team-based management enables the founder to draw on the talents and skills of the entire organization.

Team-Based Management. Although large companies have been using self-directed work teams for years to improve quality, increase productivity, raise morale, lower costs, and boost motivation, team-based management is just now beginning to catch on in small firms. In fact, a team approach may be best suited for small companies. A **self-directed work team** is a group of workers from different functional areas of a company who work together as a unit largely without supervision, making decisions and performing tasks that once belonged only to managers. Some teams may be temporary, attacking and solving a specific problem, but many are permanent components of an organization's structure. As their name implies, these teams manage themselves, performing such functions as setting work schedules, ordering raw materials, evaluating and purchasing equipment, developing budgets, hiring and firing team members, solving problems, and a host of other activities. The goal is to get people working together to serve customers better.

Managers in companies using teams don't just sit around drinking coffee, however. In fact, they work just as hard as before, but the nature of their work changes dramatically. Before teams, managers were bosses who made most of the decisions affecting their subordinates alone and hoarded information and power for themselves. In a team environment, managers take on the role of coaches who empower those around them to make decisions affecting their work and share information with workers. As facilitators, their job is to support and to serve the teams functioning in the organization and to make sure they produce results.

Companies have strong, competitive reasons for using team-based management. Companies that use teams effectively report significant gains in quality, reductions in cycle time, lower costs, increased customer satisfaction, and improved employee motivation and morale. A team-based approach is not for every organization, however. Teams are *not* easy to start, and switching from a traditional organizational structure to a team-based one is filled with potential pitfalls. Teams work best in environments in which the work is interdependent and people must interact to accomplish their goals. Although a team approach might succeed in a small plant making gas grills, it would most likely fail miserably in a real estate office, where salespeople work independently with little interaction required to make a sale. Table 19.6 describes some of the transitions a company must make as it moves from a traditional organizational structure to a team-based style.

In some cases, teams have been a company's salvation from failure and extinction; in others, the team approach has flopped. What makes the difference? What causes teams to fail? The following errors are common:

- Assigning a team an inappropriate task, one in which the team members may lack the necessary skills to be successful (lack of training and support).
- Creating work teams but failing to provide the team with meaningful performance targets.
- Failing to deal with known underperformers and assuming that being part of a group will solve the problem. It doesn't.
- Failing to compensate the members of the team equitably.

Table 19.6

Making the Transition from a Traditional Organizational Structure to a Team-Based Style

TRADITIONAL ORGANIZATION	TEAM-BASED ORGANIZATION
Management driven	Customer driven
Isolated specialists	Multiskilled workforce
Many job descriptions	Few job descriptions
Information limited	Information shared
Many management levels	Few management levels
Departmental focus	Whole-business focus
Management controlled	Team regulated
Policy and procedure based	Values and principles based
Selection-based employment	Training-based employment
Temporary changes	Ongoing changes
Seemingly organized	Seemingly chaotic
Incremental improvement	Continuous improvement
High management commitment	High worker commitment

Source: Kenneth P. De Meuse and Thomas J. Bergmann, "Managers Must Relinquish Control If They Are to Establish Effective Work Teams," *Small Business Forum*, Spring 1996, p. 86.

To ensure teams' success, entrepreneurs must:

- *Make sure that teams are appropriate for the company and the nature of the work.* A good starting point is to create a "map" of the company's work flow that shows how workers build a product or deliver a service. Is the work interdependent, complex, and interactive? Would teamwork improve the company's performance?
- *Form teams around the natural work flow and give them specific tasks to accomplish.* Teams can be effective only if managers challenge them to accomplish specific, measurable objectives. They need targets to shoot for.
- *Provide adequate support and training for team members and leaders.* Team success requires a new set of skills. Workers must learn how to communicate, resolve conflict, support one another, and solve problems as a team. Smart managers see that team members get the training they need.
- *Involve team members in determining how their performances will be measured, what will be measured, and when it will be measured.* Doing so gives team members a sense of ownership and pride about the tasks they are accomplishing.
- *Make at least part of team members' pay dependent on team performance.* Companies that have used teams successfully still pay members individually, but they make successful teamwork a major part of an individual's performance review.

Figure 19.1 illustrates the four stages teams go through on their way to performing effectively and reaching set goals.

Communicating Effectively

4. Understand the potential barriers to effective communication and describe how to overcome them.

Like all leaders, entrepreneurs constantly confront dilemmas as they operate their businesses. Frequently, they must walk the fine line between the chaos involved in encouraging creativity and maintaining control over their companies. At other times, they must steer their companies around those questionable actions that might produce large short-term gains into those that are ethical. As leaders, an important and highly visible part of their jobs is to communicate the values, beliefs, and principles for which their business stands. A leader's foremost job is to communicate the company's vision. It is a job that never ends. "The essence of leadership today is to make sure that the organization knows itself," says one entrepreneur when asked about his job as a

Figure 19.1

The Stages of Team Development

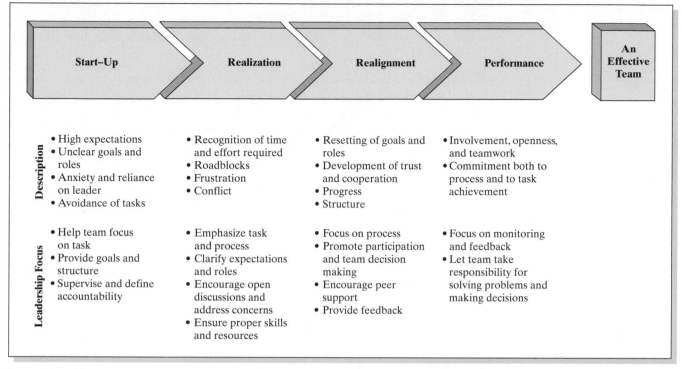

Sources: Adapted from Mark A. Frohman, "Do Teams ... But Do Them Right," *Industry Week,* April 3, 1995, p. 22; "The Stages of a Group," *Communication Briefings,* October 1997, p. 6.

leader. "There are certain durable principles that underlie an organization. The leader should embody those values. They're fundamental."[21] Nowhere is this skill more important than among entrepreneurs, whose organizations are predicated on their founders' ability to communicate a vision and a set of values that everyone in the company can embrace.

Improving Communication

Managers spend about 80 percent of their time in some form of communication. To some managers communicating means only one thing: sending messages to others. Although talking to people both inside and outside the organization is an important part of an entrepreneur's job, the other important aspect of an entrepreneur's job as chief communicator is listening.

Communicating Effectively. One of the most frustrating experiences for entrepreneurs occurs when they ask an employee to do something and nothing happens. Although entrepreneurs are quick to perceive the failure to respond as the employee's lack of motivation or weak work ethic, often the culprit is improper communication. The primary reasons employees don't do what they are expected to do have little to do with their motivation and desire to work. Instead, workers often fail to do what they are supposed to because:

- They don't know what to do.
- They don't know how to do it.
- They don't have the authority to do it.

■ They get no feedback on how well or how poorly they are doing it.

■ They are either ignored or punished for doing it right.

■ They realize that no one ever notices even if they *are* doing it right.

The common thread running through all of these causes is poor communication between business owner and employee. What barriers to effective communication must entrepreneurs overcome?

■ *Managers and employees don't always feel free to say what they really mean.* CEOs and top managers in companies of any size seldom hear the truth about problems and negative results from employees. This less-than-honest feedback results from the hesitancy of subordinates to tell the boss bad news. Over time, this tendency can paralyze the upward communication in a company.

■ *Ambiguity blocks real communication.* The same words can have different meanings to different people, especially in modern companies, where the workforce is likely to be highly diverse. For instance, a business owner may tell an employee to "take care of this customer's problem as soon as you can." The owner may have meant "solve this problem by the end of the day" but the employee may think that fixing the problem by the end of the week will meet the owner's request.

■ *Information overload causes the message to get lost.* With information from mail, telephone, faxes, e-mail, face-to-face communication, and other sources, employees in modern organizations are literally bombarded with messages. With such a large volume of information washing over workers, it is easy for some messages to get lost.

■ *Selective listening interferes with the communication process.* Sometimes people hear only what they want to hear, selectively tuning in and out on a speaker's message. The result is distorted communication.

■ *Defense mechanisms block a message.* When people are confronted with information that upsets them or conflicts with their perceptions, they immediately put up defenses. Defense mechanisms range from verbally attacking the source of the message to twisting perceptions of reality to maintain self-esteem.

■ *Conflicting verbal and nonverbal messages confuse listeners.* Nonverbal communication includes a speaker's mannerisms, gestures, posture, facial expressions, and other forms of body language. When a speaker sends conflicting verbal and nonverbal messages, research shows that listeners will believe the nonverbal message almost every time.

How can entrepreneurs overcome these barriers to become better communicators? The following tips will help:

■ *Clarify your message before you attempt to communicate it.* Before attempting to communicate your message, identify exactly what you want the receiver to think and do as a result of the message. Then focus on getting that point across clearly and concisely.

■ *Use face-to-face communication whenever possible.* Although not always practical, face-to-face communication reduces the likelihood of misunderstandings because it allows for immediate feedback and nonverbal clues.

■ *Be empathetic.* Try to put yourself in the place of those who will receive your message and develop it accordingly. Be sure to tell your audience up front what's in it for them.

■ *Match your message to your audience.* Business owners would be very unlikely to use the same words, techniques, and style to communicate their company's financial position to a group of industry analysts as they would to a group of workers on the factory floor. One study examined the importance of matching the message to the audience. RHI Consulting reports that 40 percent of chief information officers it recently polled find translating complex technical information into laypersons' terms is their greatest challenge in working with end users. Tips for ensuring effective communication with end users include avoiding buzzwords, not assuming people understand complex topics, showing empathy when confronted with confusion, coming to an employee's desk rather than trying to explain a tech-fix over the phone, and remaining patient in the face of frustration.[22]

■ *Be organized.* Effective communicators organize their messages so that their audiences can understand them easily.

■ *Encourage feedback.* Allow listeners to ask questions and to offer feedback. Sometimes employees are hesitant to ask the boss any questions for fear of "looking stupid." One useful technique, especially when giving instructions, is to ask workers to repeat the message to make sure they understand it correctly.

■ *Tell the truth.* The fastest way to destroy your credibility as a leader is to lie.

■ *Don't be afraid to tell employees about the business, its performance, and the forces that affect it.* Too often, entrepreneurs assume that employees don't care about such details. Employees *are* interested in the business that employs them and want to understand where it is headed and how it plans to get there.

Listening. When you think about communication, listening does not necessarily come to mind. Too often managers never develop effective listening skills. When entrepreneurs do develop excellent listening skills, they discover clues to improved performance and profitability. Entrepreneurs need to be conscious of what employees who are on the "firing line" are learning about customers' needs and demands.

The employees who perform the work in the company and serve its customers are the *real* experts in the company's day-to-day activities and are in closer contact with potential problems and opportunities at the operating level. By encouraging employees to develop innovative ideas and creative solutions to problems and then listening to and acting on them, business owners can make their companies more successful. *For instance, the manager of a plant making toothpaste found that the frequent need to wash out the steel holding tank interrupted the company's production schedule. One day the manager was talking to one of the operators, who suggested that the company put in a second tank. "That way we can use one tank while we wash the second one, and we don't have to stop production to do it." This simple yet effective solution that was so obvious to the worker because he dealt with the problem every day had never occurred to the plant's managers.*[23]

Improvements such as these depend on entrepreneurs' ability to listen. To improve listening skills, entrepreneurs can use the PDCH formula: identify the speaker's *purpose*, recognize the *details* that support that purpose, see the *conclusions* they can draw from what the speaker is saying, and identify the *hidden* meanings communicated by body language and voice inflections.

Company Example

The Informal Communication Network: The "Grapevine"

Despite all of the modern communication tools available, the grapevine, the informal lines of communication that exist in every company, remains an important link in a company's communication network. The grapevine carries vital information—and sometimes rumors—through every part of the organization with incredible speed. It is not unusual when management makes an important change in the organization for most employees to hear the news first by the grapevine. One study found that 46 percent of employees say they first hear about major changes at work through the grapevine. However, only 17 percent of their employers think that employees hear about changes this way.[24] One researcher describes the grapevine this way: "With the rapidity of a burning powder trail, information flows like magic out of the woodwork, past the water fountain, past the manager's door and the janitor's mop closet. As elusive as a summer zephyr, it filters through steel walls, bulkheads, or glass partitions, from office boy to executive."[25]

Knowing that employees are connected through the grapevine allows business owners to send out ideas to obtain reactions without making a formal announcement. The grapevine can be an excellent source of informal feedback when management is also connected. In many companies, training and information still flow downhill and not uphill. Over the next decade, successful companies will bring the knowledge economy full circle by making sure knowledge flows up, down, and sideways, increasing innovation and competitiveness. "The only way they're going to do that," says Mark Loschiavo, executive director of the Laurence A. Baiada Center for Entrepreneurship in Technology at Drexel University in Philadelphia, "is if they break down the barriers that say, 'Because you work for me, I can't learn from you.'" *One entrepreneur, Kim Seymour, founder and owner of Cravings, a 2-year-old Raleigh, North Carolina, retail company that sells trendy maternity clothing and accessories, has learned the value of listening to the employee grapevine for feedback. Seymour seeks advice from her three employees who have taught her about merchandising, marketing, and customer relations. One employee had spent nine years as a retail manager, experience Seymour didn't have when she started the company. "There's no way someone is going to be an expert in every aspect of running a business," says Seymour.*[26]

> **Company Example** →

The Challenge of Motivating Employees

> 5. Discuss the ways in which entrepreneurs can motivate their employees to achieve higher levels of performance.

Motivation is the degree of additional effort an employee exerts to accomplish a task; it shows up as excitement about work. Motivating workers to higher levels of performance is one of the most difficult and challenging tasks facing a small business manager. Few things are more frustrating to a business owner than an employee with a tremendous amount of talent who lacks the desire to use it. This section discusses four aspects of motivation: empowerment, job design, rewards and compensation, and feedback.

Empowerment

One of the principles underlying the team-based management style is empowerment. **Empowerment** involves giving workers at every level of the organization the authority, the freedom, and the responsibility to control their own work, to make decisions, and to take action to meet the company's objectives. Competitive forces and a more demanding workforce challenge business owners and managers to share power with everyone in the organization, whether they use a team-based approach or not.

Empowering employees requires a different style of management and leadership from that of the traditional manager. Many old-style managers were often unwilling to share power with anyone because they feared doing so would weaken their authority and reduce their influence. In fact, exactly the *opposite* is true. Business owners who share information, responsibility, authority, and power soon discover that their success (and their company's success) is magnified many times over. Even when the information being shared isn't positive, the results can be. *The business rationale of Nucor Steel under the guidance of the late F. Kenneth Iverson focused employees on driving the bottom-line performance and managers on removing obstacles from their path. Iverson's egalitarian management philosophy drove consistent, double-digit, profitable growth during his tenure. His belief in the power of employees was evident and his company's success speaks for itself: From 1966 to 1996, Nucor grew at a compound annual rate of about 17 percent, earning a profit and paying a dividend each year. One concept Iverson promoted was called "sharing the pain." Instead of lining the pockets of company executives,*

> **Company Example** →

he pushed decision-making authority down to the frontline worker, minimizing distinctions between managers and employees and paying people for their productivity.

"Painsharing" helped Nucor get through tough times without ever laying off a single employee or closing a single facility for lack of work, even when the steel industry was shedding thousands of jobs. The economy was mired in a slump during the first quarter of 1982, and Nucor production was down by nearly half. Cutbacks to four-day or even three-day workweeks reduced the average Nucor worker's earnings by 25 percent. Iverson recalled in his book Plain Talk: Lessons from a Business Maverick, *"Still, I never heard one employee complain about it. Not one. Why? Simple. No employee was being asked to carry more than his or her part of the burden. Their department heads had taken pay cuts of up to 40%, and the general managers and other officers of the company were earning 56–60% less than we'd made in previous years. We not only shared the pain, we doled out the lion's share to the people at the top."*[27]

Even in bad times, empowered workers become more successful on the job, which means the entrepreneur's firm has a better chance of survival and ultimate success. Empowerment builds on what real business leaders already know: that the people in their organizations bring with them to work an amazing array of talents, skills, knowledge, and abilities. Workers are willing—even anxious—to put these to use; unfortunately, in too many businesses, suffocating management styles and poorly designed jobs quash workers' enthusiasm and motivation. Enlightened business owners recognize their workers' abilities, develop them, and then give workers the freedom and the power to use them. Empowered employees are more likely to display creativity and initiative in problem solving when they feel that management respects their ideas and talents.

When implemented properly, empowerment can produce impressive results, not only for the business but also for newly empowered employees. For the business, benefits typically include significant productivity gains, quality improvements, more satisfied customers, improved morale, and increased employee motivation. For workers, empowerment offers the chance to do a greater variety of work that is more interesting and challenging. Empowerment challenges workers to make the most of their creativity, imagination, knowledge, and skills. This method of management encourages them to take the initiative to identify and solve problems on their own and as part of a team. As empowered workers see how the various parts of a company's manufacturing or service systems fit together, they realize their need to acquire more skills and knowledge to do their jobs well. Entrepreneurs must realize that empowerment and training go hand in hand.

Not every worker *wants* to be empowered, however. Some will resist, wanting only to "put in their eight hours and go home." Companies that move to an empowerment philosophy will lose about 5 percent of their workforce because those workers simply are unwilling or are unable to make the change. Another 75 percent of the typical workforce will accept empowerment and thrive under it, and the remaining 20 percent will pounce on it eagerly because they want to contribute their talents and their ideas. *When Peggy Finley became president of K40 Electronics, a radar detector maker with 27 employees in Elgin, Illinois, she brought in a management style based on employee empowerment, which was completely different from the fear-based style of the previous management team. When she assumed leadership of the company, employee turnover was high, and morale was low. She began transforming the company by redefining its core values to reflect the empowerment philosophy, laid off a few employees who were not willing to make the transition, and used a new hiring process to replace them with workers who embraced the new management style. Since she made the changes, employee turnover has plummeted, profits have tripled, and K40 Electronics is gaining market share even as three of the top radar detector manufacturers have filed for bankruptcy.*[28]

Company Example →

Empowerment works best when an entrepreneur:

- *Is confident enough to give workers all the authority and responsibility they can handle.* Early on, this may mean giving workers the power to tackle relatively simple assignments. But as their confidence and ability grow, most workers are eager to take on more responsibility.
- *Plays the role of coach and facilitator, not the role of meddlesome boss.* One surefire way to make empowerment fail is to give associates the power to attack a problem and then to hover over them, criticizing every move they make. Smart owners empower their workers and then get out of the way so they can do their jobs!
- *Recognizes that empowered employees will make mistakes.* The worst thing an owner can do when empowered employees make mistakes is to hunt them down and punish them. That teaches everyone in the company to avoid taking risks and to always play it safe—something no innovative small business can afford.
- *Hires people who can blossom in an empowered environment.* Empowerment is not for everyone. Owners quickly learn that as costly as hiring mistakes are, such errors are even more costly in an empowered environment. Ideal candidates are high-energy self-starters who enjoy the opportunity to grow and to enhance their skills.
- *Trains workers continuously to upgrade their skills.* Empowerment demands more of workers than traditional work methods. Managers are asking workers to solve problems and make decisions they have never made before. To handle these problems well, workers need training, especially in effective problem-solving techniques, communication, teamwork, and technical skills.
- *Trusts workers to do their jobs.* Once workers are trained to do their jobs, owners must learn to trust them to assume responsibility for their jobs. After all, they are the real experts; they face the problems and challenges every day.
- *Listens to workers when they have ideas, solutions, or suggestions.* Because they are the experts on the job, employees often come up with incredibly insightful, innovative ideas for improving them—if business owners give them the chance. Failing to acknowledge or to act on employees' ideas sends them a clear message: Your ideas really don't count.
- *Recognizes workers' contributions.* One of the most important tasks a business owner has is to recognize jobs well done. Some businesses reward workers with monetary awards; others rely on recognition and praise; still others use a combination of money and praise. Whatever system an owner chooses, the key to keeping a steady flow of ideas, improvements, suggestions, and solutions is to recognize the people who supply them.
- *Shares information with workers.* For empowerment to succeed, business owners must make sure workers get adequate information, the raw material for good decision making. Some companies have gone beyond sharing information to embrace **open-book management,** in which employees have access to *all* of a company's records, including its financial statements. The goal of open-book management is to enable employees to understand why they need to raise productivity, improve quality, cut costs, and improve customer service. Under open-book management, employees (1) see and learn to understand the company's financial statements and other critical numbers in measuring its performance; (2) learn that a significant part of their jobs is making sure those critical numbers move in the right direction; and (3) have a direct stake in the company's success through profit sharing, ESOPs, or performance-based bonuses. In short, open-book management establishes the link between employees' knowledge and their performance. Individuals' feedback on performance energizes their motivation to continue.

Job Design

Over the years, managers have learned that the job itself and the way it is designed can be a source of motivation (or demotivation!) for workers. During the industrial age (1920–1980), work was organized on the principle of **job simplification,** which involved breaking the work down into its simplest form and standardizing each task, as in some assembly-line operations. The scope of jobs organized in such a way is extremely narrow, resulting in impersonal, monotonous, and boring work that creates little challenge or motivation for workers. Job simplification invites workers to "check their brains at the door" and offers them little opportunity for excitement, enthusiasm, or pride in their work. The result can be apathetic, unmotivated workers who care little about quality, customers, or costs.

To break this destructive cycle, some companies have redesigned jobs so that they offer workers intrinsic rewards and motivation. Three job design strategies are common: job enlargement, job rotation, and job enrichment.

- **Job enlargement** (or **horizontal job loading**) adds more tasks to a job to broaden its scope. For instance, rather than having an employee simply mount four screws in computers as they come down an assembly line, the worker might assemble, install, and test the entire motherboard (perhaps as part of a team). The idea is to make the job more varied and to allow employees to perform a more complete unit of work.

- **Job rotation** involves cross-training employees so they can move from one job in the company to others, giving them a greater number and variety of tasks to perform. As employees learn other jobs within an organization, both their skills and their understanding of the company's purpose and processes increase. Cross-trained workers are more valuable because they give a company the flexibility to shift workers from low-demand jobs to those where they are most needed. As an incentive for workers to learn to perform other jobs within an operation, some companies offer **skill-based pay,** a system under which the more skills workers acquire, the more they earn.

- **Job enrichment** (or **vertical job loading**) involves building motivators into a job by increasing the planning, decision-making, organizing, and controlling functions— that is, traditional managerial tasks—workers perform. The idea is to make every employee a manager—at least a manager of his or her own job. Notice that empowerment is based on the principle of job enrichment. To enrich employees' jobs, a business owner must build five core characteristics into them:
    1. *Skill variety* is the degree to which a job requires a variety of different skills, talents, and activities from the worker. Does the job require the worker to perform a variety of tasks that demand a variety of skills and abilities, or does it force the worker to perform the same task repeatedly?
    2. *Task identity* refers to the degree to which a job allows the worker to complete a whole or identifiable piece of work. Does the employee build an entire piece of furniture (perhaps as part of a team), or does the employee merely attach four screws?
    3. *Task significance* describes the degree to which a job substantially influences the lives or work of others—employees or final customers. Does the employee get to deal with customers, either internal or external? One effective way to establish task significance is to put employees in touch with customers so that they can see how customers use the product or service they make.
    4. *Autonomy* is the degree to which a job gives a worker freedom, independence, and discretion in planning and performing tasks. Does the employee make

decisions affecting his or her work, or must the employee rely on someone else (e.g., the owner, a manager, or a supervisor) to "call the shots"?

5. *Feedback* is the degree to which a job gives workers direct, timely information about the quality of their performance. Does the job give employees feedback about the quality of their work, or does the product (and all information about it) simply disappear after it leaves the worker's station?

As the nation's workforce and employers continue to change, business is changing the way people work, moving away from a legion of full-time employees in traditional 8-to-5, on-site jobs. Organizational structures, even in small companies, are flatter than ever before, as the lines between traditional "managers" and "workers" become blurred. Rather than resembling the current pyramid, the organization of tomorrow will more closely resemble a spider's web, with a network of interconnected employee specialists working in teams and using lightning-fast communication to make decisions without having to go through three or four layers of management.

Changes in workplace design and the integration of technology have resulted in an economy where productivity per employee continues to grow. The nature of how work is done has also changed as workers demand more flexibility in their jobs. One study found that 51 percent of employees say they prefer a job that offers flexible working hours more than one that offers the opportunity for advancement.[29] Many companies are providing that flexibility in the form of flextime, job sharing, and flexplace.

Flextime is an arrangement under which employees build their work schedules around a set of "core hours," such as 11 A.M. to 3 P.M., but have flexibility about when they start and stop work. For instance, one worker might choose to come in at 7 A.M. and leave at 3 P.M. to attend her son's soccer game, while another may work from 11 A.M. to 7 P.M. Flextime not only raises levels of job satisfaction and worker morale, but it also makes it easier for companies to attract and retain high-quality young workers who want rewarding careers without sacrificing their lifestyles. One recent survey found that employees with high flexibility in their work arrangements reported more than twice the level of job satisfaction as workers with low flexibility in their work arrangements.[30] In addition, companies using flextime schedules often experience lower levels of tardiness and absenteeism.

Job sharing is a work arrangement in which two or more people share a single full-time job. For instance, two college students might share the same 40-hour-a-week job, one working mornings and the other working afternoons. Although job sharing affects a relatively small portion of the nation's workforce, it is an important job design strategy for some companies that find it difficult to recruit capable, qualified full-time workers. Job sharing has become extremely popular among retired workers who want to supplement their retirement income while remaining active, alert, and having a feeling of remaining valuable contributors to society.

Flexplace is a work arrangement in which employees work at a place other than the traditional office, such as a satellite branch closer to their homes or, in some cases, at home. Flexplace is an easy job design strategy for companies to use because of **telecommuting.** Using modern communication technology such as e-mail, the Internet, fax machines, and laptop computers, employees have more flexibility in choosing where they work. Today, it is quite simple for workers to hook up electronically to their workplaces (and to all of the people and the information there) from practically anywhere on the planet!

Telecommuting not only makes it easier for employees to strike a balance between their work and home lives, but it also leads to higher productivity. Studies show that telecommuters are from 4 percent to 12 percent more productive than office-bound workers.[31] Companies also benefit from telecommuting in other ways. Management

Figure 19.2

Number of Workers Telecommuting in the United States

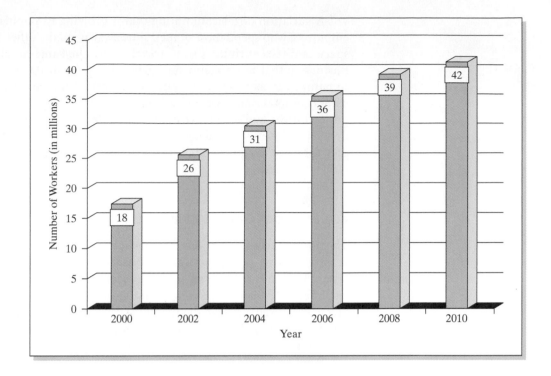

Recruiters International estimates that employers can save $10,000 annually for each telecommuting worker by reduced absenteeism and job retention costs alone.[32] Managers at Sun Microsystems say they have reduced the company's office space expense by $71 million since employees began telecommuting.[33] Figure 19.2 shows growth trends in the number of telecommuting workers in the United States.

Before shifting to telecommuting, entrepreneurs must address the following questions.

1. *Does the nature of the work fit telecommuting?* Obviously, some jobs are better suited to telecommuting than others. Positions in which employees work independently, use computers frequently, or spend a great deal of time calling on customers and clients are good candidates for telecommuting.
2. *Can you monitor compliance with federal wage and hour laws for telecommuters?* In general, employers must keep the same employment records for telecommuters that they do for traditional office workers.
3. *Which workers are best suited for telecommuting?* Those who are self-motivated, are disciplined, and have been around long enough to establish solid relationships with coworkers make the best telecommuters.
4. *Can you provide the equipment and the technical support telecommuters need to be productive?* Telecommuting often requires an investment in portable computers, fax machines, extra telephone lines or high speed Internet access, and software. Workers usually need technical training as well because they often assume the role of their own technical support staff.
5. *Are you adequately insured?* Employers should be sure that the telecommuting equipment employees use in their homes is covered under their insurance policies.
6. *Can you keep in touch?* Telecommuting works well provided long-distance employees stay in touch with headquarters. Frequent telephone conferences, regular e-mail messages, and occasional personal appearances in the office will prevent employees from losing contact with what's happening "at work."

A variation of telecommuting that is growing in popularity is **hoteling,** in which employees who spend most of their time away from the office anyway use the same office space at different times, just as travelers use the same hotel rooms on different days. Businesses that use hoteling have been able to reduce the cost of leasing office space, sometimes by as much as 50 percent. Workers can connect their laptops into the company's computer network and e-mail system, forward their telephone calls to their temporary offices, and even move mobile file cabinets in when they need them. Flexible office designs and furnishings allow workers to configure these "hot offices" (so called because they turn over so quickly that the seats are still hot from the previous user) to suit their individual needs.

Rewards and Compensation

The rewards an employee gets from the job itself are intrinsic rewards, but managers have at their disposal a wide variety of extrinsic rewards to motivate workers. The key to using rewards to motivate involves tailoring them to the needs and characteristics of the workers. Effective reward systems tap into the values and issues that are important to people. Smart entrepreneurs take the time to learn what makes their employees "tick" and then build their reward system around those issues. For instance, to a technician making $25,000 a year, a chance to earn a $3,000 bonus would most likely be a powerful motivator. To an executive earning $200,000 a year, it may not be.

One of the most popular rewards is money. Cash is an effective motivator—up to a point. Over the last 25 years, many companies have moved to **pay-for-performance compensation systems,** in which employees' pay depends on how well they perform their job. In other words, extra productivity equals extra pay. By linking employees' compensation directly to the company's financial performance, a business owner increases the likelihood that workers will achieve performance targets that are in their best interest and in the company's best interest.

Pay-for-performance systems work only when employees see a clear connection between their performance and their pay. That's where small companies actually have an advantage over large businesses. Because they work for small companies, employees can see more clearly the impact their performance has on the company's profitability and ultimate success than their counterparts at large corporations. To be successful, however, pay-for-performance systems should meet the following criteria:

- Employees' incentive pay must be clearly and closely linked to their performances. That's where most compensation systems based on simple annual raises lose their effectiveness.
- Entrepreneurs must set up the system so that employees see the connection between what they do every day on the job—selling to customers, producing a product, or anything else—and the rewards they receive under the system.
- The system must be simple enough so that employees understand and trust it. Complex systems that employees have difficulty understanding will not produce the desired results.
- Employees must believe the system is fair.
- The system should be inclusive. Entrepreneurs are finding creative ways to reward all employees, no matter what their jobs might be.
- The company should make frequent payouts to employees. A single annual payout is the worst schedule because employees have long since forgotten what they did to earn the incentive pay. Many companies pay employees the week after they have achieved an important goal. Regular and frequent feedback is an essential ingredient in any incentive-pay program.

Money isn't the only motivator business owners have at their disposal, of course. In fact, nonfinancial incentives can be more important sources of employee motivation than money. After its initial motivational impact, money loses its impact; it does not have a lasting motivational effect (and for small businesses, with their limited resources, a lasting effect is a plus). Often the most meaningful motivating factors are the simplest ones—praise, recognition, respect, feedback, job security, promotions, and others—things that any small business, no matter how limited its budget, can do. Entrepreneurs can offer praise, recognition, and demonstrations of respect for workers on a regular basis at absolutely no cost. When an employee has done an exceptional job, an entrepreneur should be the first to recognize that accomplishment and the first to say "thank you." Praise is a simple, yet powerful, motivational tool. People enjoy getting praise; it's just human nature. As Mark Twain once said, "I can live for two months on a good compliment." Praise is an easy and inexpensive reward for employees producing extraordinary work.

One of the surest ways to kill high performance is simply to fail to recognize the performance and the employees responsible for it. Failing to praise good work eventually conveys the message that the owner either doesn't care about exceptional performance or cannot distinguish between good work and poor work. In either case, through inaction, the manager destroys employees' motivation to excel.

Because they lack the financial resources of bigger companies, small business owners must be more creative when it comes to giving rewards that motivate workers. In many cases, however, using rewards other than money gives small businesses an advantage because they usually have more impact on employee performance over time. In short, rewards do *not* have to be expensive to be effective, but they should be creative and should have a direct link to employee performance. Consider how the following rewards for exceptional performance recognize the employee's contribution while also building a positive organizational culture:

- The company CEO washes the top-performing employee's car at lunchtime in front of the building.
- A small firm that historically suffered from high levels of tardiness created a poker game with a weekly $25 prize. Employees who were on time every morning received a card. The best hand on Friday won the prize.
- The best employee suggestion, as judged by an employee team, wins an evening for two with limousine service and dinner.

Whatever system of rewards they use, managers will be most successful if they match rewards to employees' interests and tastes. For instance, the ideal reward for one employee might be tickets to a hockey game; to another, it might be tickets to a musical show. Once again, because they know their employees so well, this is an area in which small business owners have an advantage over large companies. The better entrepreneurs know their employees' interests and tastes, the more effective they will be at matching rewards with performance.

For highly skilled people, work is often not just about money. Standard financial incentives—bonuses, stock options, or the lure of a raise or corner office—will not always motivate highly skilled or extremely creative individuals to do their best work. They sometimes respond more strongly to intrinsic rewards. The nature of the job and the structure of the work environment must also meet their inner needs and desires. Suppose that a young working mother is working partly for the money, but she has other strong drives and needs. You might effectively harness her energies by offering a tailored mix of intrinsic factors—perhaps a more flexible schedule, plus a willingness to look at results rather than worry so much about how she gets them. Leslie Perlow of the University of Michigan documented a major electronics company that granted this very mix to such a woman, a project team leader. Her next performance review was her best ever.[34]

In the future, managers will rely more on nonmonetary rewards—praise, recognition, car washes, letters of commendation, and others—to create a work environment where employees take pride in their work, enjoy it, are challenged by it, and get excited about it—in short, act like owners of the business themselves. The goal is to let employees know that every person is important and that the company notices, appreciates, and recognizes excellent performance.

✦ GAINING a COMPETITIVE EDGE ✦

Customizing Rewards by Generation

Like most salespeople, Jason Blumberg, a 30-year-old public relations and marketing specialist for Bold Approach, a public relations firm in Boise, Idaho, looks forward to the incentives he can earn if he achieves his sales targets each month. Blumberg, however, readily admits that some rewards get him more fired up than others. He has little use for a luxury trip to some exotic destination such as Bora-Bora. Instead, Blumberg, who is married and has young children, prefers cash. "I'd rather get a $300 check for each new client I bring in," he says. "I don't really have the time for travel incentives."

Tom Waldron, on the other hand, a single, twenty-something regional manager for Intercall, a conference services company in Chicago, goes all out so that he can qualify for the luxury trip incentives his company offers top performers. The trip, he says, "is definitely the biggest motivator for me. It's all inclusive, and it's five-star." Waldron estimates that he works 10 percent to 20 percent harder at his job simply because of the "carrot" the trip represents.

What's the difference? Why does one reward work for one employee and not another? Much of it has to do with age, lifestyle, and interests—all factors that change as a person ages. "What works for the fifties crowd doesn't work for the twenties and thirties," says one expert. With the diversity of the workforce increasing with each passing year, entrepreneurs must be able to customize the rewards they offer to recruit, retain, and motivate employees to higher levels of performance. The following suggestions will help entrepreneurs find the right incentives for employees of various ages.

For workers in their twenties

What works:

▪ Challenging work and increasing responsibilities
▪ Ongoing learning and training opportunities
▪ Praise and recognition
▪ Flexible schedules
▪ Small electronic appliances, such as MP3 players or DVD players
▪ Golf-related rewards

▪ Outdoor sports gear, such as mountain bicycles, climbing equipment, skis, and others
▪ Adventure travel

What doesn't work:

▪ State technology—deficient work environments
▪ Little or no feedback on job performance
▪ Small cash incentives
▪ Large appliances that require installation
▪ Lawn and garden equipment

For workers in their thirties

What works:

▪ A workplace that feels like family
▪ An entrepreneurial culture
▪ An environment that values, encourages, and supports creativity
▪ Rewards and praise
▪ Golf-related rewards
▪ High definition TVs
▪ Time off to spend with family

What doesn't work:

▪ Shooting down their ideas and stifling creativity
▪ Failing to keep them informed about company matters
▪ Adventure travel
▪ Lack of opportunities to improve their skills

For workers in their forties

What works:

▪ Opportunities to mentor younger workers by sharing their experience and knowledge
▪ Time off to care for aging parents or children
▪ Praise and recognition
▪ Spa visits
▪ Golf-related rewards
▪ Trips to interesting destinations such as museums, shops, and entertainment
▪ Lawn and garden equipment

What doesn't work:

- An authoritarian management style
- A lack of recognition for their contributions
- Small electronics such as MP3 players

For workers in their fifties and beyond

What works:

- Opportunities to mentor younger workers by sharing their experience and knowledge
- Cash
- Praise and recognition
- "Soft adventure" trips, such as a fly fishing trip to an exotic destination that features a luxurious lodge
- Unique trips such as Alaskan cruises or a stay at an island resort
- Upscale household appliances such as coffee makers and cookware

What doesn't work:

- Treating them as if they are "old" and of little value to the company
- Lack of opportunities to keep learning

- Small electronics such as MP3 players or DVD players

Remember: These are generalizations based on the characteristics of workers across different generations. Perhaps the two best ways for entrepreneurs to offer rewards and incentives that genuinely motivate workers are to get to know their employees well and to ask them what rewards mean the most to them. The key to higher levels of performance is customizing incentives and rewards to meet employees' needs no matter what stage of life they are in.

1. What similarities do you see across these lists? Differences?
2. What other items can you add to these lists? Explain your reasoning.
3. Interview an employee in each of these four groups (sales representatives make excellent candidates) and ask them about the incentives that motivate them most. What is their reasoning?

Source: Adapted from Jennifer Gilbert, "Motivating Through the Ages," *Sales & Marketing Management,* November 2003, pp. 31–40.

Performance Feedback

Business owners not only must motivate employees to excel in their jobs, but they must also focus their efforts on the right targets. Providing feedback on progress toward those targets can be a powerful motivating force in a company. To ensure that the link between their vision for the company and its operations is strong, entrepreneurs must build a series of specific performance measures that serves as periodic monitoring points. For each critical element of the organization's performance (e.g., product or service quality, financial performance, market position, productivity, employee development), owners should develop specific measures that connect daily operational responsibilities with the company's overall strategic direction. These measures become the benchmarks for measuring employees' performance and the company's progress. The adage "what gets measured and monitored gets done" is true for most organizations. By connecting the company's long-term strategy to its daily operations and measuring performance, entrepreneurs make clear to everyone in the company what is most important. Jack Stack, CEO of Springfield Remanufacturing Corporation, explains the importance of focusing every employee's attention on key performance targets:

> To be successful in business, you have to be going somewhere, and everyone involved in getting you there has to know where it is. That's a basic rule, a higher law, but most companies miss . . . the fact that you have a much better chance of winning if everyone knows what it takes to win.[35]

In other words, getting or giving feedback implies that business owners have established meaningful targets that serve as standards of performance for them, their employees, and the company as a whole. One characteristic successful people have in common is that they set goals and objectives, usually challenging ones, for themselves. Business owners are no different. Successful entrepreneurs usually set targets for performance that

Figure 19.3

The Feedback Loop

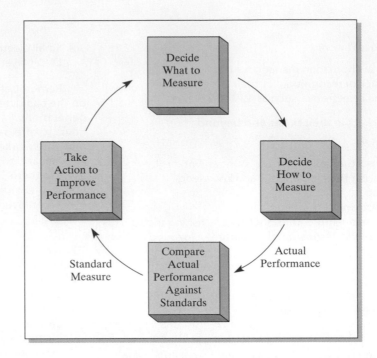

make them stretch to achieve, and then they encourage their employees to do the same. The result is that they keep their companies constantly moving forward.

For feedback to have impact as a motivating force in a business requires business owners to follow the procedure illustrated in Figure 19.3, the feedback loop.

Deciding What to Measure. The first step in the feedback loop is deciding what to measure. Every business is characterized by a set of numbers that are critical to its success, and these "critical numbers" are what entrepreneurs should focus on. Obvious critical numbers include sales, profits, profit margins, cash flow, and other standard financial measures. However, running beneath these standard and somewhat universal measures of performance is an undercurrent of critical numbers that are unique to a company's operations. In most cases, these are the numbers that actually drive profits, cash flow, and other financial measures and are the company's *real* critical numbers. *For instance, in a conversation with another business owner, a hotel franchisee said that his company's critical number was profit and that the way to earn a profit was to control costs. His managerial efforts focused on making sure that his employees knew exactly what to do, how to do it, and how much they could spend doing it. The only problem was that the hotel was losing money.*

"Tell me," said his friend, "how do you make money in this business?"

"We fill rooms," said the hotelier.

"How many rooms do you have to fill to break even?"

"Seventy-one percent," came the reply, "but we're only running at 67 percent."

"How many people know that?" asked his friend.

"Two," he said.

"Maybe that's your problem," observed his friend.

The hotel owner quickly realized that one of his company's most critical numbers was occupancy rate; that's what drove profits! His managerial focus had been misguided, and he had failed to get his employees involved in solving the problem. The hotel owner put together an incentive plan for employees based on occupancy rate. Once the rate surpassed 71 percent,

Company Example

all employees qualified for bonuses, and the higher the occupancy rate, the higher the bonuses. Working with his employees, he identified other critical numbers, such as customer satisfaction levels and retention rates, and began tracking results and posting them for everyone to see. Since then, the hotel's occupancy rate, customer satisfaction scores, customer retention rate, and profits have shot up. The hotel owner learned not only what his company's critical numbers were but also how to use them to motivate employees.[36]

Deciding How to Measure. Once business owners identify their companies' critical numbers, the issue of how to best measure them arises. In some cases, identifying the critical numbers defines the measurements the owners must make, and measuring them simply becomes a matter of collecting and analyzing data. In other cases, the method of measurement is not as obvious or as tangible. For instance, in some businesses, social responsibility is a key factor, but how should managers measure their company's performance on such an intangible concept? One of the best ways to develop methods for measuring such factors is to use brainstorming sessions involving employees, customers, and even outsiders. For example, one company used this technique to develop a "fun index," which used the results of an employee survey to measure how much fun employees had at work (and, by extension, how satisfied they were with their work, the company, and their managers).

Comparing Actual Performance Against Standards. In this stage of the feedback loop, the idea is to look for deviations *in either direction* from the performance standards the company has set for itself. In other words, opportunities to improve performance arise when there is a gap between "what should be" and "what is." The most serious deviations usually are those in which actual performance falls far below the standard. Managers and employees must focus their efforts on figuring out why actual performance is substandard. The goal is *not* to hunt down the guilty party (or parties) for punishment but to discover the cause of the poor performance and fix it. Managers should not ignore deviations in the other direction, however. When actual performance consistently exceeds the company's standards, it is an indication that the standards are set too low. The company should look closely at "raising the bar another notch" to spur motivation.

Taking Action to Improve Performance. When managers or employees detect a performance gap, their next challenge is to decide on a course of action that will eliminate it. Typically, several suitable alternatives to solving a performance problem exist; the key is finding an acceptable solution that solves the problem quickly, efficiently, and effectively.

Performance Appraisal

One of the most common methods of providing feedback on employee performance is through performance appraisal, the process of evaluating an employee's actual performance against desired performance standards. Most performance appraisal programs strive to accomplish three goals: (1) to give employees feedback about how they are doing their jobs, which can be an important source of motivation; (2) to provide business owners and employees the opportunity to create a plan for developing employee skills and abilities and for improving their performance; and (3) to establish a basis for determining promotions and salary increases. Although the primary purpose of performance appraisals is to encourage and to help employees improve their performance, too often they turn into uncomfortable confrontations that do nothing more than upset the employees, aggravate the business owners, and destroy trust and morale. Why? Because most business owners don't understand how to conduct an effective performance appraisal. Although U.S. businesses have been conducting performance appraisals for about 75 years, most companies, their managers, and their employees are dissatisfied with the entire process. A recent survey by Watson Wyatt, a global human resources company, found that 60 percent of workers say that performance appraisals do not produce any useful feedback and fail to help them set meaningful objectives.[37] Common complaints include unclear standards and objectives, managers who lack information about employees' performances, managers who are unprepared or who lack honesty and sincerity, and managers who use general, ambiguous terms to describe employees' performances.

Perhaps the biggest complaint concerning appraisals is that they happen only periodically: in most cases, just once a year. Employees do not have the opportunity to receive any ongoing feedback on a regular basis. All too often, managers save up all of the negative feedback to give employees and then dump it on them in the annual performance review. Not only does it destroy employees' motivation, but also it does *nothing* to improve employees' performance. What good does it do to tell employees that six months before, they botched an assignment that caused the company to lose a customer? Performance reviews that occur once or twice a year in an attempt to improve employees' performance are similar to working out once or twice a year in an attempt to get into top physical condition!

Lack of ongoing feedback is similar to asking employees to bowl in the dark. They can hear some pins falling, but they have no idea how many or which ones are left standing for the next frame. How motivated would you be to keep bowling? Managers should address problems when they occur rather than wait until the performance appraisal session. Continuous feedback, both positive and negative, is a much more effective way to improve employees' performance and to increase their motivation.

If done properly, performance appraisals can be effective ways to provide employee feedback and to improve workers' performance. However, it takes some planning and preparation on the business owners' part. The following guidelines can help a business owner create a performance appraisal system that actually works:

- *Link the employee performance criteria to the job description discussed earlier in this chapter.* To evaluate employees' performance effectively, managers must understand the employee's job very well.
- *Establish meaningful, job-related, observable, measurable, and fair performance criteria.* The criteria should describe behaviors and actions, not traits and characteristics. What kind of behavior constitutes a solid performance in this job?
- *Prepare for the appraisal session by outlining the key points you want to cover with employees.* Important points to include are employees' strengths and weaknesses and developing a plan for improving their performance.
- *Invite employees to provide an evaluation of their own job performance based on the performance criteria.* In one small company, workers rate themselves on a one-to-five scale in categories of job-related behavior and skills as part of the performance appraisal system. Then they meet with their supervisor to compare their evaluations with those of their supervisor and discuss them.
- *Be specific.* One of the most common complaints employees have about the appraisal process is that managers' comments are too general to be of any value. Offer employees specific examples of their desirable or undesirable behavior.
- *Keep a record of employees' critical incidents—both positive and negative.* The most productive evaluations are those based on managers' direct observation of their employees' on-the-job performance. Such records also can be vital in case legal problems arise.
- *Discuss employees' strengths and weaknesses.* Appraisal sessions are not the time to "unload" about everything employees have done wrong over the past year. Use them

as opportunities to design plans for improvement and to recognize employees' strengths, efforts, and achievements.

■ *Incorporate employees' goals into the appraisal.* Ideally, the standard against which to measure employees' performance is the goal they have played a role in setting. Workers are likely to be motivated to achieve goals that they have helped establish.

■ *Keep the evaluation constructive.* Avoid the tendency to belittle employees. Do not dwell on past failures. Instead, point out specific things they should do better and help them develop meaningful goals for the future and a strategy for getting there.

■ *Praise good work.* Avoid focusing only on what employees do wrong. Take the time to express your appreciation for hard work and solid accomplishments.

■ *Focus on behaviors, actions, and results.* Problems arise when managers move away from tangible results and actions and begin to critique employees' abilities and attitudes. Such criticism creates a negative tone for the appraisal session and undercuts its primary purpose.

■ *Avoid surprises.* If business owners are doing their jobs well, performance appraisals should contain no surprises for employees or the owners. The ideal time to correct improper behavior or slumping performance is when it happens, not months later. Managers should provide employees with continuous feedback on their performance and use the appraisal session to keep employees on the right track.

■ *Plan for the future.* Smart business owners use appraisal sessions as gateways to workers' future success. They spend only about 20 percent of the time discussing past performance; they use the remaining 80 percent of the time to develop goals, objectives, and a plan for the future. When one sales manager worked with a sales representative whose performance had been mediocre to set meaningful goals and objectives, her performance improved immediately. As a result of the productive performance appraisal, the sales representative increased her sales by 40 percent in less than a year.[38] *When Chip Prince took over as sales manager at City Wholesale, a company that sells food service products, employees underwent performance appraisals only once a year, and even then, they were not very effective. After talking with sales representatives, Prince decided to establish quarterly performance appraisals to give workers the more timely feedback they requested. In every appraisal, Prince makes it a habit to ask employees for specific things he and the company can do to improve sales representatives' performance. Then he makes sure to act on what he hears. Since making the changes in the performance appraisal process, City Wholesale's employee annual turnover rate has dropped from 50 percent to just 15 percent, and profit margins have climbed an average of 15 percent a quarter. "People are telling us they know where they're supposed to go and are more in tune with what they are supposed to be doing," says Prince.*[39]

Company Example

Many companies are encouraging employees to evaluate each others' performance in **peer reviews** or to evaluate their boss's performance in **upward feedback,** both part of a technique called **360-degree feedback.** Peer appraisals can be especially useful because employees' coworkers see others' on-the-job performance every day. As a result, peer evaluations tend to be more accurate and more valid than those of some managers. Plus, they may capture behavior that managers might miss. Disadvantages of peer appraisals include potential retaliation against coworkers who criticize others, the possibility that appraisals will be reduced to "popularity contests," and the refusal of some workers to offer any criticism because they feel uncomfortable evaluating others. Some bosses using upward feedback report similar problems, including personal attacks and extreme evaluations by vengeful subordinates.

▌▐▐ Chapter Review

1. Explain the challenges involved in the entrepreneur's role as leader and what it takes to be a successful leader.

   ■ Leadership is the process of influencing and inspiring others to work to achieve a common goal and then giving them the power and the freedom to achieve it.

   ■ Management and leadership are not the same, yet both are essential to a small company's success. Leadership without management is unbridled; management without leadership is uninspired. Leadership gets a small business going; management keeps it going.

2. Describe the importance of hiring the right employees and how to avoid making hiring mistakes.

   ■ The decision to hire a new employee is an important one for every business, but its impact is magnified many times in a small company. Every "new hire" a business owner makes determines the heights to which the company can climb or the depths to which it will plunge.

   ■ To avoid making hiring mistakes, entrepreneurs should develop meaningful job descriptions and job specifications, plan and conduct an effective interview, and check references before hiring any employee.

3. Explain how to build the kind of company culture and structure to support the entrepreneur's mission and goals and to motivate employees to achieve them.

   ■ Company culture is the distinctive, unwritten code of conduct that governs the behavior, attitudes, relationships, and style of an organization. Culture arises from an entrepreneur's consistent and relentless pursuit of a set of core values that everyone in the company can believe in. Small companies' flexible structures can be a major competitive weapon.

4. Understand the potential barriers to effective communication and describe how to overcome them.

   ■ Research shows that managers spend about 80 percent of their time in some form of communication, yet their attempts at communicating sometimes go wrong. Several barriers to effective communication

include: managers and employees don't always feel free to say what they really mean; ambiguity blocks real communication; information overload causes the message to get lost; selective listening interferes with the communication process; defense mechanisms block a message; and conflicting verbal and nonverbal messages confuse listeners.

   ■ To become more effective communicators, business owners should clarify their messages before attempting to communicate them; use face-to-face communication whenever possible; be empathetic; match their messages to their audiences; be organized; encourage feedback; tell the truth; and not be afraid to tell employees about the business, its performance, and the forces that affect it.

5. Discuss the ways in which entrepreneurs can motivate their employees to achieve higher levels of performance.

   ■ Motivation is the degree of effort an employee exerts to accomplish a task; it shows up as excitement about work. Four important tools of motivation are empowerment, job design, rewards and compensation, and feedback.

   ■ Empowerment involves giving workers at every level of the organization the power, the freedom, and the responsibility to control their own work, to make decisions, and to take action to meet the company's objectives.

   ■ Job design techniques for enhancing employee motivation include job enlargement, job rotation, job enrichment, flextime, job sharing, and flexplace (which includes telecommuting and hoteling).

   ■ Money is an important motivator for many workers but not the only one. The key to using rewards such as recognition and praise to motivate involves tailoring them to the needs and characteristics of the workers.

   ■ Giving employees timely, relevant feedback about their job performance through a performance appraisal system can also be a powerful motivator.

▌▐▐ Discussion Questions

1. What is leadership? What is the difference between leadership and management?
2. What behaviors do effective leaders exhibit?
3. Why is it so important for small companies to hire the right employees? What can small

business owners do to avoid making hiring mistakes?
4. What is a job description? A job specification? What functions do they serve in the hiring process?

5. Outline the procedure for conducting an effective interview.

6. What is company culture? What role does it play in a small company's success? What threats does rapid growth pose for a company's culture?

7. What mistakes do companies make when switching to team-based management? What can they do to avoid these mistakes? Explain the four phases teams typically go through.

8. What is empowerment? What benefits does it offer workers? The company? What must a small business manager do to make empowerment work in a company?

9. Explain the differences among job simplification, job enlargement, job rotation, and job enrichment. What impact do these different job designs have on workers?

10. Is money the "best" motivator? How do pay-for-performance compensation systems work? What other rewards are available to small business managers to use as motivators? How effective are they?

11. Suppose that a mail-order catalog company selling environmentally friendly products identifies its performance as a socially responsible company as a "critical number" in its success. Suggest some ways for the owner to measure this company's "social responsibility index."

12. What is performance appraisal? What are the most common mistakes managers make in performance appraisals? What should small business managers do to avoid making those mistakes?

Staffing and Leading a Growing Company

Business PlanPro

In many successful small companies, the key competitive weapon is *people*. The quality of a company's employees determines the heights to which it can climb or the depths to which it can plummet. Competitors may be able to duplicate a successful company's infrastructure, its strategies, and its operations, but they cannot duplicate the advantages that a carefully-selected, well-trained, highly-motivated workforce brings to a business. Assembling a team of capable, motivated employees and supporting them with the proper organizational architecture and job design is no easy task, however. It requires a great deal of thought and planning.

The exercises for Chapter 19 that accompany Business Plan Pro are designed to help you define the key components of your leadership style, describe the process you will use to staff your organization, and explain the techniques you will use to motivate employees to higher levels of performance. Once you finish these exercises, you can use the results to complete the Personnel component of the Management Summary section in Business Plan Pro.

Chapter 20

Management Succession and Risk Management Strategies in the Family Business

> *When it works right, nothing succeeds like a family firm. The roots run deep, embedded in family values. The flash of the fast buck is replaced with long-term plans. Tradition counts.*
>
> —ERIC CALONIUS

> *Walk sober off before the sprightlier age comes titt'ring on and shoves you from the stage.*
>
> —ALEXANDER POPE

Upon completion of this chapter, you will be able to:

1. Explain the factors necessary for a strong family business.
2. Understand the exit strategy options available to an entrepreneur.
3. Discuss the stages of management succession.
4. Explain how to develop an effective management succession plan.
5. Understand the four risk management strategies.
6. Discuss the basics of insurance for small businesses.

Family Businesses

1. Explain the factors necessary for a strong family business.

Nearly 90 percent of all companies in the United States, about 24 million businesses, are family owned. Yet, family-owned businesses, those in which family members control ownership and/or decision making, are often overlooked by the media that focus most of their attention on the larger firms in our economy. In reality, family businesses generate 50 percent of the U.S. gross domestic product, account for 60 percent of all employment and 78 percent of job creation, and pay 65 percent of all wages.[1] Despite common perceptions, not all family businesses are small. The average annual sales of family businesses in the United States are about $36.5 million, and 37 percent of *Fortune* 500 companies are family businesses.[2] Indeed, Sam Walton's heirs own controlling stock in the world's largest company—Wal-Mart.

When a family business works right, it is a thing of beauty. Family members share deeply rooted values that guide the company and give it a sense of harmony. Family members understand and support one another as they work together to achieve the company's mission. That harmony can produce a significant financial payoff. A study by the Family Business Center at California State University at Northridge comparing the financial performances of similar sets of family and nonfamily businesses concluded that "firms controlled by the founding family have greater value, are operated more efficiently, and carry less debt than other firms."[3] Another study of companies among the Standard & Poor's 500 Index by Ronald Anserson, David Reeb, and Sattar Mansi found that family firms financially outperformed their nonfamily counterparts.[4]

Family businesses also have a dark side, and it stems from their lack of continuity. Sibling rivalries, fights over control of the business, and personality conflicts often lead to nasty battles that can tear families apart and destroy once thriving businesses. Family relationships can be difficult, and when mixed with business decisions and the wealth family businesses can create, the result can be explosive. Unfortunately, 70 percent of first-generation businesses fail to survive into the second generation, and of those that do, only 12 percent make it to the third generation.[5] The stumbling block is management succession. Just when they are ready to make the transition from one generation of leaders to the next, family businesses are most vulnerable. As a result, the average life expectancy of a family business is 24 years, although some last *much* longer (see Table 20.1).[6] The oldest family business in the world is Kongo Gumi, a construction company in Japan that specializes in building temples. Established more than 1,400 years ago, the business has navigated management succession successfully across 40 generations of the Kongo family. The current president's son, Masakazu Kong, now in his fifties, is being groomed to take over for the forty-first generation.[7]

The best way to avoid deadly turf battles and conflicts is to develop a succession plan for the company. Although business founders inevitably want their businesses to survive them and almost 80 percent intend to pass them on to their children, they do not always support their intentions with a plan to accomplish that goal. A recent survey of family business owners by MassMutual Financial Group and Arthur Andersen found that 19 percent had not engaged in any kind of estate planning.[8] Many entrepreneurs dream of their businesses continuing in the family but take no significant steps to make their dreams a reality.

David Bork, founder of the Aspen Family Business Conference, has identified several qualities that are essential to a successful family business: shared values, shared power, tradition, a willingness to learn, family behavior, and strong family ties.[9]

Shared Values

The first, and probably most overlooked, quality is a set of shared values. What family members value and believe about people, work, and money shapes their behavior toward the business. All members of a family business should talk openly to determine, in a nonjudgmental

Table 20.1

The World's Oldest Family Businesses

William O'Hara, director of the Institute for Family Enterprise at Bryant College, and Peter Mandel have compiled a list of some of the world's oldest family businesses.

Company	Country	Nature of Business	Year Established
Kongo Gumi	Japan	Temple construction	578
Hoshi Hotel	Japan	Hotel	718
Château de Goulaine	France	Vineyard, museum, butterfly collection	1000
Barone Ricasoli	Italy	Wine and olive oil	1141
Barovier & Toso	Italy	Artistic glassmaking	1295
Hotel Pilgram Haus	Germany	Innkeeping	1304
Richard de Bas	France	High-quality paper maker	1326
Torrini Firenze	Italy	Goldsmiths	1369
Antinori	Italy	Wine	1385
Camuffo	Italy	Shipbuilding	1438
Baronnie de Coussergues	France	Wine	1495
Grazia Deruta	Italy	Ceramics	1500
Fabbrice D'Armi Beretta	Italy	Firearms production	1526
John Brooke & Sons	Great Britain	Textiles	1541
Codorniu	Spain	Wine	1551
Fonjallaz	Switzerland	Wine	1552

Source: Adapted from William T. O'Hara and Peter Mandel, "The World's Oldest Family Companies," *Family Business,* www.familybusinessmagazine.com/oldworld.html.

fashion, each one's values. Without shared values, it is difficult to create a future direction for a business.

Individual family members may share the values of the family but may be motivated to achieve personal goals that are different from those of their parents or siblings. In many cases this is an advantage when there are many children in the family. One or two of the children may elect to work in the business while the others select alternative careers.

To avoid the problems associated with conflicting values and goals, the family should consider taking the following actions:

- Make it clear to all family members that they are not required to join the business on a full-time basis. Family members' goals, ambitions, and talents should be foremost in their career decisions.
- Do not assume that a successor must always come from within the family. Simply being born into a family does not guarantee that a person will make a good business leader.
- Give family members the opportunity to work outside the business initially to learn firsthand how others conduct business. Working for others will allow family members to develop knowledge, confidence, and credibility before stepping back into the family business.

Shared Power

Shared power is not necessarily equal power. Rather, shared power is based on the simple idea that the skills and talents of each family member may run in different directions. Shared power is based on the idea that family members should allow those with the greatest expertise, ability, and knowledge in particular areas to handle decisions in those areas. Dividing responsibilities along the lines of expertise is an important way of acknowledging respect for each family member's talents and abilities. *For instance, when Thad Garner invented a concoction of red peppers and vinegar called Texas Pete Hot Sauce*

Company Example

during the Great Depression, he and his brothers, Harold and Ralph, built a business, T.W. Garner Food Company, around the product. Each assumed responsibilities in a different area of the company based on his talents and interests. Thad (known as "Mr. Texas Pete") took over the sales and marketing side of the business, while Harold managed its financial and operational aspects, and Ralph handled production. Working together, the brothers built the company into a very successful business, selling millions of dollars' worth of Texas Pete a year.[10]

Tradition

Tradition is necessary for a family business because it serves to bond family members and to link one generation of business leaders to the next. However, founders must hold tradition in check when it becomes a barrier to change. The key is to select those traditions that provide a solid foundation for positive behavior while taking care not to restrict the future growth of the business. "The companies that are successful change their strategy after each generation," says Joachim Schwass, a professor of family business at Switzerland's IMD business school. "Bringing in the new generation and saying, 'Son, do as I did,' will not work."[11] *In 1938, Lynn Cooper launched the Cooper Motor Company, a Dodge and Plymouth auto dealership in tiny Clinton, South Carolina, using $750 that he borrowed to acquire his initial inventory of three cars. Cooper was the company's only salesperson until his son, Lynn Jr., joined the business a few years later. In 1956, Lynn Jr. took over the dealership, building on the traditions of providing superior customer service and building customer loyalty established by his father but also making important changes to keep the company growing. He brought into the company as a partner a longtime friend and added Chrysler, Dodge, and Oldsmobile lines to the dealership. Lynn Jr. retired in 2000, turning the reins of Cooper Motors over to his son, Chip, and his son-in-law, Steve Lamb. The third generation of owners takes pride in sticking to the values and traditions that have served the dealership so well for more than 60 years, but they also are committed to making the changes necessary to remain competitive in the highly competitive auto market. They have added the Jeep franchise to their product offerings, made significant upgrades to the*

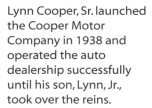

Company Example

Lynn Cooper, Sr. launched the Cooper Motor Company in 1938 and operated the auto dealership successfully until his son, Lynn, Jr., took over the reins.

Cooper Motors is now in its third generation of family ownership. In 2000, Lynn, Jr. (center) turned over leadership of the family business to his son, Chip (left), and son-in-law, Steve Lamb (right). The third generation leaders have made important changes to the company to ensure its continued success.

showroom, and built a Web site that enables the company to sell several cars online each month. "I have a lot of pride in continuing what my grandfather started and Dad continued," says Chip.[12]

A Willingness to Learn

A willingness to learn and grow is the hallmark of any successful firm, and it is essential to a family business. The family business that remains open to new ideas and techniques is likely to reduce its risk of obsolescence. The current generation of leadership must set the stage for new ideas involving the next generation in today's decisions. In many cases, a formalized family council serves as a mechanism through which family members can propose new ideas. Perhaps more important than a family council is fostering an environment in which family members trust one another enough to express their ideas, thoughts, and suggestions openly and honestly. Open discussion of the merits of new ideas is a tradition that has proved valuable for many family businesses' ability to sustain their competitive advantages.

Behaving Like Families

Families that play together operate family businesses that are more likely to stay together. Time spent together outside the business creates the foundation for the relationships family members have at work. Too often, life in a family business can degenerate into nothing but day after day of work and discussions of work at home. In some cases, work is the only way some parents interact with their children. But when a family adds activities outside the scope of the business, new relationships develop in a different arena. A family should not force members to "play together" but instead should create an environment that welcomes every member into fun family activities. Planned activities should be broad enough in scope to involve all family members. In time, trust, respect, openness, and togetherness will lead to behavior that communicates genuine caring and concern for the well-being of each family member, and that spills over into the working relationship as well.

Strong Family Ties

Strong family ties grow from one-on-one relationships. Shared time conveys the message that the family business is *more* than just a business; it is a group of people who care for one another working together for a common goal. The bond that a family business creates among relatives can be strong and enduring. "There's a love and a trust and a respect that can be very powerful when they are brought into a business environment," says Ross Nager, director of the Arthur Andersen Center for Family Business.[13]

The same emotions that hold family businesses together can also rip them apart if they run counter to the company's and the family's best interest. Emotions run deep in family businesses, and the press is filled with examples of once successful companies that have been ruined by family feuds over who controls the company and how to run it. Conflict is a natural part of any business but can be especially powerful in family businesses because family relationships magnify the passions binding family members to the company. Without a succession plan, those passions can explode into destructive behavior that can endanger the family business. *After living in a family that struggled for a meager existence in Ecuador, Luis Noboa cofounded a coffee and banana business and earned his first million by age 39. Noboa later bought out his partner, and when he died at the age of 78, his company, Fruit Shippers Ltd., held $800 million in assets. Unfortunately, Noboa had neglected to develop a management succession plan, and a lengthy and costly battle among his four children ensued. Nine years and $20 million later, Noboa's youngest son Alvaro emerged as the "winner" in the fierce battle over control of the business. However, the Noboa family was divided from the nasty accusations, underhanded tactics, and lengthy lawsuits that characterized one of the most expensive family business conflicts in history.*[14]

> Company Example

Exit Strategies

2. Understand the exit strategy options available to an entrepreneur.

Most family business founders want their companies to stay within their families, although in some cases maintaining family control is not practical. Sometimes no one in the next generation of family members has an interest in managing the company or has the necessary skills and experience to handle the job. Under these circumstances, the founder must look outside the family for leadership if the company is to survive. Whatever the case, entrepreneurs must confront their mortality and plan for the future of their companies. Having a solid management succession plan in place well before retirement is near is absolutely critical to success. Entrepreneurs should examine their options once they decide it is time to step down from the businesses they have founded. Three options are available to entrepreneurs planning to retire: sell to outsiders, sell to (nonfamily) insiders, or pass the business on to family members with the help of a management succession plan. We turn now to these three exit strategies.

Selling to Outsiders

As you learned in Chapter 5, selling a business to an outsider is no simple task. Done properly, it takes time, patience, and preparation to locate a suitable buyer, strike a deal, and make the transition. Advance preparation, maintaining accurate financial records, and timing are the keys to a successful sale. Too often, however, business owners, like some famous athletes, stay with the game too long until they and their businesses are well past their prime. They postpone selling until the last minute when they reach retirement age or when they face a business crisis. Such a "fire sale" approach rarely yields the maximum value for a business.

A straight sale may be best for those entrepreneurs who want to step down and turn the reins of the company over to someone else. However, selling a business outright is not an attractive exit strategy for those who want to stay on with the company or for those who want to surrender control of the company gradually rather than all at once. *When Paul and David Merage decided to sell their highly successful family business, Chef America, their preference was to "cash out" and leave the business behind. The brothers, émigrés from Iran, launched Chef America in 1977 when they spotted three key trends they believed would establish convenience foods as a market staple: more women joining the workforce, people eating more on the run, and people "grazing" rather than sitting down to the traditional three meals a day. After spending a great deal of money and effort on research and development, Chef America developed the predecessor to the company's hit product, the Hot Pocket, which achieved iconic status after being mentioned in an Austin Powers film. Chef America achieved market dominance in the frozen portable entrée category, making it one of the most profitable companies in the entire food industry. Recently, Swiss food giant Nestlé SA purchased Chef America for $2.6 billion!*[15]

The financial terms of a sale also influence the selling price of the business and the number of potential bidders. Does the owner want "clean, cash only, 100 percent at closing" offers, or is the owner willing to finance a portion of the sale? The 100 percent, cash-only requirement dramatically reduces the number of potential buyers. On the other hand, the owner can exit the business "free and clear" and does not incur the risk that the buyer may fail to operate the business in a profitable fashion and not able to complete the financial transition.

Selling to Insiders

When entrepreneurs have no family members to whom they can transfer ownership or who want to assume the responsibilities of running a company, selling the business to employees is often the preferred option. In most situations, the options available to owners are (1) a sale for cash plus a note, (2) a leveraged buyout, and (3) an employee stock ownership plan (ESOP).

Sales for Cash Plus a Note. Whether entrepreneurs sell their businesses to insiders, outsiders, or family members, they often finance a portion of the sales price. The buyer pays the seller a lump-sum amount of cash up-front and the seller holds a promissory note for the remaining portion of the selling price, which the buyer pays off in installments. Because of its many creative financial options, this method of selling a business is popular with buyers. They can buy promising businesses without having to come up with the total purchase price all at one time. Sellers also appreciate the security and the tax implications of accepting payment over time. They receive a portion of the sale up-front and have the assurance of receiving a steady stream of income in the future. Plus, they can stretch their tax liabilities from the capital gains on the sale over time rather than having to pay them in a single year. In many cases, sellers' risks are lower because they may even retain a seat on the board of directors to ensure that the new owners are keeping the business on track. *When Jim and Lorraine Hudson decided to retire from the successful auto dealership they had operated for 26 years, they decided to sell the business to their daughter, Lynne, and her husband, Chad Millspaugh. The founding couple was confident in turning over the decision making to Lynne and Chad, but they needed help structuring the sale so that it would give them the retirement income they sought and not put the new owners in a difficult financial position. Because the land the dealership occupied had become so valuable, they separated it from the business. They sold the dealership to the Millspaughs for $2 million, accepting a down payment and financing the balance. The Hudsons kept the real estate and will receive lease payments from it, providing them with a healthy retirement income.*[16]

Leveraged Buyouts (LBOs). In a **leveraged buyout (LBO),** managers and/or employees borrow money from a financial institution and pay the owner the total agreed-upon price at closing; then they use the cash generated from the company's operations to pay off the debt. The drawback of this technique is that it creates a highly leveraged business. Because of the high levels of debt they take on, the new management has very little room for error. Too many management mistakes or a slowing economy has led many highly leveraged businesses into bankruptcy.

If properly structured, LBOs can be attractive to both buyers and sellers. Because they get their money up front, sellers do not incur the risk of loss if the buyers cannot keep the business operating successfully. The managers and employees who buy the company have a strong incentive to make sure the business succeeds because they own a piece of the action and some of their capital is at risk in the business. The result can be a highly motivated workforce that works hard and makes sure that the company operates efficiently. *In one of the most successful LBOs in recent years, Jack Stack and a team of managers and employees purchased an ailing subsidiary of International Harvester. The new company, Springfield Remanufacturing Corporation (SRC), which specializes in engine remanufacturing for automotive, trucking, agricultural, and construction industries, began with a debt to equity ratio that was astronomically high, but the team of motivated managers and employees turned the company around. Today SRC has more than 1,000 employees and $140 million in sales.*[17]

[Company Example] →

Employee Stock Ownership Plans (ESOPs). Unlike LBOs, **employee stock ownership plans (ESOPs)** allow employees and/or managers (that is, the future owners) to purchase the business gradually, which frees up enough cash to finance the venture's future growth. With an ESOP, employees contribute a portion of their earnings over time toward purchasing shares of the company's stock from the founder until they own the company outright. (Although in leveraged ESOPs, the ESOP borrows the money to buy the owner's stock up front. Then, using employees' contributions, the ESOP repays the loan over time. Another advantage of a leveraged ESOP is that the principal and the interest the ESOP borrows to buy the business are tax deductible, which can save thousands or even millions of dollars in taxes.) Transferring ownership to employees through an ESOP is a long-term exit strategy that benefits everyone involved. The owner sells the business to the people he or she can trust the most—his or her managers and employees. The managers and employees buy a business they already know how to run successfully. Plus, because they own the company, the managers and employees have a huge incentive to see that it operates effectively and efficiently. One recent study of employee stock ownership plans in privately held companies found that the ESOPs increased sales, employment, and sales per employee by 2.4 percent a year.[18] Figure 20.1 shows the trend in the number of ESOPs and the number of employee owners.

The third exit strategy available to company founders is transferring ownership to the next generation of family members with the help of a comprehensive management succession plan.

Management Succession

3. Discuss the stages of management succession.

Experts estimate that between 2001 and 2017, $12 trillion in wealth will be transferred from one generation to the next, representing the greatest transfer of wealth ever and much of it funneled through family businesses.[19] Most of the family businesses in existence today were started after World War II, and more than 70 percent of them still are controlled by either their founders or the second generation of family members.[20] Many of the founders who have not yet transferred ownership to the next generation now are in their seventies and eighties and are ready to pass the torch of leadership. For a smooth

Figure 20.1

Employee Stock Ownership Plans

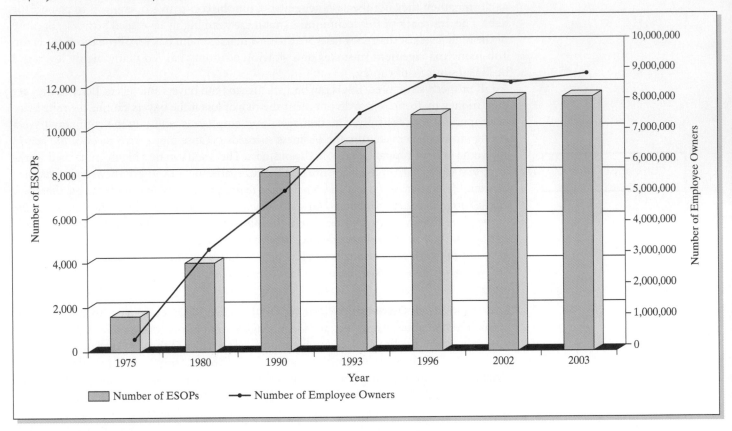

Source: National Center for Employee Ownership, 2004.

transition from one generation to the next, these companies need a succession plan. Without a succession plan, family businesses face an increased risk of faltering or failing in the next generation. Those businesses with the greatest probability of surviving are the ones whose owners prepare a succession plan well before it is time to transfer control to the next generation. Succession planning also allows business owners to minimize the impact of taxes on their businesses, their estates, and their successors' wealth as well and to avoid saddling the next generation of ownership with burdensome debt.

Why, then, do so many entrepreneurs postpone succession planning until it is too late? Many business founders hesitate to let go of their businesses because their personal identities are so wrapped up in their companies. Over time, the founder's identity becomes so intertwined in the business that, in the entrepreneur's mind, there is no distinction between the two. John Gregorian, who inherited the family Oriental rug business from his father in 1978, says that he has "thought about" succession planning but has done nothing about it even though his son, Scott, is obviously his successor in the company. Gregorian, now in his early sixties, displays an attitude typical of so many business owners. "I am the company, and the company is me," he says. "I will always have some sort of connection with the business."[21]

Another barrier to succession planning is that, in planning the future of the business, owners are forced to accept the painful reality of their own mortality. Plus turning over the reins of a business they have sacrificed for, fretted over, and dedicated themselves to for so many years is extremely difficult to do—even if the successor is a son or daughter! Paul Snodgrass, son of the founder of Pella Products, a maker of apparel for work and outdoor activities, who accepted leadership of the company from his father, explains, "Dad loves you and wants you to take over the business, but he also put heart and soul into that business, and he's not going to let anybody screw it up—not even you."[22] Finally, many family business founders believe that controlling the business also gives them a degree of control over family members and family behavior. *David Molina started Molina Health Care, a hospital and insurance company, in 1980 with just $5,000. Although the company grew to be a huge success with hundreds of millions of dollars in sales, Molina never got around to preparing a succession plan for the business. When he died, the family business faced a serious challenge. "Dad had not expressed what he wanted to happen to the company should he not be here," says son John, one of five children who worked in the family business. Ultimately, the board of directors selected Molina's oldest son, Mario, to assume the helm. The family rallied around Mario to maintain the company's success and created a family council that has put in place a succession plan for the next generation of ownership.*[23]

Company Example

Planning for management succession protects not only the founder's, successor's, and company's financial resources, but it also preserves what matters most in a successful business: its heritage and tradition. "Real succession planning involves developing a strategy for transferring the trust, respect, and goodwill built by one generation to the next," explains Andy Bluestone, who took over as president of the financial services company his father founded.[24] Management succession planning requires, first, an attitude of trusting others. It recognizes that other family members have a stake in the future of the business and want to participate in planning its future. Planning is an attitude that shows that decisions made with open discussion are more constructive than those without family input. Second, management succession as an evolutionary process must reconcile an entrepreneur's inevitable anguish and even pain with his or her successors' desire for autonomy. Owners' emotional ties to their businesses usually are stronger than their financial ties. On the other side are the successors, who desire or even crave the autonomy to run the business their way. These inherent conflicts can—and often do—result in skirmishes.

Succession planning reduces the tension and stress created by these conflicts by gradually "changing the guard." A well-developed succession plan is like the smooth, graceful exchange of a baton between runners in a relay race. The new runner still has maximum energy; the concluding runner has already spent his or her energy by running at maximum speed. The athletes never come to a stop to exchange the baton; instead, the handoff takes place on the move. The race is a skillful blend of the talents of all team members—an exchange of leadership so smooth and powerful that the business never falters, but accelerates, fueled by a new source of energy at each leg of the race.

Management succession involves a lengthy series of interconnected stages that begins very early in the life of the owner's children and extends to the point of final ownership transition (see Figure 20.2). If management succession is to be effective, it is necessary for the process to begin early in the successor's life (Stage I). For instance, the owner of a catering business recalls putting his son to work in the family owned company at age 7. On weekends, the boy would arrive at dawn to baste turkeys and was paid in his favorite medium of exchange—doughnuts![25] In most cases, family business owners involve their children in their businesses while they are still in junior high or high school. In this phase, the tasks are routine, but the child is learning the basics of how the business operates. Young adults begin to appreciate the role the business plays in the life of the family. They learn firsthand about the values and responsibilities of running the company.

While in college, the successor moves to Stage II of the continuum. During this stage, the individual rotates among a variety of job functions to both broaden his or her base of understanding of the business and to permit the parents to evaluate the child's skills. Upon graduation from college, the successor enters Stage III. At this

Figure 20.2

Stages in Management Succession

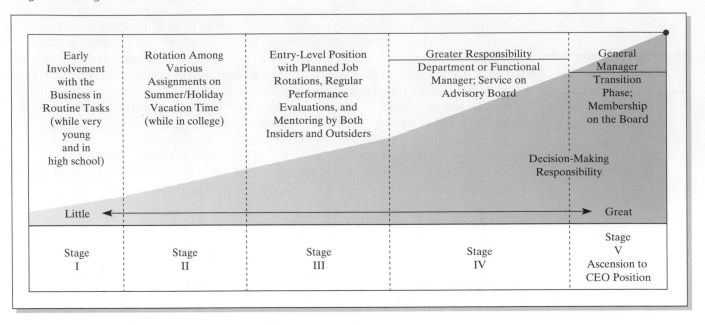

point, the successor becomes a full-time worker and ideally has already begun to earn the respect of coworkers through his or her behavior in the first two stages of the process. In some cases, the successor may work for a time outside of the family business to gain experience and to establish a reputation for competency that goes beyond "being the boss's kid." Stage III focuses on the successor's continuous development, often through a program designed to groom the successor using both family and non-family managers as mentors. *Donata Major, who, with her brothers, runs the construction and real estate development company her father launched, was working in the family business by age 12. When she graduated from college, she joined the company full time as a property manager. Although not yet teenagers, the third generation of the Russell family is already helping in the business. "The exposure is so important," says Major.*[26]

As the successor develops his or her skills and abilities, he or she moves to Stage IV, in which real decision-making authority grows rapidly. Stage IV of the succession continuum is the period when the founder makes a final assessment of the potential successor's competence and ability to take full and complete control over the firm. The skills the successor will need include the following:

- *Financial abilities.* Understanding the financial aspect of a business, what its financial position is, and the managerial implications of that position are crucial to success.
- *Technical knowledge.* Every business has its own body of knowledge, ranging from how the distribution system works to the trends shaping the industry, that an executive must master.
- *Negotiating ability.* Much of business, whether buying supplies and inventory or selling to customers, boils down to negotiating, and a business owner must be adept at it.
- *Leadership qualities.* Leaders must be bold enough to stake out the company's future and then give employees the resources, the power, and the freedom to pursue it.
- *Communication skills.* Business leaders must communicate the vision they have for their businesses; good listening skills also are essential for success as a top manager.

Company Example

- *Juggling skills.* Business owners must be able to handle multiple projects effectively. Like a juggler, they must maintain control over several important assignments simultaneously.
- *Integrity.* To be an effective leader of a family business, a successor must demonstrate honesty and integrity in business dealings.
- *Commitment to the business.* It helps if a successor has a genuine passion for the business. Leaders who have enthusiasm for what they do create a spark of excitement throughout the entire organization.[27]

The final stage in the management succession process involves the ultimate transition of organizational leadership. It is during this stage that the founder's role as mentor is most crucial. *When Debbie Bailey joined Delta Dallas Staffing, the staffing and temporary services company her mother founded, she was concerned that working for the family business might damage their mother–daughter relationship. It didn't happen. The move worked out well for mother, daughter, and the company, which under Bailey's guidance has diversified and has grown to sales of more than $11.5 million a year. "The biggest advantage of taking over a family business," says Bailey, "is that you have a built-in mentor."[28]*

| Company Example | → |

In Stage V the successor may become the organization's CEO while the former CEO retains the title of chairman of the board. In other cases, the best solution is for the founder to step out of the business entirely and give the successor the chance to establish his or her own identity within the company. "Any leader's final legacy is building the next generation," says one business consultant.[29]

IN THE FOOTSTEPS OF AN ENTREPRENEUR . . .

The Race Goes On

NASCAR, the National Association for Stock Car Auto Racing (itself a family-owned business), is the centerpiece of one of the hottest sports in the nation. Founded in 1947 by Bill France Sr., NASCAR has tapped into America's love affair with the automobile and fascination with speed. NASCAR recently closed a television deal worth nearly $2.8 billion and, despite having the highest average ticket prices of any sport ($80), consistently sells out each race. NASCAR's Nextel Cup races average more than 135,000 fans, and television ratings are climbing rapidly, unlike those of other professional sports, which are declining. Television ratings, of course, attract advertisers, and sponsors pay as much as $15 million to racing teams to get their names and logos emblazoned on a stock car. Sales of NASCAR-related products now exceed $1 billion a year.

Despite being a big business, much of NASCAR is controlled by family businesses. Many of the companies that own the teams of cars and drivers are family businesses, but few are as famous as Dale Earnhardt Inc. (DEI), headquartered in tiny Mooresville, North

Carolina. Driver of the well-known "#3 car," Dale Earnhardt Sr. and his wife Teresa worked side by side in the business he founded in 1980 until his tragic death in a crash at the Daytona 500 in 2002. Despite the loss of DEI's founder, central figure, and endorsement icon, Teresa, who now owns the company fully, says, "I never once considered walking away." Her challenge was to determine how to keep this unique family business going after Earnhardt Sr.'s death.

DEI's primary revenue streams are corporate car sponsorships, winnings from its team of three drivers (which includes Dale Earnhardt, Jr., Dale's son), product endorsements, and royalties from licensing deals. The largest portion of the company's revenue comes from the 15 companies that pay about $40 million a year for the three Nextel Cup cars and their crews and, in exchange, get their names splashed across the cars. Teresa convinced all of DEI's sponsors (the biggest are Anheuser-Busch, Napa Auto Parts, and Pennzoil) to remain with the company and added three more, including cologne maker Drakkar Noir. Maintaining sponsorships, however, requires drivers who win races, so Teresa decided to invest $3 million in new equipment and 50 new engineers and mechanics to maintain the teams' edge on the racetrack.

The trickiest issue is endorsements. Because Earnhardt was a spokesman for Coca-Cola, Chevrolet,

and Kraft, among others, Teresa had to find new ways to create marketing deals with these companies. She worked with Chevrolet, which pulled all of its Earnhardt ads after the fatal crash, produced a limited number of black Monte Carlos modeled after the one Dale Sr. drove, and sold them all. Teresa convinced Kraft to sponsor one of DEI's team cars, which means that the company now spends more with DEI than when Dale Sr. was alive. Even though DEI lost its primary salesperson in Dale Earnhardt Sr., Teresa has kept the company at the front of the pack. Annual revenues recently hit $80 million, the highest in the company's history.

1. In what ways is DEI a typical family business? In what ways is it unique?
2. Explain the qualities that are necessary for a successful family business.
3. What advice would you offer Teresa Earnhardt about keeping the family business in the family?

Sources: Adapted from Joanne Gordon, "Wife After Death," *Forbes*, February 17, 2004; Liz Clarke and Thomas Heath, "NASCAR's Owner Does It His Way," *Greenville News*, July 8, 2001, pp. 1G, 4G; "History of NASCAR," *Chatham Journal*, July 2000, www.chathamjournal.com/700nascarhistory.html; Mike Harris, "NASCAR's France Resigns," *Witchita Eagle*, November 29, 2000, web.wichitaeagle.com/content/wichitaeagle/2000/11/29/racing/nascar1128_txt.htm.

Developing a Management Succession Plan

4. Explain how to develop an effective management succession plan.

Families that are most committed to ensuring that their businesses survive from one generation to the next exhibit four characteristics: (1) They believe that owning the business helps achieve their families' missions. (2) They are proud of the values their businesses are built on and exemplify. (3) They believe that the business is contributing to society and makes it a better place to live. (4) They rely on management succession plans to assure the continuity of their companies.[30] Developing a plan takes time and dedication, yet the benefits are well worth the cost. A sound succession plan enables a company to maintain its momentum and sense of purpose and direction.

It is important to start the planning process early, well before the founder's retirement. Succession planning is not the kind of activity an entrepreneur can do in a hurry, and the sooner an entrepreneur starts, the easier it will be. Unfortunately, too many entrepreneurs put it off until it's too late. "Succession works best when parents have enough fortitude to discuss everything with their kids and resolve these issues while they're still alive," says one expert.[31] Creating a succession plan involves the following steps.

Step 1: Select the Successor

The average tenure of the founder of a family business has remained constant at 25 years for the past decade.[32] Yet, there comes a time for even the most dedicated founder to step down and hand the reins of the company to the next generation. Entrepreneurs should never assume that their children want to take control of the business, however. Above all, they should not be afraid to ask the question: "Do you really want to take over the family business?" Too often, children in this situation tell Mom and Dad what they want to hear out of loyalty, pressure, or guilt. It is critical to remember at this juncture in the life of a business that children do not necessarily inherit their parents' entrepreneurial skills and desires. By leveling with the children about the business and their options regarding a family succession, the owner will know which heirs, if any, are willing to assume leadership of the business.

One of the worst mistakes entrepreneurs can make is to postpone naming a successor until just before they are ready to step down. One study by Arthur Andersen and MassMutual found that 55 percent of family business owners age 61 or older have not yet designated a successor![33] The problem is especially acute when more than one family member works for the company and is interested in assuming leadership of it. Sometimes founders avoid naming successors because they don't want to hurt the family members who are not chosen to succeed them. However, both the business and the family will be better off if, after observing family members as they work in the business, the founder picks a successor based on skill and ability. When naming a successor, merit is a better standard to use than gender or birth order. The key is to establish standards of performance, knowledge, education, and ability and then to identify the person who best meets those standards. As part of his company's succession plan, Joe De La Torre selected his daughter Gina to take over Jaunita's Foods rather than his two sons because her financial skills and her ability to solve problems were what the company needed most.[34] Gina La Torre is part of a growing trend among family businesses; 34 percent of family business founders expect the next CEO to be a woman, quite a change from just a generation ago.[35] *When her father was ready to retire from the golf course and resort his father had founded in 1921, Victoria Ross was the natural choice to take over leadership of the business. Ross literally grew up in the family business and knew every aspect of it intimately. "I was in a waitress uniform at age 6 and have worked every position [in the business]," she says. When she was just 18, Ross assumed management positions at the resort and golf club before going on to earn a degree in business administration with a concentration in small business. She even found time to work at another resort, something she says proved to be quite helpful in managing the family business today.*[36]

<table>
<tr><td>Company Example</td><td>→</td></tr>
</table>

Step 2: Create a Survival Kit for the Successor

Once he or she identifies a successor, an entrepreneur should prepare a survival kit and then brief the future leader on its contents, which should include all of the company's critical documents (wills, trusts, insurance policies, financial statements, bank accounts, key contracts, corporate bylaws, and so forth). The founder should be sure that the successor reads and understands all the relevant documents in the kit. Other important steps the owner should take to prepare the successor to take over leadership of the business include:

- Create a strategic analysis for the future. Working with the successor, identify the primary opportunities and the challenges facing the company and the requirements for meeting them.
- On a regular basis, share with the successor the owner's vision of the business's future direction, describing key factors that have led to its success and those that will bring future success.
- Be open and listen to the successor's views and concerns.
- Teach and learn at the same time.
- Identify the industry's key success factors.
- Tie the key success factors to the company's performance and profitability.
- Explain the company's overall strategy and how it creates a competitive advantage.
- Discuss the values and philosophy of the business and how they have inspired and influenced past actions.
- Discuss the people in the business and their strengths and weaknesses.

▪ Discuss the philosophy underlying the firm's compensation policy and explain why employees are paid what they are.

▪ Make a list of the firm's most important customers and its key suppliers or vendors and review the history of all dealings with the parties on both lists.

▪ Discuss how to treat key suppliers or vendors to ensure the company's continued success and its smooth and error-free ownership transition.

▪ Develop a job analysis by taking an inventory of the activities involved in leading the company. This analysis can show successors those activities on which they should be spending most of their time.

▪ Document as much process knowledge—"how we do things"—as possible. After many years in their jobs, business owners are not even aware of their vast reservoirs of knowledge. For them, making decisions is a natural part of their business lives. They do it effortlessly because they have so much knowledge and experience. It is easy to forget that a successor will not have the benefit of those years of experience unless the founder communicates it.

▪ Include an ethical will, a document that explains to the next generation of leaders the ethical principles on which the company operates. An ethical will gives company founders the chance to bequeath to their heirs not only a business but also the wisdom and ethical lessons learned over a lifetime.

Company Example

Before Bob Waldrop, founder of Milbank Manufacturing Company, a maker of electrical meter casings with sales of $100 million, retired, he and the members of the family business drafted a "family constitution," a 20-page statement of the guiding principles on which the company was built. Drafting the document, in which Waldrop, his son Rob (company president), his daughter Katrina (executive vice president), and two other children involved in the family business, were the primary players, took 18 months and created a few disagreements, which is a normal—and healthy—part of the process. "The process is almost as important as the document," says Bill Chapman, the family business consultant who worked with the Waldrop family to create the document. The Waldrops' document covered everything from accountability and compensation to board composition and management succession plans and made the transition from one generation of leadership to the next much smoother.[37]

Pepper . . . and Salt

THE WALL STREET JOURNAL

CALDWELL.

"It's been difficult, Ray. Grooming my successor has left me with precious little time for myself."

Step 3: Groom the Successor

The process by which business founders transfer their knowledge to the next generation is gradual and often occurs informally as they spend time with their successors. Grooming the successor is the founder's greatest teaching and development responsibility, and it takes time, usually five to ten years. To implement the succession plan, the founder must be:

- Patient, realizing that the transfer of power is gradual and evolutionary and that the successor should earn responsibility and authority one step at a time until the final transfer of power takes place.
- Willing to accept that the successor will make mistakes.
- Skillful at using the successor's mistakes as a teaching tool.
- An effective communicator and an especially tolerant listener.
- Capable of establishing reasonable expectations for the successor's performance.
- Able to articulate the keys to the successor's performance.

Teaching is in reality the art of assisting discovery and requires letting go rather than controlling. When a problem arises in the business, the founder should consider delegating it to the successor-in-training. If the successor-in-training takes on responsibility for the problem, the founder must resist the tendency to wade in and fix the problem unless it is beyond the scope of the successor's ability. Most great teachers and leaders are remembered more for the success of their students and followers than for their own.

Step 4: Promote an Environment of Trust and Respect

Another priceless gift a founder can leave a successor is an environment of trust and respect. Trust and respect on the part of the founder and others fuel the successor's desire to learn and excel and they also build the successor's confidence in making decisions. Empowering the successor by gradually delegating responsibilities creates an environment in which all parties can objectively view the growth and development of the successor. Customers, creditors, suppliers, and staff members can gradually develop confidence in the successor. The final transfer of power is not a dramatic, wrenching change but a smooth, coordinated passage.

A problem for some founders at this phase is the meddling retiree syndrome, in which they continue to show up at the office after they have officially stepped down and get involved in business issues that no longer concern them. This tendency merely undermines the authority of the successor and confuses employees as to who really is in charge.

Company Example → *Helen Dragas, who succeeded her father at The Dragas Company, a residential construction business, praises her father for handing the reins of the company over to her and then trusting her to handle them. "He gave me the authority and then he stepped back," she says of the successful transfer of leadership.*[38]

Step 5: Cope with the Financial Realities of Estate and Gift Taxes

The final step in developing a workable management succession plan is structuring the transition to minimize the impact of estate, gift, and inheritance taxes on family members and the business. Entrepreneurs who fail to consider the impact of these taxes may force their heirs to sell a successful business just to pay the estate's tax bill. Still, a survey by MassMutual Financial Group and the Raymond Institute found that 19 percent of senior

Company Example → generation owners had done no estate planning at all![39] *Ella Perkins, co-owner of Perkins Flowers, and her son Gordon saw the need to develop an estate plan to minimize the impact of estate and gift taxes on the company, which Gordon was running. Each year, Ella gave Gordon $10,000 worth of stock in the company, the maximum amount the law allows without* *triggering gift taxes. She also transferred majority ownership in the company to Gordon using other estate planning tools so that estate taxes would be smaller on her minority share of the business. Gordon also purchased enough life insurance for his mother to pay the estimated estate tax bill. When Ella died at age 83, Gordon discovered that despite their attempts at estate planning, the amount of tax due was more than he had expected. "At the very least," he says, "it's going to repress the growth of my business for some significant amount of time." He says that he may have to sell a 43-acre tree farm the company owns to pay the full tax bill.*[40]

Although tax laws currently allow individuals to pass up to $2 million of assets to their heirs without incurring any estate taxes, the tax rate on transfers above that amount starts at 41 percent! Although Congress has overhauled the estate and gift tax (see Table 20.2), without proper estate planning, an entrepreneur's family members will incur a painful tax bite when they inherit the business. Entrepreneurs should be actively engaged in estate planning no later than age 45; those who start businesses early in their lives or whose businesses grow rapidly may need to begin as early as age 30. A variety of options exist that may prove to be helpful in reducing the estate tax liability. Each operates in a different fashion, but their objective remains the same: to remove a portion of business owners' assets out of their estates so that when they die, those assets will not be subject to estate taxes. Many of these estate planning tools need time to work their magic, so the key is to put them in place early on in the life of the business.

Buy/Sell Agreement. One of the most popular estate planning techniques is the buy/sell agreement. One survey by the Chartered Life Underwriters and the Chartered Life Financial Consultants found that 76 percent of small business owners who have estate plans have created buy/sell agreements.[41] A **buy/sell agreement** is a contract that co-owners often rely on to ensure the continuity of a business. In a typical arrangement, the co-owners create a contract stating that each agrees to buy the others out in case of the death or disability of one. That way, the heirs of the deceased or disabled owner can "cash

Table 20.2

Changes in Estate
and Gift Taxes

After years of complaints from family business owners, Congress finally overhauled the often punishing structures of estate and gift taxes. The federal estate tax is actually interwoven with the gift tax, but under the modified law, the impact of the two taxes began to differ starting in 2004. The estate tax is scheduled to be repealed in 2010, but under current provisions, it will reappear in 2011! The following table shows the exemptions and the minimum tax rates for the estate and gift taxes as they currently stand.

Year	Estate Tax Exemption	Gift Tax Exemption	Maximum Tax Rate
2001	$675,000	$675,000	55%
2002	$1 million	$1 million	50%
2003	$1 million	$1 million	49%
2004	$1.5 million	$1 million	48%
2005	$1.5 million	$1 million	47%
2006	$2 million	$1 million	46%
2007	$2 million	$1 million	45%
2008	$2 million	$1 million	45%
2009	$3.5 million	$1 million	45%
2010	Tax repealed	$1 million	35% (gifts only)
2011	$1 million	$1 million	55%

However the federal laws governing estate taxes may change over the next few years, entrepreneurs whose businesses have been successful must not neglect estate planning. Even though the federal estate tax burden has eased somewhat (at least for a while), many states have *increased* their estate tax rates.

Sources: Tom Herman, "Estate Taxes Will Turn Sharply Lower on Jan. 1," *Wall Street Journal*, November 20, 2003, p. D2; Jeanne Lee, "Death and Estate Taxes," *FSB*, April 2004, p. 96.

out" of the business while leaving control of the business in the hands of the remaining owners. The buy/sell agreement specifies a formula for determining the value of the business at the time the agreement is to be executed. One problem with buy/sell agreements is that the remaining co-owners may not have the cash available to buy out the disabled or deceased owner. To resolve this issue, many businesses buy life and disability insurance for each of the owners in amounts large enough to cover the purchase price of their respective shares of the business. *Partners Ray Ellis, Scott Hopkins, and John Leimbach spent six months creating a buy/sell agreement to protect themselves and their business, Mailing Concepts Inc., a direct-marketing agency, in the event of the death or disability of a partner. "When we got it done," says Leimbach, "we knew we had guaranteed the long-term survival of the company." The agreement is supported by two disability and two life insurance policies on each partner, giving them the income security they need for their families and providing the remaining partners the financial resources to buy the shares of the missing partner.*[42]

Without the support of adequate insurance policies, a buy/sell agreement offers virtually no protection.

Lifetime Gifting. The owners of a successful business may transfer money to their children (or other recipients) from their estate throughout the parents' lives. Current federal tax regulations allow individuals to make gifts of $11,000 per year, per parent, per recipient, that are exempt from federal gift taxes. Each child would be required to pay income taxes on the $11,000 gift they receive, but the children are usually in lower tax brackets than those of the giver. For instance, husband-and-wife business owners could give $1.32 million worth of stock to their three children and their spouses over a period of 10 years without incurring any estate or gift taxes at all.

Setting Up a Trust. A **trust** is a contract between a grantor (the founder) and a trustee (generally a bank officer or an attorney) in which the grantor gives to the trustee legal title to assets (e.g., stock in the company), which the trustee agrees to hold for the beneficiaries (children). The beneficiaries can receive income from the trust, or they can receive the property in the trust, or both, at some specified time. Trusts can take a wide variety of forms, but two broad categories of trusts are available: revocable trusts and irrevocable trusts. A **revocable trust** is one that the grantor can change or revoke during his or her lifetime. Under present tax laws, however, the only trust that provides a tax benefit is an **irrevocable trust,** in which the grantor cannot require the trustee to return the assets held in trust. The value of the grantor's estate is lowered because the assets in an irrevocable trust are excluded from the value of that estate. However, an irrevocable trust places severe restrictions on the grantor's control of the property placed in the trust. Business owners use several types of irrevocable trusts to lower their estate tax liabilities.

Bypass Trust. The most basic type of trust is the bypass trust, which allows a business owner to put up to $1.5 million (an amount that will increase by the amount of the estate tax exemption according to the schedule listed in Table 20.2) into trust naming his or her spouse as the beneficiary upon the owner's death. The spouse receives the income from the trust throughout his or her life, but the principal in the trust bypasses the spouse's estate and goes to the couple's heirs free of estate taxes upon the spouse's death.

Irrevocable Life Insurance Trust. This type of trust allows a business owner to keep the proceeds of a life insurance policy out of his or her estate and away from estate taxes, freeing up that money to pay the taxes on the remainder of the estate. To get the tax benefit, business owners must be sure that the business or the trust (rather than themselves) owns the insurance policy. The disadvantage of an irrevocable life insurance trust is that if the owner dies within three years of establishing it, the insurance proceeds do become part of his or her estate and are subject to estate taxes.

Company Example

Irrevocable Asset Trust. An irrevocable asset trust is similar to a life insurance trust except that it is designed to pass the assets in the parents' estate on to their children. The children do not have control of the assets while the parents are still living, but they do receive the income from those assets. Upon the parents' death, the assets in the trust go to the children without being subjected to the estate tax.

Grantor Retained Annuity Trust (GRAT). A grantor retained annuity trust (GRAT) is a special type of irrevocable trust and has become one of the most popular tools for entrepreneurs to transfer ownership of a business while maintaining control over it and minimizing estate taxes. Under a GRAT, an owner can put property in an irrevocable trust for a maximum of 10 years. While the trust is in effect, the grantor (owner) retains the voting power and receives the interest income from the property in the trust. At the end of the trust (not to exceed 10 years), the property passes to the beneficiaries (heirs). The beneficiaries are required to pay the gift tax on the value of the assets placed in the GRAT but no estate tax on them. However, the IRS taxes GRAT gifts only according to their discounted present value because the heirs did not receive use of the property while it was in trust. The primary disadvantage of using a GRAT in estate planning is that if the grantor dies during the life of the GRAT, its assets pass back into the grantor's estate. These assets then become subject to the full estate tax.

Establishing a trust requires meeting many specific legal requirements and is not something business owners should do on their own. It is much better to hire experienced attorneys, accountants, and financial advisors to assist in creating them. Although the cost of establishing a trust can be high, the tax savings they generate are well worth the expense.

Estate Freeze. An **estate freeze** attempts to minimize estate taxes by having family members create two classes of stock for the business: (1) preferred voting stock for the parents and (2) nonvoting common stock for the children. The value of the preferred stock is frozen whereas the common stock reflects the anticipated increased market value of the business. Any appreciation in the value of the business after the transfer is not subject to estate taxes. However, the parents must pay gift tax on the value of the common stock given to the children. The value of the common stock is the total value of the business less the value of the voting preferred stock retained by the parents. The parents also must accept taxable dividends at the market rate on the preferred stock they own.

Family Limited Partnership. Creating a **family limited partnership** (**FLP**) allows business-owning parents to transfer their company to their children (thus lowering their estate taxes) while still retaining control over it for themselves. To create a family limited partnership, the parents (or parent) set up a partnership among themselves and their children. The parents retain the general partnership interest, which can be as low as 1 percent, and the children become the limited partners. As general partners, the parents control both the limited partnership and the family business. In other words, nothing in the way the company operates has to change. Over time, the parents can transfer company stock into the limited partnership, ultimately passing ownership of the company to their children. One of the principal tax benefits of an FLP is that it allows discounts on the value of the shares of company stock the parents transfer into the limited partnership. Because a family business is closely held, shares of ownership in it, especially minority shares, are not as marketable as those of a publicly held company. As a result, company shares transferred into the limited partnership are discounted at 20 to 50 percent of their full market value, producing a large tax savings for everyone involved. The average discount is 40 percent, but that amount varies based on the industry and the individual company involved. A business owner should consider an FLP as part of a succession plan "when there has

Table 20.3

An Estate Planning
Checklist

> Would your estate be in order if you died unexpectedly? Would your family suffer because you hadn't planned? Would your estate be socked with high taxes? Would your business be able to continue? Answer these 12 questions to measure how well you have done your estate planning.
>
>   1. Do you have a will?
>   2. Has your will been updated within the past three years?
>   3. Do you know your net worth?
>   4. Do you know the value of your business?
>   5. Do you know who would acquire ownership of your business if you were to die tomorrow?
>   6. Do you know who would run your business if you were to die tomorrow?
>   7. Would your business be likely to survive under the ownership and leadership of the people named in questions 5 and 6?
>   8. Have you groomed your successor properly to take over the management of the business?
>   9. Have you cultivated a team of people to support your successor in running the business successfully?
> 10. Do you know how your estate would finance the applicable estate taxes if you were to die tomorrow?
> 11. Do you know how the new owner of your business would finance its purchase?
> 12. Has an attorney, an accountant, and other professionals who specialize in estate planning reviewed your estate plan?
>
> **Scoring:**
>
> Give yourself 10 points for every question you answered "yes." If your score is:
>
> ■ between 100 and 120—Your estate is in secure hands. You should talk with an estate planning professional periodically to adjust your plan as your needs change.
>
> ■ between 70 and 90—Your estate is exposed to more risk than it should be. Your family is likely to incur unnecessary expenses and trouble with your estate. See an estate planning professional for advice soon.
>
> ■ between 0 and 80—Your estate is in imminent danger! You should call an estate planning professional immediately and develop a sound plan to make sure your business survives you.
>
> *Sources:* Adapted from Carole Matthews, "Choosing a Successful Successor," *Inc.*, October 17, 2001, www.inc.com/search/23550.html; Randy Myers, "Where There's a Will ...," *Nation's Business*, April 1997, p. 26.

been a buildup of substantial value in the business and the older generation has a substantial amount of liquidity," says one expert.[43] Because of their ability to reduce estate and gift taxes, family limited partnerships have become one of the most popular estate planning tools in recent years.

Developing a succession plan and preparing a successor requires a wide variety of knowledge and skills, some of which the business founder will not have. That's why it is important to bring into the process experts when necessary. Entrepreneurs often call on their attorneys, accountants, insurance agents, and financial planners to help them build a succession plan that works best for their particular situations. Because the issues involved can be highly complex and charged with emotion, bringing in trusted advisors to help improves the quality of the process and provides an objective perspective. Table 20.3 provides an estate planning checklist for entrepreneurs.

Risk Management Strategies

5. Understand the four risk management strategies.

Insurance is an important part of creating a management succession plan because it can help business owners minimize the taxes on the estates they pass on to their heirs and can provide much needed cash to pay the taxes the estate does incur. However, insurance plays an important role in many other aspects of a successful business—from covering employee injuries to protecting against natural disasters that might shut a business down temporarily. When most small business owners think of risks such as these, they automatically think of insurance. However, insurance companies are the first to point out that insurance does not solve all risk problems. A more comprehensive strategy is risk management, which takes a proactive approach to dealing with the risks that businesses face daily. Pointing to a study showing that only 10 percent of small and midsized companies have developed plans to ensure business survival in the face of a business crisis, one expert claims, "Small companies often spend more time planning the company picnic than planning for an event that could put them out of business."[44] Dealing with risk successfully requires a combination of four risk management strategies: avoiding, reducing, anticipating, and transferring (or spreading) risk.

Avoiding risk requires a business to take actions to shun risky situations. For example, you could substantially reduce the risk of an automobile accident if you sold your car, refused to ride with others, walked to work, and carefully looked both ways before crossing the street. Such actions would be possible, but not practical, because in our busy society people depend on transportation by car or bus. However, businesspeople can avoid risk by thoughtful business practices. For instance, conducting credit checks of customers can help decrease losses from bad debts. Wise managers know that they can avoid some risks simply by taking proactive management actions. Workplace safety improves when business owners implement programs designed to make all employees aware of the hazards of their jobs and how to avoid being hurt. Business owners who have active risk identification and prevention programs can reduce their potential insurance costs as well as create a safer, more attractive work environment for their employees. Because avoiding risk altogether usually is not practical, however, a strategy of reducing risk becomes necessary.

A risk-reducing strategy takes actions that build an extra degree of safety into a situation with an identified level of risk. Businesses can reduce risk by following common safety practices, such as installing a sprinkler system to lower the threat of damage from fire. The sprinkler system cannot guarantee that a fire will not occur, but it may minimize the damage that results. Risk-reduction strategies do not eliminate the source of the risk, but they lessen the impact of its occurrence. Even with avoidance and reduction strategies, the source of the risk is still present; thus, losses can occur.

Risk-anticipation strategies promote self-insurance. Knowing that some element of risk still exists, a business owner puts aside money each month to cover any losses that might occur. For example, suppose that a business owner checks each customer's credit very carefully. The owner takes all reasonable steps to ensure that the customer can pay the bill and has a sound history of prompt payment. Shortly after the sale, however, a fire completely destroys the customer's business, and the merchandise, unpaid for, also was destroyed. The business owner also discovers that the customer's business was not insured and that the loss will cause the customer to declare bankruptcy. The owner may have done everything possible to determine that the customer's credit was solid, but that did not prevent the financial loss caused by the fire and subsequent bankruptcy. In this case, the owner's loss would be less devastating to the company if the owner had put aside cash periodically to cover such losses.

Sometimes a self-insurance fund set aside may not be large enough to cover the losses from a particular situation. When this happens, the business or individual stands to lose despite the best efforts to anticipate risk, especially in the first few years when the fund may be insufficient to cover large losses. Most individuals and businesses, therefore, include in their risk strategies some form of insurance to transfer risk. *For instance, Donald Kling, owner of General Finance, a brick manufacturing company in Concordia, Kansas, grew tired of watching the cost of health care coverage for his 125 employees climb at double-digit rates every year and decided to establish a self-insurance fund to cover his employees' health care benefits. If employees' claims were low in a given year, he would save money over what he would have paid in insurance premiums. If several workers suffered*

Company Example

catastrophic illnesses at once, however, his company could face a cash crisis. Recognizing that a self-insurance strategy alone could be risky, Kling purchased a "stop-loss" policy, which takes over payment if any individual employee's health care costs exceed $25,000 a year. Kling also hired a company to handle all of the insurance paperwork. In the first year after switching to self-insurance, Kling says the strategy saved his company 10 percent over the cost of the company's old plan while providing the same coverage.[45]

Self-insurance is not for every business owner, however. For businesses with fewer than 50 employees, self-insurance is usually not a wise choice because there is so much variation in the number of annual claims. Also, companies using self-insurance should be financially secure with a relatively stable workforce and should see it as a long-term strategy for savings. Self-insuring also is more time-consuming, requiring a business owner to take a more active role in managing the company's insurance needs.

> Company Example →

James Meier, co-owner of Herzog-Meier, a Beaverton, Oregon, car dealership, discovered the disadvantages of being small and trying to self-insure. Major illnesses among several employees in two consecutive years drained the company's self-insurance fund, forcing the dealership to dig into other accounts to pay employees' claims. Even with its stop-loss coverage, the dealership spent $280,000 in just one year, an amount much higher than its health insurance premiums would have been with full insurance coverage. The company is now fully insured again, and its owners are much more comfortable with their limited exposure.[46]

Risk transfer strategies depend on the use of insurance. Insurance is a risk transfer (or risk spreading) strategy because an individual or a business transfers some of the costs of a particular risk to an insurance company, which is set up to spread out the financial burdens of risk. During a specific time period, the insured business or individual pays money (a premium) to the insurance carrier (either a private company or a government agency). In return, the carrier promises to pay the insured a certain amount of money in the event of a loss.

The Basics of Insurance

> **6.** Discuss the basics of insurance for small business.

Insurance is the transfer of risk from one entity (an individual, a group, or a business) to an insurance company. Without insurance, many of the activities and services we take for granted would not be possible because the risk of overwhelming financial loss would be too great for a business to assume. Yet many small business owners ignore their companies' insurance needs. According to the Insurance Information Institute, 15 percent of entrepreneurs do not have any insurance to protect their businesses.[47] Many other entrepreneurs buy insurance coverage for their companies but not enough to protect them from the most basic risks such as property damage, fire, theft, and liability. Home-based business owners, in particular, put their companies at risk. According to the Independent Insurance Agents of America, only 40 percent of home-based business owners have adequate insurance coverage.[48]

To be insurable, a situation or hazard must meet the following requirements:

1. It must be possible to calculate the actual loss being insured. For example, it would probably not be possible to insure an entire city against fire because too many variables are involved. It is possible, however, to insure a specific building.
2. It must be possible to select the risk being insured. No business owner can insure against every potential hazard, but insurance companies offer a wide variety of policies. One company even offers an alien abduction policy ($150 a year for $150 million of coverage) and has actually paid one claim! Another offers werewolf insurance, but the policy pays only if the insured turns into a werewolf.[49]

3. There must be enough potential policyholders to assume the risk. If you are a tightrope walker specializing in walking between tall downtown buildings, you probably cannot be insured because there are simply not enough people engaging in this activity to spread the risk sufficiently.

Perhaps the biggest barrier facing entrepreneurs is the difficulty of understanding the nature of the risks they and their businesses face. The risk management pyramid (see Figure 20.3) can help business owners decide how they should allocate their risk management dollars. Begin by identifying the primary risks your company faces: for example, a fire in a manufacturing plant, a lawsuit from a customer injured by your company's product, an earthquake. Then rate each event on three factors:

1. *Severity*. How much would the event affect your company's ability to operate?
2. *Probability*. How likely is the event to occur?
3. *Cost*. How much would it cost your company if the event occurred?

Rate the event on each of these three factors using a simple scale: A (high) to D (low). For instance, a small company might rate a fire in its manufacturing plant as ABA. On the other hand, that same company might rank a computer system crash as CBA. Using the

Figure 20.3

The Risk Management Pyramid

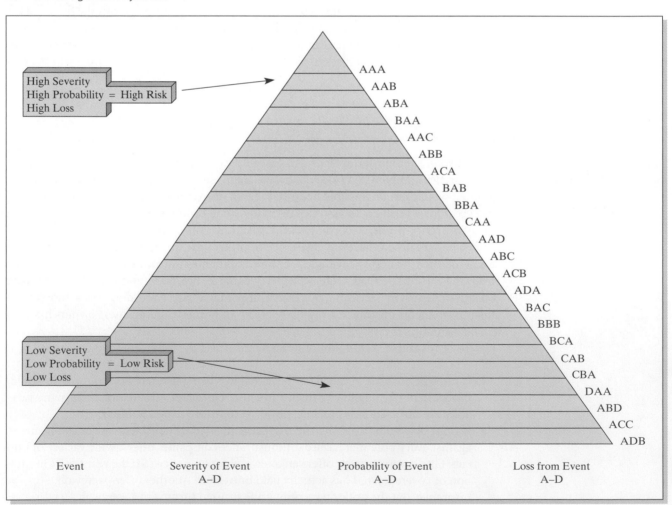

risk management pyramid, the business owner sees that the event rated ABA is higher on the risk scale than the event rated CBA. Therefore, this company would focus more of its risk management dollars on preventing a fire in its plant than on dealing with a computer system crash.

Types of Insurance

No longer is the cost of insurance an inconsequential part of doing business. Now the ability to get adequate coverage and to pay the premiums is a significant factor in starting and running a small business. Sometimes just *finding* coverage for their businesses is a challenge for entrepreneurs. *When J. Linwood Paul and Leslie Bourne launched Fulcrum Learning Systems Inc., in Redondo Beach, California, they had an extremely difficult time finding a company willing to sell them liability insurance because of the risk involved in their business. Fulcrum Learning Systems is an adventure training company that provides customers with training experiences that magnify real-life situations, such as navigating a high-ropes course or scaling a vertical rock cliff. Unfortunately, that makes the company an extremely high insurance risk. "Without insurance, there is no business," says Bourne. The entrepreneurs finally found a company willing to insure them, but for the first six years of business, Fulcrum had six different insurance companies. Although Fulcrum had a perfect safety record for its 80,000 clients and had made no claims, each insurance company decided to get out of the adventure training industry. Finally, the entrepreneurs were able to secure a policy from a more stable insurance company, and their business continues to boom.*[50]

A wide range of business, individual, and group insurance is available to small business owners, and deciding which ones are necessary can be difficult. Some types of insurance are essential to providing a secure future for the company; others may provide additional employee benefits. The four major categories of insurance are property and casualty insurance, life and disability insurance, health insurance and workers' compensation coverage, and liability insurance. Each category is divided into many specific types, each of which has many variations offered by insurance companies. Business owners should begin by purchasing a basic **business owner's policy (BOP),** which typically includes basic property and casualty insurance and liability insurance coverage. BOPs alone are not sufficient to meet most small business owners' insurance needs, however. Entrepreneurs should start with BOPs and then customize their insurance coverage to suit their companies' special needs by purchasing additional types of coverage.

Property and Casualty Insurance. Property and casualty insurance cover a company's tangible assets, such as buildings, equipment, inventory, machinery and signs that might be damaged, destroyed, or stolen. Business owners should be sure that their policies cover the replacement cost of their property, not just its value at the time of the loss, even if it costs extra. One business owner whose policy covered the replacement cost of his company's building was glad he had purchased the extra coverage when he suffered a devastating fire loss. When he began rebuilding, he discovered that the cost to comply with current building code regulations was $1 million, much higher than merely replacing the previous structure.

Specific types of property and casualty insurance include surety, marine and inland marine, crime, liability, business interruption, motor vehicle, and professional liability insurance.

Property insurance protects a company's assets against loss from damage, theft, or destruction. It applies to automobiles, boats, homes, office buildings, stores, factories, and other items of property. Some property insurance policies are broadly written to include all of an individual's property up to some maximum amount of loss, whereas other

Company Example

policies are written to cover only one building or one specific piece of property, such as a company car. Many natural disasters such as floods and earthquakes are not covered under standard property insurance; business owners must buy separate insurance policies for those specific causes of loss. Within the past decade, business owners across the United States have suffered billions of dollars in losses from natural and man-made disasters, including floods in the Midwest, hurricanes on the East Coast, earthquakes in California, and the terrorist attacks on September 11, 2001. Many of those businesses without proper insurance coverage were forced to close, and others are still struggling to recover.

A company's BOP may insure the buildings and contents of a factory for loss from fire or natural disaster, but the owner may also buy insurance, called extra expense coverage, to cover expenses that occur while the destroyed factory is being rebuilt. **Extra expense coverage** pays for the costs of temporarily relocating workers and machinery so that a business can continue to operate while it rebuilds or repairs its factory. A similar type of insurance, called **business interruption insurance,** covers business owners' lost income and ongoing expenses in case their companies cannot operate for an extended period of time. As devastating as such interruptions can be to a small company, studies show that 55 percent of small business owners do not purchase business interruption coverage and that 63 percent of them don't know how the coverage works.[51] Even more alarming is the fact that 40 percent of businesses whose operations are interrupted

Company Example

because of a disaster never recover.[52] *Four years after Al Sanabel, a bakery specializing in pita-based entrées, opened in Anaheim, California, the building housing Nick El Deek's business was damaged by a fire that started in the restaurant next door. The damage was so severe that El Deek's bakery was closed for more than five months, a devastating event because Al Sanabel finally had established a solid customer base, and sales were growing rapidly. Fortunately, El Deek had fire insurance and business interruption insurance, which provided enough money for him and his family to live on until he could reopen Al Sanabel. Extended negotiations with the insurance company required him to borrow $37,000 from friends and family to complete the repairs and renovations. Although sales have not returned to their prefire levels, El Deek is optimistic. "I can make it. It just takes time," he says philosophically.*[53]

Machinery and equipment insurance is a common addition for many businesses and covers a wide range of problems with equipment such as production machinery, electrical systems, HVAC systems, and others. For instance, a restaurant that loses thousands of dollars' worth of food when a freezer breaks would be covered for its loss under machinery and equipment insurance.

IN THE FOOTSTEPS OF AN ENTREPRENEUR...

A Bad Day at the Warehouse

Launched in 1907 by its namesake founder, Maud Borup Chocolates moved quickly from selling homemade candy through a flower shop in downtown St. Paul, Minnesota, to counting the Queen of England as a regular customer. Borup ran the company for 53 years, building it into a thriving business, until her death in 1960. After struggling through an assortment of owners, the company was sold to Kim and Mark Kalan, both of

whom are entrepreneurs who had decided to sell their respective businesses and restore the classic candy business to its former grandeur. In August 2001, they completed the sale and began upgrading the company's retail stores and equipment. A year later, they purchased a wholesale chocolate company in Perham, Minnesota, three hours northwest of Minneapolis. With its manufacturing plant and warehouse, the acquisition enabled the

Kalans to sell large orders of chocolates to corporate clients such as Caribou Coffee and Borders Books. Soon the wholesale division of Maud Borup Chocolates was generating 80 percent of the company's annual revenue. Sales were climbing, and in 2003 the company was on track to generate a profit for the first time since the Kalans had bought it.

Then disaster struck.

On October 7, Mark made the usual weekly three-hour drive from headquarters to the factory and warehouse in Perham, but this time things were different when he arrived. As he pulled up to the factory, he saw all of the workers standing outside. "Strange," he thought. The factory looked the same, but he couldn't see the warehouse behind it. Ten minutes before he had arrived, the twenty-third car in a 53-car freight train going 54 miles per hour had jumped the tracks and careened one-and-a-half blocks, smashed 30 cars in a nearby parking lot, and crashed into the company's warehouse, leveling it and destroying *everything* inside it. Had Mark not stopped for coffee on his trip, he and some of his workers would have been inside the warehouse when the 60,000-pound train car hit. Fortunately, none of the company's workers were hurt in the accident.

However, Maud Borup Chocolates' entire inventory was destroyed. All of the finished chocolates that were ready to be shipped, its ingredients, packaging, and equipment—all worth hundreds of thousands of dollars—were gone! To make matters worse, the company was gearing up for the busy holiday season and had more inventory than usual stored in the warehouse. The accident's timing could not have been worse because Maud Borup Chocolates does 80 percent of its annual sales in the fourth quarter of the year.

As experienced business owners, the Kalans were familiar with business interruption insurance. When they bought the chocolate maker, they paid $700 for a $500,000 business interruption policy. Now, they realized, that amount probably would not cover their actual losses in their busiest season; they would need twice as much insurance coverage. "If this had happened in the summer, we probably wouldn't be underinsured," says Kim.

Shifting into crisis management mode, the Kalans began dealing with the aftermath of the accident. They placed emergency calls to their suppliers in an attempt to replace as much of their lost ingredients as possible and closed their three retail stores in stages, shifting inventory from one to the other until it ran out. They also had to deal with the reams of paperwork required to file their insurance claim. Because of a lack of precise sales records and the company's rapid growth, reaching a settlement with the insurance company took four months. In early January, the Kalans received a $225,000 advance from the insurance company. By then, however, they estimate that they had missed more than $400,000 in holiday sales and were about to miss out on another peak candy season, Valentine's Day.

Burlington Northern Santa Fe, which owns the train that crashed into the Kalans' warehouse, averages just 2.5 derailments per million train miles traveled, and most of those occur in train yards at slow speeds. Speaking about the chances of their warehouse being destroyed by a runaway rail car, Kim says, "I would have had a better chance of winning the lottery."

1. What purpose does business interruption insurance serve?
2. Explain the other types of insurance you would recommend the Kalans purchase for Maud Borup Chocolates. Describe what each type of insurance protects against.
3. Use the risk management pyramid in Figure 20.3 to assess the threat posed by an event such as the one described here. What recommendations can you make?

Source: Adapted from Michele Marchetti, "Thrown Off Track," *FSB*, February 2004, pp. 66–69.

Auto insurance policies offer liability coverage that protects against losses resulting from injuries, damage, or theft involving the use of company vehicles. A typical BOP does not include liability coverage for automobiles; business owners must purchase a separate policy for auto insurance. The automobiles a business owns must be covered by a commercial policy, not a personal one. *Bob Foutz, owner of Purity Pool Service in Huntington Beach, California, counted on his auto insurance policy when a thief stole his service truck from the driveway of his home. Not only did the thief take the vehicle, but he also stole Foutz's inventory of equipment, tools, and parts, some of which were custom-fitted to his customers' pools. Without adequate coverage, Foutz knows that he would have been out of business.*[54]

Company Example

Electronic data processing (EDP) insurance covers losses from the theft or loss of computers and data, the impact of computer viruses and computer system failures, intrusion by hackers, and problems with the privacy of customer information stored in databases. EDP insurance has become more important as businesses have

Company Example ➡

moved their operations online and engage in increasing volumes of e-commerce. *Thomas Shipley, whose company sells business accessories, generates 30 percent of his sales from the company's Web site. Shipley recently purchased an EDP policy that protects his business from, among other things, hackers and viruses. The policy costs $14,000 a year, but Shipley says it is well worth the price to protect his company that now brings in more than $10 million in sales a year.*[55]

A business may also purchase **surety insurance,** which protects against losses to customers that occur when a company fails to complete a contract on time or completes it incorrectly. Surety protection guarantees customers that they will get either the products or services they purchased or the money to cover losses from contractual failures.

Businesses also buy insurance to protect themselves from losses that occur when either finished goods or raw materials are lost or destroyed while being shipped. **Marine insurance** is designed to cover the risk associated with goods in transit. The name of this insurance goes back to the days when a ship's cargo was insured against high risks associated with ocean navigation. Today, business owners can purchase marine insurance to cover property in transit and property still under their care.

Crime insurance does not deter crime, but it can reimburse the small business owner for losses from the three Ds: dishonesty, disappearance, and destruction. Business owners should ask their insurance brokers or agents exactly what their crime insurance policies do and do not cover; after-the-fact insurance coverage surprises are seldom pleasant. Premiums for such policies vary depending on the type of business, store location, number of employees, maximum cash value, quality of the business's security system, and the business's history of losses. Specific coverage may include fidelity bonds, which are designed to reimburse the business owner for losses due to embezzlement and employee theft. Forgery bonds reimburse the business owner for any loss sustained from the forgery of business checks.

Life and Disability Insurance. Unlike most forms of insurance, life insurance does not pertain to avoiding risk because death is a certainty for everyone. Rather, **life insurance** protects families and businesses against loss of income, security, or personal services that results from an individual's untimely death. Life insurance policies are usually issued in a face amount payable to a beneficiary upon the death of the insured. Life insurance for business protection, though not as common as life insurance for family protection, is becoming more popular. Many businesses insure the lives of key executives to offset the costs of having to make a hurried and often unplanned replacement of important managerial personnel.

When it comes to assets that are expensive to replace, few are more costly than the key people in a business, including the owner. What would it take to replace a company's top sales representative? Its production supervisor? Clearly, money alone would not be the answer, but it would provide the business with the funds necessary to find and train their replacements and to cover the profits lost because of their untimely deaths or disabilities. That's what key-person insurance does. It provides valuable working capital to keep a business on track while it reorganizes and searches for the right person to replace the loss of someone in a key position in the company.

Pensions and annuities are special forms of life insurance policies that combine insurance with a form of saving. With an annuity or pension plan, the insured person's premiums go partly to provide standard insurance coverage and partly to a fund that is invested by the insurance company. The interest from the invested portion of the policy is then used to pay an income to the policyholder when he or she reaches a certain age. If the policyholder dies before reaching that age, either the policy converts to income for the spouse or family of the insured or the insurance proceeds (plus interest) go to the beneficiary as they would in ordinary life insurance.

Disability insurance, like life insurance, protects an individual in the event of unexpected and often very expensive disabilities. Because a sudden disability limits a person's ability to earn a living, the insurance proceeds are designed to help make up the difference between what that person could have expected to earn if the accident had not occurred. Sometimes called income insurance, these policies usually guarantee a stated percentage of an individual's income—usually around 60 percent—while he or she is recovering and is unable to run a business. Short-term disability policies cover the 90-day gap between the time a person is injured and when workers' compensation payments begin. Long-term disability policies pay for lost income after 90 days or longer. In addition to the portion of income a policy will replace, another important factor to consider when purchasing disability insurance is the waiting period, the time gap between when the disability occurs and the disability payments begin. Although many business owners understand the importance of maintaining adequate life insurance coverage, fewer see the relevance of maintaining proper coverage for disabilities. For most people, disability represents a greater risk than death; 15 percent of workers will be unable to work for 90 days or longer due to a disability.[56]

Business owners can supplement traditional disability policies with **business overhead expense (BOE) insurance.** Designed primarily for companies with fewer than 15 employees, a BOE policy will replace 100 percent of a small company's monthly overhead expenses such as rent, utilities, insurance, and taxes if the owner is incapacitated. Payments typically begin 30 days after the owner is incapacitated and continue for two years.

Health Insurance and Workers' Compensation. One of small business owners' greatest concerns in recent years has been the skyrocketing cost of health insurance. According to the National Federation of Independent Businesses (NFIB), just 42 percent of small businesses offer health insurance to their employees.[57] The most commonly cited reason among small business owners for not offering health care coverage is cost. As health care costs have climbed and the average age of the workforce has risen, fewer small companies can afford to provide coverage for their employees. Yet, health insurance has become an extremely important benefit to most workers. Small companies that offer thorough health care coverage often find that it gives them an edge in attracting and retaining quality workers. A key to providing proper health care coverage while keeping costs in check is to offer the benefits that are most important to your employees and to avoid spending money unnecessarily on coverage that does not apply to them. Four basic options are available to employers:

Traditional Indemnity Plans. Under these plans, employees choose their own health care providers, and the insurance company either pays the provider directly or reimburses employees for the covered amounts.

Frank and Ernest

Managed Care Plans. As part of employers' attempts to put a lid on escalating health care costs, these plans have become increasingly popular. Two variations, the health maintenance organization (HMO) and the preferred provider organization (PPO) are most common. An HMO is a prepaid health care arrangement under which employees must use health care providers who are employed by or are under contract with the HMO their company uses. Although these plans lower health care costs, employees have less freedom in selecting physicians under an HMO. Under a PPO, an insurance company negotiates discounts for health care with certain physicians and hospitals. If employees choose a health care provider from the approved list, they pay only a small fee for each office visit (often just $10 to $25). The insurance company pays the remainder. Employees may select a provider outside the PPO, but they pay more for the service.

Health Savings Accounts (HSAs). Created as part of the major Medicare overhaul in 2003, health savings accounts (HSAs) are similar to IRAs except employees' contributions are used for medical expenses rather than for retirement. An HSA is a special savings account coupled with a high-deductible insurance policy (usually $3,000 to $4,500). Those with this insurance contribute pretax dollars from their paychecks into the fund and use them as they need to. Withdrawls from an HSA are not taxed as long as the money is used for approved medical expenses. Unused funds can accumulate indefinitely and earn tax-free interest. HSAs offer employees incentives to contain their health care costs, but the employer must choose both an insurance carrier to provide coverage and a custodial firm to manage employees' accounts. Although critics contend that consumer-driven plans push a greater portion of health care expenses onto employees, these plans will grow in popularity among small businesses because of their potential to rein in escalating costs. Forrester Research projects that consumer-driven plans will account for 24 percent of all health care plans by 2010, up from just 4 percent today.[58] *When Jo Ribordy-Christofferson, president of RD Systems, a manufacturer of automation equipment, received the news that premiums for her company's health care insurance (of which the company paid 100 percent) were going up 60 percent in just one year, she switched to a health savings account approach for her employees. RD Systems contributes $600 to each employee's personal medical fund to cover the $1,000 deductible on the plan, leaving employees responsible for the remaining $400. The HSA saved RD Systems $49,000 in the first year and has encouraged employees to take a more active part in controlling health care costs.*[59]

> Company Example →

Self-Insurance. As you learned earlier in this chapter, some business owners choose to insure themselves for health coverage rather than to incur the costs of fully insured plans offered by outsiders. The benefits of self-insurance include greater control over the plan's design and the coverage it offers, fewer paperwork and reporting requirements, and, in some cases, lower costs. The primary disadvantage, of course, is the possibility of having to pay large amounts to cover treatments for several employees' major illnesses at the same time, which can strain a small company's cash flow. Many self-insured businesses limit their exposure to such losses by purchasing stop-loss insurance.

Another type of health-related coverage is **workers' compensation,** which is designed to cover employees who are injured on the job or who become sick as a result of a work environment. Before passage of workers' compensation legislation, any employee injured on the job could bring a lawsuit to prove the employer was liable for the worker's injury. Because of the red tape and expenses involved in these lawsuits, many employees were never compensated for job-related accidents and injuries. Although the details of coverage vary from state to state, workers' compensation laws require employers to provide benefits and medical and rehabilitation costs for employees injured on the job. The amount of compensation an injured employee will receive is determined by a fixed schedule of payment benefits based on three factors: the wages or salary that the employee was earning at the time of the accident or injury, the seriousness of the injury, and the extent of the disability to the employee. *For instance, the producers of the hit Broadway musical The* Phantom of the Opera *experienced a large workers' compensation claim when*

> Company Example →

a maintenance worker was injured on the set. The worker was polishing the show's huge chandelier as it sat on the floor when another employee unknowingly hit the switch to retract the chandelier into the ceiling. The chandelier knocked the worker into the orchestra pit, seriously injuring him. That one claim ran "well into six figures," says the agent representing the insurance company.[60]

Only three states, New Jersey, South Carolina, and Texas, do not require companies to purchase workers' compensation coverage once they reach a certain size (usually three or more employees). Usually, the state sets the rates businesses pay for workers' compensation coverage, and business owners purchase their coverage from private insurance companies. Rapidly escalating workers' compensation rates have become a major concern for small businesses across the nation. Michael Hamman, a general contractor in San Francisco with three employees, says that he now pays 54 cents in workers' compensation premiums for every dollar in salary he pays his carpenters. Workers' compensation costs are climbing so fast that Hamman says he cannot afford to buy new equipment or hire additional workers.[61] Rates vary by industry, business size, and the number of claims a company's workers make. For instance, workers' compensation premiums are higher for a timber-cutting business than for a retail gift store.

Whatever industry they are in, business owners can reduce their workers' compensation costs by improving their employees' safety records. *In an effort to contain rising workers' compensation costs, Paul Darley, president of W.S. Darley & Company, a manufacturer of emergency equipment in Melrose Park, Illinois, hired a safety director in 1999 even though he didn't think his company "was large enough to support a permanent safety director." The new director implemented a company-wide safety initiative that included safety instruction, installing new equipment to automate the riskiest manual jobs, setting up a reward system for safety, and combing through company records looking for accident and injury patterns. The system has paid off. At last count, employees were celebrating nearly three years without an accident, and Darley says the company's "workers' comp premiums are a fraction of what they were four years ago."*[62]

Liability Insurance. One of the most common types of insurance coverage is liability insurance, which protects a business against losses resulting from accidents or injuries people suffer on the company's property, from its products or services, and damage the company causes to others' property. Most BOPs include basic liability coverage; however, the limits on the typical policy are not high enough to cover the potential losses many small business owners face. For example, one "slip-and-fall" case involving a customer who is injured by slipping and falling on a wet floor could easily exceed the standard limits on a basic BOP. Claims from customers injured by a company's product or service are also covered by its liability policy. With jury awards in product liability cases often reaching into the millions of dollars (the median product liability claim settlement cost is $7.4 million), business owners who fail to purchase sufficient liability coverage may end up losing their businesses.[63] Most insurance experts recommend purchasing a commercial general liability policy that provides coverage of at least $2 million to $3 million for the typical small business. As a result, many business owners find it necessary to purchase additional liability coverage for their companies.

Another important type of liability insurance for many small businesses is **professional liability insurance** or **"errors and omissions" coverage.** This insurance protects against damage a business causes to customers or clients as a result of an error an employee makes or an employee's failure to take proper care and precautions. For instance, a land surveyor may miscalculate the location of a customer's property line. If the landowner relies on that property line to build a structure on what he thinks is his land and it turns out to be on his neighbor's land, the surveyor would be liable for damages. Doctors, dentists, attorneys, and other professionals protect themselves through a similar kind of insurance, malpractice insurance, which protects them against the risk of lawsuits arising from errors in professional practice or judgment.

Employment practices liability insurance (EPLI) provides protection against claims arising from charges of employment discrimination, wrongful termination, sexual harassment, and violations of the Americans with Disabilities Act, the Family and Medical Leave Act, and other employment legislation. Because the number of lawsuits from these sources has climbed so dramatically in the past several years, this is one of the fastest-growing forms of insurance coverage. Although most violations of these employment laws are not intentional but are the result of either carelessness or lack of knowledge, the company that violates them is still liable. Because they often lack full-time human resources professionals, small companies are especially vulnerable to charges of improper employment practices, making this type of insurance coverage all the more important to them. *Managers at Alternative Services, a small nonprofit company that trains people to work with developmentally disabled adults, were displeased with a female employee's job performance. She came to work late, missed deadlines for assignments, and was performing her job poorly, so her manager fired her. Much to the manager's surprise, the employee filed a lawsuit against the company for more than $50,000, claiming that she had been sexually harassed. Fortunately, CEO Art Mack had purchased an EPLI policy to protect the company against such claims, and within three months, the insurance company settled the case with the disgruntled former worker for $25,000. "I'm glad we decided to purchase that insurance," says Mack.*[64]

> Company Example

Figure 20.4 shows recent trends in million-dollar verdicts for cases involving various types of liability issues.

Every business's insurance needs are somewhat unique, requiring owners to customize the insurance coverage they purchase. Entrepreneurs also must keep their insurance coverage updated as their companies grow; when companies expand, so do their insurance needs. *Davin Wedel, founder of Global Protection Corporation, a company that makes condoms, purchased a simple BOP that gave him adequate coverage for his tiny business. As sales grew and the company took on more customers and moved into foreign markets, Wedel recognized that the company's risk exposure also had changed. Today, in addition to an*

> Company Example

Figure 20.4

Trends in Million-Dollar Verdicts

Source: Current Award Trends in Personal Injury, LRP Publications, Horsham, PA, 2004.

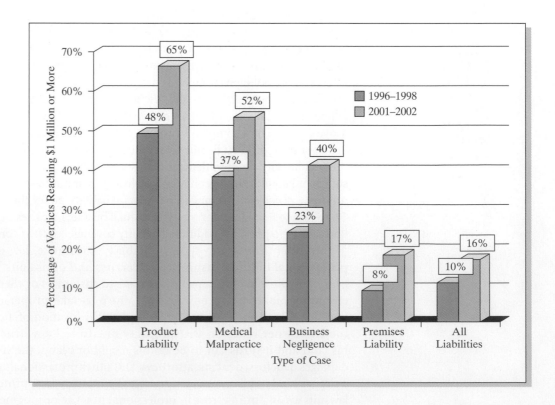

expanded BOP, Wedel has insurance policies that cover product liability, increased limits on general liability, and employment practices liability.[65]

Controlling Insurance Costs

IN THE FOOTSTEPS OF AN ENTREPRENEUR...

Facing a Difficult Decision

Over the past 20 years, Matthew Prentice has built the largest catering business in Michigan and a chain of 14 very successful restaurants in the Detroit area. Together the businesses of the Unique Restaurant Corporation (URC) generate $40 million in annual sales. When asked about his company's success, Prentice is quick to credit the fact that that he has the best managers and staff of any catering business or restaurant in the area. Not only are his employees the best in the trade, but they also are loyal to Prentice. In an industry famous for high employee turnover rates, Unique has a very low turnover rate. In fact, seven of Prentice's first 15 workers are still with the company. While most of his competitors are sending out poorly trained, temporary workers to face customers, Prentice is able to rely on dependable, seasoned veterans who understand his business philosophy and his expectations of customer service.

What is Prentice's secret? "I learned very early that in order to get the best people, I had to do things a little differently," he says, pointing to his employee benefit package, which is considered generous by restaurant industry standards. Prentice began offering health insurance for his employees 17 years ago, making the plan available to all full-time workers and to part-time workers who worked at least three shifts a week and had been with the company at least three years.

Prentice enrolled in a plan sponsored by Gerber, the baby food maker, that allowed his employees to tap into Gerber's network of HMO or PPO providers. The cost of the plan, of which Prentice paid 100 percent, was reasonable in the early days. As his company grew and added more employees, Prentice added more benefits to the health care plan. First, he added dental coverage and then a prescription drug plan that covered 100 percent of cost of the drugs. A few years ago, he began paying a portion of employees' child care costs. In addition to

their health care benefits, URC's employees also received paid vacations and a 401(k) retirement plan.

The company's generous benefit package worked just the way Prentice had envisioned. He attracted and kept the best employees on staff. Over the past few years, however, weaker sales, fewer catered parties thrown by a cost-cutting auto industry, severe winter weather, and climbing health care costs have squeezed URC's earnings. Prentice had seen insurance premiums climb anywhere from 10 percent to 23 percent a year. The cost of the company's prescription drug plan alone tripled, from $3,000 a month to $9,000 a month. Now with 800 people on his payroll, Prentice is considering the unthinkable: dropping his employees' health care coverage altogether. If he does, he wonders how his employees will react. He considers them to be the key ingredient in his company's recipe for success and fears that many will leave if he drops their insurance coverage. If he decides to pass along some of the rising cost of the health care plan to his employees, he worries that some will not be able to afford it. "The last thing I wanted to do was entertain cutting any portion of health care," says Prentice.

1. Explain the risks Prentice faces if he decides to drop his employees' health care coverage. What risks does he face if he continues to provide employees with the coverage they have now?
2. Assume the role of consultant to Matthew Prentice. Research and develop at least three courses of action that he could take concerning his employees' health care coverage.
3. Which course of action do you recommend Prentice follow? Explain.

Source: Adapted from Bobbie Gossage, "Tabling Benefits," *Inc.,* June 2003, pp. 46–48.

Small business owners face constantly rising insurance premiums. In fact, a recent study by the National Federation of Independent Businesses found that the ability to pay for insurance was the number-one concern for small business owners, ranking above taxes.[66] Business owners can take steps to lower insurance costs, however. In the property and casualty insurance area, owners should take the following steps:

1. *Pursue a loss-control program, by making risk reduction a natural part of all employees' daily routine.* As discussed earlier in the chapter, risk reduction minimizes claims and eventually lowers premiums. Establishing a loss-control program means taking steps such as installing modern fire alarms, safety programs, and sophisticated security systems.

2. *Increase their policies' deductibles.* If a business can afford to handle minor losses, the owner can save money by raising the deductible to a level that protects the business against catastrophic events but, in effect, self-insures against minor losses. Business owners must determine the amount of financial exposure they can reasonably accept.

3. *Work with qualified professional insurance brokers or agents.* Business owners should do their homework before choosing insurance brokers or agents. This includes checking their reputation, credentials, and background by asking them to supply references.

4. *Work actively with brokers to make sure they understand business owners' particular needs.* Brokers need to know about entrepreneurs' businesses and objectives for insurance coverage. They can help only if they know their clients' needs and the degree of risk they are willing to take.

5. *Work with brokers to find competitive companies that want small companies' insurance business and have the resources to cover losses when they arise.* The price of the premium should never be an entrepreneur's sole criterion for selecting insurance. The rating of the insurance company should always be a primary consideration. What good is it to have paid low premiums if, after a loss, a business owner finds that the insurance company is unable to pay? Many small business owners have learned costly lessons when their insurance companies, unable to meet their obligations, filed for bankruptcy protection.

6. *Utilize the resources of your insurance company.* Many insurers will provide risk management inspections designed to help business owners assess the level of risk in their companies either for free or for a minimal fee. Smart entrepreneurs view their insurance companies as partners in their risk management efforts.

7. *Conduct a periodic insurance audit.* Reviewing your company's coverage annually can ensure that insurance coverage is adequate and can lead to big cost savings as well. *Keith Alper, owner of Creative Products Group (CPG), a business that produces videos for Fortune 500 companies, was surprised to discover that CPG was wasting thousands of dollars on policies it did not need. Many employees were classified incorrectly for workers' compensation coverage, several policies duplicated the coverage of others, and the company was paying for auto insurance on four cars when it had only three! In all, Alper was able to shave more than $10,000 off of the company's $75,000 annual insurance bill.*[67]

Company Example →

When it comes to health insurance, the sky seems to be the limit for costs. The popular press and every national political candidate have debated the need to balance health services with the cost of providing them. Traditionally, businesses have been and continue to be the principal suppliers of health insurance in our society. To control the cost of health insurance, the small business owners should consider the following:

1. *Increase the dollar amount of employee contributions and the amount of the employee's deductibles.* Neither option is desirable, but rising medical costs will inevitably result in individuals becoming, to some degree, self-insured in order to cover the high deductibles.

2. *Switch to HMOs or PPOs.* Higher premium costs have encouraged some small business owners to reevaluate health maintenance organization (HMOs) and preferred provider organizations (PPOs) as alternatives to traditional health insurance policies. Although some employees resent being told where they must go to receive treatment, the number of businesses offering the HMO and PPO options to employees is rising.

3. *Consider joining an insurance pool.* Small businesses can lower their insurance premiums by banding together to purchase coverage. In many states, chambers of

One way small businesses can lower the cost of health care insurance is to create wellness programs that reward employees for engaging in healthy lifestyles. Companies that have created wellness programs report cost savings of $6 for every $1 they invest.

commerce, trade associations, and other groups form insurance pools that small businesses can join, spreading risk over a larger number of employees. In Pennsylvania, for example, two dozen chambers of commerce have formed an insurance pool that covers 30,000 people employed at small businesses at rates well below those that the owners could negotiate separately.[68]

4. *Conduct a yearly utilization review.* A review may reveal that your employees' use of their policies is statistically lower, which may provide you leverage to negotiate lower premiums or to switch to an insurer that wants a business with your track record and offers lower premiums.

5. *Make sure your company's health plan fits the needs of your employees.* One of best ways to keep health care costs in check is to offer only those benefits that employees actually need. Getting employee input is essential to the process.

6. *Create a wellness program for all employees.* We have all heard the old adage that an ounce of prevention is worth a pound of cure, but when it comes to the high cost of medical expenses, this is especially true! Companies that have created wellness programs report cost savings of $6 for every $1 they invest. Employees involved in wellness programs not only incur lower health care expenses, but they also tend to be more productive as well. Providing a wellness program does not mean building an expensive gym, however. Instead, it may be as simple as a providing routine checkups from a county nurse, incentives for quitting smoking, weight-loss counseling, or after-work athletic games that involve as many employees as possible. *R.D. Systems, a manufacturer of automation equipment, created a wellness program called "Vitality" that awards employees points for every visit they make to a gym, for quitting smoking, for maintaining a healthy weight, and other good health practices. Employees can redeem the points they accumulate for a variety of benefits including movie tickets, airline miles, and hotel stays.*[69]

7. *Conduct a safety audit.* Reviewing the workplace with a safety professional to look for ways to improve its safety has the potential for saving some businesses thousands of dollars a year in medical expenses and workers' compensation claims. The National Safety Council offers helpful information on creating a safe work environment.

Company Example

8. *Create a safety manual and use it.* Incorporating the suggestions for improving safety into a policy manual and then using it will reduce the number of on-the-job accidents. Training employees, even experienced ones, in proper safety procedures is also effective.

9. *Create a safety team.* Assigning the responsibility for workplace safety to workers themselves can produce amazing results. When one small manufacturer turned its safety team over to employees, the plant's lost time due to accidents plummeted to zero for three years straight! The number of accidents is well below what it was when managers ran the safety team, and managers say that's because employees now "own" safety in the plant.

The key to controlling insurance costs is aggressive prevention. Entrepreneurs who actively manage the risks that their companies are exposed to find that they can provide the insurance coverage their businesses need at a reasonable cost. Finding the right insurance coverage to protect their businesses is no easy matter for business owners. The key to dealing with those differences is to identify the risks that represent the greatest threat to a company and then to develop a plan for minimizing their risk of occurrence and insuring against them if they do.

▐ ▌ ▌ Chapter Review

1. Explain the factors necessary for a strong family business.

- More than 80 percent of all companies in the United States are family owned. Family businesses generate 50 percent of the U.S. gross domestic product, account for 60 percent of employment, and pay 65 percent of all wages. Several factors are important to maintaining a strong family business, including shared values, shared power, tradition, a willingness to learn, behaving like families, and strong family ties.

2. Understand the exit strategy options available to an entrepreneur.

- Family business owners wanting to step down from their companies can sell to outsiders, sell to insiders, or transfer ownership to the next generation of family members. Common tools for selling to insiders (employees or managers) include sale for cash plus a note, leveraged buyouts (LBOs), and employee stock ownership plans (ESOPs).

- Transferring ownership to the next generation of family members requires a business owner to develop a sound management succession plan.

3. Discuss the stages of management succession.

- Unfortunately, 70 percent of first-generation businesses fail to survive into the second generation and, of those that do, only 12 percent make it to the third generation. One of the primary reasons for this lack of continuity is poor succession planning. Planning for management succession protects not only the founder's, successor's, and company's financial

resources, but it also preserves what matters most in a successful business: its heritage and tradition. Management succession planning can ensure a smooth transition only if the founder begins the process early on.

4. Explain how to develop an effective management succession plan.

- A succession plan is a crucial element in transferring a company to the next generation. Preparing a succession plan involves five steps: (1) Select the successor. (2) Create a survival kit for the successor. (3) Groom the successor. (4) Promote an environment of trust and respect. (5) Cope with the financial realities of estate taxes.

- Entrepreneurs can rely on several tools in their estate planning, including buy/sell agreements, lifetime gifting, trusts, estate freezes, and family limited partnerships.

5. Understand the four risk management strategies.

- Four risk strategies are available to the small business: avoiding, reducing, anticipating, and transferring risk.

6. Discuss the basics of insurance for small businesses.

- Insurance is a risk transfer strategy. Not every potential loss can be insured. Insurability requires that it be possible to estimate the amount of actual loss being insured against and identify the specific risk and that there be enough policyholders to spread out the risk.

- The four major types of insurance small businesses need are property and casualty insurance, life and disability insurance, health insurance and workers' compensation coverage, and liability insurance.

- Property and casualty insurance covers a company's tangible assets, such as buildings, equipment, inventory, machinery, and signs that have been damaged, destroyed, or stolen. Specific types of property and casualty insurance include extra expense coverage, business interruption insurance, surety insurance, marine insurance, crime insurance, fidelity insurance, and forgery insurance.

- Life and disability insurance also comes in various forms. Life insurance protects a family and a business against the loss of income and security in the event of the owner's death. Disability insurance, like life insurance, protects an individual in the event of unexpected and often very expensive disabilities.

- Health insurance is designed to provide adequate health care for business owners and their employees. Workers' compensation is designed to cover employees who are injured on the job or who become sick as a result of a work environment.

- Liability insurance protects a business against losses resulting from accidents or injuries people suffer on the company's property, from its products or services, and damage the company causes to others' property. Typical liability coverage includes professional liability insurance or "errors and omissions" coverage, which protects against damage a business causes to customers or clients as a result of an error an employee makes or an employee's failure to take proper care and precautions. Doctors, dentists, attorneys, and other professionals protect themselves through a similar kind of insurance, malpractice insurance, which protects them against the risk of lawsuits arising from errors in professional practice or judgment. Employment practices liability insurance provides protection against claims arising from charges of employment discrimination, sexual harassment, and violations of the Americans with Disabilities Act, the Family and Medical Leave Act, and other employment legislation.

Discussion Questions

1. What factors must be present in a strong family business?
2. Discuss the stages of management succession in a family business.
3. What steps are involved in building a successful management succession plan?
4. What exit strategies are available to entrepreneurs wanting to step down from their businesses?
5. What strategies can business owners employ to reduce estate and gift taxes?
6. Can insurance eliminate risk? Why or why not?
7. Outline the four basic risk management strategies and give an example of each.
8. What problems occur most frequently with a risk-anticipating strategy?
9. What is insurance? How can insurance companies bear such a large risk burden and still be profitable?
10. Describe the requirements for insurability.
11. Briefly describe the various types of insurance coverage available to small business owners.
12. What kinds of insurance coverage would you recommend for the following businesses?

    - A manufacturer of steel sheets.
    - A retail gift shop.
    - A small accounting firm.
    - A limited liability partnership involving three dentists.

13. What can business owners do to keep their insurance costs under control?

Management Succession and Risk Management Strategies in the Family Business

Business Plan Pro

Family-owned businesses dominate the landscape of U.S. companies, but they face a dangerous threat from within: management succession. Most family businesses fail to survive into the second generation and beyond, and the problem usually is the result of a lack of planning for a smooth transition from one generation of management to the next.

The best way to prevent a successful family-owned business from becoming just another management succession failure statistic is to develop a management succession plan early on in the life of the company. The exercises for Chapter 20 that accompany Business Plan Pro are designed to help you identify the key management succession issues facing your company and to begin building a solid management succession plan. If your company operates as a family-owned business, you should complete these exercises. Remember: It's never too early to start building a management succession plan!

These exercises will also help you develop a risk management strategy for your company. You will identify the events that represent the greatest threats to your business and the type of insurance that you should purchase to protect against these threats. When you complete these exercises, you may want to include the description of your company's management succession plan in the Appendix section of Business Plan Pro.

Chapter 21

Values-Based Leadership: Doing the Right Thing

> *Try not to become a man of success but rather try to become a man of value.*
> —ALBERT EINSTEIN

> *If we are to go forward, we must go back and rediscover those precious values—that reality hinges on moral foundations and that all reality has spiritual control.*
> —DR. MARTIN LUTHER KING JR.

Upon completion of this chapter, you will be able to:

1. Define business ethics and describe three levels of ethical standards.
2. Determine who is responsible for ethical behavior and why ethical lapses occur.
3. Explain how to establish and maintain high ethical standards.
4. Define social responsibility.
5. Understand the nature of business's responsibility to the environment.
6. Describe business's responsibility to employees.
7. Explain business's responsibility to customers.
8. Discuss business's responsibility to investors.
9. Discuss business's responsibility to the community.

Business ethics involves the moral values and behavioral standards businesspeople draw on as they make decisions and solve problems. It originates in a commitment to do what is right. Ethical behavior—doing what is "right" as opposed to what is "wrong"—starts at the top of an organization with the entrepreneur. Entrepreneurs' personal values and beliefs influence the way they lead their companies in every decision they make, every policy they write, and every action they take. Entrepreneurs who succeed in the long term have a solid base of personal values and beliefs that they articulate to their employees and put into practice in ways that others can observe. Values-based leadership is more than attempting to follow the rules and regulations. Values-based leaders do what is right because their consciences dictate what they must do.

In some cases, ethical dilemmas are apparent. Entrepreneurs are keenly aware of the ethical entrapments awaiting them and know that society will hold them accountable for their actions. More often, ethical issues are less obvious, cloaked in the garb of mundane decisions and everyday routine. Because they can easily catch entrepreneurs off guard and unprepared, these ethical "sleepers" are most likely to ensnare business owners, soiling their reputations and those of their companies. To make proper ethical choices, entrepreneurs must first be aware that a situation with ethical implications exists.

Complicating the issue even more is that, in some ethical dilemmas, no clear-cut, right (or wrong) answers exist. There is no direct conflict between good and evil, right and wrong, or truth and falsehood. Instead, there is only the issue of conflicting interests among a company's **stakeholders**, the various groups and individuals who affect and are affected by a business. These conflicts force entrepreneurs to identify their stakeholders and to consider the ways in which entrepreneurs will deal with them (see Figure 21.1). For instance, when the founders of a small manufacturer of frozen foods make business decisions, they must consider the impact of those decisions on many stakeholders, including the team of employees who work there, the farmers and companies that supply the business with raw materials, the union that represents employees in collective bargaining, the government agencies that regulate a multitude of activities, the banks that provide the business with financing, the stockholders who own shares of the company's stock, the general public the business serves, the community in which the company operates, and the customers who buy the company's products. When making decisions, entrepreneurs often must balance the needs and demands of a company's stakeholders, knowing that whatever the final decision is, not every group will be satisfied.

Values-based leaders approach their organizational responsibilities with added dimensions of thought and action. They link ethical behaviors to organizational outcomes and incorporate social responsibility into daily decisions. They establish ethical behavior and concern for the environment as an integral part of organizational training and eventually as part of company culture. What does this mean from a practical standpoint? How does a commitment to "doing the right thing" apply to employees, customers, and other stakeholders, and how does it impact an organization's daily decision making? *Consider the situation Harry M. Jansen Kraemer Jr., chairman and CEO of Baxter International, a medical equipment and supplies company, faced when several kidney dialysis patients in Spain died mysteriously. One of the possible causes of this tragedy was a filter made by Baxter, so the company hired an independent testing company to evaluate the filters. They could find nothing wrong; yet several days later, there were more dialysis-related deaths, this time in Croatia. A team of Baxter experts finally determined a fluid (which was made by another company) that Baxter used in testing the quality of the filters during manufacturing turned to gas when heated in the bloodstream, causing a pulmonary embolism. When faced with the dilemma of what to do with this information, Kraemer and his management team had three choices: hide these findings, blame others, or step forward and "do the right thing." What did they do? The managers publicly apologized, ceased manufacturing the product, shut down the two plants that made the filters, and settled with virtually all the families affected. The company took a hit of $189 million, and Kraemer recommended to the board that because the filter problems had*

Company Example

Figure 21.1

Key Stakeholders

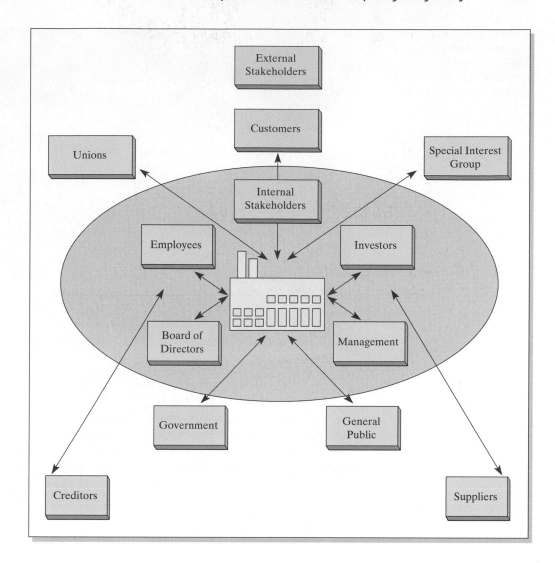

occurred on his watch, his 2001 bonus should be reduced by 40 percent and other executives' bonuses should be reduced by 20 percent. "What we try to do is do the right thing," Kraemer says. "I think there's a tendency to make things more complex than they are. If we live the values we profess, we'll add shareholder value. I don't see a conflict." His commitment to corporate values cost Kraemer, his leadership team, and the company a lot of money. But even when a commitment to values comes at great immediate cost—not only to management but to a company's shareholders—there are those who argue that this is solid business because an articulated and visible set of values that focuses on doing good by employees and customers creates a stronger company that rewards shareholders over the long term.[1]

An Ethical Perspective

1. Define business ethics and describe three levels of ethical standards.

Business ethics consists of the fundamental moral values and behavioral standards that form the foundation for the people of an organization as they make decisions and interact with stakeholders. Business ethics is a sensitive—and highly complex—issue, but it is not a new one. It is rare to find executives who explicitly use the views of Plato, Aristotle, Mill, or Kant to explain and justify their actions. But ethical theory does influence our judgments and actions. Any time we explain why we decided to act as we did, we appeal to

Corporate scandals in the early twenty-first century have placed a new emphasis on the issue of corporate and personal ethics.

certain standards. These standards must be grounded in a deep understanding of ethical values if they are to have any lasting and beneficial effect on how we live. Business is a human activity. As such, it is subject to moral evaluation, just like any other activity that we engage in. The old adage that the sole purpose of business is to maximize profits has never been relevant. It is becoming rare to find anyone who takes this view seriously. Increasingly, success in business requires an understanding of ethical theory. Because business generally is not yet structured to handle these questions and managers have not been trained to do so, there is an urgent need to find a way to determine the values that should guide a business and to set up procedures for employees to handle these issues.

Unlike the natural sciences, with their highly refined methods and well-defined theories and laws, ethical issues and practices are more complex. This has caused some to think that moral values are merely the reflection of our personal opinions and feelings and nothing more. Others view them as the standards of the culture in which we live. However one conceives of moral values, clearly there is some apprehension as to whether it is possible for a person in business to master the knowledge necessary to understand ethics. It is important, at this point, to recall Aristotle's advice:

> We must be content then, in speaking of such subjects and with such premises to indicate the truth roughly and in outline, and in speaking about things which are only for the most part true, and with premises of the same kind, to reach conclusions that are no better. In the same spirit, therefore, should each type of statement be received; for it is the mark of an educated man to look for precision in each class of things just so far as the nature of the subject admits; it is evidently foolish to accept probable reasoning from a Mathematician and to demand from a rhetorician demonstrative proofs. (Aristotle, *Nicomachean Ethics*, book 1, part 3)

Maintaining an ethical perspective is crucial to creating and protecting a company's reputation, but it is no easy task. Succumbing to unethical temptations ultimately will destroy a company's reputation, one of the most precious and most fragile possessions of any business. Building a reputation for ethical behavior typically takes a long time; unfortunately, destroying that reputation requires practically no time at all, and, like a bad

Company Example →

hangover, the effects linger for quite some time. Some businesses flounder or even fail after their owners or managers are caught acting unethically. *Martha Stewart, who built an empire out of her flair for entertaining, gardening, and crafts was convicted of lying to investigators about a personal stock sale. Stewart was forced to resign as an officer and board member of her company. After her conviction, Martha Stewart Living Omnimedia Inc. posted large quarterly losses as advertising revenue plunged and the company moved to distance itself from its founder. The company also downplayed Martha Stewart's name on the flagship magazine* Martha Stewart Living *as part of efforts to identify its brand name with overall quality instead of with an expert personality. Regardless of these actions, the stock fell about 40 percent in the weeks after a New York jury convicted Stewart.*[2]

Three Levels of Ethical Standards

There are three levels of ethical standards:

1. *The law,* which defines for society as a whole which actions are permissible and which are not. The law merely establishes the minimum standard of behavior. Laws, therefore, set a minimum standard. Actions that are legal, however, may not be ethical. Simply obeying the law is insufficient as a guide for ethical behavior; ethical behavior requires more. Few ethical issues are so simple and one dimensional that the law can serve as the acid test for making a decision.
2. *Organizational policies and procedures,* which serve as specific guidelines for people as they make daily decisions. Many colleges and universities have created honor codes, and companies rely on policies covering everything from sexual harassment and gift giving to hiring and whistleblowing.
3. *The moral stance* employees take when they encounter a situation that is not governed under levels one and two. The values people learn early in life at home, in the church or synagogue, and in school are key ingredients at this level. One primary determinant of ethical behavior is *training.* As Aristotle said thousands of years ago, you get a good adult by teaching a child to do the right thing. A company's culture can serve either to support or undermine its employees' concept of what constitutes ethical behavior.

The ethical stance employees take when faced with a difficult decision often reflects the entrepreneur's values. *Consequentialists* hold that the value of an act should be judged solely on the basis of that act's effects on others. In contrast, *deontologists* hold that the rightness of an act is derived from its logical consistency and universality. For deontologists, the right action is obligatory without regard to its consequences. *Objectivists* believe that moral values can be objectively true independently of individual, subjective feelings. In contrast, *relativists* do not believe in the existence of universal moral truth and hold that right and wrong must be defined within the context of cultural norms and mores.

To maintain high ethical standards throughout the organization, companies must hire employees who have high levels of moral development. Lawrence Kohlberg describes three levels of individual moral development, with each level having two stages.[3] The moral development of individuals generally is related to growth and maturity.

Kohlberg calls the first level of moral development the *pre-conventional level.* This level deals with the motivation of small children. In the first stage, Kohlberg notes that children typically do not have any notion of right and wrong. Avoiding punishment normally is the guiding force for their actions. In this stage, they act to avoid being scolded or spanked. In the second stage, however, they realize that their good behavior is rewarded, usually by the praise of their parents.

The second level of moral development is the *conventional level.* The first stage is known as the good boy/nice girl stage. Here young people conform to social expectations and roles because they begin to understand the importance of rules and moral norms. This stage marks the beginning of the process of socialization by which we enter the social world. We do what parents, peers, and teachers expect of us. The second stage is one in which we develop an understanding of our culture and legal structure and identify with the laws of our society. Young people begin to understand what a good citizen is and what actions society expects of them.

The final level is the *post-conventional* or *principled* level of moral development. Here individuals find themselves conforming to principles not because of the demands and expectations of others, but because it is the right thing to do. We are able to give a rational defense of our principles and do not require encouragement from society to motivate us. In fact, sometimes we find ourselves compelled to reject social norms because they are inconsistent with our moral principles. The first stage of this level is one that is governed by the ideal of the social contract. We understand the importance of living up to agreements through a "golden rule" mentality. At the final stage, though, we act on principles that we accept as our own ethical guidelines.

✦ GAINING *a* COMPETITIVE EDGE ✦

Doing the Right Things Pays Off

Entrepreneurs are willing now more than ever to come forward and express their belief that acting in ethical and socially responsible ways produces positive outcomes. Behaving in an ethical and socially responsible fashion has the following positive outcomes:

- Improves the ability to attract and retain high-quality, productive employees
- Builds long-lasting relationships with customers or clients
- Helps employees focus on positive behaviors, knowing that management supports their decisions and actions

Good corporate citizenship begins with establishing and enforcing positive internal policies, which include the basics, such as:

- Always, and in every way, obey the law
- Treat all employees fairly and with respect
- Be honest and fair to employees, customers, and suppliers
- Be aware of the impact of your actions on others and the environment
- Design your products to deliver what you promise
- Ensure high-quality and safe products

1. How could a company quantify the bottom-line value of these policies?

Source: Adapted from Rhonda Abrams, "Companies Strive to Do Well by Doing Good," *Business,* August 12, 2001, p. 3.

Establishing an Ethical Framework

To cope successfully with the many ethical decisions they face, entrepreneurs must develop a workable ethical framework to guide themselves and the organization. Although many such frameworks exist, the following four-step process can work quite well.

Step 1   *Recognize the ethical dimensions involved in the dilemma or decision.* Before entrepreneurs can make informed ethical decisions, they must recognize that an ethical situation exists. Only then is it possible to define the specific ethical issues involved. Too often business owners fail to take into account the ethical impact of a particular course of action until it is too late. To avoid ethical quagmires, entrepreneurs must consider the ethical forces at work in a situation—honesty, fairness, respect for community, concern for the environment, trust, and others—to have a complete view of the decision.

Step 2 *Identify the key stakeholders involved and determine how the decision will affect them.* Every business influences, and is influenced by, a multitude of stakeholders. Frequently, the demands of these stakeholders conflict with one another, putting a business in the position of having to choose which groups to satisfy and which to alienate. Before making a decision, managers must sort out the conflicting interests of the various stakeholders by determining which ones have important stakes in the situation. Although this analysis may not resolve the conflict, it will prevent the company from inadvertently causing harm to people it may have failed to consider.

Step 3 *Generate alternative choices and distinguish between ethical and unethical responses.* Entrepreneurs will find the questions in Table 21.1 to be helpful. Asking and answering the questions posed ensures that everyone involved understands the whole picture.

Table 21.1

Questions to Help Identify the Ethical Dimension of a Situation

---

Principles and Codes of Conduct

- Does this decision or action meet my personal standards for how people should interact?
- Does this decision or action agree with my religious teachings or beliefs (or with my personal principles and sense of responsibility)?
- How will I feel about myself if I do this?
- Do we (or I) have a rule or policy for cases like this?
- Would I want everyone to make the same decision and take the same action if faced with these circumstances?
- What are my true motives for considering this action?

Moral Rights

- Would this action allow others freedom of choice in this matter?
- Would this action involve deceiving others in any way?

Justice

- Would I feel this action was just (right) if I were on the other side of the decision?
- How would I feel if this action were done to me or someone close to me?
- Would this action or decision distribute benefits justly?
- Would it distribute hardships or burdens justly?

Consequences and Outcomes

- What will be the short- and long-term consequences of this action?
- Who will benefit from this course of action?
- Who will be hurt?
- How will this action create good and prevent harm?

Public Justification

- How would I feel (or how will I feel) if (or when) this action becomes public knowledge?
- Will I be able to explain adequately to others why I have taken the action?
- Would others feel that my action or decision is ethical or moral?

Intuition and Insight

- Have I searched for all alternatives? Are there other ways I could look at this situation? Have I considered all points of view?
- Even if there is sound rationality for this decision or action, and even if I could defend it publicly, does my inner sense tell me it is right?
- What does my intuition tell me is the ethical thing to do in this situation? Have I listened to my inner voice?

Source: Sherry Baker, "Ethical Judgement," *Executive Excellence,* March 1992, pp. 7–8.

Step 4   *Choose the "best" ethical response and implement it.* At this point, there likely will be several ethical choices from which managers can pick. Comparing these choices with the "ideal" ethical outcome may help managers make the final decision. The final choice must be consistent with the company's goals, culture, and value system as well as those of the individual decision makers.

Who Is Responsible for Ethical Behavior?

2. Determine who is responsible for ethical behavior and why ethical lapses occur.

Although companies may set ethical standards and offer guidelines for employees, the ultimate decision on whether to abide by ethical principles rests with the *individual*. In other words, companies really are not ethical or unethical; individuals are. Managers, however, can greatly influence individual behavior within the company. And that influence must start at the *top*. A founder or chief executive officer who practices ethical behavior establishes the moral tone for the entire organization. Table 21.2 summarizes the characteristics of the three ethical styles of management: immoral, amoral, and moral.

Table 21.2

Approaches to Management Ethics

ORGANIZATIONAL CHARACTERISTICS	IMMORAL MANAGEMENT	AMORAL MANAGEMENT	MORAL MANAGEMENT
Ethical norms	Management decisions, actions, and behavior imply a positive and active opposition to what is moral (ethical). Decisions are discordant with accepted ethical principles. An active negation of what is moral is implicit.	Management is neither moral nor immoral; decisions are not based on moral judgments. Management activity is not related to any moral code. A lack of ethical perception and moral awareness may be implicit.	Management activity conforms to a standard of ethical, or right, behavior. Management activity conforms to accepted professional standards of conduct. Ethical leadership is commonplace.
Goals	Profitability and organizational success at any price.	Profitability. Other goals are not considered.	Profitability within the confines of legal obedience and ethical standards.
Orientation toward law	Legal standards are barriers that management must overcome to accomplish what it wants.	Law is the ethical guide, preferably the letter of the law. The central question is: What we can do legally?	Obedience toward letter and spirit of the law. Law is a minimal ethical behavior. Prefer to operate well above what law mandates.
Strategy	Exploit opportunities for corporate gain. Cut corners when it appears useful.	Give managers free rein. Personal ethics may apply but only if managers choose. Respond to legal mandates if caught and required to do so.	Live by sound ethical standards. Assume leadership position when ethical dilemmas arise. Enlightened self-interest.

Source: Archie B. Carroll, "In Search of the Moral Manager," reprinted from *Business Horizons,* March/April 1987. Copyright 1987 by the Foundation for the School of Business at Indiana University. Used with permission.

IN THE FOOTSTEPS OF AN ENTREPRENEUR...

Does It Pay to Be a Green Company?

Paul Hawken, founder of several businesses and author of several books, including *Growing a Business, The Ecology of Commerce,* and *Natural Capitalism: Creating the Next Industrial Revolution,* holds back none of his passion for the environment when he addresses other business owners. "There is no polite way to say that business is destroying the world," he says bluntly. Explaining his view of the next industrial revolution, Hawken says, "We have to reimagine everything we do, everything we make, every process, every product in such a way that allows us to improve the quality of our lives and everybody else's." In *The Ecology of Commerce,* Hawken chronicles a thoughtful plan for business success without sacrificing the environment. Based on the model of nature itself, Hawken's book calls for controlling the creation of harmful wastes rather than focusing on their disposal. Hawken's book envisions a business system that copies nature, where everything's waste is food for something else. Nothing is wasted.

Natural capitalism is based on four principles: (1) increasing productivity of natural resources, (2) modeling industrial processes after biological systems, (3) selling service-based solutions to the environment, and (4) reinvesting in natural capital. The theory behind natural capitalism is that companies that eliminate waste and become more environmentally friendly and efficient prosper and grow, but companies that are environmentally inefficient ultimately fail. Several studies support the theory. One study by Michael Russo of the University of Oregon and Paul Fouts of Golden State University found that companies that had the highest rates of return on assets surpassed their lower-performing rivals in terms of pollution control and waste reduction. Another study by Vanderbilt University concluded that 80 percent of environmentally sound companies outperformed their higher polluting counterparts.

A new generation of entrepreneurs is taking note of these ideas, and building businesses based on them. Darren Patrick launched Rainbow Play Systems when he was just 20 years old. The company, which makes residential playground equipment from redwood and red cedar, rings up more than $6 million in annual sales and is one of the nation's largest consumers of redwood. Sensitive to the fact that many people have an interest in protecting the remaining old-growth forests and, in particular, the remaining stands of redwood trees, Patrick purchases lumber only from mills that participate in sustained-yield programs designed to protect and renew the nation's redwood forests. "Since the beginning of our business," says Patrick, "we have

been concerned about our lumber purchases and the mills that fulfill them."

Patrick also uses Rainbow's marketing program to educate its customers about the benefits sustained-yield programs produce. "These programs have been successful environmentally and for us by creating a sustainable resource. Today, we have more redwood trees than ever before."

Entrepreneurs still wrestle with the three-fold challenge of earning a profit, satisfying their social responsibility, and preserving the environment. One top manager poses a question he believes should be at the top of every CEO's agenda: How do you bring the economics together with the environmental and societal needs so that they are all part of your business strategy? That's the problem facing Eloise Gonzalez-Geller, founder of interior finishing contractor Commercial Interior Contractors Corporation (CICC). Gonzalez-Geller encourages her employees to write memos on waste paper, and the company recycles as much of the material it removes as possible. However, when she landed a contract to replace carpets in several airports, she ran into a roadblock. Because the carpets usually contain trace amounts of jet fuel, they are expensive to recycle. "It's cheaper to throw them into land fills," she says. Gonzalez-Geller, however, is committed to recycling the carpets, even though none of her clients have agreed to pay the extra cost. Frustrated, she says, "I'm losing money on the carpet recycling project."

1. One environmental marketing consultant says, "If you look at the green consumer, the consumer part is more important than the green part. People buy laundry detergent to get their clothes clean, not to save the planet." Do you agree? Explain.
2. The environmental marketing consultant in question 1 goes on to say, "The trick is, if you can clean people's clothes and the world at the same time, you'll have a real competitive edge." Do you agree? Explain.
3. What are the strategic implications of being environmentally friendly and efficient for entrepreneurs launching businesses?

Source: Adapted from Cait Murphy, "The Next Big Thing," *FSB,* June 2003, pp. 64–70; Thomas Petzinger Jr., "Business Achieves Greatest Efficiencies When at Its Greenest," *Wall Street Journal,* July 11, 1997, p. B1; Joseph Conlin, "Natural Order," *Entrepreneur,* November 2001, pp. 72–75; David Whitford, "Smith & Hawken Founder Paul Hawken Believes That Business Is Destroying the World. Maybe That's Why the Author and Environmentalist Wants You to Turn Your Small Business Upside Down," *FSB,* May 2002, pp. 41–45; Marc Gunter, "Tree Huggers, Soy Lovers, and Profits," *Fortune,* June 23, 2003, pp. 98–104.

Gaining the Benefits of Moral Management

One of the most common misconceptions about business is that there is a contradiction between earning a profit and maintaining high ethical standards. In reality, companies have learned that these two goals are consistent with one another. Many entrepreneurs launch businesses with the idea of making a difference in society. They quickly learn that to "do good," their companies must first "do well." *Jeffrey Swartz, CEO of Timberland, a company known almost as well for its ethical and socially responsible behavior as it is for its footwear and outdoor clothing, says, "I honestly believe doing good and doing well are inextricably linked." Swartz practices his belief in the way he runs Timberland. In addition to their normal vacation time, employees get a full week off with pay each year to help local charities. The company also grants four employees paid sabbaticals if they volunteer to work full-time for up to six months at a nonprofit organization. In addition, Timberland shuts down production one day a year at a cost of $2 million so its 5,400 employees can participate in company-sponsored philanthropic projects. Bonnie Monahan, a vice president at Timberland, recently took off four days from work to organize a bike-a-thon that raised $50,000 for a local charity.*[4]

Although behaving ethically has value in itself, there are many other benefits to companies that adhere to high ethical standards. First, companies avoid the extremely damaging fallout on their reputations resulting from unethical behavior. Unethical businesses usually gain only short-term advantages; over the long run, unethical decisions don't pay. It's simply not good business.

Second, a solid ethical framework guides managers as they cope with an increasingly complex network of influence from external stakeholders. Dealing with stakeholders is much easier if a company has a solid ethical foundation on which to build.

Third, businesses with solid reputations as ethical companies find it easier to attract and retain quality workers. Explaining why she came to work for Timberland, Helen Kellogg, a senior manager, says, "I was looking for a company that had a conscience." Bonnie Monahan, the Timberland vice president who organized the bike-a-thon, says that she has turned down "several lucrative job offers" from larger companies to stay with Timberland, where "you don't have to leave your values at the door."[5]

Finally, a company's ethical philosophy has an impact on its ability to provide value for its customers. The "ethics factor" is difficult to quantify, yet it is something that customers consider when deciding where to shop and which company's products to buy. "Do I want people buying Timberland boots as a result of the firm's volunteer efforts?" asks CEO Jeffrey Swartz. "You bet."[6] Entrepreneurs must recognize that ethical behavior is an investment in the company's future rather than a simple cost of doing business.

Why Ethical Lapses Occur

Even though most small business owners run their companies ethically, business scandals involving Enron, WorldCom, Tyco, and other high-profile companies have sullied the reputations of businesses of all sizes. In a recent CBS poll, less than one-third of the respondents said they believe most CEOs are honest, 79 percent said questionable business practices are widespread, and more than two-thirds said they think CEOs are commonly compensated illegally.[7] The best way for business owners to combat these negative public perceptions is to run their business ethically. When faced with an ethical dilemma, however, not every manager or employee will make the correct decision. In fact, many unethical acts are committed by normally decent people who believe in moral values. What causes these ethical lapses to occur?

Company Example

An Unethical Employee. Ethical decisions are individual decisions, and some people are corrupt. Try as they might to avoid them, organizations occasionally find that they have hired a bad apple. Eliminating unethical behavior requires the elimination of these bad apples.

An Unethical Organizational Culture. In some cases, the company culture has been poisoned with an unethical overtone; in other words, the problem is not the bad apple but the bad barrel. Pressure to prosper produces an environment that creates conditions that reward unethical behavior, and employees act accordingly. To create an environment for employees that encourages ethical behavior, entrepreneurs should:

- *Set the tone.* Someone once said, "The character of the leader casts a long shadow over the organization and can determine the character of the organization itself." What you do, how you do it, and what you say sets the tone for your employees. The values you profess must be aligned with the behaviors you demonstrate.
- *Establish and enforce policies.* Set appropriate policies for your organization. Communicate them on a regular basis, and adhere to them personally for others to see. Show zero tolerance for ethical violations—and be assured the old adage "Don't do as I do; do as I say" does *not* work. Without a demonstration of real consequence and personal accountability, policies are useless.
- *Educate and recruit.* Consider using a formal education program to enhance the understanding of and commitment to ethical behavior. Find colleges and universities that have incorporated business ethics in courses and make them a prime recruiting source.
- *Separate related job duties.* This is a classic organizational concept. Not allowing the employee who writes checks to reconcile the company bank statement is one example.
- *Reward ethical conduct.* The reward system is a large window into the values of an organization. If you reward a behavior, people have a tendency to repeat the behavior.
- *Eliminate "Undiscussables."* One of the most important things entrepreneurs can do to promote ethical behavior is to instill the belief that it is acceptable for employees to question what happens above them. Doing away with undiscussables shines a light of openness and promotes trust.[8]

Moral Blindness. Sometimes, fundamentally ethical people commit unethical blunders because they are blind to the implications of their conduct. Moral blindness may be the result of failing to realize that an ethical dilemma exists, or it may arise from a variety of mental defense mechanisms. One of the most common mechanisms is rationalization:

- "Everybody does it."
- "If they were in my place, they'd do it too."
- "Being ethical is a luxury I cannot afford right now."
- "The impact of my decision/action on (whomever or whatever) is not my concern."
- "I don't get paid to be ethical; I get paid to produce results."

Training in ethical thinking and creating an environment that encourages employees to consider the ethical impact of their decisions can reduce the problem of moral blindness.

Competitive Pressures. If competition is so intense that a company's survival is threatened, managers may begin to view what were once unacceptable options as acceptable. Managers and employees are under such pressure to produce that they may sacrifice their ethical standards to reduce the fear of failure or the fear of losing their jobs. When there does not exist a positive organizational culture that stresses ethical behavior regardless of the consequences, employees may respond to feelings of pressure and compromise personal ethical standards to ensure that a contract is not lost or that a project is completed on time.

Opportunity Pressures. When the opportunity to "get ahead" by taking some unethical action presents itself, some people cannot resist the temptation. The greater the reward or the smaller the penalty for unethical acts, the greater is the probability that such behavior will occur. If managers, for example, condone or even encourage unethical behavior, they can be sure it will occur. Those who succumb to opportunity pressures often make one of two mistakes: They overestimate the cost of doing the right thing, or they underestimate the cost of doing the wrong thing. Either error can lead to disaster.

Globalization of Business. The globalization of business has intertwined what once were distinct cultures. This cultural cross-pollination has brought about many positive aspects, but it has created problems as well. Companies have discovered that there is no single standard of ethical behavior applying to all business decisions in the international arena. Practices that are illegal in one country may be perfectly acceptable, even expected, in another. Actions that would send a businessperson to jail in Western nations are common ways of working around the system in others. *For example, as part of Russia's move to privatize formerly government-owned businesses, government officials decided to sell the 1,777-room Cosmos Hotel, originally built for the 1980 Olympics. The hotel generates revenues of $100 million a year (in hard currency) and produces profits of $10 million each year. Although such a business would sell for at least $100 million in the United States or in Western Europe, Mikhail Kharshan bought a 25 percent interest in the Cosmos for a mere $2.5 million! Getting the property at just 10 percent of its value was no easy task. As an insider, Kharshan knew the hotel would be put up for sale before most people did, and he used the extra time to scare off rival bidders for the popular hotel. He bribed journalists from two influential business papers to publish negative financial reports about the Cosmos. Then he arranged to be interviewed on Russian television, where he talked about the poor state of the Russian hotel industry. He bribed government officials to limit the Cosmos auction to just two locations and then bribed two other likely bidders not to participate in the auction. The result: Kharshan was the only serious bidder at the auction; that's how he managed to get the hotel at such a bargain. Kharshan says that his actions, although unethical by U.S. business standards, "are normal business practices in Russia. We didn't shoot anyone and we didn't violate any laws."*[9]

> Company Example

"Jackson had to skip the meeting...he's being sentenced today."

Establishing Ethical Standards

3. Explain how to establish and maintain high ethical standards.

A recent study by the Southern Institute for Business and Professional Ethics found that small companies are less likely than large ones to have ethics programs.[10] Although they may not have formal ethics programs, entrepreneurs can encourage employees to become familiar with the following ethical tests for judging behavior.

- *The utilitarian principle.* Choose the option that offers the greatest good for the greatest number of people.
- *Kant's categorical imperative.* Act in such a way that the action taken under the circumstances could be a universal law or rule of behavior.
- *The professional ethic.* Take only those actions that a disinterested panel of professional colleagues would view as proper.
- *The golden rule.* Treat other people the way you would like them to treat you.
- *The television test.* Would you and your colleagues feel comfortable explaining your actions to a national television audience?
- *The family test.* Would you be comfortable explaining to your children, your spouse, and your parents why you took this action?[11]

Although these tests do not offer universal solutions to ethical dilemmas, they do help employees identify the moral implications of the decisions they face. People must be able to understand the ethical impact of their actions before they can make responsible decisions. Table 21.3 describes 10 ethical principles that differentiate between right and wrong, thereby offering a guideline for ethical behavior.

Implementing and Maintaining Ethical Standards

Establishing ethical standards is only the first step in an ethics-enhancing program; implementing and maintaining those standards is the real challenge facing management. What can entrepreneurs do to integrate ethical principles into their companies?

Create a Company Credo. A **company credo** defines the values underlying the entire company and its ethical responsibilities to its stakeholders. It offers general guidance in ethical issues. The most effective credos capture the elusive essence of a company—what it stands for and why it's important—and they can be a key ingredient in a company's competitive edge. A company credo is especially important for a small company, where the entrepreneur's values become the values driving the business. A credo is an excellent way to transform those values into employees' ethical behavior.

Develop a Code of Ethics. A **code of ethics** is a written statement of the standards of behavior and ethical principles a company expects from its employees. Codes of ethics do not ensure ethical behavior, but they do establish minimum standards of behavior throughout the organization. A code of ethics spells out what kind of behavior is expected (and what kind will not be tolerated) and offers everyone in the company concrete guidelines for dealing with ethics every day on the job. Although creating a code of ethics does not guarantee 100 percent compliance with ethical standards, it does tend to foster an ethical atmosphere in a company. Workers who will be directly affected by the code should have a hand in developing it.

Enforce the Code Fairly and Consistently. Managers must take action whenever they discover ethical violations. If employees learn that ethical breaches go unpunished, the code of ethics becomes meaningless. Enforcing the code of ethics demonstrates to everyone that you believe that ethical behavior is mandatory.

Table 21.3

10 Ethical Principles to Guide Behavior

The study of history, philosophy, and religion reveals a strong consensus about certain universal and timeless values that are central to leading an ethical life.

1. *Honesty.* Be truthful, sincere, forthright, straightforward, frank, and candid; do not cheat, lie, steal, deceive, or act deviously.

2. *Integrity.* Be principled, honorable, upright, and courageous, and act on convictions; do not be two-faced or unscrupulous or adopt an ends-justify-the-means philosophy that ignores principles.

3. *Promise-keeping.* Be worthy of trust, keep promises, fulfill commitments, and abide by the spirit as well as the letter of an agreement; do not interpret agreements in a technical or legalistic manner in order to rationalize noncompliance or to create excuses for breaking commitments.

4. *Fidelity.* Be faithful and loyal to family, friends, employers, and country; do not use or disclose information learned in confidence; in a professional context, safeguard the ability to make independent professional judgments by scrupulously avoiding undue influences and conflicts of interest.

5. *Fairness.* Be fair and open-minded, be willing to admit error, and, when appropriate, change positions and beliefs and demonstrate a commitment to justice, the equal treatment of individuals, and tolerance for diversity; do not overreach or take undue advantage of another's mistakes or adversities.

6. *Caring for others.* Be caring, kind, and compassionate; share, be giving, serve others; help those in need and avoid harming others.

7. *Respect for others.* Demonstrate respect for human dignity, privacy, and the right to self-determination for all people; be courteous, prompt, and decent; provide others with the information they need to make informed decisions about their own lives; do not patronize, embarrass, or demean.

8. *Responsible citizenship.* Obey just laws (if a law is unjust, openly protest it); exercise all democratic rights and privileges responsibly by participation (voting and expressing informed views), social consciousness, and public service; when in a position of leadership or authority, openly respect and honor democratic processes of decision making, avoid secrecy or concealment of information, and ensure others have the information needed to make intelligent choices and exercise their rights.

9. *Pursuit of excellence.* Pursue excellence in all matters; in meeting personal and professional responsibilities, be diligent, reliable, industrious, and committed; perform all tasks to the best of your ability, develop and maintain a high degree of competence, and be well informed and well prepared; do not be content with mediocrity, but do not seek to win "at any cost."

10. *Accountability.* Be accountable; accept responsibility for decisions, for the foreseeable consequences of actions and inactions, and for setting an example for others. Parents, teachers, employers, many professionals, and public officials have a special obligation to lead by example and to safeguard and advance the integrity and reputation of their families, companies, professions, and the government; avoid even the appearance of impropriety and take whatever actions are necessary to correct or prevent inappropriate conduct by others.

Source: Michael Josephson, "Teaching Ethical Decision Making and Principaled Reasoning," *Ethics: Easier Said Than Done,* Winter 1988, pp. 28–29.

Conduct Ethics Training. Instilling ethics in an organization's culture requires more than creating a code of ethics and enforcing it. Managers must show employees that the organization truly is committed to practicing ethical behavior. One of the most effective ways to display that commitment is through ethical training designed to raise employees' consciousness of potential ethical dilemmas. Ethics training programs not only raise employees' awareness of ethical issues, but they also communicate to employees the core of the company's value system.

Hire the Right People. Ultimately, the decision in any ethical situation belongs to the individual. Hiring people with strong moral principles and values is the best insurance against ethical violations. To make ethical decisions, people must have: (1) *ethical commitment*—the personal resolve to act ethically and do the right thing; (2) *ethical consciousness*—the ability to perceive the ethical implications of a situation; and (3) *ethical competency*—the ability to engage in sound moral reasoning and develop practical problem-solving strategies.[12]

Perform Periodic Ethical Audits. One of the best ways to evaluate the effectiveness of an ethics system is to perform periodic audits. These reviews send a signal to employees that ethics is not just a passing fad.

Establish High Standards of Behavior, Not Just Rules. No one can legislate ethics and morality, but managers can let people know the level of performance they expect. It is crucial to emphasize to *everyone* in the organization the importance of ethics. All employees must understand that ethics is *not* negotiable. The role that an entrepreneur plays in establishing high ethical standards is critical; no one has more influence over the ethical character of a company than its founder. One experienced entrepreneur offers this advice to business owners: "Stick to your principles. Hire people who want to live by them, teach them thoroughly, and insist on total commitment."[13]

Set an Impeccable Ethical Example at All Times. Remember that ethics starts at the top. Far more important than credos and codes are the examples a company's leaders set. If managers talk about the importance of ethics and then act in an unethical manner, they send mixed signals to employees. Workers believe managers' *actions* more than their words.

Create a Culture That Emphasizes Two-Way Communication. A thriving ethical environment requires two-way communication. Employees must have the opportunity to report any ethical violations they observe. Such a two-way system is integral to a whistle-blowing program, in which employees anonymously report breaches of ethical behavior through proper channels.

Involve Employees in Establishing Ethical Standards. Encourage employees to offer feedback on how standards should be established. Involving employees improves the quality of a firm's ethical standards and increases the likelihood of employee compliance.

The Issue of Social Responsibility

4. Define social responsibility.

The concept of social responsibility has evolved from a nebulous "do-gooder" image to one of "social steward" with expectations that organizations will produce benefits not only for themselves but also for society as a whole. Society is constantly redefining its expectations of business and now holds all enterprises to high behavioral standards. Companies must go beyond "doing well"—simply earning a profit—to "doing good"—living up to their social responsibility. Businesses of all sizes are using their resources and sphere of influence to tackle challenging problems confronting the global economy, including pollution, habitat destruction, human rights, AIDS, hunger, poverty, and others.

In a free enterprise system, companies that fail to respond to their customers' needs and demands soon go out of business. Today, customers are increasingly demanding that the companies they buy goods and services from be socially responsible. When customers shop for "value," they no longer consider only the price-performance relationship of the product or service; they also consider the company's stance on social responsibility. A recent study by consulting firm Hill and Knowlton found that 79 percent of U.S. consumers consider a company's reputation when evaluating products, and 36 percent consider reputation to be an important factor in their purchasing decision.[14] Another study revealed that nearly 90 percent of consumers said that when price, service, and quality are equal among competitors, they will buy from the company that has the best reputation for social responsibility. The survey also revealed that 70 percent of consumers would not buy, at any price, from a company that was not socially responsible.[15]

Other studies show a connection between social responsibility and profitability. A study by the Sustainable Asset Management Group concluded that companies that embrace social responsibility as part of their corporate culture, decision making, and actions financially outperform those that do not.[16] The message is clear: Companies that incorporate social responsibility into their competitive strategies outperform those that fail to do so.

Putting Social Responsibility Into Practice

One problem facing businesses is defining just what social responsibility is. Is it manufacturing environmentally friendly products? Is it donating a portion of profits to charitable organizations? Is it creating jobs in inner cities plagued by high unemployment levels? The nature of a company's social responsibility efforts will depend on how its owners, employees, and other stakeholders define what it means to be socially responsible. Typically, businesses have responsibilities to several key stakeholders, including the environment, employees, customers, investors, and the community. **Social responsibility** is the awareness by a company's managers of the social, environmental, political, human, and financial consequences their actions produce.

Business's Responsibility to the Environment

5. Understand the nature of business's responsibility to the environment.

Driven by their customers' interest in protecting the environment, companies have become more sensitive to the impact their products, processes, and packaging have on the planet. Environmentalism has become, and will continue to be, one of the dominant issues for companies worldwide because consumers have added another item to their list of buying criteria: environmental safety. Companies have discovered that sound environmental practices make for good business. In addition to lowering their operating costs, environmentally safe products attract environmentally conscious customers and can give a company a competitive edge in the marketplace. Socially responsible business owners focus on the three Rs: *reduce, reuse,* and *recycle.*

- *Reduce* the amount of materials used in your company, from the factory floor to the copier room.
- *Reuse* whatever you can.
- *Recycle* the materials that you must dispose of.

Company Example

Grant Goodman, CEO of Rockland Materials, a Phoenix-based maker of aggregate and concrete materials used in the construction industry, wanted his company to live up to its motto, "Good business means good environmental policy." In 2001, Goodman decided to reduce Rockland's impact on the environment by converting all of the company's fleet of 120 ready-mix concrete delivery trucks to biodiesel fuel. Made from soybeans, biodiesel fuel is degradable, nontoxic, and free of sulfur, which makes it much more environmentally friendly than petroleum-based diesel fuel. "I'm not an environmentalist," insists Goodman. "I'm just attuned to business ethics." Although the biodiesel fuel costs 50 to 60 cents more per gallon than diesel fuel, Goodman made the conversion because "it was the right thing to do." He says, "As an entrepreneur, you have to have the backbone to reconcile the profit motive with the desire to make things in sync with the environment."[17]

Like Rockland Materials, progressive companies are taking their environmental policies a step further, creating redesigned, "clean" manufacturing systems that focus on *avoiding* waste and pollution. That requires a different manufacturing philosophy. These companies design their products, packaging, and processes from the start with the environment in mind, working to eliminate hazardous materials and by-products and looking for ways to turn what had been scrap into salable products. Such an approach requires an ecological evaluation of every part of the process—from the raw materials put into the product to the disposal or reuse of the packaging that surrounds it. Table 21.4 offers a list of suggestions environmentally responsible entrepreneurs should take into consideration.

Table 21.4

Enhancing Environmental Performance

Corporations looking to enhance their environmental performance would do well to focus not only on assessing current practices but also on anticipating future requirements and capacities.

Some essential first steps can be implemented easily and cost-effectively. They include:

- *Know your employees and partners.* Check references, employment history, and qualifications. Are suppliers legitimately registered companies? Who are their subcontractors? Have they met obligations for taxes, social insurance, payroll, and labor contracts?
- *Conduct preliminary assessments of facilities.* Verify security of the premises, acceptability of health and safety measures and waste management procedures, quality of accommodations, and other amenities for employees. Develop contingency plans for dealing with security breaches, employment standards violations, industrial accidents, or environmental damage.
- *Keep everyone informed.* Disseminate your environmental, health, and safety criteria. Local staff value working in companies that have high standards and practices and will be more loyal and ultimately more productive if they know they are protected.
- *Make clear your expectations.* For suppliers, make it part of their contractual obligations to comply with your standards. Explain how and why it is relevant to the production cycle and success of your and the contractor's business to meet or even exceed the criteria you set.
- *Be prepared to invest in your partners.* By and large, suppliers do value their company names and want to be seen as capable of delivering world-class products. They won't always have the means to switch to cleaner machinery, fix potential hazards in their facilities, or train employees. A short-term investment in their business could lead to savings for yours in the long run.
- *Set specific, achievable goals.* Follow up with independent audits to provide unbiased and systematic assessments. These checks should be ongoing at different times of the year, day, and production cycle. Unannounced checks ensure the opportunity to monitor the situation as it really is, rather than a cleaned-up version specially prepared for a preannounced audit.
- *Resist complacency.* Monitor progress and revise goals continually. Publicize success strategies, and acknowledge and learn from problem areas.

To complement these actions, companies can also undergo a formal certification process—such as attaining the internationally recognized ISO 14001 or SA 8000 certifications that monitor, respectively, environmental or employment practices. Ultimately, social accountability is not a test to be passed once and forgotten. It entails establishing a culture of compliance and responsibility within the corporation and throughout the supply chain.

Source: Adapted from Ian Gilcrest, "Beyond Compliance: Social Accountability Can Protect Companies and Profits," *Asia Week Magazine,* April 13, 2001, www.asiaweek.com/asiaweek/magazine/nations/ 0,8782,105424,00.html.

Business's Responsibility to Employees

6. Describe business's responsibility to employees.

Few other stakeholders are as important to a business as its employees. It is common for managers to *say* their employees are their most valuable resource, but the truly excellent ones *treat* them that way. Employees are at the heart of increases in productivity, and they add the personal touch that puts the passion in customer service. In short, employees produce the winning competitive advantage for an entrepreneur. As such, employees really are the firm's most valuable asset.

Entrepreneurs who are sensitive to the value of their employees follow a few simple procedures by:

- Listening to employees and respecting their opinions.
- Asking for their input; involving them in the decision-making process.
- Providing regular feedback—positive and negative—to employees.
- Telling them the truth—always.
- Letting them know exactly what's expected of them.
- Rewarding employees for performing their jobs well.
- Trusting them; creating an environment of respect and teamwork.

Company Example →

Starbucks Coffee Company, the successful Seattle-based coffee retailer, recognizes the special role its employees (or "partners," in company lingo) play in keeping customers coming back to its retail locations, and it shows employees that it appreciates their contributions. Reflecting on the importance of having satisfied partners interacting with customers in the retail business, CEO Howard Schultz explains, "We recognized (from the onset that) we had to build trust and confidence with customers and shareholders. But first and foremost, we had to build this trust with employees." At Starbucks, employee-partners come first. Great benefits, constant training, respect, and a team approach keep costs low and employee turnover down to just one-eighth of the industry average. Company surveys show that 82 percent of Starbucks partners, who volunteer more than 200,000 hours a year in their local communities, are either satisfied or very satisfied with their jobs.[18]

Several important issues face small business managers trying to meet their social responsibility to employees, including cultural diversity, drug testing, AIDS, sexual harassment, and privacy.

Cultural Diversity in the Workplace

The United States has always been a nation of astonishing cultural diversity, a trait that has imbued it with an incredible richness of ideas and creativity. Indeed, this diversity is one of the driving forces behind the greatest entrepreneurial effort in the world, and it continues to grow. The United States, in short, is moving toward a "minority majority," and significant demographic shifts will affect virtually every aspect of business. Nowhere will this be more visible than in the makeup of the nation's workforce. The population of Hispanics, African Americans, Native Americans, Asians and others grew 43 percent from 1990 to 2000. The Hispanic sector alone grew 58 percent and now constitutes more than 13 percent of the U.S. population.[19]

This rich mix of cultures within the workforce presents both opportunities and challenges to employers. One of the chief benefits of a diverse workforce is the rich blend of perspectives, skills, talents, and ideas employees have to offer. Also, the changing composition of the nation will change the customer base. What better way is there for an entrepreneur to deal with culturally diverse customers than to have a culturally diverse workforce? "No matter who you are, you're going to have to work with people who are different from you," says Ted Childs, vice president of global workforce diversity for IBM. "You're going to have to sell to people who are different from you, buy from people who are different from you, and manage people who are different from you."[20]

Managing a culturally diverse workforce presents a real challenge for employers, however. Molding workers with highly varied beliefs, backgrounds, and biases into a unified team takes time and commitment. Stereotypes, biases, and prejudices will present barriers that workers and managers must constantly overcome. Communication may require more effort because of language differences. In many cases, dealing with diversity causes a degree of discomfort for entrepreneurs because of the natural tendency to associate with people who are similar to ourselves. These reasons and others cause some entrepreneurs to resist the move to a more diverse workforce, a move that threatens their ability to create a competitive edge.

How can entrepreneurs achieve unity through diversity? The only way is by *managing* diversity in the workforce. In its *Best Practices of Private Sector Employers,* an Equal Employment Opportunity Commission task force suggests following a "SPLENDID" approach to diversity:

- **Study.** Business owners cannot solve problems they don't know exist. Entrepreneurs must familiarize themselves with issues related to diversity, including relevant laws.
- **Plan.** Recognizing the makeup of the local population, entrepreneurs must set targets for diversity hiring and develop a plan for achieving them.

- **Lead.** A diversity effort starts at the top of the organization with managers communicating their vision and goals to everyone in the company.
- **Encourage.** Company leaders must encourage employees at all levels of an organization to embrace the diversity plan.
- **Notice.** Entrepreneurs must monitor their companies' progress toward achieving diversity goals.
- **Discussion.** Managers must keep diversity on the company's radar screen by communicating the message that diversity is vital to business success.
- **Inclusion.** Involving employees in the push to achieve diversity helps break down barriers that may arise.
- **Dedication.** Achieving diversity in a business does not happen overnight, but entrepreneurs must be persistent in implementing their plans.[21]

The goal of diversity efforts is to create an environment in which all types of workers—men, women, Hispanic, African American, white, disabled, homosexual, elderly, and others—can flourish and can give top performances to their companies. In fact, researchers at Harvard University report that companies that embrace diversity are more productive than those that shun diversity. A distinguishing factor the companies supporting diversity share is the willingness of people to learn from their coworkers' different backgrounds and life experiences.[22]

Managing a culturally diverse workforce requires a different way of thinking, however, and that requires training. In essence, diversity training will help make everyone aware of the dangers of bias, prejudice, and discrimination, however subtle or unintentional they may be. Managing a culturally diverse workforce successfully requires a business owner to:

Assess your company's diversity needs. The starting point for an effective diversity management program is an assessment of the company's needs and problems. Surveys, interviews, and informal conversations with employees can be valuable tools. Several organizations offer more formal assessment tools—"cultural audits," questionnaires, and diagnostic forms—that also might be useful.

Learn to recognize and correct your own biases and stereotypes. One of the best ways to identify your own cultural biases is to get exposure to people who are not like you. By spending time with those who are different from you, you will learn quickly that stereotypes simply don't hold up.

Avoid making invalid assumptions. Decisions based on faulty assumptions are bound to be flawed. False assumptions made on the basis of inaccurate perceptions or personal bias have kept many qualified women and minorities from getting jobs and promotions.

Push for diversity in your management team. To get maximum benefit from a culturally diverse workforce, a company must promote nontraditional workers into top management. A culturally diverse top management team that can serve as mentors and role models provides visible evidence that nontraditional workers can succeed.

Concentrate on communication. Any organization, especially a culturally diverse one, will stumble if lines of communication break down. Frequent training sessions and regular opportunities for employees to talk with one another in a nonthreatening environment can be extremely helpful.

Make diversity a core value in the organization. For a cultural diversity program to work, top managers must "champion" the program and take active steps to integrate diversity throughout the entire organization.

Continue to adjust your company to your workers. Rather than pressure workers to conform to the company, those entrepreneurs with the most successful cultural diversity programs are constantly looking for ways to adjust their businesses to their workers. Flexibility is the key.

As business leaders look to the future, an increasingly diverse workforce stares back. People with varying cultural, racial, gender, and lifestyle perspectives are seeking opportunity and acceptance from coworkers, managers, and business leaders. With the unbridled growth of information technology, people of different backgrounds are more accessible than ever. At the dawn of the new millennium, over half of new workforce entrants were women. Furthermore, studies by the U.S. Census Bureau predict that, by the year 2010, people of color will make up 33 percent of the nation's population. Businesses that practice inclusiveness may enjoy greater employee satisfaction, commitment, retention, and productivity.[23]

Table 21.5 outlines the steps necessary to achieve diversity success in an organization.

Drug Testing. One of the realities of our society is substance abuse. Another reality, which entrepreneurs now must face head on, is that substance abuse has infiltrated the workplace. In addition to the lives it ruins, substance abuse takes a heavy toll on business and society, costing employers between $60 and $100 billion a year.[24] Drug and alcohol abuse by employees results in reduced productivity, increased medical costs, higher accident rates, and absenteeism. Unfortunately, small companies bear a disproportionate share of the burden. Approximately three-fourths of all substance abusers are employed. Because small companies are less likely to have drug-testing programs than large companies, they are more likely to hire people with substance abuse problems. Abusers who know that they cannot pass a drug test simply apply for work at companies that do not use drug tests. Also, because the practice of drug testing remains controversial, its inconsistent use can lead to a variety of legal woes for employers, including charges of invasion of privacy, discrimination, slander, or defamation of character.

An effective, proactive drug program should include the following four elements:

1. *A written substance abuse policy.* The first step is to create a written policy that spells out the company's position on drugs. The policy should state its purpose, prohibit

Table 21.5

Six Stages of Diversity Success

1. Assess need
   - Identify business objectives
   - Benchmark best practices
   - Determine business case for a diversity initiative (councils or task forces)
2. Analyze
   - Conduct a baseline survey of employee perceptions regarding diversity issues
   - Correlate results with business operational objectives
   - Develop visual descriptors (company or department-wide)
3. Be aware
   - Educate the organization to create a base of understanding of the business's need to embrace diversity (company or department-wide)
4. Evaluate and enhance business systems and processes
   - Concurrently with awareness development, evaluate human resources processes as well as marketing, community relations, product/service development, and so forth (task forces)
5. Reassess employee perceptions
   - Resurvey employees and compare results to baseline
   - Identify successes and areas needing further focus
   - Determine next steps (company or department-wide)
6. Evaluate business results
   - Compare business results to visual descriptors
   - Determine actions needed to make new behaviors part of the company culture

Source: Lenora Billings-Harris, *The Diversity Advantage: A Guide to Making Diversity Work,* cited in Hagin King, "Diversity Partnerships Celebrate the Best in Everyone," *Employment Review,* December 1999, www.employmentreview.com/1999–12/features/CNfeat07.asp.

the use of drugs on the job (or off the job if it affects job performance), specify the consequences of violating the policy, explain any drug testing procedures to be used, and describe the resources available to help troubled employees.

2. *Training for supervisors to detect drug-using workers.* Supervisors are in the best position to identify employees with drug problems and to encourage them to get help. The supervisor's job, however, is not to play "cop" or "therapist." The supervisor should identify problem employees early and encourage them to seek help. The focal point of the supervisor's role is to track employees' performances against their objectives to identify the employees with performance problems. Vigilant managers look for the following signs:
   - Frequent tardiness or absences accompanied by questionable excuses
   - Long lunch, coffee, or bathroom breaks
   - Frequently missed deadlines
   - Withdrawl from or frequent arguments with fellow employees
   - Excessive sensitivity to criticism
   - Declining or inconsistent productivity
   - Inability to focus on work

3. *A drug testing program, when necessary.* Experts recommend that business owners seek the advice of an experienced attorney before establishing a drug testing program. Preemployment testing of job applicants generally is a safe strategy to follow, as long as it is followed consistently. Testing current employees is a more complex issue.

4. *An employee assistance program (EAP).* No drug-battling program is complete without a way to help addicted employees. An **employee assistance program (EAP)** is a company-provided benefit designed to help reduce workplace problems such as alcoholism, drug addiction, a gambling habit, and other conflicts and to deal with them when they arise. Although some troubled employees may balk at enrolling in an EAP, the company controls the most powerful weapon in motivating them to seek and accept help: *their jobs.* The greatest fear that substance-abusing employees have is losing their jobs, and the company can use that fear to help workers recover.

AIDS

One of the most serious health problems to strike the world is AIDS (acquired immune deficiency syndrome). This deadly disease, for which no cure yet exists, poses an array of ethical dilemmas for business, ranging from privacy to discrimination. AIDS has had an impact on our economy in the form of billions of dollars in lost productivity and increased health care costs. For most business owners, the issue is not one of *if* one of their employees will contract AIDS but *when.*

Coping with AIDS in the workplace is not like managing normal healthcare issues because of the fear and misunderstanding the disease creates among coworkers. When confronted by the disease, many employers and employees operate on the basis of misconceptions and fear, resulting in "knee-jerk" reactions that are illegal, including firing the worker and telling other employees. Too many entrepreneurs know very little about their legal obligation to employees with AIDS. In fact, AIDS is considered a disability and is covered by the Americans with Disabilities Act. This legislation prohibits discrimination against any person with a disability, including AIDS, in hiring, promoting, discharging, or compensation. In addition, employers are required to make "reasonable accommodations" that will allow an AIDS-stricken employee to continue working. Some examples of these accommodations include; job sharing, flexible work schedules, job reassignment, sick leave, and part-time work.

Despite the fact that AIDS is becoming more common in the workplace, few businesses are adequately prepared to deal with it. Yet coping with AIDS in a socially responsible manner requires a written policy and an educational program, ideally implemented *before* the need arises. When dealing with AIDS, entrepreneurs must base their decisions on facts rather than on emotions, so they must be well informed.

As with drug testing, it is important to ensure that a company's AIDS policies are legal. In general, a company's AIDS policy should address the following:

Employment. Companies must allow employees with AIDS to continue working as long as they can perform the job.

Discrimination. Because AIDS is a disability, employers cannot discriminate against qualified people with the disease who can meet job requirements.

Employee benefits. Employees with AIDS have the right to the same benefits as those with any other life-threatening illness.

Confidentiality. Employers must keep employees' medical records strictly confidential.

Education. An AIDS education program should be a part of every company's AIDS policy. The time to create and implement one is before the problem arises. As part of its AIDS program, one small company conducted informational seminars, distributed brochures and booklets, established a print and video library, and even set up individual counseling for employees.

Reasonable accommodations. Under the ADA, employers must make reasonable accommodations for employees with AIDS. These may include extended leaves of absence, flexible work schedules, restructuring a job to require less strenuous duties, purchasing special equipment to assist affected workers, and other modifications.

Sexual Harassment

As the number of women in the workforce has increased, so has the number of sexual harassment charges filed (see Figure 21.2). One of the ugly historical truths about the work environment in some businesses was the silent acceptance of sexual harassment. Sexual harassment is a violation of Title VII of the Civil Rights Act of 1964 and is considered to be a form of sex discrimination. Studies show that sexual harassment occurs in businesses of all sizes, but small businesses are especially vulnerable because they typically lack the policies, procedures, and training to prevent it. Even cartoon strip characters are not immune to sexual harassment charges. In Mort Walker's long-running "Beetle Bailey" comic strip, Miss Buxley once filed charges against General Halftrack because of his leering stares and sexual and untoward comments.[25]

Sexual harassment is any unwelcome sexual advance, request for sexual favors, or other verbal or physical sexual conduct made explicitly or implicitly as a condition of employment. Women bring about 85 percent of all sexual harassment charges. Jury verdicts reaching into the millions of dollars are not uncommon. Retaliation against employees who file a complaint of sexual harassment occurs, unfortunately, too often. A recent study found that retaliation claims occur in 47 percent of sexual harassment cases. The most common form of employer retaliation was termination, which occurred in 61 percent of the cases of retaliation.[26]

Several types of behavior may result in sexual harassment charges:

Quid Pro Quo Harassment. The most blatant, and most potentially damaging, form of sexual harassment is *quid pro quo* ("something for something"), in which a superior conditions the granting of a benefit (promotion, raise, etc.) upon the receipt of sexual favors from a subordinate. Only managers and supervisors, not coworkers, can engage in *quid pro quo* harassment. Unfortunately, this form of harassment is all too common.

Figure 21.2

Number of Sexual
Harassment Charges
Filed

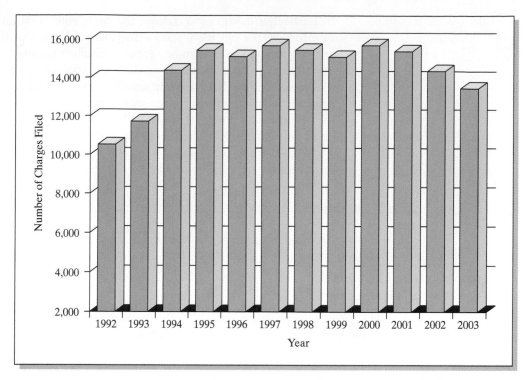

Source: Equal Employment Opportunity Commission, 2004.

Hostile Environment. Behavior that creates an abusive, intimidating, offensive, or hostile work environment also constitutes sexual harassment. A hostile environment usually requires a *pattern* of offensive sexual behavior rather than a single, isolated remark or display. In judging whether a hostile environment exists, courts base their decisions on how a "reasonable woman" would perceive the situation. (The previous standard was that of a "reasonable person.") Although not easily defined, a hostile work environment is one in which continuing unwelcome sexual conduct in the workplace interferes with an employee's work performance. Most sexual harassment charges arise from claims of a hostile environment.

Harassment by Nonemployees. An employer can be held liable for third parties (customers, sales representatives, and others) who engage in sexual harassment if the employer

Company Example → has the ability to stop the improper behavior. *For example, one company required a female employee to wear an extremely skimpy, revealing uniform. She complained to her boss that the uniform encouraged members of the public to direct offensive comments and physical contact toward her. The manager ignored her complaints, and later she refused to wear the uniform, which resulted in her dismissal. When she filed a sexual harassment claim, the court held the company accountable for the employee's sexual harassment by nonemployees because it required her to wear the uniform after she complained of the harassment.*[27]

No business wants to incur the cost of defending itself against charges of sexual harassment, but those costs can be devastating for a small business. Multimillion-dollar jury awards in such cases are becoming increasingly common because the Civil Rights Act of 1991 allows victims to collect punitive damages and emotional distress awards.

In recent rulings, the United States Supreme Court changed the nature of an employer's liability for sexual harassment, rejecting the previous standard that the employer had to be negligent somehow to be liable for a supervisor's improper behavior toward employees.

In *Burlington Industries vs. Ellerth*, the court ruled that an employer can be held liable *automatically* if a supervisor takes a "tangible employment action," such as failing to promote or firing an employee whom he has been sexually harassing. The employer is liable even if he was not aware of the supervisor's conduct. If a supervisor takes no tangible employment action against an employee but engages in sexually harassing behavior such as offensive remarks, inappropriate touching, or sexual advances, the employer is not *automatically* liable for the supervisor's conduct. An employer would be liable for such conduct if, for example, the employer knew (or should have known) about the supervisor's behavior and failed to stop it.[28]

A company's best weapons against sexual harassment are education, policy, and procedures.

✦ GAINING *a* COMPETITIVE EDGE ✦

How Much Do You Know About Sexual Harassment?

Do you know sexual harassment when you see it? Consider the following true case:

Catherine was exposed to nude photographs posted in various areas of the plant in which she worked. She eventually complained about the pictures to the plant manager, who (1) made inappropriate personal and sexual remarks to her, (2) addressed her as "honey" and "dear," and (3) insinuated that she was a troublemaker. Thereafter, some, but not all, of the pictures were removed, despite the employer's policy to remove sexually explicit materials upon discovery.

When Catherine's immediate supervisor heard of her complaint, he indicated that he disapproved of "women's liberation" and recited a story to Catherine about employees who had quit their jobs after the jobs were made intolerable. Other employees (including another supervisor) also expressed to Catherine their annoyance over her complaint, and she was subjected to catcalls and harassing whistles. These instances of harassment were also reported by Catherine to her immediate supervisor and the plant manager, who indicated to her that she was somehow encouraging the harassment. Management failed to put an end to the whistling and catcalls.

In its defense, the company cited the fact that it had instituted a policy of using gender-neutral terms in its job titles.

Did Catherine have a legitimate sexual harassment complaint?

Yes, although the company had a mechanism for employees to complain about sexual harassment, managers failed to take any action to stop the harassment. Indeed, the managers to whom she complained participated in the harassment. Catherine prevailed in court.

One of the primary causes of sexual harassment in the workplace is the lack of education concerning what constitutes harassment. The following quizzes ask you to assume the roles of an employee and of a manager when answering the questions. Perhaps these statements can help you avoid problems with sexual harassment on the job.

Test for Employees

Answer each question as true or false.

1. If I just ignore unwanted sexual attention, it will usually stop.
2. If I don't mean to sexually harass another employee, there's no way my behavior can be perceived by him or her as sexually harassing.
3. Some employees don't complain about unwanted sexual attention from another worker because they don't want to get that person in trouble.
4. If I make sexual comments to someone and that person doesn't ask me to stop, then I guess my behavior is welcome.
5. To avoid sexually harassing a woman who comes to work in a traditionally male workplace, the men simply should not haze her.
6. A sexual harasser may be told by a court to pay part of a judgment to the employee he or she harassed.
7. A sexually harassed man does not have the same legal rights as a woman who is sexually harassed.
8. About 90 percent of all sexual harassment in today's workplace is done by males to females.
9. Sexually suggestive pictures or objects in a workplace don't create a liability unless someone complains.
10. Displaying "girlie" pictures can constitute a hostile work environment even though most workers in the workplace think they are harmless.

11. Telling someone to stop his or her unwanted sexual behavior usually doesn't do any good.

Answers: (1) False, (2) False, (3) True, (4) False, (5) False, (6) True, (7) False, (8) True, (9) False, (10) True, (11) False.

A Test for Managers

Answer each question as true or false.

1. Men in male-dominated workplaces usually have to change their behavior when a woman begins working there.
2. Employers are not liable for the sexual harassment of one of their employees unless that employee loses specific job benefits or is fired.
3. Supervisors can be liable for sexual harassment committed by one of their employees against another.
4. Employers can be liable for the sexually harassing behavior of management personnel even if they are unaware of that behavior and have a policy forbidding it.
5. It is appropriate for a supervisor, when initially receiving a sexual harassment complaint, to determine if the alleged recipient overreacted or misunderstood the alleged harasser.
6. When a supervisor is telling an employee that an allegation of sexual harassment has been made against the employee, it is best to ease into the allegation instead of being direct.
7. Sexually suggestive visuals or objects in a workplace don't create a liability unless an employee complains about them and management allows them to remain.
8. The lack of sexual harassment complaints is a good indication that sexual harassment is not occurring.
9. It is appropriate for supervisors to tell an employee to handle unwelcome sexual behavior if they think that the employee is misunderstanding the behavior.
10. The *intent* behind employee A' s sexual behavior is more important than the *impact* of that behavior on employee B when determining if sexual harassment has occurred.
11. If a sexual harassment problem is common knowledge in a workplace, the courts assume that the employer has knowledge of it.

Answers: (1) False, (2) False, (3) True, (4) True, (5) False, (6) False, (7) False, (8) False, (9) False, (10) False, (11) True.

Sources: Reprinted with permission from *Industry Week,* November 18, 1991, p. 40. Copyright Penton Publishing, Cleveland, Ohio; *Sexual Harassment Manual for Managers and Supervisors* (Chicago: Commerce Clearing House, 1992), p. 22; Andrea P. Brandon and David R. Eyler, *Working Together* (New York: McGraw-Hill, 1994).

Education. Preventing sexual harassment is the best solution, and the key to prevention is educating employees about what constitutes sexual harassment. Training programs are designed to raise employees' awareness of what might be offensive to other workers and how to avoid sexual harassment altogether.

Policy. Another essential ingredient is a meaningful policy against sexual harassment that management can enforce. The policy should:

- Clearly define what behaviors constitute sexual harassment.
- State in clear language that harassment will not be tolerated in the workplace.
- Identify the responsibilities of supervisors and employees in preventing harassment.
- Define the sanctions and penalties for engaging in harassment.
- Spell out the steps to take in reporting an incident of sexual harassment.

The United States Supreme Court ruled that an employer was liable for a supervisor's sexually harassing behavior even though the employee never reported it. The company's liability stemmed from its failure to communicate its sexual harassment policy throughout the organization. This ruling makes employers' policies and procedures on sexual harassment the focal point of their defense.[29]

Procedure. Socially responsible companies provide a channel for all employees to express their complaints. Choosing a person inside the company (perhaps someone in the human

Table 21.6

Questions for Sexual
Harassment
Investigations

When an employee files a sexual harassment complaint, the Equal Employment Opportunity Commission (EEOC) recommends that you (1) question both parties in detail and (2) probe deeply for corroborative evidence. Here is a checklist to help in following these EEOC recommendations.

- Analyze the victim's story for sufficient detail, internal consistency, and believability.
- Do not attach much significance to a general denial by the accused harasser.
- Search completely and thoroughly for evidence that corroborates either side's story.
- You can do this by
  - interviewing coworkers, supervisors, and managers
  - obtaining testimony from individuals who observed the accuser's demeanor immediately after the alleged incident of harassment
  - checking out people with whom the alleged victim discussed the incident (e.g., coworkers, a doctor, or a counselor).
- Ask other employees if they noticed changes in the accusing individual's behavior at work or in the alleged harasser's treatment of him or her.
- Look for evidence of other complaints, either by the victim or other employees.
- Follow up on evidence that other employees were sexually harassed by the same person.

In order to make a fair and legal decision on a sexual harassment complaint, you need to find out as much information as you can, not only on the incident itself but also on the victim's and accuser's personalities, surroundings, and relationships. To accomplish this task, you need to not only ask many questions of the victim and accuser but also of any witnesses to the incident and the surrounding environment.

Source: Women's Studies Database at the University of Maryland, www.mith2.umd.edu/ WomensStudies/GenderIssues/SexualHarassment/questions-for-investigations.

resources area) and one outside the company (a close advisor or attorney) is a good strategy. At least one of these should be a woman. When a complaint arises, managers should:

- Listen to the complaint carefully without judging. Taking notes is a good idea. Tell the complainant what the process involves. Never treat the complaint as a joke.
- Investigate the complaint *promptly,* preferably within 24 hours. Failure to act quickly is irresponsible and illegal.
- Privately and separately, interview the accused party and any witnesses who may be aware of a pattern of harassing behavior.
- Keep findings confidential.
- Decide what action to take, relying on company policy as a guideline.
- Inform both the complaining person and the alleged harasser of the action taken.
- Document the entire investigation.[30]

Sexual harassment will continue to be an issue that business owners must address. Table 21.6 offers a list of suggestions for sexual harassment investigations recommended by the EEOC.

Privacy

Modern technology has given business owners the ability to monitor workers' performances as they never could before, but where is the line between monitoring productivity and invasion of privacy? At the touch of a button, it's possible to view e-mail messages employees send to one another, listen to voice-mail or telephone conversations, and actually see what's on their monitors while they're sitting at their computer terminals. Managers use electronic monitoring to track customer service representatives, word-processing clerks, data entry technicians, and other workers for speed, accuracy, and productivity. Even truck drivers, the lone rangers of the road, are not immune to electronic tracking. Almost two-thirds of the major trucking companies now have communications devices in their trucks. Companies use these devices to monitor drivers' exact locations at all times, to regulate their speed, to make sure they stop only at approved fueling points, and to ensure that they take the legally required hours of rest. Although many drivers support the use of these devices, others worry about their tendency to create George Orwell's "Big Brother" syndrome.

Electronic communication technology also poses ethical problems for employers. Increasingly, workers are using voice-mail and electronic-mail systems to communicate with others; however, few know just what the rules governing their use and their privacy are. A study by the Society for Human Resource Management found that, although 80 percent of all organizations communicate via e-mail, only 34 percent have written policies governing the privacy of e-mail messages.[31] Most employees simply do not know that their bosses can legally monitor their e-mail and voice-mail messages, often without notification. To avoid ethical problems, a business owner should establish a clear policy for monitoring employees' communications and establish guidelines for the proper use of the company's communication technology. The policies should be reasonable and should reflect employees' reasonable expectations of privacy.

Balancing Privacy and Security. What happens when information about one of your employees may be an issue of national security? When the FBI and local law enforcement officials requested access to databases containing personal information about employees and contractors, one entrepreneur was faced with balancing employee privacy with national security. "They wanted to be able to match records to a suspected watch list of terrorists and people wanted for violent crimes," said the entrepreneur. "How can I protect personal information while sharing our databases with who knows how many people? Yet there are valid national security reasons why the government would be interested in our workers." His attorney advised him that, as a high-profile company, a privacy breach could damage its reputation and pose risks of class-action lawsuits.

Add to this the fact that a number of the company's employees were using wireless devices such as cell phones (some with built-in digital cameras) and PDAs. The entrepreneur knew about terrorists using wireless technology to collect digital photos, plant explosives, and release remote bombing devices, but he knew that his company had yet to address the security implications of wireless equipment to which many employees and contractors now had routine access.

In the meantime, the FBI had begun surveillance because they believed terrorists might have infiltrated the business. Video cameras were installed in several discreet locations to record suspicious activity. In the interest of national security, however, employees and contractors were not told about the increased surveillance. A few months later, FBI agents were reviewing some of the tapes that had been flagged for their attention. The tape had captured two employees engaged in a compromising act during working hours. The use of video camera surveillance to protect against terrorism has created new data and privacy risks for the business. While not tipping their hands to terrorists and making them aware of the surveillance technologies in place, entrepreneurs must consider the privacy commitment of the business to citizens, contractors, and employees.

First, is the company's current privacy policy realistic? What privacy protections should the privacy policy commit to? Second, the company should determine how it will protect information gathered through surveillance from overexposure and individuals' right to privacy. In this case, security surveillance had the unintended consequence of creating a potential employee disciplinary issue for the company.

From a security perspective, wireless communication raises many new challenges in addition to those associated with traditional networking. Employees are bringing new wireless devices into the workplace. These security issues become even more critical when an organization must not only deal with potential employee abuse and negligence but also with possible terrorist attacks.

In today's environment, companies should assign a high priority to developing policies for the appropriate use of network wireless technologies. Many organizations are now prohibiting the use of these technologies in the workplace for business confidentiality and intellectual property reasons and also to prevent a security and privacy breach. The policies should define the "do's and don'ts" for everyone to follow. They should also identify clear accountability for enforcing the rules, as well as have training and assignment of roles, responsibilities, and duties to the employees and contractors who deploy, operate, administer, and maintain the organization's security on an ongoing basis.[32]

Business's Responsibility to Customers

7. Explain business's responsibility to customers.

One of the most important groups of stakeholders that a business must satisfy is its *customers*. Building and maintaining a base of loyal customers is no easy task—it requires more than just selling a product or a service. The key is to build relationships with customers. Socially responsible companies recognize their duty to abide by the Consumer Bill of Rights, first put forth by President John Kennedy. This document gives consumers the following rights.

Right to Safety

The right to safety is the most basic consumer right. Companies have the responsibility to provide their customers with safe, quality products and services. The greatest breach of trust occurs when businesses produce products that, when properly used, injure customers. Product liability cases can be controversial, such as the McDonald's hot coffee litigation in which the jury found that the coffee was "too hot" and resulted in serious injury when the store patron dropped the coffee in her lap. In many other situations, the evidence is clear that the product purchased had fundamental flaws in either design or construction and resulted in injury to its user when operated properly. Industry associations often take action to identify products that they find to be unsafe in an attempt to make buyers aware of unsafe products.

Right to Know

Consumers have the right to honest communication about the products and services they buy and the companies that sell them. In a free market economy, information is one of the most valuable commodities available. Customers often depend on companies for the information they need to make decisions about price, quality, features, and other factors. As a result, companies have a responsibility to customers to be truthful in their advertising. Unfortunately, not every business recognizes its social responsibility to be truthful in advertising. Businesses that rely on such unscrupulous tactics may profit in the short term, but they will not last in the long run.

Right to Be Heard

The right to be heard suggests that the channels of communication between companies and their customers run in both directions. Socially responsible businesses provide customers with a mechanism for resolving complaints about products and services. Some companies have established a consumer ombudsman to address customer questions and complaints. Others have created customer hot lines, toll-free numbers designed to serve customers more effectively.

Another effective technique for encouraging two-way communication between customers and companies is the customer report card. The Granite Rock Company relies on an annual report card from its customers to learn how to serve them better. Although the knowledge a small business owner gets from customer feedback is immeasurable for making improvements, only one in 12 small companies regularly schedules customer satisfaction surveys such as Granite Rock's. It's a tool that can boost a company's profitability significantly.

Right to Education

Socially responsible companies give customers access to educational programs about their products and services and how to use them properly. The goal is to give customers enough information to make informed purchase decisions. A product that is the wrong solution to the customer's needs will only result in a disappointed customer who is likely to blame the manufacturer or retailer for the mistake. Consumer education is an inexpensive investment in customer satisfaction and the increased probability that a satisfied customer is a repeat buyer.

Right to Choice

Inherent in the free enterprise system is the consumer's right to choose among competing products and services. Socially responsible companies do not restrict competition, and they abide by the United States' antitrust policy, which promotes free trade and competition in the market. The foundation of this policy is the Sherman Antitrust Act of 1890, which forbids agreements among sellers that restrain trade or commerce and outlaws any attempts to monopolize a market.

Business's Responsibility to Investors

8. Discuss business's responsibility to investors.

Companies have the responsibility to provide investors with an attractive return on their investments. Although earning a profit may be a company's *first* responsibility, it is not its *only* responsibility; meeting its ethical and social responsibility goals is also a key to success. Business owners have discovered that investors want to know what actions the organization is taking that encourage and support ethical decision making and acts of social responsibility. Investors know that such proactive steps reduce the risk of future economic loss. Ethical and socially responsible businesses seldom lose legal challenges. Maintaining high social and ethical standards translates into an environment in which a company is likely to remain profitable in the long run.

Companies also have the responsibility to report their financial performances in an accurate and timely fashion to their investors. Firms that misrepresent or falsify their financial and operating records are guilty of violating the fiduciary relationship

Company Example →

with their investors. *For example, investors in Bre-X Minerals, a tiny mineral exploration company in Calgary, Canada, saw the value of their stock skyrocket when the company announced that it had made the richest gold find of the century in its Busang mine in Borneo, Indonesia. Within two years, however, the value of the company's stock collapsed when an independent consulting firm discovered that drilling samples from the mine had been doctored with gold dust from other sources. Angry investors saw billions of dollars of their wealth evaporate when it became apparent that Bre-X's mine contained only planted gold. That none of the 268 holes that Bre-X had drilled over three years contained any gold amounts to what experts say is a scam "without precedent in the history of mining." Investors immediately filed several class-action lawsuits against the company, claiming that Bre-X executives had committed fraud and had misled shareholders about the Busang mine's potential. Within three months of the discovery, Bre-X was in bankruptcy.*[33]

Business's Responsibility to the Community

9. Discuss business's responsibility to the community.

As corporate citizens, businesses have a responsibility to the communities in which they operate. In addition to providing jobs and creating wealth, companies contribute to the local community in many different ways. Socially responsible businesses are aware of their duty to put back into the community some of what they take out as they generate profits; their goal is to become a neighbor of choice.

The following are just a few examples of ways small businesses have found to give back to their communities:

- Act as volunteers for community groups such as the American Red Cross, United Way, literacy programs, or the community food bank.
- Participate in projects that aid the elderly or economically disadvantaged.
- Adopt a highway near the business to promote a clean community.

U.S. companies devote $9 billion a year to social causes. These companies commit talent and know-how, not just dollars, to pressing but carefully chosen social needs and then tell the world about their causes and their dedication to serving them. Companies that support worthwhile causes not only make a difference in their communities, but they also find that they enhance their reputations, deepen employee loyalty, strengthen ties with business partners, and sell more products or services. *For example, cosmetics maker Avon committed itself to raising breast cancer awareness in the United States, particularly among medically underserved women. Independent sales representatives now routinely distribute educational materials on their sales calls and participate alongside customers in fund-raising walks. All told, Avon has raised and contributed $250 million for the cause. Another company, ConAgra Foods, has embraced the cause of combating child hunger by underwriting 100 after-school cafés now serving about 1 million hot meals each year. The program also encourages ConAgra employees to raise money and serve meals, donates products and trucks to food banks across the United States, and leads a national public service advertising campaign to raise public awareness of child hunger.*

In both cases, the causes have acquired not only additional funds but also a higher profile and a bigger contingent of supporters. The companies have witnessed employees' increasing commitment to the causes and to their jobs. According to a Cone/Roper Corporate Citizenship Study, 88 percent of employees aware of cause-related programs at their companies feel a "strong sense of loyalty" to their employers.

Companies such as Avon and ConAgra Foods that demonstrate a sense of social responsibility stand out in a world of increasingly undifferentiated goods and services.[34] Refer to Table 21.7 for a list of situations that can sometimes challenge an entrepreneur's desire to "do the right thing."

Company Example →

Table 21.7

Challenging Situations for Entrepreneurs

Situations that have the potential to pose ethical dilemmas for entrepreneurs:

1. Maintaining independence in vendor relationships against the pressures of personal bias, demands for reciprocity, and offers of gifts, giveaways, or stock ownership.
2. Maintaining the integrity of company databases in the face of requests to use the data inappropriately.
3. Ensuring that the necessary security and controls are incorporated and maintained in organizational systems despite pressures to reduce costs.
4. Providing truthful information on the status of projects, budgets, and profits even when there are problems.
5. Standing firm on a decision despite its unpopularity.
6. Reporting suspected unethical behavior of others despite personal discomfort.

Source: Adapted from Patricia Wallington, "Total Leadership: Honestly!?" *CIO,* May 15, 2003, www.cio.com/archive/031503/lead.html.

Conclusion

Businesses must do more than merely earn profits; they must act ethically and in a socially responsible manner. Establishing and maintaining high ethical and socially responsible standards must be a top concern of every business owner. Managing ethics and social responsibility presents a tremendous challenge, however. There is no universal definition of ethical behavior, and what is considered ethical may change over time or may be different in other cultures. Many companies are tackling the problem with education and the establishment of clearly written standards of behavior, which are consistently reinforced.

Finally, business owners and managers must recognize the key role they play in influencing their employees' ethical and socially responsible behavior. What owners and managers *say* is important, but what they *do* is even more vital. Employees throughout a small company look to the owners and managers as models; therefore, these owners and managers must commit themselves to following the highest ethical standards if they expect their organizations to do so.

▌▌▌ Chapter Review

1. Define business ethics and describe three levels of ethical standards.

   - Business ethics involves the fundamental moral values and behavioral standards that form the foundation for the people of an organization as they make decisions and interact with organizational stakeholders. Small business managers must consider the ethical and social as well as the economic implications of their decisions.
   - The three levels of ethical standards are (1) the law, (2) the policies and procedures of the company, and (3) the moral stance of the individual.

2. Determine who is responsible for ethical behavior and why ethical lapses occur.

   - Managers set the moral tone of the organization. There are three ethical styles of management: immoral, amoral, and moral. Although moral management has value in itself, companies that operate with this philosophy discover other benefits, including a positive reputation among customers and employees.
   - Ethical lapses occur for a variety of reasons:
     Some people are corrupt ("the bad apple").
     The company culture has been poisoned ("the bad barrel").
     Competitive pressures push managers to compromise.
     Managers are tempted by an opportunity to "get ahead."
     Managers in different cultures have different views of what is ethical.

3. Explain how to establish and maintain high ethical standards.

   - Philosophers throughout history have developed various tests of ethical behavior: the utilitarian principle, Kant's categorical imperative, the professional ethic, the golden rule, the television test, and the family test.
   - A small business manager can maintain high ethical standards in the following ways:
     Create a company credo.
     Develop a code of ethics.
     Enforce the code fairly and consistently.
     Hire the right people.
     Conduct ethical training.
     Perform periodic ethical audits.
     Establish high standards of behavior, not just rules.
     Set an impeccable ethical example at all times.
     Create a culture emphasizing two-way communication.
     Involve employees in establishing ethical standards.

4. Define social responsibility.

   - Social responsibility is the awareness of a company's managers of the social, environmental, political, human, and financial consequences of their actions.

5. Understand the nature of business's responsibility to the environment.

   - Environmentally responsible business owners focus on the three Rs: reduce, reuse, recycle. *Reduce* the amount of materials used in the company from the factory floor to the copier room; *reuse* whatever you can; and *recycle* the materials that you must dispose of.

6. Describe business's responsibility to employees.

   ▪ Companies have a duty to act responsibly toward one of their most important stakeholders: their employees. Businesses must recognize and manage the cultural diversity that exists in the workplace; establish a responsible strategy for combating substance abuse in the workplace (including drug testing) and dealing with AIDS; prevent sexual harassment; and respect employees' right to privacy.

7. Explain business's responsibility to customers.

   ▪ Every company's customers have a right to safe products and services; to honest, accurate information; to be heard; to education about products and services; and to choices in the marketplace.

8. Discuss business's responsibility to investors.

   ▪ Companies have the responsibility to provide investors with an attractive return on their investments and to report their financial performances in an accurate and timely fashion to their investors.

9. Describe business's responsibility to the community.

   ▪ Increasingly, companies are seeing a need to go beyond "doing well" to "doing good"—being socially responsible community citizens. In addition to providing jobs and creating wealth, companies contribute to the local community in many different ways.

▌▐▐ Discussion Questions

1. What is ethics? Discuss the three levels of ethical standards.
2. In any organization, who determines ethical behavior? Briefly describe the three ethical styles of management. What are the benefits of moral management?
3. Why do ethical lapses occur in businesses?
4. Describe the various methods for establishing ethical standards. Which is most meaningful to you? Why?
5. What can business owners do to maintain high ethical standards in their companies?
6. What is social responsibility?
7. Describe business's social responsibility to each of the following constituents:

   a. The environment
   b. Employees
   c. Customers
   d. Investors
   e. The community

8. What can businesses do to improve the quality of our environment?

9. Should companies be allowed to test employees for drugs? Explain. How should a socially responsible drug testing program operate?
10. Many owners of trucking companies use electronic communications equipment to monitor their drivers on the road. They say that the devices enable them to remain competitive and to serve their customers better by delivering shipments of vital materials exactly when their customers need them. They also point out that the equipment can improve road safety by ensuring that drivers get the hours of rest the law requires. Opponents argue that the surveillance devices work against safety. "The drivers know they're being watched," says one trucker. "There's an obvious temptation to push." What do you think? What ethical issues does the use of such equipment create? How should a small trucking company considering the use of such equipment handle these issues?
11. What rights do customers have under the Consumer Bill of Rights? How can businesses ensure those rights?

Values-Based Leadership: Doing the Right Thing

Business PlanPro

Businesses have a responsibility to both "do well" (earn a profit, remain financially sound, and stay in business) and "do good" (operate ethically and meet their responsibility to society). Unfortunately, some business owners fail to recognize their obligation to operate their businesses in an ethical and socially responsible manner. They simply do not consider these issues to be an important part of their businesses, or they assume that their employees will choose to do what is right when faced with an ethical dilemma. Values-based leaders, however, integrate the ethical dimensions of their actions and decisions as well as those of their employees into the fabric of their companies' culture. They establish ethical guidelines, conduct training sessions in ethics, and, most important, set the example for ethical behavior in the organization. These leaders understand that ethical behavior does not simply happen in an organization; it is the result of a conscious effort that involves everyone in an organization. They also recognize that their companies have a responsibility to society that extends far beyond merely earning a profit.

The exercises for Chapter 21 that accompany Business Plan Pro are designed to help you identify the key stakeholders in your company, verbalize your philosophy of business ethics, identify the best ways to establish high ethical standards in your company, and to explain the level of your company's social responsibility. When you complete these exercises, you may want to include the description of your philosophy of ethics and social responsibility plan in the Strategy and Implementation section of Business Plan Pro. Your analysis of these important issues also may lead you to modify your company's mission statement to reflect your philosophy.

Chapter 22

The Legal Environment: Business Law and Government Regulation

> *A verbal contract isn't worth the paper it's written on.*
> —Samuel Goldwyn

> *A wise and frugal government, which shall leave men free to regulate their own pursuits of industry and improvement, and shall not take from the mouth of labor the bread it has earned—this is the sum of good government.*
> —Thomas Jefferson

Upon completion of this chapter, you will be able to:

1. Explain the basic elements required to create a valid, enforceable contract.

2. Outline the major components of the Uniform Commercial Code governing sales contracts.

3. Discuss the protection of intellectual property rights using patents, trademarks, and copyrights.

4. Explain the basics of the law of agency.

5. Explain the basics of bankruptcy law.

6. Explain some of the government regulations affecting small businesses, including those governing trade practices, consumer protection, consumer credit, and the environment.

The legal environment in which small businesses operate is becoming more complex, and entrepreneurs must understand the basics of business law if they are to avoid legal entanglements. Particularly in the United States, situations that present potential legal problems arise every day in most businesses, although the majority of small business owners never recognize them. Routine transactions with customers, suppliers, employees, government agencies, and others can develop into costly legal problems. For example, a manufacturer of lawnmowers might face a lawsuit if a customer is injured while using the product. Or a customer who slips on a wet floor while shopping could sue the retailer for negligence. A small manufacturer that reneges on a contract for a needed raw material when it finds a better price elsewhere may be open to a breach of contract suit. Even when they win a lawsuit, small businesses often lose because the costs of defending themselves can run quickly into thousands of dollars. Lawsuits also are bothersome distractions that prevent entrepreneurs from focusing their energy on running their businesses. Plus, one big judgment against a small company in a legal case could force it out of business.

As we will discuss later in this chapter, judgments against a firm can actually take three forms: compensatory, consequential, and punitive damages. *Compensatory damages* cover the actual amount of loss incurred by the plaintiff. This type of damage occurs often in breach of contract cases in which the defendant is required to "make whole" the plaintiff. In cases involving *consequential damages*, the losses a plaintiff suffers go beyond simple compensatory damages because of the lasting effects of the damage. Consider the cost associated with an electrical motor and pump that are of inferior quality or improperly designed. If this equipment malfunctions and causes an entire pumping station to become inoperable for three weeks, a judge may award the plaintiff consequential damages for destruction of other equipment and the loss of revenue directly associated with the faulty engine and pump. The last form of damages is *punitive damages*, which are awarded in blatant cases of intentional neglect or reckless endangerment tied to the defendant's knowingly disregarding

| Company Example | → |

a problem with a product or a failure to provide essential services. *After Ira Gore purchased a new BMW from an Alabama dealership, he discovered that the car had been repainted and sued BMW's U.S. distributor, claiming that he had been a victim of fraud because BMW failed to tell him that the car had been repainted. At trial, a jury awarded Gore $4,000 in compensatory damages—and $4 million in punitive damages! BMW appealed the decision to the Alabama Supreme Court, arguing that the damages were "grossly excessive." The Alabama Supreme Court reduced the punitive damages to $2 million, and BMW appealed again, this time to the United States Supreme Court, which ruled that the damages awarded Gore were excessive and reduced the amount to $50,000.*[1]

Small business owners must be knowledgeable of the basics of the laws that govern business practices to ensure that their decisions and actions avoid potentially damaging outcomes. The best way for entrepreneurs to avoid legal problems that can threaten their companies is to equip themselves with a basic understanding of the principles of business

| Company Example | → |

law. *One entrepreneurial couple in Mississippi found out about certain laws in their state the hard way. Mitch and Hilda Bankston were a good example of hard work and fulfilling the American dream. After graduating from pharmacy school in 1971, Mitch fulfilled his lifelong dream of buying and operating a pharmacy in Fayette, Mississippi. He worked hard and built a solid reputation as a caring, honest pharmacist. The couple's American dream turned into a nightmare in 1991 when the Bankston Drugstore was named as a defendant in a national class-action lawsuit brought in Jefferson County, Mississippi, against one of the nation's largest drug companies, the manufacturer of Fen-Phen, an FDA-approved drug for weight loss. Although Mississippi law does not allow for class-action lawsuits, it does allow for consolidation of lawsuits as long as the case involves a plaintiff or defendant from Mississippi. Because Bankston Drugstore was the only drugstore in Jefferson County and because it had filled prescriptions for Fen-Phen (a drug whose manufacturer is headquartered in New Jersey), the plaintiffs could keep the case in a place already known for its lawsuit-friendly environment.*

They could also use Bankston's records as a virtual database of potential clients. As the Fen-Phen case drew more attention, Mitch Bankston became increasingly concerned about what his customers would think. His integrity, honor, and reputation were on the line. Overnight, the couple's work went from serving the public's health to becoming a means to an end for trial lawyers to cash in on lucrative class-action lawsuits.

Three weeks after being named in the lawsuit, Mitch, who was 58 years old, died suddenly of a massive heart attack. In the midst of her grief, the widow was called to testify in the first Fen-Phen trial. Dismayed, Hilda Bankston sold the pharmacy in 1999 but still spends countless hours retrieving records for plaintiffs and getting dragged into court again and again to testify in hundreds of national lawsuits brought in Jefferson County against the pharmacy and out-of-state manufacturers of other drugs.[2]

This chapter is not designed to make you an expert in business law or the regulations that govern business but to familiarize you with the fundamental legal issues of which every business owner should be aware. Business owners should consult their attorneys for advice on legal questions involving specific situations.

The Law of Contracts

1. Explain the elements required to create a valid, enforceable contract.

Contract law governs the rights and obligations among the parties to an agreement (contract). It is a body of laws that affects virtually every business relationship. A **contract** is simply a legally binding agreement. It is a promise or a set of promises for the breach of which the law gives a remedy, or the performance of which the law in some way recognizes as a duty. A contract arises from an agreement, and it creates an obligation among the parties involved. Although almost everyone has the capacity to enter into a contractual agreement (freedom of contract), not every contract is valid and enforceable. A *valid* contract has four separate elements:

1. *Agreement.* A valid offer by one party is accepted by the another party.
2. *Consideration.* Something of legal value is exchanged by the parties as part of a bargain.
3. *Contractual capacity.* The parties must be adults capable of understanding the consequences of their agreement.
4. *Legality.* The parties' contract must be for a legal purpose.

In addition, a contract must meet two supplemental requirements: genuineness of assent and form. *Genuineness of assent* is a test to make sure that the parties' agreement is genuine and not subject to problems such as fraud, misrepresentation, or mistakes. *Form* involves the writing requirement for certain types of contracts. Although not every contract must be in writing to be enforceable, the law does require some contracts to be evidenced by writing.

Agreement

Agreement requires a "meeting of the minds" and is established by an offer and an acceptance. One party must make an offer to another, who must accept that offer. Agreement is governed by the **objective theory of contracts,** which states that a party's intention to create a contract is measured by outward facts—words, conduct, and circumstances—rather than by subjective, personal intentions. In settling contract disputes, courts interpret the objective facts surrounding the contract from the perspective of an imaginary reasonable

Company Example →

person. *For instance, Klick-Lewis, a car dealership, offered a new Chevrolet Beretta as a prize to any person who hit a hole-in-one on the ninth hole of a golf tournament. It displayed the car at the tee box of the ninth hole with a sign saying, "HOLE-IN-ONE Wins This 1988 Chevrolet Beretta GI Courtesy of Klick-Lewis Buick-Chevrolet-Pontiac $49.00 OVER FACTORY INVOICE in Palmyra." Amos Carbaugh was playing in the East End Open Golf Tournament* *and scored a hole-in-one on the ninth hole, but when he attempted to claim the prize, Klick-Lewis refused to sell him the car at $49.00 over invoice. The dealer said that it had offered the car as a prize in another golf tournament that had taken place two days earlier and that it had simply neglected to remove the car and the sign before the tournament in which Carbaugh was playing. Carbaugh filed a lawsuit against Klick-Lewis and won the right to buy the car at $49.00 over invoice. The court said that, based on the objective theory of contracts, an imaginary reasonable person in Carbaugh's position would have believed that the dealership was making an offer, citing the presence of the sign, the car, and no mention of a specific golf tournament. Klick-Lewis's subjective intent was irrelevant.[3]*

Agreement requires that one of the parties to a contract make an offer and the other an acceptance.

Offer. An **offer** is a promise or commitment to do or refrain from doing some specified thing in the future. For an offer to stand, there must be an intention to be bound by it. The terms of the offer must be definite and reasonably certain, and the offer must be communicated to the offeree. The party making the offer must genuinely intend to make an offer, and the offer's terms must be specific not vague. The following terms must either be expressed or be capable of being implied in an offer: the parties involved; the identity of the subject matter (which goods or services), and the quantity. Other terms of the offer should specify price, delivery terms, payment terms, timing, and shipping terms. Although these elements are not required, the more terms a party specifies, the more likely it is that an offer exists.

Courts often supply missing terms in a contract for the sale of goods when there is a reliable basis for doing so. For instance, the court usually supplies a time term that is reasonable for the circumstances. It supplies a price term (a reasonable price at the time of delivery) if a readily ascertainable market price exists; otherwise, a missing price term defeats the contract. On rare occasions, the court supplies a quantity term, but a missing quantity term usually defeats a contract. For example, the small retailer who mails an advertising circular to a large number of customers is not making an offer because one major term—quantity—is missing. Similarly, price lists and catalogs sent to potential customers are not offers.

Generally, a party making an offer can revoke at any time before the offeree accepts it. One exception to this rule involves **option contracts,** which are separate contracts in which a potential buyer purchases the right to keep an offer open for a specific time period. In that case, an offeror cannot revoke an offer while the option contract is in effect. The other exception falls under the Uniform Commercial Code (UCC), which governs the sale of all goods. Under the UCC, a merchant that makes a **firm offer** in a signed writing to sell goods to another is bound by that offer for the stated period, which cannot exceed three months. For instance, suppose that Ralph Frank, owner of Wholesale Appliances sends a written offer to Payne Appliances on March 15 that says, "We will sell you 20 model X washing machines at $199 each. This offer is good through March 30. (signed) Ralph Frank." Because Wholesale Appliances is a merchant of washing machines and has put its offer in writing and signed it, the offer is a firm offer, which Wholesale Appliances cannot revoke before March 30.

An offer must always be communicated to the other party because one cannot agree to a contract unless one knows it exists. The offeror may communicate an offer by verbal expression, written word, or implied action.

Acceptance. Only the person to whom the offer is made (the offeree) can accept an offer and create a contract. The offeree must accept voluntarily, agreeing to the terms exactly as the offeror presents them. When the offeree suggests alternative terms or conditions, he or she is implicitly rejecting the original offer and making a counteroffer. Common law requires that the offeree's acceptance exactly match the original offer. This is called the **mirror image rule,** which says that an offeree's acceptance must be the mirror image of the offeror's offer.

Generally, silence by an offeree cannot constitute acceptance, even if the offer contains statements to the contrary. For instance, when an offeror claims, "If you do not respond to this offer by Friday at noon, I conclude your silence to be your acceptance," no acceptance exists even if the offeree does remain silent. The law requires an offeree to act affirmatively to accept an offer in most cases.

An offeree must accept an offer by the means of communication authorized by and within the time limits specified by the offeror. Generally, an attempt to accept an offer after the deadline specified in the offer is ineffective. If the offeror specifies no means of communication, the offeree can accept the offer in any reasonable manner using any reasonable method. If the offeror stipulates a particular method of acceptance, however, the offeree must use that method; otherwise, no contract results. According to the **mailbox rule,** if an offeree accepts by mail, the acceptance is effective when the letter is dropped in the mailbox, even if it never reaches the offeror. Also, all offers must be properly dispatched; that is, they must be properly addressed, noted, and stamped.

Consideration

Contracts are based on promises, and because it is often difficult to distinguish between promises that are serious and those that are not, courts require that consideration be present in virtually every contract. **Consideration** is something of *legal* value (*not* necessarily economic value) that the parties to a contract bargain for and exchange as the "price" for the promise given. Consideration can be money, but parties most often swap promises for promises. For example, when a buyer promises to buy an item and a seller promises to sell it, valuable consideration exists. The buyer's promise to buy and the seller's promise to sell constitute the consideration for their contract. To comprise valuable consideration, a promise must impose a liability or create a duty. This is the concept of "legal detriment." A party to a contract incurs legal detriment (and therefore provides consideration) either by doing something or promising to do something he had no prior legal duty to do or by refraining from doing something or promising not to do something he has a legal right to do.

For a contract to be binding, the two parties involved must exchange valuable consideration. The absence of consideration makes a promise unenforceable. A promise to perform something one is already legally obligated to do is not valuable consideration. Also, because consideration is what the promisor requires in exchange for his or her promise, it must be given after the promisor states what is required. In other words, past consideration is not valid. Also, under the common law, new promises require new consideration. For instance, if two businesspeople have an existing contract for performance of a service, any modifications to that contract must be supported by new consideration. Also, promises made in exchange for "love and affection" are not enforceable because this does not constitute valuable consideration.

One important exception to the requirement of exchanging valuable consideration is **promissory estoppel.** Under this rule, a promise that induces another party to act can be enforceable without consideration if the promisee substantially and justifiably relies on the promise. Thus, promissory estoppel is a substitute for consideration. A classic case illustrating promissory estoppel is *Hoffman v. Red Owl Stores, Inc. Hoffman, the plaintiff in the case, brought suit against Red Owl Stores, Inc., a company that operated grocery stores in Michigan and Wisconsin. Hoffman, who with his wife operated a bakery in Wautoma, Wisconsin, wanted to expand his business and contacted a representative of Red Owl Stores*

Company Example →

about opening a franchised grocery store in Wautoma. In meetings with Red Owl Stores' representatives, Hoffman repeatedly mentioned that he had only $18,000 to invest in a store, and the representatives repeatedly assured him that this amount would be sufficient to open a Red Owl franchise. Hoffman decided that it would be beneficial if he gained experience operating a grocery store, so he purchased a small grocery store in Wautoma. After running it for three months, Red Owl officials verified that Hoffman's store was operating at a profit and assured him that Red Owl would find a larger store for him to operate in another location. Once again, Hoffman told the Red Owl officials that he had $18,000 for "getting set up in business," and they assured him that getting a larger store would be no problem.

Hoffman sold the grocery store and purchased a site for the new store based on Red Owl's statements. He also sold his bakery, which he was still operating, when Red Owl representatives told him that owning that business was the only "hitch" remaining in the process. Subsequently, Red Owl Stores raised the price of the franchise from $18,000 to $24,100, and later to $26,100. Hoffman never opened a Red Owl store. Although Hoffman and Red Owl had never come to agreement on the specific terms of a franchise contract, Hoffman based his claim against Red Owl on the theory of promissory estoppel. Did the cases meet the three requirements of promissory estoppel: (1) a promise on which the plaintiff is likely to rely, (2) the plaintiff's reliance on that promise, and (3) injury to the plaintiff as a result of relying on that promise?

The Supreme Court of Wisconsin upheld the lower court's ruling in favor of Hoffman, saying that although the parties had not exchanged any consideration, Red Owl had made reasonable promises on which Hoffman relied. Hoffman was entitled to damages because Red Owl had breached the promises it had made to him even though those promises were not supported by consideration.[4]

In most cases, courts do not evaluate the adequacy of consideration given for a promise. In other words, there is no legal requirement that the consideration the parties exchange be of approximately equal value. Even if the value of the consideration one party gives is small compared with the value of the bargain to the other party, the bargain stands. Why? The law recognizes that people have the freedom to contract and that they are just as free to enter into "bad" bargains as they to enter into "good" ones. Only in extreme cases (e.g., cases affected by mistakes, misrepresentation, fraud, duress, and undue influence) will the court examine the value of the consideration provided in a trade.

Contractual Capacity

The third element of a valid contract requires that the parties involved in it must have contractual capacity for it to be enforceable. Not every individual who attempts to enter into a contract has the capacity to do so. Under the common law, minors, intoxicated people, and insane people either lack or have limited contractual capacity. As a result, contracts these people attempt to enter into are considered to be voidable—that is, the party can annul or disaffirm the contract at his or her option.

Minors. Minors constitute the largest group of individuals with limited contractual capacity. In most states, anyone under age 18 is a minor. With a few exceptions, any contract made by a minor is voidable at the minor's option. In addition, a minor can avoid a contract during minority and for "a reasonable time" afterward. The adult involved in the contract cannot avoid it simply because he or she is dealing with a minor.

If a minor receives the benefit of a completed contract and then disaffirms that contract, the minor must fulfill his or her duty of restoration by returning the benefit. In other words, the minor must return any consideration he or she has received under the contract to the adult, and the minor is entitled to receive any consideration he or she gave the adult under the contract. The minor must return the benefit of the contract no

Minors constitute the largest group of individuals with limited contractual capacity. Business owners who enter into contracts with minors do so at their own risk. One way to lower the risk is to have an adult cosign for the purchase.

matter what form or condition it is in. For instance, suppose that Brighton, a 16-year-old minor, purchases a mountain bike for $415 from Cycle Time, a small bicycle shop. After riding the bike for a little more than a year, Brighton decides to disaffirm the contract. Under the law, all he must do is return the mountain bike to Cycle Time, whatever condition it is in (pristine, used, wrecked, or rubble), and he is entitled to get all of his money back. In most states, he does not have to pay Cycle Time for the use of the bike or the damage done to it. Adults enter into contracts with minors at their own risk.

Parents are usually not liable for any contracts made by their children, although a cosigner is bound equally with the minor. Small business owners can protect themselves in dealing with minors by requiring an adult to cosign. If the minor disaffirms the contract, the adult cosigner remains bound by it.

Intoxicated People. A contract entered into by an intoxicated person can be either voidable or valid, depending on the person's condition when entering into the contract. If reason and judgment are impaired so that the person does not realize he or she is making a contract, the contract is voidable (even if the intoxication was voluntary) and the benefit must be returned. However, if the intoxicated person understands that he or she is forming a contract, although it may be foolish, the contract is valid and enforceable.

Insane People. A contract an insane or mentally incapacitated person enters into can be void, voidable, or valid, depending on the mental state of the person. Those who have been judged to be so mentally incompetent that a guardian is appointed for them cannot enter into a valid contract. If such a person does make a contract, it is void (i.e., it does not exist). A person who has not been legally declared insane or appointed a guardian (e.g., someone suffering from Alzheimer's disease) is bound by a contract if he or she was lucid enough at the time of the contract to comprehend its consequences. On the other hand, if at the time of entering the contract, that same person was so mentally incompetent that he or she could not realize what was happening or could not understand the terms, the contract is voidable. Like a minor, he or she must return any benefit received under the contract.

Legality

The final element required for a valid contract is legality. The purpose of the parties' contract must be legal. Because society imposes certain standards of conduct on its members, contracts that are illegal (criminal or tortuous) or against public policy are void. Examples of these situations include contracts in which the stated interest rate violates the state's usury laws; interstate gambling that is conducted in states where the type of gambling is illegal (e.g., casino games via the Internet); business transactions that violate a state's Sabbath laws (conducting business on a Sunday); performance of immoral acts or any business activities that require a state license to conduct business or, if implemented, would be a restraint of trade.

If a contract contains both legal and illegal elements, the courts will enforce the legal parts as long as they can separate the legal portion from the illegal portion. However, in some contracts, certain clauses are so unconscionable that the courts will not enforce them. Usually, the courts do not concern themselves with the fairness and equity of a contract between parties because individuals are supposed to be intelligent. But in the case of unconscionable contracts, the terms are so harsh and oppressive to one party that the courts often rule the clause to be void. These clauses, called **exculpatory clauses,** frequently attempt to free one party of all responsibility and liability for an injury or damage that might occur. For instance, suppose that Miguel Ferras signs an exculpatory clause when he leaves his new BMW with the attendant at a parking garage. The clause states that the garage is "not responsible for theft, loss, or damage to cars or articles left in cars due to fire, theft, or other causes." The attendant leaves Miguel's car unattended with the keys in the ignition, and a thief steals the car. A court would declare the exculpatory clause void because the garage owes a duty to its customers to exercise reasonable care to protect their property, a duty it breached because of gross negligence.

Genuineness of Assent and the Form of Contracts

Although a contract that contains the four elements just discussed—agreement, consideration, capacity, and legality—is valid, the contract may still be unenforceable if it fails to meet two additional tests: genuineness of assent and form. **Genuineness of assent** serves as a check on the parties' agreement, verifying that it is genuine and not subject to mistakes, misrepresentation, fraud, duress, or undue influence. The existence of a contract can be affected by mistakes that one or both parties to the contract make. Different types of mistakes exist, but only mistakes of *fact* permit a party to avoid a contract. Suppose that a small contractor submits a bid on the construction of a bridge, but the bidder mistakenly omits the cost of some materials. The client accepts the contractor's bid because it is $52,000 below all others. If the client knew or should have known of the mistake, the contractor can void the contract; otherwise, the contractor must build the bridge at the bid price.

Fraud also makes a contract unenforceable because no genuineness of assent exists. **Fraud** is the intentional misrepresentation of a material fact, justifiably relied on, that results in injury to the innocent party. The misrepresentation with the intent to deceive can result from words or conduct. Suppose a small retailer purchases a new security system from a dealer who promises it will provide 20 years of reliable service and lower the cost of operation by 40 percent. The dealer then knowingly installs a used, unreliable system. In this case, the dealer has committed fraud, and the retailer can either rescind the contract with his or her original position restored or enforce it and seek damages for injuries. "Very rarely do you find a situation where a company has set out to be a sham, to create willful fraud," says attorney Jerry C. Jones. Jones spent 17 years defending outfits accused of accounting irregularities and now heads the legal team at Acxiom Corp., a data-storage company. Instead, he says, "Trouble may start with management that decides to muscle its way through a crisis—one of several innocuous-seeming signs of danger to watch out for."[5]

Duress, forcing an individual into a contract by fear or threat, eliminates genuineness of assent. The innocent party can choose to carry out the contract or to void it. For example, if a supplier forces the owner of a small video arcade to enter a contract to lease the supplier's machines by threat of personal injury, the supplier is guilty of duress. Blackmail and extortion used to induce another party to enter a contract also constitute duress.

Generally, the law does not require contracts to follow a prescribed form; a contract is valid whether it is written or oral. Most contracts do *not* have to be in writing to be enforceable, but for convenience and protection, a small business owner should insist that every contract be in writing. If a contract is oral, the party attempting to enforce it must first prove its existence and then establish its actual terms. Although each state has its own rules, the law, called the statute of frauds, generally requires the following contracts to be in writing:

- Contracts for the sale of land.
- Contracts involving the transfer of an interest in land (e.g., rights-of-way or leases lasting more than one year).
- Contracts that cannot by their terms be performed within one year.
- Collateral contracts such as promises to answer for the debt or duty of another.
- Promises by the administrator or executor of an estate to pay a debt of the estate personally.
- Contracts for the sale of goods (as opposed to services) priced at $500 or more.

Breach of Contract

The majority of contracts are discharged by both parties fully performing the terms of their agreement. This is known as complete performance. Occasionally, however, one party fails to perform as agreed. This failure is called **breach of contract,** and the injured

Company Example	→

party has certain remedies available. *For instance, Ronald Leek, owner of a drag strip, entered into a contract with Randy Folk to resurface the 25-year-old raceway and to build several retaining walls required by Leak's insurance company. After Folk had completed the job, Leek refused to pay for the work, claiming it was of poor quality and would have to be redone. At trial, several experts testified that the surface was uneven, that it contained large dips, and that it was unsafe. One race official attended a race at which the track's poor condition caused several race cars to lose control and one to crash. The court ruled that Folk had failed to perform his obligations under the contract and ruled in Leek's favor.*[6]

A breach of contract can be either a minor breach in which substantial, but not complete, performance occurs or a material breach of contract associated with nonperformance or inferior performance. In cases in which there exists a minor breach of contract, the party "in breach" may agree to complete the terms of the contract or compensate the other party for the unperformed component of the contract. If these two remedies are not accepted, the next step is legal action to recover the cost to repair the defect.

In contrast, a *material breach* occurs when a party renders inferior performance that impairs or destroys the essence of the contract. The non-breaching party may either rescind the contract and recover restitution or affirm the contract and recover damages. Consider the following case involving breach of contract brought by Hotmail

Company Example	→

Corporation. *Hotmail Corporation provides free e-mail on the Internet, allowing its subscribers to exchange e-mail messages. To become a Hotmail subscriber, a person must agree to abide by a service agreement that prohibits subscribers from using Hotmail's services to send unsolicited commercial bulk e-mails (spam) or to send obscene or pornographic messages. Subscribers must accept the service agreement by checking the "accept" prompt on the screen.*

Hotmail Corporation brought suit against four defendants, Van $ Money Pie, Inc.; ALS Enterprises Inc.; LCGM, Inc.; and the Genesis Network, Inc., on the grounds that all four businesses were sending spam messages advertising pornography and "get-rich schemes," among other things, in violation of the Hotmail contract they accepted when they clicked the "accept" prompt. Hotmail sued the four defendants on the grounds of breach of contract and asked the court to enjoin (stop) the defendants from sending spam e-mails using Hotmail's accounts, domain name, and mark. The court agreed that the defendants were in breach of contract and issued the injunction against the defendants.[7]

Company Example →

The injunction the court issued in the Hotmail case is one of several equitable remedies available. An **injunction** is an order from the court ordering a party to stop engaging in some activity. *For example, American Family Products (AFP), an Illinois-based company, was selling barstools, dartboards, and other items bearing the logos of professional and collegiate sports teams, NASCAR drivers, and several private companies on the Internet and at trade shows without obtaining permission or paying the required licensing fees. Several of the teams and the companies whose logos AFP used illegally petitioned the court for an injunction, which it issued, halting AFP's trademark infringement. The organizations involved also filed a lawsuit against AFP for illegally using their logos, and the company agreed to settle the dispute by paying $3.1 million in damages.[8]*

In other cases in which monetary damages are inadequate to compensate the injured party for the breach of contract, the court can compensate the nonbreaching party by issuing a decree of specific performance, which is an order to perform the act promised in the contract. **Specific performance** is usually the remedy for breached contracts dealing with unique items such as antiques, land, and animals. For example, if an antique auto dealer enters a contract to purchase a rare Corvette and the other party breaches the contract, the dealer may sue for specific performance. That is, the dealer may ask the court to order the breaching party to sell the antique car. Courts rarely invoke the remedy of specific performance. Generally, contracts for performance of personal services are not subject to specific performance.

The Uniform Commercial Code (UCC)

2. Outline the major components of the Uniform Commercial Code governing sales contracts.

For many years, sales contracts relating to the exchange of goods were governed by a loosely defined system of rules and customs called the *Lex Mercatoria* (Merchant Law). Many of these principles were assimilated into the U.S. common law through court opinions, but they varied widely from state to state and made interstate commerce difficult and confusing for businesses. In 1952, the Commission on Uniform State Laws published the **Uniform Commercial Code** (or the **UCC** or the **Code**) to replace the hodgepodge collection of confusing, often conflicting state laws that governed basic commercial transactions with a document designed to provide uniformity and consistency. The UCC replaced numerous statutes governing trade when each of the states, the District of Columbia, and the Virgin Islands adopted it. (Louisiana has adopted only articles 1, 3, 4, and 5.) The Code does not alter the basic tenets of business law established by the common law; instead, it unites and modernizes them into a single body of law. In some cases, however, the Code changes some of the specific rules under the common law. The Code consists of 10 articles:

1. General Provisions
2. Sales
   a. Leases
3. Negotiable Instruments
4. Bank Deposits and Collections
   a. Wire Transfers

5. Letters of Credit
6. Bulk Transfers
7. Documents of Title, Warehouse Receipts, Bills of Lading, and Others
8. Investment Securities
9. Secured Transactions
10. Effective Date and Repealer

This section covers some of the general principles relating to sales (UCC Article 2), but small business owners should also become familiar with the basics of the other parts the Code. The UCC creates a "caste system" of merchants and nonmerchants and requires merchants to have a higher degree of knowledge and understanding of the Code.

Sales and Sales Contracts

Every sales contract is subject to the basic principles of law that govern all contracts— agreement, consideration, capacity, and legality. But when a contract involves the sale of goods, the UCC imposes rules that may vary slightly or substantially from basic contract law. Article 2 governs *only* contracts for the *sale of goods*. To be considered "goods," an item must be personal property that is tangible and moveable (e.g., not real estate), and a "sale" is the "passing of title from the seller to the buyer for a price" (UCC Sec. 2–106[1]). The UCC does *not* cover the sale of services, although certain "mixed transactions," such as the sale by a garage of car parts (goods) and repairs (a service) will fall under the Code's jurisdiction if the goods are the dominant element of the contract.

In addition to the rules it applies to the sale of goods in general, the Code imposes special standards of conduct in certain instances when merchants sell goods to one another. Usually, a person is considered a professional **merchant** if he or she "deals in goods of the kind" involved in the contract and has special knowledge of the business or of the goods; employs a merchant agent to conduct a transaction for him or her; or holds himself or herself out to be a merchant.

Although the UCC requires that the same elements outlined in common law be present in forming a sales contract, it relaxes many of the specific restrictions. For example, the UCC states that a contract exists even if the parties omit one or more terms (price, delivery date, place of delivery, quantity), as long as they intended to make a contract and there is a reasonably certain method for the court to supply the missing terms. Suppose a manufacturer orders a shipment of needed raw materials from a regular supplier without asking the price. When the order arrives, the price is substantially higher than the manufacturer expected, and the manufacturer attempts to disaffirm the contract. The Code verifies the existence of a contract and assigns to the shipment a price that was reasonable at the time of delivery.

Common law requires that acceptance of an offer be exactly the same as the offer; an acceptance that adds some slight modification is no acceptance at all, and no contract exists. Any modification constitutes a counteroffer. But the UCC states that as long as an offeree's response (words, writing, or actions) indicates a sincere willingness to accept the offer, it is judged as a legitimate acceptance even though varying terms are added. In dealings between buyers and sellers, these added terms become "proposals for addition." Between merchants, however, these additional proposals automatically become part of the contract unless they materially alter the original contract, the offer expressly states that no terms other than those in the offer will be accepted, or the offeror has already objected to the particular terms. Unless the offeror objects to the added terms, they will become part of the contract. For example, suppose an appliance wholesaler offers to sell a retailer a shipment of appliances for $5,000 plus freight. The retailer responds with acceptance but adds "Price is $5,100 including freight." A contract exists, and the addition will become part of the contract unless the wholesaler objects within a reasonable time. If the wholesaler objects, a contract still exists, but it is formed on the wholesaler's original terms of $5,000 plus freight.

The UCC significantly changes the common-law requirement that any contract modification requires new consideration. Under the Code, modifications to contract terms are binding *without* new consideration if they are made in good faith. For example, suppose a small building contractor forms a contract to purchase a supply of lumber for $1,200. After the agreement but before the lumber is delivered, a hurricane forces the price of the lumber to double, and the supplier notifies the contractor that he must raise the price of the lumber shipment to $2,400. The contractor reluctantly agrees to the additional cost but later refuses to pay. According to UCC, the contractor is bound by the modification because no new consideration is required.

The Code also has its own Statute of Frauds provision relating to the form of contracts for the sale of goods. If the price of the goods is $500 or more, the contract must be in writing to be enforceable. Of course, the parties can agree orally and then follow it with a written memorandum. The Code does not require both parties to sign the written agreement, but it must be signed by the party against whom enforcement is sought (which is impossible to tell before a dispute arises, so it's a good idea for *both* parties to sign the agreement).

The UCC includes a special provision involving the writing requirement in contracts between merchants. If merchants form a verbal contract for the sale of goods priced at more than $500 and one of them sends a written confirmation of the deal to the other, the merchant receiving the confirmation must object to it *in writing* within 10 days. Otherwise, the contract is enforceable against *both* merchants, even though the merchant receiving the confirmation has not actually signed anything.

Once the parties create a sales contract, they are bound to perform according to its terms. Both the buyer and the seller have certain duties and obligations under the contract. Generally, the Code assigns the obligations of "good faith" (defined as "honesty in fact in the conduct or transaction concerned") and "commercial reasonableness" (commercial standards of fair dealing) to both parties. *For example, Alpine Resources, Inc, contracted to buy the timber on land owned by the George Syrovy Trust over a period of two years for $140,000. At the end of the two years, Alpine Resources, Inc., paid the George Syrovy Trust just $50,000, claiming that bad weather had not allowed Alpine to harvest the timber. The George Syrovy Trust sued for the payment of the remaining $90,000. The court ruled in favor of the trust based on the fact that the conditions of the contract were clearly stated and that bad weather was a risk factor that the defendant should have considered when it created the contract.*[9]

The seller must deliver the items involved in the contract, but "delivery" is not necessarily physical delivery. The seller simply must make the goods available to the buyer. The contract normally outlines the specific details of the delivery, but occasionally the parties omit this provision. In this instance, the place of delivery will be the seller's place of business, if one exists; otherwise, it is the seller's residence. If both parties know the usual location of the identified goods, that is the place of delivery (e.g., a warehouse). In addition, the seller must make the goods available to the buyer at a reasonable time and in a reasonable manner. Unless otherwise noted, all goods covered in the contract must be tendered in one delivery.

A buyer must accept the delivery of conforming goods from the seller. Of course, the buyer has the right to inspect the goods in a reasonable manner and at any reasonable time or place to ensure before making payment that they are conforming goods. However, C.O.D. terms prohibit the right to advance inspection unless the contract specifies otherwise. Under the perfect tender rule in Section 2–601 of the Code, "if goods or tender of delivery fail, in any respect, to conform to the contract," the buyer is not required to accept them.

Company Example

A buyer can indicate acceptance of the goods in several ways. Usually the buyer indicates acceptance by an express statement that the goods are suitable. This expression can be in words or by conduct. Suppose a small electrical contractor orders a truck to use in her business. When she receives it, she equips it to suit her trade, including a company decal on each door. Later the contractor attempts to reject the truck and return it. By customizing the truck, the buyer has indicated her acceptance of the truck. Also, the Code assumes acceptance if the buyer has a reasonable opportunity to inspect the goods and has failed to reject them within a reasonable time.

A buyer has the duty to pay for the goods on the terms stated in the contract when they are received. A seller cannot require payment before the buyer receives the goods. Unless otherwise stated in the contract, payment must be in cash.

Breach of Sales Contracts

As we have seen, when a party to the sales contract fails to perform according to its terms, that party is said to have breached the contract. The law provides the innocent (non-breaching) party numerous remedies, including damage awards and the right to retain possession of the goods. The object of these remedies is to place the innocent party in the same position as if the contract had been carried out. The parties to the contract may specify their own damages in case of breach. These provisions, called **liquidated damages,** must be reasonable and cannot be in the nature of a penalty. For example, suppose that Alana Mitchell contracts with a local carpenter to build a booth from which she plans to sell crafts. The parties agree that if the booth is not completed by September 1, Mitchell will receive $500. If the liquidated damages had been $50,000, they would be unenforceable because such a large amount of money is clearly a penalty.

An unpaid seller has certain remedies available under the terms of the Code. Under a seller's lien, every seller has the right to maintain possession of the goods until the buyer pays for them. In addition, if the buyer uses a fraudulent payment to obtain the goods, the seller has the right to recover them. If the seller discovers the buyer is insolvent, the seller can withhold delivery of the goods until the buyer pays in cash. If goods are shipped to an insolvent buyer, the seller can require their return within 10 days after receipt. In some cases, the buyer breaches a contract while the goods are still unfinished in the production process. When this occurs, the seller must use "reasonable commercial judgment" in deciding whether to sell them for scrap or complete them and resell them elsewhere. In either case, the buyer is liable for any loss the seller incurs. Of course, the seller has the right to withhold performance when the buyer breaches the sales contract.

When the seller breaches a contract, the buyer also has specific remedies available. For instance, if the goods do not conform to the contract's terms, the buyer has the right to reject them. Or if the seller fails to deliver the goods, the buyer can sue for the difference between the contract price and the market price at the time the breach became known. When the buyer accepts goods and then discovers they are defective or nonconforming, the buyer must notify the seller of the breach. In this instance, damages amount to the difference between the value of the goods delivered and their value if they had been delivered as promised. If a buyer pays for goods that the seller retains, the buyer can take possession of the goods if the seller becomes insolvent within ten days after receiving the first payment. If the seller unlawfully withholds the goods from the buyer, the buyer can recover them. Under certain circumstances, a buyer can obtain specific performance of a sales contract; that is, the court orders the seller to perform according to the contract's terms. As mentioned earlier, specific performance is a remedy only when the goods involved are unique or unavailable on the market. Finally, if the seller breaches the contract, the buyer has the right to rescind the contract; if the buyer has paid any part of the purchase price, it must be refunded.

Whenever a party breaches a sales contract, the innocent party must bring suit within a specified period of time. The Code sets the statute of limitations at four years. In other words, any action for a breach of a sales contract must begin within four years after the breach occurred.

Sales Warranties and Product Liability

The U.S. economy once promulgated the philosophy of "let the buyer beware," but today the marketplace enforces a policy of "let the seller beware." Small business owners must be aware of two general categories involving the quality and reliability of the products sold: sales warranties and product liability.

Sales Warranties. Simply stated, a **sales warranty** is a promise or a statement of fact by the seller that a product will meet certain standards. Because a breach of warranty is a breach of promise, the buyer has the right to recover damages from the seller. Several different types of warranties can arise in a sale. A seller creates an **express warranty** by making statements about the condition, quality, and performance of the good that the buyer substantially relies on. Express warranties can be created by words or actions. For example, a vendor selling a shipment of cloth to a customer with the promise that "it will not shrink" clearly is creating an express warranty. Similarly, the jeweler who displays a watch in a glass of water for promotional purposes creates an express warranty that "this watch is waterproof" even though no such promise is ever spoken. Generally, an express warranty arises if the seller indicates that the goods conform to any promises of fact the seller makes, to any description of them (e.g., printed on the package or statements of fact made by salespersons), or to any display model or sample (e.g., a floor model used as a demonstrator).

Whenever someone sells goods, the UCC automatically implies certain types of warranties unless the seller specifically excludes them. These **implied warranties** take several forms. Every seller, simply by offering goods for sale, implies a **warranty of title,** which promises that the seller's title to the goods is valid (i.e., no liens or claims exist) and that transfer of title is legitimate. A seller can disclaim a warranty of title only by using very specific language in a sales contract.

An implied warranty of merchantability applies to every merchant seller, and the only way to disclaim it is by mentioning the phrase *warranty of merchantability* in a conspicuous manner. An **implied warranty of merchantability** assures the buyer that the product will be of average quality—not the best and not the worst. In other words, merchantable goods are "fit for the ordinary purposes for which such goods are used" (UCC Sec. 2–314[1-C]). For example, a refrigeration unit that a small food store purchases should keep food cold.

| Company Example | → | *Webster, a longtime New England resident, ordered a bowl* |

of fish chowder at the Blue Ship Tea Room, a Boston restaurant that overlooks the ocean. After eating three or four spoonfuls, Webster felt something caught in her throat. It turned out to be a fish bone that was in the bowl of chowder she had ordered. Webster had to undergo two surgical procedures to remove the bone from her throat and she filed a lawsuit against the restaurant, claiming that it had breached the implied warranty of merchantability. The Supreme Court of Massachusetts ruled in favor of the Blue Ship Tea Room, stating that "the occasional presence of [fish bones] in chowders is . . . to be anticipated and . . . [does] not impair their fitness or merchantability." Because the fish bone in the fish chowder was not a foreign object, but one that a person could reasonably expect to find in chowders on occasion, the court decided that the restaurant had not breached a warranty of merchantability.[10]

An implied **warranty of fitness for a particular purpose** arises when a seller knows the particular reason for which a buyer is purchasing a product and knows that the buyer is depending on the seller's judgment to select the proper item. For example, suppose a customer enters a small hardware store requesting a chemical to kill poison ivy. The owner hands over a gallon of chemical, but it fails to kill the weed; the owner has violated the warranty of fitness for a particular purpose.

The Code also states that the only way a merchant can disclaim an implied warranty is to include the words "sold as is" or "with all faults," stating that the buyer purchases the product as it is, without any guarantees. The following statement is usually sufficient to disclaim most warranties, both express and implied: "Seller hereby disclaims all warranties, express and implied, including all warranties of merchantability and all warranties of fitness for a particular purpose." Such statements must be printed in bold letters and placed in a conspicuous place on the product or its package.

✦ GAINING *a* COMPETITIVE EDGE ✦

How Hot Is "Too Hot"?

Stella Liebeck, 79, was sitting in the passenger seat of her grandson's car when they pulled up to the drive-thru window at McDonald's in Albuquerque, New Mexico. Her grandson stopped the car so she could add cream and sugar to the cup of coffee she had just ordered. Liebeck put the Styrofoam cup between her knees to remove the lid, but when she did, the coffee spilled into her lap, soaked into her sweatpants, and burned her severely. She received third-degree burns over 6 percent of her body, was hospitalized for eight days, and had to undergo skin grafts and other treatments.

Liebeck sued McDonald's under product liability law. During the trial, McDonald's documents showed more than 700 claims filed between 1982 and 1992 by people burned by its coffee. McDonald's testified that, at a consultant's advice, it held its coffee at temperatures between 180 and 190 degrees to maintain optimum taste but that it had not studied the safety implications of serving coffee at that temperature. A quality assurance manager for the chain testified that the company actively enforced a requirement that coffee be kept and served at that temperature. Evidence also revealed that other restaurants typically serve their coffee at much lower temperatures and that coffee made at home typically is between 135 and 140 degrees. In addition, attorneys pointed to a warning to the franchise industry from the Shriner's Burn Institute in Cincinnati that some chains were causing unnecessarily serious burns by serving beverages at temperatures over 130 degrees.

An expert witness for Liebeck testified that at 180 degrees liquid that comes into contact with human skin will cause third-degree burns within two to seven seconds. Liquids at 155 degrees also can produce third-degree burns but the time required to do so is about 60 seconds.

McDonald's claimed that its customers buy coffee on their way to work or home with the intent of drinking it when they arrive at their destinations. The company admitted that it did not warn customers of the risk of incurring severe burns in case of spilled coffee served at McDonald's required temperature. McDonald's argues that its customers know that its coffee is hot and that they prefer it that way. (The company sells about $1.3 million of coffee a day.)

The jury awarded Liebeck $200,000 in compensatory damages for her injuries, but that amount was reduced to $160,000 because the jury ruled that Liebeck was 20 percent responsible for the accident. The jury also awarded her $2.7 million in punitive damages, roughly the equivalent of two days' worth of McDonald's coffee sales, but that amount was reduced to $480,000. Ultimately, McDonald's and Liebeck entered into a secret postverdict settlement.

1. On what grounds could Liebeck have brought her product liability suit against McDonald's?
2. Do you agree or disagree with the jury's verdict in this case? Explain.
3. What advice would you give to a restaurant owner about serving coffee to customers and avoiding legal liabilities?

Sources: Adapted from "The McDonald's Scalding Coffee Case," The Association of Trial Lawyers of America, www.atlanet.org/CJFacts/other/mcdonald.htm; "The Actual Facts About the McDonald's Coffee Case,"'Lectric Law Library, www.lectlaw.com/files/cur78.htm; "Mythbuster! The 'McDonald's Coffee Case' and Other Fictions," Center for Justice and Democracy, www.centerjd.org/free/mythbustersfree/MB-mcdonalds.htm.

Product Liability. At one time, only the parties directly involved in the execution of a contract were bound by the law of sales warranties. Today, the UCC and the states have expanded the scope of warranties to include any person (including bystanders) incurring personal or property damages caused by a faulty product. In addition, most states allow an injured party to sue *any* seller in the chain of distribution for breach of warranty. Product liability is built on the principle that a person who introduces a product into the stream of commerce owes a duty of care, not only to the person who first purchases the product, but also to anyone else who might foreseeably come into contact with it.[11] A company that might shoulder just a small percentage of the responsibility for a person's injury may end up bearing the majority of the damage award in the case. Eight recent studies confirm that (1) the number of product liability lawsuits is an extremely small percentage of all lawsuits; (2) punitive damage awards in product liability cases are extremely rare; (3) the size of jury awards has remained stable after accounting for inflation and other factors; (4) the real litigation crisis involves business-related disputes; (5) premiums for product liability insurance are declining; and (6) overall tort cases have stabilized. However, if an entrepreneur is personally affected by a product liability lawsuit, the results can be devastating.[12]

According to a study conducted by the Department of Justice, the Bureau of Justice Statistics, and the National Center for State Courts, punitive damages were awarded in only 2 percent of all winning plaintiff cases or in just 0.8 percent of all product liability jury trials. The total amount of the punitive damage awards for these cases was $40,000. The median award was $9,000 and the average award was $12,000. In contrast, punitive damages were awarded in 169 contract cases or roughly 12 percent of all winning plaintiff contract cases. The total amount of the punitive damages awards for these cases was $169.5 million or roughly 63 percent of the total amount of punitive damages awarded in all winning plaintiff civil jury trials. The median award in these cases was $52,000, and the average award was $1,003,000. Twenty-four percent of these punitive damage awards exceeded $250,000, and 13 percent were greater than $1 million.[13]

Many customers who ultimately file suit under product liability laws base their claims on **negligence,** when a manufacturer or distributor fails to do something that a "reasonable" person would do. Typically, negligence claims arise from one or more of the following charges.[14]

> *Negligent design.* In claims based on negligent design, a buyer claims an injury occurred because the manufacturer designed the product improperly. To avoid liability charges, a company does not have to design products that are 100 percent safe, but it must design products that are free of "unreasonable" risks.
>
> *Negligent manufacturing.* In cases claiming negligent manufacturing, a buyer claims that a company's failure to follow proper manufacturing, assembly, or inspection procedures allowed a defective product to get into the customer's hands and cause injury. A company must exercise "due care" (including design, assembly, and inspection) to make its products safe when they are used for their intended purpose.
>
> *Failure to warn.* Although manufacturers do not have to warn customers about obvious dangers of using their products, they must warn them about the dangers of normal use and of foreseeable misuse of the product. (Have you ever read the warning label on a stepladder?) Many businesses hire attorneys to write the warning labels they attach to their products and include in their instructions. Table 22.1 offers a humorous look at some of the statements that have appeared on the warning labels of products.

Another common basis for product liability claims against businesses is **strict liability,** which states that a manufacturer is liable for its actions no matter what its

Table 22.1

Say What?!?

Following are some statements that actually appeared on product warning labels:

On a curling iron:
"This product for external use only."
"Warning: This product can burn eyes."

On a hair dryer:
"Do not use in shower."
"Do not use while sleeping."

On the case of a chocolate CD in a gift basket:
"Do not place this product into any electronic equipment."

On an electric rotary tool:
"This product not intended for use as a dental drill."

On a cardboard sun visor that fits inside a car's windshield:
"Do not drive with sunshield in place."

On a toner cartridge for a laser printer:
"Do not eat toner."

On a 13-inch wheelbarrow wheel:
"Not intended for highway use."

On a package of Silly Putty:
"Do not use as ear plugs."

On a folding baby stroller:
"Caution: Remove infant before folding for storage."

On the packaging of an iron:
"Do not iron clothes on body."

On a child's Superman costume:
"Wearing of this garment does not enable you to fly."

On the wrapper of a fruit roll-up snack:
"Remove plastic before eating."

On a can of pepper spray:
"May irritate eyes."

Source: "Warning Labels," *Rinkworks,* rinkworks.com/said/warnings.shtml.

intentions or the extent of its negligence. Unlike negligence, a claim of strict liability does not require the injured party to prove that the company's actions were unreasonable. The injured person must prove only that the company manufactured or sold a product that was defective and that it caused the injury. For instance, suppose the head of an axe flies off its handle, injuring the user. To sue the manufacturer under strict liability, the customer must prove that the defendant sold the axe, the axe was unreasonably dangerous to the customer because it was defective, the customer incurred physical harm to person or to property, and the defective axe was the proximate cause of the injury or damage. If these allegations are true, the axe manufacturer's liability is

Company Example ➔ virtually unlimited. *Walker Gunning was eating at a New York restaurant when the water glass he was drinking from allegedly exploded in his hand, causing serious injuries. Gunning filed a claim to recover damages against Small Feast Caterers, claiming that the restaurant had violated the Uniform Commercial Code's warranty of fitness for a particular purpose and that the restaurant was liable on the basis of strict liability. The restaurant filed a motion to dismiss the case, arguing that it should not be held liable because it is not "in the business of selling water" or the water glasses it provides to diners. Citing as precedent a similar New Jersey case involving a wine glass that broke in a customer's hand, the New York Supreme Court ruled that the glass of water was "an indispensable part of the meal" and that the implied warranty extended to the glass containing the water. In doing so, the court held the restaurant strictly liable for the glass that broke in Gunning's hand.*[15]

Protection of Intellectual Property Rights

3. Discuss the protection of intellectual property rights using patents, trademarks, and copyrights.

Entrepreneurs excel at coming up with innovative ideas for creative products and services. Many entrepreneurs build businesses around **intellectual property,** products and services that are the result of the creative process and have commercial value. New methods of teaching foreign languages at an accelerated pace, hit songs, books that bring a smile, and new drugs that fight diseases are just some of the ways intellectual property makes our lives better or more enjoyable. Entrepreneurs can protect their intellectual property from unauthorized use with the help of three important tools: patents, trademarks, and copyrights.

Patents

A **patent** is a grant from the federal government's Patent and Trademark Office (PTO) to the inventor of a product, giving the exclusive right to make, use, or sell the invention in this country for 20 years from the date of filing the patent application. The purpose of giving an inventor a 20-year monopoly over a product is to stimulate creativity and innovation. After 20 years, the patent expires and cannot be renewed. Most patents are granted for new product inventions, but **design patents,** issued for $3\ ^{1}/_{2}$, 7, or 14 years beyond the date the patent is issued, are given to inventors who make new, original, and ornamental changes in the design of existing products that enhance their sales. Inventors who develop a new plant can obtain a **plant patent** (issued for 7 years), provided they can reproduce the plant asexually (e.g., by grafting or cross-breeding rather than planting seeds). To be patented, a device must be new (but not necessarily better!), not obvious to a person of ordinary skill or knowledge in the related field, and useful. A device cannot be patented if it has been publicized in print anywhere in the world or if it has been used or offered for sale in this country prior to the date of the patent application. A U.S. patent is granted only to the true inventor, not a person who discovers another's invention. No one can copy or sell a patented invention without getting a license from its creator. A patent does not give one the right to make, use, or sell an invention but the right to exclude others from making, using, or selling it.

The "Patent of the Week" Web site offers a humorous look at the "strange, interesting, bizarre, inexplicable, wacky, useful, and sometimes just plain weird patents, issued from the U.S. and around the world." This "banana protective device" was awarded patent number 6,612,440 and is for "storing and transporting a banana carefully."

In recent years, the PTO has awarded companies, primarily Web-based businesses, patents on their business methods. Rather than giving them the exclusive rights to a product or an invention, a business method patent protects the way a company conducts business. *For instance, Amazon.com earned a patent on its "1-Click" Web-based checkout process, precluding other e-tailers from using it. Priceline.com has a patent on its business model of "buyer-driven commerce," in which customers name the prices they are willing to pay for airline tickets, hotel rooms, and other items.*

Although inventors are never assured of getting a patent, they can enhance their chances considerably by following the basic steps suggested by the PTO. Before beginning the often lengthy and involved procedure, inventors should obtain professional assistance from a patent practitioner—a patent attorney or a patent agent—who is registered with the PTO. Only attorneys and agents who are officially registered may represent an inventor seeking a patent. Approximately 98 percent of all inventors rely on these patent experts to steer them through the convoluted process. Legal fees for filing a patent application typically range from $3,000 to $10,000, depending on the complexity of the product.[16] Small businesses qualify for "small entity status," which gives them a 50 percent reduction in patent application fees. One study reports that for the typical small business, obtaining a patent and maintaining it for 20 years cost about $10,000.[17]

The Patent Process. Since George Washington signed the first patent law in 1790, the U.S. Patent and Trademark Office has issued patents on everything imaginable (and some unimaginable items, too), including mouse traps, animals (genetically engineered mice), games, and various fishing devices. To date the PTO has issued more than 7 million patents, including more than 6.7 million patents for new inventions (known as utility patents), and it receives more than 350,000 new applications each year (see Figure 22.1).

Figure 22.1

Patent Applications and Patents Granted

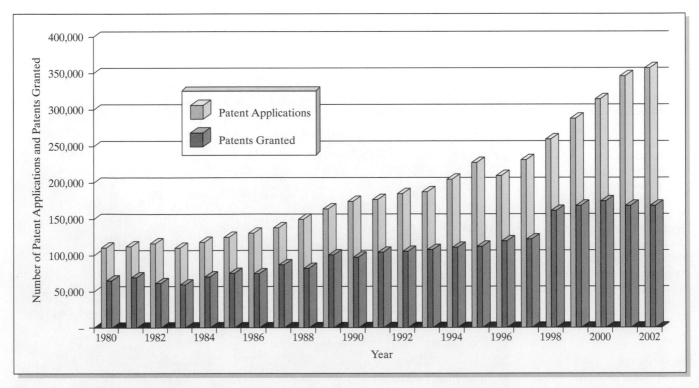

Source: U.S. Patent and Trademark Office.

Because of the high volume of applications it receives and the time it takes to process a patent, the application process grows longer each year. The proportion of patents granted within 24 months of application fell from 85 percent in the early 1990s to 70 percent by the late 1990s. The average time is expected to go as high as 27 months over the next several years.[18]

To receive a patent, an inventor must follow these steps:

Establish the invention's novelty. An invention is not patentable if it is known or has been used in the United States or has been described in a printed publication in this or a foreign country.

Document the device. To protect their patent claims, inventors should be able to verify the date on which they first conceived the idea for their inventions. Inventors can document a device by keeping dated records (including drawings) of their progress on the invention and by having knowledgeable friends witness these records. Inventors also can file a disclosure document with the PTO—a process that includes writing a letter describing the invention and sending a check for $10 to the PTO.

Search existing patents. To verify that the invention truly is new, nonobvious, and useful, inventors must conduct a search of existing patents on similar products. The purpose of the search is to determine whether the inventor has a chance of getting a patent. Most inventors hire professionals trained in conducting patent searches to perform the research.

Study search results. Once the patent search is finished, inventors must study the results of the search to determine their chances of getting a patent. To be patentable, a device must be sufficiently different from what has been used or described before and must not be obvious to a person having ordinary skill in the area of technology related to the invention.

Submit the patent application. If inventors decide to seek a patent, they must file an application describing the invention with the PTO. This description, called the patent's claims, should be broad enough so that others cannot easily engineer around the patent, rendering it useless. However, they cannot be so narrow as to infringe on patents that other inventors already hold. "The trick to getting a good patent is writing good claims," says Cort Flint, an attorney who specializes in intellectual property law.[19] Most inventors include detailed drawings, and many build and submit models of their inventions to support their patent applications. Charles Brannock, inventor of the "Brannock Device," the gizmo used in shoe stores to measure both the length and the width of a person's foot, used parts from an erector set to build the model he submitted with his patent application in 1926.[20]

Prosecute the patent application. Before the PTO will issue a patent, one of its examiners studies the application to determine whether or not the invention warrants a patent. If the PTO rejects the application, the inventor can amend his or her application so that the PTO can accept it.

In today's global economy, entrepreneurs often discover that companies based in foreign countries have stolen their intellectual property. In fact, U.S. businesses lose an estimated $200 billion a year because of counterfeit goods.[21] Bringing foreign companies to justice over intellectual property infringement often is difficult because many foreign countries' legal systems do not value individual property rights. Organizations such as the International Trade Centre, International Trade Administration, World Intellectual Property Organization, and the World Trade Organization are addressing this issue, but enforcement lags far behind the rhetoric.

Increasingly, the companies that are guilty of violating inventors' intellectual property rights are large businesses based in the United States. Protecting intellectual property against "copycat producers" can be expensive and time-consuming for entrepreneurs but often is

Company Example

necessary to protect and preserve entrepreneurs' businesses. In intellectual property lawsuits involving less than $1 million, legal costs, including attorney's fees, average $400,000, according to consulting firm Penta Advisory Services. In suits in which the amount in dispute is between $1 million and $10 million, legal costs average $1 million.[22] *While out searching for cows on a frigid night, Nebraska rancher Gerald Gohl came up with the idea for a remote-controlled spotlight that would enable him to control the light beam without having to roll down the window to hold out a hand-held spotlight. Gohl filed his application with the PTO in 1994 and received patent number 5,673,989 for a "wireless, remote-controlled portable searchlight." By 1997, Gohl had launched Golight Inc. and was selling the RadioRay through retail outlets for a retail price of more than $200. A buyer for Wal-Mart's Sam's Club stores contacted Gohl about distributing the RadioRay, but Gohl declined, concerned that selling through a discount store would dilute the product's image. Later that year, Wal-Mart began selling its own low-end version of the spotlight for just $60. The light looked nearly identical to Gohl's RadioRay with the addition of a small plastic stop that restricted the light to turning less than a full 360 degrees. Gohl filed a lawsuit against Wal-Mart, alleging that the company was in violation of his patent. Wal-Mart contended that Gohl's invention was obvious and that its light was not an exact copy of the RadioRay. Four years after filing the suit, the U.S. Court of Appeals for the Federal Circuit upheld a trail court's ruling, which concluded that Wal-Mart had infringed on Gohl's patent and awarded Gohl $464,280 in damages.*[23]

The U.S. patent system, as noted, requires that an invention (whether process, machine, manufacture, or composition of matter) satisfy certain requirements such as adequate disclosure, novelty, usefulness, and nonobviousness. However, in Europe since 1978, a single application may be submitted to the European Patent Office that specifies up to 24 national jurisdictions in which the inventor desires patent protection. The patentability requirements in Europe are broadly similar but not identical to those in the United States. In addition, the median time between application and patent issue can take up to four years in Europe.

Trademarks

A **trademark** is any distinctive word, phrase, symbol, design, name, logo, slogan, or trade dress that a company uses to identify the origin of a product or to distinguish it from other goods on the market. (A **service mark** is the same as a trademark except that it identifies and distinguishes the source of a service rather than a product.) A trademark serves as a company's "signature" in the marketplace. A trademark can be more than just a company's logo, slogan, or brand name; it can also include symbols, shapes, colors, smells, or sounds. For instance, Coca-Cola holds a trademark on the shape of its bottle, and NBC owns a trademark on its three-toned chime. Components of a product's identity such as these are part of its **trade dress,** the unique combination of elements that a company uses to create a product's image and to promote it. For instance, a Mexican restaurant chain's particular décor, color schemes, design, and overall "look and feel" would be its trade dress. To be eligible for trademark protection, trade dress must be inherently unique and distinctive to a company, and another company's use of that trade dress must be likely to confuse customers. *Joshua Wesson created Best Cellars Inc., a chain of retail stores, to make buying wine much simpler and less intimidating, and customers responded. Selling only 100 labels, all for less than $10 per bottle, the company grew quickly thanks to its unique displays and eye-catching layout. Wesson was stunned when he learned that a competitor, Grape Finds, had created a wine store that was virtually identical to Best Cellars' shops. Wesson filed a lawsuit, charging that Grape Finds had copied his company's trade dress; the court agreed, ruling in favor of Best Cellars and ordering Grape Finds to change its stores to avoid copying the distinctive look of Best Cellars' stores.*[24]

Company Example

There are 1.5 million trademarks registered in the United States, 900,000 of which are in actual use. Federal law permits a manufacturer to register a trademark, which prevents other companies from employing a similar mark to identify their goods. Before 1989, a business could not reserve a trademark in advance of use. Today, the first party that either uses a trademark in commerce or files an application with the PTO has the ultimate right to register that trademark. Unlike patents and copyrights, which are issued for limited amounts of time, trademarks last indefinitely as long as the holder continues to use it. However, a trademark cannot keep competitors from producing the same product or and selling it under a different name. It merely prevents others from using the same or confusingly similar trademark for the same or similar products.

Many business owners are confused by the use of the symbols ™ and ®. Anyone who claims the right to a particular trademark (or service mark) can use the ™ (or ℠) symbols without having to register the mark with the PTO. The claim to that trademark or service mark may or may not be valid, however. Only those businesses that have registered their marks with the PTO can use the ® symbol. Entrepreneurs do not have to register trademarks or service marks to establish their rights to those marks; however, registering a mark with the PTO does give entrepreneurs greater power in protecting their marks. Filing an application to register a trademark or service mark is relatively easy, but it does require a

| Company Example | → search of existing names. *When Barbara Allen launched a business selling an old family recipe of oils and vitamins that prevented pets from shedding, she named her product Mrs. Allen's SHED-STOP. Rather than applying for a patent for her product, however, Allen chose to register its name as a trademark. "If we went the patent route," she explains, "we'd have to divulge the formula. So we decided on the 'Coca-Cola' approach—trademark the name and keep the formula secret."*[25]

An entrepreneur may lose the exclusive right to a trademark if it loses its unique character and becomes a generic name or if the company abandons its trademark by failing to market the brand adequately. Aspirin, escalator, thermos, brassiere, super glue, yo-yo, and cellophane all were once enforceable trademarks that have become common words in the English language. These generic terms can no longer be licensed as a company's trademark.

◆ GAINING *a* COMPETITIVE EDGE ◆

A Blind by Any Other Name. . .

Early in 2004, Google was hit with a lawsuit claiming that its sale of the terms "American blind" and "American blinds" as keywords involved trademark infringement. American Blind and Wallpaper Factory filed a complaint against the search giant, as well as Google's distribution partners, AOL, Ask Jeeves, and EarthLink. The suit came shortly after AOL settled a suit with Playboy involving similar issues.

According to the suit, "Google's practice of selling text ads related to keyword search terms takes advantage of American Blind's trademarks, because competitors' ads can appear on results pages that appear when users search for 'American blinds' and 'American blind.'" American Blind asked that Google be permanently stopped from selling those keywords.

Google agreed to block advertisers from buying keywords including "American Blind Factory" and "Decorate Today," but said it could not block other phrases American Blind wanted to protect, including "American Blind."

Similar issues were addressed in the case brought by Playboy Enterprises. In 1999, Hugh Hefner's adult entertainment empire claimed Netscape (now owned by AOL) infringed and diluted Playboy's trademark by presenting ads for rival companies when users entered "playboy" or "playmate" as keywords. The words were among 400 that triggered adult ads.

"We have a federal registered trademark for American Blind and Wallpaper Factory. We do object if you go to Google and type in that exact phrase that consumers may misleadingly be directed to a competitor's link," a spokesperson said.

1. What has been the outcome of the *American Blind v. Google* case? Do you agree with the decision? Why or why not?

Source: Adapted from Janis Mara, "Google Sued for Trademark Infringement," *Internet News*, January 29, 2004, www.clickz.com/news/article.php/3305871.

Copyrights

A **copyright** is an exclusive right that protects the creators of original works of authorship such as literary, dramatic, musical, and artistic works (e.g., art, sculptures, literature, software, music, videos, video games, choreography, motion pictures, recordings). The internationally recognized symbol © denotes a copyrighted work. A copyright protects only the form in which an idea is expressed, not the idea itself. A copyright on a creative work comes into existence the moment its creator puts that work into a tangible form. Just as with a trademark, obtaining basic copyright protection does not require registering the creative work with the U.S. Copyright Office; doing so, however, gives creators greater protection over their work. When author J. K. Rowling wrote the manuscripts for the immensely popular Harry Potter series, she automatically had a copyright on her creation. To secure her works against infringement, however, Rowling registered the copyright with the U.S. Copyright Office. Copyright applications must be filed with the Copyright Office in the Library of Congress for a fee of $30 per application. A valid copyright on a work lasts for the life of the creator plus 50 years after his or her death. (A copyright lasts 75 to 100 years if the copyright holder is a business.) When a copyright expires, the work becomes public property and can be used by anyone free of charge.

Because they are so easy to duplicate, computer software programs, CDs, DVDs and videotapes are among the items most often pirated by copyright infringers. It is not uncommon for shoppers to be able to purchase a pirated DVD of a new, recently released movie on the streets of Beijing or a dozen other cities across the globe for a small price. Advances in technology have made digital piracy simple and inexpensive; the Motion Picture Association of America estimates that Web users illegally trade between 400,000 and 600,000 copies of films each day! Two weeks *before* Universal Studios released *The Hulk*, thousands of online users of popular file-swapping software were downloading the movie free of charge.[26] The legal battles that the Recording Industry Association of America (RIAA) and many recording studios have launched in recent years against companies that have created music-swapping Web sites such as Gnutella and KaZaA have focused a great deal of attention on the issue of copyright infringement. Because they have had little success in bottling up the technology that drives these file-swapping companies, the RIAA and the music studios have changed their tactics, filing copyright infringement lawsuits against individuals who offer to trade copyrighted materials illicitly. Firing the first volley in this new battle over online music downloading, the RIAA filed 261 lawsuits against individuals (including several college students) it said have used file-sharing software illegally to distribute vast quantities of copyrighted music online. The suits sought damages of as much as $150,000 per song.[27]

Protecting Intellectual Property

Acquiring the protection of patents, trademarks, and copyrights is useless unless an entrepreneur takes action to protect those rights in the marketplace. Unfortunately, not every businessperson respects others' rights of ownership to products, processes, names, and works and infringes on those rights with impunity. In other cases, the infringing behavior simply is the result of a lack of knowledge about others' rights of ownership. The primary weapon an entrepreneur has to protect patents, trademarks, and copyrights is the legal system. The major problem with relying on the legal system to enforce ownership rights is the cost of infringement lawsuits, which can quickly exceed the budget of most small businesses.

If an entrepreneur has a valid patent, trademark, or copyright, stopping an infringer often requires nothing more than a stern letter from an attorney threatening a lawsuit. Many offenders don't want to get into expensive legal battles and agree to stop their illegal behavior. If that tactic fails, the entrepreneur may have no choice but to bring an infringement lawsuit.

Legal battles can be expensive. Before bringing a lawsuit, an entrepreneur must consider the following issues:

- Can the opponent afford to pay if you win?
- Do you expect to get enough from the suit to cover the costs of hiring an attorney and preparing a case?
- Can you afford the loss of time, money, and privacy from the ensuing lawsuit?

Intellectual property has long been used by businesses as a basis for producing and marketing goods and services. The difference now is that often there are many parties whose activities overlap, and some of the parties involved may not reside in the same country. This makes it important to consider each party's rights and responsibilities. Where once a single innovator may have toiled to bring a new concept or product to market, now it is common that several different technological solutions and licenses are required to enter a particular market and this requires collaboration. According to the International Chamber of Commerce *Intellectual Property Roadmap 2004:*

> The complexity of products, specialization and reorganization of production in order to benefit from economies of scale are leading to increasingly decentralized production. Outsourcing, cooperation and collaboration become more important. The partners involved are therefore often separate legal entities in different countries. Adequate protection of intellectual property is crucial to enable the free exchange of R&D results, creativity and inventiveness among such independent partners in different jurisdictions.

The Law of Agency

4. Explain the basics of the law of agency.

An **agent** is one who stands in the place of and represents another in business dealings. Although an agent has the power to act for the principal, an agent remains subject to the principal's control. Many small business managers do not realize that their employees are agents while performing job-related tasks. Employers are liable only for those acts that employees perform within the scope of employment. For example, if an employee loses control of a flower shop's delivery truck while making a delivery and crashes into several parked cars, the owner of the flower shop (the principal) and the employee (the agent) are liable for any damages caused by the crash. Even if the accident occurred while the employee was on a small detour of his own (e.g., to stop by his house), the owner is still liable for damages as long as the employee is working "within the scope of his employment." Normally, an employee is considered to be within the scope of his employment if he is motivated in part by the principal's action and if the place and time for performing the act is not significantly different from what is authorized.

Any person, even those lacking contractual capacity, can serve as an agent, but a principal must have the legal capacity to create contracts. Both the principal and the agent are bound by the requirements of a fiduciary relationship, one characterized by trust and good faith. In addition, each party has specific duties to the other. An agent's duties include the following:

- *Loyalty.* Every agent must be faithful to the principal in all business dealings.
- *Performance.* An agent must perform his or her duties according to the principal's instructions.
- *Notification.* The agent must notify the principal of all facts and information concerning the subject matter of the agency.
- *Duty of care.* An agent must act with reasonable care when performing duties for the principal.

- *Accounting.* An agent is responsible for accounting for all profits and property received or distributed on the principal's behalf.

A principal's duties include the following:

- *Compensation.* Unless a free agency is created, the principal must pay the agent for his or her services.
- *Reimbursement.* The principal must reimburse the agent for all payments made for the principal or any expenses incurred in the administration of the agency.
- *Cooperation.* Every principal has the duty to indemnify the agent for any authorized payments or any loss or damages incurred by the agency, unless the liability is the result of the agent's mistake.
- *Safe working conditions.* The law requires a principal to provide a safe working environment for all agents. Workers' compensation laws cover an employer's liability for injuries agents receive on the job.

As agents, employees can bind a company to agreements, even if the owner did not intend for them to do so. Employees can create a binding obligation, for instance, if the business owner represents them as authorized to perform such transactions. For example, the owner of a flower shop who routinely permits a clerk to place orders with suppliers has given that employee *apparent authority* for purchasing. Similarly, employees have *implied authority* to create agreements when performing the normal duties of their jobs. For example, the chief financial officer of a company has the authority to create binding agreements when dealing with the company's bank.

Bankruptcy

5. Explain the basics of bankruptcy law.

Bankruptcy occurs when a business is unable to pay its debts as they come due. Early bankruptcy laws were designed to force debtors into court, where they were required to turn over their property to creditors. Taking debtors to court prevented them from hiding assets from creditors and escaping repayment of their debts. In 1978, Congress overhauled bankruptcy laws by passing the Bankruptcy Reform Act. That law, often criticized for making bankruptcy too easy for many, removed much of the stigma of bankruptcy. Some business owners now see bankruptcy as a viable business strategy. Fortunately, over the past several years, bankruptcy rates for business have fallen (see Figure 22.2). Unfortunately, during the same time period, the number of personal bankruptcies, which account for about 98 percent of all bankruptcy filings, has risen from 900,000 in 1992 to more than 1.6 million today.[28]

Forms of Bankruptcy

Many of those filing for bankruptcy are small business owners seeking protection from creditors under one of the eight chapters of the Bankruptcy Reform Act of 1978. Under the act, three chapters (7, 11, and 13) govern the majority of bankruptcies related to small business ownership. Usually, small business owners in danger of failing can choose from two types of bankruptcies: **liquidation** (Chapter 7: once the owner files for bankruptcy, the business ceases to exist) and **reorganization** (Chapter 11: after filing for bankruptcy, the owner formulates a reorganization plan under which the business continues to operate).

Chapter 7: Liquidation. The most common type of bankruptcy is filed under Chapter 7 (called straight bankruptcy), which accounts for 72 percent of all filings. Under Chapter 7, a debtor simply declares all of his or her firm's debts; the debtor must then turn over all assets to a trustee, who is elected by the creditors or appointed by the court. The trustee

Figure 22.2

Number of Business Bankruptcies

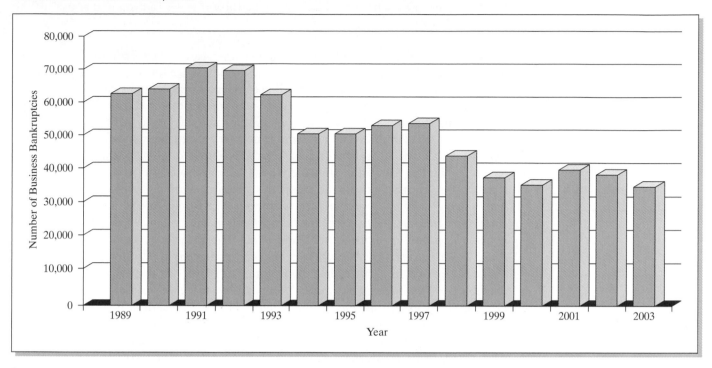

Source: American Bankruptcy Institute, 2004, www.abiworld.org/ContentManagement/ContentDisplay.cfm?ContentID=8149.

sells the assets and distributes all proceeds first to secured creditors and then to unsecured creditors (including stockholders). Depending on the outcome of the asset sale, creditors can receive anywhere between 0 and 100 percent of their claims against the bankrupt company. Once the bankruptcy proceeding is complete, any remaining debts are discharged, and the company disappears.

Straight bankruptcy proceedings can be started by filing either a voluntary or an involuntary petition. A voluntary case starts when the debtor files a petition with a bankruptcy court, stating the names and addresses of all creditors, the debtor's financial position, and all property the debtor owns. On the other hand, creditors start an involuntary petition by filing with the bankruptcy court. If there are 12 or more creditors, at least three of them whose unsecured claims total $11,625 or more must file the involuntary petition. If a debtor has fewer than 12 creditors, only one of them having a claim of $10,000 or more is required to file. As soon as a petition (voluntary or involuntary) is filed in a bankruptcy court, all creditors' claims against the debtor are suspended. Called an **automatic stay,** this provision prevents creditors from collecting any of the debts the debtor owed them before the petition was filed. In other words, no creditor can begin or continue to pursue debt collection once the petition is filed.

Not every piece of property the individual bankrupt debtor owns is subject to court attachment. According to the Code, certain assets are exempt, although each state establishes its own exemptions. Most states make an allowance for equity in a home, interest in an automobile, interest in a large number of personal items, and other personal assets. Federal law allows a $15,000 exemption for a home, a $4,000 exemption for household items and clothing, and a $400 exemption for other property.

The law does not allow a debtor to transfer the ownership of property to others to avoid its seizure in a bankruptcy. If a debtor transfers property within one year of the filing of a bankruptcy petition, the trustee can ignore the transfer and claim the assets.

In addition, any transfer of property made for the express purpose of avoiding repayment of debts (called fraudulent conveyance) will be overturned. The new law also enables a judge to dismiss a Chapter 7 bankruptcy petition if it is a "substantial abuse" of the bankruptcy code.

Chapter 11: Reorganization. For a small business weakened by a faltering economy or management mistakes, Chapter 11 provides a second chance for success. The philosophy behind this form of bankruptcy is that ailing companies can prosper again if given a fresh start with less debt. Under Chapter 11, a company is protected from creditors' legal actions while it formulates a plan for reorganization and debt repayment or settlement. In most cases, a small business and its creditors negotiate a settlement in which the company repays a percentage of its debts and is freed of the remainder. The business continues to operate under the court's direction, but creditors cannot foreclose on it, nor can they col-

Company Example →

lect any prebankruptcy debts the company owes. *Interstate Bakeries, the company that makes Twinkies, Wonderbread, and HoHos, recently filed a voluntary petition for Chapter 11 bankruptcy that showed the company's debt stands at $1.3 billion. Interstate Bakeries, the largest wholesale baker in the United States, failed to update its product line and to introduce new products to capitalize on consumers' changing eating habits. Declining sales, high fixed costs, and rising costs for ingredients, energy, and employee health care created severe cash flow problems that led to CEO James Elsesser's departure and the company's Chapter 11 filing. Industry experts say that turning around Interstate Bakeries won't be easy. Indeed, three out of four companies that file for Chapter 11 bankruptcy protection ultimately fail.*[29]

A Chapter 11 bankruptcy filing can be either voluntary or involuntary. Once the petition is filed, an automatic stay goes into effect and the debtor has 120 days to file a reorganization plan with the court. Usually, the court does not replace management with an appointed trustee; instead, the bankrupt party, called the debtor in possession, serves as trustee. If the debtor fails to file a plan within the 120-day limit, any party involved in the bankruptcy, including creditors, may propose a plan. The plan must identify the various classes of creditors and their claims, outline how each class will be treated, and establish a method to implement the plan. It also must spell out which debts cannot be paid, which can be paid, and what methods the debtor will use to repay them. In a typical reorganization plan, a debtor promises to give creditors a portion of the company's assets and to pay them a percentage of its future earnings if there are any.

Once the plan is filed, the court must decide whether or not to approve it. A court will approve a plan if a majority of each of the three classes of creditors—secured, priority, and unsecured—votes in favor of it. The court will confirm a plan if it has a reasonable chance of success, is submitted in good faith, and is "in the best interest of the creditors." If the court rejects the plan, the creditors must submit a new one for court approval.

Filing under Chapter 11 offers a weakened small business a number of advantages, the greatest of which is a chance to survive (although most of the companies that file under Chapter 11 ultimately are liquidated). In addition, employees keep their jobs (at least many do), and customers get an uninterrupted supply of goods and services. But there are costs involved in bankruptcy proceedings. Customers, suppliers, creditors, and often employees lose confidence in the firm's ability to succeed. Creditors frequently incur substantial losses in Chapter 11 bankruptcies.

Chapter 13: Individual's Repayment Plans. Chapter 13 bankruptcy is the consumer version of Chapter 11 proceedings. Individual debtors (not businesses) with a regular income who owe unsecured debts of less than $290,000 or secured debts under $872,000 may file for bankruptcy under Chapter 13. Many sole proprietors who have the choice of filing under Chapter 11 or 13 find that Chapter 13 is less complicated and less expensive. Chapter 13 proceedings must begin voluntarily. Once the debtor files the petition, creditors cannot start or continue legal action to collect payment. Under Chapter 13, only the debtor can file a repayment plan, whose terms cannot exceed five years. If the court approves the plan, the debtor may pay off the obligations—either in full or partially—on an installment basis. The plan is designed with the debtor's future income in mind, and when the debtor completes the payments under the plan, all debts are discharged.

IN THE FOOTSTEPS OF AN ENTREPRENEUR...

Do-It-Yourself Bankruptcy

In 1993, Gordon Weinberger started Top of the Tree Baking Company, a business that produced a variety of "homemade" pies that sold for $5.99 in more than 200 grocery stores near the company's Londonderry, New Hampshire, headquarters. Customers loved Top of the Tree's pies. By 1997 the company had reached annual sales of more than $400,000 thanks in large part to Weinberger's use of the "Piebus," a marketing gimmick Weinberger had created to draw attention to his company's fine pies. Weinberger decorated a school bus, transforming it into the Piebus, which he drove to weekend promotional events and to the supermarkets selling his company's pies. It drew lots of attention, especially with Weinberger, who is 6' 9" tall, at the wheel, pushing pies.

Despite Top of the Tree's rapid growth (or perhaps because of it), the company was losing money on every pie it made. Liquidity soon became a problem, and Weinberger could not convince investors or banks to put up any more capital. At that point, Top of the Tree owed 71 creditors, ranging from its insurance agent to its flour supplier, more than $225,000. Orders continued to come in at a rapid pace, but the company could not fill them because its vendors refused to ship raw materials due to lack of payment. "We couldn't ship any more pies," says Weinberger.

From a practical perspective, Top of the Tree was out of business, but being cut from the fabric of entrepreneurship, Weinberger wasn't willing to quit. Desperate to salvage the company, he contacted Pam Coleman, an attorney friend, about bankruptcy. "How often do you talk to your vendors?" she asked. "Just about every day," Weinberger answered. That gave Coleman a novel idea: Rather than file for Chapter 11 bankruptcy to get an automatic stay from a court, which means that a company is protected from its creditors while it reorganizes, Weinberger could use his close connections with his suppliers to negotiate a temporary suspension on payments while he reorganized the business. "Gordon can create his own automatic stay," says Coleman.

It was a risky strategy, but it was a risk Weinberger was willing to take to save his company and keep it out of Chapter 11 bankruptcy. His first step was to send a letter to every creditor explaining Top of the Tree's predicament. The letter was straightforward:

We have consulted with bankruptcy attorneys who have advised us that we could immediately file for Chapter 11 bankruptcy protection. However, if we file, there's no guarantee that vendors like you would get anything of note in a plan of reorganization because there is a secured lender ahead of you. We believe that it makes sense for you to wait it out with us for just a little while longer. You will be receiving a letter outlining our plan in the next several weeks.

Yours with survival in mind, (signed) Gordon Weinberger

After the letter went out, Weinberger called his creditors to answer any questions they might have. Under federal law, any three creditors could force Top of the Tree into involuntary bankruptcy, but none did. The bank to whom Weinberger owed $175,000, however, wasn't as cooperative until a courageous loan officer spoke up and said, "The guy wants to pay you back. Leave him alone."

Weinberger's first step was to close the inefficient pie-making factory he had been operating from and to outsource the production of all of the company's pies. He laid off 50 employees and sold the production equipment (but kept the Piebus, of course). Weinberger then sent his creditors another letter, offering immediate payment of 15 cents for every dollar owed or a wait of 6 months for the company to get back on its feet and pay off its debts in full. None of the creditors took the 15-cents-on-the-dollar offer. Top of the Trees was entering the fourth quarter of the year when its sales normally peak, so the timing was ideal. Weinberger hit the road in the Piebus, calling on some 500 supermarkets and closing about $1 million in sales by Thanksgiving. "That gave us a war chest," he says, which Weinberger used to pay off the company's creditors ahead of the schedule he had laid out in the earlier letters.

Weinberger's bold do-it-yourself bankruptcy plan worked, but Coleman estimates that only about 5 percent of insolvent companies attempt their own private "work out" plan with creditors. A private bankruptcy plan such as the one Weinberger used to save Top of the Tree works only if all creditors cooperate, and, according to Coleman, "That's a big if." Within a few years, Top of the Tree recovered from its cash flow woes, paid off all of its creditors in full, and generated annual sales of $5 million. Shortly after that, Weinberger sold the company to Mrs. Smith's Pies, a division of industry giant Flowers Foods, Inc.

1. What does a Chapter 11 bankruptcy filing mean for a struggling small business?
2. Is Weinberger's approach to paying Top of the Tree's creditors in full unique? If so, in what ways? What risks did Weinberger take by using this "private bankruptcy" approach?
3. What are the ethical implications of a small company declaring bankruptcy in the face of serious financial problems?

Sources: Adapted from Susan Greco, "The Lazarus Play," *Inc.,* October 2002, pp. 100–105; Jeffrey C. Shuman, "People Rarely Get the 'Rhythm' of Business Right on the First Attempt," *The Rhythm of Business,* March 27, 1998, www.rhythmofbusiness.com/LeadingThoughts/ArticlesWhitePapers.asp?newspapertype=&id=107.

Government Regulation

6. Explain some of the government regulations affecting small businesses, including those governing trade practices, consumer protection, consumer credit, and the environment.

Although most entrepreneurs recognize the need for some government regulation of business, most believe the process is overwhelming and out of control. Government regulation of business is far from new; in fact Congress created the Interstate Commerce Commission in 1887. The Great Depression of the 1930s triggered a great deal of regulation of business. Since the 1930s, laws regulating business practices and the creation of government agencies to enforce the regulations have expanded continuously. Not to be outdone by the federal regulators, most states have created their own regulatory agencies to create and enforce a separate set of rules and regulations. Small business owners often feel overwhelmed by the paperwork required to respond to all the governmental agencies trying to regulate and protect them.

The major complaint small business owners have concerning government regulation revolves around the cost of compliance. The *Code of Federal Regulations* (*CFR*) is currently 201 volumes and consists of 134,723 pages.[30] The National Federation of Independent Businesses reports that for firms with fewer than 20 employees, the cost of regulations are $5,532 per employee compared to $2,979 per employee for large businesses.[31] Larger firms can spread the cost of compliance over a larger number of employees and, consequently, have a lower per employee cost. These higher costs of compliance for small businesses place them at competitive disadvantage. In a competitive market, small companies cannot simply pass these additional costs forward to their customers and, consequently, they experience a squeeze on their profit margins. A 1996 law, the Small Business Regulatory Enforcement and Fairness Act, offers business owners some hope. Its purpose is to require government agencies to consider the impact of their regulations on small companies and gives business owners more input into the regulatory process.

Most business owners agree that some government regulation is necessary. There must be laws governing working safety, environmental protection, package labeling, consumer credit, and other relevant issues because some dishonest, unscrupulous managers will abuse the opportunity to serve the public's interest. It is not the regulations that protect workers and consumers and achieve social objectives that businesses object to but those that produce only marginal benefits relative to their costs. Owners of small firms, especially, seek relief from wasteful and meaningless government regulations, charging that the cost of compliance exceeds the benefits gained.

Trade Practices

Sherman Antitrust Act. Contemporary society places great value on free competition in the marketplace, and antitrust laws reflect this. The notion of laissez-faire—that the government should not interfere with the operation of the economy—that once dominated U.S. markets no longer prevails. One of the earliest trade laws was the Sherman Antitrust Act, which was passed in 1890 to promote competition in the U.S. economy. This act is the foundation on which antitrust policy in the United States is built and was aimed at breaking up the most powerful monopolies of the late nineteenth century. The Sherman Antitrust Act contains two primary provisions affecting growth and trade among businesses.

Section I forbids "every contract, combination in the form of trust or otherwise, or conspiracy, in restraint of trade or commerce among the several states, or with foreign nations." This section outlaws any agreement among sellers that might create an unreasonable restraint on free trade in the marketplace. For example, a group of small and medium-size regional supermarkets formed a cooperative association to purchase products to resell under private labels only in restricted geographic regions. The U.S. Supreme Court ruled that their action was an attempt to restrict competition by allocating territories and had "no purpose except stifling of competition."[32]

Section II of the Sherman Antitrust Act makes it illegal for any person to "monopolize or attempt to monopolize any part of the trade or commerce among the several states, or with foreign nations." The primary focus of Section II is on preventing the undesirable effects of monopoly power in the marketplace.

Clayton Act. Congress passed the Clayton Act in 1914 to strengthen federal antitrust laws by spelling out specific monopolistic activities. The major provisions of the Clayton Act forbid the following activities:

1. *Price discrimination.* A firm cannot charge different customers different prices for the same product, unless the price discrimination is based on an actual cost savings, is made to meet a lower price from competitors, or is justified by a difference in grade, quality, or quantity sold.
2. *Exclusive dealing and tying contracts.* A seller cannot require a buyer to purchase only the seller's product to the exclusion of other competitive sellers' products (an exclusive dealing agreement). Also, the act forbids a seller from selling a product on the condition that the buyer agrees to purchase another product the seller offers (a tying agreement). For example, a computer manufacturer could not sell a computer to a business and, as a condition of the sale, require the firm to purchase software as well.
3. *Purchasing stock in competing corporations.* A business cannot purchase the stock or assets of another business when the effect may be to substantially lessen competition. This does not mean that a corporation cannot hold stock in a competing company; the rule is designed to prevent horizontal mergers that would reduce competition. The Federal Trade Commission and the Antitrust Division of the Justice Department enforce this section, evaluating the market shares of the companies involved and the potential effects of a horizontal merger before ruling on its legality.
4. *Interlocking directorates.* The act forbids interlocking directorates—a person serving on the board of directors of two or more competing companies.

Federal Trade Commission Act. To supplement the Clayton Act, Congress passed the Federal Trade Commission Act in 1914, which created its namesake agency and gave it a broad range of powers. Section 5 gives the FTC the power to prevent "unfair methods of

✦ GAINING *a* COMPETITIVE EDGE ✦

Are Your Ads Setting You Up for Trouble?

When a Florida auto dealer offered a "free four-day, three-night vacation to Acapulco" for any customer purchasing a new car or van, he had no idea of the legal problems his advertisement would create. A customer who bought a van from the dealer felt cheated when he discovered that the "free vacation" was actually a sales promotion for a time-share condominium and was overrun with restrictions, conditions, and qualifications. Believing the ad was deceptive, the customer filed a lawsuit against the dealer. The jury ruled against the car dealer and awarded the customer $1,768 in compensatory damages and $667,000 in punitive damages.

Entrepreneurs sometimes run afoul of the laws concerning advertising because they do not know how to comply with legal requirements. The Federal Trade Commission (FTC) is the federal agency that regulates advertising and deals with problems created by deceptive ads. Under federal and state laws, an advertisement is unlawful if it misleads or deceives a reasonable customer, even if the business owner responsible for it had no intention to deceive. Any ad containing a false statement is in violation of the law although the entrepreneur may not know that the statement was false. The FTC judges an ad by the overall impression it creates and not by the technical truthfulness of its individual parts.

What can entrepreneurs do to avoid charges of deceptive advertising? The following guidelines will help:

- *Make sure your ads are accurate.* Avoid creating ads that promise more than a product or service can deliver. Take the time to verify the accuracy of every claim or statement in your ads. If a motor oil protects an engine from damage, don't claim that it will repair damage that already exists in an engine—unless you can prove that it actually does.
- *Get permission to use quotations, pictures, and endorsements.* Never use material in an ad from an outside source unless you get written permission to do so. One business owner got into trouble when he inserted a photograph of a famous athlete without his permission into an ad for his company's service.
- *Be careful when you compare competitors' products or services to your own.* False statements that harm the reputation of a competitor's business, products, or services not only may result in charges of false advertising but also in claims of trade libel. Make sure that any claims in your ads comparing your products to competitors' are fair and accurate.

- *Stock sufficient quantities of advertised items.* Businesses that advertise items for sale must be sure to have enough units on hand to meet anticipated demand. If you suspect that demand may outstrip your supply, state in the ad that quantities are limited.
- *Avoid "bait and switch" advertising.* This illegal technique involves advertising an item for sale at an attractive price when a business has no real intention of selling that product at that price. Companies using this technique often claim to have sold out of the advertised special. Their goal is to lure customers in with the low price and then switch them over to a similar product at a higher price.
- *Use the word "free" carefully and accurately.* Every advertiser knows that one of the most powerful words in advertising is *free*. However, anything you advertise as being free must actually be free. For instance, suppose a business advertises a free paintbrush to anyone who buys a gallon of a particular type of paint for $11.95. If the company's regular price for this is less than $11.95, the ad is deceptive because the paintbrush is not really free.
- *Be careful of what your ad does not say.* Omitting information in an ad that leaves customers with a false impression about a product or service and its performance is also a violation of the law.
- *Describe sale prices and "savings" carefully.* Business owners sometimes get into trouble with false advertising when they advertise items at prices that offer huge "savings" over their "regular" prices. One jeweler violated the law by advertising a bracelet for $299, a savings of $200 from the item's regular $499 price. In reality, the jeweler had never sold the item at its $499 "regular" price; the item's normal price was $299, which he advertised as the "sale" price.

1. Visit the Web site for the Federal Trade Commission at www.ftc.gov. Use the information you find there to compile a list of five suggestions to help entrepreneurs avoid charges of deceptive advertising.
2. Get a copy of a local newspaper and look for advertisements that you suspect may be false or misleading.

Sources: Adapted from *Guides Against Bait Advertising,* Federal Trade Commission (Washington, D.C.), www.gov/bcp/guides/baitads-gd.htm; *Frequently Asked Questions: A Guide for Small Business,* Federal Trade Commission (Washington, D.C.), www.ftc.gov/bcp/conline/pubs/buspubs/ad-faqs.htm; Carlotta Roberts, "The Customer's Always Right," *Entrepreneur,* November 20, 2002, www.entrepreneur.com/article/0,4621.284044.00.html; "Seven Rules for Legal Advertising," *Inc.* (no date), www.inc.com/search/20153.html; "Consumer Protection Laws," *Inc.* (no date), www.inc.com/search/19691.html.

competition in commerce and unfair or deceptive acts or practices in commerce." Recent amendments have expanded the FTC's powers. The FTC's primary targets are those businesses that engage in unfair trade practices, often brought to the surface by consumer complaints. In addition, the agency has issued a number of trade regulation rules defining acceptable and unacceptable trade practices in various industries. Its major weapon is a "cease and desist order," commanding the violator to stop its unfair trade practices.

The FTC Act and the Lanham Trademark Act of 1988 (plus state laws) govern the illegal practice of deceptive advertising. In general, the FTC can review any advertisement that might mislead people into buying a product or service they would not buy if they knew the truth. For instance, if a small business advertised a "huge year-end inventory reduction sale" but kept its prices the same as its regular prices, it is violating the law.

Company Example →

After the American Italian Pasta Company began using the advertising slogan "America's Favorite Pasta" on its Mueller's brand packaging, a competitor, New World Pasta, filed a lawsuit that claimed the phrase constituted false advertising and was a violation of the Lanham Act. A survey by New World showed that 33 percent of consumers believed that the phrase meant that the product was the best selling pasta in the United States. The Court of Appeals, however, ruled that the American Italian Pasta Company had not engaged in deceptive advertising; instead, the claim was merely "sales puffery," general sales talk that is comprised of "vague or highly subjective claims of product superiority, including bald assertions of superiority." Although some customers may believe such claims, the court ruled that puffery cannot constitute false advertising.[33]

Robinson-Patman Act. Although the Clayton Act addressed price discrimination and the Federal Trade Commission forbade the practice, Congress found the need to strengthen the law because many businesses circumvented original rules. In 1936 Congress passed the Robinson-Patman Act, which further restricted price discrimination in the marketplace. The act forbids any seller "to discriminate in price between different purchases of commodities of like grade and quality" unless there are differences in the cost of manufacture, sale, or delivery of the goods. Even if a price-discriminating firm escaped guilt under the Clayton Act, it violated the Robinson-Patman Act. Traditionally, the FTC has had the primary responsibility of enforcing the Robinson-Patman Act.

Other Legislation. The Celler-Kefauver Act of 1950 gave the FTC the power to review certain proposals for mergers so it could prevent too much concentration of power in any particular industry.

Congress created the Miller-Tydings Act in 1937 to introduce an exception to the Sherman Antitrust Act. This act made it legal for manufacturers to use fair trade agreements that prohibit sellers of the manufacturer's product from selling it below a predetermined fair trade price. This form of price fixing was outlawed when Congress repealed the Miller-Tydings Act in 1976. Manufacturers can no longer mandate minimum or maximum prices on their products to sellers.

Consumer Protection

Since the early 1960s, legislators have created many laws aimed at protecting consumers from unscrupulous sellers, unreasonable credit terms, and mislabeled or unsafe products. Early laws focused on ensuring that food and drugs sold in the marketplace were safe and of proper quality. The first law, the Pure Food and Drug Act, passed in 1906, regulated the labeling of various food and drug products. Later amendments empowered government agencies to establish safe levels of food additives and to outlaw carcinogenic (cancer-causing) additives. In 1938, Congress passed the Food, Drug, and Cosmetics Act, which created the Food and Drug Administration (FDA). The FDA is responsible for establishing standards of safe over-the-counter drugs; inspecting food and drug manufacturing operations; performing research on food, additives, and drugs; regulating drug labeling; and other related tasks.

Congress has also created a number of laws to establish standards pertaining to product labeling for consumer protection. Since 1976, manufacturers have been required to print accurate information about the quantity and content of their products in a conspicuous place on the package. Generally, labels must identify the raw materials used in the product, the manufacturer, the distributor (and its place of business), the net quantity of the contents, and the quantity of each serving if the package states the number of servings. The law also requires labels to be truthful. For example, a candy bar labeled "new, bigger size" must actually be bigger. These requirements, created by the Fair Packaging and Labeling Act of 1976, were designed to improve the customers' ability to comparison shop. A 1970 amendment to the Fair Packaging and Labeling Act, the Poison Prevention Packaging Act, required manufacturers to install childproof caps on all products that are toxic.

With the passage of the Consumer Products Safety Act in 1972, Congress created the Consumer Products Safety Commission (CPSC) to control potentially dangerous products sold to consumers, and it has broad powers over manufacturers and sellers of consumer products. For instance, the CPSC can set safety requirements for consumer products, and it has the power to ban the production of any product it considers hazardous to consumers. It can also order vendors to remove unsafe products from their shelves. In addition to enforcing the Consumer Product Safety Act, the CPSC is also charged with enforcing the Refrigerator Safety Act, the Federal Hazardous Substance Act, the Child Protection and Toy Safety Act, the Poison Prevention Package Act, and the Flammable Fabrics Act. The Consumer Product Safety Act was created to do the following:

- Protect the public against unreasonable risk of injury from consumer products.
- Help customers compare the safety features of products.
- Create safety standards for products and consolidate inconsistent state regulations.
- Research the causes and possible prevention of injuries and illness from consumer products.

The Magnuson-Moss Warranty Act, passed in 1975, regulates written warranties that companies offer on the consumer goods they sell. The act does not require companies to offer warranties; it only regulates the warranties companies choose to offer. It also requires businesses that offer written warranties on products costing $15 or more to state their warranties in easy-to-understand language and defines the conditions warranties must meet before they can be designated as "full warranties."

The Telemarketing and Consumer Fraud and Abuse Protection Act of 1994 put in place the following restrictions on telemarketers:

- Calling a person's residence at any time other than 8:00 A.M. to 8:00 P.M.
- Claiming an affiliation with a government agency when such an affiliation does not exist.
- Claiming an ability to improve a customer's credit record or obtain a loan for a person regardless of that person's credit history.
- Not telling the receiver of the call that it is a sales call.
- Claiming an ability to recover goods or money lost by a consumer.

Consumer Credit

Another area subject to intense government regulation is consumer credit. This section of the law has grown in importance since credit has become a major part of many consumer purchases. The primary law regulating consumer credit is the Truth-in-Lending Act of

1969. This law requires sellers who extend credit and lenders to fully disclose the terms and conditions of credit arrangements. The Federal Trade Commission is responsible for enforcing the Truth-in-Lending Act. The law outlines specific requirements that any firm that offers, arranges, or extends credit to customers must meet. The two most important terms of the credit arrangement that lenders must disclose are the finance charge and the annual percentage rate. The finance charge represents the total cost—direct and indirect—of the credit, and the annual percentage rate (APR) is the relative cost of credit stated in annual percentage terms.

The Truth-in-Lending Act applies to any consumer loan for less than $25,000 (or loans of any amount secured by mortgages on real estate) that includes more than four installments. Merchants extending credit to customers must state clearly the following information, using specific terminology:

- The price of the product.
- The down payment and any trade-in allowance made.
- The unpaid balance owed after the down payment.
- The total dollar amount of the finance charge.
- Any prepaid finance charges or required deposit balances, such as points, service charges, or lenders' fees.
- Any other charges not include in the finance charge.
- The total amount to be financed.
- The unpaid balance.
- The deferred payment price, including the total cash price and finance and incidental charges.
- The date on which the finance charge begins to accrue.
- The annual percentage rate of the finance charge.
- The number, amount, and due dates of payments.
- The penalties imposed in case of delinquent payments.
- A description of any security interest the creditor holds.
- A description of any penalties imposed for early repayment of principal.

Another provision of the Truth-in-Lending Act limits a credit card holder's liability in case the holder's card is lost or stolen. As long as the holder notifies the company of the missing card, he or she is liable for only $50 of any amount that an unauthorized user might charge on the card (or zero if the holder notifies the company before any unauthorized use of the card).

In 1974 Congress passed the Fair Credit Billing Act, an amendment to the Truth-in-Lending Act. Under this law, credit card holders may withhold payment on a faulty product, providing they have made a good faith effort to settle the dispute first. Credit card holders can also withhold payment to the issuing company if they believe their bill is in error. Cardholders must notify the issuer within 60 days but are not required to pay the bill until the dispute is settled. The creditor cannot collect any finance charge during this period unless there was no error.

Another credit law designed to protect consumers is the Equal Credit Opportunity Act of 1974, which prohibits discrimination in granting credit on the basis of race, religion, national origin, color, sex, marital status, or whether the individual receives public welfare payments.

In 1970, Congress created the Fair Credit Reporting Act to protect consumers against the circulation of inaccurate or obsolete information pertaining to credit applications. Under this act, the consumer can request the nature of any credit investigation, the type of information assembled, and the identity of those persons receiving the report. The law requires that any obsolete or misleading information contained in the file be updated, deleted, or corrected.

Congress enacted the Fair Debt Collection Practices Act in 1977 to protect consumers from abusive debt collection practices. The law does not apply to business owners collecting their own debts but only to debt collectors working for other businesses. The act prevents debt collectors from doing the following:

- Contacting the debtor at his or her workplace if the employer objects.
- Using intimidation, harassment, or abusive language to pester the debtor.
- Calling on the debtor at inconvenient times (before 8 A.M. or after 9 P.M.).
- Contacting third parties (except parents, spouses, and financial advisors) about the debt.
- Contacting the consumer after receiving notice of refusal to pay the debt (except to inform the debtor of the involvement of a collection agency).
- Making false threats against the debtor.

The Consumer Leasing Act of 1976 amended the Truth-in-Lending Act for the purpose of providing meaningful disclosure to consumers who lease goods. The lease period must be more than four months, and the dollar value of the lease obligation cannot exceed $25,000.

Environmental Law

In 1970, Congress created the Environmental Protection Agency (EPA) and gave it the authority to create laws that would protect the environment from pollution and contamination. Although the EPA administers a number of federal environmental statutes, three in particular stand out: the Clean Air Act, the Clean Water Act, and the Resource Conservation and Recovery Act.

The Clean Air Act. To reduce the problems associated with acid rain, the greenhouse effect, and airborne pollution, Congress passed the Clean Air Act in 1970 (and several amendments since then). The act targets everything from coal-burning power plants to automobiles. The Clean Air Act assigned the EPA the task of developing national air-quality standards, and the agency works with state and local governments to enforce compliance with these standards.

The Clean Water Act. The Clean Water Act, passed in 1972, set out to make all navigable waters in the United States suitable for fishing and swimming by 1983 and to eliminate the discharge of pollutants into those waters by 1985. Although the EPA has made progress in cleaning up many bodies of water, it has yet to achieve these goals. The Clean Water Act requires the states to establish water-quality standards and to develop plans to reach them. The act also prohibits draining, dredging, or filling wetlands without a permit. The Clean Water Act also addresses the issues of providing safe drinking water and cleaning up oil spills in navigable waters.

The Resource Conservation and Recovery Act. Congress passed the Resource Conservation and Recovery Act (RCRA) in 1976 to deal with solid-waste disposal. The RCRA sets guidelines by which solid-waste landfills must operate, and it establishes rules governing the disposal of hazardous wastes. The RCRA's goal is to prevent solid waste from contaminating the environment. But what about those waste disposal sites that are already contaminating the environment? In 1980, Congress passed the Comprehensive Environmental Response, Compensation, and Liability Act (CERCLA) to deal with those sites. The act created the Superfund, a special federal fund set up to finance and to regulate the cleanup of solid-waste disposal sites that are polluting the environment.

The Pollution Prevention Act of 1990 set forth a public policy statement that offered rewards to firms that reduced the creation of pollution. The federal government provides matching funds to states for programs that promote the use of "source reduction techniques" dealing with pollution problems. This is a milestone piece of legislation because it replaces the regulatory "stick" approach resented by business with a "carrot" approach that rewards businesses for positive actions that reduce pollution.

▌▌▌ Chapter Review

1. Explain the basic elements required to create a valid, enforceable contract.

   ▪ A valid contract must contain these elements: agreement (offer and acceptance), consideration, capacity, and legality. A contract can be valid and yet unenforceable because it fails to meet two other conditions: genuineness of assent and proper form.

   ▪ Most contracts are fulfilled by both parties performing their promised actions; occasionally, however, one party fails to perform as agreed, thereby breaching the contract. Usually, the non-breaching party is allowed to sue for monetary damages that would place him or her in the same position he or she would have been in had the contract been performed. In cases for which money is an insufficient remedy, the injured party may sue for specific performance of the contract's terms.

2. Outline the major components of the Uniform Commercial Code governing sales contracts.

   ▪ The Uniform Commercial Code (UCC) was an attempt to create a unified body of law governing routine business transactions. Of the 10 articles in the UCC, Article 2 on the sale of goods affects many business transactions.

   ▪ Contracts for the sale of goods must contain the same four elements of a valid contract, but the UCC relaxes many of the specific restrictions the common law imposes on contracts. Under the UCC, once the parties create a contract, they must perform their duties in good faith.

   ▪ The UCC also covers sales warranties. A seller creates an express warranty when he or she makes a statement about the performance of a product or indicates by example certain characteristics of the product. Sellers automatically create other warranties—warranties of title, implied warranties of merchantability, and, in certain cases, implied warranties of fitness for a particular purpose—when they sell a product.

3. Discuss the protection of intellectual property rights using patents, trademarks, and copyrights.

   ▪ A patent is a grant from the federal government that gives an inventor exclusive rights to an invention for 20 years. To submit a patent, an inventor must establish novelty, document the device, search existing patents, study the search results, submit a patent application to the U.S. Patent and Trademark Office, and prosecute the application.

   ▪ A trademark is any distinctive word, symbol, or trade dress that a company uses to identify its product or to distinguish it from other goods. It serves as the company's "signature" in the marketplace.

   ▪ A copyright protects original works of authorship. It covers only the form in which an idea is expressed, not the idea itself, and lasts for 50 years beyond the creator's death.

4. Explain the basics of the law of agency.

   ▪ In an agency relationship, one party (the agent) agrees to represent another (the principal). The agent has the power to act for the principal but remains subject to the principal's control. While performing job-related tasks, employees play an agent's role.

   ▪ An agent has the following duties to a principal: loyalty, performance, notification, duty of care, and accounting. The principal has certain duties to the agent: compensation, reimbursement, cooperation, indemnification, and safe working conditions.

5. Explain the basics of bankruptcy law.

   ▪ Entrepreneurs whose businesses fail often have no other choice but to declare bankruptcy under one of three provisions: Chapter 7, liquidations, in which the business sells its assets, pays what debts it can, and disappears; Chapter 11, reorganizations, in which the business asks that its debts be forgiven or restructured and then reemerges; and Chapter 13, straight bankruptcy, which is for individuals only.

6. Explain some of the government regulations affecting small businesses, including those governing trade practices, consumer protection, consumer credit, and the environment.

   ▪ Businesses operate under a multitude of government regulations governing many areas, including trade practices, where laws forbid restraint of trade, price discrimination, exclusive dealing and tying contracts, purchasing controlling interests in competitors, and interlocking directorates.

- Other areas subject to government regulations include consumer protection (the Food, Drug, and Cosmetics Act and the Consumer Products Safety Act) and consumer credit (the Consumer Credit Protection Act, the Fair Debt Collection Practices Act, and the Fair Credit Reporting Act), and the environment (the Clean Air Act, the Clean Water Act, and the Resource Conservation and Recovery Act.)

▌▌▌ Discussion Questions

1. What is a contract? List and describe the four elements required for a valid contract. Must a contract be in writing to be valid?
2. What constitutes an agreement?
3. Which groups of people lack or have limited contractual capacity? How do the courts view contracts that minors create? Intoxicated people? Insane people?
4. What circumstances eliminate genuineness of assent in the parties' agreement?
5. What is breach of contract? What remedies are available to a party injured by a breach?
6. What is the Uniform Commercial Code? To which kinds of contracts does the UCC apply? How does it alter the requirements for a sale contract?
7. Under the UCC, what remedies does a seller have when a buyer breaches a sales contract? What remedies does a buyer have when a seller breaches a contract?
8. What is a sales warranty? Explain the different kinds of warranties sellers offer.

9. Explain the different kinds of implied warranties the UCC imposes on sellers of goods. Can sellers disclaim these implied warranties? If so, how?
10. What is product liability? Explain the charges that most often form the basis for product liability claims. What must a customer prove under these charges?
11. What is intellectual property? What tools do entrepreneurs have to protect their intellectual property?
12. Explain the differences among patents, trademarks, and copyrights. What does each protect? How long does each last?
13. What must an inventor prove to receive a patent?
14. Briefly explain the patent application process.
15. What is an agent? What duties does an agent have to a principal? What duties does a principal have to an agent?
16. Explain the differences among the three major forms of bankruptcy: Chapter 7, Chapter 11, and Chapter 13.
17. Explain the statement "For each benefit gained by regulation, there is a cost."

The Legal Environment: Business Law and Government Regulation

Business PlanPro

Navigating the increasingly complex waters of the legal and regulatory environment is no easy task for entrepreneurs, but today's business owners must understand the basics of business law and government regulation if they are to operate successfully. Having access to a qualified attorney to serve as a business advisor is wise, but having a fundamental understanding of how to avoid potential legal entanglements every day also is important. Some entrepreneurs learn the importance of understanding business law and government regulation only after they face an expensive legal battle or heavy fine.

The exercises for Chapter 22 that accompany Business Plan Pro are designed to help you identify the major legal issues your company faces. When you complete these exercises, you may want to include this information in the Product and Service Description section of Business Plan Pro.

Case 1 A Landscape Company in Search of Green

David Knauff had no intention of having a career in the landscaping business; things just worked out that way. When he was 14, his parents told him that he had to earn some money to support the game about which he was so passionate: golf. Knauff started by mowing the lawn at a nearby church in Wilmette, Illinois, and before he knew it, he had several clients in his neighborhood for whom he handled basic landscaping work. He officially started his company, Yes, We Care Landscaping, which he ran from his bedroom throughout high school and from his dorm room at Michigan State University.

After graduating from college with a degree in horticulture and landscape design, Knauff returned home to run the business full time. "I didn't even realize it was a business until someone pointed out to me that I was helping half a dozen people support their families," he says. He borrowed heavily from his mother and from traditional lenders with her loan guarantees to buy equipment and inventory, to supply the business with working capital, and to expand the business. Much of that debt remains on the company's balance sheet. Within three years of returning home, Knauff purchased three competitors as part of his vision for growing the company. Sales climbed, but the purchases saddled Yes, We Care Landscaping with excess equipment and managerial staff, an ineffective sales force, and many money-losing landscape maintenance contracts. Before the expansion, Knauff's company generated a profit of $25,000, but three years later, it had lost nearly half a million dollars. Frustrated, he committed himself to bidding on jobs more effectively and getting rid of several expensive but less than effective employees.

Knauff, who suffers from attention deficit disorder, admits that tasks he considers dull, such as accounting and record keeping, present a challenge. "My modus operandi is procrastination," he says ruefully. His lack of attention to financial matters sometimes affects his ability to bid reasonably and accurately on jobs. On one job involving landscaping a multimillion-dollar mansion, Knauff bid—and won—the contract at $150,000. Unfortunately, he barely broke even on the job and later learned that the next highest bid was from one of his competitors for $250,000! One of Knauff's goals is to begin using project management software that will enable him to track job costs and to access actual and estimated costs on a real-time basis.

Knauff has discovered another factor affecting Yes, We Care Landscaping's ability to generate a profit. Most of the company's 38 employees are members of landscape crews. Frequently, customers would tell the crew foremen that Knauff had approved changes to their work orders—additional lighting, an extra sidewalk, a small fence, and other features—when, in reality, he had not. The crews would complete the work without checking with Knauff, who would end up footing the bill for the extra work when the customers refused to pay. "I gave away a quarter-million dollars from change orders I didn't keep track of," he laments.

Knauff's eyes light up as he describes the thrill he gets from drawing, presenting, and selling dazzling landscape designs to prospective clients. His excitement continues as he discusses his vision for his company's future. One of his goals is to increase sales from their current level of almost $2 million a year to $10 million within five years. He points out that his largest competitor already generates $20 million in annual sales, a small portion of the total potential for the local landscape market, which he estimates at $2.3 billion. Knauff also talks about other spin-off companies he hopes to launch, including businesses that would install irrigation systems, brick walls, and driveways.

Knauff also recognizes that his company needs more focus in its marketing and advertising efforts. One key target customer is upscale suburban homeowners, but Knauff's experience to date is that these customers do not respond to the direct mail ad pieces the company has tried in the past. Although Yes, We Care Landscaping has an impressive list of satisfied customers, Knauff has done little to involve them in any promotional efforts.

Although his company's annual sales are nearly $2 million, Knauff still gets most of his business advice from his mother, who runs a successful executive search firm in Chicago, and his father, a printing company executive. On several occasions, he has thought that having other business advisors would help him when making tough business decisions. With several years' experience running a business, Knauff sees many opportunities for Yes, We Care Landscaping, and he doesn't want to miss out on them. However, he recognizes the importance of getting his company in order so that he can make the most of the opportunities available.

Exercises

1. Identify the major challenges facing Yes, We Care Landscaping. Given its current business system, do you think Knauff's goal of hitting $10 million in annual sales is realistic?
2. What steps should Knauff take to improve his company's bidding process?
3. What should Knauff do to exercise better financial control over his business?
4. How can Knauff market his company's services more effectively? Generate at least five ideas for a new marketing approach.

Source: Adapted from Brian O'Reilly, "Green Dreams," *FSB*, June 2004, pp. 53–56.

▮▮▮ Case 2 Finding the Right Fit

Gavin Bromell and Tom Nathan launched Techline Studio in 1984, and the company, which occupies a unique niche in the furniture business, grew steadily from its base in downtown Manhattan. Its midtown location was ideal for serving individuals and businesses needing premade furnishings such as desks, credenzas, storage units, and wall units customized to fit the odd shapes and often cramped quarters so pervasive in New York City. Sales were strong, reaching about $4 million a year, until many of their dot-com customers began to fold and the terrorist attacks brought growth to a halt. "We had 26 employees [and a company that was] too big for two people to run and too small for middle managers," says Bromell.

To safeguard their company's future, Bromell and Nathan scaled it back. Annual revenues are about $2 million, and the staff has been cut in half. After downsizing, the company actually increased its profit margin, but Bromell and Nathan now see business rebounding. They see opportunities for growth once again and want to take advantage of them, but they want to avoid their earlier mistake of adding extensive amounts of overhead expenses to their operation. The key is to boost sales by making their current staff and business system more productive.

Complementing Techline Studio's Manhattan showroom is the company's Web site (www.techlinestudio.com), which has been a source of both sales and frustration for the cofounders. They worry that visitors to the site may not understand the unique nature of the company's approach to customizing premade furnishings and that they will lose customers to companies such as industry giant Steelcase, which sells a wide variety of office furnishings but offers no customized design services. Competing on the basis of price puts them at a distinct disadvantage. Because Techline Studio provides unique, customizing services, its prices are considerably higher, but so are its potential profit margins. Another problem is the danger of its Web site getting lost in a sea of competitors' sites, many of which use some variation of the word *techline* in their own Web sites.

Bromell and Nathan are considering redesigning Techline Studio's existing Web site. The current version of the site offers visitors a choice when they first arrive: residential solutions or business solutions. They know that many of their existing customers are former employees of large corporations who are now on their own and have never had to buy office furniture for themselves before. They suspect that many visitors to their site are looking for information because they don't know how to solve the furnishing problems their home or office spaces present. Should they change the site's content to include more interactive content that walks customers one step at a time through the process of selecting and installing appropriate furniture that suits their needs and best fits their available space? They identify the basic steps of the process as needs analysis, measurement, design, pricing, installation, and follow-up. Bromell and Nathan see an advantage in having customers view their company as the "expert" available to help them solve their furnishing needs.

Because they do not know how visitors find their site, Bromell and Nathan are not sure how to market the site most effectively. They have not yet explored the possibilities of search engine marketing and Web analytics and what these techniques might do for their business. They also wonder what portion of their customers visit the company's Web site before they enter the showroom. "We don't ask," admits Nathan.

Bromell and Nathan currently rent the space for their showroom, a converted brownstone on East 19th Street in Manhattan that was once the home of famous newspaper publisher Horace Greeley, and their warehouse in New Jersey. Those locations aren't cheap; they spend "six figures" just on rent each year. "Should we buy the building housing our showroom?" they ask. Currently, they lease the basement and first two floors of the three-story brownstone, and an architect, who serves as the absentee owner's building manager, leases the third floor. Although they understand the dangers of being burdened with a mortgage if business were to fall off again, buying the building would give them room to expand (or to contract, if necessary). If they were forced to downsize again, they could lease the unused space to another tenant. They believe that the architect would continue to serve as building manager in exchange for a reduced lease rate.

Every week, Nathan and Bromell sit down at a staff meeting with all 13 employees to update them on the company's progress and to coordinate the efficient handling of current projects. They sense that many employees see the meeting as a waste of time (but who wants to tell the boss that?). They are considering changing the focus of the meeting to more strategic issues with a problem-solving approach. They recognize that one advantage of being a small company is the ability to stay in close contact with both employees and customers and to get feedback and ideas from both of these important groups. "We are in the business of selling solutions to customers' problems, not merely selling furniture," they say. "How can we get that message across to our customers? How can we help our sales force understand that they are not selling just shelves, cabinets, and drawers?"

Exercises

1. Strategically, how would you recommend Techline Studio position itself in the broadly defined furniture market? Are there specific market segments on which the company should focus? Explain.
2. Visit the company's Web site at www.techlinestudio.com. After exploring it, develop a series of recommendations for improving the site's design and content. What steps should the company take to promote its Web site?
3. What recommendation can you make to Bromell and Nathan concerning the lease or buy decision they face for the building housing their showroom?
4. How should Bromell and Nathan restructure their weekly staff meeting? What should its focus be?

Source: Adapted from Brian O'Reilly, "Furniture That Fits," *FSB,* July/August 2004, pp. 105–110.

▌▌▌ Case 3 Doom, But Definitely *Not* Gloom

It is just a matter of weeks until id Software releases its next big computer video game, Doom 3, a sequel to its blockbuster namesake Doom, which the company released in 1994. The game, four years in the making, will be a major factor in determining the level of id's success—and perhaps its survival—in the future. With the product launch so close, the company's 20 employees are immersed in what they call "crunch mode," the chaotic period that precedes the launch of any new game. During that time, programmers, animators, and other game specialists work 80-hour weeks, sometimes sleeping on cots in their offices. "It's like being blindfolded and running flat-out through a forest, praying that you don't hit a tree," says CEO Todd Hollenshead. During this busy time, company headquarters, located just outside Dallas, is surprisingly quiet. Computer screens glow eerily, as if the game creators were inside the dark corridors of the game they are creating. Conversations interrupt the sound of tapping keyboards and clicking mice only periodically.

Everyone at id believes this version of Doom will be a monster hit, and it has to be if the company is to remain a player in the hotly competitive world of video game makers. When id first introduced Doom in 1994, the industry was made up mostly of small, independent companies that had freewheeling, creative attitudes toward gaming. Since then, the industry has undergone a transformation. Large businesses such as Microsoft and Vivendi Universal have bought up most of the small companies, leaving it as one of the few small, independently owned operations left. A recent ranking showed that of the top 50 video games, just three were created by independent developers—quite a change from the early days of the industry.

Industry consolidation has far-reaching effects for small companies such as id. Competing against giants with big budgets for developing games means that id has no room for error. The cost of developing a new video game, with its complex graphics and realistic special effects, can be as much as $30 million! Large companies that produce a game that flops see it as an expensive mistake, but to id, an unsuccessful product would be devastating, perhaps causing the company to fail. For now, id is solidly profitable on sales of $20 million a year.

Most large companies launch multiple games each year, hoping that at least one will be a big hit and knowing that some, perhaps even most, will be busts. Their strategy is to pump out lots of games and hope that one will become a blockbuster, but id does not have the capital base to use that approach. Id launched its last game, Return to Castle Wolfenstein, in 2001, and it was a huge hit. In fact, id's cofounder John Carmack and his bizarre and creative team have a perfect record of hits. Every one of the company's games, from Wolfenstein 3D to Quake III, has been a success! Can the company realistically expect to continue that nonstop stream of megahits? Given that the industry has changed so dramatically in the past decade, is such a strategy wise? Because of the huge investment of time, resources, and money, one miss for a small company such as id could spell disaster.

Carmack does not appear to be worried that with each product launch, he is, in essence, betting the company. When eager gamers ask him when the new game will be released, he responds simply, "When it's done." In other words, Carmack and his team of creative geniuses want to be sure the quality of the game they release is without question and meets the standards of those who play video games avidly. To them, the quality of the gamer's experience is more important than launching a game quickly.

When Doom came out in 1994, it revolutionized the video game industry—and generated $200 million in sales for id. It was the original "first-person shooter" game, but some people were shocked at the graphic violence the game and those that followed included. In fact, some organizations such as the National Institute on Media and the

Family have objected to the content of some games, contending that many games intended only for adult use end up with many children playing them.

With Doom, id also transformed the way the industry thought about distribution of its products. Traditionally, companies sold their games through publishers, who earned 5 percent to 10 percent of the price of each game for distributing the games. Id was the first company to use the shareware concept, cutting out the publishers and releasing the first few levels of its games for free over the Internet. Customers could purchase the remaining levels from the company and simply use their Internet connections to download the complete version of the game for about $40.

In 1996, when it released Quake, which generated sales of $214 million, id once again pioneered another industry innovation: licensing. Early on, Carmack decided to release the source code of id's computer games so that enthusiasts could design their own villains or change the settings of the games and then share their variations with friends. With Quake, he saw the opportunity to sell the game's "engine," the core technology that enables the game to process a player's moves fluidly, to other video game developers. Since 1996, these licensing agreements have generated tens of millions of dollars in sales, and they currently account for 20 percent of id's revenues. In recent years, however, licensing sales have slowed as other video game developers have begun licensing their engines. Rival developer Epic Games, which updates its engine annually, has become the popular choice among game creators looking to purchase the core technology of an engine. Id last updated its software engine in 1999 when it unveiled Quake III.

Observers note that cofounder John Carmack has been devoting an increasing amount of his time to another business he has launched, Armadillo Aerospace, which is working to develop customized rocket ships. Carmack insists that he is not leaving id, and CEO Hollenshead says that the company is bigger than just one person. Many large suitors have offered to buy id over the past decade, and estimates are that the company would sell for as much as $500 million. Carmack is not interested in selling, saying that id prefers its independence. "We like being in the driver's seat," he says.

Exercises

1. Describe the strengths that have enabled id Software to achieve the success that it has. What opportunities do you spot for the company?
2. How has the video game industry changed from its inception? Is id likely to be able to maintain its competitive advantage in the face of those changes? Explain.
3. What threats does id face? How should the company handle the complaints from parents and politicians concerned about the excessive violence of many modern video games?
4. What recommendations can you make to Carmack and Hollenshead to ensure id's success in the future?

Sources: Adapted from Kemp Powers, "Doomsday," *FSB*, July/August 2004, pp. 87–89; Brad Wright, "Sounding the Alarm on Videogame Ratings," *CNN*, February 18, 2004, www.cnn.com/2002/TECH/fun.games/12/19/games.ratings/index.html.

Case 4 Blue Man Group

Many great entrepreneurs, from Thomas Edison to Dave Hewlett and William Packard, started the businesses that would make them famous by tinkering—often in a garage. Although they were sharing a Manhattan apartment rather than a garage, Chris Wink,

Matt Goldman, and Phil Stanton began tinkering in acting, despite the fact that they had no formal training in it. In 1988, the friends, all in their mid-twenties, put on bald wigs, painted themselves blue, and held "a funeral for the '80s" in Central Park. MTV was there to record the event, and soon after, Wink, Goldman, and Stanton formed the Blue Man Group and began putting on small theatrical performances for anyone who would watch. Their persistence and a few lucky breaks landed them on *The Tonight Show* and *Live! With Regis and Kathy Lee*. For three years, they performed six days a week without a break, totaling more than 1,200 consecutive shows. Finally, their exposure enabled them to create a show called *Tubes* and perform it off Broadway. The workload was heavy, however, and the three entrepreneurs began to feel as if they were prisoners of their own success. They were so busy performing that they had little time and energy to create new shows.

One of their financial backers insisted that the group have at least one understudy, a move that proved to be helpful after Stanton cut his hand one day. The understudy stepped in, and the show never missed a beat. "It was a catalytic event," says Goldman, referring to the realization the founders of Blue Man Group had: They could create and manage the show without having to be in every performance!

Opportunities for growth were coming at the Blue Man Group rapidly and from every direction. Companies asked them to endorse their products. Disney contacted them about a movie and a theme park ride. They passed up most of the proposals and opted instead to open a second Blue Man Group show in Boston. Coordinating both shows required shuttling back and forth between New York and Boston, however, and the entrepreneurs found themselves locked tightly inside another prison: the prison of seemingly endless meetings.

That's when Wink, Goldman, and Stanton decided to write a business plan, a 132-page document that told the story of the Blue Man Group performance step-by-step from their perspective. The result was not a typical business plan (with references to wide-ranging topics such as the writings of George Bernard Shaw to the caves at Lascaux), but it also accomplished exactly what the founders had hoped: It forced them to articulate the foundation on which their business was built. It also helped the trio to focus on managing the successful brand that they had created and to learn about managing that brand.

With the help of their plan, the Blue Man Group began to focus on the opportunities that were most important to its founders. The Blue Man Group holds regular casting calls across the United States, and thousands of performers have auditioned. Only 35 performers have met the founders' standards, which means that the company has a total of 38 actors portraying the Blue Man Group in four cities across the nation—New York, Boston, Chicago, and Las Vegas. The secret ingredient, say the founders, is not just memorizing a set of movements but also truly digging into a character to understand what drives him, something they spelled out in their original business plan. Referring to the creation of their plan, Goldman says, "Everything in our project lives either before that moment or after that moment."

After opening the Boston show in 1997, the trio of founders decided to focus on marketing the Blue Man Group. In the early days, the group lacked the money to run extensive advertising campaigns; instead, their philosophy was to create unique, stimulating shows and count on their audiences to spread the word. Their initial marketing efforts were modest—a few print ads for the Chicago show—but they decided to accept an offer from Intel, the giant computer chip maker, to appear in television commercials that would run nationally. The agreement gave the Blue Man Group the clout to work directly with the ad agency to create the commercials. (The group came up with most of the ideas that actually appeared in the commercials; none of the ad agency's ideas made the cut!) Two series of commercials were produced, all involving the Blue Man Group interacting with an Intel logo. The commercials not only advertised Intel's computer chips but also promoted the Blue Man Group.

Wink, Goldman, and Stanton still enjoy their performances and creating new routines, but they also realize the importance of managing their business and marketing it effectively. "What takes place while you're gone is just as important as what's on stage—the management of it, the business of it," says Stanton. So far, the trio has managed to do what James Collins and Jerry Porras advise in their book, *Built to Last:* "Preserve the Core/Stimulate Progress." They are considering opening shows in other cities, and their DVD, *The Complex Rock Tour Live,* has gone platinum, selling more than 100,000 units. A national Blue Man Group tour, a first for the group, recently performed in 35 cities across the United States, although the founders will not be donning the blue greasepaint for any of the road performances.

Opportunities are still flying at the Blue Man Group, and the founders still handle them the same way they always have. They make decisions unanimously, and they analyze each one the same way. "Okay, that's all good and that's a nice thought," says Wink, before revealing the real issue. "But is it Blue Man?"

Exercises

1. Develop a basic marketing plan for the Blue Man Group. How should the founders use the principles of guerrilla marketing to their company's advantage?
2. Which market research techniques would be most useful to the Blue Man Group? Explain.
3. Define a unique selling proposition (USP) for the Blue Man Group.
4. Use the USP you created in question 3 to devise an advertising strategy for the Blue Man Group.
5. Visit the Blue Man Group's Web site at www.blueman.com. What suggestions can you offer for improving it?

Sources: Adapted from Blue Man Group, www.blueman.com; Rob Walker, "Brand Blue," *FSB*, March 2003, pp. 50–56.

Case 5 The Oldest Brewery in America

A sixth-generation family business founded in 1829, D.G. Yuengling & Son lives up to its billing as "America's Oldest Brewery." German immigrant David Yuengling (pronounced "YING-ling") settled in Pottsville, Pennsylvania, and opened the Eagle Brewery, but two years later, the building was destroyed by fire. Yuengling decided to rebuild the brewery a few blocks away at the corner of Mahantongo Street and 5th Street, where he could use the caves that run underneath Sharp Mountain as storerooms to aid in the fermentation process. With temperatures a constant 50 degrees year-round, the caves were the ideal place to store beer, and in the early days, many of the company's workers would gather there to socialize (and have a hearty stein of lager) before they started their shifts. With many German immigrants, Pennsylvania in the 1800s became a hub of beer-brewing activity, and D.G. Yuengling was one of many breweries serving Schuylkill County with its horse-drawn carts.

The company grew, and in 1873, David's son, Frederick, became a partner in the business, and the business was renamed D.G. Yuengling & Son. After his father retired, Frederick took over the operation and in 1895 added the brewery's first bottling line, which remains in operation today. In 1899, Frederick died suddenly at the age of 51, leaving his son, Frank, who was in his early twenties, to run the family business. Frank learned quickly and guided the company successfully, but in 1919 he confronted the greatest challenge that D.G. Yuengling had ever faced: Prohibition, when the U.S. government made the manufacture and sale of alcoholic beverages illegal. Many breweries failed, but under Frank's leadership, D.G. Yuengling managed to survive by adding a dairy to its operation, selling ice cream, and producing "near beer," a nonalcoholic concoction that the Yuengling family hoped would keep its brand name alive. Fourteen years later, Prohibition ended, and D.G. Yuengling began selling "Winner Beer," a name that jabbed at the temperance movement. Frank even sent a truckload of the beer to President Franklin Roosevelt at the White House!

Frank stayed at the helm of the brewery for 64 years before turning over the family business to his sons, Richard and Dohrman, in 1963. Dorhman died in 1972, and Richard ran the company by himself but did so without much vision for the future. He simply maintained the status quo and never expanded the brewery's operations or even upgraded the plant. Richard's son Dick began working in the brewery as a teenager in 1957, stacking crates and moving kegs. With his perspective as a worker as well as a family member, Dick saw plenty of problems in the operation of the brewery, and he was quite vocal about them to his father. "I'd force my way into other areas of the business," he recalls. "I'd try to implement changes at 18, and, of course, I'd get overruled." Being outvoted did not stop Dick from voicing his ideas for improvement, which began to cause a rift between him and his father Richard. "I wasn't getting along with my Dad," he says, which prompted him to leave the family business for a time to run his own beer distributorship. Of course, he sold Yuengling beer, which meant that he made regular runs to the brewery to fill up his trucks with cases of beer. After Richard was diagnosed with Alzheimer's disease in 1983, Dick took over as manager of the brewery.

Dick's experience and the network of contacts he made as a wholesale distributor proved to be valuable when he assumed leadership of the family business. D.G. Yuengling had always considered its lager to be "the working man's beer" and priced its products in line with that image. Although always popular in Pennsylvania, where customers simply referred to Yuengling as "the local beer," the company's products were virtually unknown and unrecognized outside the region. Because of the company's interesting history and unique local flavor, Yuengling's beer held a certain mystique among customers outside of its primary markets, and Dick began to notice this. Sales began to climb during the 1990s as the microbrewery trend reached a crescendo and customers enjoyed savoring the distinctive beers companies produced in small batches in the tradition of European breweries. To capitalize on the opportunity, Dick boosted production from 200,000 barrels to more than 300,000 barrels and began to move into new markets in the Northeast. Because the company had never embarked on a deliberate growth strategy in its entire history, this was a major strategic shift.

In 1993, Dick began to think more about Yuengling's future. He sat down with his four daughters and asked them point-blank if any of them would be interested in taking over the family business one day. Three daughters said that they were interested in running the family business (the fourth is still considering it), and they began working at the brewery right away. Jennifer, the oldest of the three, is plant coordinator, Debbie works in finance and accounting, and Sheryl helps manage distribution. They are the first women ever to take on managerial roles in the brewery. "We consider it a source of pride," says Sheryl, "that we are women and we're going to be taking this over." That day probably won't be coming in the near future, according to Dick, who acknowledges that none of his daughters is ready to assume leadership of the company. Currently, Jennifer seems to be best qualified, having completed brewing school and also having earned a graduate degree in psychology. She also has exhibited the same take-charge spirit that has enabled her father to make Yuengling the success it is today. Even though she is at work before dawn most days, she says that her father remains her best resource at the company. "He's dedicated his life to the brewing industry, and he's magical with it. The best way to learn is through interaction with him."

By 1996, the growth strategy was working. Demand climbed to 500,000 barrels a year, and the creaky old factory built in 1831 was struggling to churn out enough beer to satisfy customers' tastes. Knowing that the existing plant could not keep up the frenetic pace for much longer, Dick convened a strategy session to weigh the company's options. In a bold move, Dick decided to build a brand new brewery at a cost of $50 million (and to keep the old one) in Pottstown that would increase Yuengling's brewing capacity by 1.2 million barrels—quite a change for a business whose strategy for most of its 167 years of existence seemed to be *avoiding* growth. Then the opportunity to purchase a brewery in Florida that had been owned by the Stroh Brewery came up. Seeing the purchase as the gateway to the market in the Southeast and as an opportunity to add capacity while the new plant was under construction, Yuengling paid just $13 million for the operation. Even after spending an additional $5 million to upgrade the brewery, Yuengling knew he had gotten a real bargain. The plant was up and running within three months.

Although Florida is the nation's third largest consumer of beer, Yuengling struggled to break into the market. Because it had spent very little on marketing in its northeastern market, counting instead on the "buzz" created by satisfied customers, Yuengling's name recognition in Florida was almost nonexistent. "We became a small fish in a big pond," says one member of the company's informal board of advisors.

Although a small company by industry standards (industry giant Anheuser-Busch produces 130 gallons of beer for every one gallon Yuengling produces), Yuengling has become the nation's fifth largest brewer, generating more than $100 million in sales. The family business has 160 employees and three factories in two states. The company's size has created a multitude of managerial issues Yuengling must address. "I'm good at running a small business," he says, "but we're not a small business anymore." Dick keeps the company's organizational structure flat and informal, but management consultants have suggested that the company has grown to the point that it now needs a level of middle managers to operate efficiently. "The tipping point," says consultant Eric Flamholtz, "usually comes at either the $100 million-revenue or 500-employee mark, and failure to address the infrastructure needs can sink a company."

Dick Yuengling agrees. "You've got to get people in the proper place," he says. "Sometimes as an owner it's hard to do it. I at least recognize it." Pushing for a more formalized structure, one advisory board member says, "Dick does recognize this, but I'm not sure he's embraced it."

Family members want to maintain a balance between an organizational structure strong enough to support the company but not so large as to tie it down in a bureaucratic morass and destroy its unique culture. "It's a fine line trying to maintain the laid-back, flexible attitude and still not become corporate America," says Jennifer. "We don't have a board of directors. We don't have managerial meetings every week. There's basically one guy here who controls the whole operation. That's something that, as we do expand, we're going to have to sit down and discuss."

Yuengling recognizes the challenges that growth has brought the family business, but he remains optimistic about the future. "We fought through Prohibition," he says with a smile, "so we'll fight through anything."

Exercises

1. Identify the management succession issues D.G. Yuengling & Son faces.
2. What steps should Dick Yuengling and his family members take to develop a management succession plan?

3. What changes should the company make in its current organizational and management structure?
4. How would you recommend the company market its beer in Florida and other southeastern states?

Sources: Adapted from Rod Kurtz, "America's Oldest Brewery," *Inc.*, July 2004, pp. 64–70; "The Pennsylvania Anomaly: Healthy Old-Line Regional Brewers," *Modern Brewery Age,* December 10, 2001, www.findarticles.com/p/articles/mi_m3469/is_50_52/ai_81393558; "D.G. Yuengling & Son Is Boosting Production," *Modern Brewery Age,* December 3, 2001, www.findarticles.com/p/articles/mi_m3469/is_49_52/ai_81393530; "History," D.G. Yuengling & Son, www.yuengling.com/history2.htm.

▮▮▮ Case 6 The Checker Cab of the Skies?

For many businesspeople, travel by commercial jet has become a nightmare characterized by cramped seating, inordinate delays, security procedures that stop just short of strip searches, and inconvenient flight schedules. Who hasn't dreamed of owning a private jet plane or at least having the ability to travel by private jet for business or pleasure? Unfortunately, travel by private jet is far beyond the budget of all but the most successful small and medium-sized business executives; it remains the realm of rock stars and giant corporate executives. But if left to entrepreneur Vern Raburn, founder of Eclipse Aviation, those dreams might become reality in the near future.

In 2006, Raburn, who was one of Microsoft's first executives and later became CEO of Symantec, plans to offer the Eclipse 500 to the private aviation market. The twin-engine jet plane will seat six and will sell for less than half the price of the current least expensive jets. The targeted price will be about $1 million, a real bargain by today's standards. Raburn is aiming his jet at companies that operate jet taxis on short flights up to about 500 miles and business-people who cannot afford expensive corporate jets but who need the convenience of flexible air travel. "The new generation of very light jets will offer all the speed and safety of airline travel at a cost far below that of today's private jet," says Raburn. "These aircraft are giving rise to a new industry known as 'air taxis.' These services will cost little more than a full-fare coach ticket on many routes and will provide access to thousands of locations not served at all by airlines today." Raburn estimates that the Eclipse 500 will fly at a cost of just 69 cents per mile.

Raburn is targeting a market that has been in a nosedive; just 384 business jets were shipped in 2003, down 44 percent from 2002, according to the General Aviation Manufacturers Association. Eclipse has 2,100 orders for its budget jets, generating $75 million in deposits, and expects to ship 1,500 a year once production begins. Raburn says Eclipse will reach $1 billion in annual revenue faster than any company in history except Amazon.com.

Although the interior of the Eclipse 500 resembles the cabin of a minivan more than it does a high-tech jet, the technical details of the aircraft are impressive. A 41,000-foot ceiling avoids most severe weather, and the 67-knot stall speed makes safe landings easier. Excellent performance at high altitudes and extreme temperatures builds in an extra margin of safety. Features such as fuel tanks that are fully contained in the wings, bird-strike resistant wind-shields, and smart actuators that ensure symmetrical flap deployment are also results of a safety-conscious design. The Eclipse 500 also features the Avio computerized control system, which previously was available only in advanced military and commercial aircraft. The pilot assistance system decreases a pilot's workload and improves safety benefits by integrating most of the aircraft's major systems through its sophisticated computerized system. "I think part of what the Eclipse 500 is today is a direct, absolute reflection of my knowledge and my experience in the computer business," says Raburn. "There are things in this airplane that aren't in any other airplanes because of my [computer industry] experience."

A classic entrepreneur, Raburn has overcome many obstacles to get his company this far. Building a jet aircraft demands a great deal of capital, and Raburn had to raise $325 million in private equity capital to get the company off the ground. Raburn also has had to rescue his company from a near-fatal crash. Originally, he had planned to begin selling the Eclipse 500 in 2004, but the Michigan-based company Eclipse had contracted with to provide the engines for the aircraft failed to deliver as promised. The engines the company supplied failed safety and durability standards in short test flights, forcing Raburn to cancel the contract and to push back the delivery date of the company's first jets by two years. Raburn then approached Pratt & Whitney, a company with a solid reputation in manufacturing engines of all types, including aircraft engines, and the company agreed to design and manufacture an appropriate engine for the Eclipse 500.

Raburn also must contend with competition in the small aircraft market. Although Eclipse Aviation offers the lowest-priced jet in this segment of the market, jets such as the Adam 700, Cessna Citation Mustang, Safire Jet, Diamond D-Jet, and others also are competing for market share.

In his office, Raburn keeps a photo of a friend in an airplane recovering from a dive so low that the airplane actually is kicking up dirt. "He cheated death," says Raburn. "Our experience with the engine was like that."

Eclipse Aviation has pioneered the use of several innovative manufacturing processes that speed production and lower costs. Technologies such as stir-friction welding, an advanced process that replaces more than 60 percent of the rivets on major aircraft assemblies and fuses two metal sheets almost seamlessly, reduce assembly time drastically and produce superior joints on the aluminum aircraft.

Enamored with flying since he earned his pilot's license at age 17, Raburn's goal is to transform the aviation industry. "Developing a new aircraft isn't easy," he says. "It's full of risks." Raburn spotted an opportunity for innovation in an industry he says is consumed by convention. "[The established companies] have the attitude that there's no new market: Everything has been done that can ever be done. They believe that to take risk, do anything new, innovative, or different is just stupid."

The issue facing Eclipse Aviation may lie not in the technical specifications of the aircraft but in the skill of the firm in overcoming a resistance to a new and revolutionary product. Will potential buyers trust a plane that is so significantly less expensive than the current products? Can the company actually sell enough planes to earn a profit?

In the meantime, Vern Raburn couldn't be happier running Eclipse Aviation. "I don't see myself retiring," says the 54-year-old entrepreneur. "This isn't work. I'm having immense fun. Most people would love to combine their occupation with their avocation, and I've done it. I know how lucky I am."

Exercises

1. Does Vern Raburn fit the profile of the typical entrepreneur? Explain.
2. What unique selling proposition should Eclipse Aviation use in its marketing program?
3. What will prove to be the most difficult parts in developing an integrated marketing communication plan for Eclipse Aviation?
4. What types of salespeople must Eclipse Aviation bring on board? Explain.

Sources: Adapted from Del Jones, "Helping Bring Corporate Jets to the Masses," *USA Today,* March 9, 2004; Rich Karlgaard, "The Future of Personal Aviation," *Forbes,* November 20, 2003, www.forbes.com/2003/11/20/cz_rk_1120aviation; Jon Bonne, "Creating a Jet for the Rest of Us," *MSNBC,* May 4, 2004, www.eclipseaviation.com/inthenews/detail_04.htm?content_id=559; Karen Di Piazza, "Eclipse Aviation Founder and CEO Vern Raburn Won't Be Stopped," *Centennial Aviation and Business Journal,* March 30, 2004, www.eclipseaviation.com/inthenews/detail_04.htm?content_id=552; "In the News," Eclipse Aviation, www.eclipseaviation.com/inthenews/index.htm.

▪▮▮ Case 7 Quality Employees Are Hard to Find

T. Lynn Wilson was a man who loved his "roots." Born in Hinton, West Virginia, Lynn left to attend Marshall University in the mid-1990s. Lynn enjoyed the study of engineering because it provided him with a deeper understanding of how things worked. Lynn's mother would often comment to friends about his tendency to take almost anything apart just to see how it worked. By the time Lynn was in high school, he could fix almost any kind of mechanical or electrical appliance and made extra money repairing cars. Even the "old-timers" would comment on his abilities. Some wondered why he was going off to college when he could be earning a good living by starting a repair shop. Lynn did well in college and upon graduation returned to Hinton to work as a field engineer for the local rural electric cooperative. Many faculty members at Marshall University were disappointed in Lynn's career choice. They saw Lynn as one of the school's most technically gifted graduates and had hoped that he would attend graduate school or at least take a challenging position in research at a large corporation.

Lynn, however, was drawn back home. In his spare time, he began to experiment with new technologies and build simple prototypes of machines. The Hinton librarian would order the books and publications he requested because he was her "best customer."

In 2003, Lynn began to focus his spare-time efforts on the integration of microminiature electronics and highly sophisticated mechanical devices that had only recently been discussed in technical publications. Within eight months, Lynn had produced a life-sized doll that employed programmable computer logic to operate the electronic and mechanical components. The doll looked and moved so much like a real baby that people who saw it were amazed. Friends and relatives were astounded when they saw the first doll that Lynn gave his five-year-old niece as a Christmas gift. It could move like a real child, and it could speak; it was absolutely lifelike. By the new year, most of the residents of Hinton had either seen the doll or had heard about it. Most of Lynn's family and friends suggested that he start a business and build these dolls. However, none of them had any idea of the sophisticated components that went into this toy or how it was assembled. Lynn did enjoy the response of his niece and decided to make a few more dolls of different types. Over the winter months he built another dozen toys. In fact, each new doll was more sophisticated than the previous one.

In the spring, Lynn donated six dolls to his church for the annual auction to raise money for the church budget. Hinton was not a rich community. Frank Arnold, a visitor in town, happened to attend the auction and purchased one of the dolls. Impressed, he approached Lynn about his willingness to produce more dolls if Arnold could find a buyer for them. Lynn agreed but did not expect to ever hear from the stranger. Six weeks later, Arnold called and asked Lynn if he would be willing to make and sell 100 dolls at $175 each. Frank had a friend who owned a chain of small, highly exclusive toy stores. Frank asked for $20 per doll as a finder's fee that Lynn agreed to pay when the toy store owner paid him. Frank asked if Lynn would consider making the $20 per doll a standing contract for the next five years, and Lynn agreed.

Lynn was glad to let Frank Arnold find buyers for his dolls. He cared little about selling products; he enjoyed the challenge of creating and designing things. "I figure that the market for these dolls is very limited," Lynn told his father. Still he focused on manufacturing the 100 dolls he had promised Frank. He knew that his cost for producing the first doll was about $80; plus lots of late hours of personal labor. Lynn knew that as he produced more dolls the time to assemble each one would drop and the needed materials could be reduced to $70 per doll. His estimate of the costs to build a doll was as follows:

Parts	$ 70
Labor (3 hours × $10/hours)	$ 30
Frank Arnold's Fee	$ 20
Total Cost	$ 120
Revenues	$ 170
Profit ($170 − $120)	$ 50

Lynn knew that his cost estimates were rough, but he didn't take the needed time to refine them. "I need to produce dolls," he reasoned.

Lynn planned to hire three of his cousins to work with him to produce the dolls. They could work evenings because they, like him, had day jobs. They began almost immediately and enjoyed earning extra money. What Lynn had failed to consider was the skill level of his cousins and the learning curve for this rather complicated and detailed work. One missed connection meant that a doll did not work properly. The three men were doing their best, but it was taking the best of them five hours to complete one doll assembly. Lynn had wanted to do only final inspection and then box and ship the dolls. Instead, he had to do a lot of rework, and the men were always calling on him to show them "one more time" the way to make the more sophisticated connections. Lynn quickly realized that although the three were doing their best to produce quality dolls, they were not the answer to the company's production issues. By the time the last of the 100 dolls was completed, Lynn sat back to recalculate his cost of production:

Parts	$ 72
Labor (6 hours × $10 hours)	$ 60
Frank Arnold's Fee	$ 20
Packaging and Shipping	$ 5
Total Cost	$ 157
Revenue	$ 175
Profit ($175 − $157)	$ 18

After subtracting all of his costs, Lynn had earned just $18 per doll rather than the $50 he was expecting. He decided that $1,800 was not a great deal of money for all those hours of work. The problem, of course, was his faulty assumption about the number of hours each assembly would take. Instead of three hours per doll, it took the men six hours. The men had worked hard every evening; they simply lacked the skills to do this type of work. However, he noticed that toward the end of the production run, they *were* more productive. Each made $2,000 for the work (6 hrs × $10 × 100 dolls divided by 3 men). Lynn was glad that his dolls had helped the men's families, but he had failed to factor in a wage for himself and he earned only $1,800 on the first order of 100 dolls!

The next day, Frank Arnold called Lynn. Frank was really excited, thanked Lynn for the $2,000 check ($20 × 100 dolls), and then told Lynn his good news. "I believe I am going to get an order for 5,000 dolls from a large toy retailer," Frank announced. "When should I promise delivery?" Frank continued, "I also showed the doll to five other potential buyers and each was impressed, but no contract offers have come through yet." Lynn thanked him politely for his efforts and told Frank that he would need to get back to him on the delivery date.

Lynn had a problem. Because several large factories had closed in recent years, Hinton had plenty of people who wanted to work but lacked the skills needed to manufacture the dolls. How long, and at what cost, would it take to produce a skilled workforce in this community? These were his neighbors, friends, and relatives; he did not want to take the work to another location. Lynn also wondered, "What if we only sell five or ten thousand dolls, and the demand is satisfied? What happens to the people whom we hire then?"

The people of Hinton could use the jobs. Demand for his product was real, but as it stood, profits would not really equate with the risks Lynn would be taking if he expanded his new business. Lynn would take the weekend to evaluate this opportunity.

Exercises

1. What advice would you give Lynn?
2. How might Lynn go about training the workers in Hinton?
3. If you had to approve training these people, would you do so based on the uncertainty of continued demand for the product?
4. Can this business succeed with its current pricing and personnel policies? Explain.
5. Advise Lynn on preparing a business plan for his new business. What elements should it contain? How should Lynn use his plan?

Case 8 Triple Point Technology

Triple Point Technology (TPT), a $10 million software company that is the leading provider of commodity trading solutions for energy, power, and financial services companies around the world, signed three contracts with Transammonia, a $1.5 billion petrochemical company, in early 2000. In the contract, Triple Point promised to link all 27 of Transammonia's global offices with a state-of-the-art commodities trading platform called Tempest 2000. Triple Point also agreed to design and develop six interfaces between Tempest and Transammonia's existing PeopleSoft accounting system.

For Transammonia, this project would launch the old economy company into the twenty-first century of Internet-based, real-time, "24/7," free-flowing information. The six interfaces between Tempest and Transammonia's existing accounting software were the crux of the deal. There was no point in having a free flow of information if it didn't freely flow into the general ledger.

In its business proposal to Transammonia from September 1999, Triple Point said no fewer than three times that it had "experience building fully integrated network solutions." The contract went on to say that Triple Point would "custom-build any interfaces required." The parties talked about the interfaces shortly after Triple Point submitted the proposal and again a month later when Triple Point assured Transammonia that it was "very familiar with the nature of these interfaces, having built them for some of our existing clients." Transammonia was convinced.

Triple Point, it turned out, was rather liberal in representing its experience. The company had only managed subcontractors that developed the interfaces, and it had done that just twice. No one at Triple Point had mentioned subcontractors to anyone at Transammonia prior to the contract signing in March, even though Triple Point planned to use subcontractors all along. Shortly after the contract was signed, Triple Point hired PeopleSoft to develop the interfaces.

Several months into the project, Triple Point still hadn't provided PeopleSoft with a project plan and had failed to monitor progress on the interfaces. By the December 31, 2000, deadline, none of the six interfaces had been completed. Early in 2001, Triple Point stopped paying PeopleSoft. A few days later, Transammonia stopped all payments to Triple Point. Finally, Triple Point gave its subcontractor a firm deadline of March 9, 2001, to complete the interfaces.

PeopleSoft failed to meet that deadline and the "extended deadlines" on March 29, April 24, and April 30. Transammonia officially suspended the project on May 2, 2001. Triple Point wrote letters to Transammonia claiming it was the subcontractor's fault for not devoting the talent and resources necessary to the project—despite the fact that Triple Point was so tardy in providing a development plan and wasn't checking up on its subcontractor.

The contract stated that Transammonia would get the six interfaces in 230 days at a cost of $375,000. However, after 400 days and having been billed $635,000, Triple Point had completed only one interface. In July 2001, Transammonia gave Triple Point a 30-day ultimatum: Make everything work, or else. Transammonia also refused to pay Triple Point any more money on the contract, so Triple Point sued the company for breach of contract, demanding $795,000 for services rendered. Transammonia then countersued for breach of the agreements and asking for recission of the contract and damages.

Thus, the legal proceedings began, and they didn't end until September 25, 2003, more than two years after lawyers commenced billing the companies for their legal services and a full four years after Triple Point submitted its sunny business proposal. Judge Herman Cahn, New York Supreme Court justice, handed down a 4,408-word decision, ruling in favor of Transammonia.

Transammonia won the case, entitling it to a refund (a court-appointed special referee is still deciding the amount), but four of Transammonia's five counterclaims were thrown out. The one claim granted called for rescission—or putting things back the way they were before the parties entered their bargain. The final footnote in Cahn's decision noted, "Transammonia asserts that it has paid over $1.5 million to Triple Point under the Agreements, 'and has nothing of value to show for it.' "

Technology litigation—broadly defined as lawsuits filed over software project failures—is not new. In one notable 1979 case, Chatlos Systems, an electronics company, won a case against National Cash Register (NCR) for breach of contract. As in the Triple Point case, NCR promised systems it did not deliver. In another case, service staffers for Wang Laboratories (now Getronics Wang, a branch of Dutch company Getronics) attempted to repair a deployment of computers it had just sold to a sports injury clinic, but it accidentally destroyed five years of clinical and accounting data. Wang was found to be grossly negligent.

Like the *Transammonia v. Triple Point* case, those cases occurred in down economies. Lawyers say litigiousness in the software project world (as in the world at large) is inversely proportional to the economy. The number of software disputes coinciding with the recent recession points to more IT project court battles.

What makes software project disputes different from traditional corporate lawsuits and what shocks lawyers about this particular cottage industry is that so many of the complaints are avoidable! These suits are not about the failure of projects as much as they are about the failure of executives to prepare legally for failed projects. The contracts they create often are incomplete, lack specificity, are poorly thought out, and, as a result, are flawed. One problem is that most business owners and corporate executives do not understand the basics of contract law and do not realize the importance of a carefully crafted contract until a dispute arises.

When they fail to properly prepare contracts—any kind of contracts—business owners can expect to end up in one of three types of outcomes:

Mediation is the least offensive and most likely to save the project.
Arbitration is a more confrontational genre in which witnesses and evidence are used and in which there are "losers" and ostensible "winners."
Litigation is the last resort and the parties involved can expect to hear phrases attached to this kind of action such as "years of depositions and discovery" and "millions of dollars in fees and awards."

"Although anticipating disagreements is one of the primary functions of a contract, the written agreements for software projects don't seem to do that at all," says Hillard Sterling, a partner at Much, Shelist, Freed, Denenberg, Ament & Rubenstein in Chicago. In any other industry, many of these cases never would have made it to court because both sides would have signed a contract that accounted for what lawyers say are easily foreseeable—and avoidable—problems. Perhaps Abraham Lincoln said it best: "[In court], the nominal winner is often the real loser—in fees, expenses, and waste of time."

Exercises

1. What are the basic elements required for a contract such as the one Triple Point Technology and Transammonia created?
2. What advantages do mediation and arbitration offer over litigation? Should the parties in this case have pursued mediation or arbitration before resorting to litigation? If so, at what point should mediation or arbitration have begun? Explain.
3. Would arbitration help to resolve the issues in this situation? If so, at what cost?
4. Why would arbitration or mediation be a lower cost alternative to litigation in situations such as the one described in this case?

Sources: Adapted from Scott Berinato, "You Sue, You Lose: The High Cost of Litigation," *CIO Magazine*, February 1, 2004, www.cio.com/archive/020104/vendor.html; "Case Study: Triple Point Technology, Inc.," *Newsgator,* www.newsgator.com/casestudies/triplepoint.aspx.

Case 9 "Where Do We Stand?"

Rolley Moy was concerned. He had been managing the paint and wallpaper store his father, Sanford, had started in 1977 for the past seven years. Before his father decided to retire because of health problems, he had done everything he could think of to get Rolley ready to take over the family business. Now that his father was gone, Rolley sometimes felt isolated as a business owner. "There have been many times during the day that I wish Dad were around so I could ask his advice," he confessed to his wife. "Some issues are beyond my level of training and experience, and I don't know what to do."

"Here's a perfect example," he said, flipping a stack of financial statements onto the counter. "I've never taken an accounting or finance course in my life! I majored in art in college. How am I supposed to know what all of this means?" The frustration rang in his voice.

Walking into his office, Rolley continued, "Our accountant says that the company's financial performance has been slipping. I know we've experienced pressure from rising costs such as health insurance and increased competition from some of those big home superstores that have opened on the outskirts of town, but our customer base is strong and our sales have been going up every year."

After several years working in sales for a large paint manufacturing company, Sanford Moy formed Henderson Paint & Wallpaper (HP&W) as an S corporation. Having seen many small paint stores fail because of a lack of capital, Sanford wanted to make sure he avoided the same mistake. He invested his own money in the start-up and convinced several wealthy friends and business acquaintances to become investors in the S corporation. Over the years, HP&W has earned a solid reputation among the residents of Henderson, and its location "on the square" in the downtown business district means that the company is centrally located to its primary customer base. The company still operates on the principles on which Sanford Moy founded the business. "Never forget that this is a small business in a small town," he once told Rolley. "That means we take good care of our customers. Whatever it takes to make them happy is what we do. They may be able to find slightly lower prices at some of those mega-stores, but they cannot get the quality, personal service, individual attention, and conveniences there that we offer here. *That's* what keeps them coming back."

As he leaned back in his chair, Rolley smiled as he stared at the unusual (some say "tacky") wallpaper that hung on the office wall in front of his desk. Even though he did not like the pattern at all, he had never changed it because it was a tangible reminder of his father's customer-focused philosophy, something he had learned quite well over the years he had spent working in the business observing his father deal with many customers. He recalls the time that one hard-to-please customer requested a special order of wallpaper. When the wallpaper arrived, and HP&W's crew began installing it, the customer, a prominent socialite from an established family in Henderson, decided she did not like it at all. She demanded that Sanford "send it back and exchange it for a prettier pattern." His father explained that because it was a special order, he could not send it back. The customer was incensed. Rather than risk losing the customer, Sanford smiled and said, "If you aren't happy with this pattern, we'll get the one you want. I think I know what I can do with this paper that you don't like." The next day, he installed the paper himself on the wall opposite his desk. It matched nothing in the office décor, but everyone in the company knew that had nothing to do with why Sanford had hung the paper there. It was a tangible, daily reminder of the importance of keeping the company's customers happy. Sometimes that philosophy cost the company more money, but Rolley simply saw that as a cost of keeping longtime customers happy. Company records show that HP&W has a strong base of repeat customers.

HP&W's customer base is an interesting mix of both residential and commercial clients. Many retail and service companies in Henderson have been doing business with HP&W for years, and Rolley has continued the practice of extending sometimes generous payment terms to them. For many of these customers, HP&W will order paint and wallpaper with only a small deposit required and then will invoice the customer after the items are delivered (or the project is completed if HP&W crews do the painting or wallpaper installation).

"Our insurance company just sent us a notice that the health care premiums we pay are going up by 14 percent next year," Rolley said. "Can you believe it? 14 percent in one year! I'm not sure we can afford to continue to pay 100 percent of our employees' health care costs. We may have to pass some of the costs along to them. They won't like that change, but the accountant says that is eating into our profit margins."

Rolley turned to the financial statements he had picked up. As he flipped through them, he couldn't help but recall his first art appreciation course in college. He felt as though he were looking at the work of an artist he just couldn't understand. The financial statements for HP&W showed the following information:

Henderson Paint & Wallpaper Inc.
Income Statement
December 31, 200X

Revenue

Net Sales		$1,918,543	Credit Sales
			$1,036,013

Cost of Goods Sold

Beginning Inventory	$ 224,397		
+ Purchases	$1,105,794		
Goods Available for Sale	$1,330,191		
− Ending Inventory	$ 326,863		
Total Cost of Goods Sold		$1,003,328	
Gross Profit		$ 915,215	

(Continued)

Operating Expenses

Wages	$247,625	
Salaries	$207,893	
Mortgage Payment	$ 84,876	
Utilities	$ 42,627	
Insurance	$ 53,764	
Advertising	$ 89,525	
Supplies	$ 13,849	
Computer Expense	$ 24,158	
Depreciation Expense	$ 24,500	
Repair Expense	$ 9,107	
Travel	$ 8,543	
Other	$ 1,922	
Total		$808,389

Other Expenses

Interest Expense	$ 21,841	
Bad Debt Expense	$ 4,321	
Total		$ 26,162
Net Income (before taxes)		$ 80,664

Henderson Paint & Wallpaper Inc.
Balance Sheet
December 31, 200X

Assets

Current Assets

Cash	$ 18,105	
Short-Term Investments	$ 8,400	
Accounts Receivable (less allowance for doubtful accounts)	$187,800	
Inventory	$326,863	
Total Current Assets		$ 541,168

Fixed Assets

Plant	$547,621	
Equipment	$124,367	
Other	$ 18,964	
Total Fixed Assets		$ 690,952
Total Assets		$1,232,120

Liabilities and Stockholder's Equity

Current Liabilities

Accounts Payable	$198,257	
Note Payable	$248,500	
Income Taxes Payable	$ 24,378	
Total Current Liabilities		$ 471,135

(Continued)

Long-Term Liabilities

Bond Payable	$ 55,000	
Total Liabilities		$ 526,135
Stockholder's Equity		$ 705,985
Total Liabilities and Stockholder's Equity		$1,232,120

"I wish I knew more about finance," Rolley sighed. "What are these statements trying to tell me? Where do we stand?"

Exercises

1. For Henderson Paint & Wallpaper, calculate the 12 ratios covered in Chapter 8.
2. Compare the ratios you calculated to the following industry standards for companies of similar size drawn from the *RMA Annual Statement Studies:*

Ratio	Industry Median
Current ratio	1.7:1
Quick ratio	.7:1
Debt ratio	.503:1
Debt to net worth ratio	2.7:1
Times interest earned ratio	4.0:1
Average inventory turnover ratio	4.8 times per year
Average collection period	25.0 days
Average payable period	45.1 days
Net sales to total assets ratio	3.4:1
Net sales to working capital ratio	9.7:1
Net profit on sales ratio	3.5%
Net profit to equity ratio	15.4%

3. Which ratios are out of line? Identify them and develop a list of possible causes for each one.
4. Based on your analysis of these ratios, what recommendations can you make to Rolley about improving the financial condition of HW&P? Write a short report telling him "where his company stands."
5. What recommendations can you make to Rolley for controlling the company's health care costs?
6. Describe the advantages and the disadvantages Rolley encountered by choosing an S corporation as the company's form of ownership.

▌▌▌ Case 10 Ready for the Spotlight?

You know your company is a success when its name becomes a verb that people use all the time as in, "I'm googling for that information right now." Google, the Web's most popular search engine, was founded in 1998 by Sergey Brin and Larry Page in their Stanford University dorm room. Their goal was to make the world's information universally acceptable and usable by taking a new approach to online searches, and they've made great progress toward achieving it. Their unique approach simplified the process of searching through the billions of documents posted on the Web and changed forever the way everyone from CEOs to teenagers search for information. Its search engine technology powers major Web sites such as Yahoo!, AOL, and Amazon.

When they launched Google (the name is a takeoff on *googol,* the term for the value 10^{100}, or the numeral 1 followed by 100 zeroes, and reflects the company's mission to organize the vast amounts of information on the Web), Brin and Page created a company that reflected their unconventional style—more "graduate student" than "corporate executive." Software engineers set their own hours, often reporting to work at the "Googleplex" at noon, eating company-sponsored lunches and dinners prepared by a celebrity chef who once cooked for the Grateful Dead, and working into the wee hours of the morning. The dress code leans more toward jeans and T-shirts than business suits and ties. There is an on-site masseuse, staffers' dogs are welcome at the office, and beanbag chairs and lava lamps are prevalent. Twice weekly, staffers take to the company parking lot to have fun in roller-hockey games. (Both Brin and Page are roller-hockey enthusiasts.) Employees are free to spend up to 20 percent of their time working on projects they believe will benefit the company most. More than one thousand people apply for jobs at Google every *day*!

The democratic organizational style the founders created has produced impressive results for the company. Google's sales have grown so fast that the company has joined just a handful of companies such as Apple, Compaq, and Amazon that reached $100 million in sales in record time. In just one 18-month period, the company quadrupled in size, moving to a workforce of more than 1,300 people. Profits also have climbed rapidly, but like many fast-growing businesses, not fast enough to support the company's enormous appetite for capital.

In addition to finding the necessary growth capital, that rapid growth rate brings with it numerous challenges, including maintaining open lines of communication among employees, retaining the unique small company culture that the founders and their employees value so highly, and making sure that everyone on the crew is rowing in the same direction. Competition from strong rivals also is intensifying. Industry giant Microsoft is investing billions of dollars to build its own search engine that it will incorporate into its online services and the latest version of its operating system. Current search engine partner Yahoo! has been quietly acquiring smaller innovative search engine companies, such as Inktomi and Overture Services, and is positioning itself to distance itself from Google to become a direct competitor. Other companies such as AOL, eBay, and Amazon are considering opportunities to enter the search engine market.

One problem any search engine company faces is the lack of customer loyalty. Although many customers return to the same search engine repeatedly out of habit, most will migrate to "the next best thing," whichever search engine that may be. Google faces the challenge of keeping its current base of users in the face of growing competition from capable and deep-pocketed rivals. One way Google can combat the threat of being outdistanced by a better search engine is to invest constantly to improve the quality and the features of its search engine. In the high-tech business, innovation rarely is inexpensive, however, which adds greater urgency to Google's quest for capital.

Brin, originally from Moscow (and who once seriously considered joining the circus as a trapeze artist), and Page, a Michigan native, were doctoral students in computer science at Stanford when they teamed up to write a paper on creating a better search engine. After their project, they realized they were on to something and maxed out their credit cards to develop a prototype search engine based on their model. Rather than judge the quality of a site by the frequency with which a keyword appeared on a site (the typical method at the time), they created an algorithm to judge the relevance of a site using the number of hits it received and how many other pages were linked to it. Their system worked. Type in a word or phrase for a search today, and Google races through more than 4 billion Web pages and returns the most relevant results in less than half a second.

As Google grew from its college dorm roots, Brin and Page attracted capital from private investors, limited partners, and venture capital firms. After the cofounder of Sun Microsystems saw a demonstration of the prototype that Brin and Page had created, he invested $100,000 of his own money on the spot. (The friends had not even formed Google yet; they had to wait two weeks until the company actually existed before they could cash the check that was made out to "Google Inc"!) They convinced family members and friends to invest as well, and managed to raise $1 million in start-up capital. Later, as the company grew, two of Silicon Valley's leading venture capital firms invested $25 million in Google. Yahoo! also invested $10 million. With the help of hired manager and now CEO Eric Scmidt (who is old enough to be the founders' father), Google became one of the few companies of the dot-com era that was actually able to generate revenue from the Internet. The company created a program for advertisers called AdWords that triggers on-screen ads based on the keywords users type in. Advertisers pay Google only when a user actually clicks through to their Web sites, making advertising space on Google available to small companies as well as large businesses. Managers also pursued a globalization strategy, launching versions of the Google site in 10 different languages so users in other parts of the world could conduct Web searches in their native languages. In 2004, Google entered the e-mail business with its free Gmail service that offers users 1,000 megabytes of memory and a powerful built-in search function.

Cofounders Brin and Page believe that innovation has been the key to Google's success and that it will remain the key to the company's fortunes in the future. To keep a steady stream of innovative products and services flowing, they need more capital to ensure their company's continued growth and survival. Brin and Page are considering making an initial public offering (IPO), but they are concerned about the impact that an IPO might have on the unique culture they have created at Google, something they consider crucial to the company's tradition of innovation. They also are troubled at the prospects of losing their "small company charm" and becoming a "big business" characterized by bureaucracy and maintaining the status quo. Is Google ready for life in the spotlight and the changes that an IPO would bring to the company?

Exercises

1. Explain the advantages and disadvantages that Google will encounter if its management team decides to pursue an IPO.
2. Outline the process that Google would go through if the company chooses to make an IPO.
3. Should Google go forward with an IPO? Explain.
4. What changes in its organizational structure and management style would employees at Google be likely to experience if the company makes an IPO?

Sources: Adapted from Fred Vogelstein, "Can Google Grow Up?" *Fortune,* December 8, 2003, pp. 102–112; "Google History," Google Inc., www.google.com/corporatehistory.com; Carol Hymowitz, "Google Founders Face Wealth, Resentment and a Changed Culture," *Wall Street Journal,* May 18, 2004, p. B1; Reed Stevenson, "Google to Disclose Financials," *Reuters,* July 19, 2004, www.reuters.com/newsArticle.jhtml?type=technologyNews&storyID= 5711631&section=news; Rob Speigel, "What's So Special About Google?" *GSA Business,* May 31, 2004, p. 15.

InTote

Contents

EXECUTIVE SUMMARY

InTote is in the business of making unique, high-quality handbags at an affordable price. With the focus on remaining small to balance managing a small business while still in college, InTote has an advantage of being in constant contact with its target market of female college students. Where large companies neglect advertising their products to female college students, InTote can gain a competitive edge by offering one-of-a-kind handbags at a little over half the cost.

Using a mix of cost leadership and focus strategies gives InTote the chance to fill a niche in the market that large companies have overlooked. The ability to have direct contact with customers, who offer their opinions and feedback, gives InTote the benefit of improving its business every day. By understanding that its target market is always looking for unique accessories to add to their wardrobes, InTote offers females the option of creating a handbag that matches their style and personality.

By keeping its overhead costs to a minimum and having to spend little on advertising, InTote is able to keep most of its initial revenue. Having no employees and almost no utility, advertising, building, or equipment costs allows InTote to keep its profit margin high. As the company expands, the amount of money spent on advertising and employees will increase.

Once InTote is able to develop a Web site, its customer base will expand dramatically and InTote will be able to reach customers outside the local area. Offering 24-hour access to InTote will increase sales steadily.

To survive in an industry that is already saturated with many handbag businesses, InTote has the challenge of differentiating its product against competitors. This means focusing on outstanding customer service with high-quality products that lead to a customer's repeat business with InTote.

VISION STATEMENT

We wish to build our company around four values: remaining a small, easily mobile business; focusing on education for professional and artistic improvement; remembering that the customer comes first; and giving back to our community.

MISSION STATEMENT

We believe in the power of remaining small. Remaining small involves a desire to

1. remain focused on our unique customers, and

2. not to measure success as growing upward with market control but as growing outward by exposing more customers to our handbags. Only because of increased demand from our customers will we strive to increase the size of our operations.

We see the future in terms of growing through education. We desire to educate ourselves in the manufacturing of our bags and in business operations—all to create more value for our customers.

We always want to remember our customers, their changing desires, and their wants. For this reason, we want to develop high-quality bags at a fair price that are viewed more as an artful expression than an ordinary accessory.

We desire to build a business that is capable of giving back to our community—specifically to our college and our department.

> InTote strives to develop high-quality handbags that our customers see as an artful expression rather than an ordinary accessory.

BUSINESS AND INDUSTRY PROFILE

Stage of Growth

InTote is in its infancy. Although Ms. Ruth Ingram has been making and distributing bags as a hobby for her friends, she has never tried to start her own manufacturing/retailing business.

Goals

The **ultimate goal** of InTote is to provide a learning atmosphere for its cofounders to gain real-world practice in the operation of a business. We believe that a small-scale business, such as InTote, is the perfect way to apply the concepts and principles that we are currently learning at Presbyterian College.

This one fundamental goal is accompanied by **five** secondary goals.

➤ **First**, InTote will achieve its mission of remaining small by focusing on differently patterned and sized bags that are to be limited in quantities produced. This goal will ensure the attraction and retention of the unique customers whom we seek to gain. Customers will also have the option of customizing their own bags by meeting with the designer to obtain a one-of-a-kind handbag.

➤ **Second**, InTote must set prices efficiently, so that it may price its bags at a minimum of 100 percent over the cost of production. It is important to note that this price-setting goal is based on materials and overhead, not direct or indirect labor. InTote's owner will receive compensation from the increase over cost of production mentioned earlier.

➤ **Third**, InTote's cofounders will hold each other accountable for attending craft/trade shows (and other product-improvement programs) and continuing their college educations to improve the quality and efficiency of InTote's products and services.

➤ **Fourth**, InTote must seek as close to 100 percent customer satisfaction as possible. However, because one goal of this business is to educate ourselves in the operation of a business, nonprofitable customers will not be allowed to hamper our development.

➤ **Fifth**, within two years of start-up, InTote's cofounders must develop a system of *thanks*. This system will be twofold and will begin the process of increased investment in capital resources (*thanks* to customers) and a system of donation back to Presbyterian College (*thanks* for the knowledge and experience that it has provided us).

Objectives

To effectively apply these goals, InTote must construct an efficient framework of strategic objectives.

The first and most vital objective that we will establish is to develop a "meeting" system that requires the cofounders—from week 1—to sit down weekly and actively analyze the path that InTote is taking. Based on what we gain from these meetings, we will then begin the process of developing realistic and controllable objectives.

InTote will have the following as its initial operating **objectives** (which may be eliminated or altered at any time):

➤ Constant contact must be maintained with our customers via e-mail, so that they may have an active role in the construction, style, and size of their bags. This step is vital, because the bags must say something about those who carry them and also be a useful tool in their daily lives.

➤ InTote must keep accurate customer profiles, so that we may build customer relationships that are impossible for our competitors to duplicate.

➤ InTote must establish beginning production goals at a minimum of five bags per week.

➤ Product testing must ensure that the return of bags is not an issue. This is important for two reasons: (1) returns add costs that would destroy our ability to earn a profit, and (2) it pleases the customer to have a quality bag.

➤ InTote's cofounders must establish a networking system of friends and family that will aid the company in its word-of-mouth advertising campaign at college campuses in the surrounding area. This marketing method will be one of our most powerful tools in attracting new customers.

➤ InTote will rely heavily on the budgeted cost-of-production reports created by Mr. Cooper Strickland before production of a new line is begun. This will ensure that InTote meets its profitability goal stated previously.

INDUSTRY ANALYSIS

One important quality to note about the handbag industry is that for all practical purposes it is dependent upon the apparel industry. This dependence on the apparel industry is based on the fact that women generally like to have handbags that complement their outfits, so it makes sense that as apparel sales go up handbag sales will go up as well (likewise, if apparel sales go down, handbag sales also go down). Looking at the apparel sales figures for 2001 and 2002 shows that sales have remained relatively flat at approximately $166 billion.[1] However, New York retail consultant Walter Loeb predicts that retail sales will increase 8 percent in 2003.[2] The reason that was attributed to the "lackluster sales"[3] in 2001 and 2002 was a lack of innovation in the fashion industry. Herein lies the key to success for any fashion or handbag business— innovation that mimics the changes of individuals' fashion desires. One fashion analyst remarked about the handbag industry that "unique creations stand out from the crowd— and smaller designers seeking to retain their hold in this highly competitive industry know [that] their products must also be distinctive."[4]

Ultimately, what this translates into is an amazing opportunity for new businesses to enter the handbag industry.

According to *Entrepreneur* magazine, "Launching a handbag venture can be hard to handle, but it's probably easier today than it's ever been before [because] giants like Coach, Liz Claiborne and Ralph Lauren can't possibly meet every market demand, leaving the door wide open for self-starters."[5] Current "estimates indicate that the growth of handbag sales nationwide now exceeds 7 percent a year—a rate higher than any other category in the accessories business."[6] We believe that this means InTote is attempting to fill a niche in an industry that has plenty of room to grow. After all, Americans spend more than $4.4 billion annually on bags.[7] Based on this, we will focus on two important facts that should give us a distinct ability to capitalize on these sales. First, most businesses turn out new styles only six times a year, and at InTote we will turn out new styles bimonthly—if not more frequently.[8] Second, research and sales have shown that the most recent style trends in handbags have favored Kelly, evening, casual, shoulder, and tote bags—the latter style being the exact bag that InTote currently produces.[9]

Although these figures do not encompass a complete outlook on the handbag industry, we believe that they are promising figures to encourage the creation of a small business such as InTote, especially considering the target customer to whom we will direct our marketing efforts.

However, we also recognize that if our business grows substantially, we may purchase information from organizations that deal specifically in gathering market research on the handbag industry for more in-depth data. Currently Infomat.com (Fashion Industry Information Services and Search Engine) provides some of the most comprehensive industry research reports available: (1) *Women's Handbag Retail Buyers* at a base price of $285 and (2) *Infomat Guide: The Handbag Market from A to Z* at a price of $165.[10] Although better guides may be available by the time that this information will be useful to InTote, Infomat should provide a good starting point for further research.

POPULAR TYPES OF BAG DESIGNS

Kelly Bag—a bag with a trapezoid shape in many sizes, with a short flap and brass fastener.
Evening Bag—a small bag for evening necessities, basic or glamorous.
Casual Bag—designed for heavy use and should be a comfortable expression of yourself.
Shoulder Bag—a design that is cut in a half-moon shape to match the contour of your shoulder.
Tote Bag—a workhorse bag in almost any material.

At InTote we also value the position of the economy as a whole. Currently, the *Beige Book* reports that in the Richmond District of the Federal Reserve manufacturing had been delivered a hard blow. It states that continued contraction in the manufacturing sector is still being felt. This conclusion is based on the fact that reported "shipments, new orders, capacity utilization and employment" all fell in the month of September. The *Beige Book* also noted that "contracts in [...] textiles and apparel industries noted particularly sharp declines in shipments [...], several textile and apparel manufacturers told us that foreign manufacturers continued to gain market share to the detriment of U.S. textile and apparel companies." The only good news that InTote could look to is found in the Atlanta District, which reported that for consumer spending "contacts noted that apparel sales improved in September [...] exceed[ing] retailer's expectations."[11] Although the outlook of these data is rather bleak, we anticipate that a nationwide economic upturn is just around the corner.

However, regardless of whether the economy is poised for a turnaround or not, we must rely most on data that are specific to our industry.

In the end, we find our greatest opportunity in the fact that "there aren't many fashion luxuries left [and] handbags remain one of the most accessible—and affordable—items in a woman's luxury wardrobe."[12] If we always focus on what this statement truly means—innovation and affordability are the two most important factors in the handbag industry—then InTote should always have an opportunity in this competitive market.

BUSINESS STRATEGY

Competitive Strategy

InTote employs a mixed competitive strategy that enables the business to blend elements of a **cost leadership** and **focus** strategy. For the former, we target customers who seek InTote out because of the competitive price that they are paying compared to other handbags. For the latter, we target customers who want to play an active role in the design and production of their bags. Although this will be a challenging strategy to follow, we believe that it is the only way to break into this heavily saturated market. From our research with female college students at Presbyterian College, we know that students are always looking for unique handbags that are different from what other females are carrying, and the possibility of having a one-of-a-kind handbag gives us a competitive advantage.

InTote's Image

We believe that InTote's products will be viewed as unique, artistic, practical, of good quality, and affordable. Although many handbag businesses attempt to achieve this, we hope that through our close connection with the customer we will be able to accomplish this goal more successfully. It is this connection with our customers and desire to educate ourselves further in production and management techniques that we view as InTote's major competitive advantage. Making our customers one of our top priorities by listening to their opinions and ideas gives us a way to improve our handbags and reputation, while also delivering exactly what the customer expects.

SWOT Analysis

Strengths:

➤ A connection with our target customers—female college students—that comes from being in college ourselves.

➤ A good foundation of business knowledge that we have built while attending Presbyterian College for the past three years.

➤ The fact that InTote's cofounders share different interests and skills—one having the ability to make creative bags and market them, and the other overseeing controls, pricing, and accounting.

➤ A group of friends and supporters who are willing to sacrifice their own time helping with the success of InTote, specifically with our marketing campaign.

➤ System of production and retailing that does not require a tremendous amount of skill or prior training to implement.

➤ Our ability to avoid costly overhead expenses.

Weaknesses:

➤ A limited amount of resources that makes time-consuming, detailed planning a must for survival.

➤ InTote's cofounders lack large amounts of time and capital to expand the business quickly.

➤ InTote's cofounders lack any real prior business operation experience.

Opportunities:

➤ The lack of a business that is currently filling the niche that we want to create because of the general lack of knowledge most businesses have about our target market.

➤ The flexibility and size of the e-commerce market.

➤ The low-cost methods that can be used to market to college students effectively.

➤ The high prices of our competitors.

Threats:

➤ The sheer number of businesses on the Internet that sell handbags and, subsequently, the number of customers who are not looking for a unique product.

➤ The brand loyalty and distribution channels that established businesses such as Vera Bradley have built.

➤ Textile factories in our area are being injured by foreign competition, and without easy access to their discounted bolt remnants, our ability to set a competitive price is seriously weakened.

COMPANY PRODUCTS AND SERVICES

Purpose of Our Bags

Before we are able to look at our finished product, it is important to step back and analyze the purpose of a bag. This purpose is twofold: On one hand, it needs to be **functional,** and on the other, it must be a **form of expression**.

Functional Value:

➤ A bag should vary in size to carry what is needed.

➤ It should offer some degree of protection for that which is being carried.

➤ It should be easy to care for.

➤ It should be easily stored.

➤ Its dimensional proportions should not burden the user.

➤ It should have the ability to carry a heavy load while still maintaining its integrity and shape.

➤ It should be like everyone's favorite "old t-shirt," so that it ages well and retains memories.

Expressional Value:

➤ A bag should coordinate with a wide range of outfits.

➤ It should say something meaningful about the person who carries it.

➤ It should attract more focus and complements than any other item of apparel or accessory.

Use of InTote's Bags

Purchasers of InTote bags should not be afraid of using our product in any kind of circumstance. Once the right bag has been matched to a customer, she should be able to take it to work, to school, on a date, to piano lessons, to the beach, with her baby, or anywhere else that the owner wants to go. InTote dedicates itself to this idea, because we do not want to see our bags sitting on shelves in a closet but out being used. With the low price, the customer has the opportunity to buy a bag to match every outfit. The limited number of students at Presbyterian College who have purchased one of InTote's bags embrace this idea because you can see them taking their books to class, their towels to the pool, their instruments to practice, and their clothes for a weekend trip.

Construction and Design

In general there are two types of bags: padded and unpadded. They come in all sizes, but they share a common shape. Generally they are constructed out of two contrasting fabrics, one for the external portion of the bag and the other for the internal portion. They all have a handle that is made from the same external fabric, which is secured on the interior of the bag. All in all, the bag is simplistic in such a way that its functional usage is not sacrificed. InTote's bags focus on the sense of touch—if the fabric is not soft and comfortable on the shoulder, then it has failed in one of its major goals.

Ultimately, the bag's true expression comes from the choice of fabrics used in its construction. As a designer, Ms. Ingram is always on the lookout for colorful fabrics to create the overall uniqueness of a bag.

Production Process

The steps required to make a bag from start to finish average around 45 minutes. However, this labor requirement does go down when larger batches are made and two individuals are working. The material costs that are associated with construction of a bag are for two contrasting remnants of bolt fabric, batting (optional), thread, straight pins, and safety pins. The cost of these items varies, but fabric generally costs $1 to $6 per yard (it takes half a yard to make a bag 13 by 13 inches), $1 for the batting (in this size bag), and less than $1 for the other incidental materials. Based on past production, a typical bag will cost less than $5.00 to make.

Currently, we are able to purchase these materials from most Wal-Marts, Joann's Fabrics and Crafts (Columbia, SC), and Mary Jo's Fabrics (Gastonia, NC). All of these locations are within two hours' driving time of our location in Clinton, South Carolina.

Customer Benefits and Uniqueness

The benefits a customer of InTote receives are very simple but effective. Ultimately, an individual can buy a bag from anywhere to serve the general purpose of a handbag. However, the benefits that we provide to our customers come via some services that we have seen no other business claim—an unparalleled commitment to uniqueness, careful attention to detail, and extraordinary service. The bottom line is that we want customers to get exactly what they desire, whether it is a specific color, size, or durability—so communication between InTote and its customers is crucial. We intend to be in constant contact with our customers during the manufacturing process, so that they get a bag that not only is made *for* them but also that is made *with* them.

> **Customers get a bag that is not only made *for* them but also that is made *with* them.**

Also, just as any work of art is not copied over and over again, resulting in its diminished value, we do not want our bags to be something that everyone has a rubber-stamped copy of. For this reason, InTote will limit its production so that customers may rest assured that what they carry is truly a unique expression of themselves. Although we are the first to admit that we have not made "the bag to end all bags," we do provide customers with a benefit that they may not get from another company. Within this idea is the key to success for InTote, because the bags that our customers purchase should be the bags that they would make for themselves if they had the skill, knowledge, or time to do so.

Ultimately we want every customer to feel like beta-user Susan Fox, a junior at Presbyterian College, who stated, "Ruth takes her time when making these bags, and it shows in the workmanship and quality."

Product Protection

As a result of being small and not having the resources needed to fully protect InTote's products with the appropriate trademarks or copyrights at this time, InTote will use a system that is often employed by artists. This process includes (1) taking a picture of a new product or design, (2) sealing it in an envelope, and (3) mailing it back to our address.

Searching for the business name "InTote" online, we discovered that it was not taken as a Web site address or as a business name. For example, when our Web page is launched, we can purchase the rights to have the address www.intote.com.

Satisfaction

At InTote, we dedicate ourselves to the quality of our product, but we also know that with the creation of any new business there are going to be problems that arise with quality. That is why we are thankful that we have had the ability to test a sample batch of our product. Based on our current information, no defects have arisen with the bags that have been used by our beta-users. However, we realistically understand that they have not been put through the extremes that they will face when they are sold. For this reason, we are going to adopt a policy of 100 percent customer satisfaction, which will be judged and applied on an individual basis. It is important to note that we do not use the words *warranty* or *guarantee*, but **satisfaction**. This policy is one of the major benefits that we see in having a small employee base because we may have the option of repairing a minor flaw or replacing the product if there is a major defect. Whatever the case may be, the customer may rest assured that we will take the right action. We also believe that through this one-on-one problem-solving method, we will earn the respect and loyalty from our customers that come with satisfying their complaints.

Future of Products

We would like to see InTote expand into other apparel and accessories—like skirts, knitted scarves, and toboggans.

However, even in these new product lines we desire to carry the same commitment to uniqueness and quality that we do with our bags.

Nevertheless, InTote must always focus the majority of its resources on bags. For this reason, we will try to expand this product line by gaining the knowledge and financial resources needed to create new bag shapes, quality increasing features (strength, thickness, etc.), and fabric pattern designs of our own. Some fabric designs that we would like to find are local college fabrics (South Carolina, Clemson, etc.) and South Carolina state flag fabric—which we believe could easily be our two most successful lines. InTote will also provide a system for its customers to suggest ideas because the lack of employee base limits our

creativity, but this can be recaptured through our customers. In fact this is currently being done because we asked our initial batch of beta-users about improvements for future lines. Some of the ideas mentioned were thicker linings to make bags sturdier, an inside pocket for keys, diaper bags, ribbon straps, and reversible bags (a feature that is now being produced). We believe that this give-and-take between InTote and our customers is yet another way that we can gain loyalty from our market, while at the same time communicating the deep respect we have for customers who seek out a product that is one of a kind. Customer feedback is a vital part of InTote's continued growth and success.

MARKETING STRATEGY

The market that InTote is designed to reach is the female college student population of South Carolina, specifically those who are members of Greek organizations. In this geographic area alone there are 18 major colleges and universities that we view as potential markets with approximately 42,855 female undergraduate students.[13] During our initial research, we looked for Greek populations and found that at the University of South Carolina, 17 percent of the female undergraduate population were members of sororities, amounting to approximately 1,523 students.[14]

Likewise at Presbyterian College, we found that 46 percent of female students were members of sororities, amounting to approximately 287 students.[15]

We are confident that this test sample proves that for the amount of sales that we desire to produce there is a sufficient market to support our sales estimates. We are further encouraged by a comment of one of our beta-users, Rebecca Carpenter, who when asked if people ever commented on her bag stated, "All the time, especially at ZTA meetings [...] everyone is always dying to know where I bought it."

Nationwide College Population

Demographics and Statistics

What follows next are some of the most important statistics concerning the U.S. college student population in regard to size, location, employment, and spending that will be important to InTote's first stage of non-Internet-based selling:

➤ There are approximately 15.6 million college students in the United States alone, with women comprising 59 percent of total college graduates.[16]

➤ Young adults ages 18–24 comprise 24 percent of the nation's population, with over one-third of these being college students.[17]

➤ The average age of a full-time student is 20.5 years, with 26 percent being 22 years old or older.[18]

➤ College students are highly transient, changing addresses on average 2.3 times annually.[19]

➤ Of the 91 percent of college students who live away from home, 50 percent live on-campus and 41 percent live off-campus.[20]

➤ Of the 66 percent of students who work, 8 percent work full-time and 58 percent work part-time.[21]

➤ Furthermore, 62 percent work during the school year, and 87 percent work during the summer.[22]

➤ The average college student worker has $4,740 in annual personal earnings.[23]

➤ On average the total family income of a college student is $75,000, with 20 percent earning more than $100,000 annually.[24]

➤ In addition, 58 percent of the students get money from home, averaging $261 monthly.[25]

Female Undergraduate Enrollment in Target Market

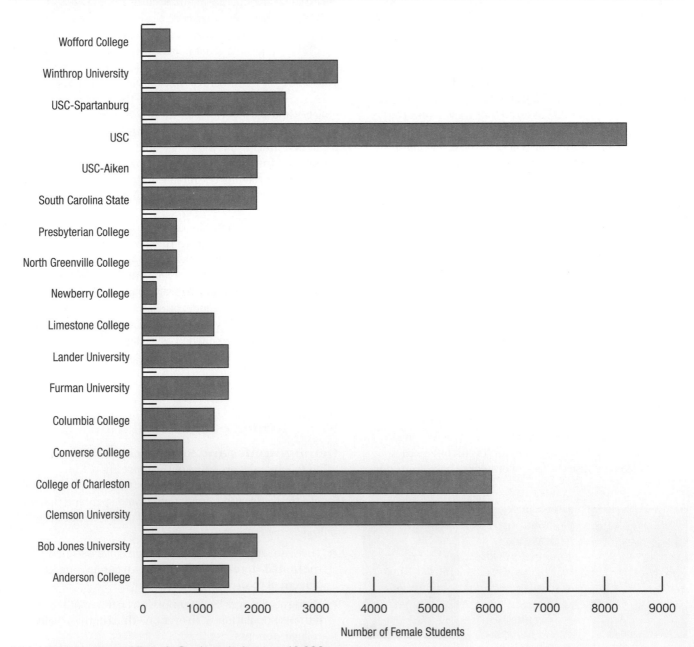

Number of Female Students

Note: Total Number of Female Students Is Approx. 43,000

➤ The annual buying power of undergraduate students is estimated to be $70 billion.[26]

➤ The average monthly buying power of an undergraduate student is estimated to be $400.[27]

➤ The annual discretionary item spending (basically items they want but do not need) of undergraduate students is approximately $19 billion.[28]

➤ Of this amount, it is estimated that undergraduate students have average monthly discretionary spending of anywhere from $133 to $287.[29]

➤ Students spend approximately $6,760 a year.[30]

These numbers show the impressive discretionary income that college students possess; in fact, college students' discretionary spending budgets are among the largest of any demographic group in the United States.[31] However, because students move so frequently, it is difficult for retailers to maintain consistent selling patterns. In the end, handbags are good items to sell because they are not items that students need but rather want, and they have the money to spend on them. Nevertheless, it is crucial to keep up-to-date records about customers' current addresses, because otherwise they may quickly slip away.

Buying Habits and Interests

College students represent an amazing opportunity for new businesses to market to, because rarely do students have firm brand loyalties.[32] For most, going to college for the first time is the biggest transition in their lives. For the first time they are on their own to pick laundry detergent, bread, and so on, and they do not remember the brands that their parents bought—so they pick their own. What is ironic about this buying pattern is that it usually rubs off onto all purchasing decisions of college students—the bottom line is that college students like trying new products. This fact provides InTote with an excellent opportunity to cash in on students' willingness to experiment. Female college students are always on the lookout for the latest products.

For the vast majority of the college population, their interests focus on music, television, movies, health-related topics, restaurants, travel, sports, and the Internet.[33] This is reflected in what generally consumes their spending: food, 32 percent; debt, 18 percent; automobile, 13 percent; clothing, 8 percent; telephone, 6 percent; and other, 23 percent.[34] Notice that 8 percent of student spending goes for clothing. If you take this percentage and apply it to the annual student spending statistic given previously, then the average student spends approximately $541 a year on clothing. If you apply this figure even further to InTote's average selling price of $15, then you find that this number will only consume a small percentage of a student's annual clothing expense. We look at this as an important percentage because buying an InTote bag is such a small monetary decision that we believe we can easily sway

college students' "nonexistent" brand loyalties toward our new product.

Student Buying Expectations and the Internet

In the course of the market research that we conducted, we have determined that students value convenience and low price.[35] This translates into a need for businesses that serve college students to have longer operating hours and the lowest prices. What these two values have done is encourage the growth of student purchases on the Internet. Internet storefronts provide students with 24-hour shopping and the ability to search for the lowest prices. That is why we have chosen to incorporate an Internet selling operation into InTote's retail plan to complement our non-Internet sales. The numbers prove that any business that desires to break into the college market is going to have to have a presence on the Web:

➤ Student shoppers reported going off-campus or online to find the most competitive pricing.[36]

➤ College students represent approximately 13 percent of all online users.[37]

➤ The average college student spends 22 hours a week online.[38]

➤ College students represent the most wired demographic, spending an average of 3 hours online per day.[39]

➤ Eighty percent of all students access the Internet at least once a day.[40]

➤ Student Internet spending amounted to $1.4 billion in 2001, a $300 million increase from 2000.[41]

➤ Nine out of ten students spend an average of $330 annually on online purchases.[42]

➤ Thirty-three percent of students say they have purchased something directly due to seeing an online ad.[43]

Ultimately, we see the Internet as a great equalizer for InTote because students like shopping on the Internet, and it provides a lower-cost retail option for our business.

Advertising

During the course of trying to discover which type of advertising reaches the college market, we also discovered why other businesses do not try to profit from such an obviously lucrative demographic group. First, the traditional middle-aged marketer remembers college very differently from the experience of most of today's college students. Prior to the late 1980s and 1990s, colleges were inhabited by students living off of sandwiches and soup. That is not the case today, but marketers still do not view colleges as potential profit areas. That is why "advertisers [only] spend about $100 million a year on campuses, [which is] a tiny fraction of the $15 billion directed at the overall young-adult market."[44] Second, there is a perception that direct marketing does not work on college-age students.[45] However, this is completely false. Direct marketing does work—it just has to be adjusted to the lifestyles of college students and their key transitional periods (remembering that the beginning of a new academic year is a crucial marketing opportunity).

Based on this information, InTote must use *word-of-mouth marketing*, which is a mix of buzz marketing and *viral marketing.* Basically, word-of-mouth marketing requires a business to remember that a student's network of friends and their influence on each other is the best way to influence sales.[46]

For example, if a small group of students discovers a product, such as mesh-backed hats, and then begins to use the product and talk about it, ultimately their friends are much more likely to go out and buy the product and continue the cycle. Word-of-mouth marketing is the number-one way that students learn about new products. Rounding out the top five are television advertising, in-store samples, radio advertising, and samples in the mail.[47]

To make this word-of-mouth marketing strategy successful, InTote must learn how to effectively use *buzz* and viral marketing. Buzz marketing is doing something so innovative that it is likely to be talked about.

Similarly, viral marketing (an approach that works best on the Internet) is based on a benefit within the product that, because of its very nature, requires it to be transmitted from one individual to another.

For InTote this translates into getting the product out and seen by target customers, so that it can be talked about.

To begin this process we have chosen three low-cost advertising methods—postering, business cards, and e-mail.[48] The process of postering (buzz marketing) will include the following steps:

1. Ms. Ruth Ingram will design posters and business cards. Posters will sometimes incorporate the feathering feature at the bottom of the poster that allows around 10 to 15 contact information tabs to be torn away.

2. We will deliver posters and business cards to friends and family who attend schools in our target market to be distributed in high traffic areas around their respective campuses (e.g., sports facilities, bulletin boards, dining halls, female dorms, student centers, etc.).

3. Based on response rate, we will ask members of our advertising team to check the condition of our posters periodically (generally they should last approximately one week).

Price Comparison: InTote Versus Vera Bradley

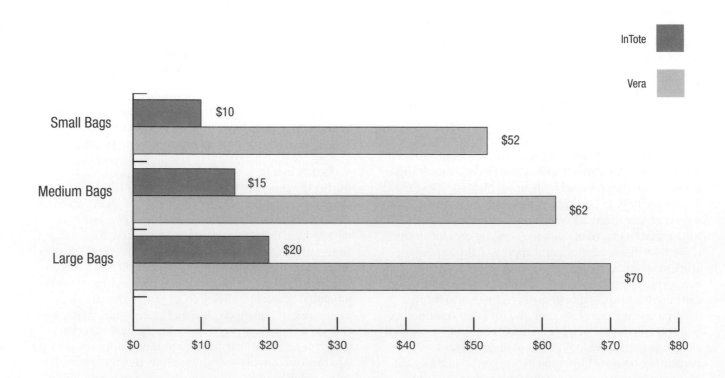

The second method, e-mailing (viral marketing), will be much easier to implement because it will require InTote to design an e-mail, send it to a pool of addressees, and ask them to forward it to their friends. In the end, we believe this will be an effective way to begin our word-of-mouth marketing approach outside of Presbyterian College.

To go along with the use of e-mail, our beta-users are also an excellent source of advertisement. The simple act of carrying an InTote bag is in essence "free advertising." Specific beta-users will be given business cards to pass out when other students ask, "Where did you get your bag?" All the beta-user has to do is hand the interested student a business card and offer a testimonial about the level of service they received.

Pricing and Collections

InTote's target customers, female college students, are extremely sensitive to pricing because they have the time and resources to find the best values. This gives InTote a distinct advantage because the costs of production for our product allow us to price our product at a very reasonable rate.

Consequently, pricing of our products will be based on InTote's previously stated goals. We have estimated that the general price range for our product will be $10 to $25 based on several factors including size, fabric, and features (shipping will be applied at a flat rate of $5 for one item and $1 for every additional item).

We desire to have the image of providing a quality product at an affordable price. We believe that this puts us in a strong position to compete with Vera Bradley, Tea Bags, and ItsMargery all of which are currently charging from $45 up to $300 for comparably sized bags.

Another benefit of the selection of our target customers is the way in which they pay for their purchases. Although the media consistently reports that students are addicted to credit, the truth of the matter is that students prefer cash to credit.

It is estimated that college students pay for 29 percent of their purchases with cash, 24 percent with checks, 30 percent with bank debit cards, and just 17 percent with credit cards.[49] This makes it feasible for InTote to avoid the expense of credit card transfers initially, because our target customers already prefer cash and debit cards for payment.

LOCATIONS AND LAYOUT

 Resulting from InTote's dual purpose of manufacturing and selling its own products, the company has a rather unique location and layout strategy. This dual purpose is further complicated by the fact that we have nominal starting capital, and we desire for InTote to remain small. This has led us to choose a low-budget method of production and retailing, the former being accomplished in our dorm rooms and homes, and the latter being accomplished through e-commerce. Our e-commerce strategy is further broken down into three phases that will be described later.

Manufacturing Location

One of the major benefits of our desire to stay small is the flexibility that it provides InTote in setting up manufacturing facilities.

1. For the amount of production equipment required for operation we need very little space.

2. InTote's facility needs only enough space to lay out, cut, and assemble fabric pieces into our final product. To prepare and finish the work we need a location to wash, dry, and iron the fabric and bags.

3. We will be maintaining low inventories and cycling them quickly—resulting from making only a few of each pattern to maintain uniqueness—so that storage is not a major concern.

Already, based on the production of a few initial batches, which will mimic our future production objectives, we have determined that a complete manufacturing operation may be run out of a Presbyterian College dorm room. This lack of demand for manufacturing space translates into an extraordinary ability to move our manufacturing operation at the beginning and end of semesters, from home (Cheraw, SC) to college (Clinton, SC) and vice versa.

Also, InTote's flexibility in location provides us with an indirect benefit—avoidance of certain manufacturing overhead costs. At home and at college, our limited use of electricity, water, heat/cooling, and Internet access will be covered by our parents in the form of their payment of room expenses at college and their payment of utility bills at home. Although it is important to note that if phone communication becomes a necessity that exceeds our cell phones' minute plans, then we intend to reimburse our parents for this expense. However, we hope to communicate primarily via e-mail.

If we make the decision to one day expand our operation because of demand or pressure for more inventory space, we will seek out the lowest-cost alternative. We see this as being able to take shape in one of two forms: (1) negotiate with our parents for more space, which we will rent, or (2) seek an outside facility that fits our minimum requirements—hopefully something as basic as a storage unit. However, even if the latter is required, remaining in our same general geographic area is a must. Our desire to stay in upstate South Carolina results from personal preference, the number of high-quality textile providers that are so near at hand, and the location of our current target market.

Retail Location

Non-Internet Format

Retailing of our product is going to be extremely complicated initially because of the nature of our word-of-mouth marketing strategy. Our number-one priority is that InTote must get its products out and be seen. For this reason, prior to the three Internet phases discussed later, we will try to sell our product in any way possible. This includes using our advertising campaign to sell by e-mail, over the phone, and through the mail to our target customers as long as payment is made in cash. Another way in which we hope to sell our product is directly to unique stores that may have an interest in InTote's bags. Already one store, The Spice of Life, located in Asheville, North Carolina's Grove Arcade, has approached us with an interest in buying one of InTote's early bags that featured a chili pepper design (The Spice of Life sells specialty spices).

We would also like to sell InTote's products at various festivals in North Carolina and South Carolina, because this would get our product before a large number of customers without requiring a large time investment.

In Ms. Ingram's hometown, the Cheraw Spring Festival takes place each year in April. InTote's bags will be sold during this festival to see how customers respond and how successful the product can be with this demographic. A list of local festivals and craft shows can be obtained through the Internet and also by contacting the town hall or chamber of commerce of the particular town or city of interest.

In January, the Greek Shop of Clinton, South Carolina, purchased an initial batch of 36 bags from InTote. The Greek Shop's owner, Mrs. Jennifer Ainsworth, was impressed with the quality and style of InTote's product. Currently the Greek Shop sells a large variety of handbags and purses ranging from $15 to $50. Mrs. Ainsworth bought InTote's bags at a $7 base price and will be selling them for $17 to $20 depending on the size of the bag and if the customer chooses to have the handbag monogrammed.

Plans were also discussed to purchase more handbags from InTote. The Greek Shop manufactures letter shirts for sororities and, with InTote's assistance, Mrs. Ainsworth could offer the customers a coordinating handbag to match the fabric chosen for their letter shirt.

A school teacher at Theodore Lester Elementary School in Florence, South Carolina, approached Ms. Ingram to create bags made from children's fabric.

Ultimately, any way that we can sell a bag we will try to use to our benefit in this early start-up stage.

Internet Format

The capital limitation of InTote has led us to choose the business location of the twenty-first century—the Internet. We also selected this format because of the numerous benefits it affords new businesses. The Web enables us to fill a niche because of the large amount of traffic that can be attracted to sites, the higher percentage of customers who are seeking a unique product, and the costs that can be avoided associated with a typical "bricks and mortar" store.

However, we do recognize the difficulties of this type of service—security, time requirements to get information posted to the Net, intellectual capital needed to operate Web storefronts, and so on. In the end, however, we believe that the benefits far outweigh the costs.

To enter into an Internet business we have developed a three-step plan that allows us to manage growth and risk at a controllable pace.

Phase One

Initially we will sell our products exclusively on an eBay account, which will serve as an extended test stage. We have made this choice for InTote because of our inexperience at business. This option will give us time to learn in the friendliest and least risky way possible. To setup a Seller's Account with eBay is simple and time effective[50] Using eBay as our initial selling outlet allows InTote to reach a pool of 42 million users who purchased $14.87 billion of goods from the online retailer in 2002—by far the highest-traffic option we can afford.[51] We already have had experience with this form of transaction and the steps involved are user friendly. Much of the work is done for you because of the system of templates that eBay uses to gather information about the user and the item for bid. However, these services come at a cost, which is based on the services you choose and the opening price of the item for sale. Based on InTote's current pricing range of $10 to $50, the fact that we want to set a reserve price for each item, and the desire to add at least one additional picture, we have determined that to sell one item will cost InTote $1.70 to $2.40.[52] InTote will factor these costs into the price of the item from the start of production. Further costs come into the selling of an item on eBay because in order to avoid as many mail orders and checks as possible, we are going to setup a PayPal account. PayPal accounts handle credit card transactions between buyers and sellers and reduce the costs associated with merchant accounts for small businesses. Also, PayPal charges only 3.3 percent per net transaction.[53] eBay does have its drawbacks; its customer service is horrible, everything has the same general appearance, bidding lasts approximately a week, and InTote will not have the ability to post as much information about our product as we would like. However, these are all outweighed by the cost–benefit advantage that eBay gives us as a small business.

Phase Two

During this stage, InTote will begin to slowly phase out of eBay auctioning in favor of a *Yahoo! Store*. Based on information that we have gathered on Yahoo! Stores and eBay Stores, it seems that Yahoo! is the best choice. To set up a Yahoo! Store is rather simple and is based on a system of templates. The costs associated with this service are a hosting charge of $39.95 a month with a one-month trial offer, 10 cents per item listed per month, 0.5 percent of each transaction, and 3.5 percent if the referral comes from the Yahoo! Network.[54] However, for these costs, InTote will have access to daily sales and visitor statistics, a merchant credit account through Yahoo!, the option of using an existing domain name (an additional $10 per year), and the potential to tap into the high traffic that Yahoo! attracts.[55] Ultimately, this is a low-cost solution for InTote, which gives us more options than an auction format at eBay. The major problem here is to avoid having our store look like everyone else's because this would take away from the unique image that we wish to convey.

Phase Three

Within two to three years, we would like to establish InTote as an independent e-commerce business. As a result of this timeline, in this proposal we would only like to hint at some of the work that will go into the creation of this type of business solution, because within those two to three years the process and costs will undoubtedly change.

First, InTote must set up a ".com" domain name with a host, probably through Network Solutions. Although many places will register a domain name for an entity, Network Solutions was the first and most knowledgeable. The current cost for this service is $25 per year.[56] Second, InTote must trademark its domain name to protect it from competition. Third, InTote must begin the process of building an attractive site, which can be expensive. Fourth, InTote must focus on the legal issues of the Web, such as users' age, copyrights, exporting, framing insurance, linking, privacy policies, user agreements, and warranties.[57] Fifth, InTote must decide whether or not to stay with PayPal or set up its own credit card merchant account.

Finally, InTote must go through the process of getting its site listed on the major search engines. This is an extremely complicated process, and by this point in our company's life we will probably seek the aid of professional search engine consultants. Although the current costs for their services is approximately $600 to $900, they are generally very good at getting sites in the top 10 search results, and this expense usually pays for itself rather quickly.[58] A much cheaper option might be to hire a college intern with extensive background knowledge of the Internet for a lower fee.

Future Phases

One day there may come a time for InTote to expand into a "click and mortar" business, but presently we have no desire to seek this option. This is a decision that will ultimately be made based on the success of InTote as an e-commerce business. However, the eventual goal of the cofounders is to build such a high level of demand for our products that InTote becomes solely a manufacturer—much like Vera Bradley.

Nevertheless, the merit of creating this business is the practice it will provide us in running a business. The layout of our manufacturing facilities and e-commerce site will at first be limited by size restrictions and the nature of eBay auction accounts. However, we believe that InTote will make the most of these limitations, and we will continue to look to the future. We are currently working with two fellow Presbyterian College students—Ms. Anne Shortall and Mr. Michael Smith— to begin the process of learning how to design a Web site, so that within two to three years we will have a unique and user-friendly portal. An initial Web site has already been designed by Ms. Anne Shortall on the design program Dreamweaver. We hope to get this site up and running, not just for retailing but also as a place where potential customers who are not in the Presbyterian College community may get information about our company and products.

InTote can expand its Web site if needed with an e-commerce service company such as Microsoft's bcentral.com, which enables a company to obtain a site hosted and managed for around $24.95 a month. Using an e-commerce service can be beneficial and a lot less expensive than hiring a professional to design a Web site, which can cost thousands of dollars.

> **The rights to www.intote.com as a domain name have not been purchased by anyone.**

Shipping

Currently most of our products do not require any shipping costs because our customers are mostly located at Presbyterian College. Based on our location, we have chosen to ship our packages through UPS or the United States Postal Service. We have estimated that for what we hope to be a typical package going from Clinton, South Carolina to Columbia, South Carolina, sent to a residential address via regular ground services, the cost will be less than $5 (including shipping materials). However, we would like to note that this is an area of our plan that we would like to revise in the near future based on further research.

COMPETITOR ANALYSIS

Breaking into the handbag market is not something that we believe will be easy to do. That is why we are taking advantage of the fact that we are in school and are not dependent on a stable income for our personal survival. This flexibility gives us the ability to start very small—guessing and checking—until we find exactly what works and how to get our product to our target customers. However, we have identified the businesses that will be our strongest competitors.

Vera Bradley

Vera Bradley started 20 years ago in much the same way that InTote is beginning today.[59] Patricia Miller and Barbara Baekgaard just happened to have a great idea at the right time. Even on Presbyterian College's campus, Vera Bradley's distinguished quilted cotton designs can be seen being used by students.

Vera Bradley's major strengths include:

➤ An amazing Web site that is not complicated but extremely tasteful.

➤ A system of store distributors.

➤ Lots of bag size options.

➤ Appearance of excellent customer service.

➤ Strong brand loyalty and recognition.

➤ A product that sends a message of strength and quality.

➤ Giving back to the community through the company's Breast Cancer Foundation.

Vera Bradley's major weaknesses include:

➤ High prices resulting from the image of the product (typically around $75).

➤ Products can only be bought in retail stores, not directly from the company.

➤ Patterns are produced for long periods—two years.

➤ All fabric patterns have the same general appearance.

Based on the perception of value in its customers' eyes, its brand loyalty, and the price that it is able to demand, Vera Bradley has chosen to use a differentiation strategy. Although this will be difficult to compete against, for obvious reasons, InTote must stay focused on providing the customer with a limited-quantity product, carrying a wide range of fabric designs, ensuring product quality, and providing a better-priced product. By focusing on these, we believe that InTote can carve a niche out of Vera Bradley's market.

Tea Bags

Tea Bags is a small handcrafted bag company that is owned and operated by Lisa Frisby.[60] Tea Bags specializes in making custom purses from quality upholstery, silk, satin, tapestry, cotton, and linen fabrics.

Tea Bags' major strengths include:

➤ The quality of the fabrics used.

➤ Posting on the company Web site the images of the bags the company has previously sold.

➤ A movie introduction to its Web site that focuses on keywords, like "special," "rare," "one," "reserved," "exceptional," and "conversational." All of these words represent ideas that Lisa Frisby wants the customer to associate with her bags.

➤ Detailed description (including size and materials) and a large, high-quality photo of each purse.

➤ An innovative brand name.

➤ Each bag is one of a kind—one made and one sold.

➤ Excellent prices for luxury bags (typically between $50 and $80).

Tea Bags' major weaknesses include:

➤ Tea Bags has a ".biz" domain name that automatically cuts down on potential customer traffic.

➤ Besides the site introduction, the site is not extremely innovative.

➤ Customers must e-mail their orders instead of ordering directly at the site.

➤ Appearance of a lack of customer service.

➤ Does not actively market to college students.

Without a doubt, Tea Bags has chosen to use a focus strategy, which poses a threat to InTote. However, Tea Bags wants customers who are looking solely for a work of art and not the daily functional quality of InTote products. Also, we would like to compete with Tea Bags by involving customers more in the manufacturing process, attracting customers who wish to pay a lower price, and making more products than Tea Bags currently offers for sale within a given period.

ItsMargery

ItsMargery started in the same way that Vera Bradley and InTote did—a friend needed a bag that was different, and ItsMargery's founder was able to make it.[61] ItsMargery focuses on making bags that are a statement of elegance, style, and fun.

ItsMargery's bags also are made out of top-quality fabrics that have unique embroidery and designs.

ItsMargery's major strengths include:

➤ An excellent Web site, which does sell bags.

➤ A step-by-step process that allows the customers to pick the fabric and size of their bag. Currently there are 11 fabric designs and 10 sizes to choose from.

➤ Great descriptions and photos of the products.

➤ A customer "Suggestion Box."

ItsMargery's major weaknesses include:

➤ Large production quantities of a fabric design.

➤ High prices (typically $100 to $300 for bags that InTote would price at $10 to $30).

As far as product quality and image, ItsMargery is the most successful of our three competitors. It has also chosen to use a differentiation strategy, because it has strong loyalty and can demand high prices. Where InTote must compete with ItsMargery is with customers who want a similarly-styled bag but cannot afford the high price of an ItsMargery product. We believe that within two to three years, when InTote does have its own Web site, we will be very successful competing with ItsMargery.

Future Competitors

The threat of future competitors is something that InTote is always going to have to face. We know this fact simply because of the way in which we started—with nothing. Unlike an automobile manufacturer, a business such as InTote can be started with very little capital or technical knowledge.

For this reason, InTote will always have to keep its guard up against new handbag companies with innovative ideas. What we must do to survive is continue to build on our knowledge of the product, forge relationships with our customers, and focus our energies on gaining the strategic capital and marketing resources that will allow us to maintain our competitive edge.

Fortunately, the odds are in our favor because rarely do look-alike businesses survive against existing competition, and as long as we can keep them at bay we should remain successful.

PLAN OF OPERATION

InTote will begin as a sole proprietorship. All final decision making will be the responsibility of Ms. Ruth Ingram. Mr. Cooper Strickland will have the ability to advise, but nothing more, unless granted by Ms. Ingram. The majority of the time and difficulties of running the business will be placed on Ms. Ingram, who will be assisted by Mr. Strickland.

MANAGEMENT TEAM

InTote's management team is made up of two Presbyterian College students, Ms. Ruth Ingram and Mr. Cooper Strickland. Both are juniors in the Business Administration Department. The former is working toward a management concentration, and the latter is working toward an accounting concentration. Although we both lack any significant business background, the hope that we will learn from this experience is one of the driving forces behind the creation of InTote.

Ms. Ruth Ingram

Ruth is the creative individual in this sole proprietorship because she is the sole creator and producer of the handbags. All aspects of InTote's business activities are her responsibility, and without her there would be no business at all. Ms. Ingram receives assistance from friends and associates with more experience as well as other applicable knowledge of running a business.

Mr. Cooper Strickland

Cooper serves as the primary business consultant for this business. His main duties include helping to produce costing report schedules for new products, balancing of the books, order processing/shipping, and other nonproduction work.

FINANCIAL STATEMENTS

InTote's financial projections are based on a simple formula because of the lack of overhead expenses, fixed expenses, and the low amount of assets required. There are actual cash flow statements for the months of operation (December 2003 to March 2004). The cash flow projections are given at pessimistic, most likely, and optimistic outcomes (April 2004 to December 2005).

InTote makes the following **assumptions** for its financial statements:

➤ Each bag will cost on average around $3 to produce and will be sold at an average price of $10.

➤ Once a Web site is developed, there will be low costs in maintaining the Web site because it will be primarily run by the founder and friends of InTote.

➤ Revenue will increase dramatically during the summer months (May to August) because of the amount of time available, as opposed to during the academic year.

➤ Advertising costs will be kept at a minimum due to word-of-mouth marketing.

Sales Tax Requirements

A new requirement for InTote beginning in April is the sales tax requirement necessitated by obtaining a retail license. We must keep accurate records to file taxes due quarterly to the South Carolina Department of Revenue.

Custom Handbag Down Payments

When customers order a customized InTote, they may be required to pay for a percentage of the handbag before the actual handbag is produced. This down payment gives InTote assurance that the customer will make full payment when payment comes due.

Balance Sheet—Actual
InTote
December 2003 – March 2004

Assets

Current Assets:

Cash	$500.00
Inventory – Materials	
Labels	$70.00
Thread	$30.00
Miscellaneous Supplies	$25.00
TOTAL CURRENT ASSETS	$625.00

Fixed Assets:

Sewing Machine	$250.00
Scissors/Incidental Manufacturing Items	$25.00
Retail License	$50.00
TOTAL FIXED ASSETS	$325.00
TOTAL ASSETS	$950.00

Liabilities and Owner's Equity

Current Liabilities:

	-
Accounts Payable	-
TOTAL CURRENT LIABILITIES	-
	-

Long-Term Liabilities:

Owner's Equity	$950.00
TOTAL LIABILITIES AND OWNER'S EQUITY	$950.00

Income Statement—Actual
InTote
December 2003 – March 2004

Net Sales Revenue	$1,819.00
Cost of Goods:	
Cost of Goods Manufactured	$528.00
Gross Margin	$1,291.00
Operating Costs	
Advertising	$25.00
Salaries	$0.00
Web site	$100.00
eBay	$25.00
Miscellaneous	$70.00
Total Operating Costs	$220.00
Operating Income	$1,071.00

Cash Flow—Actual
InTote
First Four Months of Fiscal Year

	December	January	February	March
Cash Receipts:				
Sales	$840.00	$629.00	$181.00	$169.00
Collections:				
Cash Sales	$840.00	$629.00	$181.00	$169.00
Total Cash Receipts	$840.00	$629.00	$181.00	$169.00
Cash Disbursements:				
Purchases – Materials	$210.00	$219.00	$57.00	$42.00
Rent	-	-	-	-
Utilities Expense	-	-	-	-
Shipping	-	-	-	-
Salaries	-	-	-	-
Office/Computer Supplies	-	-	-	-
Advertising	-	-	-	-
eBay	-	-	-	$25.00
Web site	-	-	-	$100.00
Miscellaneous Expenses	-	-	-	$70.00
Total Cash Disbursements	$210.00	$219.00	$57.00	$237.00
End-of-Month Balance:				
Cash (beginning of month)	$500.00	$1,130.00	$1,540.00	$1,664.00
Add: Cash Receipts	$840.00	$629.00	$181.00	$169.00
Less: Cash Disbursements	$210.00	$219.00	$57.00	$237.00
Cash (end of month)	$1,130.00	$1,540.00	$1,664.00	$1,596.00

Projected InTote Cash Flow
Last Eight Months of Fiscal Year

Most Likely	April	May	June	July	August	September	October	November	December
Cash Receipts:									
Number of handbags	30	150	150	150	150	100	25	25	25
Sales (at $12.00)	$360.00	$1,800.00	$1,800.00	$1,800.00	$1,800.00	$1,200.00	$300.00	$300.00	$300.00
Collections:									
Cash Sales	$360.00	$1,800.00	$1,800.00	$1,800.00	$1,800.00	$1,200.00	$300.00	$300.00	$300.00
Total Cash Receipts	$360.00	$1,800.00	$1,800.00	$1,800.00	$1,800.00	$1,200.00	$300.00	$300.00	$300.00
Cash Disbursements:									
Purchase – Materials	$90.00	$450.00	$450.00	$450.00	$450.00	$300.00	$75.00	$75.00	$75.00
Rent	-	-	20.00	20.00	20.00	-	-	-	-
Utilities Expense	-	-	30.00	30.00	30.00	-	-	-	-
Shipping	-	150.00	150.00	150.00	150.00	100.00	25.00	25.00	25.00
Salaries	-	-	-	-	-	-	-	-	-
Office/Computer Supplies	10.00	10.00	10.00	10.00	10.00	10.00	10.00	-	-
Advertising	-	10.00	10.00	10.00	10.00	10.00	-	-	-
eBay	10.00	10.00	10.00	10.00	10.00	10.00	-	-	-
Web site	20.00	20.00	20.00	20.00	20.00	20.00	20.00	20.00	20.00
Miscellaneous Expenses	50.00	50.00	50.00	50.00	50.00	50.00	20.00	20.00	20.00
Sales Tax (6%)	1.80	9.00	9.00	9.00	9.00	6.00	1.50	1.50	1.50
Total Cash Disbursements	$182.00	$709.00	$759.00	$759.00	$759.00	$506.00	$152.00	$142.00	$142.00
End-of-Month Balance:									
Cash (beginning of month)	$1,596.00	$1,774.00	$2,865.00	$3,906.00	$4,947.00	$5,988.00	$6,682.00	$6,830.00	$6,988.00
Add: Cash Receipts	360.00	1,800.00	1,800.00	1,800.00	1,800.00	1,200.00	300.00	300.00	300.00
Less: Cash Disbursements	182.00	709.00	759.00	759.00	759.00	506.00	152.00	142.00	142.00
Cash (end of month)	$1,774.00	$2,865.00	$3,906.00	$4,947.00	$5,988.00	$6,682.00	$6,830.00	$6,988.00	$7,146.00

WORKS CITED

1   *Trendsetters.com,* Apparel Sales.
2   *Ibid.*
3   *Ibid.*
4   Charlotte Mulhern, "Style and Substance: Success Is in the Bag," *Enterpreneur* September 1998, pp. 18–19.
5   *Ibid.*
6   *Ibid.*
7   Joanna Bober, "Going from Bag to Purse," *In Style* November 1998, p. 153.
8   "Money in the Bags," *Business Week* June 12, 2000, p. F54.
9   Bober, "Going from Bag to Purse," p. 153.
10 *Tea Bags,* Online Store, *www.teabags.biz.*
11 *The Federal Reserve Board,* The *Beige Book* for October 15, 2003, Atlanta and Richmond Districts, *www.federalreserve.gov/fomc/beigebook/2003.*
12 Dana Thomas and Anna Kuchment, "Personalizing Purses," *Newsweek International* March 18, 2002, p. 90.
13 *National Center for Educational Statistics,* College Enrollment Statistics, *www.nces.ed.gov.*
14 *University of South Carolina,* Greek Organization Statistics, *www.sc.edu.*
15 *Presbyterian College,* Greek Organization Statistics, *www.presby.edu.*
16 Campus Media Group, Media Kit, *www.campusmediagroupinc.com.*
17 *Ibid.*
18 *Eastern College Athletic Conference,* College Market Demographic Profile, *www.ecac.org/marketing/college_market_demographic_profile.pdf.*
19 Campus Media Group, Media Kit.
20 Eastern College Athletic Conference, College Market Demographic Profile.
21 *Ibid.*
22 *Purdue Online,* Advertising and Sponsorship Opportunities, *purdueonline.com/advertising.*
23 Carol Angrisani and Liza Casabona, "What's All the Buzz About? Word-of-Mouth Marketing Both on and off Campus Is Turning Students into Brand Ambassadors," *Supermarket News* April 8, 2002, p. 15S.
24 Eastern College Athletic Conference, College Market Demographic Profile.
25 Angrisani and Casabona, "What's All the Buzz About? Word-of-Mouth Marketing Both on and off Campus Is Turning Students into Brand Ambassadors," p. 15S.
26 Eastern College Athletic Conference, College Market Demographic Profile.
27 *Ibid.*
28 *Ibid.*
29 Campus Media Group, Media Kit.
30 Purdue Online, Advertising and Sponsorship Opportunities.
31 Tibbett Speer, "College Come-Ons," *American Demographics* March 1998, pp. 40–46.
32 *Ibid.*
33 Gena Hatch, "Companies Will Find Strong Consumers in College Students," *Boston Business Journal* July 6, 2001, p. 35.
34 Speer, "College Come-Ons," pp. 40–46.
35 "College Students More Inclined to Shop Online, Survey Finds," *Westchester County Business Journal,* March 12, 2001, p. 21.
36 Hatch, "Companies Will Find Strong Consumers in College Students," p. 35.
37 Campus Media Group, Media Kit.
38 Chana Schoenberger, "Campus Connection," *Forbes* September 6, 1999, p. 128.
39 Campus Media Group, Media Kit.
40 *Ibid.*
41 Angrisani and Casabona, "What's All the Buzz About? Word-of-Mouth Marketing Both on and off Campus Is Turning Students into Brand Ambassadors," p. 15S.
42 Campus Media Group, Media Kit.
43 *Ibid.*
44 Speer, "College Come-Ons," pp. 40–46.
45 Elaine Burn, "Back to School: The Benefits of Selling to the College Market," *Direct Marketing* February 1996, pp. 30–34.
46 Angrisani and Casabona, "What's All the Buzz About? Word-of-Mouth Marketing Both on and off Campus Is Turning Students into Brand Ambassadors," p. 15S.
47 *Ibid.*
48 Campus Media Group, Media Kit.
49 "College Students More Inclined to Shop Online," p. 21.
50 *Ebay.com,* How to Sell Overview, *www.pages.ebay.com/help/sell/basics.html.*
51 *Ebay.com,* Clothing, Shoes & Accessories Keyword Search "Handbag," *www.ebay.com.*
52 *Ebay.com,* Fees Overview for Selling on eBay, *www.pages.ebay.com/help/sell/basics.html.*
53 Melissa Campanelli, "It's PayPal Time," *Entrepreneur.com* February 2003, pp. 1–2.
54 Mark Henricks, "How Low?," *Entrepreneur.com* June 2003, pp. 1–4.
55 *Ibid.*
56 Dan Blacharski, "Registering Domain Names," *Entrepreneur.com* January 14, 2001, pp. 1–2.
57 Judith Silver, "A to Z of Legal Issues," *Entrepreneur.com* April 14, 2003, pp. 1–5.
58 Corey Rudl, "Getting Your Site Listed in Search Engines," *Entrepreneur.com* July 7, 2003, pp. 1–3.
59 *Vera Bradley,* Vera Bradley Design, Inc. Informational Page, *www.verabradley.com.*
60 *Infomat.com,* Fashion Industry Information Services Search Engine, *www.infomat.com.*
61 *ItsMargery,* ItsMargery Online Store, *www.itsmargery.com..*

Endnotes

Chapter 1

1. Robert A. Chernow, "The Entrepreneurial Landscape: What's Next?" Keynote Speech, 18th Annual United States Association for Small Business and Entrepreneurship National Conference, Dallas, Texas, January 15–18, 2004.
2. "Small Business Is Cool Now," *Inc. Special Report: The State of Small Business 1996*, p. 17.
3. Donald F. Kuratko, *Entrepreneurship Education: Emerging Trends and Challenges for the 21st Century*, 2003 Coleman Foundation White Paper Series for the United States Association of Small Business and Entrepreneurship, p. 3.
4. "Study: Slump in U.S. Entrepreneurial Activity Levels Off, Interest in Starting New Businesses Holds Steady," Ewing Marion Kaufman Foundation, www.emkf.org/pages/372.cfm, August 13, 2003.
5. Yochi J. Dreazen, "In Baghdad, Even Pizza Is in Allah's Hands," *Wall Street Journal*, November 10, 2003, pp. B1, B3.
6. Jeffry A. Timmons, "An Obsession with Opportunity," *Nation's Business*, March 1985, p. 68.
7. Jerry Useem, "The Risk-Taker Returns," *FSB*, May 2001, p. 70.
8. Nadine Heintz, "Media Mid-Perm," *Inc.*, November 2003, p. 25.
9. David McClellan, *The Achieving Society* (Princeton, NJ: Van Nostrand, 1961), p. 16; Nancy Michaels, "Entrepreneurship: An Alternative Career Choice," *U.S. News & World Report*, March 24, 2003, p. 45; Susan Ward, "So You Want to Start a Small Business? Part 2: The Personality of the Entrepreneur," *Small Business Canada*, http://sbinfocanada.about.com/library/weekly/aa082900b.htm.
10. Norm Brodsky, "The Road Not Taken," *Inc.*, March 2000, p. 43.
11. Ralph Waldo Emerson, "Essays: First Series," Emerson.com, www.emersoncentral.com/selfreliance.htm.
12. Julia Boorstin, "Return of the Mail-Order Man," *Fortune*, September 15, 2003, p. 48; J. Peterman Company, www.jpeterman.com.
13. Sabin Russell, "Being Your Own Boss in America," *Venture*, May 1984, p. 40.
14. Joan Caplin, Ellen McGirt, and Amy Wilson, "Fortune Hunters," *Money*, August 2003, pp. 80–85.
15. Stephanie N. Mehta, "Young Entrepreneurs Are Starting Business After Business," *Wall Street Journal*, March 19, 1997, p. B2.
16. Roger Rickleffs and Udayan Gupta, "Traumas of a New Entrepreneur," *Wall Street Journal*, May 10, 1989, p. B1.
17. "Company Information," Hewlett Packard Company, www.hp.com/hpinfo/abouthp/main.htm; James C. Collins, "Sometimes a Great Notion," *Inc.*, July 1993, pp. 90–91; Andrew E. Serwer, "Lessons from America's Fastest Growing Companies," *Fortune*, August 8, 1994, pp. 42–62.
18. John Case, "The Origins of Entrepreneurship," *Inc.*, June 1989, p. 52.
19. "Higher Purpose," *Entrepreneur*, May 2003, p. 32.
20. Justin Martin, "Here Comes the New Gold Rush," *FSB*, June 2003, pp. 72–92.
21. Roger P. Levin, "You've Got to Love It or Leave It," *Success*, December 2000/January 2001, p. 22.
22. "What Builds a Fortune?" *Money*, August 2003, p. 78.
23. Tom Fetzer, "Never Say Die," *Success*, December 2000/January 2001, p. 60.
24. Mary Diebel, "4.6 Million Americans Are Millionaires," *The Sacramento Bee*, July 16, 2001, http://24hour.sacbee.com/24hour/business/story/632161p-678117c.html; Sheryl Nance, "You Can Be a Millionaire," *Your Company*, June/July 1997, pp. 26–33.
25. Carlye Adler, "The Fresh Prince of Software," *FSB*, March 2003, pp. 42–48; "Marc Benioff," Salesforce.com, www.salesforce.com/us/company/board.jsp?name=benioff.
26. Susan Adams, "Trigger Happy," *Forbes*, May 12, 2003, pp. 160–161; "About Greg Martin Auctions," Greg Martin Auctions, http://gmartin-auctions.com/aboutus.html.
27. Gayle Sato-Stodder, "Never Say Die," *Entrepreneur*, December 1990, p. 95.
28. *NFIB Small Business Policy Guide* (Washington, D.C.: NFIB Education Foundation, 2000), p. 22.
29. Anne Fisher, "Is Your Business Ruining Your Marriage?" *FSB*, March 2003, pp. 63–71.
30. Emily Lambert, "No Free Lunch," *Forbes*, June 9, 2003, pp. 154–156.
31. Geoff Williams, "Guiding Light," *Entrepreneur B.Y.O.B.*, August 2003, p. 84.
32. Fisher, "Is Your Business Ruining Your Marriage?"
33. David Newton and Mark Henricks, "Can Entrepreneurship Be Taught?" *Entrepreneur*, April 2003, p. 63.
34. Jim Hopkins, "Venture Capital 101: Entrepreneur Courses Increase," *USA Today*, January 5, 2004, p. 1B.
35. April Y. Pennington, "What's for Dinner?" *Entrepreneur*, August 2003, p. 148; Dream Dinners, Inc., www.dreamdinners.com.
36. Anne Stuart, "A World of His Own," *Inc. Technology 2001*, No. 2, pp. 33–36.
37. *E-Commerce and Development Report 2003*, United Nations Conference on Trade and Development, United Nations (New York and Geneva: 2003), www.unctad.org/en/docs/ecdr2003ch1_en.pdf, p. 17.
38. "It All Adds Up: A National Study of Small and Medium Size Businesses with Web Sites," Interland Inc., www.vservers.com/10–03%20Interland%20Ecom%20Survey.pdf; "To Web or Not to Web," *Small Business Computing*, October 2, 2003, www.smallbusinesscomputing.com/news/print.php/3086151.
39. Mark Henricks, "Net Meeting," *Entrepreneur*, February 2003, pp. 52–55; Groomsonline, www.groomsonline.com.
40. Jack Faris, "Small Business Focus: Go West, Entrepreneurs. . . and East, North, and South," National Federation of Independent Businesses, March 7, 2003, www.nfib.com/cgi-bin/NFIB.dll/jsp/issues/newsReleaseDisplay.jsp?contentId=3733741; Joshua Kurlantzick, "Stay Home?" *Entrepreneur*, February 2003, pp. 56–59.
41. Dawn Bruno, "Marinades Make the World Taste Better," *Export America*, February 2003, pp. 6–7.
42. Meredith Bagby, "Generation X," *Success*, September 1998, pp. 22–23; Debra Phillips, "Great X-Pectations," *Business Start-Ups*, January 1999, pp. 31–33.
43. "Entrepreneurship Is Increasingly Popular Among Young Adults," *Business Education Week*, Association of Collegiate Business Schools and Programs, Vol. 1, No. 11, November 2003, p. 1.
44. Cora Daniels, "Minority Rules," *FSB*, December 2003/January 2004, pp. 65–66.
45. "Exec Bios," Handango, www.handango.com/ExecBios.jsp?siteId=1&jid=XXD7BAE3BFEX4F32E8D3F1335A463CF3; Amanda C Kooser, "Beyond Their Years: Randy Eisenman," *Entrepreneur*, November 2003, p. 82.
46. "Women Own Nearly Half of All U.S. Businesses," *Newsletter*, Center for Women's Business Research, National Federation of Women Business Owners, No. 2, 2003, p. 1, www.nfwbo.org/newsletter/CWBRNewsletter.pdf, p. 1.
47. Ibid.
48. April Y. Pennington, "Fancy Footwork," *Entrepreneur*, January 2003, p. 304; "About Us," Taryn Rose International, www.tarynrose.com/aboutus/index.html.
49. Daniels, "Minority Rules."
50. *The State of Minority Business* (Washington, D.C.: Minority Business Development Agency, 2001), www.mbda.gov/documents/mbda2.pdf, p. 2.
51. April Y. Pennington, "Beyond Their Years: Chai Ling," *Entrepreneur*, November 2003, pp. 78–81.
52. Curtis Rist, "The Small Office Home Office Update," Special Advertising Section, *Inc.*, November 2003.
53. *NFIB Small Business Policy Guide* (Washington, D.C.: NFIB Education Foundation, 2000), p. 20; Joanne H. Pratt, "Small Business Research Summary, Home-Based Business: The Hidden Economy," U.S. Small Business Administration Office of Advocacy, No. 194, March 2000, pp. 1–2.
54. Eleena De Lisser and Dan Morse, "More Men Work at Home Than Women, Study Shows," *Wall Street Journal*, May 18, 1999, p. B2; Ronaleen Roha, "Home Alone," *Kiplinger's Personal Finance Magazine*, May 1997, pp. 85–89.
55. J. Pratt, "Small Business Research Summary, Home-Based Business," p. 2.; "QuickStats," *Home Business News Report*, Fall 1994, p.1.
56. Jim Woodward, "Kitchen Table Start-Ups," *E-Merging Business*, Fall/Winter 2000, pp. 226–229.
57. "Facts and Figures on Family Business in the U.S.," The Family Firm Institute, www.ffi.org/looking/fbfacts_us.cgi.
58. Erick Calonius, "Blood and Money," *Newsweek*, Special Issue, p. 82.
59. "Facts and Perspectives on Family Business in the U.S." The Family Firm Institute, www.ffi.org/fbfacts_us.pdf.
60. Fisher, "Is Your Business Ruining Your Marriage?" p. 68.
61. "Love and the Bottom Line: Couples in Business Find High Rewards and Risks," *Nando Times News*, archive.nandotimes.com/newsroom/nt/0212bizcpl.html.
62. Fisher, "Is Your Business Ruining Your Marriage?" pp. 63–71.
63. Mark Henricks, "Back to Basics," *Entrepreneur*, September 2003, pp. 19–22.
64. Donna Kato, "Changing Course, Burning Suits," *Greenville News*, June 6, 1993, p. 1D.
65. Maggie Pouncey, "In Full Bloom," *My Generation*, January/February 2003, p. 13.
66. "Small Business FAQ," U.S. Small Business Administration, Office of Advocacy, December 2000, p. 1; *NFIB Small Business Policy Guide*, p. 25.
67. "Small Business by the Numbers," U.S. Small Business Administration, Office of Advocacy, May 2003, p. 1; "The Job Factory," *Inc. Special Report: The State of Small Business 2001*, pp. 40–43.

68. *NFIB Small Business Policy Guide*, p. 30; "Help Wanted," *Inc. Special Report: The State of Small Business 1997*, pp. 35–41; "The Job Factory," *Inc. Special Report: The State of Small Business 2001*, pp. 40–43; "The Gazelle Theory," *Inc. Special Report: The State of Small Business 2001*, pp. 28–29.

69. Preston McLaurin, "Small Businesses Are Winners," *S.C. Business Journal*, May 2000, p. 10; Erskine Bowles, "Training Ground," *Entrepreneur*, March 1994, p. 168.

70. *NFIB Small Business Policy Guide*, p. 33; "Small Business FAQ"; McLaurin, "Small Businesses Are Winners."

71. *NFIB Small Business Policy Guide*, p. 33.

72. Paul Reynolds, M. Hay, and S. M. Camp, "Global Entrepreneurship Monitor," Kauffman Center for Entrepreneurial Leadership, 1999, p. 27.

73. "Small Business by the Numbers," p. 1.

74. "Opportunity Knocks," *Inc. Special Report: The State of Small Business 2001*, pp. 94–99.

75. Lee Smith, "The Innovators," *FSB*, May 2001, pp. 43–68.

76. "Middle-Aged Spread," *Inc. Special Report: The State of Small Business 2001*, p. 54.

77. David Taymond, "Famous Flops," *Forbes ASAP*, June 2, 1997, pp. 101–103.

78. Ray Hoopes, "Mind Your Own Business," *Modern Maturity*, February–March 1991, pp. 26–33.

79. Kevin Maney, "Founder of Web-Based Grocery Store Tries Again with Online Newsstand," *USA Today*, July 23, 2003, p. 3B.

80. George Gendron, "The Failure Myth," *Inc.*, January 2001, p. 13.

81. Christopher Cooper and Erik Portanger, "Money Men Liked Boo and Boo Liked Money; Then It All Went Poof," *Wall Street Journal*, June 27, 2000, pp. A1, A8.

82. Rifka Rosenwein, "Despite Ale's Success, Brewery Loses Out," *Inc.*, October 2000, p. 37.

83. Eugene Carlson, "Spreading Your Wings," *Wall Street Journal*, October 16, 1992, p. R2.

84. Julia Angwin, "Anatomy of a Net Bookseller's Rapid Rise and Fall," *Wall Street Journal*, March 2, 2000, pp. B1, B4.

85. Norm Brodsky, "Street Smarts," *Inc.*, June 2003, pp. 55–56.

86. Jeff Bailey, "For Investors, Founders Are Short-Term CEOs," *Wall Street Journal*, October 21, 2003, p. A24.

87. Michael Warshaw, "Great Comebacks," *Success*, July/August 1995, p. 43.

88. Michael Barrier, "Entrepreneurs Who Excel," *Nation's Business*, August 1996, p. 28.

89. Clint Willis, "Try, Try Again," *Forbes ASAP*, June 2, 1997, p. 63.

90. Geoff Williams, "I Quit," *Start-Ups*, December 2000, pp. 47–49.

91. Stephanie Barlow, "Hang On!" *Entrepreneur*, September 1992, p. 156.

92. Jared Sandberg, "Counting Pizza Slices, Cutting Water Cups—You Call This a Budget?" *Wall Street Journal*, January 21, 2004, p. B1.

93. Kirsten Von Kriesler-Bomben, "The Obstacle Course," *Entrepreneur*, July 1990, p. 175.

94. Rhonda Abrams, "Building Blocks of Business: Great Faith, Great Doubt, Great Effort," *Business*, March 4, 2001, p. 2.

Chapter 2

1. Alvin Toffler, "Shocking Truths About the Future," *Journal of Business Strategy*, July/August 1996, p. 6.

2. Thomas A. Stewart, "You Think Your Company's So Smart? Prove It," *Fortune*, April 30, 2001, p. 188.

3. Thomas A. Stewart, "Intellectual Capital: Ten Years Later, How Far We've Come," *Fortune*, May 28, 2001, p. 188.

4. Gary Hamel, "Innovation's New Math," *Fortune*, July 9, 2001, p. 130.

5. Mike Steere, "A Timeless Recipe for Success," *Business 2.0*, September 2003, pp. 47–49; "History," In-N-Out, www.in-n-out.com; "Employment," In-N-Out, www.in-n-out.com.

6. Dan Morse, "Hardware Distributor Sticks to Nuts-and-Bolts Strategy," *Wall Street Journal*, July 3, 2001, p. B2; "Fastenal Company Overview," www.fastenal.com/inside/overview.asp.

7. Ray Smilor, *Daring Visionaries: How Entrepreneurs Build Companies, Inspire Allegiance, and Create Wealth* (Avon, MA: Adams Media Corporation, 2001), pp. 12–13.

8. Hermann Simon, "The World's Best Unknown Companies," *Wall Street Journal*, May 20, 1996, p. A18.

9. Thomas A. Stewart, "Why Values Statements Don't Work," *Fortune*, June 10, 1996, p. 137.

10. Paulette Thomas, "Case Study: Ramp Maker Realizes Line Is Medical Care," *Wall Street Journal*, August 5, 2003, p. B3; Mark Micheli, "Ramps Up," *Boston Business Journal*, May 16, 2003, http://boston.bizjournals.com/boston/stories/2003/05/19/smallb1.html.

11. Tom Chappell, "Heart, Soul, and Toothpaste," *Your Company*, September 1999, pp. 64–68; "The Tom's of Maine Story," Tom's of Maine, www.tomsofmaine.com/about.

12. "About Our Winery: Mission Statement," Fetzer Vineyards, www.fetzer.com/about/stor_miss.html.

13. April Y. Pennington, "Smarts," *Entrepreneur*, March 2003, p. 14; "History," Jack Black Inc., www.getjackblack.com/jackblack/home.nsf/pages/history!opendocument.

14. Stephanie Fitch, "Stringing Them Along," *Forbes*, July 26, 1999, pp. 90–91; C.F. Martin and Company, www.cfmartin.com.

15. Nicole L. Torres, "Roast of the Town," *Entrepreneur B.Y.O.B.*, March 2003, p. 118; "Retail Shops," Mayorga Coffee Roasters, www.mayorgaimports.com/html.

16. Alison Stein Wellner, "Spy vs. Spy," *Inc.*, June 2003, pp. 39–41.

17. Carolyn Z. Lawrence, "Know Your Competition," *Business Start-ups*, April 1997, p. 51.

18. "Know Thy Enemy," *Entrepreneur*, July 2003, p. 103.

19. David Whitford, "Sandwich Superheroes," *FSB*, June 2003, p. 20; "Our History," Geno's Steaks, www.genosteaks.com; "History," Pat's King of Steaks, www.patskingofsteaks.com/history.htm.

20. Julia Boorstin, "Cruising for a Bruising?" *Fortune*, June 9, 2003, pp. 143–150; Martha Brannigan, "Cruise Lines Look to the Land to Get Boomers on Board," *Wall Street Journal*, December 6, 1999, p. B4.

21. Shari Caudron, "I Spy, You Spy," *Industry Week*, October 3, 1994, p. 36.

22. Stephen D. Solomon, "Spies Like You," *FSB*, June 2001, pp. 76–82.

23. Dan Brekke, "What You Don't Know Can Hurt You," *Smart Business*, March 2001, pp. 64–76.

24. Samuel Greenguard, "Knowledge Management Can Turbocharge Your Company," *Beyond Computing*, November/December 2000, p. 28.

25. Julei Schlosser, "Looking for Intelligence in Ice Cream," *Fortune*, March 17, 2003, pp. 114–120.

26. Chris Penttila, "Who Knows?" *Entrepreneur*, April 2000, pp. 138–143.

27. Mark Henricks, "In the BHAG," *Entrepreneur*, August 1999, pp. 65–67.

28. Joseph C. Picken and Gregory Dess, "The Seven Traps of Strategic Planning," *Inc.*, November 1996, p. 99.

29. Kambiz Foroohar, "Step Ahead—and Avoid Fads," *Forbes*, November 4, 1996, pp. 172–176.

30. Rich Karlgaard, "The Cheap Decade," *Forbes*, March 31, 2003, p. 37.

31. Paul Sloan, "AirTran's Quick-Change Act," *Business 2.0*, December 2003, pp. 51–53; "JetBlue 101," JetBlue Airlines, www.jetblue.com/learnmore/air101.html.

32. Debra Phillips, "Leaders of the Pack," *Entrepreneur*, September 1996, p. 127.

33. Bridget Finn, "For Petco, Success Is a Bitch," *Business 2.0*, November 2003, p. 54.

34. Phillips, "Leaders of the Pack."

35. Emily Lambert, "Bed & Beacon," *Forbes*, May 26, 2003, pp. 194–196; "Lighthouses with Overnight Accommodations," www.lighthouse.cc/links/overnight.html#anchor859344.

36. Robert Johnson, "This Pair of Shoes Are Soles of Indiscretion; That's the Point," *Wall Street Journal*, February 25, 2000, pp. A1, A4.

37. Nichole L. Torres, "Nab Your Niche," *Entrepreneur B.Y.O.B.*, June 2003, p. 100.

38. "The Zamboni Story," Frank J. Zamboni and Company, Inc., www.zamboni.com/story; Mark Borden, "The Monopolists," *FSB*, May 2001, pp. 85–89.

39. Justin Martin, "Who Would Pay $125,000 for Stereo Speakers? Who Would Make Them?" *FSB*, July/August 2003, pp. 107–114; "History of Wilson," Wilson Audio Inc., www.wilsonaudio.com/history/index.html.

40. Joel Kurtzman, "Is Your Company Off Course? Now You Can Find Out Why," *Fortune*, February 17, 1997, p. 128.

41. Robert S. Kaplan and David P. Norton, "The Balanced Scorecard—Measures That Drive Performance," *Harvard Business Review*, January–February 1992, pp. 71–79.

42. Kevin Ferguson, "Mission Control," *Inc.*, November 2003, pp. 27–28.

43. Patricia Schiff Estes, "Survival Training," *Entrepreneur*, September 1997, pp. 78–81.

Chapter 3

1. John B. Horrigan, "Risky Business: Americans See Greed, Cluelessness Behind Dot-Coms' Comeuppance," Pew Internet & American Life Project, full report available at www.pewinternet.org, March 16, 2001.

2. Anne Marie Borrego, "These *Inc.* 500 CEOs Have Chosen Company Names That Hold a Special Meaning for Them," *Inc.*, October 2000, www.inc.com/magazine/20011015/20735.html.

3. Tracey Drury, "Reduced Loan Guaranty Worries Small Business," *Business First*, February 20, 2004, Vol. 20, No. 22, p. 4.
4. Lauren Gibbons-Paul, "A Soloist's Nightmare: Independent Contractors Often Can't Diagnose Their Own Computer Ills," *Inc.*, August 2001, www.inc.com/magazine/20010801/23232.html.
5. Ilan Mochari, "The Partners in Each of These *Inc.* 500 Businesses Knew One Another Long Before Working Together," *Inc.*, October 2000, www.inc.com/magazine/2001015/20734.html.
6. Aliza Sherman, "Partners Are from Mars: Advice for Choosing a Business Partner," *Business Start-Ups*, April 2000, p. 36.
7. Henry R. Chesseman, *Business Law*, 5th ed. (Upper Saddle River, NJ: Pearson/Prentice Hall, 2004), p. 675.
8. Mark Kind, "Actions Shed Light on Westar Plane Use," *Kansas City Business Journal*, December 26, 2003, Vol. 22, No. 16, p. 1.
9. Marjorie Griffing, "How Failure to Pay Employment Taxes Forced a Company into Bankruptcy," *IOMA's Payroll Manager's Report*, New York, September 2003, Vol. 3, No. 9, p. 3.

Chapter 4

1. Richard Gibson, "New CEO Favors Talks, Not Suits, to Settle Issues," *Wall Street Journal*, January 27, 2004, p. B3.
2. Janean Huber, "Franchise Forecast," *Entrepreneur*, January 1993, p. 72.
3. Jane R. Plitt, "Ahead of Her Time," *Success*, July/August 2000, pp. 84–87.
4. David J. Kaufmann, "The Big Bang," *Entrepreneur*, January 2004, pp. 86–101.
5. Ibid.
6. Ronaleen R. Roha, "Making It: Franchise Style," *Kiplinger's Personal Finance Magazine*, July 1996, pp. 71–72.
7. Catherine Siskos, "Franchises That Work Out," *Kiplinger's Personal Finance Magazine*, October 2003, pp. 73–75.
8. Gregory Matusky, "The Franchise Hall of Fame," *Inc.*, April 1994, pp. 86–89.
9. Mark Jones, "Down Economy Boosts Franchising," *GSA Business*, November 3, 2003, pp. 3, 6.
10. Kaufmann, "The Big Bang."
11. Ibid; "Portrait of an 'Average' Franchisee," The Franchise Store, www.thefranchisestore.com/portrait_of_an_average_franchisee.htm; "Gallup Survey of Franchise Owners Finds 92 Percent Successful," *The Info Franchise Newsletter*, April 1998, www.infonews.com/newsletters/apr98.html.
12. Siskos, "Franchises That Work Out."
13. Janean Huber, "The Buddy System," *Entrepreneur*, January 1993, p. 96.
14. Richard Landesberg, "A New Career for You Might Start at Franchise U," *Success*, July/August 2000, pp. 82–83.
15. Louise Witt, "Franchising: The Great Entrepreneurial Gambit," Special Advertising Section, *FSB*, December 2002/January 2003, pp. 51–52; Mark Jones, "Getting Hip with Plato's Closet," *GSA Business*, September 22, 2003, pp. 3, 7.
16. Bob Weinstein, "Survival of the Biggest," *Entrepreneur*, August 1999, p. 141.
17. Janean Huber, "Franchise Forecast," *Entrepreneur*, January 1993, p. 73.
18. Devlin Smith, "Uncommon Currency," *Entrepreneur B.Y.O.B.*, June 2003, pp. 96–99.
19. Niles Howard, "Cashing In," *Entrepreneur*, January 2004, p. 120.
20. Smith, "Uncommon Currency"; Julie Bawden Davis, "Financing Your Franchise," *Business Start-Ups*, September 1997, pp. 106–110; www.dunkin-baskin-togos.com.
21. "The Franchise Registry Partnership," The Franchise Registry, www.franchiseregistry.com/partnership.asp.
22. Stephanie Barlow, "Sub-Stantial Success," *Entrepreneur*, January 1993, p. 126.
23. Weinstein, "Survival of the Biggest," pp. 138–141.
24. *Vylene Enterprises vs. Naugles*, FindLaw, http://caselaw.lp.findlaw.com/cgi-bin/getcase.pl?court=9th&navby=case&no=9456470; Nicole Harris and Mike France, "Franchisees Get Feisty," *Business Week*, www.businessweek.com/1997/08/b351592.htm; Richard Gibson, "Court Decides Franchisees Get Elbow Room," *Franchise Law Update*, Luce, Forward, Hamilton, & Scripps LLP. Vol. 1, No. 6, October 1996, www.lice.com/publicat/flu_16-3.html.
25. Devlin Smith, "Want a Franchise with That?" *Entrepreneur B.Y.O.B.*, May 2002, pp. 102–106.
26. Siskos, "Franchises That Work Out."
27. Kirk Shivell and Kent Banning, "What Every Prospective Franchisee Should Know," *Small Business Forum*, Winter 1996/1997, pp. 33–42.
28. Julie Bawden Davis, "A Perfect Match," *Business Start-Ups*, July 1997, p. 45.
29. Siskos, "Franchises That Work Out"; Jones, "Down Economy Boosts Franchising."
30. Jones, "Down Economy Boosts Franchising."
31. Steve Cooper, "Creative Endeavors," *Entrepreneur*, January 2003, pp. 126–128.

32. "Notable Franchise Facts," McDonald's, www.mcdonalds.com/corporate/franchise/facts/index.html; Matusky, "The Franchise Hall of Fame."
33. Geoff Williams, "Keep Thinking," *Entrepreneur B.Y.O.B.*, January 2002, pp. 100–103.
34. Dan Morse, "Individual Owners Set Up Own E-Commerce Sites," *Wall Street Journal*, March 28, 2000, p. B2.
35. Siskos, "Franchises That Work Out."
36. Echo Montgomery Garrett, "Multi-Unit Moguls," *Inc.*, October 1999, pp. 105–111.
37. Jeannie Ralston, "Before You Bet Your Buns," *Venture*, March 1988, p. 57.
38. Siskos, "Franchises That Work Out."
39. Roberta Maynard, "Rejuvenated Sales," *Nation's Business*, July 1997, pp. 49–54.
40. Janean Chun, "Global Warming," *Entrepreneur*, April 1997, p. 156.
41. Michelle Prather, "No. 1 with Everything," *Entrepreneur*, January 2002, p. 144.
42. Asia Pacific Economic Cooperation, "Consultative Survey on Franchising in APEC Member Economies," www.strategis.ic.gc.ca/SSG/ae00275e.html.
43. Asia Pacific Economic Cooperation, "Consultative Survey on Franchising in APEC Member Economies," www.strategis.ic.gc.ca/SSG/ae00275e.html.
44. Devlin Smith, "You're the Boss," *Entrepreneur B.Y.O.B.*, September 2003, pp. 90–93.
45. Zaheera Wahid, "Twist and Shout," *Business Start-Ups*, February 2000, p. 85; Elizabeth Bernstein, "Holy Frappuccino," *Wall Street Journal*, August 31, 2001, pp. W1,W8; "Holy Fries," ABC13.com, abclocal.go.com/ktrk/news/020601_sn_holyfries.html.
46. Janean Chun, "Franchise Frenzy," *Entrepreneur*, January 1997, p. 162.
47. Richard C. Hoffman and John F. Preble, "Convert to Compete: Competitive Advantage through Conversion Franchising," *Journal of Small Business Management*, Vol. 41, No. 2, July 2003, pp. 187–204.
48. Carol Steinberg, "Instant Growth," *Success*, July/August 1996, pp. 77–83.
49. Devlin Smith, "True Conversion," *Entrepreneur*, April 16, 2001, www.entrepreneur.com/Your_Business/YB_PrinArticel/0,2361,288580,00.html.
50. "McBusiness," *Inc. Special Report: State of Small Business 2001*, pp. 34–35; Kaufmann, "The Big Bang," p. 95.
51. Peter Birkeland, "A Quiet Revolution in Franchising," Special Advertising Insert, *FSB*, June 2003, pp. S1-S3.
52. Garrett, "Multi-Unit Moguls."
53. Roberta Maynard, "Why Franchisees Look Abroad," *Nation's Business*, October 1995, pp. 65–72.
54. Dunkin Donuts/Baskin-Robbins/Togo's Franchise Opportunities, www.dunkin-baskin-togos.com; Bruce Horovitz, "The Latest Fast-Food Combo: Restaurants," *Greenville News*, March 16, 2002, p. 1D.
55. Devlin Smith, "Good as Gold," *Entrepreneur*, January 2004, pp. 106–110.
56. Janean Huber, "What's Next?" *Entrepreneur*, September 1994, p. 151.

Chapter 5

1. Julie Bawden Davis, "Buying an Existing Business? You'd Better Shop Around," *Entrepreneur*, August 1999, www.entrepreneur.com/article/0,4621,230574,00.html.
2. Lin Grensing-Pophal, "Decide Whether You'll Buy an Existing Business, a Business Opportunity, a Franchise, or Go It Alone," *Business Start-Ups*, December 2000, pp. 28–32.
3. Bill Broocke, "Buy—Don't Start—Your Own Business: Why Not Take a Common Sense Approach to Entrepreneurship, and Consider the Option of Buying an Already Established Business?" *Entrepreneur*, March 22, 2004, www.entrepreneur.com/article/0,4621,314869,00.html.
4. Nichole L. Torres, "Fixer-Upper: If You See It's Got Plenty of Potential, You Can Get That Clunker of a Business Off the Lot and Running in No Time," *Entrepreneur*, November 2001, www.entrepreneur.com/article/0,4621,293673,00.html.
5. Dennis Rodkin, "Leap of Faith: Think There's Nothing to Buying a Business? Then We've Got a Piece of the Brooklyn Bridge to Sell You," *Entrepreneur*, February 1998, www.entrepreneur.com/article/0,4621,228054,00.html.
6. Gianna Jacobson, "Misson: Acquisition," *Success*, October 1997, pp. 62–66.
7. Edward Karstetter, "How Intangible Assets Affect Business Value," *Entrepreneur*, May 6, 2002, www.entrepreneur.com/article/0,4621,299514,00.html.

Chapter 6

1. William A. Sahlman, "How to Write a Great Business Plan," *Harvard Business Review*, July/August 1997, p. 105.
2. Nicole Gull, "Plan B (and C and D and . . .)," *Inc.*, March 2004, p. 40.

3. Greg Sands, "The Return of the Business Plan," *FSB*, April 2001, p. 31.
4. Chandrani Ghosh, "Junkyard Dog," *Forbes*, April 16, 2001, pp. 34–36.
5. Paul Hawken, "Money," *Growing a Business* (San Francisco: KQED, 1988).
6. Steve Marshall Cohen, "Money Rules," *Business Start-Ups*, July 1995, p. 79.
7. "Advice from the Great Ones," *Communication Briefings*, January 1992, p. 5.
8. Don Debelak, "The Next Big Product," *Entrepreneur's Be Your Own Boss*, October 2000, pp. 163–164.
9. Robert S. Strauss, "Breaking Big," *FSB*, June 2003, p. 22; "About Us," Mitchell & Ness Nostalgia Company, www.mitchellandness.com/02aboutus.htm.
10. Edward Clendaniel, "The Professor and the Practitioner," *Forbes ASAP*, May 28, 2001, p. 57.
11. Joseph Rsoenbloom, "Space Man," *Inc.*, May 2003, pp. 42–44.
12. Anne Marie Borrego, "Big Plans," *Inc.*, January 2001, pp. 77–85.
13. Chris Penttila, "Share the Wealth," *Entrepreneur B.Y.O.B.*, May 2003, pp. 88–95; "About Us," Sunstream Corporation, www.sunstreamcorp.com/ssc/about.html.
14. Jacqueline Lynn, "Let the Bidding Begin," *Entrepreneur*, September 2003, www.entrepreneur.com/article/0,4621,310583,00.html.
15. Jeff Wuorio, "Get an 'A' in Researching a Business Idea," *Microsoft bCentral*, www.bcentral.com/articles/wuorio/140.asp.
16. C. J. Prince, "The Ultimate Business Plan," *Success*, January 2000, pp. 44–49.
17. Sahlman, "How to Write a Great Business Plan," p. 100.
18. Prince, "The Ultimate Business Plan."
19. Lynn H. Colwell, "Mapping Your Route," *Business Start-Ups*, December 1996, p. 44.
20. David Newton, "Model Behavior," *Entrepreneur*, March 2002, p. 71.
21. Sahlman, "How to Write a Great Business Plan," p. 105.
22. "Prepping Yourself for Credit," *Your Company*, April/May 1997, p. 9.
23. David R. Evanson, "Capital Pitches That Succeed," *Nation's Business*, May 1997, pp. 40–41.
24. Ibid., p. 41.
25. Jill Andresky Fraser, "Who Can Help Out with a Business Plan?" *Inc.*, June 1999, p. 115.

Chapter 7

1. Melanie Wells, "Cult Brands," *Forbes*, April 16, 2001, pp. 198–205; Victoria Neal, "Gourmet Bubbly," *Entrepreneur*, September 1999, www.entrepreneur.com/Magazines/ MA_SegArticle/0,1539,230624--1,00.html; "The Jones Soda Story," Jones Soda Company, www.jonessoda.com/ stockstuff/story.html.
2. Christopher Null, "The Check Is in the Car," *Business 2.0*, July 2003, pp. 42–43.
3. Howard Fana Shaw, "Customer Care Checklist," *In Business*, September/October 1987, p. 28.
4. Lynn Rosellini, "The High Life of Crime," *U.S. News & World Report*, November 20, 2000, pp. 76–77.
5. Chris Penttila, "Sharing the Wealth," *Entrepreneur B.Y.O.B.*, May 2003, pp. 88–95; "About DLNY," DLNY, www.dlny.com.
6. Kim T. Gordon, "Se Habla Español?" *Entrepreneur*, June 2003, pp. 83–84; Miriam Jordan, "Hispanic Magazines Gain Ad Dollars," *Wall Street Journal*, March 3, 2004, p. B2; Marci McDonald, "Madison Avenue's New Latin Beat," *U.S. News & World Report*, June 4, 2001, p. 42; James Kuhnhenn, "Mexican Influence Is Here to Stay," *Greenville News*, September 9, 2001, p. 1G; Eric Schmitt, "Census Figures Show Hispanics Pulling Even with Blacks," *New York Times*, March 8, 2001, www.nytimes.com/2001/03/08/naional/08CENS.html; Frank Solis, "The Next Big Market," *Success*, October 2000, pp. 36–38.
7. Rudolph Bell, "Mexico Natives Find Love, Success in Greenville," *Upstate Business*, November 26, 2000, pp. 1, 6–7.
8. Nicholas Kulish, "Marketers Tweak Strategies as Age Groups Realign," *Wall Street Journal*, May 15, 2001, pp. B1, B4.
9. George Anders, "The Top 10 Trends in 10 Industries," *Wall Street Journal*, February 9, 2004, p. R5.
10. Kimberly L. McCall, "Fielding Questions," *Entrepreneur*, September 2001, pp. 14–15.
11. Christina Binkley, "Soon, the Desk Clerk Will Know All About You," *Wall Street Journal*, May 8, 2003, p. D4.
12. Shari Caudron, "Right on Target," *Industry Week*, September 2, 1996, p. 45.
13. Angela Garber Wolf, "Million-Dollar Questionnaire," *Small Business Computing*, January 2002, pp. 47–48.
14. Carol Pogash, "From Harvard Yard to Vegas Strip," *Forbes ASAP*, October 7, 2001, pp. 48–52; Joe Ashbrook Nickell, "Welcome to Harrah's," *Business 2.0*, April 2002, pp. 49–54; "About Us," Harrah's Entertainment, www.harrahs.com/about_us/index.html; Christina Binkley, "Lucky Numbers: Casino Chain Mines Data on Its Gamblers and Strikes Pay Dirt," *Wall Street Journal*, May 4, 2000, pp. A1, A10.

15. Josephine Lee, "If You Build It, They Will Make You Rich," *Forbes*, November 10, 2003, pp. 130–132.
16. Nick Wreden, "From Customer Satisfaction to Customer Loyalty," *Beyond Computing*, January/February 1999, pp. 12–14.
17. Newkirk Environmental Inc., www.newkirkenv.com.
18. Roberta Maynard, "Rich Niches," *Nation's Business*, November 1993, p. 41.
19. Dale D. Buss, "Entertailing," *Nation's Business*, December 1997, p. 18.
20. Ibid., pp. 12–18.
21. Allison Fass, "Bear Market," *Forbes*, March 1, 2004, p. 88; Elizabeth Goodgold, "Talking Shop," *Entrepreneur*, September 2003, pp. 62–65; Sharon Nelton, "Building an Empire One Smile at a Time," *Success*, September 2000, pp. 34–37; Teresa F. Lindeman, "Former Payless Chief Hits Pay Dirt with Build-A-Bear," *Post-Gazette.com*, www.post-gazette.com/businessnews/20010803bears0803bnp1.asp.
22. Chris Penttila, "Battle of the Brand," *Entrepreneur*, March 2004, pp. 52–56.
23. Ibid.
24. Kimberly L. Allers, "Retail's Rebel Yell," *Fortune*, November 10, 2003, pp. 137–142; Goodgold, "Talking Shop," pp. 62–65.
25. Goodgold, "Talking Shop," pp. 62–65; ESPN Zone, www.espnzone.com.
26. Joseph R. Garber, "Know Your Customer," *Forbes*, February 10, 1997, p. 128.
27. "Deadly Game of Losing Customers," *In Business*, May 1988, p. 189.
28. Jenny C. McCune, "Becoming a Customer-Driven Company," *Beyond Computing*, May 2000, pp. 18–24.
29. David J. Wallace, "e=crm²," *Small Business Computing*, November 2000, pp. 55–57.
30. "Keeping Customers for Life," *Communication Briefings*, September 1990, p. 3.
31. Brian Caufield, "How to Win Customer Loyalty," *Business 2.0*, March 2004, pp. 77–78.
32. Rahul Jacob, "Why Some Customers Are More Equal Than Others," *Fortune*, September 19, 1994, pp. 215–224.
33. Robert B. Tucker, "Earn Your Customers' Loyalty," Economics Press Techniques, Strategies, and Inspiration for the Sales Professional, www.epic.co/SALES/selltips.htm#earn_loyalty.
34. Patricia Sellers, "Companies That Serve You Best," *Fortune*, May 31, 1993, p. 75.
35. Willian A. Sherden, "The Tools of Retention," *Small Business Reports*, November 1994, pp. 43–47.
36. Catherine Siskos, "Clothes: Fitting Pretty," *Kiplinger's Personal Finance Magazine*, June 2003, p. 24.
37. "Ways and Means," *Reader's Digest*, January 1993, p. 56.
38. "Encourage Customers to Complain," *Small Business Reports*, June 1990, p. 7.
39. Dave Zielinski, "Improving Service Doesn't Require a Big Investment," *Small Business Reports*, February 1991, p. 20.
40. Caufield, "How to Win Customer Loyalty."
41. Susan Greco, "Fanatics," *Inc.*, April 2001, pp. 36–48.
42. Ibid.
43. Max Jarman, "Business Links Quality, Service," *Greenville News*, May 18, 2003, p. 1E.
44. Mark Henricks, "Make No Mistake," *Entrepreneur*, October 1996, pp. 86–89.
45. Faye Rice, "How to Deal with Tougher Customers," *Fortune*, December 3, 1990, pp. 39–40.
46. Rahul Jacobs, "TQM: More Than a Dying Fad," *Fortune*, October 18, 1993, p. 67.
47. Ibid.
48. Kim Clark, "Customer Disservice," *U.S. News & World Report*," August 18/August 25, 2003, pp. 28–38.
49. Rory Evans, "Office Services," *Inc.*, January 2004, pp. 56–57.
50. Loree Stark, "New Twist in Lead Retrieval Tech," *Meeting News*, March 15, 2004, p. 9; "Interactive Name Badge for Networking Events," Gizmo.com.au, www.gizmo.com.au/public/News/news.asp?articleid=2543; "About Us," nTag Interactive, LLC, www.ntag.com.
51. Emily Nelson, "Marketers Push Individual Portions and Families Bite," *Wall Street Journal*, July 23, 2002, pp. A1, A6.
52. Lucy McCauley, "Measure What Matters," *Fast Company*, May 1999, p. 100.
53. Roberta Maynard, "The Heat Is On," *Nation's Business*, October 1997, pp. 14–23.
54. Matthew Maier, "Home Sweet Home Networking," *Business 2.0*, February 2003, pp. 23–24.
55. Michael Schrage, "Getting Beyond the Innovation Fetish," *Fortune*, November 13, 2000, p. 230.
56. Maynard, "The Heat Is On," p. 16.
57. Joseph R. Mancuso, "How Callaway Runs His Idea Factory," *Your Company*, April/May 1997, p. 72.
58. Alan Deutschman, "America's Fastest Risers," *Fortune*, October 7, 1991, p. 58.
59. Jonathan Karp, "Hey, You! How About Lunch?" *Wall Street Journal*, April 1, 2004, pp. B1, B5.

60. Maynard, "The Heat Is On," pp. 14–23.
61. Greco, "Fanatics," p. 38.
62. Angela R. Garber, "Hook, Line, and Sinker," *Small Business Computing*, February 2000, pp. 41–42.
63. Richard Gibson, "Can I Get a Smile with My Burger and Fries?" *Wall Street Journal*, September 23, 2003, p. D6.
64. Chris Penttila, "Brand Awareness," *Entrepreneur*, September 2001, pp. 49–51.
65. Thomas A. Stewart, "After All You've Done for Your Customers, Why Are They Still NOT HAPPY?" *Fortune*, December 11, 1995, pp. 178–182; Gile Gerretsen, "Special Tools Are Used by Super Markets," *Upstate Business*, June 14, 1998, p. 4.
66. Caufield, "How to Win Customer Loyalty," pp. 77–78; Melissa Campanelli, "At Their Service," *Entrepreneur*, July 2003, pp. 40–42.
67. Debbie Salinsky, "Insanely Great Customer Service," *Success*, September 2000, p. 61.
68. Caufield, "How to Win Customer Loyalty," pp. 77–78.
69. William C. Gillis, "Pool Sharks," *Small Business Computing*, September 2001, p. 25.
70. Ron Zemke and Dick Schaaf, "The Service Edge," *Small Business Reports*, July 1990, p. 60.
71. Brian Dumaine, "How Managers Can Succeed Through Speed," *Fortune*, February 13, 1989, pp. 54–59.
72. Mark Henricks, "Time Is Money," *Entrepreneur*, February 1993, p. 44.
73. Carlta Vitzthum, "Just-In-Time Fashion," *Wall Street Journal*, May 18, 2001, pp. B1, B4.
74. John Galvin, "Home, Home on the Web," *Smart Business*, February 2001, pp. 58–60.
75. Laura Rush, "E-Commerce Growth Will Impact SMBs," *Small Business Computing*, February 19, 2004, www.smallbusinesscomputing.com/emarketing/article.php/3314571.
76. Ibid.
77. Leigh Buchanan, "Working Wonders on the Web," *Inc.*, November 2003, pp. 77–84, 104.
78. Pratt, *E-Biz:Strategies for Small Business Success*, U.S. Small Business Administration Office of Advocacy, www.sba.gov/advo/research/rs220tot.pdf, p. 13.
79. David G. Propson, "Small Biz Gets Small Piece of the Pie," *Small Business Computing*, November 1999, p. 24.
80. Greco, "Fanatics," p. 42; Bonny L. Georgia, "Make Your Customers Love You," *PC Computing*, January 2000, pp. 105–112.
81. Buchanan, "Working Wonders on the Web," pp. 77–84, 104.
82. Stanley J. Winkelman, "Why Big Name Stores Are Losing Out," *Fortune*, May 8, 1989, pp. 14–15.
83. "Silly Putty Stretches into Cyberspace for Its 50th Anniversary," Sillyputty.com, www.sillyputty.com/campus_news/campus_news_web.htm; Deanna Hodgin, "A War Baby Bounces Back in Trendy Style," *Insight*, April 1, 1991, p. 44.
84. Brett Nelson, "Fore!-Boding," *Forbes*, April 14, 2003, p. 60.
85. Caroline Hsu, "Party Profits," *U.S. News & World Report*, October 30, 2003, pp. 36–38.
86. Shelley Branch, "Catwalk to Coffee Table," *Wall Street Journal*, November 7, 2003, pp. B1, B4.
87. Lynn Cook, "How Sweet It Is," *Forbes*, March 1, 2004, pp. 90–92; "About Blue Bell," Blue Bell Creameries, www.bluebell.com/about.htm.

Chapter 8

1. Eileen Davis, "Dodging the Bullet," *Venture*, December 1988, p. 78.
2. "Odds and Ends," *Wall Street Journal*, July 25, 1990, p. B1.
3. Richard G. P. McMahon and Scott Holmes, "Small Business Financial Management Practices in North America: A Literature Review," *Journal of Small Business Management*, April 1991, p. 21.
4. C. J. Prince, "Number Rustling," *Entrepreneur*, March 2003, pp. 43–44.
5. Daniel Kehrer, "Big Ideas for Your Small Business," *Changing Times*, November 1989, p. 57.
6. Norm Brodsky, "The Magic Number," *Inc.*, September 2003, pp. 43–46.
7. Russ Banham, "Does Dell Stack Up?" *CFO-IT*, Fall 2003, pp. 39–43.
8. Jared Sandberg, "Counting Pizza Slices, Cutting Water Cups—You Call This a Budget?" *Wall Street Journal*, January 21, 2004, p. B1.
9. Diedrich Von Soosten, "The Roots of Financial Destruction," *Industry Week*, April 5, 1993, pp. 33–34.
10. McMahon and Holmes, "Small Business Financial Management Practices in North America: A Literature Review."
11. Lori Ioannou, "He's Preaching the Power of Thrift," *Fortune*, October 30, 2000, p. 208[P].

12. Christina Binkley, "Trump's Casinos Risk Bankruptcy, Auditors Warn," *Wall Street Journal*, March 31, 2004, pp. A3, A8.
13. Herb Greenberg, "The Hidden Dangers of Debt," *Fortune*, July 21, 2003, p. 153.
14. "Analyzing Creditworthiness," *Inc.*, November 1991, p. 196.
15. Jill Andresky Fraser, "Giving Credit to Debt," *Inc.*, November 2000, p. 125.
16. Banham, "Does Dell Stack Up?"
17. Jeff Bailey, "Small Car Lots: A Basic, Gritty Loan Business," *Wall Street Journal*, July 8, 2003, p. B9.
18. Ilan Mochari, "Give Credit to the Small Business Owner," *Inc.*, March 2001, p. 88.
19. Edward Wong, "High Costs Bring Indian Motorcycle to a Halt," *New York Times*, September 23, 2003, p. C6.
20. Pat Croce, "Taking Your Own Pulse," *FSB*, December 2003/January 2004, p. 36.
21. Joshua Hyatt, "Planes, Trains, and . . . Buses," *FSB*, February 2004, p. 20.
22. Croce, "Taking Your Own Pulse."
23. Brodsky, "The Magic Number."
24. William F. Doescher, "Taking Stock," *Entrepreneur*, November 1994, p. 64.
25. Ibid.
26. Hyatt, "Planes, Trains, and . . . Buses."

Chapter 9

1. John Mariotti, "Cash Is Like Oxygen," *Industry Week*, April 21, 1997, p. 42.
2. Mike Hofman, "Archive," *Inc.*, January 2002, p. 104.
3. Paul DeCeglie, "8 Common Mistakes Entrepreneurs Make with Their Money," *Business Start-Ups*, July 1999, p. 106.
4. Aliza Sherman, "I Got the Blues," *Start-Ups*, September 2000, p. 37.
5. "Are You Ready for the Major Leagues?" *Inc.*, February 2001, p. 106.
6. Daniel Kehrer, "Big Ideas for Your Small Business," *Changing Times*, November 1989, p. 58.
7. Daniel Lyons, "Wool Gatherer," *Forbes*, April 16, 2001, p. 310.
8. Jason Leopold, "Enron But Not Forgotten," *Entrepreneur*, January 2003, p. 63.
9. Douglas Bartholomew, "4 Common Financial Mistakes . . . And How to Avoid Them," *Your Company*, Fall 1991, p. 9.
10. Karen M. Kroll, "Ca$h Wears the Crown," *Industry Week*, May 6, 1996, pp. 16–18.
11. David Armstrong, "The Segway: Bright Idea, Wobbly Business," *Wall Street Journal*, February 12, 2004, pp. B1, B6; "Segway Slump," *FSB*, March 2004, p. 12.
12. Kortney Stringer, "Neither Anthrax Nor the Economy Stops the Fruitcake," *Wall Street Journal*, December 19, 2001, pp. B1, B4; Dirk Smillie, "Signs of Life," *Forbes*, November 11, 2002, p. 160.
13. Ed Engel, "Number One with a Bullet," *Inc.*, April 2002, p. 34.
14. Bartholomew, "4 Common Financial Mistakes . . . And How to Avoid Them."
15. Jill Andresky Fraser, "Monitoring Daily Cash Trends," *Inc.*, October 1992, p. 49.
16. George Anders, "Truckers Trials: How One Firm Fights to Save Every Penny as Its Profits Plummet," *Wall Street Journal*, April 13, 1982, pp. 1, 22.
17. Mark Henricks, "Losing Stream," *Entrepreneur*, September 2003, pp. 77–78.
18. William Bak, "Make 'Em Pay," *Entrepreneur*, November 1992, p. 64.
19. C. J. Prince, "Give 'Em Credit," *Entrepreneur*, April 2004, pp. 59–60.
20. Michael Selz, "Big Customers' Late Bills Choke Small Suppliers," *Wall Street Journal*, June 22, 1994, p. B1.
21. Ilan Mochari, "Wisdom for First-Time Founders," *Inc.*, January 2001, p. 103.
22. Richard G. P. McMahon and Scott Holmes, "Small Business Financial Practices in North America: A Literature Review," *Journal of Small Business Management*, April 1991, p. 21.
23. "The Check Isn't in the Mail," *Small Business Reports*, October 1991, p. 6.
24. Howard Muson, "Collecting Overdue Accounts," *Your Company*, Spring 1993, p. 4.
25. Elaine Pofeldt, "Collect Calls," *Success*, March 1998, pp. 22–24.
26. Kimberly Stansell, "Tend to the Business of Collecting Your Money," *Inc.*, March 2, 2000, www2.inc.com/search/17568.html; Frances Huffman, "Calling to Collect," *Entrepreneur*, September 1993, p. 50.
27. "Time Shrinks Value of Debts," *Collection*, Winter 1992, p. 1.
28. "Make Them Pay!" *Inc.*, August 2003, p. 50.
29. John Gorham, "Revenge of the Lightweight," *Forbes*, March 6, 2000, p. 54.
30. C. J. Prince, "Vulture Capital," *Entrepreneur*, February 2003, pp. 47–48.
31. Russ Banham, "Does Dell Stack Up?" *CFO-IT*, Fall 2003, pp. 39–43.
32. Jill Andresky Fraser, "How to Get Paid," *Inc.*, March 1992, p. 105.
33. Elizabeth Olson, "When the Check in the Mail Is a Bill," *New York Times*, April 22, 2004, p. C5; "Protect Your Business from Phony Invoices," *GSA Business*, December 4, 2000, p. 28.

34. Donna Fenn, "A Bigger Wheel," *Inc.*, November 2000, p. 88.
35. Crystal Detamore-Rodman, "Cash In, Cash Out," *Entrepreneur*, June 2003, pp. 53–54.
36. William G. Shepherd, Jr., "Internal Financial Strategies," *Venture*, September 1985, p. 68.
37. Roberta Maynard, "Can You Benefit from Barter?" *Nation's Business*, July 1994, p. 6.
38. "33 Ways to Increase Your Cash Flow and Manage Cash Balances," *The Business Owner*, February 1988, p. 8.
39. Carol Pickering, "The Price of Excess," *Business 2.0*, February 6, 2001, pp. 38–42.
40. Kroll, "Ca$h Wears the Crown," pp. 16–18; Lynn Cook, "Requiem for a Business Model," *Forbes*, July 24, 2000, pp. 60–63.
41. Jeffrey Lant, "Cash Is King," *Small Business Reports*, May 1991, p. 49.
42. "Statistics," International Reciprocal Trade Association, www.irta.com; K. Oanh Ha, "Bartering Is Means to a Business," *Greenville News*, September 7, 2003, p. 1E.
43. Richard J. Maturi, "Collection Dues and Don'ts," *Entrepreneur*, January 1992, p. 328.
44. Ha, "Bartering Is Means to a Business."
45. "Industry Overview," Equipment Leasing Association, www.elaonline.com/industryData/overview.cfm.
46. "Small Businesses Like Leasing," *Small Business Computing*, November 18, 2003, www.smallbusinesscomputing.com/news/article/php/3110021; Juan Hovey, "The Most for the Leased," *Emerging Business*, Summer 2001, pp. 171–178.
47. Bob Violino, "What's the Deal?" *CFO-IT*, Spring 2004, pp. 15–18.
48. Tim Reason, "New Life on Lease," *CFO*, November 2000, pp. 123–126.
49. Roger Thompson, "Business Copes with the Recession," *Nation's Business*, January 1991, p. 20.
50. Ibid.
51. Bruce G. Posner, "Skipped Loan Payments," *Inc.*, September 1992, p. 40.
52. Mike Hogan, "Go Retro," *Entrepreneur*, April 2003, pp. 41–42.
53. Tom Dinome, "Power Plays," *Small Business Computing*, September 2001, pp. 29–34.
54. Ilan Mochari, "Cost-Control Diet," *Inc.*, August 2001, p. 74.
55. "Statistics on Checks," ACA International, www.collector.com/content/press/industrystats/check.html; "Fraud Statistics," FraudBAN Community, www.financialgo.net/fraud-statistics.html.
56. "How to Win the Battle of Bad Checks," *Collection*, Fall 1990, p. 3.
57. Randy Myers, "Asset Accounts Keep Cash Working," *Nation's Business*, July 1997, pp. 30–32.
58. Robert A. Mamis, "Money In, Money Out," *Inc.*, March 1993, p. 103.

Chapter 10

1. Roberta Maynard, "Take Guesswork Out of Pricing," *Nation's Business*, December 1997, pp. 27–30.
2. Jeannie Mandelker, "Pricing Right from the Start," *Profit*, September/October 1996, p. 20.
3. Erik Torkells, "Watch This," *Fortune*, June 16, 2003, pp. 123–126; Joshua Levine, "Time Is Money," *Forbes*, September 18, 2000, pp. 178–185.
4. Joann S. Lublin, "Fountain Pen Fashion: Try 5,072 Diamonds or Abe Lincoln's DNA," *Wall Street Journal*, August 14, 2001, p. A1.
5. Jeff Shulman and Richard Miniter, "Discounting Is No Bargain," *Wall Street Journal*, September 18, 2002, p. A30.
6. Brenda Biondo, "Think Your Day Care Is Expensive?" *USA Weekend*, February 4–6, 2000, p. 10.
7. Nadine Heintz, "Flexing Your Pricing Muscles," *Inc.*, February 2004, p. 25.
8. Richard Gibson, "Big Price Cut at McDonald's Seems a McFlop," *Wall Street Journal*, May 9, 1997, pp. B1, B2; Richard Gibson, "Prices Tumble on Big Macs, But Fries Rise," April 25, 1997, *Wall Street Journal*, pp. B1, B2; Cliff Edwards, "Some McDonalds Franchises Quietly Boosting Prices to Offset Cost of Promotion," *Greenville News*, April 26, 1997, p. 8D.
9. Carolyn Z. Lawrence, "The Price Is Right," *Entrepreneur*, October 1994, p. 54.
10. Rifka Rosenwein, "CEO's Regret #7: Charging Too Little for Too Long," *Inc.*, October 2000, www.inc.com/articles/2000/10/21005.html.
11. Michael Menduno, "Priced to Perfection," *Business 2.0*, March 2001, pp. 40–41; Amy Cortese, "The Power of Optimal Pricing," *Business 2.0*, September 2002, pp. 68–70; John Edwards, "Cyber Pricing," *CFO*, June 2001, p. 16.
12. Dayana Yochim, "Dump Your Duds," *Motley Fool*, May 18, 2004, http://www.fool.com/news/commentary/2004/commentary040518dy.htm?npu=y.
13. Selena Maranjian, "Living on Borrowed Dimes," *Motley Fool*, March 4, 2004, http://www.fool.com/Server/FoolPrint.asp?File=/news/commentary/2004/commentary040304sm.htm.

Chapter 11

1. Lin Grensing-Pophal, "Who Are You?" *Business Start-Ups*, September 1997, pp. 38–44.
2. Michelle Prather, "Selling Points," *Business Start-Ups*, July 1999, p. 96.
3. Melanie Wells, "Austin Powers: Call Home," *Forbes*, March 1, 2004, p. 52.
4. Donna Fenn, "Honey, Hand Me a Polygamy Porter," *Inc.*, August 2002, pp. 94–97.
5. Debra Phillips, "Fast Track," *Entrepreneur*, April 1999, p. 42.
6. Ibid.
7. Monique Harris, "Fast Pitch," *Business Start-Ups*, December 1999, pp. 71–75.
8. Maureen Tracik, "Roxy Builds TV Book Series Around Its Own Surf Wear," *Wall Street Journal*, February 19, 2003, p. B1.
9. Warren Berger, "Just Do It Again," *Business 2.0*, September 2002, pp. 77–84.
10. Landy Chase, "2000 and Beyond: The Golden Age of Professional Selling," *The Small Business Journal*, www.tsbj.com/editorials/02050501.htm.
11. Jaclyn Fierman, "The Death and Rebirth of the Salesman," *Fortune*, July 25, 1994, pp. 80–91.
12. Mark Hendricks, "Spread the Word," *Entrepreneur*, February 1998, pp. 120–125.
13. *Radio Marketing Guide and Fact Book*, Radio Advertising Bureau (New York, 2003), p. 4.
14. "Trends in Television," Television Bureau of Advertising, www.tvb.org/TVfacts/trends/TV/executive.html.
15. Ibid.
16. C. David Doran, "Station Breaks," *Entrepreneur*, September 1998, pp. 148–151.
17. Ibid.
18. Maggie Overfelt, "Hot Knots," *FSB*, May 2004, p. 57.
19. "Fact Sheets," Magazine Publishers of America, www.magazine.org/resources/fact_sheets/ed11_8_99.html.
20. "The Dynamics of Change in Markets and Media," Magazine Publishers Seminar, New York.
21. "Fact Sheets," Magazine Publishers of America, www.magazine.org/resources/fact_sheets/ed3_8_99.html.
22. "Point of Purchase (POP) Advertising," Smart Business Supersite, www.smartbiz.com/sbs/arts/hgh8.htm.
23. Francis B. Allgood, "Lindsey Named SC Restaurateur of the Year," *GSA Business*, April 5, 2004, pp. 19, 29.
24. Marc Gunther, "The Great Outdoors," *Fortune*, March 1, 1999, pp. 150–157; Outdoor Advertising of America, www.oaaa.org.
25. TAA Rate Directory of Transit Advertising, New York: Transit Advertising Association, p. 2.
26. Heidi Anderson, "Email Versus Direct Mail: A Head-to-Head Test," September 19, 2002, www.clickz.com/experts/em_mkt/case_studies/article.php/1465331.
27. Tad Simmons, "Trick of the Trade," *Presentations*, December 1998, pp. 131–135.

Chapter 12

1. Curt Cultice, "Writing the Book on Exports," *Export America*, August 2003, pp. 6–7.
2. Lowell L. Bryan and Jane N. Fraser, "Getting to Global," *The McKinsey Quarterly*, Number 4, 1999, pp. 1–9; Bradford W. Ketchum, "Going Global: East Asia-Pacific Rim," Special Advertising Section, *Inc.*, May 20, 1997.
3. Bryan and Fraser, "Getting to Global," pp. 1–2.
4. Roberta Maynard, "Trade Tide Rises Across the Pacific," *Nation's Business*, November 1995, pp. 52–56.
5. Hugh Menzies, "Export Your Way to Double-Digit Growth," *Your Company*, Forecast 1997, pp. 56–57; "International Incentive," *Small Business Reports*, June 1992, p. 5; Rob Norton, "Strategies for the New Export Boom," *Fortune*, August 22, 1994, p. 130.
6. Ted Miller, "Can America Compete in the Global Economy?" *Kiplinger's Personal Finance Magazine*, November 1991, p. 8.
7. Bernard Wysocki Jr., "Going Global in the New World," *Wall Street Journal*, September 21, 1990, p. R3.
8. Monci Jo Williams, "Rewriting the Export Rules," *Fortune*, April 23, 1990, p. 90.
9. John Ward, "A Mold Maker Finds a Mexican Match: Small Manufacturer Uses Interagency Approach to Export," *Export America*, May 2003, pp. 8–9.
10. Andy Raskin, "How to Bulletproof Your Product (Hint: Take It to Japan)," *Business 2.0*, September 2003, p. 54.
11. "Globesmanship," *Across the Board*, January/February 1990, p. 26.
12. "Our History," Montague Corporation, www.montagueco.com/aboutusourhistory.html; Ann Farnham, "Global—Or Just Globaloney?" *Fortune*, June 27, 1994, pp. 97–100.

13. Michael Barrier, "Why Small Looms Large in the Global Economy," *Nation's Business*, February 1994, p. 9; Vivian Pospisil, "Global Paradox: Small Is Powerful," *Industry Week*, July 18, 1994, p. 29.

14. Michael Barrier, "A Global Reach for Small Firms," *Nation's Business*, April 1994, p. 66.

15. Jeremy Main, "How to Go Global—And Why," *Fortune*, August 28, 1989, p. 70.

16. "Internet Usage Statistics: The Big Picture," Internet World Stats, www.internetworldstats.com/stats.htm; "Internet Users Will Top 1 Billion in 2005," *Computer Industry Almanac*, March 21, 2002, www.c-i-a.com/pr032102.htm.

17. Emily Esterson, "United Nations," *Inc. Technology*, No. 2, 1998, p. 88.

18. Roberta Maynard, "Trade Links Via the Internet," *Nation's Business*, December 1997, pp. 51–53.

19. Melissa Campanelli, "A World of Goods," *Entrepreneur*, December 2003, pp. 60–61.

20. Doug Barry, "Hair Care Company Sitting Pretty: Assistance Locating Distributors," *Export America*, January 2004, pp. 8–9.

21. "Reducing the Risk of Doing Business in China," *Nation's Business*, November 1994, p. 12.

22. Joseph E. Pattison, "Global Joint Ventures," *Overseas Business*, Winter 1990, p. 25.

23. Polly Larson, "Opening Doors to Emerging Markets," International Franchise Association, www.ifa.org/intl/News/Prjf6.asp.

24. Stephanie Hainsfurther, "Licensing Your Product," *Business Start-Ups*, January 1997, p. 50.

25. Gayle Sato Stodder, "Boxer Rebellion," *Entrepreneur*, August 1993, pp. 88–92.

26. Ian Mount, "Things Are Getting Ugly," *Inc.*, November 2003, pp. 87–90.

27. Larson, "Opening Doors to Emerging Markets."

28. Larson, "Opening Doors to Emerging Markets"; Ilan Alon, "Franchising in Emerging Markets," Franchise Chat, www.franchise-chat.com/resources/franchising_in_emerging_markets.htm.

29. Larson, "Opening Doors to Emerging Markets."

30. Lourdes Lee Valeriano, "How Small Firms Can Get Free Help from Big Ones," *Wall Street Journal*, July 30, 1991, p. B2.

31. Joshua Kurlantzick, "Stay Home?" *Entrepreneur*, February 2003, pp. 58–59.

32. Gene Sperling, "Free Free-Trade," *Inc.*, May 2003, p. 18.

33. Curt Cultice, "UAE Oil Company Keeps on Truckin': U.S. Big-Rig Wash Technology Shines Overseas," *Export America*, March 2003, pp. 8–9.

34. Geoff Williams, "It's a Small World After All," *Entrepreneur*, May 2004, pp. 39–43; Kurlantzick, "Stay Home?"

35. Paul C. Hsu, "Profiting from a Global Mind-Set," *Nation's Business*, June 1994, p. 6.

36. David Newton, "Shipping News," *Entrepreneur*, February 2004, p. 22.

37. Curt Cultice, "Making Dough Is Good for Business: San Francisco Firm Sells Better Batter to World Markets," *Export America*, June 2003, pp. 6–7.

38. Jan Alexander, "To Sell Well Overseas, Customize," *Your Company*, Fall 1995, p. 15.

39. Kurlantzick, "Stay Home?"

40. Frances Huffman, "Hello, World!" *Entrepreneur*, August 1990, p. 108.

41. Christopher Knowlton, "The New Export Entrepreneurs," *Fortune*, June 6, 1988, p. 98.

42. Alexander, "To Sell Well Overseas, Customize."

43. Cultice, "Making Dough Is Good for Business: San Francisco Firm Sells Better Batter to World Markets."

44. Jan Alexander, "How to Find an Overseas Distributor," *Your Company*, April/May 1996, pp. 52–54.

45. Inge McNeese, "Reducing the Risk of Harmful Pesticides: New Technology Wins Export Markets," *Export America*, April 2003, pp. 6–7.

46. "The Pacific Rim on a Shoestring," *Inc.*, June 1991, pp. 122–123.

47. Ward, "A Mold Maker Finds a Mexican Match: Small Manufacturer Uses Interagency Approach to Export."

48. Charlotte Mulhern, "Fast Forward," *Entrepreneur*, October 1997, p. 34.

49. Doug Barry, "There's No Place Like Dome," *Export America*, December 2003, pp. 6–7.

50. "Stronger Than Expected Growth Spurs Modest Trade Recovery," Press Release #373, World Trade Organization, April 5, 2004.

51. Neil King Jr., "Is Wolverine Human? A Judge Answers No," *Wall Street Journal*, January 20, 2003, pp. A1, A8.

52. Eric Wahlgreen, "Trade Winds," *Inc.*, November 2003, pp. 36–38.

53. Ira Carnahan, "Quota Factory," *Forbes*, April 14, 2003, p. 110.

54. Dan Morse, "Furniture Makers Seek Trade Duties," *Wall Street Journal*, November 3, 2003, p. A2; "U.S. Panel Finds Chinese Manufacturers Dumping Bedroom Furniture," *KeepMedia*, January 9, 2004, www.keepmedia.com/ShowItemDetails.do?itemID=348238.

55. Edmund Faltermayer, "Does Japan Play Fair?" *Fortune*, September 7, 1992, pp. 38–52.

56. Deb Richardson-Moore, "For Internationals, Life Here Can Be Jolting," *Greenville News*, May 25, 2003, pp. 1D, 11D.

57. Stephen J. Simurda, "Trade Secrets," *Entrepreneur*, May 1994, p. 120.

58. Edward T. Hall, "The Silent Language of Overseas Business," *Harvard Business Review*, May–June 1960, pp. 5–14.

59. Ibid.

60. Roger E. Axtell, *Gestures: The Do's and Taboos of Body Language Around the World* (New York: John Wiley & Sons, Inc., 1991).

61. Lawrence Van Gelder, "It Pays to Watch Words, Gestures While Abroad," *Greenville News*, April 7, 1996, p. 8E.

62. Anton Piëch, "Speaking in Tongues," *Inc.*, June 2003, p. 50.

63. Anton Piëch, "Lost in the Translation," *Inc.*, June 2003, p. 50.

64. Curt Cultice, "President's 'E' Awards Recognize Exporting Excellence," *Export America*, July 2002, pp. 6–7.

65. John S. McClenahen, "Sound Thinking," *Industry Week*, May 3, 1993, p. 28.

66. Jeremy Main, "How to Go Global—And Why," *Fortune*, August 28, 1989, p. 70.

67. Orit Gadiesh and Jean-Marie Pean, "Think Globally, Market Locally," *Wall Street Journal*, September 9, 2003, p. B2.

Chapter 13

1. Josef Federman, "In the Driver's Seat," *Wall Street Journal*, May 16, 2003, p. R12.

2. Nick Wingfield, "Amazon, Mail-Order Retailers Reheat Online Food Sales," *Wall Street Journal*, June 23, 2003, pp. B1, B3; Anne D'Innocenzio, "Online Grocery Hopes Fresh Take on Concept Helps Business Ripen," *Greenville News*, April 19, 2003, p. 12A; Tim Laseter, Barrie Berg, and Martha Turner, "What FreshDirect Learned from Dell," *Strategy + Business*, Spring 2003, pp. 20–25.

3. Andrew Raskin, "Setting Your Sites," *Inc. Technology*, No. 2, 1999, p. 20.

4. *E-Commerce and Development Report 2003*, United Nations Conference on Trade and Development (New York and Geneva: United Nations, 2003), p. 4.; "Global Village," *Entrepreneur*, April 2003, p. 30.

5. Jerry Useem, "Our 10 Principles of the New Economy, Slightly Revised," *Business 2.0*, August/September 2001, p. 85.

6. "Forrester Projects $6.8 Trillion for 2004," Global Reach, http://global-reach.biz/eng/index/php3.

7. Laura Rush, "E-Commerce Growth Will Impact SMBs," *Small Business Computing*, February 19, 2004, www.smallbusinesscomputing.com/emarketing/print.php/3314571.

8. "Interland Survey Finds Web Sites Are Key to Driving Credibility, Marketing, and Sales for Small Businesses," *Yahoo! Finance*, October 1, 2003, www.biz.yahoo.com/bw/031001/15400_1.html.

9. Wingfield, "Amazon, Mail-Order Retailers Reheat Online Food Sales"; "About Us," The Cheesecake Factory, www.cheesecakefactory.com.

10. "Marketing on the World Wide Web," Alaska Internet Marketing, www.alaskaoutdoors.com/Misc/info.html.

11. Laseter, Berg, and Turner, "What FreshDirect Learned from Dell."

12. Julia Angwin, "Used-Car Auctioneers, Dealers Meet Online," *Wall Street Journal*, November 20, 2003, pp. B1, B13.

13. Lorraine Farquharson, "The Web @ Work: Jos. A. Bank," *Wall Street Journal*, October 29, 2001, p. B5.

14. Leigh Buchanan, "Working Wonders on the Web," *Inc.*, November 2003, pp. 76–84, 104; "Surf's Up," *Entrepreneur*, March 2004, p. 31.

15. David G. Propson, "Small Biz Gets Small Piece of the Pie," *Small Business Computing*, November 1999, p. 24; "Survival of the Fastest," *Inc. Technology*, No.4, 1999, pp. 44–57.

16. "A Perfect Market," *The Economist*, May 15, 2004, p. 4.

17. George Mannes, "Don't Give Up on the Web," *Fortune*, March 5, 2001, pp. 184[B]–184[L].

18. "Reality Bites," *Wall Street Journal*, May 1, 2000, p. B18.

19. Robert McGarvey, "Connect the Dots," *Entrepreneur*, March 2000, pp. 78–85.

20. Karen Klein, "Netting More Business on the Web," *Business Week Online*, May 20, 2004, www.businessweek.com/smallbiz/content/may2004/sb20040520_7126_sb024.htm.

21. Joe Dysart, "Promote Your Site," *Emerging Business*, Summer 2001, pp. 29–32; Williams Nursery, www.williams-nursery.com.

22. Matthew Fogel, "Blogging for Dollars," *Inc.*, May 2003, p. 36.

23. Claire Tristram, "Many Happy Returns," *Small Business Computing*, May 1999, p. 73.

24. Douglas Gantenbein, "The Tender Digital Trap," *Small Business Computing*, May 1, 2001, www.sbcmag.com.

25. Melissa Campanelli, "E-Business Busters," *Entrepreneur*, January 2000, pp. 46–50.
26. Jodi Mardesich, "The Web Is No Shopper's Paradise," *Fortune*, November 8, 1999, pp. 188–198.
27. "Survival of the Fastest," *Inc. Technology*, No. 4, 1999, p. 57.
28. "The *Smart Business* 50: Dell Computer," *Smart Business*, September 2001, p. 74.
29. Steve Bennett and Stacey Miller, "The E-Commerce Plunge," *Small Business Computing*, February 2000, p. 50.
30. "Beyond Their Years," *Entrepreneur*, November 2003, www.entrepreneur.com/article/0,4621,311420,00.html; "Zappos.com on Pace to More Than Double Sales This Year," *Internet Retailer*, November 3, 2003, www.internetretailer.com/dailynews.asp?id=10577; "About Zappos.com," Zappos.com, www.zappos.com/about.zhtml; Jane Bennett Clark, Robert Frick, Sean O'Neill, Ronaleen Roha, and Alison Stevenson, "Point Click Buy," *Kiplinger's*, June 2003, pp. 90–93.
31. Amanda C. Kooser, "Ring My Bell," *Entrepreneur*, December 2000, p. 24.
32. Mark Henricks, "User Unfriendly," *Entrepreneur*, February 2003, p. 54.
33. Bryan Eisenberg, "20 Tips to Minimize Shopping Cart Abandonment (Part 1)," *Small Business Computing*, September 24, 2003, www.smallbusinesscomputing.com/emarketing/print.php/3081791, p. 1; Alice Hill, "5 Reasons Customers Abandon Their Shopping Carts (and What You Can Do About It)," *Smart Business*, March 2001, pp. 80–84.
34. Laura Rush, "Fear of Abandonment," *Small Business Computing*, January 28, 2004, www.smallbusinesscomputing.com/emarketing/print.php/3304551.
35. Eisenberg, "20 Tips to Minimize Shopping Cart Abandonment (Part 1)," pp. 1–2.
36. Melissa Campanelli, "It's PayPal Time," *Entrepreneur*, February 2003, pp. 42–43; John Edwards, "The New Economy," *CFO*, January 2004, pp. 19–20.
37. Bronwyn Fryer, "When Something Clicks," *Inc. Technology*, No. 1, 2000, pp. 62–72; Tristram, "Many Happy Returns," pp. 70–75; Mardesich, "The Web Is No Shopper's Paradise."
38. Melanie Trottman, "Travelocity Streamlines Its Web Site," *Wall Street Journal*, March 25, 2004, p. D5.
39. Fred Vogelstein, "A Cold Bath for Dot-Com Fever," *U.S. News & World Report*, September 13, 1999, p. 37.
40. Mardesich, "The Web Is No Shopper's Paradise."
41. Bethany McLean, "More Than Just Dot-Coms," *Fortune*, December 6, 1999, pp. 130–138.
42. "Hello Amazon," *CFO*, September 2003, p. 26.
43. "A Perfect Market," pp. 3–5.
44. The *Smart Business* 50: REI," *Smart Business*, September 2001, p. 73.
45. Harriet B. Stephenson, Diane L. Lockwood, and Peter Raven, "The Entrepreneur's Guide to the Strategic Use of the Internet," presented at United States Association of Small Business and Entrepreneurship, Hilton Head Island, South Carolina, January 2003, p. 1.
46. Robert McGarvey, "From: Business To: Business," *Entrepreneur*, June 2000, pp. 96–103.
47. Ibid.
48. "The *Smart Business* 50: Cisco Systems," *Smart Business*, September 2001, p. 80; William J. Holstein, "Rewiring the 'Old Economy,' " *U.S. News & World Report*, April 10, 2000, pp. 38–40.
49. Bronwyn Fryer and Lee Smith, ".com or Bust," *Forbes Small Business*, December 1999/January 2000, p. 41.
50. Patricia W. Pool, John A. Parnell, and Shawn Carraher, "Utilizing E-Commerce in Small Business," presented at Annual Conference of the United States Association for Small Business and Entrepreneurship, March 24–26, 2004, Albuquerque, New Mexico, p. 30.
51. "A Perfect Market," pp. 3–5.
52. Michelle Prather, "Life Online," *Business Start-Ups*, May 2000, p. 17.
53. Stephenson, Lockwood, and Raven, "The Entrepreneur's Guide to the Strategic Use of the Internet," p. 3.
54. Fogel, "Blogging for Dollars."
55. Ralph F. Wilson, "The Five Mutable Laws of Web Marketing," *Web Marketing Today*, April 1, 1999, www.wilsonweb.com/wmta/basic-principles.htm, pp. 1–7.
56. April Y. Pennington, "Through the Grapevine," *Entrepreneur*, June 2003, p. 81; Mike Wendland, "E-Mail Helps Wine Store Reach Out, Boost Profits," *Detroit Free Press*, July 1, 2002, www.freep.com/money/tech/mwend1_20020701.htm.
57. Giesla M. Pedroza, "Do Or Die," *Start-Ups*, October 2000, p. 17.
58. Jan Gardner, "10 Ideas for Growing Business Now," *Inc.*, October 29, 2001, www2.inc.com/search/23629.html.
59. Ellen Neuborne, "Taming the Beast," *Inc.*, February 2004, p. 32.
60. Melissa Campanelli, "Stand and Deliver," *Entrepreneur*, November 2003, pp. 56–57.
61. David Ernst, Tammy Halevy, Jean-Hugues Monire, and Higo Sazzarin, "A Future for e-Alliances," *The McKinsey Quarterly*, No 2, 2001, www.mckinseyquarterly.com/article_page.asp?tk=440472:1039:24&ar=1039&L2=24&L3=47.
62. Robert McGarvey, "Irreconcilable Differences," *Entrepreneur*, February 2000, p. 75.
63. Dylan Tweney, "Think Globally, Act Locally," *Business 2.0*, November 2001, pp. 120–121.
64. Ibid.
65. "Search and the Small Business: Why Mom and Pop Will Drive Search Marketing," *Sales and Marketing Management's Performance Newsletter*, March 2004, newsletter@salesandmarketing.com.
66. Joanna L. Krotz, "Rise to the Top of Search Results," *bCentral*, www.bcentral.com/articles/krotz/110.asp?.
67. Mylene Mangalindan, "Playing the Search-Engine Game," *Wall Street Journal*, June 16, 2003, pp. R1, R7.
68. Ellen Neuborne, "Finding the Right Keyword," *Inc.*, October 2003, p. 44.
69. Mangalindan, "Playing the Search-Engine Game."
70. "Design Matters," *Fortune Tech Guide*, 2001, pp. 183–188.
71. "Virtual Estate," *Entrepreneur*, May 2001, p. 28; Robert A. Mamis, "The Name Game," *Inc.'s The State of Small Business 2000*, pp. 141–144; "Name Your Price," *Start-Ups*, January 2001, p. 14.
72. Alfred Gingold, "Click Here," *My Generation*, July–August 2001, p. 51.
73. Herman Miller, www.hermanmiller.com; "Design Matters," *Fortune Tech Guide*.
74. "Santa's Helpers," *The Economist*, May 15, 2004, pp. 5–8.
75. Melissa Campanelli, "Spring Cleaning," *Entrepreneur*, April 2003, pp. 44–45.
76. Ibid.
77. Carol Stavraka, "There's No Stopping E-Business. Are You Ready?" Special Advertising Section, *Forbes*, December 13, 1999.
78. Adam Stone, "Small Business Web Analytics," *Small Business Computing*, www.smallbusinesscomputing.com/emarketing/print.php/2234491.
79. Kathleen Dooher, "Many Happy Returns," *Inc.*, November 2001, pp. 150–152; Anne Stuart, "The Best Small Business Sites in America," *Inc.*, November 2001, pp. 129–130.
80. Ann Harrison, "Privacy? Who Cares," *Business 2.0*, June 12, 2001, pp. 48–49.
81. Alix Nyberg, "Privacy Matters," *CFO*, July 2001, p. 22.
82. Ibid.
83. J. D. Tuccille, "Don't Be Big Brother," *Small Business Computing*, July 1999, pp. 42–43; Kbtoys, www.kbtoys.com.
84. Michael Bertin, "The New Security Threats," *Smart Business*, February 2001, pp. 78–86.
85. Jeremy Wagstaff, "Home Phishing: Web Scam Takes Dangerous Turn," *Wall Street Journal*, May 27, 2004, pp. B1, B5.
86. Sharon Gaudin, "Security Threats Coming from All Sides," *Small Business Computing*, March 18, 2004, www.smallbusinesscomputing.com/news/article.php/3327541.
87. Martha Mendoza, "Cybercriminals Rarely Face Jail," *Greenville News*, August 31, 2003, p. 5A; Paul Kedrosky, "You've Got 'Mydoom'!" *Wall Street Journal*, January 30, 2004, p. A12.
88. Melissa Campanelli, "A Wall of Fire," *Entrepreneur*, February 2000, pp. 48–49.
89. "Insane Stat," *Business 2.0*, March 6, 2001, p. 30.
90. Mie-Yun Lee, "Wrong Number," *Entrepreneur*, March 2001, pp. 84–85; Paul Kraaijvanger, "Don't Get Slammed If Your Business Takes Credit Cards Online," *Success*, February 2000, pp. 62–63.
91. Susan Greco, "The Fraud Bogeyman," *Inc.*, February 2001, pp. 103–104.
92. Adam Stone, "Small E-Stores Avoid Credit Card Fraud," *Small Business Computing*, December 23, 2003, www.smallbusinesscomputing.com/emarketing/print.php/3291231.

Chapter 14

1. Paul DeCeglie, "What About Me?" *Business Start-Ups*, June 2000, pp. 45–51.
2. Alison Stein Wellner, "Blood Money," *Inc.*, December 2003, pp. 48–50.
3. Elaine Pofeldt, "Six Degrees of Capitalization," *Success*, January 2000, pp. 16, 57.
4. Silva Sansoni, "Burned Angels," *Forbes*, April 19, 1999, pp. 182–185.
5. Jacquelyn Lynn, "Secret to My Financing," *Entrepreneur*, May 2000, www.Entrepreneur.com/article/o,4621,27185,00.html.
6. Carrie Coolidge, "The Bootstrap Brigade," *Forbes*, December 28, 1998, pp. 90–91.
7. Wellner, "Blood Money," p. 50.
8. Richard Breeden, "Small Talk: Informal Funding," *Wall Street Journal*, August 26, 2003, p. B8; Mabel Brecrick-Okereke, "Report to U.N. Cautions That Focus on Venture Capital Can Hinder Entrepreneurial Economy," United Nations Association of the United States of America, http://unusa.school.aol.com/newsroom/NewsReleases/ean_venture.asp.

9. Paul Kvinta, "Frogskins, Shekels, Bucks, Moolah, Cash, Simoleans, Dough, Dinero: Everybody Wants It. Your Business Needs It. Here's How to Get It," *Smart Business*, August 2000, pp. 74–89.

10. Pamela Sherrid, "Angels of Capitalism," *U.S. News & World Report*, October 13, 1997, pp. 43–45.

11. Joanne Gordon, "Wings," *Forbes*, October 30, 2001, pp. 299–300.

12. "Is He an Angel or a Beatle?" *FSB*, October 2000, p. 39.

13. Wendy Taylor and Marty Jerome, "Pray," *Smart Business*, July 2000, p. 45; John Heylar, "The Venture Capitalist Next Door," *Fortune*, November 13, 2000, pp. 293–312.

14. Sansoni, "Burned Angels."

15. Geoff Williams, "Shoot for the Stars," *Entrepreneur*, March 2004, p. 27.

16. Jennifer Keeney and Ron Orol, "Touched by an Angel," *FSB*, April 2001, p. 34.

17. Jennifer Lawton, "Making Friends: The Name of the Angel Game," *EntreWorld.org*, February 1, 2000, www.entreworld.org.

18. Suzanne McGee, "A Chorus of Angels," *Inc.*, January 2004, pp. 38–40.

19. Bonnie Azab Powell, "Angel Investors Fill Void Left by Risk Capital," *New York Times*, July 6, 2001, p. 28; Loren Fox, "Heaven Can't Wait," *Business 2.0*, March 20, 2001, pp. 123–124; Anne Ashby Gilbert, "Small Stakes in Small Business," *Fortune*, April 12, 1999, p. 162[H]; Sherrid, "Angels of Capitalism"; Heylar, "The Venture Capitalist Next Door."

20. Bruce J. Blechman, "Step Right Up," *Entrepreneur*, June 1993, pp. 20–25.

21. Heylar, "The Venture Capitalist Next Door."

22. Nancy Scarlato, "Money," *Business Start-Ups*, December 1995, pp. 50–51; Gianna Jacobson, "Raise Money Now," *Success*, November 1995, pp. 39–50.

23. *Corporate Venture Capital Report* (New York: Ernst & Young, 2002), p. 3; Alistair Christopher, "Corporate Venture Capital: Moving to the Head of the Class," *Venture Capital Journal*, November 1, 2000, www.findarticles.com/cf_dls/m0ZAL/2000_Nov_1/66502342/print.jhtml.

24. David Worrell, "The Big Guns," *Entrepreneur*, November 2003, pp. 68–69.

25. Brian Caulfield, "The Pentagon's Venture Capitalists," *Business 2.0*, April 2003, p. 28.

26. David Worrell, "Safe Bet," *Entrepreneur*, February 2004, p. 24; "About Us," Sourcefire Network Security Inc., www.sourcefire.com/about.html.

27. Roy Harris, "Capital Without the Venture," *CFO*, February 2004, pp. 31–32.

28. Brecrick-Okereke, "Report to U.N. Cautions That Focus on Venture Capital Can Hinder Entrepreneurial Economy"; Cara Cannella, "Where Seed Money Really Comes From," *Inc.*, August 2003, p. 26.

29. PricewaterhouseCoopers MoneyTree Survey, www.pwcmoneytree.com/stage.asp?year=2001&qtr=3; National Venture Capital Association, www.nvca.org.

30. Jeff Bailey, "Rethinking a Return to Venture Capital Funding," *Wall Street Journal*, September 30, 2003, p. B4.

31. D. M. Osborne, "Dear John," *Inc.*, May 2001, pp. 44–48.

32. PricewaterhouseCoopers MoneyTree Survey, www.pwcmoneytree.com/PDFS/mt_q3_2001.pdf.

33. Harris, "Capital Without the Venture."

34. Karl Rhodes, "The Venture Adventure," *Region Focus*, Fall 2003, pp. 22–26.

35. Harris, "Capital Without the Venture."

36. Tracy T. Lefteroff and Nichole L. Torres, "The Thrill of the Chase," *Entrepreneur*, July 2003, pp. 56–63.

37. Dave Pell, "What's Old Is New Again," *FSB*, July/August 2000, p. 122.

38. Kvinta, "Frogskins, Shekels, Bucks, Moolah, Cash, Simoleans, Dough, Dinero: Everybody Wants It. Your Business Needs It. Here's How to Get It," p. 87.

39. IPO.com, www.ipo.com.

40. David R. Evanson, "Tales of Caution in Going Public," *Nation's Business*, June 1996, p. 58.

41. Roberta Maynard, "Are You Ready to Go Public?" *Nation's Business*, January 1995, pp. 30–32.

42. Tim Reason, "Off the Street," *CFO*, May 2003, pp. 54–58.

43. Sally McGrane, "The Crash's Silver Lining," *Forbes*, September 10, 2001, p. 26.

44. Reason, "Off the Street," p. 58.

45. David Worrell, "Waiting in the Wings," *Entrepreneur*, January 2004, pp. 21–22.

46. Sheila Muto, "Targeting Texas," *Wall Street Journal*, March 24, 2004, p. B6; "Outdoor Sporting Goods Mecca Cabela's Announces Its IPO Terms," IPO Home, www.ipohome.com/marketwatch/iponews2.asp?article=3656.

47. Kvinta, "Frogskins, Shekels, Bucks, Moolah, Cash, Simoleans, Dough, Dinero: Everybody Wants It. Your Business Needs It. Here's How to Get It," p. 88.

48. Mirenco, Inc., www.mirenco.com/Company/SECFilings.asp; Tom Stewart-Gordon, SCOR-Report, www.scor-report.com.

49. P. B. Gray, "Drug Money," *FSB*, May 2004, p. 23; "Eximias Pharmaceutical Corporation Announces $63.5 Million Private Placement," Eximias Pharmaceutical Corporation, www.eximiaspharm.com/news/business/2004_03_31_1.htm.

50. Toni Mack, "They Stole My Baby," *Forbes*, February 12, 1996, pp. 90–91.

51. Drew Field Public Offerings: Client Summaries, Thanksgiving Coffee Company, www.dfdpo.com/clientsum11.htm; Thanksgiving Coffee Company, www.thanksgivingcoffee.com.

52. "Go Public Overseas," *Success*, September 1997, pp. 89–96.

Chapter 15

1. Cynthia E. Griffin, "Something Borrowed," *Entrepreneur*, February 1997, p. 26; Business Lenders Inc., www.businesslenders.com/q&a.htm.

2. *Small Business and Micro Business Lending in the United States 2002*, Small Business Administration Office of Advocacy (Washington, D.C.: December 2003), www.sba.gov/advo/stats/lending/2002/sbl_study.pdf, p. i.

3. Karen Axelton, "Don't Bank on It," *Business Start-Ups*, May 1998, p. 116.

4. Cynthia E. Griffin, "Money in the Bank," *Entrepreneur*, July 2000, pp. 84–89; *Small Business and Micro Business Lending in the United States 2002*, pp. 10–12.

5. Paul DeCeglie, "Funny Money," *Entrepreneur's Be Your Own Boss*, January 2001, pp. 141–146.

6. Daniel M. Clark, "Banks and Bankability," *Venture*, September 1989, p. 29.

7. "Lines of Credit," *Inc.*, July 1990, p. 96.

8. "Dispatches," *Inc.*, December 31, 2001, pp. 92–94.

9. Tim Reason, "Borrowing Big Time," *CFO*, November 2003, pp. 87–94.

10. Juan Hovey, "Want Easy Money? Look for Lenders Who Say Yes," *FSB*, November 2000, pp. 41–44.

11. Anne Ashby Gilbert, "Where to Go When the Bank Says No," *Fortune*, October 12, 1998, pp. 188[C]–188[F].

12. Jane Applegate, "Inventory-Based Lines of Credit," *Entrepreneur*, July 16, 2001, www.entrepreneur.com/article/0,4621,291071,00.html.

13. "What Is Business Credit?" National Association of Credit Management, www.nacm.org/aboutnacm/what.html; "Financing Small Business," *Small Business Reporter*, C3, p. 9.

14. Jill Andresky Fraser, "When Supplier Credit Helps Fuel Growth," *Inc.*, March 1995, p. 117.

15. *Small Business and Micro Business Lending in the United States 2002*, p. 1.

16. David Worrell, "The Other Colors of Money," *Entrepreneur*, July 2004, p. 67.

17. Patricia Fusco, "Small Businesses 'Capitalize' on UPS," *Small Business Computing*, January 13, 2004, www.smallbusinesscomputing.com/news/article.php/3298181.

18. Scott McMurray, "Personal Loans from Brokers Offer Low Rates," *Wall Street Journal*, January 7, 1986, p. 31.

19. Crystal Detamore-Rodman, "Give 'Em Credit," *Entrepreneur*, August 2003, pp. 55–56.

20. National Credit Union Administration, *2003 Mid-Year Statistics for Federally Insured Credit Unions* (Alexandria, Virginia: 2004), www.ncua.gov/ReportsAndPlans/statistics/Midyear2003.pdf, p. 23.

21. Detamore-Rodman, "Give 'Em Credit."

22. Sean P. Melvin, "Itsy-Bitsy Bonds," *Entrepreneur*, January 2002, pp. 78–81.

23. Robert McGough, "Money to Burn," *FW*, June 26, 1990, p. 18; Longview Fibre Company, www.longviewfibre.com.

24. *SBIC Program Statistical Package*, U.S. Small Business Administration (Washington, D.C., 2003), www.sba.gov/INV/stat/table1.pdf.

25. *SBIC Program Statistical Package*, U.S. Small Business Administration (Washington, D.C., 2003), www.sba.gov/INV/stat/table3.pdf.

26. Ibid.

27. *SBIC Program Statistical Package*, U.S. Small Business Administration (Washington, D.C., 2003), www.sba.gov/INV/stat/table2.pdf.

28. Crystal Detamore-Rodman, "Solid Backing," *Entrepreneur*, February 2003, pp. 49–50; "About Us," Intelliseek, www.intelliseek.com/lifeatiseek.asp.

29. *EDA RLFs Performance Evaluation*, Economic Development Administration, Department of Commerce (Washington, D.C., 2002), www.eda.gov/ImageCache/EDAPublic/documents/pdfdocs/rlf_5fperf_5feval_2epdf/v1/rlf_5fperf_5feval.pdf, p. 8.

30. "Section 108 Case Studies," U.S. Department of Housing and Urban Development, www.hud.gov/offices/cpd/communitydevelopment/programs/108/casestudies.cfm.

31. Sarah Zajaczek, "Local Manufacturer Gets Minority Ownership Funding," *Clinton Chronicle*, July 25, 2001, p. 4A.

32. "SBA Technology: Small Business Innovation Research Program (SBIR)," www.sba.gov/SBIR/sbir.html; Charles Stein, "A Sugar Daddy for Hungry Start-Ups," *FSB*, May/June 2000, pp. 41–42.

33. "SBIR/STTR Program Successes," Department of Defense, www.acq.osd.mil/sadbu/sbir/success/index.htm; "Company History," Savi Technology, www.savi.com/company/ov.company.shtml.

34. "Overview and History of the SBA," U.S. Small Business Administration, www.sba.gov/aboutsba/history.html.

35. Art Beroff and Dwayne Moyers, "SBA Guaranteed Loans," *Entrepreneur*, www.entrepreneur.com/article/0,4621,261896,00.html.

36. Laura M. Litvan, "Some Rest for the Paperwork Weary," *Nation's Business*, June 1994, pp. 38–40; Robert W. Casey, "Getting Down to Business," *Your Company*, Summer 1994, pp. 30–33.

37. *Loan Approvals*, U.S. Small Business Administration (Washington, D.C., 2004), www.sba.gov/cgi-bin/loanapprovals4.pl.

38. Julie Monahan, "Quick Fix," *Entrepreneur*, April 2004, p. 27.

39. "The History of Ruiz Food Products," Ruiz Foods, www.ruizfoods.com/aboutus/history.htm; "America's Emissary for Small Business," Special Advertising Section, *Inc.*, December 2003, pp. S1–S3.

40. Roberta Reynes, "Borrowing Tailored for Exporters," *Nation's Business*, March 1999, pp. 29–30.

41. Gwendolyn Bounds, "SBA Loan Program Remains Little Known and Underused," *Wall Street Journal*, February 10, 2004, p. B9.

42. Gwendolyn Bounds, "Risky Businesses May Find Loans Even Scarcer," *Wall Street Journal*, April 13, 2004, p. B8.

43. Ibid.

44. Anna Barron Billingsley, "Dream Weavers," *Region Focus*, Fall 1999, pp. 20–23.

45. "Small Businesses Shortchanged in Grant Program, Analysis Finds," *New York Times*, September 8, 2003, pp. A1, A16; "SBA Disaster Loan Assistance in NYC Reaches $200 Million Following September 11 Attack," Small Business Administration, www.sba.gov/news/indexheadline.html; Susan Hansen, "Ground Zero: The State of Small Business," *Inc.*, October 8, 2001, www.inc.com/search/23503.html.

46. "America's Emissary for Small Business," pp. S1–S3.

47. Crystal Detamore-Rodman, "Public Works," *Entrepreneur*, June 2004, pp. 60–62.

48. Ziona Austrian and Zhongcai Zhang, "An Inventory and Assessment of Pollution Control and Prevention Financing Programs," Great Lakes Environmental Finance Center, Levin College of Urban Affairs, Cleveland State University, www.csuohio.edu/glefc/inventor.htm#sba.

49. Sharon Nelton, "Loans That Come Full Circle," *Nation's Business*, June 1999, pp. 35–36.

50. Ibid.

51. Sean P. Melvin, "Hidden Treasure," *Entrepreneur*, February 2002, pp. 56–58.

52. Martin Mayer, "Taking the Fear Out of Factoring," *Inc.*, December 2003, pp. 90–99.

53. Bobbie Gossage, "Charging Ahead," *Inc.*, January 2004, pp. 42–43.

54. Ibid.

55. Jill Andresky Fraser, "Business Owners, Beware!" *Inc.*, January 1997, pp. 86–87.

Chapter 16

1. Vivian Wagner, "Site Management Software Deployed by Bank," *Bank Systems & Technology Online*, May 27, 2003, www.banktech.com/story/techFocus/BNK20030527S0014.

2. Kevin Potter, "NC State's Centennial Campus Doubles Corporate Partners in 1998–99," *Hot News-Press Release*, July 9, 1999, www.centennial.ncsu.edu/news/release/doubled.htm.

3. Amanda C. Kooser, "Tech Towns," *Entrepreneur*, June 2003, pp. 24–26; Kurt Badenhausen, "Wide Open for Business," *Forbes*, May 26, 2003, pp. 116–120; Paul Kaihla, "Boom Towns," *Business 2.0*, March 2004, pp. 94–102.

4. Elaine Appleton, "E-Town, USA," *Inc. Technology*, 2000, No. 3, pp. 56–61.

5. Steven Gray, "How Applebee's Is Making It Big in Small Towns," *Wall Street Journal*, August 2, 2004, pp. B1, B4.

6. Matt Rosenberg, "About Reilly's Law of Retail Gravitation," About.com, geography.about.com/cs/citiesurbangeo/a/aa041403a.htm; G. I. Thrall and J. C. del Valle, "The Calculation of Retail Market Areas: The Reilly Model," *GeoInfoSystems* Vol. 7, No. 4, 1997, pp. 46–49.

7. Chad Terhune, "Anderson, S.C., Reborn in the 90's Maintains Its Cool in Slowdown," *Wall Street Journal*, July 11, 2001, p. A1; Beth Kwon, "L.A. Renaissance," *FSB*, November 2000, pp. 100–114.

8. Kerry A. Dolan, "San DNAgo," *Forbes*, May 26, 2003, pp. 122–126.

9. Kevin Helliker, "Monster Movie Theaters Invade the Cinema Landscape," *Wall Street Journal*, May 13, 1997, pp. B1, B13.

10. Mike Ramsey, "Borders Going Places Other Stores Dare Not Go," *Business*, June 13, 2004, p. 6.

11. *Scope U.S. 2004*, International Council of Shopping Centers, www.icsc.org/srch/rsrch/scope/current/United_States04.pdf.

12. Dean Storkman, "Mall Developers Envision Shopping Paradise: It's Called Las Vegas," *Wall Street Journal*, July 11, 2001, B1.

13. Annelena Lobb, "A Decade of Super-Sized Shopping," *CNNMoney*, August 9, 2002, money.cnn.com/2002/08/08/pf/saving/q_mall_of_america/.

14. Ibid.

15. Nichole L. Torres, "No Place Like Home," *Business Start-Ups*, September 2000, pp. 38–45, "Executive Overview," National Association of Home-Based Businesses, USA. Home-Based Businesses Information Superhighway, www.ushomebusiness.com/homesite2.htm.

16. Joanna H. Pratt, "Home-Based Business: The Hidden Economy," *Small Business Research Summary*, No. 194, March 2000, U.S. Small Business Administration Office of Advocacy, www.sba.gov/ADVO/research/rs194.pdf.

17. Susan Gregory Thomas, "Home Offices That Really Do The Job," *U.S. News and World Report*, October 28, 1996, pp. 87–87.

18. Timothy Aeppel, "Still Made in the USA," *Wall Street Journal*, July 8, 2004, pp. B1, B4.

19. Veronica Byrd, "Getting Into A Zone Could Be This Year's Smart Move," *Your Company*, April/May 1997, pp. 8–10; Cynthia E. Griffin, "In The Zone," *Entrepreneur*, May 1998, pp. 16–17.

20. "Business Incubation Facts," National Business Incubation Association, 2004, www.nbia.org/resource_center/bus_inc_facts/index.php.

21. Ibid.

22. Lori Iannou, "Start-Ups with a Catch," *Fortune*, July 20, 1998, pp. 156(C)–156(D).

23. Chris Pentilla, Amanda C. Kooser, Kimberly L. McCall, Scott Bernard Nelson, and David Worrell, "Drab to Fab," *Entrepreneur*, April 2004, pp. 64–66.

24. Marci McDonald, "The Latte Connections," *U.S. News & World Report*, March 20, 1999, pp. 63–66.

25. Ron Lieber, "Creative Space," *Fast Company*, January 2001, pp. 136–146.

26. Laura Tiffany, "The Rules of . . . Retailing," *Business Start-Ups*, December 1999, p. 106; Paul Keegan, "The Architect of Happy Customers," *Business 2.0*, August 2002, pp. 85–87.

27. Elizabeth Razzi, "Retailers' Siren Song," *Kiplinger's Personal Financial Magazine*, November 2000, pp. 130–134.

28. John Galvin, "Blueprint for Success," *Smart Business*, September 2000, pp. 114–124.

29. Ibid.

30. "Proposal for an Ergonomics Program Standard," The Occupational Health and Safety Administration, www.osha-slc.gov/ergonomics-standard/ergo-trq.html.

31. Melissa J. Perenson, "Straighten Up," *Small Business Computing*, October 1999, pp. 77–80.

32. "Work Week," *Wall Street Journal*, November 16, 1999, p. A1.

33. Shane McLaughlin, "You Put Your Left Foot In," *Inc. Technology*, 1998, No. 2, p. 18.

34. Leigh Gallagher, "Get Out of My Face," *Forbes*, October 18, 1999, p. A1.

35. Alex Frangos, "Here Comes the Sun," *Wall Street Journal*, November 12, 2003, pp. B1, B8.

36. Galvin, "Blueprint for Success."

37. Frangos, "Here Comes the Sun"; Galvin, "Blueprint for Success."

38. Thomas Mucha, "Target Thinks Outside the Box Wine," *Business 2.0*, February 2003, pp. 46–47.

39. "Business Bulletin," *Wall Street Journal*, April 15, 1999, p. A1.

40. Tom Stevens, "Practice People," *Industry Week*, March 17, 1997, pp. 33–36.

41. Paul Keegan, "The Architect of Happy Customers," *Business 2.0*, August 2002, pp. 85–87; Kenneth Labich, "This Man Is Watching You," *Fortune*, July 19, 1999, pp. 131–134.

42. Razzi, "Retailers' Siren Song"; Keegan, "The Architect of Happy Customers."

43. Matthew Maier, "Redecorating the Rat Shack," *Business 2.0*, June 2003, p. 36.

44. Colleen Bazdarich, "In the Buying Mood? It's the Muzak," *Business 2.0*, March 2002, p. 100.

45. Nadine Heintz, "Play Bach, Boost Sales," *Inc.*, January 2004, p. 23.

46. "Release Me," *Entrepreneur*, January 1998, pp. 48–49.

Chapter 17

1. Ian Mount and Brian Caulfield, "The Missing Link," *eCompany*, May 2001, p. 84.

2. Ibid., pp. 82–88.

3. Donna Fenn, "Made in the USA," *Inc.*, January 2002, pp. 77–83.

4. American Society for Quality, www.asq.org.

5. Jay Heizer and Barry Render, *Principles of Operations Management* (Prentice Hall Publishing Company: Upper Saddle River, NJ, 2004), pp. 190–191.

6. Ben Worthen, "Hot Potato," *CIO*, January 15, 2003, www.cio.com/archive/011503/potato.html.

7. Ibid.

8. Jeff Bailey, "Co-Op Entrepreneur Makes Discounts a Business," *Wall Street Journal*, October 22, 2002, p. B4.

9. "The Nuts and Bolts of Supplier Relations," *Nation's Business*, August 1997, p. 11.
10. Mount and Caulfield, "The Missing Link," pp. 82–88.
11. Mount and Caulfield, "The Internet-Based Supply Chain," *ecompany*, May 2001, p. 85.
12. Russ Banham, "Everything Must Go," *CFO-IT*, Summer 2003, pp. 31–37.
13. Joel Kurtzman, "These Days, Small Manufacturers Can Play on a Level Field," *Fortune*, July 20, 1998, p. 156(F).
14. Patricia Brown, "Building the Right Partnerships: Chico's Tries on Flexible Contracts with Stable Partners," *Optimize*, November 2003, www.optimizemag.com/showArticle.jhtml?articleID=17701003.

Chapter 18

1. Carol Pickering, "The Price of Excess," *Business 2.0*, January 29, 2001, www.business2.com/b2/web/articles/0,17863,528666,00.html.
2. "With Billions of Bytes of Customer Data, How Can Retailers Be 'Starved for Information?'" *Knowledge@Wharton*, August 2000, pf.inc.com/articles/2000/08/20043.html.
3. Phaedra Hise, "Early Adoption Pays Off," *Inc.*, August 1996, p. 101.
4. Caroline Kvitka, "RFID: True Supply Chain Transparency," *Oracle Magazine*, July/August 2004, p. 25.
5. Mark Henricks, "Tell and Show," *Entrepreneur*, April 2004, pp. 77–78.
6. Alex Niemeyer, Minsok H. Pak, and Sanjay Ramaswamy, "Smart Tags for Your Supply Chain," *McKinsey Quarterly*, Number 4, 2003, www.mckinseyquarterly.com/article_page.aspx?ar=1347&L2=1&L3=26.
7. Traci Purdum, "Best Practices: Fast-Track Furniture," *Industry Week*, August 1, 2002, www.industryweek.com/currentArticles/asp/articles.asp?ArticleId=1292.
8. Mark Henricks, "On the Spot," *Entrepreneur*, May 1997, p. 80.
9. Seth Kantor, "How to Foil Employee Crime," *Nation's Business*, July 1983, p. 38.
10. Serri Pfeil, "Is There a Thief Among Us?" *Employment Review*, December 2000, pp. 37–38.
11. Sarabeth Kayton, "How to Avoid Excessive Employee Theft," *Market-Link*, Vol. 22, No. 4, Fall 2003, www.rdmanager.org/pdf/Market-Link03 fall-employeetheft.pdf.
12. Melody Vargas, "Retail Theft and Inventory Shrinkage," *Report on the 2002 Retail Security Survey*," retailindustry.about.com/library/weekly/02/aa021126a.htm.
13. Robert T. Gray, "Clamping Down on Worker Crime," *Nation's Business*, April 1997, p. 44.
14. Calmetta Coleman, "Sticky Fingers," *Wall Street Journal*, September 8, 2000, pp. A1, A6.
15. "Facts About Shoplifters," *Shoplifters Alternative*, www.shopliftersalternative.org.
16. William Ecenbarger, "They're Stealing You Blind," *Reader's Digest*, June 1996, p. 101.

Chapter 19

1. Max DePree, *Leadership Jazz* (New York: Currency Doubleday, 1992), pp. 8–9.
2. Francis Huffman, "Taking the Lead," *Entrepreneur*, November 1993, p. 101.
3. April Y. Pennington, "Big Switch," *Entrepreneur*, August 2004, p. 32.
4. William H. Miller, "The Stuff of Leadership," *Industry Week*, August 18, 1997, p. 100.
5. Carol Hymowitz, "Effective Leaders Say One Pivotal Experience Sealed Their Careers," *Wall Street Journal*, August 27, 2002, p. B1.
6. Michael Barrier, "Hiring the Right People," *Nation's Business*, June 1996, pp. 18–27.
7. Todd Datz, "Measuring Employee Quality—Not," *Darwin*, October 2000, www.darwinmag.com/read/100100/buzz_hr.html; Julie Forster, "Early Retirement May Create Worker Shortage," *Greenville News*, December 7, 2002, p. F1.
8. Richard J. Pinsker, "Hiring Winners," *Small Business Forum*, Fall 1994, pp. 66–84.
9. Jim Johnson, "Take It from Me: Write a Job Description," *Small Business Forum*, Fall 1994, pp. 10–11.
10. "Making the Most of Job Interviews," *Your Company*, Spring 1993, p. 6.
11. Chris Pentilla, "This Is a Test," *Entrepreneur*, August 2004, pp. 72–73.
12. Chris Pentilla, "Testing the Waters," *Entrepreneur*, January 2004, pp. 72–73.
13. Julai Chang, "Liar! Liar!" *Sales & Marketing Management*, November 2003, pp. 63–64.
14. Peter Weaver, "Ignoring a Résumé Can Prove Costly," *Nation's Business*, September 1997, pp. 32–34.
15. John Case, "Corporate Culture," *Inc.*, November 1996, p. 45.

16. Chang, "Balancing Act," *Sales & Marketing Management*, February 2004, p. 16.
17. Ethan Watters, "Come Here, Work, and Get Out of Here. You Don't Live Here. You Live Someplace Else," *Inc. 500*, Fall 2002, pp. 56–62.
18. Lee Smith, "The Diversity Factor," Advertising Insert, *Fortune*, October 13, 2003.
19. Ellyn Spragins, "The Best Bosses," *Inc.*, October 2003, pp. 36–46.
20. Ibid.
21. Mort Meyerson, "Everything I Know About Leadership Is Wrong," *Fast Company's Handbook of the Business Revolution* 1997, p. 9.
22. "Translating Technical Info into Simple Terms Is a Challenge for CIOs," *Wall Street Journal*, June 11, 2001, p. W12.
23. *Bits & Pieces*, February 1, 1996, pp. 10–11.
24. "Smarts," *Entrepreneur*, January 2004, p. 23.
25. E. Rogers and R. Argawala Rogers, *Communication in Organizations* (New York: Free Press, 1976), p. 82.
26. Chris Pentilla, "Live and Learn," *Entrepreneur*, June 2004, www.entrepreneur.com/article/0,4621,315690,00.html.
27. Patricia Panchak, "Executive Word: Putting Employees First Pays Off," *Industry Week*, June 1, 2001, www.industryweek.com/currentArticles/asp/articles.asp?ArticleId=1248.
28. Spragins, "The Best Bosses," pp. 36–46.
29. Magali Rahault, "On the Job," *Kiplinger's Personal Finance Magazine*, May 2001, p. 24.
30. "Flexible Work Arrangements," Ceridian Corporation, www.ceridian.com/www/content/3/10027/11028/319,32, Flexible_work_arrangements_related_to_job_satisfaction_in_2002.
31. Doug Bartholomew, "Your Place or Mine?" *CFO-IT*, Spring 2004, pp. 32–38.
32. Christine L. Romero, "Telecommuting Popular on Both Ends of the Connection," *Greenville News*, July 20, 2003, p. E1.
33. Bartholomew, "Your Place or Mine?" pp. 32–38.
34. Richard Florida, "The Rise of the Creative Class: Motivating Creative IT Workers to Give Their All Means Going Beyond Trappings of Foosball Tables and Casual Dress," *Optimize*, May 2002, www.optimizemag.com/issue/007/culture.htm.
35. Jack Stack, "That Championship Season," *Inc.*, July 1996, p. 27.
36. Jack Stack, "The Logic of Profit," *Inc.*, March 1996, p. 17.
37. John Eckeberg, "Workers Debunk Value of Their Annual Reviews," *Greenville News*, June 11, 2004, p. A18.
38. Jordana Mishory, "Frequency Matters," *Sales & Marketing Management*, July 2004, pp. 36–38.
39. Ibid.

Chapter 20

1. "Successful Family Businesses: Must the Work Come Before the Family?" More Than Money, www.morethanmoney.org/collNov5.htm; Nicholas Stein, "The Age of the Scion," *Fortune*, April 2, 2001, pp. 121–128; MassMutual Family Business Network, www.massmutual.com/fbn/index.htm; "Family Business Facts," Family Business Institute, www.ffi.org/looking/fbfacts_us.pdf.
2. James Lea, "Five Ways Family Firms Can Thrive," *Family Business Bizjournals.com*, February 2, 2004, www.bizjournals.com/extraedge/consultants/family_business/2004/02/02/column180.html.
3. Stein, "The Age of the Scion."
4. "Research Reveals: Family Firms Perform Better," *Family Business Advisor*, March 2003, Vol. 12, No. 3, p. 1.
5. "Family Business Facts," Family Business Institute, www.ffi.org/looking/fbfacts_us.pdf.
6. Ibid.
7. William T. O'Hara and Peter Mandel, "The World's Oldest Family Companies," *Family Business*, www.familybusinessmagazine.com/oldworld.html.
8. "New Nationwide Survey Points to Bright Spot in American Economy—Family-Owned Businesses," MassMutual Financial Group, www.massmutual.com/mmfg/about/pr_2003/01_22_03.html; J. K. Wall, "Trying to Keep It in the Family," *Greenville News*, August 17, 2003, p. E1; "Family Business Facts," Family Business Institute.
9. Sharon Nelton, "Ten Keys to Success in Family Business," *Nation's Business*, April 1991, pp. 44–45.
10. "Family Members Fight Over Control of Texas Pete Hot Sauce Empire," *Greenville News*, May 17, 1997, p. 11D.
11. Stein, "The Age of the Scion."
12. Greg Vandevoord, "Cooper Motor Company Founded on Loyalty," *Clinton Chronicle: Families in Business*, November 26, 2003, pp. 4, 20.

13. Ibid.

14. Michael Freedman, "Slippery Situation," *Forbes*, March 17, 2003, pp. 108–112.

15. Emily Nelson and Sarah Ellison, "Hot Pockets Started as Émigré Family Business," *Wall Street Journal*, May 8, 2002, p. B4.

16. Lori Ioannou, "Keeping the Business All in the Family," *FSB*, November 2001, p. 75.

17. Springfield Remanufacturing Corporation, www.screamn.com/index/htm.

18. "Largest Study Yet Shows ESOPs Improve Performance and Employee Benefits," National Center for Employee Ownership, www.nceo.org/library/esop_perf.html.

19. Paul J. Lim, "Putting Your House in Order," *U.S. News & World Report*, December 10, 2001, p. 38.

20. "Fast Facts," MassMutual Financial Group, www.massmutual.com/mmfg/about/pr_2003/fast_facts.html.

21. Rod Kurtz, "Family-Run Companies Face Leadership Crisis," *Inc.*, May 2003, pp. 25–27.

22. TCPN Quotations Center, www.cyber-nation.com/victory/quotations/subject/quotes_subjects_f_to_h.html#f.

23. Karen Fuller, "Healthy Transition," *Success*, June 2000, pp. 52–53.

24. Andy Bluestone, "Succession Planning Isn't Just About Money," *Nation's Business*, November 1996, p. 6.

25. Shelly Branch, "Mom Always Liked You Best," *Your Company*, April/May 1998, pp. 26–38.

26. "The Russell Family," *Black Enterprise*, June 2003, p. 243.

27. Patricia Schiff Estess, "Heir Raising," *Entrepreneur*, May 1996, pp. 80–82.

28. Linda Thieman, "When Gen-X Takes Over," *Success*, February/March 2001, pp. 44–45.

29. Jacquelyn Lynn, "What Price Successor?" *Entrepreneur*, November 1999, p. 146.

30. Craig E. Aronoff and John L. Ward, "Why Continue Your Family Business?" *Nation's Business*, March 1998, pp. 72–74.

31. Gordon Williams, "Passing the Torch," *Financial World*, January 21, 1997, p. 78.

32. Lee Smith, "The Next Generation," *Your Company*, October 1999, pp. 36–46.

33. "New Nationwide Survey Points to Bright Spot in American Economy—Family-Owned Businesses," MassMutual Financial Group.

34. Annetta Miller, "You Can't Take It with You," *Your Company*, April 1999, pp. 28–34.

35. "Family Business Facts," Family Business Institute.

36. Aliza Pilar Sheridan, "Connect the Daughters," *Entrepreneur*, December 2002, pp. 36–37.

37. Matthew Fogel, "A More Perfect Business," *Inc.*, August 2003, p. 44.

38. Sharon Nelton, "Why Women Are Chosen to Lead," *Nation's Business*, April 1999, p. 51.

39. "New Nationwide Survey Points to Bright Spot in American Economy—Family-Owned Businesses," MassMutual Financial Group.

40. Miller, "You Can't Take It With You"; Joan Pryde, "The Estate Tax Toll on Small Firms," *Nation's Business*, August 1997, pp. 20–24.

41. Amanda Walmac, "Get an Estate Plan to Protect Your Family," *Your Company*, Forecast 1997, pp. 48–54.

42. Juan Hovey, "The Ultimate Assurance of Buy-Sell Agreements," *Nation's Business*, March 1999, pp. 24–26.

43. Joan Szabo, "Spreading the Wealth," *Entrepreneur*, July 1997, pp. 62–64.

44. Daniel Tynan, "In Case of Emergency," *Entrepreneur*, April 2003, p. 60.

45. Michelle Andrews, "Heal Thyself," *FSB*, May 2004, p. 53.

46. Stephen Blakely, "The Backlash Against Managed Care," *Nation's Business*, July 1998, pp. 16–24.

47. Mark Henricks, "Risky Business," *Entrepreneur*, June 2003, pp. 73–74.

48. Jan Norman, "How To: Insure Your Home-Based Business," *Business Start-Ups*, May 1998, pp. 46–49.

49. Kimberly Lankford, "Weird Insurance," *Kiplinger's Personal Finance Magazine*, October 1998, pp. 113–116.

50. Elaine W. Teague, "Risky Business," *Entrepreneur*, May 1999, pp. 104–107.

51. Michele Marchetti, "Thrown Off Track," *FSB*, February 2004, pp. 66–69.

52. Tynan, "In Case of Emergency," pp. 58–61.

53. Jan Norman, "Business Disaster Can Strike at Any Time," *Greenville News*, April 4, 2004, p. E1.

54. Jan Norman, " Contacts Key When Disaster Hits," *Greenville News*, February 8, 2004, p. 1E.

55. Ilan Mochari, "A Security Blanket for Your Web Site," *Inc.*, December 2000, pp. 133–134.

56. Niles Howard, "It's Time for an Insurance Checkup," Advertising Insert, *Inc.*, March 2002.

57. Michael A. Morrisey, *National Small Business Poll: Health Insurance* (Washington, D.C.: Insurance, National Federation of Independent Businesses, 2003), Vol. 3, No. 4, p. 1.

58. Michelle Andrews, "Passing the Buck on Health Care Costs?" *FSB*, December 2003/January 2004, pp. 16–18.

59. Michelle Andrews, "Affordable Health Care," *FSB*, May 2004, pp. 44–53.

60. Leslie Scism, "If Disorder Strikes This 'Titanic,' Chubb Could Lose Millions," *Wall Street Journal*, April 9, 1997, pp. A1, A4.

61. Joshua Kurlantzick, "Staying Alive," *Entrepreneur*, January 2004, pp. 57–59.

62. Ibid.

63. Russ Banham, "Under Cover?" *CFO*, November 2001, pp. 49–56.

64. Jeremy Kahn, "Avoiding Judgment Day," *FSB*, April 2002, pp. 77–82.

65. Mie-Yun Lee, "Pile It On," *Entrepreneur*, February 2001, pp. 82–84.

66. Bruce D. Phillips, *Small Business Problems and Priorities* (Washington, D.C.: National Federation of Independent Businesses, 2004), p. 5.

67. Ilan Mochari, "Bug Your Broker," *Inc.*, August 2000, pp. 127–128.

68. Dale D. Buss, "Cost-Saving Tips for Health Plans," *Nation's Business*, May 1999, pp. 30–33.

69. Andrews, "Affordable Health Care."

Chapter 21

1. Michael Sisk, "Do the Right Thing," Harvard Business School: *Working Knowledge*, September 29, 2003, hbsworkingknowledge.hbs.edu/item.jhtml?id=3689&t=moral_leadership.

2. "Martha Stewart's Company Posts Loss, Shares Fall," *Forbes*, May 7, 2004, www.forbes.com/newswire/2004/05/07/rtr1364228.html.

3. Lawrence Kohlberg, *The Psychology of Moral Development: The Nature and Validity of Moral Stages*, (New York: Harper and Row, 2000).

4. Joseph Pereira, "Doing Good and Doing Well at Timberland," *Wall Street Journal*, September 9, 2003, pp. B1–B10.

5. Ibid.

6. Ibid.

7. Patricia Wallington, "Total Leadership: Honestly?!" *CIO*, March 15, 2003, www.cio.com/archive/031503/lead.html.

8. Ibid.

9. Paul Klebnikov, "Russia—The Ultimate Emerging Market," *Forbes*, February 14, 1994, pp. 88–94.

10. Joshua Kurlantzick, "Liar, Liar," *Entrepreneur*, October 2003, pp. 68–71.

11. Gene Laczniak, "Business Ethics: A Manager's Primer," *Business*, January–March 1983, pp. 23–29.

12. Michael Josephson, "Teaching Ethical Decision Making and Its Principled Reasoning," *Ethics: Easier Said Than Done*, Winter 1988, p. 28.

13. John Rutledge, "The Portrait on My Wall," *Forbes*, December 30, 1996, p. 78.

14. Lori Ioannou, "Corporate America's Social Conscience," *Fortune*, Advertising Insert, May 26, 2003, pp, S1–S10; "Americans Are Looking for Good Corporate Citizens But Aren't Finding Them," *CSR Wire*, July 3, 2001.

15. Gayle Sato Stodder, "Goodwill Hunting," *Entrepreneur*, July 1998, pp. 118–125.

16. Lori Ioannou, "Corporate America's Social Conscience," *Fortune*, pp. S1–S10.

17. Geoff Williams, "Green Machines," *Entrepreneur*, July 2003, p. 34; "Rockland Materials," *Clean Cities Success Stories*, U.S. Department of Energy, www.eere.energy.gov/cleancities/progs/new_success_ddown.cgi?140; Bill Welgoss, "Cleaning the Air in Arizona with Biofuel," *Aggregates Manager*, September 2001, www.aggman.com/0901_pages/operations.html.

18. "Starbucks Validates Commitment to Corporate Transparency in New Corporate Social Responsibility Report," *GreenMoneyJournal.com*, www.greenmoneyjournal.com/article.mpl?newsletterid=29&articleid=316; Mary Scott, "Howard Schulz," *Business Ethics*, November/December 1995, pp. 26–29.

19. J. Walker Smith and Craig Wood, "Difference Matters," *Direct*, August 1, 2003, www.directmag.com/ar/marketing_difference_matters/index.htm.

20. Keith H. Hammonds, "Difference Is Power," *Fast Company*, July 2000, p. 58.

21. *Best Practices of Private Sector Employers*, Equal Employment Opportunity Commission, (Washington, DC, 2003), www.eeoc.gov/abouteeoc/task_reports/prac2.html.

22. Martha Lagace, "Racial Diversity Pays Off," Harvard Business School: *Working Knowledge*, June 21, 2004, hbsworkingknowledge.hbs.edu/item.jhtml?id=4207&t=organizations.

23. Hagin King, "Diversity Partnerships Celebrate the Best in Everyone," *Employment Review*, December 1999, www.employmentreview.com/1999–12/features/CNfeat07.asp.

24. "What Are the Practical Issues We Should Consider Before We Implement a Drug and Alcohol Testing Program?" *HR Comply Newsletter*, July 31, 2002, www.hreducation.com/newsletter/073102/customer.html.

25. Amy Wilson, "Inappropriate Behavior Lands Beetle Bailey's General in Hot Water," *Greenville News*, November 22, 1992, p. 20D.
26. Anne C. Wendt and William M. Slonaker, "Sexual Harassment and Retaliation: A Double-Edged Sword," *SAM Advanced Management Journal*, Autumn 2002, pp. 31–36.
27. *Sexual Harassment Manual for Managers and Supervisors*, (Chicago: Commerce Clearing House, 1992), pp. 25–26.
28. *Burlington Industries v. Ellerth* (97–569) 123 F.3d 490; William H. Floyd and III and Eric C. Schweitzer, "Sexual Harassment Rules Change," *South Carolina Business Journal*, August 1998, pp. 1, 8.
29. Floyd and Schweitzer, "Sexual Harassment Rules Change."
30. Nicole P. Cantey, "High Court Rules Same Sex Harassment Is Against the Law," *South Carolina Business Journal*, August 1998, p. 3; Jack Corcoran, "Of Nice and Men," *Success*, June 1998, pp. 64–67.
31. Samuel Greengard, "Policy Matters," *Personnel Journal*, May 1996, p. 75.
32. Larry Ponemon, "Ports in a Security Storm," *Darwin*, May 2004, www.darwinmag.com/reas/050104/ponemon.html.
33. Peter Waldman and Jay Solomon, "Gold-Fraud Recipe? Bre-X Workers Saw Mine Samples Mixed," *Wall Street Journal*, May 6, 1997, pp. Al, A12; "All That Glitters Now Is the Whodunit," *Atlanta Journal/Constitution*, May 6, 1997, p. F2; Suzanne McGee and Mark Heinzl, "How Bre-X Holders Passed Warnings, Got Lost in Glitter," *Wall Street Journal*, May 16, 1997, pp. Cl, C13; Rachard Behar, "Jungle Fever," *Fortune*, June 9, 1997, pp. 116–128.
34. Carol Cone et. al., "Align Your Brand with a Social Cause," Harvard Business School: *Working Knowledge*, July 14, 2003, hbswk.hbs.edu/item.jhtml?id=3589&t=nonprofit.

Chapter 22

1. *BMW of North America v. Gore*, 517 U.S. 559, 116 S. Ct. 1589, 1996 U.S. LEXIS 3390 (1996).
2. Hilda Bankston, "My Say: The Need for Tort Reform," *My Business*, October/November 2002, www.mybusinessmag.com/fullstory.php3?sid=676.
3. *Carbaugh v. Click-Lewis*, 561 A.2d 1248 (Pa. 1989).
4. *Hoffman v. Red Owl*, 26 Wis. 2d 683; 133 N.W. 2d 267; 1965 Wisc. LEXIS 1026.
5. Daniel E. Kasron, "Getting the Goods on the Plaintiffs—And Their Lawyers," *Corporate Board Member*, March/April 2003, www.boardmember.com/issues/archive.pl?article_id=11375.
6. *Folk v. Central National Bank and Trust Co.*, 201 Ill. App. (1991).
7. *Hotmail Corporation v. Van $ Pie Inc.*, 1998 U.S. Dist. Lexis 10729; 47 U.S.P.Q.2D (BNA) 1020.
8. Dan Rozek, "Firm in Sports Logo Scam Settles for $3.1 Million," *Chicago Sun-Times*, June 5, 2004, web.lexis-nexis.com/universe/document?_m=ff9ce58a95684b9e25fa35d192f3dc4b&_docnum=12&wchp=dGLbVzb-zSkVb&_md5=1751ce3dc1ba89546aa966930d650f95.
9. *George Syrovy v. Alpine Resources, Inc.*, 122 Wn.2d 544; 859 P.2d 51; 1993 Wash. LEXIS 249; 21 U.C.C. Rep. Serv. 2d (Callaghan) 917.
10. *Webster v. Blue Ship Tea Room*, 347 Mass. 421; 198 N.E.2d 309; 1964 Mass. LEXIS 780; 2 U.C.C. Rep. Serv. (Callaghan) 161.
11. "Product Liability Basics," *Inc.*, February 22, 2000, www.inc.com/articles/2000/02/17249.html.
12. "Recent Evidence Demonstrates That There Is No Product Liability Crisis," www.smith-johnson.com/personalinjury/iabilitycrisis.htm.
13. Ibid.
14. Jeffrey F. Beatty and Susan S. Samuelson, *Business Law and the Legal Environment*, Third Edition, (Thompson-South-Western, 2004), p. 478.
15. *Gunning v. Small Feast Caterers, Inc.*, 4 Misc. 3d 209; 777 N.Y.S.2d 268; 2004 N.Y. Misc. LEXIS 535; 53 U.C.C. Rep. Serv. 2d (Callaghan) 502.
16. *General Information Concerning Patents* (Washington, D.C.: U.S. Patent and Trademark Office, 1997); Tomima Edmark, "Bright Idea," *Entrepreneur*, April 1997, p. 98; Tomima Edmark, "What Price Protection?" *Entrepreneur*, September 1998, pp. 109–110; "Attorneys and Agents," U.S. Patent and Trademark Office, www.uspto.gov/web/offices/pac/doc/general/attorney.htm.
17. "Snapshot," *Entrepreneur*, January 2003, p. 22.
18. Bronwyn H. Hall et al., "Prospects for Improving U.S. Patent System to Promote Innovation, But Some Suggest Could Place Greater Burdens on All Patent Applicants," *Southeast Tech Wire*, November 25, 2003, www.wcsr.com/CM/News%20Bites/NewsBites1802.asp.
19. Kondria B. Woods, "Security Blanket," *GSA Business*, May 31, 2004, p. 9.
20. Alaina Sue Potrikus, "Drawings Reveal Ideas That Altered Life," *Greenville News*, December 14, 2003, pp. 1D, 6D.
21. Carlye Adler, "Can You Spot the Knockoff?" *FSB*, April 2002, pp. 42–47.
22. Ibid.
23. *Golight Inc. v. Wal-Mart Stores Inc.*, 355 F.3d 1327; 2004 U.S. App. LEXIS 775; 69 U.S.P.Q.2D (BNA) 1481; Timothy Aeppel, "Brothers of Invention," *Wall Street Journal*, April 19, 2004, pp. B1, B3.
24. Rodney Ho, "Best Cellars Inc. Doesn't Think Imitation Is Flattering," *Wall Street Journal*, April 18, 2000, p. B1.
25. Lance Frazer, "A Small Business Guide to Trademarks, Patents, and Copyrights," *E-Merging Business*, Fall/Winter 2000, pp. 112–115.
26. Kenneth Terrell, "A Nation of Pirates," *U.S. News & World Report*, July 14, 2003, pp. 40–47.
27. Ibid; Bruce Orwall, Martin Peers, and Ethan Smith, "Music Industry Presses 'Play' on Plan to Save Its Business," *Wall Street Journal*, September 3, 2003, p. A1.
28. "U.S. Bankruptcy Filings 1980–2003," American Bankruptcy Institute, www.abiworld.org/ContentManagement/ContentDisplay.cfm?ContentID=8149.
29. Bruce Horovitz, "Twinkie Maker Files for Protection, Gets New CEO," *USA Today*, September 22, 2004, www.usatoday.com/money/companies/management/2004–09–22-interstate-bakeries-bankruptcy_x.htm; "Twinkies Maker Files Bankruptcy," *CNNMoney*, September 22, 2004, money.cnn.com/2004/09/22/news/fortune500/interstate_bankruptcy/.
30. *NFIB Policy Guide*, National Federation of Independent Businesses, (Washington, D.C., 2000), p. 98; Angelina Antonelli, "Regulations: Demanding Accountability and Common Sense," Heritage Foundation, 2000, www.heritage.org/.
31. *NFIB Policy Guide*, National Federation of Independent Businesses, (Washington, D.C., 2000), p. 105.
32. *United States v. Topco Associates Inc.*, 405 US 596 (1972).
33. *American Italian Pasta Company v. New World Pasta Company*, 371 F.3d 387; 2004 U.S. App. LEXIS 11072; 71 U.S.P.Q.2D (BNA) 1046; 2004–1 Trade Cas. (CCH) P74,435; Steve Seidenberg, "Appeals Court Upholds Boastful Pasta Slogan," *Corporate Legal Times*, September 2004, web.lexis-nexis.com/universe/document?_m=ffc6378464cdafd4ca78b6c763cb33a8&_docnum=1&wchp=dGLbVlb-zSkVb&_md5=ae880c1f2b6cc352dd1a81def23df251.

▮▮▮ Credits

Chapter 1

Page 6: *Non Sequitur* © 2003 Wiley Miller. Dist. By *Universal Press Syndicate*. Reprinted with permission. All rights reserved. Page 14: Courtesy of the Tupperware Corporation. Page 17: Warschawski Public Relations/Armour, Inc. Courtesy Under Armour, Inc. Page 20: Seltzer & Associates. Courtesy Nancy Seltzer & Associates.

Chapter 2

Page 41: Christina Lease/Christina Lease Photography. © Christina Lease. Page 45: Courtesy of David A. Rodgers. Page 47: © Randy Glasbergen, www.glasbergen.com. Page 61: Courtesy Frank J. Zamboni Company.

Chapter 3

Page 73: Courtesy of Linda Zimmerer. Page 82: Courtesy of CartoonStock, www.CartoonStock.com.

Chapter 4

Page 101: Courtesy of Jane Plitt. Page 112: Courtesy of Culver Franchising System, Inc.

Chapter 5

Page 131: Courtesy of CartoonStock, www.CartoonStock.com. Page 133: Courtesy of Ira Jackson/Perfect Image Printing. Page 136: Courtesy of Robert Brenner/ PhotoEdit. Page 139: Courtesy of Corbis/Bettmann.

Chapter 6

Page 169: Courtesy of American Business Systems. Page 177: Courtesy of AP Wide World Photos.

Chapter 7

Page 197: Courtesy of Getty Images/Time Life Pictures. Page 207: Courtesy of Kelly Mooney/Corbis/Bettmann. Page 211: Courtesy of Richard Cummins/Corbis/Bettmann. Page 211: Copyright, 2004, Tribune Media Services. Reprinted with permission.

Chapter 8

Page 238: From *The Wall Street Journal*—Permission, Cartoon Feature Syndicate. Page 249: Courtesy of Corbis/Bettmann. Page 251: Courtesy of Laurence Dutton/Image Bank/Getty Images.

Chapter 9

Page 271: Courtesy of H. J. Heinz Company. Page 276: Courtesy of Chuck Savage/Corbis/Bettmann. Page 286:

DILBERT reprinted by permission of United Feature Syndicate, Inc. Page 292: © Randy Glasbergen, www.glasbergen.com.

Chapter 10

Page 305: Courtesy of Lance W. Clayton. Page 312: Courtesy of Ric Brewer/Woodland Park Zoo.

Chapter 11

Page 330: From *The Wall Street Journal*—Permission, Cartoon Feature Syndicate. Page 350: Courtesy of Jeff Greenberg/ The Image Works.

Chapter 12

Page 365: Courtesy of Pelican Publishing Company, Inc. Used by permission of Pelican Publishing Company, Inc. Page 368: Courtesy of the Montague Corporation. Page 380: Courtesy of Jeff Greenberg/PhotoEdit.

Chapter 13

Page 402: © Randy Glasbergen, www.glasbergen.com. Page 413: Courtesy of REI Recreational Equipment Inc. Courtesy REI. Page 415: All-Outdoors Whitewater Rafting. Courtesy of rapidshooters.com.

Chapter 14

Page 442: From *The Wall Street Journal*—Permission, Cartoon Feature Syndicate. Page 444: Courtesy of Stacey's Café. Page 457: Courtesy of Cabela's.

Chapter 15

Page 468: © *The New Yorker* Collection 1990 Jack Ziegler from cartoonbank.com. All Rights Reserved. Page 480: Courtesy of Intelliseek, Inc. Page 480: Courtesy of Intelliseek, Inc. Page 486: Courtesy of SM Group, Inc./Ruiz Foods. Page 487: Courtesy of SM Group, Inc./Ruiz Foods. Page 494: Courtesy Karaoke Star Store and Stage.

Chapter 16

Page 506: Courtesy of Roger Winstead/Roger W Winstead Photography. Page 515: Courtesy of CartoonStock, www.CartoonStock.com. Page 528: Courtesy of Corbis/Bettmann.

Chapter 18

Page 604: Courtesy of Reuters Media/Corbis/Bettmann.

Chapter 19

Page 620: © Randy Glasbergen, www.glasbergen.com.

Chapter 20

Page 653: Courtesy of Cooper Motor Company. Page 654: Courtesy of Cooper Motor Company. Page 662: Courtesy of Robert Labere/Getty Images, Inc. Page 664: From *The Wall Street Journal*—Permission, Cartoon Feature Syndicate. Page 677: Copyright © 1999 by Thaves. All Rights Reserved. Page 683: Courtesy of Christopher J. Morris/Corbis/Bettmann.

Chapter 21

Page 690: Courtesy of Jeff Christensen/Corbis/Bettmann. Page 698: © Danscartoons.com www.danscartoons.com/business_cartoons.htm.

Chapter 22

Page 725: Courtesy of Digital Vision/Getty Images/Digital Vision. Page 738: Courtesy of Aberrant Designs, Inc./www.BananaGUARD.com.

▌▐▌ Index